FREE
Campgrounds,
U.S.A.
Revised Edition

FREE
Campgrounds,
U.S.A.
Revised Edition

Edited by Mary VanMeer

Illustrator: Ruth VanMeer
Director of Research and Development: Leo VanMeer
Editorial and Research Assistant: Michael Anthony Pasquarelli

Published by The East Woods Press
in association with VanMeer Publications, Inc.

A See America
FREE
Book

The
East Woods
Press

Library of Congress Cataloging in Publication Data

Main entry under title:

Free campgrounds, U.S.A.

   (See America free book)
   Rev. ed. of: New free campgrounds. c1976.
   1. Camp sites, facilities, etc.—United States—Directories.
I. VanMeer, Mary. II. Series.
GV198.56.F7   1983   647'.9473   83-1644
ISBN 0-914788-69-8

Editorial and Direct Mail Inquiries:
     VanMeer Publications, Inc.
     PO Box 1289
     Clearwater, FL 33517

Retail, Wholesale, and Library Orders:
     The East Woods Press
     Fast & McMillan Publishers, Inc.
     429 East Boulevard
     Charlotte, NC 28203

56,848

I travel not to go anywhere.
But to go.

I travel for travel's sake.

—Robert Louis Stevenson

TABLE OF CONTENTS

READ THIS!

All information relative to each campground and state is currently accurate to the best of the publisher's knowledge. However, non-fee status and facilities are subject to change.

If any inaccuracies in this directory are discovered, or you know of any additional FREE campgrounds, please contact: VMPI; Box 1289; Clearwater, FL 33517.

INFORMATION ON HOW TO PURCHASE ADDITIONAL COPIES OF THIS BOOK AS WELL AS QUANTITY DISCOUNT INFORMATION IS ALSO AVAILABLE AT THIS ADDRESS.

FREE CAMPGROUNDS, USA

WELCOME TO THE WONDERFUL WORLD OF

FREE CAMPING!

The United States of America has EVERYTHING! Sunshine, snow, smog; mountains, valleys, deserts, lakes, rivers, oceans. Now YOU can have it all . . . and your bank account will never know the difference! Indulge yourself and enjoy your FREEDOM!

ADDITIONAL PLACES TO CAMP FOR FREE

If you happen to be in an area where there are no free campgrounds, but you want to stop for the night, there are several free alternatives for the non-tent camper.

STUCKEY'S and NICKERSON FARMS stores will frequently allow you to spend the night in their parking lot, providing they don't also run a pay-campground concession. Ask permission first.

TRUCK STOPS: Although they tend to be noisy, truck stops can look very good to a tired camper who needs a free place to stop for the night. The advantage of truck stops is the fact that they are nearly everywhere; they generally have an economical restaurant; and the restrooms sometimes contain free showers.

CITY PARKS: Numerous city parks are discussed in this directory to free campgrounds. However, there are still many to be uncovered. If you need a place to stay for the night, and you are driving through a town, stop at one of the service stations or the police station and ask if there is a free city park nearby.

SHOPPING CENTERS and SUPERMARKETS: You will rarely be bothered if you park your RV in an obscure corner of the parking lot, so as not to obstruct traffic. Ask permission first.

24-HOUR MINI-MARKETS and SERVICE STATIONS: With the permission of the manager, you will have a reasonably-protected free place to spend the night.

PUBLIC SCHOOLS: After 5:00 p.m., the parking lots are often empty (except on Friday nights, during an athletic competition). If you choose to park here, however, keep in mind that some schools begin classes as early as 7:00 a.m. (when using double shifts). Only use this as an alternative if you are an EARLY riser.

POLICE STATION: If you want to REALLY be safe, request permission to spend the night in the far corner of the parking lot!

CHURCH: Church parking lots are generally located in quiet residential areas. If the parsonage adjoins the church, ask permission. Avoid Sunday nights and Wednesday nights, as these are the nights of most religious services. And if you plan to spend Saturday night there, leave before Sunday services begin . . . unless you plan to attend them.

GOLDEN EAGLE and GOLDEN AGE PASSPORTS

Golden Eagle Passports. This is an annual entrance permit to National Parks, National Monuments, and National Recreation Areas where a fee is charged; for persons under 62 years of age. Use fees are not covered by this permit; only entrance fees.

The cost is $10.00, and is valid for one calendar year. It can be an economical move if you plan several visits to fee areas in the Park System (which charge from 50¢ per person to $3.00 per car).

The permit may be purchased in person or by mail from National Park Service headquarters or at fee areas at the National Park System which charge entrance fees.

5

Golden Age Passport. This is a FREE LIFETIME ENTRANCE PERMIT for persons 62 years of age and older, valid in National Parks, National Monuments, and National Recreation Areas. The permit-holder also receives a 50% discount for Federal "use" fees charged for parking, camping, etc.

The Golden Age Passport may be obtained IN PERSON ONLY by bringing proof of age to the National Park headquarters in Washington, D.C., or regional offices, or at the entrance to most Federal recreation areas which honor its use.

National Park Service Offices

NPS Headquarters; Room 1013; US Dept. of the Interior; 18th and C Streets, NW; Washington, D.C. 20240.
NPS; North Atlantic Region; 15 State Street; Boston, MA 02109.
NPS; Mid-Atlantic Region; 143 South Third Street; Philadelphia, PA 19106.
NPS; National Capital Region; 1100 Ohio Drive, SW; Washington, D.C. 20242.
NPS; Southeast Region; 1895 Phoenix Blvd.; Atlanta, GA 30349.
NPS; Midwest Region; 1709 Jackson Street; Omaha, NB 68102.
NPS; Rocky Mountain Region; 655 Parfet Street; PO Box 25287; Lakewood, CO 80225.
NPS; Southwest Region; Old Sante Fe Trail; PO Box 728; Sante Fe, NM 87501.

WATER

Many campgrounds indicate that there is safe drinking water available. Although the water supply is checked quite frequently for drinkability, the quality can vary; and if you happen to drink it on an "off day," it could spoil a perfectly wonderful adventure. My suggestion is this: bring your own water supply with you just in case. Or plan to boil the water that is supplied.

PETS

Generally speaking, all National Forests permit pets, preferably on a leash or under any other-than-verbal control. In fact, MOST campgrounds in this directory allow pets. If it is not specifically indicated that pets are permitted, there is no reason to assume that they are NOT permitted. It usually means that the specific information wasn't available at the time of this printing.

WOODSY OWL and SMOKEY BEAR

Woodsy Owl and Smokey Bear are the property of the United States Government. They and their slogans ["Give a Hoot! Don't Pollute!" and "Remember, only YOU can prevent forest fires."] serve as symbols for a campaign to promote the maintenance and improvement of environmental quality. Woodsy Owl and Smokey Bear art and messages appearing in this publication are presented as a public service of SEE AMERICA FREE by permission of the U.S. Department of Agriculture, Forest Service.

IMPORTANT NOTE

All information relative to each campground and state is currently accurate to the best of the publisher's knowledge. However, non-fee status and facilities are subject to change.

If any inaccuracies in this directory are discovered, or you know of any additional FREE campgrounds, please contact: Mary VanMeer, Executive Editor; FREE CAMPGROUNDS, VanMeer Publications, Inc.; PO Box 1289; Clearwater, FL 33517.

THINK FREE, BE FREE, SEE AMERICA FREE!

ABBREVIATIONS

```
BLM.......Bureau of Land Management
cga.......campfire/grill area
COE.......Corps of Engineers
Co Hwy.......County Highway
drk wtr.......drinking water
dump.......sanitary disposal area
E.......east
elev.......elevation
f........firewood
food.......food concession
FS.......Forest Service Road
ft.......feet
jct.......junction
LD.......Labor Day
lmt.......limit
MD.......Memorial Day
mi.......miles
N.......north
NF.......National Forest
NM.......National Monument
NP.......National Park
NRA.......National Recreation Area
NWR.......National Wildlife Refuge
pets.......pets allowed, usually on leash
rd.......road
S.......south
sites.......combination trailer/RV/tent sites, unless otherwise specified
SF.......State Forest
SP.......State Park
SRA.......State Recreation Area
St Hwy.......State Highway
tbls.......tables
toil.......toilets
tr -22.......trailers less than 22 feet in length
W.......west
yr.......year
Boating
    r.......rental
    l.......launch
    d.......dock
*Not accessible by car.
```

ALABAMA

GENERAL STATE INFORMATION

Miscellaneous

Toll-Free Number for Travel Information: 1-800-633-5761 (except AL, AK, HI)
Right Turns on Red: Permitted after full stop, unless otherwise posted.
STATE CAPITOL: Montgomery
STATE NICKNAME: "The Cotton State"
STATE MOTTO: "We Dare Defend Our Rights"
STATE BIRD: Yellowhammer
STATE FLOWER: Goldenrod
STATE TREE: Longleaf Pine

State Parks

Fees range from $2.00 to $4.50 per night. Children under 6, free. Special weekly
and off-season camping rates. Pets are allowed on leash. Further information: Division of State Parks; Alabama Department of Conservation and Natural Resources; 64
North Union Street; Montgomery, AL 36130.

Rest Areas

Overnight stops are permitted in certain designated areas.

Tennessee Valley Authority

TVA designated campgrounds are no longer free. However, unimproved TVA lands may
be used for informal camping. These areas are shown on recreation maps of individual
TVA lakes. No fees or permits required. Pets are allowed. For free maps, contact:
Tennessee Valley Authority; Knoxville, TN 37902.

INFORMATION SOURCES

Maps

The following maps are available from **Forsyth Travel Library** (see order form in Appendix B):

> State of Alabama [Up-to-date, showing all principal roads,
> points of interest, sports areas, parks, airports, mileage,
> etc. Full color.]

> Completely indexed city maps, including all airports, lakes,
> rivers, etc., of: **Birmingham; Huntsville; Mobile; Montgomery; Muscle Shoals/Florence.**

Gold Mining and Prospecting

Geological Survey of Alabama; University, AL 35486

State Information

Alabama Bureau of Publicity and Information; 532 S. Perry St.; Montgomery, AL 36130
Bureau of Publicity; State of Alabama; Montgomery, AL 36130 [205/832-5510]
Division of State Parks; Alabama Department of Conservation and Natural Resources;
    64 North Union Street; Montgomery, AL 36104
Division of Game and Fish; Department of Conservation and Natural Resources; 64 North
    Union Street; Montgomery, AL 36104

City Information

Birmingham Chamber of Commerce; PO Box 10127; Birmingham, AL 35202
Huntsville Chamber of Commerce; 305 Church St.; PO Box 1087; Huntsville, AL 35807
Mobile Chamber of Commerce; 61 St. Joseph St.; PO Box 2187; Mobile, AL 36601
Montgomery Chamber of Commerce; 41 Commerce St.; PO Box 79; Montgomery, AL 36101
Tuscaloosa Chamber of Commerce; 2200 Univ. Blvd.; PO Box 430; Tuscaloosa, AL 35402

National Forests

Conecuh NF; 1765 Highland Avenue; Box 40; Montgomery, AL 36101
Talladega NF; 1765 Highland Avenue; Box 40; Montgomery, AL 36101
Tuskegee NF; 1765 Highland Avenue; Box 40; Montgomery, AL 36101
William B. Bankhead NF; 1765 Highland Ave.; Box 40; Montgomery, AL 36101

8

ALABAMA

Corps of Engineers

U.S. Army Engineer District, Mobile; PO Box 2288; Mobile, AL 33628
Resource Manager; COE; PO Box 520; Demopolis, AL 36732

FREE CAMPGROUNDS

ABBEVILLE

Abbie Creek Public Use Area (COE;George W. Andrews Lake). 14 mi S of Abbeville on St Hwy 95 to Haleburg; 2 mi E on St Hwy 12 to Jct of St Hwys 12/97; 1 mi S on St Hwy 97 to entrance road. SEASON: all yr; 14-day lmt. FACILITIES: 5 sites (tr -18), tbls, toil, cga, well drk wtr. ACTIVITIES: boating,l; fishing and swimming nearby; picnicking. MISC.: Pets.

AKRON

Old Lock 8 (COE; Warrior Lake). 5 mi W of Akron on Lock 8 Rd to sign. SEASON: Day after LD to 5/31, FREE ($3 rest of yr); 14-day lmt. FACILITIES: 10 sites (tr -18), tbls, toil, cga, drk wtr, f. ACTIVITIES: boating,l (concrete boat ramp); bank fishing; swimming; picnicking. MISC.: Pets.

ALBERTA

Chilatchee (COE; Bill Dannelly Reservoir). From Alberta on St Hwy 5, 8-1/10 mi E on Co Rd 29 to sign at gravel rd; 2 mi left to park. SEASON: Day after LD to 5/31, FREE ($2 rest of yr); 14-day lmt. FACILITIES: 14 sites (tr -30), tbls, toil, cga, drk wtr. ACTIVITIES: bank fishing; swimming; boating,l; picnicking; hiking. MISC.: Scenic overlook; trails; pets.

ARDMORE

I-16 Welcome Center. 1 mi S of Ardmore on US 65 at milepost 364. SEASON: all yr, 1-night lmt. FACILITIES: tbls, toil, cga, dump, telephone. ACTIVITIES: picnicking. MISC.: Pets.

ASHEVILLE

Northbound Rest Area. North of Asheville on I-59 at milepost 165. SEASON: all yr, 1-night lmt. FACILITIES: tbls, toil, cga, dump, telephone. ACTIVITIES: picnicking. MISC.: Pets allowed on leash.

Southbound Rest Area. South of Asheville on I-59 at milepost 168. SEASON: all yr, 1-night lmt. FACILITIES: tbls, toil, dump, telephone. ACTIVITIES: picnicking. MISC.: Pets.

ATHENS

Blue Springs Dock. 9 mi W and N of Athens on St Hwy 72. SEASON: all yr. FACILITIES: Free campsites. MISC.: Pets.

Lucy Branch Park. 9 mi W of Athens off St Hwy 72. SEASON: all yr. FACILITIES: Free campsites. MISC.: Pets.

Sportsman's Park. 9 mi NW of Athens on US 72. SEASON: all yr. FACILITIES: Free campsites. MISC.: Pets.

BAY MINETTE

Rest Area. 5 mi S of Bay Minette on US 31. SEASON: all yr, 1-night lmt. FACILITIES: tbls, toil, cga, dump, telephone. ACTIVITIES: Picnic. MISC.: Pets.

BENTON

Prairie Creek Park (COE; Woodruff Lake). From US 80, 4½ mi W on Co Rd 23 to dead end; 3½ mi left on Co Rd 40 to park entrance. SEASON: all yr, 14-day lmt. FACILITIES: 49 sites (tr -30), pull-thru spaces, tbls, flush toil, cga, dump. ACTIVITIES: swimming; picnicking; fishing; boating,l. MISC.: Pets.

BLOUNT SPRINGS

Stuckey's. On I-65, near Blount Springs. SEASON: all yr, 1-night lmt. FACILITIES: places for self-contained RVs; fd, toil, drk wtr, gas. MISC.: Pets; not in bldg.

BUTLER

McCarthy's Ferry (COE). 12 mi E of St Hwy 17, at S end of Butler, on Co Rd 23; 1-1/5 mi N on gravel rd. (Poor access rds.) SEASON: all yr,14-day lmt. FACILITIES: 6 sites (tr -18), tbls, toil, cga. ACTIVITIES: picnicking; fishing; boating,l. MISC.: Pets on leash; lake.

CAMDEN

Bridgeport Park (COE; Bill Dannelly Reservoir). 4 mi NE of Camden on St Hwy 41; exit for Reservoir; take Co Rd 37; park entrance on right. SEASON: Day after LD to 5/31, FREE ($2 rest of yr); 14-day lmt. FACILITIES: 12 sites (tr -30), tbls, toil, cga, drk wtr. Fd, store, ice and laundry facilities are nearby. ACTIVITIES: bank fishing; swimming (beach, change house); boating,l; picnicking; hiking. Golf nearby. MISC.: 300 acres; pets; foot trails; lake.

Ellis Ferry Access Area (COE; Bill Dannelly Reservoir). 2 mi N of Camden on Co Rd 29 (from St Hwy 28);1 mi to park. SEASON: all yr, 14-day lmt. FACILITIES: 3 sites (1 handicapped), tbls, toil, cga, drk wtr. ACTIVITIES: bank fishing; picnicking; boating,l. MISC.: Pets.

See page 7 for KEY TO ABBREVIATIONS.

Millers Ferry Lock & Dam (COE; Bill Dannelly Reservoir). 14 mi NW of Camden off St Hwy 28; east of Alabama River Bridge. SEASON: all yr, 14-day lmt. FACILITIES: 6 sites, tbls, toil, cga, drk wtr. ACTIVITIES: picnicking; fishing (fishing deck); boating,l; swimming. MISC.: Scenic overlook; powerhouse; manager's office; lake; pets on leash.

Portland (COE). 12 mi N of Camden on St Hwy 41; 5 mi W. SEASON: all yr, 14-day lmt. FACILITIES: Sites (tr -18), tbls, toil, cga, f. ACTIVITIES: waterskiing; boating,l; hiking; fishing. MISC.: Lake; pets on leash; trails.

CLANTON

Northbound I-65 Rest Area. On I-65 N, 1 mi N of Clanton exit; milepost 214. SEASON: all yr, 1-night lmt. FACILITIES: places for self-contained RVs to park, tbls, toil, cga, dump, telephone. ACTIVITIES: Picnicking. MISC.: Pets.

Southbound I-65 Rest Area. On I-65 S, N of Clanton exit; at milepost 214. SEASON: all yr, 1-night lmt. FACILITIES: places for self-contained RVs; tbls, toil, cga, dump, telephone. ACTIVITIES: picnicking. MISC.: Pets.

COLUMBIA

Abbie Creek Public Use Area (COE;George W. Andrews Lake). 22 mi N of Columbia on Co Hwy. SEASON: all yr, 14-day lmt. FACILITIES: 5 sites (tr -18), tbls, toil, cga, well drk wtr. ACTIVITIES: fishing and swimming nearby; boating,l;picnicking. MISC.: Pets on leash; lake.

Coheelee Creek Public Use Area (COE; George W. Andrews Lake). 10 mi N of Columbia on Co Hwy. SEASON: all yr, 14-day lmt. FACILITIES: 7 sites (tr -18), tbls, toil, cga, hand pump available. ACTIVITIES: picnicking; boating,l; fishing/swimming nearby. MISC.: Pets.

Omussee Creek (COE). 1-1/5 mi S of St Hwy 52 on St Hwy 95. SEASON: all yr, 14-day lmt. FACILITIES: 12 sites, tbls, toil, cga. ACTIVITIES: boating,l; picnicking; fishing. MISC.: Pets; river.

CUBA

Old Lock 3 Right Bank (COE). 7 mi E of Cuba on US 80; 7-4/5 mi S on St Hwy 17; 12-2/5 mi E; 2-9/10 mi E on dirt access road. SEASON: 4/1-11/15, 14-day lmt. FACILITIES: 10 sites, tbls, toil, cga. ACTIVITIES: picnicking; fishing; boating,l. MISC.: Pets.

CULLMAN

Stuckey's. On I-65, near Cullman. SEASON: all yr, 2-night lmt. FACILITIES: places for self-contained RVs; fd, toil, drk wtr, gas, telephone. MISC.: Pets allowed, but not in the builidng.

DECATUR

Rest Area. 4 mi N of Decatur on US 31 SEASON: all yr, 14-day lmt. FACILITIES: places for self-contained RVs; tbls, toil, cga. ACTIVITIES: picnicking. MISC.: Pets.

DEMOPOLIS

Forkland Public Use Area (COE; Demopolis Lake). 10 mi N of Demopolis on St Hwy 43. SEASON: day after LD to 5/31, FREE ($3 rest of yr); 14-day lmt. FACILITIES: 14 sites (tr -30), tbls, toil, cga, drk wtr. Fd, store, ice nearby. ACTIVITIES: boating,l (concrete boat ramp); bank fishing; picnicking; swimming. MISC.: 98 acres; pets.

Lock 3 (Right Bank) (COE; Coffeeville Lake). 12 mi S of Demopolis on Co Hwy 21. SEAS: 4/16-11/15, 14-day lmt. FACILITIES: 7 sites (tr -18), tbls, toil, cga. ACTIVITIES: swimming and bank fishing nearby; boating,l; hiking; picnicking. MISC.: Foot trails; pets.

EASTABOGA

Stuckey's. On I-20, near Eastaboga. SEASON: all yr, 1-night lmt. FACILITIES: places for self-contained RVs; fd, toil drk wtr, telephone, gas. ACTIVITIES: picnicking. MISC.: Pets allowed outdoors.

EUFAULA

White Oak Creek Park (COE; Walter F. George Lake). 7 mi S of Eufaula on St Hwy 431; 3 mi E on St Hwy 95. White Oak is on your left. SEASON: 9/15-3/15, FREE ($2 rest of yr); 14-day lmt. FACILITIES: 49 sites (tr -30), tbl/cga at each site, toil. ACTIVITIES: picnicking; fishing; swimming; boating,l. MISC.: 170 acres; pets; nice sand beach throughout most of park. Fd/store/ice nearby.

EUTAW

Jennings Ferry (COE; Warrior Lake). 6 mi E of Eutaw on St Hwy 14 to sign. SEASON: day after LD to 5/31, FREE ($3 rest of yr). FACILITIES: 13 sites (tr -18), tbls, toil, cga, drk wtr. ACTIVITIES: bank fishing; boating,l (concrete boat ramp). MISC.: 30 acres; pets.

EVERGREEN

Rest Area. 6 mi S of Evergreen on I-65 (both sides). SEASON: all yr; 1-night lmt. FACILITIES: places for self-contained RVs; tbls, toil, cga. ACTIVITIES: picnicking. MISC.: Pets.

FAIRFAX

Stuckey's. On I-85, near Fairfax. SEASON: all yr, 1-night lmt. FACILITIES: places for self-contained RVs; fd, toil, drk wtr, telephone, gas. MISC.: Pets are allowed outdoors only.

See page 7 for KEY TO ABBREVIATIONS.

GEORGIANA

Union Camp. 2-acre site, 2 mi N of Georgiana. This site is generally used by hunters in conjunction with the Butler Co. Wildlife Management Area. Additional directions can be obtained by calling the Union Camp Woodlands Office in Chapman, Alabama: 205/376-2241.

GILBERTOWN

Lenoir Landing (COE; Coffeeville Lake). 10 mi E of Gilbertown on Co Hwy. SEASON: all yr, 14-day lmt. FACILITIES: 5 sites (tr -18), tbls, toil, cga, drk wtr. ACTIVITIES: swimming and bank fishing nearby; boating,l; picnicking. MISC.: Pets.

GRAND BAY

I-10 Alabama Welcome Center. I-10 E; milepost 1. SEASON: all yr, 1-night lmt. FACILITIES: places for self-contained RVs; tbls, toil, cga, dump, telephone. ACTIVITIES: picnicking. MISC.: Pets.

Stuckey's. On I-10, near Grand Bay. SEASON: all yr, 1-night lmt. FACILITIES: places for self-contained RVs; fd, toil, drk wtr, telephone, gas. MISC.: Pets.

GUNTERVILLE

Marshall City Park. 1 mi N of Gunterville on US 431. SEASON: all yr. FACILITIES: 20 sites. MISC.: Pets.

LANETT

I-85 Rest Area. On I-85, S of Lanett exit; milepost 79. SEASON: all yr, 1-night lmt. FACILITIES: places for self-contained RVs; tbls, toil, cga, dump, telephone. ACTIVITIES: picnicking. MISC.: Pets.

LOWER PEACHTREE

Lower Peachtree Access Point (COE; Claiborne Lake). From jct of St Hwy 5 and Co Rd 1, turn SE on Co Rd 1; 11 mi SE on Co Rd 1 to Lower Peachtree; left on paved rd (Co Rd 35); 1 mi to end of pavement; left on gravel rd; 2 mi to park entrance. SEASON: all yr, 14-day lmt. FACILITIES: 5 sites, tbls, toil, cga, picnic shelters, drk wtr. ACTIVITIES: hiking; boating,l; bank fishing; picnicking. MISC.: Foot trails; pets.

MADRID

Rest Area. 2 mi S of Madrid on US 231, on E side (at border). SEASON: all yr, 1-night lmt. FACILITIES: spaces for self-contained RVs; tbls, toil, cga. ACTIVITIES: picnicking. MISC.: Pets.

MONROEVILLE

Bell's Landing Park (COE; Claiborne Lake). 23 mi N of Monroeville on St Hwy 41 to park entrance sign. SEASON: all yr, 14-day lmt. FACILITIES: 6 sites, tbls, toil, cga, drk wtr. ACTIVITIES: hiking; boating,l; small game hunting with permit only; bank fishing; picnicking. MISC.: Foot trails; pets on leash.

Haines Island Park (COE;Claiborne Lake). 8 mi N of Monroeville on St Hwy 41; left on Co Rd 17; 10 mi to park entrance sign; left and go 1 mi on gravel rd to park and ferry. SEASON: all yr, 14-day lmt. FACILITIES: 12 sites, tbls, toil, cga, drk wtr, group areas. ACTIVITIES: bank fishing; hiking; picnicking; boating,l. MISC.: Trails; pets.

MONTGOMERY

Prairie Creek Park (COE;Woodruff Lake). 35 mi W of Montgomery on St Hwy 80 to Benton exit; 4½ mi W on Co Rd 23 to dead end; 3½ mi left on Co Rd 40 to park entrance. SEASON: all yr, 14-day lmt. FACILITIES: 49 sites (tr -30), tbls, flush toil, cga, dump, pull-thru spaces. ACTIVITIES: swimming; boating,l; picnicking; fishing. MISC.: 50 acres; pets.

MORVIN

Bashi Creek (COE). 21¼ mi N of Morvin on St Hwy 69; 5-2/5 mi W on Co Rd 20. (Poor access rds.) SEASON: all yr, 14-day lmt. FACILITIES: 12 sites, tbls, toil, cga. ACTIVITIES: boating,l; picnicking; fishing; hiking; waterskiing. MISC.: Lake; pets.

MOULTON

Brushy Lake (Wm. B. Bankhead NF). 15 mi S of Moulton on St Hwy 33; 5 mi E on FS 245. SEASON: all yr; 14-day lmt. FACILITIES: 13 sites (tr -22), tbls, toil, cga, piped drk wtr, bath house, showers. Fd, store, ice, gas nearby. ACTIVITIES: picnicking; fishing; swimming; boating,dl; hunting nearby; hiking. MISC.: 3 acres; elev 600 ft; pets on leash; nature trails; lake.

OAKLAND

Rest Area. 1 mi N of Oakland on US 31. SEASON: all yr, 1-night lmt. FACILITIES: places for self-contained RVs; tbls, toil, cga. ACTIVITIES: picnicking. MISC.: Pets.

OPELIKA

Rest Area. 7 mi NW of Opelika on US 280. SEASON: all yr, 1-night lmt. FACILITIES: spaces for self-contained RVs; tbls, toil, cga. ACTIVITIES: picnicking. MISC.: Pets.

See page 7 for KEY TO ABBREVIATIONS.

PINE LEVEL

Rest Area. 2 mi S of Pine Level on US 231 (both sides). SEASON: all yr,1-night lmt. FACILITIES:places for self-contained RVs; tbls, toil, cga. ACTIVITIES: picnicking. MISC.: Pets.

SELMA

Six Mile Creek Park (COE; Bill Dannelly Reservoir). 6 mi S of Selma on St Hwy 41; right at sign at gravel rd; 1½ mi to fork. Boat ramp and camping is 1 mi right. Overlook and picnic area is 1 mi to the left. SEASON: all yr, 14-day lmt. FACILITIES: 14 sites, tbls, toil, cga, picnic shelter. ACTIVITIES: boating,l; hiking; fishing; small game hunting with permit only. MISC.: Trails; scenic overlook; drk wtr; pets.

SHEPHERDVILLE

Portland Access Point (COE; Bill Dannelly Reservoir). From St Hwy 41, W on gravel rd marked "Portland", midway between Selma and Camden; 5 mi to park. SEASON: all yr, 14-day lmt. FACILITIES: 2 sites, drk wtr, tbls, cga. ACTIVITIES: bank fishing;picnicking;boating,l. MISC.: Pets.

SYLACAUGA

Stuckey's. On US 231/280, near Sylacauga. SEASON: all yr, 1-night lmt. FACILITIES: places for self-contained RVs; fd, toil, drk wtr, telephone, gas. MISC.: Pets.

TUSCALOOSA

Rocky Branch (COE; Holt Lake). 5 mi N of Tuscaloosa on St Hwy 215; 10 mi N on St Hwy 216 through Peterson; 2 mi left to park....total 17 mi. SEASON: day after LD to 5/31, FREE ($3 rest of yr); 14-day lmt. FACILITIES: 25 sites (tr --18), tbls, toil, cga, drk wtr, campfire circles. ACTIVITIES: boating,l (concrete boat ramp); swimming; bank fishing; picnicking; hiking. MISC.: 340 acres; beach; foot trails; scenic overlook; pets.

TUSKEGEE

Taska (Tuskegee NF). 4 mi E of Tuskegee on US 80. SEASON: all yr, 14-day lmt. FACILITIES: 4 sites (tr -22), tbls, toil, cga, f, well drk wtr. ACTIVITIES: Picnicking; hiking. Fishing and swimming (4 mi). Hunting nearby. MISC.: Elev 400 ft; 4 acres; nature trails; William Bartram National Recreation Trail (10 mi); pets

ALASKA

GENERAL STATE INFORMATION

Miscellaneous

Right Turns on Red: Permitted after full stop, unless otherwise posted.
STATE CAPITOL: Juneau
STATE MOTTO: The Great Land
STATE BIRD: Willow Ptarmigan
STATE FLOWER: Forget-me-not
STATE TREE: Sitka Spruce

Help Woodsy spread the word.
WOODSY OWL

State Parks

There is no charge for the use of the facilities in Alaska's state park system (state parks, state recreation areas, waysides, and historic sites). HOWEVER, A PERMIT IS REQUIRED. This annual permit is $10.00 and can be purchased after visitors arrive in Alaska or by mail in advance of the visit and it is applicable to state facilities only. Contact: State of Alaska; Dept. of Natural Resources; Division of Parks; 323 East 4th Avenue; Anchorage, AK 99503. Pets permitted on leash.

Rest Areas

Overnight camping in self-contained RVs is allowed at the wayside areas in Alaska.

See page 7 for KEY TO ABBREVIATIONS.

ALASKA

Proposed New National Forests in Alaska

Several new national forests are being added to the current forest system in Alaska. For current information on progress and possible new free campgrounds and wilderness areas, contact: U.S. Forest Service; Alaska Planning Team; Suite 280; 121 W. Fireweed Lane; Anchorage, AK 99503.

THE CHILKOOT TRAIL
(Klondike Gold Rush National Historic Park)

There is free camping along the Chilkoot Trail. Keep your campsite and equipment clean. Food should be sealed in containers and hung from trees so that animals will not be attracted by food odors. Pets must be leashed, and are not recommended on this trail. Bear and moose country. Bring a campstove and adequate fuel, as there is no wood in the summit area and campfires are not allowed at all on the Canadian portion.

Hiking the trail north from Dyea is recommended because it is the historic route. Also, traveling the trail in reverse is not recommended because descending the steep summit, the "Golden Stairs" of gold rush days, is dangerous. Additional information: Klondike Gold Rush National Historic Park; PO Box 517; Skagway, AK 99840.

ARCTIC NATIONAL WILDLIFE RANGE

Wilderness camping, hiking, caribou hunting, fishing, in Alaska's far north wilderness area. For free information/maps: **Map of the Proposed Gates of the Arctic National Park** [National Park Service; 334 W. 5th Ave., Ste. 250; Anchorage, AK 99501]; **Arctic National Wildlife Range** [Bureau of Sport Fishery and Wildlife; 813 "D" St.; Anchorage, AK 99501].

BACKCOUNTRY CAMPING IN KATMAI NATIONAL MONUMENT

Katmai is brown bear country, and campers are urged to take appropriate precautions. No roads lead to the Monument, and all access is by air. Wien Air Alaska has daily flights to Brooks Camp from Anchorage at a round-trip cost of about $150. Federal regulations prohibit transporting fuel on an aircraft. Please be certain all fuel containers are empty before arriving at the airport. Use existing campsites and firesites rather than establishing new ones.

Information and a free map on hiking and camping in the Katmai backcountry can be obtained by contacting: Superintendent; Katmai National Monument; PO Box 7; King Salmon, AK 99613. Also available free of charge is the publication **Katmai--Angler's Paradise**, available from Wien Air Alaska; 4100 W. International Airport Road; Anchorage, AK 99502.

[See listing in this chapter: Anchorage -- Brooks River Campground.]

KENAI NATIONAL MOOSE RANGE

Camping

1,730,000 acres, the Moose Range was established in 1941 to protect the Kenai moose, whose antlers often exceed 6 feet. Camping is permitted throughout the Range. It is restricted to 7 consecutive days at Kenai-Russian River and Hidden Lake campgrounds, and 14 consecutive days elsewhere. Specific information on specified campgrounds can be found in this chapter under the following cities: Sterling, Cooper Landing, and Soldotna. Motorized vehicles are prohibited off established maintained roads. Boating is permitted on all waters of the Moose Range. Boats or canoes with motors are not permitted within the canoe system lakes. More than 100 miles of established, well-marked hiking trails. They vary in degree of difficulty from fairly level to quite strenuous. Additional free information, maps, and brochures: The Kenai National Moose Range; PO Box 500; Kenai, AK 99611.

Swanson River Canoe Route

This canoe route links more than 40 lakes with 46 miles of the Swanson River. The entire route (80 miles in length) can be traveled in less than one week. Canoeists can enter the headwaters of the Swanson River (via Gene Lake outlet) and float down to the Swanson River Campground, a distance of 19 miles, or continue to its terminus at the North Kenai Road Bridge, 24 miles downstream. **Camping sites are available** along the lake shores in wilderness-type surroundings. Fishing and hunting available.

ALASKA

Swan Lake Canoe Route

This canoe route connects 30 lakes with forks of the Moose River. The entire canoe route (60 miles in length) can be traveled in less than one week; however, leisurely travel will provide many additional days of excellent fishing and camping. Nearly one day's canoeing is required to reach Gavia Lake from either the East or West Entrance. Camping sites are available along the lake shores in wilderness-type surroundings. Fishing and hunting are available.

BACKCOUNTRY CAMPING IN MT. McKINLEY NATIONAL PARK

A backcountry use permit for overnight camping must be obtained and then returned when the trip is complete. Permits are issued at the Visitor Orientation Center, Eielson Visitor Center, and at any ranger station during the summer season. In winter they must be obtained at park headquarters. A stove is recommended for backpacking; do not bury or leave behind any garbage or trash.

No fishing licenses are required. Limits for each person per day: lake trout (2 fish), grayling and other fish (10 fish or 10 lbs. and 1 fish). Hunting is prohibited. Firearms must be surrendered or made inoperative upon entering the park. The hunting ban is strictly enforced. Pets must be leashed or under restraint at all times. They are not permitted with you on trails or in the backcountry.

For specific Mt. McKinley NP campground listings, see the heading "McKinley Park" in this chapter. For free information and maps, contact: Superintendent; Mt. McKinley National Park; PO Box 9; McKinley Park, AK 99755.

BACKCOUNTRY CAMPING IN GLACIER BAY NATIONAL MONUMENT

Camping and hiking is on a wilderness basis. Glacier Bay maintains only one small walk-in backcountry-type campground with 10 sites at the monument headquarters at Bartlett Cove. There are very few roads and trails. Wilderness camping is made relatively easy as campers can be dropped off by the cruise boat, other concessioner boat, Glacier Bay Airways, or bus, and can be picked up at a later date. There are commercial flights from Juneau to Gustavus during the season, May to mid-September. It is 10 miles from Gustavus to Bartlett Cove. Commercial bus service is available during the season. Air charter can provide access all year. Boat charters can also be arranged from Juneau. Camping at Bartlett Cove is on a first-come first-served basis, free of charge.

Hiking and camping in the upper reaches of Glacier Bay afford a wilderness experience difficult to have anywhere else so easily. The camper or hiker is completely on his own, and is unlikely to see anyone until he is picked up. Barren rock and gravel provide easy open hiking to spectacular views of mountains and glaciers.

Buy your own food and camping supplies before you come to Glacier Bay. There are no stores or camping services locally. Cooking stoves are recommended because no wood is available in many portions of upper Glacier Bay for campfires. All campers are requested to carry out all unburnable materials.

CAUTION: Brown and black bears may be encountered at nearly any site. Glacial streams may be small in the morning and uncrossable torrents in the afternoon after a warm or rainy day.

Fishing license is required. Boats for charter may be obtained at Bartlett Cove. No hunting. All firearms must be surrendered, or sealed, or unloaded and cased, or otherwise packed in such a way as to prevent their use while in park areas. Strictly enforced. Pets are not permitted on trails or in the backcountry. Too dangerous for your pet and the wildlife.

Obtain free information and maps by contacting: Superintendent; Glacier Bay National Monument; Box 1089; Juneau, AK 99801.

INFORMATION SOURCES

Maps

Detailed, up-to-date, completely indexed maps are available from **Forsyth Travel Library** (see order form in Appendix B) for the **State of Alaska** and the city of Ketchikan.

Gold Mining and Prospecting

Alaska Division of Mines and Minerals; State Capitol Building; Juneau, Alaska 99801

State Information

Div. of Tourism; Department of Commerce and Economic Development; Pouch E, State Capitol; Juneau, Alaska 99811 [907/465-2010]

14

ALASKA

Alaska Division of Lands; 344 - 6th Avenue; Anchorage, Alaska   99501
Fish and Wildlife Service; Information Office; 813 "D" St.; Anchorage, Alaska   99501
Dept. of Fish and Game; Subport Building; Juneau, Alaska   99801
Department of Natural Resources; 323 East 4th Avenue; Anchorage, Alaska   99501

City Information

Anchorage Visitor Center; Terminal Building; Anchorage International Airport; Anchorage, Alaska   99502   [907/277-9211]
Fairbanks Chamber of Commerce; 550 - 1st Ave.; Fairbanks, Alaska 99701
Juneau Visitor Information; Div. of Tourism; 9th Floor; State Office Building; Juneau, Alaska   99811   [907/465-2010]
Skagway Chamber of Commerce; PO Box 194; Skagway, AK 99840   [907/983-2220]

National Forests

Forest Service; U.S. Dept. of Agriculture; PO Box 1980; Sitka, Alaska   99835
Chugach NF; 2221 East Northern Lights Boulevard; Anchorage, AK   99504
North Tongass NF; 217 - 2nd Street; Juneau, Alaska   99801
South Tongass NF; Box 2278; Ketchikan, Alaska   99901

Miscellaneous

Klondike Gold Rush National Historic Park; PO Box 517; Skagway, AK   99840
Bureau of Outdoor Recreation; Information Office; 524 West Sixth Avenue; Anchorage, Alaska 99501
Mount McKinley National Park; PO Box 9; McKinley Park, AK   99755
National Park Service; Alaska Field Office; 540 W. 5th Ave., #202; Anchorage, AK 99501
Glacier Bay National Monument; PO Box 1089; Gustavus, Alaska   99801
Katmai National Monument; Box 7; King Salmon, Alaska   99613
Director; Juneau Area Office; Bureau of Indian Affairs; PO Box 3-8000; Juneau, AK   99801
Kenai National Moose Range; Box 500; Kenai, AK   99611
Alaska Area Director; NWR; 1101 Tudor Road; Anchorage, Alaska   99507
Alaska BLM; 555 Cordova Street; Anchorage, Alaska   99501

FREE CAMPGROUNDS

ANCHORAGE

Bird Creek (Chugach SP).   26 mi S of Anchorage on Seward Highway. SEASON: 5/15-9/10; 15-day lmt. FACILITIES: 25 sites (tr -20), tbls, toil, cga, no drk wtr, food nearby. ACTIVITIES: fishing (salmon, Dolly Varden); hunting; hiking; picnicking. MISC.:**Entrance permit required; 20 acres; trails; located in a densely-wooded stand of Spruce trees. Don't go out on mud flats at low tide; dangerous. Chugach SP--495,000 acres, near the eastern edge of the Anchorage metro area; rugged peaks, glaciers, open alpine valleys.

Brooks River (Katmai NM). 250 mi SW of Anchorage by plane to King Salmon (commercial flights daily). SEASON: The campground and the National Monument are open all year.   Scheduled air service is available only from June 1 to September 5.   Off-season visitors must use chartered aircraft to reach the monument. FACILITIES: 10 tent sites, including 3 with wooden shelters.   Each site holds 4-6 people.   Tents can be rented. Firewood.   Available at Brooks Camp (1/4 mi): Freeze-dried food; meals, if arrangements are made several hours

beforehand at the lodge office; rents tents, cots, stoves, white gas (blazo), propane; hot showers ($2), including soap, towel and washcloth; sells fishing licenses and tackle. ACTIVITIES: hiking; fishing; naturalist-led walks; evening naturalist programs.   All-day bus tour to the Valley of Ten Thousand Smokes ($20); reservations must be made at the lodge office the previous day. MISC.: No entrance fee to NM. Located on the shore of Naknek Lake.   No pets.

Eagle River (Chugach SP). 14 mi N of Anchorage on Glenn Hwy; at milepost 14.   SEASON: 5/15-9/10;   15-day lmt. FACILITIES: 36 sites (tr -20), tbls, toil, cga, f, drk wtr. ACTIVITIES: fishing; snowmobiling; snowskiing; swimming nearby; canoeing; hunting; hiking. MISC.:**Entrance permit required. Located amidst Birch and Spruce trees. Trails. Pets. Chugach SP--495,000 acres, near the eastern edge of the Anchorage metro area; rugged peaks, glaciers, open alpine valleys.

Eklutna Basin Recreation Area (Chugach SP).   23 mi NE of Anchorage on Glenn Hwy; 8 mi E on gravel road (a little steep).   SEASON: 5/15-9/10;   15-day lmt.

**See page 12.

FACILITIES: 30 sites (tr -20), tbls, toil, f, cga, no drk wtr. ACTIVITIES: hiking; hunting; canoeing; picnicking. MISC.: **Entrance permit required. On Eklutna Lake. Trails; pets. Chugach SP—495,000 acres, near the eastern edge of the Anchorage metro area; rugged peaks, glaciers, open alpine valleys. Scenic—waterfalls, occasional herds of mountain sheep in the mountains nearby.

Long Lake Wayside. 86 mi N of Anchorage on Glenn Hwy; at milepost 86. SEASON: 5/15-9/10, 15-day lmt. FACILITIES: 8 sites (tr -20), tbls, toil, cga, f, drk wtr. ACTIVITIES: fishing; boating,l; canoeing. MISC.:Entrance permit required;** pets permitted if on a leash.

Peters Creek Wayside. 22 mi N of Anchorage on Glenn Hwy, at milepost 21.7. SEASON: 5/15-9/10, 15-day lmt. FACILITIES: 32 sites (tr -20), tbls, toil, cga, f, drk wtr. ACTIVITIES: fishing (Dolly Varden); picnicking. MISC.: **Entrance permit required; 52 acres; pets; located in a thick stand of Birch trees.

CANTWELL

Brushkana Creek Campground (BLM). 30 mi E of Cantwell on Denali Hwy at milepost 104.5. [Approximately 60 mi from Mt. McKinley NP.] SEASON: 6/1-10/30, 7-day lmt. FACILITIES: 7 primitive sites (tr -20), tbls, toil, f, cga, well drk wtr; group shelter for picnics with firepits. ACTIVITIES: fishing; hiking; hunting; picnicking. MISC.: 47 acres; pets on leash; scenic.

Byers Lake Campground (Denali SP). E of Cantwell on St Hwy 8 and Denali Hwy. SEASON: 5/15-9/15, 15-day lmt. FACILITIES: 100 sites (tr -20), tbls, toil, f, cga, drk wtr, pull-thru spaces. ACTIVITIES: fishing, hiking, canoeing, swimming, picnicking. MISC.:**Entrance permit required; trails; pets. The SP contains 282,000 acres of mountains, forests, rivers and lakes. Located approximately 130 mi N of Anchorage. Largely undeveloped. The Anchorage-Fairbanks Hwy, which crosses the park,offers excellent views of Mt. McKinley.

CHATANIKA

Chatanika River Wayside . On Steese Hwy (gravel surfaced) at milepost 39. [39 mi N of Fairbanks.] SEASON: 5/15-9/10, 15-day lmt. FACILITIES: 25 sites (tr -20), tbls, toil, cga, f, no drk wtr, unsurfaced boat ramp. ACTIVITIES: snowskiing nearby (in season); fishing; boating,l; canoeing; gold panning. MISC.:**Entrance permit required; pets. Beginning of federal BLM Chatanika River Canoe Trail, which ends at Elliott Highway.

CHITINA

Liberty Falls Wayside (BLM). From jct Richardson Hwy, Edgerton exit; 23 mi E. SEASON: 5/1-10/30, 7-day lmt. FACILITIES: tbls, toil, f, cga, stream water must be boiled for drinking. 3 primitive sites (tr -20). ACTIVITIES: fishing; hiking; picnicking. MISC.: 10 acres; scenic, large waterfall; pets on leash.

COOPER LANDING

*Crescent Lake Campsite (Chugach NF). 3-2/5 mi E of Cooper Landing on St Hwy 1; 2-9/10 mi NE on FS 961; 6-1/5 mi SE on TRAIL 8. SEASON: 10/1-5/31, FREE ($1 rest of yr); May and September are the best FREE months. FACILITIES: 3 tent sites, toil, cga, f. ACTIVITIES: boating, fishing. MISC.: 2 acres; lake; no drk wtr; scenic.

Engineer Lake (Kenai National Moose Range, NWR). Milepost 10, Skilak Loop Road. SEASON: 5/1-10/20, 14-day lmt. FACILITIES: tbls, toil, f, cga, drk wtr. 3 sites. ACTIVITIES: fishing; hunting; hiking; berry picking; in season — ice fishing, cross-country skiing, snowshoeing, ice skating. MISC.: Seven Lakes Trail begins here. Pets on leash.

Kelly Lake (Kenai National Moose Range, NWR). 1 mi from Hwy at milepost 68, Sterling Hwy. SEASON: 5/1-10/20, 14-day lmt. FACILITIES: 3 sites, tbls, toil, cga, f, drk wtr. ACTIVITIES: fishing (trout); boating,l; hunting (moose); berry picking; in season — ice fishing, cross-country skiing, snowshoeing, ice skating; picnicking. MISC.: Access to Seven Lakes Trail; pets on leash.

Kenai-Russian River (Kenai National Moose Range , NWR). Milepost 55, Sterling Hwy, 6 mi from Cooper Landing. SEASON: 5/1-10/20, 7-day lmt. FACILITIES: 20 sites (tr -20), tbls, toil, drk wtr. ACTIVITIES: fishing; boating,r; berry picking; hunting; in season—ice fishing, cross-country skiing, snowshoeing, ice skating. MISC.: acres; pets.

Peterson Lake (Kenai National Moose Range, NWR). Milepost 68, Sterling Hwy. SEASON: 5/1-10/20, 14-day lmt. FACILITIES: 3 sites, tbls, toil, cga, f, drk wtr. ACTIVITIES: fishing (trout); hunting (moose); hiking; berry picking;boating,l; in season—ice fishing, cross-country skiing, snowshoeing, ice skating. MISC.: Access to Seven Lakes Trail; pets.

Watson Lake (Kenai National Moose Range, NWR). Milepost 71, Sterling Hwy. SEASON: 5/1-10/20, 14-day lmt. FACILITIES: 3 sites, tbls, toil, f, cga, drk wtr. ACTIVITIES: boating,l; fishing (trout, red salmon); hunting (moose); hiking; berry picking; in season — ice fishing, cross-country skiing, snowshoeing, ice skating (winter). MISC.: Pets; access to Seven Lakes Trail.

COOPER LODGE

Cooper Creek Campground (Chugach NF).
LOCATION: -4/5 mi W of Cooper Lodge on
St Hwy 1. Sites are located on both
sides of road. SEASON: 9/6-5/24, FREE
($1 rest of yr); May and September best
FREE months; 14-day lmt. FACILITIES:
26 sites (tr -22), tbls, toil, well drk
wtr, store/gas (2 mi), laundry (3 mi),
food (5 mi). ACTIVITIES: fishing (Rainbow
and Dolly Varden Trout, Silver Salmon),
picnicking. MISC.: 8 acres;Cooper Creek;
pets are permitted if on a leash.

Quartz Creek (Chugach NF). 3-2/5 mi
E of Cooper Lodge on St Hwy 1; 3/10
mi S on FS 961. SEASON: 9/6-5/24, FREE
($1 rest of yr); May and September are
best FREE months; 14-day lmt. FACILI-
TIES: 35 sites (tr -32), tbls, toil, f,
cga, piped drk wtr. ACTIVITIES: swimming (beach); picnicking; boating,l;
berry picking; fishing (Lake Trout; Dolly
Varden; Rainbow Trout). MISC.: Lake;
pets; hiking; canoeing; showers/gas/store
(1 mi). Laundry (3 mi).

Russian River Campground (Chugach NF).
3-9/10 mi W of Cooper Lodge on St Hwy
1; 4/5 mi W on FS 979. SEASON: 9/6-
5/24, FREE ($1 rest of yr); May and
September are best FREE months; 14-day
lmt. FACILITIES: 91 sites (tr -32), tbls,
flush toil, f, cga, piped drk wtr, food
(1 mi), showers/store/gas (4 mi),
laundry (5 mi). ACTIVITIES: fishing
(Red and Silver Salmon; Rainbow Trout);
hiking; picnicking. MISC.:Russian River;
pets permitted if on a leash.

CORDOVA

Cabin Lake (Chugach NF). 11 mi SE
of Cordova on St Hwy 10; 3 mi N on
FS 535. SEASON: all year, weather permitting; 14-day lmt. FACILITIES: 11
sites (tr -16), tbls, toil, f, no drk
wtr. ACTIVITIES: picnicking. MISC.:
7 acres; lake; pets permitted on leash.

CRAIG

*****Canoe Point** (Tongass NF). 9½ mi SE
of Craig BY BOAT. SEASON: 5/25-9/5.
FACILITIES: 1 tent site, tbl, toil, cga,
f. ACTIVITIES: boating; picnicking.
MISC.: 1 acre; stream; elev 100 ft.

DELTA JUNCTION

Clearwater-Alcan Wayside. 8 mi NE of
milepost 1415 on the Alaska Hwy. Good,
level, gravel access road. Adjacent
to Clearwater Creek. SEASON: 5/15-9/10,
15-day lmt. FACILITIES: 12 sites (tr
-20), tbls, toil, f, cga, no drk wtr.
ACTIVITIES: fishing (grayling, whitefish); boating,l; canoeing; picnicking.
MISC.:**Entrance permit required; pets;
herd of buffalo roams nearby.

Donnelly Creek Wayside. On Richardson
Hwy, 28 mi S of Delta Junction, at milepost 238. SEASON: 5/15-9/10, 15-day
lmt. FACILITIES: 12 sites (tr -20), tbls,
toil, cga, f, no drk wtr. ACTIVITIES:
fishing (grayling); picnicking. MISC.:
**Entrance permit required; pets. Heavy
winds can be a problem for tents.

EAGLE CITY

Liberty Creek Campground (BLM). From
jct of Alaska Hwy and Taylor, N on
Taylor to milepost 131.6. SEASON: 3/20-
10/15, 7-day lmt. FACILITIES: 7 primitive sites (tr -20), tbls, toil, f, cga,
stream water must be boiled for drinking. ACTIVITIES: fishing; hunting; picnicking. MISC.: 3 acres; scenic; pets.

FAIRBANKS

Bedrock Creek Campground (BLM). 119
mi N of Fairbanks on Steese Hwy; at
milepost 119 (near Central). SEASON:
5/15-10/15, 7-day lmt. FACILITIES: 8
primitive sites (tr -20), tbls, toil, f,
cga, stream water must be boiled for
drinking. ACTIVITIES: fishing (grayling);
rockhounding; gold panning; picnicking.
MISC.: 14 acres; Bedrock Creek; view
of Midnight Sun; pets. Take insect repellent and/or head nets during summer
(lots of mosquitoes.)

Cripple Creek Campground (BLM). At milepost 60 on Steese Hwy, near Fairbanks.
SEASON: 4/15-12/15, 7-day lmt. FACILI-
TIES: 21 primitive sites (tr -20), tbls,
toil, f, cga, well drk wtr. ACTIVITIES:
fishing; picnicking; hunting; boating;
hiking; rockhounding. MISC.: 20 acres;
scenic; pets permitted if on a leash.

Harding Lake Recreation Area (SRA).
1 mi from 321/Richardson Hwy, on side
road. SEASON: 5/15-9/10, 15-day lmt.
FACILITIES: 89 sites (tr -30), tbls, toil,
f,cga, store, food, dump, picnic shelters,
well drk wtr, surfaced boat ramp. ACTIV-
ITIES: boating,lr; picnicking; canoeing,r;
fishing (trout, pike); swimming (beach).
MISC.:**Entrance permit required;95 acres;
pets on leash. One of Alaska's best State
campgrounds.

Ketchem Creek Campground (BLM). N of
Fairbanks on Steese Hwy to milepost 128;
6 mi E on Circle Hot Springs Rd.
SEASON: 6/1-10/1, 7-day lmt. FACILITIES:
7 primitive sites (tr -20), tbls, toil,
f, cga, stream water must be boiled for
drinking. ACTIVITIES: fishing (grayling);
hunting; picnicking. MISC.: 3 acres;
pets permitted on leash; scenic.

Tolovana River Campground (BLM). 11
mi N of Fairbanks on Steese Hwy, jct
of Elliot and Fox; 57 mi W on Elliot Hwy
at milepost 57 (Elliot Hwy is gravel).
SEASON: 4/15-10/15, 7-day lmt. FACILI-
TIES: 5 primitive sites (tr -20), tbls,

toil, f, cga, stream water must be boiled for drinking. ACTIVITIES: fishing (grayling); hunting; gold panning; picnicking. MISC.: 9 acres; pets on leash; scenic.

GLENALLEN

Dry Creek Wayside. 5 mi N of Glenallen jct on Richardson Hwy. SEASON: 5/15-9/10, 15-day lmt. FACILITIES: 13 sites (tr --20), tbls, toil, f, cga, no drk wtr; store nearby. MISC.: 128 acres; pets. Once the site of an Indian village.

Lake Louise Wayside. 20 mi NW of milepost 159 on Glenn Hwy (twisting gravel access rd). Located next to Lake Louise. SEASON: 5/15-9/10, 15-day lmt. FACILITIES: 5 sites (tr -20), tbls, toil, f, cga. ACTIVITIES: fishing (grayling, trout); boating, unsurfaced ramp; canoeing; picnicking. MISC.: Access road crosses winter range of caribou herds. Heavy use during hunting season. Pets.

Little Nelchina Wayside. On Glenn Hwy, at milepost 138 (steep access rd). On the shores of Little Nelchina River. SEASON: 5/15-9/10, 15-day lmt. FACILITIES: 6 sites (tr -20), tbls, toil, cga, f, no drk wtr. ACTIVITIES: picnicking. MISC.:**Entrance permit required. 22 acres. Fossil beds are located upriver.

Tolsona Creek Wayside. On Glenn Hwy, at milepost 172. SEASON: 5/15-9/10, 15-day lmt. FACILITIES: 5 sites (tr -20), tbls, toil, cga, no drk wtr. ACTIVITIES: fishing, picnicking. MISC.:**Entrance permit required. 40 acres. Pets.

HAINES

Chilkoot Lake Wayside. 11 mi N of Haines; 5½ mi from ferry terminal. SEASON: 5/15-9/10; 15-day lmt. FACILITIES: 32 sites (tr -20), tbls, toil, cga, f, drk wtr, shelter. ACTIVITIES:fishing; swimming; boating,l; canoeing; picnicking. MISC.:**Entrance permit required. 80 acres; scenic; pets on leash.

Mosquito Lake Wayside. At milepost 26 on Haines Hwy; 35 mi from ferry terminal; 2-2/5 mi on Mosquito Lake Road. SEASON: 5/15-9/10, 15-day lmt. FACILITIES: 13 sites (tr -20), tbls, toil, cga, f, drk wtr, shelter. ACTIVITIES: picnicking; fishing (trout); canoeing; boating,l. MISC.:**Entrance permit required. 5 acres; pets permitted on leash.

Portage Cove Wayside. 1 ml S of Haines; 6 mi from ferry terminal. SEASON: 5/15-9/10, 15-day lmt. FACILITIES: 9 sites (tr -20), tbls, toil, cga, f, no drk wtr. ACTIVITIES: picnicking. MISC.:**Entrance permit required. 7 acres; scenic; pets allowed on leash.

HOMER

Anchor River Wayside. 8 mi N of Homer on Sterling Hwy; 4 mi SE of Anchor Point (on Anchor River). SEASON: 5/15-9/10, 15-day lmt. FACILITIES: 7 sites (tr -20), t˵ls, toil, cga, f, no drk wtr. ACTIVITIES: fishing (trout, salmon); picnicking. MISC.:**Entrance permit required. 57 acres; pets on leash.

Stariski Wayside. 22 mi N of Homer on Sterling Hwy; at milepost 154. SEASON: 5/15-9/10, 15-day lmt. FACILITIES: 12 sites (tr -20), tbls, toil, cga, f, no drk wtr, shelter. ACTIVITIES: fishing nearby; picnicking. MISC.: **Entrance permit required. 30 acres; pets.

HOPE

Coeur D'Alene (Chugach NF). 7-2/5 mi SE of Hope on FS 901. SEASON: 5/15-9/5, 14-day lmt. FACILITIES: 5 tent sites, tbls, toil, cga, f, no drk wtr. ACTIVITIES: moose and ptarmigan hunting; alpine hiking; berry picking; picnicking; fishing (2 mi). MISC.: 1 acre; elev 1400 ft; stream; pets on leash.

Porcupine (Chugach NF). 9/10 mi NW of Hope on FS 14. SEASON: 9/2-5/24, FREE ($2 rest of yr); 14-day lmt. May and September are best FREE months. FACILITIES: 24 sites (tr -22), tbls, toil, cga, f, well drk wtr. ACTIVITIES: picnicking; fishing (1 mi). MISC.: 10 acres; elev 100 ft; Old Hershey Mine (2 mi); food and store (1 mi); pets on leash.

JUNEAU

Auke Village Campground (Chatham Area; Tongass NF). 15-1/10 mi N of Juneau (2 mi W of Auke Bay). Located in a thick Spruce forest. SEASON: 9/15-5/15, FREE ($1 rest of yr); 14-day lmt. Reservations required during pay season. FACILITIES: 11 tent sites, tbls, flush toil, cga, f, drk wtr, store (4 mi), large community shelter with fireplace, water system, and sanitary facilities. ACTIVITIES: boating,dl; picnicking; fishing (salmon); waterskiing; swimming. MISC.: 4 acres; scenic; pets; Indian artifacts. Water shut off during free season. Located adjacent to the saltwater near the site of an old Tlinget Indian encampment.

*Bartlett Cove (Glacier Bay NM). 50 mi from Juneau BY AIR. SEASON: all year. FACILITIES: 5 primitive tent sites, f. ACTIVITIES: fishing; boating,d.

Mendenhall Lake Campground (Chatham Area; Tongass NF). 15 mi NW of Juneau, on Mendenhall Lake. SEASON: 9/15-5/15, FREE ($1 rest of yr), 14-day lmt. Reservations required during pay season. FACILITIES: 65 sites (tr -22), tbls, toil, cga, f, drk wtr, ice, food/store (5 mi).

**See page 12.

18

ACTIVITIES: hiking; swimming; boating,d; picnicking; fishing (3 mi). MISC.: 22 acres; nature trails and visitor center nearby; pets on leash. Good view of the glacier. Water is shut off during free season.

KENAI

Bernice Lake Wayside. 10 mi N of Kenai on N Kenai Rd. SEASON: 5/15-9/10, 15-day lmt. FACILITIES: 11 sites (tr -20), tbls, toil, cga, f, drk wtr, food nearby. ACTIVITIES: swimming (beach); boating,l (unsurfaced boat ramp); canoeing; picnicking. MISC.:**Entrance permit required; 7 acres.

Bishop Creek (Captain Cook Recreation Area). 24 mi N of Kenai on N Kenai Hwy. SEASON: 5/15-9/10, 15-day lmt. FACILITIES: 15 sites (tr -20), tbls, toil, cga, f, drk wtr. ACTIVITIES: hiking; picnicking. MISC.:**Entrance permit required. Trails; pets on leash.

Discovery Campground (Captain Cook Recreation Area). 24 mi N of Kenai on N Kenai Hwy. SEASON: 5/15-9/10, 15-day lmt. FACILITIES: 57 sites (tr -20), tbls, toil, cga, f, drk wtr. ACTIVITIES: picnicking. MISC.:**Entrance permit required. Pets allowed if on a leash.

Stormy Lake (Captain Cook Recreation Area). 24 mi N of Kenai on N Kenai Hwy. SEASON: 5/15-9/10, 15-day lmt. FACILITIES: 10 sites (tr -20), tbls, toil, cga, drk wtr, shelter. ACTIVITIES: hiking; boating,l; canoeing; picnicking; fishing; swimming (beach). MISC.:**Entrance permit required. Trails; pets.

KETCHIKAN

Last Chance (Tongass NF). 4-2/5 mi NW of Ketchikan on St Hwy 7; 2-4/5 mi NE on FS 39. SEASON: 5/25-9/5, 14-day lmt. FACILITIES: 23 sites (tr -22), tbls, toil, cga, no drk wtr, store/gas (3 mi). ACTIVITIES: boating,d (1 mi); swimming (1 mi); hiking; picnicking; fishing (trout and salmon). MISC.: 6 acres; elev 100 ft; stream; nature trails; pets.

*Perseverance Trail (Tongass NF). 2-1/10 mi long. Begins approx. 1/8 mi past the Forest Service Visitor Center at Ward Lake and terminates at Perseverance Lake. There is a parking area at the trailhead. The first 1/8 mi of trail is gravel, providing good footing. The remainder of the trail is boardwalk, passing through stands of Sitka spruce and western hemlock. A swinging bridge crosses Ward Creek. This trail is easy to walk, well-suited for family groups. Outstanding view at Perseverance Lake, with its mountainous backdrop. ACTIVITIES: nature study, hiking, berry picking, fishing in the lakes, and FREE CAMPING. Map/information can be obtained from the Visitor Center, or by

writing: Supt.; Tongass NF; Federal Bldg; Ketchikan, AK 99901; 907/225-6141.

Settlers Cove Campground (Tongass NF). 12½ mi NW of Ketchikan on St Hwy 7; 4-1/10 mi NE on FS 1. Located next to the beach, one of the finest sandy beaches on the island. SEASON: 5/25-9/5, 14-day lmt. FACILITIES: 9 sites (tr -22), tbls, toil, cga, f, piped drk wtr. ACTIVITIES: swimming; picnicking; fishing. MISC.: 4 acres; elev 100 ft; pets. Aug.-Sept.: hundreds of salmon spawn in the tidal zone of the stream. During early parts of their run, you can catch them by spin-casting with lures.

Signal Creek (Tongass NF). 4-2/5 mi NW of Ketchikan on St Hwy 7; 4/5 mi E on FS 39. Located beside Ward Lake. SEASON: 5/25-9/5, 14-day lmt. FACILITIES: 25 sites (tr -22), tbls, toil, cga, f, piped drk wtr, store/gas (1 mi). ACTIVITIES: swimming (1 mi); boating,d (3 mi); picnicking; fishing (salmon, trout); hiking. MISC.: 8 acres; elev 100 ft; Signal Creek; pets. During Aug. or Sept., salmon spawn in the outlet area of the lake. Entrance to Ward Lake Nature Trl (18 interpretive signs).

3 C's CG (Tongass NF). 4-2/5 mi NW of Ketchikan on St Hwy 7; 1 mi E on FS 39 [1/4 mi up the rd from Signal Creek Campground]. SEASON: 5/25-10/31, 14-day lmt. FACILITIES: 4 sites (tr -32), tbls, toil, cga, f, piped drk wtr, store/gas (1 mi). ACTIVITIES: swimming (1 mi); picnicking; fishing (1 mi); boating (3 mi). MISC.: 2 acres; elev 100 ft; nature trail; pets.

*Ward Creek Trail (Tongass NF). 3-9/10 mi long. Two access points: Connell Lake Dam parking lot; FS 39, approx. 1 mi SW of the Lake Harriet Hunt Rd jct. Combination of gravel, boardwalk and natural surfaces; a few mudholes. ACTIVITIES: hiking along Ward Creek, Talbot Lake and Connell Lake; berry picking; fishing; nature study; FREE CAMPING. Map/information can be obtained from Visitor Center or by writing to: Supt.; Tongass NF; Federal Bldg.; Ketchikan, AK 99901; 907/225-6141.

KODIAK

Camping in the Area. Hundreds of beautiful spots for camping are located along the 60-some miles of roadway from Kodiak to Chiniak, on beaches, along streams, near lakes, or along some abandoned road. These are undeveloped and one must take along all their facilities. Pets.

Fort Abercrombie. 4½ mi NE of Kodiak on Miller Point. SEASON: 5/15-9/10, 15-day lmt. FACILITIES: 7 sites (tr -20), tbls, toil, cga, f, no drk wtr. ACTIVITIES: swimming; picnicking; fishing.

MISC.:**Entrance permit required. 183
acres; pets. Ft. Abercrombie is an old
WWII fortification.

McKINLEY PARK

Igloo (Mt. McKinley NP). 33 mi from
McKinley Railroad Depot, at milepost 34.
SEASON: 5/15-9/15, 14-day lmt. FACILI-
TIES: 7 tent sites, tbls, toil, cga, boil
river water for drinking. ACTIVITIES:
picnicking. MISC.: Reservations are required and may be made in person at
Riley Creek Visitor Center beginning only
for the period of intended, continuous
use--no advance reservations. Elev
2900 ft; pets allowed on leash.

*Morino Campground (Mt. McKinley NP).
1/8 mi W of McKinley Railroad Depot BY
TRAIL. SEASON: all year, 14-day lmt.
FACILITIES: 15 tent sites, tbls, toil,
river water must be boiled for drinking.
ACTIVITIES: hiking; picnicking. MISC.:
Elev 1600 ft; pets. Walk-in campground
for backpackers arriving by train; no
parking available.   No open fires.

Sanctuary River (Mt. McKinley NP).
22 mi from McKinley Railroad Depot,
at milepost 22. SEASON: 5/15-9/15,
14-day lmt. FACILITIES: 7 sites (tr
-15), toil, stream water must be boiled
for drinking.   MISC.: Reservations are
required and may be made in person
at Riley Creek Visitor Center beginning
only for the period intended continuous
use--no advance reservations.   Elev
2400 ft.   Pets permitted on leash.

MOOSE PASS

Primrose Landing (Chugach NF). 11-2/5
mi S of Moose Pass on St Hwy 9; 1-1/5
mi N on FS 953. [At lower end of Kenai
Lake.] SEASON: 9/6-5/24, FREE ($1 rest
of yr), 14-day lmt. May and Sept. are
best FREE months. FACILITIES: 10 sites
(tr -22), tbls, toil, cga, f, drk wtr,
unsurfaced boat ramp. ACTIVITIES: picnicking; boating,dl. MISC.:3 acres;pets.

Ptarmigan Creek (Chugach NF). 5-4/5
mi S of Moose Pass on St Hwy 9; 1/10
mi E on FS 952. [24 mi N of Seward.]
On Ptarmigan Creek. SEASON: 9/6-5/24,
FREE ($1 rest of yr), 14-day lmt. FA-
CILITIES: 23 sites (tr -22), tbls, toil,
cga, f, well drk wtr. ACTIVITIES: mountain goat hunting; hiking; picnicking;
fishing (Rainbow & Dolly Varden Trout,
grayling). MISC.: 8 acres; elev 500
ft; pets permitted if on a leash.

Tenderfoot Creek Campground (Chugach
NF). 15½ mi NW of Moose Pass on St
Hwy 1; ½ mi S on FS 925. SEASON: 9/6-
5/25, FREE ($1 rest of yr), 14-day lmt.
FACILITIES: 14 sites (tr -16), tbls,
toil, cga, f, well drk wtr; food/gas/ice/
showers (1 mi). ACTIVITIES: picnicking;

fishing (Dolly Varden). MISC.: 9 acres;
elev 1300 ft; pets.   Among stands of
White Spruce.

Tern Lake (Chugach NF). 7½ mi NW of
Moose Pass on St Hwy 9. [37 mi N of
Seward.] On Tern Lake. SEASON: 9/6-
5/24, FREE ($1 rest of yr), 14-day lmt.
May and Sept. are best FREE months.
FACILITIES: 28 sites (tr -32), tbls,
toil, cga, f, well drk wtr. ACTIVITIES:
boating; picnicking.   MISC.: 8 acres;
elev 700 ft; pets. Nesting area for
Arctic Tern.   Don't get too close to
their nests or they'll attack you.

NINILCHIK

Ninilchik Wayside.   On Sterling Hwy;
at milepost 138. SEASON: 5/15-9/10, 15-
day lmt. FACILITIES: 15 sites (tr -20),
tbls, toil, cga, f, no drk wtr, food/store
nearby. ACTIVITIES: picnicking; fishing
(salmon, trout). MISC.: **Entrance permit required. 13 acres; pets on leash.
Scenic--mountains/volcanoes.

NOME

Salmon Lake Campground (BLM). 38 mi
N of Nome on Nome-Kougarok Road. SEA-
SON: 6/15-10/1, no time lmt. FACILITIES:
6 primitive sites (no size limit), toil,
lake water must be boiled for drinking.
ACTIVITIES: boating,l; fishing; hunting.
MISC.: 5 acres; scenic; pets on leash.

PALMER

Big Lake Wayside, East. 30 mi W of Palmer on St Hwy 3. On Big Lake. SEASON:
5/15-9/10, 15-day lmt. FACILITIES: 14
sites (tr -20), tbls, toil, cga, f, drk
wtr. ACTIVITIES: swimming; waterskiing;
boating,lr; canoeing; sailing; flying;
picnicking; fishing (trout); hunting.
MISC.: **Entrance permit required. 19
acres; surfaced boat ramp; pets.

Big Lake Wayside, South. 30 mi W of
Palmer on St Hwy 3. On Big Lake. SEA-
SON:5/15-9/10, 15-day lmt. FACILITIES:
13 sites (tr -20), tbls, toil, cga, f, drk
wtr, surfaced boat ramp. ACTIVITIES:
swimming; waterskiing; boating,lr; sailing; canoeing; picnicking;fishing (trout);
flying; hunting. MISC.: **Entrance permit
required.   16 acres; pets on leash.

Finger Lake Wayside. 6 mi E of Palmer
at Finger Lake. SEASON: 5/15-9/10, 15-
day lmt. FACILITIES: 36 sites (tr -20),
tbls, toil, cga, f, drk wtr. ACTIVITIES:
hiking; ice fishing during colder months;
canoeing; boating,l; picnicking; fishing
(silver salmon); nearby is golf, boat
rental. MISC.:   **Entrance permit required.   47 acres; trails; pets are permitted on leash.

King Mountain Wayside. Glenn Highway; at milepost 76. SEASON: 5/15-9/10, 15-day lmt. FACILITIES: 22 sites (tr -20), tbls, toil, cga, f, drk wtr, shelter, food nearby. ACTIVITIES: picnicking. MISC.: **Entrance permit required. 20 acres; pets permitted if on leash.

Matanuska Glacier Wayside. On Glenn Hwy; at milepost 100. SEASON: 5/15-9/10, 15-day lmt. FACILITIES: 6 sites (tr -20), tbls, toil, cga, no drk wtr. ACTIVITIES: hiking; picnicking; fishing. MISC.: **Entrance permit required. 231 acres; pets; trail leads to Matanuska Glacier.

Moose Creek Wayside. 5 mi N of Palmer on Glenn Hwy; at milepost 54.5. SEASON:5/15-9/10, 15-day lmt. FACILITIES: 10 sites (tr -20), tbls, toil, cga, f, spring drk wtr. ACTIVITIES: picnicking; fishing (Dolly Varden). MISC.: **Entrance permit required. 40 acres; pets. Fossils upstream in river bed. Historic: located on remains of coal mining area.

Nancy Lake Wayside. 25 mi NW of Palmer on St Hwy 3, at White's Crossing. Located on 700-acre Nancy Lake, which has 24 mi of shoreline. SEASON: 5/15-9/10, 15-day lmt. FACILITIES: 30 sites (tr -20), tbls, toil, cga, f, drk wtr, surfaced boat ramp. ACTIVITIES: boating,l; canoeing; hiking; picnicking; fishing (trout). MISC.: **Entrance permit required. 35 acres; pets.

Rocky Lake Wayside. 28 mi W of Palmer on St Hwy 3 (narrow access rd). SEASON: 5/15-9/10, 15-day lmt. FACILITIES: 10 sites (tr -20), tbls, toil, cga, f, drk wtr. ACTIVITIES: boating,l; canoeing; picnicking; fishing (trout). MISC.: **Entrance permit required. 19 acres; pets permitted if they are on a leash.

PAXSON

Fielding Lake Wayside (BLM). 15 mi N of Paxson on Richardson Hwy at milepost 201. Located on large Fielding Lake. SEASON: 6/1-10/30, 7-day lmt. FACILITIES: 7 primitive sites (tr-20), tbls, toil, cga, f, well drk wtr, unsurfaced boat ramp. ACTIVITIES: hunting; canoeing,l; hiking; picnicking; fishing (trout, grayling, burbot); boating,l; rockhounding. MISC.: 26 acres; pets; scenic--view of Alaska Range.

Paxson Lake Campground (BLM). 10 mi S of Paxson on Richardson Hwy; at milepost 175. SEASON: 6/1-10/31, 7-day lmt. FACILITIES: 20 sites (no size lmt), tbls, toil, cga, f, drk wtr. ACTIVITIES: hiking; canoeing,l; boating,l; swimming; picnicking; fishing. MISC.: 200 acres; pets; stream; scenic.

Paxson Lake Wayside (BLM). 5 mi S of Paxson on Richardson Hwy; at milepost 181 (narrow twisting access rd;not recommended for trailers). Located on the shore of Paxson Lake, on a sandspit. SEASON: 6/1-10/30, 7-day lmt. FACILITIES: 4 primitive sites (no size lmt), tbls, toil, cga, f, pull-thru spaces, drk wtr. ACTIVITIES: picnicking; fishing (trout, whitefish, grayling); boating,l (unsurfaced); steep access; sand can be a problem); canoeing; golf nearby. MISC.: 4 acres; Paxson Lake; pets allowed on leash.

Tangle Lakes Campground (BLM). W of Paxson on Denali Hwy to milepost 22; ½ mi on access rd. SEASON: 6/1-10/30, 7-day lmt. FACILITIES: 13 sites (tr -20), tbls, toil, cga, f, stream water must be boiled for drinking; store/food nearby. ACTIVITIES: boating,l; hunting; canoeing; hiking; rockhounding; picnicking; fishing (trout, grayling, burbot). MISC.:40 acres; unmarked trails; scenic; stream; pets permitted on leash.

Tangle River Boat Launch (BLM). 22 mi W of Paxson on Denali Hwy. SEASON: 6/1-10/30, 7-day lmt. FACILITIES: 7 primitive sites (no size lmt), tbls,toil, cga, f, well drk wtr, pull-thru spaces; store/food nearby. ACTIVITIES: boating,l; hunting; canoeing; picnicking; fishing; hiking. MISC.: 3 acres; pets; unmarked trails; scenic.

PETERSBURG

Ohmer Creek (Tongass NF). 25 mi S of Petersburg on Mitkof Hwy. SEASON: all yr, no time lmt. FACILITIES: 13 tent sites, tbls, toil, cga, no drk wtr. ACTIVITIES: berry picking; hiking; swimming (5 mi); boating,d (5 mi); picnicking; fishing (trout, salmon). MISC.: 5 acres; Ohmer Creek; pets on leash.

PORTAGE

Bertha Creek (Chugach NF). 13-3/10 mi SW of Portage on St Hwy 1. SEASON: 9/6-5/24, FREE ($1 rest of yr), 14-day lmt. May and Sept. are the best FREE months. FACILITIES: 10 sites (tr -16), tbls, toil, cga, f, well drk wtr. ACTIVITIES: hiking; picnicking. MISC.: 4 acres; trails; scenic overlook; pets.

PORTAGE JUNCTION

Beaver Pond (Chugach NF). 2-4/5 mi SE of Portage Junction on St Hwy 113. SEASON: 9/6-5/24, FREE ($1 rest of yr), 14-day lmt. May and Sept. are best FREE months. FACILITIES: 7 sites (tr -16), tbls, toil, cga, f, well drk wtr, food/showers/visitor center (2 mi), gas (3 mi). ACTIVITIES: hiking; picnicking. MISC.: 4 acres; elev 100 ft; pets. Caution: If you see foul-weather warnings on Portage Hwy, postpone visit. Winds can get up to 100 mph.

**See page 12.

ALASKA

Black Bear (Chugach NF). 3-9/10 mi SE
of Portage Junction on St Hwy 113. SEA-
SON:9/6-5/24, FREE ($1 rest of yr), 14-
day lmt. May and Sept. are best FREE
months. FACILITIES: 12 sites (tr -22),
tbls, toil, cga, f, drk wtr, visitor center
nearby, food/showers (1 mi), store (4
mi). ACTIVITIES: hiking; picnicking.
MISC.: 4 acres; pets. Caution: If you
see foul-weather warnings on Portage
Hwy, postpone visit. Winds can get up
to 100 mph.

Granite Creek (Chugach NF). 15-7/10 mi
SW of Portage Junction on St Hwy 1; ½
mi SW on FS 926. SEASON: 9/6-5/24, FREE
($1 rest of yr), 14-day lmt. May and
Sept. are best FREE months. FACILITIES:
19 sites (tr -16), tbls, toil, cga, f, well
drk wtr. ACTIVITIES: picnicking.
MISC.: 12 acres; elev 600 ft; pets; Granite Creek. Located where Bench Creek,
Center Creek, and Granite Creek meet
to form the East Fork of Six-Mile Creek.

Williwaw (Chugach NF). 4-1/5 mi SE of
Portage Junction on St Hwy 113. SEASON:
9/6-5/24, FREE ($1 rest of yr), 14-day
lmt. May and Sept. are best FREE months.
FACILITIES: 36 sites (tr -16), tbls, toil,
cga, f, well drk wtr, food/showers/visitor
center (1 mi), gas (4 mi). ACTIVITIES:
hiking; picnicking. MISC.: 22 acres;
elev 100 ft; nature trails; pets. Caution:
If you see foul-weather warnings on Portage Hwy, postpone visit. Winds can
get up to 100 mph.

SEWARD

*Johnson Pass Trail (Chugach NF). Trail-
head is approx. at milepost 64 on Seward
Hwy. The trail is 22 mi long. Access
into alpine country. Spectacular views.
Bench Lake is above timberline; so no
firewood. During winter, avalanche danger is high beyond mile 2. Pets allowed
on leash (for their own protection). Use
existing campsites and cga. Additional
information/map: Supt.; Chugach NF;
Box 275; Seward, AK 99664; 224-3023.

*Lost Lake Trail (Chugach NF). Trailhead
is at gravel pits at milepost 5 on Seward
Hwy. 7-mile-long trail. Good family trail.
Access into alpine country. Spectacular
views. See black bear in the spring.
Salmonberry patches in Aug. near Mile
4/5. Lost Lake is above timberline; no
firewood. Snowmobile trail leaves summer
trail at Mile 1.5. Use existing sites.
Pets on leash. Info/map: Supt.; Chugach
NF; Box 275; Seward, AK 99664; 224-3023.

Ptarmigan Creek Trail (Chugach NF).
Trailhead is located at milepost 23 on
Seward Hwy. Trail is 3½ mi long; good
family trail. Good chance of seeing
sheep & goats on mountain peaks/slopes.
Take insect repellent. When traveling
bear country take a .30/06 or larger
caliber rifle. Trail is closed to all

motorized vehicles 4/1-11/30; closed to
horses April, May, June. Avalanche hazards during winter. Use existing campsites and cga. Pets on leash for their
own protection. Information/maps: Supt.;
Chugach NF; Box 275; Seward, AK 99664.

*Resurrection Pass Trail System (Chugach
NF). One of the most popular trails
in Chugach NF. Several routes available:
Hope to Schooner Bend (37½ mi); Hope
to Seward Hwy via Devils Pass (30 mi);
Seward Hwy to Schooner Bend, (27½ mi).
Take insect repellent. Chances of seeing
brown bear are remote. Snowmobiling
and cross-country skiing in winter.
Devils Creek Trail not suitable in winter
due to avalanche danger; blizzards can
be expected in Resurrection Pass. Use
existing campsites and cga. Pets on
leash for their own protection. Use of
motorized vehicles is prohibited 2/15-
11/30. Information/map: Supt.; Chugach
NF; 2221 E. Northern Lights Blvd., Room
230; Anchorage, AK 99504; 274-6061.

*Russian Lakes Trail (Chugach NF).
Trailhead is the Parking Lot in Russian
Lake Campground, milepost 52, Sterling
Hwy. Trail is 20 mi long. Brown bear
country; carry a rifle of .30/06 caliber
or larger. In winter, good snowmobiling
to Lower Lake only; avalanche danger
beyond. Trail is closed to all motorized
vehicles 4/1-11/30; closed to horses
April, May, June. Use existing campsites and cga. Pets on leash for their
own protection. Information/map: Supt.;
Chugach NF; Box 275; Seward, AK 99664.

SITKA

Sawmill Creek (Tongass NF). 6 mi SE
of Sitka on FS 11 (steep access rds).
Adjacent to Sawmill Creek. SEASON: all
yr; but not maintained as consistently
in winter. 14-day lmt. FACILITIES:
11 sites (tr -32), tbls, toil, cga, f,
no drk wtr; food/gas (5 mi). ACTIVI-
TIES: swimming (water is cool); waterskiing; boating,dl; picnicking; fishing
(trout); hiking; berry picking; snow
ski on Harbor Mountain in winter (no
ski lift, so snowmobile or walking required during winter). MISC.: 4 acres;
elev 300 ft; pets. ½ mi by rd to Blue
Lake. At the beginning of the Beaver Lake
Trail.

Starrigavan (Tongass NF). 6-3/5 mi N
of Sitka on FS 11 (Halibut Point Rd).
SEASON: all yr; not maintained as consistently during winter. 14-day lmt.
FACILITIES: 24 sites (tr -32), tbls, toil,
cga, f, well drk wtr. ACTIVITIES: swimming (water is cool); boating,d (1 mi);
picnicking; fishing (1 mi); waterskiing;
berry picking; snow skiing on Harbor
Mountain (no ski lift, so snowmobile or
walking is required during winter).
MISC.: 28 acres; elev 100 ft; stream;
pets. Alaska State Ferry Terminal (½
mile from campground).

SKAGWAY

Liarsville. 1 mi E of Skagway; 1½ mi from ferry terminal (easy access rd). SEASON: 5/15-9/10, 15-day lmt. FACILITIES: 7 sites (tr -20), tbls, toil, cga, f, no drk wtr, store/food nearby. ACTIVITIES: picnicking; fishing. MISC.: **Entrance permit required. 2 acres; pets.

SOLDOTNA

Izaak Walton Wayside. 6 mi N of Soldotna on Sterling Highway. SEASON: 5/15-9/10, 15-day lmt. FACILITIES: 42 sites (tr -20), tbls, toil, cga, f, no drk wtr. ACTIVITIES: picnicking; fishing. MISC.: **Entrance permit reqd. 79 acres; pets.

Johnson Lake Wayside. 16 mi S of Soldotna on Sterling Hwy; at milepost 112. SEASON: 5/15-9/10, 15-day lmt. FACILITIES: 20 sites (tr -20), tbls, toil, cga, f, no drk wtr. ACTIVITIES: swimming; canoeing; boating,l; picnicking; fishing (salmon). MISC.: **Entrance permit required. 56 acres; pets permitted on leash.

Kasilof River Wayside. 16 mi S of Soldotna on Sterling Hwy. SEASON: 5/15-9/10, 15-day lmt. FACILITIES: 10 sites (tr -20), tbls, toil, cga, f, drk wtr. ACTIVITIES: picnicking; fishing. MISC.: **Entrance permit required. 47 acres; pets.

SOLDOTNA

Tustumena Lake Campground (Kenai National Moose Range; NWR). From milepost 112, Sterling Hwy; 6 mi E on access rd. Located on Kasilof River, 1 mi downstream from Tustumena Lake . SEASON: 5/1-10/20, 14-day lmt. FACILITIES: 10 sites (tr -20), tbls, toil, cga, f, drk wtr. ACTIVITIES: boating,l (caution small boats: high winds appear with no notice); picnicking; fishing (trout); hunting; berry picking; winter––ice fishing, cross-country skiing, snowshoeing, ice skating. MISC.: 10 acres; no motorbikes; pets permitted on leash.

SOURDOUGH

Sourdough Campground (BLM). From jct Richardson Hwy and Tok, 19 mi N on Richardson Hwy. SEASON: 5/1-10/30, 7-day lmt. FACILITIES: 8 primitive sites (tr -20); not recommended for large trailers. Tbls, toil, cga, f, stream water must be boiled for drinking. ACTIVITIES: picnicking; fishing (grayling); hunting; boating; canoeing, takeout; hiking. MISC.: 20 acres; stream; pets. Near Trans-Alaska Pipeline. Nearby (N), caribou herds use this area when migrating to and from their winter ranges. Scenic –– views of 3 mountain ranges: Chugach (SW), Wrangells (SE), Alaska Range. Food/store are nearby.

STERLING

Bottinentnin Lake Campground (Kenai National Moose Range; NWR). Milepost 20, on Skilak Lake Rd. SEASON: 5/1-10/20, 14-day lmt. FACILITIES: tbls, 3 sites, toil, cga, f, no drk wtr. ACTIVITIES: hunting; picnicking; fishing (red salmon); berry picking; boating (the lake is very shallow; 8-10 ft deep); winter –– ice fishing, cross-country skiing, snowshoeing, ice skating. MISC.: pets permitted if on a leash.

Dolly Varden Lake (Kenai National Moose Range; NWR). Milepost 14, Swanson River Rd, near Sterling. SEASON: 5/1-10/20, 14-day lmt. FACILITIES: 10 sites (tr -15), tbls, toil, cga, f, drk wtr. ACTIVITIES: swimming; boating,l; berry picking; hunting; picnicking; fishing (Dolly Varden, trout); winter –– ice fishing, cross-country skiing, snowshoeing, ice skating.

Hidden Lake (Kenai National Moose Range; NWR). Milepost 4, Skilak Lake Rd; 20 mi from Sterling. SEASON: all yr, 7-day lmt. FACILITIES: 40 sites (tr -20), tbls, toil, cga, f, drk wtr. ACTIVITIES: hunting; hiking; waterskiing; berry picking; boating,l; picnicking; fishing (trout, salmon); swimming. Winter –– ice fishing, cross-country skiing, snowshoeing, ice skating. MISC.: 15 acres, pets, trails.

Jim's Landing (Kenai National Moose Range; NWR). 18 mi E of Sterling on Skilak Lake Rd; at milepost 5. SEASON: 5/1-10/30, 14-day lmt. FACILITIES: 10 sites (tr -15), tbls, toil, cga, f, drk wtr. ACTIVITIES: picnicking; fishing. MISC.: 5 acres; no motorbikes; pets.

Lower Ohmer Lake (Kenai National Moose Range; NWR). 18 mi from Sterling on Skilak Lake Rd; at milepost 9. SEASON: 5/1-10/20, 14-day lmt. FACILITIES: 6 sites (tr -20), tbls, toil, cga, f, drk wtr. ACTIVITIES: picnicking; fishing (from boat or shore; rainbow trout); swimming; boating,l; hunting; berry picking. Winter –– ice fishing, cross-country skiing, snowshoeing, ice skating. MISC.: 2 acres; scenic: pets permitted on leash.

Lower Skilak Lake (Kenai National Moose Range; NWR). 11 mi SE of Sterling on Sterling Hwy and Skilak Lake Rd; at milepost 15 (narrow access rd). Located on 15-mi Skilak Lake. SEASON: all yr, 14-day lmt. FACILITIES: 13 sites (tr -13), tbls, toil, cga, f, drk wtr. ACTIVITIES: boating,l (caution small boats: high winds appear with no warning); hunting; hiking; berry picking; picnicking; fishing (nearby). Winter –– ice fishing, cross-country skiing, snowshoeing, ice skating. MISC.: 5 acres; no motorbikes; lake; pets on leash.

Rainbow Lake (Kenai Natl Moose Range; NWR). Swanson River Rd, near Sterling; at milepost 16. On Rainbow Lake. SEASON: 5/1–10/20, 14-day lmt. FACILITIES: 5 sites (tr –20), tbls, toil, cga, f, drk wtr. ACTIVITIES: swimming; boating,l; hunting; berry picking; fishing (trout); picnicking. Winter -- ice fishing, cross-country skiing, snowshoeing, ice skating.

Swanson River (Kenai Natl Moose Range; NWR). At the end of Swanson River Road, near Sterling, milepost 18. SEASON: 5/1–10/20, 14-day lmt. FACILITIES: 4 sites (tr –20), tbls, toil, cga, f, drk wtr. ACTIVITIES: hunting; canoeing; boating,l; picnicking; fishing. Winter - ice fishing, cross-country skiing, snowshoeing, ice skating. MISC.: 2 acres; no motorbikes; pets allowed on leash.

Upper Skilak Lake Campground (Kenai National Moose Range; NWR). Skilak Lake Rd, 18 mi from Sterling; milepost 9. SEASON: 5/1–10/20, 14-day lmt. FACILITIES: 10 sites (tr –16), tbls, toil, cga, f, drk wtr. ACTIVITIES: picnicking; fishing; boating,l (caution small boats: strong winds arise with no warning); hiking; hunting; berry picking. Winter -- ice fishing, cross-country skiing, snowshoeing, ice skating. MISC.: 5 acres; pets on leash. Nearby: rock island nesting site for gulls. Skilak Lake (15 mi).

TETLIN JUNCTION

Walker Fork Campground (BLM). From Jct of Alaska Hwy and Taylor Hwy, at Tetlin Jct, N on Taylor Hwy to milepost 82. Located where Jack Wade Creek and the Walker Fork of the Forty-Mile River meet. SEASON: 3/1–10/31, 7-day lmt. FACILITIES: 20 primitive sites (tr –20), tbls, toil, cga, f, well drk wtr. ACTIVITIES: picnicking; fishing (grayling); hunting; hiking; rockhounding; gold panning. MISC.: 5 acres; pets; scenic; stream. Trail up limestone bluff which overlooks site.

TOK

Deadman Lake Wayside. 65 mi from Tok on Alaska Hwy, at milepost 1249. SEASON:5/15–9/10, 15-day lmt. FACILITIES: 16 sites (tr –16), tbls, toil, cga, f, no drk wtr. ACTIVITIES: swimming; canoeing; picnicking; fishing (northern pike); boating,l (ramp is unsurfaced, muddy). MISC.: **Entrance permit required. 20 acres; pets on leash.

Eagle Trail Wayside. 15 mi S of Tok on Slana-Tok-Glenn Hwy, at milepost 109.5. SEASON: 5/15–9/10, 15-day lmt. FACILITIES: 40 sites (tr –30), tbls, toil, cga, f, well drk wtr, picnic shelter. ACTIVITIES: hiking; picnicking; fishing (grayling). MISC.: **Entrance permit required. Pets. Clearwater Creek.

Forty–Nine–Mile Campground (BLM). From Alaska Hwy - Tetlin Jct, N on Taylor to milepost 49. SEASON: 3/20–10/15, 7-day lmt. FACILITIES: 2 primitive sites (no size lmt), tbls, toil, cga, f, stream water must be boiled for drinking. ACTIVITIES: hunting; boating; picnicking; fishing. MISC.: 2 acres; scenic; pets on leash.

Gardiner Creek Wayside. 67 mi from Tok on Alaska Hwy, at milepost 1247 [approx. 25 mi N of border crossing point]. SEASON:5/15–9/10, 15-day lmt. FACILITIES: 6 sites (tr –20), tbls, toil, cga, f, no drk wtr. ACTIVITIES: picnicking; fishing (grayling). MISC.: **Entrance permit required. 10 acres; pets on leash.

Lakeview Wayside. 57 mi from Tok on Alaska Hwy, at milepost 1257. Okay for vans, on a slope of a hill. Okay for vans, tents, campers; not trailers. SEASON: 5/15–9/10, 15-day lmt. FACILITIES: 8 sites (tr –20), tbls, toil, cga, f, no drk wtr. ACTIVITIES: canoeing; swimming; boating,l; picnicking; fishing. MISC.: **Entrance permit required. Pets on leash.

Moon Lake Wayside. 18 mi W of Tok on Alaska Hwy, at milepost 1332. SEASON: 5/15–9/10, 15-day lmt. FACILITIES: 15 sites (tr –20), tbls, toil, cga, f, no drk wtr. ACTIVITIES: swimming (beach); boating,l (unsurfaced ramp); picnicking. MISC.: **Entrance permit required. 92 acres; pets are permitted on leash only.

Porcupine Creek Wayside. 63 mi S of Tok on Glenn Hwy. SEASON: 5/15–9/10, 15-day lmt. FACILITIES: 12 sites (no size lmt), tbls, toil, cga, drk wtr. ACTIVITIES: swimming; hiking; picnicking. MISC.: **Entrance permit required. 240 acres; pets; trails. Scenic--Wrangell Mtns (So.).

Tok River Wayside. 5 mi E of Tok on Alaska Hwy; at milepost 1309. SEASON: 5/15–9/10, 15-day lmt. FACILITIES: 10 sites (tr –20), tbls, toil, cga, f, drk wtr. ACTIVITIES: picnicking. MISC.: **Entrance permit required. 4 acres; pets are permitted if on a leash.

VALDEZ

Blueberry Lake Wayside. 22 mi N of Valdez on Richardson Hwy. SEASON: 5/15–9/10, 15-day lmt. FACILITIES: 6 sites (tr –20), tbls, toil, cga, f, no drk wtr, shelter. ACTIVITIES: picnicking; fishing (trout); birdwatching (large flocks of ptarmigan, the Alaska State Bird, live in this area). MISC.: **Entrance permit reqd. View of Keystone Canyon. Pets.

Little Tonsina Wayside. 64 mi N of Valdez on Richardson Hwy. SEASON: 5/15–9/10, 15-day lmt. FACILITIES: 6 sites (tr –20), tbls, toil, cga, f, drk wtr. ACTIVITIES: picnicking; fishing. MISC.: **Entrance permit required. 102 acres; pets. Little Tonsina River.

Squirrel Creek Wayside. 79 mi N of Valdez on Richardson Hwy; at milepost 80. Located on banks of Squirrel Creek; in Copper River Valley. SEASON: 5/15-9/10, 15-day lmt. FACILITIES: 7 sites (tr -20), tbls, toil, cga, f, drk wtr; nearby at Tonsina Lodge--showers, laundry, water, ice. ACTIVITIES: picnicking; fishing (grayling). MISC.: **Entrance permit. 30 acres; pets on leash.

Worthington Glacier Wayside. 28 mi N of Valdez on Richardson Hwy. SEASON: 5/15-9/10, 15-day lmt. FACILITIES: 6 sites (tr -20), tbls, toil, cga, f, no drk wtr, ice (glacier). ACTIVITIES: picnicking. MISC.: **Entrance permit required. Above timberline; glacier;pets.

WILLOW

South Rolly Lake Campground (Nancy Lake SRA). 3 mi S of Willow on St Hwy 3; 7 mi on side rd. Located in the Matanuska-Susitna River valleys near Wasilla and Willow. On South Rolly Lake. SEASON: 5/15-9/10, 15-day lmt. FACILITIES:

106 sites (tr -20), tbls, toil, cga, f, pull-thru spaces. ACTIVITIES: 12-mile canoe trail; picnicking; fishing. MISC.: **Entrance permit required. The entire SRA is 22,685 acres. Pets on leash.

Willow Creek Wayside. 1 mi NE of Willow on Deception Creek at the jct of Willow Creek. SEASON: 5/15-9/10, 15-day lmt. FACILITIES: 17 sites (tr -20); 3 areas of sites. Tbls, toil, cga, f, no drk wtr. ACTIVITIES: picnicking; fishing (salmon, trout, grayling). MISC.: **Entrance permit required. 90 acres; pets on leash.

WRANGELL

Pat's Creek Wayside. 20 mi S of Wrangell to end of Wrangell Hwy. [11 mi S of Ferry Terminal] SEASON: 5/15-9/10, 15-day lmt. FACILITIES: 9 sites (tr -20), tbls, toil, cga, f, no drk wtr. ACTIVITIES: picnicking; fishing (cutthroat trout, Dolly Varden); clam digging on the tide flats; hiking. MISC.: **Entrance permit required. Pat's Creek; trails; 198 acres; pets permitted if kept on a leash.

ARIZONA

GENERAL STATE INFORMATION

Miscellaneous

Toll-Free Number for Travel Information: 1-602-956-4727 (in-state)
1-800-528-6110 (out-of-state)
Right Turns on Red: Permitted after full stop, unless otherwise posted.
STATE CAPITOL: Phoenix
STATE NICKNAME: Apache State
STATE MOTTO: "God Enriches"
STATE BIRD: Cactus Wren
STATE FLOWER: Saguaro
STATE TREE: Foothill Palo Verde

Remember, only you can prevent forest fires.

I can't

State Parks

Fees range from $2.00 to $5.00 per night. Dogs are welcome but must be kept on a leash at all times; droppings are the responsibility of the owner and must be properly disposed of. There is a 15-day limit. Further information: Arizona State Parks; 1688 West Adams Street; Phoenix, AZ 85507; 602/271-4174.

Rest Areas

No "camping"; however, resting in a vehicle overnight is permitted.

WILDERNESS/BACKCOUNTRY CAMPING

Glen Canyon National Recreation Area

There are primitive areas available for free camping. Inquire at park headquarters or write: Supt.; Glen Canyon NRA; Box 1507; Page, AZ 86040. For designated free campgrounds in this NRA, see "Hanksville" and "Page" in this chapter.

**See page 12.

ARIZONA

Mount Baldy Wilderness (Apache-Sitgreaves NF)

Located on E slope of Mt. Baldy; Springerville Ranger District of Apache NF; in the White Mountains. 20 mi SW of Springerville; approx. 225 mi NE of Phoenix. Access via St Hwy 273 and FS roads. 6,975 acres; the only wilderness in Arizona to include the subalpine vegetation zone (heavy stands of fir, spruce, pine; meadows). Elev ranges from 9,000-11,500 feet. Two developed trails lead to Mt. Baldy. Trailheads: St Hwy 273 near Sheep Crossing (ascends West Fork of the Little Colorado); St Hwy 273 near Phelps Cabin (ascends East Fork of the Little Colorado). These trails converge near the top, continuing to summit. ACTIVITIES: FREE CAMPING; horseback riding; hiking; nature study; photography. Hunting during the fall (elk, mule deer, white-tailed deer, turkey, black bear). Fishing (brook/rainbow/cutthroat trout); 5 mi of fishing streams. Additional Information: District Ranger; Springerville Ranger District; Apache NF; PO Box 640; Springerville, AZ 85938. [602/333-4372]

Sycamore Canyon Wilderness

Located in three national forests: Kaibab NF, Coconino NF, and Prescott NF. Motorized vehicles are prohibited. Trailheads: Packard Place, Rd 131 (Coconino NF); Henderson Flat, Rd 181 (Prescott NF); Sycamore Pass Trailhead, Rd 525-C [and several other entrances] (Coconino NF). Vegetation ranges from cactus/mesquite to fir/pine. April-June and Sept.-Nov. are best hiking/camping months. No drinking water (during dry seasons, no water for pack/riding animals). Parson Spring to Packard Place, creek flows all year; but camping is restricted this first $2\frac{1}{2}$ mi. Campfire/smoking restrictions during dry seasons. Pack your garbage/trash out. Camp at least $\frac{1}{4}$ mi from springs or water. Elevation ranges from 3,600-7,000 feet. Approx. 19,600 acres. 14-day lmt. Additional information: See addresses of the 3 national forests listed under the heading "Information Sources" following this section.

Huachuca Recreation Area (Coronado NF)

Miles of trails. Free backcountry camping. No motorized vehicles permitted. Good roads lead to the edges of the mountains, leaving most of the range in near-wilderness condition where campers can enjoy the feeling of quiet and space and immense vistas. Water is scarce, but there are some small springs. Additional information/maps: Supt.; Coronado National Forest; 301 West Congress; Tucson, AZ 85701.

Wilderness Camping in Tonto NF

Tonto NF offers FOUR wildernesses (totalling 360,000 acres). No motorized vehicles permitted. PINE MOUNTAIN WILDERNESS: straddles Verde Rim in Prescott/Tonto NFs; small; heavily forested. MAZATZAL WILDERNESS: extends down the E side of Verde River to just N of Bartlett Lake. Also, SUPERSTITION WILDERNESS and CAVE CREEK WILDERNESS. ACTIVITIES: FREE PRIMITIVE CAMPING; horseback riding; hiking. Free wilderness permits are required. Maps of Tonto NF, Superstition Wilderness, and Cave Creek-Mazatzal Mountains Area (50¢ each), and additional information (free): Supt.; Tonto NF; 102 South 28th St.; PO Box 13705; Phoenix, AZ 85002.

Backcountry Camping in Grand Canyon NP

PERMITS are required for any hiking/camping below the rim. There is no fee, except for the $2.00 entrance fee into the NP itself (or Golden Eagle/Age Passport*). Camping below the rim is limited to 7 nights per hike, with a limit of 2 nights per campground per hike. Advance reservations are necessary to make sure you will be able to hike where you want, when you want. An early request is advised for groups and/or hikes planned for the spring break period (3/1-4/30), weekends, holidays, and other vacation periods. Reservations for overnight hiking and camping are only accepted 3 months in advance of the month requested (i.e., reservations for any day in July will only be accepted beginning April 1). Requests received more than 3 months in advance will be returned.

Easter is the most popular time of the year to hike the canyon since most schools are on break and the weather is usually ideal. If you wish to hike during the 10-day period prior to and including Easter Sunday, your request must be received between January 2-9 or called in on the telephone between January 2-9. A lottery will be held in mid-January to assign available space. There is a great demand for available space and disappointment is common. For the remainder of the year, available space will be filled on a first-come/first-served reservation basis.

RESERVATION REQUESTS must specify the number of people in your party; campgrounds or trails desired; and dates proposed for each. To make reservations, call or write: Backcountry Reservation Office; Grand Canyon NP, AZ 86023 [602/638-2474]. This office does not make reservations for group or individual campground space on the rim, river trips, mule trips, lodging, or trips into the Havasupai Indian Reservation.

26

FIRES: No wood or charcoal fires allowed. Use Sterno, a backpack stove, or carry cold foods. PETS: Not allowed below the rim. Taking an animal on the trail, especially in the summer, can be fatal. They also disturb wildlife, other hikers, and mule parties. No motorized vehicles or wheeled vehicles allowed on trails. The trails are not constructed for motorcycles, bicycles, baby buggies, and similar vehicles. FISHING: Requires a valid AZ fishing license or nonresident permit which can be obtained at Babbitts General Store inside the park. SWIMMING: In the Colorado River, it is inadvisable and highly dangerous. Strong currents, deep pools, cold. WATER: From all natural sources, must be purified before drinking. Water found in campground taps and the resthouses on the Bright Angel Trail has already been purified. Free detailed information/maps: Supt.; Grand Canyon NP; Box 129; Grand Canyon NP, AZ 86023.

Galiuro Wilderness (Safford Ranger District; Coronado NF)

Location: 35 air mi NW of Willcox; 45 air mi NE of Tucson. Trailheads (on the E side of the Galiuro Mountains): Ash Creek Rd, 40 mi from Willcox; High Creek Rd, 44 mi from Willcox; Deer Creek Rd, 57 mi from Willcox. Due to rough topography and dense vegetation, travel is limited to the forest trails. No motorized vehicles permitted. 52,717 acres. Outstanding opportunity for solitude. Scenic. Historic: remains of former mining activity include the Power's Cabin constructed around 1910, mine tunnels, a ball mill, stamp mill used for obtaining ore concentrates. Power's Garden Cabin, used by the Forest Service and the local rancher, is open for public use. Water: During late spring and early summer, water is usually limited; otherwise usually available at springs and stream. Wildlife: Desert Mule deer, Whitetail deer, javelina, bear, mountain lion, cottontail rabbits, bandtail pigeon. Fire danger high from April-July. Register at one of the registration stations. Additional information/maps: Supt.; Coronado NF; 301 W. Congress; Tucson, AZ 85701.

Chiricahua Wilderness (Douglas Ranger District; Coronado NF)

Located 35 air mi NE of Douglas. Four main entrances: Turkey Creek; Rucker Canyon; Rustler Park; Cave Creek. 111-mi trail system, of which 49 mi are within the Wilderness boundary. Due to rough topography and dense vegetation, travel is limited to the forest trails. 18,000 acres. Generally encompasses the crest of the Chiricahua Mountains. Cliffs and canyons. Includes some of the roughest country in SE Arizona. Elev ranges from 9,797-6,100 feet. Wildlife: Whitetail deer, black bear, mountain lion, Arizona gray squirrel, turkeys, chulas; Chiricahua fox squirrel (which are rare). Water: Generally available all year at seven springs. During rainy season, water is found at additional springs and in creeks. Fire danger high from April-July. Register at one of the registration stations. Additional free information/maps: Supt.; Coronado National Forest; 301 West Congress; Tucson, AZ 85701.

Backcountry Camping in Kaibab NF

Kaibab NF embraces much of Grand Canyon country; scenic. The thickly-forested high plateaus almost entirely lack in surface water. Deep canyons in the low desert country near the Colorado River is where most people hike/camp. Ample opportunity for solitude. These canyon-bottom routes can be quite hot, even intolerable in summer; water sources are uncertain and few. Spring and Fall are the most favorable times for backpacking/camping; but even so, the hiker should be well-versed in the techniques of desert travel. For detailed information, maps, free permit: Supt.; Kaibab NF; PO Box 817; Williams, AZ 86046.

INFORMATION SOURCES

Maps

The following maps are available from **Forsyth Travel Library** (see order form in Appendix B):

> **State of Arizona** [Up-to-date, showing all principal roads, points of interest, sports areas, parks, airports, mileage, etc. Full color.]

> Completely indexed city maps, including all airports, lakes, rivers, etc., of: **Phoenix/Scottsdale, Sun City/Youngtown; Tucson; Yuma.**

Gold Mining and Prospecting

Arizona Bureau of Mines; University of Arizona; Tucson, Arizona 85721

ARIZONA

State Information

Arizona State Chamber of Commerce; 3216 N. 3rd St., Suite 103; Phoenix, AZ 85012
Arizona State Parks; 1688 W. Adams Street; Phoenix, AZ 85007 [602/271-4174]
Travel Development Section; Office of Economic Planning and Development; 1645 West Jefferson, Room 428; Phoenix, AZ 85007
Arizona Office of Tourism; 1700 West Washington, Room 501; Phoenix, AZ 85007
Arizona Dept. of Game and Fish; 2222 West Greenway Road; PO Box 9099; Phoenix, AZ 85023 [602/942-3000]
National Parks and Monuments; 1115 North 1st Street; Phoenix, AZ 85004

City Information

Flagstaff Chamber of Commerce; 101 W. Santa Fe; Flagstaff, AZ 86001
Grand Canyon Chamber of Commerce; PO Box 507; Grand Canyon, AZ 86023
Phoenix Metropolitan Chamber of Commerce; 34 West Monroe, 9th Floor; PO Box 10; Phoenix, AZ 85001
Tucson Chamber of Commerce; 420 W. Congress St.; PO Box 991; Tucson, AZ 85702
Yuma County Chamber of Commerce; 200 First St.; PO Box 230; Yuma, AZ 85364

National Forests

Apache-Sitgreaves NF; PO Box 640; Federal Building; Springerville, AZ 85938
Coconino NF; 2323 E. Greenlaw Lane; Flagstaff, AZ 86001
Coronado NF; 301 West Congress; Tucson, AZ 85701
Kaibab NF; PO Box 817; Williams, AZ 86046
Prescott NF; 344 S. Cortez St.; PO Box 2549; Prescott, AZ 86302
Tonto NF; 102 S. 28th St.; PO Box 13705; Phoenix, AZ 85002

National Monuments

Canyon de Chelly NM; PO Box 588; Chinle, AZ 86503
Navajo NM; Tonalea, AZ 86044
Organ Pipe Cactus NM; Box 38; Ajo, AZ 85321
Saguaro NM; Box 17210; Tucson, AZ 85731

Miscellaneous

Grand Canyon NP; Box 129; Grand Canyon, AZ 86023
Petrified Forest NP; Holbrook, AZ 86025
Glen Canyon NRA; Box 1507; Page, AZ 86040
BLM; 2400 Valley Bank Center; Phoenix, AZ 85073
Bureau of Indian Affairs; Phoenix Area Office; PO Box 7007; Phoenix, AZ 85011
Bureau of Indian Affairs; Navajo Area Office; Window Rock, AZ 86515

GIVE A HOOT! DON'T POLLUTE

FREE CAMPGROUNDS

ALPINE

Army Canyon (Apache-Sitgreaves NF). 1-9/10 mi NW of Alpine on US 180; 9 mi W on FS 1249; 11-1/5 mi SW on FS 1276. SEASON: 4/1-11/30; 14-day lmt. FACILITIES: 4 sites (tr -22), tbls, toil, cga, f. ACTIVITIES: Picnicking; fishing. MISC.: Elev 7600 ft; stream; scenic; pets. Primitive type camping.

Aspen (Apache-Sitgreaves NF). 1-9/10 mi NW of Alpine on US 180; 9 mi W on FS 1249; 8-1/5 mi SW on FS 1276. SEASON: 4/1-11/30; 14-day lmt. FACILITIES: 5 primitive sites (tr -32), tbls, toil, cga, f. ACTIVITIES: Picnicking; fishing. MISC.: Elev 7500 ft; 2 acres; stream; scenic. Pets permitted if on a leash.

Beaver Dam (Apache-Sitgreaves NF). 1-9/10 mi NW on US 180; 9 mi W on FS 1249; 10 mi SW on FS 1276. SEASON: 4/1-11/30; 14-day lmt. FACILITIES: 4 sites (tr -16); tbls, toil, cga, f. ACTIVITIES: Picnicking; fishing. MISC.: Elev 7600 ft; 2 acres; scenic; pets. Primitive type camping.

Buffalo Crossing (Apache-Sitgreaves NF). 1-9/10 mi SW of Alpine on US 180; 9 mi W on FS 1249; 13-1/5 mi SW on FS 1276. SEASON: 4/1-11/30; 14-day lmt. FACILITIES: 20 sites (tr -16); tbls, toil, cga, f. ACTIVITIES: Picnicking; fishing. MISC.: Elev 7600 ft; stream; scenic;pets.

Deer Creek (Apache-Sitgreaves NF). 1-9/10 mi NW of Alpine on US 180; 9 mi W on FS 1249; 11-1/5 mi SW on FS 1276. SEASON: 4/1-11/30; 14-day lmt. FACILI-TIES: 4 sites (tr -16), tbls, toil, cga,

See page 7 for KEY TO ABBREVIATIONS.

Deer Creek (cont.) f. ACTIVITIES: Picnicking; fishing. MISC.: Elev 7700 ft; stream; pets; primitive camping.

Diamond Rock (Apache-Sitgreaves NF). 1-9/10 mi NW of Alpine on US 180; 9 mi W on FS 1249; 5-9/10 mi SW on FS 1276. SEASON: 4/1-11/30; 14-day lmt. FACILITIES: 14 sites (tr -22), tbls, toil, cga, f, piped drk wtr. ACTIVITIES: Picnicking, fishing. MISC.: Elev 7900 ft; 6 acres; stream; scenic. Pets allowed on leash.

Hall (Apache-Sitgreaves NF). 1-9/10 mi NW of Alpine on US 180; 9 mi W on FS 1249; 8-1/5 mi SW on FS 1276. SEASON: 4/1-11/30; 14-day lmt. FACILITIES: 4 sites (tr -16), tbls, toil, cga, f. ACTIVITIES: Picnicking; fishing. MISC.: Elev 7700 ft; 1 acre; stream; scenic; pets.

Hannagan (Apache-Sitgreaves NF). 23 mi SW of Alpine on St Hwy 666. SEASON: 5/1-11/15, 14-day lmt. FACILITIES: 8 sites (tr -32), tbls, toil, cga, f, fd, store, gas, drk wtr. ACTIVITIES: Picnicking; hiking. Fishing (4 mi). MISC.: Elev 9100 ft; 3 acres; scenic; pets. Jump-off point to Blue Primitive Area.

K.P. Cienega (Apache-Sitgreaves NF). 28 mi SW of Alpine on St Hwy 666; 1 mi SE on FS 155. SEASON: 5/1-11/15, 14-day lmt. FACILITIES: 5 sites (tr -22), tbls, toil, cga, f, piped drk wtr. ACTIVITIES: Picnicking; hiking. Fishing (2 mi). MISC.: Elev 9000 ft; 2 acres; scenic; pets. Access point to Blue Primitive Area.

Strayhorse (Apache-Sitgreaves NF). 26 mi S of Alpine on US 666. SEASON: 5/15-9/30, 14-day lmt. FACILITIES: 6 sites (tr -22), tbls, toil, cga, f, piped drk wtr. ACTIVITIES: Picnicking. Horseback riding (1 mi). MISC.: Elev 8200 ft; 2 acres. Pets permitted if on leash.

West Fork (Apache-Sitgreaves NF). 13½ mi SW of Alpine on US 666; 11½ mi NW on FS 1285; 4 mi W on FS 25; 4 mi N on FS 168. SEASON: 4/1-11/30; 14-day lmt. FACILITIES: 3 sites (tr -16), tbls, toil, cga, f, no drk wtr. ACTIVITIES: Picnicking; fishing. MISC.: Elev 7800 ft; 4 acres; stream; scenic. Pets.

AMADO

Rest Area. 35 mi S of Tucson on St Hwy 89. SEASON: All yr, 1-night lmt. FACILITIES: Undesignated spaces for self-contained RVs (no tent camping). Tbls, toil, cga. ACTIVITIES: Picnicking. MISC.: Pets allowed if on a leash.

APACHE JUNCTION

Apache Lake (Tonto NF). 31-3/5 mi SW of Apache Junction on St Hwy 88; 1 mi NW on FS 79. SEASON: All yr, 14-day lmt. FACILITIES: 12 tent sites; tbls, toil, cga, no drk wtr. Store,

ice, fd, gas -- 1 mi. ACTIVITIES: Picnicking. Boating (rld, 1 mi). Fishing; swimming; waterskiing. MISC.: Elev 1900 ft; 5 acres; lake; scenic; pets.

Coon Bluff (Tonto NF). 7-3/5 mi W of Apache Junction on US 60; 10-1/10 mi N on FS 204; 1½ mi NW on FS 204E. SEASON: All yr, 14-day lmt. FACILITIES: 8 sites (tr -16), tbls, toil, cga, no drk wtr. ACTIVITIES: Picnicking; fishing. MISC.: 4 acres; pets on leash.

Granite Reef (Tonto NF). 7-3/5 mi W of Apache Junction on US 60; 6-3/5 mi N on FS 204. SEASON: All yr, 14-day lmt. FACILITIES: 5 sites (tr -16), tbls, toil, cga, no drk wtr. ACTIVITIES: Picnicking; fishing. MISC.: Elev 1300 ft; 2 acres; river. Pets allowed on leash.

*The Point (Tonto NF). 15-7/10 mi NE of Apache Junction on St Hwy 88; 2-7/10 mi NE, BY BOAT. SEASON: All yr, 14-day lmt. FACILITIES: 3 tent sites; tbls, toil, cga, no drk wtr. 4 mi -- store, ice, gas, dump, fd. ACTIVITIES: Boating, I (2 mi), r (4 mi); swimming; waterskiing; picnicking; fishing. MISC.: Elev 1700 ft; 1 acre; pets. Canyon Lake.

Rest Area. 5 mi NE of Apache Junction on St Hwy 88. SEASON: All yr, 1-night lmt. FACILITIES: Undesignated spaces for self-contained RVs (no tent camping). Tbls, toil, cga. ACTIVITIES: Picnicking. MISC.: Pets allowed if kept on leash.

BENSON

Lions Park. 1 block N of I-10 at W edge of Benson. SEASON: All yr. FACILITIES: Undesignated sites; tbls, toil, cga. ACTIVITIES: Picnicking. MISC.: Pets.

BLUE

Blue Crossing (Apache-Sitgreaves NF). 2 mi N of Blue on FS 1285. SEASON: 3/15-12/15; 14-day lmt. FACILITIES: 4 sites (tr -22), tbls, toil, cga, f, no drk wtr. Gas (2 mi). ACTIVITIES: Hiking; picnicking; fishing. Horseback riding/rental (2 mi). MISC.: Elev 6200 ft; 1 acre; scenic; river; pets. Adjacent to Blue Range Primitive Area.

Upper Blue (Apache-Sitgreaves NF). 7-3/5 mi N of Blue on FS 12813; ¼ mi W of FS 1281A. SEASON: 3/15-12/15; 14-day lmt. FACILITIES: 3 sites (tr -22), tbls, toil, cga, f. ACTIVITIES: Picnicking; fishing. MISC.: Elev 6200 ft; 1 acre; river; scenic. Pets allowed on leash.

BOWIE

Joy Valley Rockhound Area (BLM). 16 mi NE of Bowie. Turn N at the Texaco service station in Bowie and follow the rd for ¼ mi; turn right onto graded dirt rd for approx. 8½ mi; turn E (right) again. After crossing the San Simon River, directional signs will guide you.

[Roads may be impassable in July, Aug., or Sept., due to thunderstorms and flash floods.] **SEASON:** All yr, 14-day lmt. **FACILITIES:** No designated sites; tbls, cga. **ACTIVITIES:** Hiking; hunting; picnicking; rockhounding. **MISC.:** Elev 3650 ft. Pets allowed if kept on leash.

BUCKEYE

Buckeye Hills (County Park). 5 mi SW of Buckeye on St Hwy 80. **SEASON:** All yr. **FACILITIES:** Undesignated sites; drk wtr. **MISC.:** Elev 1075 ft; pets on leash. Undeveloped.

BULLHEAD CITY

Bullhead Community Park (City Park). ¼ mi S of Bullhead City. **SEASON:** All yr. **FACILITIES:** 100 sites; tbls, toil, cga, drk wtr. **ACTIVITIES:** Swimming; boating,l; picnicking; fishing. **MISC.:** Elev 675 ft. Pets permitted if on leash.

CAREFREE

Bartlett Lake (Tonto NF). 6-3/5 mi E of Carefree on FS 24; 6-1/10 mi E on FS 205; 7 mi SE on FS 19; ½ mi SE on FS 185. **SEASON:** All yr, 14-day lmt. **FACILITIES:** 20 sites (tr -16); no tbls, no drk wtr, toil. **ACTIVITIES:** Swimming; waterskiing; boating; fishing. **MISC.:** Elev 1800 ft; 1 acre;pets. Bartlett Lake.

Cave Creek (Tonto NF). 21 mi NE of Carefree on FS 24. **SEASON:** All yr, 7-day lmt. **FACILITIES:** 12 sites (tr -16), tbls, toil, cga, piped drk wtr. **ACTIVITIES:** Picnicking. **MISC.:** Elev 3500 ft; 4 acres. Pets permitted if on leash.

Horseshoe (Tonto NF). 6-3/5 mi E of Carefree on FS 24; 15-2/5 mi NE on FS 205; 3/5 mi NE on FS 205A. **SEASON:** All yr, 7-day lmt. **FACILITIES:** 20 sites (tr -16), tbls, toil, cga, no drk wtr. **ACTIVITIES:** Picnicking; fishing. **MISC.:** Elev 1900 ft; 4 acres; river. Pets.

Riverside (Tonto NF). 6-3/5 mi E of Carefree on FS 24; 6-1/10 mi E on FS 205; 9-1/5 mi SE on FS 19; 9/10 mi SW on FS 162. **SEASON:** All yr, 7-day lmt. **FACILITIES:** 3 tent sites; no tbls, no drk wtr, toil. **ACTIVITIES:** Fishing. **MISC.:** 3 mi -- boating, waterskiing. **MISC.:** Elev 1600 ft; 1 acre; river; pets.

Seven Springs (Tonto NF). 20 mi NE of Carefree on FS 24. **SEASON:** All yr, 7-day lmt. **FACILITIES:** 23 sites (tr -16), tbls, toil, cga, piped drk wtr. **ACTIVITIES:** Picnicking. **MISC.:** Elev 3400 ft; 3 acres. Pets on leash.

CASA GRANDE

Rest Area. 10 mi N of Casa Grande. **SEASON:** All yr, 1-night lmt. **FACILITIES:** Undesignated spaces for self-contained RVs (no tent camping); tbls, toil, cga. **ACTIVITIES:** Picnicking. **MISC.:** Pets.

CHINLE

Cottonwood (Canyon de Chelly NM). 1 mi SE of Chinle on St Hwy 7, below Visitor Center. **SEASON:** All yr, 14-day lmt. **FACILITIES:** 94 sites (tr -30), pull-thru spaces; tbls, flush toil, cga, laundry, dump. Nearby -- store, ice, fd. **ACTIVITIES:** Campfire programs during summer. Hiking; picnicking. Nearby -- boating; fishing (Navajo Tribal Fishing Permit required). **MISC.:** Motorbikes prohibited. Pets are not allowed in canyon floor areas or on self-guiding White House Trail. Otherwise permitted on leash.

CLIFTON

Granville (Apache-Sitgreaves NF). 16 mi N of Clifton on US 666. **SEASON:** 5/15-9/30, 14-day lmt. **FACILITIES:** 9 sites (tr -16), tbls, toil, cga, f, piped drk wtr. **ACTIVITIES:** Picnicking. Horseback riding (1 mi). **MISC.:** Elev 6600 ft; 5 acres. Pets permitted if on a leash.

Greys Peak (Apache-Sitgreaves NF). 22 mi NW of Clifton on US 666. **SEASON:** 4/1-10/15, 14-day lmt. **FACILITIES:** 3 sites (tr -22), tbls, toil, cga, f, piped drk wtr. **ACTIVITIES:** Picnicking. **MISC.:** Elev 6000 ft; 4 acres. Pets on leash.

Honey Moon (Apache-Sitgreaves NF). 26 mi N of Clifton on US 666; 24 mi NW on FS 1217. **SEASON:** 5/15-9/30, 14-day lmt. **FACILITIES:** 4 sites (tr -16), tbls, toil, cga, f. **ACTIVITIES:** Picnicking; fishing. Horseback riding (1 mi). **MISC.:** Elev 5600 ft; 5 acres; stream. Pets on leash.

Lower Juan Miller (Apache-Sitgreaves NF). 25½ mi N of Clifton on US 666; 1½ mi E on FS 475. **SEASON:** 5/15-9/30, 14-day lmt. **FACILITIES:** 4 sites (tr -16), tbls, toil, cga, f. **MISC.:** Elev 6000 ft; 2 acres. Pets permitted if on leash.

Upper Juan Miller (Apache-Sitgreaves NF). 25½ mi N of Clifton on US 666; 1 mi E on FS 475. **SEASON:** 5/15-9/30, 14-day lmt. **FACILITIES:** 4 tent sites; tbls, toil, cga, f. **ACTIVITIES:** Picnicking. **MISC.:** Elev 6100 ft; 2 acres; pets.

DEWEY

Powell Springs (Prescott NF). 13-3/10 mi NE of Dewey on FS 372 (Cherry Rd). [Far off the beaten path.] **SEASON:** All yr, 14-day lmt. **FACILITIES:** 10 sites (tr -22), tbls, toil, cga, no drk wtr. **ACTIVITIES:** Picnicking. **MISC.:** Elev 5300 ft; 3 acres; pets. Garbage must be packed out with you.

DRAKE

Bear Siding (Prescott NF). SW of Drake at the end of FS 492A (on the Verde River). [Rough/rocky access rd; impassable during wet/winter weather.] **SEASON:** All yr (weather permitting), 14-day lmt. **FACILITIES:** Undesignated sites.

See page 7 for KEY TO ABBREVIATIONS.

Primitive camping. No drk wtr or other facilities. ACTIVITIES: Fishing (AZ fishing license is required; bass, catfish, carp). Hiking. MISC.: Quiet/beautiful spot; very popular on weekends. Patrolled regularly by Forest Service personnel and Yavapai County Sheriff's Dept. No shooting allowed. 10 acres;pets.

DUNCAN

Round Mountain Rockhound Area (BLM). Located approx. 10 mi S of Duncan. Follow US 70 out of Duncan into New Mexico and turn W (right) about 4½ mi from AZ-NM State Line. Follow this graded dirt rd about 7 mi to a BLM sign that gives further directions. [Rds may be impassable during summer rainy season.] SEASON: All yr. FACILITIES: Undesignated tent sites; tbls, toil, cga. ACTIVITIES: Hunting; hiking; rockhounding; picnicking. MISC.: Pets on leash.

EAGAR

South Fork (Apache-Sitgreaves NF). 5½ mi W of Eagar on St Hwy 260; 2½ mi SW on FS 560. SEASON: 4/15-10/15, 14-day lmt. FACILITIES: 8 sites (tr -22), tbls, toil, cga, no drk wtr. 1 mi - store, ice, fd. ACTIVITIES: Fishing; picnicking; hiking. MISC.: Elev 7600; 3 acres; stream; botanical; pets. Self clean-up area. Trailhead into South Fork Basin.

EHRENBERG

Rest Area. W of Ehrenberg on I-10. SEASON: All yr, 1-night lmt. FACILITIES: Undesignated spaces for self-contained RVs (no tent camping); tbls, toil, cga. ACTIVITIES: Picnicking. MISC.: Pets.

ELFRIDA

Sycamore (Coronado NF). 14-7/10 mi N of Elfrida on US 666; 12 mi E on St Hwy 181; 10½ mi W on FS 41. SEASON:2/1-11/30, 14-day lmt. FACILITIES: 5 sites (tr -16), tbls, toil, cga, no drk wtr. ACTIVITIES: Picnicking. MISC.: Elev 6200 ft; 3 acres; stream; scenic. Pets on leash.

West Turkey Creek (Coronado NF). 14-7/10 mi N of Elfrida on US 666; 12 mi E on St Hwy 181; 8½ mi W on FS 41. SEASON: 2/1-11/30, 14-day lmt. FACILITIES: 7 sites (tr -16), tbls, toil, cga, no drk wtr. ACTIVITIES: Picnicking. MISC.: Elev 5900 ft; 4 acres; stream; scenic; pets.

FLAGSTAFF

Ashurst Lake (Coconino NF). 1 mi SW of Flagstaff on US 66; 2 mi S on St Hwy 89A; 17-3/10 mi SE on Co Hwy FH3; 4 mi E on FS 82E. SEASON: 4/15-11/1, 7-day lmt. FACILITIES: 23 sites (tr -22), tbls, toil, cga, no drk wtr. ACTIVITIES: Picnicking. Boating,1 (8 HP motors only on lake)/swimming/fishing (1 mi). MISC.: Elev 7000 ft; 20 acres; pets. Ashurst Lake.

Forked Pine (Coconino NF). 1 mi SW of Flagstaff on US 66; 2 mi S on St Hwy 89A; 17-3/10 mi SE on Co Hwy FH3; 5-1/10 mi E on FS 82E. SEASON: 4/15-11/1, 7-day lmt. FACILITIES: 33 sites (tr -16), tbls, toil, cga, no drk wtr. ACTIVITIES: Picnicking. 1 mi -- boating,1 (8 HP motor or less on lake); swimming; fishing. MISC.: Elev 7100 ft; 20 acres; lake. Pets permitted if on a leash.

Kinnikinick (Coconino NF). 2-2/5 mi S of Flagstaff on St Hwy 89A; 25 mi SE on Co Hwy FH3; 5 mi E on FS 125; 4-3/5 mi SE on FS 82. SEASON: 5/1-10/1, 14-day lmt. FACILITIES: 13 sites (tr -22), tbls, toil, cga, no drk wtr. ACTIVITIES: Picnicking. 1 mi -- boating,1 (8 HP motor only on lake); fishing. MISC.: Elev 7000 ft; 20 acres; lake; pets.

Lakeview (Coconino NF). 1 mi SW of Flagstaff on US 66; 2 mi S on St Hwy 89A; 13-1/5 mi SE on Co Hwy FH3. SEASON: 4/15-10/15, 7-day lmt. FACILITIES: 30 tent sites; tbls, toil, cga, no drk wtr. 5 mi -- store, ice. ACTIVITIES: Picnicking. 1 mi -- boating,1; swimming; fishing; waterskiing. MISC.: Elev 6900 ft; 15 acres; lake. Pets on leash.

Meteor Crater Regional Park. 40 mi E of Flagstaff, just off I-40. SEASON: All yr. FACILITIES: Undesignated sites.

FREDONIA

Jacob Lake Annex (Kaibab NF). 29 mi S on US 89; 1/10 mi N on US 89A; 1/10 mi E on St Hwy 67. SEASON: 6/1-9/15; 14-day lmt. FACILITIES: 63 sites (tr -32); tbls, toil, cga, store, gas, ice, dump. ACTIVITIES: Picnicking; hiking. MISC.: Elev 9000 ft; 5 acres; scenic; pets; visitor center. 44 mi N of North Rim Grand Canyon.

Toroweap Point. 72 mi SW of Fredonia. SEASON: All yr, 14-day lmt. FACILITIES: 10 sites, tbls, toil, cga, no drk wtr. ACTIVITIES: Picnicking. MISC.: Elev 5600 ft; primitive. Pets on leash.

GILA BEND

Rest Area. 35 mi W of Gila Bend on I-8. SEASON: All yr, 1-night lmt. FACILITIES: Spaces for self-contained RVs (no tent camping), tbls, toil, cga. ACTIVITIES: Picnicking. MISC.: Pets.

GLOBE

City Park/Rest Area. W edge of Globe on St Hwy 60/70. SEASON: All yr, 1-night lmt. FACILITIES: Spaces for self-contained RVs (no tent camping), tbls, toil, cga. ACTIVITIES: Picnicking. MISC.: Pets permitted if on a leash.

Jackson Butte (Tonto NF). 18 mi NE of Globe on US 60. SEASON: All yr, 1-day lmt. FACILITIES: 5 sites (tr -22), tbls,

See page 7 for KEY TO ABBREVIATIONS.

toil, cga, no drk wtr. ACTIVITIES: Picnicking. MISC.: Elev 5000 ft; 1 acre; pets permitted if kept on a leash.

Jones Water (Tonto NF). 17-1/5 mi NE of Globe on US 60. SEASON: All yr, 14-day lmt. FACILITIES: 13 sites (tr -16), tbls, toil, cga, piped drk wtr. ACTIVITIES: Picnicking. MISC.: Elev 4500 ft; 7 acres. Pets permitted if on leash.

Pinal (Prescott NF). 2½ mi SW of Globe on FS 112; 2-3/5 mi SW on FS 55; 9-2/5 mi SW on FS 651. SEASON: 5/1-11/15, 14-day lmt. FACILITIES: 22 sites (tr -16), tbls, toil, cga, piped drk wtr. ACTIVITIES: Picnicking. MISC.: Elev 7500 ft; 6 acres. Pets okay on leash.

Pioneer Pass (Tonto NF). 8-3/5 mi S of Globe on FS 112. SEASON: 4/1-12/31, 1-day lmt. FACILITIES: 27 tent sites, tbls, toil, cga, piped drk wtr. ACTIVITIES: Picnicking. MISC.: Elev 6000 ft; 18 acres; pets.

GOODYEAR

Estrella Mountain County Park. 2 mi S of Goodyear. SEASON: All yr. FACILITIES: 75 sites, tbls, toil, cga, drk wtr. ACTIVITIES: Picnicking. MISC.: Elev 3650 ft.

GRAND CANYON

*Phantom Ranch--Inner Canyon (Grand Canyon NP). 7-14 mi BY TRAIL from either rim. Hike-in or Boat-in. SEASON: All yr, 2-day lmt. FACILITIES: 75 tent sites, tbls, toil, cga, drk wtr [2 mi -- flush toil]. ACTIVITIES: Hiking; boating; picnicking. MISC.: $2 entrance fee into the NP itself, or use your Golden Eagle/Age Passport.** Reservations required. Elev 730 ft; 1 acre. No pets allowed.

GREER

*Benny Creek (Apache-Sitgreaves NF). 2½ mi N of Greer on St Hwy 373; ½ mi W on Trail 870. Accessible BY FOOT. SEASON: 4/15-10/15, 14-day lmt. FACILITIES: 12 sites (tr -22), tbls, toil, cga, piped drk wtr. Store/ice/gas (2 mi). Food (3 mi). ACTIVITIES: Picnicking. Boating (l, 2 mi; r, 3 mi). Fishing/swimming/horse rental and riding (3 mi). MISC.: Eleve 8300 ft; 4 acres; nature trails; scenic; pets. Bunch Reservoir (2 mi).

Gabaldon (Apache-Sitgreaves NF). 2 mi N of Greer on St Hwy 373; 6 mi SE on FS 87; 4 mi SE on St Hwy 273. SEASON: 5/1-10/15, 14-day lmt. FACILITIES: 5 sites (tr -16), tbls, no drk wtr, f. Store (4 mi). ACTIVITIES: Mountain climbing; picnicking; fishing. Boating,d (2 mi). MISC.: Elev 8500 ft; 3 acres; botanical; stream; pets. Campground for horse users of the Mt. Baldy Wilderness Area. Limited corral facilities.

Greer (Apache-Sitgreaves NF). ½ mi N of Greer on St Hwy 373. SEASON: 4/15-10/15, 14-day lmt. FACILITIES: 10 sites (tr -22), tbls, toil, cga, piped drk wtr. l mi -- store, ice, fd, gas, dump. ACTIVITIES: Picnicking; hiking; berry-picking. Horseback riding/rental (1 mi). 2 mi -- boating,ld (1 mi, rental); fishing; swimming. MISC.: Elev 8500 ft; 8 acres; stream; self-guiding nature trails; scenic; pets. Within 2 mi of the Greer Lakes. Electric motors only, in the lake.

*Greer Lakes (Apache-Sitgreaves NF). 2½ mi N of Greer on St Hwy 373; ½ mi W on Trail 870. Accessible BY FOOT. SEASON: 4/15-10/15, 14-day lmt. FACILITIES: 12 sites (tr -22), tbls, toil, cga, piped drk wtr. Dump (1 mi). 2 mi -- store, ice, gas. Fd (3 mi). ACTIVITIES: Picnicking; berry-picking. 2 mi -- boating,l; horse rentals; hiking; swimming; fishing. 3 mi -- boat rental; horseback riding. MISC.: Elev 8300 ft; 4 acres; scenic; nature trails; pets. Self clean-up area. Within 2 mi of river, tunnel, and Bunch Reservoir. Electric motors only, on lake.

HAPPY JACK

Clints Well (Coconino NF). 15 mi SE of Happy Jack on FS FH3. SEASON: 5/15-11/15, 14-day lmt. FACILITIES: 7 sites (tr -32), tbls, toil, cga, no drk wtr. 1 mi -- store, ice, gas. ACTIVITIES: Picnicking. MISC.: Elev 7000 ft; 3 acres; pets. 9 mi -- Blue Ridge Reservoir.

Kehl Springs (Coconino NF). 15-1/5 mi SE of Happy Jack on FS FH3; 9-4/5 mi SW on St Hwy 87; 7-1/10 mi E on FS 300. SEASON: 5/15-11/15, 14-day lmt. FACILITIES: 8 sites (tr -22), tbls, toil, cga, f, no drk wtr. ACTIVITIES: Picnicking. MISC.: 6 acres; pets on leash.

HEBER

Black Canyon Rim (Apache-Sitgreaves NF). 12-3/5 mi SW of Heber on St Hwy 160; 2½ mi SE on FS 300. SEASON: 4/15-11/1, 14-day lmt. FACILITIES: 18 sites (tr -16), no tbls, no drk wtr, toil, f, cga. ACTIVITIES: 2 mi -- boating,ld; fishing (popular fishing spot, 3 mi E). MISC.: Elev 7600 ft; 3 acres; pets. Closest Forest Service campground to Black Canyon Lake.

Chevelon Crossing (Apache-Sitgreaves NF). 1½ mi W of Heber on St Hwy 260; 16½ mi NW on FS 504. SEASON: 3/1-12/31. FACILITIES: 6 tent sites; tbls, toil, cga, f, no drk wtr. ACTIVITIES: Picnicking; fishing; rockhounding. MISC.: Elev 6300 ft; 5 acres; stream; geological; pets. 34 mi S of Winslow, Arizona.

See page 7 for KEY TO ABBREVIATIONS.

Gentry (Apache-Sitgreaves NF). 12-3/5 mi SW of Heber on St Hwy 160; 4-7/10 mi SE on FS 300. SEASON: 4/1-11/1, 14-day lmt. FACILITIES: 6 sites (tr -16), tbls, toil, cga, f, no drk wtr. ACTIVITIES: Picnicking. 5 mi -- boating,ld; fishing. MISC.: Elev 7700 ft; 2 acres; pets. Approx. 5 mi to Black Canyon Lake, a popular fishing spot.

HOOVER DAM

Kingman Wash. 6½ mi NE of Hoover Dam. SEASON: All yr. FACILITIES: No designated sites. MISC.: Elev 1250 ft; pets. Not developed.

HOUCK

Rest Area. W of Houck on I-40. SEASON: All yr, 1-night lmt. FACILITIES: Spaces for self-contained RVs (no tent camping), tbls, toil, cga. ACTIVITIES: Picnicking. MISC.: Pets permitted if on a leash.

JACOB LAKE

Indian Hollow (Kaibab NF). 25-9/10 mi S of Jacob Lake on St Hwy 67; 17-4/5 mi NW on FS 422; 7-4/5 mi SW on FS 425; 4-7/10 mi W on FS 232. SEASON: 5/1-11/15, 14-day lmt. FACILITIES: 3 sites (tr -32), tbls, toil, cga, f. ACTIVITIES: Picnicking; rockhounding; hiking. MISC.: Elev 6000 ft; 2 acres; scenic; pets. Trailhead for Thunder River Trail into Grand Canyon. Snow blocks access in winter months.

JEROME

Mingus Mountain (Prescott NF). 6-3/5 mi SW of Jerome on US 89A; 2½ mi SE on FS 104. Located at the top of Mingus Mountain. SEASON: 4/1-11/30, 14-day lmt. FACILITIES: 24 sites (tr -22), tbls, toil, cga, no drk wtr. 3 mi -- store, fd. ACTIVITIES: Horseback riding; hiking; picnicking; hunting (antelope,dove, quail,deer). MISC.: Elev 7600 ft; 10 acres; hiking trails; pets. Lookout view over the Verde Valley towards the Mogollon Rim and town of Cottonwood.

Potato Patch (Prescott NF). 6½ mi SW on US 89A (on Mingus Mtn). SEASON: 3/1-11/30; 14-day lmt. FACILITIES: 14 sites (tr -22); tbls, toil, cga, no drk wtr. Store/ice/fd (1 mi). ACTIVITIES: Hiking; picnicking. MISC.: Elev 6500 ft; 4 acres; pets.

JOSEPH CITY

Cholla Lake County Park. 2 mi E of Joseph City on I-40. SEASON: All yr, 1-night lmt. FACILITIES: 5 sites for self-contained RVs (no tent camping), tbls, flush toil, cga. ACTIVITIES: Swimming; picnicking; fishing; boating,ld. MISC.: 40 acres; lake; pets on leash.

KAYENTA

*Backcountry Campground (Navajo NM). 22 mi SW of Kayenta on US 160; 9 mi N/NW on St Hwy 564 to the monument headquarters. 9 mi N of visitor center on rough Trail. SEASON: 6/1-LD, 1-night lmt. FACILITIES: Undesignated tent sites. ACTIVITIES: Hiking; horseback riding. MISC.: Elev 7300 ft; 60 acres; pets. No wood fires allowed;only charcoal/propane.

Main Campground (Navajo NM). 22 mi SW of Kayenta on US 160; 9 mi N/NW on St Hwy 564 to the monument headquarters. Campground is just beyond the Visitor Center. SEASON: May-October, 7-day lmt. FACILITIES: 30 sites (tr -25), tbls, flush toil, cga, dump, water in restrooms. ACTIVITIES: Picnicking; hiking. In the summer, campfire programs are given on the archeology, history, and natural history of the monument. MISC.: Elev 7300 ft; pets on leash. A Navajo Tribal Guild concession in the Visitor Center sells objects made by the Indians. No wood fires allowed; charcoal/propane.

Primitive Campground (Navajo NM). 22 mi W of Kayenta on US 160; 9 mi N/NW on St Hwy 564 to monument headquarters. Campground is within ½ mi of Visitor Center. SEASON: All yr (but not cleared of snow in winter; sometimes impassible), 7-day lmt. FACILITIES: 12 sites (tr -25), tbls/cga (by Visitor Center), toil, no wtr. ACTIVITIES: Picnicking; hiking. In the summer, campfire programs are given on the archeology, history, and natural history of the monument. MISC.: Elev 7300 ft; pets on leash. A Navajo Tribal Guild concession in the Visitor Center sells objects made by the Indians. No wood fires; only charcoal/propane.

KINGMAN

Bonelli Landing. 75 mi NW of Kingman. SEASON: All yr. FACILITIES: Undesignated sites, tbls, toil, cga, no drk wtr. ACTIVITIES: Fishing; swimming; picnicking; boating,l. MISC.: Elev 1230 ft; pets.

Gregg's Hideout. 70 mi N of Kingman. SEASON: All yr. FACILITIES: Undesignated sites. MISC.: Elev 1280 ft. Not developed. Pets permitted if they are kept on leash.

Monkey Cove. 70 mi N of Kingman. SEASON: All yr. FACILITIES: Undesignated sites. MISC.: Elev 1280 ft. Not developed. Pets permitted if they are kept on leash.

Wild Cow Springs (BLM). Approx. 12 mi S/E of Kingman on Hualapai Mountain Rd, to Hualapai Mountain County Park; approx. 5 mi S on winding dirt road thru County Park, to the campground. SEASON: All yr. FACILITIES: 24 sites (tr -20), no tbls, no drk wtr, toil, cga. ACTIVITIES: Hunting; hiking. MISC.: Elev 7200 ft; 10 acres; pets.

See page 7 for KEY TO ABBREVIATIONS.

Pack Saddle (BLM). 21 mi NW of Kingman; then 10 mi E on Chloride Rd. SEASON: All yr, 21-day lmt. FACILITIES: 6 sites, tbls, toil, cga, no drk wtr. MISC.: Elev 6200 ft. Pets on leash.

Windy Point - Pack Saddle (BLM). 21 mi N of Kingman on US 93; right on dirt rd located 2 mi N of St Hwy 62 (Chloride Rd) for approx. 10¼ mi to campground. SEASON: All yr. FACILITIES: 7 primitive sites (tr -20), tbls, toil, cga, no drk wtr. ACTIVITIES: Hunting; hiking; picnicking. MISC.: 13 acres. Pets permitted on leash.

KLONDYKE

Four Mile Canyon Campground (BLM). Located SW of Klondyke in Graham County, just 6 mi from the Aravaipa Canyon Primitive Area. SEASON: All year. FACILITIES: Tent and RV Sites; toil, cga. ACTIVITIES: Hiking; backpacking; birdwatching; picnicking. MISC.: Elev 3500 ft; pets.

LAGUNA DAM

Senator Wash (BLM). 6-1/5 mi N of Laguna Dam. SEASON: All yr. FACILITIES: Undesignated sites, tbls, toil, cga, no drk wtr. ACTIVITIES: Swimming; boating,l; picnicking; fishing. MISC.: Elev 160 ft. Pets on leash.

LAKE HAVASU

Rest Area. 20 mi S of Lake Havasu on US 95. SEASON: All yr, 1-night lmt. FACILITIES: Spaces for self-contained RVs (no tent camping), tbls, toil, cga. ACTIVITIES: Picnicking. MISC.: Pets.

MESA

*Bagley Flat (Tonto NF). 27 mi N of Mesa on St Hwy 87; 4 mi SE on FS 204; 1 mi E on FS 206; 5 mi E by BOAT. SEASON: All yr, 14-day lmt. FACILITIES: 30 tent sites, tbls, flush toil, cga, no drk wtr. 5 mi -- ice, fd, gas. ACTIVITIES: Swimming; waterskiing; picnicking; fishing; boating (lr, 5 mi). MISC.: Elev 1500 ft; 5 acres; lake; pets.

MORENCI

*Safford-Morenci Trail (BLM). The Eagle Creek trailhead (E end) is less than 6 mi SE of Morenci, off US 666 on Black River Rd. SEASON: All yr. FACILITIES: Primitive tent sites. ACTIVITIES: Hiking; hunting. MISC.: Informative signs; pets.

MORMON KALE

Kinnikinick (Coconino NF). 2 mi S of Mormon Kale on FS FH90; 2-1/10 mi SE on Co Hwy FH3; 4-4/5 mi E on FS 125;

4-3/5 mi SE on FS 82. SEASON: 5/1-10/1, 14-day lmt. FACILITIES: 13 sites (tr - -22), tbls, toil, cga, no drk wtr. ACTIVITIES: Picnicking. 1 mi -- fishing; boating,l (8 HP motor only on lake). MISC.: Lake. Pets permitted if on leash.

MORMON LAKE

Dairy Springs (Coconino NF). 4 mi NW on FS90; 1/10 mi W on FS 90C. SEASON: 5/15-10/1; 14-day lmt. FACILTIES: 2 sites (tr -16), tbls, toil, cga, tbls. Store/gas/ice/laundry/fd (1 mi). ACTIVITIES: Picnicking. Horse rental & riding/boating/fishing (1 mi). MISC.: Elev 7000 ft; 3 acres; lake; pets. Reservations required; contact district ranger.

NEW ORAIBI

Oraibi Wash Campground (Hopi Indian Reservation). 1 mi E of New Oraibi on St Hwy 264. SEASON: All yr, 7-day lmt. FACILITIES: 7 sites (tr -24), tbls, toil, cga, no drk wtr. Nearby -- store, ice, fd, laundry. ACTIVITIES: Picnicking. MISC.: 1 acre; reservations accepted; pets permitted if kept on a leash.

ORACLE

Peppersauce (Coronado NF). 15 mi SE of Oracle on FS 382; 1/5 mi W on FS 29. SEASON: All yr, 14-day lmt. FACILITIES: 31 sites (tr -22), tbls, toil, cga, f, piped drk wtr. ACTIVITIES: Rockhounding; picnicking. MISC.: Elev 4700 ft; 10 acres; scenic; pets. Many large Sycamore. Only campground on N side of Mt.Lemmon.

PAGE

Halls Crossing (Glen Canyon NRA). 95 mi W/SW of Blanding, Utah. SEASON: All yr, 30-day lmt. FACILITIES: 64 sites.

Lone Rock (Cedar Breaks NM). 13 mi N of Page on US 89. SEASON: All yr, 14-day lmt. FACILITIES: Undesignated primitive sites (tr -20), tbls, toil, cga. ACTIVITIES: Swimming; picnicking; fishing. MISC.: 25 acres. Pets allowed on leash.

PARKER

Take-Off Point Recreation Site (BLM). 16 mi N of Parker on St Hwy 95; W (left) onto unmarked dirt rd approx. 100 ft before turnoff into Havasu Springs Resort. SEASON: All yr. FACILITIES: 50 sites, tbls, toil, cga. ACTIVITIES: Swimming; boating,l; picnicking; fishing. MISC.: Pets permitted if kept on a leash.

PAYSON

Sycamore (Tonto NF). 6 mi N of Payson on St Hwy 87. SEASON: All yr, 14-day lmt. FACILITIES: 6 sites (tr -16), tbls,

See page 7 for KEY TO ABBREVIATIONS.

toil, cga, no drk wtr. ACTIVITIES: Picnicking. Fishing (1 mi). MISC.: Elev
4500 ft; 5 acres; stream; pets on leash.

Tonto Creek (Tonto NF). 17 mi NE of
Payson on St Hwy 260. SEASON: 5/1-11/1,
14-day lmt. FACILITIES: 27 sites (tr
-16); tbls, toil, cga, no drk wtr.
Store/ice/fd (1 mi). Gas (3 mi).
ACTIVITIES: Picnicking; fishing. Horseback rental/riding (1 mi). MISC.: Elev
5600; 13 acres; pets permitted on leash.

Upper Tonto Creek (Tonto NF). 17 mi
NE of Payson on St Hwy 260; 1 mi N
on Co Hwy 289. SEASON: 5/1-11/1, 14-
day lmt. FACILITIES: 10 sites (tr -16),
tbls, toil, cga, no drk wtr. 2 mi -
store, ice, fd. Gas (4 mi). ACTIVI-
TIES: Picnicking; fishing. Horseback
rental/riding (2 mi). MISC.: Elev 5600
ft; 7 acres; stream. Pets on leash.

PHOENIX

Rest Area. 35 mi N of Phoenix on I-
17. SEASON: All yr, 1-night lmt. FACIL-
ITIES: Spaces for self-contained RVs
(no tent camping), tbls, toil, cga. AC-
TIVITIES: Picnicking. MISC.: Pets.

White Tank Mountain Regional Park.
25 mi W of I-17 on Dunlap/Olive Avenue
in Phoenix. SEASON: All yr, 3-day lmt.
FACILITIES: 40 sites (tr -16), tbls,
toil, cga. ACTIVITIES: Picnicking.
MISC.: Elev 3600 ft. Pets on leash.

PINE

Clints Well (Coconino NF). 21-9/10 mi
N of Pine on St Hwy 87; 1/5 mi N on
FS FH3. SEASON: 5/15-11/15, 14-day lmt.
FACILITIES: 7 sites (tr -22), tbls, toil,
cga, f, no drk wtr. 1 mi --store, gas.
ACTIVITIES: Picnicking. MISC.: Elev
7000 ft; 3 acres; pets. 9 mi -- Blue
Ridge Reservoir.

Kehl Springs (Coconino NF). 13 mi N of
Pine on St Hwy 87; 7-1/10 mi E on FS
300. SEASON: 5/15-11/15, 14-day lmt. FA-
CILITIES: 8 sites (tr -22), tbls, toil,
cga, f, no drk wtr. ACTIVITIES: Picnicking. MISC.: Elev 7500 ft; 6 acres; pets.
Knoll Lake (21 mi).

PORTAL

Pinery Canyon (Coronado NF). 3/5 mi
W of Portal on Co Hwy 42; 16 mi W on
FS 42. SEASON: 4/1-11/30, 14-day lmt.
FACILITIES: 5 sites (tr -16), tbls, toil,
cga, no drk wtr. ACTIVITIES: Picnicking.
MISC.: Elev 7000 ft; 3 acres; scenic;pets.

South Fork (Coronado NF). 3/5 mi W of
Portal on Co Hwy 42; 2-7/10 mi SW on
FS 42; 1-2/5 mi SW on FS 42E. SEASON:
2/1-11/30, 14-day lmt. FACILITIES: 4

tent sites, tbls, toil, cga, no drk wtr.
5 mi -- store, fd, gas. ACTIVITIES:
Hiking; picnicking. MISC.: Elev 5300
ft; 2 acres; stream; nature trails; botanical. Pets permitted if kept on leash.

PRESCOTT

Granite Basin (Prescott NF). 5-2/5 mi
NW of Prescott on Co Hwy 255; 3-1/10
mi NW on FS 374. SEASON: All yr, 14-
day lmt. FACILITIES: 23 sites (tr -22),
tbls, toil, cga, piped drk wtr. ACTIVI-
TIES: Hunting (deer, antelope, dove,
quail); hiking; boating,d (no motors);
picnicking; fishing; horseback riding.
MISC.: Elev 5600; 14 acres; pets. Located
near Granite Basin Lake. This lake is
shallow with weeds; swimming is prohibited. Nearby: horse corral and trail.

Hilltop (Prescott NF). 4-1/10 mi E of
Prescott on St Hwy 69; 3½ mi S on Co
Hwy 197; 2/5 mi E on FS 623 (paved
access and campground rds). SEASON:
5/1-9/30 (often stays open all yr), 5-
day lmt. FACILITIES: 35 sites (tr -22),
no tbls, no drk wtr, toil, cga, f. 2
mi -- store, ice, fd. ACTIVITIES: Hunting (deer, antelope, dove, quail); hiking; boating,d (l,1 mi; r,2 mi); fishing.
MISC.: Elev 6000 ft; 25 acres; pets. Pine
trees. Lynx Lake (½ mi, by trail).

Indian Creek (Prescott NF). 4 mi SW
of Prescott on US 89; ½ mi S on FS 63.
Nestled along Indian Creek between the
White Spar Hwy and the Groom Creek
cut-off #97. SEASON: 5/15-9/15, 14-day
lmt. FACILITIES: 27 sites (tr -22), tbls,
toil, cga, well drk wtr. 4 mi -- store,
ice, gas. Food (5 mi). ACTIVITIES:
Hunting (deer, antelope, dove, quail);
hiking; picnicking. MISC.: Elev 5800
ft; 10 acres; scenic; pets. Pine and
Oak trees furnish shade in campground.

Lower Wolf Creek (Prescott NF). 7-3/5
mi S of Prescott on Co Hwy 52; 9/10
mi W on FS 97. SEASON: All yr, 14-day
lmt. FACILITIES: 20 sites (tr -22), tbls,
toil, cga, piped drk wtr. ACTIVITIES:
Hiking; picnicking; hunting (deer, antelope, dove, quail). MISC.: Elev 6000
ft; 7 acres; paved campground; pets.
Situated in the pine forest area of the
Senator Hwy.

QUARTZSITE

Crystal Hill (Dept. of Fish & Wildlife).
15 mi S of Quartzsite. SEASON: All yr,
14-day lmt. FACILITIES: 32 sites, tbls,
toil, cga, no drk wtr. ACTIVITIES:
Picnicking. MISC.: Elev 1480 ft; pets.

La Posa Recreational Area (BLM). 3
mi S of Quartzsite on US 95. [Located
on 3 gravel rds between ¼ and 5 mi
S of Quartzsite on US 95.] SEASON: All

See page 7 for KEY TO ABBREVIATIONS.

yr. FACILITIES: Undesignated sites, tbls, toil, cga, no drk wtr. ACTIVITIES: Hiking; picnicking. MISC.: Elev 875 ft; primitive. Pets on leash.

ROOSEVELT

Bachelors Cove (Tonto NF). 1-3/5 mi NW of Roosevelt on St Hwy 88; 7-3/10 mi NW on St Hwy 188. SEASON: All yr, 14-day lmt. FACILITIES: 10 sites (tr -22), no tbls, no drk wtr, toil. ACTIVITIES: Swimming; boating,l; fishing; waterskiing. MISC.: Elev 2100 ft; 5 acres; lake. Pets permitted on leash.

Burnt Corral (Tonto NF). 6-1/5 mi SW of Roosevelt on St Hwy 88; 1/5 mi W on FS 12183. SEASON: All yr, 14-day lmt. FACILITIES: 17 sites (tr -22), tbls, toil, no drk wtr. ACTIVITIES: Swimming; picnicking; fishing (1 mi); waterskiing; boating,ld (1 mi). MISC.: Elev 1900 ft; 38 acres; lake. Pets on leash.

Cholla Bay (Tonto NF). 1-3/5 mi NW of Roosevelt on St Hwy 88; 8-1/10 mi NW on St Hwy 188. SEASON: All yr, 14-day lmt. FACILITIES: 10 sites (tr -22), no tbls, no drk wtr, toil. ACTIVITIES: Swimming; boating; fishing; waterskiing. MISC.: Elev 2100 ft; 3 acres; lake; pets.

Horse Pasture (Tonto NF). 1-3/5 mi NW of Roosevelt on St Hwy 88; 8-9/10 mi NW on St Hwy 188. SEASON: 2/15-11/15, 14-day lmt. FACILITIES: 25 sites (tr -22), no tbls, no drk wtr, toil. ACTIVITIES: Swimming; fishing; waterskiing; boating,r. MISC.: Elev 2100 ft; 18 acres; lake. Pets permitted if on a leash.

Hotel Point (Tonto NF). 1-4/5 mi W of Roosevelt on St Hwy 88; 2/5 mi NW on St Hwy 188. SEASON: All yr, 14-day lmt. FACILITIES: 4 sites (tr -16), tbls, toil, cga, no drk wtr. ACTIVITIES: Swimming; waterskiing; picnicking; fishing (1 mi); boating,dr (l, 3 mi). MISC.: Elev 2200 ft; 2 acres; pets on lake.

Schoolhouse Point (Tonto NF). 7-3/10 mi SE of Roosevelt on St Hwy 88; 3½ mi NE on FS 447. SEASON: All yr, 14-day lmt. FACILITIES: 10 sites (tr -22), no tbls, no drk wtr, toil. 5 mi -- store, ice, gas, laundry, dump, fd. ACTIVITIES: Swimming; boating,l; fishing; waterskiing. MISC.: Elev 2100 ft; 35 acres; pets; stream. Access to Salt River.

Windy Hill (Tonto NF). 3-1/10 mi SE of Roosevelt on St Hwy 88; 2-1/5 mi N on FS 82. SEASON: All yr, 14-day lmt. FACILITIES: 10 sites (tr -22), no tbls, no drk wtr, toil. ACTIVITIES: Boating (ramp, 1 mi); swimming; fishing; waterskiing. MISC.: Lake. Pets on leash.

SAFFORD

Black Hills Rockhound Area (BLM). 17 mi NE of Safford, just off US 666. The access rd turns off from St Hwy 666 and continues approx. 1 mi to parking area. SEASON: All yr. FACILITIES: No designated sites, tbls, toil, cga. ACTIVITIES: Hunting; hiking; picnicking; fishing. MISC.: Drk wtr. Pets on leash.

Hospital Flat (Coronado NF). 7½ mi S of Safford on US 666; 23 mi SW on St Hwy 366. SEASON: 5/20-12/1, 14-day lmt. FACILITIES: 12 sites (tr -32), tbls, toil, cga, f. ACTIVITIES: Picnicking; horseback riding. MISC.: 2 acres; pets.

*Safford-Morenci Trail (BLM). The West Ranch trailhead is approx. 12 mi NE of Safford on the San Juan Mine Rd (W end). SEASON: All yr. FACILITIES: Primitive tent sites. ACTIVITIES: Hunting; hiking. MISC.: Pets; informative signs.

Stockton Pass (Coronado NF). 16½ mi S of Safford on US 666; 12 mi W on St Hwy 266; ½ mi NE on FS 198. SEASON: All yr. FACILITIES: 11 tent sites, tbls, toil, cga, f, piped drk wtr. ACTIVITIES: Picnicking. Riding horses (1 mi). MISC.: Elev 5600 ft; 4 acres; pets.

SEDONA

Bootlegger (Coconino NF). 8-7/10 mi N of Sedona on US 89A. SEASON: 6/1-9/1, 3-day lmt. FACILITIES: 9 sites (tr -32), tbls, toil, cga, no drk wtr. 1 mi -- store, ice, gas. ACTIVITIES: Swimming; picnicking; fishing; hiking. MISC.: Elev 5200 ft; 1 acre; stream; nature trails. Pets allowed on leash.

Halfway (Coconino NF). 7-4/5 mi N of Sedona on US 89A. SEASON: 5/15-9/15. FACILITIES: 9 tent sites, tbls, toil, cga, no drk wtr. [Handicapped toil.] 1 mi -- store, ice, gas. Fd (2 mi). ACTIVITIES: Picnicking; hiking. 1 mi -- swimming; fishing. MISC.: Elev 5000 ft; 1 acre; stream; pets. Trails (4 mi).

Red Rock Crossing (Coconino NF). 4-3/5 mi W of Sedona on US 89A; 2-3/10 mi SE on FS 216; ½ mi SE on FS 216A. SEASON: All yr, 7-day lmt. FACILITIES: 17 sites (no tr), tbls, flush toil, cga, no drk wtr. [Handicapped toil.] ACTIVITIES: Swimming; picnicking; fishing. MISC.: Elev 4000 ft; 6 acres; stream. Pets permitted if kept on a leash. Rough dirt road last 1/2 mile.

SHOW LOW

Fool Hollow (Apache-Sitgreaves NF). 1-3/5 mi SW of Show Low on US 60; 2 mi NW on St Hwy 160; ½ mi E on Co Hwy; 1½ mi N on FS 137. SEASON: 4/15-10/15. FACILITIES: 20 sites (tr -32), no tbls, no drk wtr, toil. 5 mi -- store, ice, gas, laundry, fd. ACTIVITIES: Swimming; fishing; boating. 5 mi -- Boat rental; horse rental/riding. MISC.: Elev 6300 ft; 10 acres; lake; pets.

See page 7 for KEY TO ABBREVIATIONS.

Lewis Canyon (Apache-Sitgreaves NF). 13 mi NW of Show Low on St Hwy 260; 2 mi S on FS 130. SEASON: 5/1-9/30, 14-day lmt. FACILITIES: 22 sites (tr -22), tbls, toil, cga, f. ACTIVITIES: Picnicking. MISC.: Elev 6300 ft; 5 acres; scenic. Pets permitted if on leash.

SUPERIOR

Oak Flat (Tonto NF). 4 mi NE of Superior on US 60. SEASON: All yr, 14-day lmt. FACILITIES: 27 sites (tr -22), tbls, toil, cga, no drk wtr. 4 mi -- Store, ice, fd, gas, laundry, showers. ACTIVITIES: Rockhounding; picnicking. MISC.: Elev 4200 ft; 20 acres. Pets on leash.

TACNA

Rest Area. E of Tacna on I-8. SEASON: All yr, 1-day lmt. FACILITIES: Spaces for self-contained RVs (no tent camping). Tbls, cga, toil. ACTIVITIES: Picnicking. MISC.: Pets permitted if on a leash.

TOMBSTONE

City Park. E on Allen St, follow signs; on edge of Tombstone. SEASON: All yr, 2-night lmt. FACILITIES: Undesignated sites. MISC.: Pets allowed on leash.

TONALEA

Elephant Feet (Indian). 1 mi E of US 160. SEASON: All yr. FACILITIES:3 sites, tbls, toil, cga, no drk wtr. ACTIVITIES: Picnicking. MISC.: Elev 5000 ft; pets.

TUBA CITY

*Backcountry Campground** (Navajo NM). 50 mi NE of Tuba City on US 160; 9 mi N/NW on St Hwy 564 to monument headquarters. 9 mi N of Visitor Center on rough TRAIL. SEASON: 6/1-LD, 1-night lmt. FACILITIES: Undesignated tent sites. ACTIVITIES: Hiking; horseback riding. MISC.: Elev 7300; 60 acres; pets. No wood fires; charcoal/propane.

Main Campground (Navajo NM). 50 mi NE of Tuba City on US 160; 9 mi N/NW on St Hwy 564 to monument headquarters. Campground is just beyond the Visitor Center. SEASON: May-October, 7-day lmt. FACILITIES: 30 sites (tr -25), tbls, flush toil, cga, dump, water in restrooms. ACTIVITIES: Picnicking. In summer, campfire programs on archeology, history and natural history of the monument. MISC.: Elev 7300 ft. Pets on leash. A Navajo Tribal Guild concession in the Visitor Center sells objects made by the Indians. No wood fires; only charcoal/propane.

Primitive Campground (Navajo NM). 50 mi NE of Tuba City on US 160; 9 mi N/NW on St Hwy 564 to monument headquarters.

Campground is within ½ mi of Visitor Center. SEASON: All yr (but not cleared of snow in winter; sometimes impassable), 7-day lmt. FACILITIES: 12 sites (tr -25), no water, toil. Tbls/cga by Visitor Center. ACTIVITIES: Picnicking; hiking. In summer, campfire programs on archeology, history, and natural history of the monument. MISC.: Elev 7300 ft. Pets. No wood fires; only charcoal/propane. One group site. A Navajo Tribal Guild concession in the Visitor Center sells objects made by the Indians.

TUCSON

Rest Area. 10 mi W of Tucson. SEASON: All yr, 1-night lmt. FACILITIES: Spaces for self-contained RVs (no tent camping), tbls, toil, cga. ACTIVITIES: Picnicking. MISC.: Pets permitted if kept on leash.

Rest Area. 35 mi S of Tucson on St Hwy 89. SEASON: All yr, 1-night lmt. FACILITIES: Spaces for self-contained RVs (no tent camping), tbls, toil, cga. ACTIVITIES: Picnicking. MISC.: Pets on leash.

WILLIAMS

Cataract Lake (Kaibab NF). 3/10 mi W of Williams on US 140; 1-3/10 mi W on FS 749. SEASON: All yr, 14-day lmt. FACILITIES: 4 sites (tr -16), tbls, toil, cga, no drk wtr. 1 mi -- Store, ice, gas, showers, laundry, lifeguard, dump, fd. ACTIVITIES: Boating,l; picnicking; fishing. Horseback riding (rent, 2 mi). MISC.: Elev 6800 ft; 9 acres; lake; pets; scenic. Access to FS 749 from N 6th St in Williams.

YOUNG

Rose Creek (Tonto NF). 23-2/5 mi S of Young on St Hwy 288. SEASON: 5/1-11/1, 14-day lmt. FACILITIES: 4 sites (tr -22), tbls, toil, cga, f, piped drk wtr. ACTIVITIES: Picnicking. MISC.: Elev 5400 ft; 5 acres. Pets on leash.

YUMA

Rest Area. 18 mi N of Yuma. SEASON: All yr, 1-night lmt. FACILITIES: Spaces for self-contained RVs (no tent camping), tbls, toil, cga. ACTIVITIES: Picnicking. MISC.: Pets permitted if kept on leash.

Senator Wash Reservoir Recreation Site (BLM). 26 mi NE of Yuma on Imperial County Highway (Calif. St Hwy 24). SEASON: All yr. FACILITIES: 600 sites, tbls, toil, cga. ACTIVITIES: Swimming; boating,l; picnicking. MISC.: Pets on leash.

See page 7 for KEY TO ABBREVIATIONS.

ARKANSAS

GENERAL STATE INFORMATION

Miscellaneous

Toll-Free Number for Travel Information:
1-800-482-8999 (in Arkansas)
1-800-643-8383 (out of state)
Right Turns on Red: Permitted after a full stop,
unless otherwise posted.
STATE CAPITOL: Little Rock
STATE NICKNAME: Bear State
STATE MOTTO: "The People Rule"
STATE BIRD: Mockingbird
STATE TREE: Shortleaf Pine
STATE FLOWER: Apple Blossom

State Parks

Fees range from $3.50 to $7.00 per night. Pets must be on leash and under control. Campsites are limited to 14 days occupancy within a 30-day period. State Park campgrounds are open all year. Further information: The Arkansas Department of Parks and Tourism; 149 State Capitol; Little Rock, ARK 72201.

Rest Areas

Overnight parking in self-contained RVs, or in cars, is permitted. No tent camping.

Arkansas Game & Fish Commission Campgrounds

All of the Arkansas Game & Fish Commission campgrounds are free and primitive (no facilities). The Game & Fish Commission owns about 300,000 acres of land in the State which are operated as wildlife management areas with designated, free camping areas; and also manages wildlife on more than one million acres of National Forest land that is open to the public for camping. A description of how to get to each camping area would be next to impossible (one area alone has 52 camping sites). Therefore, if you write to the Arkansas Game & Fish Commission (Little Rock, AR 72201) they will send you a state map which depicts the location of each wildlife area. Campsites are relatively easy to find, once a camper finds the wildlife area.

Buffalo National River (NPS)

Float down the Buffalo River in a canoe past massive sandstone and limestone bluffs; white water (usually floatable in spring/winter). Fishing (small/largemouth bass, catfish, panfish). For developed (though primitive) campgrounds, see the following sections in this chapter: "Jasper", "Morning Star", "Pindall", "Ponca", "Pruitt", "Yellville". For map and additional information, including a list of canoe rentals, write: Supt.; Buffalo National River; PO Box 1173; Harrison ARK 72601. [Located in New Federal Building; Erie and Walnut, Room 136.]

Camping in White River National Wildlife Refuge

Can be reached from E or N via US 70, from Little Rock or Memphis. From near Hazen turn off on St Hwy 11 to Stuttgart and follow this same route to DeWitt. Then take St Rte 1 to St. Charles. From the S, travel via US 65 to Pine Bluff and then to Stuttgart. Visitors always welcome; but stop and ask directions and road conditions at the St. Charles Headquarters, since the bottoms' roads are often impassable even during summer months. There are more than 20 designated camping areas. For details on the developed campground, see "Dewitt" (Jacks Bay Landing) in this chapter. For a map which pinpoints the other camping areas, write to: White River NWR; PO Box 308; Dewitt, AR 72042. Camping is permitted from 3/16-10/31 in designated areas; 14-day lmt. Fishing: Season, 3/16-10/31; no permit required. Hunting: Permits are required, are non-transferable, and must be on the hunter at all times. Closed areas for all hunts are shown on the above-mentioned map and posted as "closed".

WILDERNESS AREAS

Backcountry Camping in Ouachita National Forest

Hundreds of miles of scenic trails. Hunting (deer, red fox, opossum, raccoon, wild turkey, bobwhite). Fishing (striped bass, rainbow trout). Free maps/brochures available from: Supt.; Ouachita NF; PO Box 1270; Hot Springs, AR 71901 [501/623-7763].

Caney Creek Wilderness (Ouachita NF)

Headquarters: 15 mi S of Mena on US 59/71; 17 mi E on St Hwy 246; 9 mi N on FS 38 (in Mena Ranger District). 12 mi of hiking trails within 14,433 acres of secluded forest. Scenic: flowing streams; panoramic views. Largest roadless mountain area in central United States. Hunting (deer, red fox, opossum, raccoon, wild turkey, bobwhite). Fishing (striped bass, rainbow trout). Free information and map ("Caney Creek Back Country"): Supt.; PO Box 1270; Hot Springs, AR 71901 [501/623-7763]; or Supt.; Mena Ranger District; Ouachita NF; 507 Mena Street; Mena, AR 71953.

Upper Buffalo Wilderness (Ozark NF)

Wilderness hiking and camping. Fishing (smallmouth bass). Hunting (deer, raccoon, squirrel, red fox, wild turkey). Located at headwaters of Buffalo National Wild and Scenic River, an extremely picturesque canoeing route. Further information: Supt.; Ozark-St. Francis NF; PO Box 1008; Russellville, AR 72801 [501/968-2354].

Wilderness Camping/Canoeing in Ozark National Forest

Headwaters of several outstanding wildwater float streams are here: Buffalo, Illinois Bayou, Mulberry, Big Piney, King, White River. Hundreds of miles of exciting/relaxing/beautiful canoeing and wilderness camping. Further free information/map: Supt., Ozark-St. Francis NF; PO Box 1008; Russellville, AR 72801. Also, free "Float Streams of Arkansas" from Dept. of Parks & Tourism (State Capitol; Little Rock, AR 72201). The Game & Fish Commission (Game and Fish Building; Little Rock, AR 72201) publishes several free area fishing guides, which indicate roads, portage points, and other free area information.

INFORMATION SOURCES

Maps

Completely indexed, up-to-date, detailed maps of The State of Arkansas and Little Rock are available from Forsyth Travel Library (see order form in Appendix B).

State Information

Arkansas Dept. of Parks & Tourism; 149 State Capitol Building; Little Rock, AR 72201
Game & Fish Commission; Game and Fish Building; Little Rock, AR 72201

City Information

Hot Springs Chamber of Commerce; Hot Springs, AR 71901
Little Rock Chamber of Commerce; Continental Building; Markham and Main Streets; Little Rock, AR 72201
Malvern Chamber of Commerce; Malvern, AR 72104

Miscellaneous

Ouachita NF; Federal Building; PO Box 1270; Hot Springs, AR 71901 [501/623-7763]
Ozark-St. Francis NF; PO Box 1008; Russellville, AR 72801.
Buffalo National River (National Park Service); New Federal Building; Erie and Walnut, Room 136; PO Box 1173; Harrison, AR 72601
U.S. Army Engineer District, Little Rock; Corps of Engineers; 700 West Capitol; PO Box 867; Little Rock, AR 72203
White River National Wildlife Refuge; Box 308; 704 Jefferson Street; DeWitt, AR 72042 [501/946-1468]

FREE CAMPGROUNDS

ASHDOWN

Ashley's Camp (COE; Millwood Lakes). 10 mi N of Ashdown on St Hwy 71; 2 mi SE on Old Hwy 71. SEASON: All yr, 14-day lmt. FACILITIES: 7 sites (tr -32), pull-thru spaces; tbls, toil, cga. ACTIVITIES: Swimming; boating,l; picnicking; fishing. MISC.: 1 acre; pets.

Beard's Lake (COE; Millwood Lakes). 13 mi W of Ashdown. SEASON: All yr, 14-day lmt. FACILITIES: 5 sites, pull-thru spaces; tbls, toil, cga. ACTIVITIES: Horseback riding, picnicking; fishing. Swimming (1 mi). MISC.: 50 acres; pets; playground. Recreation area is upstream of the east embankment of the dam.

See page 7 for KEY TO ABBREVIATIONS.

River Run East (COE; Millwood Lakes). 10 mi E of Ashdown on St Hwy 32; ½ mi E on access rd. Below Millwood Dam. SEASON: All yr, 14-day lmt. FACILITIES: 13 sites; tbls, toil, cga. Nearby -- Store, ice, fd. ACTIVITIES: Boating,l; picnicking; fishing. Swimming (nearby). MISC.: 20 acres; pets permitted if kept on a leash.

White Cliffs (COE; Millwood Lakes). 10 mi N of Ashdown on St Hwy 71; 5 mi E on St Hwy 27; 6 mi S on St Hwy 317. SEASON: All yr, 14-day lmt. FACILITIES: 18 sites; tbls, toil, cga, drk wtr. ACTIVITIES: Swimming; boating,l; picnicking; fishing. MISC.: 58 acres; pets.

ATHENS

Bard Springs (Ouachita NF). 2 mi NW of Athens on Co Hwy 246; 6 mi N on FS 38; ½ mi E on FS 106. (Gravel access rds.) SEASON: All yr, 14-day lmt. FACILITIES: 7 sites (tr -22), tbls, toil, cga, well drk wtr, bathhouse. Showers (4 mi). ACTIVITIES: Swimming (small swim area); picnicking; fishing; hiking; hunting (nearby, in season). Horseback riding (1 mi). MISC.: Elev 1200 ft; 4 acres; pets; scenic small stream. Nature trails (3 mi).

ATKINS

Sweeden Island (COE; Lock & Dam #9). 10 mi SW of Atkins on St Hwy 105. SEASON: 11/24-3/1, FREE (rest of yr, $3); 14-day lmt. FACILITIES: 28 sites; tbls, toil, cga, drk wtr. ACTIVITIES: Boating,l; picnicking; fishing. MISC.: Pets. McClellan-Kerr Arkansas River Navigation River.

BAUCUM

Willow Beach (COE; David D. Terry Lock & Dam and Lake). 2 mi SE of Baucum; ½ mi SW on paved access road. SEASON: 11/19-4/30, FREE (rest of yr, $2); 14-day lmt. FACILITIES: 21 sites; tbls, toil, cga, drk wtr, group shelter, playground, dump. ACTIVITIES: Boating,l; picnicking. MISC.: Pets on leash.

BEAVER

Beaver Campground (COE; Table Rock Lake). At Beaver, on St Hwy 187. SEASON: 9/16-3/1, FREE ($2 rest of yr); 14-day lmt. FACILITIES: 27 sites; tbls, toil, cga, drk wtr. ACTIVITIES: Swimming; picnicking; fishing; boating,rl. MISC.: 16 acres. Pets allowed on leash.

BEE BRANCH

Sugar Loaf (COE; Greers Ferry Lake). 11 mi NE of Bee Branch. SEASON: 9/4-5/13, FREE ($3 rest of yr); 14-day lmt. FACILITIES: 83 sites; tbls, toil, cga,

drk wtr, playground, ice, dump. ACTIVITIES: Swimming; picnicking; fishing; boating,rdl. MISC.: 55 acres; pets.

BIG CEDAR

Billy Creek Campground (Ouachita NF). 6 mi W of Big Cedar on St Hwy 63; 3 mi N (at sign) on FS 22. FACILITIES: 11 sites (tr -22), tbls, toil, cga, drk wtr. ACTIVITIES: Hunting; hiking; picnicking; fishing. MISC.: Natural pool in attractive stream. Pets on leash.

BLUE MOUNTAIN

Ashley Creek (COE; Blue Mountain Lake). 2 mi S of Blue Mountain on gravel access road. SEASON: All yr, 14-day lmt. FACILITIES: 10 sites; tbls, toil, cga, drk wtr, dump. ACTIVITIES: Boating,rld; picnicking; fishing. MISC.: 8 acres; pets.

BOONVILLE

Hise Hill (COE; Blue Mountain Lake). 6 mi S of Boonville on gravel access rd to Sugar Grove; 2 mi E at crossroad. SEASON: All yr, 14-day lmt. FACILITIES: 9 sites; tbls, toil, cga, drk wtr. ACTIVITIES: Boating,rl; picnicking; fishing. MISC.: 22 acres; no motorbikes; pets.

Jack Creek (Ouachita NF). 3 mi S of Boonville on St Hwy 23; 1 mi E on St Hwy 116; 5 mi SE on FS 19; 1 mi E on FS 141. SEASON: 4/4-12/1; 14-day lmt. FACILITIES: 5 sites (tr -22), tbls, toil, cga, f, well drk wtr. ACTIVITIES: Swimming; picnicking; fishing. MISC.: Pets.

Knoppers Ford (Ouachita NF). 3 mi S of Boonville on St Hwy 23; 1 mi E on St Hwy 116; 7 mi SE on FS 19. SEASON: All yr, 14-day lmt. FACILITIES: 6 sites (tr -22), tbls, toil, cga, f, well drk wtr. ACTIVITIES: Swimming; picnicking; fishing. MISC.: Stream. Pets on leash.

BRINKLEY

Greenlee City Park. 2 mi from Business District on US 70E. SEASON: All yr.

BROWNSVILLE

Cherokee Park (COE; Greers Ferry Lake). 4 mi S of Brownsville. SEASON: All yr, 14-day lmt. FACILITIES: 33 sites; tbls, toil, cga, drk wtr. ACTIVITIES: Boating,rl; picnicking; fishing. MISC.: 20 acres. Pets allowed on leash.

BULL SHOALS

Bull Shoals Campground (COE;Bull Shoals Lake). W of Bull Shoals on St Hwy 178. SEASON: 5/15-9/15, 14-day lmt. FACILITIES: 12 sites; tbls, toil, cga, drk wtr, ice, fd. Laundry nearby. ACTIVITIES: Boating,rld; picnicking; fishing. MISC.: 9 acres. Pets permitted on leash.

Point Return (COE; Bull Shoals Lake).
½ mi NE of Bull Shoals on access rds.
SEASON: 9/4-5/13, FREE ($3 rest of yr);
14-day lmt. FACILITIES: 28 sites; tbls,
toil, cga, drk wtr, dump. ACTIVITIES:
Swimming; boating,rl; picnicking; fishing. MISC.: 38 acres. Pets on leash.

CAMDEN

Rest Area. 5 mi S of Camden on US
79. SEASON: All yr, 1-night lmt. FACIL-
ITIES: Spaces for self-contained RVs.
No tent camping. Tbls, toil, cga.
ACTIVITIES: Picnicking. MISC.: Pets.

CECIL

Citadel Bluff (COE; Ozark Lake). 1 mi
N of Cecil on Co Rd. SEASON: 9/4-5/13,
FREE ($2 rest of yr); 14-day lmt. FA-
CILITIES: 36 sites; tbls, toil, cga, drk
wtr. ACTIVITIES: Hiking; boating,l;
picnicking. MISC.: 175 acres; nature
trails. Pets on leash.

CHOCTAW

Choctaw Park (COE; Greers Ferry Lake).
4 mi E of Choctaw on St Hwy 330. SEA-
SON: 9/4-5/13, FREE ($3 rest of yr); 14-
day lmt. FACILITIES: 115 sites; tbls,
toil, cga, drk wtr, ice, dump, amphitheater, playground. ACTIVITIES: Swimming;
boating,rld; picnicking; fishing. MISC.:
63 acres; lake. Pets on a leash.

CLARKSVILLE

Spadra (COE; Dardanelle Lake). 2 mi
S of Clarksville on St Hwy 103 to Jamestown; 1 mi on access road. SEASON: 9/4-
5/13, FREE ($3 rest of yr); 14-day lmt.
FACILITIES: 31 sites; tbls, toil, cga,
drk wtr, electric hookup, dump, showers,
store, ice, fd, group shelters. ACTIVI-
TIES: Boating,rld; picnicking; fishing.
MISC.: 82 acres. Pets permitted on leash.

Wolf Pen (Ozark NF). 20 mi NW of Clarksville on St Hwy 103; 3 mi W on St Hwy
215. SEASON: All yr, 14-day lmt. FACILI-
TIES: 6 sites; tbls, toil, cga, f. 4 mi
-- Store, ice, gas. ACTIVITIES: Canoeing; picnicking; fishing. MISC.: Elev
1000 ft; 4 acres; pets. Entry point for
Mulberry River canoeists.

CLEVELAND

Driver Creek (Ozark NF). 7/10 mi N of
Cleveland on St Hwy 95; 2-3/10 mi N on
FS 1306; 7/10 mi W on FS 1335. [Caution:
Roads into Driver Creek Area may be
very rough. Cars pulling trailers should
check road conditions before entering
access road.] SEASON: All year; 14-day
lmt. FACILITIES: 1 site (tr -22), tbls,
toil, cga, f, well drk wtr. Fd (1 mi).
Store/gas (4 mi). ACTIVITIES: Hunting;
swimming; picnicking; fishing. Boating

(5 mi) ; 10 HP limit for boats. MISC.:
Elev 700 ft; 1 acre; 35-acre lake; pets.

CLINTON

South Fork (COE; Greers Ferry Lake).
3 mi E of Clinton on St Hwy 16; 7 mi
SE on gravel access road. SEASON: All
yr, 14-day lmt. FACILITIES: 13 sites;
tbls, toil, cga, drk wtr. ACTIVITIES:
Boating,rl; picnicking; fishing. MISC.:
15 acres; lake. Pets allowed on leash.

CONWAY

Toad Suck Park — West (COE; Toad
Suck Ferry Lock & Dam). 5 mi W of
Conway on US 63. SEASON: 11/24-3/1,
FREE ($3 rest of yr); 14-day lmt. FA-
CILITIES: 31 sites; tbls, toil, cga, drk
wtr, dump, showers. ACTIVITIES: Pic-
nicking; boating,l. MISC.: McClellan-
Kerr Arkansas River Navigation System.
Pets permitted if kept on a leash.

CORNING

Rest Area. 5 mi N of Corning on US
67. SEASON: All yr, 1-night lmt. FACILI-
TIES: Spaces for self-contained RVs (no
tent camping); tbls, toil, cga. ACTIVI-
TIES: Picnicking. MISC.: Pets on leash.

DARDANELLE

Dam Site West (COE; Dardanelle Lake).
1 mi N of Dardanelle. SEASON: 9/4-5/13,
FREE ($2 rest of yr); 14-day lmt. FA-
CILITIES: 22 sites; tbls, toil, cga, drk
wtr. ACTIVITIES: Picnicking; fishing.
MISC.: 73 acres; scenic overlook; pets.

DELAWARE

Delaware Campground (COE; Dardanelle
Lake). ¼ mi E of Delaware on St Hwy
22; ½ mi on access road. SEASON: 9/4-
5/13, FREE ($2 rest of yr); 14-day lmt.
FACILITIES: 15 sites; tbls, toil, cga,
drk wtr. ACTIVITIES: Boating,rl; picnicking; fishing. MISC.: 140 acres; pets.

DEWITT

Jacks Bay Landing (White River NWR).
10 mi S of Dewitt on St Hwy 1; 9 mi
E on St Hwy 44; E on Co Rd. SEASON:
3/15-10/31, 14-day lmt. FACILITIES:
Undesignated sites, tbls, flush toil,
cga, drk wtr. ACTIVITIES: Boating,l;
picnicking; fishing. MISC.:10 acres;pets.

Merrisach Lake (COE; Lock & Dam #2).
5 of Dewitt on St Hwy 1; 5 mi E on
St Hwy 44; 10 mi S at Tichnor. SEASON:
11/19-4/30, FREE ($3 rest of yr); 14-
day lmt. FACILITIES: 46 sites; tbls,
toil, cga, drk wtr, dump, playground.
ACTIVITIES: Boating,rl; picnicking;
fishing. MISC.: 102 acres. McClellan-
Kerr Arkansas River Navigation System.
Pets permitted if kept on a leash.

See page 7 for KEY TO ABBREVIATIONS.

DIERKS

Blue Ridge Public Use Area (COE; Dierks Lake). 3 mi N of Dierks on St Hwy 70. SEASON: All yr, 14-day lmt. FACILITIES: 21 self-contained RV sites; tbls, toil, cga, drk wtr. ACTIVITIES: Swimming; boating,l; picnicking; fishing. MISC.: 125 acres. Pets permitted on leash.

DRASCO

Cherokee Park (COE; Greers Ferry Lake). 7½ mi SW of Drasco on St Hwy 92; 4½ mi S on gravel access rd. SEASON: All yr, 14-day lmt. FACILITIES: 33 sites; tbls, toil, cga, drk wtr. ACTIVITIES: Boating,rl; picnicking; fishing. MISC.: 20 acres; no motorbikes. Pets on leash.

EUREKA SPRINGS

Dam Site (COE; Beaver Lake). 9 mi NW of Eureka Springs on US 62; 2½ mi S on paved St Hwy 187 to dam. SEASON: 11/1-5/13, FREE ($3 rest of yr); 14-day lmt. FACILITIES: 78 sites; tbls, flush toil, cga, drk wtr, dump, electric hookup ($). Store nearby. ACTIVITIES: Swimming; boating,rl; picnicking; fishing. MISC.: 93 acres; scenic overlook. Pets on leash.

Starkey (COE; Beaver Lake). 4 mi NW of Eureka Springs on US 62; 7 mi SW on paved St Hwy 187. SEASON: 11/1-5/13, FREE ($3 rest of yr); 14-day lmt. FACILITIES: 32 sites; tbls, toil, cga, drk wtr, fd, ice; store; electric hookup ($). ACTIVITIES: Boating,rld; picnicking. MISC.: 17 acres. Pets allowed on a leash.

FLIPPEN

City Park. E edge of Flippen on US 62. SEASON: All year.

FORT SMITH

Rest Area. On I-40, E edge of Fort Smith. SEASON: All yr, 1-night lmt. FACILITIES: Spaces for self-contained RVs (no tent camping). ACTIVITIES: Picnicking. MISC.: Pets allowed if on a leash.

GAMALIEL

Bidwell Point (COE; Norfork Lake). 6 mi SE of Gamaliel on St Hwy 101. SEASON: 11/10-3/1, FREE ($3 rest of yr); 14-day lmt. FACILITIES: 48 sites; tbls, toil, cga, drk wtr, dump, change shelter. ACTIVITIES: Swimming (beach); boating,rl; picnicking; fishing. MISC.: 34 acres. Pets permitted if on a leash.

Red Bank (COE; Norfork Lake). 3 mi SW of Gamaliel on St Hwy 101 and gravel access road. SEASON: 9/4-5/13, FREE ($2 rest of yr); 14-day lmt. FACILITIES: 12 sites; tbls, toil, cga, drk wtr. ACTIVITIES: Boating,rl; picnicking; fishing. MISC.: 8 acres. Pets on leash.

GARFIELD

Lost Bridge (COE; Beaver Lake). 6 mi SE of Garfield on St Hwy 127. SEASON: 11/1-5/13, FREE ($3 rest of yr); 14-day lmt. FACILITIES: 94 sites; tbls, toil, cga, drk wtr, electric hookup ($), ice, dump, fd, store. ACTIVITIES: Swimming; boating,rld; picnicking; fishing. MISC.: 29 acres. Pets allowed if on a leash.

Ventris (COE; Beaver Lake). 5-1/5 mi S of Garfield on paved rd; 2-3/5 mi W on gravel access road. SEASON: All yr, 14-day lmt. FACILITIES: 17 sites; tbls, toil, cga, drk wtr. ACTIVITIES: Picnicking; boating,rl. MISC.: 5 acres; pets permitted if kept on a leash.

GATEWAY

Indian Creek (Beaver Lake; COE). 1½ mi E of Gateway on US 62; 5 mi S on gravel access rd. SEASON: All yr, 14-day lmt. FACILITIES: 42 sites; tbls, toil, cga, drk wtr. ACTIVITIES: Swimming; boating,rl; picnicking; fishing. MISC.: 20 acres. Pets on leash.

GILLETT

Morgan Point (COE; Lock & Dam #2). 1 mi S of Gillett on St Hwy 1 to Pendleton; 1 mi N on paved access rd. SEASON: All yr, 14-day lmt. FACILITIES: 16 sites; tbls, toil, cga, drk wtr. ACTIVITIES: Boating,rl; picnicking; fishing. MISC.: 137 acres; pets. McClellan-Kerr Arkansas River Navigation System.

Pendleton Bend (COE; Lock & Dam #2). 10 mi S of Gillett on St Hwy 1 to Pendleton; then 1 mi N on paved access rd. SEASON: 5/1-9/30, 14-day lmt. FACILITIES: 10 sites; tbls, toil, cga, drk wtr. ACTIVITIES: Picnicking; boating,l. MISC.: Pets. McClelland-Kerr Arkansas River Navigation System.

GREEN FOREST

City Park. On West 6th Street in Green Forest. SEASON: All year.

GREERS FERRY

Mill Creek (COE; Greers Ferry Lake). 7 mi W of Greers Ferry. SEASON: All yr, 14-day lmt. FACILITIES: 27 sites; tbls, toil, cga, drk wtr. ACTIVITIES: Swimming; picnicking; fishing; boating,rl. MISC.: 30 acres. Pets on a leash.

Narrows Park (COE; Greers Ferry Lake). 2 mi SW of Greers Ferry. SEASON: 11/19-3/14, FREE ($3 rest of yr); 14-day lmt. FACILITIES: 60 sites; tbls, toil, cga, drk wtr, electric hookup ($), dump, ice. Laundry nearby. ACTIVITIES: Picnicking; fishing; boating,rld. MISC.: 50 acres. Pets permitted if kept on a leash.

See page 7 for KEY TO ABBREVIATIONS.

Shiloh Park (Greers Ferry Lake; COE).
3 mi SE of Greers Ferry. SEASON: 9/4-
5/13, FREE ($3 rest of yr); 14-day lmt.
FACILITIES: 113 sites, tbls, toil, cga,
drk wtr, ice, dump, playground. ACTIV-
ITIES: Swimming; picnicking; fishing;
boating,rld. MISC.: 72 acres; pets.

HARRISON

Lost Valley (Buffalo National River).
30 mi S of Harrison on St Hwy 43. SEA-
SON: All yr, 14-day lmt. FACILITIES:
15 sites (tr -20), tbls, toil, cga, drk
wtr. ACTIVITIES: Hiking; canoeing; swimming (no diving); picnicking; fishing.
MISC.: 200 acres; scenic; pets. Access
to floating by canoe down Buffalo River.

HARTMAN

Horsehead (COE; Dardanelle Lake). 1
mi E of Hartman on US 64; 2 mi E on
St Hwy 194; 1-3/4 mi S on access rd.
SEASON: All yr, 14-day lmt. FACILITIES:
10 sites; tbls, toil, cga, drk wtr, group
shelter. ACTIVITIES: Boating,rl; picnicking; fishing. MISC.: 107 acres; pets.

HAVANA

Mount Magazine Recreation Area (Ozark
NF). 12 mi N of Havana on St Hwy 309.
FACILITIES: 16 sites; tbls, toil, cga,
drk wtr. ACTIVITIES: Mountain climb-
ing; picnicking. Hunting/fishing nearby.
Swimming at Cove Lake (9 mi N).
MISC.: Rugged mountain scenery; cool
climate; highest point in Arkansas;pets.

HEBER SPRINGS

Dam Site Park (COE; Greers Ferry Lake).
3 mi NE of Heber Springs on St Hwy
25. SEASON: 9/4-5/13, FREE ($3 rest
of yr); 14-day lmt. FACILITIES: 269
sites; tbls, flush toil, cga, dump, showers, ice, amphitheater, drk wtr. ACTIVI-
TIES: Swimming; picnicking; fishing;
boating,rld. MISC.: 110 acres; pets.

Heber Springs Park (COE; Greers Ferry
Lake). 3 mi W of Heber Springs on St
Hwy 110. SEASON: 9/4-5/13, FREE ($3
rest of yr); 14-day lmt. FACILITIES:
140 sites; tbls, flush toil, cga, dump,
showers, ice, drk wtr. ACTIVITIES:
Swimming; picnicking; fishing; boating,rld. MISC.: 61 acres; pets.

Old Highway 25 Park (COE; Greers Ferry
Lake). 6¼ mi N of Heber Springs on
St Hwy 25; 3 mi W on old St Hwy 25.
SEASON: 9/4-5/13, FREE ($3 rest of yr).
FACILITIES: 100 sites; tbls, toil, cga,
drk wtr, dump, playground. Laundry
nearby. ACTIVITIES: Swimming; picnicking; fishing; boating,rld. MISC.: 47
acres. Pets permitted if kept on leash.

HECTOR

Bayou Bluff (Ozark NF). 3-1/10 mi N
of Hector on St Hwy 27; 2-2/5 mi NE
on FS 1303. SEASON: All year; 14-day
lmt. FACILITIES: 7 sites (tr -22), tbls,
toil, cga, f, well drk wtr, picnic shelters, camping shelters. ACTIVITIES: Hunting; wading; swimming; picnicking;
fishing. MISC.: Elev 600 ft; 6 acres;
Illinois Bayou stream; picturesque
bluffs. Pets allowed if kept on leash.

HENDERSON

Woods Point (COE; Norfork Lake). 12
mi SE of Henderson. SEASON: All yr,
14-day lmt. FACILITIES: 11 sites; tbls,
toil, cga, drk wtr. ACTIVITIES: Boating,rl; picnicking; fishing. MISC.: 10
acres. Pets permitted if kept on leash.

HOLLIS

South Fourche (Ouachita NF). 1 mi S of
Hollis on St Hwy 7. FACILITIES: 7 sites;
tbls, toil, cga, drk wtr. ACTIVITIES:
Hiking; hunting; picnicking; fishing.
MISC.: Roadside campground,on a stream.
St Hwy 7 is a popular route for viewing
autumn foliage color. Pets on leash.

HOT SPRINGS

Carpenter Dam (Arkansas Power & Light).
S of Hot Springs, just below Carpenter
Dam. SEASON: All yr, 7-day lmt. FACILI-
TIES: Free campsites, tbls, toil, cga,
hand-pumped drk wtr. ACTIVITIES: Pic-
nicking. MISC.: Pets permitted on leash.

Charlton (Ouachita NF). 13 mi W of Hot
Springs on US 270. SEASON: 5/23-10/28,
14-day lmt. FACILITIES: 22 sites (tr -
-22), tbls, toil, cga, f, drk wtr. ACTIVI-
TIES: Swimming; picnicking; fishing;
boating,rld. MISC.: 7 acres; 3-5 campsites per acre; surfaced roads; pets.

Lena Landing (COE; Lake Ouachita
[Blakely Mountain]). 10 mi NE of Hot
Springs; 11 mi W on St Hwy 298; 2 mi
S on access rds. SEASON: All yr, 14-day
lmt. FACILITIES: 6 sites; tbls, toil, cga,
drk wtr, fd, marina. ACTIVITIES: Swim-
ming; picnicking; fishing; boating,rl.
MISC.: 74 acres. Pets allowed on leash.

HOUSTON

Cypress Creek (COE; Toad Suck Ferry
Lock). 2 mi N of Houston on Co Rd. SEA-
SON: 5/1-9/30, 14-day lmt. FACILITIES:
9 sites; tbls, toil, cga, drk wtr. ACTIVI-
TIES: Boating,l; picnicking. MISC.: Pets.
McClellan-Kerr Arkansas River Navigation
System.

JASPER

Hasty (Buffalo National River). 4 mi E
of Jasper on St Hwy 74; left on the only

See page 7 for KEY TO ABBREVIATIONS.

paved rd. SEASON: All yr, 14-day lmt. FACILITIES: Undesignated sites (tents, small RVs/trailers); tbls, toil, cga. ACTIVITIES: Canoeing; picnicking; fishing; swimming (no diving); hiking. MISC.: Scenic; pets. Access to floating by canoe down Buffalo River.

Kyles Landing (Buffalo National River). Steep, rough access, not recommended for autos, off St Hwy 74, 5 mi W of Jasper. Turn-off is marked for Boy Scout Camp Orr. SEASON: All yr, 14-day lmt. Tent sites, tbls, toil, cga. ACTIVITIES: Canoeing; swimming (no diving); hiking; picnicking; fishing. MISC.: This is designed primarily for floaters. Access to floating by canoe down Buffalo River. Scenic. Pets allowed if on a leash.

JERUSALEM

Upper Brock Creek (Ozark NF). 5-9/10 mi N of Jerusalem on FS 1305; 1 mi NE on FS 1331. SEASON: All year; 14-day lmt. FACILITIES: 7 sites (tr -22), tbls, toil, cga, f, well drk wtr. ACTIVITIES: Swimming; picnicking; fishing; boating. MISC.: Elev 800 ft; 2 acres; lake; pets.

KIRBY

Bear Creek (COE; Lake Greeson). ½ mi S of Kirby on St Hwy 27; 1-3/4 mi W on access rd. FACILITIES: 10 sites; tbls, toil, cga, drk wtr. ACTIVITIES: Swimming; picnicking; fishing; boating,l; hiking. MISC.: 125 acres; pets.

KNOXVILLE

Cabin Creek (COE; Dardanelle Lake). 2 mi W of Knoxville on gravel rd. SEASON: All yr, 14-day lmt. FACILITIES: 5 sites; tbls, toil, cga, drk wtr, group shelter. ACTIVITIES: Boating,rl; picnicking; fishing. MISC.: 54 acres; pets.

LAKEVIEW

Lakeview (COE; Bull Shoals Lake). 1 mi N of Lakeview on St Hwy 178. SEASON: 11/10-3/1, FREE ($3 rest of yr); 14-day lmt. FACILITIES: 81 sites; tbls, toil, cga, drk wtr, electric hookup, dump, showers, fd, ice, playground. Laundry nearby. ACTIVITIES: Swimming (beach); picnicking; fishing; boating,rld. MISC.: 54 acres. Pets on leash.

LAVACA

Vache Grasse (COE; Ozark Lake). 4 mi W of Lavaca (at St Hwy 255) on Co Rd. SEASON: All yr, 14-day lmt. FACILITIES: 24 sites; tbls, flush toil, cga, drk wtr, group shelter. ACTIVITIES: Picnicking; boating,l. MISC.: 230 acres; pets.

LEAD HILL

Lead Hill Campground (COE; Bull Shoals Lake). 4 mi N of Lead Hill on St Hwy 7. SEASON: 11/10-3/1, FREE ($3 rest of yr); 14-day lmt. FACILITIES: 77 sites; tbls, toil. cga, electric hookup, ice, fd, dump,group shelter, playground, drk wtr. ACTIVITIES: Swimming (beach); picnicking;fishing (heated fishing dock); boating,rld. MISC.: 55 acres; pets.

Tucker Hollow (COE; Bull Shoals Lake). 7 mi NW of Lead Hill on St Hwy 14; 3 mi N on St Hwy 281. SEASON: 9/4-5/13, FREE ($3 rest of yr); 14-day lmt. FACILITIES: 30 sites; tbls, toil, cga, drk wtr, dump, fd, ice. ACTIVITIES: Swimming (beach); picnicking; fishing; boating,rld. MISC.: 16 acres. Pets allowed on leash.

LEOLA

Cox Creek (Game & Fish Commission). Cox Creek Lake near Leola, on St Hwy 46 about 18 mi from Sheridan, has been built and stocked by Game & Fish Comm. There are plenty of spots for free camping. Boat ramps are available; excellent fishing. Pets allowed if kept on a leash.

LITTLE ROCK

Maumelle (COE; Murray Lock & Dam). 3 mi E of Little Rock on St Hwy 130. SEASON: 11/24-3/1, FREE ($3 rest of yr); 14-day lmt. FACILITIES: 44 sites; tbls, flush toil, cga, drk wtr, showers, dump. ACTIVITIES: Picnicking; boating,l. MISC.: Pets allowed if on leash.

LONDON

Piney Bay (COE; Dardanelle Lake). 8 mi NW of London. SEASON: 11/24-3/1, FREE ($3 rest of yr); 14-day lmt. FACILITIES: 39 sites; tbls, toil, cga, drk wtr, group shelters, electric hookup, dump. ACTIVITIES: Boating,rl; picnicking; fishing. MISC.: 118 acres; pets.

MINERAL SPRINGS

Cottonshed Landing (COE; Millwood Lakes). 8 mi SW of Mineral Springs. SEASON: All yr, 14-day lmt. FACILITIES: 25 sites; tbls, toil, cga, dump, drk wtr. Ice nearby. ACTIVITIES: Boating,l; picnicking;fishing. MISC.:135 acres;pets.

MORNING STAR

Maumee (Buffalo National River). N on the only paved rd off St Hwy 27 at Morning Star. Rd turns to gravel and becomes steep but is well graded. SEASON: All yr, 14-day lmt. FACILITIES: Undesignated sites (tents, small RVs

and trailers), tbls, toil, cga. ACTIVI-
TIES: Hiking; canoeing; swimming (no
diving); picnicking; fishing. MISC.:
Scenic; pets. Access to floating by
canoe down Buffalo River.

MORRILTON

Point Remove (COE; Toad Suck Ferry
Lock & Dam). 2 mi SW of Morrilton.
SEASON: 9/4-5/14, FREE ($2 rest of yr);
14-day lmt. FACILITIES: 21 sites; tbls,
flush toil, cga, drk wtr, showers. AC-
TIVITIES: Boating,l; picnicking. MISC.:
Pets permitted if kept on a leash.

MOUNT IDA

Big Fir (COE; Lake Ouachita [Blakely
Mountain]). 7 mi N of Mount Ida on
St Hwy 27; 7 mi E on St Hwy 188; 4 mi
on gravel rd; 1 mi on paved access rd.
SEASON: All yr, 14-day lmt. FACILITIES:
10 sites; tbls, toil, cga, drk wtr. ACTIV-
ITIES: Swimming; picnicking; fishing;
boating,l. MISC.: 144 acres; pets.

Fulton Branch (Ouachita NF). 4-2/5 mi
NW of Mount Ida on US 270; 2/5 mi N
on FS 298; 1-3/5 mi NE on Co Hwy 621;
3/10 mi N on FS 7437 (gravel access rds).
SEASON: All yr, 14-day lmt. FACILITIES:
7 sites (tr -22), tbls, toil, cga, f, well
drk wtr. ACTIVITIES: Swimming; picnicking; fishing; boating,ld; hiking; hunting;
canoeing. Float fishing on Ouachita
River. MISC.: Elev 600 ft; 3 acres; pets;
scenic. Connects with Ouachita Trail.

Highway 27 Landing (COE; Lake Ouachita
[Blakely Mountain]). 8 mi E of Mount
Ida on US 270; 1 mi N on access rd.
SEASON: All yr, 14-day lmt. FACILITIES:
6 sites; tbls, toil, cga, fd, drk wtr,
marina. Ice nearby. ACTIVITIES: Swimming (beach); picnicking; fishing; boating,rl. MISC.: 17 acres. Pets on leash.

Little Fir (COE; Lake Ouachita [Blakely
Mountain]). 7 mi N of Mount Ida on St
Hwy 27; 9 mi NE on St Hwy 188; follow
signs. SEASON: All yr, 14-day lmt. FA-
CILITIES: 25 sites; tbls, toil, cga, drk
wtr, marina. ACTIVITIES: Swimming; picnicking; boating,rl. MISC.: 68 acres;pets.

River Bluff (Ouachita NF). 3/10 mi NW
of Mount Ida on US 270; 3/5 mi NE on
St Hwy 27; 3-7/10 mi on Co Hwy 59; 2-
4/5 mi NW on FS 138. SEASON: All yr,
14-day lmt. FACILITIES: 7 sites (tr -22),
tbls, toil, cga, f, well drk wtr. ACTIVI-
TIES: Swimming; hiking; hunting; canoeing; picnicking; fishing; boating,ld.
Float fishing in Ouachita River. MISC.:
Elev 600 ft; 2 acres; pets; Ouachita River; scenic. Connects with Ouachita Trail.

Rocky Shoals (Ouachita NF). 5-2/5 mi
NW of Mount Ida on US 270. SEASON:
All yr, 14-day lmt. FACILITIES: 7 sites

(tr -22), tbls, toil, cga, f, well drk
wtr. 3 mi -- Store, ice, fd, gas. ACTIV-
ITIES: Swimming; picnicking; fishing;
boating,ld; hiking; hunting; canoeing.
MISC.: Elev 600 ft; 4 acres; pets. Base
camp for float fishing on Ouachita River.
Trail connects with Ouachita Trail.

Twin Creek (COE; Lake Ouachita [Blakely
Mountain]). 11 mi E of Mount Ida on
US 270; 1 mi N on access rd; follow
signs. SEASON: All yr, 14-day lmt. FA-
CILITIES: 15 sites; tbls, toil, cga, drk
wtr. ACTIVITIES: Swimming; picnicking;
fishing; boating,l. MISC.:141 acres;pets.

MOUNTAIN HOME

Cranfield (COE; Norfork Lake). 5½ mi
NE of Mountain Home on US 62; 2 mi
N on paved access rd. SEASON: 11/10-
3/1, FREE ($3 rest of yr); 14-day lmt.
FACILITIES: 79 sites; tbls, toil, cga,
drk wtr, change shelter, dump, playground, electric hookup ($). ACTIVITIES:
Swimming (beach); picnicking; fishing;
boating,rld. MISC.: 78 acres; pets.

George's Cove (COE; Norfork Lake). 6½
mi SE of Mountain Home on St Hwy 5;
2½ mi E on paved St Hwy 342. SEASON:
All yr, 14-day lmt. FACILITIES: 12
sites; tbls, toil, cga, drk wtr. ACTIVI-
TIES: Swimming (beach); picnicking;
fishing; boating,rl. MISC.:20 acres;pets.

Hand Landing (COE; Norfork Lake). 16
mi E of Mountain Home on US 62; cross
lake on ferry; 9 mi SW on gravel access
road. SEASON: All yr, 14-day lmt. FA-
CILITIES: 7 sites; tbls, toil, cga, drk
wtr. ACTIVITIES: Boating,rl; picnicking;
fishing. MISC.: Free permit required.
7 acres. Pets permitted on leash.

Henderson (COE; Norfork Lake). 10 mi
NE of Mountain Home on US 62; cross
lake on ferry; turn left. SEASON: 9/4-
5/13, FREE ($3 rest of yr); 14-day lmt.
FACILITIES: 38 sites; tbls, toil, cga,
drk wtr, dump. ACTIVITIES: Swimming
(beach); picnicking; fishing; boating,rld. MISC.: 18 acres. Pets on leash.

Panther Bay (COE; Norfork Lake). 9
mi NE of Mountain Home on US 62. SEA-
SON: 9/4-5/13, FREE ($3 rest of yr);
14-day lmt. FACILITIES: 28 sites; tbls,
toil, cga, drk wtr, dump. ACTIVITIES:
Swimming (beach); picnicking; fishing;
boating,rld. MISC.: 52 acres; pets.

Pigeon Creek (COE; Norfork Lake). 6½
mi N of Mountain Home on St Hwy 201;
¼ mi E on access rd. SEASON: All yr,
14-day lmt. FACILITIES: 5 sites; tbls,
toil, cga, drk wtr. ACTIVITIES: Swimming; picnicking; fishing; boating,rld.
MISC.: 12 acres. Pets.

Robinson Point (COE; Norfork Lake). 10
mi NE of Mountain Home on US 62; 2½

mi S on paved access road. **SEASON:** 11/10–4/30, FREE ($3 rest of yr); 14-day lmt. **FACILITIES:** 102 sites; tbls, toil, cga, drk wtr, electric hookup ($), dump, showers, change shelter. **ACTIVITIES:** Swimming (beach); picnicking; fishing; boating,rl. **MISC.:** 48 acres. Pets.

Tracy (COE; Norfork Lake). 6½ mi SE of Mountain Home on St Hwy 5; 3 mi on St Hwy 341. **SEASON:** All yr, 14-day lmt. **FACILITIES:** 7 sites; tbls, toil, cga, drk wtr. **ACTIVITIES:** Boating,rld; picnicking; fishing. **MISC.:** 10 acres; pets.

Woods Point (COE; Norfork Lake). 16 mi E of Mountain Home on US 62; cross lake on ferry; 9 mi S on gravel access road. **SEASON:** All yr, 14-day lmt. **FACILITIES:** 11 sites; tbls, toil, cga, drk wtr. **ACTIVITIES:** Boating,rld; picnicking; fishing. **MISC.:** 10 acres; pets.

MOUNTAIN VIEW

Barkshed (Ozark NF). 14 mi NW of Mountain View on St Hwy 14 (paved); 3 mi NE on FS 1112 (gravel). **FACILITIES:** 1 site; tbls, toil, cga, drk wtr, picnic shelter. **ACTIVITIES:** Swimming; picnicking; fishing; hunting; hiking. **MISC.:** Clear mountain stream. Pets on leash.

MULBERRY

Vine Prairie (COE; Ozark Lake). 2 mi S of Mulberry on Co Rd. **SEASON:** 5/1–9/30, 14-day lmt. **FACILITIES:** 34 sites; tbls, flush toil, cga, dump, drk wtr, group shelter. **ACTIVITIES:** Picnicking; boating,l. **MISC.:** 185 acres; pets.

White Oak (COE; Ozark Lake). 5 mi E of Mulberry (at US 64) on Co Rd. **SEASON:** All yr, 14-day lmt. **FACILITIES:** 7 sites; tbls, toil, cga, drk wtr. **ACTIVITIES:** Picnicking;boating,l. **MISC.:**85 acres;pets.

NEW BLAINE

Shoal Bay (COE; Dardanelle Lake). 2 mi N of New Blaine on access rd. **SEASON:** 11/24–3/1, 14-day lmt. **FACILITIES:** 60 sites; tbls, toil, cga, drk wtr, group shelter, dump, store, ice. **ACTIVITIES:** Hiking; boating,rld; picnicking; fishing. **MISC.:** 93 acres; nature trail; pets.

NEWHOPE

Star of the West (COE; Lake Greeson). 2–3/4 mi E of Newhope on US 70. **SEASON:** All yr, 14-day lmt. **FACILITIES:**26 sites; tbls, toil, cga, drk wtr. **ACTIVITIES:** Swimming; picnicking; fishing. **MISC.:** 36 acres. Pets allowed if on leash.

NOBLE LAKE

Trulock Bend (COE; Lock & Dam #3). 4 mi N of Noble Lake. **SEASON:** All yr, 14-day lmt. **FACILITIES:** 15 sites; tbls, flush toil, cga, drk wtr, playground.

ACTIVITIES: Loating,rl; picnicking; fishing. **MISC.:** 41 acres. McClellan-Kerr Ark. River Navigation System. Pets.

NORFORK

Jordan (COE; Norfork Lake). 3 mi E of Norfork on St Hwy 177; 3 mi N on gravel access rd. **SEASON:** 11/10–4/30, FREE ($3 rest of yr); 14-day lmt. **FACILITIES:** 33 sites; tbls, toil, cga, drk wtr, electric hookup ($), dump, bathhouse. **ACTIVITIES:** Swimming (beach); picnicking; fishing; boating,rld. **MISC.:** 27 acres. Pets permitted if on leash.

*Matney (Ozark NF). Boat landing is ½ mi W of Norfork. Campground is 4 mi NW of Norfork on White River BY BOAT. **SEASON:** All yr, 14-day lmt. **FACILITIES:** 8 tent sites; tbls, toil, cga, well drk wtr, f. 4 mi — Store, ice, fd, laundry, gas. **ACTIVITIES:** Hiking; hunting; picnicking; fishing (outstanding fishing for rainbow trout); boating (4 mi — r,l,d). **MISC.:** Elev 400 ft; 5 acres; pets; high picturesque bluffs. On White River near Matney Fire Detection Tower.

Quarry Cove and Dam Site (COE; Norfork Lake). 3 mi NE of Norfork on St Hwy 5; 2 mi E on St Hwy 177. **SEASON:** 9/4–5/13, FREE ($3 rest of yr); 14-day lmt. **FACILITIES:** 57 sites; tbls, toil, cga drk wtr, dump, change house. **ACTIVITIES:** Swimming; picnicking; fishing; boating,rld. **MISC.:** 124 acres; pets.

NORMAN

Crystal (Ouachita NF). 1 mi N of Norman on St Hwy 27; 3 mi NE on FS 177 (gravel access rd). **SEASON:** All yr, 14-day lmt. **FACILITIES:** 9 sites (tr –22), tbls, toil, cga, well drk wtr, picnic shelter. 4 mi — Store, ice, fd, laundry, gas. **ACTIVITIES:** Swimming; picnicking; fishing; hiking; hunting; rockhounding. **MISC.:** Elev 1000 ft; 4 acres; pets; stream; nature trails; scenic drives; wooded site;flowing spring.

OAKLAND

Oakland Campground (COE; Bull Shoals Lake). 4 mi SW of Oakland. **SEASON:** 9/4–5/13, FREE ($3 rest of yr); 14-day lmt. **FACILITIES:** 34 sites; tbls, toil, cga, drk wtr, store, ice, dump. **ACTIVITIES:** Swimming (beach); picnicking; fishing; boating,rld. **MISC.:** 76 acres; pets.

Ozark Isle (COE; Bull Shoals Lake). 5 mi SW of Oakland. **SEASON:** 9/4–5/13, FREE ($3 rest of yr); 14-day lmt. **FACILITIES:** 118 sites; tbls, flush toil, cga, drk wtr, group picnic shelter, group camp area, showers, playground. **ACTIVITIES:** Swimming (beach); picnicking; fishing; boating,rld. **MISC.:** 190 acres; pets.

See page 7 for KEY TO ABBREVIATIONS.

OLA

Project Point (COE; Nimrod Lake). 9 mi SE of Ola on St Hwy 7; ½ mi on access road. SEASON: 9/4-5/13, FREE ($2 rest of yr); 14-day lmt. FACILITIES: 6 sites; tbls, toil, cga, drk wtr. ACTIVITIES: Boating,rl; picnicking; fishing. MISC.: 10 acres. Pets permitted if kept on leash.

Quarry Cove (COE; Nimrod Lake). 7 mi SE of Ola on St Hwy 7; ½ mi W on St Hwy 60 to access road. SEASON: 9/4-5/13, FREE ($2 rest of yr); 14-day lmt. FACILITIES: 31 sites; tbls, toil, cga, drk wtr, dump. ACTIVITIES: Swimming; picnicking; fishing; boating,rl. MISC.: 30 acres;pets.

River Road (COE; Nimrod Lake). 9 mi SE of Ola on St Hwy 7; 1/3 mi on River Road below dam. SEASON: 9/4-5/13, FREE ($2 rest of yr); 14-day lmt. FACILITIES: 21 sites; tbls, toil, cga, drk wtr, dump. ACTIVITIES: Boating,rl; picnicking; fishing. MISC.: 15 acres. Pets on leash.

OZARK

Dam Site South (COE; Ozark Lake). 1 mi SE of Ozark on Co Rd. SEASON: 9/4-5/13, FREE ($2 rest of yr); 14-day lmt. FACILITIES: 24 sites; tbls, flush toil, cga, drk wtr, dump. ACTIVITIES: Picnicking; boating,l. MISC.:249 acres;pets.

West Creek (COE; Dardanelle Lake). 2½ mi SE of Ozark on US 64; 5 mi S on gravel road; ½ mi W on access road. SEASON: All yr, 14-day lmt. FACILITIES: 5 sites; tbls, toil, cga, drk wtr. ACTIVITIES: Boating,rl; picnicking; fishing. MISC.: 141 acres. Pets on a leash.

OZONE

Ozone Campground (Ozark NF). 2-4/5 mi N of Ozone on St Hwy 21. SEASON: All yr, 14-day lmt. FACILITIES: 8 sites (tr -16), tbls, flush toil, cga, well drk wtr. 3 mi -- Store, ice, fd, gas. ACTIVITIES: Picnicking. Hunting nearby. 10 mi N on St Hwy 21 -- swimming, boating, fishing, waterskiing at Lake Ludwig. MISC.: 8 acres; pets. Situated in tall pine timber. Site of old Ozone CCC Camp. Elev. 1800 ft.

PARALOMA

Paraloma Landing (COE; Millwood Lake). 1½ mi S of Paraloma on Co Rd. SEASON: All yr, 14-day lmt. FACILITIES: 18 sites; tbls, toil, cga, drk wtr. ACTIVITIES: Horseback riding; swimming; picnicking; fishing; boating,rl. MISC.: 8 acres. Pets permitted if on leash.

PARIS

Cameron Bluff (Ozark NF). 1-1/10 mi S of Paris on St Hwy 109; 12-1/5 mi SE on St Hwy 309; 1-9/10 mi W on FS

1606. SEASON: All yr, 14-day lmt. FACILITIES: 16 sites (tr -16), tbls, toil, cga, well drk wtr. ACTIVITIES: Picnicking; berrypicking. MISC.: 8 acres; pets. Located on highest point in Arkansas -- Mount Magazine. Elev. 2800 ft.

Mount Magazine Recreation Area (Ozark NF). 1 mi S of Paris on St Hwy 109 (paved); 17 mi SE on St Hwy 309 (paved). FACILITIES: 16 sites; tbls, toil, cga, drk wtr. ACTIVITIES: Picnicking. Fishing and hunting nearby. Swimming at Cove Lake (9 mi N). MISC.: Rugged mountain scenery; cool climate; pets. Highest point in Arkansas.

O'Kane (COE; Dardanelle Lake). 5 mi N of Paris on St Hwy 309. SEASON: All yr, 14-day lmt. FACILITIES: 5 sites; tbls, toil, cga. ACTIVITIES: Boating,rl; picnicking; fishing. MISC.: 29 acres. Pets are permitted if kept on a leash.

PELSOR

Fairview (Ozark NF). 1½ mi N of Pelsor on St Hwy 7. SEASON: All yr, 14-day lmt. FACILITIES: 11 sites (tr -22), tbls, flush toil, well drk wtr. ACTIVITIES: Hunting; berrypicking; picnicking. Fishing (5 mi). MISC.: 4 acres. Located on Scenic Hwy Seven, one of the country's 10 most beautiful highways. Gorgeous fall colors in October and November. Abundant dogwood and redbud in early spring. Pets allowed. Elev. 2200 ft.

Haw Creek Falls (Ozark NF). 12-9/10 mi W of Pelsor on St Hwy 123; 2/5 mi SE on FS 1837 (gravel access roads). SEASON: All year; 14-day lmt. FACILITIES: 8 sites (tr -22), tbls, toil, cga, f, well drk wtr. ACTIVITIES: Wading; hunting; picnicking; fishing; boating,d. MISC.: 3 acres; pets. Big Piney Creek nearby. Small mountain stream with picturesque falls, rocks, and bluffs. Elev 800 ft.

Richland Creek (Ozark NF). 10 mi E of Pelsor on St Hwy 16; 7½ mi N on FS 1205. SEASON: All yr, 14-day lmt. FACILITIES: 4 sites; tbls, toil, cga, well drk wtr. ACTIVITIES: Hiking; picnicking; fishing; swimming. MISC.: Elev 1000 ft; 4 acres. Backpacking nearby. Pets on leash.

PENCIL BLUFF

Big Brushy (Ouachita NF). 6 mi NW of Pencil Bluff on US 270. SEASON: 3/1-11/17, 14-day lmt. FACILITIES: 11 sites (tr -22), tbls, toil, cga, f, well drk wtr. ACTIVITIES: Hunting; hiking; picnicking; fishing. MISC.: Elev 800 ft; 3 acres; pets. Attractive wooded setting on stream bank.

Shirley Creek (Ouachita NF). 6½ mi W of Pencil Bluff on St Hwy 88; ½ mi SE on Co Hwy 7991. SEASON: All yr, 14-day lmt. FACILITIES: 7 tent sites; tbls, toil, cga, f, store, ice, gas, well drk wtr. ACTIVITIES: Swimming; picnicking; fishing; boating. MISC.: Elev 700 ft;5 acres; scenic; river. Pets on leash.

PINDALL

Woolum (Buffalo National River). Access on unmarked gravel road from Pindall or St Joe. Inquire locally. SEASON: All yr, 14-day lmt. FACILITIES: Undesignated sites (tents, small RVs/trailers), tbls, toil, cga. ACTIVITIES: Swimming (no diving); hiking; picnicking; fishing; canoeing. MISC.: Access to floating by canoe down Buffalo River; pets.

PINEY

Flat Rock (COE; Dardanelle Lake). 2/3 mi E of Piney on US 64; ½ mi N on St Hwy 359; 3/4 mi W on access road. SEASON: 9/4-5/13, FREE ($2 rest of yr); 14-day lmt. FACILITIES: 15 sites; tbls, toil, cga, drk wtr, group shelter. ACTIVITIES: Boating,rl; picnicking; fishing. MISC.: 59 acres. Pets on leash.

PLAINVIEW

Carden Point (COE; Nimrod Lake). 6 mi SE of Plainview on St Hwy 60. SEASON: All yr, 14-day lmt. FACILITIES: 9 sites; tbls, toil, cga, drk wtr. ACTIVITIES: Boating,rl; picnicking; fishing. MISC.: 10 acres. Pets allowed on leash.

Carter Cove (COE; Nimrod Lake). 3 mi E of Plainview on St Hwy 60; 1 mi S on access road. SEASON: 9/4-5/13, FREE ($2 rest of yr); 14-day lmt. FACILITIES: 16 sites; tbls, toil, cga, drk wtr. ACTIVITIES: Swimming; boating,rl; picnicking; fishing. MISC.:14 acres;pets.

County Line (COE; Nimrod Lake). 6 mi SE of Plainview on St Hwy 60; ½ mi S on access road. SEASON: 9/4-5/13, FREE ($2 rest of yr); 14-day lmt. FACILITIES: 15 sites; tbls, toil, cga, drk wtr, dump. ACTIVITIES: Swimming; picnicking; fishing; boating,rld. MISC.: 17 acres. Pets permitted if on a leash.

Sunlight Bay (COE; Nimrod Lake). 1½ mi SE of Plainview on St Hwy 60; 2 mi SW on Sunlight Rd (gravel access rd). SEASON: 9/4-5/13, FREE ($2 rest of yr); 14-day lmt. FACILITIES:28 sites; tbls, toil, cga, drk wtr, dump. ACTIVITIES: Boating,rl; picnicking; fishing. MISC.: 17 acres.Pets permitted on leash.

PONCA

Lost Valley (Buffalo National River). Easy access off St Hwy 43, 1 mi S of Ponca. SEASON: All yr, 14-day lmt. FACILITIES: 15 sites (tr -20), tbls, toil, cga, drk wtr. ACTIVITIES: Hiking; swimming (no diving); canoeing; picnicking;

fishing. MISC.: 200 acres; scenic; pets. Access to floating by canoe down Buffalo River.

Steel Creek (Buffalo National River). Easy but steep access off St Hwy 74; 1 mi E of Ponca. SEASON: All yr, 14-day lmt. FACILITIES: Undesignated sites (tents and small RVs/trailers), tbls, toil, cga. ACTIVITIES: Swimming (no diving); hiking; canoeing; picnicking; fishing. MISC.: Scenic; pets. Access to floating by canoe down the river.

PRIM

Hill Creek (COE; Greers Ferry). 7 mi SW of Prim on gravel road. SEASON: All yr, 14-day lmt. FACILITIES: tbls, toil, cga, ice, drk wtr. ACTIVITIES: Swimming; boating,rld; picnicking; fishing. MISC.: 38 acres. Pets on leash.

PRUITT

Ozark (Buffalo National River). Steep access on unmarked gravel road 1 mi S of Pruitt off St Hwy 7. Inquire at Pruitt Ranger Station. SEASON: All yr, 14-day lmt. FACILITIES: Undesignated sites (tents, small RVs/trailers), tbls, toil, cga, drk wtr. ACTIVITIES: Hiking; swimming (no diving); canoeing; picnicking; fishing. MISC.: Scenic; pets. Access to floating by canoe down Buffalo River.

QUITMAN

Cove Creek (COE; Greers Ferry Lake). 6½ mi NE of Quitman on St Hwy 25; 3 mi NW on St Hwy 16; 1¼ mi on access rd. SEASON: All yr, 14-day lmt. FACILITIES: 55 sites; tbls, toil, cga, drk wtr. ACTIVITIES: Swimming; boating,rl; swimming; picnicking; fishing. MISC.: 35 acres. Pets permitted if kept on leash.

Mill Creek Park (COE;Greers Ferry Lake). 6½ mi NE of Quitman on St Hwy 25; 13½ mi N on St Hwy 16; 3 mi on gravel access road. SEASON: All yr, 14-day lmt. FACILITIES: 27 sites; tbls, toil, cga, drk wtr. ACTIVITIES: Swimming; picnicking; fishing; boating,rl. MISC.: 30 acres; pets.

REDFIELD

Tar Camp (COE; Lock & Dam #5). 6 mi E of Redfield on access road. SEASON: 11/19-4/30, FREE ($3 rest of yr); 14-day lmt. FACILITIES: 29 sites; tbls, toil, cga, drk wtr, showers, group shelter, playground, dump. ACTIVITIES: Boating,rl; picnicking; fishing. MISC.: 100 acres. Pets permitted if on leash. McClellan-Kerr Arkansas River Navigation System.

See page 7 for KEY TO ABBREVIATIONS.

ARKANSAS

REYDEL

Little Bayou Metro (COE; Lock & Dam #2). 2 mi S of Reydel on gravel road. SEASON: All yr, 14-day lmt. FACILITIES: 8 sites; tbls, toil, cga, drk wtr. ACTIVITIES: Boating,rl; picnicking; fishing. MISC.: 12 acres; pets. McClellan-Kerr Arkansas River Navigation System.

ROGERS

Horseshoe Bend (COE; Beaver Lake). 6 mi SE of Rogers on St Hwy 94. SEASON: 11/1-5/13, FREE ($3 rest of yr); 14-day lmt. FACILITIES: 108 sites; tbls, toil, cga, drk wtr, electric hookup ($), store, ice, fd, showers, dump. ACTIVITIES: Boating,rld; picnicking; fishing; swimming. MISC.: 166 acres; pets.

Prairie Creek (COE; Beaver Lake). 3½ mi E of Rogers on St Hwy 12; 1 mi on access road. SEASON: 11/1-5/13, FREE ($3 rest of yr); 14-day lmt. FACILITIES: 119 sites; tbls, toil, cga, drk wtr, ice, store, fd, electric hookup ($), showers. ACTIVITIES: Swimming; picnicking; fishing. MISC.: Pets permitted on leash.

Rocky Branch (COE; Beaver Lake). 11 mi E of Rogers on St Hwy 12; 4½ mi NE on paved St Hwy 303. SEASON: 11/1-5/13, FREE ($3 rest of yr); 14-day lmt. FACILITIES: 50 sites; tbls, toil, cga, drk wtr, store, ice, fd, dump, electric hookup ($). ACTIVITIES: Swimming; boating,rld; picnicking; fishing. MISC.: 39 acres. Pets permitted if on leash.

RUSSELLVILLE

Old Post Road Park (COE; Dardanelle Lake). 3 mi SW of Russellville on St Hwy 7. SEASON: 9/4-5/13, FREE ($3 rest of yr); 14-day lmt. FACILITIES:16 sites; tbls, flush toil, cga, drk wtr, tennis courts, dump, playground. Information Center (open in summer). ACTIVITIES: Tennis; boating,l; picnicking. MISC.: Scenic overlook. Pets permitted on leash.

SARATOGA

Saratoga Landing (COE; Millwood Lakes). 1 mi S; then 1 mi W of Saratoga. SEASON: All yr, 14-day lmt. FACILITIES: 35 sites; tbls, toil, cga, drk wtr. Nearby -- Store, ice, fd, laundry. ACTIVITIES: Horseback riding; boating,rl; swimming; picnicking;fishing. SEASON:200 acres;pets.

SCRANTON

Cane Creek (COE; Dardanelle Lake). 3½ mi NE of Scranton on St Hwy 197; 2 mi N on paved rd. SEASON: All yr, 14-day lmt. FACILITIES: 8 sites; tbls, toil, cga, drk wtr, group shelters. ACTIVITIES: Boating,rl; picnicking; fishing. MISC.: 48 acres. Pets allowed if on leash.

SHERIDAN

City Park. 1 mi E of Sheridan on US 270 West. SEASON: All yr. FACILITIES: Undesignated sites; tbls. ACTIVITIES: Picnicking. MISC.: Pets on leash.

SHIRLEY

Van Buren Park (COE;Greers Ferry Lake). 2 mi S of Shirley on St Hwy 16; 5 mi on St Hwy 330. SEASON: 9/4-5/13, FREE ($3 rest of yr); 14-day lmt. FACILITIES: 65 sites; tbls, toil, cga, drk wtr, ice, dump. ACTIVITIES: Swimming; boating,rld; picnicking; fishing. MISC.: 44 acres. Pets allowed if kept on leash.

SIMS

Dragover Float Camp (Ouachita NF). 3 mi E of Sims on St Hwy 88; 1 mi S on FS 138A (gravel access roads). SEASON: All yr, 14-day lmt. FACILITIES: 7 sites (tr -22), tbls, toil, cga, well drk wtr, f. 5 mi -- Store, ice, gas. ACTIVITIES: Canoeing; hunting; hiking; swimming; boating,ld; picnicking; fishing. Float fishing on Ouachita River. MISC.:4 acres; elev 600 ft. Pets allowed on leash.

SPRINGDALE

Blue Springs (COE; Beaver Lake). 7½ mi E of Springdale on St Hwy 68; 1 mi S on paved access road. SEASON: 9/16-5/14, FREE ($2 rest of yr); 14-day lmt. FACILITIES: 18 sites; tbls, toil, cga, drk wtr, electric hookup ($). ACTIVITIES: Boating,rl; picnicking; fishing. MISC.: 33 acres. Pets permitted if on leash.

Hickory Creek (COE; Beaver Lake). 4 mi N of Springdale on US 71 to Vogel; 6½ mi E on paved St Hwy 264. SEASON: 11/1-5/13, FREE ($3 rest of yr); 14-day lmt. FACILITIES: 38 sites; tbls, toil, cga, drk wtr, store, ice, fd, dump, electric hookup ($). ACTIVITIES: Swimming; picnicking; fishing; boating,rld. MISC.: 90 acres. Pets on leash.

War Eagle (COE; Beaver Lake). 12 mi NE of Springdale on St Hwy 68 to Nob; 3 mi NW on paved access road. SEASON: 11/1-5/13, FREE ($3 rest of yr); 14-day lmt. FACILITIES: 22 sites; tbls, toil, cga, store, ice, fd, dump, electric hookup ($). ACTIVITIES: Swimming; boating,rld; picnicking; fishing. MISC.: 29 acres. Pets permitted if on leash.

STARK

Devil's Fork Park (COE; Greers Ferry Lake). ½ mi N of Stark on St Hwy 16. SEASON: 9/4-5/15, FREE ($3 rest of yr); 14-day lmt. FACILITIES: 55 sites; tbls, toil, cga, drk wtr, dump. ACTIVITIES: Swimming; boating,rl; picnicking; fishing. MISC.: 30 acres. Pets on leash.

SUBIACO

Six Mile (COE; Dardanelle Lake). 3 mi N and 1 mi E of Subiaco on St Hwy 109; 2 mi N and 1 mi W on Co Rd. SEASON: All yr, 14-day lmt. FACILITIES: 5 sites; tbls, toil, cga, drk wtr, group shelter. ACTIVITIES: Boating,rl; picnicking; fishing. MISC.: 86 acres. Pets on leash.

TAMO

Rising Star (COE; Lock & Dam #3). 5 mi N of Tamo. SEASON: 11/19-4/30, FREE ($2 rest of yr); 14-day lmt. FACILITIES: 19 sites; tbls, toil, cga, playground, drk wtr. ACTIVITIES: Boating,rl; picnicking; fishing. MISC.: 91 acres; pets. McClellan-Kerr Arkansas River Navigation System.

VAN BUREN

Lee Creek (COE; Lock & Dam #13). 1 mi W of Van Buren. SEASON: 5/1-9/30, 14-day lmt. FACILITIES: 10 sites; tbls, flush toil, cga, showers, drk wtr. ACTIVITIES: Boating,l; picnicking. MISC.: Pets permitted if kept on a leash.

WAVELAND

Lick Creek (COE; Blue Mountain Lake). 6 mi SW of Waveland on St Hwy 309. SEASON: 5/1-9/30, 14-day lmt. FACILITIES: 7 sites; tbls, toil, cga, drk wtr. ACTIVITIES: Picnicking; boating,l. MISC.: Pets allowed if kept on leash.

Outlet Area (COE; Blue Mountain Lake). 3 mi S of Waveland on paved road. Located below the dam on Petit Jean River. SEASON: 9/4-5/13, FREE ($2 rest of yr); 14-day lmt. FACILITIES: 25 sites; tbls, toil, cga, drk wtr, dump. ACTIVITIES: Boating,r; picnicking; fishing. MISC.: Pets allowed if kept on a leash.

Waveland Park (COE; Blue Mountain Lake). 2 mi SW of Waveland on paved road. SEASON: 9/4-5/13, FREE ($2 rest of yr); 14-day lmt. FACILITIES:47 sites; tbls, toil, cga, drk wtr, dump. ACTIVITIES: Swimming; boating,rl; picnicking; fishing. MISC.: 18 acres. Pets on leash.

WRIGHTSVILLE

Wrightsville (COE; Lock & Dam #5). 1 mi N of Wrightsville on St Hwy 386; 4 mi S on gravel rd; 1½ mi E. SEASON: All yr, 14-day lmt. FACILITIES: 9 sites; tbls, toil, cga, drk wtr. ACTIVITIES: Boating,rl; picnicking; fishing. MISC.: 50 acres. Pets permitted on a leash.

YELLVILLE

Highway 125 (COE; Bull Shoals Lake). 17 mi NW of Yellville on St Hwy 14; 12½ mi N on St Hwy 125. SEASON: 11/10-3/1, FREE ($3 rest of yr); 14-day lmt. FACILITIES: 32 sites; tbls, toil, cga, drk wtr, dump, fd, ice, playground. ACTIVITIES: Swimming (beach); boating,rld; picnicking; fishing. MISC.: 25 acres; pets.

Rush (Buffalo National River). Access on unmarked gravel road off St Hwy 14 and about 10 mi S of Yellville. Inquire locally. SEASON: All yr, 14-day lmt. FACILITIES: Undesignated sites (tents and small RVs/trailers); toil, cga. ACTIVITIES: Hiking; swimming (no diving); fishing; canoeing. MISC.: Scenic; pets. Access to floating by canoe down Buffalo River.

CALIFORNIA

GENERAL STATE INFORMATION

Miscellaneous

Right Turns on Red: Permitted after full stop, unless otherwise posted.
STATE CAPITOL: Sacramento
STATE NICKNAME: Golden State
STATE MOTTO: "Eureka, I Have Found It!"
STATE BIRD: Valley Quail
STATE FLOWER: Golden Poppy
STATE TREE: Redwood

See page 7 for KEY TO ABBREVIATIONS.

CALIFORNIA

State Parks

Fees range from $2.00 to $5.00 per night. Most campsites can be reserved in advance through Ticketron computer outlets. Off-Season Camping Tickets: A booklet containing 10 tickets, each good for one night of non-reserved camping at most campgrounds during off-season (winter for most parks; summer for desert parks) is available. It can be purchased for $20 at parks where it can be used, or by mail from the Department of Parks and Recreation; PO Box 2390; Sacramento, CA 95811. Pets are allowed. There is a $1-per-dog-per-night camping fee. If your dog is over 5 months old, a license or other proof of current rabies inoculation is required. Dogs are permitted in campground and day-use areas ON LEASH; in order to protect wildlife and other campers, they are not allowed on trails or on many beaches (check with the ranger).

Rest Areas

Overnight parking is NOT permitted. The California statutes specifically state that rest areas are for short rest periods only.

Pacific Crest National Trail

When completed, the trail will be about 2500 miles long, extending through Washington, Oregon, and California, mainly along the crest of the mountain ranges of these states. The trail will be carefully designed to fit in with the wild landscape. The proposed route passes through 23 national forests (including several wildernesses), 7 national parks, other federal lands, and numerous portions of state, local government, and private lands.

The California section of the proposed trail begins at the California-Oregon border south of Observation Peak in the Siskiyou Mountain Range, and terminates at International Border at Mexico, about 2½ miles east of Tecate. It traverses some of the most scenic areas in the state. Elevations range from 500-13,200 feet. The trail passes within a few miles of 14,496-foot Mt. Whitney, the highest peak in the continental U.S.

The completed part of the proposed 1660-mile trail in California consists of existing trails where possible. New sections are being developed. On uncompleted portions, route is transferred to rural roads or other trails where feasible. Other uncompleted portions are unmarked and have no alternate. The current status of the trail should be checked before starting a pack trip.

A set of over 60 maps showing the proposed and temporary route of the trail and an index sheet to Geological Survey quadrangle maps of the route are available from national forest headquarters for a reasonable fee.

A "California Campfire Permit" is necessary and available free from most Forest Service offices. This requires that a small shovel be available at all times at the campfire site. You must also have either the National Park permit or a Forest Service Wilderness Permit in national parks along the trail.

No guns or pets are allowed. Fishing is permitted. You may camp anywhere along the trail. Many primitive campsites have been established, with more to come as the trail is developed.

Maps and information about local conditions can be obtained from local national forest headquarters. Or, write to: US Forest Service; Division of Information and Education; 630 Sansome Street, Room 531; San Francisco, CA 94111.

INFORMATION SOURCES

Maps

The following maps are available from **Forsyth Travel Library** (see order form in Appendix B):

> STATE OF CALIFORNIA [Up-to-date, showing all principal roads, points of interest, sports areas, parks, airports, mileage, etc. Full color.]

> Completely indexed city maps, including all airports, lakes, rivers, etc., of more than two dozen cities, which are listed in detail in Appendix B.

Gold Mining and Prospecting

California Division of Mines and Geology; Department of Conservation; Ferry Building; San Francisco, CA 94111.

State Information

State of California; Division of Tourism; 1400 Tenth Street; Sacramento, CA 95814

CALIFORNIA

California State Chamber of Commerce; 455 Capitol Mall; Sacramento, CA 95814
Southern California Visitors Council; 705 West 7th Street; Los Angeles, CA 90017
Department of Natural Resources; Division of Parks and Recreation; PO Box 2390; Sacramento, CA 95811
California Department of Fish and Game; 1416 Ninth Street; Sacramento, CA 95814
California Division of Forestry; 1416 Ninth Street; Sacramento, CA 95814
Automobile Club of Southern California; 2601 S. Figueroa St.; Los Angeles, CA
CALTRANS; 1120 "N" St.; Sacramento, CA 95814 [for state and county road maps, and traffic flow maps]
State of California; Business and Transportation Agency; Dept. of California Highway Patrol; PO Box 898; Sacramento, CA 95804
Sierra Club; 530 Bush Street; San Francisco, CA 94108
Far West Ski Association; 1313 West 8th Street; Los Angeles, CA 90017
Wine Institute; 717 Market Street; San Francisco, CA 94103

City Information

Anaheim Area Visitor and Convention Bureau; 800 W. Katella Ave.; Anaheim, CA 92802
Cambria Pines Chamber of Commerce; PO Box 134; Cambria, CA 93428 [Hearst Castle area]
Camp Seco: Camanche Regional Park Board; PO Box 1; Camp Seco, CA 95226
Catalina Island Chamber of Commerce; Avalon, CA 90704
Ione: Pardee Reservoir; Rte 1, Box 224B; Ione, CA 95640
Lake Tahoe Area Council; PO Box 3475; South Lake Tahoe, CA 95705
    Greater North Lake Tahoe Chamber of Commerce; PO Box 884; Tahoe City,CA 95730
Los Angeles Area Chamber of Commerce; 404 S. Bixel St.; Los Angeles, CA 90054
Monterey: Visitors and Convention Bureau of the Monterey Peninsula Chamber of Commerce; PO Box 1770; Monterey, CA 93940 [380 Alvarado Street]
Oakland: East Bay Regional Park District; 11500 Skyline Blvd.; Oakland, CA 94619
    Lafayette Reservoir; E.B.M.U.D.; PO Box 24055; Oakland, CA 94623
Palm Springs Convention and Visitors Bureau; Municipal Airport Terminal;Palm Springs, California 92262
Sacramento Convention and Visitors Bureau; 1100 - 14th Street; Sacramento, CA 95814
    Sacramento Metropolitan Chamber of Commerce; 917 Seventh St.; -- 95814
San Diego Chamber of Commerce; 233 "A" St.; San Diego, CA 92101
    Convention and Visitors Bureau; 1200 Third Avenue; Security Pacific Plaza, Suite 824; San Diego, CA 92101
San Francisco Chamber of Commerce; 420 Montgomery Street; San Francisco, CA 94104
    Convention and Visitors' Bureau; Fox Plaza, Suite 260; Market at Hayes Street; San Francisco, CA 94102
Santa Clara Tourist and Convention Bureau; 1515 El Camino Real; Santa Clara, CA 95056
Ukiah (N. Calif.): Chamber of Commerce of Mendocino County; Ukiah, CA 95482
Yreka (N. Calif.; Deadwood Ghost Town): The Inter-Counties Chamber of Commerce; Yreka, CA 96097

National Forests

Angeles NF; 150 S. Los Robles Ave., Suite 300; Pasadena, CA 91101
Cleveland NF; 3211 Fifth Ave.; San Diego, CA 92103
Eldorado NF; 100 Forni Road; Placerville, CA 95667
Inyo NF; 873 N. Main St.; Bishop, CA 93514
Klamath NF; 1215 S. Main St.; Yreka, CA 96097
Lake Tahoe Basin Management Unit; PO Box 8465;
    1052 Tata Lane; S. Lake Tahoe, CA 95731
Lassen NF; 707 Nevada St.; Susanville, CA 96130
Los Padres NF; 42 Aero Camino; Goleta, CA 93107
Mendocino NF; 420 E. Laurel St.; Willows, CA 95988
Modoc NF; PO Box 611; Alturas, CA 96101
Plumas NF; PO Box 1500; Quincy, CA 95971
San Bernardino NF; 144 N. Mountain View Avenue;
    San Bernardino, CA 92408
Sequoia NF; 900 W. Grand Ave.; Porterville, CA 93257
Shasta-Trinity NF; 2400 Washington Avenue;
    Redding, CA 96001
Sierra NF; 1130 "O" Street; Federal Building, Room
    3017; Fresno, CA 93721
Six Rivers NF; 507 "F" St.; Eureka, CA 95501
Stanislaus NF; 175 S. Fairview Lane; Sonora, CA 95370
Tahoe NF; Hwy 49 and Coyote St.; Nevada City, CA 95959
Toiyabe NF; 1555 South Wells Ave.; Reno, NV 89502

A Public Service of
The Advertising Council

CALIFORNIA

National Parks

National Park Service; PO Box 36063; 450 Golden Gate Avenue; San Francisco, CA 94012
Lassen Volcanic NP; Mineral, CA 96063
Sequoia and Kings Canyon Parks; Three Rivers, CA 93271
Yosemite NP; Box 577 (Yosemite Village); Yosemite National Park, CA 95389

Miscellaneous

California Bureau of Land Management; Federal Building, Room E-2841; 2800 Cottage Way; Sacramento, CA 95825
Channel Islands National Monument; 1699 Anchors Way Drive; Ventura, CA 93033
Death Valley National Monument; Death Valley, CA 92328
Joshua Tree National Monument; 74485 National Monument Drive; Twentynine Palms, CA 92277
Golden Gate National Recreation Area; Fort Mason; San Francisco, CA 94123
Point Reyes National Seashore; Point Reyes, CA 94956
Regional Information Office; Mid-Pacific Region; U.S. Bureau of Reclamation; 2800 Cottage Way; Sacramento, CA 95825
Corps of Engineers: US Army Engineer Division, South Pacific; 630 Sansome Street, Room 1216; San Francisco 94111. Sacramento District; 650 Capital Mall; Sacramento, CA 95814
Delevan National Wildlife Refuge; Box 66; Sutter, CA 95982
Kern National Wildlife Refuge; Box 219; Delano, CA 93215
Whiskeytown National Recreation Area; PO Box 188; Whiskeytown, CA 96095

NATIONAL FOREST WILDERNESS AND BACKCOUNTRY AREAS

Obtaining Your Wilderness Permit

A Wilderness Permit is required before entering any of the 24 special Wilderness or Primitive Areas in the National Forests in California. The permit is FREE to anyone who will agree to follow simple rules intended to protect the visitor as well as the Wilderness resource. The Wilderness Permit also authorizes building campfires. Only one permit is required for a group traveling together. A Wilderness Permit for entry into an area through a National Forest is valid for travel through a contiguous area managed by the National Park Service and vice versa. The Permits are issued at Ranger Stations and Forest Service field offices near your point of entry; or write to the address given in the following entries.

ANGELES NF: Castaic Lake Area

Free camping only at Rogers Trail Camp, which has 6 sites, access by trail only, fire permits are required, and you must pack out your own refuse. Reservations required; call 805/259-2790. ACTIVITIES: Boating, waterskiing, fishing (trout, bass, catfish), picnicking, swimming, hiking. Additional information: Supt.; Angeles NF; 150 South Los Robles; Pasadena, CA 91101 [213/577-0050; Los Angeles, 213/684-0350].

ANGELES NF: Gabrielino National Recreation Trail

In the Arroyo Seco Ranger District. The 28-mile trail forms a semi-circle from Chantry Flat (above Sierra Madre) through Big Santa Anita Canyon, the West Fork of the San Gabriel River, and the Arroyo Seco Canyon, to the city of Pasadena. FREE camping in the seven Forest Service campgrounds along the trail. Open fires not allowed; campfire permits which allow use of the stoves provided at the campgrounds are required. During periods of high fire danger in the summer and fall, trail users should check in advance with either the Oak Grove Ranger Station in Pasadena or the Chantry Flat Station at the beginning of the trail. You may also obtain your campfire permit at either of these stations. Please smoke only in posted areas. Additional information: Ranger; Arroyo Seco District; Oak Grove Park; Flintridge, CA 91011 [213/790-1151]; OR, Supt.; Angeles NF; 150 S. Los Robles; Pasadena, CA 91101 [577-0050; Los Angeles, 213/684-0350].

ANGELES NF: San Gabriel Wilderness

Rugged and scenic; 36,000 acres; elevations from 1600-8200 feet. Three trails into this area. Free trail camps accessible by foot: Narrows and Fish Fork, along West Fork Road (also accessible by bicycle); Little Jimmy, at end of Windy Gap Trail. Fires only in stoves provided or in portable stoves and braziers; no open fires. Fire permits are necessary during fire season and are available at the Information Station or the nearest Ranger Station. Glen Camp and Little Jimmy campgrounds have tables, stoves, and toilet facilities. Fishing available along Lower and Upper Bear Creek Trails. Additional information: Supt.; Angeles NF; 150 S. Los Robles; Pasadena, CA 91101 [213/577-0050; Los Angeles, 213/684-0350].

CALIFORNIA

CLEVELAND NF: Agua Tibia Wilderness

On the west slope of Mt. Palomar. Elevations from 1700–5000 feet. Summer temperatures may exceed 100 degrees F. Best travel seasons are winter and spring. Because
of high fire hazard, the area is subject to closure from July 1 to about December 1
each year. Open campfires prohibited; portable stoves permitted. Water is scarce.
No overnight use of pack or saddle stock. Additional information: Palomar Ranger
District Office; 332 South Juniper; Escondido, CA 92025; OR, Supt.; Cleveland NF; 3211
5th Avenue; San Diego, CA 92103 [714/293-5050].

CLEVELAND NF: Dispersed Overnight Camping Program

Designed to allow individuals and small groups to camp in undeveloped areas of the
forest. A Dispersed Overnight Camping Permit is required and must be obtained in
person. Information on issuing locations may be obtained from either the Descanso
Ranger District (2707 Alpine Blvd.; Alpine, CA 92001) or the Palomar Ranger District
(732 North Broadway; Escondido, CA 92025). Dispersed Day Use and Picnicking are
allowed in the national forest without a permit, except in fire closure areas. Backpack
stoves are permitted. No open fires allowed.

ELDORADO NF: Desolation Wilderness

63,475 acres of High Sierra wilderness area, with elevations from 6,500–10,000 feet.
More than 75 miles of trails. Trout fishing. Due to the high use which occurs during
the summer months, they have established a trailhead quota from June 15th through
Labor Day. Reservations can be made up to 90 days in advance of your planned visit
so PLAN AHEAD! Many small streams. About 130 lakes (some as large as 900 acres).
Alpine timber and flora. Snowmelt makes travel hazardous before July 1st. Additional
information: Supt.; Eldorado NF; 100 Forni Road; Placerville, CA 95667 [916/622-5061].

ELDORADO NF: Granite Chief Motor Vehicle Closure Area

Alpine terrain; steep, rugged ridges; glacial valleys. Trout fishing in small lakes
and streams. No developed recreational sites. In this particular instance, a Wilderness Permit is not required; but a Campfire Permit is. This can be obtained free
at any ranger station. Use existing fireplaces when available. Don't smoke while
traveling. Additional information: Big Bend Ranger Station; Eldorado NF; Soda
Springs, CA 95728 [916/426-3609]; OR, Foresthill Ranger District; Eldorado NF; Foresthill, CA 95631 [916/367-2224]; or Truckee Ranger District; Eldorado NF; Truckee, CA
95732 [916/587-3558].

ELDORADO NF: Lake Tahoe Basin

Numerous designated hiking trails of differing length and difficulty located in this
area. Wilderness camping is popular here. Pick up your Wilderness Permit at the
William Kent Visitor Center. Additional information: Supt.; Eldorado NF; 100 Forni
Road; Placerville, CA 95667 [916/622-5061].

ELDORADO/STANISLAUS NF: Mokelumne Wilderness

Located near the crest of the Sierra Nevada Range. 50,400 acres; elevation from 4,000–
10,000 feet. In shallow valleys north of Mokelumne Peak are many small lakes. Mokelumne Canyon is extremely rugged. Numerous primitive campsites. Wilderness Permits
and additional information: Supt.; Eldorado NF; 100 Forni Road; Placerville, CA 95667
[916/622-5061]. For north side entry information: PO Box 1327; Jackson, CA 95642.

KLAMATH NF: Marble Mountains Wilderness

Numerous backpacking trails. Lots of wilderness camping opportunities. 213,363 acres
(about 93,000 are forested; many meadows; easily traveled). FISHING: 79 lakes
stocked with native trout, Aug.-Oct.; large streams have steelhead and salmon. Hunting. Campbell, Cliff, Sky High, and Ukonom Lakes are heavily used. Additional information: Supt.; Klamath NF; 1215 S. Main St.; Yreka, CA 96097 [916/842-2741].

KLAMATH/SHASTA-TRINITY NFs: Salmon-Trinity Alps Primitive Area

225,000 acres; elevation from 2000–9000 feet; rugged, isolated area. Mountain ridges
and deep canyons. 55 lakes and streams. Many bears. Area accessible from mid-
June to mid-October (as much as 12 inches of snow in winter). Firewood is scarce
in many areas; portable stove recommended. Excellent fishing. Wilderness camping.
Additional information: (For north side entry) Supt.; Klamath NF; 1215 S. Main Street;
Yreka, CA 96097 [916/842-2741]. (For south side entry) Supt.; Shasta-Trinity NF;
PO Box T; Weaverville, CA 96093.

CALIFORNIA

LASSEN NF: Caribou Wilderness

Gently-rolling forested plateau. Trout periodically planted in some of the lakes. Well-maintained trails. Summer thunderstorms are common. Additional information: Supt.; Lassen NF; 707 Nevada Street; Susanville, CA 96130 [916/257-2151].

LASSEN NF: Thousand Lakes Wilderness

Elevations from 5000-9000 feet. The portion above the timberline is open with barren mountain sides and ravines. Lakes formed in lava potholes during eruptions of ancient extinct volcano. Limited trail maintenance. Much of the terrain is steep and rocky. Much opportunity for wilderness camping. Lower elevations are covered with ponderosa pine, white fir, and red fir. Brown bear country. Additional information: Supt.; Lassen NF; 707 Nevada Street; Susanville, CA 96130 [916/257-2151].

LOS PADRES NF: Backcountry Camping

Numerous unroaded backcountry areas. Good trails. Scenic: waterfalls, thermal springs. Primitive campsite facilities (some include toilets and tables). Additional information: Supt.; Los Padres NF; 42 Aero Camino; Goleta, CA 913107 [805/968-1578].

LOS PADRES NF: Ventana Wilderness

98,065 acres, approximately 120 miles south of San Francisco and 90 miles north of San Luis Obispo. Elevations from 600-4965 feet. Scenic: Santa Lucia Mountain Range; waterfalls; thermal springs; deep pools. Overnight camping is limited to designated campsites, which are identified by Forest Service stoves. If wilderness is filled, a ranger can direct you to the backcountry area which offers unlimited wilderness camping. Additional information: Monterey Ranger District Office; 406 South Mildred Avenue; King City, CA 93930 [408/385-5434].

LOS PADRES NF: Santa Lucia Wilderness

This is a new area, located east of San Luis Obispo in Lopez Canyon. Elevations from 600 feet near Lopez Reservoir to 6800 feet at Lopez Mountain. Campfires permitted only at designated locations; portable stoves advised. Additional information: Los Padres NF; 1616 North Carlotti Drive; Santa Maria, CA 93454.

LOS PADRES NF: San Rafael Wilderness

Located in the San Rafael Mountains north of Santa Barbara. Elevations from 1000-6800; 149,170 acres. 125 miles of trails. Severe fire hazard; campfires only in designated areas. Portable stoves are permitted. Two-thirds of the area is closed July 1 to November 15 because of fire danger. Best time to hike and camp here is in the spring.

MENDOCINO/SHASTA-TRINITY NFs: Yolla Bolly-Middle Eel Wilderness

113,030 acres; elevations from 2700-8083 feet. Located between North and South Yolla Bolly Mountains in rugged country of the headwaters of the Middle Fork of the Eel River. Bear and deer country. Trout fishing. Hunting. Water may be scarce in late summer. Extensive trail system. Deer hunting in late September. Numerous rustic camps with the Wilderness, usually consisting of a fireplace and a table. Pets are allowed on the trails; "however, it must be under that degree of control by you commensurate with its disposition and threat to other recreationists and to wildlife." Firearms are discouraged except during hunting seasons. This is not a prohibition however. Additional information: (For north side entry) Supt.; Shasta-Trinity NF; 2400 Washington Avenue; Redding, CA 96001 [916/246-5222]. (For south side entry) Supt.; Mendocino NF; 420 E. Laurel Street; Willows, CA 95988 [916/934-3316].

MODOC NF: South Warner Wilderness

Located in the extreme northeast corner of California in the Cascade Range. Scenic: meadows, canyons, glacial lakes. Highest peaks in northeast California. 100 miles of trails. Trout fishing; limited hunting; horseback riding. SEASON: July through September. 68,540 acres. Additional information: Modoc NF; PO Box 220; Cedarville, California 96104. No designated campgrounds within its boundaries.

PLUMAS NF: Backcountry Camping

Brochures are available to assist forest visitors in locating and planning hiking/backpacking/camping trips in Plumas NF. The information on trail conditions, hazards, restrictions, and camping information, can be obtained by writing to: Supt.; Plumas NF; 159 Lawrence Street; PO Box 1500; Quincy, CA 95971 [916/283-2050].

PLUMAS NF: Middle Fork Feather River

The entire Middle Fork of the Feather River is one of six rivers in the U.S. designated

CALIFORNIA

as a component of the National System of Wild and Scenic Rivers by an act of Congress. The Middle Fork is approximately 108 miles long. About 25,000 acres of public and private lands are within the designated narrow band along the river averaging less than ½-mile wide. About 13,200 areas (52%) of this are federally-owned....all national forest. Primitive camping is available in much of this area. Additional information: Supt.; Plumas NF; 159 Lawrence Street; PO Box 1500; Quincy, CA 95971.

SAN BERNARDINO NF: Cucamonga Wilderness

Wilderness hiking and camping. Free Wilderness Permits are available at Lytle Creek Ranger Station (Star Route; Box 100; Fontana, CA 92335 [714/887-2576, San Bernardino]) only. There is no limit to the number of people or permits. The Wilderness is located In the San Gabriel Mountain Range, bordering the San Bernardino and Angeles National Forests, administered as part of the San Bernardino NF. Los Angeles is only 50 miles west; San Bernardino Valley is 20 miles east. 8,500 acres; elevations from 5000-9000 feet. Steep mountainsides, rough terain, sharp peaks. Campfires permitted in designated spots only; portable stove recommended. Water is scarce. Heavy use of Canyon bottoms where water is available. A small part of this area is closed July 1 through December 1 due to high fire hazard. Additional information: Supt.; San Bernardino NF; 144 North Mountain View Avenue; San Bernardino, CA 92408 [714/383-5588]; OR, Lytle Creek Ranger Station (address above).

SAN BERNARDINO NF: San Gorgonio Wilderness

The largest and most popular wilderness area in the San Bernardino NF, located in the summit region of the San Gorgonio Mountain Range, the highest in Southern California. Free Wilderness Permits are available at Mill Creek Ranger Station (Route 1, Box 264; Mentone, CA 92359 [714/794-1123, Redlands]) and Barton Flats Visitor Center. 35,255 acres; elevation from 7,000-11,502 feet. Open fire prohibited in heavily-used South Fork Travel zone; portable stove recommended. Plummer meadows closed to overnight camping. Camping on Summit of San Gorgonio mountain is limited to 5 permits per day; very heavily used area. Entry quota in effect in some travel zones. Additional information: Supt.; San Bernardino NF; 144 North Mountain View Avenue; San Bernardino, CA 92408 [714/383-6688]; OR,Mill Creek Ranger Station (address above).

SAN BERNARDINO NF: San Jacinto Wilderness

The Wilderness is located in the San Jacinto Mountain Area in Riverside County. It is split into two areas, separated by the Mt. San Jacinto State Park. Free Wilderness Permits are available only at the Idyllwild Ranger Station (PO Box 518; Idyllwild, CA 92349 [714/659-2117]). 21,951 acres; elevations from 6,000-10,000 feet. Good fishing in Snow Creek. Quota on number of overnight campers. Wood fires allowed only at designated areas; portable stove recommended. Heavily-used area. Additional information: Supt.; San Bernardino NF; 144 North Mountain View Avenue; San Bernardino, CA 92408 [714/383-5588]; OR, Idyllwild Ranger Station (address given above).

SEQUOIA NF: Backcountry Camping

There is plenty of room to roam and camp in the backcountry of this national forest, which encompasses two million acres along the southern Sierras. Pets are welcome (on leash in developed areas). Fishing and hunting. NO WILDERNESS PERMIT REQUIRED; only a campfire permit. Additional information: Supt.; Sequoia NF; 900 W. Grand Ave.; Porterville, CA 93257 [209/784-1500].

SEQUOIA NF: Dome Land Wilderness

Free Wilderness Permit and campfire permit are both required. The southernmost Wilderness Area in the Sierra Nevada Range. Located at the southern end of the Kern Plateau, about 70 miles NE of Bakersfield. 62,695 acres; elevations from 3000-9000 feet. Picturesque granite domes. Semi-arid to desert country. Approximately 30 miles of trails in the Wilderness. Hunting and fishing. Pets permitted on trails; on leash in developed areas. Portable stove recommended. Lightly-used area. Best travel in spring and fall. Additional information: Cannell Meadow Ranger District; Sequoia NF; PO Box 6; Kernville, CA 93238 [714/376-2294].

SEQUOIA/INYO NFs: Golden Trout Wilderness

Free Wilderness Permit and campfire permit are both required. Located at the southern end of the Inyo NF (adjacent to the John Muir Wilderness) and the northern end of the Kern Plateau and the Little Kern Basin of the Sequoia NF. Extensive forest and meadows. Water limited in dry periods. Wood fires not encouraged above 10,000 feet elevation. Special DFG fishing rules in the area east of Kern River. Quota for entry to Sequoia National Park. New area. 306,000 acres; elevations from 4,800-12,432 feet. Pets are allowed on trails; on leash in developed areas. Additional information: (For east side entry) Inyo NF; PO Box 8; Lone Pine, CA 93545. (For west side entry)

Tule River Ranger District; Sequoia NF; 32588 Highway 190; Porterville, CA 93257. (For south side entry) Cannell Meadow Ranger District; Sequoia NF; PO Box 6; Kernville, CA 93238.

SHASTA-TRINITY NF: Shasta Lake Shoreline Camping

Shasta Lake is one of the few lakes in California where you can still camp along the shore outside of designated campgrounds. There are a few "restricted" areas, however, for obvious reasons: no public camping is permitted on private property, near the water intake system for the community of Mountain Gate, or in osprey and eagle nesting areas. Maps showing the restricted areas will be posted at all Ranger Stations, resorts, and boat ramps. It should be noted, however, that there remains literally hundreds of miles of shoreline where camping IS permitted. A free campfire permit is required for all fire use outside developed campgrounds; this includes the use of gas stoves, catalytic heaters, and lanterns. NO WILDERNESS PERMIT IS REQUIRED. Additional information, map and free campfire permit: Supt.; Shasta-Trinity NF; 1615 Continental Street; Redding, CA 96001 [916/241-7100].

SIERRA NF: Backcountry Camping

There are many unimproved sites for those who prefer solitude over conveniences. Except for areas of concentrated use such as Bass Lake, Shaver Lake, Huntington Lake and Dinkey Creek, you can usually camp wherever you choose. However, if you do select an unimproved campsite, you must obtain a free campfire permit before building a fire or cooking outdoors with a gas stove. People camping in undeveloped sites are also asked to take their unburnable garbage home with them. Where piped water is not available for cooking or drinking, you should boil or treat stream water with purification tablets. Additional information, maps, and campfire permit: Supt.; Sierra NF; Federal Building; 1130 "O" Street, Room 3017; Fresno, CA 93721 [209/487-5155].

SIERRA/SEQUOIA NFs: High Sierra Primitive Area

Extremely rugged mountainous area. Free Wilderness Permit and campfire permit are both required. This is a small wilderness (11,656 acres) lying adjacent to Kings Canyon National Park backcountry. It is part of the proposed Monarch Wilderness (30,689 acres). Elevations from 4,300 to 11,000 feet. Because of the rugged, steep character of the terrain and the absence of good fishing lakes, the Primitive Area is lightly used. Portable stove recommended. Additional information: Hume Lake Ranger District; Sierra NF; Miramonte, CA 93641 [209/336-2881].

SIERRA/INYO NFs: John Muir Wilderness

483,155 acres of high mountain lands, with thousands of lakes and streams, and snow-capped mountains. Wood-burning fires are prohibited at some sites; portable stoves recommended. Quotas for many trails; reservations advisable. Elevations from 4,000-14,496 feet. Deep canyons and beautiful meadows. No roads. The John Muir Trail traverses about 30 airline miles of this wilderness. The Pacific Crest Trail follows the same route as the John Muir Trail through this portion of the Sierra Nevada Range. Additional information: (For east side entry) Sierra NF; PO Box 306; Shaver Lake, CA 93664. (For east side entry-central portion) Inyo NF; 798 N. Main Street; Bishop, CA 93514. (For east side entry-south portion) Inyo NF; PO Box 8; Lone Pine,CA 93545. (For east side entry-north portion) Inyo NF; PO Box 148; Mammoth Lakes, CA 93546.

SIERRA NF: Kaiser Wilderness

Located just north of Huntington Lake, approximately 70 miles NE of Fresno. Driving time from Fresno to the southern trailheads near Huntington Lake is approximately two hours via State Highway 168. Named after Kaiser Ridge, whose highest point is 10,320-foot-high Kaiser Peak (which divides the wilderness into two considerably different parts). The northern part contains all but two of the twenty small lakes. Upper Twin Lake is the largest (40 acres) and most heavily used. Additional information: Supt.; Sierra NF; PO Box 306; Shaver Lake, CA 93664 [209/841-3311].

SIERRA/INYO NFs: Minarets Wilderness

Approach roads to the area are the Tioga Pass Road (on the north); Mammoth Pass and Agnew Meadow (on the east); from the road end at Clover Meadow (on the west) via Minarets Road. Wilderness is traversed north to south by Pacific Crest National Scenic Trail. Fishing; mountain climbing. Small glaciers. 102,040 acres; elevations from 7,000-14,000 feet. Heavily-used area. John Muir Trail crosses this area. Quota is in effect on several trailheads. Campfires prohibited in some areas; firewood scarce above 10,000 feet elevation; portable stove recommended. Additional information: (West side entry) Minarets Ranger District; Sierra NF; North Fork, CA 93643. (East side entry) Inyo NF; PO Box 148; Mammoth Lakes, CA 93546.

CALIFORNIA

SIX RIVERS NF: Backcountry Camping

Camping is permitted anywhere on national forest land within the Six Rivers NF.   If
you camp outside the designated campgrounds, and if you have an open fire, a member
of your party must have a valid campfire permit in his possession.   (An open fire
is any fire outside of an enclosed vehicle, and includes butane and gasoline cook
stoves, heaters, and gas lights, as well as the campfire.)   A shovel with a blade
at least 12" long is required at campfire sites when camping in nondesignated campgrounds.   Don't forget there are PRIVATE LANDS within the national forest and you
must have permission from the landowner before using his land.   Additional information
and campfire permit: Supt.; Six Rivers NF; 710 East Street; Eureka, CA 96601 [707/442-
1721].

STANISLAUS NF: Emigrant Wilderness

Located along the west slope of the Sierra Nevada Mountains, approximately 185 miles
east of San Francisco (via St Hwy 108 or 120, Forest Roads, and then trails.   Broad
expanses of glaciated granite; lava-capped peaks, alpine lakes; granite-walled canyons.   111,496 acres; elevations from 6,000-12,000 feet.   SEASON: May-October. Snowstorms may occur after October 1st.   Firewood is scarce; portable stove recommended.
Additional information: Supt.; Stanislaus NF; 175 S. Fairview Lane; Sonora, CA 95370.

STANISLAUS/ELDORADO NFs: Mokelumne Wilderness

Several primitive trails into the wilderness join St Hwy 4 at various points between
Ganns and Hermit Valley Campground.   Many small and scenic lakes.   50,165 acres;
elevations from 4,000-10,000 feet.   Rugged Mokelumne River Canyon.   Portable stove
recommended.   Additional information: Eldorado NF; PO Box 1327; Jackson, CA 95642.
(For south side entry) Stanislaus NF; PO Box 48; Arnold, CA 915223.

TAHOE NF: Backcountry Camping

Most of the forest land is open to camping, but in several areas of heavy use, camping is limited to developed campgrounds or designated campsites.   This has become
necessary to avoid problems of pollution and sanitation.   These areas are located on
portions of the North and South Yuba Rivers, Highway 89 from Sierraville to Truckee,
on the Truckee River from Truckee to Tahoe City, and in the vicinity of Bullards Bar,
French Meadows, Jackson Meadow, Stampede, Boca and Prosser Reservoirs.   The areas
are posted with signs indicating where you may camp.   Additional information: Supt.;
Tahoe NF; St Hwy 49; Nevada City, CA 95959 [916/265-4531].

TOIYABE NF: Hoover Wilderness

Extremely rugged area.   Recommended travel period: July-September (although extreme
weather conditions occur even then).   Lakes, meadows.   47,937 acres; elevations from
8,000-13,000 feet.   Trout fishing.   Campfires prohibited in 20 Lakes Basin; portable
stove recommended.   Additional information: (East side entry) Toiyabe NF; Bridgeport,
CA 913517.   (South side entry) Inyo NF; PO Box 10; Lee Vining, CA 93541. Also, Supt.;
Toiyabe NF; PO Box 1331; Reno, NV 89504.

MISCELLANEOUS BACKCOUNTRY CAMPING AREAS

Yosemite National Park

Backcountry campers must build open fires in designated firesites.   Wilderness Permit
required.   Keep a clean camp to reduce conflicts between bears and campers.   Lock
all food in vehicle trunks or suspend packs from trees while in the backcountry.
Pets are not allowed on trails.   Information, maps, permits: Supt.; Yosemite NP, CA
95389.

Lassen Volcanic National Park

A wilderness permit is required when camping anywhere other than designated campgrounds.   There is a $1.00 entrance fee, unless you have a Golden Eagle or Golden
Age Passport.*   Pets are not permitted on trails, swimming beaches, at evening programs, or in public buildings.   Information, maps, permit: Supt.; Lassen Volcanic
NP; Mineral, CA 96063.

Sequoia and Kings Canyon National Parks

There is an entrance fee of $3.00 per car per trip into the park OR the Golden Eagle
(or Golden Age) Passport.*   However, all backcountry camping is free of any additional

charge. Free Wilderness Permits are required. Between February 1st and May 31st, reservations may be made for permits for the coming summer. After May 31st, application for these permits must be made in person, no more than 24 hours in advance, at the visitor contact station nearest the proposed point of entry. Those who schedule trips on days other than weekends normally will experience lighter crowds and will have a better chance of entering the area on the day of their choice, as there are limitations on the number of people allowed on the trails during the summer. No firearms or hunting allowed. No pets on trails. Information, maps, permit: Chief Ranger's Office; Sequoia and Kings Canyon National Parks; Three Rivers, CA 93271.

Whiskeytown National Recreation Area

Backcountry camping accessible by foot OR CAR. No entrance fee to NRA. Camping can be done anywhere within the area so long as the camper is at least one mile away from the lake. A free backcountry permit is required. Pets must be kept off beaches entirely and under physical restraint in campgrounds, near boat landings, and in other areas where visitors concentrate. There are about 50 miles of backcountry roads open for your use. Most of these roads are south and west of the lake. They are graded roads of dirt and gravel and are clearly marked on a map available from Park Headquarters. Some are passable for passenger cars; others may require 4-wheel drive vehicles. Inquire at one of the visitor-contact stations prior to driving the backcountry roads in a passenger car. These roads open more territory for exploring, hiking, and camping, and for fishing and hunting in season. CAUTION: Backcountry roads are regularly patrolled only during summer. If you have car trouble and must go for help, stay on the road. Do NOT attempt to leave the road and hike crosscountry. Information and permit: NRA; PO Box 188; Whiskeytown, CA 96095 [916/241-6584].

Point Reyes National Seashore

The Wilderness Area of Point Reyes National Seashore is not open for wilderness-type camping. Camping is restricted to four hike-in campgrounds. (See "Olema, CA" for specifics.) Permits are required, but are available without charge at Bear Valley Visitor Center. Additional information and map: Supt.; Point Reyes National Seashore; Point Reyes, CA 94956.

Havasu National Wildlife Refuge

Camping is permitted on Havasu Refuge, but free camping is restricted to boat and tent camping along the Arizona shoreline below the buoy designating the south entrance to Topock Gorge area. Camping is prohibited in Mesquite Bay. All camping is limited to seven consecutive nights. Additional information: Havasu NWR; PO Box A; Needles, CA 92363.

Sacramento Valley National Wildlife Refuges

The complex of NWRs in the Sacramento Valley of Northern California includes the Sacramento, Delevan, Colusa and Sutter Refuges. These comprise a total of 23,071 acres. The largest of these, and the administrative office location for all four refuges, is the Sacramento NWR, 6 miles south of Willows. Hunting; fishing; photography. Camping is not permitted on the refuges. HOWEVER, hunters can stay overnight in the main parking areas if they are willing to sleep in their cars or campers. Additional information: Refuge Manager; Sacramento NWR; Route 1, Box 311; Willows, CA 95988 [916/934-4090].

Stanislaus River Recreation Area; Bureau of Land Management (BLM)

For information about whitewater rafting along the Stanislaus River, and camping, contact: BLM, Folsom District; 63 Natoma Street; Folsom, CA 95630 [916/985-4474]. Leave a clean camp and dead fire. Never take glass into the river corridor. Carry out what you carry in. Respect the privacy of other campers. There is a BLM comfort station at Rose Creek for your convenience.

FREE CAMPGROUNDS

ADIN

Ash Creek (Modoc NF). 2/10 mi S of Adin on St Hwy 299; 7½ mi SE on Co Rd 88 (Ash Valley Road); 3/10 mi N on FS 41N02. [Off Adin-Madeline Rd.] SEASON: 5/1-10/15. FACILITIES: 7 sites (tr -22), tbls, toil, cga, piped drk wtr. ACTIVITIES: Rockhounding; picnicking; fishing. MISC.: 7 acres; elev 4800 ft; scenic. Ash Creek. Pets on leash.

ALLEGHANY

Cornish House (Tahoe NF). 2-3/10 mi NW of Alleghany on Co Hwy 19N31; 4 mi NE on Co Hwy 19N24; 2-1/5 mi E on Co Hwy 19N03. [On Henness Rd; not advised for trailers.] SEASON: 6/15-11/1, 14-day lmt. FACILITIES: 6 sites (tr -22), tbls, toil, cga, no drk wtr. MISC.: Elev 5600 ft; 1 acre. Pets.

Middle Waters (Tahoe NF). 2-3/10 mi NW of Alleghany on Co Hwy 19N31; 4 mi NE on Co Hwy 19N24; 8-7/10 mi E on Co Hwy 19N03. [On Henness Rd; not advised for trailers.] SEASON: 7/1-10/15, 14-day lmt. FACILITIES: 4 sites (tr -22), tbls, toil, cga, no drk wtr. ACTIVITIES: Picnicking. Fishing (1 mi). MISC.: Elev 6200 ft; 1 acre; stream. Pets on leash.

ALTADENA

*Idlehour (Angeles NF). 2-9/10 mi NE of Altadena on Trail 2N453; 4/5 mi NE on Trail 2N452; 1½ mi N on Trail 12W16. SEASON: All yr; 14-day lmt. FACILITIES: 4 tent sites; tbls, toil, cga, no drk wtr. ACTIVITIES: Picnicking. MISC.: Elev 2500 ft; 2 acres; stream. Pets on leash. Closed during high fire danger; call local ranger station for details.

*Millard (Angeles NF). 1-2/5 mi N of Altadena on Lake Avenue; 1-1/5 mi W on Loma Alta Drive; 1-7/10 mi N on Co Hwy 2N65 to Cheney Trail in Millard Canyon. SEASON: All yr; 14-day lmt. FACILITIES: 7 tent sites; tbls, toil, cga, piped drk wtr. 4 mi -- Store, ice, gas, fd, laundry. ACTIVITIES: Hiking; picnicking. MISC.: Elev 1900 ft; 1 acre; stream water. Pets on leash.

*Mt. Lowe (Angeles NF). 4 mi N of Altadena on Trail 12W14; 1/5 mi N on FS 2N50. [Primitive roads.] SEASON: All yr. FACILITIES: 6 tent sites; tbls, toil, cga, piped drk wtr. ACTIVITIES: Hiking; picnicking; horseback riding. Fishing (4 mi). MISC.: Elev 4500 ft; 2 acres; pets; nature trails. Hiking and equestrian access only. Fire closure restrictions in summer.

AMBOY

City Park. Free overnight park in town. SEASON: All year.

ANGELES OAKS

Thomas Hunting Ground (San Bernardino NF). 4 mi W of Angeles Oaks on FS 1N12. SEASON: 5/15-11/30; 10-day lmt. FACILITIES: 3 sites (tr -22), tbls, toil, cga, no drk wtr. 4 mi -- Store, ice,

gas, fd. ACTIVITIES: Hiking; picnicking. MISC.: Elev 5800 ft; 15 acres; pets. 4 mi W of Camp Angelus (suitable for groups).

ARCATA

City Park. Free overnight park at 9th and "F" Streets, in town. SEASON: All year.

ARIPOSA

Summit Camp (Sierra NF). 12-3/10 mi E of Ariposa on St Hwy 49; 6-4/5 mi NE on Co Hwy 5S092. SEASON: 5/15-11/15; 14-day lmt. FACILITIES: 12 sites (tr -22); tbls, toil, cga, f, piped drk wtr. ACTIVITIES: Picnicking. MISC.: Elev 5800 ft; 2 acres; scenic; pets.

ARROYO GRANDE

Aqua Escondido (Los Padres NF). 27-3/5 mi E of Arroyo Grande on Co Hwy 32 (Arroyo Grande Huasna Rd); 1½ mi N on FS 30S07; 2 mi N on FS 30S02. SEASON: All year; 14-day lmt. FACILITIES: 2 tent sites; tbls, toil, cga, piped drk wtr. ACTIVITIES: Deer hunting; hiking; picnicking. Horseback riding (1 mi). MISC.: Open during DEER SEASON ONLY. Elev 2200 ft; 1 acre; pets.

*Balm of Gilead Trail Camp. (Los Padres NF). 19 mi NE of Arroyo Grande on Pozo-Arroyo Grande Co Rd; 6 mi E on Forest Trail 15E06. FACILITIES: Tent sites. ACTIVITIES: Hiking. MISC.: Pets on leash.

Stony Creek (Los Padres NF). 20 mi E of Arroyo Grande on Co Hwy 32 (Arroye Grande-Huasna Rd); 1-7/10 mi N on FS 30S02; 2 mi NW on FS 31S09. SEASON: 8/5-9/15 [DEER SEASON ONLY]; 14-day lmt. FACILITIES: 12 tent; tbls, toil, cga, piped spring drk wtr. ACTIVITIES: Deer hunting; hiking; picnicking. Horseback riding (1 mi). MISC.: Elev 2000 ft; 3 acres. Pets allowed if on a leash.

AZUSA

*Glenn (Angeles NF). 13 mi N of Azusa on St Hwy 39; 6 mi W on Trail 2N25 (West Fork Rd). SEASON: All yr; 14-day lmt. FACILITIES: 10 tent sites; tbls, toil, cga, no drk wtr. ACTIVITIES: Swimming; picnicking; fishing; hiking. MISC.: Elev 2000 ft; 1 acre; pets. West Fork of San Gabriel River.

*Iron Fork (Angeles NF). 11 mi N of Azusa on St Hwy 39; 6 mi E on East Fork Rd; 5 mi N on Trail. SEASON: 4/1-10/31. FACILITIES: 6 tent sites; no facilities or drk wtr. ACTIVITIES: Swimming; fishing; hiking. MISC.: Elev 3200 ft; pets. East Fork of San Gabriel River.

See page 7 for KEY TO ABBREVIATIONS.

*The Narrows (Angeles NF). 11 mi N of
Azusa on St Hwy 39; 6 mi E on East Fork
Rd; 4 mi N on Trail. **SEASON:** 4/1-10/31.
FACILITIES: 6 tent sites; no facilities
or drk wtr. **ACTIVITIES:** Fishing; swim-
ming; hiking. **MISC.:** Elev 2800 ft; pets.
East Fork of San Gabriel River.

BADGER

Eshom (Sequoia NF). 8-1/5 mi NE of Badger on Co Hwy 465. [Paved access rd.]
SEASON: 5/1-11/15; 14-day lmt. **FACILI-
TIES:** 17 sites (tr -22), tbls, toil, cga,
piped spring drk wtr. 5 mi -- Store,
gas, fd. **ACTIVITIES:** Fishing; picnicking.
MISC.: Elev 4800 ft; Eshom Creek; pets.

BAKER

City Park. Free overnight camping
on the west edge of town on the north
side of Main. **SEASON:** All year.

BAKERSFIELD

Live Oak (Sequoia NF). 23 mi NE of
Bakersfield on St Hwy 178. **SEAS.:** All
yr; 14-day lmt. **FACILITIES:** 13 sites
(no tr); tbls, toil, cga; no drk wtr.
ACTIVITIES: Picnicking; fishing.
MISC.: Elev 1400 ft; 3 acres; river;
pets.

Lower Richbar (Sequoia NF). 23½ mi
NE of Bakersfield on St Hwy 178.
SEASON: 4/1-10/31; 14-day lmt. **FACIL-
ITIES:** 9 sites (no tr); tbls, toil,
cga, piped drk wtr. **ACTIVITIES:**
Picnicking; fishing. **MISC.:** Elev 1400
ft; 4 acres; river; pets.

Upper Richbar (Sequoia NF). 23-7/10
mi NE of Bakersfield on St Hwy 178.
[Along the Kern River.] Paved access
rd. **SEASON:** All yr; 14-day lmt. **FACIL-
ITIES:** 16 tent sites, tbls, flush toil,
cga, piped drk wtr. **ACTIVITIES:** Fishing; picnicking. **MISC.:** River; pets;
elev 1400 ft; 9 acres.

BARSTOW

Afton Canyon (BLM). 43 mi E of Barstow
on US 91; 3 mi S. **SEASON:** All yr.
FACILITIES: 22 sites; cistern water.
MISC.: Elev 1400 ft; pets. Mojave River
desert site.

Rainbow Basin - Owl Canyon (BLM).
8 mi N via Camp Irwin Rd from Barstow;
US 66; then 2 mi W on Fossil Bed Rd.
SEASON: All yr. **FACILITIES:** 31 sites.
MISC.: Elev 3000 ft. Pets on leash.

BASS LAKE

Chilkoot (Sierra NF). 4-3/5 mi N of Bass
Lake on Co Hwy 434. **SEASON:** 5/21-9/30,
14-day lmt. **FACILITIES:** 14 sites (tr

-16), tbls, toil, cga, tank drk wtr. 5
mi -- Store, ice, gas, laundry. **ACTIV-
ITIES:** Picnicking. Fishing (1 mi).
5 mi -- Swimming; waterskiing; boat-
ing,rld; horseback riding/rental. **MISC.:**
Elev 4600 ft; 4 acres; stream; pets.
North Fork of Chilkoot Creek and Bass
Lake (5 mi).

Jones Beasore (Sierra NF). 18 mi SW
of Bass Lake on FS 05S07. **SEASON:** 6/15-
10/31. **FACILITIES:** 5 sites; toil, piped
drk wtr. **MISC.:** Elev 6800 ft; 2 acres;
stream. Pets permitted if kept on leash.

BEAR CITY

Pipes Canyon (San Bernardino NF).
9 mi SE of Bear City on St Hwy SH38;
7½ mi SW on FS 1N01. **SEASON:** 6/15-
9/15; 7-day lmt. **FACILITIES:** 6 sites
(no tr); tbls, toil, cga, no drk wtr.
ACTIVITIES: Picnicking. Horseback
riding (1 mi). **MISC.:** Elev 6400 ft;
3 acres; pets.

BEAR VALLEY

Bloomfield (Stanislaus NF). 15-4/5 mi
NE of Bear Valley on St Hwy 4; 4/5 mi
SE on FS 8N01; 1/10 mi S on FS 8N29.
SEASON: 6/15-10/1; 14-day lmt. **FACILI-
TIES:** 10 sites (tr -16), tbls, toil, no
drk wtr. **ACTIVITIES:** Fishing; picnicking.
Boating (3 mi). **MISC.:** Elev 8000 ft; 5
acres; river. Pets allowed if on leash.

Hermit Valley (Stanislaus NF). 12-1/10
mi NE of Bear Valley on St Hwy 4; 3/10
mi S on FS 8N22. **SEASON:** 6/15-10/1; 14-
day lmt. **FACILITIES:** 5 sites (tr -16),
tbls, toil, cga, no drk wtr. **ACTIVITIES:**
Swimming; picnicking; fishing. **MISC.:**
Elev 7500 ft; 5 acres; river; pets.

Highland Lakes (Stanislaus NF). 15-4/5
mi NE of Bear Valley on St Hwy 4; 5-
7/10 mi SE on FS 8N01; ½ mi SW on FS
8N33. **SEASON:** 7/1-10/1; 14-day lmt.
FACILITIES: 10 sites (tr -16), tbls, toil,
no drk wtr. **ACTIVITIES:** Horseback riding; swimming; picnicking; fishing; boating. **MISC.:** Elev 8600 ft; 5 acres; lake.
Pets permitted only if kept on a leash.

Pacific Valley (Stanislaus NF). 10 mi
NE of Bear Valley on St Hwy 4; 1/10 mi
S on FS 8N12. [6 mi W of Ebbetts Pass.]
SEASON: 6/15-10/1; 14-day lmt. **FACILI-
TIES:** 6 sites (tr -16), tbls, toil, cga,
no drk wtr. **ACTIVITIES:** Fishing; pic-
nicking. **MISC.:** Elev 7600 ft; 10 acres;
stream. Pets allowed if kept on leash.

Sand Flat (Stanislaus NF). 5-1/10 mi
SW of Bear Valley on St Hwy 4; 2 mi
E on FS 7N02. **SEASON:** 6/15-10/1; 14-day
lmt. **FACILITIES:** 4 tent sites, tbls, toil,
cga, no drk wtr. **ACTIVITIES:** Swimming;
picnicking; fishing. **MISC.:** Elev 5800
ft; 5 acres; river. Pets on leash.

See page 7 for KEY TO ABBREVIATIONS.

Stanislaus River (Stanislaus NF). 3-2/5 mi SW of Bear Valley on St Hwy 4; 3-3/10 mi SE on FS 6N06 (labeled Stanislaus River). [Difficult to reach and primitive.] SEASON: 6/15-10/1; 14-day lmt. FACILITIES: 5 sites (tr -16), tbls, toil, cga, no drk wtr. 5 mi -- Store, ice, fd, gas. ACTIVITIES: Swimming; hunting; picnicking; fishing. MISC.: Elev 5900 ft; 2 acres; pets. Stanislaus River. Trailers are not recommended.

BECKWORTH

Crocker (Plumas NF). 7 mi N of Beckworth on Co Hwy 111 (Beckworth Genesee Rd); 1/5 mi W on FS 24N36. SEASON: 5/1-10/1; 14-day lmt. FACILITIES: 15 sites (tr - -32), tbls, toil, piped drk wtr. 4 mi -- Store, ice. ACTIVITIES: Hunting; picnicking; boating,d (rent, 5 mi). Swimming (4 mi). Fishing (1 mi). MISC.: Elev 5800 ft; 1 acre; pets. Crock Creek/Lake Davis (4 mi).

BERRY CREEK

*Dan Beebe (Plumas NF).14 mi N of Berry Creek on Co Hwy 27562; 11 mi NE on FS 23N60; 3 mi S on Trail P2000. SEASON: 6/1-10/15; 14-day lmt. FACILITIES: 4 tent sites; tbls, toil, cga, piped drk wtr. ACTIVITIES: Swimming; picnicking; fishing; hiking. MISC.: Elev 2400 ft; 3 acres; pets; scenic. Trail camp within Middle Fork Wild River Area. On Middle Fork Feather River. Access by Hartman Bar Trail from Gravel Range Rd at a point 7 mi S of Bucks Lake. A 4-mi hike from rd to river.

Grizzly Creek (Plumas NF). 31 mi N of Berry Creek on Co Hwy 24N25 (Oroville Quincy Rd). [3 mi W of Bucks Lake.] SEASON: 6/1-10/15; 14-day lmt. FACILITIES: 8 sites (tr -22), tbls, toil, cga, no drk wtr. 3 mi (at Bucks Lake) - Store, ice, laundry. ACTIVITIES: Horseback riding; hunting; hiking; picnicking. 3 mi (at Bucks Lake) -- Fishing; swimming; waterskiing; boating,rld. MISC.: Elev 5400 ft; 2 acres;stream;pets.

Little North Fork (Plumas NF). 14 mi N of Berry Creek on Co Hwy 27562 (Oroville Quincy Rd); 5 mi NE on FS 23N60; ½ mi N on FS 23N15. SEASON: 5/15-10/15; 14-day lmt. FACILITIES: 8 sites (tr -16), tbls, toil, cga, no drk wtr. ACTIVITIES: Hunting; picnicking; fishing; hiking. MISC.: Elev 3700 ft; 3 acres; pets. Off Oroville-Bucks Lake Rd on Little North Fork of Feather River.

Rogers Cow Camp (Plumas NF). 15 mi NE of Berry Creek on Co Hwy 27562; ½ mi W on FS 23N15. [Off Oroville-Bucks Lake Rd, ½ mi W of Merrimac.] SEASON: 5/15-10/15. FACILITIES: 5 sites (tr -16), tbls, toil, cga, no drk wtr. 5 mi -- Store, gas. ACTIVITIES: Berry-picking; picnicking. MISC.: Elev 4100 ft; 1 acre; stream; pets.

BIG BAR

Big Bar (Shasta-Trinity NF). 1 mi SE of Big Bar on St Hwy 299, across bridge from Big Bar Ranger Station. SEASON: All year; 14-day lmt. FACILITIES: 3 sites (tr -16), tbls, toil, cga, piped drk wtr. 1 mi -- Store, ice, gas, fd, laundry. ACTIVITIES: Swimming; picnicking; fishing. MISC.: Elev 1200 ft; 1 acre; scenic; stream. Pets on leash.

BIG BEAR CITY

Pipes Canyon (San Bernardino NF). 9 mi SE of Big Bear City on St Hwy SH38; 7½ mi SW on FS 1N01. SEASON: 6/15-9/15; 7-day lmt. FACILITIES: 6 tent sites; tbls, toil, cga, no drk wtr. ACTIVITIES: Horseback riding; boating,d; picnicking; fishing. Swimming (5 mi). MISC.: Elev 6400 ft; 3 acres. Pets allowed on leash.

BIG BEND

Deadlun (Shasta-Trinity NF). 7 mi NW of Big Bend on FS N9M02. SEASON: 4/1-11/30; 21-day lmt. FACILITIES: 33 sites; (tr -22); tbls, toil, cga, f, hand pumped well drk wtr. ACTIVITIES: Swimming; picnicking; fishing; boating,d (l, 1 mi). MISC.: Elev 2700 ft; 5 acres; pets. Adjacent to Iron Canyon Reservoir. Unit of the Whiskeytown-Shasta-Trinity National Recreation Area.

Deep Creek (Shasta-Trinity NF). 3 mi SE of Big Bend on Co Hwy 7M01; 7 mi SE on FS N8L02. SEASON: 5/15-10/31; 21-day lmt. FACILITIES: 22 tent sites; tbls, toil, cga, no drk wtr. ACTIVITIES: Hiking; picnicking; fishing. MISC.: Elev 1200 ft; 10 acres; pets. Unit of the Whiskeytown-Shasta-Trinity NRA.

BIG CREEK

West Kaiser (Sierra NF). 20 mi NE of Big Creek on FS 8S01. SEASON: 6/1-10/30; 14-day lmt. FACILITIES: 7 sites (tr -22); tbls, toil, cga, no drk wtr. ACTIVITIES: Picnicking; fishing. MISC.: Elev 5500 ft; 15 acres; stream; scenic; pets.

BIG PINE

Baker Creek County Park. US 395 to Poplar Street, then west. SEASON: All yr. FACILITIES: 25 sites.

Birch (Inyo NF). 9½ mi SW of Big Pine on Co Hwy 1069 (Glacier Lodge Rd). SEASON: 5/1-11/1; 14-day lmt. FACILITIES: 11 tent sites; tbls, toil, cga,

See page 7 for KEY TO ABBREVIATIONS.

no drk wtr. 1 mi -- Store, ice, gas, fd. ACTIVITIES: Picnicking. Fishing and horseback riding/rental -- 1 mi. MISC.: Elev 7900 ft; 2 acres; primitive rds; pets. Big Pine Creek. Trailhead into John Muir Wilderness.

Grandview (Inyo NF). ½ mi N of Big Pine on US 395; 13 mi NE on St Hwy 168; 5½ mi N on Co Hwy 4S01 (White Mountain Rd). [Primitive rds.] SEASON: 6/15-9/15; 14-day lmt. FACILITIES: 26 sites (tr -22), tbls, toil, cga, f, no drk wtr. ACTIVITIES: Picnicking; hiking. MISC.: Elev 8600 ft; 2 acres; botanical; pets. Serves ancient bristlecone pine forest. Nature trails (5 mi).

Sage Flat (Inyo NF). 8 mi SW of Big Pine on Co Rd 1069 (Glacier Lodge Rd). [Primitive rds.] SEASON: 4/15-11/15; 14-day lmt. FACILITIES: 32 sites (tr -22), tbls, toil, cga, no drk wtr. ACTIVITIES: Hiking; picnicking; fishing. 2 mi -- Horseback riding/rental. MISC.: Elev 7400 ft; 12 acres; pets. Big Pine Creek.

*****Second Falls** (Inyo NF). 11 mi SW of Big Pine on Co Rd 1069 (Glacier Lodge Rd). [Primitive rd.] Walk-in campground. SEASON: 5/1-11/1; 14-day lmt. FACILITIES: 15 tent sites; tbls, toil, cga, no drk wtr. ACTIVITIES: Mountain climbing; hiking; picnicking; fishing. Horseback riding/rental (2 mi). MISC.: Elev 8300 ft; 6 acres; pets. Trailhead into John Muir Wilderness. North Fork of Big Pine Creek.

BIG SUR

Bottchers Gap (Los Padres NF). 12½ mi NW of Big Sur on St Hwy 1; 6½ mi SE on Palo Colorado Rd 5012; 3 mi SE on FS 18S05. SEASON: All yr; 14-day lmt. FACILITIES: 9 tent sites; tbls, toil, cga, piped drk wtr. ACTIVITIES: Hiking; picnicking. Horseback riding (1 mi). MISC.: Elev 2100 ft; 3 acres; pets. Departure point for Ventana Wilderness.

Sycamore Flats (Los Padres NF). 29 mi SE of Big Sur on St Hwy 1; 3 mi E on FS 23S01. SEASON: All yr; 14-day lmt. FACILITIES: 3 tent sites; tbls, toil, cga, no drk wtr. ACTIVITIES: Hunting; picnicking; fishing; hiking. Horseback riding (1 mi). MISC.: Elev 700 ft; 15 acres; stream. Pets on leash.

BISHOP

*****Aspen Meadow** (Inyo NF). 13 mi SW of Bishop on St Hwy 168; 2¼ mi S on Co Hwy 8S01. Walk-in camping only. SEASON: 4/15-11/15; 14-day lmt. FACILITIES: 5 tent sites; tbls, flush toil, cga, no drk wtr. 1 mi -- Store, ice, gas, showers, laundry. ACTIVITIES: Hiking; picnicking; fishing. Horseback riding/rental

(3 mi). Boating,rl (4 mi). MISC.: Elev 8500 ft; 1 acre; stream. Pets on leash.

Big Meadow (Inyo NF). 23½ mi NW of Bishop on US 395; 4 mi S on Co Rd FH89 (Rock Creek Rd). SEASON: 4/15-11/15; 14-day lmt. FACILITIES: 10 sites (tr -22), tbls, toil, cga, no drk wtr. 4 mi -- Store, ice, gas, fd. ACTIVITIES: Hiking; picnicking; fishing. Horseback riding (4 mi) and rental (5 mi). Boating,rld (4 mi). MISC.: Elev 8600 ft; 14 acres; stream. 4 mi -- Rock Creek and Rock Creek Lake. Pets on leash.

Big Trees (Inyo NF). 10½ mi SW of Bishop on St Hwy 168; 2 mi SW on Co Rd 5S20. [Primitive rds.] SEASON: 4/15-11/15; 14-day lmt. FACILITIES: 9 sites (tr -22), tbls, toil, cga, no drk wtr. ACTIVITIES: Hiking; picnicking. Fishing nearby. MISC.: Elev 7500 ft;5 acres;stream;pets.

Bishop Park (Inyo NF). 14½ mi SW of Bishop on St Hwy 168. SEASON: 4/15-11/15; 14-day lmt. FACILITIES: 18 sites (tr -22), tbls, toil, cga, no drk wtr. 3 mi -- Store, ice, fd. ACTIVITIES: Hiking; picnicking; fishing. Boating,rdl (3 mi). Horseback riding/rental (5 mi). MISC.: Elev 7500 ft; 10 acres; stream; pets. Bishop Creek/Lake Sabrina (2½ miles).

Forks (Inyo NF). 13 mi SW of Bishop on St Hwy 168. SEASON: 4/15-11/15; 14-day lmt. FACILITIES: 8 sites (tr -22), tbls, toil, cga, no drk wtr. 2 mi -- Store, ice, fd. ACTIVITIES: Picnicking. Fishing nearby. Boating,rld (4 mi). MISC.: Elev 7800 ft; 5 acres; stream; pets. 4 mi -- Bishop Creek/Lake Sabrina.

Iris Meadows (Inyo NF). 23½ mi NW of Bishop on US 395; 3-1/5 mi S on Co Rd FH89 (Rock Creek Rd). SEASON: 4/15-11/15; 14-day lmt. FACILITIES: 16 sites (tr -22), tbls, toil, cga, no drk wtr. 3 mi -- Store, ice, fd, gas. ACTIVITIES: Hiking; picnicking; fishing. Boating,rld (5 mi). MISC.: Elev 8300 ft; 12 acres; stream. Pets on leash. Rock Creek and Rock Creek Lake (5 mi).

Lower Rock Creek (Inyo NF). 22 mi NW of Bishop on US 395; 1 mi SE on Co Hwy 4S80. SEASON: 4/15-11/15; 14-day lmt. FACILITIES: 5 tent sites; tbls, flush toil, cga, no drk wtr. 3 mi -- Store, ice, fd, gas. ACTIVITIES: Hiking; picnicking; fishing. MISC.: Elev 6500 ft; 30 acres; stream. Pets on leash.

Mosquito Flat (Inyo NF). 23½ mi NW of Bishop on US 395; 9 mi S on Co Rd FH89 (Rock Creek Rd). SEASON: 5/15-10/15; 7-day lmt. FACILITIES: 15 sites (tr -22), tbls, toil, cga, no drk wtr. 2 mi -- Store, ice. ACTIVITIES: Picnicking; fishing. Boating,rld (2 mi). Horseback rental (1 mi) and riding (2 mi). MISC.: Elev 1000 ft; 8 acres;

See page 7 for KEY TO ABBREVIATIONS.

pets. 2 mi -- Rock Creek Lake. Trail-head to John Muir Wilderness.

*Mountain Glen (Inyo NF). 13 mi SW of Bishop on St Hwy 168; 2¼ mi S on Co Hwy 8S01. Walk-in camping only. SEASON: 4/15-11/15; 14-day lmt. FACILITIES: 5 tent sites; tbls, flush toil, cga, no drk wtr. 1 mi -- Store, ice, fd. ACTIVITIES: Fishing; picnicking. Horseback rental/riding (3 mi). Boating,rl (4 mi). MISC.: Elev 8400 ft; 1 acre; stream. Pets permitted if on a leash.

Ownes River Campground (County Campground). 37 mi N of Bishop on US 395; 7 mi E on Whitmore Springs Rd. SEASON: 5/1-11/15. FACILITIES: 25 sites. ACTIVITIES: Fishing. MISC.: Elev 4000 ft; 45 acres. Pets permitted on leash.

Palisade (Inyo NF). 23½ mi NW of Bishop on US 395; 5 mi S on Co Rd FH89 (Rock Creek Rd). [Primitive rds.] SEASON: 4/15-11/15; 14-day lmt. FACILITIES: 5 sites (tr -22), tbls, toil, cga, no drk wtr. 3 mi -- Store, ice. Gas (5 mi). ACTIVITIES: Fishing; picnicking. Boating,rl (3 mi). Horseback rental/riding (4 mi). MISC.: Elev 8600 ft;2 acres; stream; pets. Rock Creek Lake (2 mi).

Pine Grove (Inyo NF). 23½ mi NW of Bishop on US 395; 6-7/10 mi S on Co Rd FH89 (Rock Creek Rd). SEASON: 5/1-11/1; 14-day lmt. FACILITIES: 14 sites (tr -22), tbls, toil, cga, no drk wtr. 1 mi -- Store, ice, fd. ACTIVITIES: Fishing; picnicking. Boating,lr (2 mi). Horseback rental/riding (3 mi). MISC.: Elev 9300 ft; 1 acre; stream; pets. 1½ mi -- Rock Creek and Rock Creek Lake.

Rock Creek Lake Inlet (Inyo NF). 23½ mi NW of Bishop on US 395; 7-3/5 mi S on Co Rd FH89 (Rock Creek Rd); 3/10 mi S on FS 4S36. SEASON: 5/1-11/1; 14-day lmt. FACILITIES: 22 sites (tr -22), tbls, toil, cga, no drk wtr. 1 mi -- Store, ice, fd. ACTIVITIES: Hiking; picnicking; fishing; boating,l. 1 mi -- Boat rental; horseback rental/riding. MISC.: Elev 9600 ft; 15 acres; pets. Rock Creek Lake.

Sabrina (Inyo NF). 16½ mi SW of Bishop on St Hwy 168. SEASON: 5/1-11/1; 7-day lmt. FACILITIES: 34 sites (tr -22), tbls, toil, cga, no drk wtr. 1 mi -- Store, ice, fd. ACTIVITIES: Hiking; picnicking; fishing. Boating,lr (1 mi). Horseback riding/rental (3 mi). MISC.: Elev 9000 ft; 9 acres; stream; pets. Lake Sabrina (1 mi). North Lake (1¼ mi).

*Table Mountain (Inyo NF). 13 mi SW of Bishop on St Hwy 168; 3½ mi S on Co Hwy 8S01. Walk-in camping only. 5 tent sites; tbls, flush toil, cga, no drk wtr. 2 mi -- Store, ice, fd. ACTIVI-

TIES: Hiking; picnicking; fishing. Horseback riding/rental (2 mi). Boating,rl (3 mi). MISC.: Elev 8600 ft; 3 acres; stream. Pets permitted if on a leash.

Tuff (Inyo NF). 23 mi NW of Bishop on US 395. SEASON: 4/15-11/15; 14-day lmt. FACILITIES: 30 sites (tr -22), tbls, toil, cga, no drk wtr. 1 mi -- Store, ice, gas, fd. ACTIVITIES: Hiking; picnicking; fishing. MISC.: Elev 7000 ft; 15 acres; pets. Rock Creek.

Willow Camp (Inyo NF). 13 mi SW of Bishop on St Hwy 168; 5 mi S on Co Rd 8S01 (South Lake Rd). [Dirt access rds.] SEASON: 5/1-11/1; 7-day lmt. FACILITIES: 7 sites (tr -22), tbls, toil, cga, no drk wtr. 1 mi -- Store, ice, gas, fd. ACTIVITIES: Hiking; picnicking; fishing. Horseback riding/rental (1 mi). Boating,rl (2 mi). MISC.: Elev 9000 ft; 1 acre; stream; pets.

BLYTHE

Coon Hollow (BLM). 27 mi SW of Blythe; 12 mi S of I-10 on Wiley Well Rd. SEASON: All yr. FACILITIES: 29 sites. MISC.: Elev 700 ft. Low Desert.

Sixth Avenue County Park. On St Hwy 60, near river. SEASON: All yr. FACILITIES: 40 sites.

Wiley Well (BLM). 23 mi SW of Blythe; 8 mi S of I-10 (US 60). SEASON: All yr. FACILITIES: 20 sites; tbls, cga. ACTIVITIES: Picnicking. MISC.: Elev 593 ft. Low Desert.

BODFISH

Breckenridge (Sequoia NF). 9 mi S of Bodfish on Co Hwy P483Y; 7 mi W on FS 28S06; 1-3/5 mi SW on FS 28S07. SEASON: 5/1-11/1; 14 days. FACILITIES: 8 tent sites; tbls, toil, cga, no drk wtr. ACTIVITIES: Hiking; picnicking. MISC.: Elev 7100 ft; 3 acres; nondrinkable spring water; pets. Paved and dirt road. Mill Creek.

Saddle Spring (Sequoia NF). 2-7/10 mi S of Bodfish on Co Hwy P483Y; 7 mi SE on FS 27S02. [Paved and dirt rds.] SEASON: 5/1-11/1; 14-day lmt. FACILITIES: 8 sites (tr -16), tbls, toil, cga, piped spring drk wtr. ACTIVITIES: Picnicking. MISC.: Elev 6800 ft; 1 acre. Pets permitted if kept on a leash.

BRAWLEY

Osborne County Park (Imperial County Park). 24 mi E of Brawley on St Hwy 78. SEASON: All yr; 3-day lmt. FACILITIES: 150 sites; tbls, toil, cga, no drk wtr. ACTIVITIES: Hunting (dove, pheasant, duck); dune buggying; motorbike trail-riding; picnicking. MISC.:

See page 7 for KEY TO ABBREVIATIONS.

Elev 500 ft; 15 acres; pets on leash.
Motorbike trails. Imperial Sand Dunes.

BRIDGEPORT

Huntoon (Toiyabe NF). 5-3/5 mi N of Bridgeport on US 395; 3/10 mi NE on FS 10055. SEASON: 6/15-10/15; 14-day lmt. FACILITIES: 18 sites (tr -22), tbls, toil, cga, f, no drk wtr. 5 mi -- Store, ice, fd, laundry, gas. ACTIVITIES: Rockhounding; picnicking; fishing. Horseback riding (1 mi). MISC.: Elev 6500 ft; 6 acres; pets. Swauger Creek. Bridgeport Ranger Station (1 mi).

Virginia Creek (Toiyabe NF). 14 mi S of Bridgeport on US 395; 2-4/5 mi W on Co Hwy 10021 (Virginia Lake Rd); 2 mi W on FS. SEASON: 6/15-9/15; 16-day lmt. FACILITIES: 30 sites; toil, no drk wtr. Store (2 mi). ACTIVITIES: 2 mi -- Boating,rl; fishing. Hiking. MISC.: Elev 8500 ft; pets. Virginia Creek and Virginia Lake (2 mi). Hoover Wilderness (3 mi).

BROWN'S CANYON

Brown's Canyon (Six Rivers NF). 4 mi S of St Hwy 36 on paved Co Rd on bank of Van Duzen. SEASON: April-November; 14-day lmt. FACILITIES: 4 sites; tbls, toil, cga. ACTIVITIES: Hunting; swimming; picnicking; fishing (trout). MISC.: Elev 2560 ft; pets. Van Duzen River.

BURNEY

Big Pine (Lassen NF). 5 mi NE of Burney on US 299; 27 mi SE on St Hwy 89; 1 mi S on FS 32N13. On Hat Creek. [10 mi NE of Manzanita Lake on St Hwy 44/89; 1 mi S on FS 32N13.] SEASON: 4/15-10/31; 14-day lmt. FACILITIES: 19 sites (tr -22), tbls, toil, cga, no drk wtr. 1 mi -- Store, ice, gas, fd. ACTIVITIES: Fishing; picnicking. MISC.: Elev 4600 ft; 3 acres. Pets allowed if on leash.

Boundary (Lassen NF). 5 mi NE of Burney on US 299; 8 mi SE on St Hwy 89. On Hat Creek. SEASON: 4/15-10/31; 14-day lmt. FACILITIES: 12 sites (tr -22), tbls, toil, cga, no drk wtr. 2 mi -- Store, ice, fd, gas. ACTIVITIES: Fishing; picnicking. MISC.: Elev 3200 ft; 2 acres. Pets allowed if on a leash.

Butte Creek (Lassen NF). 5 mi NE of Burney on US 299; 23 mi SE on St Hwy 89; 10 mi E on St Hwy 44; 2½ mi S on FS 32N21. [Off St Hwy 44, 2 mi S on rd to Butte Lake and NE part of Lassen Volcanic NP.] SEASON: 5/1-10/15; 14-day lmt. FACILITIES: 14 sites (tr -22), tbls, toil, cga, no drk wtr. ACTIVITIES: Fishing; picnicking. 4 mi -- Swimming; boating,rl. MISC.: Elev 5600 ft; 2 acres. Pets allowed only if kept on a leash.

Honn (Lassen NF). 5 mi NE of Burney on US 299; 13 mi SE on St Hwy 89. On Hat Creek. SEASON: 4/15-10/31; 14-day lmt. FACILITIES: 6 tent sites; tbls, toil, cga, no drk wtr. 4 mi -- Store, ice, gas. Fd (1 mi). ACTIVITIES: Hiking; picnicking; fishing. MISC.: Elev 3400 ft; 1 acre. Pets allowed on leash.

Rocky (Lassen NF). 5 mi NE of Burney on US 299; 20 mi SE on St Hwy 89. On Hat Creek. SEASON: 4/15-10/31; 14-day lmt. FACILITIES: 8 tent sites; tbls, toil, cga, no drk wtr. 4 mi -- Store, ice, gas, fd. ACTIVITIES: Fishing; picnicking; hiking. MISC.: Elev 4200 ft; 1 acre;pets;stream. Silver Lake (¼ mi).

CALIFORNIA HOT SPRINGS

Deer Creek Mill (Sequoia NF). 2-3/10 mi E of California Hot Springs on Co Hwy 56 (Hot Springs Rd); 4 mi E on FS 23S04 (Deer Creek Mill Rd). [Narrow unsurfaced rd.] SEASON: 5/15-10/31; 14-day lmt. FACILITIES: 6 tent sites; tbls, toil, cga, piped spring drk wtr. 5 mi -- Store, ice, fd, laundry, gas. ACTIVITIES: Hiking; picnicking. Fishing (2 mi). MISC.: Elev 5400 ft; 2 acres; scenic; pets. Deer Creek. Adjacent to Deer Creek Mill is a giant sequoia grove, the southernmost redwood grove in the Sierra Nevada.

Frog Meadow (Sequoia NF). 4 mi E of California Hot Springs on Co Hwy 56; 6 mi S on FS 23S05; 5-1/5 mi SE on FS 24S06; 6 mi N on FH90. [Paved and narrow road.] SEASON: 6/1-10/31; 14-day lmt. FACILITIES: 10 sites (tr -22), tbls, toil, cga, piped spring drk wtr. ACTIVITIES: Hiking; picnicking. Fishing (1 mi). MISC.: Elev 7500 ft; 4 acres; pets. Tobias Creek (1 mi). Supplies at Glennville (26 mi).

Gooseberry (Sequoia NF). 4 mi E of California Hot Springs on Co Hwy 56; 6 mi S on FS 23S05; 3/5 mi SE on Co Hwy 9; 3 mi SE on FS 24S06. [Paved and dirt rds.] SEASON: 6/1-10/31; 14-day lmt. FACILITIES: 6 sites (tr -22), tbls, toil, cga, no drk wtr. 3 mi -- Store, ice, fd, laundry. ACTIVITIES: Picnicking. Swimming (3 mi). Fishing (5 mi). MISC.: Elev 6800 ft; 1 acre; pets. White River (3 mi).

Panorama (Sequoia NF). 4 mi E of California Hot Springs on Co Hwy 56; 6 mi S on FS 23S05; 5-1/5 mi SE on FS 24S06; 1 mi N on FS FH90. [Paved and narrow dirt rd. Not advisable for trailers.] SEASON: 6/1-10/31; 14-day lmt. FACILITIES: 10 sites (tr -22), tbls, toil, cga, no drk wtr. ACTIVITIES: Picnicking. Fishing (4 mi). MISC.: Elev 6800 ft; 4 acres; pets. Deep Creek and Capinero Creek (4 mi). Supplies at Glennville (21 mi).

See page 7 for KEY TO ABBREVIATIONS.

Sugar Loaf (Sequoia NF). 4 mi E of California Hot Springs on Co Hwy 56 (Hot Springs Rd); 6 mi S on FS 23S05; 3/5 mi SE on Co Hwy 9. [Paved and dirt rd. Not suitable for trailers.] SEASON: 6/1-10/31; 14-day lmt. FACILITIES: 5 sites (tr -22), tbls, toil, cga, no drk wtr. 1 mi -- Store, ice, fd, laundry. ACTIVITIES: Picnicking. Fishing and swimming (1 mi). MISC.: Elev 6000 ft; 2 acres; pets. White River.

White River (Sequoia NF). 2-7/10 mi S of California Hot Springs on FS 23S05, along White River. [Paved and dirt rd. Not recommended for trailers.] SEASON: 6/15-9/15; 14-day lmt. FACILITIES: 12 sites (tr -22), tbls, toil, cga, piped spring drk wtr. 5 mi -- Store, ice, laundry. ACTIVITIES: Fishing; picnicking. Swimming (5 mi). MISC.: Elev 4000 ft; 3 acres; pets. Supplies at Pine Flat.

CALLAHAN

Scott Mountain (Klamath NF). 9-1/10 mi SE of Callahan on St Hwy S3. SEASON: 5/1-10/15. FACILITIES: 7 sites (tr -22), tbls, toil, cga, piped drk wtr. ACTIVITIES: Picnicking. MISC.: Elev 5400; 4 acres; stream. Pets on leash.

Trail Creek (Klamath NF). 16-3/5 mi SW of Callahan on Co Hwy FH93; 3/10 mi S on FS 39N08. SEASON: 5/15-10/15. FACILITIES: 15 sites (tr -22); tbls, toil, cga, piped drk wtr. ACTIVITIES: Picnicking. Swimming/fishing (1 mi). MISC.: Elev 4700 ft; 4 acres; stream; pets.

CAMP CONNELL

Boards Crossing (Stanislaus NF). 1/10 mi NE of Camp Connell on St Hwy 4; 1/5 mi SE on FS 5N02; 4 mi SE on Co Hwy 5N75; 1/10 mi W on FS 5N60. SEASON: 4/15-10/1; 14-day lmt. FACILITIES: 5 tent sites; tbls, toil, no drk wtr. 3 mi -- Store, ice, gas. Fd (4 mi). ACTIVITIES: Swimming; picnicking; fishing. MISC.: Elev 3800 ft; 3 acres; pets. River. Calaveras Memorial (4 mi N).

Sour Grass (Stanislaus NF). 1/10 mi S of Camp Connell on St Hwy 4; 5 mi NE on FS 5N02; 1/10 mi N on FS 5N02R. SEASON: 4/15-10/1; 14-day lmt. FACILITIES: 3 sites (tr -16), tbls, toil, no drk wtr. 4 mi -- Store, ice, gas. Fd (5 mi). ACTIVITIES: Swimming; picnicking; fishing. MISC.: Elev 4000 ft; 2 acres; river. Pets on leash.

CAMPTONVILLE

Convict Flat (Tahoe NF). 12 mi NE of Camptonville on St Hwy 49. On North Yuba River. SEASON: 4/15-10/15; 14-day lmt. FACILITIES: 8 tent sites; toil,

no drk wtr. Store (4 mi). ACTIVITIES: Swimming; fishing; rockhounding.

Cornish House (Tahoe NF). 20 mi E of Camptonville on FS 19N03 (Henness Pass Rd). [Henness Pass Rd is a steep and winding rd; not advised for trailers.] SEASON: 6/15-11/1; 14-day lmt. FACILITIES: 6 sites (tr -22), tbls, toil, cga, no drk wtr, nondrinkable spring water. ACTIVITIES: Picnicking. MISC.: Elev 5600 ft; 1 acre. Pets allowed on leash.

Fiddle Creek (Tahoe NF). 8½ mi NE of Camptonville on St Hwy 49. SEASON: All yr; 14-day lmt. FACILITIES: 13 tent sites; tbls, toil, cga, fd, no drk wtr. 1 mi -- Store, gas, laundry. ACTIVITIES: Rockhounding; gold panning; swimming; picnicking; fishing. MISC.: Elev 2200 ft; 2 acres; river; pets.

*__Frenchy Point__ (Tahoe NF). 1½ mi SW of Camptonville on St Hwy 49; 3½ mi SW on Co Hwy 18N48; ½ mi N on Co Hwy 19N51; 3½ mi NW, BY BOAT. SEASON: 5/1-9/15; 14-day lmt. FACILITIES: 9 tent sites; tbls, toil, cga, no drk wtr at campsite. However, drk wtr and garbage collection are available at Dark Day boat ramp. ACTIVITIES: Swimming; waterskiing; boating; sailing; picnicking; fishing. MISC.: Elev 2000 ft; 3 acres; lake. Pets on leash.

*__Garden Point__ (Tahoe NF). 1½ mi SW of Camptonville on St Hwy 49; 3½ mi SW on Co Hwy 18N48; ½ mi N on Co Hwy 19N51; 1½ mi NW, BY BOAT. SEASON: 5/1-9/15; 14-day lmt. FACILITIES: 20 tent sites; tbls, toil, cga, no drk wtr at campsite. However, drk wtr and garbage collection are available at Dark Day boat ramp (2 mi). ACTIVITIES: Swimming; waterskiing; boating; picnicking; fishing. MISC.: Elev 2000 ft; 6 acres; lake. Pets on leash.

*__Madrone Cove__ (Tahoe NF). 1½ mi SW of Camptonville on St Hwy 49; 3½ mi SW on Co Rd 18N48; ½ mi N on Co Hwy 19N51; 5 mi NW, BY BOAT. SEASON: 5/1-9/15; 14-day lmt. FACILITIES: 11 tent sites; tbls, flush toil, cga, f, no drk wtr at campground. However, drk wtr and garbage collection are available at Dark Day boat ramp (5 mi). ACTIVITIES: Swimming; waterskiing; boating; sailing; picnicking; fishing. MISC.: Elev 2000 ft; 4 acres; lake. Pets on leash.

Oregon Creek (Tahoe NF). 7 mi SW of Camptonville on St Hwy 49. SEASON: All yr; 14-day lmt. FACILITIES: 20 sites (tr -22), toil. Store (3 mi). ACTIVITIES: Gold panning; rockhounding; fishing; swimming. MISC.: Elev 1500 ft; pets. Middle Yuba River.

Shenanigan Flat (Tahoe NF). 7-4/5 mi N of Camptonville on St Hwy 49; 1 mi

W on FS 19N43 (Pendola Extension). [On North Yuba River, 1 mi W of the State Hwy 49 bridge at Indian Valley.] SEASON: 4/1–11/1; 14-day lmt. FACILITIES: 8 sites (tr –16), tbls, toil, cga, showers, no drk wtr. 2 mi –– Store, ice, laundry, fd, gas. ACTIVITIES: Swimming; picnicking; fishing; rockhounding; gold panning. MISC.: Elev 2200 ft; 5 acres. Pets.

CANBY

Cottonwood Flat (Modoc NF). 4 mi SE of Canby on St Hwy 299; 4–1/10 mi W on Co Hwy 84; 3½ mi W on FS 41N44; ½ mi NW on FS 42N10. SEASON: 6/1–10/15; 14-day lmt. FACILITIES: 10 sites (tr –22), tbls, toil, cga, piped drk wtr. ACTIVITIES: Rockhounding; picnicking. Fishing (4 mi). MISC.: Elev 4700 ft; 6 acres; historic; pets. Hulbert Creek and Pit River (4 mi).

CANYON COUNTRY

Soledad (Angeles NF). 10 mi E of Canyon Country on Co Hwy 5N07. SEASON: All yr. FACILITIES: 3 sites (tr –32), tbls, toil, cga, no drk wtr. 1 mi –– Store, ice, fd. ACTIVITIES: Rockhounding; picnicking; fishing. Swimming (1 mi). MISC.: Elev 2000 ft; 2 acres; stream;pets.

CARMEL VALLEY

China Camp (Los Padres NF). 13 mi SE of Carmel Valley on Co Hwy G16 (Carmel Valley – Tularcitos Rd); 7 mi S on FS 18S02 (Tassajara Rd). SEASON: 3/1–11/30; 14-day lmt. FACILITIES:8 tent sites; tbls, toil, cga, piped drk wtr. ACTIVITIES: Hiking; picnicking. Horseback riding (1 mi). MISC.: Elev 4300; 4 acres; pets. Trailhead to Ventana Wilderness.

White Oaks (Los Padres NF). 13 mi SE of Carmel Valley on Co Hwy 18S02; 6 mi S on FS 18S02. SEASON: 3/1–11/30; 14-day lmt. FACILITIES: 8 tent sites; tbls, toil, cga, piped drk wtr. ACTIVITIES: Picnicking; hiking. Horseback riding (1 mi). MISC.: Elev 4200 ft; 4 acres. Pets allowed if on a leash.

CASTIAC

*****Rogers** (Angeles NF). 10 mi N of Castiac on I-5; 7 mi NE on Co Hwy 6N32; 2 mi E on FS 6N32; 3 mi N on TRAIL 16W02. SEASON: All yr; 14-day lmt. FACILITIES: 5 tent sites; tbls, toil, cga, f, no drk wtr. ACTIVITIES: Mountain climbing; hiking; picnicking. MISC.: Elev 2300 ft; 2 acres; stream; pets. Special campfire permit is required. Trail camp.

CECILVILLE

East Fork (Klamath NF). 2–1/10 mi

NE of Cecilville on Co Hwy FH93 (Callahan-Cecilville Rd). SEASON: 6/1-10/15; 14-day lmt. FACILITIES: 9 sites (tr –16), tbls, toil, cga, piped drk wtr. 2 mi –– Store, ice, fd, gas. ACTIVITIES: Picnicking. MISC.: Elev 2400 ft; 3 acres; pets. Salmon River.

CEDARVILLE

Stough Reservoir (Modoc NF). 5–1/10 mi W of Cedarville on St Hwy 299; ½ mi N on FS 45N39. SEASON: 5/30–10/15. FACILITIES: 8 tent sites; tbls, toil, cga, piped drk wtr. ACTIVITIES: Rockhounding; picnicking. MISC.: Elev 6300 ft; 3 acres; pets. Site may be reserved by groups.

CHESTER

Banner Creek (Lassen NF). 10 mi N of Chester on Co Rd 318. SEASON: 14-day lmt. FACILITIES: 4 tent sites; no drk wtr. MISC.: Elev 4600 ft; stream; pets.

Alder Creek (Lassen NF). 11½ mi W of Chester on St Hwy 36; 7 mi SW on St Hwy 32. SEASON: 5/1–11/1; 14-day lmt. FACILITIES: 5 tent sites; tbls, toil, cga, no drk wtr. ACTIVITIES: Hiking; picnicking; fishing. MISC.: Elev 3900 ft; 1 acre; pets on leash. Deer Creek.

Benner Creek (Lassen NF). 7 mi N of Chester on Co Hwy 318. SEASON: 5/25–10/1; 14-day lmt. FACILITIES: 4 tent sites; tbls, toil, no drk wtr. ACTIVITIES: Hiking; picnicking; fishing. MISC.: Elev 5600 ft; 1 acre; stream. Pets on leash.

High Bridge (Lassen NF). 5 mi NW of Chester on Co Rd 312 (Chester-Warner Valley Rd). [Along the North Fork of Feather River.] SEASON: 5/25–10/1; 14-day lmt. FACILITIES: 12 sites (tr –22), tbls, toil, cga, no drk wtr. 5 mi –– Store, ice, fd. MISC.: Elev 5200 ft; 5 acres; pets; Warner Creek. ACTIVITIES: Fishing; picnicking; horseback riding (rental nearby).

*****Horseshoe Lake** (Lassen Volcanic Park). 15 mi NW of Chester on Juniper Lake Rd; 1½ mi W on TRAIL. SEASON: 6/20–10/1; 7-day lmt. FACILITIES: 12 tent sites; toil. ACTIVITIES: Fishing; boating (no motor boats). MISC.: Elev 6540 ft. Snag Lake. Small pets on leash.

Juniper Lake (Lassen Volcanic NP). 13 mi NW of Chester on Juniper Lake Rd at E shore of Juniper Lake. [1 mi from Ranger Station.] Road not suitable for trailers. SEASON: Late June to October 1 (depends on snow); 7-day lmt. FACILITIES: 18 tent sites; tbls, toil, cga, no

Little Grizzly (Lassen NF). 2 mi S on St Hwy 36; 4½ mi S on St Hwy 89; 14 mi W on FS 26N32. SEASON: 5/25–10/1; 14-day lmt. FACILITIES: 6 tent sites;

See page 7 for KEY TO ABBREVIATIONS.

tbls, toil, cga, no drk wtr. **ACTIVITIES:** Picnicking. Fishing (3 mi). **MISC.:** Elev 5800 ft; 2 acres; stream; pets.

Soda Springs (Lassen NF). 11½ mi W of Chester on St Hwy 36; 20 mi SW on St Hwy 32; 2/5 mi NE on FS 26N19 (Soda Springs Rd). **SEASON:** 5/15-10/15; 14-day lmt. **FACILITIES:** 10 sites (tr -22), tbls, toil, cga, well drk wtr. **ACTIVITIES:** Fishing; picnicking. **MISC.:** Elev 3600 ft; 4 acres. Big Chico Creek.

Warner Creek (Lassen NF). 7 mi NW of Chester on Co Rd 312 (Chester-Warner Valley Rd). [Along Warner Creek.] **SEASON:** 5/25-10/1; 14-day lmt. **FACILITIES:** 11 sites (tr -22), tbls, toil, cga, no drk wtr. **ACTIVITIES:** Fishing; picnicking. **MISC.:** Elev 5000 ft; 5 acres; pets. Warner Creek.

Willow (Lassen NF). 8 mi SW of Chester on St Hwy 36; 4 mi N on FS 29N19 (Lost Creek Rd). **SEASON:** 5/25-10/1; 14-day lmt. **FACILITIES:** 8 sites (tr -22), tbls, toil, cga, no drk wtr. **ACTIVITIES:** Fishing; picnicking. **MISC.:** Elev 5100 ft; 5 acres; pets. Lost Creek.

CHICO

Soda Springs (Lassen NF). 36 mi NE of Chico on St Hwy 32. **SEASON:** 5/15-10/15; 14-day lmt. **FACILITIES:** 10 sites (tr -22), tbls, toil, cga, well drk wtr. 3 mi -- Store, ice, gas. **ACTIVITIES:** Fishing; picnicking. **MISC.:** Elev 3600 ft; 4 acres; pets. Big Chico Creek.

CHOWCHILLA

Codorniz Campground (COE;Eastman Lake). 22 mi NE of Chowchilla on Co Rd 29. **SEASON:** All yr. **FACILITIES:** 62 sites (tr -30), tbls, toil, cga, hot showers, drk wtr, dump, playground. **MISC.:** Pets.

Wildcat Campground (COE; Eastman Lake). Approximately 21 mi NE of Chowchilla on Co Rd 29. **SEASON:** May-October. **FACILITIES:** 19 sites; toil, drk wtr. **MISC.:** Pets permitted if kept on leash.

CISCO GROVE

Woodchuck (Tahoe NF). 3 mi NE of I-80 at Cisco Grove on Rattlesnake Rd. **SEASON:** 6/15-10/15; 14-day lmt. **FACILITIES:** 8 sites (tr -16), tbls, toil, cga, no drk wtr. 3 mi -- Ice, fd, gas. **ACTIVITIES:** Picnicking. Fishing/swimming (3 mi). **MISC.:** Elev 6300 ft; 5 acres; pets. Rattlesnake Creek and Sterling Lake (3 mi).

COLEVILLE

Shingle Mill Flats (County Park). 11 mi S of Coleville on US 395. **SEASON:** 4/15-11/15. **FACILITIES:** 150 sites (75 have pull-thru spaces) [tr -30], tbls,

toil, cga, f, drk wtr. **ACTIVITIES:** Swimming; picnicking; fishing. **MISC.:** Elev 6000 ft; 80 acres; river; pets. Paved access roads.

Sonora Bridge Meadow (Toiyabe NF). 17-2/5 mi S of Coleville on US 395; 2 mi NW on St Hwy 108. [Adjacent to Sonora Bridge Campground.] **SEASON:** 5/1-10/31; 1-day lmt. **FACILITIES:** 18 tent sites; toil, no drk wtr, no tbls. 5 mi -- Store, ice, fd, shower, gas. **ACTIVITIES:** Swimming; picnicking; fishing; rockhounding. Horseback rental/riding (5 mi). **MISC.:** Elev 6800 ft; 1 acre; pets. West Walker River.

COVELO

Hammerhorn Lake (Mendocino NF). 2-3/5 mi N of Covelo on US Hwy 162; 11-1/10 mi E on FS 1N02; 2/5 mi E on FS 23N01. **SEASON:** 5/1-10/1; 14-day lmt. **FACILITIES:** 8 sites (tr -16), tbls, toil, cga, no drk wtr. **ACTIVITIES:** Horseback riding; picnicking; fishing; swimming. **MISC.:** Elev 3500 ft; 2 acres; pets. 5-acre Hammerhorn Lake for trout fishing.

DARDANELLE

Arnot Bridge (Stanislaus NF). 2-4/5 mi NW of Dardanelle on St Hwy 108; 5-3/5 mi NE on FS 7N83. **SEASON:** 6/1-10/15; 14-day lmt. **FACILITIES:** 13 sites (tr -22), toil, cga, no tbls. **ACTIVITIES:** Fishing. **MISC.:** Elev 6200 ft; pets. 2½ mi from Clark Fork.

Baker (Stanislaus NF). 5-2/5 mi SE of Dardanelle on St Hwy 108. **SEASON:** 5/15-10/15; 14-day lmt. **FACILITIES:** 44 sites (tr -22), tbls, toil, cga, no drk wtr. 1 mi -- Store, ice, fd, showers, laundry, gas. **ACTIVITIES:** Hiking; mountain climbing; picnicking; fishing. Horseback riding/rental (1 mi). **MISC.:** Elev 6200 ft; 4 acres; pets; geological. Middle Fork of Stanislaus River. Point of departure to Emigrant Basin Primitive Area (1½ mi). Nature trails (3 mi).

Boulder Flat (Stanislaus NF). 1-3/10 mi NW of Dardanelle on St Hwy 108. **SEASON:** 5/15-10/15; 14-day lmt. **FACILITIES:** 23 sites (tr -22), tbls, toil, cga, no drk wtr. 1 mi -- Store, ice, fd, showers, gas. **ACTIVITIES:** Mountain climbing; hiking; picnicking; fishing. **MISC.:** Elev 5600 ft; 15 acres; pets; geological. Nature trails (3 mi). Middle Fork of Stanislaus River. Columns of the Giants (2-3/5 mi).

Brightman Flat (Stanislaus NF). 1-1/5 mi NW of Dardanelle on St Hwy 108. **SEASON:** 5/15-10/15; 14-day lmt. **FACILITIES:** 30 sites (tr -22), tbls, toil, cga, no drk wtr. 1 mi -- Store, ice, fd, showers, gas. **ACTIVITIES:** Mountain climbing; hiking; picnicking; fishing. **MISC.:** Elev 5600 ft; 5 acres; pets; geological. Middle Fork of Stanislaus River. Nature trails (3 mi). Columns of the Giants ($2\frac{1}{2}$ mi).

Chipmunk Flat (Stanislaus NF). $9\frac{1}{2}$ mi SE of Dardanelle on St Hwy 108; 1/10 mi S on FS 6N67Y. **SEASON:** 7/1-9/30; 14-day lmt. **FACILITIES:** 6 sites (tr -22), tbls, toil, cga, no drk wtr. **ACTIVITIES:** Mountain climbing; picnicking; fishing. **MISC.:** Elev 8400 ft; 2 acres; pets. Deadman Creek. Gateway to Sonora Pass.

Cottonwood (Stanislaus NF). 2-4/5 mi NW of Dardanelle on St Hwy 108; $4\frac{1}{2}$ mi NE on FS 7N83. **SEASON:** 6/1-10/15; 14-day lmt. **FACILITIES:** 17 sites (tr -22), toil, no tbls, no drk wtr. **ACTIVITIES:** Hiking; fishing. **MISC.:** Elev 5800 ft; pets. Arnot Creek trailhead (2 mi). Clark Fork ($4\frac{1}{2}$ mi).

Deadman (Stanislaus NF). 6 mi SE of Dardanelle on St Hwy 108; 6 mi SE on FS 6N012 (Kennedy Meadow Rd). **SEASON:** 5/15-10/15; 14-day lmt. **FACILITIES:** 21 sites (tr -22), tbls, toil, cga, no drk wtr. 1 mi -- Store, ice, fd, showers, laundry, gas. **ACTIVITIES:** Mountain climbing; hiking; picnicking; fishing. Horseback riding/rental (1 mi). **MISC.:** Elev 6200 ft; 3 acres; pets; geological. Stanislaus River. Gateway to Emigrant Basin Primitive Area. Trails (4 mi).

Eagle Meadow (Stanislaus NF). $7\frac{1}{2}$ mi SW of Dardanelle on St Hwy 108; 6 mi SE on FS 5N011. **SEASON:** 6/15-10/15; 14-day lmt. **FACILITIES:** 10 tent sites; toil, no drk wtr, no tbls. **MISC.:** Elev 7500 ft. Pets allowed on leash.

Fence Creek (Stanislaus NF). 2-4/5 mi NW of Dardanelle on St Hwy 108; 7/10 mi NE on FS 7N83 (Clark Fork Rd); 2/5 mi NW on FS 6N061; 1/5 mi NE on FS 6N82Y. **SEASON:** 5/15-10/15; 14-day lmt. **FACILITIES:** 8 sites (tr -22), tbls, toil, cga, no drk wtr. 4 mi -- Store, ice, fd, showers, gas. **ACTIVITIES:** Mountain climbing; picnicking. Fishing ($\frac{1}{2}$ mi). **MISC.:** Elev 5600 ft; 10 acres; pets. Fence Creek.

Lodgepole (Stanislaus NF). 5-3/5 mi SE of Dardanelle on St Hwy 108; 1/5 mi SE on FS 6N012. **SEASON:** 5/15-10/15; 14-day lmt. **FACILITIES:** 19 sites (tr -22), tbls, toil, cga. Store (1 mi). **ACTIVITIES:** Hiking; picnicking; fishing. **MISC.:** Elev 6200 ft; pets. Middle Fork of Stanislaus River. Columns of Giants (3.7 mi).

Niagara Creek (Stanislaus NF). $7\frac{1}{2}$ mi SW of Dardanelle on St Hwy 108; 3/10 mi NE on FS 5N011; $\frac{1}{2}$ mi NE on FS 6N24. **SEASON:** 6/1-10/15; 14-day lmt. **FACILITIES:** 5 sites (tr -22), tbls, toil, cga,

no drk wtr. **ACTIVITIES:** Mountain climbing; hiking; picnicking; fishing. **MISC.:** Elev 6600 ft; 3 acres; pets. Niagara Creek. Nature trails (1 mi). Trail of Ancient Dwarfs ($\frac{1}{2}$ mi).

Niagara Crossing (Stanislaus NF). $7\frac{1}{2}$ mi SW of Dardanelle on St Hwy 108; 2 mi SE on FS 5N011. **SEASON:** 6/15-10/15; 14-day lmt. **FACILITIES:** 6 sites (tr -16), tbls, toil, cga. **ACTIVITIES:** Picnicking. Fishing (1 mi). **MISC.:** Elev 7000; 5 acres; pets. Niagara Creek.

*Pigeon Flat (Stanislaus NF). 1-2/5 mi E of Dardanelle on St Hwy 108; 1/10 mi E on FS 6N43Y; 1/10 mi E on TRAIL 0. **SEASON:** 5/15-10/15; 14-day lmt. **FACILITIES:** 6 tent sites; tbls, toil, cga, no drk wtr. 2 mi -- Store, ice, showers, gas. Fd (1 mi). **ACTIVITIES:** Hiking; picnicking; fishing; mountain climbing. Horseback riding/rental (4 mi). **MISC.:** Elev 6000 ft; 2 acres; geological; pets. Middle Fork of Stanislaus River. Column of the Giants (1/5 mi). Nature trails (1 mi).

DAVIS CREEK

Plum Valley (Modoc NF). 2-2/5 mi SE of Davis Creek on FS 45N04; 1 mi SE on FS 45N35. **SEASON:** 5/30-10/15. **FACILITIES:** 13 sites (no tr); tbls, toil, cga, no drk wtr. Store/gas (3 mi). **ACTIVITIES:** Picnicking; rockhounding; fishing; boating. **MISC.:** Elev 5600 ft; 4 acres; lake; pets. South Fork of Davis Creek.

DEATH VALLEY

Emigrant Junction (Death Valley NM). Junction of St Hwy 190 and Emigrant Canyon Rd. **SEASON:** 4/15-10/15; 30-day lmt. **FACILITIES:** 20 sites (tr -30), tbls, flush toil, cga, drk wtr. **ACTIVITIES:** Picnicking. **MISC.:** Pets on leash.

DEL MAR

City Park. Free overnight camping, S of town, E side of I-5. **SEASON:** All year.

DENNY

Denny (Shasta-Trinity NF). $1\frac{1}{2}$ mi SW of Denny on FS 7N01. **SEASON:** All year; 14-day lmt. **FACILITIES:** 16 sites (tr -22), tbls, toil, cga, piped drk wtr. **ACTIVITIES:** Rockhounding; picnicking. Fishing/swimming (1 mi). **MISC.:** Elev 2000 ft; 5 acres; stream; pets. Access is poor for trailers.

DESERT CENTER

Corn Springs (BLM). 8 mi W of 4-10; SE of Desert Center. **SEASON:** All yr. **FACILITIES:** 27 sites; tbls, toil, cga.

See page 7 for KEY TO ABBREVIATIONS.

ACTIVITIES: Picnicking. MISC.: Elev 1500 ft. Chuckwalla Mountains. Native Palm site.

DINKEY CREEK

Buck Meadow (Sierra NF). 12 mi SE of Dinkey Creek on FS 11S40. SEASON: 5/25-11/1; 14-day lmt. FACILITIES: 10 sites (tr -16), tbls, toil, no drk wtr. ACTIVITIES: Swimming; picnicking; fishing. MISC.: Elev 6800 ft; 3 acres; pets. On Deer Creek, 4 mi E of McKinley Grove.

Gigantea (Sierra NF). 1-3/5 mi S of Dinkey Creek on Co Hwy PN44 (Dinkey Creek Rd); 6 mi SE on FS 11S40. SEASON: 5/15-11/1; 14-day lmt. FACILITIES: 7 sites (tr -16), tbls, toil, no drk wtr. ACTIVITIES: Picnicking. MISC.: Elev 6500 ft; 2 acres; botanical; stream; pets.

Lily Pad (Sierra NF). 16-4/5 mi SE of Dinkey Creek on FS 11S40. At Wishon Reservoir. SEASON: 5/15-11/1; 14-day lmt. FACILITIES: 16 sites (tr -16), tbls, toil, cga, no drk wtr. 1 mi -- Store, ice, fd, laundry, shower, gas. ACTIVITIES: Swimming; picnicking; fishing; boating,d (r/l, 1 mi). Horseback riding/rental (1 mi). MISC.: Elev 6500 ft; 5 acres. Pets permitted if kept on leash.

Marmont Rock (Sierra NF). 14-1/5 mi SE of Dinkey Creek on FS 11S40; 7-7/10 mi N on FS 10S16. At Courtright Reservoir. SEASON: 6/15-10/21; 14-day lmt. FACILITIES: 12 sites (tr -22), tbls, toil, cga, no drk wtr. ACTIVITIES: Swimming; picnicking; fishing; boating,ld. Horseback riding/rental (3 mi). MISC.: Elev 8300 ft; 3 acres; pets on leash; scenic.

Sawmill Flat (Sierra NF). 12-9/10 mi SE of Dinkey Creek on FS 11S40; 3-3/10 mi S on FS 11S12. SEASON: 6/15-11/1; 14-day lmt. FACILITIES: 15 sites (tr --22), tbls, toil, no drk wtr. 5 mi -- Store, ice, fd, showers, laundry, gas. ACTIVITIES: Picnicking. Horseback riding/rental (5 mi). MISC.: Elev 6700 ft; 7 acres; pets. Wishon Reservoir (6 mi).

*Voyager Rock (Sierra NF). 14 mi E of Dinkey Creek on FS 11S40; 8 mi N on FS 40S16; 3 mi N on TRAIL 28E34. [Last 3 mi via dusty vehicle way.] SEASON: 6/15-10/31; 14-day lmt. FACILITIES: 14 tent sites; tbls, toil, cga, no drk wtr. ACTIVITIES: Mountain climbing; boating,d (l, 3 mi); swimming; picnicking; fishing; hiking. Horseback riding/rental (3 mi). MISC.: Elev 8000 ft; 5 acres; pets; lake.

DORRINGTON

Boards Crossing. 4 mi S of Dorrington on Hells Half Acre Road. FACILITIES: Undesignated tent sites; toil, piped drk

wtr. Hunting (late season deer hunting); picnicking; fishing. MISC.: Elev 3800 ft. Timbered site on North Fork of Stanislaus River.

DOYLE

Meadow View (Plumas NF). 6-3/5 mi W of Doyle on Co Hwy 331 (Doyle Grade); 9/10 mi NW on Co Hwy 101. SEASON: 5/1-10/15; 14-day lmt. FACILITIES: 6 sites (tr -22), tbls, toil, cga, well drk wtr. ACTIVITIES: Picnicking. Fishing (3 mi). Hunting, big and small game (1 mi). MISC.: Elev 6100 ft; 2 acres; pets. Last Chance Creek.

EAGLEVILLE

Patterson (Modoc NF). 3-3/10 mi S of Eagleville on Co Hwy 1 (Surprise Valley Rd); 5-1/10 mi SW on FS 39N01; 4-4/5 mi W on FS 39N01; 3/10 mi E on FS 39N28 (near South Warner Wilderness). SEASON: 7/1-10/15. FACILITIES: 7 sites (tr -16), tbls, toil, cga, piped drk wtr. ACTIVITIES: Hiking; picnicking. Fishing/horseback riding (1 mi). MISC.: Elev 7200 ft; 6 acres; pets. Nature trails. East Creek. Reservations accepted. Trailhead to South Warner Wilderness.

EBBETTS PASS

Hermit Valley (Stanislaus NF). 5 mi W of Ebbetts Pass Summit on St Hwy 4. SEASON: 7/1-10/1; 14-day lmt. FACILITIES: 5 sites (tr -16), tbls, toil, cga, no drk wtr. ACTIVITIES: Swimming; picnicking; fishing; hunting (early-season deer hunting); boating,d. MISC.: Elev 7500 ft; 5 acres; pets. Mokelumne River.

Highland Lakes (Stanislaus NF). 7 mi S of St Hwy 4 near Ebbetts Pass. [Not recommended for trailers.] SEASON: 7/1-10/1; 14-day lmt. FACILITIES: 10 sites (tr -16), tbls, toil, cga, no drk wtr. ACTIVITIES: Swimming; picnicking; fishing; boating,d; early-season deer hunting. MISC.: Elev 8600 ft; 5 acres; pets. Unimproved camp area. Highland Lakes. Stream.

EL CENTRO

Earl Walker (Imperial County Park). 10 mi E of El Centro on I-8/US 80; 3 mi N on St Hwy 115 in Holtville. SEASON: All yr; 3-day lmt. FACILITIES: Undesignated sites; flush toil. MISC.: Elev, sea level. Pets permitted if on leash.

Heber Dunes County Park (Imperial County Park). 3 mi E of El Centro on I-8; 3 mi S on St Hwy 111; 7 mi E on Heber Rd. SEASON: All yr; 3-day lmt. FACILITIES: 300 sites; tbls, flush toil, drk wtr. 5 mi -- Store, fd, LP gas. ACTIV-ITIES: Hunting (dove, pheasant); frogging in ponds/swamps. Golf nearby. Hiking. MISC.: Elev -40 ft; 340 acres; pets. Nature trails; motorbike trails; sand dunes.

ELK CREEK

Board Tree (Mendocino NF). 4½ mi N of Elk Creek on Co Hwy 306; 21-3/10 mi W on Co Hwy 307; 1-4/5 mi W on Co Hwy 312. SEASON: 6/15-10/15; 14-day lmt. FACILITIES: 24 sites (tr -22), tbls, toil, cga, no drk wtr. ACTIVITIES: Picnicking. MISC.: Elev 6100 ft; 2 acres; pets; scenic. Camp in open brush area adjacent to mixed pine and fir stand. Spring water about ¼ mi S of camp at Hunter Camp.

Masterson (Mendocino NF). 4½ mi N of Elk Creek on Co Hwy 306; 30 mi NW on Co Hwy 307. SEASON: 5/25-10/15. FACILITIES: 20 sites (tr -22), tbls, toil, cga, piped drk wtr. ACTIVITIES: Picnicking. 1 mi -- Fishing; swimming; boating (power boats prohibited on lake). MISC.: Elev 6000 ft; 7 acres; pets on leash. Reservations required. Scenic.

Telephone Camp (Mendocino NF). 4½ mi N of Elk Creek on Co Hwy 306; 36 mi NW on Co Hwy 307. SEASON: 6/15-10/15; 14-day lmt. FACILITIES: 13 sites (tr --22), tbls, toil, cga, piped drk wtr. ACTIVITIES: Picnicking. 3 mi -- Swimming; fishing; boating. MISC.: Elev 6600 ft; 6 acres; pets; scenic. Located on edge of Dry Meadow in red fir timber area. Gravity water system. Pinto Creek.

EMIGRANT GAP

Carr Lake (Tahoe NF). 4-4/5 mi E of Emigrant Gap on I-80; 4-3/10 mi W on St Hwy 20; 8-2/5 mi N on FS 18N18; 2-1/10 mi E on FS 18N16. SEASON: 6/15-10/1; 14-day lmt. FACILITIES: 4 tent sites; tbls, toil, cga, no drk wtr. ACTIVITIES: Swimming; picnicking; fishing; boating,l. MISC.: Elev 6700 ft; 2 acres; pets; lake.

Fuller Lake (Tahoe NF). 4-4/5 mi E of Emigrant Gap on I-80; 4-3/10 mi W on St Hwy 20; 4-1/10 mi N on FS 18N18 (Bowman Lake Rd). SEASON: 5/23-10/15; 14-day lmt. FACILITIES: 11 tent sites; tbls, toil, cga, no drk wtr. ACTIVITIES: Boating,d (hand-off boat launching); picnicking; fishing. MISC.: Elev 5400 ft; 2 acres; pets. Fuller Lake.

Grouse Ridge (Tahoe NF). 4-4/5 mi E of Emigrant Gap on I-80; 4-3/10 mi W on St Hwy 20; 6-2/5 mi N on FS 18N18; 4-3/5 mi NE on FS 18N14 (Grouse Ridge Rd). [Near Grouse Ridge Lookout.] SEASON: 6/15-10/15; 14-day lmt. FACILITIES: 9 sites (tr -16), tbls, toil, cga, piped spring drk wtr. ACTIVITIES: Picnicking. Fishing/swimming (1 mi). MISC.: Elev

7400 ft; 3 acres; pets. Many small lakes nearby in the Grouse Lakes Area. Milk Lake and Sanford Lake (¼ mi).

North Fork (Tahoe NF). 4/5 mi E of Emigrant Gap on I-80; 6 mi SE on FS 17N25 (Texas Hill Rd). SEASON: 5/23-10/15; 14-day lmt. FACILITIES: 8 sites (tr -16), tbls, toil, cga, piped spring drk wtr. ACTIVITIES: Swimming; picnicking; fishing. MISC.: Elev 4400 ft; 4 acres; stream; pets. On the North Fork of the American River.

Sterling Lake (Tahoe NF). 8-3/10 mi E of Emigrant Gap on I-80; 6-1/10 mi NE on FS 17N16 (Fordyce Lake Rd). SEASON: 6/15-10/15; 14-day lmt. FACILITIES: 5 tent sites; tbls, toil, cga, no drk wtr. ACTIVITIES: Swimming; picnicking; fishing; boating,l (hand-off boat launching). MISC.: Elev 7000 ft; 2 acres; pets. Sterling Lake.

Tunnel Mills. 4/5 mi E of Emigrant Gap on I-80; 7-3/10 mi SE on FS 17N25 (Texas Hill Rd). SEASON: 6/1-10/15; 14-day lmt. FACILITIES: 5 sites (tr -16), tbls, toil, cga, no drk wtr. ACTIVITIES: Swimming; picnicking; fishing. MISC.: Elev 4400 ft; 2 acres; pets. East Fork of American River.

Woodchuck (Tahoe NF). 8-3/10 mi E of Emigrant Gap on I-80; 2-9/10 mi NE on FS 17N16 (Fordyce Lake Rd). SEASON: 6/15-10/15; 14-day lmt. FACILITIES: 8 sites (tr -16), tbls, toil, cga, no drk wtr. ACTIVITIES: Picnicking. 3 mi -- Ice, fd, gas. MISC.: Elev 6300 ft; 5 acres; pets. Rattlesnake Creek and Sterling Lake (3 mi).

ENCINITAS

City Park. Free overnight camping. N of town on I-5 at La Costa Rd. SEASON: All year.

ETNA

Etna (Klamath NF). 1/10 mi N of Etna on St Hwy S3. [On the N side of Etna, in town.] SEASON: 5/1-10/15. FACILITIES: 10 sites (tr -22), tbls, flush toil, cga, store, ice, laundry, gas, piped drk wtr. ACTIVITIES: Picnicking. MISC.: Elev 3000; 6 acres. Pets permitted if kept on leash.

EUREKA

Arcata (City Park). 8 mi N of Eureka via US 101 to Arcata exit, ¼ mi N on "F" Street at 9th Street in Eureka. SEASON: All yr; 2-day lmt. FACILITIES: 12 sites; dump, electric, fd. Store (¼ mi). ACTIVITIES: Picnicking. Boating,l (2 mi). MISC.: Elev 34 ft; pets on leash. Humboldt Bay. Camping sign-up at Police Department, at 7th and "F" Streets.

FALL RIVER MILLS

Cinder Cone (BLM). Plateau 6 mi SE of Fall River Mills off US 299. **SEASON:** May-October. **FACILITIES:** 13 tent sites; no drk wtr. **ACTIVITIES:** Hunting. **MISC.:** Elev 3500 ft. Boil water before using.

Dusty (Lassen NF). 6½ mi W of Fall River Mills on US 299; 5½ mi NW on Co Rd. [On N shore of Lake Britton.] **SEASON:** 4/15-10/15; 14-day lmt. **FACILITIES:** 6 sites (tr -22), tbls, toil, cga, no drk wtr. **ACTIVITIES:** Swimming; picnicking; fishing; boating,d (l, 1 mi). Waterskiing (1 mi). **MISC.:** Elev 3000 ft; 3 acres; pets permitted if on a leash.

Wiley Ranch (Lassen NF). 8 mi NE of Fall River Mills on US 299; 16 mi NW on Co Hwy 40N01. **SEASON:** 5/15-10/15; 14-day lmt. **FACILITIES:** 12 sites (tr --22), tbls, toil, cga, no drk wtr. **ACTIVITIES:** Picnicking. **MISC.:** Elev 3800 ft; 4 acres; pets on leash.

FAWNSKIN

Holcomb Valley (San Bernardino NF). 1-4/5 mi E of Fawnskin on St Hwy SH38; 3 mi N on Co Hwy 2N09; 9/10 mi E on FS 3N16. **SEASON:** 5/15-10/1; 7-day lmt. **FACILITIES:** 19 sites (tr -16), tbls, toil, cga, no drk wtr. **ACTIVITIES:** Picnicking. Fishing (4 mi). **MISC.:** Elev 7400 ft; 7 acres; pets. Holcomb Creek and Big Bear Lake (3 mi).

Horse Springs (San Bernardino NF). 2 mi NW of Fawnskin on Co Hwy 3N14; 7-3/5 mi NW on FS 3N14; 2/5 mi NE on FS 3N17. **SEASON:** 6/15-9/15; 7-day lmt. **FACILITIES:** 17 sites (tr -16), tbls, toil, cga, no drk wtr. **ACTIVITIES:** Picnicking. Fishing (2 mi). **MISC.:** Elev 5800 ft; 4 acres; pets. Coxey Creek (2 mi).

FILLMORE

*****Cow Springs** (Los Padres NF). 15 mi N of Fillmore. Accessible by TRAIL. Located within Sespe Condor Wildlife Sanctuary. **SEASON:** All yr; 14-day lmt. **FACILITIES:** 6 tent sites; tbls, toil, cga, no drk wtr. **ACTIVITIES:** Hiking; picnicking. **MISC.:** Elev 3500 ft; pets. No shooting at any time.

FISH CAMP

Big Sandy (Sierra NF). ½ mi S of Fish Camp on St Hwy 41; 5-3/10 mi E on FS 6S00. **SEASON:** 5/21-9/30; 14-day lmt. **FACILITIES:** 21 sites (tr -16), tbls, toil, cga, no drk wtr. **ACTIVITIES:** Picnicking; fishing. Horseback riding (1 mi) and rental (3 mi). **MISC.:** Elev 5800 ft; 5 acres; pets. Big Creek.

Little Sandy (Sierra NF). ½ mi S of Fish Camp on St Hwy 41; 6-9/10 mi E on FS 6S00. **SEASON:** 5/21-9/30; 14-day lmt. **FACILITIES:** 10 tent sites; tbls, toil,

cga, no drk wtr. **ACTIVITIES:** Fishing; picnicking. Horseback riding (1 mi) and rental (5 mi). **MISC.:** Elev 6100 ft; 3 acres; pets. Big Creek.

FOREST GLEN

Forest Glen (Shasta-Trinity NF). 1-1/10 mi W of Forest Glen on St Hwy 36. **SEASON:** 4/1-1/31; 14-day lmt. **FACILITIES:** 14 sites (tr -16); tbls, toil, cga, f, piped drk wtr; gas/store/ice. **ACTIVITIES:** Picnicking; swimming; fishing. **MISC.:** Elev 2300 ft; 4 acres; river; pets.

Hell Gate (Shasta-Trinity NF). 1 mi E of Forest Glen on St Hwy 36. **SEASON:** 4/1-1/31; 14-day lmt. **FACILITIES:** 16 sites (tr -22); tbls, toil, cga, f, well drk wtr. Store/gas/ice (1 mi). **ACTIVITIES:** Picnicking; swimming; fishing. **MISC.:** Elev 2300 ft; 4 acres; river; pets.

FORESTHILL

Ahart (Tahoe NF). 28½ mi E of Foresthill on FS 15N10 (Mosquito Ridge Rd); 10 mi NE on FS 15N08; 5-1/5 mi NE on FS 17N12. [Located on the Middle Fork of the American River, 1 mi above French Meadows Reservoir.] **SEASON:** 6/1-10/15; 14-day lmt. **FACILITIES:** 17 sites (tr -22), tbls, toil, cga, no drk wtr. **ACTIVITIES:** Horseback riding; swimming; boating,d (l, 1 mi); picnicking; fishing; hiking. Waterskiing (1 mi). **MISC.:** Elev 5300 ft; 7 acres; pets; game refuge. Nature trails (1 mi).

Forbes (Tahoe NF). 11-1/10 mi N of Foresthill on Co Hwy 15N34 (Iowa Hill Rd). On Forbes Creek. **FACILITIES:** No longer has facilities. Available for dispersed camping. Spring water available nearby. **ACTIVITIES:** Fishing. **MISC.:** Elev 3600 ft; pets.

*****Poppy** (Tahoe NF). 28½ mi E of Foresthill on FS 15N10; 10 mi NE on FS 15N08; 2 mi E on FS 17N12; 4/5 mi NW, by BOAT or TRAIL. Trail access is from McGuire Beach Parking Lot: 3½ mi NE of Foresthill on FS 17N12; 1 mi SW, BY FOOT. [Located on the NW shore of French Meadows Reservoir.] **SEASON:** 6/1-10/15; 14-day lmt. **FACILITIES:** 12 tent sites; tbls, toil, cga, no drk wtr. **ACTIVITIES:** Swimming; picnicking; fishing; boating (ld, 1 mi); hiking; horseback riding; waterskiing. **MISC.:** Elev 5300 ft; 4 acres; pets on leash; nature trails.

*****Robinson Flat** (Tahoe NF). 33 mi NE of Foresthill on FS 15N10 (Mosquito Ridge Rd). [Narrow, winding mountain rd; not recommended for trailers.] **SEASON:** 6/15-10/15; 14-day lmt. **FACILITIES:** 6 tent sites; tbls, toil, cga, no drk wtr (only undrinkable spring water). **ACTIVITIES:**

See page 7 for KEY TO ABBREVIATIONS.

Horseback riding; hiking; picnicking. Fishing (2 mi). MISC.: Elev 6800 ft; 5 acres; pets; nature trails. Little Duncan Creek (2 mi). Equestrian trails.

Secret House (Tahoe NF). 18-7/10 mi NE of Foresthill on Co Hwy 15N34 (Foresthill Divide Rd). [Narrow, winding mountain rd; trailers not recommended.] SEASON: 6/15-10/15; 14-day lmt. FACILITIES: 4 tent sites; tbls, toil, cga, piped drk wtr. ACTIVITIES: Hiking; picnicking. Fishing (2 mi). MISC.: Elev 5400 ft; 1 acre; pets; nature trails.

Tadpole Campground (Tahoe NF). 24 mi NE of Foresthill. [Narrow, winding mountain rd; trailers not recommended.] SEASON: 6/15-10/15; 14-day lmt. FACILITIES: No longer has facilities. Available for dispersed camping. MISC.: Elev 6400 ft. Pets.

Talbot (Tahoe NF). $28\frac{1}{2}$ mi E of Foresthill on FS 15N10 (Mosquito Ridge Rd); 10 mi NE on FS 15N08; 8-3/10 mi NE on FS 17N12. [Rough, narrow rd; trailers not recommended.] SEASON: 6/15-10/15; 14-day lmt. FACILITIES: 5 tent sites; tbls, toil, cga, no drk wtr. ACTIVITIES: Horseback riding; swimming; picnicking; fishing; waterskiing; hiking. Boating,d (3 mi). MISC.: Elev 5600 ft; 6 acres; pets. Nature trails (1 mi). On the Middle Fork of the American River, 5 mi above French Meadows Reservoir.

*Upper Hell Hole (Eldorado NF). 20 mi E of Foresthill on FS FH96; 8-4/5 mi NE on FS 15N10; 8-4/5 mi E on FS 15N08; $13\frac{1}{2}$ mi SE on FS 17N12; 3 mi BY BOAT. SEASON: 6/15-9/15. FACILITIES: 15 tent sites; tbls, toil, piped drk wtr. ACTIVITIES: Swimming; picnicking; fishing; boating (l, 3 mi); sailing; waterskiing. MISC.: Elev 4600 ft; 8 acres; pets. Hell Hole Reservoir.

FOREST RIVER

Soda Springs (Lassen NF). 15 mi NE of Forest River on St Hwy 32; 2/5 mi NE on FS 26N19. SEASON: 5/25-10/1; 14-day lmt. FACILITIES: 10 sites (tr -22); tbls, toil, cga, no drk wtr. ACTIVITIES: Picnicking; fishing. MISC.: Elev 3600 ft; 4 acres; stream; pets.

FORT JONES

Lovers Camp (Klamath NF). 18 mi W of Fort Jones on Co Rd 7F01 (Scott River Rd); 5-2/5 mi SW on FS 44N45; 1-3/5 mi SW on FS 43N45. SEASON: 6/1-10/31. FACILITIES: 10 tent sites; tbls, toil, cga, piped drk wtr, f. ACTIVITIES: Picnicking. Fishing (1 mi). Swimming (3 mi). MISC.: Elev 4300 ft; 5 acres; pets. Canyon Creek (1 mi).

FORTUNA

Mad River (Six Rivers NF). 4 mi S of Fortuna on I-101; 49 mi E on St Hwy 36; 3-7/10 mi SE on Co Hwy 501. SEASON: FREE during winter when water is turned off ($1 rest of yr); 14-day lmt. FACILITIES: 30 sites (tr -22), tbls, toil, cga, piped drk wtr. ACTIVITIES: Swimming; picnicking; fishing; boating,rld. MISC.: Elev 2600 ft; 1 acre; pets. 2 units designed for drive-thru for trailers; 5 units have double-wide spurs for 2-car parties. Good trout fishing. 4 mi N of Ruth Lake.

FRAZIER PARK

*Bear Trap 1 (Los Padres NF). 30-3/10 mi SW of Frazier Park on Co Hwy 9N03; 2 mi S on FS 7N11; 4 mi SE on TRAIL 23W02. SEASON: 5/1-11/30; 14-day lmt. FACILITIES: 7 tent sites; tbls, cga, no toil, no drk wtr. ACTIVITIES: Hiking; picnicking; fishing. Horseback riding (1 mi). MISC.: Elev 5000 ft; 1 acre; pets; scenic.

*Cedar Creek (Los Padres NF). $13\frac{1}{2}$ mi SW of Frazier Park on Co Hwy 9N03; 5 mi S on FS 7N03; 1 mi SW on FS 7N03C; $1\frac{1}{2}$ mi W on TRAIL 21W06. SEASON: 5/15-11/1; 14-day lmt. FACILITIES: 3 tent sites; tbls, toil, cga, no drk wtr. ACTIVITIES: Hiking; picnicking. MISC.: Elev 5000; 1 acre; pets; scenic; stream. Horseback riding (1 mi).

Half Moon (Los Padres NF). 3-2/5 mi W of Frazier Park on Co Hwy FH95; 10-2/5 mi SW on Co Hwy 9N03; 8-4/5 mi SE on FS 7N03. SEASON: 5/1-11/30; 14-day lmt. FACILITIES: 10 sites (tr -22), tbls, cga, f, no tbls, no drk wtr. ACTIVITIES: Picnicking. MISC.: Elev 4700 ft; 10 acres; pets on leash.

Lockwood Canyon (Los Padres NF). 3-2/5 mi W of Frazier Park on Co Hwy FH95 (Frazier Mountain Park Rd); $5\frac{1}{2}$ mi SW on 9N03; 1-3/10 mi S on FS 8N12 (subject to washout in spring and winter). SEASON: 5/15-11/15; 14-day lmt. FACILITIES: 5 tent sites; tbls, toil, cga, no drk wtr. Fd (3 mi). ACTIVITIES: Swimming; picnicking. MISC.: Elev 4600 ft; 2 acres; pets. Lockwood Creek.

Pine Springs (Los Padres NF). 3-2/5 mi W of Frazier Park on Co Rd FH95 (Frazier Mountain Park Rd); 10-2/5 mi SW on Co Rd 9N03; 2-4/5 mi S on FS 7N03; 1 mi W on FS 7N03A. [A limited area for camp trailers because of narrow dirt rd.] Not accessible during wet weather. SEASON: 5/15-11/1; 14-day lmt. FACILITIES: 12 tent sites (tr -16), tbls, toil, cga, no drk wtr. ACTIVITIES: Picnicking. MISC.: Elev 5800 ft; 10 acres. Pets permitted on leash.

See page 7 for KEY TO ABBREVIATIONS.

73

Thorn Meadows (Los Padres NF). 3-2/5 mi W of Frazier Park on Co Hwy FH95; 10-2/5 mi SW on Co Hwy 9N03; 7½ mi S on FS 7N03; 1-3/5 mi SW on FS 7N03C. SEASON: 5/15-11/1; 14-day lmt. FACILITIES: 4 sites (tr -16), tbls, toil, cga, no drk wtr. ACTIVITIES: Hiking; picnicking. MISC.: Elev 5000 ft; 3 acres; pets on leash; stream.

*Upper Reyes** (Los Padres NF). 30-3/10 mi SW of Frazier Park on Co Hwy 9N03; 2 mi S on FS 7N11; 2 mi SE on TRAIL 23W02. SEASON: 5/1-11/30; 14-day lmt. FACILITIES: 4 tent sites; no toil/drk wtr. ACTIVITIES: Hiking; picnicking; fishing. Horseback riding (1 mi). MISC.: Elev 4800 ft; 1 acre; pets; creek.

FRESNO

Camp 4 (Sequoia NF). 65 mi E of Fresno along Kings River via St Hwy 180, Piedra Rd, Trimmer Springs Rd (FS 11S12), and Davis Rd (FS 12S01). [Paved and dirt rd; not suitable for trailers.] SEASON: All yr; 14-day lmt. FACILITIES: 5 sites (tr -16), tbls, toil, cga, no drk wtr. ACTIVITIES: Swimming; picnicking; fishing. MISC.: Elev 1000 ft; 1 acre; pets; river.

Camp 4½ (Sequoia NF). 64 mi E of Fresno on Kings River via St Hwy 180, Piedra, Trimmer Springs Rd (FS 11S12), and Davis Rd (FS 12S01). [Paved and dirt rds.] SEASON: All yr; 14-day lmt. FACILITIES: 5 sites (tr -16), tbls, toil, cga, piped drk wtr. ACTIVITIES: Swimming; picnicking; fishing. MISC.: Elev 1000 ft; 3 acres; pets. Kings River. Water available at Camp 4½ Guard Station.

Mill Flat (Sequoia NF). 66 mi E of Fresno along Kings River via St Hwy 180, Piedra Rd, Trimmer Springs Rd (FS 11S12) and Davis Rd (FS 12S01). [Paved and dirt rds.] SEASON: All yr; 14-day lmt. FACILITIES: 5 sites (tr -16), tbls, toil, cga, no drk wtr. ACTIVITIES: Swimming; picnicking; fishing. MISC.: Elev 1100 ft; 2 acres; pets. Kings River.

FURNACE CREEK

Furnace Creek (Death Valley NM). ½ mi W of Furnace Creek on St Hwy 190. SEASON: April to November, FREE ($1 rest of yr). FACILITIES: 200 sites (tr -30), flush toil. ½ mi -- Store, LP gas. ACTIVITIES: Horseback riding/rental; hiking. Golf (½ mi). Nature programs. MISC.: Elev -175 ft; pets on leash. Visitor Center. Nature trails.

GARBERVILLE

Watts (Six Rivers NF). 19½ mi E of Garberville on Co Hwy 229; 17-3/10 mi E on Co Hwy 516; 4 mi N on FS 25082. SEASON: 6/15-10/31; 14-day lmt. FACILITIES:

6 sites (tr -16), tbls, toil, cga, piped drk wtr. ACTIVITIES: Hunting; picnicking. MISC.: Elev 5000 ft; 2 acres; pets; mountain scenery. 1½-acre mountain lake. Supplies at Zenia (7 mi).

GASQUET

Big Flat (Six Rivers NF). 8-1/5 mi SW of Gasquet on I-199; 17-1/10 mi SE on Co Rd 427; 1/5 mi N on Co Hwy 405. SEASON: All yr; 14-day lmt. FACILITIES: 30 sites (tr -22), tbls, toil, cga, f, piped drk wtr. ACTIVITIES: Swimming; hunting; picnicking; fishing. MISC.: FREE IN WINTER, when water is turned off ($2 rest of yr). Elev 660 ft; 8 acres; pets on leash.

GLENNVILLE

Alder Creek (Sequoia NF). 8 mi E of Glennville on St Hwy 155; 3 mi S on FS 25S04 (Alder Creek Rd). [Paved and dirt rds.] SEASON: 4/1-11/30; 14-day lmt. FACILITIES: 12 sites (tr -22), tbls, toil, cga, no drk wtr. ACTIVITIES: Fishing; picnicking. MISC.: Elev 3900 ft; 5 acres; pets. Alder Creek and Cedar Creek.

Cedar Creek (Sequoia NF). 10 mi E of Glennville on St Hwy 155. [Paved rd.] SEASON: 5/1-11/1; 14-day lmt. FACILITIES: 13 tent sites; tbls, toil, cga, piped spring drk wtr. 5 mi -- Store, ice, food, gas. ACTIVITIES: Fishing; picnicking. MISC.: Elev 4800 ft; 2 acres; pets. Cedar Creek.

Frog Meadow (Sequoia NF). 26 mi NE of Glennville via St Hwy 155 and FS FH90. [Paved and narrow rd.] SEASON: 6/1-10/31; 14-day lmt. FACILITIES: 10 sites (tr -22), tbls, toil, cga, piped spring drk wtr. ACTIVITIES: Fishing (1 mi). MISC.: Elev 7500 ft; 4 acres; pets. Tobias Creek (1 mi).

Panorama (Sequoia NF). 21 mi NE of Glennville via St Hwy 155 and FS FH90. [Paved and narrow dirt road. Not advisable for trailers.] SEASON: 6/1-10/31; 14-day lmt. FACILITIES: 10 sites (tr -22), tbls, toil, cga, no drk wtr. ACTIVITIES: Picnicking. Fishing (4 mi). MISC.: Elev 6800 ft; 4 acres; pets. Deep Creek and Capinero Creek (4 mi).

Tiger Flat (Sequoia NF). 13 mi E of Glennville on St Hwy 155; 4 mi N on FS FH90. SEASON: 5/1-11/1; 14-day lmt. FACILITIES: 6 sites (tr -22), tbls, toil, cga, piped spring drk wtr. 5 mi -- Store, ice, fd, gas. ACTIVITIES: Picnicking. MISC.: Elev 6600 ft; 2 acres. Pets on leash. Supplies at Glennville.

GORMAN

Dutchman (Los Padres NF). 1-1/10 mi W of Gorman on US 99; 9½ mi SW on

FS 8N01 (Hungry Valley Rd); 11-2/5 mi SW on FS 7N01; 1-1/10 mi S on FS 7N01C. **SEASON:** 5/15-11/1; 14-day lmt. **FACILITIES:** 8 sites (tr -16), tbls, toil, cga, no drk wtr. **ACTIVITIES:** Picnicking. **MISC.:** Elev 6800 ft; 5 acres; pets.

Hardluck (Los Padres NF). 7-1/5 mi SE of Gorman on I-5; 3 mi W on FS 8N02; 5-7/10 mi S on FS 7N08. **SEASON:** All yr; 14-day lmt. **FACILITIES:** 6 sites (tr -16), tbls, toil, cga, no drk wtr. **ACTIVITIES:** Swimming; rockhounding; picnicking; fishing. **MISC.:** Elev 2800 ft; 2 acres; pets; stream.

Horse Trail (Angeles NF). 4-3/10 mi S of Gorman on I-5; 3-4/5 mi E on St Hwy 138; 2-2/5 mi SE on Co Hwy 8N04; 3-7/10 mi E on Co Hwy 8N03. **SEASON:** All yr; 14-day lmt. **FACILITIES:** 5 sites (tr -22), tbls, toil, cga, f, no drk wtr. 3 mi -- Store, ice, fd. **ACTIVITIES:** Hiking; horseback riding; picnicking. **MISC.:** Elev 4000 ft; 1 acre; pets; nature trails.

Kings Camp (Los Padres NF). 1-1/10 mi W of Gorman on US 99; 9½ mi SW on FS 8N01 (Hungry Valley Rd); 1-1/10 mi S on FS 7N01; 1 mi E on FS 7N01A. [Not advisable for trailers.] **SEASON:** All yr (except during occasional winter storm periods); 14-day lmt. **FACILITIES:** 7 sites (tr -16), tbls, toil, cga, piped spring drk wtr. **MISC.:** Elev 4200 ft; 3 acres; pets.

*****Seven Pines** (Los Padres NF). 9/10 mi W of Gorman on St Hwy 99; 6 mi SW on FS 8N03; 13 mi SW on FS 7N03; 2½ mi E on TRAIL 19W04. [Located on upper Snowy Creek which drains into the Piru Creek. Travel to the camp is accessible by bikes, horseback and hiking. Shortest distance to any rd from the camp is 3 mi from Alamo Loop Rd.] **SEASON:** 5/15-11/1; 14-day lmt. **FACILITIES:** 3 tent sites; tbls, toil, cga, no drk wtr. **ACTIVITIES:** Hiking; horseback riding; picnicking. **MISC.:** Elev 5000 ft; 2 acres; pets; stream; scenic.

Twin Pines (Los Padres NF). 1-1/10 mi W of Gorman on US 99; 9½ mi SW on FS 8N01 (Hungry Valley Rd); 9-1/10 mi W on FS 7N01; ½ mi S on FS 7N01A. [Not advisable for trailers.] **SEASON:** 5/15-11/1; 14-day lmt. **FACILITIES:** 5 tent sites; tbls, toil, cga, no drk wtr. **ACTIVITIES:** Hiking; picnicking. **MISC.:** Elev 6600 ft; 1 acre; pets.

GRADE VALLEY

*****Cedar Creek** (Los Padres NF). Approx. 3 mi W on TRAIL 22W10 from Thorn Meadows Rd, or from Grade Valley via Fishbowls Trail, 9 mi, by foot or horseback. **FACILITIES:** Tent sites; cga, no drk wtr. **ACTIVITIES:** Hiking; horseback riding.

MISC.: Cedar Creek. Public corrals at Thorn Meadows Campground.

*****Fishbowls** (Los Padres NF). 6 mi from Grade Valley or 6 mi from the trail jct on Thorn Meadows Rd, by foot or horseback. The trailhead in Grade Valley is located just past the location of the old Grade Valley Campground. [Located deep in the Los Padres backcountry.] **FACILITIES:** Tent sites; cga, no drk wtr. **ACTIVITIES:** Hiking; horseback riding. **MISC.:** This scenic camp derives its name from the bowl-shaped pools approx. 300 yards above the camp which have been known to contain trout. Public corrals at Thorn Meadows Campground.

GRANT GROVE

Big Meadow (Sequoia NF). 1-2/5 mi S of Grant Grove on St Hwy 180; 6½ mi SE on US FH78 (The General's Hwy); 4-2/5 mi NE on FS 14S01 (Horse Corral Rd). [Paved access rds.] **SEASON:** 5/15-11/1; 14-day lmt. **FACILITIES:** 25 sites (tr -22), tbls, toil, cga, no drk wtr. Water available at Big Meadow Guard Station about 1½ mi W of campground. **ACTIVITIES:** Fishing; picnicking. Horseback riding/rental (4 mi). **MISC.:** Elev 7600 ft; 15 acres; pets. Big Meadow Creek.

Buck Rock (Sequoia NF). 1-2/5 mi S of Grant Grove on St Hwy 180; 6½ mi SE on US FH78 (The Generals Hwy); 3-1/5 mi NE on FS 14S01 (Horse Corral Rd); 1/5 mi N on FS 13S04 (Buck Rock Rd). [Paved and dirt rds.] **SEASON:** 5/15-11/1; 14-day lmt. **FACILITIES:** 5 sites (tr -22), tbls, toil, cga, no drk wtr. Water available at Big Meadow Guard Station approx. 1 mi E of campground. **ACTIVITIES:** Picnicking. Horseback riding/rental (5 mi). **MISC.:** Elev 7600 ft; 2 acres; pets; stream.

Landslide (Sequoia NF). 13 mi NE of Grant Grove via St Hwy 180 and FS 13S01 (Hume Rd). [Paved rd.] **SEASON:** 5/1-11/15; 14-day lmt. **FACILITIES:** 6 sites (tr -16), tbls, toil, cga, nondrinkable spring water. 4 mi -- Store, ice, fd, shower, gas. **ACTIVITIES:** Picnicking. Fishing (1 mi). Swimming (3 mi). Boating,rl (4 mi). Horseback riding/rental (4 mi). **MISC.:** Elev 5800 ft; 2 acres; pets. Landslide Creek and Hume Lake (3 mi).

Upper Tenmile (Sequoia NF). 1-2/5 mi S of Grant Grove on St Hwy 180 (Kings Canyon Hwy); 3 mi SE on St Hwy 198 (The General Hwy); 5 mi N on FS 13S01. [Paved rd.] **SEASON:** 5/15-11/15; 14-day lmt. **FACILITIES:** 5 sites (tr -22), tbls, toil, cga, no drk wtr. 5 mi -- Store, ice, fd, gas, shower.

See page 7 for KEY TO ABBREVIATIONS.

ACTIVITIES: Fishing; picnicking. Swimming (4 mi). Boating,rl (5 mi). Horseback riding/rental (5 mi). MISC.: Elev 5800 ft; 5 acres; stream; pets; scenic. Tenmile Creek and Hume Lake (4 mi).

GREENFIELD

Horse Bridge (Lassen NF). 18 mi SW of Greenfield on Co Hwy G16; 4 mi S on FS 19S09. SEASON: All yr; 14-day lmt. FACILITIES: 5 tent sites; tbls, toil, cga, no drk wtr. Fd (5 mi). ACTIVITIES: Hiking; horseback riding; picnicking; fishing. MISC.: 2 acres;pets.

White Oaks (Los Padres NF). 25 mi W of Greenfield on Tassajara Rd, 1 mi below top of Chews Ridge, Monterey Co. [Not recommended for trailers.] SEASON: 3/1-11/30; 14-day lmt. FACILITIES: 8 tent sites; toil, piped drk wtr. ACTIVITIES: Hiking. MISC.: Elev 4000 ft; pets. Trailhead to Ventana Wilderness.

GREENVILLE

Greenville (Plumas NF). 1 mi N of Greenville on St Hwy 89. SEASON: 5/1-9/10; 15-day lmt. FACILITIES: 23 sites (tr -32), flush toil, showers. Store (1 mi). ACTIVITIES: Fishing; boating,rld. MISC.: Round Valley Reservoir (4 mi).

GRIZZLY MOUNTAIN

Grizzly (Six Rivers NF). Turn off FS 2S08 onto FS 2S17. Drive a short distance then turn right and continue 9/10 mi up jeep road to Grizzly Mountain. FACILITIES: Tbls, cga. MISC.: Hot, dry camp in the summer. Pets on leash.

GROVELAND

Carlon (Stanislaus NF). 20-7/10 mi E of Groveland on St Hwy 120; 4/5 mi N on Co Hwy 3400 (Evergreen Rd). SEASON: 5/1-11/10; 14-day lmt. FACILITIES: 17 sites (tr -16), tbls, toil, cga, piped drk wtr (June-Sept). Store (1 mi). 5 mi -- Ice, fd, gas. ACTIVITIES: Swimming; picnicking; fishing. MISC.: Elev 4600 ft;5 acres;pets;stream through park.

Cherry Valley (Stanislaus NF). 16 mi E of Groveland on St Hwy 120; 18 mi NE on FS 1N07 (Cherry Valley Rd). SEASON: 5/10-10/15; 14-day lmt. FACILITIES: 50 sites (tr -16), tbls, toil, cga, drk wtr. ACTIVITIES: Waterskiing; boating,ld; picnicking. Swimming/fishing (1 mi). Horseback riding. MISC.: Elev 4700; 18 acres; pets. Cherry Lake (1 mi).

Lost Claim (Stanislaus NF). 10-3/5 mi E of Groveland on St Hwy 120. [10½ mi from Groveland Ranger Station.] SEASON: FACILITIES: 10 tent sites; tbls, toil, cga; drk wtr (June-Sept). 1 mi -- Store, ice, gas. ACTIVITIES: Picnicking; hiking.

Swimming/fishing (2 mi). MISC.: Elev 3100 ft; 4 acres; pets. Carry out trash. South Fork of Tuolumne River (2 mi).

Lumsden (Stanislaus NF). 7½ mi E of Groveland on St Hwy 120; 9/10 mi N on Co Hwy 6210 (Co Rd A36210, Ferrett Rd); 4-3/10 mi E on FS 1N10. [5 mi of dirt rd (one lane) are very steep and not advisable for vehicles pulling trailers or larger RVs -- use extreme caution!] 12 mi from Groveland Ranger Station. SEASON: 4/1-11/15. FACILITIES: 12 tent sites; tbls, toil, cga, no drk wtr. ACTIVITIES: Swimming; picnicking; fishing; hiking. MISC.: Elev 1500 ft; 4 acres; pets. Tuolumne River.

Lumsden Bridge (Stanislaus NF). 7½ mi E of Groveland on St Hwy 120; 9/10 mi N on Co Hwy 6210 (Co Rd A36210, Ferrett Rd); 5½ mi E on FS 1N10. [5 mi of dirt rd (one lane) are very steep and not advisable for vehicles pulling trailers or large RVs -- use extreme caution!] 16 mi from Groveland Ranger Station. SEASON: 4/11-11/15; 14-day lmt. FACILITIES: 8 sites, no trailers; tbls, toil, cga, no drk wtr. ACTIVITIES: Swimming; hiking; picnicking; fishing. MISC.: Elev 1500 ft; 2 acres; pets. Tuolumne River.

Middle Fork (Stanislaus NF). 10-7/10 mi E of Groveland on St Hwy 120; 4½ mi N on Co Hwy 3400. [Last 3 mi of rd very rough.] 25 mi from Groveland Ranger Station. SEASON: 5/1-11/10; 14-day lmt. FACILITIES: 25 sites (tr -16), tbls, toil, cga, no drk wtr. 2 mi -- Store, ice, fd, gas. ACTIVITIES: Swimming; picnicking; fishing. Horseback riding/rental (3 mi). MISC.: Elev 4400 ft; 8 acres; pets. Middle Fork of the Tuolumne River.

The Pines (Stanislaus NF). 8 mi E of Groveland on St Hwy 120. [8 mi from Groveland Ranger Station.] SEASON: All yr; 14-day lmt. FACILITIES: 14 sites (tr -22), tbls, toil, cga; piped drk wtr (June-Sept). 2 mi -- Store, ice, gas. ACTIVITIES: Picnicking. Swimming/fishing (5 mi). MISC.: Elev 3200 ft; 2 acres; pets. Carry out trash. South Fork of Tuolumne River (5 mi).

Rush Creek (Stanislaus NF). 17 mi E of Groveland on St Hwy 120. [2 mi W of Yosemite NP on old St Hwy 120.] SEASON: 5/1-10/15; 14-day lmt. FACILITIES: 7 sites (tr -16), tbls, toil, cga, f. ACTIVITIES: Swimming; picnicking; fishing. MISC.: Elev 4400 ft; pets. Rush Creek and South Fork of Tuolumne (½ mi).

South Fork (Stanislaus NF). 7½ mi E of Groveland on St Hwy 120; 9/10 mi N on Co Hwy 6210; 4-3/5 mi E on FS 1N10. SEASON: 4/1-11/15; 14-day lmt. FACILITIES: 5 tent sites; tbls, toil, cga, no

See page 7 for KEY TO ABBREVIATIONS.

drk wtr. **ACTIVITIES:** Hiking; swimming; picnicking; fishing. **MISC.:** Elev 1500 ft; 2 acres; river; pets.

Sweetwater (Stanislaus NF). 13-2/5 mi E of Groveland on St Hwy 120. [13½ mi from Groveland Ranger Station.] SEASON: All yr; 14-day lmt. FACILITIES: 9 sites (tr -22), tbls, toil, cga; piped drk wtr (June-Sept). ACTIVITIES: Picnicking. Swimming/fishing (1 mi). MISC.: Elev 3000 ft; 5 acres; pets. Unlevel sites.

HAPPY CAMP

Sulphur Springs (Klamath NF). 13-9/10 mi S on Co Rd 7C001 (Elk Creek Rd). SEASON: 5/1-10/31; 14-day lmt. FACILITIES: 6 tent sites; tbls, toil, cga, piped drk wtr. ACTIVITIES: Swimming; picnicking; fishing; horseback riding. MISC.: Elev 2400 ft; 4 acres; pets. Elk Creek.

West Branch (Klamath NF). 7-7/10 mi N of Happy Camp on Co Hwy 7C01; 5-1/5 mi NW on Co Rd 8C002; 3/10 mi NW on FS 40S07; 1-1/5 mi NW on FS 18N31. SEASON: 5/1-10/31; 14-day lmt. FACILITIES: 16 sites (tr -32), tbls, toil, piped drk wtr. ACTIVITIES: Picnicking. Swimming/fishing (1 mi). MISC.: Elev 2200 ft; 15 acres; pets.

HAWKINS BAR

Panther Creek (Shasta-Trinity NF). Off St Hwy 299, 15 mi NE of Hawkins Bar, reached from Eureka-Weaverville Hwy. [Requires careful driving.] SEASON: 6/1-9/30; 14-day lmt. FACILITIES: 4 tent sites; toil, piped drk wtr. MISC.: Elev 1200 ft. Pets allowed on leash.

HAYFORK

Cold Springs (Shasta-Trinity NF). 8 mi S of Hayfork on Co Hwy 3; 4 mi W on Co Hwy 353. [2 mi N of jct of St Hwy 3 and Temp. 36.] SEASON: 4/1-1/31; 14-day lmt. FACILITIES: 4 sites (tr -22), tbls, toil, cga, f, piped drk wtr. ACTIVITIES: Fishing (1 mi). MISC.: Elev 3200; 2 acres; pets.

Philpot (Shasta-Trinity NF). 8 mi S of Hayfork on St Hwy 3; 1/2 mi W on Co Hwy 353; 3/10 mi N on FS. SEASON: 4/1-10/31; 14-day lmt. FACILITIES: 10 sites (tr -16); tbls, toil, cga, f, piped drk wtr. ACTIVITIES: Picnicking; fishing. MISC.: Elev 2700 ft; 2 acres; stream; pets.

HELENA

Hobo Gulch (Shasta-Trinity NF). 20 mi N of Helena on FS 34N07 (Hobo Gulch Rd). [Not advisable for trailers; difficult access for trailers.] SEASON: All year; 14-day lmt. FACILITIES: 10 sites (tr -16), tbls, toil, cga, piped drk

wtr. **ACTIVITIES:** Swimming; picnicking; fishing; hiking. **MISC.:** Elev 2900 ft; 5 acres; pets. Adjoins primitive area. Trinity River.

Pigeon Point (Shasta-Trinity NF). 2-1/5 mi W of Helena on St Hwy 299, on Eureka-Weaverville Hwy. SEASON: All year; 14-day lmt. FACILITIES: 9 sites (tr -22) [limited trailer space]; tbls, toil, cga, no drk wtr. 2 mi -- Store, ice, fd, gas. ACTIVITIES: Swimming; picnicking; fishing. MISC.: Elev 1100; 3 acres; pets. Trinity River.

HESPERIA

Deep Creek (San Bernardino NF). 2 mi S of Hesperia on St Hwy SH173; 1 mi E on Co Hwy; 6 mi S on Co Hwy. SEASON: All yr; 7-day lmt. FACILITIES: 19 sites (tr -22), tbls, flush toil, cga, no drk wtr. Store (1 mi). ACTIVITIES: Picnicking. Swimming/fishing (1 mi). Horseback riding. MISC.: Elev 3300 ft; 7 acres. Pets on leash.

HOLTVILLE

Walker County Park (County Park). West edge of Holtville on I-80. SEASON: All yr; 3-day lmt. FACILITIES: 50 sites (pull-thru spaces); tbls, toil, cga, drk wtr. ACTIVITIES: Picnicking; fishing. Golf nearby. MISC.: 5 acres.

HOPLAND

Sheldon Creek (BLM). In Cow Mountain Recreation Area. Off US 101, 12 mi E of Hopland on Highland Springs Rd. SEASON: 5/1-9/1; 14-day lmt. FACILITIES: 10 tent sites; tbls, toil, cga, drk wtr. ACTIVITIES: Hunting; hiking; picnicking. MISC.: Elev 2500 ft. Mountainous terrain. Small pets. Trails.

HORNBROOK

Juniper Point Camp (Pacific Power and Light). 11 mi E of Hornbrook on Co Rd (¼ mi from Mirror Cove Campground). [Hornbrook is 12 mi N of Yreka on I-5.] SEASON: May-October. FACILITIES: 9 sites; toil. ACTIVITIES: Swimming. MISC.: Klamath River. Pets on leash.

Mirror Cove Camp (Pacific Power and Light). 11 mi E of Hornbrook on Co Rd (¼ mi from Juniper Point Campground). [Hornbrook is 12 mi N of Yreka on I-5.] SEASON: May-October. FACILITIES: 10 sites; toil. ACTIVITIES: Swimming; boating,l. MISC.: Klamath River. Pets.

HUME LAKE

Landslide (Sequoia NF). 3½ mi SE of Hume Lake on FS 13S01. [Paved road.] SEASON: 5/1-11/15; 14-day lmt. FACILITIES: 6 sites (tr -16), tbls, toil, cga, nondrinkable spring water. 4 mi -- Store, ice, fd, showers, gas. ACTIVITIES: Picnicking. Fishing (1 mi). Swimming (3 mi). 4 mi -- Boating,rl; horseback riding/rental. MISC.: Elev 5800 ft; 2 acres; pets. Landslide Creek and Hume Lake (3 mi).

Upper Tenmile (Sequoia NF). 5 mi SE of Hume Lake on FS 13S01. [Paved rd.] SEASON: 5/15-11/15; 14-day lmt. FACILITIES: 5 sites (tr -22), tbls, toil, cga, no drk wtr. 5 mi -- Store, ice, fd, gas, showers. ACTIVITIES: Picnicking; fishing. Swimming (4 mi). 5 mi -- Boating,rl; horseback riding/rental. MISC.: Elev 5800 ft; 5 acres; pets; scenic. Tenmile Creek and Hume Lake (4 mi).

HYAMPOM

Big Slide (Shasta-Trinity NF). 5 mi NW of Hyampom on Co Hwy 311. SEASON: 4/1-1/31; 14-day lmt. FACILITIES: 8 sites (tr -16); tbls, toil, cga, f, piped drk wtr. Store/ice/food/laundry (1 mi). Gas (2 mi). ACTIVITIES: Picnicking; swimming; fishing. MISC.: Elev 1200 ft; 3 acres; river; pets.

Slide Creek (Shasta-Trinity NF). 5-1/5 mi NW of Hyampom on Co Hwy 311. SEASON: 4/1-1/31; 14-day lmt. FACILITIES: 4 sites (no tr); tbls, toil, cga, f, piped drk wtr. Store/ice/laundry/food (1 mi). Gas (2 mi). ACTIVITIES: Picnicking; swimming; fishing. MISC.: Elev 1200 ft; 4 acres; river; pets.

IDYLLWILD

Bay Tree Flats (San Bernardino NF). 10 mi NW of Idyllwild on St Hwy 243 (Banning-Idyllwild Hwy); 4-4/5 mi NW on FS 4S01. SEASON: All yr; 7-day lmt. FACILITIES: 9 sites (tr -16), tbls, toil, cga, no drk wtr. Water at Bay Tree Spring. ACTIVITIES: Picnicking. MISC.: Elev 5200 ft; 5 acres; scenic; pets. No open fires.

INDEPENDENCE

Oak Creek (Inyo NF). 1½ mi NW of Independence on US 395; 3 mi W on Co Rd 13S04 (North Oak Creek Rd). SEASON: All yr; 14-day lmt. FACILITIES: 20 sites (tr -22), tbls, toil, cga, no drk wtr. ACTIVITIES: Fishing; picnicking. MISC.: Elev 5000 ft; 10 acres; pets. Oak Creek.

Sawmill Creek (Inyo County Park). 8½ mi N of Independence on US 395; 5 mi W on Black Rock Rd. [Dirt access rd.] SEASON: All yr; 14-day lmt. FACILITIES: 45 sites; tbls, toil, cga, drk wtr. ACTIVITIES: Fishing; picnicking. MISC.: Elev 4000 ft; 10 acres. Sawmill Creek.

Upper Oak Creek (Inyo NF). 1½ mi NW of Independence on US 395; 5½ mi W on Co Hwy 13S04. SEASON: All year. FACILITIES: 3 sites; tbls, toil, cga, no drk wtr. ACTIVITIES: Picnicking. MISC.: Elev 6200 ft; 1 acre; stream; pets. Trailhead Baxter Pass; John Muir Wilderness. Trail quota 25 persons per day all year.

INYOKERN

Chimney Peak (BLM). 15 mi N of Inyokern on US 395; 13 mi W on Co Hwy 152 (Nine Mile Canyon - Kennedy Meadow Rd). SEASON: 5/1-9/30; 14-day lmt. FACILITIES: 35 sites. MISC.: Elev 5500.

Fish Creek (Sequoia NF). 15 mi N of Inyokern on US 395; 23-3/5 mi NW on Co Hwy 152; 8-3/10 mi NW on FS 21S02. [Paved and dirt rd with some steep sections.] SEASON: 5/1-10/31; 14-day lmt. FACILITIES: 40 sites (tr -16), tbls, toil, cga, f, piped spring drk wtr. Store (2 mi). ACTIVITIES: Horseback riding; picnicking; fishing (in season with barbless flies only). MISC.: Elev 7400 ft; 2 acres; pets. Fish Creek. Garbage disposal not provided; pack out all waste. Supplies at Kennedy Meadows and Troy Meadows.

Kennedy (Sequoia NF). 15 mi N of Inyokern on US 395; 23-3/5 mi NW on Co Hwy 152; 2-1/5 mi N on Co Hwy 152; 2/5 mi N on FS 22S11. [Paved and dirt rd with some steep sections.] SEASON: 4/1-11/15; 14-day lmt. FACILITIES: 38 sites (tr -22), tbls, toil, cga, f, piped spring drk wtr (drk wtr available 5/15-9/30). ACTIVITIES: Swimming; picnicking; fishing. MISC.: Elev 6100 ft; 15 acres; pets; river. Store/gas (3 mi). Garbage disposal not provided; pack out all waste. On South Fork Kerr River.

Long Valley (BLM). 15 mi N of Inyokern on US 395; 26 mi NW on Co Hwy 152 (Nine Mile Canyon Rd). SEASON: 5/1-9/30; 14-day lmt. FACILITIES: 18 sites; toil. ACTIVITIES: Fishing; hiking;horseback riding/rental. MISC.: Elev 9000 ft; small pets; nature trails. Long Valley Creek. In Lamont Meadows-Long Valley Recreation Area.

Troy Meadow (Sequoia NF). 15 mi N of Inyokern on US 395; 23-3/5 mi NW on Co Hwy 152; 9-9/10 mi NW on FS 21S02. [Paved and dirt rd with some steep sections.] SEASON: 5/1-11/15; 14-day lmt. FACILITIES: 73 sites (tr -22), tbls, toil, cga, f, piped drk wtr (drk wtr available 5/15-9/30). Store (1 mi). ACTIVITIES: Picnicking; fishing (in season with barbless flies only). Horseback riding (1 mi). MISC.: Elev 7800 ft; 15 acres; pets; stream. Fish Creek

(2 mi). Garbage disposal not provided; pack out all waste.

JACUMBA

White Arrow (BLM; McCain Valley Recreation Area). 2 mi E Blvd. via Co Rd; 15 mi NW on McCain Valley Rd. **SEASON:** All yr. **FACILITIES:** 11 sites; toil, nondrinkable water. **ACTIVITIES:** Rockhounding; hiking; hunting. **MISC.:** Elev 4000; small pets on leash.

JOHNSONDALE

Long Meadow (Sequoia NF). 8-3/10 mi W of Johnsondale on FS 23S03; 3-4/5 mi N on FS FH90 (Great Western Divide Rd). [Paved rd.] **SEASON:** 5/15-10/31; 14-day lmt. **FACILITIES:** 5 sites (tr -22), tbls, toil, cga, piped drk wtr. **ACTIVITIES:** Picnicking. Fishing (2 mi). **MISC.:** Elev 6500 ft; 2 acres; pets; stream. Parker Meadow Creek (2 mi).

Redwood Meadow (Sequoia NF). 8-3/10 mi W of Johnsondale on FS 23S03; 2-4/5 mi N on FS FH90 (Great Western Divide Rd). [Paved rd.] **SEASON:** 6/15-9/15; 14-day lmt. **FACILITIES:** 15 sites (tr -22), tbls, toil, cga, no drk wtr. **ACTIVITIES:** Picnicking. Fishing (2 mi). **MISC.:** Elev 6500 ft; 4 acres; pets. Parker Meadow Creek (1 mi). Adjacent to Long Meadow giant sequoia redwood grove.

JOLON

Escondido (Los Padres NF). 16½ mi NW of Jolon on Co Rd M1L; 5½ mi NW on FS 19S09 (Milpitas Rd). **SEASON:** All yr; 14-day lmt. **FACILITIES:** 14 sites (tr -16), tbls, toil, cga, piped drk wtr, f, store. **ACTIVITIES:** Hiking; picnicking; fishing; horseback riding. **MISC.:** Elev 2300 ft; 5 acres; pets. Arroyo Seco River. Point of departure into Ventura Wilderness.

Memorial Park (Los Padres NF). 16½ mi NW of Jolon on Co Rd M1L; 5½ mi NW on FS 19S09 (Milpitas Rd). [Travel route through military reserve.] **SEASON:** All yr; 14-day lmt. **FACILITIES:** 12 sites; tbls, toil, cga, f, piped spring drk wtr. **ACTIVITIES:** Horseback riding; picnicking; fishing. **MISC.:** Elev 2100 ft; 5 acres; pets. Arroyo Seco River.

Ponderosa (Los Padres NF). 12 mi W of Jolon on I-ML; 2 mi W on FS 22S01. [First travel route is through a US Military Rd Reserve.] Paved campground rd. **SEASON:** All yr; 14-day lmt. **FACILITIES:** 22 sites (tr -16), tbls, toil, cga, piped drk wtr. **ACTIVITIES:** Hunting; hiking; horseback riding; picnicking; fishing. **MISC.:** Elev 1500 ft; 1 acre; pets on leash.

JOSHUA TREE

Hidden Valley Campground (Joshua Tree NM). 12 mi E of Joshua Tree. **SEASON:** All yr; 14-day lmt. **FACILITIES:** 62 sites (tr -33), tbls, toil, cga, no drk wtr. **ACTIVITIES:** Hiking; picnicking. Nature program (Nov.-May). **MISC.:** Elev 4200 ft; pets. Magnificent rock formations in the Wonderland of Rock.

Ryan Campground (Joshua Tree NM). 16 mi SE of Joshua Tree on Park Blvd-Quail Springs Rd. **SEASON:** All yr; 14-day lmt. **FACILITIES:** 27 sites (tr -33), tbls, toil, cga, no drk wtr. **ACTIVITIES:** Hiking; picnicking; horseback riding. Horses permitted; only campground in the monument which permits horses. **MISC.:** Elev 4300 ft; pets; trails.

JUNCTION CITY

Ripstein (Shasta-Trinity NF). 14-4/5 mi N of Junction City on Co Hwy P401 (Canyon Creek Rd). Good dirt rd. **SEASON:** All year; 14-day lmt. **FACILITIES:** 10 sites (tr -16), tbls, toil, cga, no drk wtr. **ACTIVITIES:** Hiking; picnicking; fishing. **MISC.:** Elev 3000 ft; 5 acres; pets. Canyon Creek. Trailhead of Salmon-Trinity Alps Primitive Area (2 mi).

JUNE LAKE

Big Springs (Inyo NF). 2-2/5 mi NE of June Lake on St Hwy 158 (June Lake Loop Rd); 7½ mi SE on US 395; 1½ mi NE on Co Rd 2S07. **SEASON:** 5/25-10/15; 14-day lmt. **FACILITIES:** 24 sites (tr -22), tbls, toil, cga, f, no drk wtr. 3 mi -- Store, ice, fd. **ACTIVITIES:** Picnicking; hiking. **MISC.:** Elev 7300 ft; 4 acres; pets. Deadman Creek.

Deadman (Inyo NF). 2-2/3 mi NE of June Lake on St Hwy 158; 6½ mi SE on St Hwy 395; 3 mi SW on FS 2S05. **SEASON:** 6/1-10/15; 14-day lmt. **FACILITIES:** 30 sites (tr -22); tbls, toil, cga, no drk wtr. **ACTIVITIES:** Picnicking; fishing. **MISC.:** Elev 7800 ft; 8 acres; stream; pets.

Glass Creek (Inyo NF). 2-2/5 mi NE of June Lake on St Hwy 158 (June Lake Loop Rd); 6 mi SE on US 395; 1/5 mi W on FS 2S24. **SEASON:** 5/25-10/15; 14-day lmt. **FACILITIES:** 30 sites (tr -22), tbls, toil, cga, no drk wtr. 1 mi - Store, ice, gas. **ACTIVITIES:** Hiking; picnicking; fishing. **MISC.:** Elev 7600 ft; 15 acres; pets. Glass Creek.

Hartley Springs (Inyo NF). 2 mi NE of June Lake on St Hwy 158; 2 mi SE on US 395; 1½ mi S on FS 2S78. **SEASON:** 6/1-10/15; 14-day lmt. **FACILITIES:** 20 sites (tr -16), tbls, toil, cga, no drk wtr. Gas (4 mi). ACTIVITIES: Picnicking. 5 mi -- Fishing; swimming; boating. MISC.: Elev 8400 ft; 18 acres; pets on leash.

Lower Deadman (Inyo NF). 2-2/5 mi NE of June Lake on St Hwy 158 (June Lake Loop Rd); 6½ mi SE on St Hwy 395; 3 mi SW on FS 2S05 (Deadman Creek Rd). SEASON: 6/1-10/15; 14-day lmt. FACILITIES: 30 sites (tr -22), tbls, toil, cga, no drk wtr. 4 mi -- Store, ice, fd, gas. ACTIVITIES: Picnicking; fishing. MISC.: Elev 7800 ft; 8 acres; pets. Deadman Creek.

KERNVILLE

Brush Creek (Sequoia NF). 20 mi N of Kernville on Co Hwy PM99 (along Kern River). [Paved rd.] SEASON: All yr; 1-day lmt. FACILITIES: 12 sites (tr -22), toil, cga, f, no tbls/drk wtr. 3 mi -- Store, ice, fd, gas. ACTIVITIES: Fishing (use barbless flies only in Brush Creek). MISC.: Elev 3800 ft; 3 acres; pets. Brush Creek. Campfire permit required. Well-suited for self-contained RVs. Supplies at Roads End and Fairview.

Chico Flat (Sequoia NF). 6 mi NW of Kernville on Co Hwy PM99 (Sierra Hwy) along Kern River. [Paved rd.] SEASON: All yr; 14-day lmt. FACILITIES: 35 sites (tr -32), tbls, f, toil, no drk wtr. 3 mi -- Store, ice, gas. ACTIVITIES: Fishing; picnicking. MISC.: Elev 3000 ft; 18 acres; pets. Campfire Permit required. On Kern River. Well suited for self-contained RVs.

Corral Creek (Sequoia NF). 8-9/10 mi N of Kernville on Co Hwy PM99. SEASON: All year; 14-day lmt. FACILITIES: 10 sites (tr -22); tbls, toil, cga, f, no drk wtr. ACTIVITIES: Picnicking; swimming; fishing. MISC.: Elev 3000 ft; 5 acres; river; pets. Firewood available from local businesses. Commercial rafting available May-October, on Kern River.

Eastside Campground (COE; Isabella Lake). 5 mi S of Kernville on Sierra Way. SEASON: All yr; 14-day lmt. FACILITIES: No designated sites (enough room for about 150 campers); tbls, toil, cga, drk wtr, dump. ACTIVITIES: Fishing; picnicking. MISC.: Elev 2600 ft; pets. Fish cleaning area. Off-road motorcycle area nearby. Isabella Lake (½ mi). Boating, l.

Fairview (Sequoia NF). 15-3/5 mi NW of Kernville on Co Hwy PM99 (Sierra Hwy), along Kern River. [Paved rd.] SEASON: 4/1-11/15; 14-day lmt. FACILITIES: 55 sites (tr -27), toil, f, no tbls/drk wtr. Store, ice, fd, gas. ACTIVITIES: Fishing. MISC.: Elev 3500 ft; 20 acres; pets. On Kern River.

Horse Meadow (Sequoia NF). 21-3/10 mi N of Kernville on Co Hwy PM99; 6 mi E on FS 22S05; 8-9/10 mi SE on FS 52S01; 1-2/5 mi S on FS 23S10.* [Paved rds.] SEASON: 5/1-11/15; 14-day lmt. FACILITIES: 41 sites (tr -22), tbls, toil, cga, f, piped drk wtr. ACTIVITIES: Picnicking; fishing (in season, barbless flies). MISC.: Elev 7600 ft; 20 acres; pets. Salmon Creek. Garbage disposal not provided; pack out all waste. Supplies at Roads End.

Limestone (Sequoia NF). 20 mi NW of Kernville on Co Hwy PM99 (Sierra Hwy), along Kern River. [Paved rd.] SEASON: 4/1-11/15; 14-day lmt. FACILITIES: 22 sites (tr -22), tbls, toil, cga, f, no drk wtr. 3 mi -- Store, ice, fd, gas. MISC.: Elev 3800 ft; 5 acres; pets. Brush Creek. Kern River. Near Lake Isabella. Supplies at Roads End. Firewood available from local businesses. Commercial rafting available May-October.

Shirley Meadow (Sequoia NF). 4-1/5 mi S of Kernville on Co Hwy to Wofford Heights; 8 mi W on St Hwy 155; 2-2/5 mi SW on Co Hwy 25S03. SEASON: 5/1-11/1; 14-day lmt. FACILITIES: 5 sites (tr -22), tbls, toil, cga, no drk wtr. 3 mi -- Store, ice, fd, gas. ACTIVITIES: Picnicking. MISC.: Elev 6500 ft; 2 acres; pets. Gravel access rd.

KETTENPOM

Salt Creek (Six Rivers NF). 7 mi E of Kettenpom via gravel Co Rd on bank of Salt Creek. SEASON: All yr (though not recommended in mid-summer); 14-day lmt. FACILITIES: 4 sites; tbls, toil, cga, no drk wtr. ACTIVITIES: Fall deer hunting; late spring swimming; steelhead fishing; picnicking. MISC.: Elev 2000 ft; pets.

KIDD LAKE

City Park. 1 mi S of Kidd Lake on Serene Lakes Rd; 3 mi W on Pahatsi Rd. SEASON: All yr; 1-night lmt.

KING CITY

Lion Den (Los Padres NF). 18 mi S of King City on Co Hwy G14; 18 mi W on FS 22S01; 16 mi S on FS 20S05. SEASON: All yr; 14-day lmt. FACILITIES: 3 tent sites; tbls, toil, cga, no drk wtr. ACTIVITIES: Picnicking; hiking. MISC.: Elev 3000 ft; 1 acre; pets on leash.

Nacimiento (Los Padres NF). 18 mi SW of King City on Co Rd G16; 15 mi W on FS 22S01. SEASON: All yr; 14-day lmt. FACILITIES: 9 tent sites; tbls, toil, piped drk wtr. ACTIVITIES: Fishing; picnicking. MISC.: Elev 1600 ft; 3 acres; pets. Nacimiento River.

*Prewett Ridge (Los Padres NF). 18 mi SW of King City on Co Rd G14; 20 mi W on FS 22S01; 3½ mi S on FS 20S05; 1½ mi W on TRAIL 5E12. SEASON: All yr; 14-day lmt. FACILITIES: 3 tent sites; tbls, toil, cga. ACTIVITIES: Picnicking; fishing. MISC.: Elev 2500 ft; 1 acre; scenic; pets.

KLAMATH RIVER

Beaver Creek (Klamath NF). 7-1/10 mi NE of Klamath River on St Hwy 96; 4-9/10 mi N on FS 48N01 (Beaver Creek Rd). SEASON: 5/1-11/15; 14-day lmt. FACILITIES: 8 sites (tr -16); tbls, toil, cga, no drk wtr. ACTIVITIES: Berry-picking; picnicking; hiking. MISC.: Elev 2400 ft; 2 acres; pets; Beaver Creek; trout fishing.

KYBURZ

Rat Castle (Eldorado NF). 2-3/10 mi S of Kyburz on FS 11N40; 1/5 mi SW on FS 11N44. SEASON: 5/15-10/15; 14-day lmt. FACILITIES: 10 sites (tr -16), tbls, toil, cga, drk wtr. ACTIVITIES: Swimming; picnicking; fishing. MISC.: pets; 3 acres.

LaCANADA

*Bear Canyon (Angeles NF). 10 mi NE of LaCanada on St Hwy 2; ¼ mi S on FS 2N57; 1½ mi SW on TRAIL 11W14; 3 mi SW on TRAIL 12W08. SEASON: All yr; 14-day lmt. FACILITIES: 3 tent sites; cga, tank drk wtr, no toil. ACTIVITIES: Boating; picnicking; fishing; hiking. MISC.: Elev 3400 ft; 2 acres; pets.

*DeVore (Angeles NF). 4/5 mi NW of LaCanada on St Hwy 118; 14-3/10 mi NE on St Hwy 2 (Angeles Crest Hwy); 5-3/5 mi SE on FS 2N24;1-1/5 mi E on TRAIL 11W12. SEASON: All yr; 14-day lmt. FACILITIES: 5 tent sites; tbls; no toil/drk wtr. ACTIVITIES: Picnicking; hiking; horseback riding. MISC.: Elev 2900 ft; 2 acres; stream; pets.

*Oakwilde (Angeles NF). 4/5 mi NW of LaCanada on St Hwy 118; 6-1/5 mi NE on St Hwy 2 (Angeles Crest Hwy); 3½ mi SE on TRAIL 12W17. SEASON: All yr; 14-day lmt. FACILITIES: 6 tent sites; tbls, toil, cga, no drk wtr. ACTIVITIES: Boating; picnicking; hiking. Fishing (1 mi). MISC.: Elev 1800 ft; 1 acre; pets. Dark Canyon Creek. Closed during high fire danger; see local ranger station for details. Hiking or equestrian access only, by Gabrielino N.R.T.

*Shangraw's Rest (Angeles NF). 2½ mi E on St Hwy 118; 3/5 mi N on Co Hwy;

1/2 mi N on Trail 11W14. SEASON: All year; 14-day lmt. FACILITIES: 2 sites (no tr); tbls; no drk wtr. ACTIVITIES: Picnicking; fishing; horseback riding. MISC.: Elev 1900 ft; 1 acre; stream; pets. Hiking or equestrian access by Gabrielino N.R.T.

West Fork (Angeles NF). 4/5 mi NW of LaCanada on St Hwy 118; 14-3/10 mi NE on St Hwy 2 (Angeles Crest Hwy); 5-3/5 mi SE on FS 2N24. SEASON: 7 sites, no trailers; tbls, toil, cga, no drk wtr. ACTIVITIES: Hiking; picnicking; fishing. Horseback riding (1 mi). MISC.: Elev 3000 ft; 2 acres;pets;stream.

LAKE ALPINE

Bloomfield (Stanislaus NF). 13-4/5 mi NE of Lake Alpine on St Hwy 4; 4/5 mi SE on FS 8N01 (Highland Lake Rd). SEASON: 7/1-10/1; 14-day lmt. FACILITIES: 10 sites (tr -16), tbls, toil, cga, no drk wtr. ACTIVITIES: Hiking; picnicking. 4 mi -- Swimming; fishing; boating,d. MISC.: Elev 8000 ft;5 acres; pets. Mokelumne River and Highland Lakes (4 mi).

Hermit Valley (Stanislaus NF). 10-1/10 mi NE of Lake Alpine on St Hwy 4; 3/10 mi S on FS 8N21. SEASON: 7/1-10/1; 14-day lmt. FACILITIES: 5 sites (tr -16), tbls, toil, cga, no drk wtr. ACTIVITIES: Early-season deer hunting; picnicking; fishing; boating,d; swimming. MISC.: Elev 7500 ft; 5 acres; pets. Mokelumne River.

Highland Lakes (Stanislaus NF). 13-4/5 mi NE of Lake Alpine on St Hwy 4; 5-7/10 mi SE on FS 8N01 (Highland Lakes Rd). [Not recommended for trailers.] SEASON: 7/1-10/1; 14-day lmt. FACILITIES: 10 sites (tr -16), tbls, toil, cga, no drk wtr. ACTIVITIES: Swimming; picnicking; fishing; early-season deer hunting. MISC.: Elev 8600 ft; 5 acres; pets; stream. Highland Lakes. Unimproved camp area.

Mosquito Lake (Stanislaus NF). 6-3/5 mi NE of Lake Alpine on St Hwy 4. SEASON: 7/1-11/15; 14-day lmt. FACILITIES: 8 sites; toil, no drk wtr. ACTIVITIES: Fishing; picnicking. MISC.: Elev 8000 ft; pets. Mosquito Lake.

Pacific Valley (Stanislaus NF). 8 mi NE of Lake Alpine on St Hwy 4; 1/10 mi S on FS 8N12. [Not recommended for trailers.] SEASON: 7/10-10/1; 14-day lmt. FACILITIES: 6 sites; tbls, toil, cga, no drk wtr. ACTIVITIES: Early-season deer hunting; picnicking; fishing. MISC.: Elev 7600 ft; 1 acre; pets. Pacific Creek,

Stanislaus River (Stanislaus NF). 6 mi SW of Lake Alpine on St Hwy 4; 4 mi

SE on FS 7N01. [Difficult to reach.] SEASON: 6/15-10/1; 14-day lmt. FACILITIES: 5 sites (tr -16) [trailers not recommended], tbls, toil, cga, no drk wtr. 5 mi -- Store, ice, fd, gas. ACTIVITIES: Hunting; swimming; picnicking; fishing. MISC.: Elev 5900 ft; 2 acres; pets. Stanislaus River.

LAKEHEAD

*Gooseneck Cove (Shasta-Trinity NF). 1 mi S of Lakehead on I-5; 3 mi SW, BY BOAT. [9 mi NW of Pitrina Bridge (located on I-5). SEASON: 4/1-10/31; 14-day lmt. FACILITIES: 10 tent sites; tbls, toil, cga, no drk wtr.   3 mi -- Store, ice, fd, gas, dump. ACTIVITIES: Swimming; picnicking; fishing; boating,d (rl, 3 mi); waterskiing. MISC.: Elev 1100 ft; 4 acres; pets. On Sacramento River Arm. Unit of the Whiskeytown-Shasta-Trinity National Recreation Area.

Point McCloud (Shasta-Trinity NF). 4½ mi SE of Lakehead on I-5; 17 mi NE on Co Hwy 7H01 (Gilman Rd); ½ mi W on FS 35N64. SEASON: 5/1-10/15; 21-day lmt. FACILITIES: 36 sites (tr -32), tbls, flush toil, piped drk wtr, store, ice, gas, shower, dump, laundry, fd. ACTIVITIES: Swimming; waterskiing; picnicking; fishing; boating,rld. MISC.: Elev 1200 ft; 15 acres; pets. At Shasta Lake, within Shasta-Trinity NRA, adjacent to resort.

*Salt Creek Point (Shasta-Trinity NF). 1-1/10 mi S of Lakehead on I-5; 2½ mi S, BY BOAT. [2 mi W of Low Salt Creek Campground.] SEASON: 4/1-10/31; 14-day lmt. FACILITIES: 7 tent sites; tbls, toil, cga, no drk wtr. 1 mi -- Store, ice, fd, gas, dump. Laundry (3 mi). ACTIVITIES: Swimming; waterskiing; picnicking; fishing; boating,rld. MISC.: Elev 1100 ft; 2 acres; pets. On Salt Creek Arm of Sacramento Arm of Shasta Lake. Unit of Whiskeytown-Shasta-Trinity NRA.

LAKE HUGHES

Atmore Meadows (Angeles NF). 5-4/5 mi W of Lake Hughes on Co Rd 8N03 (Elizabeth Lake - Pine Canyon Rd); 6-1/10 mi W on FS 7N23; 2-2/5 mi S on FS 7N19. SEASON: 3/15-11/30; 14-day lmt. FACILITIES: 6 sites (tr -22), tbls, toil, cga, f, no drk wtr. ACTIVITIES: Picnicking. MISC.: Elev 4300 ft; 2 acres; pets; scenic; stream.

Bear Camp (Angeles NF). 5-4/5 mi W of Lake Hughes on Co Rd 8N03 (Elizabeth Lake - Pine Canyon Rd); 9-1/10 mi W on FS 7N23. SEASON: 3/15-11/30; 14-day lmt. FACILITIES: 8 sites (tr -22), tbls, toil, cga, f, no drk wtr. ACTIVITIES: Picnicking. MISC.: Elev 5400 ft; 2 acres; pets; scenic. Remote area.

Cottonwood (Angeles NF). 4-9/10 mi SW on Co Hwy 7N09. SEASON: All yr; 14-day lmt. FACILITIES: 1 site (no tr); tbls, toil, cga. Store/gas/ice/ food (5 mi). ACTIVITIES: Picnicking. Boating/swimming; fishing; waterskiing (5 mi). MISC.: Elev 2700 ft; 1 acre; stream; scenic; pets. Reservations available at Saugus Ranger Sta.

*Lion Trail (Angeles NF). 5-4/5 mi W of Lake Hughes on Co Hwy 8N03; 6-1/10 mi W on FS 7N23; 2-2/5 mi S on FS 7N19; 3-7/10 mi S on TRAIL 16W05. SEASON: All yr; 14-day lmt. FACILITIES: 4 tent sites; tbls, toil, cga, f, no drk wtr. ACTIVITIES: Hiking; picnicking. MISC.: Elev 2700 ft; 1 acre; pets; scenic. Special campfire permit required. Trail camp.

Lower Shake (Angeles NF). 5-1/5 mi W of Lake Hughes on Co Rd 8N03 (Elizabeth Lake - Pine Canyon Rd); 3/10 mi S on FS 7N34. SEASON: 3/1-12/30; 14-day lmt. FACILITIES: 5 sites, no trailers; tbls, toil, cga, drk wtr. ACTIVITIES: Hiking; picnicking. MISC.: Elev 4300 ft; 1 acre; pets on leash.

Manzanita Hills (Angeles NF). 1-9/10 mi E of Lake Hughes on Co Rd 8N03 (Elizabeth Lake - Pine Canyon Rd). [Paved rds.] SEASON: All yr; 14-day lmt. FACILITIES: 6 sites (tr -32), tbls, flush toil, cga, drk wtr. Store/ice (2 mi). ACTIVITIES: Swimming; picnicking; fishing; boating,rd. MISC.: pets; 2 acres.

Sawmill (Angeles NF). 5-4/5 mi W of Lake Hughes on Co Rd 8N03 (Elizabeth Lake - Pine Canyon Rd); 4-3/10 mi W on FS 7N23. SEASON: 3/15-11/30; 14-day lmt. FACILITIES: 8 sites (tr -22), tbls, toil, cga, f, no drk wtr. ACTIVITIES: Picnicking. MISC.: Elev 5200 ft; 4 acres; pets on leash; scenic.

Upper Shake (Angeles NF). 5-4/5 mi W of Lake Hughes on Co Rd 8N03 (Elizabeth Lake - Pine Canyon Rd); 1-4/5 mi W on FS 7N23;4/5 mi SE on FS 7N23B. SEASON: 3/1-12/30; .14-day lmt. FACILITIES: 28 sites (tr -22), tbls, toil, cga.

LAKE ISABELLA

Auxiliary Dam Area Campground (COE; Lake Isabella). 1 mi E of Lake Isabella on St Hwy 178. SEASON: All yr; 14-day lmt. FACILITIES: Undesignated sites; flush toil, cga, hot showers. Store/fd (2 mi). ACTIVITIES: Swimming; picnicking; fishing; boating,l. MISC.: Elev 2600 ft; pets on leash. Isabella Lake (1 mi). Kern River (1½ mi).

Main Dam Campground (COE; Isabella Lake). 1½ mi N of Lake Isabella on St Hwy 155. SEASON: 4/1-11/1; 14-day lmt. FACILITIES: 84 sites (tr -30), tbls, flush

See page 7 for KEY TO ABBREVIATIONS.

toil, cga, f. Store/fd/LP gas (2 mi). Drk wtr. **ACTIVITIES:** Swimming; waterskiing; hiking; picnicking; fishing (large and small-mouth bass, crappie, bluegill, catfish, trout). Boating,rl (1 mi). **MISC.:** Elev 2600 ft; 18 acres; pets. Dump. Pull-thru spaces. Kern River. Isabella Lake.

Paradise Cove Campground (COE; Lake Isabella). 4 mi NE of Lake Isabella on St Hwy 178. **SEASON:** All yr; 14-day lmt. **FACILITIES:** Undesignated sites; toil, cga, dump. Store/fd/LP gas (5 mi). Marina nearby. **ACTIVITIES:** Swimming; fishing; boating,l (r, 1 mi). **MISC.:** Elev 2600 ft; pets. Fish cleaning area. Isabella Lake.

Pioneer Campground (COE; Isabella Lake). Approximately 3 mi N of Lake Isabella on St Hwy 155. **SEASON:** 10/1-3/31; 14-day lmt. **FACILITIES:** 77 sites (tr -30), toil, cga, drk wtr, playground. **MISC.:** Pets on leash.

Tillie Creek Campground (COE; Isabella Lake). Approximately 6 mi N of Lake Isabella on St Hwy 155. **SEASON:** 10/1-3/31; 14-day lmt. **FACILITIES:** 105 sites (tr -30), toil, cga, drk wtr, dump, playground. **MISC.:** Pets.

LAKESHORE

Badger Flat (Sierra NF). 7/10 mi E of Lakeshore on Co Hwy M2710; 5 mi NE on FS 4S01; 1/5 mi S on FS 4S01M. **SEASON:** 6/15-9/15; 14-day lmt. **FACILITIES:** 10 sites (tr -22), tbls, toil, cga, no drk wtr. Store/ice/fd/gas (4 mi). Shower (5 mi). **ACTIVITIES:** Fishing; picnicking. Swimming/boating,rld/horseback rent and riding/waterskiing (4 mi). **MISC.:** Elev 8200 ft; 5 acres; pets; scenic. Rancheria Creek and Huntington Lake (4 mi). Visitor Center (4 mi). Stream.

Bolsillo (Sierra NF). 7/10 mi E of Lakeshore on Co Rd M2710; 17 mi NE on FS 4S01. **SEASON:** 6/1-10/15; 14-day lmt. **FACILITIES:** 4 sites; tbls, toil, cga, piped drk wtr. Store/ice/fd/gas/showers (3 mi). **ACTIVITIES:** Fishing; picnicking. Horseback riding (1 mi). **MISC.:** Elev 7400 ft; 1 acre; pets; stream. Visitor center (1 mi).

Sample Meadow (Sierra NF). 7/10 mi E of Lakeshore on Co Hwy M2710; 9-4/5 mi NE on FS 4S01; 3 mi NW on FS 7S05. [Low standard access rd last 3 mi.] **SEASON:** 6/15-10/31; 14-day lmt. **FACILITIES:** 16 sites (tr -16), tbls, toil, cga, no drk wtr. **ACTIVITIES:** Fishing; picnicking. **MISC.:** Elev 7800 ft; 7 acres; pets; scenic. Kaiser Creek.

LAKEVIEW TERRACE

*__Pappy Keef__ (Angeles NF). 9 mi NE of Lakeview Terrace on FS 3N37. [Limited parking; hike to campsites 100 yards.] **SEASON:** All yr; 14-day lmt. **FACILITIES:** 9 tent sites; tbls, toil, cga, no drk wtr. **ACTIVITIES:** Picnicking; hiking; target practice. **MISC.:** Elev 3100 ft; 2 acres; pets; stream. Near legal target shooting area.

LaPORTE

*__Cleghorn Bar__ (Plumas NF). 15 mi N of LaPorte on Co Hwy 511; 9½ mi W on FS 23N24; 2½ mi N on TRAIL 9E10. [4-wheel drive or foot access.] **SEASON:** 6/15-10/15; 14-day lmt. **FACILITIES:** 4 tent sites; tbls, toil, cga, no drk wtr. **ACTIVITIES:** Hiking; picnicking; fishing. **MISC.:** Elev 3100 ft; 1 acre; pets. On Middle Fork of Feather River.

LEE VINING

Aspen Grove (Mono County Park). 7 mi W of Lee Vining on St Hwy 120. **SEASON:** May-October. **FACILITIES:** 25 sites (tr -20), toil. **ACTIVITIES:** Fishing. **MISC.:** Elev 8000 ft; pets. Lee Vining Creek.

Junction (Inyo NF). 10 mi W of Lee Vining on St Hwy 120; 1/10 mi N on FS 1N04. [1 mi E of Yosemite NP.] **SEASON:** 6/1-10/15; 7-day lmt. **FACILITIES:** 12 sites (tr -22), tbls, toil, cga, no drk wtr. Store/ice/gas/fd (1 mi). **ACTIVITIES:** Mountain climbing; picnicking; fishing; hiking. Boating,ld (1 mi). **MISC.:** Elev 9600 ft; 5 acres; stream; scenic; pets. Tioga Lake. Nature trails (1 mi).

Lee Vining Creek (Mono County Park). 1 mi W of Lee Vining on St Hwy 120. **SEASON:** May-October; 14-day lmt. **FACILITIES:** 17 sites (tr -22), toil, f, drk wtr. **ACTIVITIES:** Fishing. **MISC.:** Elev 7200 ft; 30 acres; pets. Lee Vining Creek.

*__Sawmill__ (Inyo NF). 10 mi SW of Lee Vining on St Hwy 120; 1½ mi NW on Co Hwy 1N04. [Walk-in campground.] **SEASON:** 6/15-10/15; 14-day lmt. **FACILITIES:** 5 tent sites; tbls, toil, no drk wtr. Store/fd (1 mi). **ACTIVITIES:** Mountain climbing; hiking; picnicking; fishing. Boating,rl (1 mi). **MISC.:** Elev 9800 ft; 2 acres; pets. Saddlebag Lake.

LIKELY

Soup Spring Campground (Modoc NF). 8-3/5 mi E on Co Hwy 64; 2-2/5 mi N on Co Hwy 64; 1 mi N on FS 42N0S; 6-2/5 mi E on FS 40N24. **SEASON:** 6/15-10/15. **FACILITIES:** 14 sites (tr -22); tbls, toil, cga, piped drk wtr. **ACTIVITIES:** Picnicking. Horseback riding (1 mi). Fishing (2 mi). **MISC.:** Elev 6800 ft; 2 acres; stream; pets.

See page 7 for KEY TO ABBREVIATIONS.

LITTLEROCK

Little Cedars (Angeles NF). 2-3/5 mi W of Littlerock on Co Hwy 138; 4 mi S on Co Hwy; 8 mi SW on FS 5N04. [High water over crossing, Dec.-April.] SEASON: All yr; 14-day lmt. FACILITIES: 3 sites; tbls, toil, cga, no drk wtr. ACTIVITIES: Hiking; picnicking; fishing. MISC.: Elev 4200 ft; 1 acre; pets; stream.

Little Sycamore (Angeles NF). 2-3/5 mi W of Littlerock on Co Hwy 138; 4 mi S on Co Hwy; 7 mi S on FS 5N04 (Barrel Springs Rd). [High water over crossings, Dec.-April.] SEASON: All yr; 14-day lmt. FACILITIES: 9 sites (tr -16), tbls, toil, cga, no drk wtr. ACTIVITIES: Fishing; picnicking. MISC.: Elev 3900 ft; 2 acres; pets; stream.

LONE PINE

Road's End (Inyo NF). 3½ mi W of Lone Pine on Co Hwy 15S02 (Whitney Portal Rd); 18½ mi SW on Co Hwy 15S01. SEASON: 6/15-10/15; 14-day lmt. FACILITIES: 15 sites (tr -16); flush toil; no tbls/drk wtr. ACTIVITIES: Picnicking; hiking; fishing. Horseback riding/rental (1 mi). MISC.: Elev 9400 ft; 2 acres; pets. Cottonwood Creek. Trailhead into Golden Trout area.

LONG BARN

Hull Creek (Stanislaus NF). 9 mi E of Long Barn on FS 3N01. SEASON: 6/1-10/15; 14-day lmt. FACILITIES: 11 sites; tbls, toil, cga, no drk wtr. ACTIVITIES: Hiking; picnicking; fishing (trout). MISC.: Elev 5600 ft; 5 acres; pets. Hull Creek (dries up in summer). Ranger Stat. (11 mi).

LOOKOUT

Lava Camp (Modoc NF). 15 mi N of Lookout on Co Hwy 91; 9-1/5 mi NW on FS 42N03. SEASON: 5/15-10/30. FACIL: 12 sites (tr -22), tbls, toil, cga, no drk wtr. ACTIVITIES: Rockhounding; picnicking. MISC.: Elev 4400 ft; 9 acres. Pets on leash. Scenic.

LUCERNE

Lakeview (Mendocino NF). 2 mi NW of Lucerne on St Hwy 20; 5 mi NE on Co Hwy FH8; 3 mi S on Co Hwy 15N09. SEASON: 5/1-10/15; 14-day lmt. FACILITIES: 8 sites (tr -16), tbls, toil, cga, drk wtr. ACTIVITIES: Picnicking. MISC.: Elev 3200 ft; 3 acres; pets; scenic. Check at Upper Lake Ranger Station regarding crossing at Rice Fork.

LYTLE CREEK

Big Tree (San Bernardino NF). 1/5 mi N of Lytle Creek on Co Hwy; 7 mi SE on Co Hwy; 10½ mi NW on FS 1N34. [Site located in fire closure; no entry from 7/1 to end of fire season.] SEASON: 11/20-6/30; 7-day lmt. FACILITIES: 3 sites; toil, f, cga, no tbls. ACTIVITIES: Mountain climbing; hiking. MISC.: Elev 5800 ft; 1 acre; pets; scenic. Horseback riding.

*Coldwater (San Bernardino NF). 1/5 mi N of Lytle Creek on Co Hwy 02N55; 1/5 mi NW on Co Hwy 03N06; 4 mi NW on FS 03N06; 1 mi SW on FS 3N06A. [4-wheel drive access only.] SEASON: All yr; 7-day lmt. FACILITIES: 4 tent sites; toil, cga, f, no tbls/drk wtr. ACTIVITIES: Hiking; rockhounding. MISC.: Pets; scenic. Horseback riding.

*Paiute (San Bernardino NF). 2/10 mi N of Lytle Creek on Co Hwy; 1/5 mi NW on Co Hwy; 5-1/5 mi NW on FS 03N06; 2-3/10 mi NW on TRAIL 07W03. [Access by 4-wheel drive or foot only.] SEASON: All yr; 7-day lmt. FACILITIES: 6 tent sites; tbls, toil, cga, f, no drk wtr. ACTIVITIES: Rockhounding; hiking;horseback riding. MISC.: Pets; scenic.

San Sevaine Flat (San Bernardino NF). 1/5 mi N of Lytle Creek on Co Hwy; 7 mi SE on Co Hwy; 7 mi W on FS 1N34. [Site located in fire closure area; no entry from 7/1 to end of fire season.] SEASON: 11/20-6/30; 7-day lmt. FACILITIES: 6 sites; toil, cga, f, piped drk wtr, no tbls. ACTIVITIES: Hiking; horseback riding. MISC.: Elev 5500 ft; 1 acre; pets. Special permit required; obtain at Lytle Creek Ranger Station (free).

Stockton Flats (San Bernardino NF). ½ mi NW of Lytle Creek on Co Hwy; 5-1/5 mi NW on FS 3N06; 7/10 mi W on FS 3N01. SEASON: 14-day lmt. FACILITIES: 15 sites (tr -16), toil, cga. MISC.: Elev 5700 ft. Pets permitted if kept on a leash.

*Stone House Crossing (San Bernardino NF). 1/5 mi N of Lytle Creek on St Hwy 03N06; 3 mi S on Co Hwy 02N55; 7 mi W on FS 02N58;9/10 mi W on TRAIL 06W01. SEASON: All yr; 7-day lmt. FACILITIES: 6 tent sites; toil, cga, f, no tbls/drk wtr. ACTIVITIES: Rockhounding; hiking; horseback riding. MISC.: Elev 4400 ft; 3 acres; scenic; pets. Middle Fork of Lytle Creek. Access to ¼ mi of Cucamonga Wilderness.

MacDOEL

Martins Dairy (Klamath NF). 12 mi S of MacDoel on St Hwy 97; 11 mi NW on FS 46N10; 2 mi NW on FS 46N12; 1/5 mi NE on FS 46N09. SEASON: 6/1-10/15; 14-day lmt. FACILITIES: 7 sites (tr -32), tbls, toil, cga, piped drk wtr. ACTIVITIES: Hunting; picnicking; fishing. MISC.: Elev 6000 ft; 8 acres; pets. Little Shasta Spring.

See page 7 for KEY TO ABBREVIATIONS.

Shafter (Klamath NF). 6–2/5 mi S of Mac-Doel on Co Hwy 8001. SEASON: 5/1–10/15; 14–day lmt. FACILITIES: 10 sites (tr – –32), tbls, toil, cga, piped drk wtr, store, ice, gas. ACTIVITIES: Swimming; boating; picnicking; fishing. MISC.: Elev 4400 ft; 11 acres; pets; stream.

MAD RIVER RIDGE

Oak Grove (Six Rivers NF). 4 mi S of St Hwy 36 via gravel FS 1N03 on Mad River Ridge. SEASON: June–November. FACILITIES: 3 sites; tbls, cga, no drk wtr. ACTIVITIES: Hunting; hiking; picnicking. MISC.: Elev 3800 ft; pets; privacy. Spring water (100 yds).

MADERA

Hidden View Campground (COE; Hensley Lake). Take any of the 4 exits off St Hwy 99 to Yosemite Avenue in Madera. E on Yosemite Avenue; E on Co Rd 400 (River Rd); left on Co Rd 603 (Daulton Rd); right on Co Rd 407 (Hensley Rd) for approx. 1½ mi. SEASON: All yr; 14–day lmt. FACILITIES: 51 sites (tr –40), toil, cga, drk wtr, hot showers, dump. MISC.: Pets permitted if on leash.

MAMMOTH LAKES

Benton Crossing (Mono County Park). 3 mi E on St Hwy 203; 5 mi SE on US 395; 5½ mi NE on a paved, 2-lane county road. SEASON: All year. FACILITIES: Undesignated tent/RV sites; toil, no drk wtr. ACTIVITIES: Hunting; fishing. MISC.: Elev 7000 ft; pets on leash. Owens River and Crowley Lake (2 mi).

McGee Creek (Inyo NF). 3 mi SE of Mammoth Lakes on St Hwy 203; 7½ mi SE on US 395; 1½ mi S on Co Rd 4S06 (McGee Creek Rd). SEASON: 5/1–11/1; 14–day lmt. FACILITIES: 18 sites (tr –22), tbls, toil, cga, no drk wtr. Store/ice/fd/gas/laundry (2 mi). ACTIVITIES: Fishing; picnicking. Horseback rental/riding (2 mi). MISC.: Elev 7600 ft; 3 acres; pets. McGee Creek.

MARICOPA

Caballo (Los Padres NF). 9 mi S of Maricopa on St Hwy 166; 15 mi SE on Co Rd FH95 (Cerro Noroeste Rd); 1 mi N on FS 9N27. SEASON: 5/15–11/15; 14–day lmt. FACILITIES: 5 sites (tr –16), tbls, toil, cga. ACTIVITIES: Picnicking. MISC.: Elev 5800 ft; 2 acres; pets. Mt. Abel (10 mi S).

Campo Alto (Los Padres NF). 9 mi S of Maricopa on St Hwy 166; 27 mi SE on Co Rd FH95 (Cerro Noroeste Rd). SEASON: 5/15–11/15; 14–day lmt. [Open during winter for winter sports––tow rope––when rd is plowed.] FACILITIES: 17 sites (tr –22), tbls, toil, cga, drk wtr available in tank at the lodge. ACTIVITIES: Hiking;

picnicking; mountain climbing. MISC.: Elev 8200 ft; 10 acres; pets. Located at the summit of Cerro Norreste Mountain (Mt. Abel). Operated by Kern County. Nearest supplies in Lake–of–the–Woods, approx. 15 mi.

Marian (Los Padres NF). 9 mi S of Maricopa on St Hwy 166; 15 mi SE on Co Rd P364J; 1½ mi N on FS 9N27. [Not recommended for trailers.] SEASON: 5/15–11/15; 14–day lmt. FACILITIES: 5 sites (tr –16), tbls, toil, cga, no drk wtr. ACTIVITIES: Mountain climbing nearby; hiking; picnicking. MISC.: Elev 6600 ft; 4 acres; pets. 11½ mi N of Mt. Abel.

*Sheep Camp (Los Padres NF). 9 mi S of Maricopa on St Hwy 166; 26½ mi SE on Co Hwy FH95; 2½ mi SE on TRAIL 21W03. [Many campers hike to this camp from Mt. Abel and Mt. Pinos. From Mt. Pinos: take the trail at the Condor Observation Point (21W03) for 2 mi. From Mt. Abel: take the Mt. Abel-Mt. Pinos Trail (21W03) for 3 mi. From Lockwood Valley: take the trail which runs past the Three Falls Boy Scout Camp approx. 7 mi.] SEASON: 5/15–11/15; 14–day lmt. FACILITIES: 4 tent sites; cga, no drk wtr, no tbls, no toil. ACTIVITIES: Hiking; horseback riding. MISC.: Elev 8400 ft; 1 acre; pets; scenic. Located under a stand of Jeffrey pines. Hikers should be in good condition before taking this hike because of the high elevation and the steep pitches in the trail.

Toad Springs (Los Padres NF). 9 mi S of Maricopa on St Hwy 166; 15 mi SE on Co Hwy P364J; ½ mi SW on FS 9N09. SEASON: 5/1–11/15; 14–day lmt. 7 sites (tr –16), tbls, toil, cga, f, no drk wtr. ACTIVITIES: Picnicking. MISC.: Elev 5700 ft; 2 acres; pets.

Valle Vista (Los Padres NF). 9 mi S of Maricopa on St Hwy 166; 12 mi S on Co Rd FH95. [Suitable for small trailers.] SEASON: all yr; 14–day lmt. FACILITIES: 10 sites (tr –32), tbls, toil, cga, no drk wtr. ACTIVITIES: Picnicking. MISC.: Elev 4800 ft; 4 acres; pets. Operated by Kern County.

MARIPOSA

Crows Foot (Sierra NF). 12¼ mi E of Mariposa on St Hwy 49 (Bootjack Rd); 5¼ mi NE on FS 5S092; 3 mi W on FS 4S041. SEASON: 6/15–10/1; 14–day lmt. FACILITIES: 8 sites; toil. MISC.: Elev 6200 ft. Pets on leash.

Signal (Sierra NF). 17 mi E of Mariposa on Co Hwy 49; 9–4/5 mi NW on Co Hwy 5S092. SEASON: 5/15–11/15; 14–day lmt. FACILITIES: 20 sites; toil, cga, f, piped drk wtr, no tbls. ACTIVITIES: Picnicking. MISC.: Elev 6400 ft; 3 acres; pets; scenic. Trailers not recommended.

See page 7 for KEY TO ABBREVIATIONS.

Summit Camp (Sierra NF). 12-3/10 mi E of Mariposa on St Hwy 49; 6-4/5 mi NE on Co Hwy 5S092. SEASON: 6/15-10/15; 14-day lmt. FACILITIES: 12 sites (tr -22), tbls, toil, cga, piped drk wtr. ACTIVITIES: Picnicking. MISC.: Elev 5800 ft; 2 acres; pets on leash.

MARYSVILLE

Englebright (COE; Eastman Lake). About 15 mi E of Marysville on St Hwy 20 to the Englebright Dam turnoff at Mooney Flat Rd. The lake is about 5 mi N on this rd. Accessible BY BOAT. SEASON: All yr. FACILITIES: 85 sites; toil, cga, drk wtr. Marina on lake.

McARTHUR

Wiley Ranch (Lassen NF). 5 mi NE of McArthur on St Hwy 299; 15 mi NW on FS 40N01 (Day Rd). SEASON: 5/15-10/15; 14-day lmt. FACILITIES: 12 sites (tr -22), tbls, toil, cga, piped drk wtr. ACTIVITIES: Picnicking. MISC.: Elev 3800 ft; 4 acres; pets on leash.

Willow Springs (Lassen NF). 2 mi E of McArthur on US 299; 15 mi SE on Co Rd 111 (Little Valley Rd); 3 mi SE on FS 35N63. SEASON: 5/15-10/15; 14-day lmt. FACILITIES: 5 sites (tr -22). Tbls, cga, nondrinkable spring Hwy 89, 4 mi S of Lake McCloud.] SEASON: 5/1-11/1; 14-day lmt. FACILITIES: 16 sites (tr -16); tbls, toil, cga, f, piped drk wtr. ACTIVITIES: Picnicking; swimming; fishing. Boating,d (5 mi). MISC.: Elev 2200 ft; 30 acres; pets. Lake McCloud (4½ mi). Access is narrow dirt road and not used by lake users; road not advised for large trailers.

Algoma (Shasta-Trinity NF). 13 mi E on St Hwy 89; 1/2 mi S on FS 39N06. SEASON: 5/1-10/15; 14-day lmt. FACILITIES: 8 sites; toil, no drk wtr. Tables. MISC.: Pets. Area East of Mt. Shasta. (Tr -32).

Cattle Camp (Shasta-Trinity NF). 9½ mi E on St Hwy 89; ½ mi S on FS 40N44. SEASON: 5/1-11/1; 14-day lmt. FACILITIES: 10 sites (tr -32); well drk wtr, f; no tbls/toil. ACTIVITIES: Picnicking; fishing. Swimming (1 mi). MISC.: Elev 3700 ft; 7 acres; river; pets. Area East of Mt. Shasta.

Harris Spring (Shasta-Trinity NF). 16-1/5 mi E of McCloud on St Hwy 89; 16 mi N on FS 43N15. SEASON: 6/1-10/15. FACILITIES: 11 sites (tr -22), tbls, toil, cga, f, piped drk wtr. ACTIVITIES: Picnicking. MISC.: Elev 4800 ft; 3 acres; pets. McCloud River. Approx. 10 mi S of proposed Medicine Lake Highlands Recreation Area. E of Mt. Shasta.

MERRIMAC

Rogers Cow Camp (Plumas NF). Off Oroville-Bucks Lake Rd, ½ mi W of Merrimac. SEASON: 5/15-10/15. FACILITIES: 5 sites (tr -16), tbls, toil, cga, no drk wtr. Store/gas (5 mi). ACTIVITIES: Berry-picking; picnicking. Fishing (5 mi). MISC.: Elev 4100 ft; 1 acre; pets; stream.

MILFORD

Conklin Park (Plumas NF). 5½ mi SE of Milford on Co Hwy 336; 6 mi S on FS 26N70; 1/5 mi NE on FS 26N91, on Willow Creek. SEASON: 5/1-10/15; 14-day lmt. FACILITIES: 9 sites (tr -22), tbls, toil, cga, no drk wtr. ACTIVITIES: Picnicking; hiking. Fishing and big game hunting (1 mi). MISC.: Elev 5900 ft; 2 acres; pets allowed if kept on leash.

Laufman (Plumas NF). 2½ mi SE of Milford on Co Hwy 326 from Milford. SEASON: 5/1-10/15; 14-day lmt. FACILITIES: 8 sites (tr -22), tbls, toil, cga, piped drk wtr. Store/ice/gas/laundry (2 mi). ACTIVITIES: Hiking; picnicking. Big and small game hunting (1 mi). Fishing (5 mi). MISC.: Elev 5100 ft; 4 acres; pets. East McDermott Creek.

MILL CREEK

Mill Creek (Lassen NF). ½ mi E of Mill Creek on St Hwy 172. SEASON: 5/25-10/1; 14-day lmt. FACILITIES: 12 sites (tr -22), tbls, toil, cga, piped drk wtr. Store/ice/fd/gas (1 mi). ACTIVITIES: Fishing; picnicking. MISC.: Elev 4700 ft; 3 acres; pets. Horseback riding/rental. Mill Creek.

MINERAL KING

Atwell Mill (Sequoia NP). 6 mi W of Mineral King on St Hwy 276 (Mineral King Rd). SEASON: 5/25-9/25; 14-day lmt. FACILITIES: 23 sites, no trailers; toil, no drk wtr. ACTIVITIES: Fishing. MISC.: Elev 6645 ft; pets on leash. Atwell Creek and East Fork of Kaweah River (1 mi).

MONO HOT SPRINGS

*Boulder Creek (Sierra NF). 1 mi SW of Mono Hot Springs on FS 4S01; 5-1/5 mi SE on FS 7S01; 2½ mi SE on Florence Lake BY BOAT. SEASON: 6/1-9/15; 14-day lmt. FACILITIES: 5 tent sites; toil. No drk wtr. ACTIVITIES: Fishing; swimming; boating (rl, 1 mi). MISC.: Elev 7600 ft; pets. San Joaquin River. Florence Lake Inlet.

Florence Lake (Sierra NF). 1-1/10 mi SW of Mono Hot Springs on FS 4S01; 5-1/5 mi SE on FS 7S01. SEASON: 6/1-9/15; 14-day lmt. FACILITIES: 14 sites, no trailers; tbls, toil, cga, no drk wtr.

Store/gas (1 mi). **ACTIVITIES:** Swimming; hiking; picnicking; fishing; boating,d (rl, 1 mi). Horseback riding/rental (1 mi). **MISC.:** Elev 7400 ft; 2 acres; pets. Trailhead into John Muir Wilderness. Florence Lake. Scenic.

Jackass Meadow (Sierra NF). 1-1/10 mi SW of Mono Hot Springs on FS 4S01; 5-3/10 mi SE on FS 7S01. **SEASON:** 6/1-10/15; 14-day lmt. **FACILITIES:** 15 sites (tr -16), tbls, toil, cga, well drk wtr. Gas (1 mi). **ACTIVITIES:** Swimming; picnicking; fishing; boating,d (rl, 1 mi). Horseback riding/rental (1 mi). **MISC.:** Elev 7200 ft;3 acres;pets;scenic. San Joaquin River and Florence Lake (1 mi).

Mond Creek (Sierra NF). 3-1/5 mi N of Mono Hot Springs on FS 4S01. **SEASON:** 6/1-10/15; 14-day lmt. **FACILITIES:** 18 sites (tr -16), tbls, toil, cga, no drk wtr. Store/ice/fd/gas/showers (2 mi). **ACTIVITIES:** Swimming; picnicking; fishing. Boating,rl (2 mi). Horseback riding/rental (2 mi). **MISC.:** Elev 7400 ft; 3 acres; pets; scenic; stream. Visitor center (5 mi).

Mono Diversion (Sierra NF). 3-1/5 mi N of Mono Hot Springs on FS 4S01. **SEASON:** 6/1-9/15; 14-day lmt. **FACILITIES:** 18 sites (tr -16), toil, cga, no drk wtr. Store (2 mi). **ACTIVITIES:** Fishing; swimming; boating (rl, 2 mi). **MISC.:** Elev 7400 ft; pets. Mono Creek and Lake Edison (2 mi).

Portal Forebay (Sierra NF). 4 mi SW of Mono Hot Springs on FS 4S01. **SEASON:** 6/1-10/15; 14-day lmt. **FACILITIES:** 9 sites (tr -16), tbls, toil, cga, no drk wtr. Store/ice/fd/gas/showers (5 mi). **ACTIVITIES:** Swimming; picnicking; fishing. Horseback riding (5 mi). **MISC.:** Elev 7200 ft; 3 acres; pets; scenic; lake. Visitor center (2 mi).

Ward Lake (Sierra NF). 1½ mi SW of Mono Hot Springs on FS 4S01; 3-1/5 mi SE on FS 7S01. **SEASON:** 6/1-10/15; 14-day lmt. **FACILITIES:** 17 sites (tr -16), tbls, toil, cga, no drk wtr. Store (4 mi). Ice/fd/gas (5 mi). **ACTIVITIES:** Swimming; boating (rl, 4 mi); picnicking; fishing. Horseback rental/riding (4 mi). **MISC.:** Elev 7300 ft; 3 acres; scenic; pets; lake. Visitor center (5 mi).

MONO LAKE

Mill Creek (Municipal Park). 2 mi N of Mono Lake on US 395; 2 mi W on Lundy Lake Rd. **SEASON:** 5/15-10/15. **FACILITIES:** 30 sites (tr -20), tbls, toil, cga, f. **ACTIVITIES:** Picnicking; fishing. **MISC.:** Elev 8000 ft; 40 acres; pets on leash. Mill Creek and Lunday Lake (2 mi).

MONTGOMERY CITY

Chirpchatter (Shasta-Trinity NF). 2 mi

SW of Montgomery City on US 299 W; 2½ mi SW on Co Hwy 6L005; 23 mi NW on FS N8G01. [Located next to Squaw Creek, 1 mi S of Squaw Creek Guard Station on Fender Ferry Rd.] **SEASON:** 5/15-10/31; 21-day lmt. **FACILITIES:** 4 sites, no trailers; tbls, toil, cga, no drk wtr. **ACTIVITIES:** Picnicking. Fishing (1 mi). **MISC.:** Elev 1300 ft; 2 acres; pets; creek. Unit of the Whiskeytown-Shasta-Trinity NRA.

Madrone (Shasta-Trinity NF). 2 mi SW of Montgomery City on US 299; 2½ mi W on Co Hwy 6L005 (Fenders Ferry Rd); 17 mi NW on FS N8G01. **SEASON:** 5/15-10/31; 21-day lmt. **FACILITIES:** 13 sites (tr -16), tbls, toil, cga, no drk wtr. **ACTIVITIES:** Fishing; picnicking. **MISC.:** Elev 1200 ft; 6 acres; pets. On Squaw Creek. Unit of the Whiskeytown-Shasta-Trinity Natl Recreation Area.

MOUNT BALDY

*Kelly's Camp (Angeles NF). 2 mi NE of Mt. Baldy on Co Hwy 3N01 (Mills-Mt. Baldy Rd); 6 mi SE on TRAIL 7W07. **SEASON:** 4/1-10/30. **FACILITIES:** 5 tent sites; cga, no tbls. **ACTIVITIES:** Hiking; mountain climbing. **MISC.:** Elev 8900 ft; 3 acres; pets. On the boundary of Cucamonga Wilderness Area.

MOUNT LAGUNA

Laguna (Cleveland NF). 2-4/5 mi NW of Mt. Laguna on Co Rd S-1; 1/10 mi S on Co Rd J31B. [14 mi N of Laguna Jct on Sunrise Hwy (S-1/I-8).] **SEASON:** 4/15-11/1; 14-day lmt. **FACILITIES:** 105 sites (tr -22), tbls, toil, cga, f, piped drk wtr. **ACTIVITIES:** Horseback riding; picnicking. Swimming (4 mi). **MISC.:** Elev 5600 ft; 5 acres; pets. Reached by 1 mi of oiled rd from hwy.

MOUNT SHASTA

Gumboot (Shasta-Trinity NF). 3½ mi SE of Mounta Shasta on Co Hwy 2M002; 11-1/10 mi SW on FS 40N30; 3/5 mi S on FS 40N37. **SEASON:** 6/1-10/30; 14-day lmt. **FACILITIES:** 4 sites (tr -16), tbls, toil, piped spring drk wtr. **ACTIVITIES:** Swimming; picnicking; fishing. **MISC.:** Elev 6200 ft; 10 acres; pets; lake. Campfire permit required.

Panther Meadow (Shasta-Trinity NF). 13-2/5 mi NE of Mt. Shasta on Co Hwy FH98. **SEASON:** 6/15-9/30; 7-day lmt. **FACILITIES:** 4 sites (tr -16), tbls, toil, cga, no drk wtr. **ACTIVITIES:** Mountain climbing; picnicking; hiking. **MISC.:** Elev 7400 ft; 5 acres; pets; scenic; stream. Mt. Shasta Ski Bowl (2 mi N).

MOUNTAIN CENTER

Thomas Mountain (San Bernardino NF). 6 mi SE of Mountain Center on St Hwy 74; 5 mi W on FS 6S13 (Little Thomas

Mountain Rd); 3 mi SE on FS 5S16. SEA-SON: 4/15-11/15; 7-day lmt. FACILITIES: 6 sites, no trailers; tbls, toil, cga, no drk wtr. Water is available at Tool Box Spring. ACTIVITIES: Hiking; picnicking. MISC.: Elev 6800 ft; 5 acres; pets.

Tool Box Springs (San Bernardino NF). 11 mi SE of Mountain Center on St Hwy 74; 7 mi NW on FS 5S15. SEASON: 4/15-11/15; 7-day lmt. FACILITIES: 6 sites, no trailers; tbls, toil, cga, no drk wtr. Water available at Tool Box Spring. ACTIVITIES: Picnicking. MISC.: Elev 6500 ft; 5 acres; pets on leash.

MURRIETTA

Fishermans Camp (Cleveland NF). 12 mi W of Murrietta on Co Rd 7S01; 4 mi NW on FS 6S082; 2 mi W on FS 7S07. SEASON: All yr; 14-day lmt. FACILITIES: 5 sites, no trailers; tbls, toil, cga, no drk wtr. ACTIVITIES: Picnicking. Horseback riding (1 mi). MISC.: Elev 1200 ft; 12 acres; pets; stream.

NEVADA CITY

Bowman (Tahoe NF). 23-1/5 mi E of Nevada City on St Hwy 20; 16-1/5 mi N on FS 18N18. SEASON: 6/15-10/15; 14-day lmt. FACILITIES: 7 sites (tr -22), tbls, toil, cga, no drk wtr. ACTIVITIES: Swimming; boating,d; waterskiing; picnicking; fishing. MISC.: Elev 5600 ft; 3 acres; pets. Bowman Lake.

Canyon Creek (Tahoe NF). 23-1/5 mi E of Nevada City on St Hwy 20; 17-1/5 mi N on FS 18N18; 2-3/10 mi SE on FS 18N13. SEASON: 6/15-10/15; 14-day lmt. FACILITIES: 20 sites (tr -22); tbls, toil, cga, piped drk wtr. ACTIVITIES: Picnicking; fishing. Swimming/boating,l (1 mi). MISC.: Elev 6000 ft; 5 acres; stream; pets.

Jackson Creek (Tahoe NF). 23-1/5 mi E of Nevada City on St Hwy 20; 17-1/5 mi N on FS 18N18. [On Jackson Creek, 1 mi above Bowman Lake.] SEASON: 6/15-10/15; 14-day lmt. FACILITIES: 14 sites (tr -22), tbls, toil, cga, no drk wtr. ACTIVITIES: Picnicking. Swimming/water-skiing/boating,d/fishing (1 mi). MISC.: Elev 5600 ft; 7 acres; pets; creek.

*South Yuba Trail Camp (BLM). 10 mi N of Nevada City on North Bloomfield Rd; BY FOOT. SEASON: All yr; 14-day lmt. FACILITIES: 17 tent sites; toil, no drk wtr. ACTIVITIES: Hiking; hunting; fishing. MISC.: Elev 2500 ft; small pets on leash. 6-mi riding/hiking trail. South Yuba River.

NEW CUYAMA

Aliso (Los Padres NF). 3 mi W of New Cuyama on St Hwy 166; 4 mi S on Co Rd AL1S0 (Alison Canyon Rd); 1 mi S on FS 11N02. SEASON: All yr; 14-day lmt. FACILITIES: 11 sites (tr -22), tbls, toil, cga, no drk wtr. Well water should be boiled before drinking. ACTIVITIES: Horseback riding; picnicking. MISC.: Elev 3200 ft; 3 acres; pets. Operated by county.

Ballinger (Los Padres NF). 10 mi E of New Cuyama on St Hwy 166; 4 mi S on St Hwy 33; 3 mi E on FS 9N100 (Ballinger Canyon Rd). [Mainly used by motorcycles; but trailers are okay.] SEASON: All yr; 14-day lmt. FACILITIES: 20 sites (tr -32), tbls, toil, cga, no drk wtr. MISC.: Elev 3000 ft; 8 acres; pets.

Bates Canyon (Los Padres NF). 10 mi W of New Cuyama on St Hwy 166; 8 mi S on FS 11N01. SEASON: All year; 14-day lmt. FACILITIES: 6 sites (tr -16), tbls, toil, cga, piped spring wtr. MISC.: Elev 2900 ft; 1 acre; pets.

*Bear Trap (Los Padres NF). 5 mi S on 23W02 from Reyes Creek Campground, which is located 10 mi E of New Cuyama on St Hwy 166; 20 mi S on St Hwy 33; 3½ mi E on Co Rd 9N03; 2 mi S on FS 7N11. FACILITIES: 3 tent sites; toil, cga, no drk wtr. ACTIVITIES: Hiking; horseback riding. MISC.: Creek; scenic. Nearest supplies at Camp Scheideck adjacent to Reyes Creek Campground.

Dome Springs (Los Padres NF). 10 mi E of New Cuyama on St Hwy 166; 20 mi S on St Hwy 33; 6 mi E on Co Hwy 9N03; 3 mi NE on FS 9N03C. [3 mi of dirt rd N of Lockwood/Ozena Rd.] SEASON: All yr; 14-day lmt. FACILITIES: 4 sites, no trailers; toil, cga, no drk wtr. ACTIVITIES: Hiking. Horseback riding (1 mi). MISC.: Elev 4800 ft; 1 acre; pets. Tables; picnicking.

*Hog Pen Springs (Los Padres NF). 3 mi W of New Cuyama on St Hwy 166; 4 mi S on Co Rd AL1S0 (Aliso Canyon Rd); 1 mi S on FS 11N02; 2 mi S on TRAIL 27W01. SEASON: 5/1-11/30; 14-day lmt. FACILITIES: 7 tent sites; tbls, toil, cga, piped drk wtr. ACTIVITIES: Hiking; picnicking. Horseback riding (1 mi). MISC.: Elev 3600 ft; 1 acre; pets. BY FOOT OR JEEP.

*Mine Camp (Los Padres NF). 10 mi E of New Cuyama on St Hwy 166; 20-3/5 mi S on St Hwy 33; ¼ mi W on FS 7N04A; 5½ mi E on TRAIL 24W04. SEASON: All yr; 14-day lmt. FACILITIES: 3 tent sites; cga, nondrinkable spring water, no tbls/toil. ACTIVITIES: Hiking; horseback riding. MISC.: Elev 3600 ft; 1 acre; pets.

Miranda Pine (Los Padres NF). 25-3/10 mi NW of New Cuyama on St Hwy 166; 7½ mi SE on FS 32S13. SEASON: All yr; 14-day lmt. FACILITIES: 3 sites (tr -16), tbls, toil, cga, piped drk wtr. ACTIVITIES: Picnicking. MISC.: Elev 4000 ft; 1 acre; pets; scenic.

Nettle Spring (Los Padres NF). 10 mi E of New Cuyama on St Hwy 166; 16 mi S on St Hwy 33; 8 mi NE on FS 8N06. [8 mi up dirt rd in Apache Canyon.] SEASON: All yr; 14-day lmt. FACILITIES: 9 sites (tr -22), tbls, toil, cga, piped drk wtr. ACTIVITIES: Picnicking; hiking. MISC.: Elev 4400 ft; 4 acres; pets. Not recommended for trailers.

*__Painted Rock__ (Los Padres NF). Take Co Hwy 11N02 4 mi S; TRAIL 26W01 for 1 mi S; TRAIL 27W04, 5 mi SW. SEASON: 5/1-11/1; 14-day lmt. FACILITIES: 3 tent sites; tbls, toil, cga. ACTIVITIES: Hiking; horseback riding; picnicking. MISC.: Elev 4600 ft; 1 acre; pets.

Tinta Camp (Los Padres NF). 10 mi E of New Cuyama on St Hwy 166; 19 mi S on St Hwy 33; 2 mi NW on FS 7N04; 2 mi NW on FS 7N04J. [Not suitable for trailers.] SEASON: 4/1-11/30; 14-day lmt. FACILITIES: 3 sites (tr -22), tbls, toil, cga, no drk wtr. ACTIVITIES: Picnicking. Horseback riding (1 mi). MISC.: Elev 3600 ft; 1 acre; pets;stream.

*__Upper Rancho Nuevo__ (Los Padres NF). 10 mi E of New Cuyama on St Hwy 166; 16-7/10 mi S on St Hwy 33; 1½ mi W on FS 7N04A; 5 mi W on TRAIL 24W03. SEASON: 5/1-11/30; 14-day lmt. FACILITIES: 4 tent sites; cga, no toil/drk/drk wtr. ACTIVITIES: Hiking; horseback riding. MISC.: Elev 4500 ft; 1 acre; pets; stream. This camp is surrounded by pinion pines, yucca and chaparral in a beautiful secluded canyon.

Upper Tinta (Los Padres NF). 10 mi E of New Cuyama on St Hwy 166; 13-1/5 mi S on St Hwy 33; 4 mi W on FS 8N07. SEASON: 5/1-11/30; 14-day lmt. FACILITIES: 3 sites, no trailers; cga, no tbls/toil/drk wtr. ACTIVITIES: Hiking. Horseback riding (1 mi). MISC.: Elev 4500 ft; 1 acre; pets.

*__Yellowjacket__ (Los Padres NF). 10 mi E of New Cuyama on St Hwy 166; 13-3/5 mi S on St Hwy 33; 5¼ mi NE on FS 8N06; 4 mi S on TRAIL 23W44. SEASON: All yr; 14-day lmt. FACILITIES: 1 tent site; tbls, cga, undrinkable water, no toil. ACTIVITIES: Hiking; horseback riding; picnicking. MISC.: Elev 4200 ft; 1 acre; pets.

NEW PINE CREEK

Cave Lake (Modoc NF). 6-1/5 mi SE on FS 48N01. SEASON: 7/1-10/15. FACILITIES: 6 sites (tr -16); tbls, toil, cga, piped drk wtr. ACTIVITIES: Picnicking; boating; swimming; fishing. MISC.: Elev 6600 ft; 8 acres; lake; pets.

NEW PINE CREEK

Lily Lake (Modoc NF). 6-1/10 mi SE of New Pine Creek on FS 48N01. SEASON: 7/1-10/15. FACILITIES: 6 sites, no trailers; tbls, toil, cga, no drk wtr. ACTIVITIES: Swimming; picnicking; fishing; boating; rockhounding. MISC.: Elev 6600 ft; 4 acres; pets. Lily Lake.

NORTH FORK

Bowler (Sierra NF). 42 mi N of North Fork on FS 5S05; 55 mi NE on FS 4S81. SEASON: 6/15-10/15; 14-day lmt. FACILITIES: 30 sites, no trailers; tbls, toil, cga, no drk wtr. Store/fd/gas (4 mi). ACTIVITIES: Hiking; picnicking. Horseback riding/rental (4 mi). MISC.: Elev 7000 ft; 5 acres; pets. Reservations are required.

*__China Bar__ (Sierra NF). 4-3/5 mi SE of North Fork on Co Hwy 225; 33-1/5 mi NE on FS 4S81; 1½ mi S on FS 6S25; 3½ mi NE, BY BOAT. SEASON: 6/15-9/15; 14-day lmt. FACILITIES: 6 tent sites; tbls, toil, cga, no drk wtr. Store/ice/fd/gas (5 mi). ACTIVITIES: Swimming; picnicking; fishing; boating (r, 3 mi; l, 4 mi). Horseback riding/rental (5 mi). MISC.: Elev 3400 ft; 3 acres; pets. Boat camp on San Joaquin River inlet to Mammoth Pool Reservoir.

Clover Meadow (Sierra NF). 4-3/5 mi SE of North Fork on Co Hwy 225; 50-3/10 mi NE on FS 4S81; 1-2/5 mi N on FS 5S30; 2 mi NE on FS 5S071. SEASON: 6/15-10/15; 14-day lmt. FACILITIES: 7 sites (tr -16), tbls, toil, piped drk wtr. Fd/gas (4 mi). ACTIVITIES: Picnicking. Horseback riding/rental (4 mi). MISC.: Elev 7000 ft; 4 acres; pets.

Fish Creek (Sierra NF). 4-3/5 mi SE of North Fork on Co Hwy 225; 18-7/10 mi NE on FS 4S81. SEASON: 4/20-11/15; 14-day lmt. FACILITIES: 7 sites, no trailers; tbls, toil, no drk wtr. ACTIVITIES: Hiking; picnicking; fishing. MISC.: Elev 4600 ft; 2 acres; pets. Fish Creek.

Gaggs Camp (Sierra NF). 15-4/5 mi N of North Fork on FS 5S07. SEASON: 6/1-10/30. FACILITIES: 9 sites (tr -16), tbls, toil, no drk wtr. Store/fd/gas (3 mi). ACTIVITIES: Picnicking; swimming. Fishing (4 mi). MISC.: Elev 5800 ft; 2 acres; pets. Sand Creek.

Granite Creek (Sierra NF). 4-3/5 mi SE of North Fork on Co Hwy 225; 50-3/10 mi NE on FS 4S81; 1-2/5 mi N on FS 5S30; 3-2/5 mi NE on FS 5S071. SEASON: 6/15-10/15; 14-day lmt. FACILITIES: 18 sites, no trailers; tbls, toil, cga, no drk wtr. Fd/gas (5 mi). ACTIVITIES: Hiking; picnicking; fishing. Horseback riding/rental (5 mi). MISC.: Elev 6900 ft; 5 acres; pets. Granite Creek.

See page 7 for KEY TO ABBREVIATIONS.

Lower Chiquito (Sierra NF). 4-3/5 mi SE of Co Hwy 225; 35-4/5 mi NE on FS 4S81; 3 mi N on FS 6S71; 1 mi NE on FS 6S01. SEASON: 5/1-10/15; 14-day lmt. FACILITIES: 7 sites (tr -22), tbls, toil, cga, no drk wtr. ACTIVITIES: Fishing; picnicking. MISC.: Elev 4900 ft; 2 acres; pets on leash. Chiquito Creek.

Placer (Sierra NF). 4-3/5 mi SE of North Fork on Co Hwy 225; 33-1/5 mi NE on FS 4S81; 1-2/5 mi S on FS 6S25; 1-4/5 mi W on FS 6S61Y. SEASON: 4/20-11/15; 14-day lmt. FACILITIES: 7 sites, no trailers; tbls, toil, piped drk wtr. Store/fd/ice/gas (4 mi). ACTIVITIES: Picnicking. Swimming/fishing/boating,rl (5 mi). MISC.: Elev 4100 ft; 30 acres; pets. Mammoth Pool Reservoir (5 mi).

Soda Springs (Sierra NF). 4-3/5 mi SE of North Fork on Co Hwy 225; 30-1/5 mi NE on FS 4S81. SEASON: 4/20-11/15; 14-day lmt. FACILITIES: 18 sites (tr -22), tbls, toil, cga, no drk wtr. ACTIVITIES: Fishing; picnicking. MISC.: Elev 4400 ft; 4 acres; pets. West Fork of Chiquito Creek.

Sweet Water (Sierra NF). 10 mi SE of North Fork on Co Hwy 04S8; 33-1/5 mi NE on FS FH100; 2 mi S on FS 6S25. SEASON: 4/20-11/15; 14-day lmt. FACILITIES: 10 sites (tr -16), tbls, toil, cga, no drk wtr. Store/ice/fd/gas (3 mi). ACTIVITIES: Fishing; picnicking. Swimming/boating,rld/waterskiing (4 mi). MISC.: Elev 3800 ft; 4 acres; stream; pets. Mammoth Pool Reservoir (2 mi).

Upper Chiquito (Sierra NF). ½ mi E of North Fork on Co Hwy 225; 9 mi NE on Co Hwy 274; 11-7/10 mi NE on FS 6S05; 12-2/5 mi NE on FS 5S07. SEASON: 6/15-10/15; 14-day lmt. FACILITIES: 20 sites, toil, cga, no drk wtr. ACTIVITIES: Fishing; picnicking. MISC.: Elev 6800 ft; 6 acres; pets on leash. Chiquito Creek.

OAKHURST

Fresno Dome (Sierra NF). 1/5 mi N of Oakhurst on Co Hwy 426; 4 mi N on St Hwy 41; 11 mi NE on FS 6S10; 1-3/5 mi N on FS 6S08. SEASON: 5/15-9/30; 14-day lmt. FACILITIES: 12 sites (tr -16), tbls, toil, cga, no drk wtr. ACTIVITIES: Fishing; picnicking. Horseback riding (1 mi). MISC.: Elev 6400 ft; 3 acres; pets on leash. Big Creek.

Greys Mountain (Sierra NF). 1/5 mi N of Oakhurst on Co Hwy 426; 4 mi N on St Hwy 41; 7-4/5 mi NE on FS 6S10; 2-3/10 mi N on FS 4S04. SEASON: 5/21-9/30, 14-day lmt. FACILITIES: 12 sites (tr -16), tbls, toil, cga, no drk wtr. ACTIVITIES: Fishing; picnicking. Swimming/horseback riding (1 mi). MISC.: Elev 5200 ft; 3 acres; pets. Willow Creek.

Kelty Meadow (Sierra NF). 1/5 mi N of Oakhurst on Co Hwy 426; 4 mi N on St Hwy 41; 10-7/10 mi NE on FS 6S10; 1/5 mi W on FS 6S10C. SEASON: 5/21-9/30; 14-day lmt. FACILITIES: 14 sites (tr --16), tbls, toil, cga, no drk wtr. ACTIVITIES: Horseback riding; picnicking; fishing. MISC.: Elev 5800 ft; 4 acres; pets. Big Creek. Equestrian camp.

Nelder Grove (Sierra NF). 1/5 mi N of Oakhurst on Co Hwy 426; 4 mi N on St Hwy 41; 8-1/10 mi NE on FS 6S10; 10-3/10 mi NW on FS 4S04. [Steep,narrow entrance rd.] SEASON: 5/21-9/30; 14-day lmt. FACILITIES: 10 sites (tr -16), tbls, toil, cga, no drk wtr. ACTIVITIES: Hiking; picnicking; fishing. MISC.: Elev 5300 ft; 3 acres; pets; scenic; nature trails. California Creek. Located within Nelder Grove of Giant Sequoias.

Soquel (Sierra NF). 1/5 mi N of Oakhurst on Co Hwy 426; 4 mi N on St Hwy 41; 7-4/5 mi NE on FS 6S10; 1-1/5 mi S on FS 4S04. SEASON: 5/21-9/30; 14-day lmt. FACILITIES: 14 sites (tr -16), tbls, toil, cga, no drk wtr. ACTIVITIES: Fishing; picnicking. Horseback riding/swimming (1 mi). MISC.: Elev 5400 ft; 5 acres; pets. Willow Creek.

Texas Flat (Sierra NF). 1/5 mi N of Oakhurst on Co Hwy 426; 4 mi N on St Hwy 41; 9-1/5 mi NE on FS 6S10; 1½ mi E on FS 6S38. SEASON: 5/21-9/30; 14-day lmt. FACILITIES: 4 sites (tr -16); tbls, toil, cga, no drk wtr. ACTIVITIES: Picnicking; fishing; horseback riding. MISC.: Elev 5500 ft; 5 acres; pets; stream. Approved for horses.

O'BRIEN

Lower Salt Creek (Shasta-Trinity NF). 2 mi NW of O'Brien on I-5; 1/5 mi N on Co Hwy 7H005 (Gilman Rd); 1 mi W on Co Hwy 7H001. SEASON: All yr; 14-day lmt. FACILITIES: 12 sites; no trailers. Hand-pumped well drk wtr, tbls, toil, cga, dump. Store/ice/fd/gas (1 mi). ACTIVITIES: Swimming; picnicking; fishing; waterskiing; boating,ld (r, 1 mi). MISC.: Elev 1100 ft; 3 acres; pets; At Shasta Lake within the Shasta-Trinity National Recreation Area.

Wintoon (Shasta-Trinity NF). 1½ mi E of O'Brien on Co Hwy 6H200. SEASON: All year; 14-day lmt. FACILITIES: 11 sites; no trailers. Piped drk wtr, tbls, toil, cga. Dump/store/ice/fd/gas (1 mi). ACTIVITIES: Swimming; waterskiing; picnicking; fishing; boating,d (rl, 1 mi). MISC.: Elev 1100 ft; 4 acres; pets; geological. Lifeguard (4 mi). Located on McCloud Arm of Shasta Lake. Unit of the Whiskeytown-Shasta-Trinity NRA.

CALIFORNIA

OJAI

Bear Creek (Los Padres NF). 1 mi W of Ojai on St Hwy 150; 14-4/5 mi NW on St Hwy 33; 9½ mi E on FS 7N03 (Sespe River Rd). SEASON: 4/1-11/30; 14-day lmt. FACILITIES: 12 sites; no trailers. No drk wtr, tbls, toil, cga. ACTIVITIES: Picnicking; fishing. Horseback riding (1 mi). MISC.: Elev 2800 ft; 5 acres; pets; scenic. Bear Creek; Sespe Creek.

Beaver Camp (Los Padres NF). 1 mi W of Ojai on St Hwy 150; 15-7/10 mi NW on St Hwy 33; ½ mi E on FS 22W04. SEASON: All yr; 14-day lmt. FACILITIES: 7 sites (tr -16), tbls, toil, cga, no drk wtr. ACTIVITIES: Swimming; picnicking; fishing. MISC.: Elev 3000 ft; 3 acres; pets; scenic. Sespe Creek.

Cherry Creek (Los Padres NF). 1 mi W of Ojai on St Hwy 150; 23½ mi NW on St Hwy 33; 2-4/5 mi S on FS 6N01. SEASON: All yr (closed during fire season, 7/1-10/31), 14-day lmt. FACILITIES: 4 sites; no trailers. Cga. No tbls/toil/drk wtr. ACTIVITIES: Swimming; fishing. MISC.: Elev 4500 ft;2 acres;pets;stream.

*****Chorro Springs Trail Camp** (Los Padres NF). 1 mi W of St Hwy 150; 23-4/5 mi NW on St Hwy 33;4 mi N on TRAIL 23W05. SEASON: All yr; 14-day lmt. FACILITIES: 6 tent sites, cga; no tbls/toil/drk wtr. ACTIVITIES: Hiking. MISC.: Elev 4800 ft; 3 acres; pets on leash.

*****East Fork Lions Trail Camp** (Los Padres NF). 6 mi NE of Ojai. 1 mi W of St Hwy 150; 14½ mi NW on St Hwy 33; 5½ mi E on FS 7N03; 2½ mi SE on TRAIL 22W06. SEASON: All yr; 14-day lmt. FACILITIES: 3 tent sites; no tbls/toil/drk wtr. ACTIVITIES: Hiking. MISC.: Elev 4000 ft; pets permitted if kept on a leash.

Howard Creek (Los Padres NF). 1 mi W of Ojai on St Hwy 150; 14-4/5 mi NW on St Hwy 33; 2-1/5 mi E on FS 7N03 (Sespe River Rd); 1-1/5 mi NE on FS 5N03. SEASON: All yr; 14-day lmt. ACTIVITIES: Hiking; picnicking; fishing. FACILITIES: 6 sites; no trailers. No tbls/drk wtr. Toil, cga. MISC.: Elev 3200 ft; 2 acres; geological; pets. Howard/Sespe Creeks.

Matilija (Los Padres NF). 1 mi W of Ojai on St Hwy 150; 5 mi NW on St Hwy 33; 7-3/10 mi NW on FS 5N13; 1-1/5 mi N on TRAIL 23W07. [Located along trail, 3 mi from the end of a 5-mi spur (Matilija Reservoir Rd).] SEASON: All yr (closed during fire season, 9/1-7/1), 14-day lmt. FACILITIES: 5 tent sites, toil, cga. No tbls/drk wtr. ACTIVITIES: Hiking; swimming; picnicking; fishing. MISC.: Elev 2000 ft; 2 acres; pets. On Upper North Fork of Matilija Creek.

Middle Lion (Los Padres NF). 1 mi W of Ojai on St Hwy 150; 14-4/5 mi NW on

St Hwy 33; 5-2/5 mi E on FS 7N03 (Sespe River Rd); 1 mi S on FS 22W06. SEASON: All yr; 14-day lmt. FACILITIES: 10 sites (tr -16), tbls, toil, cga, no drk wtr. ACTIVITIES: Hiking; picnicking; fishing. Horseback riding (1 mi). MISC.: Elev 3300 ft;5 acres; scenic; pets. Lion Creek.

*****Murietta Trail Camp** (Los Padres NF). Located along trail 1½ mi from the end of a 5-mi spur (Matilija Reservoir Rd); 7 mi N of Ojai on St Hwy 33. SEASON: 11/15-6/30; 14-day lmt. FACILITIES: 5 tent sites; toil, cga. No tbls/drk wtr. ACTIVITIES: Hiking. MISC.: Elev 1850 ft. Pets allowed if kept on leash. Creek water available.

*****Oak Flat Trail Camp** (Los Padres NF). 1 mi W of Ojai on St Hwy 150; 14½ mi NW on St Hwy 33; 11½ mi E on FS 7N04; 1 block SE on TRAIL. SEASON: 4/1-11/31; 14-day lmt. FACILITIES: 3 tent sites; tbls, cga. No toil/drk wtr. ACTIVITIES: Hiking; swimming; picnicking; fishing; horseback riding. MISC.: Elev 2700 ft; scenic. Pets on leash.

*****Piedra Blanca Trail Camp** (Los Padres NF). 1 mi W of Ojai on St Hwy 150; 14-4/5 mi NW on St Hwy 33; 6½ mi E on FS 7N03; 2-1/10 mi N on TRAIL 22W03. SEASON: All yr; 14-day lmt. FACILITIES: 4 tent sites; cga. No tbls/toil/drk wtr. ACTIVITIES: Hiking; fishing. MISC.: Elev 3700 ft; 2 acres; stream; pets.

Pine Mountain (Los Padres NF). 1 mi W of Ojai on St Hwy 150; 29-1/5 mi NW on St Hwy 33; 5 mi E on FS 6N06. SEASON: 4/1-11/31; 14-day lmt. FACILITIES: 8 sites; no trailers. No drk wtr, tbls, toil, cga. ACTIVITIES: Hiking; fishing. Horseback riding (1 mi). MISC.: Elev 6700 ft; 5 acres; pets. Located in large timber. Dry camp; water available ¼ mi down trail at Raspberry Spring.

*****The Pines Trail Camp** (Los Padres NF). 5 mi E of Ojai on St Hwy 150; 1 mi NE on Co Hwy; 1 mi NE on Co Hwy; 1-4/5 mi NE on TRAIL 22W08. SEASON: All yr; 14-day lmt. FACILITIES: 3 tent sites; cga. No tbls/toil/drk wtr. ACTIVITIES: Hiking. MISC.: Elev 3400 ft; 3 acres. Pets on leash.

Reyes Peak Campground (Los Padres NF). 1 mi W of Ojai on St Hwy 150; 29-1/5 mi NW on St Hwy 33; 6 mi E on FS 6N06. SEASON: 4/1-12/31; 14-day lmt. FACILITIES: 7 sites; no trailers. Tbls, cga. No toil/drk wtr. ACTIVITIES: picnicking. Horseback riding (1 mi). MISC.: Elev 6800 ft; 15 acres; scenic; pets on leash.

Rose Valley Falls (Los Padres NF). 1 mi W of Ojai on St Hwy 150; 14-4/5 mi NW on St Hwy 33; 2-7/10 mi E on FS 7N03 (Sespe River Rd); ½ mi S on FS 7N03R

See page 7 for KEY TO ABBREVIATIONS.

(Rose Valley Rd). SEASON: All yr; 14-day lmt. FACILITIES: 42 sites (tr -16), tbls, toil, cga, no drk wtr. ACTIVITIES: Hiking; picnicking; fishing. Horseback riding (1 mi). MISC.: Elev 3400 ft; 10 acres; scenic; pets. Rose Valley Creek.

*Sespe Hot Springs Trail Camp (Los Padres NF). 1 mi W of Ojai on St Hwy 150; 14-4/5 mi NW on St Hwy 33; 21 mi E on FS 7N03 (Sespe River Rd); 1 mi N on TRAIL 20W12. [Access by foot or 4-wheel drive.] SEASON: 4/1-12/31; 14-day lmt. FACILITIES: 5 tent sites; tbls, toil, cga, no drk wtr. ACTIVITIES: Hiking; swimming; picnicking; fishing. Horseback riding (1 mi). MISC.: Elev 3200 ft; 2 acres; scenic; pets. Sespe Creek.

Teacher (Los Padres NF). Located on Sespe Creek approx. 18 mi on good dirt rd and 15 mi on St Hwy 33 from Ojai. SEASON: 11/15-6/30; 14-day lmt. FACILITIES: Sites, cga, no drk wtr. ACTIVITIES: Hiking; fishing. MISC.: Creek;pets.

*West Fork Lions Trail Camp (Los Padres NF). 1 mi W of Ojai on St Hwy 150; 14-4/5 mi NW of St Hwy 33; 6-3/10 mi E on FS 7N03; 2-3/10 mi SE on TRAIL 22W06. SEASON: All yr; 14-day lmt. FACILITIES: 4 tent sites; cga. No tbls/drk wtr. ACTIVITIES: Hiking; swimming; fishing. MISC.: Elev 3400 ft; 2 acres; stream;pets.

OLANCHA

Dirty Sock Campground (County Park). 4 mi E of US 395 on Death Valley exit, St Hwy 190; located in Olancha. SEASON: All yr; 14-day lmt. FACILITIES: 21 sites; tbls, toil, cga, drk wtr. ACTIVITIES: Swimming; picnicking. MISC.: Elev 3600 ft; 10 acres; pets on leash.

OLEMA

*Coast Camp (Point Reyes National Seashore). ½ mi NW of Olema on Bear Valley Rd to park headquarters; 8 mi BY FOOT to campground on nearly level trails; or 6 mi via Inverness Ridge on steeper trails. [Accessible BY FOOT or BY HORSEBACK.] SEASON: All yr; 1-night lmt. FACILITIES: 14 tent sites; tbls, toil, cga, drk wtr. Only gas stoves, charcoal, or canned heat may be used for cooking. Wood fires are prohibited. Store is ½ mi from trailhead. ACTIVITIES: Hiking; horseback riding; picnicking; fishing; swimming (in ocean). MISC.: Hitchrail for horses. Nature trails. The camp is on an open, grassy bluff about 200 yards above the beach. No trees. CAMPING PERMIT is required; obtain it free at park headquarters. Reservations are recommended. NOT PETS ALLOWED.

*Glen Camp (Point Reyes National Seashore). ½ mi NW of Olema on Bear Valley Rd to park headquarters; 4½ mi BY FOOT to campground, on nearly level trails. SEASON: All yr; 1-night lmt. FACILITIES: 12 tent sites; tbls, toil, cga, drk wtr. Only gas stoves, charcoal, or canned heat may be used for cooking. Wood fires are prohibited. ACTIVITIES: Hiking; swimming; picnicking; fishing. MISC.: Elev 85 ft; nature trails. Store is ½ mi from trailhead. Tomales Bay (2 mi). Free CAMPING PERMIT REQUIRED; available at park headquarters. No motorbikes. NO PETS. Reservations are recommended. It is located in a small, wooded valley about 2 mi from the ocean.

*Sky Camp (Point Reyes National Seashore). ½ mi NW of Olema on Bear Valley Rd to park headquarters; 3 mi BY FOOT to campground. [2-4/5 mi from the Bear Valley Trailhead on the western side of Mt. Wittenberg.] SEASON: All yr; 1-night lmt. FACILITIES: 12 tent sites; toil. No tbls/drk wtr. Only gas stoves, charcoal, or canned heat may be used for cooking. Wood fires prohibited. Store is 1 mi from trailhead. ACTIVITIES: Hiking; swimming; fishing. MISC.: Elev 1025 ft; nature trails. No motorbikes. NO PETS. Tomales Bay (3 mi). Free CAMPING PERMIT REQUIRED; available at park headquarters. Reservations are recommended. It commands a view of Drakes Bay and the surrounding hills of Point Reyes.

*Wildcat Group Camp (Point Reyes National Seashore). ½ mi NW of Olema on Bear Valley Rd to park headquarters; 7 mi BY FOOT to campground from trailhead. SEASON: All yr; 3-night lmt. FACILITIES: 12 tent sites, each accommodating up to 10 people. Hitchrail for horses; tbls, toil, cga, drk wtr. Only gas stoves, charcoal, or canned heat may be used for cooking. Wood fires are prohibited. ACTIVITIES: Hiking; horseback riding; swimming in ocean; picnicking; fishing. MISC.: Organized juvenile groups must have one adult supervisor for each eight juveniles. It lies in a grassy meadow near a small stream that flows into the sea. No trees; easy beach access. No motorbikes. NO PETS. Free CAMPING PERMIT REQUIRED; available at park headquarters. Reservations are recommended. Nature trails.

ORLAND

Buckhorn (COE; Black Butte Lake). 14 mi W of Orland off Co Hwy 200. SEASON: 4/1-10/1; 14-day lmt. FACILITIES: 65 sites (tr -30), tbls, toil, cga, hot showers, dump, playground, pull-thru spaces. Marina nearby. ACTIVITIES: Boating,rl; picnicking; fishing (large and smallmouth bass, crappie, bluegill, catfish). MISC.: 150 acres. Pets on leash.

Orland Buttes (COE; Black Butte Lake). Approximately 5 mi W of Orland on Co

See page 7 for KEY TO ABBREVIATIONS.

Rd; 3 mi left on Co Rd 206 to campground. **SEASON:** All yr; 14-day lmt. **FACILITIES:** 35 sites (tr -20), tbls, toil, cga, drk wtr, hot showers. **ACTIVITIES:** Boating, l; picnicking; fishing (large and small-mouth bass, crappie, bluegill, catfish). **MISC.:** 120 acres; pull-thru spaces; pets.

ORLEANS

Pearch Creek (Six Rivers NF). 1-1/10 mi NE of Orleans on St Hwy 96. **SEASON:** All yr; 14-day lmt. **FACILITIES:** 11 sites (tr -22), tbls, toil, cga, piped drk wtr. Store/ice/fd/laundry/gas (1 mi). **ACTIVI-TIES:** Swimming; picnicking; fishing (salmon, steelhead). **MISC.:** Elev 400 ft; 2 acres; pets. Adjacent to Klamath River.

PACIFIC VALLEY

Pacific Valley (Stanislaus NF). $\frac{1}{4}$ mi S of St Hwy 4 at Pacific Valley, midway between Lake Alpine and Ebbetts Pass. [Not recommended for trailers.] **SEASON:** June-September; 14-day lmt. **FACILITIES:** 6 sites; no trailers. No drk wtr; tbls, toil, cga. **ACTIVITIES:** Early-season deer hunting; picnicking. Fishing (2 mi). Hiking. **MISC.:** Elev 7600 ft; 1 acre; pets. 3/5 mi W of Ebbetts Pass. Pacific Creek/Mokelumne River (2 mi).

PALMDALE

Mount Pacifico (Angeles NF). 5-2/5 mi S of Palmdale on St Hwy 14; 9$\frac{1}{2}$ mi S on Co Rd N3 (Angeles Forest Hwy); 6$\frac{1}{2}$ mi E on FS 3N17. **SEASON:** 3/1-10/31; 14-day lmt. **FACILITIES:** 10 sites (tr -22), tbls, toil, cga, f, no drk wtr. **ACTIVITIES:** Picnicking. Horseback riding (1 mi). **MISC.:** Elev 7100 ft; 1 acre; pets. Good weather may lengthen season.

Roundtop Ridge (Angeles NF). 5-2/5 mi S of Palmdale on US 14; 9$\frac{1}{2}$ mi S on Co Hwy N3; 6$\frac{1}{2}$ mi E on FS 3N17; 2 mi S on FS 3N90. [Steep winding dirt rd may be difficult for trailers.] **SEASON:** 3/1-12/15; 14-day lmt. **FACILITIES:** 4 sites (tr -16), tbls, toil, cga, no drk wtr. **ACTIVITIES:** Hiking; picnicking. **MISC.:** Elev 6100 ft; 3 acres; pets on leash. Scenic pine forest.

PALO VERDE

Palo Verde County Park (Imperial County Park). 3 mi S of Palo Verde on St Hwy 78. **SEASON:** All yr; 3-day lmt. **FACILI-TIES:** 50 sites; tbls, toil, cga, no drk wtr. Store/fd/LP gas (3 mi). **ACTIVITIES:** Swimming; picnicking; fishing (catfish, bass); hunting (pheasant, dove, duck). Boating, l (no motor boats). **MISC.:** Elev 100 ft; 10 acres; pets on leash. Oxbow Lagoon/Colorado River (3 mi).

Palo Verde Oxbow Recreation Site (BLM). 3$\frac{1}{2}$ mi S of Palo Verde on St Hwy 78; E on unmarked gravel rd between mileposts 77 and 78, and follow gravel rd for 1 mi to Colorado River. **FACILITIES:** 50 sites; tbls, toil, cga, no drk wtr. **ACTIVITIES:** Hiking; hunting; picnicking; fishing; boating, l. **MISC.:** Pets on leash.

PASKENTA

Dead Mule (Mendocino NF). 28 mi W of Paskenta. S of Paskenta on Rd 23N02; right on Rd 23N50; left on Rd 23N54 to campground. **SEASON:** 5/15-11/1. **FACILI-TIES:** Sites; tbls, toil, cga. Water is located W of camp. **MISC.:** Elev 5000 ft. Pets allowed if kept on leash.

Del Harleson (Mendocino NF). 21 mi SW of Paskenta. S of Paskenta on Rd 23N02; left on Rd 23N69; left on Rd 23N03; left on Rd 23N74 to campground. **SEASON:** 4/1-11/1. **FACILITIES:** Sites; tbls, toil, cga. **MISC.:** Elev 4200 ft; pets on leash.

Kingsley Glade (Mendocino NF). 22 mi W of Paskenta. W of Paskenta on Rd 23N01; left on Rd 24N01 to campground. **SEASON:** 5/1-11/1. **FACILITIES:** Sites; toil. **MISC.:** Elev 4500 ft; pets.

Mud Flat (Mendocino NF). 10 mi SW of Paskenta. S of Paskenta on Rd 23N02; right on Rd 23N69 to campground. **SEASON:** 4/1-11/1. **FACILITIES:** Sites; tbls, toil, cga. Gravity water system. **ACTIVITIES:** Hiking; picnicking. **MISC.:** Elev 2200 ft. Pets permitted on leash.

Rocky Cabin (Mendocino NF). 24 mi NE of Paskenta. Dirt roads. W of Paskenta on Rd 23N01; right on Rd 24N04; left on Rd 24N41; right on Rd 24N38 to campground. **SEASON:** 5/15-11/1. **FACILI-TIES:** Sites; tbls, toil, cga, spring water. **ACTIVITIES:** Hiking; picnicking. **MISC.:** Elev 6250 ft. Pets on leash.

Sugar Springs (Mendocino NF). 35 mi W of Paskenta. S of Paskenta on Rd 23N02; right on Rd 23N69; right on Rd 23N41 to campground. **SEASON:** 5/15-11/1. **FACILITIES:** Sites; tbls, toil, cga. Water located W of camp. **ACTIV-ITIES:** Hiking; picnicking. **MISC.:** Elev 5400 ft. Pets permitted if on leash.

Three Prong (Mendocino NF). 25 mi W of Paskenta. W of Paskenta on Rd 23N01; left on Rd 24N13 to campground. [Dirt rds.] **SEASON:** 5/1-11/1. **FACILITIES:** Sites; tbls, toil, cga. Water piped to campground. **ACTIVITIES:** Hiking; picnicking. **MISC.:** Elev 4800 ft; pets.

Whitlock (Mendocino NF). 3-3/10 mi NW of Paskenta on Co Rd 23N01; 10-1/5 mi NW on FS 23N01; 7/10 mi NW on Co Rd 24N41. [Dirt rds.] **SEASON:** 5/1-11/1. 14-day lmt. **FACILITIES:** 5 sites (tr -22), tbls, toil, cga. Gravity water system. **ACTIVITIES:** Hiking; picnicking. **MISC.:** Elev 4300 ft; 2 acres. **Pets.**

PAYNES CREEK

Black Rock (Lassen NF). 8½ mi SE of Paynes Creek on Co Hwy 202; 22 mi SE on Co Hwy 28N29. **SEASON:** 5/1-11/1; 14-day lmt. **FACILITIES:** 4 sites; no trailers. No drk wtr; tbls, toil, cga. **ACTIVITIES:** Hiking; picnicking; fishing. **MISC.:** Elev 2100 ft; 1 acre; stream. Pets on leash.

South Antelope (Lassen NF). 8½ mi SE of Paynes Creek on Co Rd 202 (Plum Creek Rd); 11 mi SE on Co Rd 28N29 (Ponderosa Rd). **SEASON:** 5/1-11/1; 14-day lmt. **FACILITIES:** 5 sites; no trailers. No drk wtr; tbls, toil, cga. **ACTIVITIES:** Hiking; picnicking; fishing. **MISC.:** Antelope Creek. Pets permitted if on a leash. On South Antelope Creek on Ponderosa Way.

PIEDRA

Black Rock (Sierra NF). 30 mi NE of Piedra on Co Hwy N88; 12-7/10 mi NE on FS 11S12; 2/5 mi E on FS 11S07; ½ mi E on FS 11S50. **SEASON:** 4/15-11/15; 14-day lmt. **FACILITIES:** 7 sites (tr -16), tbls, toil, no drk wtr. **ACTIVITIES:** Picnicking. Fishing (1 mi). Swimming (2 mi). Boating,d (1 mi). **MISC.:** Elev 4200 ft; 2 acres; pets. Williams Creek. Black Rock Reservoir.

Camp 4 (Sequoia NF). 25 mi E of Piedra on Co Rd N0002; 2 mi SE on FS 12S01. [Not suitable for trailers.] Paved and dirt rds. **SEASON:** All yr; 14-day lmt. **FACILITIES:** 5 sites (tr -16), tbls, toil, cga, no drk wtr. **ACTIVITIES:** Swimming; picnicking; fishing. **MISC.:** Elev 1000 ft; 1 acre; pets; river; Kings River.

Camp 4½ (Sequoia NF). 25 mi E of Piedra on Co Rd N0002; 1 mi SE on FS 12S01. [Paved and dirt rds.] **SEASON:** All yr; 14-day lmt. **FACILITIES:** 5 sites (tr -16), tbls, toil, cga, piped drk wtr. Water available at the Camp 4½ Guard Station. **ACTIVITIES:** Swimming; picnicking; fishing. **MISC.:** Elev 1000 ft; 3 acres; pets. Kings River.

Duff Creek (Sierra NF). 22-2/5 mi NE of Piedra on Co Hwy N88; 7-9/10 mi N on FS 10S69; 5-1/10 mi N on FS 10S02. **SEASON:** 2/15-12/15; 14-day lmt. **FACILITIES:** 7 sites (tr -16), tbls, toil, cga, no drk wtr. **ACTIVITIES:** Swimming; picnicking; fishing. **MISC.:** Elev 3200 ft; 2 acres; pets. Big Creek.

Garnet Dike (Sierra NF). 34-3/10 mi E of Piedra on Co Hwy N88; 8½ mi E on FS 12S01. [10 mi E of Pine Flat Reservoir on middle fork of Kings River.] **SEASON:** All yr; 14-day lmt. **FACILITIES:** 4 sites (tr -16), tbls, toil,

cga, no drk wtr. **ACTIVITIES:** Swimming; whitewater rafting; picnicking; fishing. **MISC.:** Elev 1200 ft; 1 acre; pets; river.

Island Park Campground (COE; Pine Flat Lake). 7 mi E of Piedra on Trimmer Springs Rd. **SEASON:** 9/30-4/1; 14-day lmt. **FACILITIES:** 50 sites; tbls, toil, cga, drk wtr. Marina nearby. **ACTIVITIES:** Waterskiing; boating; picnicking. **MISC.:** Pets on leash. Six houseboat mooring areas are located around the lake: shore camping is not allowed in these areas; however, restrooms and garbage cans are available on shore. The locations of these areas changes as the lake level fluctuates and houseboaters wishing to moor in one of the areas should check with the park ranger.

Kirch Flat (Sierra NF). 30-3/5 mi NE of Piedra on Co Hwy N88 (Trimmer Springs Rd). **SEASON:** All yr; 14-day lmt. **FACILITIES:** 19 sites (tr -22), tbls, toil, cga, no drk wtr. **ACTIVITIES:** Swimming; picnicking; fishing. **MISC.:** Elev 1100 ft; 6 acres; pets. On Kings River at end of Pine Flat Reservoir.

Mill Flat (Sequoia NF). 25 mi E of Piedra on Co Rd N0002; 2½ mi SE on FS 12S01 (Davis Rd). [Paved and dirt rds.] **SEASON:** All yr; 14-day lmt. **FACILITIES:** 5 sites (tr -16), tbls, toil, cga, no drk wtr. **ACTIVITIES:** Swimming; picnicking; fishing. **MISC.:** Elev 1100 ft; 2 acres; pets. On Kings River.

Sycamore Flat #1 (Sierra NF). 18-9/10 mi NE of Piedra on Co Hwy N88 (Trimmer Springs Rd). **SEASON:** All yr; 14-day lmt. **FACILITIES:** 12 sites (tr -22), tbls, toil, cga, piped drk wtr. **ACTIVITIES:** Hiking; picnicking. Fishing/swimming (1 mi). Boating,rl/waterskiing (5 mi). **MISC.:** Elev 1200 ft; 6 acres; pets;lake.

Sycamore Flat #2 (Sierra NF). 19-1/10 mi NE of Piedra on Co Hwy N88. **SEASON:** All yr; 14-day lmt. **FACILITIES:** 20 sites toil, cga, piped drk wtr. **ACTIVITIES:** Hiking; picnicking. Swimming/fishing (1 mi). Boating,rl/waterskiing (5 mi). **MISC.:** Elev 1200 ft; 10 acres; pets; lake. Trimmer Springs Road.

Trimmer Campground (COE; Pine Flat Lake). 12 mi E of Piedra on Trimmer Springs Road. **SEASON:** All yr; 14-day lmt. **FACILITIES:** 23 sites; tbls, toil, cga, drk wtr, f, store, playground. Marina nearby. Fd (2 mi). **ACTIVITIES:** Waterskiing; boating,d (rl, 2 mi); picnicking; fishing (catfish, trout, bass). Swimming (2 mi). **MISC.:** Access rd steep grade. Pine Flat Dam. 5 acres; pets.

PIERPOINT

Peppermint (Sequoia NF). 26½ mi E of Pierpoint on St Hwy 190; 3 mi S on

See page 7 for KEY TO ABBREVIATIONS.

Co Hwy FH90; 3/5 mi E on Co Hwy 21S07. SEASON: 5/1-10/31; 14-day lmt. FACILITIES: 19 sites (tr -22); tbls, toil, cga, no drk wtr. Store/gas/ice/ food (2 mi). ACTIVITIES: Picnicking; swimming; fishing. Horseback riding/ rental (2 mi). MISC.: Elev 7100 ft; 10 acres; stream; pets.

PINEHURST

Eshom (Sequoia NF). 15 mi SE of Pinehurst on Eshom Creek via St Hwy 245 and Red Hill Rd. [Paved rd.] SEASON: 5/1-11/15; 14-day lmt. FACILITIES: 17 sites (tr -22), tbls, toil, cga, piped spring drk wtr. Store/fd/gas (5 mi). ACTIVITIES: Fishing; picnicking. MISC.: Elev 4800 ft; 23 acres; pets; scenic. Eshom Creek.

PINE SPRINGS

Halfmoon (Los Padres NF). 12 mi S of Pine Valley on I-8; 9 mi S on Co Hwy S1; 1½ mi NW on Co Hwy F24; 5-3/5 mi SW on FS 17S07. SEASON: All yr; 14-day lmt. FACILITIES: 6 sites; no trailers. Toil, f; no drk wtr. MISC.: Elev 1600 ft. Pets permitted if kept on a leash.

PINE VALLEY

Boulder Oaks (Cleveland NF). 7-4/5 mi SE of Pine Valley on US 8. [Located just off US 8 (Cameron Station Exit) at Boulder Oaks Resort, 53 mi E of San Diego.] FAC-ILITIES: 12 sites (tr -22), tbls, toil, cga, piped drk wtr, store, gas, ice, fd. [Supplies at Boulder Oaks Resort ad-jacent to campground.] ACTIVITIES: Pic-nicking. SEASON: All yr; 14-day lmt. MISC.: Elev 3500 ft; 3 acres; pets; botan-ical. Kitchen Creek.

Hauser Creek (Cleveland NF). 4¼ mi SE of Pine Valley on I-8; 9 mi S on Co Hwy S1; 1½ mi NW on Co Hwy F24; 5-3/5 mi SW on FS 17S07. SEASON: All yr; 14-day lmt. FACILITIES: 6 sites; no trailers. Toil, f; no drk wtr. MISC.: Elev 1600 ft. Pets permitted if kept on a leash.

PIONEER

Lumberyard (Eldorado NF). 19-9/10 mi NE of Pioneer on St Hwy 88; 1/10 mi SW on FS 8N25A. SEASON: 6/1-11/1; 14-day lmt. FACILITIES: 8 sites (tr -16), tbls, toil, cga, f, piped drk wtr. Store/ ice/gas (4 mi). ACTIVITIES: Boating,rl; picnicking. Swimming/fishing/waterski-ing (4 mi). MISC.: Elev 6500 ft; 2 acres; pets. Bear Reservoir (4 mi).

Mokelumne (Eldorado NF). 19-9/10 mi NE of Pioneer on St Hwy 88; 4½ mi S on FS 8N25 (Ellis Rd); 2 mi SE on FS 8N05; 2-3/5 mi SW on FS 8N50. SEASON: 5/1-11/1; 14-day lmt. FACILITIES: 8 sites; no trailers. No drk wtr; tbls, toil, cga. ACTIVITIES: Swimming; pic-nicking; fishing. Boating,ld (4 mi).

Reservoir boating potentially dangerous due to steep narrow canyon. MISC.: Elev 3200 ft; 2 acres; pets. Mokelumne River/Salt Springs Reservoir (4 mi).

Moore Creek (Eldorado NF). 20 mi NE of Pioneer on St Hwy 88; 4½ mi S on FS 8N25 (Ellis Rd); 2 mi SE on FS 8N05; 2-3/4 mi SE on FS 8N50. SEASON: 6/1-11/30. FACILITIES: 8 sites (tr -16), tbls, toil, cga, no drk wtr. ACTIVITIES: Picnicking. Swimming/fishing/boating,ld (4 mi). Reservoir boating potentially dangerous due to steep narrow canyon. MISC.: Elev 3200 ft; 5 acres; pets. Mokelumne River and Salt Springs Reser-voir (4 mi).

Pipi (Eldorado NF). 26-3/10 mi NE of Pioneer on US 88; 4/5 mi NW on Co Hwy 8N21; 5-9/10 mi N on FS 9N45. SEASON: 5/1-10/30; 14-day lmt. FACILITIES: 60 sites (tr -16), tbls, toil, cga, no drk wtr. ACTIVITIES: Swimming; picnicking; fishing. MISC.: Elev 3900 ft; 45 acres; pets on leash; river.

White Azalea (Eldorado NF). 19-9/10 mi NE of Pioneer on St Hwy 88; 4½ mi S on FS 8N25 (Ellis Rd); 2 mi SE on FS 8N05; 4 mi SE on FS 8N50. SEASON: 5/1-11/1; 14-day lmt. FACILITIES: 6 sites; no trailers. No drk wtr; tbls, toil, cga. ACTIVITIES: Swimming; pic-nicking; fishing. Boating,ld (3 mi). Reservoir potentially dangerous due to steep narrow canyon. MISC.: Elev 3500 ft; 2 acres; pets. Mokelumne River and Salt Springs Reservoir (3 mi).

PIRU

Blue Point (Los Padres NF). 8½ mi N of Piru on Co Hwy; 6-9/10 mi N on FS 4N13 (Piru Canyon Rd). SEASON: All yr; 14-day lmt. FACILITIES: 8 sites (tr -16), tbls, toil, cga, no drk wtr. ACTIVITIES: Fishing; picnicking; swimming. Boating,d/water-skiing (2 mi). Horseback riding (1 mi). MISC.: Elev 1000 ft; 11 acres; pets;creek. Piru Creek and Lake Piru (2 mi).

PLATINA

Basin Gulch (Shasta-Trinity NF). 5 mi W of Platina on St Hwy 36; 1-1/5 mi S on FS 29N13. SEASON: 4/1-11/30; 14-day lmt. FACILITIES: 15 sites (tr -22), tbls, toil, cga, piped drk wtr. ACTIVITIES: Fishing; picnicking. MISC.: Elev 2600 ft; 9 acres; pets. On middle fork of Cottonwood Creek.

Beegum Gorge (Shasta-Trinity NF). 1/5 mi E of Platina on St Hwy 36; 1-9/10 mi S on Co Hwy 1C001; 4-1/5 mi SW on FS 28N06. [Rd from St Hwy 36 unsafe for trailers.] SEASON: 4/15-11/30; 14-day lmt. FACILITIES: 3 sites; no trailers. No drk wtr; tbls, toil, cga. ACTIVITIES:

Swimming; picnicking; fishing. **MISC.:** Elev 2100 ft; 1 acre; pets. Beegum Creek.

Knob Peak (Shasta-Trinity NF). 2-7/10 mi W of Platina on St Hwy 36; 4-1/10 mi N on FS 29N02 (Cow Gulch Rd). SEASON: 4/1-11/30; 14-day lmt. FACILITIES: 8 sites; no trailers. Piped drk wtr; tbls, toil, cga, f. ACTIVITIES: Picnicking. **MISC.:** Elev 4400 ft; 3 acres; pets. Near Knob Peak Lookout.

North Fork of Beegum (Shasta-Trinity NF). 5 mi W of Platina on St Hwy 36; 4½ mi S on FS 29N13; ½ mi SW on FS 29N44 (Stuart Gap Rd). [Rd impassable to trailers; restricted turn-around.] SEASON: 4/1-11/30; 14-day lmt. FACILITIES: 3 sites; no trailers. No drk wtr; tbls, toil, cga, f. ACTIVITIES: Fishing; picnicking. MISC.: Elev 2900 ft; 1 acre; stream; pets.

White Rock (Shasta-Trinity NF). 5 mi W of Platina on St Hwy 36; 14-2/5 mi S on FS 29N13; 5-3/5 mi S on FS 29N19. SEASON: 5/15-10/31; 14-day lmt. FACILITIES: 3 sites; no trailers. No drk wtr; tbls, toil, cga, f. ACTIVITIES: Picnicking. MISC.: Elev 4800 ft; 1 acre; pets; stream. Adjacent to White Oak Guard Station.

POLLOCK PINES

*****Pleasant** (Eldorado NF). 8½ mi E of Pollock Pines on US 50; 23 mi N on Co Hwy 17N12; 5 mi NE on Co Hwy 14N01; 3-3/10 mi NE on TRAIL 15E03. [Accessible BY FOOT and BY BOAT.] SEASON: 6/15-9/15-; 14-day lmt. FACILITIES: 10 tent sites; tbls, toil, cga, f, no drk wtr. ACTIVITIES: Boating; swimming; hiking; picnicking; fishing. **MISC.:** Elev 6400 ft; 4 acres; pets. Waterskiing; sailing. Leon Lake and Spider Lake (1 mi).

Silver Creek (Eldorado NF). 8½ mi E of Pollock Pines on US 50; 7 mi NE on Co Rd 17N12 (Ice House Rd). SEASON: 6/1-10/15; 14-day lmt. FACILITIES: 11 sites; no trailers. No drk wtr; tbls, toil, cga. Store/fd/ice/gas (3 mi). ACTIVITIES: Hiking; swimming; picnicking; fishing; boating (l, 3 mi). **MISC.:** Elev 5200 ft; 2 acres; pets. Silver Creek and Ice House Reservoir (2 mi).

South Fork (Eldorado NF). 8½ mi E of Pollock Pines on US 50; 20½ mi on Co Rd 17N12 (Ice House Rd); ½ mi NW on FS 13N28; ½ mi NE on FS 13N29. SEASON: 6/1-10/15; 14-day lmt. FACILITIES: 17 sites (tr -22), tbls, toil, cga, no drk wtr. ACTIVITIES: Hiking; picnicking. Swimming/fishing/boating,d (4 mi). MISC.: Elev 5200 ft; 6 acres; pets; stream. Gerle Creek Reservoir and Rubicon River (4 mi).

Wentworth Springs (Eldorado NF). 8½ mi E of Pollock Pines on US 50; 24½ mi N on Co Rd 17N12; 3½ mi N on FS 17N12

(Ice House Rd); 3 mi E on FS 14N02. SEASON: 6/15-10/15; 14-day lmt. FACILITIES: 8 sites; no trailers. No drk wtr; tbls, toil, cga. ACTIVITIES: Hiking; swimming; picnicking; fishing. **MISC.:** Elev 6200 ft; 2 acres; pets; stream. Gerle Creek and Loon Lake (1 mi). Point of departure for NW end of Desolation Wilderness Area.

PORTERVILLE

Long Meadow (Sequoia NF). 57 mi SW of Porterville via St Hwy 190 and Western Divide Hwy. SEASON: 5/15-10/31; 14-day lmt. FACILITIES: 5 sites (tr -22), tbls, toil, cga, piped drk wtr. ACTIVITIES: Picnicking. Fishing (2 mi). MISC.: Elev 6500 ft; 2 acres; pets; stream. Parker Meadow Creek (2 mi).

Redwood Meadow (Sequoia NF). 58 mi SE of Porterville via St Hwy 190 and Western Divide Hwy. [Paved rd.] SEASON: 6/15-9/15; 14-day lmt. FACILITIES: 15 sites (tr -22), tbls, toil, cga, no drk wtr. ACTIVITIES: Picnicking. Fishing (2 mi). MISC.: Elev 6500 ft; 4 acres; pets. Parker Meadow Creek (1 mi). Adjacent to Long Meadow giant sequoia redwood grove.

Rocky Hill (COE; Success Lake). 5 mi E of Porterville on St Hwy 190. SEASON: All yr; 14-day lmt. FACILITIES: Undesignated sites, with room for about 300 campers; tbls, toil, cga, drk wtr. ACTIVITIES: Swimming; picnicking; fishing; boating,rld. MISC.: 100 acres; pets.

Tule Recreation Area Campground (COE; Success Lake). 6 mi E of Porterville on St Hwy 190. SEASON: 10/1-3/31; 14-day lmt. FACILITIES: 104 sites (tr -35), tbls, flush toil, cga, drk wtr, hot showers. Marina nearby. ACTIVITIES: Swimming; picnicking; fishing (large and smallmouth bass, crappie, bluegill, catfish); boating (rl, nearby). MISC.: Pets.

PORTOLA

Crocker (Plumas NF). 5½ mi E of Portola on St Hwy 70; 7-1/5 mi N on Co Hwy 111 (Beckworth Genesee Rd); 1/5 mi W on FS 24N06. SEASON: 5/1-10/1; 14-day lmt. FACILITIES: 15 sites (tr -32), tbls, toil, cga, piped drk wtr. Store/ice (4 mi). ACTIVITIES: Hunting (in season); picnicking. Fishing (1 mi). Swimming (4 mi). Boating,rd (5 mi). MISC.: Elev 5800 ft; 1 acre; pets. Crocker Creek and Lake Davis (4 mi).

PORTOLA

Lightning Tree (Plumas NF). 2½ mi E of Portola on St Hwy 70; 9-9/10 mi NW on Co Hwy 112. SEASON: 5/1-11/15; 7-day lmt. FACILITIES: 55 sites (tr -32). Dump (4 mi). Store/ice/food (5 mi). ACTIVITIES: Picnicking. Swimming/fishing/boating,l (1 mi). Boat rental (4 mi). MISC.: Elev 5900 ft; 12 acres; pets. For self-contained units only.

POTTER VALLEY

Oak Flat (Mendocino NF). 18-1/10 mi NE of Potter Valley on Co Hwy 240; 3 mi NE on FS 20N01. SEASON: All year; 14-day lmt. FACILITIES: 12 sites (tr -22), tbls, toil, cga, no drk wtr. Store/ice/gas/laundry/showers (1 mi). ACTIVITIES: Swimming; picnicking; fishing; sailing. Boating,rld/hiking/waterskiing (1 mi). MISC.: Elev 1800 ft; 4 acres; pets; lake.

PROJECT CITY

*Allie Cove (Shasta-Trinity NF). 5½ mi N of Project City on I-5; 2 mi E, BY BOAT. [2 mi E of Pit River Bridge, which is located on I-5.] SEASON: 4/1-10/31; 14-day lmt. FACILITIES: 4 tent sites; tbls, toil, cga; no drk wtr. Food/ice/gas (2 mi). Store (5 mi). ACTIVITIES: Picnicking; swimming; fishing; waterskiing; boating (rl, 2 mi). MISC.: Elev 1100 ft; 2 acres; pets. Dump (2 mi). On shore of Shasta Lake. Unit of the Whiskeytown-Shasta-Trinity National Recreation Area.

*Arbuckle Flat (Shasta-Trinity NF). 5½ mi N of Project City on I-5; 15 mi E BY BOAT. [15 mi E of Pit Bridge, located on I-5.] SEASON: 4/1-10/31; 14-day lmt. FACILITIES: 11 tent sites; tbls, toil, cga, no drk wtr. ACTIVITIES: Swimming; picnicking; fishing; waterskiing; boating,d. MISC.: Elev 1100 ft; 4 acres; pets. On shore of Lake Shasta. Unit of the Whiskeytown-Shasta-Trinity NRA.

*Greens Creek (Shasta-Trinity NF). 5½ mi N of Project City on I-5; 5 mi E, BY BOAT. [5 mi from Pit River Bridge (located on I-5).] SEASON: 4/1-10/31; 14-day lmt. FACILITIES: 11 tent sites; tbls, toil, cga, no drk wtr. Store/fd/ice/gas (2 mi). ACTIVITIES: Swimming; picnicking; fishing; boating,d (rl, 2 mi); waterskiing. MISC.: Elev 1000 ft; 6 acres; pets; geological. On McCloud River Arm of Shasta Lake. Unit of the Whiskeytown-Shasta-Trinity NRA.

Mariners Point (Shasta-Trinity NF). 1½ mi N of Project City on I-5; 2½ mi SE on Co Hwy 3H02; 5 mi NE on Co Hwy 5H100; 1 mi NW on Co Hwy 5J050. SEASON: All yr; 14-day lmt. FACILITIES: 7 sites; no trailers; tbls, toil, cga, piped well drk wtr. ACTIVITIES: Swimming; picnicking; fishing; waterskiing; boating,d (rl, 1 mi). FACILITIES: Store/fd/ice/gas (1 mi). Dump (2 mi). MISC.: Elev 1100 ft; 4 acres; pets. Narrow and

rough road. At Shasta Lake. Unit of the Whiskeytown-Shasta-Trinity NRA.

*Rend Island (Shasta-Trinity NF). 5½ mi N of Project City on I-5; 10 mi E, BY BOAT. [10 mi E of Pit River Bridge (located on I-5).] SEASON: 4/1-10/31; 14-day lmt. FACILITIES: 18 tent sites; tbls, toil, cga, no drk wtr. Store/ice/fd/gas/dump (4 mi). ACTIVITIES: Swimming; waterskiing; picnicking; fishing; boating,d (rl, 4 mi). MISC.: Elev 1100 ft; 6 acres; pets. On shore of Shasta Lake. Unit of the Whiskeytown-Shasta-Trinity National Recreation Area.

*Ski Island (Shasta-Trinity NF). 4 mi N of Project City on I-5; 12 mi NE on Co Hwy 4G100; 1/10 mi NW, BY BOAT. [Located 3 mi E of Pit River Bridge, which is on I-5.] SEASON: 4/1-10/31; 14-day lmt. FACILITIES: 29 tent sites; tbls, toil, cga, piped well drk wtr. Store/fd/ice/gas (1 mi). ACTIVITIES: Swimming; waterskiing; picnicking; fishing; boating,ld (r, 1 mi). MISC.: Elev 1100 ft; 9 acres; pets. Amphitheater. On shore of Lake Shasta. Unit of the Whiskeytown-Shasta-Trinity National Recreation Area.

*Slaughterhouse Island (Shasta-Trinity NF). 4½ mi NW of Project City on St Hwy 151; 1½ mi N on Co Hwy A18; 3-1/10 mi N, BY BOAT. [3 mi W of Pit River Bridge (located on I-5).] SEASON: 4/1-10/31; 14-day lmt. FACILITIES: 13 tent sites; tbls, toil, cga, hand-pumped well drk wtr. Store/ice/fd/gas (3 mi). ACTIVITIES: Swimming; waterskiing; picnicking; fishing; boating,d (rl, 3 mi). MISC.: Elev 1100 ft; 4 acres; pets. On Sacramento River Arm, at Shasta Lake. Unit of the Whiskeytown-Shasta-Trinity NRA.

*Stein Creek (Shasta-Trinity NF). 5½ mi N of Project City on I-5; 17 mi E, BY BOAT. [17 mi from Pit River Bridge (located on I-5).] SEASON: 4/1-10/31; 14-day lmt. FACILITIES: 5 tent sites; tbls, toil, cga, no drk wtr. ACTIVITIES: Swimming; waterskiing; picnicking; fishing; boating,d. MISC.: Elev 1100 ft; 2 acres; pets. On upper pit arm of Shasta Lake. Unit of the Whiskeytown-Shasta-Trinity National Recreation Area.

QUINCY

Brady's Camp (Plumas NF). 9 mi E of Quincy on St Hwy 70; 12 mi N on FS 25N09. SEASON: 5/15-11/1; 14-day lmt. FACILITIES: 4 sites (no tr); tbls, toil, cga, no drk wtr. ACTIVITIES: Picnicking; fishing. MISC.: Elev 7200 ft; 4 acres; scenic; stream; pets. Argentine Lookout.

Deanes Valley (Plumas NF). 5-4/5 mi W of Quincy on Co Hwy 414 (Quincy Spanish Ranch Rd); 4 mi S on FS 24N29; 1 mi

See page 7 for KEY TO ABBREVIATIONS.

97

S on FS 24N28. SEASON: 4/1-11/1; 14-day lmt. FACILITIES: 7 sites (tr -22), tbls, toil, cga, no drk wtr. ACTIVITIES: Swimming; picnicking; fishing; horseback riding; hiking. MISC.: Elev 4400 ft; 7 acres; pets; nature trails. South fork of Rock Creek.

Grizzly Creek (Plumas NF). 20 mi SW of Quincy on Co Hwy PL414. SEASON: 6/1-10/15; 14-day lmt. FACILITIES: 8 sites (tr -22), tbls, toil, cga, no drk wtr. Store/fd/ice/gas/laundry (3 mi). ACTIVITIES: Hiking; picnicking. Swimming/fishing/waterskiing/sailing/boating,rl/horseback rental & riding (3 mi). MISC.: Elev 5400 ft; 2 acres; pets; stream. Near Bucks Lake.

Meadow (Plumas NF). 5-4/5 mi W of Quincy on Co Hwy 414; 1-3/5 mi S on FS 24N29. SEASON: 4/1-11/1; 14-day lmt. FACILITIES: 3 sites; no trailers. No drk wtr; tbls, toil, cga. ACTIVITIES: Hunting; swimming; picnicking; fishing. MISC.: Elev 3800 ft; 3 acres; pets; stream. Not a developed site.

Quincy (Plumas NF). 1½ mi E of Quincy on St Hwy 70; 1½ mi N on Co Hwy. SEASON: 5/1-10/15; 14-day lmt. FACILITIES: 16 sites (tr -32), flush toil,dump. Ice, laundry, store. ACTIVITIES: Swimming; fishing. MISC.: Elev 3500 ft; pets; Greenhorn Creek. Operated by county.

Rock Creek (Plumas NF). 5-4/5 mi W of Quincy on Co Hwy 414; 4 mi S on FS 24N29; 1/10 mi N on FS 24N28. SEASON: 4/1-11/1; 14-day lmt. FACILITIES: 3 sites; no trailers. No drk wtr; tbls, toil, cga. ACTIVITIES: Swimming; picnicking; fishing; hunting; hiking. MISC.: Elev 4200 ft; 5 acres; pets; nature trails; stream.

Silver Lake (Plumas NF). 5-7/10 mi W of Quincy on Co Hwy 414 (Quincy Spanish Ranch Rd); 8-2/5 mi W on FS 24N30. SEASON: 5/1-11/1; 14-day lmt. FACILITIES: 6 sites (tr -22), tbls, toil, cga, no drk wtr. ACTIVITIES: Horseback riding; picnicking; fishing; boating,ld; hiking. MISC.: Elev 5800 ft; 5 acres; stream; scenic; pets. Silver Lake. Gold Lake trailhead.

Snake Lake (Plumas NF). 5-3/10 mi W of Quincy on Co Hwy 414; 2-2/5 mi N on FS 25N20. SEASON: 4/1-11/1; 14-day lmt. FACILITIES: 4 sites; no trailers. No drk wtr; tbls, toil, cga. ACTIVITIES: Fishing; picnicking. MISC.: Elev 4200 ft; 5 acres; pets. Snake Lake.

RED BLUFF

Saddle Camp (Shasta-Trinity NF). 13 mi W of Red Bluff on St Hwy 36; 5 mi SW on Co Hwy 181 (Cannon Rd); 19 mi W on Co Hwy 146; 1-1/10 mi SW on FS 27N04. SEASON: 4/1-11/30; 14-day lmt.

FACILITIES: 5 sites (tr -16), tbls, toil, cga, f, piped drk wtr. ACTIVITIES: Hiking; picnicking. MISC.: Elev 3700 ft; 2 acres; pets. 3 mi from trailhead into Yolla Bolly Wilderness.

Tomhead Saddle (Shasta-Trinity NF). 13 mi W of Red Bluff on St Hwy 36; 5 mi SW on Co Hwy 181 (Cannon Rd); 19 mi W on Co Hwy 146; 4-4/5 mi SW on FS 27N04. SEASON: 4/15-10/31. 5 sites; no trailers. Tbls, toil, cga, f, no drk wtr. ACTIVITIES: Hiking; picnicking; horseback riding. MISC.: Elev 5700 ft; 2 acres; pets; horse corral. Adjacent to Yolla-Bolla Wilderness.

REDDING

Brandy Creek (Whiskeytown NRA). 11 mi NW of Redding on St Hwy 299; 5 mi W on S Shore Rd (JFK Dr). SEASON: All yr; 14-day lmt. FACILITIES: 40 sites (tr -30), tbls, toil, cga, drk wtr, dump, ice. ACTIVITIES: Swimming; picnicking; fishing (trout, bass); deer hunting; boating,rld; horseback riding; waterskiing. MISC.: Elev 1210 ft; 20 acres; pets. Whiskeytown Lake.

Deadlun (Shasta-Trinity NF). 34 mi E of Redding on 299E; 17 mi N on paved rd to Big Bend; 9 mi NW to campground on Iron Canyon Reservoir. [Exit from I-5 at St Hwy 299F, N of Redding.] SEASON: 5/15-10/31; 21-day lmt. FACILITIES: 33 sites (tr -22), tbls, toil, cga, f,handpumped well drk wtr. ACTIVITIES: Swimming; picnicking; fishing; boating,d (l, 1 mi). MISC.: Elev 2700 ft; 5 acres; pets. Iron Canyon Reservoir. Unit of the Whiskeytown-Shasta-Trinity NRA.

RUTH

Barry Creek (Six Rivers NF). 8 mi S of Ruth on oiled rd; on Barry Creek. SEASON: April-November. FACILITIES: 2 sites; tbls, cga. Creek dry late in season. ACTIVITIES: Fall deer hunting; horseback riding; hiking. MISC.: Elev 3000 ft. Pets permitted if kept on leash.

Littlefield Creek (Six Rivers NF). 2½ mi SE of Ruth via paved Co Rd and gravel FS 2S02. SEASON: April-November. FACILITIES: 3 sites suitable for tenting or pickup camper; tbls, toil, cga, piped water. ACTIVITIES: Hunting; picnicking; hiking. MISC.: Elev 2800 ft; 14-day lmt. Pets; privacy. Relief from summer heat. Within short drive to Mad River and Ruth Lake.

SALYER

Denny (Shasta-Trinity NF). 4½ mi E of Salyer on St Hwy 299; 1½ mi N on Co Rd; 15 mi NE on FS 7N01 (Denny Rd). [Difficult access for trailers. Requires careful driving.] SEASON: 5/1-10/31; 14-day lmt. FACILITIES: 16 sites (tr

-22), tbls, toil, cga, piped drk wtr. AC-
TIVITIES: Rockhounding; picnicking.
Fishing/swimming (1 mi). MISC.: Elev
1400 ft; 5 acres; pets on leash.

SAN FRANCISCO

Battery Alexander (Golden Gate NRA).
The Marin Headlands are just across
the Golden Gate Bridge from San Francisco (US 101). Take the Alexander Exit
½ mi, turn left on Bunker Rd, through
the tunnel, 4 mi to the Marin Headlands
Ranger Station. SEASON: All yr. FACILI-
TIES: Environmental living GROUP CAMP-
SITE in a converted military gun bunker. Maximum group size is 65 persons;
minimum 15 persons. Electricity, water,
chemical toil, sleeping shelter, sleeping
bunks, tbls, cga. MISC.: Reservations
are required. Reservations can be obtained by writing the Marin Headlands
Ranger Station, Bldg 1050, Fort Cronkhite, Sausalito, CA 94965, or by phoning
415/561-7612. All groups are required
to check in at the Marin Headlands Ranger Station upon arrival in the park.

Hill 88 (Golden Gate NRA). The Marin
Headlands are just across the Golden
Gate Bridge from San Francisco (US 101).
Take the Alexander Exit ½ mi, turn
left on Bunker Rd, through the tunnel,
4 mi to the Marin Headlands Ranger
Station. SEASON: All yr. FACILITIES:
GROUP CAMPGROUND, maximum 25 persons.
This is an indoor facility with chemical
toil, bunks, picnic tbls, cga. No water
or f. MISC.: Reservations are required.
Reservations can be obtained by writing
the Marin Headlands Ranger Station,
Bldg 1050, Fort Cronkhite, Sausalito,
CA 94965; or by phoning 415/561-7612.
All groups are required to check in
at the Marin Headlands Ranger Station
upon arrival in the park. Hill 88 overlooks San Francisco Bay and is often
foggy or windy.

SAN LUIS OBISPO

*Sulphur Pot Trail Camp (Los Padres NF).
18 mi N of San Luis Obispo on St Hwy
101; 11 mi E on Pozo-Arroyo Grande Co
Rd; 8½ mi N on Lopez Canyon Rd; 2½
mi on TRAIL 13E03. FACILITIES: 1 tent
site; tbl, cga. ACTIVITIES: Hiking, picnicking. MISC.: Pets on leash.

*Upper Lopez Trail Camp (Los Padres NF).
18 mi N of San Luis Obispo on St Hwy
101; 11 mi E on Pozo-Arroyo Grande Co
Rd; 8½ mi N on Lopez Canyon Rd; 2½
mi on TRAIL 13E03. FACILITIES: 1 tent
site; tbl, cga, drk wtr. MISC.: Pets.

SAN MARGARITA

American Canyon (Los Padres NF). 1-1/10
mi E of San Margarita on St Hwy 58;
17-1/5 mi E on Co Hwy 21; 7 mi SE on

FS 30S02; 2-1/10 mi NE on FS 30S04.
SEASON: All year; 14-day lmt. FACILITIES:
14 sites, no trailers; tbls, toil, cga,
piped drk wtr. ACTIVITIES: Hiking; picnicking. Horseback riding (1 mi). MISC.:
Elev 1700 ft; 3 acres; pets on leash.

Navajo (Los Padres NF). 1-1/10 mi E
of San Margarita on St Hwy 58; 21½
mi E on Co Hwy 21; 4-1/10 mi NE on
FS 29S02. SEASON: All yr; 14-day lmt.
FACILITIES: 4 sites (no trailers); tbls,
toil, cga, piped drk wtr. ACTIVITIES:
Hiking; picnicking. MISC.: Elev 2200
ft; 1 acre; pets on leash.

Queen Bee (Los Padres NF). 1-1/10 mi
E of San Margarita on St Hwy 58; 15-
4/5 mi E on Co Hwy 21; 10 mi NE on
FS 29S01; 1 mi SE on FS 29S18. SEASON:
All yr; 14-day lmt. FACILITIES: 5 sites
(no trailers); tbls, toil, cga, piped
drk wtr. ACTIVITIES: Hiking; picnicking. MISC.: Elev 2400 ft; 1 acre; pets.

SAN SIMEON

Alder Creek (Los Padres NF). 24½ mi
N of San Simeon on St Hwy 1; 8 mi E
on FS 23S01. SEASON: All yr; 14-day
lmt. FACILITIES: 5 sites (no trailers);
tbls, toil, cga, no drk wtr. ACTIVITIES:
Hiking; picnicking; fishing. MISC.: Elev
2300 ft; 3 acres; pets. Alder Creek.

SANTA BARBARA

*Blue Canyon (Los Padres NF). 8 mi N
of Santa Barbara on St Hwy 154; 22
mi E on FS 5N12; 7/10 mi E on FS 5N15;
1-2/5 mi N on TRAIL 26W14. SEASON:
All yr; 14-day lmt. FACILITIES: 1 tent
site; tbls, cga, f; no toil/drk wtr. AC-
TIVITIES: Horseback riding; hiking;
boating (no motors). MISC.: Elev 1700
ft; 1 acre; stream; pets on leash.

*Hidden Potrero (Los Padres NF). 13½ mi
N of Santa Barbara on St Hwy 154; 2
mi E on FS 5N18; 4-9/10 mi NE on TRAIL
5N15. [TRAIL 5N15 is open to foot, horse,
and motorcycle travel only.] SEASON:
11/15-6/30; 14-day lmt. FACILITIES: 1
tent site; tbls, cga, f, no drk wtr.
No toil. ACTIVITIES: Hiking; picnicking;
horseback riding. Horse rental (4 mi).
MISC.: Elev 2700 ft; 1 acre; pets.
Closed during fire season.

*Indian Creek Trail Camp (Los Padres
NF). 10 mi N of Santa Barbara on St
Hwy 154; 6½ mi E on FS 5N18; 14½ mi
NE on FS 9411; 6 mi SE on TRAIL 26W08.
SEASON: End of fire season to June 30.
FACILITIES: Nondrinkable stream water.
ACTIVITIES: Hiking. MISC.: Elev 2300
ft. Pets.

Juncal (Los Padres NF). 8 mi N of Santa
Barbara on St Hwy 154; 22 mi E on FS
5N12 (East Camino Cielo Rd); 5-3/5 mi

E on FS 5N15. [Narrow mountain dirt rds. Rd not advisable in wet weather or for trailers.] SEASON: All yr; 14-day lmt. FACILITIES: 6 sites (no trailers); tbls, toil, cga, f. Piped water, must be boiled for drinking. ACTIVITIES: Hiking; picnicking; fishing. Horseback riding (2 mi). MISC.: Elev 1800 ft;2 acres; pets. Mono Creek. Closed during fire season. Nature trails (2 mi). Travel via San Marcos Pass Road.

Lower Oso (Los Padres NF). 5½ mi NW of Santa Barbara on US 101; 10 mi NW on St Hwy 154; 5-3/5 mi E on FS 5N18 (Paradise Rd). SEASON: All yr; 14-day lmt. FACILITIES: 8 sites (no trailers); tbls, toil, cga, no drk wtr. ACTIVITIES: Horseback riding; picnicking; fishing. MISC.: Elev 1000 ft; 4 acres; pets. Santa Ynez River. Store (5 mi).

Middle Santa Ynez (Los Padres NF). 8 mi N of Santa Barbara on St Hwy 154; 22 mi E on FS 5N12; 8-4/5 mi N on FS 5N15. [¼ mi W of Pendola Guard Station.] Rd not advisable in wet weather or for trailers. SEASON: All yr; 14-day lmt. FACILITIES: 6 sites (no trailers); tbls, toil, cga, no drk wtr. ACTIVITIES: Hiking; picnicking; fishing. Horseback riding (1 mi). MISC.: Elev 1800 ft;3 acres; pets; stream. Nature trails (2 mi). Travel via San Marcos Pass Road.

Mono (Los Padres NF). 8 mi N of Santa Barbara on St Hwy 154; 22 mi E on FS 5N12 (E Camino Cielo Rd); 13-1/10 mi E on FS 5N15. [5 mi W of Pendola Guard Station.] Narrow mountain, dirt rds; not advisable to travel in wet weather or for trailers. SEASON: All yr (closed during fire season); 14-day lmt. FACILITIES: 9 sites (no trailers); tbls, toil, cga, f, no drk wtr. ACTIVITIES: Hiking; picnicking; fishing. MISC.: Elev 1400 ft; 4 acre; pets. Mono Creek.

P-Bar Flat (Los Padres NF). 8 mi N of Santa Barbara on St Hwy 154; 22 mi E on FS 5N12; 9-7/10 mi N on FS 5N15. [1 mi W of Pendola Guard Station.] Narrow mountain, dirt rds. Not advisable to travel in wet weather or for trailers. [Travel via San Marcos Pass Road.] SEASON: All yr; 14-day lmt. FACILITIES: 3 sites (no tr); tbls, toil, cga, no drk wtr. ACTIVITIES: Hiking; picnicking. Fishing (1 mi). MISC.: Elev 1500 ft; 1 acre; stream; pets. Nature trails (2 mi).

*****Santa Cruz Trail Camp** (Los Padres NF). 10 mi NW of Santa Barbara on St Hwy 154; 5-3/5 mi E on FS 5N18 (Paradise Rd); 1½ mi N on FS 5N15; 10 mi N on TRAIL 27N09. SEASON: 11/15 (end of fire season) to 6/30; 14-day lmt. FACILITIES: 6 tent sites; tbls, toil, cga, f, no drk wtr. ACTIVITIES: Hiking; picnicking.

Upper Oso (Los Padres NF). 10 mi NW of Santa Barbara on St Hwy 154; 5-3/5 mi E on FS 5N18 (Paradise Rd); 1½ mi N on FS 5N15. [High river flows block rd in winter.] Paved rd. Parking area. SEASON: All yr; 14-day lmt. FACILITIES: 27 sites (tr -16), tbls, toil, cga, f, drk wtr. 12 horse corrals for individual use. Parking for 17 horse-trailers. ACTIVITIES: Hiking; horseback riding; picnicking. Horse rental (2 mi). MISC.: Elev 1200 ft; 8 acres; pets; nature trails. Santa Ynez River (1 mi). End of public rd, trails lead N to Santa Cruz and San Rafael Wilderness. Swimming (3 mi).

SANTA MARGARITA

American Canyon (Los Padres NF). 1-1/10 mi E of Santa Margarita on St Hwy 58; 17-1/5 mi E on Co Rd 21 (Pozo Rd); 7 mi SE on FS 30S02; 2-1/10 mi NE on FS 30S04. SEASON: Deer hunting season only; 8/5-9/15; 14-day lmt. FACILITIES: 17 sites (limited trailer space); tbls, toil, cga, piped spring drk wtr. ACTIVITIES: Deer hunting; horseback riding; hiking; MISC.: Elev 1700 ft; 3 acres; pets.

Friis (Los Padres NF). 22½ mi E of Santa Margarita on Margarita-Pozo Co Rd (321); 4 mi NE on FS 29S02; 1 mi N on undesignated FS. SEASON: All yr; 14-day lmt. FACILITIES: 5 sites (no trailers); toil, cga, spring water. ACTIVITIES: Hiking. MISC.:Elev 2200 ft;pets.

Navajo (Los Padres NF). 21 mi SE of Santa Margarita on Pozo-Santa Margarita Rd (#21); 4 mi E on FS 29S02. SEASON: All yr; 14-day lmt. FACILITIES: 4 sites (no trailers); tbls, toil, cga, spring water. ACTIVITIES: Hiking; picnicking. MISC.: Elev 2200 ft; pets on leash.

Queen Bee (Los Padres NF). 1-1/10 mi E of Santa Margarita on St Hwy 58; 27-1/10 mi E on Co Rd 21; 1-1/10 mi SE on FS 29S18. SEASON: All yr; 14-day lmt. FACILITIES: 5 sites (some trailer spaces); tbls, toil, cga, spring drk wtr. ACTIVITIES: Hiking; picnicking. MISC.: Elev 2400 ft; 1 acre; pets.

SANTA MARIA

Barrel Springs (Los Padres NF). 3 mi N of Santa Maria on I-101; 15 mi E on St Hwy 166; 8 mi S on Co Rd; 8 mi SE on FS 11N04. SEASON: All year; 14-day lmt. FACILITIES: 5 sites (no trailers); tbls, toil, cga, piped drk wtr. ACTIVITIES: Hiking; picnicking. MISC.: Elev 1000 ft;2 acres;stream;pets.

Colson Canyon (Los Padres NF). 3 mi N of Santa Maria on I-101; 15 mi E on St Hwy 166; 8 mi S on Co Hwy; 8 mi SE on FS 11N04. SEASON: 3/15-11/15; 14-day lmt. FACILITIES: 3 sites (tr -16), tbls, toil, cga, piped drk wtr.

See page 7 for KEY TO ABBREVIATIONS.

ACTIVITIES: Hiking; picnicking. **MISC.:** Elev 1000 ft; 2 acres; stream; pets.

Brookshire Springs (Los Padres NF). 3 mi N of Santa Maria on I-101; 15 mi E on St Hwy 166; 6 mi E on FS 11N04. **SEASON:** All year; 14-day lmt. **FACILITIES:** 1 sites (tr -16), tbls, toil, cga, piped drk wtr. ACTIVITIES: Hiking; picnicking. **MISC.:** Elev 1500 ft; pets.

Colson Canyon (Los Padres NF). 3 mi N of Santa Maria on I-101; 15 mi E on St Hwy 166; 8½ mi S on Buckhorn Canyon Rd; 4 mi E on FS 11N64. [Trailers not advised because of narrow, steep dirt rd.] Road impassable in wet weather. **SEASON:** All yr; 14-day lmt. **FACILITIES:** 9 sites (limited trailer space); tbls, toil, cga, spring water. ACTIVITIES: Hiking; picnicking. **MISC.:** Elev 2000 ft; pets.

Horseshoe Springs (Los Padres NF). 3 mi N of Santa Maria on I-101; 15 mi E on St Hwy 166; 4½ mi SE on FS 11N04. **SEASON:** All year; 14-day lmt. **FACILITIES:** 4 sites (tr -16), tbls, toil, cga, piped drk wtr. ACTIVITIES: Hiking; picnicking. **MISC.:** Elev 1500 ft; 1 acre;pets.

Sierra Madre (Los Padres NF). 3 mi N of Santa Maria on US 101; 22½ mi NE on St Hwy 166; 2½ mi SW on FS 12N03. **SEASON:** All yr; 14-day lmt. **FACILITIES:** 30 sites (no trailers); tbls, f. No toil or drk wtr. ACTIVITIES: Hiking; picnicking. **MISC.:** Elev 1500 ft; 2 acres; pets. Primitive.

SANTA MIRANDA

Miranda Pines (Los Padres NF). 25 mi NE of Santa Miranda on St Hwy 166; 7½ mi SW on FS 32S13. **SEASON:** All yr; 14-day lmt. **FACILITIES:** 3 sites (no trailers); tbls, toil, cga. Water available at lower campsite only. ACTIVITIES: Hiking; picnicking. **MISC.:** Elev 4000 ft; pets on leash.

SANTA PAULA

*__Big Cone Trail Camp__ (Los Padres NF). On Santa Paula Creek, approx. 6 mi by St Hwy 150, and 4 mi by TRAIL, from Santa Paula. **SEASON:** 11/1-6/30; 14-day lmt. **FACILITIES:** 6 tent sites; tbls, toil, cga, stream water. ACTIVITIES: Hiking; picnicking. **MISC.:** Elev 1750 ft; pets.

SANTA YNEZ

Cachuma (Los Padres NF). 2 mi E of Santa Ynez on St Hwy 246; 2 mi SE on St Hwy 154; 12 mi NE on FS 7N07 (Happy Canyon Rd). [Narrow mountain rd, not advisable for travel with trailers.] **SEASON:** All yr; 14-day lmt. **FACILITIES:** 7 sites (tr -32), tbls, toil, cga, f, no drk wtr. ACTIVITIES: Picnicking. Horseback riding (1 mi). **MISC.:** Elev

2100 ft; 2 acres; stream; pets. Figueroa Mountain area.

*__Manzana Schoolhouse Trail Camp__ (Los Padres NF). 13 mi NE of Santa Ynez on FS 7N07; 5 mi NW on Co Rd 10N08; 2 mi N on TRAIL 30W07; 2½ mi N on TRAIL 30W13. **SEASON:** All yr; 14-day lmt. **FACILITIES:** 8 tent sites; tbls, toil, cga, no drk wtr. ACTIVITIES: Hiking; picnicking; fishing. **MISC.:** Elev 1200 ft; 2 acres; pets. Sisquoc River.

Nira (Los Padres NF). 10 mi NE of Santa Ynez on Co Rd 3350; 6 mi N on FS 7N07; 5 mi N on FS 8N09 (Figueroa Mountain Rd). **SEASON:** All year; 14-day lmt. **FACILITIES:** 5 sites (tr -22), tbls, toil, cga, no drk wtr. ACTIVITIES: Hiking; picnicking; fishing. **MISC.:** Elev 2000 ft; 3 acres; pets. Manzana River. Entrance into San Rafael Wilderness.

SAUGUS

Artesian Spring (Angeles NF). 18-1/10 mi NE of Saugus on Co Rd 6N05 (Bouquet Canyon Rd); 2-3/5 mi S on FS 6N08. **SEASON:** All yr; 14-day lmt. **FACILITIES:** 6 sites (tr -16), tbls, toil, cga, piped drk wtr. ACTIVITIES: Hiking; picnicking. **MISC.:** Elev 3800 ft; 3 acres; pets.

Chaparral (Angeles NF). 14-2/5 mi NE of Saugus on Co Rd 6N05 (Bouquet Canyon Rd). **SEASON:** All yr; 14-day lmt. **FACILITIES:** 8 sites (tr -16), tbls, toil, cga, no drk wtr. Store/fd/gas (1 mi). ACTIVITIES: Fishing; picnicking. **MISC.:** Elev 2400 ft; 1 acre; pets. Located in Bouquet Canyon. Bouquet Canyon Creek and Reservoir (2 mi).

Hollow Tree (Angeles NF). 14 mi NE of Saugus on Co Hwy 6N05. **SEASON:** All yr; 14-day lmt. **FACILITIES:** 5 sites (no trailers); tbls, toil, cga, no drk wtr. Store/fd/gas (1 mi). ACTIVITIES: Picnicking; fishing. **MISC.:** Elev 2400 ft; 1 acre; pets; stream. Located in Bouquet Canyon.

South Portal (Angeles NF). 18½ mi NE of Saugus on Co Hwy 6N05; 5-2/5 mi NW on Co Hwy 6N11; 1-3/5 mi SW on Co Hwy 7N28; 3/5 mi NW on FS 7N02. **SEASON:** **FACILITIES:** 10 sites (tr -22), tbls, toil, cga, no drk wtr. Store/ice/fd/gas (3 mi). ACTIVITIES: Picnicking. **MISC.:** Elev 2800 ft; 4 acres; pets; stream.

SAWYERS BAR

Little North Fork (Klamath NF). 3-3/5 mi NW of Sawyers Bar on Co Hwy 1001. **SEASON:** 6/1-10/31; 14-day lmt. **FACILITIES:** 4 sites (no trailers); tbls, toil, cga, no drk wtr. Store/fd/gas (4 mi). ACTIVITIES: Swimming; picnicking; fishing. **MISC.:** Elev 2000 ft; 2 acres; pets; river.

Red Bank (Klamath NF). 7-2/5 mi W of Sawyers Bar on Co Hwy 1C01. **SEASON:**

6/1-10/31; 14-day lmt. FACILITIES: 4 sites (tr -16), tbls, toil, cga, piped drk wtr. ACTIVITIES: Fishing; picnicking. MISC.: Elev 1700 ft; 1 acre; pets; Winding narrow road; hazardous for campers and trailers.

SCOTT BAR

Lovers Camp (Klamath NF). 13-3/5 mi SW of Scott Bar on Co Rd 7F01; 5-2/5 mi SW on FS 44N45; 1-7/10 mi SW on FS 43N45. SEASON: 6/1-10/31. FACILITIES: 10 sites (no trailers); tbls, toil, cga, f, piped drk wtr. ACTIVITIES: Picnicking. Fishing (1 mi). Swimming (3 mi). MISC.: Elev 4300 ft; 5 acres; pets. Canyon Creek (1 mi).

SEIAD VALLEY

Fort Goef (Klamath NF). 4-7/10 mi NW of Seiad Valley on St Hwy 96. SEASON: 5/1-10/31; 14-day lmt. FACILITIES: 5 sites (no trailers); tbls, toil, cga,piped drk wtr. Fd/ice/laundry/store/gas (5 mi). ACTIVITIES: Fishing; picnicking. MISC.: Elev 1400 ft; 4 acres; pets; on banks of scenic Klamath River.

O'Neil Creek (Klamath NF). 5-1/10 mi SE of Seiad Valley on St Hwy 96. SEASON: 5/1-11/15; 14-day lmt. FACILITIES: 24 sites (tr -22); tbls, toil, cga, piped drk wtr. Store/gas/ice/ showers/laundry (3 mi). ACTIVITIES: Picnicking; mountain climbing. Fishing (1 mi). MISC.: Elev 1500 ft; 9 acres; scenic; stream; pets. Close to Klamath River. Steelhead and Salmon fishing.

SHAVER LAKE

Duff Creek (Sierra NF). 5-3/5 mi SW of Shaver Lake on St Hwy 168; 10 mi E on FS 10S02 (Big Creek Rd). SEASON: 5/1-11/15; 14-day lmt. FACILITIES: 7 sites (tr -16), tbls, toil, cga, no drk wtr. ACTIVITIES: Swimming; picnicking; fishing. MISC.: Elev 3200 ft; 2 acres; pets. Big Creek.

Swanson (Sierra NF). 3 mi E of Shaver Lake on Co Hwy M2440 (Dinkey Creek Rd). SEASON: 5/15-10/30; 14-day lmt. FACILITIES: 14 sites (tr -22), tbls, toil, cga, no drk wtr. Store/fd/ice/gas (3 mi). ACTIVITIES: Picnicking; boating (rl, 3 mi). Horseback riding/rental (3 mi). MISC.: Elev 5600 ft; 4 acres; pets; scenic. Visitor Center (4 mi). Shaver Lake (3 mi).

SIERRA CITY

Berger Creek (Tahoe NF). 5 mi NE of Sierra City on St Hwy 49; 1-3/10 mi NW on Co Hwy F424 (Gold Lake Rd); 2-2/5 mi NW on Co Rd 20N16. SEASON:

6/15-10/15; 14-day lmt. FACILITIES: sites (tr -22), tbls, toil, cga, no drk wtr. ACTIVITIES: Fishing; picnicking. Boating,rd (2 mi). Swimming (3 mi). MISC.: Elev 5900 ft; 5 acres; pets. Packer Lake.

Loganville (Tahoe NF). 1½ mi W of Sierra City on St Hwy 49. SEASON: 5/15-10/15; 14-day lmt. FACILITIES: 10 sites (tr -22), tbls, toil, cga, f, no drk wtr. Store/fd/ice/gas/laundry (1 mi). ACTIVITIES: Picnicking. MISC.: Elev 3800 ft; 20 acres; river; pets on leash.

Salmon Creek (Tahoe NF). 5 mi NE of Sierra City on St Hwy 49; 1-3/10 mi NW on Co Hwy FH24. SEASON: 6/1-10/15; 14-day lmt. FACILITIES: 29 sites (tr -22), tbls, toil, cga, no drk wtr. Store/fd/ice/ gas/showers (1 mi). Laundry (4 mi). ACTIVITIES: Picnicking. Boating,rld (1 mi). MISC.: Elev 5800 ft; 10 acres; pets. Salmon Creek.

Sierra (Tahoe NF). 7 mi NE of Sierra City on St Hwy 49. SEASON: 6/15-10/15; 14-day lmt. FACILITIES: 15 sites (tr -22), tbls, toil, cga, no drk wtr. Store/ ice/fd/gas (2 mi). Showers/laundry (5 mi). ACTIVITIES: Swimming; picnicking; fishing. Boating,rld (5 mi). MISC.: Elev 5600 ft; 5 acres; pets. On North Yuba River. Sardine Lake (5 mi).

Snag Lake (Tahoe NF). 5 mi NE of Sierra City on St Hwy 49; 5-3/10 mi N on Co Rd FH24 (Gold Lake Rd). SEASON: 6/15-10/15; 14-day lmt. FACILITIES: 16 sites (tr -22), tbls, toil, cga, no drk wtr. Store/fd/ice/gas (4 mi). Spring water. ACTIVITIES: Swimming; picnicking; fishing. Waterskiing (1 mi). Boating,rld (2 mi, at Gold Lake; no motor boats). MISC.: Elev 6600 ft; 5 acres; pets. Adjacent to Snag Lake. Gold Lake (2 mi).

SIERRA MADRE

*Hoegees (Angeles NF). 1-2/10 mi E of Sierra Madre on Co Hwy SMDR; 4-1/5 mi N on Co Rd 2N41; 3 mi W on TRAIL 11W15; 3 mi NW on TRAIL 11W15. SEASON: All yr; 14-day lmt. FACILITIES:15 tent sites; tbls, toil, cga, no drk wtr. ACTIVITIES: Hiking; picnicking. MISC.: Elev 2600 ft; 3 acres; stream. Closed during high fire danger; see local ranger station for details. Pets. Horseback riding.

*Spruce Grove (Angeles NF). 1-1/5 mi E of Sierra Madre on Co Hwy SMDR; 4-1/5 mi N on Co Hwy 2N41; 4 mi NW on TRAIL 11W14. SEASON: All yr; 14-day lmt. FACILITIES: 6 tent sites; tbls, toil, cga, no drk wtr. ACTIVITIES: Picnicking; horseback riding; hiking. MISC.: Elev 3000 ft; 1 acre; stream; pets. Closed during high fire danger; see local ranger station for details.

See page 7 for KEY TO ABBREVIATIONS.

102

SIERRAVILLE

Bear Valley (Tahoe NF). 3/10 mi E of Sierraville on St Hwy 49; 7-3/10 mi E on FS 20N04 (Lemon Canyon Rd). [Rd not recommended for trailers.] SEASON: 6/1-11/1; 14-day lmt. FACILITIES: 6 sites (tr -16), tbls, toil, cga, piped drk wtr. ACTIVITIES: Fishing; picnicking. MISC.: Elev 6700 ft; 1 acre; pets. At the head of Bear Valley Creek.

Lower Little Truckee (Tahoe NF). 8 mi SE of Sierraville on St Hwy 89. SEASON: 5/15-11/1; 2-day lmt. FACILITIES: 15 sites (tr -22), tbls, toil, cga, no drk wtr. ACTIVITIES: Swimming; picnicking; fishing. MISC.: Elev 6200 ft; 4 acres; pets. On Little Truckee River.

SOMERSET

Capps Crossing (Eldorado NF). 12-7/10 mi E of Somerset on Co Hwy 100 (Grizzly Flat Rd); 9 mi E on FS 9N03; 1/5 mi NW on FS 10N55. SEASON: 6/15-10/31; 14-day lmt. FACILITIES: 8 sites (no trailers); tbls, toil, cga, no drk wtr. ACTIVITIES: Swimming; picnicking; fishing. MISC.: Elev 5200 ft; 5 acres; pets. North Fork Cosumnes River.

SPRINGVILLE

Coy Flat (Sequoia NF). 17 mi E of Springville on St Hwy 190; 1 mi S on Co Hwy 20S94. SEASON: 5/1-10/31; 14-day lmt. FACILITIES: 15 sites (tr -22), tbls, toil, cga, no drk wtr. Store/fd/ice/gas/shower (1 mi). ACTIVITIES: Picnicking. Fishing/swimming/horseback riding & rental (1 mi). MISC.: Elev 5000 ft; 2 acres; pets. Trailers may be parked where space is available. Campfire permit required. Near S fork of middle fork of Tule River. 1 mi S of Camp Nelson.

Frasier Mill (SF). 25 mi E of Springville on Co Rds. [Difficult access for trailers.] SEASON: 6/1-10/31; 14-day lmt. FACILITIES: 82 sites (tr -20), tbls, f. ACTIVITIES: Horseback riding; picnicking; fishing. MISC.: 40 acres; pets on leash.

*Grasshopper (Sequoia NF). 26½ mi E of Springville on St Hwy 190; 4 mi NE on FS 21S50; 15 mi NE on TRAIL 33E01. [Trail open to hikers, horses, and trailbikes.] SEASON: 5/1-10/31; 14-day lmt. FACILITIES: 6 tent sites; tbls, toil, cga, no drk wtr. ACTIVITIES: Hiking; horseback riding; picnicking; fishing. MISC.: Elev 5700 ft; 4 acres; pets. Campfire permit required. Grasshopper Creek.

*Kern Flat (Sequoia NF). 26½ mi E of Springville on St Hwy 190; 4 mi N on FS 21S50; 8 mi NE on TRAIL 33E01; 4 mi on TRAIL 33E10. [Trail open to hikers, horses, and trailbikes.] SEASON: 5/1-10/31; 14-day lmt. FACILITIES: 5

tent sites; tbls, toil, no drk wtr. ACTIVITIES: Hiking; horseback riding; picnicking; fishing (in season). MISC.: Elev 5000 ft; 4 acres; pets. Campfire permit required. E Fork of Kern River. Although unburned, Kern Flat is located in the center of the 17,000-acre Flat Fire which burned in 1975.

Moses Gulch (SF). 3 mi N of Springville on St Hwy 190; 22 mi E on Bear Creek Rd. SEASON: 6/1-10/31; 14-day lmt. FACILITIES: 11 sites (tr -16), tbls, toil, f, drk wtr. ACTIVITIES: Hiking; picnicking. MISC.: 20 acres; pets.

Mt. Home (SF). 25 mi E of Springville on Co Rds. [Difficult trailer access.] SEASON: 6/1-10/31; 14-day lmt. FACILITIES: 68 sites (tr -20), tbls, toil, cga, f, drk wtr. ACTIVITIES: Hiking; horseback riding; swimming; picnicking; fishing. MISC.: Pets on leash.

Peppermint (Sequoia NF). 26½ mi E of Springville on St Hwy 190; 3 mi S on Co Hwy FH90 (Great Western Divide Rd); 3/5 mi E on Co Hwy 21S07. [Paved and dirt rd; difficult for trailers.] SEASON: 5/1-10/31; 14-day lmt. FACILITIES: 19 sites (tr -22), tbls, toil, cga, no drk wtr. Store/fd/ice/gas (2 mi). ACTIVITIES: Swimming; picnicking; fishing. Horseback riding/rental (2 mi). MISC.: Elev 7100 ft; 10 acres; pets. Campfire permit required. Supplies at Ponderosa. Peppermint Creek.

*Rifle Creek (Sequoia NF). 21 mi N of Quaking Aspen Campground (which is 27 mi E of Springville at jct of St Hwy 190 and Western Divide Hwy) via FS 21S50 and TRAILS 32E11/32E02. [Trail open to hikers and horses only.] SEASON: 5/1-10/31; 14-day lmt. FACILITIES: 3 tent sites; toil, no drk wtr. ACTIVITIES: Hiking; horseback riding; fishing (in season). MISC.: Elev 7500 ft; pets. Camping permit required. Spring water. 4-stock corral but no pasture.

Shake Camp (SF). 3 mi N of Springville on St Hwy 190; 22 mi E on Bear Creek Rd. SEASON: 6/1-10/31; 14-day lmt. FACILITIES: 11 sites (tr -20), tbls, toil, f, drk wtr. ACTIVITIES: Hiking; picnicking. MISC.: Pets on leash.

Sunset Point (SF). 3 mi N of Springville on St Hwy 190; 22 mi E on Bear Creek Rd. SEASON: 6/1-10/31; 14-day lmt. FACILITIES: 4 sites (no trailers); tbls, toil, f, drk wtr. ACTIVITIES: Hiking; picnicking. MISC.: Pets on leash.

STIRLING

Philbrook (Lassen NF). 11 mi N of Stirling on Co Rd 91513; 4 mi E on Co Rd 92523 (Philbrook Rd). SEASON: 6/1-10/1; 14-day lmt. FACILITIES: 7 sites (no trailers); tbls, toil, cga, piped drk wtr.

ACTIVITIES: Swimming; picnicking; fishing; boating,d. MISC.: Elev 5500 ft; 2 acres; pets. On N side of Philbrook Reservoir.

STONYFORD

Cedar Camp (Mendocino NF). 6½ mi W of Stonyford on Co Hwy 18N01 (Fouts Spring Rd); 10-7/10 mi S on FS 18N07 (John Smith Rd); 2 mi SW on FS 17N02. [Access up Trough Ridge or Little Stony Rd is poor for trailers.] SEASON: 5/1-10/15; 14-day lmt. FACILITIES: 6 sites (no trailers); tbls, toil, cga, no drk wtr. ACTIVITIES: Picnicking. Fishing/swimming/boating (5 mi). Power boats prohibited on lake. MISC.: Elev 4300 ft; 2 acres; pets. Little Stony Creek (5 mi). Located in timber area, mature stand of mixed fir and pine.

Digger Pine (Mendocino NF). 6-1/10 mi S of Stonyford on Co Hwy 32 (Lodoga Stonyford Rd); 3-4/5 mi SW on Co Rd 42 (Goat Mountain Rd). SEASON: All yr. FACILITIES: 7 sites (tr -16), tbls, toil, cga, no drk wtr. ACTIVITIES: Swimming; picnicking; fishing. MISC.: Elev 1500 ft; 2 acres; pets. Botanical area (5 mi). Located in Little Stony Creek drainage. Site very popular in winter when stream is in full flow.

Diversion Dam (Mendocino NF). 3 mi W of Stonyford on Rd 18N01. SEASON: All yr. FACILITIES: 5 sites (no trailers); tbls, toil, cga, no drk wtr. ACTIVITIES: Hiking; picnicking. MISC.: Elev 1300 ft; pets. In open grove of oaks. Very dry site in the summer.

Fouts Campground (Mendocino NF). 8-4/5 mi W of Stonyford on Co Rd 18N01 (Fouts Spring Rd); 3/10 mi N on Co Rd 18N03. SEASON: All yr; 14-day lmt. FACILITIES: 8 sites (tr -22), tbls, toil, cga, no drk wtr. ACTIVITIES: Swimming; picnicking; fishing; rockhounding. MISC.: Elev 1600 ft; 7 acres; pets. Stony Creek. Snow Mountain Jasper (5 mi). Digger pine trees in north end of camp.

Mill Creek (Mendocino NF). 8-7/10 mi W of Stonyford at Mill Creek on Co Rd 18N01 (Fouts Spring Rd). SEASON: All 14-day lmt. FACILITIES: 6 sites (tr -22), tbls, toil, cga, no drk wtr. ACTIVITIES: Rockhounding; swimming; picnicking; fishing. MISC.: Elev 1600 ft; 2 acres; pets. Small roadside campground. In winter and early spring streamflow is up. Snow Mountain Jasper is at the site.

Mill Valley Campground (Mendocino NF). 9 mi W of Stonyford on Co Rd 18N01; 6 mi SW on FS 18N01 (Fouts Springs Rd); 1-3/5 mi S on FS 17N02. SEASON: 4/15-11/1; 14-day lmt. FACILITIES: 18 sites (tr -16), tbls, toil, cga, piped drk wtr. ACTIVITIES: Boating,d; sailing; picnicking. (No motor boats.) Fishing/swimming (2 mi). Hiking. MISC.: Elev 4000 ft; 5 acres; pets. Nature trails (2 mi). Lower Letts Lake (2 mi).

North Fork (Mendocino NF). 9 mi W of Stonyford on Co Rd 18N01 (Fouts Spring Rd); 2-3/10 mi N on Co Rd 18N03. SEASON: All yr; 14-day lmt. FACILITIES: 8 sites (tr -16), tbls, toil, cga, no drk wtr. ACTIVITIES: Swimming; picnicking; fishing; rockhounding. MISC.: Elev 1700 ft; 3 acres; pets. Adjacent to yearlong stream (Stony Creek). Camp is located in open grove of oak trees. Snow Mountain Jasper is at the site.

Old Mill (Mendocino NF). 6½ mi W of Stonyford on Co Hwy 18N01 (Fouts Spring Rd); 7-1/10 mi S on FS 18N07 (John Smith Rd). SEASON: 5/1-11/1; 14-day lmt. FACILITIES: 10 sites (tr -16), tbls, toil, cga, gravity piped drk wtr. ACTIVITIES: Rockhounding; picnicking. Fishing (5 mi). MISC.: Elev 3600 ft; 3 acres; pets. Located in mature stand of mixed pine and fir. Small trailers can use the site, but main access rd up Trough Ridge is narrow. Mill Creek (2 mi). Snow Mountain Jasper is within 5 mi of camp.

STOVE PIPE WELLS

Mahogany Flats (Death Valley NM). 9 mi SW of Stove Pipe Wells on St Hwy 190; 29 mi SE on Wildrose Canyon Rd. [Difficult rd access.] SEASON: 4/15-10/15; 30-day lmt. FACILITIES: 10 sites (no trailers); tbls, toil, cga, no drk wtr. ACTIVITIES: Hiking; picnicking. MISC.: Elev 8200 ft; pets. 9 mi SE of Wildrose Ranger Station (Death Valley NM).

Thorndike Camp (Death Valley NM). 9 mi SW of Stove Pipe Wells on St Hwy 190; 29 mi SE on Wildrose Canyon Rd. SEASON: 4/15-10/15; 30-day lmt. FACILITIES: 10 sites (no trailers); tbls, toil, cga, no drk wtr. ACTIVITIES: Hiking; picnicking. MISC.: Elev 7500 ft; pets. 8 mi SE of Wildrose Ranger Station.

Wildrose (Death Valley NM). 9 mi SW of Stove Pipe Wells on St Hwy 190; 21 mi S on Wildrose Canyon Rd at ranger station. SEASON: All yr; 30-day lmt. FACILITIES: 38 sites (no trailers); tbls, toil, cga, no drk wtr. ACTIVITIES: Hiking; picnicking. MISC.: Elev 4000 ft; pets.

STRAWBERRY

Cascade Creek (Stanislaus NF). 9-1/10 mi NE of Strawberry on St Hwy 108; 1/5 mi NE on FS 5N28. SEASON: 6/1-10/15; 14-day lmt. FACILITIES: 6 sites (tr -22), tbls, toil, cga, no drk wtr. ACTIVITIES: Hiking; mountain climbing; picnicking. MISC.: Elev 6000 ft; 3 acres;

pets. Cascade Creek. 4-3/5 mi from the Trail of the Ancient Dwarfs.

Herring Creek Reservoir (Stanislaus NF). 1-1/10 mi N of Strawberry on St Hwy 108; 7½ mi NE on FS 5N11. SEASON: 6/15-10/15; 14-day lmt. FACILITIES: 6 sites (tr -16), tbls, toil, cga, no drk wtr. ACTIVITIES: Hiking; picnicking; fishing. MISC.: Elev 7400 ft; 5 acres; pets. Herring Creek Reservoir.

Mill Creek (Stanislaus NF). 11-1/5 mi NE of Strawberry on St Hwy 108; 2/5 mi NE on FS 5N21; ½ mi N on FS 5N26. SEASON: 6/1-10/15; 14-day lmt. FACILITIES: 12 sites (tr -22), tbls, toil, cga, f, no drk wtr. ACTIVITIES: Hiking; mountain climbing; picnicking; fishing. MISC.: Elev 6200 ft; 3 acres; pets. Nature trails (3 mi). Mill Creek. Donnell Vista (3-3/5 mi). Rock Garden Nature Trail (2-4/5 mi). Trail of the Ancient Dwarfs (2-4/5 mi).

SUNLAND

Pappy Keef (Angeles NF). 5 mi NW of Sunland on St Hwy 118; 6 mi NE on FS 4N47 (Little Tujunga Rd); 4 mi NE on FS 3N37; 1 mi E on FS 3N23. SEASON: All yr; 14-day lmt. FACILITIES: 9 sites (no trailers); tbls, toil, cga, no drk wtr. ACTIVITIES: Hiking; picnicking. Near legal target shooting area. MISC.: Elev 3100 ft; 2 acres; pets; stream. Limited parking. Hike to campsites 100 yds.

*__Tom Lucas__ (Angeles NF). 6 mi NE of Sunland on Co Rd 2N78 (Big Tujunga Rd); 3½ mi NE on TRAIL 13W03. SEASON: 3/1-11/30; 14-day lmt. FACILITIES: 6 tent sites; tbls, toil, cga, no drk wtr. ACTIVITIES: Horseback riding; hiking; picnicking. MISC.: Elev 2900 ft; 1 acre; pets; scenic; stream. Obtain free required fire permit at Big Tujunga Station.

SUSANVILLE

Eagle Lake (BLM). 33 mi N of Susanville on St Hwy 139. SEASON: June-October. FACILITIES: 17 sites; water. ACTIVITIES: Swimming; fishing; boating; hunting. MISC.: Elev 5100 ft; pets. Volcanic formation.

Ramshorn Spring (BLM). Countryside 50 mi N of Susanville; 2-3/5 mi E of US 395 on Post Camp Rd. SEASON: June-Oct. FACILITIES: 3 sites (no trailers); water. ACTIVITIES: Hunting. MISC.: Elev 6000 ft; pets.

TAHOE CITY

Deerpark. ½ mi W of Tahoe City on St Hwy 28; 4½ mi NW on ST Hwy 89. [Located along Truckee River.] SEASON: 5/1-10/31; 14-day lmt. FACILITIES: 10 sites (no trailers); tbls, toil, no drk wtr.

Store/ice/laundry/gas/shower (5 mi). Fd (1 mi). ACTIVITIES: Swimming; picnicking; fishing. Horseback riding/rental (1 mi). Boating,l/waterskiing (5 mi). MISC.: Elev 6200 ft; 3 acres; pets. Dump station (5 mi).

TEMECULA

Fishermans Camp (Cleveland NF). 2 mi N of Temecula on US 395; 2 mi NW on St Hwy 71; 12 mi W on Co Hwy 7S01; 4 mi NW on FS 6S082; 2 mi W on FS 7S07. SEASON: All yr; 14-day lmt. FACILITIES: 5 sites (no trailers); tbls, toil, cga, no drk wtr. ACTIVITIES: Hiking; picnicking. Horseback riding (1 mi). MISC.: Elev 1200 ft; 12 acres; pets; stream.

THORN MEADOWS (Los Padres NF)

Thorn Meadows Campground. 3-2/5 mi W of Thorn Meadows on Co Hwy 95; 10-2/5 mi SW on Co Hwy 9N03C; 7½ mi S on FS 7N03; 1-3/5 mi on FS 7N03C. [Not recommended for house trailers because of difficult rd.] SEASON: 5/15-11/1; 14-day lmt. FACILITIES: 3 sites (no trailers); tbls, toil, cga, no drk wtr. Nearest supplies at Lake-of-the-Woods (19 mi). ACTIVITIES: Hiking; horseback riding; picnicking. MISC.: Elev ranges from 5000-6935 ft; pets; creek. The Thorn Point Trail is approx. 3 mi long. It starts at Thorn Meadows Campground and terminates at the Thorn Point Lookout. There is no water on the trail. The majority of the trail is a steep uphill climb. However, fine conifer forest and excellent views reward the trail traveler. Thorn Point Lookout is manned from approx. 7/1-11/1. Travelers are welcome to visit the Lookout. On a clear day, the Pacific Ocean is in view. Purify all water before drinking. For the horse enthusiast, public corrals are available at the campground.

THREE RIVERS

Atwell Mill (Sequoia and Kings Canyon NPs). 24 mi SE of Three Rivers on St Hwy 198. [Rd to campground is steep, narrow and winding.] SEASON: June-Sept. FACILITIES: 23 sites (no trailers); tbls, toil, cga, piped drk wtr. ACTIVITIES: Picnicking. Fishing nearby. MISC.: Elev 6645 ft; pets. Store at Silver City (2 mi).

Horsecreek Recreation Area (COE). 5 mi SW of Three Rivers on St Hwy 198. SEASON: All yr; 14-day lmt. FACILITIES: 76 sites; flush toil. ACTIVITIES: Swimming; fishing (trout, catfish, bass); waterskiing (ski rentals). Boating,rl (1 mi). MISC.: Elev 650 ft; pets. Lake Kaweah.

See page 7 for KEY TO ABBREVIATIONS.

105

Sunny Point (Sequoia NF). 3½ mi NE of Three Rivers on St Hwy 198; 27 mi E on Co Rd 276 (Mineral King Rd) in Mineral King Valley. [Paved and narrow dirt rd.] SEASON: 6/1-10/31; 7-day lmt. FACILITIES: 5 sites (no trailers); toil, no drk wtr. Supplies at Silver City from June to LD only (1 mi). ACTIVITIES: Fishing; hunting. MISC.: Elev 7800 ft; 2 acres. E fork of Kaweah River. Located in Mineral King area, designated as the Sequoia National Game Refuge. Dogs must be on a leash at all times. Only deer and bear hunting are allowed.

South Fork (Sequoia NP). 15 mi SE of Three Rivers on S Fork Rd. SEASON: All yr; 14-day lmt. FACILITIES: 12 sites; toil, no drk wtr. ACTIVITIES: Fishing. MISC.: Elev 3650 ft; pets on leash. South fork of Kaweah River.

TINTA CANYON

*Deal Junction (Los Padres NF). Located up Tinta Canyon off St Hwy 33 where you can drive 1½ mi to Rancho Nuevo Campground. From there hike 1½ mi on TRAIL 24W03 through chapparal to the camp. FACILITIES: Tent sites; cga, no drk wtr. Mineral Springs are located along the trail. ACTIVITIES: Hiking; horseback riding. MISC.:Elev 3700 ft;pets.

TOM'S PLACE

Benton Crossing (Mono County Park). 9 mi N of Tom's Place on US 395; 7 mi E on Benton Crossing Rd. SEASON: All yr. FACILITIES: Undesignated sites; toil, no drk wtr. ACTIVITIES: Hunting; fishing. MISC.: Elev 7000 ft; pets on leash. Ghost Town of Bodie. Owens River and Crowley Lake (2 mi).

Big Meadow (Inyo NF). 4 mi S of Tom's Place on Co Hwy FH89 (Rock Creek Rd). SEASON: 4/15-11/15; 14-day lmt. FACILITIES: 5 sites (tr -22), tbls, toil, cga, no drk wtr. Store/fd/ice/gas (4 mi). ACTIVITIES: Fishing; picnicking. Boating, rl (4 mi). Horseback riding (4 mi) and rental (5 mi). MISC.: Elev 8600 ft; 14 acres; pets. Rock Creek and Rock Creek Lake (4 mi). Stream.

Iris Meadows (Inyo NF). 3-1/5 mi S of Tom's Place on Co Hwy FH89 (Rock Creek Rd). SEASON: 4/15-11/15; 14-day lmt. FACILITIES: 16 sites (tr -22), tbls, toil, cga, no drk wtr. Store/food/gas (3 mi). ACTIVITIES: Picnicking; fishing. Boating,rl (5 mi). MISC.: Elev 8300 ft; 12 acres; pets; stream. Rock Creek and Rock Creek Lake (5 mi).

Mosquito Flat (Inyo NF). 9 mi S of Tom's Place on Co Hwy FH89 (Rock Creek Rd). SEASON: 5/15-10/15; 7-day lmt. FACILITIES: 15 sites (tr -22), tbls, toil, cga, no drk wtr. Store/ice (2 mi). ACTIVITIES: Horseback riding (rental, 1 mi); picnicking; fishing. Boating,rl

(2 mi). MISC.: Elev 1000 ft; 8 acres; pets; stream. Trailhead into John Muir Wilderness. Rock Creek and Rock Creek Lake (2 mi).

Palisade (Inyo NF). 5 mi S of Tom's Place on Co Hwy FH89 (Rock Creek Rd). SEASON: 4/15-11/15; 14-day lmt. FACILITIES: 5 sites (tr -22), tbls, toil, cga, no drk wtr. Store/fd/ice (3 mi). Gas (5 mi). ACTIVITIES: Fishing; picnicking. Boating,rl (3 mi). Horseback riding/rental (4 mi). MISC.: Elev 8600 ft; 2 acres; pets; stream. Rock Creek and Rock Creek Lake (3 mi).

Rock Creek Lake Inlet (Inyo NF). 7-3/5 mi S of Tom's Place on Co Hwy FH89 (Rock Creek Rd); 3/10 mi S on FS 36. SEASON: 5/1-11/1; 14-day lmt. FACILITIES: 22 sites (tr -22), tbls, toil, cga, no drk wtr. Store/fd/ice (1 mi). ACTIVITIES: Boating,l (r, 1 mi); picnicking; fishing; horseback riding. MISC.: Elev 9600 ft; 15 acres; pets. Rock Creek Lake.

Tuff (Inyo CG). ½ mi E of Tom's Place on US 395. SEASON: 4/15-11/15; 14-day lmt. FACILITIES: 15 sites (tr -22), tbls, toil, cga, no drk wtr. Store/fd/ice/gas (1 mi). ACTIVITIES: Fishing; picnicking. MISC.: Elev 7000 ft; 15 acres; pets; Rock Creek.

TRINITY CENTER

Big Flat (Klamath NF). 8 mi N of Trinity Center on St Hwy 3; 22 mi W on Co Rd P104 (Coffee Creek Rd). SEASON: 7/1-9/30; 14-day lmt. FACILITIES: 5 sites (tr -16), tbls, toil, cga, no drk wtr. ACTIVITIES: Mountain climbing; horseback riding; picnicking. Fishing (1 mi). MISC.: Elev 5000 ft; 10 acres; pets. Salmon River.

Eagle Creek (Shasta-Trinity NF). 12-1/5 mi N of Trinity Center on St Hwy 3; 3-4/5 mi NE on Co Hwy 1089. [Accessible to trailers from Weaverville and Callahan but not from Castella.] Good rd. SEASON: 5/1-10/15; 21-day lmt. FACILITIES: 17 sites (tr -16), tbls, toil, cga, piped drk wtr. Store/fd/ice/laundry/gas (5 mi). ACTIVITIES: Swimming; picnicking; fishing; berry-picking. Horseback riding/rental (2 mi). MISC.: Elev 2800 ft; 10 acres; river; pets. 5 mi N of Coffee Creek Ranger Station. Limited trailer space.

Horse Flat (Shasta-Trinity NF). 12-1/5 mi N of Trinity Center on St Hwy 3; 1½ mi N on Co Hwy 1089; 2-4/5 mi NW on FS 38N27. SEASON: 6/1-9/30; 14-day lmt. FACILITIES: 14 sites (tr -16), tbls, toil, cga, piped drk wtr. ACTIVITIES: Hiking; picnicking; fishing; berry-picking. Swimming (3 mi). Horseback riding/rental (5 mi). MISC.: Elev 3000 ft; 12 acres; pets. On Eagle Creek. Trailhead to Salmon Trinity Alps Primitive Area. 7 mi N of Coffee Creek Ranger Station. Fd (5 mi).

See page 7 for KEY TO ABBREVIATIONS.

TRUCKEE

Alpine Meadow Campground (COE; Martis Creek Lake). Approx. 5 mi SE of Truckee on St Hwy 267. SEASON: May–October; 14-day lmt. FACILITIES: 25 sites (tr -25), tbls, toil, cga, drk wtr. ACTIVITIES: Boating (no launching ramps; no motor-powered boats on lake). Swimming; picnicking; fishing (trout). MISC.: Elev 5838 ft; pets. Season varies depending on weather conditions.

Annie McLoud (Tahoe NF). 2 mi N of Truckee on St Hwy 89; 3½ mi NE on Co Hwy 18N03 (Boca Rd). SEASON:5/15-10/15; 14-day lmt. FACILITIES: 25 sites (tr -22), toil, f, no drk wtr. ACTIVITIES: Swimming; fishing. Boating,ld (2 mi). MISC.: Elev 5800 ft; 10 acres; pets. Prosser Reservoir.

Boca (Tahoe NF). 6-4/5 mi E of Truckee on US 180; 2-1/5 mi NW on FS 18N03 (Boca Rd). SEASON: 5/1-10/30; 14-day lmt. FACILITIES: 10 sites (tr -16), toil, cga, no drk wtr. ACTIVITIES: Waterskiing; swimming; fishing. Boating,ld (1 mi). MISC.: Elev 5700 ft; 7 acres; pets. On SW shore of Boca Reservoir. A multi-lane concrete boat ramp, with toil and parking is available 1 mi W of the campground.

Boca Rest (Tahoe NF). 7 mi E of Truckee on US 80; 2½ mi N on Co Hwy 18N03. SEASON: 4/1-10/31; 14-day lmt. FACILITIES: 25 sites (tr -32), tbls, toil, cga, no drk wtr. ACTIVITIES: Swimming; fishing; waterskiing. Boating (ld, 4 mi). MISC.: Elev 5700 ft; 10 acres; pets. On Boca Reservoir.

Boyington Mill (Tahoe NF). 7 mi E of Truckee on US 18; 3-1/10 mi N on Co Hwy 21N03. SEASON: 4/1-10/31; 14-day lmt. FACILITIES: 10 sites (tr -32); tbls, toil, cga, f, no drk wtr. ACTIVITIES: Picnicking; swimming; fishing. Waterskiing (1 mi). Boating (1 mi); boat launch (4 mi). MISC.: Elev 5700 ft; 3 acres; river; pets.

Davies Creek (Tahoe NF). 7 mi E of Truckee on US 80; 9 mi N on Co Hwy 21N03 (Stampede Dam Rd); 2 mi W on Co Rd 19N03 (Henness Pass Rd). SEASON: 5/1-10/31; 14-day lmt. FACILITIES: 10 sites (tr -22), tbls, toil, cga, f, no drk wtr. ACTIVITIES: Fishing; picnicking. Boating,ld/swimming/waterskiing (1 mi). MISC.: Elev 6000 ft; 4 acres; pets. Davies Creek and Stampede Reservoir (1 mi). Historic immigrant trail.

Dead Jeffrey (Tahoe NF). 7 mi E of Truckee on US 80; 7 mi N on Co Hwy 21N03; 1½ mi W on Co Hwy 19N04. SEASON: 5/1-10/31; 14-day lmt. FACILITIES: 24 sites (tr -22), tbls, toil, f. ACTIVITIES: Fishing; picnicking. MISC.: Elev 6000 ft; pets; lake.

Goose Meadow (Tahoe NF). 1-3/10 mi W on US 18; 4-4/5 mi S on St Hwy 89. SEASON: 5/1-10/31; 14-day lmt. FACILITIES: 25 sites (tr -22); tbls, toil, cga, no drk wtr. Store (3 mi). Gas (4 mi). Ice/laundry (5 mi). ACTIVITIES: Picnicking; swimming; fishing. MISC.: Elev 6000 ft; 7 acres; lake; pets.

*__Jackson Point__ (Tahoe NF). 17-2/5 mi N of Truckee on St Hwy 89; 15-4/5 mi W on FS 19N07 (Henness Pass Rd); ½ mi SW, BY BOAT. [On the shore of Jackson Meadow Reservoir; about ½ mi SW of the Pass Creek boat ramp.] SEASON: 6/1-11/1; 14-day lmt. FACILITIES: 10 tent sites; tbls, toil, cga, no drk wtr. ACTIVITIES: Boating,d (l, 1 mi); swimming; waterskiing; picnicking; fishing. MISC.: Elev 6100 ft; 4 acres; pets; lake. Visitor Center (5 mi).

Lakeside (Tahoe NF). 4-3/10 mi N of Truckee on St Hwy 89; 2/5 mi E on FS 18N47. SEASON: 4/1-10/31; 14-day lmt. FACILITIES: 30 sites (tr -22); toil, no drk wtr. Store/gas/ice/laundry (5 mi). ACTIVITIES: Picnicking; fishing; swimming. Boating (l, 1 mi). MISC.: Elev 5700 ft; 15 acres; lake; pets. Boat speed limit 10 mph.

Polaris (Tahoe NF).4-1/10 mi E of Truckee on Co Hwy 17N45. [On the Truckee River, old Hwy 40.] SEASON: 5/1-10/15; 14-day lmt. FACILITIES: 6 sites (tr -22), tbls, toil, cga, no drk wtr. ACTIVITIES: Swimming; picnicking; fishing. MISC.: Elev 5800 ft; 6 acres; pets. Store/fd/ice/gas/ laundry (5 mi). Minimum development. Martis Creek.

Sagehen Creek (Tahoe NF). 9 mi N of Truckee on St Hwy 89; 1-3/5 mi SW on FS 18N11. SEASON: 5/15-10/15; 14-day lmt. FACILITIES: 9 sites (tr -16), tbls, toil, cga, no drk wtr. ACTIVITIES: Fishing; picnicking. MISC.: Elev 6500 ft; 10 acres; pets. On Sagehen Creek.

TUOLUMNE

Hacienda (Stanislaus NF). 4-3/5 mi NE on FS 1N01 (Buchanan Rd). [10 mi from Mi-Wok Ranger Station.] SEASON: 5/1-10/15; 14-day lmt. FACILITIES: 6 sites (tr -22), tbls, toil, cga, no drk wtr. Store/fd/ice/ laundry/gas (5 mi). ACTIVITIES: Fishing; picnicking. MISC.: Elev 2700 ft; 5 acres; pets. N fork of Tuolumne River.

TWENTYNINE PALMS

*__Belle Campground__ (Joshua Tree NM). ½ mi E of Twentynine Palms on St Hwy 62; 9 mi S on Utah TRAIL. SEASON: All yr; 14-day lmt. FACILITIES: 20 tents sites, among rock formations; tbls, toil, cga, no drk wtr. ACTIVITIES: Hiking; picnicking. MISC.: Elev 3800 ft; pets on leash.

Indian Cove (Joshua Tree NM). 6 mi W of Twentynine Palms on St Hwy 62; 3 mi S. SEASON: All yr; 14-day lmt. FACILITIES: 114 sites (tr -27), tbls, toil, cga, no drk wtr. Store (3 mi). Fd (5 mi). ACTIVITIES: Nature program (May-Nov.); picnicking. MISC.: Elev 3200 ft; pets on leash. North edge of the Wonderland of Rocks.

*__Jumbo Rocks Campground__ (Joshua Tree NM). 1 mi E of Twentynine Palms on St Hwy 62; 11 mi S on Utah TRAIL. SEASON: All yr; 14-day lmt. FACILITIES: 130 tent sites; tbls, toil, cga, no drk wtr. ACTIVITIES: Hiking; picnicking. Nature program (November-May). MISC.: Elev 4400 ft; pets on leash. Trails.

Ryan Campground (Joshua Tree NM). 15 mi SE of Twentynine Palms on St Hwy 62 to Joshua Tree; 16 mi SE on Park Blvd.-Quail Springs Rd. SEASON: All yr; 14-day lmt. FACILITIES: 27 sites (tr -27), tbls, toil, cga, no drk wtr. ACTIVITIES: Hiking; horseback riding; picnicking. MISC.: Elev 4300 ft; pets. Horses permitted; the only campground in Joshua Tree NM which permits horses.

*__White Tank Campground__ (Joshua Tree NM). ½ mi E of Twentynine Palms on St Hwy 62; 10 mi S on Utah TRAIL. SEASON: All yr; 14-day lmt. FACILITIES: 20 tent sites; tbls, toil, cga, no drk wtr. ACTIVITIES: Hiking; picnicking. MISC.: Elev 3800 ft; pets; hiking trails. Sites among rock formations.

TWIN BRIDGES

39 Mile (Eldorado NF). 4-9/10 mi W of Twin Bridges on US 50; 1/10 mi S on FS 11N95. SEASON: 5/15-10/15; 14-day lmt. FACILITIES: 4 sites (tr -22), toil, cga, piped drk wtr. Store/fd/ice/gas/laundry (3 mi). Showers (5 mi). ACTIVITIES: Picnicking. Swimming/fishing (1 mi). MISC.: Elev 5400 ft; 3 acres; pets.

UKIAH

Mayacamas (BLM). 9 mi E of Ukiah on Talmage Rd. [Off US 101.] SEASON: 5/1-10/1; 14-day lmt. FACILITIES: 7 sites (no trailers); toil, water. ACTIVITIES: Hunting; hiking; fishing. MISC.: Elev 2500 ft; pets. At McClure Creek. Cow Mountain Recreation Area. Mountainous terrain. Russian River.

Sheldon Creek (BLM). 14 mi S of Ukiah on US 101 to Hopland; 4½ mi E on St Hwy 175 (Hopland Rd); 8 mi SE on Younce Rd. SEASON: 5/1-9/1; 14-day lmt. FACILITIES: 10 sites (no trailers); toil, water. ACTIVITIES: Hunting; hiking. MISC.: Elev 2500 ft; small pets on leash. In Cow Mountain Recreation Area. Mountainous terrain.

South Red Mountain (BLM). 1½ mi S of Ukiah on US 101; 1-3/5 mi E on Talmadge Rd; 2 mi E on Mill Creek Rd; 6 mi E on New Cow Mountain Rd. SEASON: May-October; 14-day lmt. FACILITIES: 12 sites (no trailers); toil, no drk wtr. Boil water before use. ACTIVITIES: Fishing; hunting; hiking. MISC.: Elev 2500 ft; small pets on leash. Mendocino Lake and Russian River (2 mi). Mountainous terrain.

Willow Creek (BLM). 1½ mi S of Ukiah on US 101; 1-3/5 mi E on Talmadge Rd; 2 mi E on Mill Creek Rd; 4 mi E on New Cow Mountain Rd. SEASON: 5/1-10/1; 14-day lmt. FACILITIES: 20 sites (no trailers). ACTIVITIES: Fishing. MISC.: Elev 2500 ft; pets. Russian River and Mendocino Lake (2 mi).

UPPER LAKE

Bear Creek (Mendocino NF). 17 mi N of Upper Lake on Co Hwy 1N02; 6 mi E on Co Hwy 18N01; 1½ mi E on FS 17N33. SEASON: 5/1-10/15; 14-day lmt. FACILITIES: 16 sites (tr -16), tbls, toil, cga, no drk wtr. ACTIVITIES: Swimming; picnicking; fishing. MISC.: Elev 2300 ft; 6 acres; pets; creek.

Deer Valley (Mendocino NF). 12 mi N of Upper Lake on Co Rd 1N02; 4½ mi E on FS 16N01. SEASON: 4/1-10/30; 14-day lmt. FACILITIES: 11 sites (tr -16), tbls, toil, cga, no drk wtr. ACTIVITIES: Picnicking. MISC.: Elev 3700 ft; 4 acres; pets.

Lower Nye (Mendocino NF). 17 mi N of Upper Lake on Co Hwy 1N02; 6 mi E on Co Hwy 18N01; 14 mi N on FS 18N04. SEASON: 5/1-9/15; 14-day lmt. FACILITIES: 6 sites (no trailers); tbls, toil, cga, no drk wtr. ACTIVITIES: Picnicking. MISC.: Elev 3300 ft; 2 acres; stream; pets.

VALLEY SPRINGS

Acorn Campground (COE; New Hogan Lake). 1 mi S of Valley Springs on St Hwy 26; 1 mi left on Hogan Dam Rd; 2 mi left on N Shore Recreation Area Rd to campground. SEASON: 10/1-3/31; 14-day lmt. FACILITIES: 121 sites (tr -30), tbls, toil, cga, drk wtr. Marina nearby. ACTIVITIES: Hiking; boating; picnicking; fishing. MISC.: Hot showers; pets on leash.

Oak Knoll Campground (COE; New Hogan Lake). 1 mi S of Valley Springs on St Hwy 26; 1 mi left on Hogan Dam Rd; 2 mi left on N Shore Recreation Rd; adjacent to Acorn Campground. SEASON: 10/1-3/31; 14-day lmt. FACILITIES: 70 sites; tbls, toil, cga, drk wtr. Marina nearby. ACTIVITIES: Hiking; picnicking; fishing; boating. MISC.: Pets on leash.

VALYERMO

Big Rock (Angeles NF). 1–2/5 mi SE of Valyermo on Co Rd; 5–7/10 mi SE on Co Rd 4N11; 1/10 mi S on FS 4N11B. SEASON: All yr; 14–day lmt. FACILITIES: 9 sites (no trailers); tbls, toil, cga, no drk wtr. ACTIVITIES: Picnicking. Fishing (4 mi). MISC.: Elev 5500 ft; 1 acre; pets. Big Rock Creek.

VENTURA

*Anacapa Island (Channel Islands NM). This is the closest island to the mainland, approx. 11 mi S of Oxnard. Camping is confined to a campground on East Island, which has fireplaces and tbls. Latrines are also located at the East Anacapa Campground and at Frenchy's Cove. The campground is on a first-come, first-served basis. There is a limit to the number of persons which may use the campground -- therefore, everyone must register in advance with Monument Headquarters in Ventura. Do this before you make further arrangements. Campers must bring their own fd, fuel, wtr, and shelter. A tent (one which can be anchored securely) is good protection from the occasional heavy winds that blow over the island. In general, treat camping here as you would backpacking. Initially, from the Landing Cove to the top of the cliff, there is a climb of more than 150 steps, followed by a further ¼–mi walk to the campground...so pack light! ACTIVITIES: Swimming; picnicking; fishing; diving; hiking; boating. MISC.: Reach the island via commercial boat service. For directions from mainland to island, other information, and a map, contact: Supt., Channel Islands NM Headquarters; 1699 Anchors Way Dr.; Ventura, CA 93003; 805/644–8157.

*Santa Barbara Island (Channel Islands NM). A small, 259–hectare (approx. 640–acre) triangular island about 38 mi W of San Pedro Harbor in Los Angeles. Primitive camping is allowed in the vicinity of the ranger's quarters. Latrines are also located in this area. Campers must bring their own fd, fuel, shelter, and water. There will be some days when the ranger deems it necessary to prohibit open fires entirely because of the fire danger. Remember to pack light! There is a vertical climb of more than 100 ft to the camping area. Pack out all trash. Camping is limited to 4 days. It is safer to land and camp here when a ranger is present. Campers must register in advance with Monument Headquarters in Ventura. ACTIVITIES: Swimming; diving; picnicking; fishing; boating; hiking. MISC.: Reach the island via commercial boat service or private boat. For directions from mainland to island, other information, and a map, contact: Supt.;

Channel Islands NM Headquarters; 1699 Anchors Way Drive; Ventura, CA 93003; 805/644–8157.

VERDI

Crystal Park (Toiyabe NF). 8–2/5 mi NW of Verdi on FS 20002; 1/10 mi SW on FS 20008. SEASON: 6/1–10/15; 14–day lmt. FACILITIES: 21 sites (tr –16); tbls, toil, cga, f, piped drk wtr. ACTIVITIES: Picnicking; hiking; horseback riding. MISC.: Elev 6700 ft; 12 acres; pets; nature trails.

Dog Valley (Toiyabe NF). 6–3/10 ml NW of Verdi on FS 10002; 4/5 mi W on FS 10030. SEASON: 6/1–10/15; 14–day lmt. FACILITIES: 10 sites (tr –16); tbls, toil, cga, f, piped drk wtr. ACTIVITIES: Picnicking. Horseback riding (1 mi). Hiking (3 mi). MISC.: Elev 6300 ft; 5 acres; pets. Nature trails (3 mi).

VISALIA

Horse Creek Campground (COE; Lake Kaweah). 28 mi E of Visalia on St Hwy 198. SEASON: All yr; 14–day lmt. FACILITIES: 80 sites (tr –40), tbls, flush toil, hot showers, cga, drk wtr. Marina nearby. ACTIVITIES: Swimming; picnicking; fishing (large and small–mouth bass, crappie, bluegill, catfish); hiking; boating,l. MISC.: 60 acres; pets. Dump station.

WEAVERVILLE

Bridge Camp (Shasta–Trinity NF). 13–3/5 mi NE of Weaverville on St Hwy 3; 1½ mi NW on Co Hwy 112; 2 mi NW on FS 35N33. SEASON: 5/15–10/1; 14–day lmt. FACILITIES: 8 sites (no trailers); tbls, toil, cga, f, piped drk wtr. ACTIVITIES: Hiking; picnicking. Horseback riding/rental (1 mi). Swimming/fishing/boating,l/d/waterskiing/nature trails (5 mi). MISC.: Elev 2700 ft; 6 acres; stream; pets. Trailhead into Salmon–Trinity Alps Primitive Area. Clair Engle Lake Area.

*Mariners Roost (Shasta–Trinity NF). 13–3/10 mi NE of Weaverville on St Hwy 3; 5–1/5 mi E, BY BOAT, on Clair Engle Lake. SEASON: 6/1–9/1; 14–day lmt. FACILITIES: 7 tent sites; tbls, toil, cga, f, no drk wtr. Ice (2 mi). ACTIVITIES: Swimming; picnicking; fishing; boating,d (rl, 2 mi). MISC.: Elev 2400 ft; 3 acres; pets. A lakeshore camp on E Fort Stuart fork arm of Clair Engle Lake, E shore. Trinity Unit of Whiskeytown–Shasta–Trinity NRA.

*Ridgeville (Shasta–Trinity NF). 13–3/10 mi NE of Weaverville on St Hwy 3; 3–3/5 mi E, BY BOAT, on Clair Engle Lake. SEASON: 6/1–9/1. FACILITIES: 22 tent sites; tbls, toil, cga, f, no

drk wtr. Store/fd/ice/gas (1 mi). ACTI-
VITIES: Waterskiing; swimming; picnick-
ing; fishing; boating,d (rl, 1 mi).
MISC.: Elev 2400 ft; 6 acres; pets. A
lakeshore camp on Stuart Fork Arm of
Clair Engle Lake, N shore. Trinity
Unit of Whiskeytown-Shasta-Trinity NRA.

*Ridgeville Island (Shasta-Trinity NF).
13-3/5 mi NE of Weaverville on St Hwy
3 to Clair Engle Lake; 4 mi E, BY BOAT.
SEASON: 6/1-9/1. FACILITIES: Undesignated tent sites; toil, f. Store (2 mi).
ACTIVITIES: Swimming; waterskiing;
fishing; boating,d (rl, 2 mi). MISC.:
Elev 2400 ft; pets.

Rush Creek (Shasta-Trinity NF). 8-4/5
mi NE of Weaverville on St Hwy 3; ½
mi N on FS 34N97. SEASON: 6/1-9/15;
14-day lmt. FACILITIES: 11 sites (tr
-22), tbls, toil, cga, f. ACTIVITIES:
Fishing; picnicking. MISC.: Elev 2700
ft; 25 acres; pets; stream. Clair Engle
Lake (4 mi).

Stoney Creek (Shasta-Trinity NF). 14½
mi NE of Weaverville on St Hwy 3. SEA-
SON: 6/15-9/1; 1-day lmt. FACILITIES:
10 sites (no trailers); flush toil, f.
Store (3 mi). ACTIVITIES: Swimming;
waterskiing; boating (l, 1 mi; r, 2
mi). Fishing (1 mi). MISC.: Elev 2400
ft; pets. Clair Engle Lake.

WEST POINT

Moore Creek (Eldorado NF). 9½ mi E
of West Point on FS 7N03; 2½ mi E on
FS 7N06; 7 mi N on FS 7N07. SEASON:
5/1-11/15. FACILITIES: 18 sites (tr
-16), tbls, toil, no drk wtr. ACTIVI-
TIES: Swimming; picnicking; fishing;
sailing. Waterskiing (1 mi). Boating,l
(4 mi). Boating on Salt SPS Reservoir
often hazardous due to steep narrow
canyon. MISC.: Elev 3200 ft; 5 acres;
pets; river.

WHISKEYTOWN

Brandy Creek (Whiskeytown NRA). 6 mi
W of Whiskeytown on US 299; 6 mi on
Kennedy Memorial Dr. SEASON: All yr;
14-day lmt. FACILITIES: 40 sites (tr
-30), tbls, toil, cga, dump, drk wtr.
ACTIVITIES: Swimming; picnicking; fishing
(trout, bass); deer hunting; boating,rld.
MISC.: Elev 1210 ft; 20 acres; pets.
Whiskeytown Lake. Horseback riding;
waterskiing.

WILDWOOD

Grasshopper (Shasta-Trinity NF). 4/5
mi W of Wildwood on FS 29N29; 1/10 mi
W on St Hwy 36; 11½ mi S on FS 29N30;
11-9/10 mi E on FS 28N10. SEASON: 5/1-
10/31; 14-day lmt. FACILITIES: 3 sites
(tr -16), tbls, toil, cga, f, no drk wtr.
ACTIVITIES: Hiking; picnicking. MISC.:
Elev 4700 ft; 1 acre; pets. Trailhead
into Yolla Bolly Wilderness (1 mi).

WILLOW CREEK

Boise Creek (Six Rivers NF). 1-4/5 mi
W of Willow Creek on St Hwy 299. SEASON:
FREE in winter when water is shut off
(rest of yr, $2); 14-day lmt. FACILITIES:
12 sites (tr -22), tbls, toil, cga, piped
drk wtr. Store/ice (2 mi). ACTIVITIES:
Picnicking; fishing (trout, salmon, steelhead). Swimming (2 mi). MISC.: Elev
800; 4 acres; pets; stream. Trinity
River (3 mi).

WINTERHAVEN

Senator Wash (BLM). 19-3/4 mi N of Win-
terhaven on Co Hwy S24. SEASON: All
yr; 14-day lmt. FACILITIES: Undesignated
sites; toil, no drk wtr. Dump. ACTIVI-
TIES: Swimming; fishing (catfish, bass);
boating,l; waterskiing. MISC.: Elev 180
ft; pets on leash. Senator Wash Reservoir.

WOFFORD HEIGHTS

Davis (Sequoia NF). 8 mi W of Wofford
Heights on St Hwy 155; 10-4/5 mi SW on
Co Hwy 25S03 (Rancheria Rd). SEASON:
5/1-11/1; 14-day lmt. FACILITIES: 6 sites
(tr -22), tbls, toil, cga, piped spring
drk wtr. ACTIVITIES: Picnicking. MISC.:
Elev 5200 ft; 1 acre; pets on leash.

Evans Flat (Sequoia NF). 8 mi W of
Wofford Heights on St Hwy 155; 8 mi
SW on Co Hwy 25S03 (Rancheria Rd).
[Gravel rd.] SEASON: 5/1-11/1; 14-day
lmt. FACILITIES: 5 sites (tr -22), tbls,
flush toil, cga, no drk wtr. ACTIVITIES:
Picnicking. MISC.: Elev 6200 ft; 1 acre;
pets on leash.

Rhymes Camp (Sequoia NF). 8 mi W of
Wofford Heights on St Hwy 155; 4-1/5
mi SW on Co Rd 25S03 (Rancheria Rd).
[Gravel rd.] SEASON: 5/1-11/1; 14-day
lmt. FACILITIES: 5 sites (tr -22), tbls,
toil, cga, no drk wtr. Store/fd/ice/gas
(5 mi). ACTIVITIES: Picnicking. MISC.:
Elev 6500 ft; 1 acre; pets on leash.

Shirley Meadow (Sequoia NF). 8 mi W
of Wofford Heights on St Hwy 155; 2-
2/5 mi SW on Co Rd 25S03 (Rancheria
Rd). [Gravel rd.] SEASON: 5/1-11/1;
14-day lmt. FACILITIES: 5 sites (tr
-22), tbls, toil, cga, no drk wtr. Store/
fd/ice/gas (3 mi). ACTIVITIES: Picnicking. MISC.: Elev 6500 ft; 2 acres; pets.

Tiger Flat (Sequoia NF). 8 mi W of Wofford Heights on St Hwy 155; 4 mi N on
FH90. SEASON: 5/1-11/1; 14-day lmt.
FACILITIES: 6 sites (tr -22), tbls, toil,
cga, piped spring drk wtr. Store/fd/ice/
gas (5 mi). ACTIVITIES: Picnicking;
boating. MISC.: Elev 6600 ft; 2
acres; pets.

WRIGHTWOOD

Blue Ridge (Angeles NF). 5-3/5 mi W
of Wrightwood on St Hwy 2 (Angeles

Crest Hwy); 3-4/5 mi SE on FS 3N06. SEASON: 5/15-10/15; 14-day lmt. [Snow Dec.-April; access rd closed.] FACILITIES: 8 sites (tr -16), tbls, toil, cga, no drk wtr. ACTIVITIES: Hiking; picnicking. MISC.: Elev 7900 ft; 3 acres; pets; nature trails.

Cabin Flat (Angeles NF). 5-3/5 mi W of Wrightwood on St Hwy 2 (Angeles Crest Hwy); 14-9/10 mi SE on FS 3N06. SEASON: 5/15-10/15; 14-day lmt. [Snow Dec.-April; access rd closed.] FACILITIES: 11 sites (tr -16), tbls, toil, cga, f, no drk wtr. ACTIVITIES: Picnicking; fishing. MISC.: Elev 5400 ft; 2 acres; pets. Prairie Fork of San Gabriel River.

Cooper Canyon (Angeles NF). 26-7/10 mi W of Wrightwood on St Hwy 2; 1½ mi NE on FS 3N02. SEASON: 5/15-10/31; 14-day lmt. FACILITIES: 3 sites (no trailers); tbls, toil, cga, no drk wtr. ACTIVITIES: Picnicking. Fishing (1 mi). MISC.: Elev 6300 ft; 2 acres;pets;stream.

Grassy Hollow (Angeles NF). 6 mi W of Wrightwood on St Hwy 2 (Angeles Crest Hwy); 1/10 mi NW on FS 3N26. SEASON: All yr; 14-day lmt. [Snow, Dec.-March.] FACILITIES: 15 sites (tr -16), tbls, toil, cga, no drk wtr. ACTIVITIES: Hiking; picnicking. Horseback riding (4 mi). MISC.: Elev 7400 ft; 4 acres; pets. Visitor Center (3 mi). Nature trails (1 mi).

Guffy (Angeles NF). 5-3/5 mi W of Wrightwood on St Hwy 2 (Angeles Crest Hwy); 7-1/5 mi SE on FS 3N06. SEASON: 5/15-10/15; 14-day lmt. [Snow Dec.-April; access rd closed.] FACILITIES: 6 sites (tr -16), tbls, toil, cga, no drk wtr. ACTIVITIES: Hunting; hiking; picnicking. MISC.: Elev 8300 ft; 2 acres; pets.

*Little Jimmy (Angeles NF). 19-4/5 mi SW of Wrightwood on St Hwy 2 (Angeles Crest Hwy); 2-7/10 mi SE on TRAIL 9W03. SEASON: 5/15-10/15; 14-day lmt. FACILITIES: 5 tent sites; tbls, toil, no drk wtr. ACTIVITIES: Hiking; picnicking. MISC.: Elev 7400 ft; 6 acres; pets. Free required fire permit can be obtained from Valyerma Ranger District; 34146 Longview Rd; Pearblossom, CA 93553.

Lupine (Angeles NF). 5-3/5 mi W of Wrightwood on St Hwy 2 (Angeles Crest Hwy); 12 mi SE on FS 3N06. SEASON: 5/15-10/15; 14-day lmt. [Snow Dec.-April; access rd closed.] FACILITIES: 11 sites (tr -16), tbls, toil, cga, f, piped drk wtr. ACTIVITIES: Hunting; picnicking; fishing. MISC.: Elev 6600 ft; 3 acres; pets. Prairie Fork of San Gabriel River.

*Mine Gulch (Angeles NF). 5-3/5 mi NW of Wrightwood on St Hwy 2; 14-9/10 mi SE on FS 3N06; 2-1/10 mi W on TRAIL 8W091. SEASON: 5/15-10/15; 14-day lmt. [Snow Dec.-April; access rd closed.] FACILITIES: 5 tent sites; toil, cga.

No tbls/drk wtr. ACTIVITIES: Hiking; picnicking; fishing. MISC.: Elev 4500 ft; 1 acre; pets; stream.

YREKA

Copco Reservoir (BLM). 33 mi NE of Yreka on US 99 (North Central Valley). On Klamath River. SEASON: May-Nov. FACILITIES: 3 sites (no trailers); water. ACTIVITIES: Water sports; boating,l; fishing; hunting. MISC.: Elev 2500 ft; pets. Cooperative area; BLM/Pacific Power & Light Company.

Humbug (Klamath NF). 2-1/5 mi NE of Yreka on St Hwy 263; 2-1/10 mi NW on Co Rd 7J02 (Humbug Rd); 7½ mi W on FS 45N39; 9/10 mi W on Co Hwy 7J03. SEASON: 6/1-10/15; 14-day lmt. FACILITIES: 8 sites (no trailers); tbls, toil, cga, piped drk wtr. ACTIVITIES: Mountain climbing; picnicking; fishing. MISC.: Elev 3000 ft; 2 acres; pets; stream. On W Fork of Humbug Creek.

Juniper Point Camp (Pacific Power and Light Company). 12 mi N of Yreka on I-5; 11 mi E of Hornbrook on Co Rd (½ mi from Mirror Cove Campground). SEASON: May-October. FACILITIES: 9 sites; toil. ACTIVITIES: Swimming. MISC.: Klamath River. Pets on leash.

Mirror Cove Campground (Pacific Power and Light Company). 12 mi N of Yreka on I-5; 11 mi E of Hornbrook on Co Rd (½ mi from Juniper Point Camp). SEASON: May-October. FACILITIES: 10 sites; toil. ACTIVITIES: Boating,l; swimming. MISC.: On Klamath River. Pets on leash.

ZENIA STATION

Bear Wallow (Six Rivers NF). 3½ mi N of Zenia Station on oiled logging rd. SEASON: January-October. FACILITIES: 3 sites; tbls, toil, cga, piped drk wtr. [Toil located below middle unit.] ACTIVITIES: Fall deer hunting. MISC.: Elev 4900 ft; pets. Pleasant summer climate and good scenery.

READ THIS!

See page 7 for KEY TO ABBREVIATIONS.

COLORADO

GENERAL STATE INFORMATION

Miscellaneous

Toll-Free Number for Travel Information:
1-800-525-3083 (from out of state)

STATE CAPITOL: Denver
STATE NICKNAME: Centennial State
STATE MOTTO: "Nothing Without God"
STATE BIRD: Lark Bunting
STATE FLOWER: Columbine
STATE TREE: Blue Spruce

State Parks

Parks Pass: Visitors to the State Parks and Recreation Areas are required to display a current Colorado State Parks pass on their vehicle. Two types are available. A daily pass costs $1.00. The annual pass, $10.00, is valid at any State Park or Recreation Area for the remainder of the calendar year. Passes may be purchased at major park entrances, visitor centers, campgrounds, and most sporting goods outlets. Aspen Leaf Passport: To Colorado's senior citizens, 65 and over, the Division of Parks offers the Aspen Leaf Passport, a lifetime admission to all State Parks, Campgrounds, and Recreation Areas. The passport costs $2.00. No renewal is needed. CAMPGROUND FEES: In addition to the parks pass, a fee for each night's use of a campground is required which ranges from $2.00 to $3.00 per night. Further information: Colorado Division of Parks and Outdoor Recreation; Department of Natural Resources; 1313 Sherman, Room 618; Denver, CO 80203.

Rest Areas

No overnight stops are permitted in Colorado's rest areas.

INFORMATION SOURCES

Maps

The following maps are available from Forsyth Travel Library (see order form in Appendix B):

> State of Colorado [Up-to-date, showing all principal roads, points of interest, sports areas, parks, airports, mileage, etc. Full color.]

> Completely indexed city maps, including all airports, lakes, rivers, etc., of: Alamosa/Monte Vista; Broomfield; Cortez; Denver/Colorado Springs/Pueblo/Boulder; Fort Collins; Grand Junction; Loveland; Salida.

Gold Mining and Prospecting

Colorado Mining Industrial Development Board; 204 State Office Building; Denver, CO 80202.

State Information

Travel Marketing Section; Colorado Division of Commerce and Development; 602 State Capitol Annex; Denver, CO 80203. [303/892-3045]

Colorado Visitors Bureau; 225 West Colfax Avenue; Denver, CO 80202. [303/892-1112]
AAA Auto Club; 4100 East Arkansas; Denver, CO 80222.
Colorado State Patrol; 4201 East Arkansas Avenue; Denver, CO 80222. [303/757-9011]
Colorado Highway Department; 4201 East Arkansas Avenue; Denver, CO 80222.
Colorado Division of Wildlife; 6060 Broadway; Denver, CO 80216. [303/825-1192]
U.S. Geological Survey; Topographical Map Sales; Denver Federal Center, Building 41; Denver, CO 80225. [303/234-3832]
Planimetric Map Sales; Forest Service, USDA; Denver Federal Center; Building 46; Denver, CO 80225.
Wilderness Society; Western Regional Office; 5850 East Jewell Avenue; Denver, CO 80222.

City Information

Aspen Chamber and Visitors Bureau; PO Box 739; Aspen, CO 81611
Boulder Chamber of Commerce; 1001 Canyon Boulevard; Boulder, CO 80302
Colorado Springs Chamber of Commerce; PO Drawer B; Colorado Springs, CO 80901

COLORADO

Denver Convention and Visitors Bureau; 225 West Colfax Avenue; Denver, CO 80202
Denver Chamber of Commerce; 1301 Welton Street; Denver, CO 80204
Denver City Parks; East 23rd Avenue and York; Denver, CO 80205
Denver Mountain Parks; 1445 Cleveland Place, Room 304A; Denver, CO 80202
Denver City Map Dept.; City and County Building; 1445 Cleveland Place, Room 376; Denver, CO 80202

Fort Collins Area Chamber of Commerce; PO Box D; Fort Collins, CO 80521
Grand Junction Chamber of Commerce; PO Box 1330; Grand Junction, CO 81501
Greeley Chamber of Commerce; PO Box CC; Greeley, CO 80631
Pueblo Chamber of Commerce; Third and Santa Fe; Pueblo, CO 81002

National Forests

Arapaho-Roosevelt NF; Federal Building; 301 S. Howes Street; PO Box 1366; Fort Collins, CO 80522
Gunnison-Grand Mesa-Uncompahgre NF; 216 North Colorado; Gunnison, CO 81230
Pike NF; 320 West Fillmore; Colorado Springs, CO 80907
Rio Grande NF; 1803 West Hwy 160; Monte Vista, CO 81144
Roosevelt NF; 211 Canyon; Fort Collins, CO 80521
Routt NF; Hunt Building; PO Box 1198; Steamboat Springs, CO 80477
San Isabel NF; 910 Hwy 50 W; PO Box 5808; Pueblo, CO 81002
San Juan NF; Oliger Bldg; PO Box 341; Durango, CO 81301
White River NF; 733 Main; Meeker, CO 81641

National Monuments

Black Canyon of the Gunnison NM; PO Box 1648; Montrose, CO 81401
Colorado NM; Fruita, CO 81521
Dinosaur NM; Box 210; Dinosaur, CO 81610
Great Sand Dunes NM; Box 60; Alamosa, CO 81101
Hovenweep NM; McElmo Route; Cortez, CO 81321

Miscellaneous

Bureau of Outdoor Recreation; PO Box 2587; Denver Federal Center, Bldg 41; Denver, CO 80225
Facility Manager; Corps of Engineers; John Martin Resident Office; Star Route; Hasty, CO 81044
Mesa Verde NP; Mesa Verde National Park, CO 81330
Rocky Mountain NP; Estes Park, CO 80517
Colorado Bureau of Land Management; Colorado State Bank Building; 1600 Broadway, Room 700; Denver, CO 80202
Curecanti NRA; PO Box 1040; Gunnison, CO 81230
Shadow Mountain NRA; PO Box 100; Grand Lake, CO 80447
Chatfield SRA; 4201 South Parker Rd; Denver, CO 80232
Cherry Creek SRA; 4201 South Parker Road; Denver, CO 80232
Browns Park NWR; c/o Ouray NWR; 447 East Main Street, Suite 4; Vernal, Utah 84078
Browns Park NWR; Greystone, CO 81635

BACKCOUNTRY CAMPING

BUREAU OF LAND MANAGEMENT PRIMITIVE CAMPING

Although camping on the public lands outside improved campsites is not prohibited, it is not encouraged (except in designated primitive areas) because of sanitary, fire, litter, and surface damage problems. For specific developed BLM campgrounds in this chapter, see "Canon City" and "Grand Junction". Further information: BLM; Colorado State Office; Room 700; Colorado State Bank Building; 1600 Broadway; Denver, CO 80202.

COLORADO NATIONAL MONUMENT BACKCOUNTRY CAMPING

Backcountry camping is permitted free of charge, and encouraged. Such activity is allowable in any area lying more than $\frac{1}{4}$ mile from a road. No fees or advance registration is necessary, but they would appreciate your letting a ranger know your backcountry plans. Open fires are prohibited, and hikers must pack in enough drinking water to meet their personal needs. Further information: Superintendent; Colorado NM; Fruita, CO 81521. See "Fruita" for a developed campground in the NM.

DINOSAUR NATIONAL MONUMENT BACKCOUNTRY CAMPING

There are a number of free backcountry river sites at various locations. These sites are reserved EXCLUSIVELY for whitewater river trips, for which a free boating permit is required. These are not available to the casual visitor. For specific information on developed free campgrounds within the monument, see: "Dinosaur," "Maybell," and "Quarry." Further information: Superintendent; Dinosaur NM; Box 120; Dinosaur, CO 81610; 303/374-2216.

FLAT TOPS WILDERNESS; White River/Routt NFs

Lies on the White River Plateau, approximately 20 mi N of Glenwood Springs and 30 mi SW of Steamboat Springs; accessible from US Hwys 40, 6 and 24, and St Hwys 131 and 132. The Flat Tops are a concentration of flat-topped headlands dominated by the White River Plateau, a flattened dome of geological strata capped with lava. Travel in the silver forest can be difficult and dangerous. As increasing numbers of dead trees decay and fall, overland movement will become more difficult and dangerous and may be impossible in some areas. About 160 miles of trails cross the Wilderness. If you are experienced in backcountry travel, you will use these merely as starting points from which you will venture into the untracked valleys and plateaus. Hunting, fishing, hiking, camping. Further information: Supervisor; White River NF; 733 Main; Meeker, CO 81641.

GORE RANGE - EAGLES NEST PRIMITIVE AREA; Arapaho NF

61,000 acres; sharp knife-like ridges; glacial cirques; many lakes. Extremely rough terrain in some regions. Elevation ranges from 11,000-13,534 (on Mount Powell). Fishing, hunting, hiking, mountain climbing, camping. Further information: Superintendent; Arapaho NF; 1010 - 10th Street; Golden, CO 80401.

GREAT DUNES NATIONAL MONUMENT BACKCOUNTRY CAMPING

15 mi E of Alamosa on St Hwy 160; 16 mi N on St Hwy 150. Two sites along the Medano Pass Jeep Road are set aside for backpackers. These sites require a walk of 4 and 4-1/5 mi along the jeep trail. Fires are prohibited. Water is usually available; boil/purify before drinking. Trailheads leading into the Sangre do Cristo Mountains in Rio Grande NF begin within the NM. A free backcountry permit is required for overnight camping. These permits and topographic maps are available at the Visitor Center. Fishing; hiking; camping. WEATHER: Summer, from 40's to 90's. Snowstorms can occur any month of the year. Afternoon thunderstorms are common in July and August. Fall and spring, moderate temperatures. Winter can fall as low as -25 F with high winds. Mosquitos in summer. Self-guided nature trails near Visitor Center. ENTRANCE FEES: None collected mid-November to mid-March. Rest of year, $1 per vehicle per day. Hikers, bicyclists and bus passengers, 50¢ per day. Under 15 and over 62, free. Or Golden Eagle/Age Passport. Special 4-wheel drive road available. Further information: Superintendent; Great Dunes NM; PO Box 60; Alamosa, CO 81101; 303/378-2312.

LA GARITA WILDERNESS; Rio Grande/Gunnison NFs

49,000 acres of undeveloped solitude for the hiker, camper, horseback rider. Elevation goes to more than 14,000 ft. Lies along the Continental Divide, acting as a natural border between the two forests. Hunting, fishing, mountain climbing, hiking. No developed campsites; camp anywhere. Usually accessible June-October. Further information: Superintendent; Rio Grande NF; 1803 West Highway 160; Monte Vista, CO 81144.

LOST CREEK SCENIC AREA; Pike NF

Located within an hour's drive of Denver and of Colorado Springs. This is the most rugged and spectacular part of Pike NF. 15,120 acres on the NE slopes of the Tarryall Mountain Range, home of Colorado's most famous Bighorn sheep herd. The largest of three designated Scenic Areas on the Pike. Cross-country travel off the constructed trails is virtually impossible due to the rugged rocky terrain, and can be quite difficult even for experienced foot travelers. Recreationists may camp wherever they like within the Scenic Area. Camping or fire permits are not required. The McCurdy Park Trail Shelter is available for anyone on a "first-come" basis, but it's ·wise to carry a tent with you since the shelter may be occupied when you arrive. Further information: Superintendent; Pike NF; 320 West Fillmore; Colorado Springs, CO 80907.

MAROON BELLS-SNOWMASS WILDERNESS; White River NF

Located in the central Elk Range of White River NF. 66,380 acres; elevation ranges from 12,000-14,259 feet. 130 miles of trails, much of which is above timberline. Hiking, camping, mountain climbing, big-game hunting, trout fishing. Further information: Superintendent; White River NF; 733 Main; Meeker, CO 81641.

MOUNT ZIRKEL WILDERNESS; Routt NF

72,500 acres straddling the Park Range of the Continental Divide, in NW Colorado.
14 peaks which reach an elevation near 12,000 ft, the highest of which is Mt. Zirkel
(12,180 ft). In addition, there are more than 65 lakes, 30 of which are named. Snow
persists over most of the area until late June and many snowbanks remain all summer.
Deer/elk hunting; trout fishing; hiking; camping. For hiking and camping, wilderness
permits are not required, but you are requested to register at the boundary. Further
information: Superintendent; Routt NF; PO Box 1198; Steamboat Springs, CO 80477.

RAWAH WILDERNESS; Roosevelt NF

Approximately 14 mi long and 3 mi wide, the Wilderness is located in the NW corner
of Roosevelt NF. Elevations range from 9,500–13,000 ft. Rawah features many high,
alpine lakes and streams, noted for quality trout fishing. Horseback riding, hiking,
camping, mountain climbing. Some primitve sites are available; however, you may
camp anywhere. Register at trailhead registration boxes. Further information: Superintendent; Roosevelt NF; 211 Canyon; Fort Collins, CO 80521.

ROCKY MOUNTAIN NATIONAL PARK BACKCOUNTRY CAMPING

Only about 10% of the backcountry campsites are available between April and June.
Much of the park remains snowed in for 2 months after flowers have begun blooming
at lower elevations. Information on current road and weather conditions is available
at Park Headquarters west of Estes Park (303/586-2371; or 586-2385, a recording); also
at the West District Office north of Grand Lake (303/627-3471). PERMITS: Necessary
for any overnight travel in the backcountry. Campers need to know the name of the
campsite(s) where they wish to spend each night. (This information will be discussed
with you at headquarters.) Permits are good only at the location and date listed
on the permit. Permits may be obtained in advance or upon arrival at the Park;
however, the number issued is limited. Permits are FREE, but are mandatory before
entering the backcountry, and may be obtained at the East or West Side Park Headquarters, and some Ranger Stations in season. A permit tag is issued to the party
leader and should be attached to his pack. The tag must be shown to backcountry
personnel upon request. When camp is established, the tag is attached to the tent.
A permit is also required for all technical climbing. If you are not going to use
your permit, please call 303/586-2371, or write the Backcountry Office, so sites can
be released to other campers. Demand exceeds the sites available. Contact: Reservations, Backcountry Office; Rocky Mountain NP; Estes Park, CO 80517. CAMPSITES:
Several sites may make up one camp area. The directions to the campsites are marked
by a wood sign with the campsite name. Individual sites are marked by a metal arrowhead marker, and campers are required to set up camp in the immediate vicinity
of the metal arrowhead marker. They are accessible by maintained Park trails. Parties are limited to no more than 7 people. Length of stay, 3 nights at one campsite.
There is a limit of 7 nights camping, June–Sept., and 15 nights more Oct.–May per
person per year. Wood fires are permitted ONLY in metal fire rings. Where metal rings
are not provided, campers must use containerized fuel stoves. These campsites are
designated "stoves only", and fires of any type, except stoves, are not allowed. Pets
are not allowed in the backcountry. WINTER CAMPING: Permit system is still in effect.
Possible avalanche hazard. Call previously-mentioned phone numbers for weather conditions. For information on developed free NP campground, see "Estes Park".

SPANISH PEAKS AREA; San Isabel NF

Hiking, camping, horseback riding, trout fishing, big-game hunting, berry-picking,
mushroom hunting, and collecting specimens of gnarled wood shaped by wind action
at timberline. Scenic; beautiful fall colors. No developed back area camps. Rocky
Mountain bighorn sheep, bear, antelope, and mountain lion can be seen. Further information: Superintendent; San Isabel NF; 1210 Royal Gorge Boulevard; Canon City,
CO 81212.

UNCOMPAHGRE WILDERNESS; Uncompahgre NF

Trout fishing, big-game hunting, hiking, camping, mountain climbing. Uncompahgre
Peak reaches 14,309 ft in elevation. Further information: Superintendent; Uncompahgre
NF; 1063 Main; Delta, CO 81416.

WEMINUCHE WILDERNESS; San Juan NF

Encompassing 401,000 acres, this is the largest Wilderness in Colorado. The average
elevation is 10,000 ft. Three peaks in the area, Mt. Aeoulus, Sunlight, and Windom,
reach more than 14,000 ft and many are more than 13,000 ft. Over 400 miles of trails
traverse the area; many lead to mountain lakes and meadows. Mountain climbing,

COLORADO

hiking, camping, horseback riding, trout fishing, big-game hunting. RESTRICTIONS:
No camping within $\frac{1}{4}$ mi of Emerald Lake, except at designated campgrounds. Saddle
and pack stock are not allowed to graze or remain overnight within $\frac{1}{4}$ mi of the lake.
No camping within 300 yards of Flint Lake. Saddle and pack stock are not allowed
to graze or remain overnight within 300 yards of the lake. Further information: Superintendent; San Juan NF; PO Box 341; Durango, CO 81301.

WEST ELK WILDERNESS; Gunnison NF

This 1,733,589-acre Wilderness offers big-game hunting, trout fishing, hiking, and
unlimited camping. No wilderness permits or campfire permits are required. Elevations
vary from 8,000-13,035 ft (at West Elk Peak). Further information: Superintendent;
Gunnison NF; 216 North Colorado; Gunnison, CO 81230.

WILSON MOUNTAINS PRIMITIVE AREA; San Juan NF

27,000 acres; interesting scenic trips. San Miguel Mountains consist of two distinct
clusters of peaks ranging from 13,000 to over 14,000 ft. Hunting, fishing, hiking,
camping. Short cool summers and long severe winters. There are several permanent
snowfields and snow patches remain in sheltered areas throughout the summer. Be
prepared for freezing weather at all times of the year. Further information: Superintendent; San Juan NF; PO Box 341; Durango, CO 81301.

FREE CAMPGROUNDS

ALAMOSA

Mosca Creek Picnic Area (Great Sand
Dunes NM). 15 mi E of Alamosa on St
Hwy 160; 16 mi N on St Hwy 150; 1 mi
NW of Visitor Center. SEASON: November
-March; 14-day lmt. [Snowstorms can
occur any month. Temperature sometimes
drops as low as -25 degrees F in the
winter.] FACILITIES: 20 sites; tbls,
toil, cga, f, drk wtr. ACTIVITIES: Hiking; picnicking; fishing. MISC.: Firewood is $1.25/bundle at the Visitor Cen-
ter. Self-guided nature trail. Used
as secondary camping to Pinyon Flats
Campground which is open April-October,
and charges $3.00 per vehicle per night.
Pets on leash. ENTRANCE FEES: $1.00
per vehicle per day. Hikers, bicyclists,
and bus passengers - 50¢ per day.
15 and under, 62 and older, FREE.
OR, Golden Age/Gold Eagle Passports.**

ALMA

Kite Lake (Pike-San Isabel NF). 6 mi
NW of Alma on Co Rd 8. SEASON: 6/15-
9/27; 10-day lmt. FACILITIES: 3 sites,
no trailers; tbls, toil, no drk wtr. ACTI-
VITIES: Mountain climbing; picnicking;
fishing. MISC.: Elev 12,000 ft; 3 acres;
pets; lake. Historic mining area. 3 peaks
over 14,000 feet (2 mi).

ALMONT

Cold Spring (Gunnison-Grand Mesa-Uncompahgre NF). 16-1/10 mi NE on FS
742. SEASON: 6/4-9/5; 14-day lmt. FACIL-
ITIES: 6 sites (tr -16), tbls, toil, cga,
piped drk wtr. ACTIVITIES: Fishing;
picnicking. MISC.: Elev 9000 ft; 2 acres.

Dorchester (Gunnison-Grand Mesa-Uncompahgre NF). 39½ mi NE of Almont on
FS 742. SEASON: 6/4-9/5; 14-day lmt.
FACILITIES: 10 sites (tr -32); tbls,
toil, cga, well drk wtr. ACTIVITIES:
Fishing; picnicking. MISC.: Elev 9800
ft; 4 acres; scenic; stream; pets.

Lodgepole (Gunnison-Grand Mesa-Uncompahgre). 14-7/10 mi NE of Almont on
FS 742. SEASON: 5/28-10/30; 14-day lmt.
FACILITIES: 16 sites (tr -32), tbls,
toil, cga, piped drk wtr. ACTIVITIES:
Fishing; picnicking. MISC.: Elev 8800
ft; 4 acres; scenic; stream; pets.

Mirror Lake (Gunnison-Grand Mesa-Uncompahgre NF). 26-3/5 mi NE of Almont
on FS 742; 7-3/5 mi SE on FS 765; 3-
1/10 mi E on FS 211. SEASON: 6/4-9/30;
14-day lmt. FACILITIES: 10 sites (tr
-22), tbls, toil, cga, piped drk wtr.
Store/gas (3 mi). ACTIVITIES: Fishing;
picnicking. MISC.: Elev 11,000 ft; 4
acres; stream; pets; geological. On shore
of Mirror Lake (36 surface acres).
Historic Tincup Townsite (3 mi E).

Mosca (Gunnison-Grand Mesa-Uncompahgre
NF). 7-1/5 mi NE of Almont on FS 742;
12-1/10 mi N on FS 744. SEASON: 6/4-
10/15; 14-day lmt. FACILITIES: 11 sites
(tr -22), tbls, toil, cga, piped drk
wtr. ACTIVITIES: Boating, ld; picnicking;
fishing. MISC.: Elev 10,000 ft; 6 acres;
lake; scenic; pets. On SE shore of
Spring Creek Reservoir (89 surface
acres).

North Bank (Gunnison-Grand Mesa-Uncompahgre NF). 7-4/5 mi NE of Almont on
FS 742. SEASON: 5/28-10/15; 14-day lmt.

FACILITIES: 17 sites (tr -22), tbls, toil, cga, well drk wtr. Store/fd/gas (1 mi). ACTIVITIES: Fishing; picnicking. Horseback riding/rental (1 mi). MISC.: Elev 8600 ft; 6 acres; river; scenic; pets on leash.

Rosy Lane (Gunnison-Grand Mesa-Uncompahgre NF). 8-4/5 mi NE of Almont on FS 742. SEASON: 5/28-10/30; 14-day lmt. FACILITIES: 14 sites (tr -22); tbls, toil, cga, no drk wtr. Food/gas (2 mi). ACTIVITIES: Picnicking; fishing. Horseback riding/rental (2 mi). MISC.: Elev 8600 ft; 8 acres; river; scenic; pets.

Spring Creek (Gunnison-Grand Mesa-Uncompahgre NF). 7-1/5 mi NE of Almont on FS 742; 2 mi N on FS 744. SEASON: 6/4-10/15; 14-day lmt. FACILITIES: 11 sites (tr -32), tbls, toil, cga, no drk wtr. Store/fd/gas (2 mi). ACTIVITIES: Fishing; picnicking. Horseback riding/rental (2 mi). MISC.: Elev 8600 ft; 4 acres; scenic; stream; pets on leash.

ANTONITO

Lake Fork (Rio Grande NF). 23 mi W of Antonito on St Hwy 17; 16 mi NW on FS 250. SEASON: FREE and accessible, 5/15-MD and LD-11/15 (MD-LD, $2); 14-day lmt. FACILITIES: 20 sites (tr -22), tbls, toil, cga, f, dump, water. ACTIVITIES: Horseback riding; picnicking. Fishing (1 mi). MISC.: During free season, no garbage collection, but water is available. Pets on leash. Located along the Conejos River.

Mix Lake (Rio Grande NF). 23 mi W of Antonito on St Hwy 17; 21-3/5 mi NW on FS 250; 4/5 mi W on FS 2506B. Located about 6 mi past Lake Fork Campground just W of the small resort community of Platoro. SEASON: FREE and accessible, 5/15-MD and LD-11/15 (MD-LD, $2); 14-day lmt. FACILITIES: 22 sites (tr -22), tbls, toil, cga, f. Store/ice/laundry/showers/food (1mi). ACTIVITIES: Horseback riding; boating,rld; picnicking; fishing. MISC.: During free season, no garbage collection or drk wtr. Pets.

Mogote (Rio Grande NF). 13 mi W of Antonito on St Hwy 17. SEASON: 6/1-9/1. FACILITIES: 5 sites (tr -22); tbls, toil, cga, no drk wtr. Store/ice/laundry/gas/showers (1 mi). ACTIVITIES: Fishing; picnicking. MISC.: Elev 8700 ft;22 acres; pets. Located on banks of Conejos River.

Rio de Pinos (Rio Grande NF). 3 mi S of Antonito on US 285; 12 mi W on FS 284. [Rough rd.] SEASON: 5/15-10/30; 14-day lmt. FACILITIES: 4 sites (tr -16), toil, f. ACTIVITIES: Fishing; hiking. MISC.: Elev 8000 ft; pets on leash.

Trujillo Meadows (Rio Grande NF). 30 mi W of Antonito on St Hwy 17; 4 mi N

on FS 118. SEASON: 6/1-9/1; 14-day lmt. FACILITIES: 17 sites (tr -22), tbls, toil, cga, piped drk wtr. ACTIVITIES: Boating,d; picnicking; fishing. MISC.: Elev 10,000 ft; 18 acres; lake; pets on leash.

ASPEN

East Maroon (White River NF). 1 mi NW of Aspen on St Hwy 82; 9-3/5 mi SW on Co Hwy 15125. SEASON: 6/1-10/1; 1-day lmt. FACILITIES: 13 sites (no trailers); tbls, toil, cga, f, no drk wtr. ACTIVITIES: Horseback riding; hiking; boating,d; picnicking; fishing. MISC.: Elev 8700 ft; 2 acres; river;pets.

Lincoln Gulch (White River NF). 12-1/5 mi SE of Aspen on St Hwy 82; ½ mi SW on FS 15106; 1/5 mi W on FS 15106. [On Lincoln Gulch Rd at mouth of Lincoln Creek.] SEASON: 6/25-9/10; 5-day lmt. FACILITIES: 6 sites (tr -16), tbls, toil, cga, no drk wtr. ACTIVITIES: Hiking; picnicking; fishing. MISC.: Elev 9700 ft; 2 acres; pets. Nature trails (1 mi). Grizzly Reservoir, by jct of Lincoln Creek and Roaring Fork River (6 mi SE).

Portal (White River NF). 12-1/10 mi SE of Aspen on St Hwy 82; 6-3/5 mi SE on FS 15106. SEASON: 6/25-11/1; 10-day lmt. FACILITIES: 7 sites (tr -16), tbls, toil, cga, f, no drk wtr. ACTIVITIES: Fishing; picnicking. MISC.: Elev 10,700 ft; 4 acres; scenic; pets; stream. On Grizzly Reservoir.

Lostman (White River NF). 16-9/10 mi SE of Aspen on St Hwy 82; 1/5 mi S on FS 15105. SEASON: 7/1-9/10; 10-day lmt. FACILITIES: 9 sites (tr -22), tbls, toil, cga, f, no drk wtr. ACTIVITIES: Hiking; picnicking. Boating,d/fishing (1 mi). MISC.: Elev 10,700 ft; 3 acres; pets. Nature trails (3 mi). Lostman Reservoir (½ mi).

Silver Bar (White River NF). 1-7/10 mi W of Aspen on St Hwy 82; 6-1/5 mi SW on FS 15125 (Maroon Lake Rd). SEASON: 5/25-9/10; 1-day lmt. FACILITIES: 4 sites (no trailers); tbls, toil, cga, f, no drk wtr. Store/fd/gas/laundry (4 mi). Showers/ice (3 mi). ACTIVITIES: Mountain climbing; picnicking; fishing; hiking. Boating (5 mi). Horseback riding/rental (2 mi). MISC.: Elev 8300 ft; 2 acres; stream; pets. Nature trails (5 mi). Dump (5 mi). Maroon Lake (4-9/10 mi).

Silver Queen (White River NF). 1-7/10 mi W of Aspen on St Hwy 82; 7-7/10 mi SW on FS 15125. SEASON: 5/25-9/10; 2-day lmt. FACILITIES: 6 sites; tbls, toil, cga, f, no drk wtr. ACTIVITIES: Mountain climbing; picnicking; fishing. Boating; no motors (3 mi). Horseback riding (3 mi). MISC.: Elev 9100 ft; 2 acres; pets. Adjacent to Maroon Creek.

See page 7 for KEY TO ABBREVIATIONS.

Snowmass Creek (White River NF). 5-1/10 mi NW of Aspen on St Hwy 82; 5-4/5 mi SW on Co Rd 10-11; 1/5 mi W on FS 15120. SEASON: 6/1-11/1; 10-day lmt. FACILITIES: 7 sites (tr -16), tbls, toil, cga, f, no drk wtr. Store/fd/ice/laundry/gas (5 mi). ACTIVITIES: Picnicking. Fishing (1 mi). Horseback riding/rental (5 mi). MISC.: Elev 8800 ft; 2 acres; scenic; pets.

Weller Lake (White River NF). 11-2/5 mi SE of Aspen on St Hwy 82; 1/10 mi S on FS 15104. SEASON: 6/25-9/10; 5-day lmt. FACILITIES: 11 sites (tr -16), tbls, toil, cga, f, no drk wtr. ACTIVITIES: Hiking; picnicking. Fishing (1 mi). MISC.: Elev 9200 ft; 3 acres; scenic; pets. Federal Entrance Permit required. Nature trails (4 mi). Adjacent to Roaring Fork River.

BASALT

Elk Wallow (White River NF). 23 mi E of Basalt on Co Hwy 15105; 3-3/10 mi E on FS 15501. SEASON: 5/25-11/1; 14-day lmt. FACILITIES: 8 sites (tr -22), tbls, toil, cga, no drk wtr. Store/ice/fd/laundry/gas (5 mi). ACTIVITIES: Fishing; picnicking. Horseback riding (3 mi), rental (4 mi). MISC.: Elev 9000 ft; 2 acres; river; pets. Ruedi Dam (12.7 mi).

BAYFIELD

Pine River (San Juan NF). 25 mi NE of Bayfield on Co Hwy 501. SEASON: 5/1-11/1; 14-day lmt. FACILITIES: 4 sites (tr -22), tbls, toil, cga, piped drk wtr. ACTIVITIES: Hiking; picnicking. Fishing/boating,r/waterskiing/horseback riding & rental (4 mi). MISC.: Elev 8100 ft; 2 acres; pets. Store (4 mi). Trailhead into Weninuche Wilderness.

BRIGGSDALE

Crow Valley Educational Site (Arapaho-Roosevelt NF). ¼ mi W of Briggsdale on St Hwy 14; ½ mi N on Co Hwy 77. SEASON: 4/15-9/15. FACILITIES: 10 sites; tbls, toil, cga, electricity in camp, piped drk wtr. Store/fd/gas (1 mi). ACTIVITIES: Picnicking; hiking. Horseback riding (1 mi). MISC.: Elev 4800 ft; 1 acre; pets; botanical; rockhounding. Nature trails (1 mi). Use is restricted to groups with educational goals. RESERVATIONS REQUIRED.

Crow Valley Park (Arapaho-Roosevelt NF). ¼ mi W of Briggsdale on St Hwy 14; ½ mi N on Co Hwy 77. SEASON: 4/15-9/15. FACILITIES: 4 sites (tr -32), tbls, toil, cga, piped drk wtr. ACTIVITIES: Rockhounding; picnicking. Horseback riding (1 mi). Hiking. MISC.: Elev 4800 ft;3 acres;pets.Store/fd/gas (1 mi).

BRUSH

Memorial Park (County Park). In Brush, 2 blocks S of traffic light on Clayton Street. SEASON: 4/1-10/31. FACILITIES: 32 sites; tbls, flush toil, cga, drk wtr, dump, shower, shelters, playground. ACTIVITIES: Swimming; picnicking. Elev 4300 ft; pets on leash.

Prewitt Reservoir Campground (SRA). 15 mi NE of Brush on US 6; 1 mi E on Sandy Rd. SEASON: All yr; 14-day lmt. FACILITIES: 25 sites (no trailers); tbls, toil, cga, drk wtr. ACTIVITIES: Swimming; hiking; waterskiing; picnicking; fishing; boating,l. MISC.: Elev 4100 ft; 50 acres; lake; beach; pets on leash. Primitive sites.

BUFFALO CREEK

Top of the World (Pike-San Isabel NF). 2-7/10 mi SE of Buffalo Creek on Co Hwy 126; 3/10 mi SE on FS 537; 1-3/10 mi N on FS 538. SEASON: 5/1-10/15. FACILITIES: 7 sites (tr -16), tbls, toil, cga, no drk wtr. Store/gas (4 mi). Picnicking. Fishing (4 mi). MISC.: Elev 7500 ft; 9 acres; pets. Observation site.

BURNS

Sweetwater Lake (White River NF). 14-1/10 mi SW of Burns on Co Hwy 37; 9-4/5 mi NW on Co Hwy 17; 3/5 mi S on FS 15607. SEASON: 5/1-10/31; 14-day lmt. FACILITIES: 9 sites (tr -22), tbls, toil, cga, f, piped drk wtr. Store/fd/ice (1 mi). ACTIVITIES: Swimming; picnicking; fishing; boating,d (rl, 1 mi). Hiking. Horseback riding/rental (1 mi). MISC.: Elev 7700 ft; 2 acres; river; nature trails; pets on leash.

CANON CITY

Five Points (BLM). 17 mi W of Canon City on US 50 along Arkansas River. SEASON: All yr; 14-day lmt. FACILITIES: 14 sites (tr -22), tbls, toil, piped drk wtr. ACTIVITIES: Hiking; picnicking; fishing. MISC.: Elev 6000 ft; 3 acres; pets. International kayak races nearby. Near Sangre De Cristo Mountains.

Oak Creek (Pike-San Isabel NF). 12-3/10 mi SW of Canon City on Co Hwy CR277. SEASON: 5/11-11/1; 10-day lmt. FACILITIES: 17 sites; tbls, toil, cga, piped drk wtr. ACTIVITIES: Picnicking; hiking. MISC.: Elev 7600 ft; 9 acres; pets.

CAPULIN

La Jara Reservoir (SRA). 15 mi W of Capulin on Co Rd. SEASON: 5/1-11/1. FACILITIES: 50 sites (no trailers); tbls, toil, cga, no drk wtr. ACTIVITIES: Boating,l; picnicking; fishing. MISC.: Pets.

See page 7 for KEY TO ABBREVIATIONS.

CARBONDALE

Avalanche (White River NF). 10-2/5 mi S of Carbondale on St Hwy 133; 2-3/5 mi E on FS 15310. SEASON: 5/25-11/1; 14-day lmt. FACILITIES: 10 sites (tr --16), tbls, toil, cga, no drk wtr. ACTIVITIES: Hiking; picnicking; fishing. Horseback riding (2 mi). MISC.: Elev 7400 ft; 3 acres; pets; stream. Trailhead into Maroon Bells-Snowmass Wilderness.

Janeway (White River NF). 10-2/5 mi S of Carbondale on St Hwy 133; 3/5 mi E on FS 15310. SEASON: 5/25-11/1; 14-day lmt. FACILITIES: 9 sites (tr -22), tbls, toil, cga, no drk wtr. ACTIVITIES: Picnicking. Horseback riding (1 mi). MISC.: Elev 6800 ft; 3 acres; stream; pets. Store/ice/gas (5 mi).

CASTLE

Clark Cabin (White River NF). 9 mi NW of Castle on Co Hwy 245; 17-1/5 mi NE on FS F244. SEASON: 6/1-10/31; 14-day lmt. FACILITIES: 4 sites (tr -16), tbls, toil, cga, f, no drk wtr. ACTIVITIES: Picnicking. MISC.: Elev 9500 ft; 1 acre; pets on leash.

Cliff Lakes (White River NF). 9 mi NW of Castle on Co Hwy 245; 20-2/5 mi NE on FS F244; 3 mi E on FS F601. SEASON: 6/10-10/31; 14-day lmt. FACILITIES: 4 sites (no trailers); tbls, toil, cga, f, no drk wtr. ACTIVITIES: Swimming; picnicking; fishing; boating (no motors). MISC.: Elev 9700 ft; 2 acres; pets; lake.

CEDAREDGE

Fish Hawk (Gunnison-Grand Mesa-Uncompahgre NF). 16 mi N of Cedaredge on St Hwy 65; 6 mi E on FS 121. SEASON: 6/20-9/15; 14-day lmt. FACILITIES: 3 sites (tr -16), tbls, toil, cga, piped drk wtr. Store/fd/gas (2 mi). ACTIVITIES: Picnicking. Fishing (1 mi). Boating (1 mi), r (2 mi). Horseback riding (1 mi) and rental (2 mi). MISC.: Elev 10,200 ft; 1 acre; pets. Visitor Center (4 mi).

Kiser Creek (Gunnison-Grand Mesa-Uncompahgre NF). 16 mi N of Cedaredge on St Hwy 65; 3 mi E on FS 121; 1/10 mi S on FS 123. SEASON: 6/20-9/15; 14-day lmt. FACILITIES: 12 sites (tr -16), tbls, toil, cga, no drk wtr. Store/gas (1 mi). ACTIVITIES: Boating,rd; picnicking; fishing. Horseback riding/rental (1 mi). MISC.: Elev 10,100 ft; 4 acres; pets. On Kiser Creek. Nature trails (4 mi).

Trickle Park (Gunnison-Grand Mesa-Uncompahgre NF). 17 mi N of Cedaredge on St Hwy 65; 8 mi E on FS 121. SEASON: 6/20-9/15; 14-day lmt. FACILITIES: 4 sites (tr -22), tbls, toil, cga, no drk wtr. ACTIVITIES: Picnicking. Fishing/boating (1 mi). MISC.: Elev 10,100 ft; 2 acres; lake; pets.

Twin Lake (Gunnison-Grand Mesa-Uncompahgre NF). 16 mi N of Cedaredge on St Hwy 65; 10 mi E on Fs 121; 2 mi E on FS 126. SEASON: 6/20-9/15; 14-day lmt. FACILITIES: 13 sites (tr -22), tbls, toil, cga, no drk wtr. ACTIVITIES: Boating (hand-propelled craft only on lake). Fishing; picnicking. MISC.: Elev 10,300 ft; 3 acres; pets; on Sackett Reservoir. Hand-propelled craft only.

Weir and Johnson (Gunnison-Grand Mesa-Uncompahgre NF). 16 mi N of Cedaredge on St Hwy 65; 11 mi E on FS 121; 3 mi E on FS 126. SEASON: 6/20-10/15; 14-day lmt. FACILITIES: 12 sites (tr -22), tbls, toil, cga, no drk wtr. ACTIVITIES: Boating,d; picnicking; fishing. MISC.: Elev 10,500 ft; 10 acres; pets. Between Sackett and Weir and Johnson Reservoirs.

CHIMNEY ROCK

First Fork Hunter Camp (San Juan NF). $\frac{1}{2}$ mi E of Chimney Rock on US 160; 10$\frac{1}{2}$ mi N on FS 622. SEASON: 5/15-11/25; 14-day lmt. FACILITIES: 10 sites (tr -22), tbls, toil, cga, f, no drk wtr. ACTIVITIES: Rockhounding; hunting; picnicking; fishing. MISC.: Elev 7100 ft; 2 acres; pets. Piedra River.

Lower Piedra (San Juan NF). 1 mi N of Chimney Rock on FS 621. SEASON: 5/1-10/31; 14-day lmt. FACILITIES: 18 sites (tr - 32), tbls, toil, cga, drk wtr. Store/ice (1 mi). ACTIVITIES: Horseback riding; picnicking; fishing; hiking. MISC.: Elev 6000 ft; 6 acres; pets.

Ute (San Juan NF). 5$\frac{1}{2}$ mi SE of Chimney Rock on US 160. SEASON: 10/14-11/25; 14-day lmt. FACILITIES: 32 sites (tr -32), tbls, toil, cga, f, piped drk wtr. Ice/fd/gas (1 mi). Store (5 mi). ACTIVITIES: Picnicking. Fishing (1 mi). MISC.: Elev 6900 ft; 60 acres; pets. Chimney Rock (13 mi).

CIMARRON

Cimarron Creek Campground (Curecanti NRA). Located in Cimarron. SEASON: May-September; 1-night lmt. FACILITIES: 10 sites (individual sites indicated by picnic tbls and firepits); tbls, toil, cga, drk wtr. MISC.: Pets allowed on leash.

CLARK

Box Canyon (Routt NF). 1 mi N of Clark on Co Hwy 129; 9 mi NE on FS 400. SEASON: 6/15-11/15; 14-day lmt. FACILITIES: 11 sites (tr -16), tbls, toil, cga, no drk wtr. ACTIVITIES: Hiking; picnicking; fishing. MISC.: Elev 7900 ft; 6 acres; pets; stream. Nature trails (3 mi).

Twin Lake (Gunnison-Grand Mesa-Uncompahgre NF). 16 mi N of Cedaredge on St Hwy 65; 10 mi E on Fs 121; 2 mi E on FS 126. SEASON: 6/20-9/15; 14-day drk wtr. ACTIVITIES: Picnicking. Fishing/boating (1 mi). MISC.: Elev 10,100 ft; 2 acres; lake; pets.

COALDALE

Hayden Creek #1 (Pike-San Isabel NF). 5-1/10 mi SW of Coaldale on FS 249. **SEASON:** 5/18-11/1; 7-day lmt. **FACILITIES:** 11 sites (tr -16), tbls, toil, cga, well drk wtr. Showers/laundry (2 mi). Store/gas (5 mi). **ACTIVITIES:** Hiking; picnicking; fishing. Horseback riding/ rental (2 mi). **MISC.:** Elev 8000 ft; 4 acres; pets. Hayden Creek.

Hayden Creek #2 (Pike-San Isabel NF). 4-1/10 mi SW of Coaldale on FS 249. **SEASON:** 5/18-11/1; 7-day lmt. **FACILITIES:** 7 sites (tr -16), tbls, toil, cga, no drk wtr. Showers/laundry (1 mi). Store (4 mi). **ACTIVITIES:** Hiking; picnicking; fishing. **MISC.:** Elev 7800 ft; 4 acres; pets. Hayden Creek.

COLLBRAN

Big Creek (Gunnison-Grand Mesa-Uncompahgre NF). 15 mi S of Collbran on FS 121; 1 mi W on FS 121A. **SEASON:** 6/20-10/15; 14-day lmt. **FACILITIES:** 23 sites; tbls, toil, cga, no drk wtr. **ACTIVITIES:** Boating,l; picnicking; fishing. **MISC.:** Elev 10,100 ft; 20 acres; pets; lake.

Bonham Lake (Gunnison-Grand Mesa-Uncompahgre NF). 12 mi S of Collbran on FS 121; 1/10 mi W on FS 257. **SEASON:** 6/20-9/5; 14-day lmt. **FACILITIES:** 11 sites (tr -16), tbls, toil, cga, no drk wtr. **ACTIVITIES:** Boating,d; picnicking; fishing. **MISC.:** Elev 9800 ft; 6 acres; pets. Bonham Lake.

COMO

Selkirk (Pike-San Isabel NF). 3½ mi NW of Como on Co Hwy 33; ½ mi NW on Co Hwy 50; 1-4/5 mi NW on FS 406. **SEASON:** 5/20-10/27; 10-day lmt. **FACILITIES:** 15 sites (tr -22), tbls, toil, cga. **ACTIVITIES:** Picnicking. Fishing (1 mi). **MISC.:** Elev 10,500 ft; 2 acres; pets; historic. Boreas Pass (6 mi).

CORTEZ

Hovenweep Campground (Hovenweep NM). Main access is via McElmo Canyon to the south. Drive S of Cortez on US 666 for 4 mi to the Amoco-Standard truck stop (across Hwy on N-bound side); turn right at crossrd to Cortez-Montezuma County airport rd. You are now on McElmo Canyon route. The rd is paved for about the first 15 miles; the remainder is a county-maintained graded and graveled rd. Travel W to McElmo Canyon. 25 mi along McElmo route you will come to Ismay Trading Post. This marks the Utah-Colorado border. The rd drops down about 50 ft to a dry wash which is crossed by means of a narrow steel bridge. Once over this bridge you are in Utah.

Approximately 4 mi W of Ismay, and on the NE boundary of the Aneth oil field, you will arrive at the first major rd jct. A right turn here will take you to Hovenweep. The jct is clearly marked with a large brown sign with white lettering. The remaining 10 mi to Hovenweep can be EXTREMELY hazardous in bad weather. USE CAUTION! (This jct is approximately ½ mi from the first oil wells you will notice, and some oil field outbuildings located directly across from the Hovenweep NM mailbox -- a large standing mailbox painted a distinctive brown.)

4 mi after this jct, and after having passed several Navajo indian homes (you are now on the Navajo Indian Reservation), you will climb a gentle rise of about 50 ft and come to another jct. A rt turn here will take you directly to the Monument. The jct is marked by a small green reflective rd sign. Nearby brush and/or snow can occasionally obscure it. This is the WORST stretch of rd you will have to negotiate. It is a poorly maintained dirt rd approximately 6 mi long. After negotiating this stretch of rd, you will have arrived at the Monument entrance gate. It would be advisable to call Mesa Verde NP to inquire after rd conditions.

SEASON: All yr. **FACILITIES:** 31 sites at the Square Tower Group; flush toil; drk wtr (a pumped-storage system maintained by the Monument, with a water softening and chlorinating facility). **ACTIVITIES:** Self-guiding trail leads through the prehistoric ruins of Square Tower Group. **MISC.:** Park ranger on duty all year. No entrance fee. Pets.

CRAIG

Elkhead Lake (SRA). 2 mi E of Craig and 3½ mi N off US 40. **SEASON:** All yr. **FACILITIES:** 50 sites; tbls, toil, cga, f, drk wtr. **ACTIVITIES:** Boating,l; picnicking; fishing. Golf nearby. Snowmobiling in winter. **MISC.:** Pets on leash.

Freeman (Routt NF). 13-1/5 mi NE of Craig on St Hwy 13; 9 mi NE on FS 112. **SEASON:** 6/15-11/15; 14-day lmt. **FACILITIES:** 12 sites (tr -22); tbls, toil, cga, no drk wtr. **ACTIVITIES:** Fishing; picnicking. **MISC.:** Elev 8800 ft; 5 acres; pets. Freeman Reservoir.

Sawmill Creek (Routt NF). 13 mi N of Craig on St Hwy 13; 12-3/5 mi NE on FS 110. **SEASON:** 6/15-11/15; 14-day lmt. **FACILITIES:** 5 sites (tr -16), tbls, toil, cga, piped drk wtr. **ACTIVITIES:** Mountain climbing; picnicking. Fishing (1 mi). **MISC.:** Elev 9000 ft; 4 acres; pets.

CRAWFORD

Mesa (Gunnison-Grand Mesa-Uncompahgre NF). 18 mi SE of Crawford on St Hwy 92. **SEASON:** 5/24-11/15; 14-day lmt. **FACILITIES:** 5 sites (tr -32); tbls, toil,

See page 7 for KEY TO ABBREVIATIONS.

cga, piped drk wtr. ACTIVITIES: Picnicking. MISC.: Elev 9000 ft; 2 acres; pets. Blue Mesa Reservoir (22 mi).

North Rim Campground (Black Canyon of Gunnison NM). 14 mi SE of Crawford on graded St Hwy 92. SEASON: FREE, mid-May to mid-Sept. ($1 entrance fee, 6/1-LD). FACILITIES: 13 sites (tr -24); tbls, toil, cga, f, store, food. ACTIVITIES: Picnicking; fishing. MISC.: Pets.

CREEDE

Crooked Creek (Rio Grande NF). $20\frac{1}{2}$ mi SW of Creede on St Hwy 149; 1-4/5 mi SW on FS 520. SEASON: 6/15-9/15. FACILITIES: 3 sites (tr -32), toil, cga, f. No tbls/drk wtr. Store/ice/gas (2 mi). ACTIVITIES: Fishing; picnicking. Horseback riding/rental (2 mi). Boating,l (3 mi). MISC.: Elev 9200 ft; 11 acres; pets; stream.

Ivy Creek (Rio Grande NF). $6\frac{1}{2}$ mi SW of Creede on St Hwy 149; 4 mi SW on FS 523; 2-7/10 mi SW on FS 528; 2 mi SW on FS 526. SEASON: 6/15-9/15. FACILITIES: 4 sites (no trailers); tbls, toil, cga, no drk wtr. ACTIVITIES: Rockhounding; picnicking; fishing; hiking. MISC.: Elev 9200 ft; 9 acres; pets; stream. No garbage collection. Trailhead to Weminuche Wilderness Area.

Lost Trail Campground (Rio Grande NF). $20\frac{1}{2}$ mi SW of Creede on St Hwy 149; $16\frac{1}{2}$ mi SW on FS 520. SEASON: 6/15-9/15;. FACILITIES: 7 sites (tr -32), tbls, toil, cga, well drk wtr. ACTIVITIES: Hiking; picnicking; fishing. Horseback riding/rental (1 mi). MISC.: Elev 9500 ft; 3 acres; scenic; pets; stream. No garbage collection.

Rio Grande (Rio Grande NF). 10 mi SW of Creede on St Hwy 149; 1 mi S on FS 529. SEASON: 6/15-9/15. FACILITIES: 4 sites (tr -32); tbls, toil, cga, f, well drk wtr. ACTIVITIES: Fishing; picnicking. Horseback riding/rental (4 mi). MISC.: Elev 8900 ft; 8 acres; river; pets. Located on Rio Grande River.

Road Canyon (Rio Grande NF). $20\frac{1}{2}$ mi SW of Creede on St Hwy 149; 6 mi SW on FS 520. SEASON: 6/15-9/15. FACILITIES: 5 sites (tr -32), tbls, toil, cga, no drk wtr. Store/ice (5 mi). ACTIVITIES: Horseback riding; boating,ld; picnicking; fishing. MISC.: Elev 9300 ft; 9 acres; pets. No garbage collection. Road Canyon Reservoir.

CRESTONE

North Crestone Creek (Rio Grande NF). 1-1/5 mi N of Crestone on FS 950. SEASON: 5/15-11/15. FACILITIES: 14 sites (tr -16); tbls, toil, cga, f, well drk wtr. Food/gas/ice/laundry/store (1 mi). ACTIVITIES: Picnicking; fishing; mountain climbing; hiking. Horseback riding/rental (1 mi). MISC.: Elev 8300 ft; 8 acres; stream; horse unloading facilities. Trailhead North Crestone Lake. Pets.

CRESTED BUTTE

Avery Peak (Gunnison-Grand Mesa-Uncompahgre NF). 7-3/10 mi N of Crested Butte on Co Hwy 3; $1\frac{1}{2}$ mi N on FS 317. SEASON: 6/4-9/5; 14-day lmt. FACILITIES: 10 sites (tr -16), tbls, toil, cga, piped drk wtr. ACTIVITIES: Picnicking. Fishing (1 mi). Horseback riding/rental (2 mi). MISC.: Elev 9600 ft; 4 acres; pets; scenic; stream. Rocky Mountain Biological Lab/historic gothic townsite (2 mi S).

Cement Creek (Gunnison-Grand Mesa-Uncompahgre NF). $7\frac{1}{2}$ mi SE of Crested Butte on St Hwy 135; 4 mi NE on FS 740. SEASON: 5/15-11/4; 14-day lmt. FACILITIES: 12 sites (tr -32); tbls, toil, cga, drk wtr. ACTIVITIES: Fishing; picnicking. MISC.: Elev 9000 ft; 4 acres; pets on leash.

Lake Irwin (Gunnison-Grand Mesa-Uncompahgre NF). 7-1/5 mi W of Crested Butte on Co Hwy 2; 2-3/5 mi N on FS 826. SEASON: 6/4-9/5; 14-day lmt. FACILITIES: 27 sites (tr -32), tbls, toil, cga, piped drk wtr. ACTIVITIES: Boating,d; picnicking; fishing. MISC.: Elev 10,200 ft; 10 acres; pets; scenic. On NW shore of Lake Irwin. Historic Irwin-Ruby Townsite (1 mi). Irwin Cemetery (2 mi).

Lost Lake (Gunnison-Grand Mesa-Uncompahgre NF). 15 mi W of Crested Butte on St Hwy 135; 3 mi S on FS 706. SEASON: 6/15-9/30; 14-day lmt. FACILITIES: 10 sites (tr -32), tbls, toil, cga, piped drk wtr. ACTIVITIES: Boating,d; picnicking; fishing; hiking. MISC.: Elev 9600 ft; 3 acres; pets; lake. West Elk Wilderness ($3\frac{1}{2}$ mi).

DILLON

Blue River (White River NF). 4 mi W of Dillon on US 6; 8-3/5 mi NW on St Hwy C09. SEASON: 5/1-11/15; 10-day lmt. FACILITIES: 20 sites (tr -32), tbls, toil, cga, no drk wtr. ACTIVITIES: Hiking; picnicking; fishing. Horseback riding/rental (4 mi). MISC.: Elev 8400 ft; 9 acres; pets. Nature trails (4 mi).

Prairie Point (White River NF). 22-1/10 mi NW of Dillon on St Hwy C09. SEASON: 5/15-10/15; 14-day lmt. FACILITIES: 30 sites; tbls, toil, cga, f, no drk wtr. ACTIVITIES: Swimming; sailing; boating; waterskiing; picnicking. MISC.: Elev 8200 ft; 13 acres; pets; scenic; fishing.

Windy Point (White River NF). 6 mi E of Dillon on US 6; 2½ mi SW on Co Hwy CH001; 1 mi NW on FS FH210. SEASON: 5/25–9/10; 10-day lmt. FACILITIES: 61 sites (tr -32); tbls, toil, cga, no drk wtr. Store/food/ice/gas (4 mi). ACTIVITIES: Hiking; sailing; picnicking; fishing; boating,d (1, 3 mi). MISC.: Elev 9100 ft; 10 acres; pets; lake; nature trails.

DINOSAUR

Echo Park (Dinosaur NM). 2 mi E of Dinosaur on US 40; 25 mi N on Scenic Drive; 13 mi NE on unpaved Echo Park Road. [13-mi steep terrain; no oversize vehicles or trailers recommended. Extremely scenic, however. Worth the effort.] SEASON: 5/15–10/15; 15-day lmt. FACILITIES: 20 primitive sites; water faucets (no water from early fall to late spring due to potential damage to pipes from freezing). ACTIVITIES: Boating, earth boat launch; special permit required for boating; whitewater running craft only. Fishing. NO SWIMMING; ice cold water; unexpected currents. MISC.: 5 acres; pets on leash; ranger station.

DOLORES

Fish Creek Campground (State Fish/Game Commission). 15 mi NE of Dolores on St Hwy 145; 12 mi N. SEASON: All yr; 14-day lmt. FACILITIES: 10 primitive sites; tbls, toil, cga, drk wtr. ACTIVITIES: Fishing; picnicking. MISC.: Elev 8200 ft; 100 acres; pets.

DURANGO

Lemon Dam (State Fish/Game Commission). 20 mi from Durango on Co Hwy 284. SEASON: 5/15–10/31. FACILITIES: 25 sites; tbls, toil, cga, f, drk wtr. ACTIVITIES: Boating,l; picnicking. Fishing (1 mi). Snowmobiling in winter. MISC.: Florida River. Pets permitted if on a leash.

Vallecito Reservoir (State Fish/Game Commission). 10 mi N of Bayfield, off US 160. SEASON: 6/5–10/15. FACILITIES: 50 sites; tbls, toil, cga, store, ice, laundry, drk wtr, playground. ACTIVITIES: Horseback riding; boating,rl; picnicking; fishing. MISC.: Lake; pets.

EAGLE

Adam (White River NF). 12–1/10 mi S of Eagle on Co Hwy 307; 5 mi SE on FS 400. SEASON: 5/1–10/31; 14-day lmt. FACILITIES: 4 sites; tbls, toil, no drk wtr. ACTIVITIES: Hiking; picnicking; fishing. Boating, no motors (1 mi). MISC.: Elev 8600 ft; 3 acres; scenic; pets; nature trails. Sylvan Lake (5 mi). Stream.

Fulford Cave (White River NF). 12–1/10 mi S of Eagle on Co Hwy 307; 6 mi E on FS 15415. SEASON: 5/15–10/31; 14-day lmt. FACILITIES: 6 sites (tr -32), tbls, toil, cga, f, piped drk wtr. ACTIVITIES: Hiking; picnicking; fishing; mountain climbing. Horseback riding (1 mi). MISC.: Elev 9600 ft; 3 acres; pets; stream; nature trails. Trailhead to Lake Charles. Fulford Cave (1 mi).

Yeoman Park (White River NF). 12–1/10 mi S of Eagle on Co Hwy 307; 6 mi SE on FS 15415; 1/10 mi S on FS 15416. SEASON: 6/1–10/31; 14-day lmt. FACILITIES: 15 sites (tr -32), tbls, toil, cga, f, piped drk wtr. ACTIVITIES: Hiking; picnicking; fishing; mountain climbing. Horseback riding (1 mi). MISC.: Elev 9000 ft; 20 acres; pets; stream; geological; nature trails.

EMPIRE

Mizpah (Arapaho NF). 6 mi W of Empire on US 40. SEASON: 6/15–9/15; 14-day lmt. FACILITIES: 11 sites (tr -16), tbls, toil, cga, f, piped drk wtr. Store/food/ice/gas (1 mi). ACTIVITIES: Mountain climbing; picnicking; fishing. Horseback riding (1 mi). MISC.: Elev 9600 ft; 5 acres; pets; stream; scenic. Continental Divide (7 mi).

ESTES PARK (Rocky Mountain NP)

Aspenglen Campground. 5 mi W of Estes Park on US 34 (near the Fall River Entrance). SEASON: Day after LD to 5/31, FREE campground, and $1 entrance fee (or Golden Eagle/Golden Age Passport).** [Rest of year, $4.00 for campground; $2.00 for entrance fee, or Passport**]. FACILITIES: 70 sites (no trailers); tbls, flush toil, f($), drk wtr, telephone, campfire amphitheater. [During free season, no water or firewood. Water is available at the Fall River Entrance Station near the campground during that time. Pit toilets are available.] ACTIVITIES: Fishing; picnicking. MISC.: Elev 8230; pets on leash.

EVERGREEN

Mount Evans Campground (State Fish/Game Commission). 10 mi W of Evergreen on St Hwy 74 to Upper Bear Creek Rd. SEASON: 5/1–10/1. FACILITIES: 15 sites (no trailers); tbls, toil, cga, no drk wtr. ACTIVITIES: Fishing; picnicking. MISC.: Elev 9100 ft; 15 acres; pets on leash.

FAIRPLAY

Buffalo Springs (Pike–San Isabel NF). 14½ mi S of Fairplay on US 285; ½ mi W on FS 431. SEASON: 5/10–10/24; 10-day lmt. FACILITIES: 17 sites (tr -22); tbls, toil, cga, well drk wtr. ACTIVITIES: Rockhounding; picnicking. MISC.: Elev 9000 ft; 9 acres; pets on leash.

Fourmile (Pike-San Isabel NF). 1-3/10 mi S of Fairplay on US 285; 8 mi W on Co Hwy 18. SEASON: 5/10-10/24; 10-day lmt. FACILITIES: 14 sites (tr -22), tbls, toil, cga, piped drk wtr. ACTIVITIES: Mountain climbing; rockhounding; picnicking. Fishing (1 mi). MISC.: Elev 10,600 ft; 6 acres; stream; pets. Historic mining area. 14,000-ft Mt. Sherman nearby.

Weston Pass (Pike-San Isabel NF). 5 mi S of Fairplay on US 285; 7 mi SW on Co Hwy 5; 4-1/10 mi SW on Co Hwy 22. SEASON: 5/10-10/14; 10-day lmt. FACILITIES: 14 sites (tr -22); tbls, toil, cga, well drk wtr. ACTIVITIES: Picnicking. Fishing (1 mi). MISC.: Elev 10,200 ft; 6 acres; stream; pets. Nearby Weston Pass Rd was former historic Toll Road.

FLAGLER

Flagler City Park. In Flagler, 1 block off I-70. SEASON: All yr; 1-night lmt. FACILITIES: Sites; toil. MISC.: Pets.

FLORISSANT

Wildhorn (Pike-San Isabel NF). 12-1/5 mi N of Florissant on Co Hwy 1; 7/10 mi W on FS 361. SEASON: 5/1-9/30; 14-day lmt. FACILITIES: 10 sites (tr -22), tbls, toil, cga, well drk wtr. ACTIVITIES: Rockhounding; picnicking; horseback riding/rental; hiking. Fishing (2 mi). MISC.: Elev 9100 ft; 4 acres; scenic; pets.

FRASER

Byers Creek (Arapaho-Roosevelt NF). 6½ mi SW of Fraser on FS 160 (St. Louis Creek Rd). SEASON: 6/20-9/15; 14-day lmt. FACILITIES: 6 sites (tr -32), tbls, toil, cga, f, no drk wtr. ACTIVITIES: Horseback riding; hiking; picnicking; fishing. MISC.: Elev 9400 ft; 2 acres; pets; scenic.

St. Louis Creek (Arapaho-Roosevelt NF). 3 mi SW of Fraser on FS 160 (St. Louis Creek Rd). SEASON: 6/15-9/15; 14-day lmt. FACILITIES: 18 sites (tr -32), tbls, toil, cga, f, well drk wtr. Store/food/ice/gas/laundry/dump (3 mi). ACTIVITIES: Fishing; picnicking. Horseback rental/riding (3 mi). MISC.: Elev 9000 ft; 6 acres; pets. St. Louis Creek.

FRISCO

Black Lakes Campground (State Fish/Game Commission). 18 mi W of Frisco on US 6. SEASON: 5/1-10/1. FACILITIES: 25 sites; tbls, toil, cga, drk wtr. ACTIVITIES: Boating; picnicking; fishing. MISC.: Elev 10,470 ft; 25 acres; pets.

Blue River Inlet (White River NF). 3 mi SE of Frisco on St Hwy C09. SEASON: 6/1-10/1; 10-day lmt. FACILITIES: 48 sites (tr -32), toil, cga. No tbls/drk wtr.

Store/gas (1 mi). Ice/laundry (3 mi). ACTIVITIES: Sailing; boating,rld; picnicking; fishing. Horseback riding/rental (5 mi). MISC.: Elev 9000 ft; 1 acre; pets. Adjacent to Lake Dillon.

Frisco Bay (White River NF). 1 mi E of Frisco on St Hwy C09. SEASON: 5/25-9/10; 10-day lmt. FACILITIES: 55 sites (tr -32), toil, cga. No tbls/drk wtr. ACTIVITIES: Sailing; boating,rld; picnicking; fishing. MISC.: Elev 9000 ft; 5 acres; pets. Adjacent to Lake Dillon. Store/food/ice/gas/laundry (1 mi).

Giberson Bay (White River NF). 2 mi N of Frisco on US 6. SEASON: 6/1-9/1; 10-day lmt. FACILITIES: 40 sites (tr -32), toil, cga, piped drk wtr. No tbls. Electric hookup. Ice/gas (1 mi). Store/laundry (2 mi). ACTIVITIES: Sailing; boating (1, 2 mi; r, 3 mi); picnicking; fishing. MISC.: Elev 9000 ft; 2 acres; pets; lake. Nature trails (3 mi).

Officers Gulch (White River NF). 3-4/5 mi SW of Frisco on I-70. SEASON: 5/25-11/1; 10-day lmt. FACILITIES: 4 sites (tr -32), tbls, toil, cga, well drk wtr. Store/gas/dump/ice/laundry/food (5 mi). ACTIVITIES: Fishing; picnicking. Sailing/boating,l (5 mi). MISC.: Elev 9700 ft; 9 acres; pond; pets. Lake Dillon (5 mi).

Rainbow Lake (White River NF). 2 mi E of Frisco on St Hwy C09; 1 mi SW on FS FH219. SEASON: 6/1-10/1; 10-day lmt. FACILITIES: 10 sites (tr -32), tbls, toil, cga, no drk wtr. ACTIVITIES: Sailing; boating,d (1, 2 mi); picnicking; fishing. MISC.: Elev 9100 ft; 10 acres; lake; pets. Store/food/ice/gas/laundry/dump (2 mi).

***Sentinel Island** (White River NF). ½ mi E of Frisco on US 6; 2 mi NE, BY BOAT. SEASON: 6/1-10/1; 10-day lmt. FACILITIES: 13 tent sites, tbls, toil, cga, f, no drk wtr. Store/ice/food/gas/laundry/dump (2 mi). ACTIVITIES: Sailing; boating,dr (1, 1 mi); hiking; picnicking; fishing. Horseback rental/riding (3 mi). No swimming or body contact sports allowed. MISC.: Elev 9000 ft; 45 acres; pets. Nature trails (1 mi). Island in Lake Dillon.

FORT COLLINS

Belleair Lake Camp (Roosevelt NF). 46 mi W of Ft. Collins on St Hwy 200 and Red Feather Lakes Rd. SEASON: 5/20-9/20; 14-day lmt. FACILITIES: 12 sites (tr -30), tbls, toil, cga, drk wtr. ACTIVITIES: Swimming; picnicking; fishing. MISC.: Elev 8200 ft; 6 acres; pets.

Chambers Lake Camp (Roosevelt NF). 65 mi W of Ft. Collins on St Hwy 14. SEASON: 5/20-9/20. FACILITIES: 53 sites (tr -30), toil, cga, drk wtr. ACTIVITIES: Boating; swimming; picnicking; fishing; waterskiing. MISC.: Elev 9000.

Kelly Flats Camp (Roosevelt NF). 35 mi W of Ft. Collins on St Hwy 14. SEASON: 5/20-9/20; 14-day lmt. FACILITIES: 23 sites (tr -30), tbls, toil, cga, no drk wtr. ACTIVITIES: Fishing; picnicking. MISC.: Elev 6600 ft; pets.

Tunnel Camp (Roosevelt NF). 10 mi N of Ft. Collins on US 287; 45 mi W on St Hwy 14; 6 mi N on FS 190. SEASON: 5/20-9/20; 14-day lmt. FACILITIES: 49 sites (tr -30), tbls, toil, cga, drk wtr. ACTIVITIES: Hiking; picnicking; fishing. MISC.: Elev 8600 ft; pets.

FRUITA

Saddle Horn Campground (Colorado NM). 3½ mi S of Fruita on St Hwy 340. SEASON: FREE, Oct.-April ($2 rest of yr); 7-day lmt. FACILITIES: 83 sites. Each site has a charcoal grill (wood fires are prohibited), a picnic table, and parking. As demand lessens during the cooler (free) months, they usually shut down all but about 30 sites, and when it's really cold they may be forced to close comfort stations to prevent freeze damage. Flush toil; drk wtr; pull-thru spaces. ACTIVITIES: Picnicking. MISC.: Visitor Center at Saddlehorn (4 mi from Fruita entrance) is open all year.

GEORGETOWN

Clear Lake (Arapaho-Roosevelt NF). 4 mi S of Georgetown on Co Hwy 118. SEASON: 6/15-9/15; 14-day lmt. FACILITIES: 8 sites (tr -32), tbls, toil, cga, no drk wtr. Store/food/ice/gas/laundry/showers (4 mi). ACTIVITIES: Hiking; picnicking. Fishing (1 mi). Horseback riding (1 mi), rental (4 mi). MISC.: Elev 10,000 ft; 3 acres; nature trails; stream; pets.

Guanella Pass (Arapaho-Roosevelt NF). 8 mi S of Georgetown on Co Hwy 281. SEASON: 6/15-9/15; 14-day lmt. FACILITIES: 9 sites (tr -22), tbls, toil, cga, no drk wtr. ACTIVITIES: Hiking; mountain climbing; picnicking; fishing. Horseback riding (1 mi). MISC.: Elev 10,900 ft; 9 acres; scenic; stream; pets.

GLADE PARK

Miracle Rock (BLM). 10 mi SW of Glade Park on Co Rd. SEASON: All yr; 14-day lmt. FACILITIES: 23 sites (tr -22), tbls, toil. ACTIVITIES: Rockhounding; hiking; picnicking. MISC.: Elev 6600 ft; 6 acres; pets on leash.

Mud Springs (BLM). 6 mi S of Glade Park on Co Rd. SEASON: 5/1-10/31; 14-day lmt. FACILITIES: 23 sites (tr -22), tbls, toil, cga, f. ACTIVITIES: Rockhounding; hiking; picnicking. MISC.: Elev 8100 ft; 8 acres; pets on leash.

GLENDEVEY

Browns Park (Arapaho-Roosevelt NF). 4 mi S of Glendevey on Laramie River Rd. SEASON: 5/20-9/20; 14-day lmt. FACILITIES: 28 sites (tr -30), tbls, toil, cga, no drk wtr. ACTIVITIES: Picnicking. Fishing (1 mi). MISC.: Elev 8600 ft; 1 acre; pets.

GLENWOOD SPRINGS

Coffee Pot Springs (White River NF). 18 mi E of Glenwood Springs on US 6/24; 2 mi N on Co Hwy 301; 20-3/5 mi NW on FS 15600. SEASON: 6/15-10/31; 14-day lmt. FACILITIES: 4 sites (tr -22), tbls, toil, cga, f, piped drk wtr. ACTIVITIES: Picnicking. Horseback riding (1 mi). Fishing (5 mi). MISC.: Elev 10,100 ft; 20 acres; pets.

Deep Lake (White River NF). 16-9/10 mi E of Glenwood Springs on US 6/24; 2 mi N on Co Hwy 301; 26½ mi NW on FS 600. SEASON: 6/15-10/31; 14-day lmt. FACILITIES: 12 sites (tr -22), tbls, toil, cga, f, no drk wtr. ACTIVITIES: Boating,ld; picnicking; fishing. MISC.: Elev 10,500 ft; 8 acres; lake; pets.

Klines Folly (White River NF). 16-9/10 mi E of Glenwood Springs on US 6/24; 2 mi N on Co Hwy 301; 25½ mi NW on FS 15600; 9/10 mi W on FS 15601. SEASON: 6/15-10/31; 14-day lmt. FACILITIES: 4 sites (tr -22), tbls, toil, cga, f, no drk wtr. ACTIVITIES: Boating; picnicking; fishing. MISC.: Elev 10,200 ft; 1 acre; lake; historic; pets.

Supply Basin (White River NF). 16-9/10 mi E of Glenwood Springs on US 6/24; 2 mi N on Co Hwy 301; 25½ mi NW on FS 15600; 1-7/10 mi W on FS 15601. SEASON: 6/15-10/31; 14-day lmt. FACILITIES: 6 sites (tr -22), tbls, toil, cga, f, no drk wtr. ACTIVITIES: Boating,d; picnicking; fishing. MISC.: Elev 10,200 ft; 2 acres; lake; historic; pets.

White Owl (White River NF). 16-9/10 mi E of Glenwood Springs on US 6 & 244; 2 mi N on Co Hwy 301; 24 mi NW on FS 15600; 4/5 mi W on FS 6002D. SEASON: 6/15-10/31; 14-day lmt. FACILITIES: 5 sites (tr -22), tbls, toil, cga, f, no drk wtr. ACTIVITIES: Picnicking; fishing; boating. MISC.: 10,200 ft; 1 acre; scenic; lake; pets.

GOULD

Aspen (Routt NF). 9/10 mi SW of Gould on FS 740; 1/10 mi W on FS 741. SEASON: 6/15-9/8; 14-day lmt. FACILITIES: 7 sites (tr -22), tbls, toil, cga, well drk wtr. Store/ice/food/gas (1 mi). ACTIVITIES: Fishing; picnicking. MISC.: Elev 8900 ft; 4 acres; stream; pets.

See page 7 for KEY TO ABBREVIATIONS.

Pines (Routt NF). 3 mi SE of Gould on FS 740. **SEASON:** 6/15-9/8; 14-day lmt. **FACILITIES:** 10 sites (tr -22), tbls, toil, cga, well drk wtr. **ACTIVITIES:** Picnicking. Fishing (1 mi). **MISC.:** Elev 9200 ft; 5 acres; pets; stream.

Rangers Lake Campground (State Fish/Game Commission). E of Gould on St Hwy 14 to State Forest Headquarters. **SEASON:** 5/1-10/1; 14-day lmt. **FACILITIES:** 15 primitive sites (no trailers); tbls, toil, cga, drk wtr. **ACTIVITIES:** Fishing; picnicking. **MISC.:** Elev 8100 ft;2 acres;pets.

GRANBY

Denver Creek (Arapaho-Roosevelt NF). 3 mi NW of Granby on US 40; 11-9/10 mi NW on St Hwy 125. **SEASON:** 6/10-9/15; 14-day lmt. **FACILITIES:** 24 sites (tr -32), tbls, toil, cga, drk wtr. **ACTIVITIES:** Horseback riding; picnicking; fishing. **MISC.:** Elev 8600 ft; 9 acres; pets.

Sawmill Gulch (Arapaho-Roosevelt NF). 3 mi NW of Granby on US 40; 9-9/10 mi NW on St Hwy 125. **SEASON:** 6/10-10/20; 14-day lmt. **FACILITIES:** 5 sites (tr -32). Well drk wtr; tbls, toil, cga, f. **ACTIVITIES:** Horseback riding; picnicking; fishing. **MISC.:** Elev 8500 ft; 2 acres; pets; stream; scenic.

GRAND JUNCTION

Hay Press (Gunnison-Grand Mesa-Uncompahgre NF). 10 mi SW of Grand Junction on St Hwy 340; 20 mi S on Co Hwy 400. **SEASON:** 5/20-10/20. **FACILITIES:** 8 sites (tr -16), tbls, toil, cga, piped drk wtr. **ACTIVITIES:** Picnicking. **MISC.:** Elev 9300 ft; 2 acres; pets. Colorado NM (14 mi).

Miracle Rock Recreation Site (BLM). 25 mi SW of Grand Junction on Co Rd 141 (gravel rd); 10 mi SW of Glade Park on Co Rd. **SEASON:** All yr; 14-day lmt. **FACILITIES:** 23 sites (tr -22), tbls, toil. **ACTIVITIES:** Rockhounding; hiking; picnicking. **MISC.:** Elev 6600 ft; 6 acres; well wtr; pets. Near Colorado NM; scenic.

Mud Springs Recreation Site (BLM). 20 mi SW of Grand Junction on gravel Co Rd 141; 6 mi S of Glade Park on gravel Co Rd. **SEASON:** 5/1-10/31; 14-day lmt. **FACILITIES:** 25 sites (tr -22), toil, cga, f, piped drk wtr. **ACTIVITIES:** Hiking; rockhounding; picnicking. **MISC.:** Elev 8100 ft; 8 acres; pets.

GRANT

Burning Bear (Pike-San Isabel NF). 5-1/5 mi NW of Grant on FS 118. **SEASON:** 5/1-10/15; 14-day lmt. **FACILITIES:** 13 sites (tr -16), tbls, toil, cga, well drk wtr. **ACTIVITIES:** Picnicking. **MISC.:** Elev 9500 ft; 6 acres; stream; pets.

Hall Valley (Pike-San Isabel NF). 3-1/10 mi W of Grant on US 285; 4-7/10 mi NW on FS 120. **SEASON:** 5/1-10/15; 14-day lmt. **FACILITIES:** 9 sites (tr -16), tbls, toil, cga, well drk wtr. **ACTIVITIES:** Fishing; picnicking. **MISC.:** Elev 9900 ft; 4 acres; stream; pets.

GUNNISON

Commissary (Gunnison-Grand Mesa-Uncompahgre NF). 26-1/10 mi W of Gunnison on US 50; 3/5 mi NW on St Hwy 92; 9-1/5 mi N on FS 721. **SEASON:** 6/4-9/5; 14-day lmt. **FACILITIES:** 7 sites (tr -16), tbls, toil, cga, piped drk wtr. **ACTIVITIES:** Fishing; picnicking. **MISC.:** Elev 7900 ft; 2 acres; pets; stream. Curecanti NRA (approx. 10 mi S).

Elk Creek (Curecanti NRA). 16 mi W of Gunnison on US 50. **SEASON:** FREE and accessible, 4/1-MD and LD-12/1, depending on weather (heavy snowfalls generally close the campground from December to March); $2, MD-LD. 14-day lmt. **FACILITIES:** 175 sites (tr -30), flush toil, dump. Store/ice nearby. **ACTIVITIES:** Boating,rld; picnicking. Swimming and fishing nearby. Snowmobiling in winter.

Lake Fork Campground (Curecanti NRA). 27 mi W of Gunnison on US 50. **SEASON:** May-October; 14-day lmt. **FACILITIES:** 150 sites (limited number of sites available for tents); flush toil, dump, fish cleaning station, drk wtr. **ACTIVITIES:** Boating,l; picnicking; fishing. **MISC.:** Located near Blue Mesa Dam.

Soap Creek (Gunnison-Grand Mesa-Uncompahgre NF). 26-1/10 mi W of Gunnison on US 50; 3/5 mi NW on St Hwy 92; 7-1/5 mi N on FS 721; 3/5 mi NE on FS 824. **SEASON:** 6/4-9/5; 14-day lmt. **FACILITIES:** 13 sites (tr -22), tbls, toil, cga, piped drk wtr. **ACTIVITIES:** Fishing; picnicking. **MISC.:** Elev 7700 ft; 8 acres; pets. Curecanti NRA (approx. 9 mi S).

Stevens Creek Campground (Curecanti NRA). 12 mi W of Gunnison on US 50. **SEASON:** June-September; 14-day lmt. **FACILITIES:** No designated sites; accommodates 75 Rvs/tents. Toil, no wtr. **MISC.:** Easy lakeshore access; an overflow campground.

GYPSUM

Lede Reservoir (NF). 17-1/10 mi SE of Gypsum on Co Hwy 301. **SEASON:** 6/1-10/31; 14-day lmt. **FACILITIES:** 3 sites (tr -22), tbls, toil, cga. **ACTIVITIES:** Boating; picnicking; fishing. [No boat launching facilities.] **MISC.:** Elev 9500 ft; 3 acres; pets. Piped drk wtr. Lede Reservoir.

HASTY

John Martin Reservoir (COE). 3 mi S of Hasty below Dam. **SEASON:** 5/1-10/1; 14-

day lmt. FACILITIES: Primitive sites; tbls, toil, cga, dump. ACTIVITIES: Free movies (p.m.). Hiking; picnicking. Boating,I (1 mi). MISC.: Elev 3755 ft; 80 acres; pets.

Lake Hasty Recreation Area (COE; John Martin Reservoir). 4 mi S of Hasty on access rd. SEASON: All yr; 14-day lmt. FACILITIES: 82 sites; 16 fresh drk wtr hydrants, Nov.-March; tbls, toil, cga. Dump (April-October). Playground. The area is well-lighted at night. ACTIVITIES: Swimming; hunting (winter goose); boating; picnicking; fishing (trout). Ice fishing in winter. MISC.: Elev 3750 ft; 300 acres; pets.

HIDEAWAY PARK

Idlewild (Arapaho-Roosevelt NF). 1 mi NW of Hideaway Park on US 40. SEASON: 6/10-9/15. FACILITIES: 24 sites (tr -32); tbls, toil, cga, f, drk wtr. Store/ice/laundry (1 mi). ACTIVITIES: Picnicking; fishing. MISC.: Elev 9000 ft; 1 acre; river; scenic; pets.

HILLSIDE

Lake Creek (Pike-San Isabel NF). 3 mi W of Hillside on FS 300. SEASON: 5/18-10/25; 10-day lmt. FACILITIES: 11 sites (tr -16); tbls, toil, cga, no drk wtr. Store/food/gas (3 mi). ACTIVITIES: Fishing; picnicking. MISC.: Elev 8300 ft; 4 acres; pets; stream.

HOT SULPHUR SPRINGS

Hot Sulphur Springs Campground (State Fish/Game Commission). 3 mi W of Hot Sulphur Springs on US 40. SEASON: All yr; 14-day lmt. FACILITIES: 50 sites (tr -22), tbls, toil, cga, drk wtr. ACTIVITIES: Fishing; picnicking. MISC.: Elev 7600 ft; 5 acres; pets.

IDAHO SPRINGS

Mizpah (Arapaho-Roosevelt NF). 17 mi W of Idaho Springs on US 40. SEASON: 6/15-9/15; 10-day lmt. FACILITIES: 11 sites (tr -16), tbls, toil, cga, f, drk wtr. Store/ice (1 mi). ACTIVITIES: Fishing; picnicking. MISC.: Elev 9600 ft; 5 acres; pets.

Robbers Roost Camp (Arapaho-Roosevelt NF). 18 mi W of Idaho Springs on US 40. SEASON: 6/20-9/15. FACILITIES: 11 sites (tr -32), tbls, toil, cga, f. ACTIVITIES: Fishing (1 mi). Picnicking. MISC.: Elev 9700 ft; 3 acres; pets.

West Chicago Creek (Arapaho-Roosevelt NF). 6 mi S of Idaho Springs on St Hwy 103; 4 mi S on Co Hwy (at end of W Chicago Rd). SEASON: 6/15-9/15; 14-day lmt. FACILITIES: 9 sites (tr -16), tbls, toil, cga, piped drk wtr. ACTIVITIES:

Mountain climbing; picnicking; fishing; hiking. MISC.: Elev 9600 ft; 5 acres; stream; pets; nature trails; scenic.

JEFFERSON

Kenosha Pass (Pike-San Isabel NF). 4-1/5 mi NE of Jefferson on US 285. [Kenosha Pass Summit.] SEASON: 5/1-10/15; 14-day lmt. FACILITIES: 25 sites (tr -16), tbls, toil, cga, f, no drk wtr. Store/gas/ice (4 mi). ACTIVITIES: Picnicking. Fishing (4 mi). MISC.: Elev 10,000 ft; 11 acres; pets.

Lost Park Camp (Pike-San Isabel NF). 1-1/5 mi NE of Jefferson on US 285; 19-7/10 mi E on FS 127; 4 mi E on FS 134. SEASON: 5/20-10/27; 10-day lmt. FACILITIES: 10 sites (tr -22), tbls, toil, cga, f, no drk wtr. ACTIVITIES: Fishing; picnicking. MISC.: Elev 10,000 ft; 4 acres; scenic; river; pets.

Michigan Creek Camp (Pike-San Isabel NF). 3 mi NW of Jefferson on Co Hwy 35 (Jefferson Lake Rd); 2-1/10 mi NW on Co Hwy 54; 1 mi NW on FS 400. SEASON: 5/10-10/24; 10-day lmt. FACILITIES: 13 sites (tr -22), tbls, toil, cga, no drk wtr. ACTIVITIES: Fishing; picnicking. MISC.: Elev 10,000 ft; 6 acres; pets. Michigan Creek.

KREMMLING

Cataract Creek (White River NF). 1/5 mi E of Kremmling on US 40; 12-3/10 mi S on St Hwy C09; 4-7/10 mi SE on Co Rd CH030; 2-1/10 mi SW on Co Hwy 1725. SEASON: 6/1-10/1; 10-day lmt. FACILITIES: 8 sites (tr -16), tbls, toil, cga, well drk wtr. Store/food/gas (2 mi). Ice (3 mi). ACTIVITIES: Hiking; picnicking; fishing. Boating,rld (3 mi). MISC.: Elev 8600 ft; 4 acres; stream; pets. Nature trails (1 mi). Trailhead to Gore Range Eagles Nest Primitive Area.

LA GARITA

Poso Campground (Rio Grande NF). 10 mi NW of La Garita on Co Rd 690; 1½ mi W on FS 675; 1-1/10 mi SW on FS 671. SEASON: 5/15-11/15; 14-day lmt. FACILITIES: 11 sites (tr -16), tbls, toil, cga, f, well drk wtr. Garbage collection. ACTIVITIES: Rockhounding; picnicking; fishing. MISC.: Elev 9000 ft; 4 acres; stream; pets.

Stormking Campground (Rio Grande NF). 10 mi NW of La Garita on Co Rd 690; 4½ mi N on FS 6902A. SEASON: 6/1-10/30; 14-day lmt. FACILITIES: 11 sites (tr -16), tbls, toil, cga, f, well drk wtr, garbage collection. ACTIVITIES: Picnicking; rockhounding. MISC.: Elev 9200 ft; 4 acres; stream; pets.

See page 7 for KEY TO ABBREVIATIONS.

LAKE GEORGE

Riverside (Pike NF). 2½ mi SW of Lake George on FS 245. SEASON: 5/16-9/25; 10-day lmt. FACILITIES: 12 sites (tr -16), tbls, toil, cga, no drk wtr. Store/ice (2 mi). ACTIVITIES: Fishing; picnicking. MISC.: Elev 8000 ft; 2 acres; river; pets.

Wagon Tongue (Pike NF). 6-3/5 mi S of Lake George on FS 245; 3/10 mi E on FS 244 (in Eleven Mile Canyon). SEASON: 5/16-9/25. FACILITIES: 15 sites; tbls, toil, cga. ACTIVITIES: Rockhounding; picnicking. MISC.: Elev 8400 ft; stream; pets.

LAMAR

John Martin Reservoir Campground (COE; John Martin Reservoir). 20 mi W of Lamar on dirt rd. SEASON: All yr; 14-day lmt. FACILITIES: 41 sites (tr -35), toil, drk wtr, dump, 2 playgrounds. ACTIVITIES: Boating (no motors); swimming; fishing (catfish, trout, crappie, pike); picnicking; waterskiing; hunting (waterfowl). MISC.: Elev 3800 ft. Southeastern Colorado plains. 70-acre Lake Hasty. Intermittant irrigation pool behind dam. Some shade. Pets on leash. No motorbikes. 3500-ft graded landing strip. Historic markers.

LaPORTE

Big Bend (Arapaho-Roosevelt NF). 4 mi N of LaPorte on US 287; 41 mi W on St Hwy 14. SEASON: 5/20-9/20; 14-day lmt. FACILITIES: 12 sites (tr -32), tbls, toil, cga, dump, no drk wtr. ACTIVITIES: Fishing; picnicking. MISC.: Elev 7600 ft; 11 acres; river; pets.

Big South (Arapaho-Roosevelt NF). 4 mi N of LaPorte on US 287; 51 mi W on St Hwy 14. SEASON: 5/15-11/12; 14-day lmt. FACILITIES: 3 sites (tr -32); tbls, toil, cga, no drk wtr. Food/ice/gas/store (4 mi). Visitor Center (2 mi). ACTIVITIES: Picnicking; fishing. Swimming/boating,l (4 mi). MISC.: Elev 8400 ft; 1 acre; lake; scenic; pets. Confluence Big South Poudre River and Joe Wright Creek. Pets.

Browns Park (Arapaho-Roosevelt NF). 4 mi N of LaPorte on US 287; 55 mi W on St Hwy 14; 21 mi N on FS 190. SEASON: 5/15-11/12; 5-day lmt. FACILITIES: 28 sites (tr -32), tbls, toil, cga, no drk wtr. Store/gas (1 mi). ACTIVITIES: Hiking; picnicking. Horseback riding/rental (1 mi). Fishing (1 mi). MISC.: Elev 8400 ft; 10 acres; pets; stream. Trailhead to Rawah Wilderness. McIntyre and Link Trailhead. Beside Jinks Creek; scenic.

Chambers Lake (Arapaho-Roosevelt NF). 4 mi N of LaPorte on US 287; 56 mi W on St Hwy 14. SEASON: 5/15-11/12; 14-day lmt. FACILITIES: 53 sites (tr -22), tbls, toil, cga, no drk wtr. ACTIVITIES: Hiking; swimming; waterskiing; boating,ld; picnicking; fishing. Horseback riding (1 mi). Sailing. MISC.: Elev 9200 ft; 30 acres; pets; geological. Trailhead to Bluelake, Rawah Wilderness.

Crown Point-Pingree (Arapaho-Roosevelt NF). 4 mi N of La Porte on US 287; 21 mi W on St Hwy 14; 8 mi S on Co Hwy 131. SEASON: 5/20-9/20; 14-day lmt. FACILITIES: 12 sites (tr -32); tbls, toil, cga, no drk wtr. ACTIVITIES: Picnicking; fishing. MISC.: Elev 8000 ft; 19 acres; river; pets. Individual site alone Co Hwy 131.

Eggars (Arapaho-Roosevelt NF). 4 mi N of LaPorte on US 287; 27 mi W on St Hwy 14. SEASON: 5/20-9/20; 14-day lmt. FACILITIES: 4 sites (tr -32), toil. No tbls/drk wtr. Store/ice/gas (4 mi). ACTIVITIES: Fishing. MISC.: Elev 6200 ft; 2 acres; pets; river.

Grandview (Arapaho-Roosevelt NF). 4 mi N on US 287; 61 mi W on St Hwy 14; 14 mi SE on FS 156. SEASON: 6/15-9/30; 1-day lmt. FACILITIES: 6 sites (no tr); tbls, toil, cga, no drk wtr. ACTIVITIES: Picnicking; boating; fishing. MISC.: Elev 10,000 ft; 4 acres; scenic; pets. At inlet of Long Draw Reservoir.

Hooligan Roost (Arapaho-Roosevelt NF). 4 mi N of LaPorte on US 287; 54 mi W on St Hwy 14; 22 mi N on FS 190; 1 mi W on FS 197. SEASON: 5/20-9/20; 10-day lmt. FACILITIES: 4 sites (no trailers), tbls, toil, cga. ACTIVITIES: Hiking; picnicking; fishing. MISC.: Elev 8600 ft; pets; stream. Trailhead to Rawah Wilderness.

Link Trailhead (Arapaho-Roosevelt NF). 4 mi N of La Porte on US 287; 5 mi W on St Hwy 14; 21 mi N on FS 190. SEASON: 5/15-11/12; 14-day lmt. FACILITIES: 28 sites (tr -32); tbls, toil, cga, no drk wtr. Food/gas/store (1 mi). ACTIVITIES: Picnicking; fishing. Horseback riding (1 mi). MISC.: Elev 8400 ft; 1 acre; stream; scenic; pets.

Little South (Arapaho-Roosevelt NF). 4 mi N of LaPorte on US 287; 21 mi W on St Hwy 14; 8 mi S on Co Hwy 131. SEASON: 5/20-9/20; 14-day lmt. FACILITIES: 12 sites (tr -32); individual sites along Co Hwy 131. Tbls, toil, cga, no drk wtr. ACTIVITIES: Fishing; picnicking. MISC.: Elev 8000 ft; 19 acres; pets.

See page 7 for KEY TO ABBREVIATIONS.

McIntyre Trailhead (Arapaho–Roosevelt NF). 4 mi N of LaPorte on US 287; 55 mi W on St Hwy 114; 21 mi N on FS 190. SEASON: 5/15–11/12; 14-day lmt. FACILITIES: 28 sites (tr –32); tbls, toil, cga. Food/gas/store (1 mi). ACTIVITIES: Picnicking; fishing. Horseback riding (1 mi). MISC.: Elev 8500 ft; 1 acre; stream; scenic; pets. Visitor Center (1 mi).

Narrows Cooperative (Arapaho–Roosevelt NF). 4 mi N of LaPorte on US 287; 23½ mi W on St Hwy 287. SEASON: 5/20–9/20; 14-day lmt. FACILITIES: 12 sites (tr –32), tbls, toil, cga, no drk wtr, dump. ACTIVITIES: Fishing; picnicking. MISC.: Elev 6500 ft; 6 acres; pets; river.

Skyline (Arapaho–Roosevelt NF). 4 mi N of LaPorte on US 287; 55 mi W on St Hwy 14; 4 mi N on FS 190. SEASON: 5/15–11/12; 14-day lmt. FACILITIES: 8 sites (tr –22), tbls, toil, cga, no drk wtr. Dump (2 mi). ACTIVITIES: Fishing; picnicking. Boating (5 mi). MISC.: Elev 8600 ft; 2 acres; pets; stream.

Stevens Gulch (Arapaho–Roosevelt NF). 4 mi N of LaPorte on US 287; 20 mi W on St Hwy 14. SEASON: 5/20–9/20; 14-day lmt. FACILITIES: 7 sites (tr –32), tbls, toil, cga, no drk wtr. Store/ice/gas (3 mi). Dump (4 mi). Toilet suitable for handicapped. MISC.: River; pets.

Stove Prairie Landing (Arapaho–Roosevelt NF). 4 mi N of LaPorte on US 287; 17 mi W on St Hwy 14. SEASON: 5/20–9/20; 14-day lmt. FACILITIES: 7 sites (tr –32), tbls, toil, cga, no drk wtr. Store/ice/gas (3 mi). Dump (4 mi). ACTIVITIES: Fishing; picnicking. MISC.: Elev 6000 ft; 3 acres; pets; river.

Tom Bennett (Arapaho–Roosevelt NF). 4 mi N of LaPorte on US 287; 27 mi W on St Hwy 14; 11 mi S on Co Hwy 131; 5 mi W on FS 145. SEASON: 5/20–9/20; 14-day lmt. FACILITIES: 5 sites (tr –16), tbls, toil, cga, no drk wtr. ACTIVITIES: Fishing; picnicking. MISC.: Elev 9000 ft; 3 acres; pets; stream. Near Pin Gree Park.

Tunnel (Arapaho–Roosevelt NF). 4 mi N of LaPorte on US 287; 55 mi W on St Hwy 14; 6 mi N on FS 190. SEASON: 5/15–11/12; 14-day lmt. FACILITIES: 49 sites (tr –32), tbls, toil, cga, no drk wtr. Store/gas/ice (3 mi). Dump (1 mi). ACTIVITIES: Hiking; picnicking; fishing. Boating,d (5 mi). Horseback riding (1 mi), rental (5 mi). MISC.: Elev 8600 ft; 18 acres; pets; stream; scenic. West Branch Trailhead to Rawah Wilderness.

Upper Landing (Arapaho–Roosevelt NF). 4 mi N of LaPorte on US 287; 19 mi W on St Hwy 14. SEASON: 5/20–9/20; 14-day lmt. FACILITIES: 6 sites (tr –32), toil, cga, no tbls/drk wtr. Store/ice/gas/dump (4 mi). ACTIVITIES: Fishing; picnicking. MISC.: Elev 6000 ft; 2 acres; pets on leash; river.

Zimmerman Lake Trailhead (Arapaho–Roosevelt NF). 4 mi N of LaPorte on US 287; 55 mi W on St Hwy 114; 21 mi N on FS 190. SEASON: All year; 14-day lmt. FACILITIES: 28 sites (tr –32); tbls, toil, cga. Food/gas/store (1 mi). No drk wtr. ACTIVITIES: Picnicking; fishing. Horseback riding and rental (1 mi). MISC.: Elev 10,000 ft; 1 acre; stream; scenic; pets. Visitor Center (1 mi).

LAS ANIMAS

John Martin Reservoir Campground (COE; John Martin Reservoir). 18 mi E of Las Animas on US 50; 3 mi S of Hasty on St Hwy 260. SEASON: All yr; 14-day lmt. FACILITIES: 41 sites (tr –35),some shade; Dump; 2 playgrounds; drk wtr; toil. ACTIVITIES: Boating (no motors); swimming; picnicking; fishing (catfish, trout, crappie, pike); waterskiing; hunting (waterfowl). MISC.: Elev 3800 ft; pets. Southeastern Colorado plains. 70-acre Lake Hasty. Intermittant irrigation pool behind dam. No motorbikes. 3500-ft graded landing strip. Historic markers.

LEADVILLE

Belle of Colorado (Pike–San Isabel NF). 4-1/5 mi SW of Leadville on FS 105; 3/5 mi NE on FS 104. SEASON: 5/31–9/6; 10-day lmt. FACILITIES: 15 tent sites (TENT CAMPING ONLY); tbls, flush toil, electricity in restrooms, cga, piped drk wtr. Dump (1 mi). ACTIVITIES: Picnicking. Hiking/boating/fishing (1 mi). MISC.: Elev 9900 ft; 6 acres; pets; lake. Nature trails (1 mi). At Turquoise Lake Recreation Area.

Elbert Creek (Pike–San Isabel NF). 6 mi SW of Leadville on FS 110. SEASON: 5/30–9/30; 10-day lmt. FACILITIES: 20 sites; tbls, toil, cga, well drk wtr. ACTIVITIES: Picnicking. Fishing (1 mi). Horseback rental/riding (5 mi). MISC.: Elev 10,100 ft; 12 acres; pets; stream.

Halfmoon (San Isabel NF). 3–7/10 mi W of Leadville on US 24; 4/5 mi W on St Hwy 300; 5-3/5 mi SW on FS 110. SEASON: 5/30–9/30; 14-day lmt. FACILITIES: 6 sites (tr –16), tbls, toil, cga, no drk wtr. ACTIVITIES: Mountain climbing; picnicking; fishing. MISC.: Elev 9900 ft; 14 acres; pets; stream.

Tennessee Pass (Pike–San Isabel NF). 9-4/5 mi N of Leadville on US 24. SEASON: 5/25–9/28; 14-day lmt. FACILITIES: 5 sites (tr –16), tbls, toil, cga, piped drk wtr. ACTIVITIES: Picnicking. Fishing (1 mi). MISC.: Elev 10,900 ft;

COLORADO

LOVELAND

Lonetree Reservoir Campground (State Fish/Game Commission). 5 mi SW of Loveland on US 287 to Champion; 4 mi W; 1 mi S at sign. **SEASON:** All yr. **FACILITIES:** 5 sites (no trailers); toil, cga, no tbls/drk wtr. **ACTIVITIES:** Boating,l; fishing. **MISC.:** Elev 5200 ft; 5 acres; pets on leash. Lake.

LYONS

Camp Dick (Arapaho–Roosevelt NF). 15 mi W of Lyons on St Hwy 7; 6 mi S on St Hwy 72; 1 mi W on FS 92. **SEASON:** 5/1–10/31; 14-day lmt. **FACILITIES:** 34 sites (tr –32); tbls, toil, cga, piped drk wtr. Gas/ice (2 mi). **ACTIVITIES:** Picnicking. Horseback riding/rental (2 mi). **MISC.:** Elev 8600 ft; 14 acres; stream; pets. In middle of St. Vrain Canyon.

Peaceful Valley (Arapaho–Roosevelt NF). 15-1/5 mi W of Lyons on St Hwy 7; 6 mi S on St Hwy 72; 1/5 mi W on FS 92. **SEASON:** 5/1–10/31; 14-day lmt. **FACILITIES:** 15 sites (tr –32); tbls, toil, cga, piped drk wtr. Gas/ice (1 mi). **ACTIVITIES:** Picnicking; fishing. Horseback riding/rental (1 mi). **MISC.:** Elev 8500 ft; 16 acres; stream; pets. In middle of St. Vrain Canyon.

MANCOS

Mancos Wayside City Campground (Municipal Park). East side of town, in Mancos. **SEASON:** All yr; 14-day lmt. **FACILITIES:** Undesignated sites; tbls, toil, cga, drk wtr, dump. **ACTIVITIES:** Hiking; picnicking; fishing; horseback riding. **MISC.:** Elev 7000 ft; pets.

Transfer (San Juan NF). 1/5 mi N of Mancos on St Hwy 184; 11-7/10 mi NE on Co Hwy FH561. **SEASON:** 6/1–11/15. **FACILITIES:** 13 sites (tr –16), tbls, toil, cga, well drk wtr, f. **ACTIVITIES:** Picnicking. Fishing (1 mi). **MISC.:** Elev 8500 ft; 4 acres; pets.

MASONVILLE

Buckhorn Canyon (Arapaho–Roosevelt NF). 4 mi N of Masonville on US 287; 15 mi W on St Hwy 14; 10 mi S on Co Hwy 27. **SEASON:** 5/20–9/20; 14-day lmt. **FACILITIES:** 12 sites (tr –32), tbls, toil, cga, no drk wtr. [Individual sites along rd.] **ACTIVITIES:** Fishing; picnicking. **MISC.:** Elev 8300 ft; 17 acres; pets; river.

MAYBELL

Deerlodge Park (Dinosaur NM). 18 mi SW of Maybell on US 40; 14 mi W to campground. **SEASON:** 5/15–10/15; 15-day lmt. **FACILITIES:** 8 sites; tbls, toil, cga, no drk wtr. **ACTIVITIES:** Boating,l (earth launch); whitewater running craft only (rafting permit required). Fishing; picnicking. **NO SWIMMING**; ice cold water and unexpected currents. **MISC.:** Elev 5000 ft; 2 acres; pets. Ranger Station. The launching area for Yampa River Trips.

Gates of Lodore (Dinosaur NM). 41 mi NW of Maybell on St Hwy 318; 4 mi SW on unpaved rds. **SEASON:** 5/1–11/1; 15-day lmt. **FACILITIES:** 17 sites (tr –22), tbls, toil, cga. Water faucets [no water from early fall to late spring due to potential damage to pipes from freezing]. **ACTIVITIES:** Boating, concrete launch; whitewater running craft only (special rafting permit required). Fishing; picnicking. **NO SWIMMING**; ice cold water; unexpected currents. **MISC.:** Elev 5600 ft; 6 acres; pets on leash; river; primitive sites. N portal to Lodore Canyon.

MEEKER

East Marvine (White River NF). 2 mi E of Meeker on St Hwy 13; 29 mi E on Co Hwy 8; 4 mi SE on FS 15240. **SEASON:** 5/25–11/10; 10-day lmt. **FACILITIES:** 7 sites (tr –22), tbls, toil, cga, f, no drk wtr. **ACTIVITIES:** Hiking; picnicking; fishing. Horseback riding (1 mi), rental (4 mi). **MISC.:** Elev 8200 ft; 2 acres; pets; stream; scenic. Marvine Lakes (6 mi). Adjacent to Flattops Primitive Area.

Hill Creek (White River NF). 2 mi E of Meeker on St Hwy 13; 23 mi E on Co Hwy 8; 8 mi SE on Co Hwy 12; ½ mi NE on FS 15228. **SEASON:** 5/25–11/10; 14-day lmt. **FACILITIES:** 10 sites; tbls, toil, cga, no drk wtr, f. **ACTIVITIES:** Hiking; picnicking; fishing. Horseback riding (1 mi). Swimming (3 mi). **MISC.:** Elev 8000 ft; 3 acres; stream; pets; scenic. Next to Flattops Wilderness.

Himes Peak (White River NF). 2 mi E of Meeker on St Hwy 13; 41 mi E on Co Hwy 8; 5 mi SE on FS 15205. **SEASON:** 5/25–11/10; 10-day lmt. **FACILITIES:** 8 sites (tr –16), tbls, toil, cga, f, no drk wtr. Store/gas/food/ice (4 mi). Dump/ shower (4 mi). **ACTIVITIES:** Hiking; picnicking; fishing. Boating,rd/swimming (5 mi). Horseback riding (1 mi), rental (4 mi). **MISC.:** Elev 9500 ft; 5 acres; river; scenic; pets. Big Fish Lake (3 mi). Adjacent to Flattops Wilderness

Marvine (White River NF). 2 mi E of Meeker on St Hwy 13; 29 mi E on Co Hwy 8; 4½ mi SE on FS 15240. **SEASON:** 5/25–11/10; 10-day lmt. **FACILITIES:** 18 sites (tr –22), tbls, toil, cga, f, no drk wtr. **ACTIVITIES:** Hiking; picnicking; fishing. Horseback riding (1 mi), rental (5 mi). **MISC.:** Elev 8200 ft; 5 acres; pets;stream; scenic. Marvine Lakes.

See page 7 for KEY TO ABBREVIATIONS.

129

South Fork (White River NF). 2 mi E of Meeker on St Hwy 13; 23 mi E on Co Hwy 8; 9½ mi S on Co Hwy 12; ½ mi SE on FS 15200. SEASON: 5/25–11/10; 10-day lmt. FACILITIES: 17 sites (tr –16), tbls, toil, cga, f, no drk wtr. ACTIVITIES: Rockhounding; swimming; picnicking; fishing. Horseback riding (1 mi). MISC.: Elev 8000 ft; 6 acres; pets; scenic; river. Spring Cave (½ mi). Next to Flattops Wilderness.

MINTURN

Half Moon (White River NF). 3–1/10 mi S of Minturn on US 24; 8 mi SW on FS 707. SEASON: 6/15–9/30; 10-day lmt. FACILITIES: 7 sites (tr –16), tbls, toil, cga, piped drk wtr. ACTIVITIES: Hiking; mountain climbing; picnicking; fishing. MISC.: Elev 10,000 ft; 3 acres; pets; stream; scenic. Trailhead to Notch Mountain, Mountain of the Holy Cross, and High Lakes.

MONTE VISTA

Alamosa (Rio Grande NF). 12 mi S of Monte Vista on St Hwy 15; 17–2/5 mi W on FS 250 (Alamosa River Rd). SEASON: Open all yr, but usually accessible only 5/1–11/15. FACILITIES: 10 sites (tr –16), tbls, toil, cga, f, well drk wtr. ACTIVITIES: Picnicking. Horseback riding (1 mi). No fishing in the Alamosa River. MISC.: Elev 8600 ft; 3 acres; pets. No garbage collection.

Comstock (Rio Grande NF). 2 mi S of Monte Vista on St Hwy 15; 16½ mi SW on FS 265 (Rock Creek Rd). SEASON: Open all yr, but usually accessible 5/15–11/15. FACILITIES: 8 sites (tr –16), tbls, toil, cga, f, well drk wtr. ACTIVITIES: Fishing; picnicking. Horseback riding (1 mi). MISC.: Elev 9500 ft; 3 acres; stream; pets. No garbage collection.

Rock Creek (Rio Grande NF). 2 mi S of Monte Vista on St Hwy 15; 13½ mi SW on FS 265 (Rock Creek Rd). SEASON: Open all yr; usually accessible 5/1–11/15. FACILITIES: 9 sites (tr –16), tbls, toil, cga, no drk wtr. ACTIVITIES: Fishing; picnicking. Horseback riding (1 mi). MISC.: Elev 9400 ft; 6 acres; pets. Rock Creek. FS 265 is gravel to within 1 mi of the campground. No garbage collection.

Stunner Campground (Rio Grande NF). 12 mi S of Monte Vista on St Hwy 15; 33–7/10 mi W on FS 250; 1/5 mi SW on FS 380. [Approximately 14 mi W of Alamosa Campground.] SEASON: Open all yr, but accessible only from 5/15–11/15. FACILITIES: 10 sites (tr –16), tbls, toil, cga, no drk wtr, f. ACTIVITIES: Picnicking. Horseback riding (1 mi). Fishing (1 mi). MISC.: Elev 9800 ft; 3 acres; pets; stream. No garbage collection.

MONTROSE

Antone Spring (Gunnison–Grand Mesa–Uncompahgre NF). 24 mi SW of Montrose on St Hwy 90; 1 mi W on FS 402. SEASON: 6/10–10/30. FACILITIES: 8 sites (tr –22), tbls, toil, cga, piped drk wtr. ACTIVITIES: Picnicking. MISC.: Elev 9700 ft; 4 acres; pets.

Beaver Lake (Gunnison–Grand Mesa–Uncompahgre NF). 20 mi E of Montrose on US 50; 20 mi S on Co Hwy 69. SEASON: 6/5–10/30; 7-day lmt. FACILITIES: 11 sites (tr –22), tbls, toil, cga, piped drk wtr. ACTIVITIES: Boating,d (no motors); picnicking; fishing. MISC.: Elev 8800 ft; 2 acres; pets. Only hand-propelled craft allowed on Beaver Lake.

Big Cimarron (Gunnison–Grand Mesa–Uncompahgre NF). 20 mi E of Montrose on US 50; 20 mi S on Co Hwy 69. SEASON: 6/5–10/30; 14-day lmt. FACILITIES: 16 sites (tr –22), tbls, toil, cga, piped drk wtr. ACTIVITIES: Fishing; picnicking. MISC.: Elev 8600 ft; 2 acres; pets.

Cimarron Creek Campground (Curecanti NRA). 20 mi E of Montrose on US 50 at Cimarron. SEASON: May–September, 1-night lmt. FACILITIES: 10 sites (individual sites indicated by picnic tables and firepits); drk wtr. MISC.: Pets.

East Portal Campground (Curecanti NRA). 8 mi E of Montrose on US 50; 7 mi on St Hwy 347; 6 mi on East Portal access rd. [Buses, trailers and motor homes are prohibited on the last 6 mi. This portion of the rd is a steep (12% grade), narrow, hazardous descent into the Black Canyon of the Gunnison] SEASON: May–October, 5-day lmt. FACILITIES: Undesignated sites (accommodates 5 tents); toil, no water.

Iron Spring (Gunnison–Grand Mesa–Uncompahgre NF). 24 mi SW of Montrose on St Hwy 90. SEASON: 6/10–10/30. FACILITIES: 7 sites (tr –22), tbls, toil, cga, drk wtr. ACTIVITIES: Picnicking. MISC.: Elev 9500 ft; 4 acres; pets on leash.

NATHROP

Iron City (Pike–San Isabel NF). ½ mi S of Nathrop on US 285; 15 mi W on St Hwy 162; ½ mi NE on FS 212. SEASON: 6/8–9/20; 7-day lmt. FACILITIES: 17 sites (tr –16), tbls, toil, cga, no drk wtr. ACTIVITIES: Fishing; picnicking. MISC.: Elev 9900 ft; 21 acres; pets; stream. Historic St. Elmo Townsite and Mining Area.

NEDERLAND

Rainbow Lakes (Arapaho–Roosevelt NF). 6½ mi N of Nederland on St Hwy 72; 5 mi W on Co Hwy 116. SEASON: 6/20–10/15; 7-day lmt. FACILITIES: 18 sites (tr –16); tbls, toil, cga, piped

drk wtr. ACTIVITIES: Picnicking.
Fishing (1 mi). MISC.: Elev 10,000
ft; 10 acres; lake; pets. West of
Peak-to-Peak Highway.

OHIO CITY

Comanche (Gunnison-Grand Mesa-Uncompahgre NF). 2-1/10 mi N of Ohio City on FS 771 (Gold Creek Rd). SEASON: 5/25-10/31; 14-day lmt. FACILITIES: 4 sites (no trailers); toil, cga, f, no drk wtr. Store/ice/gas (2 mi). ACTIVITIES: Fishing; picnicking. MISC.: Elev 9100 ft; 2 acres; stream; pets.

Gold Creek (Gunnison-Grand Mesa-Uncompahgre NF). 7-9/10 mi NE of Ohio City on FS 771. SEASON: 5/25-10/31; 14-day lmt. FACILITIES: 6 sites (tr -16), tbls, toil, cga, piped drk wtr. ACTIVITIES: Mountain climbing; picnicking; hiking. Fishing (1 mi). MISC.:Elev 10,000 ft; 2 acres; pets; scenic.

PAGOSA SPRINGS

Blanco River (San Juan NF). 13-1/10 mi SE of Pagosa Springs on US 84; 1-4/5 mi E on FS 656. SEASON: 5/15-11/15; 14-day lmt. FACILITIES: 6 sites (tr -16), tbls, toil, cga, no drk wtr. FACILITIES: Community picnic areas with ball diamond, horseshoe pits, and volleyball court. ACTIVITIES: Softball, volleyball, horseshoes; picnicking; fishing. MISC.: Elev 7200 ft; 8 acres; pets; stream.

Echo Canyon Lake (SRA). 5 mi S of Pagosa Springs on US 84. SEASON: 5/1-10/31. FACILITIES: 50 sites; tbls, toil, cga, drk wtr. ACTIVITIES: Boating,l; picnicking; fishing. MISC.: Pets on leash.

Mesa Spring Hunter Camp (San Juan NF). 19 mi W of Pagosa Springs on US 160; 12 mi N on FS 626. [FS 626 is a poor rd.] SEASON: 6/1-11/25; 14-day lmt. FACILITIES: 3 sites (tr -16), tbls, toil, cga, f, no drk wtr. ACTIVITIES: Hunting; berry-picking; picnicking. MISC.: Elev 9700 ft; 2 acres; pets. Devil Mountain (1 mi).

Middle Fork Hunter Camp (San Juan NF). 2 mi W of Pagosa Springs on US 160; 16½ mi NW on Co Hwy 631; 5 mi NE on FS 636. SEASON: 5/15-11/25; 14-day lmt. FACILITIES: 10 sites (tr -22), toil, cga, f. No tbls/drk wtr. Store/ice/showers/gas (5 mi). ACTIVITIES: Rockhounding; hunting; hiking; picnicking. Fishing (1 mi). MISC.: Elev 8500 ft; 5 acres; pets;stream. Weminuche Wilderness (2 mi).

Turkey Springs Hunter Camp (San Juan NF). 2 mi W of Pagosa Springs on US 160; 6½ mi NW on Co Hwy 631; 4½ mi SW on FS 629. SEASON: 10/1-11/25; 14-day lmt. FACILITIES: 5 sites (tr -32), tbls, toil, cga, f, no drk wtr. ACTIVITIES: Hunting; picnicking; hiking. MISC.: Elev 8200 ft; 2 acres; pets.

PAONIA

Paonia Reservoir Area (SRA). 10 mi NE of Paonia on St Hwy 135, at jct St Hwy 133. SEASON: All yr. FACILITIES: 30 sites; tbls, toil, cga, drk wtr. ACTIVITIES: Boating,l; waterskiing; picnicking; fishing. MISC.: Elev 6000 ft; 100 acres; pets on leash. Lake.

PARADOX

Buckeye (Manti Lasal NF). 11-4/5 mi NW of Paradox on FS 10071. SEASON: 6/1-9/10; 16-day lmt. FACILITIES: 5 sites (tr -22), tbls, toil, cga, f, no drk wtr. ACTIVITIES: Boating,d; swimming; picnicking; fishing. Horseback riding (1 mi). MISC.: Elev 7600 ft; 10 acres; pets; lake.

PARSHALL

Horseshoe (Routt NF). 16-4/5 mi SE of Parshall on Co Hwy 3. SEASON: 5/25-11/15. FACILITIES: 6 sites (tr -32), tbls, toil, cga, f, well drk wtr. ACTIVITIES: Horseback riding; picnicking; fishing. MISC.: Elev 8700 ft; 2 acres; stream; pets.

Hot Sulphur Springs Campground (SRA). 2 mi E of Parshall on US 40. SEASON: All yr; 14-day lmt. FACILITIES: 50 sites (tr -22), tbls, toil, cga, drk wtr. ACTIVITIES: Fishing; picnicking. MISC.: Elev 7600 ft; 5 acres; pets.

Williams Fork Reservoir Area (SRA). 5 mi S of Parshall. [On W side of lake.] SEASON: 5/25-11/15; 14-day lmt. FACILITIES: 100 sites (no trailers); toil, cga, drk wtr. ACTIVITIES: Boating,l; picnicking; fishing. MISC.: Elev 8000 ft; 300 acres; lake; pets.

PHIPPSBURG

Vaughn Lake (Routt NF). 3/10 mi S of Phippsburg on St Hwy 131; 28-1/5 mi W on FS 16. SEASON: 6/15-11/15; 14-day lmt. FACILITIES: 8 sites (tr -22), tbls, toil, cga, no drk wtr. ACTIVITIES: Boating,d; picnicking; fishing. MISC.: Elev 9500 ft; 4acres; pets.

PITKIN

Middle Quartz (Gunnison-Grand Mesa-Uncompahgre NF). 1½ mi NE of Pitkin on FS 765; 5½ mi E on FS 767. SEASON: 5/25-10/31; 14-day lmt. FACILITIES: 7 sites (tr -16), tbls, toil, cga, piped drk wtr. ACTIVITIES: Mountain climbing; picnicking; fishing. MISC.: Elev 10,200 ft; 3 acres; stream; historic; pets.

PONCHA SPRINGS

North Fork Reservoir (Pike-San Isabel NF). 6 mi W of Poncha Springs on US 50; 10-1/5 mi NW on FS 214. SEASON:

See page 7 for KEY TO ABBREVIATIONS.

6/8-9/20; 10-day lmt. FACILITIES: 8 sites (tr -16), tbls, toil, cga, piped drk wtr. Dump. ACTIVITIES: Boating; picnicking; fishing. [No motor boats permitted on adjacent Reservoir.] MISC.: Elev 11,000 ft; 3 acres; lake; pets.

Shavano (Pike-San Isabel NF). 6 mi W of Poncha Springs on US 50; 6 mi NW on FS 214. SEASON: 6/8-9/20; 7-day lmt. FACILITIES: 4 sites (no trailers); tbls, toil, cga, piped drk wtr. ACTIVITIES: Mountain climbing; picnicking; fishing. Horseback riding/rental (5 mi). MISC.: Elev 10,600 ft; 3 acres; stream; pets. Mount Shavano [14,229 ft] (5 mi).

POWDERHORN

Cebolla Creek Campground (SRA). 17 mi SW of St Hwy 149 in Powderhorn on Co Rd. SEASON: 5/1-10/1; 14-day lmt. FACILITIES: 5 sites (tr -22), tbls, toil, cga, drk wtr. ACTIVITIES: Swimming; picnicking; fishing. MISC.: Elev 8800 ft;5 acres; pets on leash.

QUARRY

Rainbow Park (Dinosaur NM). Located N of Quarry on a series of unmarked gravel county roads. Persons interested should inquire directly from a Park Ranger. (Or, for more detailed information, contact: Supt.; Dinosaur NM; Box 210; Dinosaur, CO 81610; 303/374-2216.) FACILITIES: Undesignated primitive sites; tbls, toil, cga, no drk wtr. ACTIVITIES: Whitewater rafting (special permit required); no swimming (unexpected currents).

REDCLIFF

Blodgett (White River NF). 3 mi S of Redcliff on US 24; 3/5 mi SW on FS 703. SEASON: 6/1-9/30; 10-day lmt. FACILITIES: 6 sites (tr -16), tbls, toil, cga, no drk wtr. Store/food/gas (4 mi). ACTIVITIES: Fishing; picnicking. MISC.: Elev 8900 ft; 2 acres; stream; pets.

Gold Park (White River NF). 3 mi S of Redcliff on US 24; 9 mi SW on FS 703. SEASON: 6/1-9/30; 10-day lmt. FACILITIES: 11 sites (tr -22), tbls, toil, cga, well drk wtr. ACTIVITIES: Fishing; picnicking. Boating,ld (4 mi). MISC.: Elev 9300 ft; 4 acres; stream; pets. Homestake Reservoir (4 mi).

Homestake (White River NF). 2 mi S of Redcliff on US 24. SEASON: 6/1-9/30; 10-day lmt. FACILITIES: 6 sites (tr -16), tbls, toil, cga, no drk wtr. Store/food/gas (2 mi). ACTIVITIES: Fishing; picnicking. MISC.: Elev 8800 ft; 2 acres; stream; pets.

Hornsilver (White River NF). 2½ mi S of Redcliff on US 24. SEASON: 6/1-9/30; 10-day lmt. FACILITIES: 12 sites (tr -16), tbls, toil, cga, piped drk wtr.

Store/food/gas (2 mi). ACTIVITIES: Fishing; picnicking. MISC.: Elev 8800 ft; 3 acres; pets. Near Homestake Creek.

REDFEATHER

Bellaire Lake (Roosevelt NF). 1 mi S of Redfeather on Co Hwy 4; 3 mi S on FS 162; 1 mi W on FS 163. SEASON: 5/20-9/20; 10-day lmt. FACILITIES: 5 sites (tr -22), tbls, toil, cga, no drk wtr. Store/ice/laundry/showers. ACTIVITIES: boating,d; swimming; horseback riding; picnicking; fishing. MISC.: Elev 8200 ft; 6 acres; pets. Red Feather Lakes area.

* Creedmore Lake (Arapaho-Roosevelt NF). 14-9/10 mi NW of Redfeather on FS 188; 2-1/10 mi NE on FS 180; 1 mi N on FS 181. [½-mi walk-in area.] FACILITIES: 10 tent sites; tbls, toil, cga, no drk wtr. ACTIVITIES: Boating,d; swimming; picnicking; fishing. MISC.: Elev 8300 ft; 5 acres; pets; lake.

North Fork Poudre (Arapaho-Roosevelt NF). 1 mi S of Redfeather on Co Hwy 4; 7 mi W on FS 162. SEASON: 6/1-11/12; 14-day lmt. FACILITIES: 9 sites (tr -32), tbls, toil, cga, no drk wtr. ACTIVITIES: Fishing; picnicking. MISC.: Elev 9200 ft; 3 acres; pets; stream.

REDSTONE

McClure (Gunnison-Grand Mesa-Uncompahgre NF). 8½ mi SW of Redstone on St Hwy 133. SEASON: 6/15-11/15; 14-day lmt. FACILITIES: 19 sites (tr -32), tbls, toil, cga, piped drk wtr. ACTIVITIES: Picnicking. MISC.: Elev 9100 ft; 8 acres; pets; stream.

RIFLE

Little Box Canyon (White River NF). 3 mi N of Rifle on St Hwy 13; 11-1/5 mi NE on St Hwy 325; 2-1/5 mi N on Co Hwy C217; 25 mi NE on FS 825. SEASON: 5/15-10/31; 10-day lmt. FACILITIES: 4 sites (tr -16), tbls, toil, cga, f, piped drk wtr. ACTIVITIES: Fishing; picnicking. MISC.: Elev 7600 ft; 1 acre; pets; stream; scenic.

Rifle Mountain Park (White River NF). 3 mi NE of Rifle on St Hwy 5789; 11-1/5 mi NE on St Hwy 5325; 2 mi N on Co Hwy C217. SEASON: 5/1-10/31; 14-day lmt. FACILITIES: 18 sites (tr -16), tbls, toil, cga, f, piped drk wtr. ACTIVITIES: Fishing; picnicking. MISC.: Elev 7000 ft; 20 acres; pets; scenic; stream. Co-operated by FS and City of Rifle.

Three Forks (White River NF). 3 mi N of Rifle on St Hwy 13; 11-1/5 mi NE on St Hwy 325; 2-1/5 mi N on Co Hwy C217; 20 mi N on FS 825. SEASON: 5/15-10/31; 10-day lmt. FACILITIES: 4 sites (tr -16), tbls, toil, cga, f, piped drk wtr. ACTIVITIES: Rockhounding; picnicking; fishing.

MISC.: Elev 7600 ft; 1 acre; stream; pets; scenic.

SAGUACHE

Buffalo Pass Campground (Rio Grande NF). 27-3/5 mi NW of Saguache on St Hwy 114; 1-7/10 mi S on FS 775. **SEASON:** 5/15-11/15. **FACILITIES:** 31 sites (tr -22); tbls, toil, cga, f, drk wtr. **ACTIVITIES:** Picnicking. **MISC.:** Elev 9100 ft; 37 acres; pets. Garbage collection. Located at old Indian camp site and on old stage route.

Luder's Creek Campground (Rio Grande NF). 22 mi NW of Saguache on St Hwy 114; 11 mi NW on FS 750. **SEASON:** 6/1-11/15. **FACILITIES:** 6 sites (tr -16); tbls, toil, cga, f, drk wtr. **ACTIVITIES:** Picnicking. **MISC.:** Elev 9200 ft; 2 acres.

SALIDA

Mt. Shavano Hatchery Lake (SRA). SE of Salida on US 50. **SEASON:** 5/1-10/31. **FACILITIES:** 15 sites; tbls, toil, cga, drk wtr. **ACTIVITIES:** Fishing; picnicking. Golf nearby. **MISC.:** Pets on leash.

SARGENTS

Agate (Gunnison-Grand Mesa-Uncompahgre NF). 3 mi NE of Sargents on US 50. **SEASON:** 6/15-9/15; 14-day lmt. **FACILITIES:** 8 sites (tr -16), tbls, toil, cga, piped drk wtr. Store/food/ice/gas (3 mi). **ACTIVITIES:** Mountain climbing; picnicking. Fishing (2 mi). **MISC.:** Elev 9000 ft; 13 acres; scenic; pets.

Snowblind (Gunnison-Grand Mesa-Uncompahgre NF). 1-1/10 mi NE of Sargents on US 50; 6-9/10 mi N on FS 888. **SEASON:** 5/25-10/31; 14-day lmt. **FACILITIES:** 23 sites (tr -22), tbls, toil, cga, piped drk wtr. **ACTIVITIES:** Mountain climbing; picnicking; fishing. **MISC.:** Elev 9800 ft; 10 acres; stream; scenic; pets.

SEDALIA

Jackson Creek (Pike-San Isabel NF). 10 mi W of Sedalia on St Hwy 67; 13-9/10 mi S on FS 300; 1½ mi NE on FS 502. **SEASON:** 5/1-10/15. **FACILITIES:** 9 sites (tr -16), tbls, toil, cga, no drk wtr. **ACTIVITIES:** Fishing; picnicking. **MISC.:** Elev 8100 ft; 3 acres; pets; stream.

SILVERTON

Lime Creek (San Juan NF). 11 mi SW of Silverton on US 550; 5 mi S on FS 2591. **SEASON:** 6/15-9/15; 14-day lmt. **FACILITIES:** 6 sites (tr -32), toil, cga, f. **ACTIVITIES:** Fishing. **MISC.:** Elev 9000 ft; pets on leash.

Sig Creek (San Juan NF). 21 mi SW of Silverton on US 550; 6 mi W on FS 2578. **SEASON:** 5/15-11/1; 14-day lmt. **FACILITIES:** 9 sites (tr -32), tbls, toil, cga,

f, well drk wtr. **ACTIVITIES:** Picnicking. Fishing (1 mi). Horseback riding/rental (5 mi). **MISC.:** Elev 9400 ft; 4 acres; pets; stream. 26 mi from Durango on US 550 and 6 mi on FS 2578.

South Mineral (San Juan NF). 4 mi NW of Silverton on US 550; 5 mi SW on FS 2585. **SEASON:** 6/15-9/15; 14-day lmt. **FACILITIES:** 23 sites (tr -32), tbls, toil, cga, drk wtr. **ACTIVITIES:** Fishing; picnicking. **MISC.:** Elev 9800 ft; 12 acres; pets on leash.

SOMERSET

Erikson Springs (Gunnison-Grand Mesa-Uncompahgre NF). 6-3/5 mi E of Somerset on St Hwy 133; 7 mi E on St Hwy 135. **SEASON:** 5/15-11/15; 14-day lmt. **FACILITIES:** 9 sites (tr -32), tbls, toil, cga, piped drk wtr. **ACTIVITIES:** picnicking. **MISC.:** Elev 7800 ft; 4 acres; river. Paonia Reservoir (7 mi). Lost Lake Campground (10 mi). Pets.

SOUTH FORK

Beaver Creek Campground (Rio Grande NF). 2-2/5 mi SW of South Fork on US 160; 3 mi S on FS 360. **SEASON:** FREE and accessible, 5/1-MD and LD-11/15 ($2, MD-LD). 14-day lmt. **FACILITIES:** 20 sites (tr -22), f; drk wtr. Store/food/ice/laundry (4 mi). **ACTIVITIES:** Boating,d; horseback riding. **MISC.:** During free season, no garbage collection or drk wtr. Pets. 7 acres.

Big Meadows Campground (Rio Grande NF). 12½ mi SW of South Fork on US 160; 1-4/5 mi SW on FS 410. **SEASON:** FREE and accessible, LD-11/15 ($2, MD-LD). **FACILITIES:** 50 sites (tr -32); during free season, part of the campground may be closed, but usually at least 20 units are open. Drk wtr, f. **ACTIVITIES:** Boating,d; horseback riding; fishing. **MISC.:** 16 acres; pets. During free season, no water or garbage collection.

Cross Creek Campground (Rio Grande NF). 2-2/5 mi SW of South Fork on US 160; 6-1/10 mi S on FS 360. **SEASON:** 6/15-9/10; 14-day lmt. **FACILITIES:** 7 sites (tr -16), tbls, toil, cga, piped drk wtr. **ACTIVITIES:** Rockhounding; picnicking. Boating,d/fishing/swimming (1 mi). **MISC.:** Elev 8900 ft; 3 acres; stream; no garbage collection.

Highway Springs Campground (Rio Grande NF). 5-1/5 mi SW of South Fork on US 160. **SEASON:** 6/10-9/10; 3-day lmt. **FACILITIES:** 11 sites (tr -22), tbls, toil, cga, f, piped drk wtr. Store/food/ice/gas/showers/dump (2 mi). Laundry (4 mi). **ACTIVITIES:** Fishing; picnicking. Horseback riding/rental (2 mi). **MISC.:** Elev 8400 ft; 4 acres; pets.

Tucker Ponds Campground (Rio Grande NF). Approx. 11 mi W of South Fork on US 160; 3 mi S on FS 390. **SEASON:** 6/25–9/5; 14–day lmt. **FACILITIES:** 16 sites (tr –22), tbls, toil, cga, f, no drk wtr. **ACTIVITIES:** Berry-picking; picnicking; fishing. **MISC.:** Elev 9700 ft; 16 acres; lake; pets on leash.

Upper Beaver Campground (Rio Grande NF). 2–2/5 mi SW of South Fork on US 160; 4 mi S on FS 360. [1 mi further S on FS 360 past Beaver Creek Campground.] **SEASON:** FREE and accessible, 5/1–MD and LD–11/15 ($2, MD–LD). **FACILITIES:** 15 sites (tr –22), drk wtr, f. Store/food/ice/laundry/showers (5 mi). **ACTIVITIES:** Boating,d; horseback riding; fishing. **MISC.:** 5 acres; pets. Free season, no garbage collection or drk wtr.

SPRINGFIELD

Two Buttes Reservoir (SRA). 16 mi N of Springfield on US 385/287; 6 mi E on Co Hwy. **SEASON:** 5/1–10/31. **FACILITIES:** 75 sites; tbls, toil, cga, drk wtr. Store (1 mi). **ACTIVITIES:** Boating,rl; picnicking. Swimming/fishing (1 mi). **MISC.:** Pets on leash.

STEAMBOAT SPRINGS

Dry Lake (Routt NF). 4 mi N of Steamboat Springs on Co Hwy 36; 3–3/5 mi E on FS 60. **SEASON:** 5/30–11/15; 14–day lmt. **FACILITIES:** 8 sites (tr –16), tbls, toil, cga, no drk wtr. Gas/ice/store (4 mi). Food (5 mi). **ACTIVITIES:** Picnicking; fishing. Horseback riding and rental (5 mi). **MISC.:** Elev 8000 ft; 4 acres; Dry Lake; pets.

Granite (Routt NF). 4 mi N of Steamboat Springs on Co Hwy 36; 11–3/5 mi E on FS 11060; 4–9/10 mi S on FS 11309. **SEASON:** 7/15–11/15; 14–day lmt. **FACILITIES:** 6 sites (no trailers); tbls, toil, cga, no drk wtr. **ACTIVITIES:** Boating,d; picnicking; fishing. **MISC.:** Elev 9900 ft; 2 acres; lake; pets.

Summit Lake (Routt NF). 4 mi N of Steamboat Springs on Co Hwy 36; 11–3/5 mi E on FS 60. **SEASON:** 7/1–11/15; 14–day lmt. **FACILITIES:** 17 sites (tr –22), tbls, toil, cga, no drk wtr. **ACTIVITIES:** Fishing; picnicking. **MISC.:** Elev 10,300 ft.

Walton Creek (Routt NF). 17 mi SE of Steamboat Springs on US 40. **SEASON:** 7/1–9/8; 14–day lmt. **FACILITIES:** 14 sites (tr –22), tbls, toil, cga, no drk wtr. **ACTIVITIES:** Fishing; picnicking. **MISC.:** Elev 9400 ft; 6 acres; stream; pets.

STERLING

Pioneer Park (Municipal Campground). 1 mi W of Sterling on St Hwy 14. **SEASON:** 5/1–9/1; 14–day lmt. **FACILITIES:** 60 sites; tbls, flush toil, cga, f, drk wtr, playground. **ACTIVITIES:** Swimming (pool–$).

SYLVAN LAKE

Sylvan Lake Recreation Area (SRA). 16 mi S of Sylvan Lake on W Brush Creek. **SEASON:** 5/1–10/1. **FACILITIES:** 50 sites; toil, cga, drk wtr. **ACTIVITIES:** Boating,l; fishing. **MISC.:** Pets.

TABERNASH

Meadow Creek (Arapaho–Roosevelt NF) 15 mi E of Tabernash on US 40; 2½ mi NE on FS 129. **SEASON:** 6/1–10/15; 14–day lmt. **FACILITIES:** 5 sites (tr –32), tbls, toil, cga, f, no drk wtr. Store/food/ice/gas (4 mi). **ACTIVITIES:** Picnicking. Fishing/horseback riding (1 mi). **MISC.:** Elev 8500 ft; 2 acres; scenic; stream; pets on leash.

Tabernash (Arapaho–Roosevelt NF). 3½ mi NW of Tabernash on US 40. **SEASON:** 6/1–11/15; 14–day lmt. **FACILITIES:** 30 sites (tr –32), tbls, toil, cga, f, no drk wtr. Store/food/ice/gas (4 mi). **ACTIVITIES:** Horseback riding; picnicking. Fishing (5 mi). **MISC.:** Elev 8600 ft; 13 acres; scenic; pets.

TOPONAS

Gore Pass (Routt NF). ½ mi S of Toponas on St Hwy 131; 15½ mi E on St Hwy 134. **SEASON:** 6/10–11/15; 14–day lmt. **FACILITIES:** 12 sites (tr –22), tbls, toil, cga, no drk wtr. **ACTIVITIES:** Picnicking. Fishing (1 mi). **MISC.:** Elev 9500 ft; 5 acres; pets.

Lynx Pass (Routt NF). ½ mi S of Toponas on St Hwy 131; 9 mi E on St Hwy 134; 2½ mi N on FS 270. **SEASON:** 5/20–11/15; 14–day lmt. **FACILITIES:** 12 sites (tr –22), tbls, toil, cga, no drk wtr. **ACTIVITIES:** Picnicking. Fishing (1 mi). **MISC.:** 9000 ft; 8 acres; pets.

VAIL

Black Lakes (White River NF). 13½ mi SE of Vail on I–70; 1 mi NW on US 6. **SEASON:** 6/15–9/30; 10–day lmt. **FACILITIES:** 6 sites (tr –16), tbls, toil, cga, piped drk wtr. **ACTIVITIES:** Fishing; picnicking. **MISC.:** Elev 10,500 ft; 1 acre; pets; lake.

WALDEN

Buttes Lakes Management Area (SRA). 10 mi W of Walden; take right rd W side of town; follow signs. **SEASON:** All yr; 14–day lmt. **FACILITIES:** 150 sites (tr –22), tbls, toil, cga, drk wtr. **ACTIVITIES:** Boating,rl; waterskiing; picnicking; fishing. **MISC.:** Elev 8100 ft; 300 acres; pets.

Grizzly Creek (Routt NF). 13 mi SW of Walden on St Hwy 14; 10½ mi W on Co Hwy 24; ½ mi W on FS 60. **SEASON:** 6/15–9/8; 14–day lmt. **FACILITIES:** 12 sites

(tr -22), tbls, toil, cga, well drk wtr.
ACTIVITIES: Picnicking. Fishing (1
mi). MISC.: Elev 8500 ft; 5 acres; pets.

Hidden Lakes (Routt NF). 13 mi SW of
Walden on St Hwy 14; 10½ mi N on Co
Hwy 24; 1-1/5 mi N on FS 60; 3-9/10
mi S on FS 20. SEASON: 6/15-9/8; 14-
day lmt. FACILITIES: 9 sites (tr -22),
tbls, toil, cga, well drk wtr. ACTIVI-
TIES: Boating (no motors); picnicking.
Fishing (1 mi). MISC.: Elev 8900 ft;
5 acres; pets; lake.

WALSENBURG

Huerfano River Management Area (SRA).
26 mi NW of Walsenburg on St Hwy 69
to Gardner. Then 15 mi SW on Co Rd.
SEASON: 14-day lmt. FACILITIES: Sites
(tr -22); tbls, toil, cga. ACTIVITIES:
Fishing; picnicking. MISC.: Pets.

WESTCLIFFE

Alvarado (Pike-San Isabel NF). 3½ mi
S of Westcliffe on St Hwy 69; 5-1/5 mi
W on Co Hwy 302; 1-3/10 mi SW on FS
302. SEASON: 5/18-10/25; 10-day lmt.
FACILITIES: 30 sites (tr -16), tbls, toil,
cga, drk wtr. ACTIVITIES: Picnicking.
Fishing (1 mi). MISC.: Elev 9000 ft; 2
acres; pets.

WHITEWATER

Carson Hole (Gunnison-Grand Mesa-Uncompahgre NF). 13 mi SW of Whitewater on
St Hwy 141; 7 mi SW on FS 402. SEASON:
5/20-10/20. FACILITIES: 5 sites (tr -16),
tbls, toil, cga, no drk wtr. ACTIVITIES:
Picnicking. MISC.: Elev 8400 ft; 3 acres;
pets on leash.

Divide Fork (Gunnison-Grand Mesa-Uncompahgre NF). 13 mi SW of Whitewater on
St Hwy 141; 15 mi SW on FS 402. SEASON:
6/20-10/15. FACILITIES: 11 sites (tr
-16), tbls, toil, cga, piped drk wtr.
ACTIVITIES: Picnicking. MISC.: Elev 9200
ft; 4 acres; pets.

WINTER PARK

Idlewild (Arapaho-Roosevelt NF). 1 mi
S of Winter Park on US 40. SEASON: 6/10-
9/15; 14-day lmt. FACILITIES: 26 sites
(tr -32); tbls, toil, cga, f, no drk wtr.
Store/gas/ice/laundry/dump (1 mi). ACTIV-
ITIES: Fishing; picnicking. Horseback
riding/rental (1 mi). MISC.: Elev 9000
ft; 10 acres; pets; scenic; river. Visitor
Center.

Robbers Roost (Arapaho-Roosevelt NF).
5 mi S of Winter Park on US 40. SEASON:
6/20-9/15; 14-day lmt. FACILITIES: 10
sites; tbls, toil, cga, f, no drk wtr.
Store/gas/ice/laundry/fd. ACTIVITIES:
Picnicking. Fishing (1 mi). Horseback
riding/rental (5 mi). MISC.: Elev 9700
ft; 3 acres; pets; stream; scenic.

Trestle (Arapaho-Roosevelt NF). 1/10
mi S of Winter Park on FS 12022; 9-7/10
mi W on Co Hwy 149. SEASON: 7/4-9/1.
FACILITIES: 6 sites (tr -32), tbls, toil,
cga, f. ACTIVITIES: Picnicking. MISC.:
Elev 11,000 ft; pets.

WOODLAND PARK

Big Turkey (Pike-San Isabel NF). 11-
3/5 mi NW of Woodland Park on St Hwy
67; 4/5 mi SW on FS 200; 3-9/10 mi SW
on FS 360. SEASON: 5/1-10/15. FACILI-
TIES: 10 sites (tr -16); tbls, toil, cga,
well drk wtr. ACTIVITIES: Fishing; picnicking. MISC.: Elev 8000 ft; 4 acres;
stream; pets.

Goose Creek (Pike-San Isabel NF). 24
mi NW of Woodland Park on St Hwy 67;
2-9/10 mi SW on Co Hwy 126; 12 mi SW
on FS 211. SEASON: 5/1-10/15. FACI-
LITIES: 7 sites (tr -16); tbls, toil,
cga, well drk wtr. ACTIVITIES: Hiking;
picnicking; fishing. MISC.: Elev 8100
ft; 4 acres; scenic; pets. Nature trail
(1 mi). Lost Creek Scenic Area (1 mi).
Unloading ramp and corrals on site.
Horseback riding.

Redrocks (Pike-San Isabel NF). 4 mi
N of Woodland Park on St Hwy 67. SEA-
SON: 5/12-10/1. FACILITIES: 11 sites
(no trailers); toil, cga. ACTIVITIES:
Picnicking. MISC.: Elev 8200 ft; pets.

Springdale (Pike-San Isabel NF). 4½
mi NE of Woodland Park on FS 3931;
1 mi SW on FS 300. SEASON: 5/1-9/30;
14-day lmt. FACILITIES: 8 sites (tr
-22), tbls, toil, cga, no drk wtr.
ACTIVITIES: Picnicking. MISC.: Elev
9100 ft; 5 acres; scenic; pets.

Wildhorn (Pike-San Isabel NF). 7 mi SE
of Woodland Park on US 24; 9 mi NW on
FS 359; 3 mi NE on FS 200; 7/10 mi W
on FS 361. SEASON: 6/1-9/15; 14-day lmt.
FACILITIES: 10 sites (tr -22), tbls, toil,
cga, drk wtr. ACTIVITIES: Horseback
riding/rental; rockhounding; picnicking.
Fishing (2 mi). MISC.: Elev 9100 ft; 4
acres; pets.

WRAY

Beecher Island (Municipal Park). 5 mi
S of Wray on US 385; 13 mi SE on Co
Hwy 61. SEASON: All yr. FACILITIES:
30 sites; tbls, flush toil, cga, f, showers, drk wtr, playground. MISC.: Pets.

READ THIS!

All information relative to each campground and state is currently
accurate to the best of the publisher's knowledge. However, non-
fee status and facilities are subject to change.

If any inaccuracies in this directory are discovered, or you know
of any additional FREE campgrounds, please contact: VMPI; Box
1289; Clearwater, FL 33517.

INFORMATION ON HOW TO PURCHASE ADDITIONAL COPIES OF THIS
BOOK AS WELL AS QUANTITY DISCOUNT INFORMATION IS ALSO AVAIL-
ABLE AT THIS ADDRESS.

See page 7 for KEY TO ABBREVIATIONS.

CONNECTICUT

Miscellaneous

Toll-Free Number for Travel Information:
   1-800-243-1685 (calling from New
      England States, Maine to Virginia)
   1-800-842-7492 (in Connecticut)
STATE CAPITOL: Hartford
STATE NICKNAME: Nutmeg State
STATE MOTTO: "He Who Transplanted
                  Still Sustains"
STATE BIRD: American Robin
STATE FLOWER: Mountain Laurel
STATE TREE: White Oak

State Parks

A fee is charged at all areas, ranging from $2.00-4.00 per night. The fee covers a camping party of 4 persons. Reservations are available during the active seasons of 5/15-LD. Pets are NOT permitted in State Park (only State Forest) campgrounds. They have informally started boat camping on some of their areas on the Connecticut and Housatonic Rivers. For further information: State of Connecticut; Department of Environmental Protection; Parks and Recreation Unit; State Office Building; Hartford, CT 06115.

Rest Areas

The State of Connecticut allows overnight parking in their rest areas ON AN EMERGENCY BASIS ONLY. A map/brochure pinpointing the rest areas can be obtained free of charge from: Connecticut Department of Economic Development; 210 Washington Street; Hartford, CT 06106.

Appalachian Trail

More than 2000 miles long, the Appalachian Trail (from Maine to Georgia) is the longest continuous marked trail in the world. CAMPING: More than 200 open-front shelters/lean-tos are spaced approximately 10 miles apart on the Trail (one-day intervals). As they are occupied on a first-come first-served basis, carry a tent in case the shelters are full. Potable spring water is usually available at each site, but should be purified by tablets or boiling. And always, "pack it in, pack it out." PERMITS: No permit is required to hike the Trail. However, camping permits must be obtained for overnight stays in Shenandoah NP (Luray, VA 22835) and Great Smoky Mountains NP (Gatlinburg, TN 37733). These are free of charge and available from the ranger stations or by mail. A free camping permit must be obtained for overnight stays in White Mountain National Forest Restricted Use Area (PO Box 638; Laconia, NH 03246). APPALACHIAN TRAIL CONFERENCE: A private, non-profit, national organization which represents citizen's interest in the Appalachian Trail. They offer detailed guidebooks and maps for sale, as well as the AT Data Book which gives the location and distances between shelters and certain post offices, supply points, water sources, loding and meals. For more information on this organization, write to them at: PO Box 236; Harpers Ferry, WV 25425.

Camping Along Connecticut Hiking Trails

Overnight camping along hiking trails is not allowed except along the Appalachian Trail which is heavily used for this purpose. Since most of Connecticut's trails are on private lands, they have secured permission for hiking only and have made no arrangements for camping. In addition, public agencies have not been able to develop trailside camping because of budgetory considerations. For further information on hiking, as well as numerous publications, contact: Connecticut Forest and Park Association, Inc.; PO Box 389; 1010 Main Street; East Hartford, CT 06108. [203/289-3637]

INFORMATION SOURCES

Maps

The following maps are available from Forsyth Travel Library (see order form in Appendix B):

CONNECTICUT

State of Connecticut [Up-to-date, showing all principal roads, points of interest, sports areas, parks, airports, mileage, etc. Full color.]

Completely indexed city maps, including all airports, lakes, rivers, etc., of: Bridgeport/Westport; Danbury; Hartford; New Britain/Bristol; New Haven; Stamford/Norwalk/Greenwich/ New Canaan/Wilton/Darien; Waterbury.

State Information

Parks and Recreation Unit; Department of Environmental Protection; State Office Building; Hartford, CT 06115.

Connecticut Department of Commerce; 210 Washington Street; Hartford, CT 06106.

Wildlife Unit; Department of Environmental Protection; State Office Building; Hartford, CT 06115.

Connecticut Forest and Parks Association; 1010 Main Street; East Hartford, CT 06108.

Corps of Engineers; Thames River Basin Office; Buffumville Lake; Box 155; Oxford, MA 01540.

City Information

Greater New Haven Chamber of Commerce; 152 Temple Street; New Haven, CT 06506.

New London and Groton; Chamber of Commerce of Southeastern Connecticut; 105 Huntington Street; New London, CT 06320.

FREE CAMPGROUNDS

AVON

MacDonald Memorial (Rest Area). US 44, near Avon. SEASON: All yr; 1-night lmt. [Overnight on an emergency basis only.] FACILITIES: Spaces for self-contained units; tbls, toil, cga, no drk wtr. ACTIVITIES: Picnicking. MISC.: Pets allowed if kept on leash.

BARKHAMSTED

Hitchcock Chair (Rest Area). St Hwy 20, near Barkhamsted. SEASON: All yr; 1-night lmt. [Overnight on emergency basis only.] FACILITIES: Spaces for self-contained units; tbls, toil, cga, no drk wtr. ACTIVITIES: Picnicking. MISC.: Pets allowed on leash.

BOZRAH

Gay Hill (Rest Area). St Hwy 163, near Bozrah. SEASON: All yr; 1-night lmt. [Overnight on emergency basis only.] FACILITIES: Spaces for self-contained units; tbls, toil, cga, no drk wtr. ACTIVITIES: Picnicking. MISC.: Pets.

BRANFORD

New Haven 95 East Truck Stop. At Exit 56 from I-95. SEASON: All yr; 1-night lmt. FACILITIES: Space for self-contained units; toil, dump, food, phone, mechanic, gas, drk wtr.

BRIDGEWATER

Lili-No-Nah (Rest Area). St Hwy 67, near Bridgewater. SEASON: All yr; 1-night lmt. [Overnight on emergency basis only.] FACILITIES: Spaces for self-contained units; tbls, cga, no drk wtr. ACTIVITIES: Picnicking. MISC.: Pets on leash.

BROOKLYN

Blackwell's View (Rest Area). US 6, near Brooklyn. SEASON: All yr; 1-night lmt. [Overnight on an emergency basis only.] FACILITIES: Spaces for self-contained units; tbls, toil, cga, no drk wtr. ACTIVITIES: Picnicking. MISC.: Pets allowed if kept on leash.

BURLINGTON

Woodruff Hill (Rest Area). St Hwy 4, near Burlington. SEASON: All yr; 1-night lmt. [Overnight on an emergency basis only.] FACILITIES: Spaces for self-contained units; tbls, toil, cga, no drk wtr. ACTIVITIES: Picnicking. MISC.:Pets.

CANAAN

Housatonic Rest (Rest Area). US 7, near Canaan. SEASON: All yr; 1-night lmt. [Overnight on an emergency basis only.] FACILITIES: Spaces for self-contained units; tbls, toil, cga, no drk wtr. ACTIVITIES: Picnicking. MISC.: Pets.

CHAPLIN

Button Ball Brook (Rest Area). US 6, near Chaplin. SEASON: All yr; 1-night lmt. [Overnight on an emergency basis only.] FACILITIES: Spaces for self-contained units; tbls, toil, cga, no drk wtr. ACTIVITIES: Picnicking. MISC.:Pets.

See page 7 for KEY TO ABBREVIATIONS.

COLUMBIA

Columbia (Rest Area). US 6, near Columbia. SEASON: All yr; 1-night lmt. [Overnight on an emergency basis only.] FACILITIES: Spaces for self-contained units; tbls, toil, cga, no drk wtr. ACTIVITIES: Picnicking. MISC.: Pets.

CORNWALL

Furnace Brook (Rest Area). St Hwy 4, near Cornwall. SEASON: All yr; 1-night lmt. [Overnight on an emergency basis only.] FACILITIES: Spaces for self-contained units; tbls, toil, cga, no drk wtr. ACTIVITIES: Picnicking. MISC.:Pets.

Fishing Area #1 (Rest Area). St Hwy 4, near Cornwall. SEASON: All yr; 1-night lmt. [Overnight on an emergency basis only.] FACILITIES: Spaces for self-contained units; tbls, cga. No toil or drk wtr. ACTIVITIES: Picnicking. MISC.: Pets permitted if kept on leash.

General Sedgewick (Rest Area). St Hwy 43, near Cornwall. SEASON: All yr; 1-night lmt. [Overnight on an emergency basis only.] FACILITIES: Spaces for self-contained units; tbls, toil, cga, no drk wtr. ACTIVITIES: Picnicking. MISC.: Pets.

Cobblestone (Rest Area). St Hwy 128, near Cornwall. SEASON: All yr; 1-night lmt. [Overnight on an emergency basis only.] FACILITIES: Spaces for self-contained units; tbls, cga, no drk wtr. ACTIVITIES: Picnicking. MISC.: Pets.

DANBURY

Colonial Truck Stop. Exit 1 from I-84, at 113 Millplain Rd. SEASON: All yr; 1-night lmt. [Overnight on an emergency basis only.] FACILITIES: Spaces for self-contained units; toil, drk wtr, food, phone, gas, mechanic. MISC.: Pets.

Kiss 'N Brook (Rest Area). US 7, near Danbury. SEASON: All yr; 1-night lmt. [Overnight on an emergency basis only.] FACILITIES: Spaces for self-contained units; tbls, cga. No toil/drk wtr. ACTIVITIES: Picnicking. MISC.: Pets on leash.

Rest Area. 4 mi E of Danbury on I-84. SEASON: All yr: 1-night lmt. [Overnight on an emergency basis only.] FACILITIES: Spaces for self-contained units; tbls, toil, cga, drk wtr. ACTIVITIES: Picnicking. MISC.: Pets permitted on leash.

EASTFORD

Frog Rock (Rest Area). US 44, near Eastford. SEASON: All yr; 1-night lmt. [Overnight on an emergency basis only.] FACILITIES: Spaces for self-contained units; tbls, toil, cga, no drk wtr. ACTIVITIES: Picnicking. MISC.: Pets on leash.

EAST LYME

Apple Tree Rest (Rest Area). St Hwy 156, near East Lyme. SEASON: All yr; 1-night lmt. [Overnight on an emergency basis only.] FACILITIES: Spaces for self-contained units; tbls, toil, cga, no drk wtr. ACTIVITIES: Picnicking. MISC.: Pets.

Blue Star Memorial (Rest Area). I-95, near East Lyme. SEASON: All yr; 1-night lmt. [Overnight on an emergency basis only.] FACILITIES: Spaces for self-contained units; tbls, toil, cga, drk wtr. ACTIVITIES: Picnicking. MISC.: Pets.

FAIRFIELD

Howard Johnson Rest Area. On I-95 in Fairfield. SEASON: All yr; 1-night lmt. FACILITIES: Space for self-contained vehicles to stay for one night. Restaurant, toil, drk wtr, gas. MISC.: Pets.

FARMINGTON

Shade Swamp (Rest Area). US 6, near Farmington. SEASON: All yr; 1-night lmt. [Overnight on an emergency basis only.] FACILITIES: Spaces for self-contained units; tbls, toil, cga, no drk wtr. ACTIVITIES: Picnicking. MISC.:Pets.

GOSHEN

Wadham's Grove (Rest Area). St Hwy 63, near Goshen. SEASON: All yr; 1-night lmt. [Overnight on an emergency basis only.] FACILITIES: Spaces for self-contained units; tbls, toil, cga, drk wtr. ACTIVITIES: Picnicking. MISC.: Pets.

GRANBY

East Branch Salmon Brook (Rest Area). St Hwy 20, near Granby. SEASON: All yr; 1-night lmt. [Overnight on an emergency basis only.] FACILITIES: Spaces for self-contained units; tbls, toil, cga, no drk wtr. ACTIVITIES: Picnicking. MISC.: Pets allowed if kept on leash.

GRISWOLD

Pachaug Pond (Rest Area). St Hwy 165. SEASON: All yr; 1-night lmt. [Overnight on an emergency basis only.] FACILITIES: Spaces for self-contained units; tbls, toil, cga, no drk wtr. ACTIVITIES: Picnicking. MISC.: Pets on leash.

GROTON

Gray Rock (Rest Area). St Hwy 184, near Groton. SEASON: All yr; 1-night lmt. [Overnight on an emergency basis only.] FACILITIES: Spaces for self-contained units; tbls, toil, cga, no drk wtr. ACTIVITIES: Picnicking. MISC.:Pets.

See page 7 for KEY TO ABBREVIATIONS.

CONNECTICUT

HADDAM

Steven Falls (Rest Area). St Hwy 9A, near Haddam. SEASON: All yr; 1-night lmt. [Overnight on an emergency basis only.] FACILITIES: Spaces for self-contained units; tbls, toil, cga, drk wtr.

HARTFORD

Halprin's Service Center (Truck Stop). 131 Brainard Rd; Exit 27 from I-91. SEASON: All yr; 1-night lmt. FACILITIES: Space for self-contained units; drk wtr, toil, gas, mechanic, phone. ACTIVITIES: Picnicking. MISC.: Pets on leash.

HARWINTON

Cooks Dam (Rest Area). St Hwy 4, near Harwinton. SEASON: All yr; 1-night lmt. [Overnight on an emergency basis only.] FACILITIES: Spaces for self-contained units; tbls, cga, no drk wtr. ACTIVITIES: Picnicking. MISC.: Pets on leash.

HEBRON

Raymond Hills (Rest Area). St Hwy 85, near Hebron. SEASON: All yr; 1-night lmt. [Overnight on an emergency basis only.] FACILITIES: Spaces for self-contained units; tbls, cga, no drk wtr. ACTIVITIES: Picnicking. MISC.: Pets.

LEBANON

Lebanon Town Pond (Rest Area). St Hwy 207, near Lebanon. SEASON: All yr; 1-night lmt. [Overnight on an emergency basis only.] FACILITIES: Spaces for self-contained units; tbls, cga, no drk wtr. ACTIVITIES: Picnicking. MISC.: Pets.

LITCHFIELD

Picnic Area (Rest Area). St Hwy 8, near Litchfield. SEASON: All yr; 1-night lmt. [Overnight on an emergency basis only.] FACILITIES: Spaces for self-contained units; no facilities. ACTIVITIES: Picnicking. MISC.: Pets allowed on a leash.

Schermehorn Grove (Rest Area). St Hwy 63. SEASON: All yr; 1-night lmt. [Overnight on an emergency basis only.] FACILITIES: Spaces for self-contained units; tbls, cga, no drk wtr. ACTIVITIES: Picnicking. MISC.: Pets on leash.

NEW HARTFORD

Satan's Kingdom (Rest Area). US 44, near New Hartford. SEASON: All yr; 1-night lmt. [Overnight on an emergency basis only.] FACILITIES: Spaces for self-contained units; tbls, toil, cga, no drk wtr. ACTIVITIES: Picnicking. MISC.: Pets.

LYME

Roaring Brook (Rest Area). St Hwy 82, near Lyme. SEASON: All yr; 1-night lmt. [Overnight on an emergency basis

only.] FACILITIES: Spaces for self-contained units; tbls, toil, cga, no drk wtr. ACTIVITIES: Picnicking. MISC.:Pets.

MADISON

Madison Pines (Rest Area). St Hwy 79, near Madison. SEASON: All yr; 1-night lmt. [Overnight on an emergency basis only.] FACILITIES: Spaces for self-contained units; tbls, toil, cga, no drk wtr. ACTIVITIES: Picnicking. MISC.:Pets.

MIDDLEBURY

Shepardson Haven (Rest Area). St Hwy 64, near Middlebury. SEASON: All yr; 1-night lmt. [Overnight on an emergency basis only.] FACILITIES: Spaces for self-contained units; tbls, toil, cga, drk wtr. ACTIVITIES: Picnicking. MISC.: Pets allowed if kept on a leash.

William H. Bristol (Rest Area). St Hwy 64, near Middlebury. SEASON: All yr; 1-night lmt. [Overnight on an emergency basis only.] FACILITIES: Spaces for self-contained units; no facilities. ACTIVITIES: Picnicking. MISC.: Pets.

MILFORD

Liberty Grove (Rest Area). US 1, near Milford. SEASON: All yr; 1-night lmt. [Overnight on an emergency basis only.] FACILITIES: Spaces for self-contained units; tbls, toil, cga, drk wtr. ACTIVITIES: Picnicking. MISC.: Pets on leash.

MILLDALE

American Eagle 76 Plaza (Truck Stop). I-84 and St Hwy 66, in Milldale. SEASON: All yr, 1-night lmt. FACILITIES: Space for self-contained units; toil, drk wtr, dump, food, gas, mechanic, phone. MISC.: Pets on leash.

MONTVILLE

Roadside Birches (Rest Area). St Hwy 161, near Montville. SEASON: All yr; 1-night lmt. [Overnight on an emergency basis only.] FACILITIES: Spaces for self-contained units; tbls, cga. ACTIVITIES: Picnicking. MISC.: Pets on leash.

NEWTOWN

The Berkshire (Rest Area). St Hwy 34, near Newtown. SEASON: All yr; 1-night lmt. [Overnight on an emergency basis only.] FACILITIES: Spaces for self-contained units; tbls, cga; no toil/drk wtr. ACTIVITIES: Picnicking. MISC.: Pets.

Pleasant Valley Rest (Rest Area). US 6, near Newtown. SEASON: All yr; 1-night lmt. [Overnight on an emergency basis only.] FACILITIES: Spaces for self-contained units; tbls, toil, cga, no drk wtr. ACTIVITIES: Picnicking. MISC.: Pets.

See page 7 for KEY TO ABBREVIATIONS.

139

CONNECTICUT

Pootatuck (Rest Area). Old U.S. 6, near Newtown. SEASON: All yr; 1-night lmt. [Overnight on an emergency basis only.] FACILITIES: Spaces for self-contained units; tbls, cga. No toil/drk wtr. ACTIVITIES: Picnicking. MISC.: Pets on leash.

NORFOLK

Albany Turnpike (Rest Area). US 44, near Norfolk. SEASON: All yr; 1-night lmt. [Overnight on an emergency basis only.] FACILITIES: Spaces for self-contained units; tbls, toil, cga, no drk wtr. ACTIVITIES: Picnicking. MISC.: Pets on leash.

NORTH CANAAN

Garden Shadows (Rest Area). US 44, near North Canaan. SEASON: All yr; 1-night lmt. [Overnight on an emergency basis only.] FACILITIES: Spaces for self-contained units; tbls, toil, cga, no drk wtr. ACTIVITIES: Picnicking. MISC.: Pets.

NORTH HAVEN

Harten's Pond (Rest Area). St Hwy 17, near North Haven. SEASON: All yr; 1-night lmt. [Overnight on an emergency basis only.] FACILITIES: Spaces for self-contained units; no facilities. ACTIVITIES: Picnicking. MISC.: Pets on leash.

NORTH STONINGTON

Indiantown Rest (Rest Area). St Hwy 2, near Stonington. SEASON: All yr; 1-night lmt. [Overnight on an emergency basis only.] FACILITIES: Spaces for self-contained units; tbls, toil, cga, no drk wtr. ACTIVITIES: Picnicking. MISC.: Pets allowed on leash.

Lantern Hill Rest (Rest Area). St Hwy 2, near North Stonington. SEASON: All yr; 1-night lmt. [Overnight on an emergency basis only.] FACILITIES: Spaces for self-contained units; tbls, toil, cga, no drk wtr. ACTIVITIES: Picnicking. MISC.: Pets allowed if kept on leash.

Republic Auto/Truck Plaza (24-hour Truck Stop). Clarks Falls Exit (St Hwy 216) off I-95. SEASON: All yr, 1-night lmt. FACILITIES: Space for self-contained units; toil , drk wtr, food, gas, mechanic, phone. MISC.: Pets on a leash.

Rest Area. I-95, near Stonington. SEASON: All yr; 1-night lmt. [Overnight on an emergency basis only.] FACILITIES: Spaces for self-contained units; tbls, toil, cga, drk wtr. ACTIVITIES: Picnicking. MISC.: Pets on leash.

OLD LYME

Shore Road Rest (Rest Area). St Hwy 156, near Old Lyme. SEASON: All yr; 1-night lmt. [Overnight on an emergency basis only.] FACILITIES: Spaces for self-contained units; tbls, toil, cga, drk wtr. ACTIVITIES: Picnicking. MISC.: Pets allowed on a leash.

ORANGE

Wilbur L. Cross (Rest Area). St Hwy 15, near Orange. SEASON: All yr; 1-night lmt. [Overnight on an emergency basis only.] FACILITIES: Spaces for self-contained units; tbls, toil, cga, no drk wtr. ACTIVITIES: Picnicking. MISC.: Pets allowed if kept on leash.

OXFORD

John Griffin Wayside (Rest Area). St Hwy 67, near Oxford. SEASON: All yr; 1-night lmt. [Overnight on an emergency basis only.] FACILITIES: Spaces for self-contained units; tbls, toil, cga, no drk wtr. ACTIVITIES: Picnicking. MISC.: Pets allowed if kept on a leash.

Marion's Grove (Rest Area). St Hwy 188, near Oxford. SEASON: All yr; 1-night lmt. [Overnight on an emergency basis only.] FACILITIES: Spaces for self-contained units; tbls, cga. No toil/drk wtr. ACTIVITIES: Picnicking. MISC.: Pets.

PLAINFIELD

Hilltop View (Rest Area). St Hwy 12, near Plainfield. SEASON: All yr; 1-night lmt. [Overnight on an emergency basis only.] FACILITIES: Spaces for self-contained units; tbls, cga. No toil/drk wtr. ACTIVITIES: Picnicking. MISC.:Pets.

PORTLAND

Wangunk Meadows (Rest Area). St Hwy 17A, near Portland. SEASON: All yr; 1-night lmt. [Overnight on an emergency basis only.] FACILITIES: Spaces for self-contained units; tbls, cga. No drk wtr/toil. ACTIVITIES: Picnicking. MISC.: Pets permitted if kept on a leash.

PRESTON

Folly Works Brook (Rest Area). St Hwy 165, near Preston. SEASON: All yr; 1-night lmt. [Overnight on an emergency basis only.] FACILITIES: Spaces for self-contained units; tbls, toil, cga, drk wtr. ACTIVITIES: Picnicking. MISC.: Pets permitted if kept on a leash.

PUTNAM

Five Mile River (Rest Area). US 44, near Putnam. SEASON: All yr; 1-night lmt. [Overnight on an emergency basis only.] FACILITIES: Spaces for self-contained units; tbls, toil, cga, no drk wtr. ACTIVITIES: Picnicking. MISC.: Pets allowed if kept on a leash.

CONNECTICUT

REDDING

Riverside (Rest Area). US 7, near Redding. SEASON: All yr; 1-night lmt. [Overnight on an emergency basis only.] FACILITIES: Spaces for self-contained units; tbls, cga. No toil/drk wtr. ACTIVITIES: Picnicking. MISC.: Pets.

The Oaks (Rest Area). US 7, near Redding. SEASON: All yr; 1-night lmt. [Overnight on an emergency basis only.] FACILITIES: Spaces for self-contained units; tbls, cga. No toil/drk wtr. MISC.: Pets permitted if kept on a leash.

ROXBURY

Hodge Park (Rest Area). St Hwy 67, near Roxbury. SEASON: All yr; 1-night lmt. [Overnight on an emergency basis only.] FACILITIES: Spaces for self-contained units; tbls, cga. No toil/drk wtr. ACTIVITIES: Picnicking. MISC.: Pets permitted if kept on a leash.

SALEM

Music Vale Road (Rest Area). St Hwy 82, near Salem. SEASON: All yr; 1-night lmt. [Overnight on an emergency basis only.] FACILITIES: Spaces for self-contained units; tbls, cga. No toil/drk wtr. ACTIVITIES: Picnicking. MISC.:Pets.

Shady Brook (Rest Area). St Hwy 85, near Salem. SEASON: All yr; 1-night lmt. [Overnight on an emergency basis only.] FACILITIES: Spaces for self-contained units; tbls, toil, cga, no drk wtr. ACTIVITIES: Picnicking. MISC.: Pets permitted if kept on a leash.

SALISBURY

Gateway Rest (Rest Area). St Hwy 41, near Salisbury. SEASON: All yr; 1-night lmt. [Overnight on an emergency basis only.] FACILITIES: Spaces for self-contained units; tbls, cga. No toil/drk wtr. ACTIVITIES: Picnicking. MISC.:Pets.

SHARON

Grist Mill (Rest Area). St Hwy 4, near Sharon. SEASON: All yr; 1-night lmt. [Overnight on an emergency basis only.] FACILITIES: Spaces for self-contained units; tbls, toil, cga, no drk wtr. ACTIVITIES: Picnicking. MISC.: Pets.

STERLING

Pitch Pine Grove (Rest Area). St Hwy 14, near Sterling. SEASON: All yr; 1-night lmt. [Overnight on an emergency basis only.] FACILITIES: Spaces for self-contained units; tbls, toil, cga, no drk wtr. ACTIVITIES: Picnicking. MISC.: Pets permitted if kept on leash.

Ye Olde Voluntown Pound (Rest Area). St Hwy 14, near Sterling. SEASON: All yr; 1-night lmt. [Overnight on an emergency basis only.] FACILITIES: Spaces for self-contained units; tbls, cga. No toil/drk wtr. ACTIVITIES: Picnicking. MISC.: Pets permitted if kept on leash.

SOUTHINGTON

Southington Rest Area. I-84, near Southington. SEASON: All yr; 1-night lmt. [Overnight on an emergency basis only.] FACILITIES: Spaces for self-contained units; tbls, toil, cga, drk wtr. ACTIVITIES: Picnicking. MISC.: Pets on leash.

THOMPSON

French River (Rest Area). St Hwy 12, near Thompson. SEASON: All yr; 1-night lmt. [Overnight on an emergency basis only.] FACILITIES: Spaces for self-contained units; tbls, cga. No drk wtr/toil. ACTIVITIES: Picnicking. MISC.: Pets.

Knollwood (Rest Area). St Hwy 131, near Thompson. SEASON: All yr; 1-night lmt. [Overnight on an emergency basis only.] FACILITIES: Spaces for self-contained units; tbls, toil, cga, no drk wtr. ACTIVITIES: Picnicking. MISC.: Pets.

Quinebaug Rest (Rest Area). St Hwy 197, near Thompson. SEASON: All yr; 1-night lmt. [Overnight on an emergency basis only.] FACILITIES: Spaces for self-contained units; tbls, cga, no drk wtr/toil. ACTIVITIES: Picnicking. MISC.: Pets.

TORRINGTON

Still River (Rest Area). St Hwy 800, near Torrington. SEASON: All yr; 1-night lmt. [Overnight on an emergency basis only.] FACILITIES: Spaces for self-contained units; tbls, cga. No toil/drk wtr. ACTIVITIES: Picnicking. MISC.: Pets on leash.

UNION

Goodhall's Garage (24-hour Truck Stop). Exit 106 from I-86. SEASON: All yr, 1-night lmt. FACILITIES: Spaces for self-contained units; toil, drk wtr, food, mechanic, gas, phone. MISC.: Pets.

WALLINGFORD

The Glen (Rest Area). St Hwy 15, near Wallingford. SEASON: All yr; 1-night lmt. [Overnight on an emergency basis only.] FACILITIES: Spaces for self-contained units; tbls, toil, cga, drk wtr. ACTIVITIES: Picnicking. MISC.: Pets on leash.

Wallingford Rest Area. I-91, near Wallingford. SEASON: All yr; 1-night lmt. [Overnight on an emergency basis only.] FACILITIES: Spaces for self-contained units; tbls, toil, cga, drk wtr. ACTIVITIES: Picnicking. MISC.: Pets on leash.

See page 7 for KEY TO ABBREVIATIONS.

WASHINGTON

Bee Brook (Rest Area). St Hwy 47, near Washington. SEASON: All yr; 1-night lmt. [Overnight on an emergency basis only.] FACILITIES: Spaces for self-contained units; tbls, cga. No toil/drk wtr. ACTIVITIES: Picnicking. ACTIVI-Pets permitted if kept on a leash.

East Aspetuck (Rest Area). St Hwy 25, near Washington. SEASON: All yr; 1-night lmt. [Overnight on an emergency basis only.] FACILITIES: Spaces for self-contained units; tbls, cga. No toil/drk wtr. ACTIVITIES: Picnicking. MISC.: Pets permitted if kept on a leash.

WESTBROOK

Rest Area. I-95, near Westbrook. SEASON: All yr; 1-night lmt. [Overnight on an emergency basis only.] FACILITIES: Spaces for self-contained units; tbls, toil, cga, drk wtr. ACTIVITIES: Picnicking. MISC.: Pets permitted on leash.

WILLINGTON

Rest Area. I-86, near Willington. SEASON: All yr; 1-night lmt. [Overnight on an emergency basis only.] FACILITIES: Spaces for self-contained units; tbls, toil, cga, drk wtr. ACTIVITIES: Picnicking. MISC.: Pet on leash.

WILTON

Zion Hill (Rest Area). US 7, near Wilton. SEASON: All yr; 1-night lmt. [Overnight on an emergency basis only.] FACILITIES: Spaces for self-contained units; tbls, cga, no drk wtr. ACTIVITIES: Picnicking. MISC.: Pets permitted if on a leash.

WINDHAM

Mansfield Hollow Dam (Rest Area). US 6, near Windham. SEASON: All yr; 1-night lmt. [Overnight on an emergency basis only.] FACILITIES: Spaces for self-contained units; tbls, toil, cga, no drk wtr. ACTIVITIES: Picnicking. MISC.: Pets.

WOODBRIDGE

Woodbridge Rest (Rest Area). St Hwy 15, near Woodbridge. SEASON: All yr; 1-night lmt. [Overnight on an emergency basis only.] FACILITIES: Spaces for self-contained units; tbls, cga. No toil/drk wtr. ACTIVITIES: Picnicking. MISC.: Pets.

WOODBURY

Toll Gate (Rest Area). St Hwy 47, near Woodbury. SEASON: All yr; 1-night lmt. [Overnight on an emergency basis only.] FACILITIES: Spaces for self-contained units; tbls, cga. No toil/drk wtr. ACTIVITIES: Picnicking. MISC.: Pets on leash.

DELAWARE

GENERAL STATE INFORMATION

Miscellaneous

STATE CAPITOL: Dover
STATE NICKNAME: Diamond State
STATE MOTTO: "Liberty and Independence"
STATE BIRD: Blue Hen Chicken
STATE FLOWER: Peach Blossom
STATE TREE: Longleaf Pine

State Parks

With the exception of Fort Delaware, all state parks are open for public use year round. (Fort Delaware, mid-April to mid-October.) However, there is no camping from October to mid-May. Fees range from $5.00-8.00 per night. Pets are permitted on leash. For further information: State of Delaware; Department of Natural Resources and Environmental Control; Division of Parks and Recreation; Edward Tatnall Building; PO Box 1401; Dover, Delaware 19901.

Rest Areas

Overnight stops are not permitted in Delaware's rest areas.

See page 7 for KEY TO ABBREVIATIONS.

DELAWARE

INFORMATION SOURCES

Maps

The following maps are available from **Forsyth Travel Library** (see order form in Appendix B):

State of Delaware [Up-to-date, showing all principal roads, points of interest, sports areas, parks, airports, mileage, etc. Full color.]

Completely indexed city maps, including airports, lakes, rivers, etc., of: **Wilmington/New Castle Co.; Newark.**

State Information

Bureau of Travel Development; Division of Economic Development; Department of Community Affairs and Economic Development; 630 State College Rd; Dover, Delaware 19901.
State Park Commission; 3300 Faulkland Road; Wilmington, DE 19808.
Delaware State Chamber of Commerce; 1102 West Street; Wilmington, DE 19801.
Division of Economic Development; 45 The Green; Dover, DE 19901.
Division of Fish and Wildlife; Department of Natural Resources and Environmental Control; PO Box 1401; Edward Tatnell Building; Dover, DE 19901.

FREE CAMPGROUNDS

GEORGETOWN

Redden (SF). 3 mi N of Georgetown on US 113; ½ mi E on Co Hwy 565. SEASON: All yr; 3-day lmt. FACILITIES: 20 sites (no trailers); tbls, toil, cga, f, drk wtr. Store nearby. ACTIVITIES: Picnicking; horseback riding; hiking. MISC.: Pets permitted if kept on a leash.

LAUREL

Glenn's 76 Truck Stop. US 13, northbound, at Laurel. SEASON: All yr; 1-night lmt. FACILITIES: Space for self-contained units; toil, drk wtr, food, mechanic, gas, phone. MISC.: Pets.

SEAFORD

Seaford Municipal Park. Foot of Porter Street and Nanticoke Avenue, in Seaford. SEASON: All yr. FACILITIES: Sites. ACTIVITIES: Boating,l. MISC.: Pets on leash.

SMYRNA

Blackbird (SF). 5 mi N of Smyrna on US 13; 2 mi W on Co Hwy 471. SEASON: All yr; 3-day lmt. FACILITIES: 8 sites (no trailers); tbls, toil, cga, f, drk wtr. ACTIVITIES: Picnicking; horseback riding; hiking. MISC.: Pets on leash.

FLORIDA

GENERAL STATE INFORMATION

Miscellaneous

Toll-Free Number for Travel Information:
    1-800-342-3558 (calling in Florida)
    1-800-874-8660 (calling out of state)
STATE CAPITOL: Tallahassee
STATE NICKNAME: Sunshine State
STATE MOTTO: "In God We Trust"
STATE BIRD: Mockingbird
STATE FLOWER: Orange Blossom

See page 7 for KEY TO ABBREVIATIONS.

State Parks

Fees range from $4.00-5.00 per night plus $1.00 for electricity. Florida citizens are entitled to use the Annual Family Camping Permit costing $100 + tax. Holders of the permit may camp in state parks with camping areas, but must pay $1.00/night for electricity, if used. The permits are not reduced if purchased in later months. Pets are not permitted in the camping areas or on the beaches. For further information: Division of Recreation and Parks; Department of Natural Resources; 3900 Commonwealth Boulevard; Tallahassee, FL 32303

Rest Areas

Overnight stops are not permitted in Florida's rest areas.

Florida Trail

The Florida Trail will be a 1300-mile footpath which will run the length of the State, when it is completed. Long stretches of trail are already open. Maps are available for these sections. Anyone can hike the Florida Trail across public property such as national forests and state parks and forests. However, only Florida Trail members may hike across private property. Membership dues are $7.50/single; $11.00/family, annually, PLUS $1.00 handling fee for lapsed and new members. Map sets are $3.00. Out-of-State visitors may prefer the temporary 60-day user permit for $5.00. All along the trail is available wilderness camping. The prime hiking season in north Florida is October to April, although hunting curtails hiking in many areas during November and December. In the Big Cypress the hiking is best in January and February. There are no shelters and few pumps so surface water must be purified. For further information and maps that provide descriptive data, restrictions, and INFORMATION ABOUT CAMPSITES, water and supply points: Florida Trail Association, Inc.; PO Box 13708; Gainesville, FL 32604; 904/378-8823.

Fish Camps

A map of fish camps can be obtained by writing to: Office of Informational Services; South Florida Region; 2202 Lakeland Hills Boulevard; Lakeland, FL 33801.

Hunt Camps

The Game and Fresh Water Fish Commission puts out special HUNT MAPS, available free upon request, which indicate campsites available during hunting season for hunters only. A Wildlife Management Area Permit Stamp, in addition to regular hunting license requirements, is required of any person except residents 65 years of age and over to hunt or possess a gun on the area. A Wildlife Management Area quota permit, issued from the Game and Fresh Water Fish Commission, is required of any person to hunt or possess a gun on the area from 11/10-11/18. A quota of hunters has been set for each hunting area for the first nine days of hunting season (November 10-18). Hunters wishing to participate during the first nine days must submit a written application, available at any county tax collector's office or their subagents, to the Game and Fresh Water Fish Commission, Tallahassee Office. The quota will be filled on a first-come first-served basis as received by mail in the Tallahassee office. Write to the Game and Fresh Water Fish Commission; Farris Bryant Building; Tallahassee, Fl 32304. Request the series of hunt maps. Also request their free Wildlife Management Areas map, which indicates 30 additional free campgrounds.

Canoeing/Camping in Florida

The three National Forests in Florida (Apalachicola, Ocala, and Osceola) contain more than 700 lakes and ponds, and four major rivers. But it is the numerous streams that offer the most challenge to the canoeist. There is no "whitewater" such as you will find in the mountains, but there is a variety of streams, which are kept in their natural condition. No roads parallel the streams. For further information and a map: National Forests in Florida; PO Box 13549; 2586 Seagate Drive; Tallahassee, FL 32308.

The 1979 Florida Legislature has set up a new canoe trail program. For information on this (including camping): Department of Natural Resources; Division of Education and Information; Crown Building; 202 Blount Street; Tallahassee, FL 32301.

If you don't have your own canoe, you might be interested in Canoe Outpost Wilderness Canoe Trips, providing downstream canoe trips on hundreds of miles of primitive rivers throughout Florida. Although not free, they are very reasonably priced. Write: Canoe Outpost Wilderness Canoe Trips; Route 2, Box 330J; Sarasota, FL 33582.

Corps of Engineers Free Campgrounds

In addition to the developed campgrounds specified under Chattahoochee and Sneads, there are a number of other free campgrounds located at Seminole Lake which are accessible by car, free year round, and pinpointed on a map which you can get from: COE; Lake Seminole; PO Box 96; Chattahoochee, FL 32324; 912/662-2814.

BACKCOUNTRY CAMPING

Apalachicola NF

Apalachicola is the largest National Forest in Florida. The area abounds with wildlife, including black bear and panther. Excellent fishing. Lesser developed areas located throughout the forest are available free of charge for swimming, tent camping, picnicking, and access to fishing waters. Pets are permitted. Further information: Superintendent; Apalachicola NF; PO Box 578; Florida Highway 20; Bristol, FL 32321; 904/643-2477; OR, District Ranger, Wakulla Ranger District; US Forest Service; PO Box 68; US Hwy 319; Crawfordville, FL 32327; 904/926-3561.

Blackwater River State Forest

40 primitive campsites for overnight camping are available at Bear Lake, Hurricane Lake, and Karick Lakes. These sites offer running water, a dumping station, picnicking, tables, and flush toilets. Season, May-November. More primitive sites without facilities are at Juniper Bridge, Kennedy Bridge, Red Rock, Bryant Bridge, and Camp Lowery. Camping is allowed on the forest property but is discouraged since adequate primitive campsites are available. Further information: Superintendent; Blackwater River SF; Route 1; Box 77; Milton, FL 32570.

Everglades National Park

A Backcountry Use Permit may be obtained free of charge from any Ranger Station. (Permits are not available by phone or mail.) Campsites are first-come first-served, and permits do not constitute a reservation. Most backcountry sites are chickees (wooden platforms with a roof but no walls), equipped with pit toilet, charcoal grill, and picnic table. They are accessible only BY BOAT, with no fee charged, and open year-round. During the rainy season mosquitoes and other biting insects make backcountry use very uncomfortable, and campers should be armed with adequate supplies of insect repellent and appropriate clothing. Chickee platforms can accommodate two small tents, or approximately six persons, in reasonable comfort. The park entrance is $2.00 per vehicle, charged year-round [or Golden Age/Golden Eagle Passport**].

PETS: Pets are permitted in the backcountry but MUST BE LEASHED when on land. Unless under physical control, pets can disturb reptiles and nesting birds and may themselves be seriously injured. Very few National Parks allow pets in the backcountry and by keeping them on a leash you may help preserve this privilege in Everglades NP.

FISHING: All waters of the Wilderness Waterway are brackish, so no fishing license is required. Fresh water areas of the Park require a Florida fishing license (unless you are a Florida resident and older than 65 or under 15 years of age). Certain areas are posted, "Closed to Fishing." Salt water limits conform to Florida State regulations. Oyster beds are common and oysters may be taken by hand from 9/1-4/30, provided they are at least 3". Blue crabs are also plentiful but only the males may be taken. A hook and line gaff or landing net are the only legal fishing equipment on the Wilderness Waterway. Spearguns, nets, seines, sharksticks and other devices for killing or trapping fish may not be possessed on Park waters. Along the Main Park Road, all areas from Nine Mile Pond northward are considered fresh water. You may sport fish in any of the fresh water areas of the park except the areas in the vicinity of the Main Park Visitor Center, Taylor Slough, Shark Valley Rd, and Royal Palm Visitor Center. Only hand-propelled watercraft are permitted on fresh water lakes. Spring and summer are the most productive times for fishing, but most species can be caught the year round. Main salt water species are sea trout (weakfish), mangrove snapper, redfish, snook and tarpon. Principal fresh water species are large-mouth bass and bream.

SWIMMING: General conditions are not conducive to enjoyable swimming in the park. The fresh water ponds have alligators and occasionally water moccasins. Salt water areas accessible by car are usually shallow and flat, edged by mangrove trees. Sharks and barracudas are found in most Florida waters.

For further information: Superintendent; Everglades NP; Box 279; Homestead, FL 33030.

Ocala NF

Primitively developed sites are scattered throughout the National Forest and are available year round, free of charge. Pets are permitted. Ocala NF is east of Ocala between the Oklawaha and St. Johns Rivers. This forest has the largest area of sand pine in the world. A fishing paradise year round, the forest also has one of the largest deer herds in Florida. Further information: District Ranger; Lake George Ranger District; Ocala NF; PO Box 1206; Federal Building; Ocala, FL 32670; 904/622-6577. OR, District Ranger; Seminole Ranger District; Ocala NF; 1551 Umatilla Rd; Eustis, FL 32726; 904/357-3721.

Osceola NF

For those who prefer less development and more solitude, Osceola NF offers backwoods streams, trails, and campsites. The partially-completed Osceola Trail, a part of the Florida Trail System, provides hiking enthusiasts a chance to rough it in the backcountry. During the summer season, June-September, canoeists can enjoy the designated canoe trail on an 11-mile segment of the Middle Prong of the St. Marys River. Fish; hunting. Further information: District Ranger; Osceola Ranger District; Osceola NF; PO Box 1649; US Hwy 80 East; Lake City, FL 32302; 904/752-2577.

Withlacoochee State Forest

Primitive camping is allowed only during hunting season in areas which are indicated on the map, available free of charge from: Withlacoochee SF; 7255 US 41 North; Brooksville, FL 33512. The length of continuous stay in any camping area per individual is limited to two weeks.

INFORMATION SOURCES

Maps

The following maps are available from **Forsyth Travel Library** (see order form in Appendix B):

> **State of Florida** [Up-to-date, showing all principal roads,
> points of interest, sports areas, parks, airports, mileage,
> etc. Full color.]
>
> Completely indexed city maps, including all airports, lakes,
> rivers, etc., of numerous Florida cities.

Individual details County Maps cost 30¢/chart ($\frac{1}{2}$":1 mi) or $1.50/chart (1":1 mi). They are available from: Library; Room 57; Department of Transportation; Hayden Burns Building; Tallahasse, Fl 32304.

State Information

Division of Tourism; Florida Department of Commerce; 107 West Gaines Street, Room 505; Tallahassee, FL 32304.
Florida Department of Natural Resources; Bureau of Education and Information; Larson Building, Room 664; Tallahassee, FL 32304.
Florida Department of Natural Resources; Crown Building; 202 Blount Street; Tallahassee, FL 32304. [Bureau of Education and Information: canoeing information. Division of Recreation and Parks: State Park information.]
Florida State Chamber of Commerce; Jacksonville, FL 32211.
Game and Fresh Water Fish Commission; 620 South Meridian; Tallahassee, FL 32304.

City Information

Coral Gables Chamber of Commerce; Miami, FL 33134.
Greater Miami Chamber of Commerce; 1300 Biscayne Blvd.; Miami, FL 33131.
Miami Beach Chamber of Commerce; Miami Beach, FL 33139.
St. Petersburg Chamber of Commerce; 4th St. & Third Ave. S.; St. Petersburg, FL 33701
Greater Tampa Chamber of Commerce; 801 E. Kennedy Blvd.; Tampa, FL 33601.
Sarasota County Chamber of Commerce; 1551 Second Street; Sarasota, FL 33577.

National Forests

Apalachicola NF; 214 S. Bronough St.; Box 1050; Tallahassee, FL 32302.
Ocala NF; 214 S. Bronough St.; Box 1050; Tallahassee, FL 32302.
Osceola NF; 214 S. Bronough St.; Box 1050; Tallahassee, FL 32302.
National Forests in Florida; PO Box 13549; 2586 Seagate Drive; Tallahassee, FL 32308. [904/878-1131]

Miscellaneous

Biscayne National Monument; PO Box 1369; Homestead, FL 33030.
Everglades NP; Box 279; Homestead, FL 33030.

FLORIDA

Corps of Engineers; Lake Seminole; PO Box 96; Chattahoochee, FL 32324.
Corps of Engineers; Jacksonville District; PO Box 4970; Jacksonville, FL 32201.
Gulf Islands National Seashore; PO Box 100; Gulf Breeze, FL 32561.
St. Marks NWR; PO Box 68; St. Marks, FL 32355.
St. Vincent NWR; Box 447; Apalachicola, FL 32320.
Blackwater River State Forest; Route 1, Box 77; Milton, FL 32570.
Withlacoochee SF; 7255 US 41 North; Brooksville, FL 33512.

FREE CAMPGROUNDS

ALTOONA

Big Scrub (Seminole NF). 5½ mi N of Altoona on St Hwy 19; 7 mi W on FS 73. SEASON: All yr; 14-day lmt. FACILITIES: 33 sites (tr -22); tbls, toil, cga, piped drk wtr. ACTIVITIES: Picnicking. Fishing (3 mi). Boating (4 mi). MISC.: Elev 100 ft; 9 acres; pets. Sand pines.

Island Ponds (Seminole NF). 10 ml W of Altoona on St Hwy 42; 3 mi NE on FS 88; 1 mi S on FS 87A. SEASON: All year; 14-day lmt. FACILITIES: Undesignated sites (tr -16); well drk wtr, tbls, toil, cga, f. ACTIVITIES: Picnicking; boating; fishing. MISC.: Elev 100 ft; 4 acres; lake; pets.

Lake Catherine (Ocala NF). 11 mi W of Altoona on St Hwy 42; 4 mi N on Co Hwy 200E; 3/10 mi NE on FS 73; 2 mi N on FS 91. SEASON: All yr; 14-day lmt. FACILITIES: Undesignated sites (tr -22); tbls, toil, no drk wtr. ACTIVITIES: Swimming; picnicking; fishing; boating. MISC.: Elev 200 ft; 2 acres; pets; lake.

APALACHICOLA

St. Vincent National Wildlife Refuge. The only camping available here is during the hunting program for hunt participants only with the proper hunting licenses and a refuge permit. For information on their hunt camps and hunting program, write to: St. Vincent NWR; PO Box 447; Apalachicola, FL 32320.

BRISTOL

Camel Lake (Apalachicola NF). 12-1/10 mi S of Bristol on St Hwy 12; 2 mi E on FS 105. SEASON: All yr. FACILITIES: 11 sites (tr -22), tbls, flush toil, cga, piped drk wtr. ACTIVITIES: Swimming; picnicking; fishing; boating,l. MISC.: Elev 100 ft; 4 acres; lake; pets.

Cotton Landing (Apalachicola NF). 12 mi S of Bristol on St Hwy 12; 16-1/5 mi S on St Hwy 379; 2-4/5 mi SW on FS 123; 7/10 mi W on FS 123B. SEASON: All yr. FACILITIES: 12 sites (tr -22), tbls, toil, cga, well drk wtr. ACTIVITIES: Boating,ld; picnicking; fishing.

MISC.: Elev 100 ft; 7 acres; pets. Access to Apalachicola River. Located on East bank of Kennedy Creek.

Hickory Landing (Apalachicola NF). 12-4/5 mi S of Bristol on St Hwy 12; 22 mi S on St Hwy 379; 2 mi S on St Hwy 65; 1-4/5 mi SW on FS 101. SEASON: All yr. FACILITIES: 6 sites (tr -22); tbls, toil, cga, piped drk wtr. ACTIVITIES: Boating,ld; picnicking; fishing. Swimming (1 mi). MISC.: Elev 100 ft; 2 acres; pets. Located on East bank of Owl Creek. Access to Apalachicola River.

Hitchcock Lake (Apalachicola NF). 11-2/5 mi E of Bristol on St Hwy 20; 3-1/5 mi S on St Hwy 65; 22-4/5 mi SE on St Hwy 67; 1½ mi E on FS 125B. SEASON: All yr. FACILITIES: 10 sites (tr -16), tbls, toil, cga, no drk wtr. ACTIVITIES: Boating,ld; picnicking; fishing. No swimming allowed. MISC.: Elev 100 ft; 3 acres; pets; scenic. On Hitchcock Lake, a backwater of the Ochlockonee River.

Magnolia Landing (Apalachicola NF). 21-3/5 mi S of Bristol on St Hwy 12; 3 mi SE on FS 13; 6-3/10 mi SE on FS 114; 7/10 mi E on FS 119. SEASON: All yr. FACILITIES: 2 sites (tr -22), tbls, toil, cga, well drk wtr. ACTIVITIES: Fishing; picnicking. MISC.: Elev 100 ft; 1 acre; pets. Located on a river.

Porter Lake (Apalachicola NF). 11-2/5 mi E of Bristol on St Hwy 20; 3-1/5 mi S on St Hwy 65; 16-9/10 mi SW on St Hwy 67; 2-9/10 mi E on Fs 13. SEASON: All yr. FACILITIES: 4 sites (no trailers); tbls, toil, cga, well drk wtr. ACTIVITIES: Boating; picnicking; fishing. MISC.: Elev 100 ft; 2 acres; pets. On the West bank of the Ochlockonee River.

Whitehead Lake (Apalachicola NF). 11-2/5 mi E of Bristol on St Hwy 20; 3-1/5 mi S on St Hwy 65; 15-1/10 mi SE on St Hwy 67; 3-1/5 mi E on FS 111. SEASON: All yr. FACILITIES: 6 sites (tr -22); tbls, toil, cga, piped drk wtr. ACTIVITIES: Boating,l; picnicking; fishing.

See page 7 for KEY TO ABBREVIATIONS.

No swimming allowed. **MISC.:** Elev 100 ft; 2 acres; pets; scenic. Located on backwater of the Ochlockonee River.

Wright Lake (Apalachicola NF). 12-4/5 mi S of Bristol on St Hwy 12; 22 mi S on St Hwy 379; 2 mi S on St Hwy 65; 2 mi W on FS 101. **SEASON:** All yr. **FACILITIES:** 21 sites (tr -22), tbls, flush toil, cga, piped drk wtr. **ACTIVITIES:** Swimming; picnicking; fishing. **MISC.:** Elev 100 ft; 8 acres; pets. Open, scenic area, in a stand of pines. Boating,l (1 mi).

BROOKSVILLE

*Croom Hiking Trail** (Withlacoochee SF). Located in the center tract of the 113,000-acre SF. Access is at Tucker Hill Fire Tower, 5 mi E of Brooksville on Croom Rd. [Take St Hwy 50 exit off I-75, enter Croom Motorcycle area and continue N on TRAIL 11 until Croom Rd is reached. Turn left to the tower.] **SEASON:** Closed during modern and antique firearms portion of the general hunting season. For specific dates, contact Forest Supervisor at 7255 US 41 North; Brooksville, FL 32512 [904/796-4958]. **FACILITIES:** Overnight camping is permitted only at the designated camp zone located North of Tucker Hill Tower. The zone is marked by 6"-wide white bands on trees located around the perimeter. Drk wtr is piped to camp zone from Tucker Hill tower site. Only cooking fires are permitted. No warming or bonfires. Fires may be prohibited during periods of fire danger alert. Notice of a fire danger alert will be posted on the main information sign at trail entrance. **MISC.:** Obtain a free map from Supervisor's office. Parking for vehicles is provided at trail entrance, East of Tucker Hill Tower. Dry-to-damp, all-weather trail.

CHATTAHOOCHEE

River Junction (Decatur Co., Ga.; Bainbridge, Ga., operated). Approximately 3½ mi N on eastern shore of Lake Seminole. **SEASON:** All year. **FACILITIES:** No designated sites; tbls, toil, cga, showers, drk wtr. **ACTIVITIES:** Boating,l; picnicking. **MISC.:** Lake Seminole.

CHIPLEY

City Park. At west entrance of town. **SEASON:** All yr. **FACILITIES:** Sites. **MISC.:** Pets allowed if kept on leash.

CRAWFORDVILLE

Buckhorn (Apalachicola NF). 6-2/5 mi N of Crawfordville on US 319; 12 mi NW on St Hwy 267; 2 mi S on FS 350. **SEASON:** 11/1-1/31. [Hunting season.]

FACILITIES: 10 sites (tr -22), toil, well drk wtr. No tbls. **ACTIVITIES:** Hunting; hiking. **MISC.:** Elev 100 ft; 8 acres; pets. Area serves primarily as a hunt camp.

DADE CITY

*Richloam Hiking Trail** (Withlacoochee SF). Located in the SF, 10 mi N of Dade City, and 19 mi E of Brooksville, on St Hwy 50. Acess is at the Richloam Fire Tower, 3/5 mi SW of St Hwy 50 on Clay Sink Rd. **SEASON:** Closed during 1st 9 days of the general hunting season as well as Thanksgiving, Christmas, and New Years holidays. Exercise extreme caution during the Spring Gobbler Hunt. [Specific dates from: Forest Supervisor; Withlacoochee SF; 7255 US 41 N; Brooksville, FL 33512.] **FACILITIES:** Camping is permitted at Megg's Hole and South Grade Barrow Pit. These are unimproved public campgrounds. Potable wtr may be obtained at the Tower site and at Megg's Hole campsite. Only cooking fires are permitted. **MISC.:** Parking for vehicles at Tower site. Map available from Supervisor. Keep alert for poisonous snakes, especially during wet season.

EBRO

Pine Log (SF). 1 mi S of Ebro on St Hwy 79. **SEASON:** All yr; 14-day lmt. **FACILITIES:** 20 sites (tr -20), tbls, flush toil, showers, cga, f, dump. Store/ice/food/LP gas nearby. **ACTIVITIES:** Swimming; boating,l; picnicking; fishing. **MISC.:** Pets on leash.

EVERGLADES CITY

There is a small pull-off area on Jane's Scenic Drive, 7 mi NW of the fire tower, where sometimes the Fakatchie Strand ranger will give permission for camping. It is for "self-contained units and neatniks ONLY."

FORT MYERS

Ortona Lock (COE; Okeechobee Waterway). 30 mi E of Ft. Myers on St Hwy 78 to Ortona. **SEASON:** All yr; 7-day lmt. **FACILITIES:** 12 sites (tr -30), tbls, flush toil, cga, drk wtr. **ACTIVITIES:** Boating,l; picnicking; fishing (pier fishing; bank fishing). **MISC.:** Pets on leash.

W.P. Franklin Lock and Dam (COE; Okeechobee Waterway). 10 mi E of Ft. Myers on St Hwy 78. **SEASON:** All yr; 7-day lmt. **FACILITIES:** 12 sites (tr -30), tbls, flush toil, cga, drk wtr, playground. **ACTIVITIES:** Boating,l; picnicking; fishing (bank fishing; pier fishing).

See page 7 for KEY TO ABBREVIATIONS.

GAINESVILLE

Orange Springs (COE; Cross Florida Barge Canal). 25 mi E of Gainesville on St Hwy 20; 9 mi S on St Hwy 315 to Orange Springs. SEASON: All yr; 7-day lmt. FACILITIES: No designated sites; no facilities. ACTIVITIES: Boating,l; fishing. MISC.: Pets.

HOMESTEAD

*Elliot Key Park (Biscayne NM). 9 mi E on N. Canal Dr. to Homestead Bayfront Park and launch ramp; 7½ mi E, BY BOAT. [An island park.] SEASON: All yr; 30-day lmt. FACILITIES: 50 tent spaces; 64 free dock slips; tbls, flush toil, cga, no drk wtr. A snack bar concession is available on weekends. Emergency gasoline is available throughout the week but is very limited and is expensive. Saltwater showers. ACTIVITIES: Swimming; picnicking; fishing; boating,d; hiking. MISC.: Interpretive trails. Free BY RESERVATION on 1st-come 1st-served basis; call 305/371-0743.

*Garden Key (Fort Jefferson NM). 68 mi W of Key West, BY BOAT. [Information: PO Box 279; Homestead, FL 33030; 305/247-6211.] Accessible by private plane or boat, or charter services from several locations in the Keys. SEASON: All yr; 14-day lmt. FACILITIES: 6 tent sites; each site has a picnic tbl and charcoal grill. Camping is permitted in the grassy area near the beach outside the Fort walls. Flush toil are available at the dockhouse. No drk wtr. MISC.: Boat,d.

*Everglades NP — WILDERNESS WATERWAY. IMPORTANT NOTE: This information and the following 17 campgrounds are accessible only BY BOAT.

The Wilderness Waterway winds 88 nautical miles through creeks, rivers, and open bays, from Everglades City on the Gulf of Mexico to Flamingo on Florida Bay, through mangrove wilderness. A free backcountry permit must be filed at either the Everglades City or Flamingo Ranger Stations, listing what nights will be spent at which sites. As the mangroves are virtually impenetrable, missing or not reaching a site means spending the night in your boat.

Familiarity with local poisonous plants, such as poisonwood and manchineel, is helpful. Perhaps the greatest obstacles to the trip are the sand gnats and the mosquitos. In the wet season, from May-Sept., the bugs are unbearable. In winter they don't seem to be as bad during the day when you are moving, but when you stop to camp or explore a hammock, they can be

fierce. A tent with good mosquito netting is a must and so is insect repellent.

Making the trip from Oct.-May is ideal. It seldom rains and temperatures generally stay above 60 degrees F. An occasional cold front will bring near freezing temperatures, so one really needs to be prepared for either rain or cold.

The Wilderness Waterway offers the opportunity to see and appreciate the Everglades as few people ever do. On this trip you have the chance to see orchids, tropical vegetation, beautiful and often rare bird life; elusive wildlife such as bobcat, bear and panther; porpoise, alligators and possibly even a rare mantee may swim by your boat.

Before you begin the trip, it is recommended that you read and take along a copy of A GUIDE TO THE WILDERNESS WATERWAY, by William Truesdell, published by the Everglades Natural History Association. You will need three nautical charts: 11433 (Whitewater Bay), 11432 (Shark River to Lostmans), and 11430 (Lostmans River to Wiggins Pass).

The following 17 campgrounds include only backcountry sites between Everglades City and Flamingo, both Wilderness Waterway and Coastal. Other water access campsites are available in the Hell's Bay, Cape Sable and Florida Bay areas. In addition, cross-country camping is allowed with a backcountry use permit. For further information on backcountry camping contact: Everglades NP; PO Box 279; Homestead, FL 33030 [305/247-6211]. Information and assistance are also available at any Ranger Station: Everglades City (813/695-3311); Flamingo (813-695-3101); Key Largo (305/852-5119); Pine Island (305/247-6211); Tamiami (305/221-8457).

*Broad River (Everglades NP; Wilderness Waterway). Located on the Waterway near Marker #25. Accessible at all tides. FACILITIES: Ground space is suitable for only one party of 4; tbls, toil, cga, no drk wtr. No ground fires permitted. ACTIVITIES: Boating,d. MISC.: Campsite is slightly elevated on S bank of Broad River. Pets permitted on leash.

*Camp Lonesome (Everglades NP; Wilderness Waterway). Locate by leaving Waterway at Marker #26, Broad River Bay, and travel 2-2/5 mi E. Site can be approached at all tides. FACILITIES: Ground space is available for one party of 4; tbls, toil, cga, no drk wtr. No ground fires permitted. ACTIVITIES: Boating,d (small dock); picnicking; hiking. MISC.: This is one of the few campsites on the waterway where the sawgrass is accessible on foot. The Seminoles had

See page 7 for KEY TO ABBREVIATIONS.

a hunting camp located here when the Park was established in 1947, and tropical trees still abound. MISC.: Pets.

*Canepatch (Everglades NP; Wilderness Waterway). Locate by leaving Waterway at Marker #9 and travel 3-4/5 mi E through Tarpon Bay and Avocado Creek. FACILITIES: Space is adequate for two parties of 4; tbls, toil, cga, no drk wtr. No ground fires permitted. ACTIVITIES: Boating,d; picnicking. MISC.: Pets permitted on leash. Wild sugarcane, bananas, limes and papayas can be found on this Indian mound site in the Shark Valley Slough drainage. In winter, alligators/freshwater birds are abundant.

*Graveyard Creek (Everglads NP; Wilderness Waterway; Coastal Campsite). Located on Shark Point at Ponce de Leon Bay. Approach with caution at low water. FACILITIES: Ground space for three parties of 4; tbls, toil, cga, no drk wtr. No ground fires permitted. ACTIVITIES: Boating,d; picnicking; fishing (excellent). MISC.: An open view of the Gulf. Graveyard creek derived its name from the outcome of a feud between rival pairs of racoon hunters who were supplying pelts for the coat craze of the Roaring 20's. Pets on leash.

*Indian Key (Everglades NP; Wilderness Waterway; Coastal Campsite). Located on Gulf entrance of Indian Key Pass. Accessible from the west at all tides. FACILITIES: Space is available for three parties of 4; tbls, toil, cga, no drk wtr. No ground fires permitted. ACTIVITIES: Boating; picnicking. MISC.: Boats must be beached or anchored. Approaching channel has good depth. Site is located on sand spit at NE end of Key. Pets permitted if kept on a leash.

*Joe River Chickee (Everglades NP; Wilderness Waterway). Located by (traveling south) departing Waterway at Marker #2 heading SW across Oyster Bay. Chickee is on N bank of mouth of Joe River. Continue to Flamingo via Joe River east. FACILITIES: Platform provides space for one party of 4; tbls, toil, cga, no drk wtr. No ground fires permitted. No fresh water available. ACTIVITIES: Picnicking; boating. MISC.: This chickee is situated on an alternate route south of the main Waterway. Traveling Joe River affords some protection from the gusty winds and water common on Whitewater Bay in winter. Pets on leash.

*Lopez River (Everglades NP; Wilderness Waterway). Located between Markers #127 and #126 on the Lopez River. This site is the closest to Everglades City of all Waterway camps. Accessible at all tides. FACILITIES: There is no dock, but landing will accommodate two boats and ground space is adequate for two

parties of 4 persons; tbls, toil, cga, no drk wtr. No ground fires permitted. No fresh water is available. ACTIVITIES: Picnicking; boating. MISC.: Site is an Indian mound on S bank of Lopez River. Concrete cistern remains, located near landing, marks the homesite of the Lopez family circa 1900. Pets on leash.

*Lostman's Five (Everglades NP; Wilderness Waterway). Located on the Wilderness Waterway near Marker #60. (On the eastern side of Lostman's Five Bay.) Accessible at all tides. FACILITIES: Accommodates 1 party of 4; tbls, toil, cga, no drk wtr. No ground fires permitted. No fresh water available. ACTIVITIES: Picnicking; boating,d (large floating dock with room for 2 boats). MISC.: A recent homesite. This site is typical of the several "inholdings" originally privately owned within Park boundaries. The buildings and remains seen in the NW section of Everglades are presently being acquired and the sites returned to a natural appearance. Pets on leash.

*New Turkey Key (Everglades NP; Wilderness Waterway; Coastal Campsite). Located 1 mi S of Chatham River mouth. At low tides approach should be made from the south. FACILITIES: 2 camping areas are located on the mainland side of this medium-sized island. Each site will accommodate one party of 4; tbls, toil, cga, no drk wtr. No ground fires permitted. No fresh water available. ACTIVITIES: Picnicking; boating (no dock). MISC.: The sand beach site on the NE tip is usually more pleasant in summer than the more shaded camp 150 yards away in the center of the Key. Pets on leash.

*Plate Creek Bay Chickee (Everglades NP; Wilderness Waterway). Located within sight of Waterway near Marker #63. Accessible at all tides. FACILITIES: An elevated platform provides space for one party of 4; tbls, toil, cga, no drk wtr. No ground fires permitted. No fresh water available. ACTIVITIES: Picnicking; boating (long dock which provides space for several boats). MISC.: The chickee (wooden platform with roof but no walls) is relatively free of insects even in the summer. Pets allowed on leash.

*South Lostman's (Everglades NP; Wilderness Waterway; Coastal Campsite). Located on island in mouth of South Lostman's River. Numerous oyster bars and mud flats require cautious approach at all tides. FACILITIES: Sand beach provides ground space for two parties of 4; tbls, toil, cga, no drk wtr. No ground fires permitted. No fresh water available. ACTIVITIES: Boating (no dock); picnicking. MISC.: Coming out from Lostman's River is preferable to the Gulf route when water is low. Pets permitted on leash.

See page 7 for KEY TO ABBREVIATIONS.

FLORIDA

*Rabbit Key (Everglades NP; Wilderness Waterway; Coastal Campsite). Located on Gulf entrance of Rabbit Key Pass. Approach with caution at low tides. FACILITIES: Space available for three parties of 4; tbls, toil, cga, no drk wtr. No ground fires permitted. No fresh water available. ACTIVITIES: Picnicking; boating (no dock). MISC.: Situated on a sand spit on NE end of island with mangrove cover to S offering protection from Gulf weather. Pets on leash.

*Shark River Chickee (Everglades NP; Wilderness Waterway). Locate by leaving Waterway 3/10 mi S of Marker #6, travel 1/10 mi off Waterway on river flowing into Shark on the SE. Accessible at all tides. FACILITIES: Platform provides space for one party of 4; tbls, toil, cga, no drk wtr. No ground fires permitted. No fresh water available. MISC.: Mangroves nearby reach height of 75'. Pets permitted if kept on a leash.

*Watson River Chickee (Everglades NP; Wilderness Waterway). Located off Waterway 2½ mi NE of Coast Guard marker #36 in Whitewater Bay. Accessible at all tides. FACILITIES: Platform provides space for one party of 4. This 10x12 foot platform is well-protected from prevailing winds and rough seas. Tbls, toil, cga; no drk wtr. No ground fires permitted. No fresh water available. ACTIVITIES: Picnicking; boating. MISC.: Situated on the NE tip of a large island surrounded by low mangroves. Pets.

*Watson's Place (Everglades NP; Wilderness Waterway). Is located 1-3/10 mi S of Waterway on Chatham River. Accessible at all tides. FACILITIES: Ground space is available for three parties of 4; tbls, toil, cga, no drk wtr. No ground fires. No fresh water is available. ACTIVITIES: Picnicking; boating (a 20-foot dock will accommodate two boats; a canoe slide is built nearby). MISC.: An Indian mound on the north bank of the Chatham River served as home for Ed Watson, sugar plantation owner and local legend, until 1910. The campsite now located there is surrounded by the remains of his cistern and sugarcane refining equipment. Pets.

*Wedgepoint (Everglades NP; Wilderness Waterway). Located 2/5 mi N of Coast Guard marker #20 in Whitewater Bay. This is the campsite nearest Flamingo. FACILITIES: A small sandy beach on a narrow peninsula offers ground space for two parties of 4; tbls, toil, cga, no drk wtr. No ground fires permitted. No fresh water available. ACTIVITIES: Picnicking; boating (no dock). MISC.: Pets permitted if kept on leash.

*Willy Willy (Everglades NP; Wilderness Waterway). Located 2-1/5 mi off Waterway

E of Marker #39. [NOTE: Location of Willy Willy is not accurate on nautical chart 11432. Bear left, not right, after entering Rocky Creek Bay.] FACILITIES: Campsite is an Indian mound of 2-3 feet in elev, small, and will accommodate one party of 4; tbls, toil, cga, no drk wtr. No ground fires permitted. No fresh water is available. ACTIVITIES: Picnicking; boating (small dock will provide mooring for one boat). MISC.: It is some distance off the Waterway and as a result is less used. Hardwoods and vegetation normally associated with higher ground are found here. Pets are permitted if on leash.

Flamingo (Everglades NP). 50 mi SW of Homestead on St Hwy 27. SEASON: May-October ($3 rest of yr). [However, the area is subject to severe infestations of mosquitoes during free season, and all visitors are warned of this condition.] FACILITIES: 308 sites; tbls, flush toil, cga, dump, showers. Store/ice/food/bottled gas (nearby). ACTIVITIES: Boating,rld; picnicking. MISC.: Elev 100 ft; pets. $2.00 ENTRANCE FEE (or Golden Eagle/Age** Passport) in force all year.

Long Pine Key (Everglades NP). 16 ml SW of Homestead on St Hwy 27. SEASON: May-October, FREE ($3.00 rest of yr); 14-day lmt. FACILITIES: 107 sites; tbls, flush toil, cga, dump. ACTIVITIES: Picnicking. MISC.: Pets on leash; elev 100 ft. NOTE: The area is subject to severe infestations of mosquitos during free season, and all visitors are warned of this condition. Entrance fee of $2.00 (or Golden Eagle/Age Passport**) is charged all year.

INVERNESS

*Citrus Hiking Trail (Withlacoochee SF). Access to trail is at Holder Mine Recreation Area, 2 mi W from St Hwy 581; 2½ mi S of St Hwy 44. SEASON: Closed during the gun hunt portion of the general hunting season. FACIL: Camping is permitted only at Holder Mine and Perryman Place. Basic sanitary facilities are provided at Perryman Place. The overnight camping zone is located along the 0.6 mile side trail to Perry Place. The zone itself is marked by the 6" white bands painted on trees at eye level approximately 50 paces from the trail on both sides for a distance of 0.5 miles. Continued use of the camping zone depends upon the care with which campers use it. The only water on the trail is located at Holder Mine Recreation Area and Perryman Place which is located on the west side of Loop B. MISC.: Parking for vehicles is provided at the day use portion of the Holder Mine Recreation Area. A dry all-weather trail.

LAKE CITY

Olustee Beach (Osceola NF). 12-7/10 mi E of Lake City on US 90; 3/10 mi N on Co Hwy 231. SEASON: All yr. FACILITIES: Undesignated sites; tbls, flush toil, cga, electricity in restrooms, piped drk wtr. Store/ice/showers/gas (1 mi). ACTIVITIES: Swimming; picnicking; fishing; hunting; boating,l. MISC.: Elev 200 ft; 5 acres; lake; lifeguard; pets. 1-night lmt. Trailers less than 22 feet.

Sandhill Hunt Camp (Osceola NF). 17-1/10 mi NE of Lake City on FS FH237. SEASON: 11/1-1/15; 14-day lmt. FACILITIES: Undesignated sites (tr -22); toil, f. No tbls/drk wtr. ACTIVITIES: Hunting; picnicking; fishing. MISC.: Elev 200 ft; 5 acres; pets on leash.

West Tower Hunt Camp (Osceola NF). 12-1/2 mi NE of Lake City on FS FH233. SEASON: 11/1-1/15 (hunting season). 14-day lmt. FACILITIES: Undesignated sites (tr -22); flush toil, f, piped drk wtr. ACTIVITIES: Swimming; picnicking; fishing; hunting. MISC.: Elev 200 ft; 5 acres; stream; pets on leash.

Wiggins Hunt Camp (Osceola NF). 9-3/10 mi NE of Lake City on St Hwy 250. SEASON: 11/1-1/15 (hunting season); 14-day lmt. FACILITIES: Undesignated sites; toil, f. No tbls/drk wtr. ACTIVITIES: Swimming; hunting; picnicking. MISC.: Elev 200 ft; 5 acres; pets on leash.

MELBOURNE

*Grange Island North (Municipal Park). 12 mi S of Melbourne BY BOAT. SEASON: All yr; 21-day lmt. Reservations accepted. FACILITIES: 20 tent sites; tbls, flush toil, cga, drk wtr. ACTIVITIES: Swimming; picnicking; fishing; boating,d. MISC.: Pets allowed if kept on leash.

MIAMI

Camp Buttonwood. In Greynolds Park, 17530 West Dixie Highway, Miami. SEASON: All year. FACILITIES: Primitive sites. MISC.: Prefer organized groups (nonprofit organizations only) by prior arrangement. Maximum 48 campers.   Call: 949-3134.

MUNSON

Blackwater River SF. Located in Santa Rosa and Okaloosa Counties, Blackwater River SF is the largest state forest in Florida (183,153 acres). Activities include: hunting (bow-hunting and primitive rifle hunting, in season); picnicking; fishing; hiking; swimming; boating; canoeing; horseback riding (trails and stable). CAMPING: Within a 10-mile radius of Munson (located at the junc-

tion of St Hwy 191 and 4), are the following campgrounds (for exact directions request a free, easy-to-follow map from State Forest Headquarters, Rte 1, Box 77, Milton, FL 32570; 957-4111.

Bear Lake (Blackwater River SF). Approximately 2½ mi E of Munson on St Forest Rds. SEASON: 5/1-11/30. FACILITIES: 40 primitive sites; tbls, flush toil, dump, running water. ACTIVITIES: Hiking; picnicking; fishing; canoeing; boating,ld. MISC.: Hiking trail. Pets.

Bryant Bridge (Blackwater River SF) Approximately 12 mi SE of Munson on SF rds. SEASON: All yr. FACILITIES: Primitive sites; tbls. ACTIVITIES: Swimming; picnicking; fishing; canoeing; horseback riding (stable by reservation only). MISC.: Pets on leash.

Camp Lowry (Blackwater River SF). Approximately 6 mi NW of Munson on SF rds. SEASON: All yr. FACILITIES: Primitive sites; tbls. ACTIVITIES: Swimming; picnicking; fishing; horseback riding (stable by reservation only). MISC.:Pets.

Hurricane Lake (Blackwater River SF). SEASON: 5/1-11/30. FACILITIES: 40 primitive sites; tbls, flush toil, running water, dump. ACTIVITIES: Canoeing; boating,l/pier; picnicking; fishing; horseback riding (stable by reservation only). MISC.: Pets on leash.

*Jackson Trail Shelters (Blackwater River SF). The 21-mile Andrew Jackson Red Ground Trail has been designated a link in the Florida Trail which will eventually run the full 600-mi length of Florida. It retraces the earliest trade route of Indians and settlers. Ideal for spring and fall hiking. There are two shelters along the trail. The SF map shows the exact locations. They contain chemical toilets, but no running water. Horseback riding (stable by reservations only). All year.

Juniper Bridge (Blackwater River SF). Approximately 2 mi SW of Munson on St Hwy 191. SEASON: 5/1-11/30. FACILITIES: Primitive sites; tbls. ACTIVITIES: Swimming; picnicking; fishing. MISC.: Pets permitted if kept on a leash.

Karick Lake (Blackwater River SF). Approximately 14 mi NE of Munson on SF rds. SEAS.: 5/1-11/30. FAC.: 40 prim. sites; tbls, toil, running wtr; dump. ACTIVITIES: Hiking; horseback riding (stable by reservation only); picnicking; fishing; canoeing; boating,l/pier. MISC.: Pets on leash.

Kennedy Bridge (Blackwater River SF). Approximately 8 mi NE of Munson on SF rds. SEASON: All yr. FACILITIES: Primitive sites; tbls. ACTIVITIES: Swimming; picnicking; fishing; canoeing; horseback riding (stable by reservation only).

Red Rock (Blackwater River SF). Approximately 6 mi S of Munson on SF rds. SEASON: All yr. FACILITIES: Primitive sites; tbls, toil, running water. ACTIVITIES: Hiking; horseback riding (stable by reservation only); swimming; picnicking; fishing. MISC.: Pets on leash.

OCALA

Grassy Pond (Ocala NF). 11 mi E of Ocala on St Hwy 40; 19-4/5 mi NE on St Hwy 314; 5-1/5 mi NW on St Hwy 316; 3/5 mi N on FS 88E. SEASON: All yr; 14-day lmt. FACILITIES: 6 sites (tr -32), tbls, toil, cga, f, well drk wtr. ACTIVITIES: Fishing; picnicking. MISC.: Elev 100 ft; 2 acres; pets; lake. Deep sand in access road.

Halfmoon Lake (Ocala NF). 21 mi E of Ocala on St Hwy 40; 1/2 mi SE on FS 79; 1/2 mi S on FS 79D. SEASON: All yr; 14-day lmt. FACILITIES: Undesignated sites (tr -16); tbls, toil, cga, well drk wtr. Store/ice/food/gas (4 mi). ACTIVITIES: Picnicking; fishing; boating,l (r, 4 mi). MISC.: Elev 200 ft; 2 acres; pets; lake.

Hopkins Prairie (Ocala NF). 24-1/5 mi E of Ocala on St Hwy 40; 6-3/10 mi N on FS 88; 4-3/5 mi E on FS 86; 3/5 mi N on FS 51. SEASON: All yr; 14-day lmt. FACILITIES: 6 sites (no trailers); toil, well drk wtr. No tbls/cga. ACTIVITIES: Boating,l; picnicking; fishing. MISC.: Elev 100 ft; 5 acres; lake; pets. Difficult access due to poor roads.

Lake Delancy (Ocala NF). 11 mi E of Ocala on St Hwy 40; 19-4/5 mi NE on St Hwy 314; 5-7/10 mi N on St Hwy 19; 2 mi W on FS 75. SEASON: All yr; 14-day lmt. FACILITIES: 8 sites (tr -32); tbls, toil, cga, well drk wtr. ACTIVITIES: Boating,d (rl, 2 mi); picnicking; fishing. MISC.: Elev 100 ft; 88 acres; lake. Pets on leash.

OLUSTEE

Boat Basin Hunt Camp (Osceola NF). 5-2/5 mi NE on FS 241. SEASON: 11/1-1/15; 14-day lmt. FACILITIES: Undesignated sites; toil, f. No tbls/drk wtr. ACTIVITIES: Boating; swimming; picnicking; fishing; waterskiing; hunting. MISC.: Elev 200 ft; 5 acres; pets; lake.

PAISLEY

Clay Lake (Seminole NF). 6 mi NE of Paisley on St Hwy 42; 1 mi N on FS 40; 1/5 mi E on TRAIL. SEASON: All year; 14-day lmt. FACILITIES: Primitive sites; tbls; no drk wtr, no toil. ACTIVITIES: Picnicking; boating; fishing. MISC.: Elev 100 ft; 6 acres.

PALATKA

Johnson Field (Ocala NF). 17-1/5 mi SW of Palatka on St Hwy 19; 3/10 mi W on FS 77. SEASON: All yr; 10-day lmt. FACILITIES: 20 sites (no trailers); tbls, toil, cga, piped drk wtr. ACTIVITIES: Picnicking. Boating,l/fishing (1 mi). MISC.: Elev 100 ft; 5 acres; pets on leash.

Kenwood (COE;Cross Florida Barge Canal). 9 mi S of Palatka on St Hwy 19; 8 mi to St Hwy 315; left 1 mi to Kenwood sign. SEASON: All yr; 7-day lmt. FACILITIES: Undesignated sites; tbls, toil, no drk wtr. ACTIVITIES: Boating,l; picnicking; fishing. MISC.: Pets on leash.

PERRY

Reptile Gardens. 14 mi S of Perry on US 19. SEASON: All yr; 1-night lmt. FACILITIES: Spaces for self-contained units; no facilities. ACTIVITIES: Touring Reptile Gardens. MISC.: Pets.

SANDERSON

East Tower Hunt Camp (Osceola NF). 10-1/10 mi NW of Sanderson on St Hwy 229. SEASON: 11/1-1/15 (hunting season); 14-day lmt. FACILITIES: Undesignated sites; flush toil, f, piped drk wtr, store, ice, gas. No tbls. ACTIVITIES: Fishing; hunting; swimming; hiking. MISC.: Elev 200 ft; 5 acres; pets on leash.

17-Mile Hunt Camp (Osceola NF). 10-7/10 mi NW of Sanderson on St Hwy 229. SEASON: 11/1-1/15; 14-day lmt. FACILITIES: Undesignated sites (tr -22); toil, f. No tbls/drk wtr. ACTIVITIES: Hunting; fishing; hiking; picnicking. MISC.: Pets; elev 200 ft; 5 acres. River.

SEBRING

Rodgers Creek Park. Located in town. SEASON: All yr. FACILITIES: Sites.

SILVER SPRINGS

Lake Eaton (Lake George NF). 17-1/5 mi N of Silver Springs on St Hwy 40; 4-1/5 mi N on Co Hwy 314A; 2/5 mi E on FS 79A; 1 mi N on FS 96. SEASON: All yr; 14-day lmt. FACILITIES: 6 sites; tbls, toil, cga, no drk wtr. ACTIVITIES: Boating; fishing. MISC.: Elev 100 ft; 2 acres; lake; pets.

SNEADS

Neals Landing (COE; Lake Seminole). Approximately 19 mi N, up Co Hwy 271, then E on St Hwy 2 to the Herman Talmadge Bridge on the Chattahoochee River. SEASON: All year. FACILITIES: No designated sites; tbls, toil, cga, dump, showers, drk wtr. ACTIVITIES: Boating,l; picnicking. MISC.: Pets.

See page 7 for KEY TO ABBREVIATIONS.

SOPCHOPPY

Mack Landing (Apalachicola NF). 10-1/10 mi W of Sopchoppy on St Hwy 375; 9/10 mi W on FS 375D. SEASON: All yr; 14-day lmt. FACILITIES: 5 sites (tr -22); tbls, toil, cga, well drk wtr. ACTIVITIES: Boating,l; picnicking; fishing. MISC.: Pets; river. Located on east bank of Ochlockonee River. Elev 100 ft; 3 acres.

Wood Lake (Apalachicola NF). 1-1/5 mi W of Sopchoppy on St Hwy 375; 2-9/10 mi SW on St Hwy 299; 1 mi W on FS 345; 2-1/10 mi S on FS 345B. SEASON: All yr. FACILITIES: 4 sites (tr -22); tbls, toil, cga, well drk wtr. ACTIVITIES: Boating,l; picnicking; fishing. MISC.: Located on Ochlockonee River. Elev 100 ft; 3 acres; pets. Gas (5 mi).

STUART

St. Lucie Lock and Dam (COE; Okeechobee Waterway). 8 mi S of Stuart on St Hwy 76. SEASON: All yr; 7-day lmt. FACILITIES: 10 sites (tr -30); tbls, flush toil, cga. ACTIVITIES: Boating,l; picnicking; fishing (bank fishing). MISC.: Pets allowed if kept on leash.

UMATILLA

Big Bass Lake (Ocala NF). 8 mi NW of Umatilla on St Hwy 450; 1-9/10 mi W on St Hwy 42; 3/5 mi N on FS 88.

SEASON: All yr; 30-day lmt. FACILITIES: 8 sites (tr -16), toil, well drk wtr. No tbls. ACTIVITIES: Boating,d; fishing. MISC.: Elev 100 ft; 1 acre; lake.

Buck Lake (Ocala NF). 11½ mi N of Umatilla on St Hwy 19; 2 mi W on FS 95; ½ mi S on FS 14. SEASON: All yr. FACILITIES: Undesignated sites; toil, well drk wtr. No tbls. ACTIVITIES: Picnicking; boating,l; fishing. MISC.: Elev 200 ft; 1 acre; pets; lake.

Farles Prairie (Ocala NF). 11½ mi N of Umatilla on St Hwy 19; 3-4/5 mi NW on FS 95. SEASON: All yr; 14-day lmt. FACILITIES: 5 sites (tr -22); toil, well drk wtr. No tbls. ACTIVITIES: Picnicking; swimming; fishing; boating,ld. MISC.: Elev 200 ft; 3 acres; pets; lake.

VERO BEACH

Dale Wimbrow Park. 15 mi N of Vero Beach on US 1; 2½ mi W on Roseland Rd (located on beautiful Sebastian River). SEASON: All yr. FACILITIES: Undesignated sites; tbls, cga, water. ACTIVITIES: Boating; swimming; picnicking. MISC.: The river opens into the Indian River and the Inland Waterway, directly west of Sebastian Inlet and the Atlantic Ocean.

GEORGIA

GENERAL STATE INFORMATION

Miscellaneous

STATE CAPITOL: Atlanta
STATE NICKNAME: Empire State of the South
STATE MOTTO: "Wisdom, Justice, Moderation"
STATE BIRD: Brown Thrasher
STATE FLOWER: Cherokee Rose
STATE TREE: Live Oak

State Parks

Overnight fee is $3.00. No reservations are accepted. 14-day limit per campsite. Pets are allowed in all Georgia State Parks, on leash; but not in swimming areas, cottages, or park buildings. FREE CAMPING: There are special areas at some of the state parks where they allow "pioneer camping". This is only available for properly supervised groups. Reservations are required. INFORMATION: State Parks and Historic Sites of Georgia; Georgia Dept. of Natural Resources; Parks, Recreation, and Historic Sites Division; 270 Washington Street, SW; Atlanta, GA 30334; 656-3530.

Rest Areas

Overnight stops are not permitted in Georgia's rest areas.

See page 7 for KEY TO ABBREVIATIONS.

Corps of Engineers Free Campgrounds

In addition to the developed campgrounds specified under Bainbridge and Donalsonville, there are a number of other free campgrounds located at Seminole Lake which are accessible by car, free year round, and pinpointed on a map which you can get from: COE; Lake Seminole; PO Box 96; Chattahoochee, FL 32324; 912-662-2814.

The Alapaha River Canoe Trail

The Alapaha River runs through some of the most remote areas of South Georgia. It is considered an easy river to float, having high sand banks, bends frequently, and occasional small rapids with waves. Four primitive campsites available for use by canoeists. Also available is a hunting preserve for bowhunters and trailer campsites. If your group plans to canoe the entire 83-mile section, notify the Tourism Council the date you plan to put in and take out, to qualify for the Alapaha Canoe Trail Award. For further information: Coastal Plain Area Tourism Council; Box 1223; Valdosta, GA; 912/247-3454.

CAMPING IN NATIONAL WILDLIFE REFUGES

Blackbeard Island NWR (within Savannah NWR Complex). The camping facilities (restrooms, showers, and picnic shelter) are provided only for archery hunters participating in the refuge's managed hunts and for authorized conservation-oriented groups. The hunting permit (free) which archery hunters obtain from the Savannah NWR Complex headquarters serves as a permit to camp on Blackbeard for the duration of the hunt. Requests for permits for group camping (also free) are directed to the Savannah NWR Complex office. Scheduled activities of groups planning to camp on the refuge will be closely reviewed to insure compatibility with refuge wildlife objectives. Contact: Savannah NWR Complex Hunts; PO Box 8487; Savannah, GA 31412; 912/232-4321.

Wassaw Island NWR (within Savannah NWR Complex). Camping on Wassaw Island NWR is permitted only in conjunction with the bow and gun hunts for deer. Only hunters with permits issued by the Savannah Complex office are authorized to camp during the managed hunts. Camping is restricted to Pine Island and there are no sanitary or water facilities available. All applicants for archer hunts are issued free permits; but only a limited number of free permits, selected by drawing, are issued for the Wassaw gun hunt. Contact: Savannah NWR Complex Hunts; PO Box 8487; Savannah, GA 31412; 912/232-4321.

Okefenokee NWR

PRIMITIVE CAMPING: There are 3 entrances. Using the Stephen C. Foster State Park entrance, located approximately 18 mi NE of Fargo; this entrance is administered by the Georgia Park and Historic Sites Division under an agreement with the US Fish and Wildlife Service. This is the only entrance where overnight facilities are available. The only FREE camping are two primitive campgrounds (one administered by the Fish and Wildlife Service and one administered by the State) which are both for organized youth groups only (i.e., Scouts).

CANOEING/CAMPING: Overnight canoe trips into the interior of the Swamp may be enjoyed. Canoe trips may be reserved for two to six-day trips through the swamp. There is no charge for a canoeing permit. However, reservations must be made in advance. Overnight camping is permitted only at designated overnight stops. You must register at each stop. Since firm land is not available at all overnight stops, a 20x28' wooden platform is provided. Pop tents are recommended. No nails should be used and no trees or limbs should be cut. Open fires are not permitted except at specified areas, so gasoline, bottle gas, or similar types of stoves will be required if you plan to cook meals. You must remain at the designated overnight area between sunset and sunrise. You may camp only one night per rest stop. Portable toilets with disposable bags are required.

FURTHER INFORMATION: Okefenokee NWR; Federal Building, Room 109; 601 Tebeau Street; PO Box 117; Waycross, GA 31501; 912/283-2580.

THE APPALACHIAN TRAIL

More than 2000 miles long, the Appalachian Trail (from Maine to Georgia) is the longest continuous marked trail in the world.

GEORGIA

Camping

More than 200 open-front shelters/lean-tos are spaced approximately 10 miles apart on the Trail (one-day intervals). As they are occupied on a first-come first-served basis, carry a tent in case the shelters are full. Potable spring water is usually available at each site, but should be purified by tablets or boiling. And always, "pack it in, pack it out".

Permits

No permit is required to hike the Trail. However, camping permits must be obtained for overnight stays in Shenandoah NP (Luray, VA 22835) and Great Smoky Mountains NP (Gatlinburg, TN 37733). These are free of charge and available from the ranger stations or by mail. A free camping permit must be obtained for overnight stays in White Mountain National Forest Restricted Use Area (PO Box 638; Laconia, NH 03246).

Appalachian Trail Conference

A private, non-profit, national organization which represents citizens' interest in the Appalachian Trail. They offer detailed guidebooks and maps for sale, as well as the AT Data Book which gives the location and distances between shelters and certain post offices, supply points, water sources, loding and meals. For more information on this organization, write to them at: PO Box 236; Harpers Ferry, WV 25425.

Information

For regional information on the Trail, contact: Supervisor; Chattahoochee-Oconee NF; PO Box 1437; Gainesville, GA 30501; 404/536-0541. Ask for free CHATTAHOOCHEE NATIONAL FOREST APPALACHIAN TRAIL MAP AND GUIDE.

BACKCOUNTRY CAMPING

Chattahoochee NF

Primitive camping is allowed anywhere in the national forest unless posted otherwise. Permits are not needed for camping or campfires. Hunting and fishing are allowed under Georgia Regulations; obtain appropriate permits and licenses from Georgia Dept. of Natural Resources; Game and Fish Division; 270 Washington St., SW; Atlanta, GA 30334. Additional information/map: Superintendent; Chattahoochee NF; 601 Broad Street; PO Box 1437; Gainesville, GA 30501.

Cohutta Wilderness; Chattahoochee NF

34,100 acres of wilderness in NW Georgia and SE Tennessee. The area contains rugged S end of Appalachian Mountains, and 2 of the best wild trout streams in Georgia. Bear, wild boar, whitetailed deer. Access to the interior is by footpath only. It is an ideal place for the backpacker and hardy outdoorsperson. For further information: District Ranger; Cohutta Ranger District; Chattahoochee NF; 401 Old Ellijay Road; Chatsworth, GA 30705; 404/695-6736. Pets are allowed.

Oconee NF

Primitive camping is allowed anywhere in the NF unless posted otherwise. Permits are not needed for camping or campfires. Hunting and fishing are allowed under Georgia Regulations; obtain appropriate permits and licenses from: Georgia Dept. of Natural Resources; Game and Fish Division; 270 Washington Street, SW; Atlanta, GA 30334. Further information: Superintendent; Oconee NF; 601 Broad Street; PO Box 1437; Gainesville, GA 30501; 404/536-0541. Pets are allowed.

INFORMATION SOURCES

Maps

The following maps are available from Forsyth Travel Library (see order form in Appendix B):

> State of Georgia [Up-to-date, showing all principal roads, points of interest, sports areas, parks, airports, mileage, etc. Full color.]
>
> Completely indexed city maps, including all airports, lakes, rivers, etc., of: Athens, Atlanta, Augusta, Columbus/Fort Benning, Macon, Savannah.

Gold Mining and Prospecting

Georgia Department of Mines, Mining and Geology; State Division of Conservation; 19 Hunter Street, SW; Atlanta, GA 30303.

State Information

Tourist Division; Georgia Department of Community Development; PO Box 38097; Atlanta, GA 30334.
Georgia Dept. of Natural Resources; Parks, Recreation, and Historic Sites Division; 270 Washington Street, SW; Atlanta, GA 30334.
Department of Transportation; 2 Capitol Square, SW; Atlanta, GA 30334.
U.S. Fish and Wildlife Service; 17 Executive Park Drive, NE; Atlanta, GA 30309.
Game and Fish Division; Department of Natural Resources; 270 Washington Street, SW; Atlanta, GA 30334.

City Information

Atlanta Chamber of Commerce; Tourist Department; 1300 Commerce Building; Atlanta, GA 30303.
Jekyll Island Authority; 270 Washington St., SW; Atlanta, GA 30334.
Savannah Area Chamber of Commerce; PO Box 530; Savannah, GA 31402.
Stone Mountain Memorial Association; PO Box 778; Stone Mountain, GA 30083.

Miscellaneous

U.S. Forest Service; 1720 Peachtree Road, NE; Atlanta, GA 30309.
Chattahoochee-Oconee NF; 601 Broad St.; PO Box 1437; Gainesville, GA 30501.
Allatoona Lake Project; US Army Corps of Engineers; Mobile District; PO Box 2288; Mobile, AL 36628. [Has campgrounds in GA.]
Public Affairs Office; US Army Corps of Engineers; Savannah District; PO Box 889; Savannah, GA 31402.
US Army Corps of Engineers; South Atlantic Division; 510 Title Building; 30 Pryor St., SW; Atlanta, GA 30303.
Cumberland Island National Seashore; PO Box 806; St. Marys, GA 31558.
Blackbeard Island NWR; c/o Savannah NWR Complex; Box 8487; Savannah, GA 31402.
Okefenokee NWR; Box 117; Waycross, GA 31501.
Piedmont NWR; Round Oak, GA 31080.
Wassaw Island NWR; c/o Savannah NWR Complex; Box 8487; Savannah, GA 31402.

TENNESSEE VALLEY AUTHORITY

TVA designated campgrounds are no longer free. However, unimproved TVA lands may be used for informal camping. No fees or permits are required. These areas are shown on recreation maps of individual TVA lakes. For map, contact: TVA; Knoxville, TN 37902. Ask for the map showing Georgia's TVA lakes.

FREE CAMPGROUNDS

APPLING

*Bussey Point (COE; Clark Hill Lake). 4 mi SE of Appling on St Hwy 47; 12 mi SE; 4 mi BY TRAIL or BY BOAT. SEASON: All yr; 14-day lmt. FACILITIES: 10 tent sites; tbls, toil, cga, f, drk wtr. ACTIVITIES: Picnicking; swimming; fishing; boating,l; hiking. MISC.: Pets. Lake.

ASHBURN

Rest Area. 1 mi N of Ashburn on St Hwy 159 in Ashburn on I-75 N (paved access rds). SEASON: All yr; 1-night lmt. FACILITIES: Spaces for self-contained units; tbls, toil, cga, dump, phone, playground. ACTIVITIES: Picnicking. MISC.: Pets.

BAINBRIDGE

Faceville Landing (COE; Lake Seminole). 10 mi SW of Bainbridge on St Hwy 97. SEASON: All yr; 14-day lmt. FACILITIES: 18 sites; tbls, toil, cga, f, drk wtr. ACTIVITIES: Swimming; picnicking; fishing; boating,l. MISC.: Pets; lake.

Hale's Landing (COE; Lake Seminole). SW of Bainbridge on St Hwy 253; S on Co Rd. SEASON: All yr; 14-day lmt. FACILITIES: 10 sites (no trailers). ACTIVITIES: Boating,l; picnicking; fishing. FACILITIES: Tbls, toil, cga, drk wtr. MISC.: Pets on leash. Lake Seminole.

Ray's Lake (COE; Lake Seminole). 20 mi SW of Bainbridge on St Hwy 253; N at Sealy Point sign. SEASON: All yr;

See page 7 for KEY TO ABBREVIATIONS.

14-day lmt. FACILITIES: 6 sites; tbls, toil, cga, drk wtr. Store nearby. ACTIVITIES: Swimming; picnicking; fishing; boating,l. MISC.: Pets on leash. Lake.

Sealy Point (COE; Lake Seminole). Approximately 17 mi W of Bainbridge on St Hwy 253; 16 mi S of Donalsonville, GA, on Co Hwy 374. Landing is at the S end of Co Hwy 374 on the N side of Lake Seminole. SEASON: Sept.-April, FREE ($2 rest of yr). FACILITIES: Undesignated sites; tbls, toil, cga, drk wtr. ACTIVITIES: Boating,l; picnicking. MISC.: Pets on leash. Lake Seminole.

BLAKELY

Coheelee Creek Public Use Area (COE; George W. Andrews Lake). 10 mi SW of Blakely on St Hwy 62 to Hilton, GA; turn N, follow signs approx. 2 mi to the park. SEASON: All yr; 14-day lmt. FACILITIES: 7 sites (tr -18); hand pump is available. ACTIVITIES: Boating,l. Fishing/swimming nearby. MISC.: Pets.

CALHOUN

Hidden Creek Recreation Area (Chattahoochee-Oconee NF). 7-4/5 mi W of Calhoun on St Hwy 156; 1-9/10 mi NW on FS 231; 3-3/10 mi N on FS 228; 9/10 mi N on FS 955. SEASON: 5/24-9/02; 14-day lmt. FACILITIES: 16 sites (tr -22), tbls, toil, cga, drk wtr. ACTIVITIES: Picnicking. MISC.: Elev 900 ft; 9 acres; pets on leash. On Hidden Creek.

CARTERSVILLE

Macedonia Campground (COE; Allatoona Lake). 2-2/5 mi N of Cartersville on St Hwy 41; 8-3/10 mi E on St Hwy 20; 1-4/5 mi right on Old Macedonia Rd; 2-3/5 mi right and follow signs to campground. SEASON: October-April, FREE ($3 rest of yr); 14-day lmt. FACILITIES: 26 sites; tbls, toil, cga, f, drk wtr. ACTIVITIES: picnicking; fishing; boating,l. MISC.: Isolated area. Pets permitted on leash.

Upper Stamp Creek Campground (COE; Allatoona Lake). 2-2/5 mi N of Cartersville on St Hwy 41; 6-3/10 mi E on St Hwy 20; 1-3/10 mi right on Wilderness Camp Rd; bear left on dirt rd and go 9/10 mi to campground. SEASON: March-October; 14-day lmt. FACILITIES: 9 sites; tbls, toil, cga, f, drk wtr. ACTIVITIES: Hunting; picnicking; fishing; swimming; boating,l; waterskiing. MISC.: Allatoona Lake. Pets on leash.

CLAYTON

Rabun Beach (Chattahoochee-Oconee NF). 6-3/5 mi S of Clayton on US 444; 1/10 mi W on Co Hwy 10; 1-7/10 mi S on St Hwy 15; 4-4/5 mi W on Co Hwy 10. SEASON: 6/1-9/10. FACILITIES: Undesignated

sites (no trailers); flush toil, tbls, cga, showers, piped drk wtr, dump. Store/ice/gas (1 mi). Food (5 mi). ACTIVITIES: Swimming; picnicking; fishing; sailing; boating,l (r, 5 mi); waterskiing; hiking. MISC.: Elev 1700 ft; 2 acres; lifeguard; pets; nature trails. On 834-acre lake.

Warwoman Dell (Chattahoochee-Oconee NF). 2 mi E of Clayton on Co Hwy 5. SEASON: 3/28-12/1. FACIL.: Undesig. sites; tbls, toil, cga, no drk wtr, store, ice, gas, laundry, food. ACTIVITIES: Hiking; picnicking; fishing; swimming. MISC.: Elev 1900 ft; 8 acres; scenic; pets; nature trails. Stream.

CUMMING

Two Mile Creek (COE; Lake Sidney Lanier). For exact directions/map, contact: Resource Manager; PO Box 567; Buford, GA 30518; 404/945-9531. SEASON: 9/19-4/13, FREE ($5 rest of yr); 14-day lmt. FACILITIES: 39 sites (tr -15); tbls, toil, cga, drk wtr. ACTIVITIES: Boating,l; picnicking; fishing (bank fishing). MISC.: Pets; lake.

DAHLONEGA

Waters Creek Recreation Area (Chattahoochee-Oconee NF). 12-3/10 mi NE of Dahlonega on US 19; 9/10 mi NW on FS 34. SEASON: All yr; 14-day lmt. FACILITIES: 10 sites (tr -22), tbls, toil, cga, f, well drk wtr. Store/ice/gas (2 mi). Food (3 mi). ACTIVITIES: Hiking; picnicking; fishing; rockhounding. MISC.: Elev 1600 ft; 2 acres;pets. Waters Creek.

DESSER

Ray's Lake (COE; Lake Seminole). 20 mi SW of Desser on St Hwy 253; N at Sealy Point sign. SEASON: All yr; 14-day lmt. FACILITIES: 6 sites; tbls, toil, cga, drk wtr. ACTIVITIES: Swimming; picnicking; fishing; boating,l. MISC.: Pets on leash. Lake Seminole.

Sealy Point (COE; Lake Seminole). 20 mi Sw of Desser on St Hwy 25; S at Sealy Point sign. SEASON: All yr; 14-day lmt. FACILITIES: 14 sites; tbls, toil, cga, drk wtr. ACTIVITIES: Swimming; picnicking; fishing; boating,l. MISC.: Pets permitted on leash; lake.

DONALSONVILLE

Cummings Landing (COE; Seminole Lake). 17 mi S of Donalsonville on St Hwy 39. SEASON: Sept.-April, FREE ($2 rest of yr). FACILITIES: No designated sites; tbls, toil, cga, drk wtr. ACTIVITIES: Boating,l; picnicking. MISC.: Pets.

DOUBLE BRANCHES

Mosely Creek (COE; Clark Hill Lake). SE of Double Branches on access rd.

SEAS.: All year; 14-day lmt. **FAC.**: 15 sites (tr -30), tbls, flush toil, cga, f, drk wtr. **ACTIVITIES**: Swimming; picnicking; fishing; boating,l. **MISC.**: Pets.

ELLIJAY

Doll Mountain (COE; Carter Lake). 4 mi S of Ellijay on St Hwy 5 to Flat Creek Rd; turn right, go 7 mi to Doll Mountain Park sign; turn right and go 1 mi to park entrance. **SEASON**: Week after LD to MD weekend, FREE ($2 rest of yr). 14-day lmt. **FACILITIES**: Sites; toil, flush toil, cga, shower, laundry, water fountains. **ACTIVITIES**: Hiking; boating,l; picnicking. **MISC.**: Electric and water hookups. Pets on leash.

Oak Hill (COE; Carter Lake). 4 mi S of Ellijay on St Hwy 5; 5 mi right on Flat Creek Road; 2½ mi right at Oak Hill Park sign to park entrance. **SEASON**: 4/1-10/1; 14-day lmt. **FACILITIES**: 7 sites (no trailers); tbls, toil, cga, f, hand-pumped wells. **ACTIVITIES**: Swimming; picnicking; fishing. **MISC.**: Pets on leash.

Ridgeway (COE; Carter Lake). 7½ mi W on St Hwy 282; 3 mi S on park access rd. **SEASON**: All yr; 14-day lmt. **FACILITIES**: 31 sites (no trailers), pull-thru spaces; tbls, toil, cga, f, hand-pumped well. **ACTIVITIES**: Hiking; picnicking; swimming; fishing; boating,l. **MISC.**: Hiking trails; pets.

Woodring Branch (COE; Carter Lake). 8 mi W of Ellijay on St Hwy 282; 4 mi S on park access rd. **SEASON**: Week after LD through MD weekend, FREE ($2 rest of yr); 14-day lmt. **FACILITIES**: 39 sites; tbls, toil, cga, group picnic shelter; hand-pumped wells. **ACTIVITIES**: Hiking; boating,l; swimming; picnicking; fishing. **MISC.**: Hiking trails; pets; boat camping.

EUFAULA

White Oak Park (COE; Walter F. George Lake). 10 mi S on St Hwy 95. **SEASON**: March-October; 14-day lmt. **FACILITIES**: 67 sites; tbls, toil, cga, drk wtr. **ACTIVITIES**: Swimming; fishing; boating,l. **MISC.**: Lake; pets on leash.

FACEVILLE

Faceville Landing (COE; Lake Seminole). 10 mi SW of Faceville on St Hwy 97. **SEASON**: All yr; 14-day lmt. **FACILITIES**: 18 sites; tbls, flush toil, cga, f, showers, drk wtr. **ACTIVITIES**: Swimming; picnicking; fishing; boating,l. **MISC.**: Pets on leash. Lake Seminole.

FORT GAINES

Cotton Hill Park (COE; Walter F. George Lake). 4 mi N on St Hwy 39. **SEASON**: All yr; 14-day lmt. **FACILITIES**: 90 sites; tbls, toil, cga, drk wtr. **ACTIVITIES**: Swimming; fishing; boating,l.

Sandy Creek Public Use Area (Walter F. George Lake; COE). 4 mi N of Ft. Gaines on St Hwy 39. **SEASON**: All yr; 14-day lmt. **FACILITIES**: 30 sites (tr -30), tbls, toil, cga, drk wtr. **ACTIVITIES**: Boating,l; picnicking; fishing. **MISC.**: Pets on leash. Lake.

GAINESVILLE

Bolling Mill (COE; Lake Sidney Lanier). For exact directions/map: Resource Manager; PO Box 567; Buford, GA 30518; 404/945-9531. **SEASON**: All yr; 14-day lmt. **FACILITIES**: 14 sites (tr -15), primitive camping only; tbls, toil, cga, drk wtr. **ACTIVITIES**: Boating,l; picnicking; fishing (bank fishing); swimming. **MISC.**: Lake; pets on leash.

Keith Bridge (COE; Lake Sidney Lanier). For exact directions/map: Resource Manager; PO Box 567; Buford, GA 30518; 404/945-9531. **SEASON**: 9/19-4/1, FREE ($4 rest of yr); 14-day lmt. **FACILITIES**: 20 sites (tr -15), tbls, toil, cga, f, drk wtr. **ACTIVITIES**: Boating,l; picnicking; fishing (bank fishing). **MISC.**: Pets on leash. Lake.

Little Hall Park (COE; Lake Sidney Lanier). Exact directions/map: Resource Manager; PO Box 567; Buford, GA 30518; 404/945-9531. **SEASON**: 9/19-4/13, FREE ($5 rest of yr); 14-day lmt. **FACILITIES**: Boating,l; picnicking; fishing (bank fishing).

GREENSBORO

Oconee River Recreation Area (Chattahoochee-Oconee NF). 12-3/10 mi NW of Greensboro on St Hwy 15. **SEASON**: All yr; 14-day lmt. **FACILITIES**: 7 sites (tr -22), tbls, toil, cga, well drk wtr. **ACTIVITIES**: Boating,d; hiking; picnicking; fishing. **MISC.**: Elev 400 ft; 4 acres; nature trails; historic. On Oconee River. Adjacent to the hwy, in gently rolling hill country of the Piedmont. Pets.

HARTWELL

River (COE; Hartwell Lake). 5 mi N on US 29 (between Hartwell, GA, and Anderson, SC). **SEASON**: 9/16-4/30, FREE ($4, rest of yr). **FACILITIES**: 15 sites (tr -30), tbls, flush toil, cga, drk wtr. Dump nearby. **ACTIVITIES**: Fishing; picnicking. **MISC.**: Pets on leash.

Island Point (COE; Hartwell Lake). Approximately 4 mi N of Hartwell Dam on US 29 in Anderson County, SC. **SEASON**: March-September (closed the remainder of the year); 14-day lmt. **FACILITIES**: 3 sites (tr -30); tbls,

flush toil, drk wtr, cga. **ACTIVITIES:**
Swimming;fishing;picnicking;boating,r.

Watsadler's (COE; Hartwell Lake). 4 mi
E of Hartwell on US 29 (between Hartwell,
GA, and Anderson, SC). **SEASON:** Oct.-
March, FREE ($3 rest of yr); 14-day lmt.
FACILITIES: 37 sites (tr -30), tbls, flush
toil, showers, drk wtr, dump. **ACTIVI-
TIES:** Swimming; picnicking; fishing;
boating,l. **MISC.:** Pets on leash.

LaGRANGE

Ringer Campground (COE; West Point
Lake). Approximately 10 mi N on US
27. **SEASON:** All yr; 14-day lmt. **FA-
CILITIES:** 38 sites; toil, cga, drk wtr
(hand pump), dump. **ACTIVITIES:** Fishing; waterskiing; boating,l. Picnicking
nearby. **MISC.:** This is the only free
camping area at West Point Lake. Pets.

LINCOLNTON

***Bussey Point** (COE; Clark Hill Lake).
This campground is accessible only BY
BOAT or BY TRAIL. By land, the entrance
can be reached by following St Hwy 47
towards Lincolnton from Phinizy, and
following the signs for Bussey Point after
crossing the Keg Creek arm of the lake.
By water, the area is 3 mi upstream
from the dam. **SEASON:** All yr; 14-day
lmt. **FACILITIES:** 10 tent sites; tbls,
toil, cga, f, drk wtr. **ACTIVITIES:** Swimming; boating,l; picnicking; fishing.
MISC.: Pets on leash. Lake.

MONTICELLO

Hillsboro Lake (Chattahoochee-Oconee
NF). 9-4/5 mi S of Monticello on St Hwy
11; 3-3/10 mi SE on Co Hwy 1036. **SEA-
SON:** All yr. **FACILITIES:** Undesignated
sites (no trailers); tbls, toil, cga,
piped drk wtr. Store/gas/ice (2 mi).
ACTIVITIES: Fishing; picnicking. **MISC.:**
Elev 600 ft; 12 acres; pets; lake.

MOUNT AIRY

Lake Russell (Chattahoochee-Oconee NF).
2/5 mi S of Mt. Airy on US 123; 2-3/5
mi on FS 59. **SEASON:** 5/18-9/30. **FACILI-
TIES:** No designated sites (no trailers);
tbls, flush toil, cga, piped drk wtr,
electricity in restrooms, showers, dump.
Store/ice/food/gas/laundry (3 mi). **MISC.:**
Elev 1000 ft; 9 acres; pets. On 100-acre
lake. Nature trails; lifeguard. **ACTIVI-
TIES:** Swimming; hiking; picnicking;
fishing; boating,l (no motors).

PHINIZY

***Bussey Point** (COE; Clark Hill Lake).
Reached via BOAT or FOOT. By land,

the entrance can be reached by follow-
ing St Hwy 47 towards Lincolnton, from
Phinizy, and following the signs for
Bussey Point after crossing the Keg
Creek arm of the lake, 4 mi. By water,
the area is 3 mi upstream from the dam.
SEASON: All yr; 14-day lmt. **FACILITIES:**
10 sites; drk wtr.   Hiking; boating.

REYNOLDSVILLE

Spring Creek #3 (COE; Lake Seminole).
SW of Bainbridge on St Hwy 253; follow
the signs to campground. **SEASON:** All
yr; 14-day lmt. **FACILITIES:** 5 sites
(no trailers); tbls, toil, cga, drk wtr.
ACTIVITIES: Swimming; boating,r/d;
picnicking; fishing. **MISC.:** Pets.

ST. MARYS

Cumberland Island National Seashore.
The National Seashore has hiking trails
and four primitive camping areas. Backpackers must make reservations for the
tour boat for both arrival and departure
trips, and adhere to the dates requested. Plan supplies carefully; none
are available on the island. A tent
and backpacking equipment are advisable. All trash must be packed out.
Camping limit is 7 days. Ground fires
not permitted in the backcountry, so
you must have a stove. When you arrive
on the island, you will be greeted by
a park ranger who will issue you a
camping permit and hiking trail map.
Bring insect repellent. You are invited
to participate in the guided tour and
other interpretive activities while on
the island.

The Seashore has a small 16-site developed campground with water and restrooms. Campers must make reservations
and adhere to the dates requested.
Camping limit is 7 days. All food and
camping equipment must be hand-car-
ried by each camper about $\frac{1}{2}$ mi from
the dock to the campsite, so be frugal
about the amount of equipment you
bring. No pets on the boat or island.

There is a boat user fee of $2/adults.
Senior citizens (62 and older) and children (15 and under) will be charged
$1. Purchase tickets on the day of the
tour. Ferry reservations are advisable
and can be made by calling 912/882-
4335, or by writing to the superintendent at PO Box 806; St. Marys,GA 31558.
Don't miss the ferry from the island.
It leaves as scheduled. If you miss
the boat, you must camp or charter
a boat to transport you to the mainland.
The ferry does not transport cars, bicycles, or pets.

See page 7 for KEY TO ABBREVIATIONS.

HAWAII

Miscellaneous

Right Turns on Red: Permitted after full stop, unless otherwise posted.

STATE CAPITOL: Honolulu
STATE NICKNAME: The Aloha State
STATE MOTTO: "The life of the land is perpetuated in righteousness."
STATE BIRD: Hawaiian Goose
STATE FLOWER: Hibiscus
STATE TREE: Candlenut Tree

State Parks

Camping in Hawaii's State Parks is FREE! Camping reservations are required; and free permits are granted for a maximum of 5 nights. Applications for permits must be received by the Department at least seven days in advance of the date the permit is to be in effect. Pets are not permitted to run at large in park grounds and buildings. Further information: State of Hawaii; Department of Land and Natural Resources; 1151 Punchbowl Street; Honolulu, Hawaii 96813.

Rest Areas

Overnight stops are not permitted in Hawaii's rest areas.

Quarantine of Dogs and Cats Entering Hawaii

All dogs and cats entering Hawaii, except those from Australia, New Zealand, and Guam, are subject to quarantine and are confined in the Animal Quarantine Station in Honolulu for a period of 120 days. The purpose of the quarantine is to prevent the introduction of rabies which has a variable and often prolonged incubation period. On arrival in Hawaii, your pet will be delivered to the Hawaii Airport Holding Facility where it will be received by an inspector of the Division and, subsequently, transported to the Animal Quarantine Station. It will be released to you upon approval of the State Veterinarian at the expiration of the quarantine period, or with advance notice it can be released for export. Housing, food, and attendants for the dogs and cats held in quarantine are provided by the State. Fees are at present $2.45/day for dogs and $2.05/day for cats, plus a $10 entry fee for each animal. Fees are subject to change without notice. Further information: Department of Agriculture; PO Box 22159; Honolulu, HI 96822; 488-8461.

Camping on the Island of Lanai

This island is privately owned. There are no public lands where camping is permitted. Subsidiary of Castle & Cooke handles reservations for six individual campsites at Hulupoe Beach. The island has some fine trails, but overnight camping is not permitted. Fee. Further Information: Koele Company; PO Box L; Lanai City; Lanai, HI 96763; 565-7125.

Camping on Oahu's Beaches

Camping Permits: Camping for up to one week is allowed on certain public beach parks. Camping permits can be obtained from the Department of Parks and Recreation; Honolulu Municipal Building; Honolulu, HI 96813; from 8:00-4:00, Monday-Friday, except holidays; and at Satellite City Halls: 46-108 Kam Hwy, Kaneohe, HI 96744, 235-4571; 302 Kuulei Rd, Kailua, HI 96734, 261-8575; 830 California Avenue, Wahiawa, HI 96786, 621-0791; 85-555 Farr. Hwy, Waianae, HI 96792, 696-6371; 1290 Aala St., Honolulu, HI 96817, 523-2405; 1865 Kam IV Rd, Honolulu, HI 96819, 847-4688; 2nd floor, Koko Marina Shopping Center; Honolulu, HI 96825, 395-4418; 91-923 Ft. Weaver Rd, Ewa Beach, HI 96706, 689-7914; Waipahu Shopping Plaza, Waipahu, HI, 671-5638; Hauula Kai Shopping Center, 54-316 Kam Hwy, Hauula, HI, 293-8551. Camping permits are not issued earlier than 2 weeks before the weekend of camp. No fires of any kind may be built on the ground outside of a fire pit. Drinking or displaying intoxicating beverages is prohibited in public parks of Oahu, except in golf clubhouses. Some specific beach parks are listed under: Haleiwa, Hauula, Kaawa, Maili, Makaha, Nanakuli, Punaluu, Waialua, Waimanolo.

161

Kauai State Forest Reserve Trail/Camping

Camping is limited to 4 nights within a 30-day period, of which no more than 2 nights may be spent at the same campsite. Registration (free) at a trailhead is required upon entering and leaving a forest reserve overnight use area. For a complete trail information packet (including free camping information), send $1.00 IN STAMPS (to cover shipping and handling charges; do not send check or money order or SASE): Dept. of Land and Natural Resources; Division of Forestry; Kauai District; PO Box 1671; Lihue, Kauai, HI 96766.

BACKCOUNTRY CAMPING

Haleakala National Park

To camp within the Haleakala Crater, please stop by the Park Headquarters located on the way to the crater. Telephone: 572-7749 or 572-9306; or write, PO Box 537, Makawai, Maui, HI 96768. Camping in the crater is by permit only and restricted to cabins and campgrounds. There are two "crater campgrounds" -- one near Holua cabin and the other near Paliku cabin [see: Haleakala Crater; Maui, HI]. These are primitive campsites. Haleakala Crater is a 3-hour round-trip drive from Kahului via St Hwys 37/377/378. Park Headquarters is 1½ kilometers (1 mi) from the park entrance. Here park personnel furnish general information, permits, and publications. Information/map: Superintendent; Haleakala NP; PO Box 537; Makawao, Maui, HI 96768; 572-7749 or 572-9306.

Hawaii Volcanoes National Park

All overnight backcountry users must register at either the Kilauea or Wahaula Visitor Centers when beginning their trip. No charge. Hawaii Volcanoes NP is a geologically active area. It is important for park rangers to know the locations of backcountry users in the event of strong earthquakes, tsunamis, or volcanic eruptions.

MAUNA LOA TRAIL CABINS (free): The NPS maintains two patrol cabins on Mauna Loa which may be used free of charge by hikers. One is located at Puu Ulaula (Red Hill) at an elevation of 10,000 ft. It is 7 mi from the end of the Mauna Loa Strip Road. The other cabin is located on the SW side of Mokuaweoweo, the summit caldera, at an elevation of 13,250 ft. Each cabin has bunks with mattresses, blankets, Coleman stove and lantern, and cooking and eating utensils. Hikers must provide their own fuel.

PEPEIAU CABIN: Another patrol cabin which may be used by hikers is on the Ka'u Desert Trail at Kipuka Pepeiau. It has bunks with mattresses (no bedding), Coleman stove and lantern, and cooking and eating utensils. Fuel for the stove and lantern are not provided.

These three cabins may NOT be reserved in advance. When you register, the NPS will, on request, advise you if others have registered for the cabins. Large groups should notify Park Headquarters by mail or telephone in advance of their intended dates of use. The Park Service can then advise you if other large groups intend to use the cabins on the same dates.

COASTAL FACILITIES: See "Hilo."

Camping is allowed along trails in backcountry locations throughout the park. Be sure to register at either Visitor Center before starting your trip. Information/map: Superintendent; Hawaii Volcanoes NP; Hawaii Volcanoes NP, HI 96718.

INFORMATION SOURCES

Maps

A detailed, up-to-date, full color map of **Hawaii/Honolulu** is available from **Forsyth Travel Library** (see order form in Appendix B).

State Information

Hawaii Visitors Bureau; 2270 Kalakaua Avenue, Suite 801; Honolulu, HI 96815.
Department of Land and Natural Resources; 1151 Punchbowl St.; PO Box 621; Honolulu, HI 96809.
Chamber of Commerce of Hawaii; Dillingham Building; Honolulu, HI 96813.

State Information (cont.)

Division of Fish and Game; Department of Land and Natural Resources; 1179 Punchbowl Street; Honolulu, HI 96813.
Department of Planning and Economic Development; PO Box 2359; Honolulu, HI 96804.

Regional Information

Department of Parks and Recreation; 4191 Hardy Street; Lihue, Kaui, HI 96766.
Division of Parks and Division of Forestry; State Building, 2nd Floor; 3060 Eiwa Street, Room 207; Lihue, Kauai, HI 96766.
Koele Company; PO Box 486; Lanai City, Lanai, HI 96763.
Department of Parks and Recreation; 25 Aupuni Street; Hilo, HI 96720.
Division of Parks and Division of Forestry; 75 Aupuni Street; Hilo, HI 96720.
Department of Parks and Recreation; 650 South King Street; Honolulu, HI 96813.
Division of Parks and Division of Forestry; 1151 Punchbowl Street, Room 310; Honolulu, HI 96813.
Department of Parks and Recreation; War Memorial Gym, Room 102; Kaahumanu Avenue; Wailuku, Maui, HI 96793.
Division of Parks and Division of Forestry; 54 High Street; Wailuku, Maui, HI 96793.
County Agent; Molokai Island; c/o Department of Public Works; Kaunakakai, Molokai, HI 96748.
Division of Parks and Division of Forestry; PO Box 627; Kaunakakai, Molokai, HI 96748.

Miscellaneous

National Park Service; 300 Ala Moana; Honolulu, HI 96813.
Haleakala NP; Box 537; Makawao, Maui, HI 96768.
Hawaii Volcanoes NP; Hawaii Volcanoes NP, HI 96718.
Hanalei NWR; c/o Hawaiian Islands National Wildlife Refuges; Box 87; Kilauea, HI 96754.

FREE CAMPGROUNDS

<u>ISLAND OF HAWAII</u>

HILO

*Kalue (Hawaii Volcanoes NP). 2½ mi S of Hilina Park Overlook, BY TRAIL. SEASON: All yr; 7-day lmt. FACILITIES: Primitive nondesignated tent sites; boil drk wtr; no tbls. Water catchment shelters are provided, offering little protection in inclement weather; no stoves, utensils, bunks. During summer months, water tanks may be empty. Current information on the water supply is available at the visitor centers. Water should be purified before drinking. ACTIVITIES: Hiking. MISC.: 2 acres; NO PETS.

Kamoamoa (Hawaii Volcanoes NP). 10 mi S of Hilo on St Hwy 11; 26 mi SW on St Hwy 130. SEASON: All yr; 7-day lmt. FACILITIES: 12 sites; eating shelters; cga, toil, water. MISC.: 3 acres; Wahaula Visitor Center (1 mi).

Namakani Paio (Hawaii Volcanoes NP). 33 mi S of Hilo on St Hwy 11, 2½ mi W of park headquarters. SEASON: All yr; 7-day lmt. FACILITIES: Undesignated sites (no trailers); eating shelters; flush toil, cga, drk wtr. ACTIVITIES: Golf nearby; picnicking. MISC.: 2 acres.

HILO (cont.)

*Keauhou (Hawaii Volcanoes NP). 7 mi S of Ainahou Rd, BY TRAIL. SEASON: All yr; 7-day lmt. FACILITIES: Primitive undesignated tent sites; no tbls; boil drk wtr. Water catchment shelters are provided, offering little protection in inclement weather; no stoves, utensils, bunks. During summer months, water tanks may be empty. Current information on the water supply is available at the visitor centers. Water should be purified before drinking. MISC.: 2 acres; NO PETS.

Kipuka Nene (Hawaii Volcanoes NP). 30 mi SW of Hilo on St Hwy 11; 11 mi S of NP headquarters on Hilina Pali Road. SEASON: All yr; 7-day lmt. FACILITIES: 9 sites (no trailers); eating shelter, cga, toil, water (must be boiled before drinking). MISC.: 2 acres.

HONOKAA

Kalopa Recreation Area (SRA). 5 mi SE of Honokaa on St Hwy 19. SEASON: All yr; 7-day lmt. FACILITIES: 6 sites (no trailers); tbls, flush toil, cga, showers, drk wtr. ACTIVITIES: Picnicking. MISC.: Partially developed, forested area. RESERVATIONS REQUIRED.

See page 7 for KEY TO ABBREVIATIONS.

KAWAIHAE

Hapuna Beach (SRA). 2 mi S of Kawaihae.
SEASON: All yr. FACILITIES: 6 camping
shelters; tent sites; tbls, toil, cga,
drk wtr. ACTIVITIES: Picnicking; swimming. MISC.: Partially developed.

PAHOE

MacKenzie Recreation Area (SP). 10 mi
E of Pahoe on St Hwy 137, in Puna District. SEASON: All yr; 7-day lmt. FACILITIES: 6 sites; tbls, toil, cga, drk
wtr. ACTIVITIES: Hiking; good shore
fishing; picnicking. MISC.: Ironwood
grove area along a rugged coastline.
RESERVATIONS REQUIRED. Historical interest: Hawaiian trail.

ISLAND OF KAUAI

KEKAHA

Kokee Park (SP). 15 mi N of Kekaha
on St Hwy 55. SEASON: All yr; 7-day
lmt. FACILITIES: 24 sites; tbls, flush
toil, showers, laundry, food, phone,
drk wtr. ACTIVITIES: Trout fishing;
hiking; horseback riding; picnicking.
Seasonal fruit picking and hunting nearby. MISC.: Elev 3600 ft; 4600 acres;
RESERVATIONS REQUIRED. Adjoining Waimea Canyon SP. Forested mountain park.
Spectacular scenic overlook into Kalalau Valley.

*****Milolii Area (Na Pali Coast SP).** Western
coast of Kauai, approximately 5 mi from
Polihale landing. Barking Sands. Accessible by boat or helicopter. SEASON: 5/15-
9/5; 7-day lmt. FACILITIES: 4 camping
shelters; undesignated tent sites; tbls,
flush toil, cga, drk wtr. ACTIVITIES:
Good fishing; hunting access; boating,l;
swimming. MISC.: Beach with small boat
access. RESERVATIONS REQUIRED.

Polihale Park (SP). 5 mi N of Bonham
Air Force Base. [A desert-like beach area
located at the NW end of the island.]
SEASON: All yr; 7-day lmt. FACILITIES:
12 sites (no trailers); tbls, flush toil,
showers, drk wtr; no cga. ACTIVITIES:
picnicking; fishing. MISC.: Partially
developed, scenic beach. RESERVATIONS
REQUIRED. Good swimming in summer;
may be hazardous in winter and high
surf.

LIHUE

Wailua River Park -- Lydgate Area (SP).
6 mi N of Lihue on St Hwy 56. SEASON:
All yr; 7-day lmt. FACILITIES: 20 sites
(no trailers or RVs. Tbls, flush toil,
showers, cga, drk wtr. Store/food/laundry nearby. ACTIVITIES: Swimming; boating,rl; picnicking; fishing. Golf nearby.
MISC.: Beach area. Historic interest:

heiau-city of refuge, petroglyphs. RESERVATIONS REQUIRED.

ISLAND OF MAUI

HALEAKALA CRATER

*****Holua Campground (Haleakala NP).** 4 mi
BY FOOT, in the Haleakala Crater. SEASON: All yr; 2-day lmt. FACILITIES: 5
tent sites; toil. A limited water supply
is usually available behind the nearby
cabins. No tables; no wood fires. ACTIVITIES: Hiking. MISC.: A permit is required
for overnight stays and must be acquired
before entering the crater at Park Headquarters. NO PETS.

*****Paliku Campground (Haleakala NP).** 10
mi BY FOOT, in the Haleakala Crater.
SEASON: All yr; 2-day lmt. FACILITIES:
5 tent sites; toil. A ltd water supply
usually avail. behind nearby cabins.
ACTIVITIES: Hiking. MISC.: A permit
is required for overnight stays and
must be acquired (free) before entering
the crater at Park Headquarters. NO
PETS.

HANA

Waianapanapa Caves Park (SP). 4 mi
N of Hana on St Hwy 36; approximately
52 mi from Kahului Airport. SEASON:
All yr; 7-day lmt. FACILITIES: 12 tent
sites; tbls, flush toil, showers, cga,
drk wtr. ACTIVITIES: Shore fishing;
picnicking. MISC.: Legendary caves,
rocky coast, forests. Ancient trail and
heiau. RESERVATIONS REQUIRED.

KAHULUI

Hosmer's Grove (Haleakala NP). 26 mi
SE of Kahului Airport on St Hwys 37/377/
378; 1-3/10 mi below Park Headquarters.
[On the slope of Haleakala.] SEASON:
All yr; 3-night lmt per month. FACILITIES: Capacity 25 people; 5 tent sites;
room for about 3 self-contained RVs to
park on the pavement. Tbls, toil, cga,
drk wtr, f, small open picnic shelter.
ACTIVITIES: Hiking; picnicking. MISC.:
Elev 7000 ft. Register at campground.

Kaumahina Wayside (SP). 25 mi E of
Kahului on St Hwy 36 to Hana. Approximately 28 mi from the Kahului Airport.
SEASON: All yr; 7-day lmt. FACILITIES:
2 camping shelters; tbls, toil, cga,
drk wtr. ACTIVITIES: Hiking; picnicking. Swimming/fishing nearby. MISC.:
'7-3/5 acres. RESERVATIONS REQUIRED.
Rain forest area overlooking rugged
Hana coastline. Scenic overlook. Not
near any beach areas.

See page 7 for KEY TO ABBREVIATIONS.

KIPAHULU

Seven Sacred Pools (Oheo Pools Campground) (Haleakala NP). Jct St Hwys 36/31, in Haleakala NP. [An undeveloped roadside campground located at sea level in an open pasture ¼ mi S of Oheo Strem. SEASON: All yr; 3-day lmt. (3 nights per month.) FACILITIES: Capacity 50 people; 10 sites. No f or drk wtr. ACTIVITIES: Swimming; fishing. MISC.: A permit is not required. Near the ocean. Pets allowed on leash.

KIPUKA NENE

*Halape (Haleakala NP). 7 mi S of Kipuka Nene, BY FOOT. SEASON: All yr; 7-day lmt. FACILITIES: Undesignated sites (no trailers); toil, boil drk wtr. No tbls. ACTIVITIES: Hiking. MISC.: Free permit required. Near ocean.

WAIAKOA

Poli Poli Springs Recreation Area (SRA). 9 mi S of Waiakoa on St Hwy 37/377. [On the W slope of Haleakala Crater.] SEASON: All yr; 7-day lmt. FACILITIES: 2 sites (no trailers); tbls, flush toil, cga, no drk wtr (spring water). ACTIVITIES: Hiking; picnicking. MISC.: Wooded area; sweeping view. Elev 6200 ft. RESERVATIONS REQUIRED.

ISLAND OF MOLOKAI

KUALAPUU

Palaau Park (SP). 3 mi N of Kualapuu on St Hwy 47. SEASON: All yr; 7-day lmt. FACILITIES: 6 sites (no trailers); tbls, flush toil, cga, drk wtr. ACTIVITIES: Picnicking; hiking. MISC.: Forested mountain area with impressive overlook of Kalaupapa Settlement. Historic interest: phallic rocks. Arboretum of exotic and indigenous trees. Scenic overlook. RESERVATIONS REQUIRED.

ISLAND OF OAHU

AIEA

Keaiwa Heiau Recreation Area (SRA). 3 mi from St Hwy 72 (near Aiea) on Aiea Rd to end of rd. SEASON: All yr; 7-day lmt. FACILITIES: 12 sites (no trailers); tbls, flush toil, showers, cga, drk wtr, playground. ACTIVITIES: Hiking; picnicking. MISC.: Forested mountain area. Good hiking trails. Historic interest. Medicinal heiau and plant collection. Scenic overlooks. RESERVATION REQUIRED.

HALEIWA

Haleiwa Beach Park. In town of Haleiwa. SEASON: All yr; 14-day lmt. FACILITIES: Undesignated sites; pavilion, food, emergency phone. ACTIVITIES: Basketball and volleyball courts; baseball and softball fields; fair swimming, snorkeling and surfing (coral). MISC.: For free camping permit (must be gotten in advance), map, additional information: Hauula City Hall; Hauula Kai Shopping Center; 54-316 Kam Hwy; Kauula, Oahu, HI; 293-8551.

HAUULA

Hauula Beach Park (Municipal Park). ½ mi from Hauula on St Hwy 83. SEASON: MD-LD; 14-day lmt. FACILITIES: 30 sites; flush toil, showers, food, pavilion, emergency phone. Store/f nearby. ACTIVITIES: Fishing; swimming; horseback riding; fair snorkeling. (Swimming is poor; fishing is good). MISC.: Near ocean. NO PETS. For free camping permit (must be gotten in advance), map, additional information: Hauula City Hall; Hauula Kai Shopping Center; 54-316 Kam Hwy; Kauula, Oahu, HI; 293-8551.

KAAWA

Kaawa Beach Park (Municipal Park). In Kaawa on St Hwy 83. SEASON: MD-LD; 14-day lmt. FACILITIES: 4 sites (no trailers); tbls, flush toil, showers, emergency phone. ACTIVITIES: Good swimming and snorkeling; picnicking; fishing. MISC.: Near ocean; NO PETS. For free camping permit (must be gotten in advance), map, additional information: Hauula City Hall; Hauula Kai Shopping Center; 54-316 Kam Hwy; Kauula, Oahu, HI; 293-8551.

Kahana Bay Beach Park (Municipal Park). On St Hwy 38, near Kaawa. SEASON: MD-LD; 14-day lmt. FACILITIES: 26 sites; tbls, flush toil, showers, emergency phone. Store nearby. ACTIVITIES: Boating,l; picnicking; fishing; good swimming; fair beginner's surfing. MISC.: Near ocean. NO PETS. For free camping permit (must be gotten in advance), map, additional information: Hauula City Hall; Hauula Kai Shopping Center; 54-316 Kam Hwy; Kauula, Oahu, HI; 293-8551.

Swanzy Beach Park (Municipal Park). Near Kaawa on St Hwy 83. SEASON: MD-LD; 14-day lmt. FACILITIES: 30 sites; tbls, flush toil, showers, emergency phone, playground. Store/food nearby. ACTIVITIES: Basketball and volleyball courts; softball field; poor swimming (exposed coral); picnicking; fishing. MISC.: Near ocean; NO PETS. For free camping permit (must be gotten in advance), map, additional information:

See page 7 for KEY TO ABBREVIATIONS.

Hauula City Hall; Hauula Kai Shopping Center; 54-316 Kam Hwy; Kauula, Oahu, HI; 293-8551.

LAIE

Malaekahana (SP). 1 mi. N of Laie on St Hwy 83. SEASON: All yr; 7-day lmt. FACILITIES: 20 sites (no trailers); tbls, flush toil; cga; drk wtr. ACTIVITIES: Swimming; picnicking; fishing. Golf nearby. MISC.: Reservation required; NO PETS.

MAILI

Lualualei Beach Park (Municipal Park). 7 mi N of Maili on St Hwy 90. SEASON: MD-LD; 14-day lmt. FACILITIES: 10 sites (no trailers); tbls, flush toil; showers; emergency phone. Store nearby. ACTIVITIES: Poor swimming (coral); good fishing; picnicking. MISC.: Near ocean. NO PETS. For free camping permit (must be gotten in advance), map, additional information: Waianae City Hall; 85-555 Farr Hwy; Waianae, HI 96792; 696-6371.

MAKAHA

Keaau Beach Park (Municipal Park). 10 mi N of Makaha on St Hwy 90. SEASON: MD-LD; 14-day lmt. FACILITIES: 55 sites; tbls, flush toil, showers, emergency phone. Food nearby. ACTIVITIES: Good swimming; snorkeling; skin diving; picnicking; fishing. Good paipo and body surfing. MISC.: Near ocean; NO PETS. Free camping permit (must be gotten in advance), map, additional information: Waianae City Hall; 85-555 Farr Hwy; Waianae, HI 96792; 696-6371.

NANAKULI

Kahe Point Beach Park (Municipal Park). On St Hwy 90, near Nanakuli. SEASON: 2/1-12/31; 14-day lmt. FACILITIES: 16 sites; tbls, flush toil, showers, drk wtr, emergency phone. ACTIVITIES: Good swimming and surfing nearby. Good snorkeling and fishing. Good scuba diving. Picnicking. MISC.: Tbls, flush toil, showers, drk wtr. MISC.: Free camping permit (must be gotten in advance), map, additional information: Ewa City Hall; 91-923 Ft. Weaver Road; Ewa Beach, HI 96706; 689-7914. NO PETS.

Nanakuli Beach Park (Municipal Park). On St Hwy 90, in town of Nanakuli. SEASON: 2/1-12/31; 14-day lmt. FACILITIES: 26 sites; tbls, flush toil, showers, playground, drk wtr. ACTIVITIES: Good swimming, snorkeling, fishing, and surfing, but beware of exposed reefs. Fair scuba diving. Picnicking. MISC.: Lifeguard; NO PETS. Emergency phone at Waianae and Honolulu ends and center of park. Store/food nearby. Free camping permit (must be gotten in advance), map, additional information: Waianae

City Hall; 85-555 Farr Hwy; Waianae, HI 96792; 696-6371.

PUNALUU

Punaluu Beach Park (Municipal Park). 2 mi S of Punaluu on St Hwy 83. SEASON: MD-LD; 14-day lmt. FACILITIES: 10 sites; tbls, flush toil, showers, drk wtr. Store/food nearby. ACTIVITIES: Good swimming, snorkeling, and fishing. Picnicking. MISC.: Near ocean; NO PETS. For free camping permit (must be gotten in advance), map, additional information: Hauula City Hall; Hauula Kai Shopping Center; 54-316 Kam Hwy; Kauula, Oahu, HI; 293-8551.

WAIALUA

Mokuleia Beach Park (Municipal Park). On St Hwy 99, near Dillingham Air Force Base. SEASON: MD-LD; 14-day lmt. FACILITIES: 30 sites; tbls, flush toil, showers, drk wtr. Emergency phone. ACTIVITIES: Good snorkeling, skin diving, and fishing; poor swimming (coral); fair surfing nearby, but beware of dangerous reefs and currents. MISC.: Near ocean; NO PETS. For free camping permit (must be gotten in advance), map, additional information: Waianae City Hall; 85-555 Farr Hwy; Waianae, HI 96792; 696-6371.

WAIMANOLO

Bellows Beach Park (Municipal Park). 6 mi from jct of St Hwy 61/72. SEASON: Weekends only (from Friday noon to Sunday midnight), and all national holidays. FACILITIES: 30 sites; tbls, flush toil, showers, drk wtr. Store nearby. ACTIVITIES: Fair beginners' surfing; good body surfing; paipo air mattress surfing. Good swimming; boating,l. Fishing; picnicking. MISC.: Near ocean; NO PETS; lifeguard. For free camping permit (must be gotten in advance), map, and additional information: Kailua City Hall; 302 Kuulei Rd; Kailua, Oahu, HI 96734; 261-8575.

Kaiona Beach Park (Municipal Park). S of Waimanalo on St Hwy 72. SEASON: MD-LD; 14-day lmt. FACILITIES: 15 sites (no trailers); tbls, flush toil, showers, drk wtr, playground, emergency phone. Store/food nearby. ACTIVITIES: Fair swimming; snorkeling; picnicking; fishing; boating,l. MISC.: Near ocean; NO PETS; for free camping permit (must be gotten in advance), map, additional information: Kailua City Hall; 302 Kuulei Rd; Kailua, Oahu, HI 96734; 261-8575.

Makapuu Beach Park (Municipal Park). On St Hwy 72, in town of Waimanalo. SEASON: 6/1-8/31; 14-day lmt. FACILITIES: 12 sites; tbls, flush toil, showers, drk wtr, emergency phone. ACTIVITIES: Excellent body surfing and paipo surfing, but swells of 4 ft plus may bring dan-

See page 7 for KEY TO ABBREVIATIONS.

gerous currents for swimmers. No boards allowed at the body surfing beach. Site of the annual Makapuu Body Surfing Championship. Boating,I. **MISC.:** Near ocean; NO PETS; lifeguard. For free camping permit (must be gotten in advance), map, and additional information: Kailua City Hall; 302 Kuulei Rd; Kailua, Oahu, HI 96734; 261-8575.

Waimanalo Beach (Municipal Park). SEASON: MD-LD; 14-day lmt. **FACILITIES:** 23 sites; tbls, flush toil, showers, drk wtr. Store/food nearby. **ACTIVITIES:** Basketball and volleyball courts; baseball and softball fields. Excellent swimming, sailing and snorkeling. Boating,I. **MISC.:** Free camping permit: Kailua City Hall; 302 Kuulei Rd; Kailua, Oahu. HI.

GENERAL STATE INFORMATION

Miscellaneous

Right Turns on Red: Permitted after full stop, unless otherwise posted.

STATE CAPITOL: Boise
STATE NICKNAME: Gem State
STATE MOTTO: "Exist Forever"
STATE BIRD: Mountain Bluebird
STATE FLOWER: Syringa
STATE TREE: White Pine

State Parks

Campsites are $3.00-4.00/night in season; $2.00 off-season; $\frac{1}{2}$ price for Idaho Resident Senior Citizens (65 or older) and Disabled Citizens on Social Security. Idaho Resident Camping Coupon: $7.50 for $10.00 worth of camping; not accepted toward $\frac{1}{2}$-price Senior Citizen/Disabled rates. Pets are welcome; not permitted to run loose at any time. Further information: Idaho Parks and Recreation Department; 2177 Warm Springs; Boise, Idaho 83720; 384-2154.

Rest Areas

Overnight stops are not permitted in Idaho's rest areas.

INFORMATION SOURCES

Maps

An up-to-date map of the **State of Idaho**, showing all principal roads, points of interest, sports areas, parks, airports, mileage, etc., in full color, is available from **Forsyth Travel Library** (see order form in Appendix B).

Gold Mining and Prospecting

Idaho Bureau of Mines and Geology; University of Idaho; Moscow, Idaho 83844.

State Information

Idaho Department of Fish and Game; 600 South Walnut Street; PO Box 25; Boise, ID 83707.
Idaho Division of Highways; 3311 West State Street; Boise, ID 83707.
Idaho Historical Society; 610 North Julia Davis Drive; Boise, ID 83706.
Idaho Parks & Recreation Department; 2177 Warm Springs; Boise, ID 83720.
Idaho State Library; 325 West State Street; Boise, ID 83720.
Division of Tourism & Industrial Development; Room 108; Statehouse; Boise, ID 83720.

City Information

Association of Idaho Cities; 3314 Grace Street; Boise, ID 83703.

See page 7 for KEY TO ABBREVIATIONS.

IDAHO

National Forests

Bitterroot NF; Hamilton, MT 59840.
Boise NF; 1075 Park Blvd.; Boise, ID 83706.
Caribou NF; 427 North Sixth Avenue; PO Box 4189; Pocatello, ID 83201.
Challis NF; Forest Service Building; PO Box 247; Challis, ID 83226.
Clearwater NF; Route 3; Ahsahka Road; Orofino, ID 83544.
Coeur d'Alene NF; Idaho Panhandle NFs; 218 N. 23rd; Coeur d'Alene, ID 83814.
Kaniksu NF; Idaho Panhandle NFs; 218 N. 23rd; Coeur d'Alene, ID 83814.
Nezperce NF; 319 E. Main; Grangeville, ID 83530.
Payette NF; Forest Service Building; PO Box 1026; McCall, ID 83638.
Salmon NF; Forest Service Building; PO Box 729; Salmon, ID 83467.
Sawtooth NF; 1525 Addison Avenue East; Twin Falls, ID 83301.
St. Joe NF; Idaho Panhandle NFs; 218 N. 23rd; Coeur d'Alene, ID 83814.
Targhee NF; 420 North Bridge Street; St. Anthony, ID 83445.

Miscellaneous

Idaho Bureau of Land Management; Federal Building, Room 398; 550 West Fort Street; PO Box 042; Boise, ID 83724.
Idaho Bureau of Reclamation; 550 West Fort Street; Boise, ID 83724.
Idaho Department of Lands; Room 121, Statehouse; Boise, ID 83720.
Craters of the Moon National Monument; Box 29; Arco, ID 83213.

BACKCOUNTRY AND WILDERNESS CAMPING

BIGHORN CRAGS AREA; Idaho Primitive Area; Salmon NF

A remote section of the Idaho Primitive Area. Hiking/camping in this area requires detailed planning and/or a guide. Primitive campsites with toilet facilities are located at: Crags Camp (main trailhead); Big Clear Lake, Birdbill Lake, Heart Lake, Terrace Lake, Welcome Lake. Big-game hunting (special permit required for hunting goat or sheep); trout fishing. Be prepared for rain and cold weather. Further information and map: Superintendent; Salmon NF; Forest Service Building; PO Box 729; Salmon, ID 83467.

CARIBOU NF BACKCOUNTRY CAMPING

Due to a change in Forest boundaries, the Idaho portion of the old Cache NF has been incorporated into the Caribou NF. There are no specified backcountry/wilderness camping areas there. However, camping in any unimproved campsite anywhere within the Forest is regulated only by a 14-day limit, hauling out all garbage, and not leaving campfires unattended. If the mode of transportation into any of the Forest areas is other than by foot or horseback, off-road vehicle regulations must be observed. Further information: Superintendent; Caribou NF; 427 North Sixth Avenue; PO Box 4189; Pocatello, ID 83201.

HELLS CANYON - SEVEN DEVILS SCENIC AREA

This 130,000-acre area is located within three National Forests: Nezperce NF (Idaho), Payette NF (Idaho), and Wallowa-Whitman NF (Oregon). Much of this area is accessible only by trail or river. Primitive campsites area available throughout the area. Elevations range from 1,335 feet to 9,393 feet. Trout fishing in 40 mountain lakes. Horseback riding/camping permitted. Big-game hunting. The white sturgeon is protected by law and must be thrown back unharmed if accidentally caught. Further information: Superintendent; Nezperce NF; 319 East Main; Grangeville, ID 83530. Superintendent; Payette NF; Forest Service Building; PO Box 1026; McCall, ID 83638.

IDAHO PRIMITIVE AREA

Located in the geographical center of Idaho (partially within the Payette NF), the Idaho Primitive Area covers 1¼ million acres. In-season big-game hunting: mule deer, whitetail deer, moose, elk, mountain goat, mountain sheep, black bear. Long trout and Chinook salmon fishing season. More than 1600 miles of trails. Further information: Superintendent; Intermountain Region; US Forest Service; 324 - 25th Street; Ogden, Utah 84401.

MALLARD-LARKINS PIONEER AREA

24 mi SE of Avery; accessible by secondary roads from US 10/12 and Alternate 95. 30,500 acres; elevation ranges from 2,600 to more than 7,000 feet (Black Mountain).

No roads and few trails. Excellent hiking, camping, fishing, and hunting. Groves of ancient cedars. Further information: District Ranger; Canyon Ranger District; Clearwater NF; Orofino, ID 83544. District Ranger; Red Ives Ranger District; St. Joe NF; Avery, ID 83802.

MIDDLE FORK OF THE SALMON RIVER

Designated as part of the National Wild and Scenic River System, it flows for 106 miles through the Idaho Primitive Area. Excellent trout and Chinook salmon fishing. Big-game hunting (bighorn sheep, elk, moose, mountain goat, whitetail and mule deer. July, August, and September are the best months for float trips. Caution: rattlesnake country. Free campsites are available all along the river. A primitive trail parallels the river a great deal of the way. Further information/map: Superintendent; Challis NF; Forest Service Building; PO Box 247; Challis, ID 83226. ALSO: Intermountain Region, Forest Service; 324 – 25th Street; Ogden, UT 84401 (MIDDLE FORK OF THE SALMON; free guide which includes a map showing river campsites and campgrounds accessible by car. Free THE SALMON, RIVER OF NO RETURN, which includes a "Mileage Log".). BUREAU OF LAND MANAGEMENT; Federal Building, Room 398; 550 West Fort St.; PO Box 042; Boise, ID 83724 (LOWER SALMON RIVER GUIDE, free). IDAHO DEPT. OF FISH AND GAME; 600 South Walnut Street; Boise, ID 83707 (special regulations for fishing in this area).

ST. JOE WILD AND SCENIC RIVER; St. Joe NF

Contains more than 120 miles of free-flowing river, offering a challenge to canoers, kayakers, and rafters. All types of water can be encountered, from raging whitewater suitable only for teams of expert kayakers, to placid meanderings for beginning canoeists. Ideal wilderness camping area. Primitive designated campsites are by Meadow Creek and near Gospel Hill. Horseback riding; hiking; camping; fishing; hunting. In this area you can see one of Idaho's largest bands of mountain goats. Elevations range from 2600 to more than 7000 feet. Further information: Superintendent; St. Joe NF; Idaho Panhandle NFs; 218 N. 23rd; Coeur d'Alene, ID 83814.

SAWTOOTH NATIONAL RECREATION AREA: Sawtooth NF

Headquarters are at the North Fork of the Wood River, 7 mi N of Ketchum, on US 93. ACTIVITIES: Hunting at lower elevations; fishing; wilderness camping; hiking; horseback riding; mountain climbing. Approximately 230,000 acres. No campfire permit is necessary at this time. Take insect repellent; a bug-proof tent is advisable for overnight outings. A permit is required for travel from 11/15-5/15; avalanches are common in the winter. Further information: Superintendent; Sawtooth NF; 1525 Addison Avenue East; Twin Falls, ID 83301 (Sawtooth NRA/Wilderness Map/Brochure). Superintendent; Sawtooth NRA; Ketchum Office (Hdqtrs); Ketchum; ID 83340 (White Cloud-Boulder Mountains Map/Brochure).

SAWTOOTH WILDERNESS; Sawtooth NRA; Sawtooth NF

Located within the Sawtooth NRA, it encompasses 216,000 acres of wilderness area. More than 200 alpine lakes (trout fishing). 300 miles of trails; also several designated "Trailless Areas". At the major entrances you will find a registration box with maps, litterbags, and rules for wilderness travel. Please register. Peak use is 7/15 through August. A FREE use permit is required for: groups of 10-20 persons; all stock use; winter travel between 11/15 and 5/15. This is for your own protection. Hunting and trout fishing. Mountain climbing. No rattlesnakes, poison ivy, or poison oak in the Wilderness. Take insect repellent; a bug-proof tent is advisable for overnight outings. Further information: Superintendent; Sawtooth NF; 1525 Addison Avenue East; Twin Falls, ID 83301.

FREE CAMPGROUNDS

ALBION

Brackenbury (Sawtooth NF). 5½ mi SE of Albion on St Hwy 77; 9-3/5 mi W on FS 70549. SEASON: 7/10-9/30; 14-day lmt. FACILITIES: 9 sites (tr -16); tbls, toil, cga, f, piped drk wtr. ACTIVITIES: Hiking; picnicking; fishing. Horseback riding (1 mi). MISC.: Elev 8200 ft; 6 acres; pets; lake; scenic.

Lake Cleveland (Sawtooth NF). 5½ mi SE of Albion on St Hwy 77; 10 mi W on FS 70549. SEASON: 7/10-9/30; 14-day lmt. FACILITIES: 9 sites (tr -16); tbls, toil, cga, f, piped drk wtr. ACTIVITIES: Hiking, picnicking; fishing. Horseback riding (1 mi). MISC.: Elev 9000 ft; 2 acres; pets; scenic. Lake Cleveland.

See page 7 for KEY TO ABBREVIATIONS.

Thompson Flat (Sawtooth NF). 5½ mi
SE of Albion on St Hwy 77; 8 mi W on
FS 70549. SEASON: 6/16-10/10; 14-day
lmt. FACILITIES: 16 sites (tr -22);
tbls, toil, cga, f, piped drk wtr.
ACTIVITIES: Picnicking. Horseback rid-
ing (1 mi). Fishing (2 mi). MISC.:
Elev 8000 ft; 15 acres; pets; scenic.

ALPINE

Hoffman (Caribou NF). 5 mi W of Alpine on US 89; 6 mi NW on FS 20058.
SEASON: 6/1-9/15; 16-day lmt. FACIL-
ITIES: 20 sites (tr -22); tbls, toil,
cga, f. Piped drk wtr. ACTIVITIES:
Picnicking. Swimming/fishing/horse-
back riding (1 mi). Boating, ld (2
mi). MISC.: Elev 5500 ft; 6 acres;
pets; lake.

McCoy Creek (Caribou NF). 5 mi S of
Alpine on US 89; 7 mi NW on FS 20058.
SEASON: 6/1-9/15; 16-day lmt. FACIL-
ITIES: 20 sites (tr -32); tbls, toil,
cga, f, piped drk wtr. ACTIVITIES:
Picnicking; swimming; fishing; water
skiing; boating, ld. Horseback riding
(1 mi). MISC.: Elev 5500 ft; lake; pets.

ALPINE

Hoffman (Caribou NF). 5 mi W of
Alpine on US 89; 6 mi NW on FS 20058.
SEASON: 6/1-9/15. FACILITIES: 19 sites
sites (tr -16); tbls, toil, cga, f.
ACTIVITIES: Swimming; picnicking; fish-
ing; horseback riding; boating, ld.
MISC.: 6 acres; pets on leash.

McCoy Creek (Caribou NF). 5 mi S of
Alpine on US 89; 7 mi NW on FS 20058.
SEASON: 6/1-9/15. FACILITIES: 19 sites
sites (tr -32); tbls, toil, cga, f.
ACTIVITIES: Swimming, picnicking;
fishing; horseback riding; boating, ld.
MISC.: 4 acres; pets on leash.

ASHTON

Cave Falls (Targhee NF). 5 mi N of
Ashton on St Hwy 47; 7 mi E on Co Hwy
36; 14 mi E on FS 36. SEASON: 6/1-9/30.
FACILITIES: 23 sites (tr-16); f. ACTIVI-
TIES: Fishing; swimming; horseback
riding. MISC.: 16 acres.

Grandview (Targhee NF). 15 mi E of
Ashton on St Hwy 47. SEASON: 6/1-9/30.
FACILITIES: 5 sites (tr -22); tbls, toil,
cga; f; no drk wtr. ACTIVITIES: Horse-
back riding; picnicking; fishing (1 mi).
MISC.: Elev 6200 ft; 6 acres; 47 mi to
W. Yellowstone; pets on leash.

Pole Bridge (Targhee NF). 12 mi NE of
Ashton on US 47; 3-1/2 mi N on Co Hwy
294; 2-1/2 mi E on FS 80156; 4-1/2 mi
N on FS 80150. SEASON: 6/30-10/31.
FACILITIES: 10 sites (tr -22); tbls, toil,
cga; f; fishing; picnic; well drk wtr.
ACTIVITIES: Fishing; picnicking.

West End (Targhee NF). 18 mi N of Ashton on US 191; 15 mi NW on FS 167. SEA-
SON: 5/27-9/30. FACILITIES: 19 sites (tr
-32); tbls, toil, cga, f, piped drk wtr.
ACTIVITIES: Swimming; boating, ld;
picnicking; fishing; waterskiing; berry-
picking. Horseback riding (1 mi). MISC.:
Elev 6200 ft; 15 acres; lake; pets.

ATHOL

Highway Rest Area. 3 mi N of Athol on
St Hwy 95 (gravel access rds). SEASON:
All yr; 16-hr lmt. FACILITIES: Spaces
for self-contained RVs; tbls, toil, dump.
ACTIVITIES: Picnicking. MISC.: Pets.

ATLANTA

Deer Park (Boise NF). 21 mi W of Atlanta on FS. SEASON: 6/15-10/15; 14-
day lmt. FACILITIES: 3 sites (no tr);
tbls, toil, cga, f. ACTIVITIES: Picnicking; fishing. Horseback riding (1
mi). MISC.: Elev 4500 ft; 1 acre; river; pets on leash.

Idaho Outdoor Association (Boise NF).
26 mi W of Atlanta on FS 10268.
SEASON: 6/15-9/30; 14-day lmt. FACILI-
TIES: 6 sites (tr -16); tbls, toil, cga,
f. ACTIVITIES: Picnicking; fishing.
Horseback riding (1 mi). MISC.: Elev
3800 ft; 3 acres; river; pets on leash.

Neinmeyer (Boise NF). 27 mi W of Atlanta on FS 10268. SEASON: 6/15-9/30;
14-day lmt. FACILITIES: 8 sites (tr
-22); tbls, toil, cga, f. ACTIVITIES:
picnicking; fishing. Horseback riding
(1 mi). MISC.: Elev 3800; 2 acres;
pets on leash. Adjacent to middle fork
of Boise River.

Power Plant (Boise NF). 2-1/2 mi NE
of Atlanta on FS 10268. SEASON: 6/15-
9/30; 14-day lmt. FACILITIES: 25 sites
(tr -22); piped drk wtr, tbls, toil,
cga, f. ACTIVITIES: Horseback riding
(1 mi); rental (2 mi). MISC.: Hiking; picnicking; fishing. MISC.: Elev 5800 ft;
18 acres; pets; river. Store/gas/food/
ice (2 mi). Gateway to Sawtooth Wilderness Area.

Queens River (Boise NF). 6 mi W of
Atlanta on FS 10268. SEASON: 6/15-9/30;
14-day lmt. FACILITIES: 4 sites (no
trailers); tbls, toil, cga, f, no drk
wtr. ACTIVITIES: Horseback riding (1
mi). Picnicking; fishing. MISC.: Elev
4000 ft; 2 acres; river; pets on leash.

Riverside (Boise NF). 3/5 mi NW of Atlanta on FS 10206. SEASON: 6/5-9/30;
14-day lmt. FACILITIES: 7 sites (tr
-22); tbls, toil, cga, f, no drk wtr.
ACTIVITIES: Fishing; picnicking.
Horseback riding/rental (1 mi). MISC.:
Elev 5600 ft; 4 acres. Store/gas/food/
ice (1 mi). River. Pets. Within historical Atlanta mining area.

AVERY

Beaver Creek (Idaho Panhandle NF). 3-4/5 mi E of Avery on FS 218. SEASON: 6/1-11/30; 14-day lmt. FACILITIES: 3 sites (tr -22); tbls, toil, cga, f. No drk wtr. ACTIVITIES: Fishing, picnicking. Swimming (1 mi). MISC.: Elev 3600 ft; 1 acre; pets; stream.

Conrad Crossing (Idaho Panhandle NF). 29 mi E of Avery on FS 218. SEASON: 6/1-10/30; 14-day lmt. FACILITIES: 3 sites (tr -16); tbls, toil, cga; well drk wtr. ACTIVITIES: Fishing, picnicking. Swimming (1 mi). MISC.: Elev 3600 ft; 5 acres; River. Pets on leash. Historic Montana trail.

Fly Flat (Idaho Panhandle NF[St. Joe NF]). 35 mi E of Avery on FS 218. SEASON: 6/1-10/30; 14-day lmt. FACILITIES: 14 sites (tr -16); tbls, toil, cga, f. No drk wtr. ACTIVITIES: Picnicking, fishing. Swimming (1 mi). MISC.: Elev 3500 ft; 6 acres; Pets on leash. River. 5 mi N of Red Ives Ranger Station.

Heller Creek (Idaho Panhandle NF). 40 mi E of Avery on FS 218; 13-7/10 mi E on FS 320. SEASON: 6/15-9/30; 14-day lmt. FACILITIES: 4 sites (tr -22); tbls, toil, cga. No drk wtr. ACTIVITIES: Picnicking, fishing. MISC.: Elev 4700 ft; 4 acres; stream. Pets on leash. Memorial.

Mammouth Springs (Idaho Panhandle NF [St. Joe NF]). 22 mi E of Avery on FS 218; 13-7/10 mi SW on FS 509 (Bluff Creek Rd); 2-1/2 mi S on FS 201 (Timber Creek Rd). SEASON: 6/15-10/1; 14-day lmt. FACILITIES: 6 sites (tr -22); tbls, toil, cga. Piped drk wtr. ACTIVITIES: Swimming/fishing (2 mi). Picnicking, berry-picking. MISC.: Elev 5700 ft; 5 acres; scenic. 1 mi Dismal Lake. Pets on leash.

Slate Creek. 20-9/10 mi N of Avery on Co Hwy 456; 5½ mi W on FS 225; 3/5 mi N on FS 745. SEASON: 6/15-11/15. FACILITIES: 5 sites (tr -22); toil, cga, f. MISC.: Elev 3300 ft. Pets on leash.

Spruce Tree (Idaho Panhandle NF [St. Joe NF]). 43 mi E of Avery on FS 218. SEASON: 6/1-10/15; 14-day lmt. FACILITIES: 7 sites (tr -32); tbls, toil, cga, f, well drk wtr. ACTIVITIES: Hiking; picnicking; fishing; swimming (1 mi). MISC.: Elev 3800 ft; 4 acres; hiking to virgin backcountry. 2 mi S of Red of Red Ives Ranger Station. Pets on leash.

Squaw Creek (Idaho Panhandle NF). 4-4/5 mi N of Avery on Co Hwy 456. SEASON: 5/30-11/30. FACILITIES: 9 sites (tr -22); tbls, toil, cga, f. No drk wtr. Store/food/gas (5 mi). ACTIVITIES: Picnicking; fishing. MISC.: Elev 2600 ft; 2 acres. Stream. North Fork St. Joe River. Pets on leash.

Tin Can Flat (Idaho Panhandle NF [St Joe NF]). 11 mi E of Avery on FS 218. SEASON: 6/1-10/30; 14-day lmt. FACILITIES: 8 sites (tr -22); tbls, toil, cga, f, piped drk wtr. ACTIVITIES: Picnicking; fishing. MISC.: Elev 2600 ft; 4 acres; river; pets on leash.

Turner Flat (Idaho Panhandle NF). 7-9/10 mi E of Avery on FS 218 (scenic drive up the shadowy St Joe River). SEASON: 6/1-10/30; 14-day lmt. FACILITIES: 9 sites (tr -22); tbls, toil, cga, f, piped drk wtr. ACTIVITIES: Hiking, nature trails; picnicking; fishing. MISC.: Elev 2600 ft; 5 acres. River. Permit reqd for group picnics. Pets.

BANKS

Big Eddy (Boise NF). 11 mi N of Banks on St Hwy 55. SEASON: 5/1-10/15, 14-day lmt. FACILITIES: 3 sites (tr -32); tbls, toil, cga, f. ACTIVITIES: Picnicking; fishing. MISC.: Elev 4400; 2 acres; River. Pets permitted if kept on leash.

BLISS

Roadside Rest (SRA). 10 mi S of Bliss on US 20-30 & 26. SEASON: All yr, 1-day lmt. FACILITIES: 15 sites; toil; no tents.

Roadside Rest. W bound I-80; 5 mi W, access rds good. SEASON: All yr, 16-hr lmt. FACILITIES: 10 sites; toil; dump; some pull-thru; phone. MISC.: Pets permitted if kept on leash.

BOISE

Badger Creek (Boise NF). 16 mi E of Boise on St Hwy 21; 26 mi E on FS 10168 SEASON: 6/1-9/5, 14-day lmt. FACILITIES: 5 sites (no tr); tbls, toil, cga, f; no drk wtr. ACTIVITIES: Picnicking; fishing; horses (1 mi). MISC.: Elev 3400 ft; 1 acre; Badger Creek. On the middle fork of the Boise River. Pets.

Bald Mountain (Boise NF). 29 mi NE of Boise on St Hwy 21; 13 mi E on FS 10304. SEASON: 7/15-9/15; 14-day lmt. FACILITIES: 4 sites (tr -16); tbls, toil, cga, f; no drk wtr. ACTIVITIES: Picnicking; horseback riding (1 mi). MISC.: Elev 7400 ft; 2 acres. Stream. High alpine country, within 2 mi of Thorn Creek, Butte Lookout (visitors welcome). Pets permitted if kept on a leash.

Cottonwood (Boise NF). 16 mi E of Boise on St Hwy 21; 18 mi E on FS 10168. SEASON: 6/1-9/5, 14-day lmt. FACILITIES: 3 sites (no trailers); tbls, toil, cga, f. ACTIVITIES: Boating/waterski/horseback riding (1 mi); picnicking; fishing.

See page 7 for KEY TO ABBREVIATIONS.

MISC.: Elev 3300 ft; 2 acres. Within 1 mi of the Cottonwood Ranger Station. Pets permitted if kept on a leash.

Smiths Ferry (Boise Cascade Corp.). 60 mi N of Boise on St Hwy 15. (Mtnous terrain). SEASON: 5/1–10/31; 14-day lmt. FACILITIES: 10 sites; tbls, toil, cga, f, drk wtr. Store/bottled gas (nearby) ACTIVITIES: Picnicking; snowmobiling; fishing/swimming (nearby). MISC.: 4 acres; Payette River nearby. Pets permitted on leash.

State Roadside Rest. 10 mi E of Boise on I-80 at 62 Mile Post (paved access roads). SEASON: All yr; 16-hr lmt. FACILITIES: Dump. MISC.: Pets permitted if kept on leash.

Tipton Flat (Boise NF). 16 mi E of Boise on St Hwy 21; 25 mi E on FS 10168; 15 mi SE on FS 10213. SEASON: 6/15–9/5; 14-day lmt. FACILITIES: 7 sites (tr –22); tbls, toil, cga, f; no drk wtr. ACTIVITIES: Picnicking; fishing. Horseback riding (1 mi). MISC.: Elev 4900 ft; 4 acres; stream; pets; out of the way and secluded.

Troutdale (Boise NF). 16 mi E of Boise on St Hwy 68; 16 mi NE on FS 10168. SEASON: 6/1–9/10; 14-day lmt. FACILITIES: 7 sites (tr –22); tbls, toil cga, f; no drk wtr. ACTIVITIES: Picnicking; fishing. Horseback riding (1 mi). MISC.: Elev 3600 ft; 2 acres. On middle fork of Boise River. Pets allowed on leash.

Willow Creek (Boise NF). 16 mi E of Boise on St Hwy 21; 16 mi E on FS 10168. SEASON: 6/1–6/9; 14-day lmt. FACILITIES: 10 sites (tr –16); tbls, toil, cga, well drk wtr. ACTIVITIES: Picnicking; fishing. Horseback riding (1 mi). MISC.: Elev 3200 ft; 7 acres. Adjacent to the middle fork of Boise River Inlet to Arrowrock Reservoir. Pets permitted if kept on leash.

BONNERS FERRY

Meadow Creek (Idaho Panhandle NF [Kaniksu NF]). 5 mi E of Bonners Ferry on US 2; 10 mi N on FS 229; 26 mi N on I-95; 12 mi S on FS 211 (on Moyie River). SEASON: 5/15–10/1; 14-day lmt. FACILITIES: 23 sites (tr –32); tbls, toil, cga, f, well drk wtr. ACTIVITIES: Berry-picking (huckleberries); hiking; picnicking; fishing. MISC.: Elev 2400; 9 acres; river. Pets. Accessible from North & South.

Moyle River Roadside Park. 8 mi E of Bonners Ferry on St Hwy 2 (paved access roads). SEASON: All yr; 16-hr lmt. FACILITIES: Toil. MISC.: Scenic overview. Pets permitted if kept on leash.

Smith Lake (Idaho Panhandle NF [Kaniks NF]). 5 mi N of Bonners Ferry on US 95; 1–1/5 mi E on FS 1005. FACILITIES: 7 sites (tr –16); tbls, toil, cga, f, well drk wtr. Store/food/gas/ice (3 mi). SEASON: 5/15–10/1; 14-day lmt. ACTIVITIES: Picnicking; fishing; boat,l. MISC.: Elev 2300 ft; 6 acres; pets permitted if kept on leash. On Smith Lake.

BRUNEAU

Cove Recreation Area (BLM). 2 mi W of Bruneau on St Hwy 51; 5 mi N on Co Rd. SEASON: 4/15–10/31; 14-day lmt. FACILITIES: 26 sites (tr –25); tbls, toil, cga, f. Ice nearby. ACTIVITIES: Boating,l; picnicking; fishing; swimming; water skiing; hiking. MISC.: Elev 3000 ft; 40 acres; pets permitted if kept on leash.

CALDER

Big Creek (Idaho Panhandle NF [St Joe NF]). 6 mi E of Calder on Co Hwy 347; 3 mi NW on FS 537. SEASON: 5/15–10/31; 14-day lmt. FACILITIES: 6 sites (tr –16); tbls, toil, cga, f, no drk wtr. ACTIVITIES: Hiking; picnicking; fishing. MISC.: Elev 2400; 3 acres; stream; pets.

Donkey Creek (Idaho Panhandle NF). 11 mi E of Calder on Co Hwy FH 50; 8 mi S on FS 321. SEASON: 6/1–11/15; 7-day lmt. FACILITIES: 3 sites (tr –22); tbls, toil, cga, f. ACTIVITIES: Berry picking; picnicking; fishing. MISC.: Elev 2800 ft; 2 acres; historic site; pets.

Lower Big Creek (Idaho Panhandle NF). 4–3/5 mi E on Co Hwy 347; 1–3/5 mi NW on Co Hwy 537. SEASON: 6/1–10/15; 14-day lmt. FACILITIES: 5 sites (tr –22); tbls, toil, cga, f. ACTIVITIES: Picnicking; fishing. MISC.: Elev 2300; 3 acres; pets. Local name is CCC Camp.

CAMBRIDGE

Brownlee (Payette NF). 17–1/10 mi NW of Cambridge on St Hwy 71; 1 mi E on FS 50055. SEASON: 6/1–10/31; 16-day lmt. FACILITIES: 11 sites (tr –16); tbls, toil, cga. ACTIVITIES: Horseback riding; picnicking; fishing. MISC.: Elev 4400; 4 acres; pets permitted if kept on leash. 9 mi NW to Brownlee Dam. Piped drk wtr.

CAREY

Copper Creek (Sawtooth NF). 26 mi N of Carey on Co Hwy. SEASON: 6/1–10/15. FACILITIES: 7 sites (tr –22); tbls, toil, cga, f, no drk wtr. ACTIVITIES: Horseback riding; picnicking; fishing; rockhounding. MISC.: Elev 6400 ft; 6 acres;

stream nearby. Agates 2 mi W of CG; pets permitted if kept on leash.

Little Wood River Reservoir (Bur. of Rec.). 10 mi W and N of Carey on Co Hwy. SEASON: All yr. FACILITIES: 16 sites; tbls, toil, cga. ACTIVITIES: Swimming; picnicking; fishing; boating,l. MISC.: 1206 acres. Pets permitted if kept on leash.

CASCADE

Pen Basin (Boise NF). 1 mi N of Cascade on St Hwy 55; 24 mi NE on FS FH 22; 12½ mi SE on FS 10579. SEASON: 6/15-8/31; 14-day lmt. FACILITIES: 6 sites (tr -22); tbls, toil, cga, f. ACTIVITIES: Picnicking; horseback riding; fishing. MISC.: Elev 6700 ft; 9 acres; stream; pets.

Penny Springs (Boise NF). 1 mi N of Cascade on St Hwy 55; 23½ mi NE on FS FH 22; 4½ mi N on FS 10401. SEASON: 6/1-9/3; 14-day lmt. FACILITIES: 4 sites (tr -16); tbls, toil, cga, no drk wtr. ACTIVITIES: Picnicking. Fishing (1 mi). MISC.: Elev 5200; 4 acres. Pets allowed if kept on leash.

Smith's Ferry (Boise Cascade Corp.). 18 mi S of Cascade on St Hwy 15. SEASON: 5/1-10/31; 14-day lmt. FACILITIES: 10 sites; tbls, toil, cga, f, water hookup. Store/food/btld gas/ice (nearby). ACTIVITIES: Picnicking. Swimming/fishing (nearby). MISC.: River nearby; pets okay; mountainous terrain.

Summit Lake (Boise NF). 1 mi N of Cascade on St Hwy 15; 24 mi NE on FS FH 22; 7 mi SE on FS 10579. SEASON: 6/20-9/31; 14-day lmt. FACILITIES: 3 sites (tr -16); tbls, toil, cga, f, no drk wtr. Store/food/gas (5 mi). ACTIVITIES: Picnicking. Fishing (1 mi). Boating,l/water skiing (5 mi). Swimming (1 mi). MISC.: Elev 7200 ft; 1 acre. Pets.

CHALLIS

Bayhorse Lake (Challis NF). 8 mi S of Challis on US 93; 9 mi N on FS 40051. SEASON: 7/1-9/10. FACILITIES: 7 sites (tr -32); tbls, toil, cga, f, well drk wtr. ACTIVITIES: Horseback riding; picnicking; fishing; rockhounding. MISC.: Elev 8600 ft; 12 acres. Trailers not advised; steep-narrow road. Pets allowed.

East Fork Salmon River (BLM). 18 mi S of Challis on US 93. SEASON: 5/15-10/31; 14-day lmt. FACILITIES: 15 sites (tr -25); water hookup; tbls, toil, cga, f, drk wtr. ACTIVITIES: Swimming; picnicking; fishing; hunting; hiking; rockhounding. MISC.: Elev 5376; 6 acres. Pets permitted if kept on leash.

Mill Creek (Challis NF). 4½ mi W of Challis on Co Hwy 70; 11 mi W on FS 70 (narrow road). SEASON: 6/15-9/30. FACILITIES: 15 sites (tr -16); tbls, toil, cga, f, piped drk wtr. ACTIVITIES: Rockhounding; picnicking; fishing. Horseback riding (1 mi). Boating/swimming/waterskiing (4 mi). MISC.: Elev 7500 ft; 3 acres; pets.

Sleeping Deer Transfer Camp (Challis NF). 6 mi NW of Challis on Co Hwy 80. 5 mi NW on FS 80; 34 mi NW on FS 86. SEASON: 7/1-10/10; 16-day lmt. FACILITIES: 4 sites (tr -16); f. ACTIVITIES: Picnicking. Fishing/horseback riding (1 mi). MISC.: Elev 9000 ft; pets.

St Hwy Rest Area (SRA). 9 mi N of Challis on St Hwy 93. SEASON: All yr. FACILITIES: 9 sites; tbls, toil, cga, f. ACTIVITIES: Hiking; bike trails; picnicking; fishing; hunting. MISC.: Elev 5200; Salmon River. Small pets on leash.

CLARKFORK

Porcupine Lake (Idaho Panhandle NF). 3 mi N of Clarkfork on FS 4191; 5½ mi N on FS 4192; 2½ mi N on FS 4193; 6 mi SW on FS 632. SEASON: 7/1-9/15; 14-day lmt. FACILITIES: 4 sites (tr -24); tbls, toil, cga, no drk wtr. ACTIVITIES: Swimming; picnicking; fishing; boating,l. MISC.: Elev 4800; 2 acres; scenic; lake; pets allowed on leash.

CLARKIA

Cedar Creek (Idaho Panhandle NF). 3¼ mi N of Clarkia on St Hwy 3. SEASON: 4/15-11/30; 14-day lmt. FACILITIES: 3 sites (no trailers); tbls, toil, cga, f, well drk wtr. Store/food/gas (4 mi). ACTIVITIES: Swimming; picnicking; fishing. MISC.: Elev 2800 ft; 1 acre; pets.

Emerald Creek (Idaho Panhandle NF [St Joe NF]). 5-3/10 mi NW of Clarkia on St Hwy 3; 5½ mi S on FS 447. SEASON: 12/1-5/14, FREE ($2.00 rest of yr); 14-day lmt. FACILITIES: 18 sites (tr -22); tbls, toil, cga, f, piped drk wtr. ACTIVITIES: Picnicking. Rockhounding for garnets. Fishing (2 mi). MISC.: Elev 2500; 10 acres. Water shut off during free season. 7¼ mi across to Clarkia. Pets permitted on leash.

CLAYTON

East Fork (BLM). 4 mi E of Clayton on US 93. SEASON: 6/15-9/15, 10-day lmt. FACILITIES: 12 sites (some pull-thru sp); tbls, toil, cga, piped drk wtr.

See page 7 for KEY TO ABBREVIATIONS.

ACTIVITIES: Hiking; trailbiking; picnicking; fishing; hunting. MISC.: Elev 5500 ft; scenic; pets allowed on leash.

COBALT

Crags (Salmon NF). 9 mi SW of Cobalt on FS 60055; 7 mi NW on FS 112; 13 mi N on FS 113; 2 mi N on FS 114. SEASON: 7/1-10/15. FACILITIES: 24 sites (tr -16); tbls, toil, cga, f, piped drk wtr. ACTIVITIES: Picnicking. Horseback riding (1 mi). Fishing (2 mi). MISC.: Elev 8400 ft; 27 acres. Entrance to Bighorn Crag & Idaho prim. area. Stream. Pets okay.

Deep Creek (Salmon NF). 3½ mi N of Cobalt on FS 60055. SEASON: 6/1-11/15. FACILITIES: 3 sites (tr -22); tbls, toil, cga, f, piped drk wtr. Gas (4 mi). ACTIVITIES: Picnicking; fishing. Horseback riding (1 mi). MISC.: Elev 4900 ft; 2 acres. Pets okay. Panther Creek polluted by mine wastes.

Lost spring (Salmon NF). 13-3/10 mi S of Cobalt on FS 60055; 9-3/10 mi W on FS 60108. SEASON: 5/25-10/15. FACILITIES: 12 sites (tr -22); tbls, toil, cga, f, piped drk wtr. ACTIVITIES: Picnicking; fishing. Horseback riding (1 mi). MISC.: Elev 5200; 4 acres. Chinook fishing in season. Pets okay on leash.

McDonald Flat (Salmon NF). 5 mi SW of Cobalt on FS 60055. SEASON: 6/1-11/15. FACILITIES:. 4 sites (tr -22); tbls, toil, cga, f. ACTIVITIES: Picnicking; fishing. Horseback riding (1 mi). MISC.: Elev 5400 ft; 6 acres. Stream. Pets okay.

Middle Fork Peak (Salmon NF). 9 mi S of Cobalt on FS 60055; 24 mi W on FS 60112. SEASON: 7/4-11/10. FACILITIES: 5 sites (tr -16); tbls, toil, cga, f, piped drk wtr. ACTIVITIES: Picnicking. Horseback riding (1 mi). MISC.: Elev 9000 ft; 2 acres. Pets okay. Trail entrance to Idaho prim. area.

Yellowjacket Lake (Salmon NF). 9 mi S of Cobalt on FS 60055; 7 mi W on FS 60112; 16 mi N on FS 60113. SEASON: 7/1-9/5. FACILITIES: 7 sites (tr -16); tbls, toil, cga, f, piped drk wtr. ACTIVITIES: Picnicking; fishing; boating,d (no motors). Horseback riding (1 mi). MISC.: Elev 8000 ft; 5 acres. Adjacent to Small Cold Water Lake. Pets permitted if on leash.

COEUR D'ALENE

Bell Bay (Idaho Panhandle NF [Coeur D'Alene NF]). 7 mi E on I-90; 25 mi S on St Hwy 97 (exit 22); 3 mi W on East Point Road (314). SEASON: 4/15-11/1; 14-day lmt. FACILITIES: 40 sites (tr -22); tbls, toil, cga, f, piped drk wtr. Store/food/gas/ice (5 mi). ACTIVITIES: Nature trails; hiking; picnicking; fishing; water skiing; boating,rld; swimming; beach area; sailing. MISC.: Elev 2600 ft; 23 acres. On Coeur D'Arlene Lake, East Shore. Pets.

Beauty Creek (Idaho Panhandle NF [Coeur D'Alene NF]). 7 mi E on I-90; 2½ mi W on St Hwy 97 (exit 22); 3/5 mi SE on FS 438. The road is just before you cross the bridge over Beauty Creek. SEASON: 4/15-11/1; 14-day lmt. FACILITIES: 11 sites (tr -22); tbls, toil, cga, f, piped drk wtr. Store/food/gas/ice (2 mi). ACTIVITIES: Picnicking; fishing. Boating,ld (1 mi); (r, 2 mi). MISC.: Elev 2200; 7 acres. 1 mi from Beauty Bay Inlet, scenic trail nearby. Pets permitted on leash.

Honeysuckle (Idaho Panhandle NF [Coeur D'Alene NF]). 11½ mi NE of Coeur D'Alene on FS 268; 11-1/10 mi E on FS 612. SEASON: 5/15-10/15; 14-day lmt. FACILITIES: 9 sites (tr -16); tbls, toil, cga, f, well drk wtr. ACTIVITIES: Hunting; picnicking; fishing; berry-picking. MISC.: Elev 2800 ft; 2 acres. On north fork of Coeur D'Alene River. Pets okay on leash.

COUNCIL

Bear (Payette NF). 34 mi NW of Council on Co Hwy 50002; 2½ mi NE on FS 50105. SEASON: 6/15-10/15; 16-day lmt. FACILITIES: 6 sites (tr -16); toil; no drk wtr. ACTIVITIES: Picnicking; berry-picking; fishing; horseback riding. MISC.: Elev 4500 ft; 3 acres; pets; adjacent to Bear Creek.

Big Flat (Payette NF). 20 mi SE of Council on FS 50106. SEASON: 5/30-10/30; 16-day lmt. FACILITIES: 8 sites (tr -16); tbls, toil, cga, f. ACTIVITIES: Picnicking; fishing; Horseback riding; berry-picking. MISC.: Elev 4500 ft; 3 acres. Pets. No drk wtr. Adjacent to Little Weiser River.

Black Lake (Payette NF). 34 mi N of Council on Co Hwy 50002; 7 mi N on FS 50105; 16 mi N on FS 50112; 1/10 mi E on FS 50114. SEASON: 7/20-9/30. FACILITIES: 4 sites (tr -22); tbls, toil, cga, f, piped drk wtr. ACTIVITIES: Boating; swimming; picnicking; fishing; boating; rockhounding; hiking; nature trails. Horseback riding (1 mi). MISC.: Elev 7200 ft; 25 acres; scenic. In Hills Canyon NRA (non-wilderness). Pets okay. Adjacent to Black Lake.

Cabin Creek (Payette NF). 4 mi S of Council on US 95; 10 mi E on FS 50186. SEASON: 5/30-10/31; 16-day lmt. FACILITIES: 12 sites (tr -22); tbls, toil, cga. ACTIVITIES: Picnicking; horseback riding. Fishing (1 mi). MISC.: Elev 4200; 5 acres. Pets. Piped drk wtr. Adjacent to Middle Fork Weiser River.

Huckleberry (Payette NF). 34 mi NW of Council on Co Hwy 50002; 2½ mi NE on FS 50105. SEASON: 6/15-10/15; 16-day lmt. FACILITIES: 6 sites (tr -16); tbls, toil, cga. ACTIVITIES: Horseback riding; picnicking; fishing. MISC.: Elev 4800 ft; 4 acres. Pets permitted on leash. Near Hells Canyon-Seven Devils scenic area and stream.

Lafferty Camp (Payette NF). 24 mi NW of Council on Co Hwy 50002. SEASON: 6/1-10/15; 16-day lmt. FACILITIES: 8 sites (tr -16); tbls, toil, cga, f. ACTIVITIES: Horseback riding; picnicking; fishing. MISC.: Elev 4300 ft; 3 acres. Pets. Piped drk wtr. Crooked River.

DEARY

Little Boulder Creek (Clearwater NF). 4 mi E of Deary on St Hwy 8; 2-7/10 mi SE on Co Hwy 1963. SEASON: 5/15-10/15; 14-day lmt. FACILITIES: 8 sites (tr -16); tbls, toil, cga. Store/gas/food ice (3 mi); laundry (5 mi). Well drk wtr. ACTIVITIES: Berry-picking; picnicking; fishing. MISC.: Elev 2600 ft; 7 acres. Permit required for group picnics. Located next to Pottatch Creek. Pets okay.

DIXIE

Halfway House (Nezperce NF). 5 mi SW of Dixie on FS 222; 1½ mi S on FS 2221. SEASON: 6/15-10/31; 14-day lmt. FACILITIES: 4 sites (tr -16); tbls, toil, cga, no drk wtr. Store/food/gas/ice (5 mi); shower (5 mi). ACTIVITIES: Picnicking; fishing. Horseback riding (1 mi); rental (5 mi). MISC.: Elev 5000 ft; 4 acres. 1 mi from Dixie Guard Station & Airfield. Pets allowed if on leash.

DONNELLY

Donnelly Lakeside Park (City Park). ½ mi SW of Donnelly. SEASON: All yr. FACILITIES: 5 sites (tr -20); tbls, toil, cga, f, sanitary station, playground. Store nearby. ACTIVITIES: Swimming; picnicking; fishing; boating,rd. MISC.: Pets permitted if kept on a leash.

Kenally Creek (Boise NF). 3 mi N of Donnelly on St Hwy 55; 17 mi E on FS 50388. SEASON: 6/15-10/1. FACILITIES: 8 sites (tr -22); tbls, toil, cga, no drk wtr. ACTIVITIES: Hiking; berry-picking; picnicking; fishing. Horseback riding (1 mi). MISC.: Elev 6000 ft; 5 acres. Adjacent to Kenally Lakes Trailhead and Kenally Creek. Pets okay.

Tamarack Falls (Boise NF). 4 mi SW of Donnelly on Co Hwy. SEASON: 6/1-10/1. FACILITIES: 5 sites (no trailers); toil; store. ACTIVITIES: Fishing. MISC.: Elev 4800 ft. Pets allowed on leash.

DOWNEY

Cherry Creek (Caribou NF). 4 mi SW of Downey on Co Hwy 80N; 6 mi S on FS 20047. SEASON: 6/1-9/15. FACILITIES: 4 sites (no trailers); tbls, toil, cga, f, piped drk wtr, no garbage service-pack out litter. ACTIVITIES: Picnicking; fishing. Horseback riding (1 mi). MISC.: Elev 6000 ft; 5 acres. Pets okay.

Summit (Caribou NF). 10 mi SW of Downey on US 80 N; 1½ mi W on Co Hwy; 1 mi W on FS 41. SEASON: 6/1-9/15. FACILITIES: 10 sites (tr -32); tbls, toil, cga, f. ACTIVITIES: Picnicking; fishing; horseback riding. MISC.: Elev 5400 ft; 1 acre. Reservations accepted. Pets allowed if on leash.

DRIGGS

Teton Canyon (Targhee NF). 4-1/5 mi E of Driggs on Co Hwy; 2 mi E on Co Hwy; 4-7/10 mi E on FS 2009. SEASON: 7/1-9/30. FACILITIES: 9 sites (tr -32). ACTIVITIES: Fishing. MISC.: 12 acres; pets permitted if on a leash.

DUBOIS

Dubois City Park. Center of Dubois off St Hwy 15-91 (gravel access roads). SEASON: All yr. FACILITIES: Trailer sites (no tents); toil. MISC.: Pets okay.

Hwy Rest Area. On St Hwy 15-91 at Dubois exit (paved access roads). SEASON: All yr; 1-day lmt. FACILITIES: Trailer sites (no tents); toil, dump. MISC.: Pets allowed if kept on leash.

Webber Creek (Targheee NF). 25 mi NW of Dubois on Co Hwy A3; 2-3/10 mi W on FS 80196. SEASON: 6/15-9/15. FACILITIES: 4 sites (tr -16); tbls, toil, cga, f, no drk wtr. ACTIVITIES: Picnicking; fishing. Horseback riding (1 mi). MISC.: Elev 7000 ft; 5 acres; Scenic. Pets permitted if kept on leash.

EASTPORT

Copper Creek (Idaho Panhandle NF [Kanisksu NF]). 2 mi S of Eastport on I-95 (on Moyie River). SEASON: 5/15-10/1; 14-day lmt. FACILITIES: 16 sites (tr -32); tbls, toil, cga, f, well drk wtr. Store/food/gas/ice (2 mi). ACTIVITIES: Picnicking; fishing; berry-picking. Horseback riding (1 mi). MISC.: Elev 2500 ft; 8 acres; river; Copper Falls; pets permitted if kept on leash.

Robinson Lake (Idaho Panhandle NF [Kaniksu NF]). 6½ mi S of Eastport on US 95. SEASON: 5/15-10/1; 14-day lmt. FACILITIES: 10 sites (tr -32); tbls, toil, cga, f, well drk wtr. Store/food/gas/

ice /showers (2 mi). ACTIVITIES: Hiking; berry-picking; picnicking; fishing; boating,d. MISC.: Elev 2800 ft; 2 acres; 25 mi N of Bonners Ferry, Idaho. Pets okay.

ELK CITY

Bridge Creek (Nezperce NF). 3 mi Sw of Elk city on St Hwy 14; 14 mi SE on Co Hwy 222; 12 mi NE of Red River Ranger Station on Co Hwy 234. SEASON: 6/1-10/31; 14-day lmt. FACILITIES: 5 sites (tr -16); tbls, toil, cga, f, no drk wtr. Store/food/gas/showers/dump/lifeguard (1 mi). ACTIVITIES: Picnicking; fishing. Swimming (1 mi). Horseback riding (1 mi); rental (2 mi). MISC.: Elev 4800 ft; 3 acres. 1 mi from Red river Hot Spgs. Pets permitted if kept on leash.

Ditch Creek (Nezperce NF). 3 mi SW of Elk City on St Hwy 14; 14 mi SE on Co Hwy 222; 4 mi NE on Co Hwy 234. SEASON: 6/1-10/31; 14-day lmt. FACILITIES: 4 sites (tr -16); tbls, toil, cga, no drk wtr. ACTIVITIES: Berry-picking; picnicking. Fishing/horseback riding (1 mi). MISC.: Elev 4500 ft; 3 acres; stream; pets.

Granite Springs (Nezperce NF). 3 mi SW of Elk City on St Hwy 14; 15 mi SE on Co Hwy 222; 17 mi E on FS 468. SEASON: 7/15-10/15; 14-day lmt. FACILITIES: 4 sites (tr -16); piped drk wtr; toil; no tables. ACTIVITIES: Horseback riding (1 mi). MISC.: Elev 6700 ft; 4 acres. Primarily a developed hunter's camp. Pets permitted if kept on leash.

Poet Creek (Nezperce NF). 3 mi SW of Elk City on St Hwy 14; 15 mi SE on Co Hwy 222; 25 mi E on FS 468. SEASON: 7/15-10/15; 14-day lmt. FACILITIES: 4 sites (tr -16); tbls, toil, cga, f, no drk wtr. ACTIVITIES: Picnicking. Fishing/horseback riding (1 mi). MISC.: Elev 5100 ft; 5 acres. Trailhead into Salmon River. Breaks Primitive Area. Pets permitted if kept on leash.

Red River (Nezperce NF). 3 mi SW of Elk City on St Hwy 14; 14 mi SE on Co Hwy 222; 6 mi NE of Red River Ranger Station on Co Hwy 234. SEASON: 6/1-10/31; 14-day lmt. FACILITIES: 16 sites (tr -16); tbls, toil, cga, f, piped drk wtr. ACTIVITIES: Berry-picking; picnicking; fishing. Horseback riding (1 mi). Swimming (5 mi). MISC.: Elev 4600 ft; 25 acres; river; pets.

Table Meadows (Nezperce NF). 4-9/10 mi N of Elk City on FS 283 (Ericson Ridge Rd); 5-1/10 mi NW on FS 443. SEASON: 6/15-10/15. FACILITIES: 6 sites (tr -16); toil, cga, no drk wtr. ACTIVITIES: Berry-picking; horseback riding;

MISC.: Elev 4500 ft; 7 acres. West Fork American River adjacent to site. Pets.

Wild Horse Lake (Nezperce NF). 10 mi W of Elk City on St Hwy 14; 25 mi SW on FS 233. SEASON: 7/1-9/30; 14-day lmt. FACILITIES: 6 sites (tr -16); tbls, toil, cga, f, no drk wtr. ACTIVITIES: Picnicking. Fishing/swimming/boating/horseback riding (1 mi). MISC.: Elev 7500 ft; 10 acres. Trailhead into Gospel-Hump Wilderness. Pets permitted if on leash.

FAIRFIELD

Five Points (Sawtooth NF). 5-9/10 mi N on FS 70093; 11-2/5 mi N on FS 70094. SEASON: 6/15-9/10; 14-day lmt. FACILITIES: 3 sites (tr -16); tbls, toil, cga, f, no drk wtr. ACTIVITIES: Picnicking. Fishing/horseback riding (1 mi). MISC.: Elev 5500 ft; 1 acre; pets.

Pioneer (Sawtooth NF). 11-2/5 mi N of Fairfield on FS 70093. SEASON: 6/15-9/10; 14-day lmt. FACILITIES: 4 sites (tr -16); tbls, toil, cga, f, piped drk wtr. ACTIVITIES: Picnicking. Fishing/horseback riding (1 mi). MISC.: Elev 6500 ft; 5 acres; stream. Pets permitted if kept on leash.

FEATHERVILLE

Abbot (Sawtooth NF). 2-1/10 mi E of Featherville on FS 70000. SEASON: 6/15-9/10; 14-day lmt. FACILITIES: 5 sites (tr -16); tbls, toil, cga, f, no drk wtr. Store/food/gas (2 mi). ACTIVITIES: Picnicking; fishing. Horseback riding (1 mi). Swimming (5 mi). MISC.: Elev 4400 ft; 6 acres; river; pets okay.

Big Smoky (Sawtooth NF). 22-1/5 mi E of Featherville on FS 70000. SEASON: 6/15-9/10; 20-day lmt. FACILITIES: 3 sites (tr -16); tbls, toil, cga, f. ACTIVITIES: Picnicking. MISC.: Elev 5600 ft. Pets permitted if kept on leash.

Bighorn (Sawtooth NF). 11 mi E of Featherville on FS 70000. SEASON: 6/15-9/10. FACILITIES: 3 sites (tr -16); tbls, toil, cga, f. ACTIVITIES: Picnicking; fishing. MISC.: Elev 5200 ft. Pets.

Bird Creek (Sawtooth NF). 5-1/5 mi E of Featherville on FS 70000. SEASON: 6/15-9/10; 14-day lmt. FACILITIES: 5 sites (tr -16); tbls, toil, cga, f, no drk wtr. Store/food/gas (5 mi). ACTIVITIES: Picnicking; fishing. Horseback riding (1 mi). Swimming (3 mi). MISC.: Elev 5000 ft; 5 acres. Pets okay on leash. River.

Bounds (Sawtooth NF). 23-1/5 mi E of Featherville on FS 70000. SEASON: 6/15-9/10; 14-day lmt. FACILITIES: 12 sites

(tr -16); tbls, toil, cga, f, well drk
wtr. Dump (1 mi). ACTIVITIES: Picnicking. Fishing/horseback riding (1 mi).
MISC.: Elev 5500: 6 acres; strm; pets.

Canyon (Sawtooth NF). 23-4/5 mi E of
Featherville on FS 70000; 1-1/5 mi NE
on FS 70085. SEASON: 6/15-9/10; 14-day
lmt. FACILITIES: 6 sites (tr -16); tbls,
toil, cga, f, piped drk wtr. Store/food/
gas/dump (1 mi). ACTIVITIES: Picnicking. Fishing/horseback riding (1 mi).
MISC.: Elev 5500 ft; 2 acres; stream.
Pets permitted if kept on leash.

Skeleton Creek (Sawtooth NF). 14 mi
E of Featherville on FS 70000. SEASON:
6/15-9/10; 14-day lmt. FACILITIES: 4
sites (tr -16); tbls, toil, cga, f, no
drk wtr. ACTIVITIES: Picnicking; fishing. Horseback riding (3 mi). Swimming
(4 mi). MISC.: Elev 5300 ft; 4 acres;
river. Pets permitted if kept on leash.

South Boise (Sawtooth NF). 23-7/10 mi
E of Featherville on FS 70000; 10 mi N
on FS 70077. SEASON: 6/15-9/10; 14-day
lmt. FACILITIES: 4 sites (tr -16); tbls,
toil, cga, f, no drk wtr. ACTIVITIES:
Picnicking. Fishing/horseback riding (1
mi). MISC.: Elev 6000 ft; 4 acres; river.
Pets permitted if kept on leash.

Willow Creek (Sawtooth NF). 7 mi
E of Featherville on FS 70000. SEASON:
6/15-9/10; 14-day lmt. FACILITIES: 5
sites (tr -16); tbls, toil, cga, f, no
drk wtr. ACTIVITIES: Picnicking; fishing. Swimming/horseback riding (1 mi).
MISC.: Elev 5100 ft; 5 acres; stream.
Pets permitted if kept on leash.

FISH HAVEN

Beaver Creek (Caribou NF). 18-4/5 mi
SW of Fish Haven on US 89; 4-4/5 mi N
on FS 20011. SEASON: 6/15-9/5; 14-day
lmt. FACILITIES: 5 sites (tr -16); tbls,
toil, cga, f, piped drk wtr. ACTIVITIES:
Picnicking; berry-picking. Fishing/horse-
back riding (1 mi). MISC.: Elev 7800 ft;
2 acres; stream. Pets okay on leash.

FREEDOM

Pinebar (Caribou NF). 1 mi N of Freedom
on Co Hwy 34; 9-1/2 mi W on St Hwy 34.
SEASON: 6/15-9/30; 14-day lmt. FACILI-
TIES: 5 sites (tr -16); tbls, toil, cga,
f. ACTIVITIES: Horseback riding; picnicking; fishing. MISC.: 4 acres. Pets.

GARDEN VALLEY

Beaver Creek (Boise NF). 12-1/5 mi W
of Garden Valley on US 89; 4-4/5 mi N
on FS 20011. SEASON: 6/1-9/15; 7-day
lmt. FACILITIES: 5 sites (no trailers);
tbls, toil, cga, f. ACTIVITIES: Picnicking. MISC.: Elev 7800 ft; pets permitted.

Boiling Springs (Boise NF). 2-1/2 mi
W of Garden Valley on St Hwy 17; 22
mi N on FS 10398. SEASON: 6/1-10/15;
14-day lmt. FACILITIES: 15 sites (tr
-22); tbls, toil, cga, f, no drk wtr.
ACTIVITIES: Picnicking; fishing. Horseback riding (1 mi). MISC.: Elev 4000
ft; 3 acres. Adjacent to middle fork
Payette River. Pets permitted on leash.

Hardscrabble (Boise NF). 2-1/2 mi W
of Garden Valley on St Hwy 17; 12 mi
N on FS 10398. SEASON: 5/15-10/15. FA-
CILITIES: 6 sites (tr -22); tbls, toil,
cga, f, no drk wtr. ACTIVITIES: Picnicking; fishing. Horseback riding (1
mi). MISC.: Elev 3400 ft; 2 acres. Adjacent to middle fork of Payette River.
Pets permitted if kept on leash.

Pine Creek (Boise NF). 12 mi E of
Garden Valley on St Hwy 17; 2 mi N
on FS 10555. SEASON: 6/1-10/15; 14-day
lmt. FACILITIES: 4 sites (tr -16); tbls,
toil, cga, f, no drk wtr. ACTIVITIES:
Picnicking; fishing. Horseback riding
(1 mi). MISC.: Elev 4000 ft; 3 acres;
stream. Pets permitted if on leash.

Rattlesnake (Boise NF). 2½ mi W on St
Hwy 17; 14 mi N on FS 10398. SEASON:
5/15-10/15; 14-day lmt. FACILITIES:
16 sites (tr -22); tbls, toil, cga, f,
no drk wtr. ACTIVITIES: Picnicking;
fishing. Horseback riding (1 mi).
MISC.: Elev 3800 ft; 7 acres. Adjacent
to middle fork of Payette River. Pets.

Silver Creek (Boise NF). 2½ mi W of
Garden Valley on St Hwy 17; 23 mi N
on FS 10571. SEASON: 6/1-10/15. FACIL-
ITIES: 5 sites (tr -22); tbls, toil, cga,
f, well drk wtr. ACTIVITIES: Picnicking; fishing. Horseback riding (1 mi).
Swimming/lfgrd (2 mi). MISC.: Elev
4600 ft; 5 acres; stream nearby. Pets
permitted if kept on a leash.

Tie Creek (Boise N F). 2½ mi W of
Garden Valley on St Hwy 17; 9 mi N on
FS 10398. SEASON: 5/1-10/30; 14-day lmt.
FACILITIES: 6 sites (tr -16); tbls, toil,
cga, f, well drk wtr. ACTIVITIES: Pic-
nicking; fishing. Horseback riding (1
mi). MISC.: Elev 3200 ft; 4 acres; river.
Adjacent to middle fork Payette River.
Pets permitted if kept on leash.

Trail Creek (Boise NF). 2½ mi W of
Garden Valley on St Hwy 17; 15 mi N
on FS 10398. SEASON: 5/15-10/15. FACILI-
TIES: 11 sites (tr -22); tbls, toil, cga,
f, piped drk wtr. ACTIVITIES: Picnicking; fishing. Horseback riding (1 mi).
MISC.: Elev 3800 ft; 5 acres. Adjacent
to middle fork of Payette River. Pets.

See page 7 for KEY TO ABBREVIATIONS.

GEORGETOWN

Summit View (Caribou NF). 2-2/5 mi E of Georgetown on Co Hwy 20102; 6 mi N on FS 20095. SEASON: 6/15-9/5. FACIL-ITIES: 20 sites (tr -32); tbls, toil, cga, f. ACTIVITIES: Horseback riding; picnicking; fishing. MISC.: Elev 7200 ft; 17 acres. Pets permitted if kept on leash.

GIBBONSVILLE

Twin Creek (Salmon NF). 5 mi NW of Gibbonsville on St Hwy 93; ½ mi NW on FS 60079. SEASON: 6/1-9/15. FACILITIES: 46 sites (tr -32); tbls, toil, cga, f, piped drk wtr. Store/food/gas/ice/showers (5 mi). ACTIVITIES: Horseback riding; picnicking; fishing; hiking; berry-picking. MISC.: Elev 5100 ft; 21 acres. Pets permitted if kept on leash.

GRANGEVILLE

Fish Creek Meadows (Nezperce NF). 1 mi E of Grangeville on St Hwy 13; 1 mi S on Co Hwy 17; 6-4/5 mi SE on FS 221. SEASON: 6/15-9/15; 10-day lmt. FACILITIES: 8 sites (tr -16); tbls, toil, cga, f, well drk wtr. ACTIVITIES: Picnicking; berry-picking. Fishing (1 mi). MISC.: Elev 5000 ft; 3 acres; stream. Pets okay.

South Fork (Nezperce NF). 1 mi E of Grangeville on St Hwy 13; 9-9/10 mi SE on Co Hwy 17; 6 mi SE on st Hwy 14. SEASON: 6/1-10/1; 10-day lmt. FACILITIES: 4 sites (tr -22); tbls, toil, cga, f, dump. ACTIVITIES: Picnicking. MISC.: Elev 2300 ft; pets.

HAGERMAN

Roadside Rest. 4 mi S of Hagerman on Us 20-30 & 26 (good access rds). SEASON: All yr; 16-hr lmt. FACILITIES: 8 sites (no trailers); toil, dump.

HAILEY

Bridge Camp (Sawtooth NF). 2-3/5 mi N of Hailey on St Hwy 75; 9 mi W on FS 70097. SEASON: 6/1-10/15. FACILITIES: 3 sites (no trailers); tbls, toil, cga, f, no drk wtr. ACTIVITIES: Picnicking; fishing. Horseback riding (1 mi). MISC.: Elev 5600 ft; 2 acres. Douglas fir seed production area. Pets.

Deer Creek (Sawtooth NF). 2-7/10 mi N of Hailey on St Hwy 75; 9-4/5 mi W on FS 70097. SEASON: 6/10-10/15. FACILITIES: 3 sites (no trailers); tbls, toil, cga, f, no drk wtr. ACTIVITIES: Swimming (5 mi). Picnicking; fishing. Horseback riding (1 mi). MISC.: Elev 5500 ft; 2 acres; stream nearby. Pets.

Federal Gulch (Sawtooth NF). 6-1/10 mi N of Hailey on St Hwy 75; 11 ½ mi E on FS 70118. SEASON: 5/20-10/20. FACILITIES: 6 sites (tr -22); tbls, toil, cga, f, piped drk wtr. ACTIVITIES: Hiking; picnicking; fishing. Horseback riding (1 mi). MISC.: Elev 5700 ft; 2 acres; stream nearby. 17 mi SE of Sun Valley. Trailhead to Pioneer Mtns. Pets.

Sawmill (Sawtooth NF). 6-1/10 mi N of Hailey on St Hwy 75; 10-9/10 mi E on FS 70118. SEASON: 5/20-10/15. FACILITIES: 5 sites (no trailers); tbls, toil, cga, f, piped drk wtr. ACTIVITIES: Picnicking; fishing; horseback riding. MISC.: Elev 5600 ft; 2 acres. 16 mi SE of Sun Valley. Pets.

Wolftone Camp (Sawtooth NF). 2-3/5 mi N of Hailey on St Hwy 75; 8-1/10 mi W on FS 70097. SEASON: 6/1-10/15. FACILITIES: 3 sites (no trailers); tbls, toil, cga, f, no drk wtr. Shower (3 mi). ACTIVITIES: Picnicking; fishing. Horseback riding (1 mi). Swimming (3 mi). MISC.: Elev 5500 ft; 1 acre. Hot spring swimming pools 3 mi E. Pets permitted if kept on leash.

HANSEN

Bear Gulch (Sawtooth NF). 35-4/5 mi S of Hansen on FS 70515. SEASON: 5/1-10/31; 14-day lmt. FACILITIES: 6 sites (tr -16); tbls, toil, cga, f, piped drk wtr. ACTIVITIES: Picnicking. Horseback riding (1 mi). MISC.: Elev 4900 ft; 3 acres. Pets permitted if kept on leash.

Lower Penstemon (Sawtooth NF). 24 mi S of Hansen on FS 70515. SEASON: 6/15-10/15; 16-day lmt. FACILITIES: 10 sites (tr -16); tbls, toil, cga, f, piped drk wtr. ACTIVITIES: Picnicking; fishing. Horseback riding (1 mi). MISC.: Elev 6400 ft; 7 acres. Pets.

Pettit (Sawtooth NF). 28 mi S of Hansen on FS 70515. SEASON: 6/1-9/30; 16-day lmt. FACILITIES: 7 sites (tr -16); tbls, toil, cga, f, piped drk wtr. ACTIVITIES: Picnicking; fishing. Horseback riding (1 mi). MISC.: Elev 6700 ft; 10 acres. Pets permitted if kept on leash.

Steer Basin (Sawtooth NF). 18-4/5 mi S of Hansen of FS 70515. SEASON: 5/15-10/30. FACILITIES: 5 sites (no trailers); tbls, toil, cga, f, no drk wtr. ACTIVITIES: Picnicking; fishing. Horseback riding (1 mi). MISC.: Elev 5500 ft; 3 acres; stream. Pets okay on leash.

Upper Penstemon (Sawtooth NF). 24-1/10 mi S of Hansen on FS 47051. SEASON: 6/15-10/15; 16-day lmt. FACILITIES: 7 sites (tr -16); tbls, toil, cga, f, piped drk wtr ACTIVITIES:

Picnicking; fishing. Horseback riding (1 mi). MISC.: Elev 6500 ft; 8 acres; pets; stream.

HAYDEN LAKE

Mokins Bay (Idaho Panhandle NF[Coeur d'Alene NF]). 12 mi E of Hayden Lake. SEASON: 4/15-11/1; 14-day lmt. FACILI-TIES: 16 sites (tr -22); tbls, toil, cga,f, piped drk wtr. ACTIVITIES: Pic-nicking. Fishing (1 mi). Boating,d (1 mi); (l, 5 mi); waterskiing (1 mi). MISC.: Elev 2300 ft; 6 acres. Nearest public boat launch is 5 mi by rd at N end of Lake. Pets.

HEADQUARTERS

Aquarius (Clearwater NF). 42 mi NE of Headquarters on St Hwy 11; 25 mi NE on FS 247. SEASON: 5/1-10/31; 14-day lmt. FACILITIES: 7 sites (tr -22); tbls, toil, cga, f, piped drk wtr. ACTIVITIES: Picnicking; fishing; berry-picking. MISC.: Elev 1700 ft; 3 acres; scenic. Located on N fork Clearwater River. Pets permitted if on leash.

E. C. Rettig Area (Potlatch Corp). From Headquarters, 2 mi S on St Hwy 11. SEASON: 6/1-11/15; 14-day lmt. FACILI-TIES: 9 sites (tr -20). This area is divided by St Hwy 11, having 4 tables above the rd to be used for camping while the area below the rd has 5 tbls for picnicking. Spg & creek drk wtr must be boiled. ACTIVITIES: Hiking; picnicking; fishing. MISC.: Elev 3250 ft; 4 acres; no motorbikes; pets.

HILL CITY

Lime Creek (Sawtooth NF). 5-3/10 mi NW of Hill City on Co Hwy HP; 10-7/10 mi NW on FS 70055. SEASON: 6/15-10/15; 14-day lmt. FACILITIES: 3 sites (tr -22); tbls, toil, cga. ACTIVITIES: Picnicking; fishing. Horseback riding (1 mi). MISC.: Elev 5500 ft; 5 acres; stream. Pets.

HOLBROOK

Holbrook (Caribou NF). 8 mi NW of Holbrook on St Hwy 37. SEASON: 6/1-9/15. FACILITIES: 5 sites (tr -32); toil, cga. MISC.: Elev 5400 ft. Historic area near-by. Pets permitted if kept on a leash.

Twin Springs (Caribou NF). 8 mi NW of Holbrook on St Hwy 37. SEASON: 6/1-9/15. FACILITIES: 5 sites (tr -32); tbls, toil, cga, drk wtr. No garbage service; pack out your litter. ACTIVITIES: Pic-nicking. Horseback riding (1 mi). MISC.: Elev 5400 ft; 3 acres. Historic area nearby. Pets okay if kept on leash.

HOPE

Samowen (Idaho Panhandle NF). 2-4/5 mi SE of Hope on St Hwy SH200; 2 mi W on Co Hwy 1002. SEASON: 10/16-5/31, Free ($2.00 rest of yr); 14-day lmt. FA-CILITIES: 56 sites (tr -22); tbls, flush toil, cga, f, piped drk wtr, dump. Store/food/gas/ice (5 mi). ACTIVITIES: Swimming; picnicking; fishing. Boating,l (r, 4 mi). MISC.: Elev 2000 ft; 38 acres. On NE shore of Lake Pend Orielle. Pets permitted if kept on leash. No water during free season.

IDAHO CITY

Black Rock (Boise NF). 3 mi NE of Idaho City on St Hwy 21; 15 mi E on FS. SEA-SON: 6/15-10/31; 14-day lmt. FACILITIES: 11 sites (tr -22); tbls, toil, cga, f, well drk wtr. ACTIVITIES: Picnicking; fishing. Horseback riding (1 mi). MISC.: Elev 4200 ft; 4 acres. Adjacent to N fork of Boise River. Pets.

Pine Creek (Boise NF). 1 mi from St Hwy 21. SEASON: All yr. FACILITIES: Camp sites (no trailers); tbls, toil, drk wtr. ACTIVITIES: Picnicking. MISC.: Elev 4100 ft. Pets permitted if kept on a leash.

IDAHO FALLS

Northgate Tourist Area NE on US 26-91 to Lincoln St & N Yellowstone Hwy (paved access rds). SEASON: All yr; 1-day lmt. FACILITIES: 20 sites, toil; near city golf course and large shopp-ing center. MISC.: Elev 4710 ft. Pets permitted if kept on leash.

Riverside (Co. Park). Take US 26-91 exit off I-15; 2½ mi to Southside rest area at S Yellowstone. SEASON: All yr; 1-day lmt. FACILITIES: 3 sites, tbls, toil. ACTIVITIES: Picnicking; fishing; boat-ing,l. MISC.: Elev 4600 ft; pets.

Roadside Park Rest Area. Intersec. of St Hwy 26 & 191. SEASON: All yr; 16-hr lmt. FACILITIES: Spaces for self-contained RVs; dump, phone. Pets.

IRWIN

Palisades (Targhee NF). 3-7/10 mi SE of Irwin on US 26; 2 mi NE on FS 80255. SEASON: 5/25-9/5. FACILITIES: 7 sites (tr -16); tbls, toil, cga, f, no drk wtr. ACTIVITIES: Horseback riding; picnicking; fishing. MISC.: Elev 5600 ft; 6 acres. Store (2 mi). Pets okay.

KETCHUM

Baker Creek (Sawtooth NF). 15 mi N of Ketchum on St Hwy 75. SEASON: 6/1-10/15; 16-day lmt. FACILITIES: Un-designated sites; tbls, toil, f, no drk wtr, store, showers, lifeguard (Tr

-32.) ACTIVITIES: Picnicking; fishing; swimming. MISC.: Elev 6600 ft; 75 acres; stream; pets.

Caribou (Sawtooth NF). 7 mi N of Ketchum on St Hwy 75; 3 mi E on FS 146. SEASON: 6/1-10/15; 16-day lmt. FACILITIES: Undesignated sites (tr -22); tbls, toil, cga, no drk wtr. Gas/store/ice, visitor center. ACTIVITIES: Picnicking; fishing; hiking. MISC.: Elev 6100 ft; 60 acres; stream; nature trails; pets.

Murdock (Sawtooth NF). 7 mi N of Ketchum on St Hwy 75; 1 mi E on FS 146. SEASON: 6/1-10/15; 16-day lmt. FACILITIES: Undesignated sites (tr -22); tbls, toil, cga, f, store/ice/gas, visitor center. ACTIVITIES: Picnicking; fishing; hiking. MISC.: Elev 6000 ft; 60 acres; stream; nature trails.

Prairie Creek (Sawtooth NF). 18 mi N of Ketchum on FS 75. SEASON: 6/1-10/15; 16-day lmt. FACILITIES: Undesignated sites (tr -32); tbls, toil, cga, f, no drk wtr. Store/ice; lifeguard. ACTIVITIES: Picnicking; swimming; fishing. MISC.: Elev 6800 ft; 60 acres; river; pets.

KINGSTON

Berlin Flats (Idaho Panhandle NF). 22½ mi NE of Kingston on FS FH9; 6 mi N on FS 208; 8 mi N on FS 412. SEASON: 5/15-10/15; 14-day lmt. FACILITIES: 9 sites (tr -22); tbls, toil, cga, f. ACTIVITIES: Picnicking; fishing; berry-picking. MISC.: Elev 2600 ft; 3 acres. Located on Shoshone Creek, 8 mi above Shoshone Work Center. Pets. Piped drk wtr. Stream.

Big Hank (Idaho Panhandle NF). 22½ mi NE of Kingston on FS FH9; 19 mi NW on FS 208; 1-1/10 mi NE on FS 306. SEASON: 10/2-5/29, FREE ($2.00 rest of yr); 14-day lmt. FACILITIES: 29 sites (tr -22); tbls, toil, cga, piped drk wtr. ACTIVITIES: Picnicking; fishing. Boating,l (3 mi). Hiking (1 mi). MISC.: Elev 2700 ft; 10 acres; scenic; pets okay; water shut off during free season. On Coeur d'Alene River.

Bumblebee (Idaho Panhandle NF [Coeur d'Alene NF]). 7 mi NE of Kingston on FS FH9; 3 mi NW on FS 209. SEASON: 4/15-11/1; 14-day lmt. FACILITIES: 11 sites (tr -16); tbls, toil, cga, f, piped drk wtr. ACTIVITIES: Picnicking; fishing; berry-picking. MISC.: Elev 2200 ft; 10 acres. Site is on N fork of Coeur d'Alene River. Pets.

Kit Price (Idaho Panhandle NF). 22½ mi NE of Kingston on FS FH9; 9½ mi NW on FS 208. SEASON: 10/16-5/29, FREE ($2.00

rest of yr); 14-day lmt. FACILITIES: 21 sites (tr -22); tbls, toil, cga, f, piped drk wtr, dump. ACTIVITIES: Berry-picking; picnicking; fishing. MISC.: Elev 2600 ft; 10 acres. On Coeur d'Alene River. Water shut off during free season. Pets.

Senator Creek (Idaho Panhandle NF). 22½ mi NE of Kingston on FS9; 24½ mi NW on FS 208. SEASON: 6/15-9/15; 14-day lmt. FACILITIES: 6 sites (tr -22); tbls, toil, cga, f. ACTIVITIES: Hunting; picnicking; fishing. MISC.: Elev 3000 ft. Coeur d'Alene River. Pets.

KOOSKIA

Boyd Creek (Nezperce NF). 23½ mi E on US 12; 11-1/5 mi SE on FS 223. SEASON: 5/24-11/7; 10-day lmt. FACILITIES: 7 sites (tr -22); tbls, toil, cga, piped drk wtr. ACTIVITIES: Picnicking; fishing; boating,d. MISC.: Elev 1600 ft; 5 acres; scenic; Selway River; pets.

Johnson Bar (Nezperce NF). 23½ mi E of Kooskia on US 12; 4 mi SE on FS 223. SEASON: 5/24-11/7; 14-day lmt. FACILITIES: 4 sites (tr -22); tbls, toil, cga, f, no drk wtr. Store/food/gas/ice/laundry (4 mi). Visitor ctr (1 mi). ACTIVITIES: Swimming; picnicking; fishing; boating. Horseback riding (2 mi). MISC.: Elev 1600 ft; 5 acres; scenic; river. Pets okay if kept on leash.

Knife Edge (Clearwater NF). 1 mi N of Kooskia on St Hwy 13; 33-1/2 mi E on US 12. SEASON: 5/30-9/10; 10-day lmt. FACILITIES: tbls, toil, cga, f, no drk wtr. ACTIVITIES: Berry-picking; picnicking; fishing. MISC.: Elev 1800 ft; 2 acres; scenic. Middle fork of Clearwater Wild and Scenic River. Pets.

Ohara Bar (Nezperce NF). 23½ mi E of Kooskia on US 12; 7 mi SE on FS 223; 1/10 mi S on FS 651. SEASON: 5/28-11/7; 10-day lmt. FACILITIES: 34 sites (tr -22); tbls, toil, cga, f, piped drk wtr. Store/food/gas/ice (4 mi). ACTIVITIES: Swimming; picnicking; fishing; boating,l (r, 4 mi). MISC.: Elev 1600 ft; 7 acres; Visitor Center (2 mi); Selway River. Pets.

Race Creek (Nezperce NF). 23½ mi E of Kooskia on US 12; 20½ mi SE on FS 223 (gravel rd for 13 mi). SEASON: 5/24-11/16; 14-day lmt. FACILITIES: 3 sites (tr -22); tbls, toil, cga, f, piped drk wtr. ACTIVITIES: Swimming; picnicking; fishing (Meadow Creek); boating. Horseback riding/feedrack/hitching rails/loading ramp (1 mi). MISC.: Elev 1800 ft; 4 acres. End of road facility for Bitterroot Wilderness Trailhead portal area. Pets.

Rackliff (Nezperce NF). 23½ mi E of Kooskia on US 12; 8 mi SE on FS 223. SEASON: 5/24-11/7; 14-day lmt. FACILITIES: 6 sites (tr -22); tbls, toil, cga, f, piped drk wtr. Store/food/gas/ice (5 mi). ACTIVITIES: Hiking; picnicking; fishing; swimming; boating,d (r, 5 mi). MISC.: Elev 1600 ft; 5 acres; scenic; Selway River. Visitor Center (3 mi). Pets.

Selway Falls (Nezperce NF). 23½ mi E of Kooskia on US 12; 21 mi SE on FS 223; 1 mi S on FS 290. SEASON: 5/25-11/16; 14-day lmt.. FACILITIES: 6 sites (tr -16); tbls, toil, cga, f, piped drk wtr. ACTIVITIES: Hiking; picnicking; fishing. Horseback riding (1 mi). Swimming/boating,d (2 mi). MISC.: Elev 1800 ft; 12 acres; scenic; stream; pets.

Slims (Nezperce NF). 23½ mi E of Kooskia on US 12; 21 mi SE on FS 223; 2 mi S on FS 290. SEASON: 5/24-11/16; 14-day lmt. FACILITIES: 3 sites (tr -16); tbls, toil, cga, f, no drk wtr. ACTIVITIES: Picnicking; fishing; hiking; Horseback riding. Swimming/boating (3 mi). MISC.: 1800 ft; 4 acres; scenic;stream. End of road facilities for Meadow Creek Country Pets permitted if kept on a leash.

Twenty Mile Bar (Nezperce NF). 23½ mi E of Kooskia on US 12; 10½ mi SE on FS 223. SEASON: 5/24-11/7; 14-day lmt. FACILITIES: 4 sites (tr -22); tbls, toil, cga, f, no drk wtr. ACTIVITIES: Boating; swimming; picnicking; fishing. MISC.: Elev 1700 ft; 1 acre; scenic; geological; river; pets.

Two Shadows (Clearwater NF). 1 mi N of Kooskia on St Hwy 13; 17½ mi E on US 12. SEASON: 6/15-9/5; 10-day lmt. FACILITIES: 3 sites (no trailers); toil, cga, f. ACTIVITIES: Fishing. MISC.: Elev 1500 ft; pets.

LEADORE

Big Eightmile (Salmon NF). 6-7/10 mi W of Leadore on Co Hwy; 1-1/5 mi SW on Co Hwy; 5 mi SW on FS 60096. SEASON: 6/15-9/30. FACILITIES: 8 sites (tr -16); tbls, toil, cga, f, no drk wtr. ACTIVITIES: Picnicking; fishing. Horseback riding (1 mi). MISC.: Elev 6500 ft; 1 acre. Stream. Pets.

Meadow Lake (Salmon NF). 16-4/5 mi SE of Leadore on St Hwy 28; 1-9/10 mi W on Co Hwy; 3-9/10 mi SW on FS 60002. SEASON: 7/1-9/5. FACILITIES: 9 sites (tr -16); tbls, toil, cga, f, piped drk wtr. ACTIVITIES: Boating; picnicking; fishing. Horseback riding (1 mi). MISC.: Elev 9100 ft; 5 acres; Meadow Lake. Pets.

LEMHI

Hayden Creek (Salmon NF). 1-1/10 mi N of Lemhi on St Hwy 28; 6-1/10 mi SW on Co Hwy; 2½ mi SW on FS 60008. SEASON: 6/1-11/30. FACILITIES: 4 sites (no trailers); tbls, toil, cga, f. ACTIVITIES: Picnicking; fishing. Horseback riding (1 mi). MISC.: Elev 6000 ft; 1 acre; stream. Pets. No drk wtr.

LEWISTON

Black Pine Cabin Area (Potlatch Corp.). 25 mi SE of Lewiston on Co Rd P2, near Soldiers Meadow Reservoir (gravel access rds). SEASON: 6/1-11/15; 14-day lmt. FACILITIES: 10 sites (tr -20); tbls, toil, cga, drk wtr must be boiled (sm creek & spg). ACTIVITIES: Picnicking. Hiking/fishing nearby. MISC.: Elev 4800 ft; 1 acre. No motorbikes. Pets permitted if kept on leash.

St Hwy Rest Area. 20 mi E of Lewiston on St Hwy 12 (paved access rds). SEASON: All yr; 1-day lmt. FACILITIES: Trailers okay; dump station. No tents. ACTIVITIES: Boating,l. MISC.: Pets.

Sweetwater Creek Rec. Area (Potlatch Corp.). 21 mi SE of Lewiston on Co Rd P2; 1-3/10 mi E of Lake Waha on rd to Webb Ridge; take left branch 1-3/10 mi E of Waha Store. SEASON: 6/1-10/1; 14-day lmt. FACILITIES: 13 sites (tr -20); tbls, toil, cga, drk wtr must be boiled. ACTIVITIES: Picnicking; fishing nearby in Waha Lake. MISC.: Elev 3385 ft; 2 acres. Located in the Orchards Tree Farm. Pets permitted on leash.

LOLO

Jerry Johnson (Clearwater NF). 55-4/5 mi SW of Lolo on US 12. SEASON: 6/1-9/15; 10-day lmt. FACILITIES: 15 sites (tr -22); tbls, toil, cga, f. ACTIVITIES: Picnicking; fishing. MISC.: Elev 3100 ft; 6 acres; river. Pets permitted if kept on a leash.

Powell (Clearwater NF). 44-1/2 mi SW of Lolo on US 12; 1/5 mi S on FS 111. SEASON: 6/1-10/1; 10-day lmt. FACILITIES: 37 sites (tr -22); tbls, flush toil, cga, f. Store/showers/ice (1 mi). ACTIVITIES: Picnicking; fishing. MISC.: Elev 3400 ft; 12 acres; river. Pets.

Wendover (Clearwater NF). 48 mi SW of Lolo on US 12. SEASON: 6/1-10/15; 10-day lmt. FACILITIES: 28 sites (tr -22); tbls, toil, cga, f. Store/shower laundry/ice (3 mi). ACTIVITIES: Picnicking; fishing. MISC.: Elev 3200 ft; 15 acres; river. Pets permitted on leash.

Whitehouse (Clearwater NF). 47-4/5 mi SW of Lolo on US 12. SEASON: 7/1-9/5;

10-day lmt. FACILITIES: 14 sites (tr -22); tbls, toil, cga, f. Store/showers/ice/laundry (3 mi). ACTIVITIES: Picnicking; fishing. MISC.: Elev 3200 ft; 1 acre; river. Pets permitted on leash.

LOWMAN

Bear Valley (Boise NF). 29 mi N of Lowman on FS FH082; 1 mi NW on FS FH579. SEASON: 6/15-9/30; 14-day lmt. FACILITIES: 9 sites (tr -22); tbls, toil, cga, no drk wtr. ACTIVITIES: Picnicking; fishing. Horseback riding (1 mi). MISC.: Elev 6400 ft; 20 acres; stream. Pets permitted if kept on leash.

Boundary Creek (Challis NF). 32 mi NE of Lowman on FS FH182; 13 mi N on FS FH668. SEASON: 6/15-9/10. FACILITIES: 14 sites (tr -22); tbls, toil, cga, f, piped drk wtr. ACTIVITIES: Picnicking. Fishing/horseback riding (1 mi). MISC.: Elev 5800 ft; 6 acres. Pets permitted if kept on a leash.

Bummer Town (Boise NF). 29 mi N on FS FH082; 14 mi W on FS FH579; 9 mi S on FS FH492. SEASON: 6/15-10/15; 14-day lmt. FACILITIES: 11 sites (tr -22); tbls, toil, cga, f, no drk wtr. ACTIVITIES: Boating,d; picnicking; fishing. Horseback riding (1 mi). MISC.: Elev 5200 ft; 12 acres. Adjacent to Deadwood Reservoir. Lake. Pets permitted on leash.

Cozy Cove (Boise NF). 29 mi N of Lowman on FS FH082; 14 mi W on FS FH579; 11 mi S on FS FH492. SEASON: 6/15-10/15; 14-day lmt. FACILITIES: 9 sites (tr -16); tbls, toil, cga, f, no drk wtr. ACTIVITIES: Boating,d; picnicking; fishing; waterskiing. Horseback riding (1 mi). MISC.: Elev 5200 ft; 15 acres. Adjacent to Deadwood Reservoir. Pets permitted if kept on a leash.

* **Daggar Falls #1** (Challis NF). 32 mi NE of Lowman on FS FH082; 13 mi N on FS FH668; 1/5 mi E on TRAIL 1068. SEASON: 6/15-9/10. FACILITIES: 4 tent sites, tbls, toil, cga, piped drk wtr. ACTIVITIES: Picnicking. Boating/fishing/horseback riding (1 mi). MISC.: elev 5800 ft; 1 acre. Pets permitted if on leash.

Daggar Falls #2 (Challis NF). 32 mi NE of Lowman on FS FH082; 13 mi N on FS FH668. SEASON: 6/15-9/10. FACILITIES: 10 sites (tr -22); tbls, toil, cga, f, piped drk wtr. ACTIVITIES: Picnicking. Fishing/horseback riding (1 mi). MISC.: Elev 5800 ft; 6 acres. Pets.

Deadwood (Boise NF). 3 mi W of Lowman on St Hwy 17. SEASON: 5/15-10/15; 14-day lmt. FACILITIES: 7 sites (tr -16); tbls, toil, cga, f, no drk wtr. Store/food/gas/ice (3mi). ACTIVITIES: Picnicking; fishing. Horseback riding (1 mi). MISC.: Elev 4800 ft; 2 acres. Adjacent to South form of Payette and Deadwood Rivers. Pets permitted if on a leash.

Deer Flat (Boise NF). 29 mi N of Lowman on FS FH082; 10 mi W on FS FH579. SEASON: 6/15-9/30; 14-day lmt. FACILITIES: 7 sites (tr -32); tbls, toil, cga, f, no drk wtr. ACTIVITIES: Picnicking. Fishing/horseback riding (1 mi). MISC.: Elev 6400 ft; 3 acres; stream. Pets.

Elk Creek (Boise NF). 29 mi N of Lowman on FS FH082; 6 mi W on FS FH 579. SEASON: 6/15-9/30; 14-day lmt. FACILITIES: 5 sites (tr -22); tbls, toil, cga, f, no drk wtr. ACTIVITIES: Picnicking. Fishing/horseback riding (1 mi). MISC.: Elev 6500 ft; 2 acres; stream. Pets permitted if on a leash.

Fir Creek (Boise NF). 33 mi NE of Lowman on FS FH082; 1 mi NE on FS FH470. SEASON: 6/15-9/30; 14-day lmt. FACILITIES: 4 sites (tr -22); tbls, toil, cga, f, no drk wtr. ACTIVITIES: Picnicking; fishing. Horseback riding (1 mi). MISC.: Elev 6300 ft; 2 acres; stream. Pets permitted if on a leash.

Fir Springs (Boise NF). 29 mi N of Lowman on FS FH082; 14 mi W on FS FH579; 5 mi S on FS FH492. SEASON: 6/15-10/15; 14-day lmt. FACILITIES: 3 sites (tr -16); tbls, toil, cga, f, no drk wtr. ACTIVITIES: Picnicking; fishing. Horseback riding (1 mi); boating (2 mi). MISC.: Elev 5400 ft; 3 acres. Adjacent to Deadwood River. Pets.

Four Mile (Boise NF). 11 mi S of Lowman on St Hwy 21; 16 mi SE on FS. SEASON: 6/15-10/31; 14-day lmt. FACILITIES: 5 sites (no trailers); tbls, toil, cga, f, no drk wtr. ACTIVITIES: Picnicking; fishing. Horseback riding (1 mi). MISC.: Elev 4600 ft; 2 acres. Adjacent to North fork of Boise River. Pets permitted if kept on a leash.

Graham Bridge (Boise NF). 11 mi S of Lowman on St Hwy 21; 3 mi E on FS FH484; 33½ mi SE on FS FH522 (poor road last 14 mi). SEASON: 7/15-9/30; 14-day lmt. FACILITIES: 4 sites (no trailers); tbls, toil, cga, f, no drk wtr. ACTIVITIES: Picnicking; fishing. Horseback riding (1 mi). MISC.: Elev 5600 ft; 2 acres; stream. Pets.

Grandjean (Sawtooth NF). 21 mi E of Lowman on St Hwy 21; 6 mi E on FS FH824. SEASON: 6/15-9/15; 10-day lmt. FACILITIES: 34 sites (tr -22); tbls, toil, cga, f, well drk wtr. Store/gas/ice (1 mi). ACTIVITIES: Picnicking;

fishing; mountain climbing; hiking.
Swimming; horseback riding/rental (1
mi). MISC.: Elev 5200 ft; 32 acres.
Trailhead to Sawtooth Wilderness. Pets.

Helende (Boise NF). 8 mi E of Lowman
on St Hwy 21. SEASON: 6/15-10/15; 14-
day lmt. FACILITIES: 10 sites (tr -16);
tbls, toil, cga, f, no drk wtr. ACTIVI-
TIES: Picnicking; fishing. Horseback
riding (1 mi). MISC.: Elev 4000 ft; 3
acres; river. Pets permitted on leash.

Johnson Creek (Boise NF). 11 mi S of
Lowman on St Hwy 21; 3 mi E on FS FH
484; 35 mi SE on FS FH522 (poor rd last
16 mi). SEASON: 7/15-9/30; 14-day lmt.
FACILITIES: 3 sites (no trailers); tbls,
toil, cga, f, no drk wtr. ACTIVITIES:
Picnicking; fishing. Horseback riding
(1 mi). MISC.: Elev 5600 ft; 2 acres;
river. Pets permitted if on leash.

Packsaddle (Boise NF). 8 mi W of
Lowman on St Hwy 17; 13 mi N on FS
FH555. SEASON: 6/15-9/10; 14-day lmt.
FACILITIES: 6 sites (tr -16); tbls, toil,
cga, f, no drk wtr. ACTIVITIES: Mtn
Climbing; picnicking; fishing. Horseback
riding (1 mi). MISC.: Elev 5600 ft; 1
acre; stream. Pets.

Pine Flats (Boise NF). 5 mi W of Lowman
on St Hwy 17. SEASON: 5/1-11/15. FACIL-
ITIES: 27 sites (tr -32); tbls, toil, cga,
f. Store/ice (5 mi). ACTIVITIES: Picnicking; fishing; horseback riding. MISC.:
Elev 4400 ft; 22 acres; river. Adjacent
to south form Payette River. Pets permitted if kept on a leash.

Poker Meadows (Boise NF). 32 mi N of
Lowman on FS FH082; 1 mi N on FS FH688.
SEASON: 6/15-9/30; 14-day lmt. FACILI-
TIES: 8 sites (tr -22); tbls, toil, cga,
no drk wtr. ACTIVITIES: Picnicking.
Fishing/horseback riding (1 mi). MISC.:
Elev 6300 ft; 3 acres; stream. Pets.

Riverside (Boise NF). 29 mi N of Lowman
on FS FH082; 14 mi W on FS FH579; 7
mi S on FS FH492. SEASON: 6/15-10/15;
14-day lmt. FACILITIES: 8 sites (tr -22);
tbls, toil, cga, f, well drk wtr. ACTIV-
ITIES: Picnicking; fishing.·Boating (1
mi). MISC.: Elev 5200 ft; 3 acres. Adjacent to Deadwood Reservoir. Pets okay
if kept on a leash.

Robert E. Lee (Boise NF). 11 mi S of
Lowman on St Hwy 21; 17 mi SE on FS.
SEASON: 6/15-10/31; 14-day lmt. FACIL-
ITIES: 6 sites (no trailers); tbls, toil,
cga, f no drk wtr. ACTIVITIES: Picnicking; fishing. Horseback riding (1
mi). MISC.: Elev 4800 ft; 3 acres. Adjacent to north fork of Boise River.
Pets permitted if kept on leash.

Warm Springs Creek (Boise NF). 18 mi
E of Lowman on St Hwy 21; 4/5 mi N
on FS FH251. SEASON: 6/15-10/31; 14-

day lmt. FACILITIES: 8 sites (tr -16);
tbls, toil, cga, f, no drk wtr. ACTIVI-
TIES: Picnicking; fishing. Horseback
riding (1 mi). MISC.: Elev 4400 ft; 2
acres; stream. Pets.

Willow Creek (Boise NF). 11 mi S of
Lowman on St Hwy 21; 7 mi E on FS.
SEASON: 6/15-9/30; 14-day lmt. FACILI-
TIES: 4 sites (no trailers); tbls, toil,
cga, f, no drk wtr. ACTIVITIES: Picnicking; fishing. Horseback riding (1
mi). MISC.: Elev 5400 ft; 1 acre;
stream. Pets permitted if on leash.

MACKAY

Iron Bog (Challis NF). 10 mi SE of
Mackay on US 93; 10 mi SW on Co Hwy;
7-1/5 mi SW on FS 40137. SEASON: 6/30-
9/15. FACILITIES: 13 sites (tr -32);
tbls, toil, cga, f, well drk wtr.
ACTIVITIES: Horseback riding; picnicking; fishing; rockhounding. MISC.: Elev
6500 ft; 30 acres; stream. Pets.

Mackay Reservoir (BLM). 4 mi NW of
Mackay on US 93A. SEASON: 5/1-11/30;
7-day lmt. FACILITIES: 48 sites; tbls,
toil, cga, f, drk wtr, dump. ACTIVI-
TIES: Swimming; picnicking; fishing;
hunting; hiking; boating,rl. MISC.:
Elev 6000 ft; 40 acres; pets.

MALTA

Sublett (Sawtooth NF). 20-4/5 mi E of
Malta on FS 70568. SEASON: 6/1-11/5;
14-day lmt. FACILITIES: 7 sites (tr -22);
tbls, toil, cga, f, no drk wtr. ACTIVI-
TIES: Picnicking. Horseback riding (1
mi). Fishing/swimming/boating,ld/water-
skiing (2 mi). MISC.: Elev 5500 ft; 10
acres. 2 mi E of Sublet Reservoir. Pets.

MAY

Big Creek (Challis NF). 17½ mi SE of
May on Co Hwy 22; 3-9/10 mi SE on FS
97. SEASON: 6/15-9/30. FACILITIES: 3
sites (no trailers); tbls, toil, cga, f,
no drk wtr. ACTIVITIES: Picnicking;
fishing. Horseback riding (1 mi). MISC.:
Elev 6600 ft; 1 acre; stream. Co Hwy
leaves US 93 at Ellis. Pets permitted
if kept on leash.

Timber Creek (Challis NF). 42 mi SE of
May on Co Hwy; 6-7/10 mi N on FS 40101.
SEASON: 6/15-9/15. FACILITIES: 12 sites
(tr -32); tbls, toil, cga, f, well drk
wtr. ACTIVITIES: Picnicking; fishing.
Horseback riding (1 mi). MISC.: Elev
8000 ft; 6 acres; stream; pets allowed
if kept on a leash.

MCCALL

Black Lee (Payette NF). 14 mi NE of McCall on FS. **SEASON:** 7/1–10/1. **FACIL-ITIES** 4 sites (tr –22); tbls, toil. **ACTIVITIES:** Picnicking; fishing. **MISC.:** Elev 5800 ft; pets permitted if on leash.

Buckhorn Bar (Payette NF). 39 mi NE of McCall on Co Hwy FH48; 7½ mi S on FS 6742. **SEASON:** 6/1–11/15. **FACILITIES:** 20 sites; tbls, toil, cga, f, piped drk wtr. **ACTIVITIES:** Horseback riding; picnicking; fishing. **MISC.:** Elev 3800 ft; 5 acres; stream. Adjacent to south fork of Salmon River. Pets.

Camp Creek (Payette NF). 39 mi NE of McCall on Co Hwy FH48; 11½ mi S on FS 6742. **SEASON:** 6/1–11/7. **FACILITIES:** 6 sites; toil, no drk wtr. **ACTIVITIES:** Horseback riding; picnicking; fishing. **MISC.:** Elev 4000 ft; 3 acres; stream. Pets permitted if kept on leash.

Four Mile (Payette NF). 39 mi NE of McCall on Co Hwy FH 48; 15½ mi S on FS 6742. **SEASON:** 6/1–11/15. **FACILITIES:** 12 sites; tbls, toil, cga, f, no drk wtr. **ACTIVITIES:** Horseback riding; picnicking; fishing; hiking. **MISC.:** Elev 4200 ft; 3 acres; stream. Adjacent to Four Mile Creek and Trailhead. Pets allowed.

Lake Fork (Payette NF). 9½ mi E of McCall on FS FH48. **SEASON:** 6/15–10/15; 16–day lmt. **FACILITIES:** 9 sites (tr –22); tbls, toil, cga, piped drk wtr. **ACTIVITIES:** Berry–picking; picnicking; fishing. Horseback riding (1 mi). **MISC.:** Elev 5600 ft; 8 acres; stream. Adjacent to Lake Fork Creek. Pets.

Lodgepole (Payette NF). 39 mi NE of McCall on Co Hwy FH48; 14½ mi S on FS 6742. **SEASON:** 6/1–11/7. **FACILITIES:** 6 sites; tbls, toil, cga, f, no drk wtr. **ACTIVITIES:** Horseback riding; picnicking; fishing. **MISC.:** Elev 4000 ft; 5 acres; stream. Adjacent to south fork of Salmon River. Pets allowed on leash.

North Fork Lick Creek (Payette NF). 29 mi NE of McCall on Co Hwy FH48. **SEASON:** 6/1–10/30. **FACILITIES:** 4 sites; toil, cga, f, no drk wtr. **ACTIVITIES:** Horseback riding; fishing. **MISC.:** Elev 4200 ft; 2 acres; stream. Pets permitted.

Poverty Flat (Payette NF). 39 mi NE of McCall on Co Hwy FH48; 18½ mi S on FS 6742. **SEASON:** 6/1–11/15. **FACILITIES:** 12 sites; tbls, toil, cga, no drk wtr. **ACTIVITIES:** Horseback riding; picnicking; fishing. **MISC.:** Elev 4300 ft; 5 acres; stream. Adjacent to Blackmare Trailhead. Adjacent to south fork of Salmon River. Pets permitted on leash.

Salmon Point (Payette NF). 39 mi NE of McCall on Co Hwy FH48; 6 mi S on FS 672. **SEASON:** 6/1–11/7. **FACILITIES:** 8 sites; tbls, toil, cga, f, no drk wtr.

ACTIVITIES: Horseback riding; picnicking; fishing. **MISC.:** Elev 4100 ft; 3 acres; stream. Adjacent to south fork of Salmon River. Pets permitted on leash.

Teepee Creek (Payette NF). 39 mi NE of McCall on Co Hwy FH48; 7 mi S on FS 6742. **SEASON:** 6/1–11/15. **FACILITIES:** 12 sites; tbls, toil, cga, f, no drk wtr. **ACTIVITIES:** Horseback riding; picnicking; fishing. **MISC.:** Elev 3800 ft; 2 acres; stream. Adjacent to south fork of Salmon River. Pets permitted if kept on a leash.

Upper Payette Lake (Payette NF). 18½ mi N on FS FH21; 1 mi N on FS 495. **SEASON:** 7/1–10/1; 16–day lmt. **FACILITIES:** 9 sites (tr –22); tbls, toil, cga, piped drk wtr. **ACTIVITIES:** Berry–picking; picnicking; fishing; boating, ld. Horseback riding (1 mi). **MISC.:** Elev 5600 ft; 12 acres; lake. On upper Payette Lake. Pets.

MONTPELIER

Whitman Hollow (Caribou NF). 5–4/5 mi E of Montpelier on US 89. **SEASON:** 5/25–9/5; 14–day lmt. **FACILITIES:** 4 sites (tr –22); tbls, toil, cga, f, no drk wtr. **ACTIVITIES:** Picnicking; fishing. **MISC.:** Elev 6300 ft; 2 acres; stream. Pets permitted if kept on leash.

MOSCOW

Kiwanis Rest Area. 4 mi N of Moscow on St Hwy 95 (paved rd access). **SEASON:** all yr; 16–hr lmt. **FACILITIES:** Toil/dump **MISC.:** Elev 2575; pets.

MT. HOME

Big Roaring River Lake (Boise NF). 24 mi NE of Mt. Home on St Hwy 68; 6 mi N on FS 10134; 9 mi NE on FS 10113; 19 mi NW on FS 10123. **SEASON:** 7/1–10/1; 14–day lmt. **FACILITIES:** 10 sites (tr –22); tbls, toil, cga, f, no drk wtr. **ACTIVITIES:** Boating (no motors); picnicking; fishing. Horseback riding (1 mi). **MISC.:** Elev 8200 ft; 7 acres; lake 4 high alpine lakes nearby. Pets.

Big Trinity Lake (Boise NF). 24 mi NE of Mt. Home on St Hwy 68; 6 mi N on FS 10134; 9 mi NE on FS 10113; 20 mi NW on FS 10123. **SEASON:** 7/1–10/1; 14–day lmt. **FACILITIES:** 17 sites (tr –22); tbls, toil, cga, f, piped drk wtr. **ACTIVITIES:** Boating (no motors); picnicking; fishing. Horseback riding (1 mi). **MISC.:** Elev 7900 ft; 7 acres; 4 high alpine lakes nearby. Pets.

Cove (BLM). 20 mi S of Mt. Home off US 51 between Bruneau and Grandview, on C.J. Strike Reservoir. **SEASON:** All yr; 14–day lmt. **FACILITIES:** 26 sites;

tbls, toil, cga, drk wtr. **ACTIVITIES:** Hiking; picnicking; fishing; hunting; boating. **MISC.:** Elev 3000 ft; 20 acres. Pets permitted if kept on a leash.

Cow Creek (Boise NF). 29 mi NE of Mt. Home on St Hwy 68; 9 mi NW on FS 10113. **SEASON:** 5/15-10/1; 14-day lmt. **FACILITIES:** 4 sites (tr -22); tbls, toil, cga, no drk wtr. **ACTIVITIES:** Picnicking; fishing. Horseback riding (1 mi). **MISC.:** Elev 3700 ft; 2 acres; river. 9 mi to Anderson Ranch Reservoir. Pets permitted if kept on a leash. No individual parking spaces; central parking.

Dog Creek (Boise NF). 29 mi NE of Mt. Home on St. Hwy 68; 13 mi NE on FS 10163; 14 mi N on FS 10156. **SEASON:** 6/1-10/1; 14-day lmt. **FACILITIES:** 11 sites (tr -22); tbls, toil, cga, f, piped drk wtr. Store/gas (4 mi). **ACTIVITIES:** Picnicking. Fishing/horseback riding (1 mi). Boating,l/waterskiing (5 mi). **MISC.:** Elev 4400 ft; 6 acres. Within a mile of south fork of Boise River. Pets.

Granite Creek (Boise NF). 29 mi NE of Mt. Home on St Hwy 68; 11 mi NW on FS 10113. **SEASON:** 5/15-10/1; 14-day lmt. **FACILITIES:** 4 sites (tr -16); tbls, toil, cga, piped drk wtr. **ACTIVITIES:** Picnicking. Fishing/horseback riding (1 mi). **MISC.:** Elev 3800 ft; 1 acre. 11 mi to Anderson Ranch Reservoir. Pets.

Ice Springs (Boise NF). 29 mi NE of Mt. Home on St Hwy 68; 5 mi NE on FS 10134 9 mi NE on FS 10113; 5 mi N on FS 10125. **SEASON:** 6/1-10/1; 14-day lmt. **FACILITIES:** 7 sites (tr -16); tbls, toil, cga, f, well drk wtr. Store/food/gas (5 mi). **ACTIVITIES:** Picnicking. Fishing/boating,l/swimming (5 mi); horseback riding (1 mi). **MISC.:** Elev 5000 ft; 4 acres. Pets permitted if kept on a leash.

Little Roaring River Lake (Boise NF). 24 mi NE of Mt. Home on St Hwy 68; 6 mi N on FS 10134; 9 mi NE on FS 10113; 20 mi NW on FS 10123. **SEASON:** 7/1-10/1; 14-day lmt. **FACILITIES:** 4 sites (tr -16 tbls, toil, cga, f, no drk wtr. **ACTIVITIES:** Picnicking; fishing. Horseback riding (1 mi). **MISC.:** Elev 7900 ft; 2 acres; no motor boats. Pets allowed.

Little Trinity Lake (Boise NF). 24 mi NE of Mt. Home on St Hwy 68; 6 mi N on FS 10134; 9 mi NE on FS 10113; 21 mi NW on FS 10123. **SEASON:** 7/1-10/1; 14-day lmt. **FACILITIES:** 3 sites (no trailers); tbls, toil, cga, f. **ACTIVITIES:** Picnicking; fishing; boating (no motors). Horseback riding (1 mi). **MISC.:** Elev 7900 ft; 1 acre; lake. 4 high alpine lakes nearby. Pets.

NAF

Clear Creek (Sawtooth NF). 5-9/10 mi S of Naf on FS 60006. **SEASON:** 6/1-10/15; 14-day lmt. **FACILITIES:** 7 sites (tr -16); tbls, toil, cga, f, piped drk wtr. **ACTIVITIES:** Picnicking; fishing; hunting. Horseback riding (1 mi). **MISC.:** Elev 5300 ft; 8 acres; stream; scenic; pets.

NEW MEADOWS

Cold Springs (Payette NF). 8 mi SW of New Meadows on US 95; 3 mi W on FS 50089; 1/5 mi W on FS 50091. **SEASON:** 6/1-10/31. **FACILITIES:** 31 sites (tr -22); tbls, toil, cga, f. Store/ice/gas/food (4 mi). Piped drk wtr. **ACTIVITIES:** Picnicking. Fishing/swimming/waterskiing/horseback riding/boating,d (1 mi). **MISC.:** Elev 4800 ft; 21 acres. Near Lost Valley Reservoir. Pets permitted if kept on a leash.

Grouse (Payette NF). 6 mi E of New Meadows on St Hwy 55; 10½ mi N on FS 50257; ½ mi W on FS 50273; 1/10 mi N on FS 50278. **SEASON:** 7/1-9/15. **FACILITIES:** 6 sites (tr -22); tbls, toil, cga, f, well drk wtr. **ACTIVITIES:** Berry-picking; picnicking; fishing; boating,d; waterskiing. Horseback riding (1 mi). **MISC.:** Elev 6500 ft; 4 acres; scenic. Adjacent to Goose Lake. Pets permitted if kept on a leash.

Hazard Lake (Payette NF). 9 mi E of New Meadows on St Hwy 55; 19 mi N on FS 50257; 1/10 mi E on FS 50259. **SEASON:** 7/1-9/15. **FACILITIES:** 12 sites (tr -22); tbls, toil, cga, f, piped drk wtr. **ACTIVITIES:** Picnicking; fishing; boating,d. Horseback riding (1 mi). **MISC.:** Elev 7100 ft; 5 acres; scenic. Adjacent to Hazard Lake. Pets.

Last Chance (Payette NF). 4 mi E of New Meadows on St Hwy 55; 2 mi N on FS 50453; 1/5 mi N on FS 50091. **SEASON:** 6/1-10/30. **FACILITIES:** 15 sites (tr -22); tbls, toil, cga, f, piped drk wtr, dump. Store/gas/ice (3 mi). **ACTIVITIES:** Berry-picking; picnicking; fishing. Horseback riding (1 mi). **MISC.:** Elev 4600 ft; 10 acres. Adjacent to Goose Creek. Pets are permitted if kept on a leash.

Smokey (Payette NF). 11 mi N of New Meadows on US 95; 8 mi NW on FS 50074; 1/10 mi N on FS 50076. **SEASON:** 6/1-10/30 **FACILITIES:** 6 sites (tr -22); tbls, toil, cga, f, no drk wtr. **ACTIVITIES:** Picnicking; fishing; berry-picking. Horseback riding (1 mi). **MISC.:** Elev 4600 ft; 5 acres; stream. Near Boulder Creek. Pets permitted if kept on a leash.

NORTH FORK

Deadwater Spring (Salmon NF). 3-3/5 mi W of North Fork on FS 60030. **SEASON:**

See page 7 for KEY TO ABBREVIATIONS.

4/1-10/31; 16-day lmt. FACILITIES: 4 sites (tr -32); tbls, toil, cga, well drk wtr. Store/gas/ice/laundry/shower/food (4 mi). ACTIVITIES: Picnicking; fishing. Boating,l (1 mi). MISC.: Elev 3500 ft; 1 acre. Pets permitted on leash.

OAKLEY

Bostetter (Sawtooth NF). 19-7/10 mi W of Oakley on FS 70500. SEASON: 6/1-10/15 16-day lmt. FACILITIES: 18 sites (tr - 16); tbls, toil, cga, f, piped drk wtr. ACTIVITIES: Picnicking; fishing. Horseback riding (1 mi). MISC.: Elev 7100 ft; 20 acres; stream. Pets permitted.

Father and Sons (Sawtooth NF). 21 mi W of Oakley on FS 70500. SEASON: 6/1-10/15; 16-day lmt. FACILITIES: 19 sites (tr -16); tbls, toil, cga, f, piped drk wtr. ACTIVITIES: Picnicking. Fishing/horseback riding (1 mi). MISC.: Elev 7100 ft; 13 acres; stream. Pets.

Porcupine (Sawtooth NF). 27-3/10 mi W of Oakley on FS 70500. SEASON: 6/1-10/15. FACILITIES: 5 sites (tr -16); tbls, toil, cga, f, piped drk wtr. ACTIVITIES: Picnicking; fishing. Horseback riding (1 mi). MISC.: Elev 6800 ft; 44 acres; stream. Pets permitted if kept on a leash.

OLDTOWN

Albeni Cove (COE; Albeni Falls Project) 3 mi E of Oldtown, S side of the dam, via US Hwy 2 and 195. (forested area). SEASON: 5/25-9/16; 14-day lmt. FACILITIES: 13 sites (tr -20); tbls, flush toil cga, f, drk wtr, bath house. ACTIVITIES: Boating,ld; picnicking; fishing; swimming (with floating dive platform); waterskiing. MISC.: Elev 2080 ft; 20 acres. Pets permitted if on leash.

OBSIDIAN

Tin Cup Hikier Transfer Campa (Sawtooth NF). 5-2/5 mi S of Obsidian on St Hwy 75; 2 mi SW on FS 70208. SEASON: 6/15-9/15; 10-day lmt. FACILITIES: 6 sites (no trailers) tbls, toil, cga, f, well drk wtr. ACTIVITIES: Boating, d; picnicking; fishing; swimming; water skiing; mtn climbing; hiking. MISC.: Elev 7000 ft; 4 acres; lake; scenic. 1 mi E of Sawtooth Wilderness. Pets permitted if kept on a leash.

OROFINO

City Park. N end of River Bridge on St Hwy 7 & US 12. SEASON: All yr; 1-day lmt. FACILITIES: 25 sites; tbls, toil. ACTIVITIES: Picnicking; fishing.

Dent Acres (COE; Dworshak Project). 20 mi N of Orofino on Orofino-elk River Road (on Dworshak Lake). SEASON: 11/2-4/30, FREE ($3.00 rest of yr). FACILITIES: 50 sites (tr -24) (all pull-thru); water/sewer/elec hookups (50¢); paved site/tent pads; tbls, flush toil, cga, f, drk wtr, dump, showers, handicapped fac, ACTIVITIES: Boating; picnicking; fishing; waterskiing. MISC.: Elev 1500 ft; pets. Horses/hunting prohibited. Subject to winter closure due to heavy snow.

Mini-Camps (COE; Dworshak Project [Walla Walla, Wash. COE Dist.]). 20 mi N of Orofino on Orofino-Elk River Road to reach Dworshak Lake. There are 75 of these mini-camps scattered along the entire length of the Dworshak Reservoir near the shoreline. Each mini-camp is designed for 1-3 camping units. Some mini-camps are accessible by car or by foot, but most are only accessible practically by boat and by this mode only in the summer and fall when the reservoir is nearly full or full. Chemical toilets are closed in winter. 75 sites around 184 miles of shoreline; TENT ONLY; tent pads, shade, tables, fire area, tables, picnic, boating, chemical toilets, no boat ramps, pool fluctuation: (1445-1600 ft) 155 ft; seas - summer/fall. 14-day lmt.; Hunting prohibited. Local Park Address: PO Box 147; Ahsahka, ID 83520. 208/476-3294.

PALISADES

Bear Creek (Targhee NF). 2-3/5 mi SE of Palisades on US 26; 1½ mi S on FS 20076; 4½ mi on FS 20058. FACIL.: 6 sites (tr -22); tbls, toil, cga, f, piped drk wtr. ACTIVITIES: Picnicking; fishing. Boating/swimming/horseback riding (1 mi). MISC.: Elev 5800 ft; 3 acres; scenic; stream. Pets permitted if kept on a leash. SEASON: 6/1-10/31; 16-day.

Palisades (Targhee NF). 2 mi NE of Palisades on FS 80255. SEASON: 5/25-9/5; 16-day lmt. FACILITIES: 7 sites (tr -16); tbls, toil, cga, f. Store/food/gas/shower/laundry (2 mi). ACTIVITIES: Hiking; picnicking; fishing. Horseback riding (1 mi); rental (2 mi). MISC.: Elev 5600 ft; 6 acres; scenic. 55 mi from Idaho Falls. Pets permitted on leash.

PIERCE

Cedars (Clearwater NF). ½ mi S of Pierce on St Hwy 11; NE on FS 250. SEASON: 5/31-10/30; 14-day lmt. FACILITIES: 5 sites (tr -16); tbls, toil, cga, f, no drk wtr. ACTIVITIES: Swimming; picnicking; fishing. MISC.: Elev 3600 ft; 5 acres; scenic. On upper north fork of the Clearwater River. Pets permitted.

See page 7 for KEY TO ABBREVIATIONS.

Campbell's Pond Area (Potlatch Corp.).
6 mi N of Pierce on St Hwy 11 to Hollywood Jct; 2½ mi W on Hollywood Grange-
ment Road; turn left at Campbell's
Pond turnoff & go ½ mi S on Co Rd
(gravel access rds). SEASON: 6/1-11/15;
14-day lmt. FACILITIES: 10 sites (tr
-20); tbls, toil, cga, drk wtr (must
be boiled). ACTIVITIES: Hiking; picnicking; fishing. MISC.: Elev 3330 ft;
4 acres. This is a large area & allows
adequate rm for camping. Small pond
has been stocked with fish. No motor
bikes. Pets permitted if kept on leash.

Hemlock (Clearwater NF). 9 mi NE of
Pierce on FS 250; 5 mi E on FS 547;
10 mi E on FS 535; 16 mi N on FS 555.
SEASON: 7/10-10/30; 14-day lmt. FACIL-
ITIES: 5 sites (no trailers); toil, cga,
f. ACTIVITIES: Fishing. MISC.: Elev
2700 ft; on Weitas Creek near Weitas
guard station. Pets permitted on leash.

Hidden Creek (Clearwater NF). ½ mi
S of Pierce on St Hwy 11; 58 mi NE on
FS 250. SEASON: 6/15-10/30;14-day lmt.
FACILITIES: 13 sites (tr -22); tbls,
toil, cga, f, well drk wtr. ACTIVITIES:
Berry-picking; picnicking; fishing.
MISC.: Elev 3500 ft; 5 acres; scenic;
stream. Located on north fork of Clear-
water River. Pets permitted if on leash.

Hollywood CG (Potlatch Corp.). 6½ mi
N of Pierce on St Hwy 11. SEASON: 6/1-
11/15; 14-day lmt. FACILITIES: 12 sites
(tr -20); tbls, toil, cga, drk wtr (must
be boiled). ACTIVITIES: Picnicking;
fishing/hiking (nearby). MISC.: Elev
3400 ft; 5 acres; This is a large area
and allows adequate room for camping.
Pets permitted if kept on a leash.
No motorbikes.

Kelly Forks (Clearwater NF). ½ mi S
of Pierce on St Hwy 11; 49 mi NE on
FS 250. SEASON: 5/31-10/30; 14-day lmt.
FACILITIES: 14 sites (tr -22); tbls,
toil, cga, well drk wtr. ACTIVITIES:
Picnicking; berry-picking. Fishing/
boating,d (1 mi). MISC.: Elev 2900 ft;
5 acres; scenic. Located on north fork
of Clearwater River. Pets permitted.

Noe Creek (Clearwater NF). 42 mi NE
of Pierce on FS 250. SEASON: 5/31-10/30;
14-day lmt. FACILITIES: 7 sites (tr
-22); tbls, toil, cga, f, piped drk wtr.
ACTIVITIES: Berry-picking; picnicking.

Washington Creek (Clearwater NF). 29
mi NE of Pierce on FS 250; 6 mi NW on
FS 249. SEASON: 6/1-10/31; 14-day lmt.
FACILITIES: 23 sites (tr -22); tbls, toil,
cga, f, piped drk wtr. ACTIVITIES: Hiking; picnicking; fishing. MISC.: Elev
2200 ft; 8 acres; scenic. Located on N
fork of Clearwater River. Pets permitted.

Weitas (Clearwater NF). 34 mi NE of
Pierce on FS 250. SEASON: 5/31-10/30; 14-
day lmt. FACILITIES: 6 sites (no
trailers); tbls, toil, cga, f, no drk wtr.
ACTIVITIES: Picnicking; fishing; berry-
picking; boating,d. MISC.: Elev 2500
ft; 4 acres; scenic. Located on N fork
of Clearwater River. Pets permitted.

PINEHURST

* **Mirror Lake Recreation** (BLM). 9 mi S
of Pinehurst on Rochat Div. Rd; 5 mi E
on Boise Park Rd; ½ mi BY TRAIL. SEA-
SON: 7/1-11/1; 7-day lmt. FACILITIES:
4 sites (no trailers); tbls, toil, cga.
ACTIVITIES: Swimming; picnicking; fishing. MISC.: 2 acres. Pets permitted on
leash.

PONDS LODGE

Mill Creek (Targhee NF). 2 mi N of
Ponds Lodge on US 191; 3 mi NW on
Co Hwy 30. SEASON: 5/7-10/30. FACIL-
ITIES: Undesignated sites (tr -16); f,
toil, no drk wtr. Store/food/gas/
showers/laundry (3 mi). ACTIVITIES:
Picnicking; boating,l; swimming; fishing; waterskiing. Horseback riding
(1 mi). MISC.: Elev 6200 ft; 5 acres.

PRIEST RIVER

* **Navigation** (Idaho Panhandle NF
[Kanikau NF]). 35 mi N of Priest River
on St Hwy 57; 3 mi E on FS 1339; 1/8
mi N on FS 237; 5 mi N on TRAIL 291
(located on W side of upper Priest Lake
at N end). SEASON: 6/15-8/31. FACILI-
TIES: 5 tent sites; tbls, toil, cga, f,
drk wtr (must be boiled). ACTIVITIES:
Berry-picking; picnicking; fishing; boating,d. MISC.: Elev 2400 ft; 6 acres;
lake; scenic. Pets permitted on leash.

* **Rocky Point** (Idaho Panhandle NF
[Kanikau NF]). 31 mi N of Priest River
on St Hwy 57; 1 mi E on FS 1338; 1/5
mi SE on FS 237; 2 mi NE, BY BOAT
(located on NE side of Kalispell Island
in Priest Lake). SEASON: 5/25-9/15; 10-
day lmt. FACILITIES: 6 tent sites;
tbls, toil, cga, drk wtr (must be
boiled). Store/ice/gas/food (2 mi). Dump
(3 mi). ACTIVITIES: Picnicking; fishing; swimming; waterskiing; sailing;
boating,l; (rental, 2 mi). Hiking (5
mi). MISC.: Elev 2400 ft; 4 acres;
sandy beach; scenic view; Priest Lake;
pets permitted if kept on a leash.

* **Schneider** (Idaho Panhandle NF
[Kaniskau NF]). 31 mi N of Priest River
on St Hwy 57; 1 mi E on FS 1338; 1/5
mi SE on FS 237; 1 mi NE, BY BOAT.
(At the S end of Kalispell Island in
Priest Lake.) SEASON: 5/25-9/15. FACIL-
ITIES: 5 tent sites; tbls, toil, cga;

See page 7 for KEY TO ABBREVIATIONS.

drk wtr (must be boiled). Store/ice/food/gas (1 mi). Dump (2 mi). ACTIVITIES: Picnicking; fishing; swimming; sailing; waterskiing; boating,l; (rental, 1 mi). MISC.: Elev 2400 ft; 7 acres; sandy beaches; scenic; nature trails (5 mi). Pets. 10-day lmt.

* Silver (Idaho Panhandle NF [Kaniskau NF]). 31 mi N of Priest River on St Hwy 57; 1 mi E on FS 1338; 1/5 mi SE on FS 237; 1 mi NE, BY BOAT. (Located at N end of Kalispell Island in Priest Lake.) SEASON: 5/25-9/15. FACILITIES: 9 tent sites; tbls, toil, cga, drk wtr (must be boiled). Store/food/gas (1 mi). ACTIVITIES: Picnicking; fishing; swimming; sailing; boating,l; (rental, 1 mi). Waterskiing. Hiking (5 mi). MISC.: Elev 2400 ft; 11 acres; Priest Lake; pets. 10-day lmt.

Stagger Inn (Idaho Panhandle NF). 36 mi N of Priest Lake on St Hwy 57; 14 mi NW on FS 302. SEASON: 6/1-8/31. FACILITIES: 4 sites (no trailers); tbls, toil, cga. ACTIVITIES: Picnicking; fishing; hiking; berry-picking; hiking. MISC.: Elev 3200 ft; 1 acre; scenic. 1/2 mi SE of Roosevelt Grove of Ancient Cedars. Pets permitted if kept on leash.

* Strong's Island (COE; Albeni Falls Project). 2 mi upstream from Albeni Falls Dam, BY BOAT, from Priest River. SEASON: All yr; 14-day lmt. FACILITIES: 10 tent sites; tbls, toil, cga, drk wtr. ACTIVITIES: Boating,d; swimming; waterskiing; picnicking; fishing. MISC.: Elev 2070 ft; 18 acres. Forested Island with open meadows at one end. Pets permitted if kept on a leash.

* Three Pines (Idaho Panhandle NF). 31 mi N of Priest River on St Hwy 57; 1 mi E on FS 1338; 2/10 mi SE on FS 237; 1½ mi NE, BY BOAT (on Kalispell Island). SEASON: 5/25-9/15; 10-day lmt. FACILITIES: 7 tent sites; tbls, toil, cga, no drk wtr. Store/gas/food/ice (2 mi). Dump (3 mi). ACTIVITIES: Picnicking; fishing; swimming; waterskiing; sailing; boating,l (rental 2 mi); hiking (5 mi). MISC.: Elev 2400 ft; 2 acres; sandy beach, no docks, scenic view, Priest Lake. Pets permitted.

REXBURG

Beaver Dick. 6 mi W of Rexburg on St Hwy 88 at Henry's Fork. SEASON: All yr. FACILITIES: 20 sites (no tents); tbls, toil, cga. ACTIVITIES: Picnicking; fishing; hunting; boating,l; waterskiing; bike trails. MISC.: Pets permitted.

RIGGINS

Seven Devils (Nezperce NF). 1-1/5 mi S of Riggins on US 95; 16 ½ mi SW on

FS 517 (Squaw Creek Rd). Not recommended for trailers due to narrow maneuvering conditions thru trees & lack of parking space. SEASON: 7/4-10/30. FACILITIES: 8 sites (tr -16); tbls, toil, cga, no drk wtr. ACTIVITIES: Hiking; picnicking; fishing. MISC.: Elev 8000 ft; 9 acres. Adjacent to Seven Devils Lake. Within Hells Canyon-Seven Devils Scenic Area, end of road facility. Pets.

Sheep Crest Rest Area. 6 mi SW of Riggins on US 95. (Good access rds.) SEASON: All yr; 1-day lmt. FACILITIES: 15 sites (no tents); tbls, toil, cga, dump, drk wtr. ACTIVITIES: Picnicking. MISC.: Pets permitted if kept on leash.

Spring Bar (Nezperce NF). 1½ mi S on Riggins on US 95; 11 mi E on FS 1614 (Salmon Rvr Rd). SEAS:All yr. FAC:17 sites (tr -16); tbls, toil, cga, f, piped drk wtr. ACTIVITIES: Rockhounding; picnicking; fishing; boating,ld. MISC.: Elev 2000 ft; 4 acres; scenic. On River of No Return. Popular take-out point for float trips. Pets permitted if on leash.

RIRIE

Table Rock (Targhee NF). 2½ mi E of Ririe on St Hwy 26; 1-1/5 mi N on Co Hwy; 3½ mi E of Co Hwy; 4-1/5 mi E on FS. SEASON: 5/25-9/5; 16-day lmt. FACILITIES: 9 sites (tr -12); tbls, toil, cga, f, piped drk wtr. ACTIVITIES: Picnicking. Horseback riding (1 mi). Fishing/swimming/boating (2 mi). MISC.: Elev 5800 ft; 2 acres. Pets permitted.

ROBERTS

Hwy Rest Area & Weigh Station. 9 mi N of Roberts at 142 mile marker. SEASON: All yr; 1-day lmt. FACILITIES: sites; no tents; dump. MISC.: Elev 4910 ft. Pets permitted if kept on a leash.

ROGERSON

Salmon Dam (BLM). 7 mi W of Rogerson adjacent to Salmon Falls Dam. SEASON: 5/1-11/30; 14-day lmt. FACILITIES: 14 sites (tr -25); tbls, toil, cga, drk wtr. ACTIVITIES: Horseback riding; picnicking; fishing; hunting; hiking; boating,ld. MISC.: Elev 5100 ft; 20 acres. Pets permitted if kept on a leash.

ST. MARIES

Al Vanderpoel Area (Potlatch Corp.). 15 mi SW of St. Maries at jct of US 95 and St Hwy 30. SEASON: 5/1-11/15; 14-day lmt. FACILITIES: 4 sites (tr -20); tbls, toil, cga, drk wtr (must be boiled). ACTIVITIES: Picnicking; fishing; hunting; bike trls; hiking. MISC.:

Elev 2700 ft; 6 acres. Santa Creek wtr only; **safe if boiled.** Small pets on leash only.

⋆ **Crystal Lake** (BLM). 9 mi N of St. Maries on US 95A; 10 mi on Rochat Rd., 2 mi BY TRAIL. SEASON: 6/1-9/30; 7-day lmt. FACILITIES: 4 tent sites (no trailers); tbls, toil, cga. ACTIVITIES: Swimming; picnicking; fishing; hunting; hiking. MISC.: Elev 5300 ft; 2 acres. Pets permitted if kept on a leash.

Shadowy St. Joe (Idaho Panhandle NF). 1/2 mi E of St. Maries on US 95A; 11 mi E on Co Hwy FH 50. SEASON: 5/1-11/30; 14-day lmt. FACILITIES: 14 sites (tr -22); tbls, toil, cga, well drk wtr. ACTIVITIES: Swimming; boating,l; picnicking; fishing. MISC.: Elev 2100 ft; 9 acres; pets.

Tingley Springs (BLM). 6 mi E of St. Maries on St. Joe River Hwy; 9 mi N on St. Joe Baldy Rd. SEASON: 6/1-9/30; 7-day lmt. FACILITIES: 5 sites (no trailers); tbls, toil, cga, drk wtr. ACTIVITIES: Hunting; hiking; picnicking; fishing. MISC.: Elev 5200 .ft; 10 acres. Pets.

SALMON

Cougar Point (Salmon NF). 5 mi S of Salmon on US 93; 12 mi W on FS 60021. SEASON: 6/1-10/15. FACILITIES: 12 sites (tr -22); tbls, toil, cga, f, piped drk wtr. ACTIVITIES: Picnicking; fishing. Horseback riding (1 mi). MISC.: Elev 6600 ft; 15 acres. Pets permitted.

Iron Lake (Salmon NF). 5 mi S of Salmon on US 93; 20 mi W on FS 60021; 21 mi S on FS 60020. SEASON: 7/15-9/30. FACILITIES: 8 sites (tr -16); tbls, toil, cga, f, piped drk wtr. ACTIVITIES: Picnicking; fishing; boating,ld (no motors). Horseback riding (1 mi). MISC.: Elev 8800 ft; 8 acres; Iron Lake. Pets.

Wallace Lake (Salmon NF). 3-1/5 mi N of Salmon on US 93; 14 mi NW on FS 60023; 4 mi S on FS 60020. SEASON: 6/15-9/30. FACILITIES: 12 sites (tr -16); tbls, toil, cga, f, piped drk wtr. ACTIVITIES: Picnicking; fishing; boating,d (no motors). Horseback riding (1 mi). MISC.: Elev 8200 ft; 11 acres. Pets.

SANDPOINT

Pack River Viewpoint (BLM). 18 mi E of Sandpoint on US 10A. SEASON: 5/1-9/30; 14-day lmt. FACILITIES: 5 sites (tr -25); tbls, toil, cga, drk wtr. ACTIVITIES: Hunting; hiking; picnicking. Fishing (nearby). MISC.: Elev 2300 ft; 1-1/4 acres. Pets permitted if on leash.

SHOUP

Cache Bar (Salmon NF). 23-3/5 mi W of Shoup on FS 60030. SEASON: 5/25-9/5; 16-day lmt. FACILITIES: 3 sites (tr -16); tbls, cga. ACTIVITIES: Picnicking; fishing. MISC.: Elev 3000 ft; float boat trips down the river. Pets permitted.

Corn Creek (Salmon NF). 28-4/5 mi W of Shoup on FS 60030. SEASON: 5/25-10/31; 16-day lmt. FACILITIES: 22 sites (tr -22); tbls, toil, cga, piped drk wtr. ACTIVITIES: Picnicking; fishing; mtn climbing. Boating,ld/horseback riding (1 mi). MISC.: Elev 2800 ft; 10 acres. Pets permitted if kept on leash.

Ebenezer Bar (Salmon NF). 15-3/5 mi SW of Shoup on FS 60030. SEASON: 5/25-9/5; 16-day lmt. FACILITIES: 11 sites (tr -22); tbls, toil, cga, piped drk wtr. Store/food/gas (2 mi). ACTIVITIES: Picnicking; horseback riding. Fishing (1 mi). MISC.: Elev 3100 ft; 3 acres. Pets permitted if kept on a leash.

Hourse Creek Hot Springs (Salmon NF). 1½ mi NE of Shoup on FS 60030; 11-1/5 mi NW on FS 60038; 5 mi NW on FS 60044; 2 mi SW on FS 60065. SEASON: 7/1-9/15. FACILITIES: 6 sites (tr -22); tbls, toil, cga, f, piped drk wtr. ACTIVITIES: Horseback riding; picnicking; fishing. MISC.: Elev 6200 ft; 11 acres. stream. Pets permitted if kept on leash.

SPENCER

Beaver Creek (Targhee NF). Leave I-15 at Spencer; 1/2 mi E of I-15. SEASON: All yr. FACILITIES: 12 sites (tr -30); toil, cga. ACTIVITIES: Fishing; hiking. MISC.: Elev 4870; river. Pets permitted.

Stoddard Creek (Targhee NF). 3-1/2 mi N of Spencer on US 15; 1-1/5 mi NW on FS 80003. SEASON: 6/15-9/15. FACILITIES: 7 sites (tr -22); tbls, toil, cga, f, piped drk wtr. Store/gas/food (5 mi). ACTIVITIES: Picnicking; hiking; hunting. Fishing/horseback riding (1 mi). MISC.: Elev 6200 ft; 6 acres. Pets permitted.

STANLEY

Banner Creek (Challis NF). 22 mi W of Stanley on St Hwy 21. SEASON: 6/15-9/15. FACILITIES: 3 sites (tr -22); tbls, toil, cga, f, well drk wtr. ACTIVITIES: Picnicking; fishing. Horseback riding (1 mi). MISC.: Elev 6500 ft; 1 acre; stream. Pets permitted if kept on a leash.

Beaver Creek (Challis NF). 17 mi NW of Stanley on St Hwy 21; 2 mi N on FS 40172. SEASON: 6/15-9/15. FACILITIES: 4 sites (no trailers); tbls, toil, cga, f, no drk wtr. ACTIVITIES: Picnicking;

fishing. Horseback riding (1 mi). **MISC.:** Elev 7000 ft; 3 acres; stream. Pets.

Bench Creek (Challis NF). 24 mi W of Stanley on St Hwy 21. **SEASON:** 6/15-9/15. **FACILITIES:** 5 sites (tr -16); tbls, toil, cga, f, well drk wtr. **ACTIVITIES:** Picnicking; fishing. Horseback riding (1 mi). **MISC.:** Elev 6500 ft; 2 acres; stream. Pets permitted if kept on leash.

Blind Creek (Challis NF). 14-9/10 mi NE of Stanley on US 93; 1 mi N on FS FH13. **SEASON:** 9/11-6/14 FREE; ($2.00 rest of yr). **FACILITIES:** 5 sites (tr -32); tbls, toil, cga, f, well drk wtr. Store/ice (1 mi). **ACTIVITIES:** Picnicking; fishing; horseback riding. **MISC.:** Elev 6000 ft; 4 acres. No water during FREE season. Pets permitted if kept on a leash.

Dutchman Flat (Sawtooth NF). 15-4/5 mi NE of Stanley on St Hwy 75. **SEASON:** 6/15-9/15; 10-day lmt. **FACILITIES:** 5 sites (tr -16); tbls, toil, cga, f, well drk wtr. Store/food/gas/ice (1 mi). **ACTIVITIES:** Rockhounding; hiking; picnicking; fishing. Horseback riding (1 mi). **MISC.:** Elev 5800 ft; 3 acres; historic; river. **Pets.**

Flat Rock (Challis NF). 14-9/10 mi NE of Stanley on US 93; 3 mi N on FS FH13. **SEASON:** 6/15-9/10. **FACILITIES:** 9 sites (tr -32); tbls, toil, cga, f, piped drk wtr. Store/gas/food/ice (2 mi). **ACTIVITIES:** Picnicking; fishing; rockhounding. Horseback riding (1 mi). **MISC.:** Elev 6200 ft; 4 acres; stream. Pets.

Iron Creek (Sawtooth NF). 2 mi W of Stanley on St Hwy 21; 4 mi S on Fs 40019. **SEASON:** 6/30-9/15; 10-day lmt. **FACILITIES:** 12 sites (tr -22); tbls, toil, cga, f, well drk wtr. **ACTIVITIES:** Rockhounding; picnicking; fishing; hiking; mtn climbing. **MISC.:** Elev 6600 ft; 39 acres; scenic; stream nearby; trailhead to Sawtooth Wilderness; pets.

Jerry's Creek (Challis NF). 15 mi E of Stanley on US 93; 5 mi N on FS 40013. **SEASON:** 7/1-9/10; 16-day lmt. **FACILITIES:** 3 sites (tr -22); tbls, toil, cga, f, no drk wtr. **ACTIVITIES:** Picnicking; fishing. **MISC.:** Elev 6300 ft; 2 acres. Pets permitted if kept on leash.

Lola Creek (Challis NF). 17 mi NW of Stanley on St Hwy 21; 2 mi NW on FS 40083. **SEASON:** 6/15-9/15. **FACILITIES:** 27 sites (tr -16); tbls, toil, cga, piped drk wtr. **ACTIVITIES:** Picnicking; fishing. Horseback riding (1 mi). **MISC.:** Elev 6400 ft; 12 acres; river. **Pets.**

Lower O'Brien (Sawtooth NF). 16-9/10 mi E of Stanley on St Hwy 75; 2/5 mi S on FS 40054. **SEASON:** 6/15-9/15; 10-day lmt. **FACILITIES:** 12 sites (tr -22); tbls, toil, cga, f, piped drk wtr. Store/ice/gas/food (2 mi). **ACTIVITIES:** Rockhounding; hiking; picnicking; fishing. Horseback riding (1 mi). **MISC.:** Elev 5800 ft; 4 acres; river; historic. Pets.

Mayfield Creek Transfer Camp (Challis NF). 15 mi E of Stanley on US 93; 10 mi N on FS 40013; 14 mi N on FS 40172. **SEASON:** 6/15-9/30; 16-day lmt. **FACILITIES:** 30 sites (tr -22); toil, cga, f, no drk wtr. **ACTIVITIES:** Horseback riding; hiking. **MISC.:** Elev 6300 ft; 2 acres; stream. Trailhead facility. Pets.

Pole Flat (Challis NF). 14-9/10 mi NE of Stanley on US 93; 3 mi N on FS FH13. **SEASON:** 9/11-6/14 FREE; ($2.00 rest of yr). **FACILITIES:** 17 sites (tr -32); tbls, toil, cga, f, well drk wtr. Store food/ice (3 mi). **ACTIVITIES:** Picnicking; fishing; horseback riding. **MISC.:** Elev 6200 ft; 8 acres. No water during FREE season. Pets permitted on leash.

★**Redfish Inlet Transfer Camp** (Sawtooth NF). 5 mi S of Stanley on Hwy 75; 1-7/10 mi SW on FS 70214; 4-3/10 mi SW on Trail 7101. **SEASON:** 6/15-9/15; 10-day lmt. **FACILITIES:** 6 tent sites; tbls, toil, cga, f, no drk wtr. Store/ice/gas/showers/laundry/visitor center (5 mi). **ACTIVITIES:** Swimming; picnicking; fishing; hiking; mtn climbing. Waterskiing/boating,rld (5 mi). **MISC.:** Elev 6500 ft; 5 acres; stream; scenic; nature trails (5 mi); pets permitted.

Sheep Trail (Sawtooth NF). 7 mi NW of Stanley on St Hwy 21. **SEASON:** 6/30-9/15; 10-day lmt. **FACILITIES:** 4 sites (tr -22); tbls, toil, cga, f, well drk wtr. **ACTIVITIES:** Hiking; picnicking; fishing. Horseback riding (1 mi). **MISC.:** Elev 7000 ft; 2 acres; stream. Pets permitted if kept on a leash.

Thatcher Creek (Challis NF). 15 mi NW of Stanley on St Hwy 21. **SEASON:** 6/15-9/15. **FACILITIES:** 4 sites (tr -22); tbls, toil, cga, f, well drk wtr. **ACTIVITIES:** Picnicking. Horseback riding (1 mi). **MISC.:** Elev 6400 ft; 3 acres; stream. Pets permitted if kept on leash.

Tin Cup (Challis NF). 12 mi NE of Stanley on US 93; 11 mi NW on FS FH13; 20 mi N on FS 40172 (narrow rd). **SEASON:** 6/15-9/30. **FACILITIES:** 17 sites 6/15-9/30. **FAC:** 17 sites (tr -32); toil, cga, f, piped drk wtr. **ACTIVITIES:** Rockhounding; picnicking; fishing. Horseback riding (1 mi). **MISC.:** Elev 5600 ft; 4 acres; stream. Trailers over 16' not advised. Pets permitted on leash.

Upper O'Brien (Sawtooth NF). 16-9/10 mi E of Stanley on St Hwy 75; 1/5 mi E on FS 40054. **SEASON:** 6/15-9/15; 10-day lmt. **FACILITIES:** 11 sites (tr -22); tbls, toil, cga, f, well drk wtr. Store/

ice/gas/food (2 mi). **ACTIVITIES:** Rock-hounding; picnicking; fishing. Horseback riding (1 mi). **MISC.:** Elev 5800 ft; 2 acres; river; historic. Pets permitted.

STONE

Curlew (Caribou NF). 3 mi N of Stone on Co Hwy; 1/2 mi N on FS 20. **SEASON:** 5/1–8/30. **FACILITIES:** 4 sites (tr –32); tbls, toil, cga, f, piped drk wtr. Store/gas/ice/food (5 mi). **ACTIVITIES:** Swimming; picnicking; fishing; boating,l; waterskiing. Horseback riding (3 mi). **MISC.:** Elev 4600 ft; 3 acres; lake. No garbage service; pack out your litter. Pets permitted if kept on a leash.

SUN VALLEY

Park Creek (Challis NF). 12 mi NE of Sun Valley on St Hwy 75. **SEASON:** 6/30–9/15. **FACILITIES:** 17 sites (tr –32); tbls, toil, cga, f, piped drk wtr. **ACTIVITIES:** Picnicking; horseback riding (1 mi). **MISC.:** Elev 7700 ft; 10 acres; pets permitted if kept on a leash.

Phi Kappa (Challis NF). 15 mi NE of Sun Valley on St Hwy 75. **SEASON:** 6/30–9/15. **FACILITIES:** 21 sites (tr –32); tbls, toil, cga, f, piped drk wtr. **ACTIVITIES:** Picnicking. Horseback riding (1 mi). **MISC.:** Elev 7100 ft; 8 acres; stream. Pets permitted.

Wildhourse (Challis NF). 20 mi NE of Sun Valley on St hwy 75; 7 mi S on FS 40135. **SEASON:** 6/30–9/15. **FACILITIES:** 15 sites (tr –32); tbls, toil, cga, f, piped drk wtr. **ACTIVITIES:** Rock-hounding; picnicking; fishing. Horseback riding (1 mi). **MISC.:** Elev 7400 ft; 30 acres; stream. Pets permitted.

VICTOR

Mike Harris (Targhee NF). 4 mi SE of Victor on St Hwy 33; 1/2 mi SE on FS 80330. **SEASON:** 6/1–9/15. **FACILITIES:** 12 sites (tr –32); tbls, toil, cga, f, piped drk wtr. Store/gas/food/ice/showers/laundry (5 mi). **ACTIVITIES:** Hiking; picnicking. Fishing/horseback riding (1 mi). **MISC.:** Elev 6200 ft; 5 acres; stream. Pets. Nature trails.

Pine Creek (Targhee NF). 6-1/5 mi W of Victor on St Hwy 31. **SEASON:** 6/1–9/30. **FACILITIES:** 11 sites (tr –32); tbls, toil, cga, f, piped drk wtr. **ACTIVITIES:** Picnicking; fishing. **MISC.:** Elev 6600 ft; 3 acres; stream. Pets.

Trail Creek (Targhee NF). 5-3/5 mi E of Victor on St Hwy 333; 3/10 mi E on St Hwy 22. **SEASON:** 6/1–9/30. **FACILITIES:** 11 sites (tr –32). **ACTIVITIES:** Fishing; hunting. **MISC.:** Pets permitted.

WAYAN

Gravel Creek (Caribou NF). 2 mi SW of Wayan on Co Hwy 34; 1-1/2 mi SE on FS 20191. **SEASON:** 6/15–9/30; 14-day lmt. **FACILITIES:** 8 sites (tr –22); tbls, toil, cga, f, piped drk wtr. Store/gas (4 mi). **ACTIVITIES:** Hunting; picnicking; fishing; hiking; berry-picking. Horseback riding (1 mi). **MISC.:** Elev 6500 ft; 7 acres; stream; river. Pets.

WEIPPE

Lolo (Clearwater NF). 9 mi E of Weippe on Co Hwy; 10 mi S on FS 100. **SEASON:** 5/1–10/15; 14-day lmt. **FACILITIES:** 5 sites (no trailers); tbls, toil, cga, f, no drk wtr. **ACTIVITIES:** Picnicking; fishing. **MISC.:** Elev 2800 ft; 4 acres; stream. On Lewis & Clark Trail; historic; berry-picking. Pets.

WEISER

Justrite (Payette NF). 12½ mi N of Weiser on US 95; 11½ mi N on Co Hwy 50004; 3-1/5 mi N on FS 50009. **SEASON:** 6/1–10/30; 16-day lmt. **FACILITIES:** 4 sites (no trailers); tbls, toil, cga, piped drk wtr. **ACTIVITIES:** Picnicking; fishing; horseback riding (1 mi). **MISC.:** Elev 4200 ft; 1 acre; stream. 12 mi N of Mann Creek Reservoir adjacent to Mann Creek. Pets permitted if kept on a leash.

Lower Spring Creek (Payette NF). 12½ mi N of Weiser on US 95; 11½ mi N on Co Hwy 50009; 5-3/10 mi N on FS 50009. **SEASON:** 6/1–10/30; 16-day lmt. **FACILITIES:** 12 sites (tr –16); tbls, toil, cga, piped drk wtr. **ACTIVITIES:** Picnicking; fishing. Horseback riding (1 mi). **MISC.:** Elev 4800 ft; 10 acres. 14 mi N of Mann Creek Reservoir. Pets permitted.

Mann Creek Reservoir (Bur. of Rec.). 9 mi N of Weiser on US 95; 3 mi W on reservoir access rd. **SEASON:** All yr. **FACILITIES:** 18 sites; pull-thru; flush toil, tbls. **ACTIVITIES:** Swimming; picnicking; fishing; boating,ld. **MISC.:** 653 acres. Pets permitted if on leash.

Paradise (Payette NF). 12½ mi N of Weiser on US 95; 11½ mi N on Co Hwy 50009; 3-4/5 mi N on FS 50009. **SEASON:** 6/1–10/30; 16-day lmt. **FACILITIES:** 4 sites (no trailers); tbls, toil, cga, piped drk wtr. **ACTIVITIES:** Picnicking; fishing. Horseback riding (1 mi). **MISC.:** Elev 4200 ft; 1 acre; stream. 12 mi N of Mann Creek Reservoir adjacent to Mann Creek. Pets permitted.

Steck (BLM). 22 mi W of Weiser on St Hwy 70, to Olds Ferry Rd. **SEASON:** 5/1–10/31; 14-day lmt. **FACILITIES:** 33 sites (tr –25); tbls, toil, cga, water hookup; drk wtr. **ACTIVITIES:** Swimming; picnicking; fishing; boating,ld; hunting;

hiking; waterskiing. MISC.: Elev 2028 ft; 12 acres. Pets permitted if on leash.

WHITE BIRD

North Fork Slate Creek (Nezperce NF). 11 mi S of White Bird on US 95; 10 mi E on FS 233. SEASON: 6/15-10/15. FACILITIES: 5 sites (no trailers); tbls, toil, cga, f, no drk wtr. ACTIVITIES: Picnicking; fishing. Horseback riding (1 mi). MISC.: Elev 3000 ft; 2 acres; stream. 1/2 mi N of Slate Creek Ranger Station. Pets permitted if on leash.

Rest Area. 11 mi SW of White Bird on US 95. SEASON: All yr. FACILITIES: Tbls, toil, cga, dump. MISC.: Pets.

Skookumchuck (BLM). 6 mi S of White Bird on US 95. SEASON: All yr; 7-day FACILITIES: 5 sites (tr -22); tbls, toil, cga. ACTIVITIES: Swimming; picnicking.

YELLOW PINE

Buck Mtn (Boise NF). 24 mi S of Yellow Pine on FS 10413. SEASON: 6/15-8/31; 14-day lmt. FACILITIES: 4 sites (tr -16); tbls, toil, cga, f. ACTIVITIES: Picnicking; fishing. MISC.: elev 6500 ft; 1 acre. Adjacent to Johnson Creek. Pets permitted.

Trout Creek (Boise NF). 17 mi S of Yellow Pine on FS 10413. SEASON: 6/15-8/31; 14-day lmt. FACILITIES: 8 sites (tr -16); tbls, toil, cga, f, no drk wtr. ACTIVITIES: Horseback riding; picnicking; fishing. MISC.: Elev 6200 ft; 2 acres; stream. Pets permitted on leash.

Twin Bridges (Boise NF). 12 mi S of Yellow Pine on FS 10413. SEASON: 6/15-8/31; 14-day lmt. FACILITIES: 6 sites (tr -16); tbls, toil, cga, f, no drk wtr. ACTIVITIES: Picnicking; fishing; horseback riding. MISC.: Elev 5300 ft; 5 acres; river. Adjacent to Johnson Creek. Pets permitted if kept on a leash.

ILLINOIS

GENERAL STATE INFORMATION

Miscellaneous

Toll-Free Number for Travel Information:
    1-800-637-8560 (outside of Illinois)
    1-800-637-8560 (within Illinois)
Right Turns on Red: Permitted after full stop, unless otherwise posted.
STATE CAPITOL: Springfield
STATE NICKNAME: Prairie State
STATE MOTTO: "State Sovereignty, National Union"
STATE BIRD: Cardinal
STATE FLOWER: Butterfly Violet
STATE TREE: Bur Oak

State Parks

Overnight fees range from $1.00-5.00 per night. People 65 years of age or over, as well as persons who are disabled or blind, may camp FREE OF CHARGE at all state parks. Further information: Illinois Office of Tourism; 222 South College Street; Springfield, IL 62706. Pets are allowed on leash in MOST parks.

Rest Areas

Overnight stops are not permitted at Illinois Rest Areas.

Canoeing/Camping in Illinois

Request the free book ILLINOIS CANOEING GUIDE, which includes maps and campsites along the waterways, from: Department of Conservation; 605 State Office Building; Springfield, IL 62706.

Backpacking/Camping in Shawnee NF

The Shawnee has quite a few opportunities for hiking and backcountry camping. The best long-distance area is the River to River Trail which is about 80 miles in length starting at Camp Cadiz on the east side of the Forest and ending at St Hwy 45. Only about ⅓ of the trail appears on the Shawnee NF Recreation Map, but the other half is clearly marked on the ground. The LaRue-Pine Hills Wilderness has more than 19,000 acres of natural area to explore. Further information: Forest Supervisor; Shawnee NF; 317 East Poplar Street; Harrisburg, IL 62946.

INFORMATION SOURCES

Maps

The following maps are available from Forsyth Travel Library (see order form in Appendix B):

State of Illinois [Up-to-date, showing all principal roads, points of interest, sports areas, parks, airports, mileage, etc. Full color.]

Completely indexed city maps, including all airports, lakes, rivers, etc., of: Chicago, Joliet, Bolingbrook, Peoria, Springfield, and Waukegan/Lake County.

State Information

Division of Tourism; Department of Business and Economic Development; 222 South College; Springfield, IL 62706.
Division of Tourism, Adventure Center; 160 North LaSalle Street, Room 100; Chicago, IL 60601.
Department of Conservation; 605 State Office Building; 400 South Spring Street; Springfield, IL 62706.

City Information

Chicago Association of Commerce and Industry; 130 South Michigan Avenue; Chicago, IL 60603.
Tourism Council of Greater Chicago; Civic Center; Chicago, IL 60603.
Springfield Association of Commerce and Industry; 325 East Adams Street; Springfield, IL 62701.

Miscellaneous

Shawnee NF; 317 East Poplar Street; Harrisburg, IL 62946.
Upper Mississippi River Wild Life & Fish Refuge; District Refuge Manager; PO Box 250; Savanna, IL 60174.
Corps of Engineers, St. Louis District; 210 North 12th Street; St. Louis, MO 63101. [Their free campgrounds are in Illinois.]
Corps of Engineers, North Central; 536 Clark Street; Chicago, IL 60605.
Corps of Engineers, Rock Island; Clock Tower Building; Rock Island, IL 61201.

FREE CAMPGROUNDS

ALTAMONT

Rest Area. 5 mi E of Altamont on I-70. SEASON: All yr; 1-day lmt. FACILITIES: 18 sites for self-contained RVs. Tbls, toil, drinking fountains, dump, phone. ACTIVITIES: Picnicking. MISC.: Pets permitted if kept on a leash.

ANDALUSIA

Andalusia Slough (COE; Mississippi River Public Use Area). 2 mi W of Andalusia off St Hwy 92. SEASON: All yr; 14-day lmt. FACILITIES: 30 sites; tbls, toil, cga, drk wtr. Store/food/ice/laundry nearby. ACTIVITIES: Swimming; picnicking; fishing; boating,l. MISC.: Pets.

CARLYLE

*Boulder Access Area (COE; Carlyle Lake). 6 mi E on US 50 from Carlyle; 5 mi N on Boulder-Ferrin Rd to CG. SEASON: 4/15-9/30; 14-day lmt. FACIL-

ILLINOIS

ITIES: 20 walk-in tent sites; tbls, cga, flush toil. ACTIVITIES: Fishing; hiking; boating; waterskiing; picnicking.

CARTHAGE

Carthage City Park. On the W side of Carthage, off St Hwy 136. SEASON: All yr. FACILITIES: Sites. MISC.: Pets.

CLINTON

Cattail Slough (COE; Mississippi River Public Use Area). ¼ mi SW of East Clinton. SEASON: All yr; 14-day lmt. FACILITIES: 15 sites; tbls, toil, cga, drk wtr. ACTIVITIES: Swimming; picnicking; fishing; boating,l. MISC.: Pets on leash.

EFFINGHAM

Rest Area. 5 mi W of Effingham on I-70. SEASON: All yr; 1-night lmt. FACILITIES: 18 sites; tbls, toil, cga, drinking fountains, dump. ACTIVITIES: Picnicking. MISC.: Elev 500 ft; pets on leash; phone.

FULTON

Lock and Dam 13 (Mississippi River Public Use Area; COE). 2 mi N of Fulton on St Hwy 84; turn W at sign. SEASON: All yr; 14-day lmt. FACILITIES: 14 sites; tbls, toil, cga. ACTIVITIES: Boating,l. MISC.: Pets.

GORHAM

Turkey Bayou (Shawnee NF). ½ mi SE of Gorham on Co Hwy TR913; 2 mi S on St Hwy 3; 3-9/10 mi E on FS 786; 7/10 mi N on FS 786A. SEASON: 4/15-12/31; 14-day lmt. FACILITIES: 17 sites (tr -32); tbls, toil, cga, no drk wtr. ACTIVITIES: Swimming; boating (ld, 1 mi); picnicking; fishing; berry-picking. MISC.: Elev 300 ft; 5 acres; pets; lake.

Turkey Bayou Overflow Campground (Shawnee NF). ½ mi SE of Gorham on Co Hwy TR913; 2 mi S on St Hwy 3; 3-9/10 mi E on FS FR786; 1/5 mi N on FS 786E. SEASON: 4/15-12/31; 14-day lmt. FACILITIES: 13 sites (tr -32); tbls, toil, cga, f, well drk wtr. ACTIVITIES: Fishing; picnicking. Boating,ld (1 mi). MISC.: Elev 300 ft; 5 acres; river; pets.

HAMPTON

Fisherman's Corner (COE; Mississippi River Public Use Area). 1 mi N of Hampton on St Hwy 84. [Adjacent to Lock and Dam 14.] SEASON: All yr; 14-day lmt. FACILITIES: 20 sites; tbls, toil, cga, drk wtr. ACTIVITIES: Swimming; picnicking; fishing; boating,l. MISC.: Pets permitted if kept on a leash.

HANNIBAL

John Hay (COE; Mississippi River Public Use Area). E end of US 36, near Hannibal. SEASON: All yr; 14-day lmt. FACILITIES: 50 sites; tbls, toil, cga, f, drk wtr. Store/food/ice/laundry/bottled gas nearby. ACTIVITIES: Swimming; picnicking; fishing; boating,ld. Golf nearby. MISC.: Pets on leash.

HANOVER

Blanding Landing (COE; Mississippi River Public Use Area). W off St Hwy onto the first road N of Apple River Bridge in Hanover; take first RR crossing. SEASON: All yr; 14-day lmt. FACILITIES: 50 sites; tbls, toil, cga, drk wtr, dump. Store/ice/food nearby. ACTIVITIES: Horseback riding; picnicking; fishing; swimming; boating,rl; hiking. Snowskiing nearby (in winter). MISC.: Pets.

HULL

Park-N-Fish (COE; Mississippi River Public Use Area). 7/10 mi W of Hull on US 36; 6-1/5 mi S on paved road. SEASON: All yr; 14-day lmt. FACILITIES: 10 sites; tbls, toil, cga, drk wtr. ACTIVITIES: Swimming; picnicking; fishing; horseback riding. MISC.: Pets allowed on leash.

JACKSONVILLEL

Ebaugh Park. 17 mi W of Jacksonville on US 36. SEASON: All yr. FACILITIES: Sites. MISC.: Pets allowed if on leash.

MARCELLINE

Bear Creek (COE; Mississippi River Public Use Area). 1½ mi W of St Hwy 96 in Marcelline on Bolton Rd; ½ mi on gravel rd; 3 mi W across the levee to the campground. SEASON: All yr; 14-day lmt. FACILITIES: 75 sites; tbls, toil, cga, drk wtr. ACTIVITIES: Swimming; picnicking; fishing; boating,l; horseback riding. MISC.: Pets allowed if on a leash.

McCLURE

Grapevine Trail (Shawnee NF). 4-4/5 mi E of McClure on Co Hwy 13. SEASON: All yr; 14-day lmt. FACILITIES: 6 sites (tr -22); tbls, toil, cga, f. Store/ice/gas/food (3 mi). Laundry (5 mi). MISC.: Elev 600 ft; 4 acres; pets. No drk wtr.

MUSCATINE

Blanchard Island (COE; Mississippi River Public Use Area). Turn S off St Hwy 92; 1½ mi E of Muscatine Bridge, proceed 4 mi S; turn right on 2nd Co Rd past Copperas Creek Bridge, and proceed W to levee. SEASON: All yr; 14-day lmt. FACILITIES: 35 sites; tbls, toil, cga, drk wtr. ACTIVITIES: Swimming; picnicking; fishing; boating,l; horseback riding.

OBLONG

Oblong City Park. On the East side of Oblong, North of St Hwy 33. SEASON: All yr. MISC.: Pets allowed if on a leash.

PRINCETON

Rest Area. 3 mi W of Princeton on I-80, on both sides of the highway. [Paved access roads.] SEASON: All yr; 1-night lmt. FACILITIES: 10 sites; toil, dump.

RIPLEY

LaGrange Lock and Dam Camping Area (COE). 2 mi E of Ripley on St Hwy 103; S on gravel road. There is a large

READ THIS!

sign at this crossroad directing travelers to LaGrange Lock and Dam. Bear left at all intersections until you reach the lock and dam. It is located on the Illinois River at river mile 80.3. SEASON: All yr. FACILITIES: 12 sites; tbls, flush toil, cga, electric/water/sewer hookups. ACTIVITIES: Boating,1; picnicking; fishing. MISC.: Pets.

ROBINSON

City Park. On St Hwy 33, the south side of Robinson. SEASON: All yr. FACILITIES: Sites. MISC.: Pets.

WINDSOR

Whitley Creek (COE; Lake Shelbyville). 5 mi N on St Hwy 32; 1 mi W; 1 mi N to CG. SEASON: 4/1-10/30; 14-day lmt. FACILITIES: 26 sites; tbls, flush toil, cga, drk wtr, showers. ACTIVITIES: Swimming; picnicking; fishing; boating. MISC.: Pets on leash.

INDIANA

GENERAL STATE INFORMATION

Miscellaneous

Right Turns on Red: Permitted after full stop, unless otherwise posted.
STATE CAPITOL: Indianapolis
STATE NICKNAME: Hoosier State
STATE MOTTO: "Crossroads of America"
STATE BIRD: Cardinal
STATE FLOWER: Peony
STATE TREE: Tulip

State Parks

Campground fees range from $1.00-3.00 per night. Camping fees are collected all year. Pets on leash are permitted. Admission Fee: $10 per Annual Entrance Permit; or $1.25 per single vehicle daily. Further information: Department of Natural Resources; Division of State Parks; 616 State Office Building; Indianapolis, IN 46204.

Rest Areas

Overnight parking is not permitted in Indiana Rest Areas.

Off-Season Camping at Wayne-Hoosier NF Developed Campgrounds

All campgrounds in the national forest charge fees varying from $2.00-3.00 per night. Most of the campgrounds remain open to limited use after they turn off water supplies and terminate fee collection, but this is determined by weather rather than date. Therefore, if you are in the national forest area, contact headquarters and see what the status of FREE OFF-SEASON CAMPGROUNDS is at the time of your visit. Further information/map: Forest Supervisor; Wayne-Hoosier NF; 1615 "J" Street; Bedford, IN 47421.

See page 7 for KEY TO ABBREVIATIONS.

INDIANA

Backcountry Camping/Hiking in Wayne-Hoosier NF

Free backcountry camping is permitted anywhere throughout the national forest. The Nebo Ridge area, although not technically a "wilderness", is a fairly large block of national forest land which is rather rugged and picturesque. You can purchase a booklet, "Hiker's Guide to Nebo Ridge", from the Student Committee of Indiana Sassafras Audubon Society; Room 48-M; Indiana Memorial Union; Bloomington, IN 47401. Free maps and brochures on hiking and camping throughout the forest in general can be obtained from: Forest Supervisor; Wayne-Hoosier NF; 1615 "J" Street; Bedford, IN 47421.

INFORMATION SOURCES

Maps

The following maps are available from **Forsyth Travel Library** (see order form in Appendix B):

> **State of Indiana** [Up-to-date, showing all principal roads, points of interest, sports areas, parks, airports, mileage, etc. Full color.]
>
> Completely indexed city maps, including all airports, lakes, rivers, etc., of: **Evansville; Fort Wayne; Indianapolis.**

State Information

Division of Tourism; Department of Commerce; State House, Room 336; Indianapolis, IN 46204.
Department of Natural Resources; Division of State Parks; 616 State Office Building; Indianapolis, IN 46204.
Department of Natural Resources; Fish and Game Division; 608 State Office Building; Indianapolis, IN 46204.
Indiana State Chamber of Commerce; Board of Trade Building; Indianapolis, IN 46204.

City Information

Fort Wayne Chamber of Commerce; 826 Ewing Street; Fort Wayne, IN 46802.
Convention and Visitor's Bureau; 1201 Roosevelt Building; Indianapolis, IN 46204.
Indianapolis Chamber of Commerce; 320 North Meridian Street; Indianapolis, IN 45204.
Lafayette Chamber of Commerce; PO Box 348; Lafayette, IN 47902.
South Bend Chamber of Commerce; PO Box 1677; South Bend, IN 46601.

National Forests

Wayne-Hoosier NF; 1615 "J" Street; Bedford, IN 47421.

FREE CAMPGROUNDS

BERNE

Linn Grove Park (City Park). 4 mi W of Berne on St Hwy 218; 1 mi S on Rd 500W. SEASON: All yr. FACILITIES: Sites, including tent pads; tbls, toil, cga, well drk wtr. ACTIVITIES: Fishing (crappies and bass). The site includes fishing pads for wheelchairs. Boating,l; picnicking; fishing. MISC.: Adjacent to the Wabash River; a pond; a deep pit quarry. Pets on leash.

ORIOLE

Buzzard Roost Overlook (Hoosier NF). 1 mi S of Oriole on St Hwy 66; 4 mi SE on Co Hwy 1012; ½ mi E on FS 1960. SEASON: 4/1-10/15; 14-day lmt. FACILITIES: 10 sites (tr -22); tbls, toil, cga, f, tank drk wtr. ACTIVITIES: Hiking; picnicking. Fishing (1 mi). MISC.: Elev 600 ft; 6 acres; river.

PLYMOUTH

Centennial Park. On the N edge of Plymouth on US 31 (City Route). SEASON: All year. FACILITIES: Sites. MISC.: Pets.

ST. CROIX

Celina Lake (Hoosier NF). 1½ mi S of St. Croix on St Hwy 37; 1½ mi W on FS 501. SEASON: All yr; 14-day lmt. FACILITIES: 26 sites (tr -22); tbls, toil, cga, no drk wtr. ACTIVITIES: Boating,ld; picnicking. Fishing (1 mi). MISC.: Elev 800 ft; 11 acres; lake; scenic; pets.

NOTICE TO CAMPERS

See page 5 for additional places to camp for free.

See page 7 for KEY TO ABBREVIATIONS.

IOWA

Miscellaneous

Toll-Free Number for Travel Information:
1-800-362-2843, ext. 3679 [the call
must be made within the State]
Right Turns on Red: Permitted after
full stop, unless otherwise posted.
STATE CAPITOL: Des Moines
STATE NICKNAME: Hawkeye State
STATE MOTTO: "Our Liberties We Prize
and Our Rights We
Will Maintain"
STATE BIRD: Eastern Goldfinch
STATE FLOWER: Wild Rose

State Parks

Camping rates range from $2.50-4.00 per night.   Camping fees do not include the use
of boat and beach facilities which are operated by concessionaires under contract with
the commission.   Mushroom hunting is permitted in all state parks!   Fishing, boating,
swimming, picnicking.   Pets permitted on leash.   Further information: Iowa Conservation Commission; Wallace State Office Building; Des Moines, IA 50319.

INFORMATION SOURCES

Maps

The following maps are available from **Forsyth Travel Library** (see order form in Appendix B):

State of Iowa [Up-to-date, showing all principal roads,
points of interest, sports areas, parks, airports, mileage,
etc. Full color.]

Completely indexed city maps, including all airports, lakes,
rivers, etc., of: **Davenport; Rock Island; Moline; Des
Moines; Sioux City.**

State Information

Iowa Development Commission; Tourism and Recreational Development Division; 250 Jew-
ett Building; Des Moines, Iowa 50309.
State Conservation Commission; Wallace State Office Building; 300 - 4th Street; Des
Moines, IA 50319.
Fish and Game Department; State Conservation Commission; State Office Building; 300
Fourth Street; Des Moines, IA 50319.
State of Iowa Chamber of Commerce; Hotel Burlington; Burlington, IA 52601.

City Information

Ames Chamber of Commerce; 205 Clark, Suite 2; Ames, IA 50010.
Cedar Rapids Chamber of Commerce; 127 - 3rd Street NE; Cedar Rapids, IA 52401.
Greater Des Moines Chamber of Commerce; 8th and High Streets; Des Moines, IA 50307.

Miscellaneous

Upper Mississippi River Wildlife and Fish Refuge; PO Box 250; Guttenberg, IA 52052.
Corps of Engineers, Kansas City District; 700 Federal Building; Kansas City, MO 64106.
[Has a free campground in Iowa.]

FREE CAMPGROUNDS

AINSWORTH

Marr Park (Municipal Park). 1 mi
W of Ainsworth on St Hwy 92. (On
the S side of the road). SEASON: All
yr; 4-day lmt. FACILITIES: tbls,
toil, cga, f, drk wtr. Store/laundry/
food concession nearby. ACTIVITIES:
Picnicking; fishing; playground.

See page 7 for KEY TO ABBREVIATIONS.

ALBIA

Georgetown Rest Area. 9 mi W of Albia on US 34. SEASON: All yr; 1-night lmt. FACILITIES: Spaces for self-contained vehicles; tbls, toil, cga, f. ACTIVITIES: Picnicking. MISC: Pets on leash.

ALDEN

Bessman Kemp. 1/2 mi W of Main St in Alden. SEASON: All yr; 1-night lmt. FACILITIES: Spaces for self-contained vehicles; toil; elec. lighting (no hookups). MISC: Pets.

ALGONA

Kossuth–Lake Smith (County Park). 3 mi N of jct St Hwys 18 & 169 (paved access road). SEASON: All yr; 14-day lmt. FACILITIES: 20 sites tbls, toil, cga, phone, playground. ACTIVITIES: Picnicking; fishing; boating,ld. MISC: Recreational Hall. Pets on leash.

AMES

I-35 Rest Area. 8 mi N of Ames, exit on I-35 (paved access roads). SEASON: All yr; 1-night lmt. FACILITIES: Spaces for self-contained vehicles; toil, tbls. ACTIVITIES: Picnicking. MISC: Pets.

AUDUBON

Albert The Bull Park. On St Hwy 71, S of Audubon. SEASON: All yr; 1-night lmt. FACILITIES: Spaces for self-contained vehicles; tbls, toil, cga, drk wtr. ACTIVITIES: Picnicking fishing; swimming (pool); golf nearby. MISC: Playground. Pets on leash.

BAXTER

Ashton Wildwood Park. 8 mi W of Baxter. SEASON: All yr; 1-night lmt. FACILITIES: Spaces for self-contained vehicles. MISC: Pets.

BELLEVUE

Bellevue Roadside Park (County Park). 5 mi N of Bellevue on US 52 (paved access roads). SEASON: All yr; 1-night lmt. FACILITIES: Spaces for self-contained vehicles; tbls, toil, cga. ACTIVITIES: Picnicking; hiking. MISC: Pets.

Duck Creek Park (County Park). 5 mi S of Bellevue on US 67 (park on W side of hwy). Walk-in camping. SEASON: All yr; 1-night lmt. FACILITIES: Tent sites, tbls, toil, cga, ACTIVITIES: Picnicking; fishing; hiking. MISC: Mississippi River. Pets.

Pleasant Creek (COE: Mississipi River Public Use Area). 3-1/2 mi S of Bellevue off St Hwy 52 (on E side of the road). SEASON: All yr; 14-day lmt. FACILITIES: 55 sites; tbls, toil, cga, dump, drk wtr. ACTIVITIES: Picnicking; fishing; swimming; boating,l. MISC: Miss. River. Pets on leash.

BENTONSPORT

Bentonsport River Front Park. N edge of Bentonsport. SEASON: All yr; 1-night lmt. FACILITIES: Spaces for self-contained vehicles. ACTIVITIES: Fishing. MISC: Pets.

BLOOMFIELD

Drakesville City Park (City Park). 3 mi N of Bloomfield on US 63; 4 mi W on St Hwy 273. SEASON: All yr. FACILITIES: 40 sites, tbls, toil, cga, showers, ice, fd concession, store, playground. Bottled gas nearby. ACTIVITIES: Picnicking; fishing; horseback riding. MISC: Pets.

BROOKLYN

City Park. 1 mi N of Brooklyn off I-80. SEASON: All yr; 1-night lmt. Spaces for self-contained vehicles. MISC: Pets on leash.

BUFFALO CENTER

Thompson Roadside Park (Municipal Park). 10 mi W of Buffalo Center on St Hwy 9. SEASON: All yr. FACILITIES: tbls, toil, cga, f, elec hookup; drk wtr. Food concession/store/laundry nearby. ACTIVITIES: Picnicking; golf nearby. MISC: Pets.

BURLINGTON

City Park. In Burlington. SEASON: All yr; 1-night lmt. FACILITIES: Spaces for self-contained vehicles. MISC: Pets on leash.

CENTERVILLE

Glenwood (COE: Rathbun Lake). 7 mi W of Centerville on St Hwy 2; 6 mi N on S70. SEASON: All yr; 14-day lmt. FACILITIES: 5 sites, tbls, toil, cga, drk wtr. ACTIVITIES: Picnicking; fishing; swimming; boating,l. MISC: Pets on leash.

Lelah Bradley Park (Municipal Park). 16 blocks S of St Hwy 2 in Centerville on Main Street; W on West Cottage. SEASON: 5/30-9/30; 6-day lmt. FACILITIES: 10 sites, tbls, toil, cga, f, elec/wtr/swr hookup, drk wtr. Bottled gas/ice/laundry/food concession/store nearby. ACTIVITIES: Picnicking; fishing; boating,l; playground. MISC: Pets.

Outlet (COE: Rathbun Lake). 4 mi N of Centerville on St Hwy 5; 3 mi NW on St Hwy 278. SEASON: All yr; 14-day lmt. FACILITIES: 8 sites, tbls, toil, cga. ACTIVITIES: Picnicking; fishing; boating,l. Swimming nearby. MISC: Pets.

CHARITON

Stephens Forest (SF). NE of jct of US 65/34 in Chariton off 34. SEASON: All yr; 7-day lmt. FACILITIES: 50 primitive sites, tbls, toil, cga, f, drk wtr. ACTIVITIES: Picnicking; fishing; hiking; hunting; horseback riding. MISC: Pets.

CLARINDA

Clarinda City Park. On St Hwy 2, E of business district, in Clarinda. SEASON: All yr; 1-night lmt. FACILITIES: Spaces for self-contained vehicles. MISC: Pets on leash.

Nodaway Valley Park (Municipal Park). 2-1/2 mi N of Clarinda on US 71. SEASON: 4/1-11/15; 10-day lmt. FACILITIES: 10 sites, tbls, toil, cga, f, playground, drk wtr. ACTIVITIES: Picnicking; fishing; hiking. MISC: Pets on leash.

Pioneer Park (Municipal Park). 10 mi W of Clarinda on St Hwy 2. SEASON: 4/15-10/15; 10 day lmt. FACILITIES: 10 sites (tr -28), tbls, flush toil, cga, drk wtr, elec hookup ($), showers, playground. ACTIVITIES: Picnicking; fishing. MISC: Pets.

CLEMONS

French Wild Life Area 1-1/2 mi S of Clemons on paved rd;1-1/2 mi W of Clemons. SEASON: All yr; 1-night lmt. FACILITIES: Spaces for self-contained vehicles. MISC: Pets.

CLINTON

Bulger's Hollow (COE: Mississippi River Public Use Area). 4 mi N of Clinton on US 67; 1 mi E on Co Rd. SEASON: All yr; 14-day lmt. FACILITIES: 30 sites, tbls, toil, cga, f, drk wtr. ACTIVITIES: Picnicking; fishing; boating,l; horseback riding MISC: Pets on leash.

DES MOINES

I-80 Rest Area. 10 mi W of Des Moines on I-80 (paved access roads). SEASON: All yr; 1-night lmt. FACILI-

TIES: Spaces for self-contained vehicles, toil, dump. MISC: Pets on leash.

Fishermans COG (COE: Saylorville Lake). 4 mi N of Des Moines on St Hwy R6F; 2 mi E at entrance sign. SEAS: All yr; 14-day lmt. FAC: 22 sites, tbls, toil, cga, drk wtr. Dump station nearby. ACTIVITIES: Picnicking; fishing; swimming; boating,l; snowmobiling; golfing nearby. MISC: Snowmobile trails. Pets on leash.

DRAKESVILLE

Drakesville Park. W end of town, in Drakesville. SEASON: All yr; 1-night lmt. FACILITIES: Spaces for self-contained vehicles. MISC: Pets.

DUBUGUL

Mud Lake Lagoon. 6 mi N of Dubugul on US 52; 4 mi E on Co Rd (paved access roads). SEASON: 5/1-11/1; 10-day lmt. FACILITIES: 80 sites, tbls, toil, cga, f, gas, elec hookup ($). ACTIVITIES: Picnicking; fishing; hiking; boating,ld; waterskiing. MISC: Pets on leash.

FAIRPORT

Shady Creek (COE: Mississippi River Public Use Area). 1-1/2 mi N of Fairport; turn off St Hwy 22 at sign. SEASON: All yr; 14-day lmt. FACILITIES: 50 sites, tbls, toil, cga, f. ACTIVITIES: Picnicking; boating,ld. MISC: Pets.

FARMINGTON

Shimek (SF). 1 mi E of Farmington on St Hwy 2. SEASON: All yr; 7-day lmt. FACILITIES: 50 sites, tbls, toil, cga, f, drk wtr. ACTIVITIES: Picnicking; fishing; horseback riding. MISC: Pets.

Shimek Donnellson Unit. 5 mi E of Farmington on St Hwy 2 (paved access roads). SEASON: All yr; 1-night lmt. Spaces for self-contained vehicles;tbls, toil, cga. ACTIVITIES: Picnicking; hiking. MISC: Nature trails. Pets.

FLOYD

City Park. St Hwy 218 in Floyd. SEASON: All yr; 1-night lmt. FACILITIES: Spaces for self-contained vehicles. MISC: Pets.

FOREST CITY

Ambroson Park (Municipal Park). 3 mi N of Forest City on US 69. SEASON: All yr. FACILITIES: 10 sites;

See page 7 for KEY TO ABBREVIATIONS.

tbls, toil, cga, drk wtr, playground.
Store/food concession/laundry nearby.
ACTIVITIES: Picnicking; fishing.
MISC: Pets permitted on leash.

GARNER

Ell Town Roadside. 2-1/2 mi S of
Garner on US 69. SEASON: All yr;
1-night lmt. FACILITIES: Spaces for
self-contained vehicles, tbls, toil,
cga. ACTIVITIES: Picnicking. MISC:
Pets on leash.

GAZA

Wall Park (City Park). North edge
of Gaza. SEASON: All yr; 2-day lmt.
FACILITIES: 6 sites (tr -30); tbls,
toil, cga, elec hookup, drk wtr,
playground. ACTIVITIES: Picnicking.
MISC: Pets permitted on leash.

GLIDDEN

Dickson Timber (County Park). 2 mi
E of Glidden on St hwy 30; 5 mi N.
SEASON: All yr; 1-night lmt. FACILI-
TIES: Spaces for self-contained vehic-
les, tbls, toil, cga, f. ACTIVITIES:
Picnicking; hunting; hiking. MISC:
Nature trails. Pets on leash.

Merrit Access (County Park). 2 mi
E of Glidden on St Hwy 30; 8 mi N.
SEASON: All yr; 14-day lmt. FACILI-
TIES: Spaces for self-contained vehic-
les, tbls, toil, cga, f, well drk wtr
ACTIVITIES: Picnicking; fishing; hik-
ing. MISC: River. Pets on leash.

GRAND RIVER

Shewmaker Park (County Park). 1/2
mi S of Grand River on St Hwy 294;
1 mi E. SEASON: All yr; 1-night lmt.
FACILITIES: 10 sites (tr -25), toil.
ACTIVITIES: Fishing. MISC: River.
Pets permitted on leash.

GRANGER

Jester County Park. St Hwy 141, in
Granger (follow signs). SEASON: All
yr; 14-day lmt. FACILITIES: 300
sites, tbls, toil, cga, f, phone. AC-
TIVITIES: Picnicking; fishing; golfing; softball. MISC: Pets on leash.

Thomas Mitchell Park. 2-1/2 mi S &
1/2 mi W of I-80 to park. SEASON:
All yr; 1-night lmt. FACILITIES: 30
sites, tbls, toil, cga, f, playground
ACTIVITIES: Picnicking; softball.
MISC: Pets permitted on leash.

GRANT

Pilot Grove Park. 3 mi W of Grant.
SEASON: All yr; 1-night lmt. FACILI-
TIES: 16 sites; tbls, toil, cga, f,

playground. ACTIVITIES: Picnicking;
fishing; hiking. MISC: Scenic; river.
Pets on leash.

HAMPTON

Handorf Conservation Park (County
Park). 8 mi E of Hampton on St Hwy
3. SEASON: All yr; 2-day lmt.
FACILITIES: 15 sites (tr -30); tbls,
toil, cga, f, playground. ACTIVI-
TIES: Picnicking (shelter). MISC:
Pets on leash.

WKW Conservation Park
(County Park). 1 mi N of
Hampton; 1 mi E. SEASON: 4/15-10/15;
4-day lmt. FACILITIES: Sites (tr -
32), tbls, toil, cga, f, playground.
ACTIVITIES: Picnicking; fishing;
horseback riding; hiking. MISC:
River; nature trails; shelters. Located on heavily ambered ground. A
hiking-horseback-snowmobile trail
1-4/5 mi in length winds through the
timber. Pets.

HUDSON

Sargent Memorial Roadside Park (Municipal Park). 1 mi N of Hudson on
St Hwy 63. SEASON: All yr; 14-day
lmt. FACILITIES: 10 sites (tr -30);
tbls, toil, cga, f, drk wtr. Store/
ice/food concession/laundry nearby.
ACTIVITIES: Picnicking. MISC: Pets.

HUMESTON

Humeston Lake Side Park. 1 mi N of
Humeston. SEASON: All yr; 14-day
lmt. FACILITIES: 15 sites, tbls, toil,
f, playground. ACTIVITIES: Picnicking. MISC: Pets.

IOWA CITY

I-80 Rest Stop (West Bound). 8 mi
W of Iowa City. SEASON: All yr; 1-
night lmt. FACILITIES: Spaces for
self-contained vehicles; tbls, toil,
cga. ACTIVITIES: Picnicking. MISC:
Pets permitted on leash.

Linder Point/West Overlook (COE:
Coraville Reservoir). 2 mi N of Iowa
City on St Hwy W66; 1 mi E at Coraville Lake sign (follow signs). SEA-
SON: All yr; 14-day lmt. FACILITIES:
100 sites; tbls, toil, cga. Store/food
concession/ice nearby. ACTIVITIES:
Picnicking; fishing; boating,1; hiking; playground. MISC: Nature
trails; bike trails; lake. Pets.

Tailwater East (COE: Coraville Reservoir). 2 mi N of Iowa City on St Hwy
W66; E at Coraville Lake sign; follow

signs until across Coralville Dam; turn right. **SEASON:** All yr; 14-day lmt. **FACILITIES:** 28 sites; tbls, toil, cga, drk wtr. **ACTIVITIES:** Picnicking; fishing; boating,l; hiking. **MISC:** Bike trails. Pets on leash.

Tailwater West (COE: Coralville Reservoir). 2 mi N of Iowa City on st Hwy W66; 1-1/4 mi E at Coralville Lake sign (follow signs). Paved access roads. **SEASON:** All yr; 14-day lmt. **FACILITIES:** 50 sites; tbls, toil, cga, drk wtr. Store/food concession/ ice nearby. **ACTIVITIES:** Picnicking; fishing; boating,rl; hiking; swimming. **MISC:** Bike trails; lake; beach. Pets permitted on leash.

Turkey Creek Heights (COE: Coralville Reservoir). At Headquarters; off St Hwy 1 N on Prairie Du Chien Rd (paved access rd). **SEASON:** All yr; 14-day lmt. **FACILITIES:** 35 sites; tbls, toil, cga, f, phone, drk wtr. **ACTIVITIES:** Picnicking; fishing; hiking; hunting; boating,rld; waterskiing; rockhounding. **MISC:** Bike trails; lake; river; nature trails. Pets.

St Hwy 20 Rest Area. On St Hwy 20; W edge of Iowa Falls. **SEASON:** All yr; 1-night lmt. **FACILITIES:** Spaces for self-contained vehicles; tbls, toil. **ACT.:** Picnicking. **MISC.:** Pets.

JEFFERSON

Chautauqua Park. 510 W Russell St, in Jefferson. **SEASON:** All yr; 1-night lmt. **FACILITIES:** Spaces for self-contained vehicles; toil. **ACTIVITIES:** Swimming. **MISC:** Pets.

LAKE CITY

Rainbow Bend Access (County Park). 1/2 mi W of S edge of Lake City; 2-1/2 mi S. **SEASON:** All yr; 14-day lmt. **FACILITIES:** Sites; tbls, toil, cga, f, well drk wtr. **ACTIVITIES:** Picnicking; fishing. **MISC:** River. Pets on leash.

LE MARS

City Park. On St Hwy 3/5/60; NE edge of Le Mars. **SEASON:** All yr; 1-night lmt. **FACILITIES:** Spaces for self-contained vehicles. **MISC:** Pets.

LIBERTY

Mid River Park (COE: Coralville Reservoir). 3 mi NW of North Liberty on St Hwy 153. **SEASON:** All yr; 14-day lmt. **FACILITIES:** 30 sites, tbls, toil, cga. Food concession nearby. **ACTIVITIES:** Picnicking; fishing; boating,rl; swimming. **MISC:** Pets.

LOHRVILLE

University "40". 1/2 mi E of Lohrville on St Hwy 175; 1 mi S; 1/2 mi W. **SEASON:** All yr; 14-day lmt. **FACILITIES:** Sites; tbls, toil, cga, f. **ACTIVITIES:** Picnicking; fishing; hiking. **MISC:** River. Pets on leash.

LUCAS

Spehens State Forest. 1 mi W of Lucas; 1 mi S. **SEASON:** All yr; 14-day lmt. **FACILITIES:** Sites; toil, f. **ACTIVITIES:** Fishing; hunting; hiking. **MISC:** Nature trails. Pets.

LYNNVILLE

Old Settlers Park. 7 mi off I-80. **SEASON:** All yr; 1-night lmt. **FACILITIES:** 12 sites; toil. **MISC:** Pets.

MENLO

Menlo Park (City Park). N edge of Menlo by RR track. **SEASON:** All yr; 14-day lmt. **FACILITIES:** 10 sites; tbls, toil, cga. **ACTIVITIES:** Picnicking. **MISC:** Pets on leash.

MERIDEN

Meriden Roadside Park. 1/2 mi W of Meriden on St Hwy 3. **SEASON:** All yr; 14-day lmt. **FACILITIES:** Sites; tbls, toil, cga. **ACTIVITIES:** Picnicking. **MISC:** Pets on leash.

MILES

Miles Roadside Park. On St Hwy 64; N edge of Miles. **SEASON:** All yr; 5-day lmt. **FACILITIES:** Sites, tbls, toil. **ACTIVITIES:** Picnicking. **MISC:** Pets permitted on leash.

MONTICELLO

Monticello City Park (City Park). 700 N Maple, in Monticello (within the Great Jones County Fairgrounds). **SEASON:** 4/1-10/1; 1-day lmt. **FACILITIES:** 25 sites; tbls, toil, cga, f, drk wtr, showers, playground. Ice/ bottled gas/laundry/food concession nearby. **ACTIVITIES:** Picnicking; golfing nearby. **MISC:** Pets on leash.

Picture Rocks (Municipal Park). 5 mi SE of Monticello on St Hwy 38; 2 mi E. **SEASON:** 5/1-10/15; 14-day lmt. **FACILITIES:** 20 sites; tbls, toil, cga, f, drk wtr, playground. **ACTIVITIES:** Picnicking; fishing; boating,ld. **MISC:** Pets on leash.

MONTPELIER

Montpelier (COE: Mississippi River Public Use Area). At the S edge of Montpelier. SEASON: All yr; 14-day lmt. ACTIVITIES: 55 sites; tbls, toil, cga, f, dump, drk wtr. Ice/food concession/store nearby. ACTIVITIES: Picnicking; fishing; boating,l. MISC: Pets permitted on leash.

MOUNT AYR

Fifes Grove Park (County Park). 1 mi N of Mount Ayr on St Hwy 169. SEASON: All yr; 14-day lmt. FACILITIES: Sites; tbls, toil, cga. ACTIVITIES: Picnicking; fishing; hiking. MISC: Pets on leash.

Poe Hollow Park (County Park). 1-1/2 mi E of Mount Ayr. FACILITIES: Sites; tbls, toil, cga, f, playground. SEASON: All yr; 14-day lmt. ACTIVITIES: Picnicking (shelters); hiking. MISC: Pets on leash.

MT. PLEASANT

Mud Creek Recreation Area. 2 mi SW of Mt Pleasant. SEASON: All yr; 14-day lmt. FACILITIES: Sites; tbls, toil, cga, f. ACTIVITIES: Picnicking; hiking. MISC: Pets.

MUSCATINE

Kilpeck Landing (COE: Mississippi River Public Use Area). 12 mi S of Muscatine on Co Hwy X61; 1 mi E. SEASON: All yr; 14-day lmt. FACILITIES: 20 sites; tbls, toil, cga, f, drk wtr. Store/ice nearby. ACTIVITIES: Picnicking; fishing; swimming; boating,l; horseback riding. MISC: Pets on leash.

Shady Creek (COE: Mississippi River Public Use Area). 10 mi NE of Muscatine on St Hwy 22. SEASON: All yr; 14-day lmt. FACILITIES: 100 sites; tbls, toil, cga, f, dump, drk wtr. ACTIVITIES: Picnicking; fishing; swimming; boating,l. MISC.: Pets.

NEW MARKET

Windmill Lake (County Park). 6 mi E of New Market on St Hwy 2; 1 mi N. SEASON: All yr; 14-day lmt. ACTIVITIES: Fishing. FACILITIES: Sites; toil. MISC: Pets.

NEW PROVIDENCE

J. L. Reece Memorial Park. (County Park). 2-1/2 mi SW of New Providence SEASON: All yr; 14-day lmt. FACILITIES: Sites; tbls, toil, cga. ACTIVITIES: Picnicking; hunting; hiking.

MISC: Facilities for handicapped persons. Pets.

ORIENT

Orient Park (County Park). 1 mi W of Orient. SEASON: All yr; 7-day lmt FACILITIES: 17 sites; tbls, toil, cga, ACTIVITIES: Picnicking; fishing; boating,ld. MISC: Pets.

OTTUMWA

City Park. Jct at St Hwys 63 & 34, in Ottumwa. SEASON: All yr; 1-night lmt. FACILITIES: Spaces for self-contained vehicles. MISC: Pets on leash.

PELLA

Tailwater Recreation Area (COE: Lake Red Rock). SW of Pella (follow signs) SEASON: 5/15-9/30; 14-day lmt. FACILITIES: 50 sites; tbls, toil, cga, drk wtr, dump stat nearby. ACTIVITIES: Picnicking; swimming; fishing; boating,l. MISC: Pets on leash.

PERRY

Pattee (City Park). 2 blks S of St Hwy 141 on W 3rd St, in Perry. SEASON: 4/15-10/15; 7-day lmt. FACILITIES: 30 sites; tbls, toil, cga, phone, playground, recreation hall. ACTIVITIES: Picnicking; swimming; tennis; softball. MISC: 2-ton load lmt; unmarked route for heavier vehicles 1 blk W of park. Pets.

ROCK RAPIDS

Island Park (Municipal Park). From St Hwy 9, 1 blk N at Marshall St; 1/2 block E of the Rock Rapids post office, in Rock Rapids. SEASON: 4/1-9/30. FACILITIES: 10 sites; tbls, toil, cga, f, elec/wtr hookup, showers, playground. Dump/bottle gas/ice/laundry/food concession/store nearby. ACTIVITIES: Picnicking; fishing; boating,l. MISC: Pets.

Westside Park (City Park). W edge of Rock Rapids at St Hwy 9 & US 75. SEASON: All yr; 1-night lmt. FACILITIES: 20 sites; tbls, toil, cga, f, elec/wtr hookup, dump, showers, drk wtr. Bottled gas/ice/laundry/food concession/store nearby. ACTIVITIES: Picnicking; fishing; snowmobiling. Golfing nearby. MISC: Playground. Pets on leash.

SANBORN

Douma's Park (Municipal Park). 2 mi W of Sanborn on Us 18; 1-1/2 mi

S on Co Rd. SEASON: 5/1-10/1; 14-day lmt. FACILITIES: 9 sites; tbls, toil, cga, f, elec/wtr hookup, drk wtr. ACTIVITIES: Picnicking; fishing; swimming; playground. MISC: No motorbikes. Pets on leash.

Petersen Park (Municipal Park). 2 mi E of Sanborn at Jct of US 18 & 59. SEASON: All yr; 2-day lmt. FACILITIES: 15 sites (tr -30); tbls, toil, cga, f, playground, drk wtr. ACTIVITIES: Picnicking. MISC: Pets.

SCHLESWIG

City Park. On US 59; in Schleswig. SEASON: All yr; 1-night lmt. FACILITIES: Spaces for self-contained vehicles. MISC: Pets on leash.

SHEFFIELD

Calvin Park (County Park). S edge of Sheffield. SEASON: All yr; 14-day lmt. FACILITIES: Spaces for self-contained vehicles; tbls, toil, cga, f. ACTIVITIES: Picnicking. MISC: Pets.

SHUEYVILLE

Sandy Beach (COE: Coralville Reservoir). 1 mi E of Shueyville on St Hwy F12; 4 mi S at sign (follow signs). SEASON: All yr; 14-day lmt. FACILITIES: 30 sites; tbls, toil, cga, drk wtr. ACTIVITIES: Picnicking; swimming; fishing; boating,l; horseback riding. MISC: Pets on leash.

SIDNEY

Pinky Glen (Municipal Park). US 275 to Tabor County Road. SEASON: 3/1-11/30. FACILITIES: 200 sites; tbls, toil, cga, f, dump, drk wtr. ACTIVITIES: Picnicking; fishing; horseback riding. MISC: No motorbikes. Pets.

SIGOURNEY

Lake Yenrougis (County Park). 2 mi from Sigourney. SEASON: All yr; 14-day lmt. FACILITIES: Sites; tbls, toil, cga, f. ACTIVITIES: Picnicking; fishing; hunting; boating,l; hiking. MISC: Beach. Pets on leash.

SLOAN

City Park (City Park). On US 75, off I-29, in Sloan. SEASON: All yr; 1-night lmt. FACILITIES: Sites; tbls, toil, cga, playground, elec hkup. ACTIVITIES: Picnicking; tennis.

SOLON

Sugar Bottom (COE: Coralville Reservoir). 2 mi on W 5th St in Solon;

2 mi S on paved rd; 2 mi S. SEASON: All yr; 14-day lmt. FACILITIES: 300 sites; tbls, toil, cga, showers, dump, drk wtr. ACTIVITIES: Picnicking; swimming; fishing; boating,l; horseback riding. MISC: Pets.

STEAMBOAT ROCK

Steamboat Rock Tower (County Park). 1/2 mi S of Steamboat Rock. SEASON: All yr; 14-day lmt. FACILITIES: Sites; tbls, toil, cga, f. ACTIVITIES: Picnicking; fishing; hiking. MISC: Nature trails; Pioneer Keystone Bridge. Tower Rock. Pets on leash.

UNION

Longs Memorial Park (County Park). 1 mi E of Union. SEASON: All yr; 14-day lmt. FACILITIES: 12 sites; tbls, toil, cga, f, facilities for handicapped. ACTIVITIES: Picnicking; fishing; boating,l. MISC: Pets.

WAPELLO

Ferry Landing (COE: Mississippi River Public Use Area). SE of Wapello on St Hwy 99 to Oakville; 6 mi E on Co Rd. SEASON: All yr; 14-day lmt. FACILITIES: 200 sites; tbls, toil, cga, dump, drk wtr. ACTIVITIES: Picnicking; fishing; swimming; boating,l; horseback riding. MISC: Pets on leash.

WEBSTER

Webster City Park. In Webster on US 20. SEASON: All yr; 1-night lmt. FACILITIES: Sites; tbls, toil, cga, elec/swr hkups. ACTIVITIES: Picnicking; fishing. MISC: Pets.

WHAT CHEER

Griffin County Park. S edge of What Cheer. SEASON: All yr; 1-night lmt. FACILITIES: Spaces for self-contained vehicles; toil. ACTIVITIES: Fishing; hiking. MISC: Pets on leash.

READ THIS!

All information relative to each campground and state is currently accurate to the best of the publisher's knowledge. However, non-fee status and facilities are subject to change.

If any inaccuracies in this directory are discovered, or you know of any additional FREE campgrounds, please contact: VMPI; Box 1289; Clearwater, FL 33517.

INFORMATION ON HOW TO PURCHASE ADDITIONAL COPIES OF THIS BOOK AS WELL AS QUANTITY DISCOUNT INFORMATION IS ALSO AVAILABLE AT THIS ADDRESS.

See page 7 for KEY TO ABBREVIATIONS.

KANSAS

GENERAL STATE INFORMATION

Miscellaneous

Right Turns on Red: Permitted after
    full stop, unless otherwise posted.
STATE CAPITOL: Topeka
STATE NICKNAME: Sunflower State
STATE MOTTO: "To the Stars
                through Difficulties"
STATE BIRD: Western Meadowlark
STATE FLOWER: Sunflower
STATE TREE: Eastern Cottonwood

State Parks

Fees per night are $2.00–3.00. Pets are permitted when secured on leash, except on bathing beaches, either in the water or on shore. Further information: State of Kansas Department of Economic Development; Travel and Tourism Division; 503 Kansas Avenue, 6th Floor; Topeka, KS 66603.

Rest Areas

Overnight self-contained camping is permitted. These locations and facilities are listed throughout this chapter of the directory for your convenience.

Arkansas River Canoe Trail

The Arkansas River, from Raymond to Sterling, is a beautiful sand-hills stream. The river has a sand bottom and, except for a few holes, is shallow enough for tubing, safe swimming, and wading. There are numerous clean sandbars for sunbathing, camping, and picnics. Campsites shown on the free map are usually large, clean sandbars with no facilities; potential campsites occur more frequently than are shown on the map. There are also some private campgrounds located on the map. No fees are presently charged for these facilities, but you will need to ask permission. Carry your drinking water. For further information and free map: Travel Division; Kansas Department of Economic Development; 503 Kansas Avenue, 6th Floor; Topeka, KS 66603.

INFORMATION SOURCES

Maps

The following maps are available from **Forsyth Travel Library** (see order form in Appendix B):

> State of Kansas [Up-to-date, showing all principal roads, points of interest, sports areas, parks, airports, mileage, etc. Full color.]

> Completely indexed city maps, including all airports, lakes, rivers, etc., of: **Hutchinson; Junction City; Liberal; Olathe; Topeka.**

State Information

Travel Division; Kansas Department of Economic Development; 503 Kansas Avenue, 6th Floor; Topeka, KS 66603.
Kansas Turnpike Authority; Box 18007, SE Station; Wichita, KS 67218.
Kansas Parks and Resources Authority; PO Box 977; Topeka, KS 66601.
Fish and Game Commission; PO Box 1028; Pratt, KS 67124.

Miscellaneous

Dodge City Chamber of Commerce; PO Box 939; Dodge City, KS 67801.
Kirwin National Wildlife Refuge; Kirwin, KS 67644.
Kansas (Wyoming & Nebraska) BLM; PO Box 1828; Cheyenne, WY 82001.
Corps of Engineers, Kansas City District; 700 Federal Building; Kansas City, MO 64106.
    [Free campground in Kansas.]

FREE CAMPGROUNDS

ALEXANDER

Rest Area. At Alexander on St Hwy 96. SEASON: All yr; 1-night lmt. FACILITIES: Spaces for self-contained RVs; tbls, toil, cga, drk wtr. ACTIVITIES: Picnicking. MISC.: Pets.

ALMA

Rest Area. At Alma on St Hwy 99. SEASON: All yr; 1-night lmt. FACILITIES: Spaces for self-contained RVs; tbls, toil, cga, drk wtr. ACTIVITIES: Picnicking. MISC.: Pets.

ALMENA

Rest Area. At Almena on US 383. SEASON: All yr; 1-night lmt. FACILITIES: Spaces for self-contained RVs; tbls, toil, cga, drk wtr. ACTIVITIES: Picnicking. MISC.: Pets permitted.

ARKANSAS CITY

Cowley County Park (SRA). 13 mi E of Arkansas City on US 166. SEASON: All yr; 3-day lmt. FACILITIES: Undesignated sites, tbls, toil, cga, drk wtr. ACTIVITIES: Picnicking; fishing; boating,rl. MISC.: Pets permitted if kept on leash.

ASHLAND

Rest Area. E of Ashland on US 160. SEASON: All yr; 1-night lmt. FACILITIES: Spaces for self-contained RVs; tbls, toil, cga, drk wtr. ACTIVITIES: Picnicking. MISC.: Pets permitted.

ATCHISON

Atchison County Park (SRA). 4 mi N & 2 mi W of Jct US 59 & St Hwy 7 in Atchison. SEASON: All yr; 3-day lmt. FACILITIES: Undesignated sites; tbls, toil, cga, drk wtr. ACTIVITIES: Boating,l; picnicking; fishing. MISC.: Pets.

Monroe Brown Memorial (City Park). 3 mi E of Atchison on US 59; 1 mi S on gravel rd; 1/2 mi E. SEASON: All yr; 1-night lmt. FACILITIES: 16 sites, tbls, toil, cga, f, elec hkup. ACTIVITIES: Picnicking; fishing; swimming. MISC.: Lake. Pets permitted.

Rest Area 9 mi S of Atchison on US 73. SEASON: All yr; 1-night lmt. FACILITIES: Spaces for self-contained RVs; tbls, toil, cga, no drk wtr. ACTIVITIES: Picnicking. MISC.: Historical marker. Pets.

ATWOOD

Rest Area. At Atwood on US 36. SEASON: All yr; 1-night lmt. FACILITIES: Spaces for self-contained RVs; tbls, toil, cga, drk wtr. ACTIVITIES: Picnicking; fishing; boating,l. MISC.: Pets permitted.

AUGUSTA

Rest Area. 6 mi E of Augusta on US 54 and St Hwy 96. SEASON: All yr; 1-night lmt. FACILITIES: Spaces for self-contained RVs; tbls, toil, cga, drk wtr. ACTIVITIES: Picnicking. MISC.: Pets.

AXTELL

Rest Area. 2 mi S of Axtell on US 36. SEASON: All yr; 1-night lmt. FACILITIES: Spaces for self-contained RVs; tbls, toil, cga, drk wtr. ACTIVITIES: Picnicking. MISC.: Pets.

BALDWIN

Douglas County Park (SRA). 1-1/2 mi N of Baldwin; 1 mi E to campground. SEASON: All yr; 3-day lmt. FACILITIES: Undesignated sites; tbls, toil, cga, f, drk wtr. ACTIVITIES: Picnicking; fishing; boating,rl. MISC.: Pets permitted.

Rest Area. At jct of US 59/56; on US 56. SEASON: All yr; 1-night lmt. FACILITIES: Spaces for self-contained RVs. MISC.: Pets permitted if kept on leash.

Rest Area. 3 mi E of Baldwin on US 56. SEASON: All yr; 1-night lmt. FACILITIES: Spaces for self-contained RVs; tbls, toil, cga, drk wtr. MISC.: Historical marker. Pets permitted.

BATESVILLE

Rest Area. W of Batesville on US 54. SEASON: All yr; 1-night lmt. FACILITIES: Spaces for self-contained RVs; tbls, toil, cga, drk wtr. ACTIVITIES: Picnicking. MISC.: Historical marker. Pets permitted if kept on leash.

See page 7 for KEY TO ABBREVIATIONS.

BAXTER SPRINGS

Rest Area. 2 mi N of Baxter Springs on US 66. SEASON: All yr; 1-night lmt. FACILITIES: Spaces for self-contained RVs; tbls, toil, cga, drk wtr. ACTIVITIES: Picnicking. MISC.: Historical marker. Pets.

BELLEVILLE

Rest Area. 4 mi W of Belleville on US 36. SEASON: All yr; 1-night lmt. FACILITIES: Spaces for self-contained RVs; tbls, toil, cga. ACTIVITIES: Picnicking. MISC.: Pets.

Rest Area. 5 mi S of Belleville on US 81. SEASON: All yr; 1-night lmt. FACILITIES: Spaces for self-contained RVs; tbls, toil, cga, drk wtr. ACTIVITIES: Picnicking. MISC.: Pets.

BELOIT

Rest Area. N of Beloit on US 24. SEASON: All yr; 1-night lmt. FACILITIES: Spaces for self-contained RVs; tbls, toil, cga, drk wtr. ACTIVITIES: Picnicking. MISC.: Pets permitted.

BELPRE

Rest Area. 3-1/2 mi W of Belpre on US 50. SEASON: All yr; 1-night lmt. FACILITIES: Spaces for self-contained RVs; tbls, toil, cga, drk wtr. ACTIVITIES: Picnicking. MISC.: Pets.

BELVUE

Rest Area. W of Belvue on US 24. SEASON: All yr; 1-night lmt. FACILITIES: Spaces for self-contained RVs; tbls, toil, cga, drk wtr. ACTIVITIES: Picnicking. MISC.: Historical marker. Pets.

BLOOM

Rest Area. At Bloom on US 54. SEASON: All yr; 1-night lmt. FACILITIES: Spaces for self-contained RVs; tbls, toil, cga, drk wtr. ACTIVITIES: Picnicking. MISC.: Historical marker. Pets permitted.

BLUE RAPIDS

Rest Area. NE of Blue Rapids on US 77 and St Hwy 9. SEASON: All yr; 1-night lmt. FACILITIES: Spaces for self-contained RVs; tbls, toil, cga. ACTIVITIES: Picnicking. MISC.: Historical marker. Pets.

BOGUE

Rest Area. N of Bogue on St Hwy 18. SEASON: All yr; 1-night lmt. FACILITIES: Spaces for self-contained RVs; tbls, toil, cga, drk wtr. ACTIVITIES: Picnicking. MISC.: Pets permitted.

BUFFALO

Wilson County Park. 1-1/2 mi SE of Buffalo on US 75. SEASON: All yr; 3-day lmt. FACILITIES: Undesignated sites; tbls, toil, cga, drk wtr. ACTIVITIES: Picnicking; fishing; boating,l. MISC.: Ice/food nearby. Pets permitted.

BURLINGAME

City Park. On St Hwy 56, in Burlingame. SEASON: All yr. FACILITIES: Spaces for self-contained RVs. MISC.: Pets.

BURLINGTON

Hartford (COE: John Redmond Lake). SEASON: All yr; 14-day lmt. FACILITIES: 11 sites, tbls, toil, cga, drk wtr. Store/food/ice/laundry nearby. ACTIVITIES: Picnicking, fishing; boating,l. MISC.: Pets.

Hickory Creek West (COE: John Redmond Lake). On John Redmond Lake. SEASON: All yr; 14-day lmt. FACILITIES: 6 sites; tbls, toil, cga, no drk wtr. ACTIVITIES: Picnicking; fishing. MISC.: Pets permitted.

Otter Creek (COE: John Redmond Lake). On John Redmond Lake. SEASON: All yr; 14-day lmt. FACILITIES: 10 sites; tbls, toil, cga, no drk wtr. ACTIVITIES: Picnicking; fishing; boating,l. MISC.: Pets.

Redmond Cove North (COE: John Redmond Lake). On John Redmond Lake. SEASON: All yr; 14-day lmt. FACILITIES: 30 sites; tbls, toil, cga, drk wtr. Store/food/ice/laundry nearby. ACTIVITIES: Picnicking; fishing; boating,l. MISC.: Pets.

Riverside East (COE: John Redmond Lake). On John Redmond Lake. SEASON: All yr; 14-day lmt. FACILITIES: 14 sites; tbls, toil, cga, drk wtr. ACTIVITIES: Picnicking; swimming; fishing; boating,ld. MISC.: Pets permitted.

CALDWELL

Rest Area. At Caldwell on US 81. SEASON: All yr; 1-night lmt. FACILITIES:

Spaces for self-contained RVs; tbls, toil, cga, drk wtr. ACTIVITIES: Picnicking. MISC.: Pets permitted if kept on leash. Historical marker.

CANEY

Rest Area. 3 mi N of Caney on US 166/75. SEASON: All yr; 1-night lmt. FACILITIES: Spaces for self-contained RVs; tbls, toil, cga, drk wtr. ACTIVITIES: Picnicking. MISC.: Pets.

CHANUTE

Rest Area. S of Chanute on US 169. SEASON: All yr; 1-night lmt. FACILITIES: Spaces for self-contained RVs; tbls, toil, cga, drk wtr. ACTIVITIES: Picnicking. MISC.: Pets.

Safari Campground (Municipal Park). 1 mi S of Chanute on US 169. SEASON: All yr. FACILITIES: 22 sites; tbls, flush toil, cga, f, drk wtr, elec/wtr hkup, showers. Store/ice/food/laundry nearby. ACTIVITIES: Picnicking; fishing; boating,ld; golfing; swimming. MISC.: Pets permitted if kept on leash.

CHAUTAUQUA

Boulanger Landing (COE: Hulah Lake). 7 mi S of Chautauqua on St Hwy 99; 1 mi on access road to campground. SEASON: All yr; 14-day lmt. FACILITIES: 7 sites; tbls, toil, cga, no drk wtr. ACTIVITIES: Picnicking; hunting; fishing (catfish); waterskiing. MISC.: Pets permitted if kept on leash.

Caney River (COE: Hulah Lake). 8 mi S of Chautauqua on St Hwy 99; 1-1/2 mi E and S. SEASON: All yr; 14-day lmt. FACILITIES: 10 sites; tbls, toil, cga, no drk wtr. ACTIVITIES: Picnicking; hunting; boating,l; fishing (catfish); waterskiing. MISC.: Pets.

Pond Creek (COE: Hulah Lake). 9 mi S of Chautauqua on St Hwy 99; E on Co Rd. SEASON: All yr; 14-day lmt. FACILITIES: 7 sites; tbls, toil, cga, no drk wtr. ACTIVITIES: Picnicking; fishing (catfish); hunting; waterskiing. MISC.: Pets permitted if kept on leash.

Turkey Creek (COE: Hulah Lake). 15 mi SE of Chautauqua on co rd and access rd. SEASON: All yr; 14-day lmt FACILITIES: 20 sites; tbls, toil, cga, drk wtr. Store/laundry/food nearby. ACTIVITIES: Picnicking; fishing (catfish); hunting; boating,l; waterskiing. MISC.: Pets permitted if kept on leash.

CHEYENNE BOTTOMS

Rest Area. At Cheyenne Bottoms on US 156. SEASON: All yr; 1-night lmt. FA-

KANSAS

CILITIES: Spaces for self-contained RVs; tbls, toil, cga, drk wtr. ACTIVITIES: Picnicking; boating,l; fishing nearby. MISC.: Pets.

CIMARRON RIVER

Rest Area. At Cimarron River on US 54. SEASON: All yr; 1-night lmt. FACILITIES: Spaces for self-contained RVs; tbls, toil, cga, drk wtr. ACTIVITIES: Picnicking. MISC.: Pets.

CLAY CENTER

Rest Area. 2-1/2 mi E of Clay Center on US 24. SEASON: All yr; 1-night lmt. FACILITIES: Spaces for self-contained RVs; tbls, toil, cga, drk wtr. ACTIVITIES: Picnicking. MISC.: Pets permitted if kept on leash.

COLBY

Rest Area. At Colby on US 24. SEASON: All yr; 1-night lmt. FACILITIES: Spaces for self-contained RVs; tbls, toil, cga, drk wtr. ACTIVITIES: Picnicking. MISC.: Pets permitted if kept on leash.

Rest Area. 5 mi SW of Colby on I-70. SEASON: All yr; 1-night lmt. FACILITIES: Spaces for self-contained RVs; tbls, toil, cga, drk wtr. ACTIVITIES: Picnicking. MISC.: Pets permitted.

COLDWATER

Rest Area. 2 mi S of Coldwater on US 160/183. SEASON: All yr; 1-night lmt. FACILITIES: Spaces for self-contained RVs; tbls, toil, cga, drk wtr. ACTIVITIES: Picnicking. MISC.: Pets.

COLONY

Rest Area. W of Colony on US 169. SEASON: All yr; 1-night lmt. FACILITIES: Spaces for self-contained RVs; tbls, toil, cga, drk wtr. ACTIVITIES: Picnicking. MISC.: Pets permitted.

COTTONWOOD FALLS

Chase County (SRA). 3 mi W of Cottonwood on Co Rd to campground. SEASON: All yr; 3-day lmt. FACILITIES: Undesignated sites, tbls, toil, cga, drk wtr. ACTIVITIES: Picnicking; fishing; swimming; boating,l. MISC.: Pets.

COUNCIL GROVE

Dam Site (COE: Council Grove Lake). 4 mi N of Council Grove on St Hwy

177. SEASON: All yr; 14-day lmt. FA-CILITIES: 10 sites; tbls, toil, cga, no drk wtr. ACTIVITIES: Picnicking; fishing. MISC.: Pets permitted if kept on leash.

Richey Cove North (COE: Council Grove Lake). 4 mi N of Council Grove on St Hwy 177. SEASON: All yr; 14-day lmt. FACILITIES: Undesignated sites; tbls, toil, cga, drk wtr. ACTIVITIES: Picnicking; fishing; boating,l. MISC.: Pets.

DIGHTON

Rest Area. 2 mi E of Dighton on St Hwy 96. SEASON: All yr; 1-night lmt. FACIL-ITIES: Spaces for self-contained RVs; tbls, toil, cga. drk wtr. ACTIVITIES: Picnicking. MISC.: Pets permitted if kept on leash.

DODGE CITY

Ford County Lake. 7 mi NE of Dodge City off US 283. SEASON: All yr. FACIL-ITIES: Spaces for self-contained RVs; MISC.: Pets permitted if kept on leash.

Rest Area. 7 mi E of Dodge City on US 50/56/283. SEASON: All yr; 1-night lmt. FACILITIES: Spaces for self-contained RVs; tbls, toil, cga, drk wtr. ACTIVI-TIES: Picnicking. MISC.: Historical marker. Pets.

DOUGLASS

Rest Area. E of Douglass on US 77. SEA-SON: All yr; 1-night lmt. FACILITIES: Spaces for self-contained RVs; tbls, toil, cga, drk wtr. ACTIVITIES: Pic-nicking. MISC.: Pets.

DOWNS

Rest Area. At Downs on US 24. SEASON: All yr; 1-night lmt. FACILITIES: Spaces for self-contained RVs; tbls, toil, cga, drk wtr. ACTIVITIES: Picnicking. MISC.: Pets permitted if kept on leash.

EDMOND

Rest Area. At Edmond on St Hwy 9. SEA-SON: All yr; 1-night lmt. FACILITIES: Spaces for self-contained RVs; tbls, toil, cga, drk wtr. ACTIVITIES: Pic-nicking. MISC.: Pets permitted.

ELK CITY

Oak Ridge (COE: Elk City Lake). 2 mi E of Elk City on St Hwy 39; 3 mi S to campground. SEASON: All yr; 14-day lmt. FACILITIES: 35 sites; flush toil, tbls, cga, drk wtr. ACTIVITIES: Picnicking; fishing; swimming; boat-ing,l. MISC.: Pets.

ELKHART

Rest Area. 6 mi N of Elkhart on St Hwy 27. SEASON: All yr; 1-night lmt. FA-CILITIES: Spaces for self-contained RVs; tbls, toil, cga, drk wtr. ACTIVI-TIES: Picnicking. MISC.: Pets.

ELLSWORTH

Rest Area. At Ellsworth at Jct of US 156 and St Hwy 140. SEASON: All yr; 1-night lmt. FACILITIES: Spaces for self-contained RVs; tbls, flush toil, cga, drk wtr. ACTIVITIES: Picnicking MISC.: Pets permitted.

Rest Area. 2 mi E of E Jct St Hwy 14, on I-70. SEASON: All yr; 1-night lmt. FACILITIES: Spaces for self-con-tained RVs; flush toil. ACTIVITIES: MISC.: Pets permitted if kept on leash.

ELSMORE

Bourbon County Park (SRA). 4 mi E of Us 59 in Elsmore on Co Rd to CG. SEASON: All yr; 3-day lmt. FACILI-TIES: Undesignated sites; tbls, toil, cga, drk wtr. ACTIVITIES: Picnicking; fishing; boating,l. MISC.: Pets.

EMPORIA

Rest Area. 1 mi E of Emporia on US 50. SEASON: All yr; 1-night lmt. FA-CILITIES: Spaces for self-contained RVs; tbls, toil, cga. ACTIVITIES: Pic-nicking. MISC.: Pets permitted if kept on leash.

Sun Dance (COE: Melvern Lake). 18 mi E of Emporia on I-35. SEASON: All yr; 14-day lmt. FACILITIES: 70 sites; tbls, toil, cga, drk wtr. ACTIVITIES: Picnicking; fishing; swimming; boat-ing,l. MISC.: S of Melvern Lake. Pets.

ERIE

Rest Area. N of Erie on US 59 and St Hwy 57. SEASON: All yr; 1-night lmt. FACILITIES: Spaces for self-contained RVs; tbls, toil, cga, drk wtr. ACTIVI-TIES: Picnicking. MISC.: Historical marker. Pets permitted if kept on leash.

FAIRVIEW

Rest Area. 3 mi W of Fairview on US 36/75. SEASON: All yr; 1-night lmt. FACILITIES: Spaces for self-contained RVs; tbls, flush toil, cga, drk wtr. ACTIVITIES: Picnicking. MISC.: Pets.

See page 7 for KEY TO ABBREVIATIONS.

FLORENCE

Rest Area. At Florence on US 50/77. SEASON: All yr; 1-night lmt. FACILITIES: Spaces for self-contained RVs; tbls, toil, cga, drk wtr. ACTIVITIES: Picnicking. MISC.: Pets permitted.

FORT SCOTT

Rest Area. 3 mi W of Fort Scott on US 54. SEASON: All yr; 1-night lmt. FACILITIES: Spaces for self-contained RVs; tbls, cga. ACTIVITIES: Picnicking. MISC.: Pets.

FREDONIA

Rest Area. 2 mi N of Fredonia on St Hwy 39. SEASON: All yr; 1-night lmt. FACILITIES: Spaces for self-contained RVs; tbls, toil, cga, drk wtr. ACTIVITIES: Picnicking. MISC.: Pets.

GARDEN CITY

Rest Area. W of Garden City on US 50. SEASON: All yr; 1-night lmt. FACILITIES: Spaces for self-contained RVs; tbls, toil, cga, drk wtr. ACTIVITIES: Picnicking. MISC.: Pets permitted if kept on leash.

Rest Area. Juct of St Hwy 23 and US 156; on US 156. SEASON: All yr; 1-night lmt. FACILITIES: Spaces for self-contained RVs. MISC.: Pets.

GARDNER

Rest Area. 2 mi SE of Gardner on I-35. SEASON: All yr; 1-night lmt. FACILITIES: Spaces for self-contained RVs; tbls, flush toil, cga, drk wtr. ACTIVITIES: Picnicking. MISC.: Pets permitted.

GARFIELD

Rest Area. At Garfield on US 56. SEASON: All yr; 1-night lmt. FACILITIES: Spaces for self-contained RVs; tbls, toil, cga, drk wtr. ACTIVITIES: Picnicking. MISC.: Pets permitted if kept on leash.

GIRARD

Rest Area. 1 mi E of Girard on St Hwy 57. SEASON: All yr; 1-night lmt. FACILITIES: Spaces for self-contained RVs; tbls, toil, cga, drk wtr. ACTIVITIES: Picnicking. MISC.: Pets permitted.

GLADE

Kirwin NWR. 6 mi E of Glade on St Hwy 9; 1 mi S to Hdqtrs. SEASON: All yr;

7-day lmt. FACILITIES: 300 sites; tbls, toil, cga, drk wtr, elec/wtr hkups. Store/laundry nearby. ACTIVITIES: Picnicking; fishing; swimming; boating,rl. MISC.: Pets permitted if kept on leash.

GOODLAND

Rest Area. At Goodland on US 24. SEASON: All yr; 1-night lmt. FACILITIES: Spaces for self-contained RVs; tbls, toil, cga, drk wtr. ACTIVITIES: Picnicking. MISC: Pets permitted if kept on leash.

Sherman County Park (SRA). 10 mi S of Goodland on St Hwy 27; 2 mi W; 3 mi S to Campground. SEASON: All yr; 3-day lmt. FACILITIES: 12 sites, tbls, toil, cga, drk wtr. ACTIVITIES: Picnicking; fishing; boating,l. MISC: Pets permitted if kept on leash.

GOVE

Rest Area. At Gove on St Hwy 23. SEASON: All yr; 1-night lmt. FACILITIES: Spaces for self-contained RVs; tbls, toil, cga, drk wtr. ACTIVITIES: Picnicking. MISC: Pets.

GRAINFIELD

Rest Area. 2-1/2 mi E of Grainfield on I-70. SEASON: All yr; 1-night lmt. FACILITIES: Spaces for self-contained RVs; tbls, toil, cga, drk wtr. ACTIVITIES: Picnicking. MISC: Pets.

GREAT BEND

Cheyenne Bottoms Inlet (SRA). SEASON: All yr; 3-day lmt. FACILITIES: Undesignated sites; no drk wtr. ACTIVITIES: Fishing. MISC: Pets.

Rest Area. E of Great Bend on US 56. SEASON: All yr; 1-night lmt. FACILITIES: Spaces for self-contained RVs; tbls, toil, cga, drk wtr. ACTIVITIES: Picnicking. MISC: Historical marker. Pets permitted if kept on leash.

GREENSBURG

Rest Area. E of Greensburg on US 54. SEASON: All yr; 1-night lmt. FACILITIES: Spaces for self-contained RVs; tbls, toil, cga, drk wtr. ACTIVITIES: Picnicking. MISC: Pets permitted.

HAMILTON

Rest Area. 1-1/2 mi N of Hamilton on St Hwy 99. SEASON: All yr; 1-night lmt. FACILITIES: Spaces for self-contained RVs; tbls, toil, cga, no drk wtr. ACTIVITIES: Picnicking. MISC: Pets permitted if kept on leash.

HARPER

Rest Area. W of Harper on US 160. SEASON: All yr; 1-night lmt. FACILITIES: Spaces for self-contained RVs; tbls, toil, cga, drk wtr. ACTIVITIES: Picnicking. MISC: Pets permitted.

HAYS

Rest Area. 2 mi E of Hays on I-70. SEASON: All yr; 1-night lmt. FACILITIES: Spaces for self-contained RVs; tbls, flush toil, cga, drk wtr. ACTIVITIES: Picnicking. MISC: Pets.

HIAWATHA

Brown County (SRA). 7-1/2 mi E of Hiawatha on US 36; 1 mi S to Campground. SEASON: All yr; 3-day lmt. FACILITIES: Undesignated sites; tbls, toil, cga, drk wtr, food. ACTIVITIES: Picnicking; fishing; boating,rl. MISC: Pets permitted if kept on leash.

Rest Area. 1/2 mi W of Hiawatha on US 36. SEASON: All yr; 1-night lmt. FACILITIES: Spaces for self-contained RVs; tbls, toil, cga, drk wtr. ACTIVITIES: Picnicking. MISC: Pets permitted.

HIGHLAND

Rest Area. W of Highland on US 36. SEASON: All yr; 1-night lmt. FACILITIES: Spaces for self-contained RVs; tbls, toil, cga, drk wtr. ACTIVITIES: Picnicking. MISC: Pets permitted.

HILL CITY

Rest Area. At Hill City on US 24. SEASON: All yr; 1-night lmt. FACILITIES: Spaces for self-contained RVs; tbls, toil, cga, drk wtr. ACTIVITIES: Picnicking. MISC: Pets permitted if kept on leash.

HILLSBORO

Memorial City Park (City Park). Ash and "D" St., one block W on St Hwy 56 in town. SEASON: All yr. FACILITIES: 8 sites for self-contained units; elec ($), drk wtr, toil, pool, golf course, shelter house. ACTIVITIES: Picnicking; swimming. Arts & Crafts Fair in September. MISC.: Lighted and patrolled. Pets on leash.

HOISINGTON

Rest Area. At Hoisington on US 281. SEASON: All yr; 1-night lmt. FACILITIES: Spaces for self-contained RVs; tbls, toil, cga, drk wtr. ACTIVITIES: Picnicking. MISC: Pets permitted.

HOLTON

Rest Area. 7 mi N of Holton on US 75. SEASON: All yr; 1-night lmt. FACILITIES: Spaces for self-contained RVs; tbls, toil, cga, drk wtr. ACTIVITIES: Picnicking. MISC: Historical marker. Pets permitted if kept on leash.

HOMEWOOD

I-35 West Rest Area. 4 mi W of Homewood exit, on I-35 (paved access roads). SEASON: All yr; 1-night lmt. FACILITIES: Spaces for self-contained RVs; tbls, toil, cga, dump, drk wtr. ACTIVITIES: Picnicking. MISC: Pets.

HOXIE

Rest Area. At Hoxie on US 24. SEASON: All yr; 1-night lmt. FACILITIES: Spaces for self-contained RVs; tbls, toil, cga, drk wtr. ACTIVITIES: Picnicking. MISC: Pets permitted if kept on leash.

Sheridan County. 12 mi E of Hoxie on US 24; 3/4 mi N. SEASON: All yr. FACILITIES: Sites, tbls, toil, cga. ACTIVITIES: Picnicking; fishing; boating,l. MISC: Pets permitted.

INDEPENDENCE

Montgomery County Park (SRA). 3 mi S & 1 mi E of Jct of US 75 & 160 (in Independence) on Co Road to Campground. SEASON: All yr; 3-day lmt. FACILITIES: Undesignated sites, tbls, toil, cga, f, drk wtr, food. ACTIVITIES: Picnicking; fishing; swimming; boating,rl. MISC: Pets.

Rest Area. 2 mi E of Independence on US 160. SEASON: All yr; 1-night lmt. FACILITIES: Spaces for self-contained RVs; tbls, toil, cga, drk wtr. ACTIVITIES: Picnicking. MISC: Historical marker. Pets.

INGALLS

Rest Area. 3 mi W of Ingalls on US 50. SEASON: All yr; 1-night lmt. FACILITIES: Spaces for self-contained RVs; tbls, toil, cga, drk wtr. ACTIVITIES: Picnicking. MISC: Pets.

JENNINGS

Rest Area. At Jennings on US 383. SEASON: All yr; 1-night lmt. FACILITIES: Spaces for self-contained RVs; tbls, toil, cga, drk wtr. ACTIVITIES: Picnicking. MISC: Pets.

JETMORE

Hodgeman (SRA). 5 mi E of Jct of US 156 & 283 (in Jetmore); 2 mi S. SEASON: All yr; 3-day lmt. FACILITIES:

Undesignated sites; tbls, toil, cga, drk wtr. ACTIVITIES: Picnicking. MISC: Pets permitted if. kept on leash.

JUNCTION CITY

Gearney County Park (SRA). 8-1/2 mi S of Junction City on US 77. SEASON: All yr; 3-day lmt. FACILITIES: Undesignated sites; tbls, toil, cga, drk wtr. ACTIVITIES: Picnicking; fishing; boating,ld. MISC: Pets permitted.

Rest Area. E of Junction City on St Hwy 57; SEASON: All yr; 1-night lmt. FACILITIES: Spaces for self-contained RVs; tbls, toil, cga, drk wtr. ACTIVITIES: Picnicking. MISC: Pets permitted.

Rest Area. 4 mi W of St Hwy 177 jct, on I-70. SEASON: All yr; 1-night lmt. FACILITIES: Spaces for self-contained RVs; tbls, flush toil, cga. ACTIVITIES: Picnicking. MISC: Pets permitted.

Rest Area. 1 mi NE of Junction City on St Hwy 18. SEASON: All yr; 1-night lmt. FACILITIES: Spaces for self-contained RVs; tbls, toil, cga, drk wtr. ACTIVITIES: Picnicking. MISC: Pets.

Rest Area. 2 mi W of Junction city on I-70. SEASON: All yr; 1-night lmt. FACILITIES: Spaces for self-contained RVs; tbls, flush toil, cga, drk wtr. ACTIVITIES: Picnicking. MISC: Historical marker. Pets permitted if kept on leash.

KANSAS CITY

Leavenworth Co. State Lake. 4 mi N of Kansas City on St Hwy 16; 2 mi E on St Hwy 90 to park. SEASON: All yr. FACILITIES: 60 sites; toil. ACTIVITIES: Fishing; hiking. MISC: Pets permitted if kept on leash.

Rest Area. 12 mi W of Kansas City on US 24. SEASON: All yr; 1-night lmt. FACILITIES: Spaces for self-contained RVs; tbls, cga. ACTIVITIES: Picnicking. MISC: Historical marker. Pets permitted if kept on leash.

KENSINGTON

Rest Area. At Kensington on US 36. SEASON: All yr; 1-night lmt. FACILITIES: Spaces for self-contained RVs; tbls, toil, cga, drk wtr. ACTIVITIES: Picnicking. MISC: Pets.

KINGSDOWN

Clark County Park (SRA). 10 mi S of Kingsdown on St Hwy 94; 1 mi W on Co Rd to Campground. SEASON: All yr; 3-day lmt. FACILITIES: Undesignated sites, tbls, toil, cga, drk wtr. ACTIVITIES: Picnicking; fishing; boating,rl. MISC: Pets permitted.

KINGMAN

Kingman County Park (SRA). 8 mi W of Kingman on US 54. SEASON: All yr; 3-day lmt. FACILITIES: Undesignated sites; tbls, toil, cga, drk wtr ACTIVITIES: Picnicking; fishing; boating,l. MISC: Pets permitted.

KINGSLEY

Rest Area. At Kingsley on US 50/56. SEASON: All yr; 1-night lmt. FACILITIES: Spaces for self-contained RVs; tbls, toil, cga, drk wtr. ACTIVITIES: Picnicking. MISC: Pets permitted if kept on leash.

Rest Area. 5 mi N of US 56 on US 183. SEASON: All yr; 1-night lmt. FACILITIES: Spaces for self-contained RVs; tbls, toil, cga. ACTIVITIES: Picnicking. MISC: Pets.

KIRWIN

Kirwin National Wildlife Refuge. Refuge headquarters are located 4 mi W and 1 mi S of Kirwin via St Hwy 9. Camping is permitted free of charge in designated areas. Limited to 7 days. There are 6 developed CGs, designated on a map that you can pick up from refuge hdqtrs. Each has picnic tbls, grills, pit-type toil, and trash cans. CGs are open year round, 24 hours a day. No water is available at the CGs on the N side.

Fishing, boating, waterskiing, hunting, hiking; picnicking in designated areas. Pets are permitted but must be kept on a leash or under the owner's immediate control at all times.

For info/map: Refuge Mgr, Kirwin NWR Box 125, Kirwin, KS 67644.

LACROSSE

Grass Park City Park. 1 mi S of Jct St Hwys 4 & US 183 on US 183, in LaCrosse. SEASON: All yr; 3-day lmt. FACILITIES: 20 sites; tbls, toil, cga, drk wtr, elec ($); wtr hkup. Store/ice/laundry/food nearby. ACTIVITIES: Picnicking. MISC: Pets permitted if kept on leash.

Rest Area. At LaCrosse on US 183. SEASON: All yr; 1-night lmt. FACILITIES: Spaces for self-contained RVs; tbls, toil, cga, drk wtr. ACTIVITIES: Picnicking. MISC: Pets.

LAKIN

Kearney County Park (SRA). 1-1/2 mi NE of Lakin on US 50; 2 mi E to campground. SEASON: All yr; 3-day lmt. FACILITIES: Undesignated sites; ACTIVITIES: Fishing; swimming; boating,l. MISC: Pets permitted if kept on leash.

Rest Area. At Lakin on US 50. SEASON: All yr; 1-night lmt. FACILITIES: Spaces for self-contained RVs; tbls, toil, cga, drk wtr. ACTIVITIES: Picnicking. MISC: Historical marker. Pets.

LAMED

Rest Area. 6 mi W of Lamed on US 156. SEASON: All yr; 1-night lmt. FACILITIES: Spaces for self-contained RVs; tbls, toil, cga, drk wtr. ACTIVITIES: Picnicking. MISC: Historical marker. Pets permitted if kept on leash.

LARNED

Rest Area. 6 mi W of Larned on US 156. SEASON: All yr; 1-night lmt. FACILITIES: Spaces for self-contained RVs. MISC: Pets permitted if kept on leash.

LATHAM

Butler County park (SRA). 2 mi W of Latham and 1 mi N on Co Rd to campground. SEASON: All yr; 3-day lmt. FACILITIES: Undesignated sites; tbls, toil, cga, drk wtr. ACTIVITIES: Picnicking; fishing; boating,l. MISC: Food nearby. Pets .

LECOMPTON

Rest Area. S of Lecompton on US 40. SEASON: All yr; 1-night lmt. FACILITIES: Spaces for self-contained RVs; tbls, toil, cga, drk wtr. ACTIVITIES: Picnicking. MISC: Historical marker. Pets permitted if kept on leash.

LEHIGH

McPherson County Park (SRA). W of Lehigh on US 56 to Canton; 9-1/2 mi NW on Co Rd to Campground. SEASON: All yr; 3-day lmt. FACILITIES: Undesignated sites; tbls, toil, cga, f, drk wtr. ACTIVITIES: Picnicking; fishing; boating,l. MISC: Pets .

LENORA

Rest Area. At Lenora on St Hwy 9. SEASON: All yr; 1-night lmt. FACILI-

TIES: Spaces for self-contained RVs; tbls, toil, cga, no drk wtr. ACTIVITIES: Picnicking. MISC: Pets.

LEOTI

Rest Area. 6 mi E of Leoti on St Hwy 96. SEASON: All yr; 1-night lmt. FACILITIES: Spaces for self-contained RV's; tbls, toil, cga, drk wtr. ACTIVITIES: Picnicking. MISC.: Pets.

LIBERAL

Rest Area. At Liberal on US 54. SEASON: All yr; 1-night lmt. FACILITIES: Spaces for self-contained RVs; tbls, toil, cga, drk wtr. ACTIVITIES: Picnicking. MISC: Pets permitted .

LINCOLN

Rest Area. E of Lincoln on St Hwy 18. SEASON: All yr; 1-night lmt. FACILITIES: Spaces for self-contained RVs; tbls, toil, cga, drk wtr. ACTIVITIES: Picnicking. MISC: Pets permitted.

LOGAN

Rest Area. At Logan on St Hwy 9. SEASON: All yr; 1-night lmt. FACILITIES: Spaces for self-contained RVs; tbls, toil, cga, drk wtr. ACTIVITIES: Picnicking. MISC: Pets.

LUCAS

Lucas Park (COE: Wilson Lake). SEASON: All yr; 14-day lmt. FACILITIES: 40 sites; tbls, toil, cga, drk wtr. ACTIVITIES: Picnicking; fishing; swimming; boating,ld. MISC: Pets permitted.

LURAY

Rest Area. At Luray on St Hwy 18. SEASON: All yr; 1-night lmt. FACILITIES: Spaces for self-contained RVs; tbls, toil, cga, drk wtr. ACTIVITIES: Picnicking. MISC: Pets .

LYNDON

Rest Area. 5 mi N of Lyndon on US 75 SEASON: All yr; 1-night lmt. FACILITIES: Spaces for self-contained RVs; tbls, toil, cga, no drk wtr.

LYONS

Rest Area. 4 mi W of Lyons on US 56 SEASON: All yr; 1-night lmt FACILITIES: Spaces for self-contained RVs; tbls, toil, cga, drk wtr. ACTIVITIES: Picnicking. MISC: Pets permitted.

MANHATTAN

Baldwin Creek (COE: Tuttle Creek Lake). SEASON: All yr; 14-day lmt. FACILITIES: 18 sites; tbls, toil, cga drk wtr. ACTIVITIES: Picnicking; swimming; fishing; boating,l. MISC: Pets permitted if kept on leash.

Carnahan Creek (COE: Tuttle Creek Lake). 13 mi W of Manhattan on St Hwy 13. SEASON: All yr; 14-day lmt. FACILITIES: 22 sites; tbls, toil, cga, drk wtr. ACTIVITIES: Picnicking; fishing; swimming; boating,ld. MISC: Lake. Pets.

Pohawatomie County Park, No 2 (SRA). 2-1/2 mi E of Manhattan on US 24; 2 mi N; 2 mi NW to campground. SEASON: All yr; 3-day lmt. FACILITIES: Undesignated sites; tbls, toil, cga, drk wtr. ACTIVITIES: Picnicking; fishing; boating,rl. MISC: Pets.

MANKATO

Jewell County Park (SRA). 1 mi W on US 36; 6 mi S of Mankato on Co Rd; 4 mi W on Co Rd. SEASON: All yr; 3-day lmt. FACILITIES: Undesignated sites; tbls, toil, cga, drk wtr. ACTIVITIES: Picnicking; fishing; boating,l. MISC: Pets permitted if kept on leash.

Rest Area. 10 mi W of Mankato on US 36. SEASON: All yr; 1-night lmt. FACILITIES: Spaces for self-contained RVs; tbls, toil, cga. ACTIVITIES: Picnicking. MISC: Pets.

MARION

French Creek Cove (West) COE: Marion Lake). On W side of Marion Lake. SEASON: All yr; 14-day lmt. FACILITIES: 20 sites; tbls, toil, cga, drk wtr. ACTIVITIES: Picnicking; fishing; boating,l. MISC: Pets permitted if kept on leash.

Marion County Cove (COE: Marion Lake). On Marion Lake. SEASON: All yr; 14-day lmt. FACILITIES: 20 sites; tbls, toil, cga, no drk wtr. ACTIVITIES: Picnicking; fishing; boating,l. MISC: Pets permitted if kept on leash.

MCDONALD

Rest Area. At McDonald On US 36. SEASON: All yr; 1-night lmt. FACILITIES: Spaces for self-contained RVs; tbls, toil, cga, drk wtr. ACTIVITIES: Picnicking. MISC: Pets.

MCPHERSON

McPherson County Park (SRA). 14 mi E of McPherson on US 56 to Canton;

7 mi N; 2 mi W. SEASON: All yr. FACILITIES: Sites; tbls, toil, cga. ACTIVITIES: Picnicking; fishing; boating,l. MISC: Pets permitted if kept on leash.

Rest Area. 8 mi N of McPherson on I-35W. SEASON: All yr; 1-night lmt. FACILITIES: Spaces for self-contained RVs; tbls, flush toil, cga, drk wtr. ACTIVITIES: Picnicking. MISC: Pets.

MEADE

Meade City Park. E side of Meade on St Hwy 54E. SEASON: All yr. FACILITIES: Sites; toil. MISC: Pets permitted.

MEDICINE LODGE

Barker County Park (SRA). At the Jct of US 160 & 281, on the N edge of Medicine Lodge. SEASON: All yr; 3-day lmt. FACILITIES: Undesignated sites; tbls, toil, cga; store/food/laundry nearby. ACTIVITIES: Picnicking; fishing; boating,l. MISC: Pets.

Rest Area. W of Medicine Lodge on US 160/281. SEASON: All yr; 1-night lmt. FACILITIES: Spaces for self-contained RVs; tbls, toil, cga, drk wtr. ACTIVITIES: Picnicking. MISC: Pets.

MILTONVALE

Rest Area. 2 mi W of Miltonvale on US 24. SEASON: All yr; 1-night lmt. FACILITIES: Spaces for self-contained RVs; tbls, cga. ACTIVITIES: Picnicking. MISC: Pets permitted if kept on leash.

MINNEOLA

Rest Area. At Minneola on US 283. SEASON: All yr; 1-night lmt. FACILITIES: Spaces for self-contained RVs; tbls, cga, drk wtr. ACTIVITIES: Picnicking. MISC: Pets permitted if kept on leash.

MORAN

Bourbon County Park (SRA). 9 mi S of Moran on st Hwy 6 to Elsmore; 4 mi E on Co Rd to campground. SEASON: All yr; 3-day lmt. FACILITIES: Undesignated sites; tbls, toil, cga, f, drk wtr. ACTIVITIES: Picnicking; fishing; boating,l. MISC: Pets.

Rest Area. 1 mi E of Moran on US 54 SEASON: All yr; 1-night lmt. FACILITIES: Spaces for self-contained RVs; tbls, toil, cga, drk wtr. ACTIVITIES: Picnicking. MISC: Pets permitted.

NATOMA

Rest Area. 4 mi W of Natoma on St Hwy 18. SEASON: All yr; 1-night lmt. FACILITIES: Spaces for self-contained RVs; tbls, cga. ACTIVITIES: Picnicking. MISC: Pets.

NEODESHA

Rest Area. At Neodesha on US 75. SEASON: All yr; 1-night lmt. FACILITIES: Spaces for self-contained RVs; tbls, toil, cga, drk wtr. ACTIVITIES: Picnicking. MISC: Historical marker. Pets permitted if kept on leash.

Rest Area. 2 mi NE of Neodesha on US 75. SEASON: All yr; 1-night lmt. FACILITIES: Spaces for self-contained RVs; tbls, flush toil, cga, drk wtr. ACTIVITIES: Picnicking. MISC: Pets.

NEWTON

Rest Area. 6 mi E of Newton on US 50. SEASON: All yr; 1-night lmt. FACILITIES: Spaces for self-contained RVs; tbls, toil, cga, drk wtr. ACTIVITIES: Picnicking. MISC: Pets permitted.

Rest Area. 7 mi S of Newton on I-35W. SEASON: All yr; 1-night lmt. FACILITIES: Spaces for self-contained RVs; tbls, toil, cga, drk wtr. ACTIVITIES: Picnicking. MISC: Pets permitted if kept on leash.

NICODEMUS

Rest Area. At Nicodemus on US 24. SEASON: All yr; 1-night lmt. FACILITIES: Spaces for self-contained RVs; tbls, toil, cga, drk wtr. ACTIVITIES: Picnicking. MISC: Historical marker. Pets.

NORTON

Rest Area. 2 mi S of US 36 on US 383, at Norton Reservoir. SEASON: All yr; 1-night lmt. FACILITIES: Spaces for self-contained RVs; flush toil. ACTIVITIES: Swimming; fishing nearby. MISC: Pets permitted if kept on leash.

Rest Area. At Norton on US 36. SEASON: All yr; 1-night lmt. FACILITIES: Spaces for self-contained RVs; tbls, toil, cga, drk wtr. ACTIVITIES: Picnicking. MISC: Pets permitted.

Rest Area. At Norton Reservoir on US 383. SEASON: All yr; 1-night lmt. FACILITIES: Spaces for self-contained RVs; flush toil, tbls, cga, drk wtr. ACTIVITIES: Picnicking. MISC: Pets.

OAKLEY

Rest Area. 1-1/2 mi E of Oakley on US 40. SEASON: All yr; 1-night lmt. FA-CILITIES: Spaces for self-contained RVs; tbls, toil, cga, drk wtr. ACTIVITIES: Picnicking. MISC: Pets.

Rest Area. 3 mi NE of Oakley on I-70. SEASON: All yr; 1-night lmt. FACILITIES: Spaces for self-contained RVs; tbls, toil, cga, drk wtr, phone ACTIVITIES: Picnicking. MISC: Pets.

OBERLIN

City Park. NE on US 36, just off US 83. SEASON: All yr. FACILITIES: Sites; toil. MISC: Pets permitted if kept on leash.

Decatur County Lake. 1 mi E of Oberlin; 1 mi N to campground. SEASON: All yr. FACILITIES: Spaces for self-contained RVs. MISC: Pets.

Rest Area. At Oberlin on US 36. SEASON: All yr; 1-night lmt. FACILITIES: Spaces for self-contained RVs; tbls, toil, cga, drk wtr. ACTIVITIES: Picnicking. MISC: Pets permitted.

Rest Area. S of Oberlin on US 83. SEASON: All yr; 1-night lmt. FACILITIES: Spaces for self-contained RVs; tbls, toil, cga, drk wtr. ACTIVITIES: Picnicking. MISC: Pets permitted.

OSBORNE

Rest Area. N of Osborne on US 24/281 SEASON: All yr; 1-night lmt. FACILITIES: Spaces for self-contained RVs; tbls, toil, cga, drk wtr. ACTIVITIES: Picnicking. MISC: Historical marker.

OSKALOOSA

Paradise Point (COE: Perry Lake). 6 mi W of Oskaloosa on St Hwy 92; 2 mi N on Co Rd. SEASON: All yr; 14-day lmt. FACILITIES: 76 sites; tbls, toil, cga. ACTIVITIES: Picnicking; fishing; swimming; boating, ld.

OSWEGO

Kamp Siesta (Municipal Park). 1 mi N of US 59 in Oswego on Kansas St. SEASON: 4/1-11/1; 14-day lmt. FACILITIES: 30 sites (tr -30); tbls, toil, cga, showers. Store/food/ice/laundry/nearby. ACTIVITIES: fishing; swimming. MISC: Pets permitted if kept on leash.

OTTAWA

Rest Area. S of Ottawa on US 50 and US 59. SEASON: All yr; 1-night lmt. FACILITIES: Spaces for self-contained RVs; tbls, toil, cga, drk wtr. ACTIVITIES: Picnicking. MISC: Pets permitted.

Rest Area. 7-1/2 mi SW of Ottawa on I-35. SEASON: All yr; 1-night lmt.

FACILITIES: Spaces for self-contained RVs; tbls, flush toil, cga, drk wtr. ACTIVITIES: Picnicking. MISC: Pets.

OXFORD

Rest Area. At Oxford on US 160. SEASON: All yr; 1-night lmt. FACILITIES: Spaces for self-contained RVs; tbls, flush toil, cga, drk wtr. ACTIVITIES: Picnicking. MISC: Pets permitted.

PAGE CITY

Logan County Park. 2 mi W of Page City on US 40; 11 mi S on St Hwy 25; 2-1/2 mi W to campground. SEASON: All yr. FACILITIES: Sites; tbls, toil, cga. ACTIVITIES: Picnicking; fishing; boating,1. MISC: Pets.

PARSONS

City Park. Rte 59-160. SEASON: All yr. FACILITIES: Spaces for self-contained RVs; dump. MISC: Pets permitted.

Neosho County Park (SRA). 5 mi N of Parsons on US 59; 3 mi E. SEASON: All yr; 3-day lmt. FACILITIES: Undesignated sites; flush toilets, tbls, drk wtr. ACTIVITIES: Picnicking; fishing; boating,ld. MISC: Pets permitted.

Rest Area. 10 mi W of Parsons on US 160. SEASON: All yr; 1-night lmt. FACILITIES: Spaces for self-contained RVs; tbls, toil, cga, drk wtr. ACTIVITIES: Picnicking. MISC: Historical marker. Pets.

PAXICO

I-70 Rest Area. 4 mi E of Paxico exit (paved access rds). SEASON: All yr. FACILITIES: Sites; tbls, toil, cga, dump. ACTIVITIES: Picnicking. MISC: Pets permitted if kept on leash.

PERRY

Outlet (COE: Perry Lake). 1/2 mi W of Perry on US 24; 3-1/2 mi N to campground. SEASON: All yr; 14-day lmt. FACILITIES: 50 self-contained sites; tbls, toil, cga, drk wtr. ACTIVITIES: Picnicking; swimming nearby; fishing. MISC: Pets permitted.

PITTSBURGH

Crawford County Park No. 1 (SRA). 4 mi N of Pittsburgh on US 69. SEASON: All yr; 3-day lmt. FACILITIES: Undesignated sites; tbls, toil, cga, drk wtr. ACTIVITIES: Picnicking; fishing; boating,1. MISC: Pets.

Rest Area. 2 mi S of Pittsburgh on US 69. SEASON: All yr; 1-night lmt. FACILITIES: Spaces for self-contained RVs; tbls, flush toil, cga, drk wtr. ACTIVITIES: Picnicking. MISC: Pets.

PLAINVILLE

Rest Area. E of Plainville on St Hwy 18. SEASON: All yr; 1-night lmt. FACILITIES: Spaces for self-contained RVs; tbls, toil, cga, drk wtr. ACTIVITIES: Picnicking. MISC: Pets.

PLEASANTON

Rest Area. 2-1/2 mi S of Pleasanton on US 69. SEASON: All yr; 1-night lmt. FACILITIES: Spaces for self-contained RVs; tbls. toil, cga, drk wtr. ACTIVITIES: Picnicking. MISC: Historical marker. Pets.

PRATT

Rest Area. 13 mi E of Pratt on US 54. SEASON: All yr; 1-night lmt. FACILITIES: Spaces for self-contained RVs; tbls, toil, cga, drk wtr. ACTIVITIES: Picnicking. MISC: Pets.

PRESTON

Rest Area. At Preston on St Hwy 61. SEASON: All yr; 1-night lmt. FACILITIES: Spaces for self-contained RVs; tbls, toil, cga, drk wtr. ACTIVITIES: Picnicking. MISC: Pets permitted.

READING

Lyon County Park (SRA). 5 mi W of Reading on St Hwy 170; 1-1/2 mi N to campground. SEASON: All yr; 3-day lmt. FACILITIES: Undesignated sites; tbls, toil, cga, f, drk wtr. ACTIVITIES: Picnicking; fishing; swimming; boating,1. MISC: Pets.

REXFORD

Rest Area. W of Rexford on US 83/383. SEASON: All yr; 1-night lmt. FACILITIES: Spaces for self-contained RVs; tbls, toil, cga. ACTIVITIES: Picnicking. MISC: Pets.

RILEY

Rest Area. N of Riley on US 24/77. SEASON: All yr; 1-night lmt. FACILITIES: Spaces for self-contained RVs; tbls, toil, cga, drk wtr. ACTIVITIES: Picnicking. MISC: Pets permitted.

ROLLA

Rest Area. At Rolla on US 56. SEASON: All yr; 1-night lmt. FACILITIES:

Spaces for self-contained RVs; tbls, flush toil, cga, drk wtr. ACTIVITIES: Picnicking. MISC: Pets.

ROSALIA

Rest Area. 2 mi W of Rosalia on US 54. SEASON: All yr; 1-night lmt. FACILITIES: Spaces for self-contained RVs; tbls, toil, cga, drk wtr. ACTIVITIES: Picnicking. MISC: Pets.

RULETON

Rest Area. 7 mi E of Colo. State Line on I-70. SEASON: All yr; 1-night lmt. FACILITIES: Spaces for self-contained RVs; tbls, flush toil, cga. ACTIVITIES: Picnicking. MISC: Pets.

RUSSELL

Rest Area. At Russell on Alt. US 40. SEASON: All yr; 1-night lmt. FACILITIES: Spaces for self-contained RVs; tbls, flush toil, cga, drk wtr. ACTIVITIES: Picnicking. MISC: Historical marker. Pets permitted.

Rest Area. 2 mi SE of Russell on I-70. SEASON: All yr; 1-night lmt. FACILITIES: Spaces for self-contained RVs; flush toil, phone, tbls, cga, drk wtr. ACTIVITIES: Picnicking. MISC: Historical marker. Pets.

SALINA

Ottawa County Park (SRA). 18 mi N of Salina on US 81; 4 mi E on St Hwy 93. SEASON: All yr; 3-day lmt. FACILITIES: Undesignated sites; tbls, toil, cga, f, drk wtr, food. ACTIVITIES: Picnicking; fishing; swimming; boating,rl. MISC: Pets.

Rest Area. N of Salina on US 81. SEASON: All yr; 1-night lmt. FACILITIES: Spaces for self-contained RVs; tbls, flush toil, cga, drk wtr. ACTIVITIES: Picnicking. MISC: Pets permitted.

Thomas Park. 1 mi S of I-70 on US 81. SEASON: All yr. FACILITIES: Sites; toil, dump. MISC: Pets permitted.

Tunnel Outlet (COE: Kanopolis Lake). 25 mi W of Salina on St Hwy 140; 10 mi S on St Hwy 141. SEASON: All yr; 14-day lmt. FACILITIES: 80 sites; flush toil. Store/ice/food nearby. ACTIVITIES: Picnicking; swimming nearby. MISC: Pets.

SCANDIA

Rest Area. At Scandia on US 36. SEASON: All yr; 1-night lmt. FACILITIES: Spaces for self-contained RVs; tbls,

toil, cga, drk wtr. ACTIVITIES: Picnicking. MISC: Pets permitted if kept on leash. Historical marker.

SCRANTON

Osage County (SRA). 1 mi E of Jct on US 56 & US 75; 1/2 mi S to Campground. SEASON: All yr; 3-day lmt. FACILITIES: Undesignated sites; tbls, toil, cga, f, drk wtr. ACTIVITIES: Picnicking; fishing; boating,l. MISC: Pets permitted if kept on leash.

SELDEN

Rest Area. At Selden on US 383. SEASON: All yr; 1-night lmt. FACILITIES: Spaces for self-contained RVs; tbls, toil, cga, drk wtr. ACTIVITIES: Picnicking. MISC: Pets permitted.

SENECA

Nemaha County Park (SRA). 1 mi E of Seneca and 4 mi S on St Hwy 63. SEASON: All yr; 3-day lmt. FACILITIES: Undesignated sites; tbls, toil, cga, f. ACTIVITIES: Picnicking; fishing; boating,l. MISC: Pets.

Rest Area. E of Seneca on US 36. SEASON: All yr; 1-night lmt. FACILITIES: Spaces for self-contained RVs; tbls, toil, cga, drk wtr. ACTIVITIES: Picnicking. MISC: Pets permitted.

SILVER LAKE

Shawnee (SRA). 7 mi N of US 24 in Silver Lake; 2 mi E to Campground. SEASON: All yr; 3-day lmt. FACILITIES: Undesignated sites. ACTIVITIES: Fishing; boating,l. MISC: Pets.

SIMPSON

Rest Area. At jct of US 81 and 24; on US 24. SEASON: All yr; 1-night lmt. FACILITIES: Spaces for self-contained RVs; tbls, toil, cga, no drk wtr. ACTIVITIES: Picnicking.

SMITH CENTER

Rest Area. At Smith Center on US 36. SEASON: All yr; 1-night lmt. FACILITIES: Spaces for self-contained RVs; tbls, toil, cga, drk wtr. ACTIVITIES: Picnicking. MISC: Pets.

SOLOMON

Rest Area. 1-1/2 mi NW of Solomon on I-70. SEASON: All yr; 1-night lmt. FACILITIES: Spaces for self-contained RVs; tbls, toil, cga, drk wtr, phone. ACTIVITIES: Picnicking. MISC: Historical marker. Pets permitted.

KANSAS

ST· FRANCIS

Rest Area. At St Francis on US 36.
SEASON: All yr; 1-night lmt. FACILI-
TIES: Spaces for self-contained RVs;
tbls, toil, cga, drk wtr, showers.
ACTIVITIES: Picnicking. MISC: Pets.

ST. PAUL

Rest Area. E of St Paul on St Hwy 57.
SEASON: All yr; 1-night lmt. FACILI-
TIES: Spaces for self-contained RVs;
tbls, toil, cga, drk wtr. ACTIVITIES:
Picnicking. MISC: Historical marker.

STAFFORD

Rest Area. 6 mi W of Stafford on US
50. SEASON: All yr; 1-night lmt. FA-
CILITIES: Spaces for self-contained
RVs; tbls, toil, cga, drk wtr. ACTIVI-
TIES: Picnicking. MISC: Pets permitted.

STOCKTON

Rest Area. At Stockton on US 24. SEA-
SON: All yr; 1-night lmt. FACILITIES:
Spaces for self-contained RVs; tbls,
toil, cga, drk wtr. ACTIVITIES: Picnicking. MISC: Pets.

Rooks County Park (SRA). 1/2 mi S
of Stockton on US 183; 2 mi W; 2 mi
S to park. SEASON: All yr; 3-day lmt.
FACILITIES: Undesignated sites; tbls,
toil, cga, f, drk wtr. ACTIVITIES:
Picnicking; fishing; boating,l. MISC:
Pets permitted if kept on leash.

STUDLEY

Sheridan (SRA). 2-1/2 mi W of US 24
in Studley; 1/2 mi N to campground.
SEASON: All yr; 3-day lmt. FACILI-
TIES: Undesignated sites; no drk wtr
ACTIVITIES: Fishing; boating,l. MISC:
Pets permitted if kept on leash.

SUBLETTE

Rest Area. W of Sublette on US 56/83/
160. SEASON: All yr; 1-night lmt. FA-
CILITIES: Spaces for self-contained
RVs; tbls, toil, cga, drk wtr. ACTIVI-
TIES: Picnicking. MISC: Pets permitted.

SYRACUSE

Hamilton County Park (SRA). 3 mi W
of Syracuse on US 50; 2 mi N to Campground. SEASON: All yr; 3-day lmt.
FACILITIES: Undesignated sites; tbls,
toil, cga, drk wtr. ACTIVITIES: Picnicking; fishing; boating,l. MISC:
Pets permitted if kept on leash.

Rest Area. S of Syracuse on US 270.
SEASON: All yr; 1-night lmt. FACILI-
TIES: Spaces for self-contained RVs;

tbls, toil, cga, drk wtr. ACTIVITIES:
Picnicking. MISC: Pets.

TONGANOXIE

Leavenworth (SRA). 4 mi NW of.
Tonganoxie on St Hwy 16. SEASON:
All yr; 3-day lmt. FACILITIES: Undesignated sites; tbls, toil, cga, f,
drk wtr. ACTIVITIES: Picnicking;
fishing; boating,rl. MISC: Pets.

TOPEKA

Cedar Park (COE; Pomona Lake).
20 mi S of Topeka on US 75; 8 mi
E on Co Rd. SEASON: All yr; 14-day
lmt. FACILITIES: 46 sites; tbls, toil,
cga, drk wtr. ACTIVITIES: Picnicking; fishing; swimming; boating,l.
MISC: Pets.

Rest Area. 25 mi W of Topeka on I-
70. SEASON: All yr; 1-night lmt. FA-
CILITIES: Spaces for self-contained
RVs; tbls, flush toil, cga, drk wtr.
ACTIVITIES: Picnicking. MISC: Pets
permitted if kept on leash. Historical
marker.

TORONTO

Woodson County Park (SRA). From
US 54, S on St Hwy 105 to Toronto;
5 mi E on Co Rd. SEASON: All yr;
3-day lmt. FACILITIES: Undesignated
sites; tbls, toil, cga, f, drk wtr,
food. ACTIVITIES: Picnicking; fishing; boating,rl. MISC: Pets permitted.

TRIBUNE

Rest Area. 2 mi E of Tribune on St Hwy
96. SEASON: All yr; 1-night lmt. FA-
CILITIES: Spaces for self-contained
RVs; tbls, toil, cga, drk wtr. ACTIVI-
TIES: Picnicking. MISC: Pets permitted.

Rest Area. 2 mi E of Tribune on St Hwy
96. SEASON: All yr; 1-night lmt. FA-
CILITIES: Spaces for self-contained
RVs; tbls, toil, cga. ACTIVITIES:
Picnicking. MISC: Pets.

TROY

Rest Area. 2 mi E of Troy on US 36.
SEASON: All yr; 1-night lmt. FACILI-
TIES: Spaces for self-contained RVs;
tbls, toil, cga, drk wtr. ACTIVITIES:
Picnicking. MISC: Pets.

VIOLA

Rest Area. 1 mi E of Jct of St Hwy 42
& St Hwy 2, on St Hwy 2. SEASON:
All yr; 1-night lmt. FACILITIES:
Spaces for self-contained RVs; tbls,
toil, cga. ACTIVITIES: Picnicking.

See page 7 for KEY TO ABBREVIATIONS.
217

WAKEENEY

Rest Area. 4 mi E of WaKeeney on I-70. SEASON: All yr; 1-night lmt. FACILITIES: Spaces for self-contained RVs; tbls, toil, cga, drk wtr. ACTIVITIES: Picnicking. MISC: Pets.

Rest Area. S of WaKeeney on US 283. SEASON: All yr; 1-night lmt. FACILITIES: Spaces for self-contained RVs; tbls, toil, cga, drk wtr. ACTIVITIES: Picnicking. MISC: Pets.

WALLACE

Rest Area. At Wallace on US 40. SEASON: All yr; 1-night lmt. FACILITIES: Spaces for self-contained RVs; tbls, toil, cga, drk wtr. ACTIVITIES: Picnicking. MISC: Historical marker. Pets.

WASHINGTON

Rotary Park. 1/2 mi E of Washington on St Hwy 36. SEASON: All yr. FACILITIES: Undesignated sites; tbls, no toil, well drk wtr. ACTIVITIES: Picnicking. MISC: Pets permitted.

Washington (SRA). 7 mi N of US 36 (in Washington), and 3 mi W to campground. SEASON: All yr; 3-day lmt. FACILITIES: Undesignated sites; tbls, toil, cga, drk wtr. ACTIVITIES: Picnicking; fishing; boating,l. MISC: Pets permitted if kept on leash.

WEBSTER

Rest Area. At Webster on US 24. SEASON: All yr; 1-night lmt. FACILITIES: Spaces for self-contained RVs; tbls, toil, cga. ACTIVITIES: Picnicking; boating,l/fishing/swimming nearby. MISC: Pets.

WESKAN

Rest Area. At Weskan on US 40. SEASON: All yr; 1-night lmt. FACILITIES: Spaces for self-contained RVs; tbls, toil, cga, drk wtr. ACTIVITIES: Picnicking. MISC: Pets permitted.

WESTMORELAND

Pohawatomie County Park No. 1 (SRA). 5 mi N of Westmoreland on St Hwy 99. SEASON: All yr; 3-day lmt. FACILITIES: Undesignated sites; tbls, toil, cga, f, drk wtr. ACTIVITIES: Picnicking; fishing; boating,l. MISC: Pets permitted if kept on leash.

WHITEWATER

Rest Area. 5 mi E of Whitewater on St Hwy 196. SEASON: All yr; 1-night lmt. FACILITIES: Spaces for self-contained RVs; tbls, toil, cga, drk wtr. ACTIVITIES: Picnicking. MISC: Pets.

WICHITA

Rest Area. 10 mi N of Wichita on I-35 W (paved access rds). SEASON: All yr; 1-night lmt. FACILITIES: Spaces for self-contained RVs; tbls, toil, cga. ACTIVITIES: Picnicking. MISC: Pets.

WILSON

I-70 Rest Stop. 10 mi E of Wilson on I-70 (paved access rds). SEASON: All yr; 1-night lmt. FACILITIES: Sites; tbls, toil, cga. ACTIVITIES: Picnicking. MISC: Pets.

WINONA

Rest Area. At Winona on US 40. SEASON: All yr; 1-night lmt. FACILITIES: Spaces for self-contained RVs; tbls, toil, cga, drk wtr. ACTIVITIES: Picnicking. MISC: Pets.

YATES CENTER

Rest Area. 5 mi N of Yates Center on US 75. SEASON: All yr; 1-night lmt. FACILITIES: Spaces for self-contained RVs; tbls, toil, cga, drk wtr. ACTIVITIES: Picnicking. MISC: Pets permitted.

Wilson County Park. 15 mi S of Yates Center on US 75. SEASON: All yr. FACILITIES: Sites; tbls, toil, cga. ACTIVITIES: Picnicking; fishing; boating,l. MISC: Pets.

Woodson County Park. 8 mi W of Yates Center on US 54; 3 mi S. SEASON: All yr. FACILITIES: 10 sites; tbls, toil, cga. ACTIVITIES: Picnicking; fishing; boating,rl. MISC: Pets permitted if kept on leash.

KENTUCKY

GENERAL STATE INFORMATION

Miscellaneous

Right Turns on Red: Permitted after full stop, unless otherwise posted.
STATE CAPITOL: Frankfort
STATE NICKNAME: Bluegrass State
STATE MOTTO: "United We Stand, Divided We Fall"
STATE BIRD: Cardinal
STATE FLOWER: Goldenrod
STATE TREE: Tulip Tree

State Parks

Per-night camping fee: $4.00. No extra charge for electricity. 4/1-10/31 is the Kentucky State Park camping season. No reservations. Special camping rates for Kentucky's senior citizens. Pets are allowed if kept on a leash. Further information: Kentucky Department of Parks; Department of Public Information; Capitol Annex; Frankfort, KY 40601.

Rest Areas

No overnight parking is permitted at Kentucky Rest Areas unless otherwise posted.

Mammoth Cave National Park

If you have any questions or need assistance, contact a park ranger. Coin-operated telephones are located in the breezeway at the service station. Telephone numbers to call: (day) 758-2251; (night) 758-2351. Further information: Superintendent; Mammoth Cave NP; PO Box 68; Mammoth Cave, KY 42259. For specific information on campgrounds, see: "Brownsville" and "Bowling Green" under the "FREE CAMPGROUNDS" heading.

Cumberland Gap National Historical Park

There are three backcountry campgrounds, which are elaborated on under "Middlesboro". A free Backcountry Permit is required. Reservations are available up to six months in advance. Further information/map: Cumberland Gap NHP; PO Box 840; Middlesboro, KY 40965.

Daniel Boone National Forest

There are over 140 miles of trails scattered throughout the Forest. In addition to these trails, there is the Sheltowee Trace Trail which was officially designated the 100th National Recreation Trail in June 1979. This trail runs the entire length of the Forest. Total trail distance is about 254 miles. When camping in areas other than developed recreation areas, you should contact the District Ranger in charge of the area in which you wish to camp. In the Red River Gorge, there are restricted areas where camping is not permitted. Fire permits are not required. Topographic maps are available from Kentucky Geological Survey (Room 311; Breckenridge Hall; University of Kentucky; Lexington, KY 40506). Ask for free issue of INDEX TO TOPOGRAPHIC MAPS FOR KENTUCKY. From this form, you can determine which quadrangles to purchase. In the Beaver Creek area, you could hike for about $\frac{1}{2}$ day to a secluded and primitive area, and be near a stream. The Beaver Creek Area consists of about 4790 acres, and is located in northern McCreary County, approximately 17 miles SE of Somerset, KY. The area is noted for its rugged terrain and remote, wild atmosphere. Except for the Forest Service system road that crosses over main Beaver Creek in the north-central portion of the area, access is limited. Hunting is permitted throughout the Forest, except in developed recreation areas and certain Wildlife Management Areas. Check with District Rangers for specific information. All streams and rivers in the NF are open to the public for fishing. Pets are permitted in the backcountry. Further information: Forest Supervisor; Daniel Boone NF; 100 Vaught Road; Winchester, KY 40391.

Tennessee Valley Authority

TVA designated campgrounds are no longer free   However, unimproved TVA lands may be used for informal camping. No fees or permits are required. These areas are shown on recreation maps of individual TVA lakes   Further information/map: TVA; Knoxville, TN 37902.

KENTUCKY

INFORMATION SOURCES

Maps

The following maps are available from Forsyth Travel Library (see order form in Appendix B):

> State of Kentucky [Up-to-date, showing all principal roads, points of interest, sports areas, parks, airports, mileage, etc. Full color.]

> Completely indexed city maps, including all airports, lakes, rivers, etc., of: Lexington; Louisville; Paducah.

State Information

Division of Travel and Promotion; Department of Public Information; Capitol Annex; Frankfort, KY 40601.
TVA; Land Between The Lakes; Golden Pond, KY 42231.
Kentucky Department of Fish and Wildlife Resources; Capital Plaza Tower; Frankfort, KY 40601.

Miscellaneous

Louisville Area Chamber of Commerce; 300 West Liberty; Louisville, KY 40202.
Daniel Boone NF; 100 Vaught Road; Winchester, KY 40391.
Mammoth Cave NP; PO Box 68; Mammoth Cave, KY 42259.
Cumberland Gap NHP; Box 840; Middlesboro, KY 40965.
Corps of Engineers, Louisville District; PO Box 59; Louisville, KY 40201.
Corps of Engineers, Nashville District; Lake Cumberland Resource Manager's Office; Somerset, KY 42501.

FREE CAMPGROUNDS

ALBANY

Grider Hill Recreation Area (COE: Lake Cumberland). 8 mi N of Albany on St Hwy 734; N on St Hwy 1266 to Grider Hill. (On Lake Cumberland.) SEASON: 4/1-11/1; 14-day lmt. FACILITIES: 10 sites; tbls, toil, cga, f, drk wtr; playground. Store/food concession nearby. ACTIVITIES: Picnicking; fishing; boating,l; hiking. MISC: Pets on leash.

BEREA

S-Tree Campground (Daniel Boone NF). 5-1/2 mi E of Berea on St Hwy 21; 11 mi SE on St Hwy 421 to Sandgap; 5-1/2 mi S on Co Hwy 20; 3-1/2 mi SE on FS 20. SEASON: All yr; 14-day lmt. FAC.: 10 sites (tr -22); tbls, toil, cga, drk wtr. ACTIVITIES: Picnicking (shelters). MISC: Pets.

BOWLING GREEN

* **Bluffs Backcountry Campground** (Mammoth Cave NP). 32 mi NE of Bowling Green on I-65; 10 mi W on St Hwy 70; approx. 6 mi NW at sign to Park Headquarters. SEASON: All yr; 14-day lmt. FACILITIES: Hike-in sites. 25 persons max. per site. Established fire ring per site. No water. A Backcountry Use Permit (free) must be obtained before camping. Permits may be obtained at the Ranger's Office at Headquaters or at the Main Campground Entrance Station after hours and on weekends. More complete directions will be given at that time.

* **Boat Access Sites** (Mammoth Cave NP). 32 mi NE of Bowling Green on I-65; 10 mi W on St Hwy 70; approx 6 mi NW at sign to park headquarters. Camping is at personal discretion along the banks and islands of the Green River. Stop at Park Headquarters for a map and additional information, or at the Main Campground Entrance Station after hours and on weekends.

Bowling Green Roadside Rest. I-65 Southbound, at Mile Marker 30. SEASON: All yr; 1-night lmt. FACILITIES: Spaces for self-contained vehicles; tbls, toil, cga, drk wtr, phone. ACTIVITIES: Picnicking. MISC: Pets on leash.

* **Collie Ridge Backcountry Campground** (Mammoth Cave NP). 32 mi NE of Bowling Green on I-65; 10 mi W on St Hwy 70; approx. 6 mi NW at sign to Park Headquarters. SEASON: All yr; 14-day lmt. FACILITIES: Hike-in sites. 25 persons max. per site.

See page 7 for KEY TO ABBREVIATIONS.
220

Established fire ring per site, no water. A Backcountry Use Permit (free) must be obtained before camping. Permits may be obtained at the Ranger's Office at Headquarters or at the Main Campground Entrance Station after hours and on weekends. More complete directions will be given at that time.

BROWNSBORO

Brownsboro Roadside Rest. 1-3/10 mi S of Brownsboro exit on Northbound 1-71. SEASON: All yr; 1-night lmt. FACILITIES: Spaces for self-contained vehicles; toil, tbls, drk wtr, phone. ACTIVITIES: Picnicking. MISC: Pets.

BROWNSVILLE

Houchins Ferry (Mammoth Cave NP). Turn right onto Houchins Ferry Road off of St Hwy 259 just before entering Brownsville. Approx. 1-1/2 mi to Park boundary; becomes gravel road at boundary; follow to Green River; cross ferry to campground. SEASON: All yr; 14-day lmt. FACILITIES: 12 primitive sites (8 persons max. per site); tbl and fireplace at each site. No water. Pit toil. ACTIVITIES: Picnicking; fishing; boating,1

CADIZ

Prizer Point Recreation Area (COE; Lake Barley). 12 mi NW of Cadiz on St Hwy 276. SEASON: 4/1-11/1; 14-day lmt. FACILITIES: 20 sites; tbls, toil, cga, drk wtr. ACTIVITIES: Picnicking; fishing; boating,1; hiking. MISC: Food concession nearby. Pets.

CAMPBELLSVILLE

Pike's Ridge (COE; Green River Lake) 3 mi E of Campbellsville on St Hwy 70; 3 mi SE on St Hwy 76; S at sign on Pike's Ridge Road. (On Green River Lake) SEASON: 4/1-11/1; depending on weather conditions. FACILITIES: 100 sites; tbls, toil, cga, drk wtr. ACTIVITIES: Picnicking; fishing; swimming; boating,1. MISC: No motorbikes. Pets on leash.

CAVE CITY

Cave City Roadside Rest. I-65 Southbound at Mile Marker 55. SEASON: All yr; 1-night lmt. FACILITIES: Spaces for self-contained vehicles; toil, drk wtr, phone. ACTIVITIES: Picnicking. MISC: Pets.

CEDAR SPRINGS

Bailey's Point (COE; Barren River Lake). 1 mi W of Cedar Springs on St Hwy 1533; 2 mi N on St Hwy 517. SEASON: 10/1-5/17, FREE ($3.50 rest of yr). FACILITIES: 217 sites; tbls, toil, cga, showers, drk wtr. ACTIVITIES: Picnicking; fishing; swimming; boating,1d. MISC: Pets.

COLUMBIA

Holmes Bend (COE; Green River Lake). 4 mi N of Columbia on Holmes Bend Road; follow signs. (On Green River Lake) SEASON: 10/1-5/17, FREE (rest of yr, $3.50). FACILITIES: 125 sites; tbls, toil, cga, showers, drk wtr. ACTIVITIES: Picnicking; fishing; swimming; boating,rld. Food/store nearby. MISC: Pets.

CORBIN

Corbin 76 Truck Stop. I-75, exit 29. SEASON: All yr; 1-night lmt. FACILITIES: Spaces for self-contained vehicles; toil, food, drk wtr, mechanic.

★ Star Creek (Daniel Boone NF). 8 mi S of Corbin on US 25W; 7-3/5 mi NW on St hwy 1277; 5½ mi S, BY BOAT. SEASON: All yr; 14-day lmt. FACILITIES: 3 tent sites; 200-square-foot Appalachian-type shelter is on the site; tbls, toil, cga, no drk wtr. ACTIVITIES: Picnicking; fishing; hiking; boating. MISC: Lake Cumberland Moonbow Trail. Pets on leash.

EDDYVILLE

Eddy Creek Recreation Area (COE; Lake Barkley). 5 mi S of Eddyville on St Hwy 93. SEASON: 4/1-11/1; 14-day lmt. FACILITIES: 35 sites; tbls, flush toil, cga, showers, drk wtr. Ice/store/food concession nearby. ACTIVITIES: Picnicking; fishing; swimming; boating,1. MISC: Pets.

FALLS OF ROUGH

Cave Creek (COE; Rough River Lake). 2 mi S of Rough River Dam State Resort Park, on St Hwy 79 (On Rough River lake). SEASON: All yr; 14-day lmt. FACILITIES: 75 primitive sites; tbls, toil, cga, drk wtr. Store/ice/firewood nearby. ACTIVITIES: Picnicking; swimming; boating,1d. MISC: No motorbikes. Pets on leash.

FLORENCE

Florence 76 Truckstop. I-75, Florence exit. SEASON: All yr; 1-night lmt. FACILITIES: Spaces for self-contained vehicles; 24-hr, LP gas, food, gas, mechanic.

GEORGETOWN

Georgetown Roadside Rest (Northbound). I-75, 1-1/2 mi N of exit 126 (northbound). SEASON: All yr; 1-night lmt. FACILITIES: Spaces for self-contained vehicles; toil, drk wtr, phone, food. MISC: Pets.

Georgetown Roadside Rest (southbound). I-75, 1-1/2 mi N of exit in Southbound Lane. SEASON: All yr; 1-night lmt. FACILITIES: Spaces for self-contained vehicles; toil, drk wtr, phone. MISC: Pets on leash.

GLASCOW

Austin (Barren River Lake; COE). 13 mi S of Glasgow on US 31 E; 7 mi SE on st Hwy 87. SEASON: All yr; 14-day lmt. FACILITIES: 10 sites; tbls, toil, cga, drk wtr. ACTIVITIES: Picnicking; fishing; swimming; boating,ld. MISC: Pets.

Bailey's Point. 15 mi SW of Glasgow on St Hwy 34E; 4 mi NW on St Hwy 1533. SEASON: All yr; 1-night lmt. FACILITIES: Spaces for self-contained vehicles. MISC: Pets.

Beaver Creek (COE; Barren River Lake). 5 mi S of Glasgow on US 31E; 3 mi W on St Hwy 252; follow signs (On Barren River Lake). SEASON: All yr; 14-day lmt. FACILITIES: 33 sites; tbls, toil, cga, drk wtr. ACTIVITIES: Picnicking; swimming; fishing; boating,ld. MISC: Pets.

Narrows (COE; Barren River Lake). 12 mi SE of Glasgow on US 31E; 6 mi W on St Hwy 1318. SEASON: 10/1-5/17, FREE ($2 rest of yr). FACILITIES: 54 sites. ACTIVITIES: Picnicking; fishing; swimming; boating,ld. MISC: Playground. Pets.

Tailwater (COE; Barren River Lake). 5 mi S of Glasgow on US 31E; W on St Hwy 252. SEASON: 10/1-5/17, FREE ($2 rest of yr). FACILITIES: 48 sites; Ice/food/store nearby. ACTIVITIES: Picnicking; fishing; swimming; boating,l. MISC: Pets.

GLENDALE

Cecil Key Truckstop. I-65, exit 86. SEASON: All yr; 1-night lmt. FACILITIES: Spaces for self-contained vehicles; food, gas, drk wtr, mechanic.

GRAND RIVERS

Grand Rivers Recreation Area (COE; Lake Barkley). I-1/4 mi S of Grand Rivers on St Hwy 453. SEASON: 4/1-11/1; 14-day lmt. FACILITIES: 44 sites; tbls, toil, cga, showers, dump, drk wtr. Store/ice/food concession nearby. ACTIVITIES: Picnicking; fishing; boating,l. MISC: Playground. Pets on leash.

HAZARD

Buckhorn Dam (COE; Buckhorn Lake). 10 mi W of Hazard on St Hwy 15; 18 mi W on St Hwy 28 to Buckhorn; 1/4 mi off St Hwy 28. SEASON: 10/1-5/17, FREE; ($1 rest of yr). FACILITIES: 29 sites; drk wtr. Ice/food/store nearby. ACTIVITIES: Fishing; swimming; boating,l. MISC: Pets.

Irishman Creek Recreational Area (COE; Carr Fork Lake). Approx. 17 mi E of Hazard on St Hwy 15. SEASON: 10/1-5/17, FREE; ($ rest of yr). FACILITIES: Sites; tbls, toil, cga, showers, bath house, marina. ACTIVITIES: Picnicking; swimming; boating,l. MISC: Overlook. Pets.

Littcarr Recreational Area (COE; Carr Fork Lake). Approx. 19-1/2 mi E of Hazard on St Hwy 15; approx. 2-1/2 mi NE on St Hwy 160; turn W at sign. SEASON: 10/1-5/17, FREE ($ rest of yr); 14-day lmt. FACILITIES: Sites; tbls, toil, cga, drk wtr. ACTIVITIES: Picnicking; boating,l. MISC: Pets.

HENDERSON

Busler Truck Stop. St Hwy 41 N and Racetrack Road, at Henderson. SEASON: All yr; 1-night lmt. FACILITIES: Spaces for self-contained vehicles; drk wtr, food, gas, toil, mechanic.

HORSE CAVE

Kentucky Caverns Park. I-65 at Horse Cave exit 58. Open all yr. Drinking water, electricity, 2 elec hookups, 8 sites with no hookups for tents or RVs; additional unimproved sites available. Pit toilets, grocery, picnic tables, picnic shelter, grills. Pets allowed. Free to cave customers. Limit one night.

Veterans Park. 4 miles north on US 31W. Open all year. Drinking water, electricity, 10 sites for tents or RVs. Pit toilets, grocery, ice, bottled gas, playground, picnic tables, picnic shelter, grills, firewood. Pets.

HYDEN

Confluence (COE; Buckhorn Lake). 16 mi N of Hyden on St Hwy 257 to Dry Hill Bridge; 4 mi W on gravel and dirt roads. SEASON: All yr; 14-day lmt. FACILITIES: Undesignated sites; tbls, toil, cga, drk wtr. ACTIVITIES: Picnicking; boating,l. MISC: Pets on leash.

Trace Branch (COE; Buckhorn Lake). 15 mi N of Hyden on St Hwy 257 to Dry Hill Bridge; 5 mi W on gravel & dirt roads. SEASON: All yr; 14-day lmt. FACILITIES: 31 sites; tbls, toil, cga, drk wtr. ACTIVITIES: Picnicking; fishing; swimming; boating,l. MISC: Store/ice nearby. Pets.

KUTTAWA

Boyds Landing Recreational Area (COE; Lake Barkley). 1 mi W of Kuttawa on US 641; 8 mi S on St Hwy 810. SEASON: All yr; 14-day lmt. FACILITIES: 20 primitive sites; tbls, toil, cga, drk wtr. ACTIVITIES: Picnicking; fishing; boating,l. MISC: Pets.

Eureka Recreation Area (COE; Lake Barkley). 1 mi W of Kuttawa on US 641; 3 mi S on St Hwy 1271. (Follow signs.) SEASON: All yr; 14-day lmt. FACILITIES: 35 sites; tbls, toil, cga, no drk wtr. ACTIVITIES: Picnicking; fishing; boating,l; hiking; waterskiing. MISC: Nature trails. On Lake Barkley. Pets on leash.

LEITCHFIELD

Brier Creek (COE; Nolin River Lake). 17 mi S of Leitchfield on St Hwy 259; E at the drive-in on Co Hwy 728 (follow signs). SEASON: All yr; 14-day lmt. FACILITIES: 50 sites; tbls, toil, cga, drk wtr, store. ACTIVITIES: Picnicking; fishing; swimming; boating,ld. MISC: On Nolin River Lake. Pets.

Dog Creek (COE; Nolin River Lake). 4 mi E of Leichtfield on US 62; 12 mi SE on St Hwy 88 (follow signs). SEASON: 4/1-10/31; 14-day lmt. FACILITIES: 25 sites; tbls, toil, cga, drk wtr. ACTIVITIES: Picnicking; fishing; swimming; boating,ld. MISC: Pets on leash.

Moutardier (COE; Nolin River Lake). 15 mi S of Leitchfield on St Hwy 259; 2 mi SE on Moutardier Rd. SEASON: 10/1-5/17, FREE · ($3.50 rest of yr). FACILITIES: 176 sites; tbls, toil, cga, showers, ice, laundry, store. ACTIVITIES: Picnicking; swimming; fishing; boating,rld. MISC: Pets.

Peter Cave (Rough River Lake; COE). 10 mi NW of Leichtfield on St Hwy 737 (follow signs). SEASON: All yr; 14-day lmt. FACILITIES: 25 developed sites, plus unlimited undeveloped sites; tbls, toil, cga. Store/ice/firewood nearby. ACTIVITIES: Picnicking; swimming; fishing; boating,ld. MISC: Pets on leash.

LEXINGTON

Lexington 76 Auto Truck Stop. I-75, exit 97. SEASON: All yr; 1-night lmt. FACILITIES: Spaces for self-contained vehicles; food, mechanic, drk wtr, toil, gas.

LONDON

Craigs Creek Campground (Daniel Boone NF). 15 mi W of London on St Hwy 192; 2 mi S on FS 62. SEASON: 4/1-10/31; 14-day lmt. FACILITIES: 45 sites (tr -32); tbls, toil, cga, well drk wtr. ACTIVITIES: Picnicking; fishing (1 mi); boating,ld (1 mi); waterskiing (1 mi). MISC: Pets. On Laurel River Lake. Elev 1100 ft; 12 acres.

*White Oak (Daniel Boone NF). 17 mi W of London on St Hwy 192; 2 mi S on FS 772; 3/5 mi S, BY BOAT. SEASON: All yr; 14-day lmt. FACILITIES: 51 tent sites; tbls, toil, cga, piped drk wtr. Food/gas/ice/dump (1 mi). ACTIVITIES: Picnicking; swimming; fishing; waterskiing; boating (l,r - 1 mi). MISC.: Elev 1100 ft; 145 acres. Laurel River Lake Pets. Boat-in camping only.

* White Oak Boat Access Campground (Accessible only by boat.) 15 mi W on Ky-192, then south 2 mi on FS 62 to Craigs Creek boat launch, then 1-1/2 mi NE on Laurel River Lake by boat; on Laurel River Lake in Daniel Boone National Forest. Open all yr. FACILITIES: 35 primitive sites for tents; no drk wtr; flush toil. Limit 14 days. ACTIVITIES: Fishing; waterskiing; boating. MISC: Pets on leash.

LOUISVILLE

Roadside Rest. 14 mi NE of Louisville on I-71. SEASON: All yr; 1-night lmt. FACILITIES: Spaces for self-contained vehicles; drk wtr, toil, phone. ACTIVITIES: Picnicking. MISC: Pets on leash.

Truckers World. I-65, exit 117; 1/5 mi W on St Hwy 144. SEASON: All yr; 1-night lmt. FACILITIES: Spaces for self-contained vehicles; food, drk wtr, LP gas, toil, gas, mechanic.

MCKEE

S Tree (Daniel Boone NF). 3-4/5 mi SW of McKee on St Hwy 89; 1-3/10 mi W on FS 43; 1-7/10 mi S on FS 20. SEASON: All yr; 14-day lmt. FACILITIES: 10 sites; tbls, toil, cga, well drk wtr. Store/gas/laundry (5 mi). ACTIVITIES: Picnicking; hiking. MISC: On Sheltowee Trace. Pets. Nature trails; elev 1500 ft; 3 acres; trailers less than 22 feet.

Turkey Foot (Daniel Boone NF). 3 mi N of McKee on St Hwy 89; 1-1/2 mi E on Co Rd; 1-4/5 mi E on FS 4; 1/5 mi N on FS 482. SEASON: 4/1-11/1; 14-day lmt. FACILITIES: 15 sites (tr -16) ; tbls, toil, cga, well drk wtr. Store/gas/laundry (5 mi). ACTIVITIES: Picnicking; fishing; hiking. MISC: This site is on Old Indian Warrior Trail, on Sheltowee Trace. Pets; elev 900 ft; 10 acres.

MIDDLESBORO

* Martins Fork Campground and Cabin (Cumberland Gap NHP). Located in the valley between Brush Mountain and Cumberland Mountain 2/10 mi below Chadwell Gap. The Chadwell Gap Trail is the most direct route to the campground. The trail can be reached by turning left, off US Hwy 58, at a point 9-2/5 mi E of US Hwy 25-E, on to St Hwy 690 at Caylor, VA; drive until the road forks; take the right fork for about a half mile. There will be a sign on the left side of the road at the trail head. The trail crosses privately owned land to reach the Park boundary. Please respect the privilege extended by the land owner. FACILITIES: 6 sites (max of 10 persons per site); cga, toil, cleared camping site; water must be purified (sometimes water is not available). CABIN: rustic, stone-floored cabin furnished with tbl only. 3-night maxmum use. A Backcountry Use Permit (free) is required of all persons staying overnight in the backcountry. The permit may be picked up at the Visitor Center desk up to 24 hours prior to beginning of trip. The Visitor Center is open 8-5 daily except Christmas. It may be open later during the summer months. Sites may be reserved up to 6 months in advance. Reservations may be made by telephone, by letter, or in person. Write: PO Box 840, Middlesboro, 40965.

MIDDLETOWN

Middletown Roadside Rest. 4-1/2 mi E of Middletown on I-64. SEASON: All yr; 1-night lmt. FACILITIES: Spaces for self-contained vehicles; drk wtr, toil, phone. ACTIVITIES: Picnicking. MISC: Pets.

MONTICELLO

Fall Creek (COE; Lake Cumberland). Take St Hwy 90 E to St Hwy 1275; St Hwy 1275 N to Tate Road; W on Tate Road to Fall Creek. SEASON: 4/1-11/1; 14-day lmt. FACILITIES: 10 sites; tbls, flush toil, cga, dump, showers, playground, drk wtr. ACTIVITIES: Picnicking; fishing; boating,l; hiking. MISC: Pets.

MOOREHEAD

* Claylick Boat-In Campground (Daniel Boone NF). 1/2 mi W of Moorehead on US 60; 7 mi S on St Hwy 519; 3/5 mi W on St Hwy 801; 1 mi S on St Hwy 1274. SEASON: All yr; 14-day lmt. FACILITIES: 20 sites; tbls, toil, cga, f, well drk wtr. Store/gas/ice/food (4 mi). ACTIVITIES: Picnicking; fishing, Sailing. Boating,d (l, 1 mi; r, 4 mi). Swimming/waterskiing (1 mi). MISC: Elev 800 ft; 42 acres. Cave Run Lake. Facility designed for boat in use. Scenic; lake. Pets.

Rodburn Recreation Area (Daniel Boone NF). 2 mi NE of Moorehead on US 60; 1 mi NW on FS 13. SEASON: 4/4-11/1; 14-day lmt. FACILITIES: 11 sites (tr -22); tbls, flush toil, cga, f, piped drk wtr. Ice/food concession/store/gas (1 mi). Dump (4 mi). ACTIVITIES: Picnicking; fishing (1 mi); hiking; boating, r (3 mi); swimming (2 mi). MISC: Nature trails; stream. Within city limits of Moorehead. Pets; elev 900 ft; 3 acres.

MORGANFIELD

Higginson-Henry Wildlife Management Area. 6 mi E on Ky-56, then S and follow signs; on Lake Mauzy. Open all yr. 100 unimproved sites for tents only, no RVs. Pit toil, tbls, grills, ACTIVITIES: Picnicking; fishing; boating,l. MISC: Limit 14-days. Pets.

MORTON'S GAP

Madisonville 76 Auto/Truck Plaza. St Hwy 813 and PA Parkway, in Morton's Gap. SEASON: All yr; 1-night lmt. FACILITIES: Spaces for self-contained vehicles; gas, food, drk wtr, toil, mechanic, 24-hrs. ACTIVITIES: Picnicking. MISC: Pets on leash.

PARKER LAKE

*Straight Creek (Daniel Boone NF). 7/10 mi S on US 27; 8 mi W on St Hwy 927; 3-7/10 mi SE, BY BOAT. SEASON: All yr; 14-day lmt. FACILITIES: Undesignated tent sites; tbls, toil, cga, f; no drk wtr. One shelter. ACTIVITIES: Picnicking; fishing; boating;

waterskiing. MISC.: Elev 1100 ft; 3 acres; pets. 12 mi S of Burnsides on US 27; 8 mi W on St Hwy 927; 4 mi SE by boat. No road.

RICHMOND

Richmond Roadside Rest (Northbound). 2-1/2 mi N of Richmond Exit on I-75. SEASON: All yr; 1-night lmt. FACILI-TIES: Spaces for self-contained vehicles; drk wtr, toil, phone, tbls. AC-TIVITIES: Picnicking. MISC: Pets.

Richmond Roadside Rest (Southbound). 2-1/2 mi N of Richmond on I-75. SEA-SON: All yr; 1-night lmt. FACILI-TIES: Spaces for self-contained vehicles; drk wtr, toil, phone, tbls. AC-TIVITIES: Picnicking. MISC: Pets.

ROFF

Axtel (COE; Rough River Lake). 2 mi S of Roff on St Hwy 259; 1 mi W on St Hwy 79. SEASON: 10/1-5/17, FREE ($3.50 rest of yr) ; 14-day lmt FACILITIES: 163 sites; flush toil, showers, drk wtr. Ice/food nearby. ACTIVITIES: Picnicking; fishing; swimming; boating,rld. Golfing nearby. MISC.: Pets.

Laurel Branch (COE: Rough River Lake). 3 mi S of Roff on St Hwy 259; 1 mi W on St Hwy 110. SEASON: 10/1-5/17, FREE ($2.50 rest of yr). FACILITIES: 72 sites; 14-day lmt. Store/food/ice nearby. ACTIVI-TIES: Swimming; fishing; boating,ld, MISC: Pets on leash.

North Fork (COE: Rough River Lake). 1-1/2 mi S of Roff on St Hwy 259. SEASON: 10/1-5/17, FREE ($3.50 rest of yr); 14-day lmt. FACILITIES: 107 sites, showers. Food/store/ice nearby. ACTIVITIES: Fishing; swimming; boating,rld. MISC: Pets.

SALT LICK

Clear Creek (Daniel Boone NF). 3-3/5 mi S on St Hwy 211; 1 mi E on Co Hwy 1118; 1¼ mi SE on FS FH129. At site of old iron furnace. SEASON: 4/4-1/2; 14-day lmt. FACILITIES: 24 sites (tr -22); tbls, toil, cga, f, well drk wtr. Store/gas/ice/food (3 mi). ACTIVI-TIES: Picnicking; boating (r, 4 mi; l, 5 mi); hiking; berry-picking. Fishing (5 mi). MISC.: Elev 900 ft; 10 acres; historic; pets.

SAUL

Leatherwood Creek (COE; Buckhorn Lake). Approx 1/2 mi N of Saul on St Hwy 484 (off Hwy 1482). SEASON:

All yr; 14-day lmt. FACILITIES: Primitive undesignated sites; tbls, toil, cga, drk wtr. ACTIVITIES: Pic-nicking; boating,l. MISC: Pets.

SAWYER

*Sam's Branch (Daniel Boone NF). 2¼ mi NE of Sawyer on St Hwy 896; 5 mi W, BY BOAT. SEASON: All yr. FACIL-ITIES: Undesignated tent sites; tbls, toil, cga; no drk wtr. Food/gas/ice (1 mi). ACTIVITIES: Picnicking; boating (l,r, 1 mi); fishing; water-skiing. MISC.: Elev 800 ft; 5 acres. Access by boat only. 29 mi from Burnside by water. 16 mi NW from Cumberland Falls. Pets.

Sawyer Lake (Daniel Boone NF). 1-3/5 mi NE of Sawyer on St Hwy 896; 1-7/10 mi N on FS 1609 (on Lake Cum-berland). SEASON: 4/1-11/1; 14-day lmt. FACILITIES: 19 sites (no tr); tbls, toil, cga, piped drk wtr. Store/gas (4 mi). ACTIVITIES: Picnicking; fishing; boating,ld; hiking; water-skiing. MISC: Shelters; lake. Pets. Elev 800 ft; 8 acres.

SCOTTSVILLE

Brown's Ford (COE; Barren River Lake). E of Scottsville on St Hwy 98 (follow signs). SEASON: All yr; 14-day lmt. FACILITIES: 6 sites; tbls, toil, cga, drk wtr. ACTIVITIES: Picnicking; fishing; swimming; boat-ing,ld. MISC: Pets on leash.

SMITH'S GROVE

Smith's Grove Roadside Rest. On I-65 northbound at mile marker 37. SEASON: All yr; 1-night lmt. FACILI-TIES: Spaces for self-contained vehic-les, drk wtr, phone. MISC: Pets.

SOMERSET

Bee Rock Campground (Daniel Boone NF). 1-1/2 mi NE of Somerset on St Hwy 80; 17-1/5 mi SE on St Hwy 192; 1/2 mi SE on Fs 623 (On Rockcastle River). SEASON: 4/1-11/1; 14-day lmt FACILITIES: 19 sites (tr -22), tbls, toil, cga, no drk wtr. Store/gas (4 mi). Food concession (3 mi). ACTIVI-TIES: Picnicking; fishing, Boating,ld (1 mi). MISC: Boat ramp across river approx 400 yds foot travel. Pets. Elev 700 ft; 10 acres.

Little Rock (Daniel Boone NF). 13 mi SE of Somerset on St Hwy 192; 3-3/10 mi S on Co Hwy 122; 1 mi S on FS 816; 2 mi S on FS 8163. SEASON: 4/1-11/15; 14-day lmt. FACILITIES:

See page 7 for KEY TO ABBREVIATIONS.

7 sites (tr -22); tbls, toil, cga, well drk wtr. **ACTIVITIES:** Picnicking. **MISC.:** Elev 1100 ft; 3 acres; pets.

SONORA

Sonora Roadside Rest (Northbound). SEASON: All yr; 1-night lmt. **FACILITIES:** Spaces for self-contained vehicles; drk wtr, toil, phone. **MISC:** Pets.

Sonora Roadside Rest (Southbound). I-65 Southbound at mile marker 82. **SEASON:** All yr; 1-night lmt. **FACILITIES:** Spaces for self-contained vehicles; drk wtr, toil, phone. **MISC:** Pets.

STEARNS

Great Meadow (Daniel Boone NF). 6 mi W of Stearns on St Hwy 92; 12 mi SW on St Hwy 1363; 5 mi SW on FS 137 (on Rock Creek). **SEASON:** 4/1-11/1; 14-day lmt. **FACILITIES:** 8 sites (tr -22); tbls, toil, cga, well drk wtr. **ACTIVITIES:** Picnicking; fishing; hiking. **MISC:** Nature trails; streams. Near Ky-Tenn State Line. Within 2 mi of Arch Trail on Rock Creek a favorite trout stream. Pets; scenic. Elev 1000 ft; 2 acres.

VEECHDALE

Veechdale Roadside Rest. 1-1/5 mi W of Veechdale on I-64. **SEASON:** All yr; 1-night lmt. **FACILITIES:** Spaces for self-contained vehicles; drk wtr, toil, phone. **MISC:** Pets on leash.

WALTON

Arnold's Sonoco Auto/Truck Stop. I-75, exit 171. **SEASON:** All yr; 1-night lmt. **FACILITIES:** Spaces for self-contained vehicles; drk wtr. toil, gas, 24-hrs, mechanic.

Walton 76 Truck Stop. I-75, exit 171. **SEASON:** All yr; 1-night lmt. **FACILITIES:** Spaces for self-contained vehicles; drk wtr, toil, gas, food, 24-hrs, mechanic.

WAX

Wax (COE; Nolin River Lake). 4 mi mi E of Wax on US 62; 9 mi S on St Hwy 88 (on Nolin Lake). **SEASON:** 10/1-5/17, FREE ($2.50 rest of yr). 14-day lmt. **FACILITIES:** 44 sites (tr -35); tbls, toil, cga. Store/ice nearby. Drk wtr available approx. 4/1-11/1, depending on weather conditions. **ACTIVITIES:** Picnicking; fishing; boating,rld; hiking. **MISC:** Pets.

WHITLEY CITY

Alum Ford (Daniel Boone NF). 2 mi N of Whitley City on US 27; 5 mi W on St Hwy 700. **SEASON:** 4/1-11/1; 14-day lmt. **FACILITIES:** 7 sites (tr -16); tbls, toil, cga, piped drk wtr. Store/gas (4 mi). Ice/food concession (5 mi). **ACTIVITIES:** Picnicking; fishing; boating,ld; hiking; waterskiing. **MISC:** Nature trails; scenic. Trail to Yahoo Falls scenic area & Cotton Patch Shelter. Pets. Lake Cumberland.

WILLIAMSBURG

Kentucky I-75 Welcome Center. I-75 North, Mile Marker 1. **SEASON:** All yr; 1-night lmt. **FACILITIES:** Spaces for self-contained vehicles; drk wtr, toil, phone. **ACTIVITIES:** Picnicking. **MISC:** Pets.

Williamsburg Roadside Rest. I-75 southbound, Mile Marker 1. **SEASON:** All yr; 1-night lmt. **FACILITIES:** Spaces for self-contained vehicles; drk wtr, toil, phone. **ACTIVITIES:** Picnicking. **MISC:** Pets.

LOUISIANA

GENERAL STATE INFORMATION

Miscellaneous

Right Turns on Red: Permitted after full stop, unless otherwise posted.
STATE CAPITOL: Baton Rouge
STATE NICKNAME: Pelican State
STATE MOTTO: "Union, Justice, and Confidence"

See page 7 for KEY TO ABBREVIATIONS.

STATE BIRD: Brown Pelican
STATE FLOWER: Magnolia
STATE TREE: Bald Cypress

State Parks

Entrance Fee: $1.00/day [FREE entrance to senior citizens over 62, as well as all persons accompanying them in a private, non-commercial vehicle; and to disabled veterans]. PLUS CAMPING FEE: $5.00 per night (with electricity); $3.00 per night (no electricity). No reservations. Pets are permitted if kept on a leash. Further information: Louisiana State Parks and Recreation Commission; PO Drawer 1111; Baton Rouge, LA 70821.

Rest Areas

Overnight stops are not permitted in Louisiana Rest Areas.

Wildlife Management Areas

Although the Wildlife Management Areas that allow free camping are discussed in detail in this chapter, we suggest that you send for the free book A GUIDE TO WILDLIFE MANAGEMENT AREAS, which includes maps for each area, pinpointing camping site. Write: Louisiana Department of Wildlife and Fisheries; PO Box 44095; Capitol Station; Baton Rouge, LA 70804.

Canoeing in Louisiana

Lafayette Natural History Museum (Planetarium & Nature Station; 637 Girard Park Dr.; Lafayette, LA 70503) offers a detailed guide entitled CANOEING IN LOUISIANA for $3.63, including postage and handling.

KISATCHIE NATIONAL FOREST

Caney Lakes Recreation Area

Recreation includes waterskiing, swimming, fishing, and boating in Upper Caney Lake (165 surface acres) and Lower Caney Lake (226 surface acres). Also available are hunting, hiking, picnicking, birdwatching, and FREE CAMPING. Further information and a map: District Ranger; Kisatchie NF; PO Box 479; Homer, LA 71040.

Wild Azalea Trail

Designated as a National Recreation Trail, it lies south and west of Alexandria, LA, connecting the Valentine Lake Recreation Area and a roadside area on US 165, just south of Alexandria. For foot travel only, it is approximately 31 miles long. The trail crosses seven major creeks over log bridges, and several wet areas on cordoroy tread built up of four foot bolts of timber. A log cabin shelter lies immediately west of Route 279. Trailhead parking and trash disposal containers are on Route 273, at Valentine Lake Recreation Area and the roadside rest area on US 165. FREE CAMPING is permitted adjacent to the trail. Poisonous snakes, spiders, ticks, chiggers, poison ivy and other hazards may be encountered in the area: CAUTION. Further information: District Ranger; Kisatchie NF; 3727 Government Street; Alexandria, LA 71301.

Backpacking in Kisatchie NF

Backpacking/camping is permitted in any area of the Forest except for a few well-marked sections that are reserved for military or other special use. Abundant opportunity for hunting and fishing. Further information: Forest Supervisor; Kisatchie NF; 2500 Shreveport Highway; Pineville, LA 71360.

National Catahoula Wildlife Management Preserve
National Red Dirt Wildlife Management Preserve

Hunting, fishing, trapping, and camping are permitted on the Preserves in accordance with Federal and State regulations. Each person desiring to hunt, fish, or trap (as well as camp) on the Preserves must obtain and be in possession of a seasonal permit that can be obtained FREE OF CHARGE from any of the offices listed below:

Caney Ranger District
Kisatchie NF
324 Beardsley
PO Box 479
Homer, LA 71040
Office Hours: 8:00-4:30

Evangeline Ranger District
Kisatchie NF
3727 Government Street
Alexandria, LA 71301
Office Hours: 7:30-4:00

LOUISIANA

Vernon Ranger District
Kisatchie NF
PO Box 678
Leesville, LA 71446
Office Hours: 7:30–4:00

Kisatchie Ranger District
Kisatchie NF
PO Box 2128
Natchitoches, LA 71457
Office Hours: 7:00–3:30

Forest Supervisor
Kisatchie NF
2500 Shreveport Highway
Pineville, LA 71360
Office Hours: 8:00–4:45

Catahoula Ranger District
Kisatchie NF
PO Box 207
Pollock, LA 71467
Office Hours: 8:00–4:30

Winn Ranger District
Kisatchie NF
PO Box 30
Winnfield, LA 71483
Office Hours: 7:00–4:30

The permit is valid for the entire legal season. Copies of the Federal Regulations in effect on the Preserves may be obtained at any of the above offices.

INFORMATION SOURCES

Maps

The following maps are available from **Forsyth Travel Library** (see order form in Appendix B):

State of Louisiana [Up-to-date, showing all principal roads, points of interest, sports areas, parks, airports, mileage, etc. Full color.]

Completely indexed city maps, including all airports, lakes, rivers, etc., of: **Baton Rouge; Port Allen; New Orleans; Shreveport.**

State Information

Louisiana Department of Wildlife and Fisheries; PO Box 44095; Capitol Station; Baton Rouge, LA 70804.
Louisiana Tourist Development Commission; PO Box 44291, Capitol Station; Baton Rouge, LA 70804.
Lafayette National History; Museum and Planetarium; 637 Girard Park Drive; Lafayette, LA 70501.
Office of State Parks; Department of Culture, Recreation and Tourism; PO Drawer 1111; Baton Rouge, LA 70821.

Miscellaneous

Chamber of Commerce of the New Orleans Area; PO Box 30240; New Orleans, LA 70130.
Greater New Orleans Tourist and Convention Commission; 400 Royal Street; New Orleans, LA 70130.
Kisatchie NF; 2500 Shreveport Highway; Pineville, LA 71360.

FREE CAMPGROUNDS

ALEXANDRIA

Evangeline Camp (Kistachie NF). 8 mi W on St Hwy 28; 4-4/5 mi S on FS 273. SEASON: All yr. FACILITIES: Undesignated sites (no tr); tbls, toil, cga, well drk wtr. ACTIVITIES: Hiking; picnicking. MISC.: Elev 200 ft; 10 acres. Developed for organized groups only. General use not encouraged. Area not signed.

BERNICE

Corney Lake (Kistachie NF). 1 mi N of Bernice on US 167; 12 mi NW on St Hwy Alt. 2; 2½ mi NE on St Hwy 9; 2-3/10 mi SE on FS 900. SEASON: All yr; 14-day lmt. FACILITIES: 10 sites (tr -16); tbls, toil, cga, f, piped drk wtr. ACTIVITIES: Fishing; picnicking. Boating,rd (1 mi). MISC.: Elev 200 ft; 4 acres; lake. Pets on leash.

DERRY

Lotus Camp (Kisatchie NF). 5 mi S on St Hwy 119; 12 mi NW on FS 59. SEASON: All yr. FACILITIES: Undesignated sites; piped drk wtr, flush toil. ACTIVITIES: Picnicking. MISC.: Elev 200; 2 acres; geological; pets.

DODSON

Cloud Crossing (Kisatchie NF). 15 mi W of Dodson on St Hwy 126; 2½ mi S on St Hwy 1233; 1 mi W on FS 513. SEASON: All yr; 14-day lmt. FACILITIES: 13 sites (tr -22); tbls, toil, cga, f, well drk wtr. ACTIVITIES: Boating,rd; picnicking; fishing. MISC.: Elev 100 ft; 7 acres; stream. Pets on leash.

HOMER

Bucktail Campground (Kisatchie NF). 1-1/5 mi N on St Hwy 79; 5-4/5 mi NE on St Hwy 520. SEASON: All yr. FACILITIES: Undesignated sites; piped drk wtr, f. Portable toilet on site only during hunting season. ACTIVITIES: Picnicking. Fishing (2 mi). MISC.: Elev 200 ft; 5 acres.

KISATCHIE

Dogwood (Kisatchie NF). 3 mi N of Kisatchie on St Hwy 117. SEASON: All yr; 14-day lmt. FACILITIES: 11 sites (tr -22); tbls, flush toil, cga, f, piped drk wtr. Store/gas (2 mi). ACTIVITIES: Picnicking. MISC.: Elev 200 ft; 6 acres; pets. 26 mi S of Natchitoches, oldest town in the Louisiana Purchase.

LAFAYETTE

Four Way Truck Stop. 2821 St Hwy 167 North, in Lafayette. SEASON: All yr; 1-night lmt. FACILITIES: Spaces for self-contained RVs; food, toil, drk wtr, gas. MISC.: Emergency parking only.

OPEUOUSAS

Seven Flags Auto/Truck Center. 4 mi E of Opeuousas on US 190. SEASON: All yr; 1-night lmt. FACILITIES: Spaces for self-contained RVs; food, toil, drk wtr, gas, mechanic.

PITKIN

Fullerton Lake (Kisatchie NF). 6 mi W of Pitkin on St Hwy 10; 3½ mi NE on St Hwy 399. SEASON: All yr; 14-day lmt. FACILITIES: 8 sites (tr -22); tbls, toil, cga, f, piped drk wtr. ACTIVITIES: Hiking; picnicking; fishing; boating,d. MISC.: Elev 200 ft; 3 acres; historic; nature trails; lake. Pets on leash.

SHREVEPORT

South Abutment East (COE). 13 mi NE of Shreveport on St Hwys 79/80; 8 mi N on St Hwy 157 to Bellevue; 2 mi E to campground. SEASON: All yr; 14-day lmt. FACILITIES: 10 sites; tbls, flush toil, cga, drk wtr. ACTIVITIES: Boating,l; picnicking; fishing. MISC.: Pets.

SLIDELL

Slidell Union 76 Auto/Truck Plaza. I-10; US 190 exit. SEASON: All yr; 14-day lmt. FACILITIES: Spaces for self-contained RVs; food, toil, drk wtr, dump, mechanic

WINNFIELD

Gum Springs (Kisatchie NF). 8 mi W of Winnfield on US 84. SEASON: All yr; 14-day lmt. FACILITIES: 13 sites (tr -22); tbls, toil, cga, f, piped drk wtr. Store/gas (3 mi). Ice (5 mi). ACTIVITIES: Picnicking. MISC.: Elev 200 ft; 10 acres. Pets permitted if on a leash.

MAINE

GENERAL STATE INFORMATION

Miscellaneous

Right Turns on Red: Permitted after full stop, unless otherwise posted.
STATE CAPITOL: Augusta
STATE NICKNAME: Pine Tree State
STATE MOTTO: "I Direct"
STATE BIRD: Chickadee
STATE FLOWER: Pine Cone and Tassel
STATE TREE: Eastern White Pine

See page 7 for KEY TO ABBREVIATIONS.

MAINE

State Parks

Fees range from $2.00-5.00 per night. Pets must be on a leash not to exceed 4 feet in length. No special rates for senior citizens. Further information: Maine Department of Conservation; Bureau of Parks and Recreation; State House; Augusta, ME 04333.

Rest Areas

Overnight stops are not permitted in Maine Rest Areas.

State Forests

Although Maine Forest Service campgrounds are specified within this chapter, the free map available from the Forest Service would be helpful. Write: Maine Forest Service; Department of Conservation; State Office Building; Augusta, ME 04333.

Georgia-Pacific Corporation

A free map of the expansive multiple-use recreation area offered by Georgia-Pacific can be obtained from: Georgia-Pacific Corporation; Woodland, ME 04694; 207/427-3311. Ask for their SPORTSMEN'S MAP AND TOUR GUIDE TO THE WOODLAND DIVISION OF GEORGIA-PACIFIC.

Acadia National Park

Because the Park is so small and receives a great number of campers, overnight backpacking cannot be allowed. All camping must be in designated areas only. For information on the free areas, see: "Bar Harbor" and "Stonington" in this chapter. The Visitor Center is open 5/1-10/31. Pets on leash are permitted. No fishing license is required for saltwater fishing. A freshwater fishing license may be obtained in Bar Harbor. For additional information/map: Superintendent; Acadia NP; RFD #1; Box 1; Bar Harbor, ME 04609.

North Maine Woods

This is a gigantic 2½-million-acre region of forest land jointly owned and operated by private owners and Maine's natural resource agencies. Camping and wilderness-type recreation is available here, but a fee is charged: Maine Residents, $1.50/night for camping; Non-residents, $3.00/night. Season, 5/1-11/30. Within its boundaries are two of the most famous wild rivers of the northeast.....the St. John and the Allagash. The North Maine Woods completely surrounds the Allagash Wilderness Waterway. Further information and a map: North Maine Woods; Box 552; Presque Isle, ME 04769.

Central Maine Power Company

The power company will send you, free of charge, a GUIDE TO OUTDOOR RECREATIONAL OPPORTUNITIES, including free campgrounds which are pinpointed on the map. Write: Central Maine Power Company; 9 Green Street; Augusta, ME 04330.

Maine Turnpike Authority

Overnight parking in its service areas is not permitted except in emergencies, and then only if the attendant or attendants on duty permit the parking. In any event, it would not be feasible to allow such parking during winter storms as there would be interference with snow removal and sanding of areas.

Canoe Trails/Camping

The following canoe maps have been specially-prepared for canoe enthusiasts and indicate suggested canoe trip areas including locations of campsites and campsite fire permit areas along with portage, rapids, and other information of interest:

Maine Forestry Department; State Office Building; Augusta, ME
Maine Forestry Department; Northern Regional Headquarters; Island Falls, ME
Maine Forestry Department; Eastern Regional Headquarters; Oldtown, ME
Maine Forestry Department; Western Regional Headquarters; Greenville, ME
Maine Forestry Department; Southern Regional Headquarters; RFD K#6; Bolton Hill; Augusta, ME

The Appalachian Trail

More than 2000 miles long, the Appalachian Trail (from Maine to Georgia) is the longest continuous marked trail in the world.

CAMPING: More than 200 open-front shelters/lean-tos are spaced approximately 10 miles apart on the Trail (one-day intervals). As they are occupied on a first-come first-served basis, carry a tent in case the shelters are full. Potable spring water is

MAINE

usually available at each site, but should be purified by tablets or boiling. And always "pack it in, pack it out"

PERMITS: No permit is required to hike the Trail. However, camping permits must be obtained for overnight stays in Shenandoah NP (Luray, VA 22835) and Great Smoky Mountains NP (Gatlinburg, TN 37733). These are free of charge and available from the ranger stations or by mail A free camping permit must be obtained for overnight stays in White Mountain National Forest Restricted Use Area (PO Box 638; Laconia, NH 03246).

APPALACHIAN TRAIL CONFERENCE: A private, nonprofit, national organization which represents citizen's interest in the Appalachian Trail. They offer detailed guidebooks and maps for sale, as well as the A.T. Data Book which gives the location and distances between shelters and certain post offices, supply points, water sources, lodging and meals. For more information on this organization, write to them at: PO Box 236; Harpers Ferry, WV 25425.

INFORMATION SOURCES

Maps

The following maps are available from **Forsyth Travel Library** (see order form in Appendix B):

> **State of Maine** [Up-to-date, showing all principal roads, points of interest, sports areas, parks, airports, mileage, etc. Full color.]

> Completely indexed map, including all airports, lakes, rivers, etc., of the city of **Bangor**.

State Information

Promotion Division; Department of Commerce and Industry; State House; Augusta, ME 04330.
Maine Turnpike Authority; PO Box 839; Portland, ME 04104.
North Maine Woods; Box 552; Presque Isle, ME 04769.
Department of Inland Fisheries and Wildlife; 284 State Street; Augusta, ME 04333.
Bureau of Parks and Recreation; Department of Conservation; Augusta, ME 04333.
Maine Bureau of Forestry; Ray Building; Augusta, ME 04333.
Maine Vacations; State of Maine Publicity Bureau; Gateway Circle; Portland, ME 04102.

City Information

Kennebunk Chamber of Commerce; 41 Main Street; Kennebunk, ME 04043.
Greater Portland Chamber of Commerce; 142 Free Street; Portland, ME 04101.
Presque Isle Chamber of Commerce; PO Box 672; Presque Isle, ME 04769.
Van Buren Chamber of Commerce; Main Street; Municipal Building; Van Buren, ME 04785.

Miscellaneous

Arcadia National Park; RFD #1, Box 1; Bar Harbor, ME 04609.
Refuge Manager; Moosehorn National Wildlife Refuge; Calais, ME 04619.

FREE CAMPGROUNDS

BANGOR

Hogan Road Exxon Auto/Truck Stop. I-95, Hogan Road Exit. SEASON: All yr; 1-night lmt. FACILITIES: Spaces for self-contained vehicles; drk wtr, toil, food, gas, mechanic, emergency parking.

BAY HARBOR

Blackwoods Campground (Acadia NP). 5 mi S of Bay Harbor on St Hwy 3; 1/2 mi E. SEASON: Mid-Oct until May, FREE ($4 rest of yr). FACILITIES: 34 sites; tbls, toil, cga, f. ACTIVITIES: Picnicking. MISC: Pets on leash,

BEDDINGTON

Bracey Pond (SF; Narraguagus River Dist.). 10-1/2 mi N of St Hwy 9 from Beddington on W side of C.C.C. Rd. (Information: Cherryfield; 207/546-2346.) SEASON: All yr. FACILITIES: Sites ; tbls, toil, cga, drk wtr should be boiled. Free permit required for fires in non-designated areas. ACTIVITIES: Picnicking; fishing. MISC: Pets on leash.

Deer Lake (SF; Narraguagus River Dist.). 13 mi N of St Hwy 9 from Beddington on S side of C.C.C. rd. SEASON: All yr. FACILITIES: Sites; tbls, toil, cga, drk wtr should be boiled; free fire permit required for fires in non-designated areas. ACTIVITIES: Picnicking; fishing. MISC: Pets on leash.

BRIDGEWATER

Number 9 Lake (SF; Number Nine Dist.). 14 mi W of Bridgewater on NE shore of Number 9 Lake. (Information: 207/435-6975.) SEASON: All yr. FACILITIES: Sites; tbls, toil, cga, drk wtr should be boiled; free fire permit required for fires in non-designated areas. ACTIVITIES: Picnicking; fishing. MISC: Pets.

BRIGHTON

Smith Pond (SF; Parlin Pond District). East side of St Hwy 151; N of Brighton. FACILITIES: Sites; tbls, toil, cga, drk wtr should be boiled; free fire permit required for fires in non-designated areas. ACTIVITIES: Picnicking; fishing. MISC: Pets

CARRABASSET

Big Eddy (SF; Dead River District). 15 mi N of Carrabasset on Spring Lake Road; E shore of Dead River. FACILITIES: Sites; tbls, toil, cga, drk wtr should be boiled; free fire permit required for fires in non-designated areas. ACTIVITIES: Picnicking; fishing. MISC: Pets.

CUPSUPTIC

* **Canoe Pool** (SF; Rangeley District). BOAT OR TRAIL ACCESS; 10 mi N of Cupsuptic on E shore of Kennebago River. (Information: 207/864-5545) FACILITIES: Tent sites, tbls, toil, cga, drk wtr should be boiled; free fire permit required for fires in non-designated areas. ACTIVITIES: Picnicking; fishing. MISC: Pets on leash.

EUSTIS

Alder Stream (SF; Dead River District). 4-1/2 mi N of Eustis on the W side of St Hwy 27. (Information: 207/246-3411) FACILITIES: Sites, tbls, toil, cga, drk wtr should be boiled; free fire permit required for fires in non-designated areas. ACTIVITIES: Picnicking; fishing. MISC: Pets on leash.

Flagstaff Lake (SF; Dead River District). FACILITIES: Sites, tbls, toil, cga, drk wtr should be boiled; free fire permit required for fires in non-designated areas. ACTIVITIES: Picnicking; fishing. MISC: Pets.

* **Hurricane Narrows** (SF; Dead River District). ACCESS BY BOAT; In Flagstaff Lake, on island in narrows. (Information: 207/246-3411) FACILITIES: Sites, tbls, toil, cga, drk wtr should be boiled; free fire permit required for fires in non-designated areas. ACTIVITIES: Picnicking; fishing; swimming (beach). MISC: Pets.

Rock Pond (SF; Dead River District). 20 mi W of St Hwy 201; on N shore of Rock Pond. (Information: 207/246-3411) FACILITIES: Sites, tbls, toil, cga, drk wtr should be boiled; free fire permit required for fires in non-designated areas. ACTIVITIES: Picnicking; fishing. MISC: Pets.

GREENVILLE

Bear Brook (SF; Moosehead District). 27 mi NE of Greenville on the S side of Ripogenus Dam Road. (Information: 207/695-2281) FACILITIES: Tent sites tbls, toil, cga, drk wtr should be boiled; free fire permit required for fires in non-designated areas. ACTIVITIES: Picnicking; fishing.

Big Squaw (SF; Moosehead District). 5 mi N of Greenville on St Hwy 15. (Information: 207/695-2281). FACILITIES: Tent/tr sites, tbls, toil, cga, drk wtr should be boiled; free fire permit required for fires in non-designated areas. ACTIVITIES: Picnicking; fishing; boating. MISC: Pets.

* **Boom House** (SF; Moosehead Dist.). ACCESS BY BOAT; At mouth of W Branch of Penobscot River, N end of Chesuncook Lake. (Information: 207/695-2281) FACILITIES: Tent sites, tbls, toil, cga, drk wtr should be boiled; free fire permit required for fires in non-designated areas. ACTIVITIES: Picnicking; fishing.

See page 7 for KEY TO ABBREVIATIONS.

∗ Cardesa Point (SF; Moosehead Dist). ACCESS BY BOAT; 3 mi above outlet; W shore of Chesuncook Lake. (Information: 207/695-2281) FACILITIES: Tent sites, tbls, toil, cga, drk wtr should be boiled; free fire permit required for fires in non-designated areas. ACTIVITIES: Picnicking; fishing. MISC: Pets on leash.

∗ Cunningham Brook (SF; Moosehead District). ACCESS BY BOAT; 14 mi above outlet, on the W shore of Chesuncook Lake, mouth of brook. (Information: 207/695-2281) FACILITIES: Tent sites, tbls, toil, cga, drk wtr should be boiled; free fire permit required for fires in non-designated areas. ACTIVITIES: Picnicking; fishing; swimming (beach). MISC: Pets on leash.

∗ Doughnut Cove (SF; Moosehead Dist.). BOAT ACCESS; E shore of Moosehead Lake, in Doughnut Cove on high bank. (Information: 207/695-2281) FACILITIES: Tent sites, tbls, toil, cga, drk wtr should be boiled; free fire permit required for fires in non-designated areas. ACTIVITIES: Picnicking; fishing; swimming (beach); boating. MISC: Pets.

∗ Fox Island (SF; Moosehead District). BOAT ACCESS; E shore of Moosehead Lake, E side of Spencer Bay, N side of island. (Information: 207/695-2281) FACILITIES: Tent sites, tbls, toil, cga, drk wtr should be boiled; free fire permit required for fires in non-designated areas. ACTIVITIES: Picnicking; fishing; boating. MISC: Pets.

∗ Galusha Cove (SF; Moosehead Dist). BOAT ACCESS; NE side of Sugar Island, in Galusha Cove (Moosehead Lake). (Information: 207/695-2281) FACILITIES: Tent sites, tbls, toil, cga, drk wtr should be boiled; free fire permit required for fires in non-designated areas. ACTIVITIES: Picnicking; fishing; boating. MISC: Pets.

∗ Hardscrabble Point (SF; Moosehead District). BOAT ACCESS; NW point of Mt Kineo, Moosehead Lake. (Information: 207/695-2281) FACILITIES: Tent sites; tbls, toil, cga, drk wtr should be boiled; free fire permit required for fires in non-designated areas. ACTIVITIES: Picnicking; fishing; swimming (beach); boating. MISC: Pets.

∗ John's Pond Pool (SF; Rangeley District). BOAT OR TRAIL ACCESS; 8 mi N of Cupsuptic on E shore of Kennebago River. (Information: 207/864-

5545) FACILITIES: Tent sites, tbls, toil, cga, drk wtr should be boiled; free fire permit required for fires in non-designated areas. ACTIVITIES: Picnicking; fishing; boating. MISC: Pets on leash.

Little Wilson Stream (SF; Moosehead District). 1 mi N of Big Wilson Stream Bridge at end of road. (Information: 207/695-2281) FACILITIES: Sites, tbls, toil, cga, drk wtr should be boiled; free fire permit required for fires in non-designated areas. ACTIVITIES: Picnicking; fishing. MISC: Pets on leash.

∗ Lucky Point (SF; Moosehead District). BOAT ACCESS; E shore of Moosehead Lake, NE side of Spencer Bay on W side of point. (Information: 207/695-2281) FACILITIES: Tent sites, tbls, toil, cga, drk wtr should be boiled; free fire permit required for fires in non-designated areas. ACTIVITIES: Picnicking; fishing; boating. MISC: Pets on leash.

∗ Mauser's Island (SF; Moosehead Dist)· ACCESS BY BOAT; 4 mi above outlet; island off E shore of Chesuncook Lake. (Information: 207/695-2281) FACILITIES: Tent sites, tbls, toil, cga, drk wtr should be boiled; free fire permit required for fires in non-designated areas. ACTIVITIES: Picnicking; fishing; boating. MISC: Pets.

∗ Moose Island (SF; Moosehead District) BOAT ACCESS; In cove at N end of Moose Island (Moosehead Lake). (Information: 207/695-2281) FACILITIES: Tent sites, tbls, toil, cga, drk wtr should be boiled; free fire permit required for fires in non-designated areas. ACTIVITIES: Picnicking; fishing; swimming; boating. MISC: Pets.

Old Duck Pond Storehouse (SF; Moosehead District). 6 mi N of Ripogenus Dam, on Nesowadnehunk Rd. (Information: 207/695-2281) FACILITIES: Sites, tbls, toil, cga, drk wtr should be boiled; free fire permit required for fires in non-designated areas. ACTIVITIES: Picnicking; fishing. MISC: Pets on leash.

∗ Poverty Point (SF; Moosehead District). BOAT ACCESS; Poverty Point, E side of Moose Island (Moosehead Lake) on ledge· (Information: 207/695-2281) FACILITIES: Tent sites, tbls, toil, cga, drk wtr should be boiled; free fire permit required for fires in non-designated areas. ACTIVITIES: Picnicking; fishing; boating. MISC: Pets on leash.

See page 7 for KEY TO ABBREVIATIONS.

Ragged Dam (SF; Moosehead District). 30 mi NE of Greenville; N of Ripogenus Dam Road; Ragged Lake. FACILITIES: Sites, tbls, toil, cga, drk wtr should be boiled; free fire permit required for fires in non-designated areas. ACTIVITIES: Picnicking; fishing. MISC: Pets.

* **Rand Beach** (SF; Moosehead District). BOAT ACCESS; Rand Beach, NE side of Deer Island Moosehead Lake in cove. (Information: 207/695-2281) FACILITIES: Tent sites, tbls, toil, cga, drk wtr should be boiled; free fire permit required for fires in non-designated areas. ACTIVITIES: Picnicking; fishing; swimming (beach); boating. MISC: Pets on leash.

* **Ronco Farm Wharf** (SF; Moosehead District). BOAT ACCESS; E shore of Moosehead Lake, N end of Ronco Cove. (Information: 207/695-2281) FACILITIES: Tent sites, tbls, toil, cga, drk wtr should be boiled; free fire permit required for fires in non-designated areas. ACTIVITIES: Picnicking; fishing; swimming (beach); boating. MISC.: Pets.

* **Spencer Bay** (SF; Moosehead District). BOAT ACCESS; E shore of Moosehead Lake, E side of Spencer Bay at mouth of Roach River. (Information: 207/695-2281) FACILITIES: Tent sites, tbls, toil, cga, drk wtr should be boiled; free fire permit required for fires in non-designated areas. ACTIVITIES: Picnicking; fishing. MISC: Pets on leash.

* **Spencer Bay Narrows** (SF; Moosehead District). BOAT ACCESS; E shore of Moosehead Lake, W side of point on N side of entrance to Spencer Bay. (Information: 207/695-2281) FACILITIES: Tent sites, tbls, toil, cga, drk wtr should be boiled; free fire permit required for fires in non-designated areas. ACTIVITIES: Picnicking; fishing. MISC: Pets.

GUERETTE

***High Bank** (SF; Fish River District). NW shore of Square Lake; 1/2 mi N of Eagle Lake thoroughfare; access BY BOAT. (Information: 207/435-6644) FACILITIES: Tent sites, tbls, toil, cga, drk wtr should be boiled; free fire permit required for fires in non-designated areas. ACTIVITIES: Picnicking; fishing; boating. MISC: Pets on leash.

* **Limestone Point** (SF; Fish River District). Access BY BOAT; W shore of Square Lake 1-1/2 mi S of Eagle Lake thoroughfare. (Information: 207/435-6644) FACILITIES: Tent sites, tbls,

toil, cga, drk wtr should be boiled; free fire permit required for fires in non-designated areas. ACTIVITIES: Picnicking; fishing; swimming (beach); boating. MISC: Pets.

* **Salmon Point** (SF; Fish River Dist.). Access BY BOAT; E shore of Square Lake, 3-1/2 mi S of Cross Lake thoroughfare. (Information: 207/435-6644) FACILITIES: Tent sites, tbls, toil, cga, drk wtr should be boiled; free fire permit required for fires in non-designated areas. ACTIVITIES: Picnicking; fishing; boating. MISC: Pets.

Square Lake-NE (SF; Fish River Dist.). Access BY CAR; landing on NE shore. Information: 207/435-6644) FACILITIES: Tent sites, tbls, toil, cga, drk wtr should be boiled; free fire permit required for fires in non-designated areas. ACTIVITIES: Picnicking; fishing; boating,l.

HAINES LANDING

Big Falls (SF; Rangeley District). 8 mi N of Cupsuptic Lake, on Cupsuptic River. (Information: 207/864-5545) FACILITIES: Tent sites, tbls, toil, cga, drk wtr should be boiled; free fire permit required for fires in non-designated areas. ACTIVITIES: Picnicking; fishing. MISC.: Pets.

* **Cupsuptic Lake** (SF; Rangeley Dist). BOAT ACCESS; Big Birch Island, off W shore of Cupsuptic Lake. (Information: 207/864-5545) FACILITIES: Tent sites, tbls, toil, cga, drk wtr should be boiled; free fire permit required for fires in non-designated areas. ACTIVITIES: Picnicking; fishing. MISC: Pets.

* **Guides** (SF; Rangeley District). BOAT ACCESS; SE shore of Students Island, Mooselookmeguntic Lake. (Information: 207/864-5545) FACILITIES: Tent sites tbls, toil, cga, drk wtr should be boiled; free fire permit required for fires in non-designated areas. ACTIVITIES: Picnicking; fishing; boating. MISC: Pets on leash.

ISLAND FALLS

***Mattawamkeag Lake** (SF; Mattawamkeag District). ACCESS BY BOAT; 4 mi S of thoroughfare; SE shore above dam. (Information: 207/463-2214) FACILITIES: Tent sites, tbls, toil, cga, free fire permit required for fires in non-designated areas; drk wtr should be boiled. ACTIVITIES: Picnicking; fishing. MISC: Pets.

Molunkus Lake (SF; Mattawamkeag District). ACCESS BY ROAD OR BOAT. SW arm at end of road. (Information: 207/364-2214) FACILITIES: Sites, tbls, toil, cga, drk wtr should be boiled; free fire permit required for fires in non-designated areas. ACTIVITIES: Picnicking; fishing; boating. MISC: Pets on leash.

LAKE PARLIN

Lone Jack (SF; Parlin Pond Dist). E side chain of ponds, 10 mi S of St Hwy 15 on Scott Paper Company. (Information: 207/672-3761) FACILITIES: Sites, tbls, toil, cga, drk wtr should be boiled; free fire permit required for fires in non-designated areas. ACTIVITIES: Picnicking; fishing. MISC: Pets on leash.

MASARDIS

Cold Spring (SF; Number Nine Dist.). 1-1/2 mi W of St Hwy 11, on Oxbow Road. (Information: 207/435-6975) FACILITIES: Sites, tbls, toil, cga, drk wtr should be boiled; free fire permit required for fires in non-designated areas. ACTIVITIES: Picnicking; fishing. MISC: Pets ·

MOOSEHEAD

Indian Pond (SF; Seboomook Dist.). (Road access) N shore of Indian Pond at end of MEC R.R. r/w 9 mi SW of St Hwy 15 at West outlet. (Information: (Greenville) 207/695-2281) FACILITIES: Sites, tbls, toil, cga, drk wtr should be boiled; free fire permit required for fires in non-designated areas. ACTIVITIES: Picnicking; fishing. MISC: Pets on leash.

Seven Mile Hill (SF; Seboomook Dist.). South side of Seboomook Dam Road. (road access) (Information: (Greenville) 207/695-2281) FACILITIES: Tent sites, tbls, toil, cga, drk wtr should be boiled; free fire permit required for fires in non-designated areas. ACTIVITIES: Picnicking; fishing. MISC: Pets on leash.

RANGELEY

Cold Spring (SF; Rangeley Dist). 7 mi N of Rangeley on W side of St Hwy 16; S branch of Dead River. (Information: 207/864-5545) FACILITIES: Sites, tbls, toil, cga, drk wtr should be boiled; free fire permit required for fires in non-designated areas. ACTIVITIES: Picnicking; fishing. MISC: Pets on leash.

ROCKWOOD

Big Bog (SF; Seboomook District). Road or Boat access. 20 mi N of Pittston Farm, at S end of Big Bof flowage off North Branch Road. (Information: (Greenville) 207/695-2281) FACILITIES: Tent sites, tbls, toil, cga, drk wtr should be boiled; free fire permit required for fires in non-designated areas. ACTIVITIES: Picnicking; fishing; boating. MISC: Pets.

* **Jackson Cove** (SF; Seboomook District). BOAT ACCESS; Lobster Lake, Jackson Cove, in Little Claw on SW shore of cove. (Information: (Greenville) 207/695-2281) FACILITIES: Tent sites, tbls, toil, cga, drk wtr should be boiled; free fire permit required for fires in non-designated areas. ACTIVITIES: Picnicking; fishing; swimming (beach); boating. MISC: Pets.

* **Lobster Lake - SW** (SF; Seboomook District). BOAT ACCESS; SW end of Little Claw at Log Landing (Lobster Lake). (Information: (Greenville) 207/695-2281) FACILITIES: Tent sites, tbls, toil, cga, drk wtr should be boiled; free fire permit required for fires in non-designated areas. ACTIVITIES: Picnicking; fishing; swimming (beach); boating. MISC: Pets.

* **Lobster Lake - West** (SF; Seboomook District). BOAT ACCESS; W shore of Little Claw near large rock ledge (Lobster Lake). (Information: (Greenville) 207/695-2281) FACILITIES: Tent sites, tbls, toil, cga, drk wtr should be boiled; free fire permit required for fires in non-designated areas. ACTIVITIES: Picnicking; fishing; swimming (beach); boating. MISC: Pets on leash.

* **Ogden Point - NW** (SF; Seboomook District). BOAT ACCESS; Lobster Lake, Ogden Point, NW side of point. (Information: (Greenville) 207/695-2281) FACILITIES: Tent sites, tbls, toil, cga, drk wtr should be boiled; free fire permit required for fires in non-designated areas. ACTIVITIES: Picnicking; fishing; swimming (beach); boating. MISC: Pets.

Snake Camp (SF; Seboomook District). Access by road or boat. 13 mi N of Pittston Farm, on N Branch of Penobscot River. (Information: (Greenville) 207/695-2281) FACILITIES: Tent sites tbls, toil, cga, drk wtr should be boiled; free fire permit required for fires in non-designated areas. ACTIVITIES: Picnicking; fishing; boating. MISC: Pets on leash.

See page 7 for KEY TO ABBREVIATIONS.

SHERMAN

Kathahdin Valley Texaco Truck Stop.
I-95; Sherman exit. **SEASON:** All yr;
1-night lmt. FACILITIES: Spaces for
self-contained vehicles; food, toil,
drk wtr, LP gas, emergency parking,
mechanic, gas.

SHIN POND

Camp Colby (SF; East Branch District). At MFS camp, 5 mi N of Grand
Lake Road on Scraggly Lake Road.
(Information: 207/463-2214) FACILI-
TIES: Sites, tbls, toil, cga, drk wtr
should be boiled; free fire permit
required for fires in non-designated
areas. ACTIVITIES: Picnicking; fishing. MISC: Pets on leash.

Crommet Spring (SF; East Branch District). 4 mi W of Shin Pond on Grand
Lake Road. (Information: 207/463-2214)
FACILITIES: Tent sites, tbls, toil,
cga, drk wtr should be boiled; free
fire permit required for fires in non-
designated areas. ACTIVITIES: Picnicking; fishing. MISC: Pets.

Sawtelle Brook (SF; East Branch District). 1-1/2 mi N of Grand Lake Rd
on Scraggly Lake Rd. (Information:
207/463-2214) FACILITIES: Sites,
tbls, toil, cga, drk wtr should be
boiled; free fire permit required for
fires in non-designated areas. ACTIV-
ITIES: Picnicking; fishing.

Scraggly Lake (SF; East Branch District). On W shore of Scraggly Lake;
1/2 mi above outlet. (Information:
207/463-2214) FACILITIES: Sites,
tbls, toil, cga, drk wtr should be
boiled; free fire permit required for
fires in non-designated areas. ACTIV-
ITIES: Picnicking; fishing; boating,l.

Sebqeis Stream (SF; East Branch District). E shore of Sebqeis Stream,
6 mi W of Shin Pond via the Grand
Lake Road. (Information: 207/463-
2214). Sites, tbls, toil, cga, drk wtr
should be boiled; free fire permit
required for fires in non-designated
areas. ACTIVITIES: Picnicking; fishing. MISC: Pets on leash.

STACYVILLE

Lunksoos Camp (SF; Mattawamkeag
District). 7-1/2 mi W of Stacyville
on E shore of E Branch of Penobscot
River. ACCESS BY ROAD OR BOAT.
(Information: 207/463-2214) FACILI-
TIES: Sites, tbls, toil, cga, drk wtr
should be boiled; free fire permit
required for fires in non-designated
areas. ACTIVITIES: Picnicking; fishing; boating. MISC: Pets on leash.

Whetstone Falls (SF; Mattawamkeag
District). 7 mi W of Stacyville on
the E shore of the E Branch of
Penobscot River. (Information: 207/
463-2214) Access by road or boat.
FACILITIES: Sites, tbls, toil, cga,
drk wtr should be boiled; free fire
permit required for fires in non-
designated areas. ACTIVITIES: Picnicking; fishing. MISC: Pets.

STONINGTON

* **Duck Harbor Campground** (Isle Au
Haut; Acadia NP). Passenger service
to the island from Stonington is provided by mailboat. No auto ferry
service exists. Fares are presently
$2.50/person each way. Baggage is
extra. Ferry schedules may be obtained by contacting Capt. Herbert
Aldrich, Stonington, ME.

Isle au Haut, one of the larger outlying islands of Penobscot Bay, is
approx 6 mi long and 3 mi wide.
Acadia NP on Isle au Haut encompasses 2800 acres of the 4500 acres
of the island.

To the avid hiker, numerous trails
offer passage through the scenic and
natural beauty of the island. Day
visitors should be prepared to hike
several miles from the boat landing
on gravel roads or primitive trails
in order to enjoy the natural beauty
of the park lands.

CAMPING of a primitive nature is allowed at Duck Harbor Campground,
where three Adirondack shelters are
available. BY RESERVATION ONLY.
A maximum of 6 persons per shelter
and a maximum of 5 days is allowed.
Campers should be prepared to carry
their gear the 5 mi to the Campground. Since camping is restricted
to the shelters ONLY, campers need
not bring a tent. Reservations for
camping are handled through Acadia
NP, RFD #1, Box 1, Bar Harbor, ME
04609 (207/288-3338). The camping
season is mid-May thru mid-October.

A PO and grocery store are the only
services on the Island. No organized
activities, no sandy beaches, or developed facilities for swimming in
either fresh or salt water.

TOPSFIELD

Clifford Lake (SF; St Croix District).
Accessible by car; E shore of E arm
W side of gravel road from Princeton
to Wesley. Near Topsfield. (For map,
write, Maine Forest Service, Dept. of
Cons.; State Office Bldg; Augusta

ME 04333; or call (Topsfield) 207/796–2643.) FACILITIES: Sites, tbls, toil, cga, drk wtr should be boiled; free fire permit required for fires in non-designated areas. ACTIVITIES: Picnicking; fishing; swimming (beach); boating,l. MISC: Pets.

Junior Lake (St. Croix District). By Boat; the southernmost of Big Islands (near Topsfield). (For map, write: Maine Forest Service; Dept. of Conservation; State Office Bldg.; Augusta ME 04333; or call: (Topsfield) 207/796-2643.) FACILITIES: Tent sites; tbls, toil, cga, drk wtr should be boiled; free fire permit required for fires in non-designated areas. ACTIVITIES: Picnicking; fishing; swimming (beach); boating. MISC: Pets.

Middle Oxhead Lake (SF; St Croix District). Accessible by car on gravel road, near Topsfield. (For map, write: Maine Forest Service; Dept. of Conservation; State Office Bldg; Augusta, ME 04333; or call (Topsfield) 207/796-2643.) FACILITIES: Site; tbls, toil, cga, drk wtr should be boiled; free fire permit required for fires in non-designated areas. ACTIVITIES: Picnicking; fishing; boating,l. MISC: Pets on leash.

* St. Croix River (SF; St. Croix District). Accessible BY BOAT, at W shore at Little Falls, near Topsfield. (For map, write: Maine Forest Service; Dept. of Conservation; State Office Bldg; Augusta, ME 04333; or call (Topsfield) 207/796-2643.) FACILITIES: Tent sites, tbls, toil, cga, drk wtr should be boiled. ACTIVITIES: Picnicking; fishing; boating. MISC: Pets on leash.

St. Croix River (SF; St Croix Dist.). Accessible by car at W shore of Loon Bay, near Topsfield. (For map, write Maine Forest Service; Dept. of Conservation; State Office Bldg; Augusta ME 04333; or call (Topsfield) 207/796-2643.) FACILITIES: Sites, tbls, toil, cga, drk wtr should be boiled; free fire permit required for fires in non-designated areas. ACTIVITIES: Picnicking; fishing. MISC: Pets.

* Scraggley Lake (SF; St. Croix District). Accessible BY BOAT; island at E end. Near Topsfield. (For map write to: Maine Forest Service; Dept. of Conservation; State Office Bldg; Augusta or call (Topsfield) 207/796-2643.) FACILITIES: Tent sites, tbls, toil, cga drk wtr should be boiled; free fire permit required for fires in non-designated areas. ACTIVITIES: Picnicking; fishing; boating. MISC: Pets.

Wabassus Lake (SF; St. Croix District). 6 mi W of Grand Lake Stream via gravel road; near Topsfield. (For map, write: Maine Forest Service Service; Dept. of Conservation; State Office Bldg; Augusta, Maine 04333; or call (Topsfield); 207/796-2643.) FACILITIES: Tent sites, tbls, toil, cga, drk wtr should be boiled; free fire permit required for fires in non-designated areas. ACTIVITIES: Picnicking; fishing; boating,l.

WEST BETHEL

* Caribou Shelter (White Mtn NF). 5-3/10 mi SW on US 2; 1-3/10 mi W; Co Hwy, 2-3/5 mi SW on FR FH6; 7/10 mi SW; Trail 247; 2-3/5 mi SW.SEASON: 6/1-10/15; 5-day lmt. FACILITIES: Sites, tbls, toil, cga, f, (no trailers). ACTIVITIES: Picnicking; fishing (2 mi); mtn climbing.

MARYLAND

GENERAL STATE INFORMATION

Miscellaneous

Right Turns on Red: Permitted after
    full stop, unless otherwise posted.
STATE CAPITOL: Annapolis
STATE NICKNAME: Old Line State
STATE BIRD: "Many Deeds, Womanly Words"
STATE BIRD: Oriole
STATE FLOWER: Black-eyed Susan
STATE TREE: White Oak

See page 7 for KEY TO ABBREVIATIONS.

MARYLAND

State Parks

Overnight camping fees range from $2.50-4.50. Pets are prohibited in state park camping areas with the exception of two designated pet areas....one at Elk Neck and one at Pocomoke River. Hunting and fishing. Further information: Maryland Park Service; Department of Natural Resources; Tawes State Office Building; 580 Taylor Avenue; Annapolis, MD 21401.

Rest Areas

Overnight stops are not permitted in Maryland Rest Areas.

Assateague Island National Seashore

During certain hours, bikers and hikers can have Wildlife Drive to themselves. Boating: Public boat ramp at Chincoteague Memorial Park. Boat rentals in Chincoteague, Virginia. Oversand Vehicles: Obtain a beach access permit for oversand travel, and stay on marked oversand vehicle routes. Chincoteague NWR: No camping; no pets permitted. The National Seashore headquarters and visitor center is on the mainland just before you cross the bridge to the north end of Assateague Island. Pets are prohibited in Assateague State Park, the NWR, the Virginia section of the National Seashore, and in the hike-in and canoe-in campsites. However, pets are permitted in the rest of the Maryland section if on a leash (10 feet or less). Hunting and fishing; clamming and crabbing; hiking. For specific campgrounds, see "Berlin" in this chapter. Further information: Superintendent; Assateague Island National Seashore; Route 2, Box 294; Berlin, MD 21811; 301/641-1441.

C&O Canal National Historic Park

CANOEING: Canoeing on the Potomac River is for experienced adult canoeists. Maps can be obtained from the U.S. Geological Survey (Branch of Distribution; 1200 Eads Street; Arlington, VA 22202. Or by phoning: 703/557-2751.) For current weather conditions, telephone 202/899-3210 (U.S. Weather Bureau taped message).

PARK HEADQUARTERS: Located 3 miles west of Sharpsburg, Maryland, on St Hwy 34. Additional information: Superintendent; C&O Canal NHP; PO Box 4; Sharpsburg, MD 21782; or telephone 301/432-2231 or 301/948-5641.

For information on specific campgrounds, see: "Clear Springs", "Cumberland", "Hancock", and "Sharpsburg".

INFORMATION OFFICES: 108 West Main Street; Hancock, MD [301/678-5463]; 8 mi S of Cumberland, off St Hwy 51 [301/777-8667]; Great Falls Tavern, MD [301/299-3613]; Georgetown, D.C., visitor center in Foundry Mall on the canal between 30th and Thomas Jefferson Street [202/337-6652].

The Appalachian Trail

More than 2000 miles long, the Appalachian Trail (from Maine to Georgia) is the longest continuous marked trail in the world.

CAMPING: More than 200 open-front shelters/lean-tos are spaced approximately 10 miles apart on the Trail (one-day intervals). As they are occupied on a first-come first-served basis, carry a tent in case the shelters are full. Potable spring water is usually available at each site, but should be purified by tablets or boiling. And always "pack it in, pack it out".

PERMITS: No permit is required to hike the Trail. However, camping permits must be obtained for overnight stays in Shenandoah NP (Luray, VA 22835) and Great Smoky Mountains NP (Gatlinburg, TN 37733). These are free of charge and available from the ranger stations or by mail. A free camping permit must be obtained for overnight stays in White Mountain National Forest Restricted Use Area (PO Box 638; Laconia, NH 03246).

APPALACHIAN TRAIL CONFERENCE: A private, nonprofit, national organization which represents citizen's interest in the Appalachian Trail. They offer detailed guidebooks and maps for sale, as well as the A.T. Data Book which gives the location and distances between shelters and certain post offices, supply points, water sources, lodging and meals. For more information on this organization, write to them at: PO Box 236; Harpers Ferry, WV 25425.

INFORMATION SOURCES

Maps

The following maps are available from Forsyth Travel Library (see order form in Appendix B):

State of Maryland [Up-to-date, showing all principal roads, points of interest, sports areas, parks, airports, mileage, etc. Full color.]

Completely indexed map, including all airports, lakes, rivers, etc., of the city of **Baltimore.**

State Information

Maryland Park Service; Department of Natural Resources; Tawes State Office Building; 580 Taylor Avenue; Annapolis, MD 21401.
Department of Economic and Community Development; Office of Tourist Development; 1748 Forest Drive; Annapolis, MD 21401.
Division of Fish and Game; Department of Natural Resources; Tawes State Office Building; Annapolis, MD 21401.
Maryland Chamber of Commerce; 60 West Street, Suite 405; Annapolis, MD 21401.

Miscellaneous

Baltimore Area Convention and Visitors Council; 102 St. Paul Street; Baltimore, MD 21202.
Assateague Island National Seashore; Route 2, Box 294; Berlin, MD 21811.
Chesapeake and Ohio Canal National Historical Park; Box 4; Sharpsburg, MD 21782.
Catoctin Mountain Park; Thurmont, MD 21788.
Corps of Engineers, Baltimore District; PO Box 1715; Baltimore, MD 21203.
Bureau of Land Management; Eastern States Office; 7981 Eastern Avenue; Silver Spring, MD 20910.

FREE CAMPGROUNDS

BERLIN

Bayside Campground (Assateague Island Natl Seashore). (Stop at headquarters in Berlin and get a map of the island.) Located W of the day-use parking lot, some 400 yards from the beach. **SEASON:** Mid-April to mid-June; from LD-10/31, FREE (From mid-June-LD, $2.50). Closed winter; 14-day lmt. during free season; 7-day lmt. during peak summer season. **FACIL:** toil, 40 sites (tr –22), tbls, cga, cold outdoor showers, dump, hard-surface parking pads. **ACTIVITIES:** Picnicking; fishing; clamming; crabbing along shore, except where prohibited; swimming in designated areas; hiking. **MISC:** REGISTRATION: 6/15-LD, register at CG reservation office on the S side of day-use parking lot. Cross the Route 611 bridge, take 1st rt, drive 3 mi to fee collection station in the middle of the road The Ranger will direct you to CG reservation office.

During free period, self-register at the box provided at the entrance of the campground.

Pets on leash no more than 10 ft long. Fires must be contained in the grills provided. No firearms except in designated areas during hunting season.

Bring plenty of insect repellent and long wooden tent pegs to anchor your tent in sand during winds. Do not touch or feed wild ponies. Addl info/map: Rte 2, Box 294, Berlin, MD 21811.

* **Hike-In Campsite #1** (Assateague Island Natl Seashore). This hike-in site is 4-1/2 mi S of the NPS North Beach parking area and is immediately W of the sand-fenced frontal dune. A triangular hiking symbol is located on the beach near the frontal dune, and another symbol is on the "back trail."

Reservations are required, but they will not be accepted prior to 30 days before the camping date. 2-night lmt per site from LD-6/15; 1-night lmt 6/15-LD. Maximum occupancy – 20 campers per site. April-Oct., weekends are often booked to capacity.

FACILITIES: Tent sites, tbls, toil, cga, trash can, no drk wtr. Insect repellent is a necessity, particularly at night from 5/15 to the first killing frost. CAUTION: This trail can be unexpectedly rugged even for the most experienced hiker. Do not touch/feed wild ponies. Snakes in this area are harmless.

Tents should be pitched within 15 ft of the blue and white posts located within the campsites. Do not camp on sand dunes or sleep on the

See page 7 for KEY TO ABBREVIATIONS.

beach. No camping in the refuge.

Pets are not permitted in any hike-in sites, in any of the Chincoteague NWR, or the Va. portion of the Natl Seashore.

RESERVATIONS and Registration of Site: Advance reservations may be made by writing; Supt., Assateague Island Natl Seashore, Rt 3, Box 294, Berlin, MD 21811; or call 301/641-1441. ACTIVITIES: Fishing; clamming; crabbing along shore, except where prohibited by signs. Swimming in designated areas; hiking. MISC: No firearms except in designated areas during hunting season.

* **Jim's Gut Canoe Campsite** (Assateague Island National Seashore). Located near Md-Va State Line on Assateague Island. Advance reservations must be made in person, by letter, or by phone, with Supt. Assateague Island NS, Rt 2, Box 294, Berlin, MD 21811; 301/641-1441. They will supply you with a map and a free backcountry use permit. The tear-off stub must be left plainly visible on the dashboard of the vehicle parked where the canoe is launched, and the rest of the permit should be carried in the canoe. SEASON: April 1 - October 31. Not open rest of year due to public hunting program and winter sanctuary needs of waterfowl. FACILITIES: Tent sites, tbls, toil, cga, no drk wtr. Pack out trash.

Canoeists may stay a max. of 3 nights on the trail system. These nights may be spent at the same campsite or at the individual three sites (Tingles Island Campground, Jim's Gut Campground, and Pope Bay Campground). 5/15-9/15, Jim's Gut is the only CG open, due to limited use during insect season.

All camping is in vicinity of the fire ring, which is located within a grove of pine trees. Fires should be built only in the fire rings provided. Pets are prohibited.

A public landing is available in West Ocean City at the N end of the island; cars may be left overnight. Boats may be landed in the Chincoteague Memorial Park, but no cars overnight. Nominal fee, cars may be parked over night and canoes landed in the commercial Toms Cover CG located S of Memorial Park. Canoes may be landed at or launched from the 2nd parking area on Toms Cove Drive within the National Seashore; cars left overnight.

FEES: No fees for use of the public landing in West Ocean City. During

summer only, a $1/car fee is charged at North Beach Entrance Station.

A canoe may land on the Chincoteague NWR only under a genuine emergency.

CAUTION: Rapid weather changes are common. Insect repellent necessary. Do not touch/feed wild ponies. Snakes are harmless. Watch for poison ivy.

North Beach Campground (Assateague Island National Seashore). (Stop at headquarters in Berlin and get a map of the island.) Located S of the large, day-use parking lot and just west of the high primary dune. This CG is located about 100 yards from the beach, and there is no view of the ocean from any campsite.

FACILITIES: 86 sites, tbls, toil, cga, cold outdoor showers, dump. 21 walk-in sites are "tent only" and located near the dunes a short distance from the required parking area. SEASON: FREE, mid-April to mid-June and from LD to 10/31. From mid-June to LD, $2.50. Closed in winter. 14-day lmt during free season, 7-day lmt during peak summer season.

REGISTRATION: 6/15-LD, register at CG reservation office on the S side of the day-use parking lot. Cross the Route 611 bridge, take the 1st rt, and drive 3 mi to the fee collection station in the middle of the road The ranger will direct you to CG reservation office.

During free period, self-register at the box provided at the entrance of the campground.

Pets on leash no more than 10 ft long. Open fires should be in ashes of previous campfires. No firearms except in designated areas during the hunting season.

Bring plenty of insect repellent and long wooden tent pegs to anchor your tent in sand during winds. Do not touch or feed wild ponies. ACTIVITIES: Swimming in designated areas; hiking; fishing; clamming & crabbing along shore except where prohibited.

CLEAR SPRINGS

* **McCoy's Ferry** (Chesapeake & Ohio CI NHD; Natl Park). Take Clear Springs exit off I-70; 5 mi SE on St Hwy 68; W on St Hwy 56; 3 mi on 4 Lock Road. Located at Mile 110.4 on C&O Towpath. SEASON: 5/1-10/15; 14-day lmt. FACILITIES: 20 primitive sites (tr -24), tbls, toil, cga, no drk wtr. ACTIVITIES: Picnicking; fishing; hiking; boating,l. MISC: No motorbikes; no hunting.

CUMBERLAND

Spring Gap (Chesapeake & Ohio CI NHD; Natl park). 11 mi E of Cumberland on St Hwy 51. SEASON: 5/15-10/15; 14-day lmt. FACILITIES: 20 primitive sites (tr -24), tbls, toil, cga, no drk wtr. ACTIVITIES: Picnicking; fishing; amphitheater.

HANCOCK

Fifteen Mile Creek (Chesapeake & Ohio CI NHD; Natl Park). 2-1/2 mi W of Hancock on US 40; 10 mi S on Woodmont Road. SEASON: 5/1-10/15; 14-day lmt. FACILITIES: 16 sites (tr -24), tbls, toil, cga, drk wtr. ACTIVITIES: Picnicking; fishing; boating,l.

LA PLATA

Earl's Truck Stop. 30 mi from Washington DC on US 301 at La Plata. SEASON: All yr; 1-night lmt. FACILITIES: Spaces for self-contained vehicles, drk wtr, food, toil, mechanic, emergency parking.

MILLERSVILLE

Transit Truck Stop. 10 mi S of Baltimore exit 14 and 14A at Millersville. SEASON: All yr; 1-night lmt. FACILITIES: Spaces for self-contained vehicles, drk wtr, food, toil, 24-hr, emergency parking; mechanic.

SHARPSBURG

Towpath Camping (C&O Canal NHP). "Hiker-Biker" tent campsites are spaced approx every 5 mi along the 162-mile section from Seneca to Cumberland. These are first-come first-served.

Rangers regularly patrol this area. In case of emergency, call 301/432-2233. (From Seneca to Georgetown, the US Park Police patrol the area; for emergencies in this area, call 205/426-6600.)

CAUTION: The towpath is narrow, close to the water's edge, and rocky, from Guard Lock 4 at Mile 85.6 to Lock 41 at Mile 88.9. Hiking not recommended in this section when the river level is high. Horseback riding and bicycling can be hazardous in this area. Also, watch for poison ivy. Horseback riding is permitted only under special restrictions. (Discuss this with Park Supt.)

ADDITIONAL INFO/MAPS: The C&O NHP Headquarters is located 3 mi W of Sharpsburg, MD on st Hwy 34. Write to the Supt. at PO Box 4, Sharpsburg MD 21782; or telephone 301/432-2231 or 301/948-5641.

FOR UP-TO-DATE INFO ON TOWPATH CONDITIONS, call the Distric Ranger Offices: Palisades Dist. - Mile)-31, 301/299-3613. Piedmont Dist. - Mile 31-106, 301/432-2136. Allegheny Distric - Mile 106-184, 301/678-5463.

* **Marsden Tract** (C&O Towpath). This is the only campsite which is not on a first-come first-served basis. Campsite must be reserved by calling 301/299-3613. It will also accommodate groups. Located at Mile 11.0. FACILITIES: Tent sites, tbls, toil, fire grill, drk wtr (except during winter). ACTIVITIES: Picnicking; fishing; hiking. MISC: No motorbikes; no hunting. Pets on leash.

* **Horsepen Branch** (C&O Towpath). Located at Mile 26.1. Access point, Sycamore Landing off River Road. Walk-in distance, 1-1/10 mi downstream. FACILITIES: Tent sites, tbls, toil, fire grill, drk wtr (except during winter). ACTIVITIES: Picnicking; fishing; hiking. MISC: No motorbikes; no hunting. Pets on leash.

* **Chisel Branch** (C&O Towpath). Located at Mile 30.5. Access point, Edwards Ferry Road. Walk-in distance, 3/10 mi downstream. FACILITIES: Tent sites, tbls, toil, fire grill, drk wtr (except during winter). ACTIVITIES: Picnicking; fishing; hiking. MISC: No motorbikes; no hunting. Pets.

* **Turtle Run** (C&O Towpath). Located at Mile 34.4. Access Point, White's Ferry Road. Walk-in distance 1-1/10 mi downstream. FACILITIES: Tent sites, tbls, toil, fire grill, drk wtr (except during winter). ACTIVITIES: Picnicking; fishing; hiking. MISC: No motorbikes; no hunting. Pets on leash.

*er **Marble Quarrry** (C&O Towpath). Located at Mile 38.2. Access point, White's Ferry Road. Walk-in distance 2-7/10 mi upstream. FACILITIES: Tent sites, tbls, toil, fire grill, drk wtr (except during winter). ACTIVITIES: Picnicking; fishing; hiking. MISC: No motorbikes; no hunting. Pets.

* **Indian Flats** (C&O Towpath). Located at Mile 42.5. Access Point, St Hwy 28, S on Monocacy River Road to Aqueduct. Walk-in distance, 3/10 mi upstream. FACILITIES: Tent sites, tbls, toil, fire grill, drk wtr (except during winter). ACTIVITIES: Picnicking; fishing; hiking. MISC: No motorbikes; no hunting. Pets on leash.

* **Calico Rocks** (C&O Towpath). Located at Mile 47.6. Access point, off US Hwy 15 Railroad Track at Point of Rocks. Walk-in distance, 1-1/10 mi downstream. FACILITIES: Tent sites, tbls, toil, fire grill, drk wtr (except during winter). ACTIVITIES: Picnicking; fishing; hiking. MISC: No motorbikes; no hunting. Pets.

* **Bald Eagle Island** (C&O Towpath). Located at Mile 49.9. Access point, off Trail 464 to Lander Road Cross Railroad Track. Walk-in distance, 1 mi downstream. FACILITIES: Tent sites, tbls, toil, fire grill, drk wtr (except during winter). ACTIVITIES: Picnicking; fishing; hiking. MISC: No motorbikes; no hunting. Pets.

* **Blue Ridge** (C&O Towpath). Located at Mile 59.4. Access point, off US 340 to Sandy Hook; walk across track. FACILITIES: Tent sites, tbls, toil, fire grill, drk wtr (except during winter). ACTIVITIES: Picnicking; fishing; hiking. MISC: No motorbikes; no hunting. Pets on leash.

* **Huckleberry Hill** (C&O Towpath). Located at Mile 62.5. Access point, off Harpers Ferry Road to Shinham Road to Boat Ramp. Walk-in distance, 2 mi downstream. FACILITIES: Tent sites, tbls, toil, fire grill, drk wtr (except during winter). ACTIVITIES: Picnicking; fishing; hiking. MISC: No motorbikes; no hunting. Pets.

* **Mountain Lock** (C&O Towpath). Located at Mile 67.2. Access point, S of Sharpsburg on Harpers Ferry Road to Limekiln Road; 1/2 mi to parking lot. (Adjacent vehicle parking; but CG is walk-in.) Stay is limited to 14-days. Picnic area. 11 sites. FACILITIES: Tent sites, tbls, toil, fire grill, drk wtr (except during winter). ACTIVITIES: Picnicking; fishing; hiking. MISC: No motorbikes; no hunting. Pets on leash.

* **Antietam Creek** (C&O Towpath). Located at Mile 69.3. Access point, 3 mi S of Sharpsburg on Harpers Ferry Road; 1/4 mi on Canal Road to parking lot. (Adjacent vehicle parking; but CG is walk-in). Stay is limited to 14 days. Picnic area. 44 sites. Amphitheatre. FACILITIES: Tent sites, tbls, toil, fire grill, drk wtr (except during winter). ACTIVITIES: Picnicking; fishing; hiking. MISC: No motorbikes; no hunting. Pets on leash.

* **Killiansburg Cave** (C&O Towpath). Located at Mile 75.2. Access point, off St Hwy 65 to Snyders Landing Boat Ramp. Walk-in distance, 4/5 mi downstream. FACILITIES: Tent sites, tbls, toil, fire grill, drk wtr (except during winter). ACTIVITIES: Picnicking; fishing; hiking. MISC: No motorbikes; no hunting. Pets.

* **Horseshoe Bend** (C&O Towpath). Located at Mile 79.6. Access point, off St Hwy 65 to Taylors Landing Boat Ramp. Walk-in distance, 1-1/5 mi Downstream. FACILITIES: Tent sites, tbls, toil, fire grill, drk wtr (except during winter). ACTIVITIES: Picnicking; fishing; hiking. MISC: No motorbikes; no hunting. Pets.

* **Big Woods** (C&O Towpath). Located at Mile 82.7. Access point, on Taylors Landing Road. Walk-in distance, 1-4/5 mi upstream. FACILITIES: Tent sites, tbls, toil, fire grill, drk wtr (except during winter). ACTIVITIES: Picnicking; fishing; hiking. MISC: No motorbikes; no hunting. Pets.

* **Opequon Junction** (C&O Towpath). Located at Mile 90.9. Access point, off Falling Waters Road. Walk-in distance, 3-1/2 mi downstream. FACILITIES: Tent sites, tbls, toil, fire grill, drk wtr (except during winter). ACTIVITIES: Picnicking; fishing; hiking. MISC: No motorbikes; no hunting. Pets on leash.

* **Cumberland Valley** (C&O Towpath). Located at Mile 95.2. Access point, off Falling Waters Road. Walk-in distance, 4/5 mi downstream. FACILITIES: Tent sites, tbls, toil, fire grill, drk wtr (except during winter). ACTIVITIES: Picnicking; fishing; hiking. MISC: No motorbikes; no hunting. Pets on leash.

* **Jordan Junction** (C&O Towpath). Located at Mile 101.2. Access point, from Williamsport take Bottom Road to Hagerstown Water Works. FACILITIES: Tent sites, tbls, toil, fire grill, drk wtr (except during winter). ACTIVITIES: Picnicking; fishing; hiking. MISC: No motorbikes; no hunting. Pets on leash.

* **North Mountain** (C&O Towpath). Located at Mile 109.5. Access point, from Big Spring take St Hwy 56 W to McCoy Ferry Road. Walk-in distance, 2/5 mi downstream. FACILITIES: Tent sites, tbls, toil, fire grill, drk wtr (except during winter). ACTIVITIES: Picnicking; fishing; hiking. MISC: No motorbikes; no hunting. Pets on leash.

McCoys Ferry (C&O Towpath). Located at Mile 110.4. Access point, take Clear Springs exit from I-70 5 mi SE on St Hwy 68; W on St Hwy 56; 3 mi on 4 Lock Road (or, from Big Spring take St Hwy 56 to McCoy Ferry Road). This is a drive-in area which has 20 primitive tent and trailer sites. Stay is limited to 14 days. No drk wtr. Boat,l. FACILITIES: Tent sites, tbls, toil, fire grill, drk wtr (except during winter). ACTIVITIES: Picnicking; fishing; hiking. MISC: No motorbikes; no hunting. Pets on leash.

* **Licking Creek** (C&O Towpath). Located at Mile 116.0. Access point, on US 40 to Licking Creek, cross I-70 to Aqueduct. FACILITIES: Tent sites, tbls, toil, fire grill, drk wtr (except during winter). ACTIVITIES: Picnicking; fishing; hiking. MISC: No motorbikes; no hunting. Pets on leash.

* **Millstone Point** (C&O Towpath). Located at Mile 118.9. No drk wtr. FACILITIES: Tent sites, tbls, toil, fire grill, drk wtr (except during winter). ACTIVITIES: Picnicking; fishing; hiking. MISC: No motorbikes; no hunting. Pets on leash.

* **Little Pool** (C&O Towpath). Located at Mile 120.6. Access point, off I-70, park near Tonoloway Aqueduct. Walk-in distance, 2-3/10 mi downstream. FACILITIES: Tent sites, tbls, toil, fire grill, drk wtr (except during winter). ACTIVITIES: Picnicking; fishing; hiking. MISC: No motorbikes; no hunting. Pets on leash.

* **White Rock** (C&O Towpath). Located at Mile 126.4. Access point, off I-70 or US 40 to Hancock to Canal Road. Walk-in distance, 1-1/2 mi upstream. FACILITIES: Tent sites, tbls, toil, fire grill, drk wtr (except during winter). ACTIVITIES: Picnicking; fishing; hiking. MISC: No motorbikes; no hunting. Pets on leash.

* **Leopards Mill** (C&O Towpath). Located at Mile 129.8. Access point, on Deneen Rd to Cohill Station Vehicle Bridge across Canal. Walk-in Distance, 1-2/5 mi downstream. FACILITIES: Tent sites, tbls, toil, fire grill, drk wtr (except during winter). ACTIVITIES: Picnicking; fishing; hiking. MISC: No motorbikes; no hunting. Pets on leash.

* **Cacapon Junction** (C&O Towpath). Located at Mile 133.6. Access point, on Deneen Road to Lock 54. Walk-in distance, 2/5 mi downstream. FACILITIES: Tent sites, tbls, toil, fire grill, drk wtr (except during winter). ACTIVITIES: Picnicking; fishing; hiking. MISC: No motorbikes; no hunting. Pets on leash.

* **Indigo Neck** (C&O Towpath). Located at Mile 139.2. Access point, on Zeigler Road to Little Orleans. Walk-in distance, 1-3/5 mi downstream. FACILITIES: Tent sites, tbls, toil, fire grill, drk wtr (except during winter). ACTIVITIES: Picnicking; fishing; hiking. MISC: No motorbikes; no hunting. Pets on leash.

Fifteen Mile Creek (C&O Towpath). Located at Mile 140.9. Access point, 2-1/2 mi W of Hancock on US 40; 10 mi S on Woodmont Road. This is a drive-in area which has 16 tent and trailer sties. Stay is limited to 14 days. Boating,l. FACILITIES: Tent sites, tbls, toil, fire grill, drk wtr (except during winter). ACTIVITIES: Picnicking; fishing; hiking. MISC: No motorbikes; no hunting. Pets.

* **Devils Alley** (C&O Towpath). Located at Mile 144.5. Access point, from Little Orleans. Walk-in distance, 3-7/10 mi upstream. FACILITIES: Tent sites, tbls, toil, fire grill, drk wtr (except during winter). ACTIVITIES: Picnicking; fishing; hiking. MISC: No motorbikes; no hunting. Pets on leash.

* **Stickpile Hill** (C&O Towpath). Located at Mile 149.4. No close access point. FACILITIES: Tent sites, tbls, toil, fire grill, drk wtr (except during winter). ACTIVITIES: Picnicking; fishing; hiking. MISC: No motorbikes; no hunting. Pets on leash.

* **Surrel Ridge** (C&O Towpath). Located at Mile 154.1. No close access point. FACILITIES: Tent sites, tbls, toil, fire grill, drk wtr (except during winter). ACTIVITIES: Picnicking; fishing; hiking. MISC: No motorbikes; no hunting. Pets on leash.

* **Paw Paw Tunnel** (C&O Towpath). Located at Mile 156.0. Canoeist camping only. No drk wtr. FACILITIES: Tent sites, tbls, toil, fire grill, drk wtr (except during winter). ACTIVITIES: Picnicking; fishing; hiking. MISC: No motorbikes; no hunting. Pets on leash.

* **Purslane Rune** (C&O Towpath). Located at Mile 157.4. Access point, off St Hwy 51 to Towpath. Walk-in distance, 9/10 mi upstream. FACILITIES: Tent sites, tbls, toil, fire grill, drk wtr (except during winter). ACTIVITIES: Picnicking; fishing; hiking. MISC: No motorbikes; no hunting. Pets on leash.

* **Town Creek** (C&O Towpath). Located at Mile 162.1. Access point, follow St Hwy 51 W to Town Creek.

See page 7 for KEY TO ABBREVIATIONS.

Walk-in distance, 1/10 mi downstream. FACILITIES: Tent sites, tbls, toil, fire grill, drk wtr (except during winter). ACTIVITIES: Picnicking; fishing; hiking. MISC: No motorbikes; no hunting. Pets on leash.

* **Potomac Forks** (C&O Towpath). Located at Mile 164.8. No close access point. FACILITIES: Tent sites, tbls, toil, fire grill, drk wtr (except during winter). ACTIVITIES: Picnicking; fishing; hiking. MISC: No motorbikes; no hunting. Pets.

* **Pigmans Ferry** (C&O Towpath). Located at Mile 169.1. No close access point. FACILITIES: Tent sites, tbls, toil, fire grill, drk wtr (except during winter). ACTIVITIES: Picnicking; fishing; hiking. MISC: No motorbikes; no hunting. Pets.

Spring Gap (C&O Towpath). Located at Mile 173.3. Access point, 11 mi E of Cumberland on St Hwy 51. This is a drive-in area which has 20 primitive tent and trailer sites. Stay is limited to 14 days. No drk wtr. Amphitheatre. FACILITIES: Tent sites, tbls, toil, fire grill, drk wtr (except during winter). ACTIVITIES: Picnicking; fishing; hiking. MISC: No motorbikes; no hunting. Pets.

* **Iron Mountain** (C&O Towpath). Located at Mile 175.3. Access point follow St Hwy 51 to North Branch. Walk-in distance, 1/5 mi downstream. FACILITIES: Tent sites, tbls, toil, fire grill, drk wtr (except during winter). ACTIVITIES: Picnicking; fishing; hiking. MISC: No motorbikes; no hunting. Pets on leash.

* **Evitts Creek** (C&O Towpath). Located at Mile 179.9. Access point, follow St Hwy 51 towards Cumberland. Walk-in distance, 3/5 mi from Evitts Creek Aqueduct. FACILITIES: Tent sites, tbls, toil, fire grill, drk wtr (except during winter). ACTIVITIES: Picnicking; fishing; hiking. MISC: No motorbikes; no hunting. Pets.

THURMONT

* **Hike-In Campsites** (Catoctin Mtn Park; NPS). Two Adirondack Shelters are located approx. 2-1/2 mi from Owens Creek Campground (which is located 6 mi W of Thurmont on St Hwy 77; 2 mi N on Foxville-Deerfield Road).

These shelters are a hike-in area and tents are not allowed.

MASSACHUSETTS

GENERAL STATE INFORMATION

Miscellaneous

Right Turns Are NOT Permitted On
   a Red Light, even after a full stop.
   STATE CAPITOL: Boston
STATE NICKNAME: Bay State
STATE MOTTO: "By the Sword She Seeks Peace,
            but Peace Only Under Liberty"
STATE BIRD: Chickadee
STATE FLOWER: Mayflower
STATE TREE: American Elm

State Parks

Overnight fees range from $3.00-5.00. Pets are permitted if kept on a leash. Further information: Massachusetts Department of Commerce and Development; Division of Tourism; Box 1775; Boston, MA 02105.

Rest Areas

Overnight stops are not permitted in Massachusetts Rest Areas.

See page 7 for KEY TO ABBREVIATIONS.

MASSACHUSETTS

State Forests

There is no free backcountry camping in Massachusetts State Forests.

The Appalachian Trail

More than 2000 miles long, the Appalachian Trail (from Maine to Georgia) is the longest continuous marked trail in the world.

CAMPING: More than 200 open-front shelters/lean-tos are spaced approximately 10 miles apart on the Trail (one-day intervals). As they are occupied on a first-come first-served basis, carry a tent in case the shelters are full. Potable spring water is usually available at each site, but should be purified by tablets or boiling. And always, "pack it in, pack it out".

PERMITS: No permit is required to hike the Trail. However, camping permits must be obtained for overnight stays in Shenandoah NP (Luray, VA 22835) and Great Smoky Mountains NP (Gatlinburg, TN 37733). These are free of charge and available from the ranger stations or by mail. A free camping permit must be obtained for overnight stays in White Mountain National Forest Restricted Use Area (PO Box 638; Laconia, NH 03246).

APPALACHIAN TRAIL CONFERENCE: A private, nonprofit, national organization which represents citizen's interest in the Appalachian Trail. They offer detailed guidebooks and maps for sale, as well as the A.T. Data Book which gives the location and distances between shelters and certain post offices, supply points, water sources, lodging and meals. For more information on this organization, write to them at: PO Box 236; Harpers Ferry, WV 25425.

INFORMATION SOURCES

Maps

The following maps are available from **Forsyth Travel Library** (see order form in Appendix B):

> **State of Massachusetts** [Up-to-date, showing all principal roads, points of interest, sports areas, parks, airports, mileage, etc. Full color.]
>
> Completely indexed city maps, including all airports, lakes, rivers, etc., of: **Amherst; Northampton; Boston; Holyoke; Worcester.**

State Information

Visitor Information Center; Boston Common; One Tremont Street; Boston, MA.
Massachusetts Department of Natural Resources; Division of Forests and Parks; State Office Building; 100 Cambridge Street; Boston, MA 02202.
Massachusetts Department of Commerce and Development; Division of Tourism; 100 Cambridge Street; Boston, MA 02202.

City Information

Greater Boston Chamber of Commerce; 125 High Street; Boston, MA 02110.
Bedford Chamber of Commerce; PO Box 452; Bedford, MA 01730.
Cambridge Chamber of Commerce; 859 Massachusetts Avenue; Cambridge, MA 02139.
Concord Chamber of Commerce; ½ Main Street; Concord, MA 01742.
Cape Cod Chamber of Commerce; Junction US Rt. 6 and Route 132; Hyannis, MA 02601.
Martha's Vineyard Chamber of Commerce; Vineyard Haven, MA 02568.

FREE CAMPGROUNDS

NORTHFIELD

*__Munn's Ferry__ (Northeast Utilities; Northfield Mountain Recreation). A few miles upstream on the Connecticut River from the Riverview Picnic Area, BY BOAT. SEASON: MD to end of October; 3-day lmt. FACILITIES: 6 sites and an Adirondack Shelter; tbls, toil, hibachis, pumped well water (should be boiled before drinking). ACTIVITIES: Boating; picnicking. MISC.: No pets allowed. Additional information: Northfield Mountain Visitor's Center; RR 1, Box 377; Northfield, MA 01360.

```
NOTICE TO CAMPERS
See page 5 for additional places to camp
for free.
```

MICHIGAN

GENERAL STATE INFORMATION

Miscellaneous

Toll-Free Number for Travel Information:
1-800-248-5404 [from outside Michigan]
1-800-248-5708 [within Michigan]
372-0080 [Chicago area residents]
771-1956 [Cleveland area residents]

Right Turns on Red: Permitted after full
stop, unless otherwise posted.
STATE CAPITOL: Lansing
STATE NICKNAME: Wolverine State
STATE MOTTO: "If You Seek A Pleasant
Peninsula, Look About You"
STATE BIRD: Robin
STATE FLOWER: Apple Blossom
STATE TREE: White Pine

State Parks

Entrance fee is $2.00; PLUS $2.00-5.00 per night for camping. Pets are permitted if
kept on a leash. Further information: Michigan Department of Commerce; Travel Bureau; PO Box 30226; Law Building; Lansing, MI 48909.

Rest Areas

Overnight stops are not permitted in any areas.

State Game Areas

Camping is allowed anywhere withing the State Game Areas from 10/2 to 3/31. Camping
is allowed only in designated, and posted, campsites from 4/1-10/1. Further information: State Game Areas Division; Department of Natural Resources; Forest Management
Division; PO Box 30028; Lansing, MI 48909.

Public Access Sites; Boat Launching Ramp Areas

Camping is allowed, where posted, on a number of access sites, mostly in northern
Michigan. Further information: Department of Natural Resources; PO Box 30028; Lansing, MI 48909.

Michigan's Shore to Shore Riding-Hiking Trail

The Trail stretches from the Lake Michigan shore on the west to the Lake Huron shore
on the east. Its route across the northern Lower Peninsula traverses some of the most
scenic country in the state. Parts of the Trail parallel two of the country's most
beautiful rivers, the Boardman and the Au Sable. Its path lies through stately pines
and hardwoods, along forest trails and scenic highways. Public trail camps (free),
as well as private facilities and services, are available for trail users A booklet
containing detailed maps of Michigan's Riding-Hiking Trail is available for $5 00 from
the Michigan Trail Riders Association (2864 Beitner Road; Traverse City, MI 49684);
the $5.00 includes a family membership in the association.

WILDERNESS AND BACKCOUNTRY CAMPING

Isle Royale National Park

The national park is a ½-million-acre wilderness island retreat in Lake Superior.

TRANSPORTATION TO PARK: Public transportation is available by boat or floatplane.
Reservations are recommended. Contact: Superintendent; Isle Royale NP; 87 North Ripley Street; Houghton, MI 49931 [for NPS boat Ranger III, from Houghton to Rock Harbor, May-October]; Isle Royale Queen II, Copper Harbor, MI 49918 [Copper Harbor to
Rock Harbor, late June to LD, and pre- and post-season chartered trips]; Isle Royale
Seaplane Service, Box 371, Houghton, MI 49931 [Houghton to Windigo via Rock Harbor,
late June to LD]. Private boats over 20 feet in length can go to the island. Boats

246

under 20 feet (water is too rough for them) can be transported to Isle Royale on the Ranger III. The private boat operators will transport small runabouts and canoes. Gas for your boat cannot be carried on commercial boats/planes but may be purchased at Rock Harbor and Windigo.

PETS and FIREARMS are prohibited.

WATER: The only safe drinking water is from spigots of Rock Harbor, Daisy Farm and Windigo Campgrounds. Halizone tablets will not kill tapeworms; boil water for at least 5 minutes.

FIRES: Fires are permitted only in designated areas within designated campgrounds. Backpacking stoves are preferable.

ACTIVITIES: No swimming; too cold, leeches. A fishing license is required in Lake Superior waters but not required for Isle Royale's inland lakes and streams. Fishing equipment is available at the Rock Harbor store or Windigo. Guided fishing trips are offered at Rock Harbor. A free fishing folder is available at the ranger stations. There is a marina at Rock Harbor Lodge (June-LD). Holding-tank pump-out stations for boats are at Mott Island and Windigo. There are more than 160 miles of foot trails.

CAMPING: For specific campsites, see "Houghton" in this chapter.

Further information: Superintendent; Isle Royale National Park; 87 North Ripley Street; Houghton, Michigan 49931.

Pictured Rocks National Lakeshore

The Lakeshore contains an extensive network of old logging roads and trails. Few of these roads and trails are marked with directional signs, so take a map and a compass. Hikers planning overnight camps must have a camping permit, which is available at Park Headquarters or from any Park Ranger. Bring insect repellent during the summer. From the lower peninsula take I-75 to US 2 north to St Hwy 28 to the Lakeshore. For information on Lakeshore designated campgrounds, see "Grand Marais" and "Melstrand" in this chapter. Further information/map: Pictured Rocks National Lakeshore; PO Box 40; Munising, MI 49862.

Sleeping Bear Dunes National Lakeshore

SOUTH MANITOU ISLAND: Backcountry permits are available from Rangers on the island and the ferry service operator. No open fires; bring backpack stove. No pets. Hiking. Pack all trash off the island. The only public transportation to the island is provided by the Manitou Mail Service (Leland, MI 49654; 616-256-9116/9061).

MAINLAND: Information on specific campgrounds are under "Empire" and "Frankfort" in this chapter.

GENERAL INFORMATION: Visitor Center is 2 mi S of the Dunes on St Hwy 109; open mid-June through October, and weekends thereafter.

Further information: Superintendent; Sleeping Bear Dunes National Lakeshore; 400 Main Street; Frankfort, MI 49635; 616/352-9611.

National Forests

You may camp anywhere on National Forest land, except in a few areas that are posted. No permit is required. Use dead wood for campfires and poles. If you want to cut firewood for your personal use at home, a free permit must be obtained at one of three Ranger Stations. All single-track trails and unroaded areas are closed to vehicle use unless posted open.

Big Island Lakes Wilderness (Hiawatha NF)

This area is best enjoyed by those who wish to hike, snowshoe, canoe, fish, camp (without facilities) and view the scenery. Bring plenty of insect repellent. Further information: Forest Supervisor; Hiawatha NF; 2727 North Lincoln Road; Escanaba, MI 49829.

Canoeing in Hiawatha NF

AU TRAIN RIVER (Alger County; 10 miles, 4-6 hours): This river flows through wild and scenic country, has smooth rapids and turns, and is portage free. Free camping is available all along the river. Put in at the US Forest Service campground and boat launching site on the SE side of Au Train Lake. Enter the river after crossing the N edge of the lake. Go through to Lake Superior, or take out at any of several bridges along the way. Another put-in spot is at the bridge on FS 2276.

CARP RIVER (Mackinac County; 20 miles, 1-2 days): Put in at M-123 Bridge about 5½ mi N of Moran. Good free camping spots are found all along the stream. The short rapids below Platz Lake Outlet may have to be portaged. Take out at St. Martin Bay.

WHITEFISH RIVER (Delta County; 12 miles, 1 day): Take Co Rd 509 (Whitefish Forest Road) N from US 2 at Rapid River. Travel about 12 mi to US 2236 and take this road ½ mi W to the East Branch of the Whitefish River. It's a pleasant short trip with only a few short portages, and none during the high waters of early spring. Take out at the bridge on US 2, a few miles east of Rapid River.

STURGEON RIVER (Delta County; 15 miles, 1 day): Put in about 10 mi N of US 2 on Federal Highway 13. Below US 2, three logjams will require portage. Several free campgrounds are found along the way before reaching the take-out at Nahma, near the river's mouth in Big Bay De Noc.

INDIAN RIVER (Schoolcraft County; 50 miles, 2-3 days): No fast water on this trip, and entry-exit sites are numerous. Put in at US Forest Service Widewater Campground. The trip ends at the boat landing on Indian Lake.

Further information: Forest Supervisor; Hiawatha NF; 2727 N. Lincoln Rd; Escanaba, MI 49829.

Sylvania Recreation Area (Ottawa NF)

This tract of approximately 21,000 acres is predominantly virgin timber and pristine lakes. Travel through the area is by foot or canoe; no motorized equipment is permitted. Primitive camping is permitted at designated sites, which provide only the minimum facilities needed to protect the fragile resources of the area. Camping is by permit only and all campers must register for campsites either at the Sylvania Visitors Center (at the corner of US 2 and US 45 in Watersmeet, MI) or at the Visitor Information Station, at the entrance to Sylvania, off FS 535. If you are interested in fishing in Sylvania, check the special regulations which apply to fishing in the Area. Fires are allowed only in metal rings and grills at designated sites. Camping and cooking is only allowed at designated sites. No more than 5 persons assigned to a campsite. Pets are allowed on leash. Further information: Forest Supervisor; Ottawa NF; East US 2; Ironwood, MI 49938.

INFORMATION SOURCES

Maps

The following maps are available from Forsyth Travel Library (see order form in Appendix B):

> State of Michigan [Up-to-date, showing all principal roads, points of interest, sports areas, parks, airports, mileage, etc. Full color.]

> Completely indexed city maps, including all airports, lakes, rivers, etc., of: Detroit; Kalamazoo.

State Information

Michigan Tourist Council; Department of Commerce; 300 South Capitol Avenue, Suite 102; Lansing, MI 48926.

Department of Natural Resources; Forest Management Division; PO Box 30028; Lansing, MI 48909. [State Forest information]

Fish and Game Division; Department of Natural Resources; Box 30028; Lansing,MI 48926.

Michigan Department of Commerce; Travel Bureau; PO Box 30226; Law Building; Lansing, MI 48909.

Western Michigan Tourist Association; Grand Rapids, MI 49503. [616/456-8557]

East Michigan Tourist Association; One Wenonah Park; Bay City, MI 48706. [517/895-8823]

Southeastern Michigan Travel and Tourist Association; American Center Building, Room 350; 2777 Franklin Road; Southfield, MI 48034. [313/357-1663]

Upper Michigan Tourist Association; PO Box 400; Iron Mountain, MI 49801. [906/774-5480]

Department of State Highways and Transportation; Bike Maps Division; Drawer K; Lansing, MI 48904. [Bike maps; individual county maps; ask for free list of counties.]

Michigan State Highway Department; Highway Building; PO Box 30050; Lansing,MI 48909.

CB Channel 9 (KMI-0911). Broad Emergency Assistance Radio (Project BEAR). To report emergencies to the State Police.

City Information

Alma Chamber of Commerce; 608 Wright Avenue; PO Box 506; Alma, MI 48801,
Ann Arbor Chamber of Commerce; 207 East Washington; Ann Arbor, MI 48108.
Greater Detroit Board of Commerce; 150 Michigan Avenue; Detroit, MI 48226.
Convention Bureau; 626 Book Building; Detroit, MI 48226.

Miscellaneous

Manistee NF; 421 South Mitchell Street; Cadillac, MI 49601.
Huron NF; 421 South Mitchell Street; Cadillac, MI 49601.
Hiawatha NF; 2727 North Lincoln Road; Escanaba, MI 49829.
Ottawa NF; PO Box 498; Ironwood, MI 44938.
Isle Royale NP; 87 North Ripley Street; Houghton, MI 49931.
Sleeping Bear Dunes National Lakeshore; 400 Main Street; Frankfort, MI 49635.
Pictured Rocks National Lakeshore; Munising, MI 49862.
Corps of Engineers; Detroit District; PO Box 1027; Detroit, MI 48231.

FREE CAMPGROUNDS

ALLEGAN

Ely Lake (State Game Area). 9 mi W of Allegan on Monroe Rd; 1 mi S to campground. SEASON: All yr. FACILITIES: 80 sites (tr -30), tbls, toil, cga, drk wtr. ACTIVITIES: Picnicking; fishing; swimming; boating,l MISC: Pets permitted if kept on a leash.

Lakeview (State Game Area). 5 mi W of Allegan on Monroe Rd; 1/2 mi N to S shore of the Kalamazoo River. SEASON: All yr. FACILITIES: 10 sites (tr -30), tbls, toil, cga, drk wtr. ACTIVITIES: Picnicking; fishing; boating,l. MISC: Pets permitted.

Pine Point (State Game Area). 6 mi W of Allegan on Monroe Rd; 1/2 mi S on 44th St. SEASON: All yr. FACILITIES: 50 sites (tr -30), tbls, toil, cga, f, drk wtr. ACTIVITIES: Picnicking; fishing; boating,l; hunting. MISC: Pets.

* **Swan Creek** (State Game Area). 7 mi W of Allegan on Monroe Road; 1 mi N on Woods Trail. SEASON: All yr. FACILITIES: 10 sites (tr -30), tbls, toil, cga, drk wtr, f. ACTIVITIES: Picnicking; fishing; boating,l; horseback riding/rental; hunting; rockhounding; hiking; swimming; dog sledding. MISC: Pets permitted.

BALDWIN

Bowman Bridge Recreation Area (Huron-Manistee NF). 4½ mi W of Baldwin on Co Hwy 56. SEASON: 5/25-12/1; 14-day lmt. FACILITIES: 20 sites (tr -32); well drk wtr, toil, cga, tbls. Store/gas/ice/laundry/food (5 mi). ACTIVITIES: Picnicking; boating (lr, 5 mi); swimming; fishing. MISC.: Elev 700 ft; 10 acres; pets. Pere Marquette River; canoe launch.

* **Old Grade Trail Camp** (Huron Manistee NF). 11 mi N of Baldwin on St Hwy 37; 2/5 mi W on FS; 3/10 mi N, BY TRAIL. SEASON: 5/1-12/1; 14-day lmt. FACILITIES: 4 tent sites, tbls, toil, cga, well drk wtr. Store/gas (3 mi). Food/laundry (4 mi). ACTIVITIES: Picnicking; fishing; berrypicking. Boating/swimming/waterskiing (4 mi). Horseback riding/rental (5 mi). MISC.: Pets; elev 900; 2 acres.

BANAT

Campsite #3 (Wisc. Mich. Power Co.). 5 mi E of Banat; 7/10 mi N to campground on Menominee River. SEASON: All yr (probably not plowed out in winter). FACILITIES: Primitive sites, tbls, toil, cga, no drk wtr. ACTIVITIES: Picnicking; fishing; hunting in season (whitetail deer, ruffed grouse); ice fishing and cross-country skiing in winter; boating,l. MISC: Pets permitted.

Campsite #4 (Wisc. Mich. Power Co.). 5 mi W of Banat; 1-9/10 mi N to campground; on Menominee River. SEASON: All yr (probably not plowed out in winter). FACILITIES: Primitive sites, tbls, toil, cga, no drk wtr. ACTIVITIES: Picnicking; fishing; hunting in season (whitetail deer, ruffed grouse); ice fishing and cross-country skiing in winter; boating,l. MISC: Pets permitted if kept on a leash.

BRANCH

Timber Creek (Huron-Manistee NF). 2-1/5 mi E of Branch on US 10. SEASON: All yr; 10-day lmt. FACILITIES: 9 sites (tr -22); well drk wtr, tbls, toil, cga, f. Store/gas/ice/food (2 mi). ACTIVITIES: Picnicking; berry-picking. Fishing/boating (4 mi). MISC.: Elev 800 ft; 5 acres. Botanical; pets.

CADILLAC

Long Lake (Pere Marquette). 8 mi NE of Cadillac on US 131 & Campground Road. SEASON: All yr; 15-day lmt. FACILITIES: 5 sites (tr -30), tbls, toil, cga, drk wtr. ACTIVITIES: Picnicking; fishing; boating,l; swimming. MISC: Warmwater fishing. Nestled in the hilly hardwood. Pets.

Ravine (Huron-Manistee NF). 10-1/5 mi W of Cadillac on St Hwy 55; 1 mi S on FS 5181; 2-2/5 mi W on FS 5182; 1 mi S on FS 5334. SEASON: All yr; 14-day lmt. FACILITIES: 7 sites (tr -22); well drk wtr, tbls, toil, cga. Store/gas/ice (4 mi). ACTIVITIES: Picnicking; fishing. MISC.: Elev 1000 ft; 2 acres; pets.

CHANNING

Campsite #13 (Wisc. Mich. Power Co.). 1/2 mi N of Channing on St Hwy 95; 1/5 mi N on Co Rd; 5-3/5 mi W on Co Rd; S 1/2 mi on Co Rd; 1-3/10 mi W to campground; on Michigamme Reservoir. SEASON: All yr (probably no plowed out in winter). FACILITIES: Primitive sites, tbls, toil, cga, no drk wtr. ACTIVITIES: Picnicking; fishing; hunting in season (whitetail deer, ruffed grouse); ice fishing and cross-country skiing in winter; boating,l. MISC: Pets.

Campsite #14 (Wisc. Mich. Power Co.). 1/2 mi N of Channing on St Hwy 95; 1/5 mi N on Co Rd; 4-4/5 mi W on Co Rd; 1-3/10 mi N on Co Rd; 1 mi W on Co Rd to Campground; on Michigamme Reservoir. SEASON: All yr (probably not plowed out in winter). FACILITIES: Picnicking; fishing; hunting in season (whitetail deer, ruffed grouse); ice fishing and cross-country skiing in winter; boating,l. MISC: Pets permitted.

COMMONWEALTH

Campsite #34 (Wisc. Mich. Power Co.). 3-3/5 mi S of Commonwealth on Co Rd; 1-3/10 mi W on Co Rd; 3-1/2 mi S on Co Rd to campground; on Pine River. SEASON: All yr (probably not plowed out in winter). FACILITIES: Primitive sites, tbls, toil, cga, no drk wtr. ACTIVITIES: Picnicking; fishing; hunting in season (whitetail deer, ruffed grouse); ice fishing and cross-country skiing in winter; boating,l.

CRYSTAL FALLS

Campsite #17 (Wisc. Mich. Power Co.). 6-3/5 mi N of Crystal Falls on Co Rd; 2-1/5 mi NW on Co Rd to campground; on Michigamme Reservoir. FACILITIES: Primitive sites; tbls, toil, cga, no drk wtr. SEASON: All yr (probably not plowed out in winter). ACT: Picnicking; fishing; hunting in season (whitetail deer, ruffed grouse); ice fishing and cross-country skiing in winter; boating,l. MISC: Pets permitted if kept on a leash.

Campsite #18 (Wisc. Mich. Power Co.). 6-3/5 mi N of Crystal Falls on Co Rd; 4/5 mi NW on Co Rd to campground on Michigamme Reservoir. SEASON: All yr (probably not plowed out in winter). FACILITIES: Primitive sites, tbls, toil, cga, no drk wtr. ACTIVITIES: Picnicking; fishing; hunting in season (whitetail deer, ruffed grouse); ice fishing and cross-country skiing in winter; boating,l. MISC: Pets permitted.

Campsite #19 (Wisc. Mich. Power Co.). 6-3/5 mi N of Crystal Falls on Co Rd; 3/5 mi NE on Co Rd to campground; on Michigamme Reservoir. SEASON: All yr (probably not plowed out in winter). FACILITIES: Primitive sites, tbls, toil, cga, no drk wtr. ACTIVITIES: Picnicking; fishing; hunting in season (whitetail deer, ruffed grouse); ice fishing and cross-country skiing in winter; boating,rl. MISC: Pets.

Campsite #22 (Wisc. Mich. Power Co.). 3-9/10 mi E of Crystal Falls on St Hwy 69; 3-3/5 mi S on Co Rd: 2 mi W and SW on Co Rd to campground; on Peavy Falls Pond. SEASON: All yr (probably not plowed out in winter). FACILITIES: Primitive sites, tbls, toil, cga, no drk wtr. ACTIVITIES: Picnicking; fishing; hunting in season (whitetail deer; ruffed grouse); ice fishing and cross-country skiing in winter; boating,l. MISC: Pets permitted if kept on a leash.

Campsite #27 (Wisc. Mich. Power Co.). 3-9/10 mi E of Crystal Falls on St Hwy 69; 4-9/10 mi S on Co Rd to campground; on Peavy Falls Pond. SEASON: All yr (probably not plowed out in winter). FACILITIES: Primitive camp sites, tbls, toil, cga,· no drk wtr. ACTIVITIES: Picnicking; fishing; hunting in season (whitetail deer, ruffed grouse); ice fishing and cross-country skiing in winter; boating,l. MISC: Pets.

See page 7 for KEY TO ABBREVIATIONS.

Deer Lake (Copper County SF). 17 mi N of Crystal Falls on US 141 and Deer Lake Road. SEASON: All yr; 15-day lmt. FACILITIES: 12 sites (tr -30), tbls. ACTIVITIES: Picnicking; fishing (warmouth); swimming; boating,l. MISC: Secluded area. Pets. permitted if kept on a leash.

DAGGETT

Campsite #1 (Wisc. Mich. Power Co.). 5-3/10 mi W on Co Rd 358; 2 mi S on Co Rd 577; 4-1/2 mi NW on Co Rd 536 to campground (on Menominee River. SEASON: All yr (probably not plowed out in winter). FACILITIES: Primitive sites, tbls, toil, cga, no drk wtr. ACTIVITIES: Picnicking; fishing; hunting in season (whitetail deer, ruffed grouse); ice fishing and cross-country skiing in winter; boating,l. MISC: Pets permitted.

DEARBORN

City Park. Directly behind city Police Dept. in Dearborn. SEASON: All yr; 1-night lmt. FACILITIES: Spaces for self-contained RVs. MISC: Pets.

DEXTER

Wolverine Truck Plaza. Baker Road exit, off I-94. SEASON: All yr; 1-night lmt. FACILITIES: Spaces for self-contained RVs; drk wtr, gas, emergency pking; mechanic; Union 76; 24-hour; food.

EAST TAWAS

Gordon Creek (Huron Manistee NF). 12 mi NW of East Tawas. SEASON: All yr. FACILITIES: 20 sites, well drk wtr, toil, f. Gas (1 mi). Store/ice (4 mi). ACTIVITIES: Fishing (2 mi); Boating (4 mi). MISC: Pets permitted if kept on a leash.

EMPIRE

Platte River Campground (Sleeping Bear Dunes Natl Lakeshore). 8 mi S of Empire on St Hwy 22. SEASON: Dee.-Mar.,FREE; ($2 rest of yr); 14-day lmt. FACILITIES: 150 sites, tbls, toil, cga, wtr pump, dump. ACTIVITIES: Picnicking; hiking; climbing dunes; cross-country skiing and snowshoeing in winter; canoeing; hang gliding in certain locations. MISC: Limited facilities in winter. Pets permitted if kept on a leash.

+ **White Pine Campground** (Sleeping Bear Dunes Natl Lakeshore). 8 mi S of Empire on St Hwy 22; 2-3/10 mi NE on Platte Plains Trail - ON FOOT.

SEASON: All yr; 14-day lmt. FACILITIES: 6 sites, toil. ACTIVITIES: Hiking; climbing dunes; cross-country skiing and snowshoeing in winter; canoeing; hang gliding in certain locations. MISC: Backcountry permit required. Pets.

EWEN

Matchwood (Ottawa NF). 5½ mi W on St Hwy 28; 5 mi S on Co Hwy; ¼ mi S on FS 178. SEASON: 5/1-12/1; 14-day lmt. FACILITIES: 5 sites (tr -22); well drk wtr, tbls, toil, cga, f. ACTIVITIES: Picnicking; berry-picking. Fishing (2 mi). MISC.: Elev 1300 ft; 2 acres; pets. Good grouse and whitetail deer area. Popular hunting and camping area.

FORESTVILLE

Forester Cath. Campground. Off US 25, 1/2 mi from Lake Huron. SEASON: All yr. FACILITIES: Spaces for self-contained RVs. MISC: Pets permitted if kept on a leash.

FRANKFORT

D H Day Campground (Sleeping Bear Dunes Natl Lake Shore. For directions, ask a ranger or check at 400 Main Street, Frankfort 49635. SEASON: Dec-Mar, FREE ($2 rest of yr); 14-day lmt. FACILITIES: 125 sites, toil. ACTIVITIES: Hiking; climbing dunes; cross-country skiing and snowshoeing in winter; canoeing; hang gliding in certain locations. MISC: Pets.

GRAND MARAIS

Hurricane River Campground (Pictured Rocks Natl Seashore). From Lower Peninsula, take I-75 to US 2 N to St Hwy 28 to the Natl Seashore. SEASON: 5/15-11/15; 14-day lmt. FACILITIES: 13 sites (no trailers), tbls, toil, cga, stream water only. ACTIVITIES: Picnicking; fishing. MISC: Free, but registration is required. Bring insect repellent in summer. Pets permitted.

12-Mile Beach Campground (Pictured Rocks Natl Seashore). From Lower Peninsula, take I-75 to US 2 N to St Hwy 28 to the Natl Seashore. SEASON: 5/15-11/15; 14-day lmt. FACILITIES: Picnicking; fishing. MISC: Free, but registration is required. Bring insect repellent in summer.

See page 7 for KEY TO ABBREVIATIONS.

251

HAMILTON

Silver Creek (County Park). 25 mi W of St Hwy 40 on 134th Ave., just S of Hamilton River, in Hamilton. SEASON: All yr. FACILITIES: Primitive sites (120), on 360 acres, tbls, toil, cga, well drk wtr. ACTIVITIES: Picnicking. MISC: Separate horseman camping area. MISC: Pets permitted if kept on a leash.

HARTLAND

Oasis Truck Plaza. Jct of St Hwy 59 and US 24. SEASON: All yr; 1-night lmt. FACILITIES: Spaces for self-contained RVs, toil, food, gas, 24-hr mechanic, drk wtr.

HOUGHTON

*ISLE ROYALE NP. Public transportation is available by boat or floatplane. Reservations are recommended. Contact: Superintendent; Isle Royale NP; 87 North Ripley Street; Houghton, MI 49931 (for NPS boat Ranger III, from Houghton to Rock Harbor, May-October); **Isle Royale Queen II**, Copper Harbor. MI 49918 (Copper Harbor to Rock Harbor, late June to LD, and pre- and post-season chartered trips); **Isle Royale Seaplane Service.** Box 371, Houghton, MI 49931 (Houghton to Windigo via Rock Harbor, late June to LD). Private boats over 20 feet in length can go to the island. Boats under 20 feet (water is too rough for them) can be transported to Isle Royale on the Ranger III. The private boat operators will transport small runabouts and canoes. Gas for your boat cannot be carried on commercial boats/planes but may be purchasd at Rock Harbor and Windigo.

CAMPING: All campsites are reached by foot or by boat. Most of the 31 CGs have fireplaces, tables, and tent sites. All campers must obtain a CAMPING PERMIT. In CGs, use designated fireplaces. Outside of CGs use backpack stoves.

SEASON: 6/15-LD; 15-day lmt. (which applies to a single stay or to combined separate periods, on boats, CG docks, or on land).

Bring insect repellent.

Camping must be at designated campsites except by special permit.

No pets or firearms.

Addl info/map: Supt, Isle Royale NP, 87 N. Ripley St., Houghton, Mich. 49931.

10x16-foot shelters, enclosed on 3 sides, with a wooden floor, and a screen front with screen door (accompanied by tables, fireplaces, refuse containers, and privy), are scattered throughout the Park for use up to 14 days; no reservation required.

Inland Camps Area (Isle Royale NP). Central portion of island.

Chickenbone Lake. Trail access only. SEASON: 6/15-LD; 2-day lmt. FACILITIES: 5 sites; group campsites available; no drk wtr.ACTIVITIES: Hiking; fishing. MISC: No pets.

East Chickenbone Lake. Trail access only. SEASON: 6/15-LD; 2-day lmt. FACILITIES: 6 sites; group campsites available; no drk wtr. ACTIVITIES: Hiking; fishing. MISC: No pets allowed.

Feltman Lake. Trail access only. SEASON: 6/15-LD; 3-day lmt. FACILITIES: 3 sites; group campsites available; no drk wtr. ACTIVITIES: Hiking; fishing. MISC: No pets allowed.

Hatchet Lake. Trail access only. SEASON: 6/15-LD; 2-day lmt. FACILITIES: 4 sites; group campsites available; no drk wtr. ACTIVITIES: Hiking; fishing. MISC: No pets allowed.

Island Mine. Trail access only. SEASON: 6/15-LD; 2-day lmt. FACILITIES: 6 sites; group campsites available; no drk wtr. ACTIVITIES: Hiking; fishing. MISC: No pets allowed.

Lake Richie. Trail access only. SEASON: 6/15-LD; 2-day lmt. FACILITIES: 3 sites; group campsites available; no drk wtr. ACTIVITIES: Hiking; fishing. MISC: No pets allowed.

North Lake Desor. Trail access only. SEASON: 6/15-LD; 2-day lmt. FACILITIES: 4 sites; group campsites available; no drk wtr. ACTIVITIES: Hiking; fishing. MISC: No pets.

South Lake Desor. Trail access only. SEASON: 6/15-LD; 2-day lmt. FACILITIES: 4 sites; group campsites available; no drk wtr. ACTIVITIES: Hiking; fishing. MISC: No pets.

North Shore Area (Isle Royale NP). North shore of island.

Belle Isle. Boat access only. SEASON: 6/15-LD; 7-day lmt. FACILITIES: 12 sites; no drk wtr. ACTIVITIES: Boating,d; fishing. MISC: No pets allowed.

Birch Island. Boat access only. SEASON: 6/15-LD; 3-day lmt. FACILI-

TIES: 1 site; no drk wtr. ACTIVI-
TIES: Boating,d; fishing. MISC: No
pets allowed.

Duncan Bay. Boat access only.
SEASON: 6/15-LD; 7-day lmt. FACILI-
TIES: 3 sites; no drk wtr. ACTIVI-
TIES: Boating,d; fishing. MISC: No
pets allowed.

Duncan Narrows. Boat access
only. SEASON: 6/15-LD; 7-day lmt.
FACILITIES: 2 sites; no drk wtr. AC-
TIVITIES: Boating,d; fishing. MISC:
No pets allowed.

Huginnin Cove. Boat or trail
access only. SEASON: 6/15-LD; 2-day
lmt. FACILITIES: 5 sites; no drk
wtr. ACTIVITIES: Hiking; fishing.
MISC: No pets allowed.

Lane Cove. Boat or trail access.
SEASON: 6/15-LD; 2-day lmt. FACILI-
TIES: 3 sites; no drk wtr. ACTIVI-
TIES: Hiking; fishing. MISC: No pets
allowed.

Little Todd Harbor. Boat or trail
access; group campsites available;
no drk wtr. ACTIVITIES: Hiking;
fishing; boating,d. MISC: No pets
allowed.

McCargoe Cove. Boat or trail
access. SEASON: 6/15-LD; 3-day lmt.
FACILITIES: 8 sites; group campsites
available; no drk wtr. ACTIVITIES:
Hiking; fishing; boating,d. MISC:
No pets allowed.

Todd Harbor. Boat or trail
access. SEASON: 6/15-LD; 3-day lmt.
FACILITIES: 7 sites; group campsites
available; no drk wtr. ACTIVITIES:
Hiking; fishing; boating,d. MISC:
No pets allowed.

Rock Harbor Area. (Isle Royale NP).
NE end of island.

Caribou Island. Boat access only
SEASON: 6/15-LD; 3-day lmt. FACILI-
TIES: 4 sites; no drk wtr.ACTIVI-
TIES: Fishing; boating,rd. MISC: No
pets allowed.

Daisy Farm. Boat or trail access
only. SEASON: 6/15-LD; 3-day lmt.
FACILITIES: 23 sites; group campsites
available; treated drk wtr. ACTIVI-
TIES: Hiking; fishing; boating,rd.
MISC: No pets allowed.

Merritt Lane. Boat access only.
SEASON: 6/15-LD; 3-day lmt. FACILI-
TIES: 2 sites; no drk wtr. ACTIVI-
TIES: Fishing; boating,rd. MISC: No
pets allowed.

Moskey Basin. Boat or trail access. SEASON: 6/15-LD; 3-day lmt.
FACILITIES: 10 sites; group campsites
available; no drk wtr. ACTIVITIES:

Hiking; fishing; boating,rd. MISC:
No pets allowed.

Rock Harbor. Boat or trail access.
SEASON: 6/15-LD; 1-day lmt. FACILI-
TIES: 20 sites; group campsites
available; treated drk wtr. ACTIVI-
TIES: Hiking; fishing; boating.rd.
MISC: No pets allowed.

Three Mile. Boat or trail access.
SEASON: 6/15-LD; 1-day lmt. FACILI-
TIES: 12 sites; group campsites
available; no drk wtr. ACTIVITIES:
Hiking; fishing; boating, rd. MISC:
No pets allowed.

Tookers Island. Boat access only.
SEASON: 6/15-LD; 3-day lmt. FACILI-
TIES: 2 sites; no drk wtr.ACTIVI-
TIES: Hiking; fishing; boating,rd.
MISC: No pets allowed.

South Shore Area. (Isle Royale NP).
South shore of island.

Camp Siskiwit. Boat or trail
access. SEASON: 6/15-LD; 3-day lmt.
FACILITIES: 4 sites; group campsites
available; no drk wtr. ACTIVITIES:
Hiking; fishing; boating,d. MISC:
No pets allowed.

Chippewa Harbor. Boat or trail
access. SEASON: 6/15-LD; 3-day lmt.
FACILITIES: 4 sites; group campsites
available; no drk wtr. ACTIVITIES:
Hiking; fishing; boating,d. MISC:
No pets allowed.

Hay Bay. Boat access only. SEA-
SON: 6/15-LD; 3-day lmt. FACILITIES:
2 sites; no drk wtr. ACTIVITIES:
Boating,d; fishing. MISC: No pets
allowed.

Malone Bay. Boat or trail access.
SEASON: 6/15-LD; 7-day lmt. FACILI-
TIES: 8 sites; group campsites available; no drk wtr. ACTIVITIES: Hiking; fishing; boating,d. MISC: No
pets allowed.

Windigo Area. (Isle Royale NP). SW
end of island.

Beaver Island. Boat access only.
SEASON: 6/15-LD; 3-day lmt. FACILI-
TIES: 3 sites; no drk wtr. ACTIVI-
TIES: Fishing; boating,rd. MISC: No
pets allowed.

Grace Island. Boat access only,
SEASON: 6/15-LD; 3-day lmt. ACTIVI-
TIES: 6/15-LD; 3-day lmt. ACTIVI-
TIES: Boating,rd; fishing. MISC: No
pets allowed.

Washington Creek. Boat or trail
access. SEASON: 6/15-LD; 2-day lmt.
FACILITIES: 16 sites; group campsites
available; treated drk wtr. ACTIVI-
TIES: Hiking; fishing; boating,rd.
MISC: No pets allowed.

See page 7 for KEY TO ABBREVIATIONS.

HOUGHTON LAKE

D&J Truck and Car Plaza. Snowball Road, in Houghton Lake. SEASON: All yr; 1-night lmt. FACILITIES: Spaces for self-contained vehicles; toil, drk wtr, gas, 24-hr, emergency parking; mechanic; food.

IRON RIVER

Blockhouse (Ottawa NF). 2½ mi S of Iron River on US 2; 14 mi N on Co Rd 657; 3½ mi SE on FS 347. SEASON: 4/25-11/30; 14-day lmt. ACTIVITIES: Picnicking; fishing. FACILITIES: 2 sites; no drk wtr; tbls, toil, cga, f. MISC: Elev 1400 ft; 3 acres; canoe camp; trout fishing; pets; tr -22.

Paint River Forks (Ottawa NF). 2½ mi W of Iron River on US 2; 10-1/10 mi N on Co Hwy 657. SEASON: 4/25-11/30; 14-day lmt. FACILITIES: 4 sites (tr -22); tbls, toil, cga; no drk wtr. ACTIVITIES: Picnicking. Fishing (1 mi). MISC.: Starting point for Paint River Forks Canoe Route. Pets; elev 1400 ft; 3 acres.

JACKSON

Adkins and Son Truck Stop. 6100 Ann Arbor Road (I-94, exit 145/Sargent Road). SEASON: All yr; 1-night lmt. FACILITIES: Spaces for self contained vehicles; drk wtr, toil, food, 24-hr, emergency, mechanic.

LAKE ORION

Square Lake Kelly Park 4 mi W of Lake Orion. SEASON: All yr; 1-night lmt. FACILITIES: Spaces for self-contained vehicles. MISC: Pets.

LELAND

* **Bay Campground; S. Manitore Island** (Sleeping Bear Dunes Natl Lakeshore). Take ferry from Leland ($7 for 32-mile round-trip; 10am daily, summer). Campground is located near boat dock. SEASON: All yr. FACILITIES: 45 sites, toil, pumped drk wtr in summer; marina concession provides light meals. No vehicles of any kind. Fires in fire rings only. ACTIVITIES: Picnicking; hiking. MISC: Backcountry permit required. Ferry info: (616)256-9116/9061. No pets allowed.

* **Popple Camp; S. Manitore Island** (Sleeping Bear Dunes Natl Lakeshore). Take ferry from Leland ($7 for 32-mi round trip; 10am daily, summer). Campground is located 3 mi NW of dock; use trail/road system.

SEASON: All yr. FACILITIES: 7 sites, wtr pump in summer; marina concession provides light meals; fires in fire rings only. ACTIVITIES: Picnicking; hiking. MISC: Backcountry permit required. No vehicles of any kind. No pets allowed. Ferry info: (616) 256-9116/9061.

* **Weather Station Campground; S. Manitou Island** (Sleeping Bear Dunes Natl Lakeshore). Take ferry from Leland ($7 for 32-mi round trip; 10am daily, summer). Campground is located 1½ mi S of dock; use trail/road system. SEASON: All yr. FACILITIES: 36 sites, toil, wtr pump in summer; marina concession provides light meals; fires in fire rings only. ACTIVITIES: Picnicking; hiking. MISC: Backcountry permit required. No vehicles of any kind. No pets allowed. Ferry info: (616)256-9116/9061.

LUZERNE

***Luzerne Trail Camp** (Huron-Manistee NF). 1½ mi SW on Co Hwy 490; ½ mi S on FS 4477. SEASON: 5/15-10/30. FACILITIES: 65 sites (tr -32); toil; no drk wtr. Store/gas/ice/food (2 mi). ACTIVITIES: Picnicking; horseback riding. Fishing (2 mi). MISC.: Elev 1200 ft; 31 acres; pets.

MANISTIQUE

Camp Cooks (Hiawatha NF). 10-3/5 mi W of Manistique on Co Hwy 442; 7-4/5 mi W on Co Hwy 2222; 3-7/10 mi N on Co Hwy L3; 3-1/10 mi NE on Co Hwy 442. SEASON: 5/15-9/15; 14-day lmt. FACILITIES: 12 sites (tr -32), toil, well drk wtr. ACTIVITIES: Fishing; hiking. Swimming/waterskiing; boating,ld (3 mi). MISC: CCC Campsite. Pets; elev 800 ft; 11 acres.

MELSTRAND

Little Beaver Lake Campground (Pictured Rocks Natl Seashore). From Lower Peninsula take I-75 to US 2 N to St Hwy 28 to the Natl seashore; 5 mi NE of Melstrand on Co Rd H58; 3 mi N to campground. SEASON: 5/15-11/15; 14-day lmt. FACILITIES: 8 sites (no trailers), tbls, toil, cga, drk wtr. ACTIVITIES: Picnicking; fishing. MISC: Free, but registration is required. Bring insect repellent in summer. Pets permitted on leash.

MUNISING

Hovey Lake (Hiawatha NF). 7½ mi SW of Munising on St Hwy 94; 3-3/5 mi SE on Co Hwy 2254; 3/10 mi S on FS 2473. SEASON: 5/30-9/15; 14-day lmt. **FACILITIES:** 5 sites (tr –16); well drk wtr, tbls, toil, cga, f. Food/gas (1 mi). **ACTIVITIES:** Picnicking; boating; fishing. **MISC.:** Elev 900 ft; 5 acres; pets.

NAHMA JUNCTION

Flowing Well (Hiawatha NF). 1½ mi E on US 2; 3 mi N on Co Hwy FH13. SEASON: 4/15–11/30; 14-day lmt. FACILITIES: 10 sites (tr –22); well drk wtr, tbls, toil, cga. Food (3 mi). Store/gas (4 mi). ACTIVITIES: Picnicking; fishing. MISC.: Elev 700 ft; 3 acres; pets. On the Sturgeon River.

PAULDING

Bond Falls Park (Upper Peninsula Power Co.) 4 mi E of Paulding off US 45. FACILITIES: Sites; tbls, toil, cga, drk wtr at the concession stand. Obtain camping permit (free from the concession stand). ACTIVITIES: Picnicking; Hiking (well-marked trail leads you to Bond Falls, below Bond Falls, 2 foot bridges permit scenic views of the falls from all angles). Hunting in season. Fishing (brown and rainbow trout fishing in the river north of the falls. Panfish, walleye, large northern pike in the 2,200 acre flowage). MISC: Bait/souvenirs/food at concession stand. All 50,000 acres is open to public for camping. Pets permitted on leash.

Pauling Pond (Ottawa NF). 1-1/2 mi S of Pauling on US 45. SEASON: 5/1–12/1; 14-day lmt. FACILITIES: 4 sites (tr –22), tbls, toil, cga, well drk wtr. Store/gas/ice (2 mi). ACTIVITIES: Picnicking; fishing; boating,l; berry-picking. Swimming (5 mi). MISC: Trout pond. Carry down boat launch. Pets; elev 1500 ft; 2 acres.

Robbins Pond (Ottawa NF). 1/5 mi N of Paulding on US 45; 2-1/2 mi W on Co Hwy 527; 1-3/5 mi S on FS 181. SEASON: 5/1–12/1; 14-day lmt. FACILITIES: 3 sites (tr –22), tbls, toil, cga, well drk wtr. Store/gas/ice/food (4 mi). ACTIVITIES: Picnicking; fishing; berry-picking. MISC: Trout pond; historic site; old lumbering town. Pets; elev 1300 ft; 2 acres.

RANDVILLE

Campsite #8 (Wisc· Mich· Power Co.). 2-3/10 mi S of Randville on Co Rd 607; 7-2/5 mi W on Co Rd to Campground; at Michigamme Falls on Michigamme River. SEASON: All yr (probably not plowed out in winter). FACILITIES: Primitive sites; no drk wtr, tbls, toil, cga. ACTIVITIES:

Picnicking; fishing; hunting in season (whitetail deer, ruffed grouse); ice fishing and cross-country skiing in winter; boating,l. MISC: Pets·

Campsite #9 (Wisc· Mich· Power Co.). 2-3/10 mi S of Randville on Co Rd 607; 5-3/5 mi W on Co Rd; 2-7/10 mi N on Co Rd; 2-3/5 mi E on Co Rd to campground; at Peavy Falls on Michigamme River. SEASON: All yr (probably not plowed out in winter). FACILITIES: Primitive sites; no drk wtr, tbls, toil, cga. ACTIVITIES: Picnicking; fishing; hunting in season (whitetail deer, ruffed grouse); ice fishing and cross-country skiing in winter; boating,l. MISC: Pets.

RAPID RIVER

Haymeadow Creek (Hiawatha NF). 3/10 mi E on US 2; 9-2/5 mi NE on Co Hwy 509. SEASON: 4/15–11/30; 14-day lmt. FACILITIES: 16 sites (tr –22); well drk wtr, tbls, toil, cga. ACTIVITIES: Picnicking; hiking; fishing. Horseback riding (1 mi). MISC.: Elev 800 ft; 8 acres; pets. Trail to Falls on Haymeadow Creek.

SAGOLA

Campsite #10 (Wisc. Mich. Power Co). 7-1/5 mi W of Sagola on Co Rd; 3-3/5 mi S on Co Rd; 1-2/5 mi SE on Co Rd to Campground; on Peavy Falls Pond. SEASON: All yr (probably not plowed out in witner). FACILITIES: Primitive sites; no drk wtr, tbls, toil, cga. ACTIVITIES: Picnicking; fishing; hunting in season (whitetail deer, ruffed grouse); ice fishing and cross-country skiing in winter. MISC: Pets permitted if kept on leash.

Campsite #20 (Wisc. Mich. Power Co). 2-4/5 mi W of Sagola on St Hwy 69; 4-3/10 mi N on Co Rd; 2/5 mi N on Co Rd; 1-3/10 mi W on Co Rd to campground; on Michigamme Reservoir. SEASON: All yr (probably not plowed out in winter). FACILITIES: Primitive sites; no drk wtr, tbls, toil, cga. ACTIVITIES: Picnicking; fishing; hunting in season (whitetail deer, ruffed grouse); ice fishing and cross-country skiing in winter; boating,l. MISC.: Pets.

ST IGNACE

St. Ignace Union 76 Truck Stop. 1/4 mi W of jct I-75 and US 2, on US 2. SEASON: All yr; 1-night lmt. FACILITIES: Spaces for self-contained vehicles, toil, drk wtr, gas.

SAWYER

Sawyer Truck Plaza. I-94, exit 12. SEASON: All yr; 1-night lmt. FACILITIES: Spaces for self-contained vehicles; food, toil, drk wtr, gas, 24-hr, emergency parking, mechanic.

STANDISH

Marathon Truck Stop. Jct of US 23 and St Hwy 13. SEASON: All yr; 1-night lmt. FACILITIES: Spaces for self-contained vehicles; toil, drk wtr, gas, food, mechanic, 24-hr.

TEKONSHA

Tekon Truck Plaza. Jct of St Hwy 60 and I-69, exit 25. SEASON: All yr; 1-night lmt. FACILITIES: Spaces for self-contained vehicles; toil, drk wtr, gas, food, mechanic.

WATERSMEET

* **Ash Campsite** (Ottawa NF). 1/2 mi S of Watersmeet on US 45; 4 mi W on US 2; 5-1/2 mi W on Co Hwy 535; 3/5 mi SE, BY BOAT. SEASON: 5/15-10/1; 14-day lmt. FACILITIES: 3 tent sites, tbls, toil, cga, f, no drk wtr. ACTIVITIES: Picnicking; fishing; boating. MISC: Scenic. NO MOTORS ALLOWED ON LAKE. In Sylvania; on E shore of Clark Lake. Pets.

* **Badger Campsite** (Ottawa NF). 1/2 mi S of Watersmeet on Us 45; 4 mi W on US 2; 5-1/2 mi W on Co Hwy 535; 2-3/5 mi S, BY BOAT. SEASON: 5/15-10/1; 14-day lmt. FACILITIES: 3 tent sites, tbls, toil, cga, f, no drk wtr. ACTIVITIES: Picnicking; fishing; boating. MISC: Elev 1700 ft; 2 acres; scenic. NO MOTORS ALLOWED ON LAKE. In Sylvania; on S shore of Crooked Lake. Pets.

* **Balsam Campsite** (Ottawa NF). 1/2 mi S of Watersmeet on US 45; 4 mi W on US 2; 5-1/2 mi W on Co Hwy 535; 9/10 mi SE, BY BOAT. SEASON: 5/15-10/1; 14-day lmt. FACILITIES: 3 tent sites, tbls, toil, cga, f, no drk wtr. ACTIVITIES: Picnicking; fishing; boating. MISC: Elev 1700 ft; 2 acres; scenic. NO MOTORS ALLOWED ON LAKE. In Sylvania; on E shore of Clark Lake. Pets.

* **Bass Campsite** (Ottawa NF). 1/2 mi S of Watersmeet on US 45; 4 mi W on US 2; 5-1/2 mi W on Co Hwy 535; 4-1/2 mi SW, BY BOAT. SEASON: 5/15-10/1; 14-day lmt. FACILITIES: 3 tent sites; tbls, toil, cga, f, no drk wtr. ACTIVITIES: Picnicking; fishing; boating. MISC: Elev 1700 ft; 2 acres; scenic. NO MOTORS ALLOWED ON LAKE. In Sylvania; on S shore of Whitefish Lake. Pets on leash.

* **Bear Campsite** (Ottawa NF). 1/2 mi S of Watersmeet on US 45; 4 mi W on US 2; 5-1/2 mi W on US 535; 3-9/10 mi S, BY BOAT. SEASON: 5/15-10/1; 14-day lmt. FACILITIES: 3 tent sites, tbls, toil, cga, f, no drk wtr. ACTIVITIES: Picnicking; fishing; boating. MISC: Elev 1700 ft; 2 acres; scenic. NO MOTORS ALLOWED ON LAKE. In Sylvania; S and E via Crooked and Mountain Lakes. Pets.

* **Beaver Campsite** (Ottawa NF). 1/2 mi S of Watersmeet on US 45; 4 mi W on US 2; 5-1/2 mi W on Co Hwy 535; 3-2/5 mi S, BY BOAT. SEASON: 5/15-10/1; 14-day lmt. FACILITIES: 3 tent sites, tbls, toil, cga, f, no drk wtr. ACTIVITIES: Picnicking; fishing; boating. MISC: Elev 1700 ft; 2 acres; scenic. NO MOTORS ALLOWED ON LAKE. In Sylvania; S and E via Crooked and Mountain Lakes. Pets permitted on leash.

* **Birch Campsite** (Ottawa NF). 1/2 mi S of Watersmeet on US 45; 4 mi W on US 2; 5-1/2 mi W on Co Hwy 535; 2-1/2 mi S, BY BOAT. SEASON: 5/15-10/1; 14-day lmt. FACILITIES: 3 tent sites, tbls, toil, cga, f, no drk wtr. ACTIVITIES: Picnicking; fishing; boating. MISC: Elev 1700 ft; 2 acres; scenic. NO MOTORS ALLOWED ON LAKE. In Sylvania; on W side of Clark Lake. Pets on leash.

* **Bobcat Campsite** (Ottawa NF). 1/2 mi S of Watersmeet on US 45; 4 mi W on US 2; 5-1/2 mi W on Co Hwy 535; 1 mi SE, BY BOAT. SEASON: 5/15-10/1; 14-day lmt. FACILITIES: 3 tent sites, tbls, toil, cga, f, no drk wtr. ACTIVITIES: Picnicking; fishing; boating. MISC: Elev 1700 ft; 2 acres; scenic. NO MOTORS ALLOWED ON LAKE. In Sylvania; via Crooked Lake and portage trail to High Lake.

Burned Dam (Ottawa NF). From Watersmeet 6-1/10 mi E on Co 208; 1-1/5 mi N on FS 169. SEASON: 5/15-12/1; 14-day lmt. FACILITIES: 6 sites (tr -22), tbls, toil, cga, f. ACTIVITIES: Picnicking; fishing; berry-picking. Swimming/boating/waterskiing (5 mi). MISC: Elev 1500 ft; 3 acres; historical interest; site of eary log drives. Pets permitted if on leash.

* **Cedar Campsite** (Ottawa NF). 1/2 mi S of Watersmeet on US 45; 4 mi W on US 2; 5-1/2 mi W on Co Hwy 535; 4/5 mi SW, BY BOAT. SEASON: 5/15-10/1; 14-day lmt. FACILITIES: 3 tent sites, tbls, toil, cga, f, no drk wtr. ACTIVITIES: Picnicking; fishing; boating. MISC: Elev 1700 ft; 2 acres; scenic. NO MOTORS ALLOWED ON LAKE. In Sylvania; on W shore of Lake Clark. Pets on leash.

* **Chipmunk Campsite** (Ottawa NF). 1/2 mi S of Watersmeet on US 45; 4 mi W on US 2; 5-1/2 mi W on Co Hwy 535; 2-7/10 mi S, BY BOAT. SEASON: 5/15-10/1; 14-day lmt. FACILITIES: 3 tent sites, tbls, toil, cga, f, no drk wtr. ACTIVITIES: Picnicking; fishing; boating. MISC: Elev 1700 ft; 2 acres; scenic. NO MOTORS ALLOWED ON LAKE. In Sylvania on shore of Crooked Lake. Pets.

* **Deer Campsite** (Ottawa NF). 1/2 mi S of Watersmeet on US 45; 4 mi W on Us 2; 5-1/2 mi W on co Hwy 535; 4-3/5 mi S, BY BOAT. SEASON: 5/15-10/1; 14-day lmt. FACILITIES: 3 tent sites, tbls, toil, cga, f, no drk wtr. ACTIVITIES: Picnicking; fishing; boating. MISC: Elev 1700 ft; 1 acre; scenic. NO MOTORS ALLOWED ON LAKE. In Sylvania; south, east, and north via Crooked and Mountain Lakes and portage to East Bear Lake. Pets.

* **Eagle Campsite** (Ottawa NF). 1/2 mi S of Watersmeet on US 45; 4 mi W on Us 2; 5-1/2 mi W on Co Hwy 535; 3-4/5 mi SE, BY BOAT. SEASON: 5/15-10/1; 14-day lmt. FACILITIES: 3 tent sites, tbls, toil, cga, f, no drk wtr. ACTIVITIES: Picnicking; fishing; boating. MISC: Elev 1700 ft; 2 acres; scenic. NO MOTORS ALLOWED ON LAKE. In Sylvania; via Clark Lake, portage trail and Loon Lake. Pets.

* **Ermine Campsite** (Ottawa (NF). 1/2 mi S of Watersmeet on US 45; 4 mi W on US 2; 5-1/2 mi W on Co Hwy 535; 3-9/10 mi S, BY BOAT. SEASON: 5/15-10/1; 14-day lmt. FACILITIES: 3 tent sites, tbls, toil, cga, f, no drk wtr. ACTIVITIES: Picnicking; fishing; boating. MISC: Elev 1700 ft; 2 acres; scenic. NO MOTORS ALLOWED ON LAKE. In Sylvania; on NW shore of Mountain Lake. Pets.

* **Fisher Campsite** (Ottawa NF). 1/2 mi S of Watersmeet on US 45; 4 mi W on US 2; 5-1/2 mi W on Co Hwy 535; 2-4/5 mi S, BY BOAT. SEASON: 5/15-10/1; 14-day lmt. FACILITIES: 3 tent sites, tbls, toil, cga, f, no drk wtr. ACTIVITIES: Picnicking; fishing; boating. MISC: Elev 1700 ft; 2 acres; scenic. NO MOTORS ALLOWED ON LAKE. In Sylvania; on S shore of Crooked Lake. Pets on leash.

* **Loon Campsite** (Ottawa NF). 1/2 mi S of Watersmeet on US 45; 4 mi W on US 2; 5-1/2 mi W on Co Hwy 535; 3-1/2 mi SE, BY BOAT. SEASON: 5/15-10/1; 14-day lmt. FAC: 3 tent sites; tbls, toil, cga, no drk wtr. ACTIVITIES: Picnicking; fishing; boating. MISC: Elev 1700 ft; 2 acres; scenic. NO MOTORS ALLOWED ON LAKE. In Sylvania, via Clark Lake, portage trail and Loon Lake. Pets.

* **Lynx Campsite** (Ottawa NF). 1/2 mi S of Watersmeet on Us 45; 4 mi W on US 2; 5-1/2 mi W on Co Hwy 535; 3-9/10 mi S, BY BOAT. SEASON: 5/15-10/1; 14-day lmt. FACILITIES: Tbls, toil, cga, f, no drk wtr. ACTIVITIES: Picnicking; fishing; boating. MISC: Elev 1700 ft; 2 acres; scenic. NO MOTORS ALLOWED ON LAKE. In Sylvania on N end of Mountain Lake. Pets.

* **Mallard Campsite** (Ottawa NF). 1/2 mi S of Watersmeet on US 45; 4 mi W on US 2; 5-1/2 mi SE, BY BOAT. SEASON: 5/15-10/1; 14-day lmt. FAC: 2 tent sites; tbls, toil, cga, no drk wtr. ACTIVITIES: Picnicking; fishing; boating. MISC: Elev 1700 ft; 2 acres; scenic. NO MOTORS ALLOWED ON LAKE. In Sylvania; via Clark Lake, portage trail and Loon Lake. Pets.

* **Mink Campsite** (Ottawa NF). 1/2 mi S of Watersmeet on US 45; 4 mi W on US 2; 5-1/2 mi W on Co Hwy 535; 2-4/5 mi S, BY BOAT. SEASON: 5/15-10/1; 14-day lmt. FAC: 3 tent sites; tbls, toil, cga, no drk wtr. ACTIVITIES: Picnicking; fishing; boating. MISC: Elev 1700 ft; 2 acres; scenic. NO MOTORS ALLOWED ON LAKE. In Sylvania; on shore of Crooked River.

* **Osprey Campsite** (Ottawa NF). 1/2 mi S of Watersmeet on US 45; 4 mi W on US 2; 5-1/2 mi W on Co Hwy 535; 3-1/10 mi SE; BY BOAT. SEASON: 5/15-10/1; 14-day lmt. FAC: 3 tent sites; tbls, toil, cga, no drk wtr. ACTIVITIES: Picnicking; fishing; boating. MISC: Elev 1700 ft; 2 acres; scenic. NO MOTORS ALLOWED ON LAKE. In Sylvania; via Clark Lake, portage trail and Loon Lake. Pets.

* **Perch Campsite** (Ottawa NF). 1/2 mi S of Watersmeet on US 45; 4 mi W on US 2; 5-1/2 mi W on Co Hwy 535; 3-1/2 mi SW, BY BOAT. SEASON: 5/15-10/1; 14-day lmt. FAC: 3 tent sites; tbls, toil, cga, no drk wtr. ACTIVITIES: Picnicking; fishing; boating. MISC: Elev 1700 ft; 2 acres; scenic. NO MOTORS ALLOWED ON LAKE. In Sylvania; on north shore of Whitefish Lake. Pets permitted on leash.

Taylor Lake (Ottawa NF). From Watersmeet 1/2 mi S on US 45; 6-1/5 mi E on US 2; 1-3/5 mi N on FS 346. SEASON: 5/15-12/1; 14-day lmt. FACILITIES: 21 sites (tr -22), tbls, toil, cga, f, well drk wtr. ACTIVITIES: Picnicking; fishing; boating, ld. MISC: Elev 1600 ft; 14 acres; lake. 20 mi from Sylvania Recreation Area; good bass and panfish fishing.

MINNESOTA

GENERAL STATE INFORMATION

Miscellaneous

Toll-Free Number for Travel Information:
    1-800-328-1410 [calling from IA, IL, KS,
              MI, MO, NB, ND, SD, WI]
    1-800-652-9747 [calling within MN]
Right Turns on Red: Permitted after full
    stop, unless otherwise posted.
STATE CAPITOL: St. Paul
STATE NICKNAME: Gopher State
STATE MOTTO: "Star of the North"
STATE BIRD: Loon
STATE FLOWER: Moccasin Flower
STATE TREE: Norway Pine

State Parks

The entrance fee is $1.50. The camping fees range from $3.00-4.00 per night. Pets are NOT allowed overnight. Further information: Minnesota Division of Parks and Recreation; Centennial Office Building; St. Paul, MN 55155 [612/296-4776].

Rest Areas

Overnight stops are permitted in Minnesota Rest Areas.

Boise Cascade Corporation

Boise Cascade owns about 2 million acres of timberlands in Minnesota, California, Oregon, Washington and Idaho, and with Boise Southern Company in Louisiana. Hunting (deer, elk, birds); fishing (salmon, trout, whitefish, walleye, northern pike, bass or pan fish, depending on the area); horseback riding; hiking; canoeing; snowmobiling in winter. For information on specific Boise Cascade campgrounds in Minnesota, see "International Falls", "Grand Rapids", and "Jacobson". For additional information and a map: Boise Cascade Corporation; Big Falls, MN 56649.

Minnesota Canoe Routes and Camping

There are 18 state-designated canoe and boating routes in Minnesota. Pocket-size canoe route maps of the rivers are available free of charge, and show free campsites, accesses, rest areas, river miles, hazards, and general information. Free maps and further information: Minnesota Department of Natural Resources; Division of Parks and Recreation; Canoe and Boating Route Program; 196 Centennial Office Building; St. Paul, MN 55155; 612/296-4776.

Boundary Waters Canoe Area (Superior NF)

In this vast area of 1,080,500 acres, there are nearly 2,000 managed campsites available for your use free of charge. Most have been provided with very simple camping facilities, including at least one tent site, a fireplace, and a pit toilet. There is a 14-day limit unless otherwise posted. Travel permits must be obtained (free) before entering the B.W.C.A. These are available from Superior National Forest offices. Travel permits must be in your possession at all times while in the B.W.C.A. Fishing and hunting. Further information and map: Forest Supervisor; Superior NF; Box 338; Duluth, MN 55801; 218/727-6692.

Voyageurs National Park Backcountry Camping

One of the few National Parks with no entrance fee. A trail system is being planned that will include over 100 miles of trails when completed in the early 1980's. The trail system will be designed for both summer and winter use. Access to trailheads will be by boat. Campsites within the park are accessible by boat or boat and trail. No drive-in campsites. Camping should be limited to designated sites. Canoeing; fishing; fishing; hiking; skiing; snowshoeing. Taking pets into the backcountry not recommended. Whenever pets are not in a boat or vehicle they must be leashed. For details on developed campgrounds, see "International Falls" in this chapter. Further information: Superintendent; Voyageurs NP; PO Box 50; International Falls.

MINNESOTA

Isle Royale National Park

Isle Royale NP is a ½-million-acre wilderness island retreat in Lake Superior, just 20 miles off the Minnesota shore of the world's largest fresh water lake.

TRANSPORTATION TO PARK: Public transportation is available by boat. Contact Sivertson Brothers; 366 Lake Avenue South; Duluth, MN 55802 [Grand Portage to Windigo, late June to LD; and Grand Portage to Rock Harbor via Windigo, May–October]. One boat circumnavigates Isle Royale and will discharge and pick up passengers at various points. Private boats over 20 feet in length can go to the island (water is too rough for smaller boats). Sivertson Brothers will transport small runabouts and canoes. Gas for your boat cannot be carried on commercial boats but may be purchased at Rock Harbor and Windigo.

PETS and FIREARMS are prohibited.

WATER: Only safe drinking water is from spigots of Rock Harbor, Daisy Farm, and Windigo campgrounds. Halizone tablets will not kill tapeworms; boil water for at least 5 minutes.

FIRES: Permitted only in designated areas within designated campgrounds. Backpacking stoves in other areas.

SWIMMING: No swimming. Too cold; leeches.

FISHING: License is required in Lake Superior waters but not required for Isle Royale's inland lakes and streams. Fishing equipment available at the Rock Harbor store or Windigo. Guided fishing trips offered at Rock Harbor. Free fishing folder available at ranger stations.

BOATING: Marina at Rock Harbor Lodge (June–LD). Holding-tank pump-out stations at Mott Island and Windigo.

HIKING: More than 160 miles of foot trails.

CAMPING: For specific campsites, see "Grand Portage" in this chapter.

Further information: Superintendent; Isle Royale National Park; 87 North Ripley Street; Houghton, MI 49931.

Upper Mississippi Wildlife and Fish Refuge

There are no specific campgrounds within the refuge. However primitive camping is permitted along the main channel of the Mississippi River. The refuge is located along nearly 300 miles of river channel between Wabasha, Minnesota, and Rock Island, Illinois. Primitive camping is allowed free of charge. The use on refuge lands of motorized vehicles of any type is prohibited except on designated public roads and routes of travel. There is a 14-day limit for camping at any one site or within 300 feet of such site. Further information: Refuge Manager; Upper Miss. Wildlife and Fish Refuge; 122 West 2nd Street; Winona, MN 55987 [507/452-4230].

Chippewa National Forest

Backcountry camping, hiking, and cross-country skiing (in season) are available here. Further information: Forest Supervisor; Chippewa NF; Cass Lake, MN 56633.

INFORMATION SOURCES

Maps

Detailed up-to-date maps of the State of Minnesota and the cities of Minneapolis and St. Paul are available from Forsyth Travel Library (see order form in Appendix B).

State Information

Vacation Information Center; Minnesota Department of Economic Development; Hanover Building; 480 Cedar; St. Paul, MN 55101.
Minnesota Department of Natural Resources; Division of Parks and Recreation; 196 Centennial Office Building; St. Paul, MN 55155.
Minnesota Wildlife Lands; Minnesota Department of Natural Resources; Division of Fish and Wildlife; 390 Centennial Building; St. Paul, MN 55155.

City Information

Greater Minneapolis Chamber of Commerce; 15 South Fifth Street; Minneapolis, MN 55402.
Rochester Chamber of Commerce; 212 First Avenue, SW; Rochester, MN 55901.
St. Paul Area Chamber of Commerce; Suite 300, Osborn Building; St. Paul, MN 55102.

MINNESOTA

Miscellaneous

Grand Portage National Monument; Box 666; Grand Marais, MN 55604.
Voyageurs National Park; PO Box 50; International Falls, MN 56649.
Minnesota BLM [and all states east of the Mississippi River]; Eastern States Office; 7981 Eastern Avenue; Silver Springs, MD 20910.
Minneapolis Area Office; Bureau of Indian Affairs; 831 Second Avenue South; Minneapolis, MN 55402.
Superior NF; Box 338; Duluth, MN 55801 [218/727-6692].
Chippewa NF; Route, Box 25; Cass Lake, MN 56633.
Corps of Engineers, St. Paul District; 1135 USPO and Custom House; St. Paul, MN 55101.
Agassiz NWR; Middle River, MN.
Upper Mississippi River Wildlife and Fish Refuge; 405 Exchange Building; Winona, MN 55987.
Upper Mississippi River Wildlife and Fish Refuge; 122 West 2nd Street; Winona, MN 55987.

FREE CAMPGROUNDS

ASH LAKE

*Namakan Island CG (Boise Cascade Corp; Namakan Lake). Boat access only. 20 mi N of Ash Lake on St Hwy 53; E on Ash River Trail Co Rd; 765 to end of Trail; 10 mi ENE of the end of Ash River Trail. FACILITIES: 6 primitive tent sites, tbls, toil, cga, drk wtr. ACTIVITIES: Snowmobiling in winter; hunting; fishing; berry-picking; rockhounding; swimming; boating; trapping.

ASKOV

D.A.R. (D.A.R. SF). 2 mi NE of Askov on St Hwy 23. SEASON: 5/5-9/9; 24-day lmt. FACILITIES: 6 primitive sites (tr -20), tbls, toil, cga, drk wtr (hand pump). ACTIVITIES: Picnicking. MISC: Pets permitted if kept on leash.

ATKIN

Bergland Park (Municipal Park). 10 mi W of St Hwy 65 on St Hwy 232. SEASON: 5/1-10/30; 7-day lmt. FACILITIES: 10 sites, tbls, toil, cga, f, elec hkup ($). Store/ice/food concession nearby. ACTIVITIES: Picnicking; fishing; boating,l. MISC: Pets permitted if kept on leash.

ATWATER

City Park In Atwater. SEASON: All yr; 1-night lmt. FACILITIES: Spaces for self-contained RVstbls, toil, cga. ACTIVITIES: Picnicking. MISC: Pets.

AUSTIN

Driesner Park (City Park). On the edge of Austin at Jct of St Hwys 116 & US 218 (paved access rds). SEASON: 5/1-10/1; 3-day lmt. FACILITIES: 15 sites, tbls, toil, cga, drk wtr. Store/laundry/food nearby. ACTIVITIES: Picnicking; boating,l; tennis; hiking; playground. Swimming nearby. MISC: Pets permitted if kept on leash.

*BALL CLUB

Gambler's Point Landing Campground (State Forest). 1-1/2 mi S of Ball Club on Co Rd 18 to Bridge; 2 mi BY BOAT on Mississippi. SEASON: 5/1-9/9; 14-day lmt. FACILITIES: 6 sites, tbls, toil, cga, drk wtr (hand pump). ACTIVITIES: Picnicking; fishing. MISC: Pets.

BECIDA

*Pine Point Landing Campground (Miss. Headwaters SF). 3 mi N of Becida on Co Rd 3; 2-1/2 mi N on Stecker Forest Rd. (on Mississippi River). BOAT ACCESS BY PORTAGE. SEASON: 5/5-9/9; 14-day lmt. FACILITIES: 2 sites, tbls, toil, cga, drk wtr (hand pump). ACTIVITIES: Picnicking. MISC: Canoe route. Pets permitted if kept on leash.

BELLE PLAINE

Lawrence Wayside On Us Hwy 169, between Belle Plaine and Jordan. FACILITIES: Primitive campsites, tbls, toil, cga. ACTIVITIES: Picnicking; fishing; cross-country skiing and snowmobiling in winter; hiking; horseback riding. MISC: Pets permitted if kept on leash.

See page 7 for KEY TO ABBREVIATIONS.

BENA

Richard's Townsite (Chippewa NF). 2-4/5 mi NW on US 2; 3/10 mi N on FS 2167; 1 mi NE on FS 2074. (1½ mi N of Big Fish Restaurant.) SEASON: 5/1-12/15; 14-day lmt. FACILITIES: 7 sites (tr -22); tbls, toil, cga, f, well drk wtr. Store/gas/ice/visitor center (4 mi). Food (1 mi). ACTIVITIES: Picnicking; fishing; boating,l; waterskiing; berry-picking. MISC.: Pets; elev 1300 ft; 1 acre.

Six Mile (Chippewa NF). 1-1/2 mi E of Bena on US 2; 3-4/5 mi SE on FS 2127. SEASON: 5/15-9/15; 14-day lmt. FACILITIES: 11 sites (tr -22), tbls, toil, cga, well drk wtr. Store/gas/ice (1 mi). ACTIVITIES: Picnicking; fishing; boating,lr (r, 1 mi); waterskiing; berry-picking. MISC: Pets; elev 1300 ft; 3 acres.

BERTHA

City Park. In Bertha. SEASON: All yr. FACILITIES: Spaces for self-contained RVs. MISC: Pets.

BIG FALLS

Big Fork River Campground (Boise Cascade Corp.). 13-1/2 mi S of Big Falls on St Hwy 6; 1/2 mi SW on gravel rd to river. SEASON: 5/1-11/15; 14-day lmt. FACILITIES: 3 sites, tbls, toil, cga, drk wtr, mechanical boat lift. ACTIVITIES: Picnicking; fishing; hunting; hiking; boating,l. MISC: On marked river float trip route. Pets.

City Park. In Big Falls. SEASON: All yr. FACILITIES: Spaces for self-contained RVs. MISC: Pets permitted if kept on leash.

First River Access. 13-1/2 mi S of Big Falls on St Hwy 6; 1/2 mi SW on logging road (watch for small sign at jct). SEASON: All yr. FACILITIES: 3 sites, tbls, toil, cga. ACTIVITIES: Picnicking; fishing; boating,l. MISC: River. Pets.

Giant Pine Campground (Pine Island SF). 9 mi W of Big Falls on Co Rd 30; 10 mi on Twomey Williams Rd; 3 mi N on Mannila Forest Road (not on lake or river). SEASON: 5/5-9/9; 14-day lmt. FACILITIES: 3 sites, tbls, toil, cga, drk wtr (hand pump). ACTIVITIES: Picnicking. MISC: Pets permitted if kept on leash.

BIWABIK

Whiteface River Campground (Cloquet Valley SF). 17 mi S of Biwabik on Co Rd 4. (On Whiteface Reservoir.) SEASON: 5/5-9/9; 14-day lmt. FACILITIES: 4 sites, tbls, toil, cga, drk wtr (hand pump). ACTIVITIES: Picnicking; fishing. MISC: Pets.

BLUE EARTH

Blue Earth Fairgrounds (City Park). 2 blocks N of Jct of US 169 & 16, on US 169, N edge of town (paved access roads). SEASON: 4/1-11/30; 2-day lmt. FACILITIES: 5 sites, tbls, toil, cga, f, drk wtr, dump, elec/wtr hookup. Store/ice/food/laundry nearby. ACTIVITIES: Picnicking; fishing; softball, horseshoes. Golfing nearby. MISC: River; playground. Pets.

BOVEY

City Park. In Bovey. SEASON: All yr; 1-night lmt. FACILITIES: Spaces for self-contained RVs. MISC: Pets.

BOY RIVER

City Park. In Boy River. SEASON: All yr; 1-night lmt. FACILITIES: Spaces for self-contained RVs. MISC: Pets permitted if kept on leash.

BOYD

City Park. In Boyd. SEASON: All yr; 1-night lmt. FACILITIES: Spaces for self-contained RVs. MISC: Pets permitted if kept on leash.

BRAINERD

City Park. In Brainerd. SEASON: All yr; 1-night lmt. FACILITIES: Spaces for self-contained RVs. MISC: Pets.

BROWNS VALLEY

Traverse County Public Park (Co. Park). 6 mi N of Browns Valley on St Hwy 27. SEASON: All yr. FACILITIES: 25 sites, tbls, toil, cga, f, drk wtr, elec hookup. ACTIVITIES: Picnicking; fishing; swimming; boating,l; playground; snowskiing nearby; snowmobile trails. MISC: Pets.

Village Park (City Park). 2 blocks S of Main Street in Browns Valley. SEASON: All yr. FACILITIES: 15 sites (tr -22), tbls, toil, cga, drk wtr. Store/food/laundry/gas/ice/bottled gas nearby. ACTIVITIES: Picnicking; playground. MISC: Pets permitted if kept on leash.

BUHL

City Park • In Buhl. SEASON: All yr; 1-night lmt. FACILITIES: Spaces for self-contained RVs. MISC: Pets permitted if kept on leash.

BUYCK

Lake Jeanette (Superior NF). 4 mi N of Buyck on Co Hwy 24; 12 mi E on Co Hwy 116. SEASON: 5/15-10/5; 14-day lmt. FACILITIES: 9 sites (tr -16), tbls, toil, cga, well drk wtr. ACTIVITIES: Picnicking; fishing; boating,1; hiking; berry-picking. MISC.: Nature trails; lake; elev 1500 ft; 9 acres; pets. Crane Lake (21 mi).

CASS LAKE

Cass Lake Campground At E Edge of Cass Lake on US 2. SEASON: All yr; 1-night lmt. FACILITIES: Spaces for self-contained RVs; tbls, toil, cga. ACTIVITIES: Picnicking. MISC: Pets.

CLEARWATER

Clearwater Truck Plaza I-94, Exit 178 (St Hwy 24). SEASON: All yr; 1-night lmt. FACILITIES: Spaces for self-contained RVs, tbls, toil, cga, gas, drk wtr, food, LP bottles, 24-hr mechanic.

Erv's Truck Stop I-94, Exit 183. SEASON: All yr; 1-night lmt. FACILITIES: Spaces for self-contained RVs, toil, drk wtr, gas, food 24-hr mechanic.

COOK

* **Hinsdale Island Campground.** BOAT ACCESS ONLY. 2 mi N of Cook on Co Rd 24; 6 mi E on Co Rd 78; 2 mi E on Co Rd to public access. (In Vermilion Lake). SEASON: 5/5-9/9; 14-day lmt. FACILITIES: 11 sites, tbls, toil, cga, drk wtr (hand pump). ACTIVITIES: Picnicking; fishing; boating. MISC: Pets permitted if kept on leash.

COTTONWOOD

City Park. In Cottonwood. SEASON: All yr; 1-night lmt. FACILITIES: Spaces for self-contained RVs. MISC: Pets permitted if kept on leash.

CROOKSTON

City Park. In Crookston. SEASON: All yr; 1-night lmt. FACILITIES: Spaces for self-contained RVs, toil, shower, elec hkup. MISC: Pets.

CROSSLAKE

City Park. In Crosslake. SEASON: All yr; 1-night lmt. FACILITIES: Spaces for self-contained RVs. MISC: Pets permitted if kept on leash.

DEER RIVER

Fur Farm Overflow (Chippewa NF). 1 mi NW of Deer River on US 2; 15-1/10 mi NW on St Hwy 46; 1-4/5 mi NW on Co Hwy 148. SEASON: 5/15-9/15; 14-day lmt. FACILITIES: 60 sites (tr -22), toil, no drk wtr. Showers/ice/store/gas (4 mi). Visitor center/dump (3 mi). ACTIVITIES: Hiking; boating,1 (r, 1 mi); horseback riding/rental/swimming/fishing/waterskiing (1 mi). MISC: Scenic. Pets; elev 1300 ft; 2 acres.

Lake Winnibigoshish Rec. Area (COE: St. Paul District). 12 mi NW of Deer River on St Hwy 46; 2 mi W on Co Hwy 9. SEASON: 5/15-11/30; 14-day lmt. FACILITIES: 20 sites (tr -32), tbls, toil, cga, dump, drk wtr. ACTIVITIES: Picnicking; fishing; playground. MISC: Pets

West Seeleye Overflow (Chippewa NF). 1 mi NW of Deer River on St Hwy 2; 19-3/10 mi NW on St Hwy 46; 3 mi SW on Co Hwy 33. SEASON: 5/15-9/15; 14-day lmt. FACILITIES: 60 sites (tr -22), tbls, toil, cga, no drk wtr. Store/gas/ice (1 mi). Visitor center/dump (5 mi). ACTIVITIES: Picnicking; hiking. Swimming/fishing/waterskiing (1 mi). MISC.: Nature trails (2 mi). Pets; elev 1300 ft; 3 acres.

DULUTH

* **Dr. Barney's Landing Campground** (Cloquet Valley SF). 17 mi N of Duluth on Co Rd 4; 4 mi E on Cloquet River BOAT ACCESS ONLY. SEASON: 5/5-9/9; 14-day lmt. FACILITIES: 4 sites, tbls, toil, cga, drk wtr (hand pump). ACTIVITIES: Picnicking; fishing; canoeing (canoe route). MISC: Pets permitted if kept on leash.

* **Highway 70 Campground** (St. Croix Natl Scenic Riverway). S of Duluth on I-35 to jct with St Hwy 70, near Pine City. 10 mi E on St Hwy 70. The CG is on your right after you cross the river on the Wisc. side of the river. Accessible by FOOT, or by traveling downriver BY CANOE. Ovenight parking of vehicles at the CG is not allowed. SEASON: 4/1-10/31; 14-day lmt. FACILITIES: 15 sites, tbls, toil, cga; drk wtr avail across the river at a Ranger Station, a distance of about 1/4 mi. ACTIVITIES: Picnicking. MISC: Pets.

EFFIE

Bass Lake Campground (Boise Cascade Corp.). 12 mi E of Effie on St Hwy 1; 2 mi S on logging rd. SEASON: 5/1-11/15; 14-day lmt. FACILITIES: 26 sites, tbls, toil, cga, drk wtr, dump. ACTIVITIES: Picnicking; hunting; hiking; boating; waterskiing. MISC: Pets permitted if kept on leash.

ELY

Fenske Lake (Superior NF). 2 mi E of Ely on St Hwy 169; 2-2/5 mi N on Co Hwy 88; 8-3/10 mi N on Co Hwy 116. SEASON: 5/15-11/15; 14-day lmt. FACILITIES: 16 sites (tr -16), tbls, toil, cga. no drk wtr. ACTIVITIES: Picnicking; fishing; swimming; hiking; boating,rld; waterskiing. MISC.: Nature trails. Pets.

ERSKINE

City Park. In Erskine. SEASON: All yr; 1-night lmt. FACILITIES: Spaces for self-contained RVs. MISC: Pets permitted if kept on leash.

FARIBAULT

Sakatah Singing Hills 48-mile, multiple-use trail which follows an abandoned RR right-of-way from Farbault to Mankato. SEASON: All yr; 1-night lmt. FACILITIES: 12 sites. ACTIVITIES: Picnicking; hiking; snowmobiling; biking.' MISC: Pets.

FEDERAL DAM

City Park. In Federal Dam. SEASON: All yr; 1-night lmt. FACILITIES: Spaces for self-contained RVs. MISC: Pets permitted if kept on leash.

FRANKLIN

Franklin Campsite Park (City Park). In Franklin, off St Hwy 19. SEASON: 5/1-10/1; 14-day lmt. FACILITIES: 10 sites (tr -30), tbls, toil, cga, dump, f, drk wtr, elec & wtr hookup. ACTIVITIES: Picnicking; boating,l; swimming nearby. MISC: Pets permitted if kept on leash. Playground.

GONVICK

Gonvick Park (City Park). 3 blocks N of St Hwy 92 in N Gonvick. SEASON: All yr. FACILITIES: 10 sites (tr -18), tbls, toil, cga, drk wtr. Store/food/bottled gas/laundry nearby. ACTIVITIES: Picnicking; golfing nearby. MISC: Pets permitted if kept on leash.

GRAND MARAIS

.* **Backcountry Campground** (Grand Portage NM). The Grand Portage Trail winds through the woods (8-1/2 mi) from the reconstructed North West Company Stockade on Lake Superior to the site of Fort Charlotte on the Pigeon River. The backcountry CG is located at Fort Charlotte.

No entrance fee to Natl Mon; free backcountry permit required for camping. Trail users may park at the intersection of the Trail and Old US 61. This hwy is not maintained and should be used with caution. Watch for potholes, bumps, and washouts. Trailbikes or other vehicles are not permitted on the Trail.

Pit toil, fire grates are provided but use of backpacking stoves is recommended. No water (and Pigeon River water is not potable).

Camping along the Trail is NOT permitted.

Take insect repellent.

INFO/map: Supt.; Grand Portage NM; Box 666; Grand Marais, MN 55604; 218/387-2788.

Cascade River (Superior NF). 1/2 mi N of Grand Marais on Co Hwy 12; 4 mi W on Co Hwy 7; 9 mi NW on FS 158. SEASON: 6/1-9/15; 14-day lmt. FACILITIES: 3 sites, tbls, toil, cga, piped drk wtr, f. Store/gas/food (4 mi). ACTIVITIES: Picnicking; boating,lr; fishing. MISC: Elev 1800 ft; 1 acre; river; scenic. Eagle Mtn; scenic. 2-1/2 mi by road, 3 mi by trail, 11-1/2 mi to BWCA entry on Buile Lake. Pets permitted if kept on leash.

GRAND PORTAGE

***ISLE ROYALE NP.** Public transportation is available by boat. Contact Sivertson Brothers; 366 Lake Avenue South; Duluth, MN 55802 (Grand Portage to Windigo, late June to LD; and Grand Portage to Rock Harbor via Windigo, May-October). One boat circumnavigates Isle Royale and will discharge and pick up passengers at various points. Private boats over 20 feet in length can go to the island (water is too rough for smaller boats). Sivertson Brothers will transport small runabouts and canoes. Gas for your boat cannot be carried on commercial boats but may be purchased at Rock Harbor and Windigo.

CAMPING: All campsites are reached by foot or by boat. Most of the 31

CGs have fireplaces, tables, and tent sites. All campers must obtain a CAMPING PERMIT. In CGs, use designated fireplaces. Outside of CGs use backpack stoves.

SEASON: 6/15–LD; 15–day lmt. (which applies to a single stay or to combined separate periods, on boats, CG docks, or on land).

Bring insect repellent.

Camping must be at designated campsites except by special permit.

No pets or firearms.

Addl info/map: Supt; Isle Royal NP; 87 N. Ripley St.; Houghton, Mich. 49931.

10x16–foot shelters, enclosed on 3 sides, with a wooden floor, and a screen front with screen door (accompanied by tables, fireplaces, refuse containers, and privy), are scattered throughout the Park for use up to 14 days; no reservations required.

Inland Camps Area (Isle Royale NP). Central portion of island.

Chickenbone Lake. Trail access only. SEASON: 6/15–LD; 2–day lmt. FACILITIES: 5 sites; group campsites available. No drk wtr. ACTIVITIES: Hiking; fishing. MISC: No pets.

East Chickenbone Lake. Trail access only. SEASON: 6/15–LD; 2–day lmt. FACILITIES: 6 sites; group campsites available, no drk wtr. ACTIVITIES: Hiking; fishing. MISC: No pets allowed.

Feltman Lake. Trail access only. SEASON: 6/15–LD; 3–day lmt. FACILITIES: 3 sites; group campsites available, no drk wtr. ACTIVITIES: Hiking; fishing. MISC: No pets allowed.

Hatchet Lake. Trail access only. SEASON: 6/15–LD; 2–day lmt. FACILITIES: 4 sites; group campsites available, no drk wtr. ACTIVITIES: Hiking; fishing. MISC: No pets allowed.

Island Mine. Trail access only. SEASON: 6/15–LD; 2–day lmt. ACTIVITIES: Hiking; fishing. FACILITIES: 6 sites; group campsites available; no drk wtr. MISC: No pets allowed.

Lake Richie. Trail access only. SEASON: 6/15–LD; 2–day lmt. FACILITIES: 3 sites; group campsites available; no drk wtr. ACTIVITIES: Hiking; fishing. MISC: No pets allowed.

North Lake Desor. Trail access only. SEASON: 6/15–LD; 2–day lmt. FACILITIES: 4 sites; group campsites available; no drk wtr. ACTIVITIES: Hiking; fishing. MISC: No pets.

South Lake Desor. Trail access only. SEASON: 6/15–LD; 2–day lmt. FACILITIES: 4 sites; group campsites available; no drk wtr. ACTIVITIES: Hiking; fishing. MISC: No pets.

North Shore Area (Isle Royale NP). North shore of island.

Belle Isle. Boat access only. SEASON: 6/15–LD; 7–day lmt. FACILITIES: 12 sites; no drk wtr. ACTIVITIES: Boating,d; fishing. MISC: No pets allowed.

Birch Island. Boat access only. SEASON: 6/15–LD; 3–day lmt. FACILITIES: 1 site; no drk wtr. ACTIVITIES: Boating,d; fishing. MISC: No pets allowed.

Duncan Bay. Boat access only. SEASON: 6/15–LD; 7–day lmt. FACILITIES: 3 sites; no drk wtr. ACTIVITIES: Boating,d; fishing. MISC: No pets allowed.

Duncan Narrows. Boat access only. SEASON: 6/15–LD; 7–day lmt. FACILITIES: 2 sites; no drk wtr. ACTIVITIES: Boating,d; fishing. MISC: No pets allowed.

Huginnin Cove. Boat or trail access only. SEASON: 6/15–LD; 2–day lmt. FACILITIES: 5 sites; no drk wtr. ACTIVITIES: Hiking; fishing. MISC: No pets allowed.

Lane Cove. Boat or trail access. SEASON: 6/15–LD; 2–day lmt. FACILITIES: 3 sites; no drk wtr. ACTIVITIES: Hiking; fishing. MISC: No pets allowed.

Little Todd Harbor. Boat or trail access; group campsites available; no drk wtr. ACTIVITIES: Hiking; fishing; boating,d. MISC: No pets allowed.

McCargoe Cove. Boat or trail access. SEASON: 6/15–LD; 3–day lmt. FACILITIES: 8 sites; group campsites available; no drk wtr. ACTIVITIES: Hiking; fishing; boating,d. MISC: No pets allowed.

Todd Harbor. Boat or trail access. SEASON: 6/15–LD; 3–day lmt. FACILITIES: 7 sites; group campsites available; no drk wtr. ACTIVITIES: Hiking; fishing; boating,d. MISC: No pets allowed.

Rock Harbor Area. (Isle Royale NP), NE end of island.

Caribou Island. Boat access only. SEASON: 6/15–LD; 3–day lmt. FACILITIES: 4 sites; no drk wtr. ACTIVITIES: Fishing; boating,rd. MISC: No pets allowed.

See page 7 for KEY TO ABBREVIATIONS.

Daisy Farm. Boat or trail access only. SEASON: 6/15–LD; 3–day lmt. FACILITIES: 23 sites; group campsites available; treated drk wtr. ACTIVITIES: Hiking; fishing; boating,rd. MISC: No pets allowed.

Merritt Lane. Boat access only. SEASON: 6/15–LD; 3–day lmt. FACILITIES: 2 sites; no drk wtr. ACTIVITIES: Fishing; boating,rd. MISC: No pets allowed.

Moskey Basin. Boat or trail access. SEASON: 6/15–LD; 3–day lmt. FACILITIES: 10 sites; group campsites available; no drk wtr. ACTIVITIES: Hiking; fishing; boating,rd. MISC: No pets allowed.

Rock Harbor. Boat or trail access. SEASON: 6/15–LD; 1–day lmt. FACILITIES: 20 sites; group campsites available; treated drk wtr. ACTIVITIES: Hiking; fishing; boating,rd. MISC: No pets allowed.

Three Mile. Boat or trail access. SEASON: 6/15–LD; 1–day lmt. FACILITIES: 12 sites; group campsites available; no drk wtr. ACTIVITIES: Hiking; fishing; boating,rd. MISC: No pets allowed.

Tookers Island. Boat access only SEASON: 6/15–LD; 3–day lmt. FACILITIES: 2 sites; no drk wtr. ACTIVITIES: Fishing; boating,rd. MISC: No pets allowed.

South Shore Area. (Isle Royale NP). South shore of island.

Camp Siskiwit. Boat or trail access. SEASON: 6/15–LD; 3–day lmt. FACILITIES: 4 sites; group campsites available; no drk wtr. ACTIVITIES: Hiking; fishing; boating,d. MISC: No pets allowed.

Chippewa Harbor. Boat or trail access. SEASON: 6/15–LD; 7–day lmt. FACILITIES: 4 sites; group campsites available; no drk wtr. ACTIVITIES: Hiking; fishing; boating,d. MISC: No pets allowed.

Hay Bay. Boat access only. SEASON: 6/15–LD; 3–day lmt. FACILITIES: 2 sites; no drk wtr. ACTIVITIES: Boating,d; fishing. MISC: No pets allowed.

Malone Bay. Boat or trail access SEASON: 6/15–LD; 7–day lmt. FACILITIES: 8 sites; group campsites available; no drk wtr. ACTIVITIES: Hiking; fishing; boating,d. MISC: No pets allowed.

Windigo Area. (Isle Royale NP). SW end of island.

Beaver Island. Boat access only. SEASON: 6/15–LD; 3–day lmt. FACILI-

TIES: 3 sites; no drk wtr. ACTIVITIES: Fishing; boating,rd. MISC: No pets allowed.

Grace Island. Boat access only. SEASON: 6/15–LD; 3–day lmt. FACILITIES: 2 sites; no drk wtr. ACTIVITIES: Boating,rd; fishing. MISC: No pets allowed.

Washington Creek. Boat or trail access. SEASON: 6/15–LD; 2–day lmt. FACILITIES: 16 sites; group campsites available; treated drk wtr. ACTIVITIES: Hiking; fishing; boating,rd. MISC: No pets allowed.

GRAND RAPIDS

Pokegama Rec. Area (COE; St. Paul District). 2 mi W of Grand Rapids on US 2; S on access rd. SEASON: 5/15–11/30; 5–day lmt. FACILITIES: 15 sites (tr –32); tbls, toil, cga, f, dump, drk wtr. Store/food/ice/ bait/fishing tackle/outboard motors for rent nearby. ACTIVITIES: Hiking; fishing; picnicking; boating,ld; waterskiing. MISC: Pets.

Prig Hole Lake. 14 mi N of Grand Rapids on St Hwy 38. SEASON: All yr. FACILITIES: Spaces for self–contained RVs. MISC: Pets permitted.

Raddison & Blind Pete Lakes (Blandin Paper Co.). 35 mi N by Co Rd 7 & Co Rd 52 & then to various identified woods roads. SEASON: All yr. FACILITIES: Spaces for self–contained RVs. ACTIVITIES: Hunting; berry–picking; snowmobiling. MISC: Rustic camping and unimproved lake access. Pets permitted if kept on a leash.

Shingle Mill Management Unit (Blandin Paper Co.). Blandin's largest forest management unit containing 44,000 acres is located in the SW corner of Itasca County. The main trails into the unit area, the Shingle Mill Rd running S off Co Rd 449 & the Smith Creek Trail located 9-1/2 mi S of Grand Rapids on Hwy 169. Both access rds are marked by signs. SEASON: All yr. FACILITIES: Spaces for self–contained RVs. ACTIVITIES: Berry–picking; hiking; snowmobiling. MISC: 70 mi of snowmobile trails. Pets permitted if kept on a leash.

GRANITE FALLS

City Park. In Granite Falls. SEASON: All yr. FACILITIES: Spaces for self–contained RVs. MISC: Pets permitted.

GUTHRIE

* **LeGrande Landing Campground** (State Forest). 2 mi E of Guthrie on Co Rd

16; 2 mi S on Steamboat River. BOAT ACCESS. SEASON: 5/5-9/9; 14-day lmt FACILITIES: 2 sites, tbls, toil, cga, drk wtr (hand pump). ACTIVITIES: Picnicking; fishing. MISC: Pets.

HALLOCK

City Park. Off Route 75 in center of town. SEASON: All year. FACILI-TIES: Spaces for self-contained RVs. MISC: Pets permitted if kept on a leash.

HALSTAD

City Park. In Halstad. SEASON: All yr. FACILITIES: Spaces for self-contained RVs. MISC: Pets permitted if kept on a leash.

HENDRICKS

Lake Hendricks Park (City Park). 8 mi W of US 75 on St Hwy 19; 3 mi N on St Hwy 271; on W edge of Hendricks. SEASON: 4/15-11/1. FACIL-ITIES: 30 sites, tbls, toil, cga, drk wtr, elec hookup, food concession. ACTIVITIES: Fishing; swimming; boating,ld; picnicking. Golfing nearby. MISC: Playground. Pets permitted.

HERMAN

Herman Municipal Campground. From jct St Hwys 27 & 9, 2 blks W, 2 blks N in Herman. SEASON: 5/15-9/1. FACILITIES: 8 sites, tbls, toil, cga, drk wtr, elec/wtr hkups. Store/food/laundry/bottled gas nearby. ACTIVI-TIES: Picnicking. MISC: Pets.

HIBBING

City Park. In Hibbing. SEASON: All yr. FACILITIES: Spaces for self-contained RVs. MISC: Pets permitted if kept on a leash.

HILL CITY

City Park. In Hill City. SEASON: All yr. FACILITIES: Spaces for self-contained RVs. MISC: Pets permitted if kept on a leash.

HINCKLEY

*Howell Bridge Cag (St. Croix Natl Scenic Riverway). E of I-35 in Hinckley on St Hwy 48 into Wisc. where the road number changes to St Hwy 77; stay on St Hwy 77 for 19 mi; 2 mi S (right) on Burian Road until you reach the Namekagon River. CG accessible by foot or by canoe.

SEASON: 4/1-10/31. FACILITIES: 8 sites, tbls, toil, cga, treated well drk wtr. ACTIVITIES: Picnicking. MISC: Pets permitted if kept on a leash.

HOWARD LAKE

City Park. In Howard Lake. SEASON: All yr. FACILITIES: Spaces for self-contained RVs. MISC: Pets permitted.

HOYT LAKES

Hoyt Lakes City Park. In Hoyt Lakes SEASON: All yr. FACILITIES: Spaces for self-contained RVs. MISC: Pets.

INTERNATIONAL FALLS

*Agnes Lake. (Boise Cascade Corp; Kabetogama Peninsula, Interior). BOAT ACCESS ONLY. 12 mi E of International Falls on St Hwy 11 to end of hwy; portage trail (3/4 mi) begins on most easterly end of Kab. (Lost Bay). SEASON: All yr. FACILITIES: Primitive tent sites, tbls, toil, cga, drk wtr. ACTIVITIES: Picnicking; snowmobiling in winter; hunting; fishing; berry-picking; rockhounding; swimming; boating; trapping. MISC: Pets permitted if kept on a leash.

Clark's Park (City Park). 5 mi E of International Falls on St Hwy 11 E and Co Rd 20 (across from Langdon's Greenhouse). SEASON: All yr. FACILITIES: Spaces for self-contained RVs, toil. MISC: Pets.

*Cranberry Creek Picnic Area (Boise Cascade Corp; Rainy Lake). BOAT ACCESS ONLY. 12 mi E of International Falls on St Hwy 11; 1 mi up Cranberry Creek SE from Cranberry Bay of Rainy Lake, approx. 7 mi E of end of St Hwy 11. SEASON: All yr. FACILITIES: Primitive tent sites; tbls, toil, cga, drk wtr. ACTIVITIES: Picnicking; snowmobiling in winter; hunting; fishing; berry-picking; rockhounding; swimming; boating; trapping.

*Cranberry Lake (Boise Cascade Corp; Kabetogama Peninsula, Interior) BOAT ACCESS ONLY. 12 mi E of International Falls on St Hwy 11 to end of hwy; by water from S shore of Rainy Lake SE out of Cranberry Bay up to Cranberry Creek. SEASON: All yr. FACILITIES: Primitive tent sites; tbls, toil, cga, drk wtr. ACTIVITIES: Picnicking; snowmobiling in winter; hunting; fishing; berry-picking; rockhounding; swimming; boating; trapping. MISC: Pets.

See page 7 for KEY TO ABBREVIATIONS.

*East Oslo (Boise Cascade Corp; Kabetogama Peninsula, Interior). BOAT ACCESS ONLY. 12 mi E of International Falls on St Hwy 11 to end of hwy; 20 mi E on Rainy Lake to Browns Bay; portage 1/2 mi S. SEASON: All yr. FACILITIES: Primitive tent sites; tbls, toil, cga, drk wtr. ACTIVITIES: Picnicking; snowmobiling in winter; hunting; fishing; berrypicking; rockhounding; swimming; boating; trapping. MISC: Pets.

*Jorgen's Lake (Boise Cascade Corp; Kabetogama Peninsula, Interior). BOAT ACCESS ONLY. 12 mi E of International Falls on St Hwy 11 to end of hwy; 3/4 mi portage E of Little Shoepack or 1 mi portage N from Lost Bay of Kabetogama. SEASON: All yr. FACILITIES: Primitive tent sites, tbls, toil, cga, drk wtr. ACTIVITIES: Picnicking; snowmobiling in winter; hunting; fishing; berry-picking; rockhounding; swimming; boating; trapping. MISC: Pets permitted if kept on a leash.

*Kawawia Island Campground (Boise Cascade Corp; Rainy Lake). BOAT ACCESS ONLY. 12 mi E of International Falls on St Hwy 11; 17 mi E of end of St Hwy 11. SEASON: All yr. FACILITIES: 6 sites, tbls, toil, cga, drk wtr. ACTIVITIES: Picnicking; snowmobiling in winter; hunting; fishing; berry-picking; rockhounding; swimming; boating; trapping. MISC: Pets permitted if kept on a leash.

*King Williams Narrows (Voyageurs NP). BOAT ACCESS; boat in from Crane Lake. (N end of Crane Lake). SEASON: 5/15-9/15; 14-day lmt. FACILITIES: 5 tent sites, tbls, toil, cga, no drk wtr. ACTIVITIES: Picnicking; fishing; swimming; boating,ld; snowskiing nearby. MISC: Pets permitted if kept on a leash.

* Lief Lake (Boise Cascade Corp; Kabetogama Peninsula, Interior). BOAT ACCESS ONLY. 12 mi E of International Falls on St Hwy 11 to end of hwy; portage trail (700 ft) begins on N shore of Lost Bay 3/4 mi from NE end of Kab. from Gappa's Landing ENE 10 mi by water or from the end of Ash River Trail, 8 mi by water NW then NE. SEASON: All yr. FACILITIES: Primitive tent sites, tbls, toil, cga, drk wtr. ACTIVITIES: Picnicking; snowmobiling in winter; hunting fishing; berry-picking; rockhounding; swimming; boating; trapping. MISC: Pets permitted if kept on a leash.

*Little Shoepack (Boise Cascade Corp; Kabetogama Peninsula, Interior).

BOAT ACCESS ONLY. 12 mi E of International Falls on St Hwy 11 to end of hwy; W of Shoepack then S to 1/4 mi portage SE; 1/2 mi on Little Shoepack to South Shore campsite. SEASON: All yr. FACILITIES: Primitive tent sites, tbls, toil, cga, drk wtr. ACTIVITIES: Picnicking; snowmobiling in winter; hunting; fishing; berrypicking; rockhounding; swimming; boating; trapping. MISC: Pets.

* Locator Lake (Boise Cascade Corp; Kabetogama Peninsula-Interior). BOAT ACCESS ONLY. 12 mi E of International Falls on St Hwy 11; by water from S shore of Rainy Lake SE out of Cranberry Bay up to Cranberry Creek. SEASON: All yr. FACILITIES: Primitive tent sites, tbls, toil, cga, drk wtr. ACTIVITIES: Picnicking; snowmobiling in winter; hunting; fishing; berry-picking; rockhounding; swimming; boating; trapping. MISC.: Pets.

*Loiten Lake (Boise Cascade Corp; Kabetogama Peninsula, Interior). BOAT ACCESS ONLY. 12 mi E of International Falls on St Hwy 11 to end of hwy; by water from S shore of Rainy Lake SE out of Cranberry Bay up to Cranberry Creek. SEASON: All yr. FACILITIES: Primitive tent sites tbls, toil, cga, drk wtr. ACTIVITIES: Picnicking; snowmobiling in winter; hunting; fishing; berry-picking; rockhounding; swimming; boating; trapping. MISC: Pets.

* Lost Bay Campground (Boise Cascade Corp; Rainy Lake). BOAT ACCESS ONLY. 12 mi E of International Falls on St Hwy 11; 9 mi E of end of St Hwy 11. SEASON: All yr. FACILITIES: 6 tent sites, tbls, toil, cga, drk wtr. ACTIVITIES: Picnicking; snowmobiling in winter; hunting; fishing; berry-picking rockhounding; swimming; boating, trapping. MISC: Pets.

* McDevitt Lake (Boise Cascade Corp; Kabetogama Peninsula, Interior). BOAT ACCESS ONLY. 12 mi E of International Falls on St Hwy 11 to end of hwy; 21 mi E of end of hwy; S of Anderson Bay of Rainy Lake. SEASON: All yr. FACILITIES: Primitive tent sites, tbls, toil, cga, drk wtr. ACTIVITIES: Picnicking; snowmobiling in winter; hunting; fishing; berrypicking; rockhounding; swimming; boating; trapping. MISC: Pets.

*Mukooda Lake (Voyageurs NP). BOAT ACCESS; Boat in from Crane Lake. SEASON: 5/15-9/15; 14-day lmt. FACILITIES: 5 tent sites, tbls, toil,

See page 7 for KEY TO ABBREVIATIONS.

cga, no drk wtr. ACTIVITIES: Picnicking. MISC: Pets.

* **Peary Lake** (Boise Cascade Corp; Kabetogama Peninsula, Interior). BOAT ACCESS ONLY. 12 mi E of International Falls on St Hwy 11 to end of hwy; 22 mi E of Rainy Lake to portage; 3/8 mi S to E Bay of Peary. SEASON: All yr. FACILITIES: Primitive tent sites, tbls, toil, cga, drk wtr. ACTIVITIES: Picnicking; snowmobiling in Winter; hunting; fishing; berry-picking; rockhounding; swimming; boating; trapping. MISC. Pets.

* **Quarter Line Lake** (Boise Cascade Corp; Kabetogama Peninsula, Interior). BOAT ACCESS ONLY. 12 mi E of International Falls on St Hwy 11 to end of hwy; portage trail (1/2 mi) begins on most northerly water of Lost Bay (Kab). SEASON: All yr. FACILITIES: Primitive tent sites, tbls, toil, cga, drk wtr. ACTIVITIES: Picnicking; snowmobiling in winter; hunting; fishing; berry-picking; rockhounding; swimming; boating; trapping. MISC: Pets.

* **Rainy River Public Campground** (Boise Cascade Corp). Approx. 14 mi W of International Falls on St Hwy 11 W (7 mi W of Pelland Jct . and 4 mi E of Loman). SEASON: All yr. FACILITIES: Sites, barbeque pits, tbls, toil. ACTIVITIES: Picnicking. MISC: Boise Experimental Forest - Trail 4 mi long on Co Rd 1, S of entrance to Rainy River Camp. MISC: Pets.

* **Ryan Lake** (Boise Cascade Corp; Kabetogama Peninsula, Interior). BOAT ACCESS ONLY. 12 mi E of International Fall on St Hwy 11 to end of hwy; 23 mi E of end of St Hwy 11; 3/4 mi S of Virgin Island CG's SW tip by portage. FACILITIES: Primitive tent sites, tbls, toil, cga, drk wtr. ACTIVITIES: Picnicking; snowmobiling in winter; hunting; fishing; berry-picking; rockhounding; swimming; boating; trapping. MISC: Pets .

* **Saginaw Bay Campground** (Boise Cascade Corp; Rainy Lake). BOAT ACCESS ONLY. 12 mi E of International Falls on St Hwy 11; 12 mi E of end of St Hwy 11. SEASON: All yr. FACILITIES: 6 tent sites, tbls, toil, cga, drk wtr. ACTIVITIES: Picnicking; snowmobiling in winter; hunting; fishing; berry-picking; rockhounding; swimming; boating; trapping. MISC: Pets .

* **Voyageurs NP** (Voyageurs NP). BOAT ACCESS ONLY. Boat in from Crane Lake, Ash River, Kabetogama or Island View. SEASON: 5/15-9/15; 14-day lmt. FACILITIES: 125 dispersed campsites; no drk wtr; tbls, toil, cga. ACTIVITIES: Picnicking. MISC: Pets permitted if kept on a leash.

* **War Club Lake** (Boise Cascade Corp; Kabetogama Peninsula, Interior). BOAT ACCESS ONLY. 12 mi E of International Falls on St Hwy 11 to end of hwy; by water from S shore of Rainy Lake SE out of Cranberry Bay up to Cranberry Creek. SEASON: All yr. FACILITIES: Primitive tent sites; tbls, toil, cga, drk wtr. ACTIVITIES: Picnicking; snowmobiling in winter; hunting; fishing; berry-picking; rockhounding; swimming; boating; trapping. MISC: Pets.

* **Weir Lake** (Boise Cascade Corp; Kabetogama Peninsula, Interior). BOAT ACCESS ONLY. 12 mi E of International Falls on St Hwy 11 to end of hwy; portage trail (1/2 mi) begins S shore of W end of Mica Bay of Namakan Lake. SEASON: All yr. FACILITIES: Primitive tent sites, tbls, toil, cga, drk wtr. ACTIVITIES: Picnicking; snowmobiling in winter; hunting; fishing; berry-picking; rockhounding; swimming; boating; trapping. MISC: Pets .

* **Shoepack Canoe Route** (Boise Cascade Corp; Kabetogama Peninsula, Interior). BOAT ACCESS ONLY. 12 mi E of International Falls on St Hwy 11 to end of hwy; 20 mi E on Rainy Lake to Shoepack Creek; SW to Shoepack Lake. SEASON: All yr. FACILITIES: Primitive tent sites, tbls, toil, cga, drk wtr. ACTIVITIES: Picnicking; snowmobiling in winter; hunting; fishing; berry-picking; rockhounding; swimming; boating; trapping. MISC: Pets.

* **Virgin Island Campground** (Boise Cascade Corp; Rainy Lake). BOAT ACCESS ONLY. 12 mi E of International Fall on St Hwy 11; 23 mi E of end of St Hwy 11 (6-1/4 mi NW of Kettle Falls Hotel). SEASON: All yr. FACILITIES: 6 primitive tent sites, tbls, toil, cga, drk wtr. ACTIVITIES: Picnicking; snowmobiling in winter; hunting; fishing; berry-picking; rockhounding; swimming; boating; trapping. MISC: Pets.

* **West Oslo** (Boise Cascade Corp; Kabetogama Peninsula, Interior). BOAT ACCESS ONLY. 12 mi E of International Falls on St Hwy 11 to end of hwy; 20 mi E on Rainy Lake to Browns Bay; Portage 1/2 mi S; 1/2 mi SSW. SEASON: All yr. FACILITIES: Primitive tent sites, tbls, toil, cga, drk wtr. ACTIVITIES: Picnicking; snowmobiling in winter; hunting;

fishing; berry-picking; rockhounding; swimming; boating; trapping. MISC: Pets

ISABELLA

Divide Lake (Superior NF). 7/10 mi NW of Isabella on St Hwy 1; 5 mi E on FS 172. SEASON: 6/1-9/10; 14-day lmt. FACILITIES: 3 sites (no tr), no drk wtr, tbls, toil, cga. ACTIVITIES: Picnicking; fishing; boating; berry-picking. MISC: Boat launch (1 mi). Store/gas/ice/food (5 mi). Pets; elev 1700 ft; 3 acres.

JACOBSON

Ball Bluff Park (Blandin Paper Co.). On Hwy 65, 6 mi S of Jacobson. SEASON: All yr; 1-night lmt. FACILITIES: Self-contained units only. ACTIVITIES: Picnicking. MISC: Area is surrounded by approx. 900 acres of Blandin Paper Co. spruce plantations. Primarily a picnic rest stop, but many mobile campers use it as an overnite stopping point. Pets permitted if kept on a leash.

JORDAN

Lawrence Wayside. On US Hwy 169, between Jordan and Belle Plaine. SEASON: All yr. FACILITIES: Primitive campsites; tbls, toil, cga. ACTIVITIES: Picnicking; fishing; crosscountry skiing and snowmobiling in winter; hiking; horseback riding. MISC: Pets permitted if kept on a leash.

LAKE GEORGE

Gulch Lakes Rec. Area (Paul Bunyan SF). 2-1/2 mi S of Lake George on Co Hwy 4; 3 to 9 mi E on forest rds. SEASON: 5/5-9/9; 14-day lmt. FACILITIES: 8 primitive sites (tr -20), tbls, toil, cga, drk wtr (hand pump). ACTIVITIES: Picnicking; fishing; swimming; boating,l; hiking. MISC: Portages. Comprised of 6 individual units on different lakes. Pets.

LANCASTER

Lancaster Roadside Park N of Lancaster on US 59. SEASON: 5/1-9/30. FACILITIES: 12 sites, tbls, toil, cga, drk wtr, elec hkup. Store/ice/food/bottled gas nearby. ACTIVITIES: Picnicking; playground. Golfing nearby MISC: Pets permitted if kept on a leash.

LAUREL

Rainy River (Boise Cascade). 1 mi W of bridge crossing Big Fork River, W of town on St Hwy 11. SEASON: All

yr. FACILITIES: 6 sites, tbls, toil, cga. ACTIVITIES: Picnicking; hunting; boating; hiking. MISC: In Boise Cascade Experimental Forest. Self-guided car tour from campground. Pets permitted if kept on a leash.

LeSUEUR

* Minnesota Valley Trail. 72-mi, multiple-use trail from Fort Snelling State Park to LeSueur. SEASON: All yr. FACILITIES: 9 campsites. Boat access. ACTIVITIES: 20 mi hiking and snowmobiling; 12 mi ski touring; 10 mi horse trails. MISC: Pets.

MARCELL

Caribou Lake (Chippewa NF). 6 mi SE on St Hwy 38. SEASON: 5/15-11/15; 14-day lmt. FACILITIES: 3 sites (no tr); tbls, toil, cga; well drk wtr. Food/gas (1 mi). Dump (3 mi). ACTIVITIES: Picnicking; swimming; fishing. Boating,l (rental, 3 mi); waterskiing; berry-picking. MISC.: Pets; elev 1400 ft; 7 acres.

Rice River (Chippewa NF). 1/2 mi NE of Marcell on St Hwy 38; 5-1/2 mi E on Co Hwy 45; 1-1/2 mi N on FS 2181; 1 mi E on FS 3758. SEASON: 5/30-10/30; 14-day lmt. FACILITIES: 3 sites (no trailsers), toil, cga, f, no drk wtr. ACTIVITIES: Boating,l nearby. MISC: Pets.

MARSHALL

Redwood River 1 mi SW of Marshall on St Hwy 23. SEASON: All yr. FACILITIES: Sites, tbls, toil, cga, facilities for handicapped. ACTIVITIES: Picnicking. MISC: Pets permitted.

MENAHGA

City Park. In Menahga. SEASON: All yr. FACILITIES: Self-contained sites. MISC: Pets permitted if kept on a leash.

MERRIFIELD

City Park. In Merrifield. SEASON: All yr. FACILITIES: Self-contained sites. MISC: Pets permitted if kept on a leash.

MILACA

City Park. In Milaca. SEASON: All yr. FACILITIES: Spaces for self-contained sites. MISC: Pets permitted if kept on a leash.

MINNESOTA

MINNEAPOLIS–ST. PAUL

* **Highway 70 Campground.** N of Minneapolis–St. Paul on I-35 until you come to St Hwy 70 near Pine City. 10 mi E on St Hwy 70. The campground is on your right after you cross the river on the Wisc. side of the river. Accessible by FOOT, or by traveling downriver by CANOE. Overnight parking of the campground is not allowed. SEASON: 4/1-10/31; 14-day lmt. FACILITIES: 15 sites, tbls, toil, cga, drk wtr available across the river at a Ranger Station, a distance of about 1/4 mi. ACTIVITIES: Picnicking. MISC: Pets.

MONTICELLO

Monticello River Park (City Park). W of bridge on St Hwy 25; 1 blk N of business district in Monticello. SEASON: 5/15-10/1; 1-day lmt. FACILITIES: 5 sites, flush toil, tbls, cga. Food/store/laundry/ice/bottled gas nearby. ACTIVITIES: Picnicking; fishing; golf nearby. MISC: Pets.

MORA

Knife Lake. 7 mi N of Mora on St Hwy 65. SEASON: All yr. FACILITIES: Sites for self-contained RVs. MISC: Pets permitted if kept on a leash.

NEW BRIGHTON

* **Minnesota–Wisconsin Boundary Trail.** 220-mi, multiple-use trail from New Brighton to Taylors Falls to St Croix State Park to Jay Cooke State Park. 60 mi of trail between St. Croix State park and Nemadji State Forest is developed for hiking and snowmobiling; 30 mi for horseback riding. 8 sites for tent camping; 15 picnic sites.

NEWFOLDEN

City Park. In Newfolden. SEASON: All yr. FACILITIES: Spaces for self-contained RVs. MISC: Pets permitted if kept on a leash.

ORR

City Park. In Orr. SEASON: All yr. FACILITIES: Spaces for self-contained RVs. MISC: Pets permitted if kept on a leash.

ORTONVILLE

City Campground (City Park). 1/2 mi from downtown Ortonville at the foot of Big Stone Lake and the headwaters of the Mn. River. SEASON: All yr. FACILITIES: Primitive sites, toil, drk wtr. ACTIVITIES: A neatly-kept lakeside park and playground; fishing; swimming; golfing (1-1/2 mi). MISC: Pets permitted if kept on a leash.

PALISADE

City Park. In Palisade. SEASON: All yr. FACILITIES: Spaces for self-contained RVs. MISC: Pets.

PARK RAPIDS

* **Arrow Point Campground** (White Earth SF). 17 mi N of Park Rapids on St Hwy 71; 19 mi W on St Hwy 113; 5 mi N on Height of Land Forest Road; walk 1/2 mi E (on Big Rock Lake). ACCESS BY BOAT. SEASON: 5/5-9/9; 14-day lmt. FACILITIES: 6 sites, tbls, toil, cga, drk wtr (hand pump). ACTIVITIES: Picnicking. MISC: Pets permitted if kept on a leash.

PEQUST LAKES

City Park. In Pequst Lakes. SEASON: All yr. FACILITIES: Spaces for self-contained RVs. MISC: Pets permitted if kept on a leash.

PIPESTONE

City Park. In Pipestone. SEASON: All yr. FACILITIES: Spaces for self-contained RVs. MISC: Pets permitted if kept on a leash.

RAINY RIVER

Rainy River Campground & Nature Trail (Boise Cascade Corp). Hwy 11, 8 mi W of Hwy 71 at jct with Co Rd 1. SEASON: All yr. FACILITIES: Spaces for self-contained RVs, tbls, toil, cga, drk wtr. ACTIVITIES: Picnicking; snowmobiling. MISC: Pets.

RED LAKE FALLS

Riverside Park (Municipal Park). 1 blk W of St Hwy 32 on Bottineau Ave in Red Lake Falls. SEASON: 5/1-10/30 FACILITIES: 20 sites, tbls, toil, cga, f, elec hkup. Dump/bottle gas/ice/food/laundry/store nearby. ACTIVITIES: Picnicking; swimming; golfing.

RED WING

Sturgeon Lake (COE). 18 mi W of Red Wing on US 61 to Lock & Dam 3 sign; N on township road. SEASON: 5/15-11/30; 14-day lmt. FACILITIES: 10 sites, tbls, toil, cga, drk wtr. Bottled gas nearby. ACTIVITIES: Picnicking; swimming; boating,l. Golfing nearby. MISC: Pets.

MINNESOTA

RICHVILLE

City Park. In Richville. SEASON: All yr. FACILITIES: Spaces for self-contained RVs. MISC: Pets permitted if kept on a leash.

ROCHESTER

High Forest Truck Stop. 3 mi N of I-90 on US 63. SEASON: All yr. FACILITIES: Spaces for self-contained RVs, toil, LP gas, food, drk wtr, gas, 24-hr mechanic.

ROSEAU

Roadside Park. 2 mi W of Roseau on St Hwy 11. SEASON: All yr; 1-night lmt. FACILITIES: Spaces for self-contained RVs. MISC: Pets permitted if kept on a leash.

SEBEKA

City Park. In Sebeka. SEASON: All yr; 1-night lmt. FACILITIES: Spaces for self-contained RVs. MISC: Pets.

SHELVIN

Shelvin Village Park (City Park). On N side of US 2 in Shelvin. SEASON: 5/1-9/30. FACILITIES: 15 sites (tr -20), tbls, toil, cga, drk wtr. Store/laundry nearby. ACTIVITIES: Picnicking. MISC: Playground. Pets.

SLEEPY EYE

Sportmen's Park (Municipal Park). 1/2 mi N of Jct US 14 on Sleepy Eye Lake. SEASON: All yr. FACILITIES: 30 sites, tbls, toil, cga, f, elec hookup. Bottled gas/ice/laundry/food/store nearby. ACTIVITIES: Picnicking; fishing; swimming; boating,rl; playground; snowmobile trails. MISC: Pets permitted if kept on a leash.

SQUAW LAKE

Middle Pigeon (Chippewa NF). 3-2/5 mi S of Squaw Lake on St Hwy 46; 3 mi W on FS 2196. SEASON: 5/15-9/15; 14-day lmt. FACILITIES: 3 sites, tbls, toil, cga, well drk wtr. ACTIVITIES: Picnicking; fishing; boating,l; berry-picking; waterskiing. MISC: Scenic; lake. Pets.

STEWARTVILLE

High Forest. 6 mi SW of Stewartville on Eastbound lane of I-90. SEASON: All yr. 1-night lmt. FACILITIES: Spaces for self-contained RVs. MISC: Pets permitted if kept on a leash.

STRANDQUIST

City Park. In Strandquist. SEASON: All yr. 1-night lmt. FACILITIES: Spaces for self-contained RVs. MISC: Pets permitted if kept on a leash.

TOFTE

Baker Lake (Superior NF). 1/2 mi NE of Tofte on St Hwy 61; 17 mi N on Co Hwy 2; 5 mi NE on Fs 165; 1/2 mi N on FS 1272. SEASON: 5/10-10/31; 14-day lmt. FACILITIES: 4 sites (tr -22), tbls, toil, cga, well drk wtr. ACTIVITIES: Picnicking; fishing . Boating,l; rental (3 mi). Berry-picking. MISC: Elev 1700 ft; 21 acres. Entrance to Boundary Waters Canoe Area. Pets.

Kawishiwi Lake (Superior NF). 1/2 mi NE of Tofte on St Hwy 61; 1/2 mi N on St Hwy 2; 10 mi W on Co Hwy 3; 4 mi NW on FS 354. SEASON: 5/10-10/31. FACILITIES: 5 sites (tr -16), tbls, toil, cga, drk wtr. ACTIVITIES: Picnicking; fishing; swimming; boating,l (no motors); berry-picking. MISC.: Elev 1700 ft; 2 acres; pets. Entrance point to Boundary Waters Canoe Area.

Poplar River (Superior NF). 1/2 mi NE of Tofte on st Hwy 61; 11 mi N on Co Hwy 2; 6 mi E on FS 164. SEASON: 5/10-10/31; 14-day lmt. FACILITIES: 4 sites (tr -16), tbls, toil, cga, no drk wtr. ACTIVITIES: Picnicking; fishing. MISC: Elev 1600 ft; 3 acres; Poplar River. Pets permitted if kept on a leash.

Temperance River (Superior NF). 1/2 mi NE of Tofte on St Hwy 61; 11 mi N on Co Hwy 2. SEASON: 5/10-10/31; 14-day lmt. FACILITIES: 9 sites (tr -22), tbls, toil, cga, drk wtr, f. ACTIVITIES: Picnicking; fishing. MISC: Elev 1500 ft; 6 acres. Pets.

TWO HARBORS

City Park. In Two Harbors. SEASON: All yr. FACILITIES: Spaces for self-contained RVs. MISC: Pets. permitted if kept on a leash.

Roadside Park. SW of Two Harbors on St Hwy 61. SEASON: All yr; 1-night lmt. FACILITIES: Spaces for self-contained RVs. MISC: Pets.

Rocky Shores Campground (Finland SF). 40 mi N of Two Harbors on Co Rd 2. SEASON: 5/5-9/9; 14-day lmt. FACILITIES: 4 sites, tbls, toil, cga; drk wtr (hand pump). ACTIVITIES: Picnicking; fishing; boating,l. MISC: Pets permitted if kept on a leash.

WAHKON

Nille Laco Lake Campground St Hwy 27 at Nille Laco Lake. SEASON: All yr; 1-night lmt. FACILITIES: Spaces for self-contained RVs. MISC: Pets.

WALKER

Shingobee Group Camp (Chippewa NF). 5 mi Sw of Walker on St Hwy 34; 1/2 mi NE on FS 2110. SEASON: 3/15-12/1; 14-day lmt. FACILITIES: 1 campsite limited to 75 campers, maximum (no trailers). Tbls, toil, cga, well drk wtr. Store/gas/ice/laundry/food (4 mi). ACTIVITIES: Picnicking. Fishing; swimming; boating,rl. Waterskiing (3 mi). Hiking (1 mi). MISC: Nature trails (1 mi). Pets; elev 1300 ft; 5 acres. Reservations required.

WARBA

Roadside Area. 2-1/2 mi W of Warba on St Hwy 2. SEASON: All yr; 1-night lmt. FACILITIES: Spaces for self-contained RVs. MISC: Pets.

WARREN

City Park. In Warren. SEASON: All yr; 1-night lmt. FACILITIES: Spaces for self-contained RVs. MISC: Pets permitted if kept on a leash.

WARROAD

Bemis Hill Campground (Beltrami Island SF). 12 mi S of Warroad on Co Rd 5 to ranger station; 7 mi W on gravel road. SEASON: 5/5-9/9; 14-day lmt. FACILITIES: 4 primitive sites (tr -20), tbls, toil, cga, drk wtr (hand pump). ACTIVITIES: Picnicking; snowmobiling; hiking; toboggan slide; snowskiing. MISC: Pets permitted if kept on a leash.

City Park. In Warroad. SEASON: All yr; 1-night lmt. FACILITIES: Spaces for self-contained RVs. MISC: Pets.

WILLIAMS

Blueberry Hill Campground (Beltrami Island SF). 4 mi W of Williams on St Hwy 11. SEASON: 5/5-9/9; 14-day lmt. FACILITIES: 8 primitive sites (tr -20), tbls, toil, cga, drk wtr (hand pump). ACTIVITIES: Picnicking. MISC: Pets.

WINONA

John A. Latsch State Wayside. 14 mi NW of Winona. SEASON: All yr. FACILITIES: 8 primitive sites, tbls, toil, cga. ACTIVITIES: Picnicking; hiking; fishing. MISC: 2 mi of foot trails; limestone bluffs and panoramic view of Mississippi River. Pets.

WORTHINGTON

City Park. On St Hwy 16, in Worthington. SEASON: All yr; 1-night lmt. FACILITIES: Spaces for self-contained RVs. MISC: Pets.

Olson Park (City Park). In Worthington; W end of Lake Okabena (paved access roads). SEASON: 5/1-10/31; 1-day lmt. FACILITIES: 65 sites (tr -26), tbls, toil, cga, drk wtr, elec hookup. Dump/bottled gas/laundry/food concession/store nearby. ACTIVITIES: Picnicking; fishing; boating,l; playground. Golfing nearby. MISC: Pets permitted if kept on a leash.

WAUBUN

Tulaky Lake. 15 mi E of Waubun on St Hwy 113. SEASON: All yr; 1-night lmt. FACILITIES: Spaces for self-contained RVs. MISC: Pets permitted if kept on a leash.

WEST OSLO

* Cruiser Lake. (Boise Cascade Corp; Kabetogama Peninsula, Interior). Boat access only. 1 mi S of West Oslo; 1/2 mi W by water. SEASON: All yr. FACILITIES: Primitive tent sites, tbls, toil, cga, drk wtr. ACTIVITIES: Picnicking; snowmobiling in winter; hunting; fishing; berry-picking; rockhounding; swimming; boating; trapping. MISC: Pets.

READ THIS!

If any inaccuracies in this directory are discovered, or you know of any additional FREE campgrounds, please contact: VMPl; Box 1289; Clearwater, FL 33517.

INFORMATION ON HOW TO PURCHASE ADDITIONAL COPIES OF THIS BOOK AS WELL AS QUANTITY DISCOUNT INFORMATION IS ALSO AVAILABLE AT THIS ADDRESS.

See page 7 for KEY TO ABBREVIATIONS.

MISSISSIPPI

GENERAL STATE INFORMATION

Miscellaneous

Right Turns on Red: Permitted after full
  stop, unless otherwise posted.
STATE CAPITOL: Jackson
STATE NICKNAME: Magnolia State
STATE MOTTO: "By Valor and Arms"
STATE BIRD: Mockingbird
STATE FLOWER: Magnolia Blossom
STATE TREE: Magnolia Tree

State Parks

Overnight camping fees range from $3.75-4.50. Pets are permitted if kept on a leash.
Further information: Mississippi Park Commission; 717(T) Robert E. Lee Building;
Jackson, MS 39201. No entrance fee. Senior citizen discount available.

Rest Areas

Overnight stops are permitted in Mississippi Rest Areas.

Tennessee Valley Authority

TVA designated campgrounds are no longer free. However, unimproved TVA lands may
be used for informal camping. No fees or permits are required. These areas are
shown on recreation maps of individual TVA lakes. For free map, contact: TVA; Knoxville, TN 37902.

Upper Mississippi River Wildlife and Fish Refuge

Primitive camping is permitted, free of charge, on the refuge islands and beaches.
14-day limit. Further information/map: Refuge Manager; Upper Mississippi River Wildlife and Fish Refuge; PO Box 226; Winona, MN 55987.

Black Creek Float Trip (DeSoto NF)

The longest float trip in this area is down Black Creek, from the landing at Big Creek
to Old Alexander Bridge, a distance of 42 miles. There are several developed campsites (for details on some of them see "Brooklyn" in this chapter), and more are
planned for the near future. Drinking water is generally not available at landings.
Fishing: bass, bream, catfish. Further information/map: District Ranger; Route 1,
Box 62; McHenry, MS 39561.

Delta National Forest Primitive Camping

One of the largest remaining blocks of bottomland hardwoods in the Mississippi Delta.
CAMPING: 90 primitive free campsites are scattered along hard-surfaced roads throughout the Forest. HUNTING: Squirrel, duck, deer, raccoon; 1700-acre greentree reservoir
offers waterfowl hunting. ACTIVITIES: Fishing, bird-watching, frog hunting, crawfish-
ing, picnicking, hiking. Further information: Forest Supervisor; Delta NF; Box 1291;
Jackson, MS 39205.

INFORMATION SOURCES

Maps

Detailed, up-to-date maps are available for the **State of Mississippi** and the cities
of **Jackson** and **Clinton** from **Forsyth Travel Library** (see order form in Appendix B).

State Information

Travel and Tourism Department; **Mississippi Agricultural and Industrial Board**; PO Box
22825; Jackson, MS 39205.
Mississippi Park Commission; 717(T) Robert E. Lee Building; Jackson, MS 39201.
Game and Fish Commission; Department of Conservation; PO Box 451; Jackson, MS 39205.
Natchez Pilgrimage Headquarters; PO Box 347; Natchez, MS 39120.

273

MISSISSIPPI

National Forests

Bienville NF; 350 Milner Building; Box 1291; Jackson, MS 39205.
Delta NF; 350 Milner Building; Box 1291; Jackson, MS 39205.
DeSoto NF; 350 Milner Building; Box 1291; Jackson, MS 39205.
Holly Springs NF; 350 Milner Building; Box 1291; Jackson, MS 39205.
Homochitto NF; 350 Milner Building; Box 1291; Jackson, MS 39205.
Tombigbee NF; 350 Milner Building; Box 1291; Jackson, MS 39205.

Miscellaneous

Natchez-Adams County Chamber of Commerce; PO Box 725; Natchez, MS 39120.
Natchez Trace Parkway; RR #1, NT-143; Tupelo, MS 38801.
Gulf Islands National Seashore; 4000 Hanley Road; Ocean Springs, MS 39564.
Corps of Engineers, Vicksburg District; PO Box 60; Vicksburg, MS 39180.
Corps of Engineers; Okatibbee Lake [Mobile, AL, District]; PO Box 98; Collinsville, MS 39325.
Refuge Manager; NWR; Route 1; Brooksville, MS 39739.
Refuge Manager; Upper Mississippi Wildlife and Fish Refuge; PO Box 226; Winona, MN 55987. [Free campgrounds in MS.]

FREE CAMPGROUNDS

ARKABUTLA

Outlet Channel (COE; Arkabutla Lake) 4-1/2 mi N of Arkabutla on paved road; 1/2 mi W. SEASON: All yr; 14-day lmt. FACILITIES: 47 sites, tbls, flush toil, cga, f, drk wtr. ACTIVITIES: Picnicking; fishing. MISC: Pets.

BATESVILLE

Pat's Bluff (COE; Sardis Lake). 11 mi E of Batesville on St Hwy 6; 3/4 mi N on St Hwy 315; 7 mi NE. SEASON: All yr; 14-day lmt. FACILITIES: 10 sites, tbls, toil, cga, f, drk wtr ACTIVITIES: Picnicking; fishing; swimming; boating, l. MISC: Pets.

Tedford's. Jct of 1-55 & 1-6, at Batesville. FACILITIES: All yr; 1-night lmt. FACILITIES: Spaces for self-contained vehicles. MISC: Pets.

BROOKLYN

Ash Lake (DeSoto NF). 2-3/1 mi SE on St Hwy 308. SEASON: All yr; 14-day lmt. FACILITIES: 4 sites, tbls, toil, cga, piped drk wtr. Store/gas/ice/laundry/food (2 mi). ACTIVITIES: Picnicking; fishing; hiking; hunting MISC: Elev 200 ft; 5 acres. Just N of Ashe Nursery; S side of Ash Lake. Pets. Horseback riding (1 mi).

Cypress Creek (DeSoto NF). 10-1/5 mi E of Brooklyn on Co Hwy 301; 1/5 mi E on St Hwy 29; 3-3/5 mi SE on FS 305; 1-2/5 mi S on 305B. SEASON: All yr; 14-day lmt. FACILITIES: 7 sites (tr -22), tbls, toil, cga, piped drk wtr. Store/gas/food concession (5 mi). ACTIVITIES: Picnicking; fish-

ing; boating, ld; horseback riding (1 mi); canoeing. MISC: Located on the Black Creek Float Trip. Pets. Elev 200 ft; 3 acres.

Janice (DeSoto NF). 10-1/5 mi E of Brooklyn on Co Hwy 301; approx. 2-1/2 mi S on St Hwy 29 (on E side of road). Located on the Black Creek Float Trip. SEASON: All yr; 14-day lmt. FACILITIES: Sites, tbls, toil, cga, drk wtr. ACTIVITIES: Picnicking; fishing; boating; horseback riding; hiking; canoeing. MISC: On stream. Pets permitted if on leash.

Moody's Landing (DeSoto NF). Approx. 5-2/5 mi E of Brooklyn on Co Hwy 301 (on S side of rd). Located on the Black Creek Float Trip. SEASON: All yr; 14-day lmt. FACILITIES: Sites; tbls, toil, cga, drk wtr. ACTIVITIES: Picnicking; fishing; boating; horseback riding; hiking; canoeing. MISC.: On stream; nature trails; pets.

COFFEEVILLE

Skuna-Turkey Creek (COE; Grenada Lake). 4-1/5 mi SE of Coffeeville on St Hwy 330; 2-1/10 mi S on paved road; 1-1/2 mi W; 2-4/5 mi S; 1-1/2 mi W on gravel road. SEASON: All yr; 14-day lmt. FACILITIES: 16 sites, tbls, toil, cga, drk wtr, f. ACTIVITIES: Picnicking; fishing; boating, lr MISC: Pets on leash.

COLDWATER

South Abutment (COE; Arkabutla Lake). 9-1/2 mi W of Coldwater on paved rd; 4 mi N on paved rd. SEASON: 9/4-5/13, FREE; ($4 rest of yr); 14-day lmt. FACILITIES: 41 sites, tbls, toil, cga, f, drk wtr. Store/ice nearby. ACTIVITIES: Picnicking; fishing; swimming; hunting. MISC; Pets on leash.

COMO

Teckville (COE ; Sardis Lake). 16 mi E of Como on St Hwy 310; 3 mi SE on gravel road. SEASON: All yr; 14-day lmt. FACILITIES: 12 sites, tbls, toil, cga, f, drk wtr. ACTIVITIES: Picnicking; fishing; swimming; boating,lr. MISC: Pets on leash.

FOREST

Schckaloe Trail Base Camp 2 (NF). 5½ mi W of Forest on US 80; 5 mi N on FS 513 SEASON: All yr; 14-day lmt. FACILITIES: 3 sites, tbls, toil, cga, f, piped drk wtr. Store/gas/ice (3 mi). ACTIVITIES: Picnicking; hiking; horseback riding. MISC: Located on National Recreation Trail (horse). Pets; elev 500 ft; 2 acres,

GAUTIER

Ford's Truck Stop. 2 mi E of St Hwy 57 on US 90. SEASON: All yr; 1-night lmt. FACILITIES: Spaces for self-contained vehicles, food, drk wtr, toil, 24-hr.

GRENADA

Grenada Landing (COE; Grenada Lake). 2-1/10 mi NE of Grenada on St Hwy 8; 1-1/2 mi NE on paved rd, (follow signs). SEASON: All yr; 14-day lmt. FACILITIES: 45 sites, tbls, flush toil, cga, f, food concession. Store/ice nearby. ACTIVITIES: Picnicking; fishing; swimming; boating,l. MISC: Pets on leash.

Gum's Crossing (COE; Grenada Lake). 12 mi E of Grenada on St Hwy 8; 11-1/2 mi N. SEASON: All yr; 14-day lmt. FACILITIES: 10 sites, tbls, toil, cga, f, drk wtr. ACTIVITIES: Picnicking; fishing; boating,l; store nearby. MISC: Pets on leash.

GULFPORT

Big Biloxi (NF). 14 mi N of Gulfport on US 49; 1/2 mi W on Co Hwy 416. SEASON: 3/1-11/30; 14-day lmt. FACILITIES: 10 sites (tr -22), tbls, toil, cga, drk wtr. Store/gas/ice (2 mi). ACTIVITIES: Picnicking; fishing. MISC.: Elev 100 ft; 10 acres; river; pets.

HATTIESBURG

Seago-Sullivan-Kilrain Truck Stop. I-59, exit 12 (US 11 South). SEASON:

All yr; 1-night lmt. FACILITIES: Spaces for self-contained vehicles, food, drk wtr, toil, mechanic, food, ^4-hr.

HERNANDO

Pleasant Hill (COE ; Arkabutla Lake). 5 mi W of Hernando on St Hwy 304; 5 mi S on Fogg Rd. SEASON: All yr; 14-day lmt. FACILITIES: 11 sites, tbls, toil, cga, drk wtr. ACTIVITIES: Picnicking; fishing; swimming; boating,l. MISC.: Pets.

Welcome Station. 1 mi S of Hernando on I-55 Milepost 279. SEASON: All yr; 1-night lmt. FACILITIES: Spaces for self-contained vehicles, tbls, toil, cga, drk wtr, phone. ACTIVITIES: Picnicking. MISC: Pets.

HOLLY BLUFF

Barge Lake (Delta NF). Approx. 1 mi S and then 3-1/4 mi W of Holly Bluff on St Hwy 16 to its jct with FS 703; 2 mi W on FS 703; 3 mi N on FS 715 to campground. SEASON: All yr; 14-day lmt. FACILITIES: Site tbls, toil, cga, drk wtr. ACTIVITIES: Picnicking; fishing; boating. MISC: On lake. Pets on leash.

Blue Lake (Delta NF). Approx.1 mi S and then 3-1/4 mi W of Holly Bluff on St Hwy 16 to its jct with FS 703; 2 mi W on FS 703; 1 mi N on FS 715 to campground. SEASON: All yr; 14-day lmt. FACILITIES: Sites, tbls, toil, cga, no drk wtr (available 2 mi N at Barge Lake Campground). ACTIVITIES: Picnicking; fishing; boating. MISC: On lake. Pets.

INDIANOLA

Weber's Truck Stop. US 49 and 82, in Indianola. SEASON: All yr; 1-night lmt. FACILITIES: Spaces for self-contained vehicles, food, drk wtr, toil, mechanic, 24-hr.

JACKSON

I-20 and 49 Truck Plaza. I-20, exit 19: S on St Hwy 49. SEASON: All yr; 1-night lmt. FACILITIES: Spaces for self-contained vehicles, food, drk wtr, toil, gas, mechanic, 24-hr.

LEMON

Shongelo (Bienville NF). Approx. 5 mi S of Lemon on St Hwy 35; SE on access rd. SEASON: All yr; 14-day lmt. FACILITIES: 4 sites, tbls, toil, cga, drk wtr. ACTIVITIES: Picnicking; swimming; fishing; hiking. MISC: Nature trails; fish for bass and bream. A beautiful 5-acre lake. Pets on leash.

LUCEDALE

Oakwood Truck Center. Jct St Hwy 26 and 63. SEASON: All yr; 1-night lmt. FACILITIES: Spaces for self-contained vehicles, food, drk wtr, toil, gas, 24-hr.

MATHISTON

Jeff Busby Campground (Natchez Trace Parkway). 10 mi SW of Mathiston on Parkway (2 mi S of St Hwy 9). SEASON: All yr; 14-day lmt. FACILITIES: 18 sites, tbls, toil, cga, drk wtr. Store nearby. ACTIVITIES: Picnicking. MISC: Little Mountain, on this site, is 603 ft above sea level, and its summit is the highest point on the parkway in MS. Pets,

MCCOMB

Fernwood Truck Stop. I-55, exit 5. SEASON: All yr; 1-night lmt. FACILITIES: Spaces for self-contained vehicles, food, drk wtr, toil, gas, 24-hr.

MCHENRY

* Airey Lake (DeSoto NF). SHORT TRAIL ACCESS. Approx. 4 mi E of Jct of US 49 and Co Rd 401 to jct of Co Rd 401 and FS 36 (St Hwy 67) on Co Rd 401; approx. 1 mi S on FS 36 Airey Tower Road (across the road from the Lookout Tower), on the E side of the road. SEASON: All yr; 14-day lmt. FACILITIES: 4 tent sites, tbls, toil, cga, drk wtr. ACTIVITIES: Picnicking; bass and bream fising; hiking; hunting (deer, squirrel, turkey). MISC: 5-acre lake. 1 mi, Airey Fire Tower. Airey Tower Road serves as a pickup route for those who hike only the 1st 5-mile segment of the Tuxachanie Trail. The tower is manned during the fire season, Oct-June. The Tuxachanie Trail entrance is on St Hwy 49. The trail is 18 miles (SE) long and ends at the old German POW camp. Approx. hiking time from US 49 to Airey Camp 2-1/2 hours from Airey Camp to POW camp, 3 hours.

Additional information/map: District Ranger, Route 1, Box 62, McHenry, MS 39561.

* P.O.W. Camp (DeSoto NF). SHORT TRAIL ACCESS. Approx. 4 mi E of Jct of US 49 and Co Rd 401 to Jct of Co Rd 401 and FS 46 (St Hwy 67 ; Airey

Tower Road) on Co Rd 401; approx. 3 mi S on FS 36 to Jct with FS 402; approx. 3-1/2 mi E on FS 402 to campground (on N side of road).

An open grassy camping area in the shade of longleaf pines. This is the end of the Tuxachanie Trail, whose entrance is on St Hwy 49. The trail is 18 mi (SE) long. Approx. hiking time from US 49 to Airey Camp: 2-1/2 hrs; from Airey Camp to POW camp, 3 hours.

SEASON: All yr; 14-day lmt. ACTIVITIES: Hiking; hunting (deer, squirrel, turkey). MISC: Pets on leash. Additional Information/map: District Ranger, Route 1, Box 62, McHenry, MS 39561.

Trailriders Camp (Desoto NF). The Big Foot Horse Trail system is located on the DeSoto NF about 5 mi E of McHenry. The campground is located at the beginning of the system on FS 440. (Info/map: District Ranger Biloxi Ranger Dist., Route 1, Box 62, McHenry, MS 39561).

FACILITIES: Sites, parking areas which facilitate parking of trailers with as little backing as possible; hitching rails; stock pond; and an unloading ramp; toil. SEASON: All yr; 14-day lmt. MISC: Trail consists of 4 loops ranging in length from 5-11 mi. Most trails run parallel to roads; easy access.

MCNEILL

McNeill Truck Stop. I-59, exit 5. SEASON: All yr; 1-night lmt. FACILITIES: Spaces for self-contained vehicles, drk wtr, toil, food, mechanic, 24-hr. MISC: Pets on leash.

MORTON

* Shockaloe National Recreation Trail. (Bienville NF). Located approx. 5 mi E of Morton and 5 mi W of Forest.

Traversing the full length of the Trail requires 8-10 hours on foot or 5-6 hours on horseback. A ride of almost any desired length (1-1/5 mi to more than 23 miles) can be made due to the trail's crossing of 9 all-weather roads.

The campgrounds are made available through cooperation with the Pearl River Basin Development District.

Additional info/map: District Ranger, US Forest Service, Gaddis Bldg; Forest, MS 39764; 469-3811.

Base Camp 1 (Shockaloe Trail; Bienville NF). 1/4 mi N of US Hwy 870 on FS 513. SEASON: 11/1-3/31;

14-day lmt. **FACILITIES:** Sites, tbls, toil, cga, drk wtr, shelter, parking area; hitching rails. **ACTIVITIES:** Picnicking; hiking; horseback riding **MISC:** The parking area is designed to facilitate parking of trucks and trailers. Open area for camping. Pets·

Base Camp II (Shockaloe Trail; Bienville NF). 5-1/4 mi N of US Hwy 80 on FS 513. **SEASON:** All yr; 14-day lmt. **FACILITIES:** Sites, tbls, toil, cga, drk wtr, shelter, parking area. **ACTIVITIES:** Picnicking; hiking; horseback riding. **MISC:** Open area for camping. Pets on leash.

NEWTON

Beverly Hills Truck Stop. I-20 at St Hwy 15. **SEASON:** All yr; 1-night lmt. **FACILITIES:** Spaces for self-contained vehicles, food, drk wtr, gas, toil, 24-hr, mechanic.

OAKLAND

Long Branch (COE; Enid Lake). 3-4/5 mi NE of I-55 on St Hwy 32; 2 mi N. **SEASON:** All yr; 14-day lmt. **FACILITIES:** 8 sites, tbls, toil, cga, drk wtr, f. **ACTIVITIES:** Picnicking; fishing; swimming; boating,rl. **MISC:** Pets on leash.

Point Pleasant (COE; Enid Lake). 6-1/2 mi NE of I-55 on St Hwy 32; 3 mi NW on paved access road. **SEASON:** All yr; 14-day lmt. **FACILITIES:** 5 sites, tbls, toil, cga, drk wtr. **ACTIVITIES:** Picnicking; fishing; swimming; boating,l. **MISC:** Pets.

OCEAN SPRINGS

* **Horn Island** (Gulf Islands National Seashore). BOAT ACCESS. Camping is suggested at the following locations: Western tip, Chimney area, Ranger station area, One mile east of barge, Eastern tip.

Water is available at 2 locations, the Ranger Station and the Chimney area. Pets are allowed, except in swimming areas. Fishing; swimming, but watch for Sea Nettles and Portugese Man-of-War, June-Aug. No hunting.

In case of emergency, contact a ranger. They have a 24-hr radio communication with headquarters. Their cabin is located in the middle of Horn Island, directly inland from the tidal gauge platform on the N side of the island.

Info/map: Park Mgr, Gulf Islands natl Seashore 4000 Hanley Road; Ocean Springs, MS 39564.

* **Ship Island** (Gulf Islands National Seashore). Camping is permitted on East Ship Island ONLY. Access to Ship Island is provided by concession boats from Gulfport and Biloxi, MS, twice daily, May-Sept. In April, less frequent service. Private boats may dock at Fort Mass. in the daytime.

Camp in the vicinity of the old quarantine station. Water is available through 2 artesian wells. Pets are allowed, except in swimming areas. Fishing; swimming, but watch for Sea Nettles and Portugese Man-of-War, June-Aug. No hunting.

In case of emergency, contact a ranger. They have a 24-hr radio communication with headquarters. Their cabin is located in the middle of Horn Island, directly inland from the tidal gauge platform on the N side of the island.

Info/map: park Mgr, Gulf Islands Natl Seashore, 4000 Hanley Rd; Ocean Springs, MS 39564

* **Petit Bois Island** (Gulf Islands Natl Seashore). BOAT ACCESS. Camping is suggested at the following locations: Western tip, along inside beach near trees, eastern tip.

Water is not available. No established campsites. Pets are allowed, except in swimming areas. Fishing; swimming; but watch for Sea Nettles and Portuguese Man-of-War, June-Aug. No hunting.

In case of emergency, contact a ranger. They have a 24-hr radio communication with headquarters. Their cabin is located in the middle of Horn Island, directly inland from the tidal gauge platform on the N side of the island.

Info/map: Park Mgr, Gulf Islands Natl Seashore, 4000 Hanley Road; Ocean Springs, MS 39564.

OXFORD

Hurricane Landing (COE ; Sardis Lake). 11 mi N of Oxford on St Hwy 7. **SEASON:** All yr; 14-day lmt. **FACILITIES:** 12 sites, tbls, toil, cga, f, drk wtr. **ACTIVITIES:** Picnicking; fishing; boating,l. **MISC:** Pets on leash.

Puskus Lake (Holly Springs NF). 1-1/2 mi NE of Oxford on St Hwy 7; 9-3/10 mi E on St Hwy 30; 2-4/5 mi N on FS 838. **SEASON:** All yr; 14-day lmt. FACILITIES: 21 sites (tr -22), tbls, toil, cga, f, piped drk wtr. Store/gas (5 mi). ACTIVITIES: Picnicking; fishing; boating,rl; hiking; waterskiing; swimming; hunting (deer, squirrel, turkey). MISC.: Pets; elev 400 ft; 8 acres.

PICAYUNE

Welcome Station. 3 mi N of Picayune on I-59. SEASON: All yr; 1-night lmt. FACILITIES: Spaces for self-contained vehicles, tbls, toil, cga, phone. ACTIVITIES: Picnicking. MISC: Pets on leash.

PICKENS

Skelly's Truck Stop. I-55, exit 144 (St Hwy 17); W side. SEASON: Spaces for self-contained vehicles, drk wtr, toil, food, gas, 24-hr.

POPE

Plum Point (COE; Enid Lake). 7-1/2 mi SE of Pope on paved rd; 1/2 mi S on access rd. SEASON: All yr; 14-day lmt. FACILITIES: 15 sites, tbls, toil, cga, f, drk wtr. ACTIVITIES: Picnicking; fishing; swimming; boating,l. MISC: Pets on leash.

PORT GIBSON

Rocky Springs (Natchez Trace Parkway). 17 mi NE of Port Gibson on Parkway. (11 mi S of St Hwy 27). SEASON: All yr; 14-day lmt. FACILITIES: 22 sites (tr -30), tbls, toil, cga, pull-thru spaces, drk wtr. ACTIVITIES: Picnicking. MISC: Campfire program: Fri and Sat evenings during summer. Conducted walks: Sat and Sun during summer. Pets.

RALEIGH

Shongelo (NF). 5 mi N of Raleigh on St Hwy 35. SEASON: 4/1-10/31; 14-day lmt. FACILITIES: 4 sites (tr -22), tbls, toil, cga, piped drk wtr. Food/gas (2 mi); store (3 mi); ice/laundry (5 mi). ACTIVITIES: Picnicking; swimming; fishing; hiking. MISC: Nature trails. Pets; elev 500; 2 acres.

SARDIS

Wyatt Crossing (COE; Sardis Lake). 21-1/2 mi E of I-55 on St Hwy 310; 3-3/10 mi SE on gravel road. SEASON: All yr; 14-day lmt. FACILITIES: 10 sites; tbls, toil, cga, f, drk wtr. ACTIVITIES: Picnicking; fishing; boating,l. MISC.: Pets.

SENATOBIA

4-55 Truck Stop. I-55, exit 63. SEASON: All yr; 1-night lmt. FACILITIES: Spaces for self-contained vehicles, food, drk wtr, toil, gas, 24-hr, mechanic.

TILLATOBA

Griffis All American Truck Stop. I-55, exit 56 (Tillatoba). SEASON: All yr; 1-night lmt. FACILITIES: Spaces for self-contained vehicles, food, drk wtr, gas.

TOOMSUBA

Welcome Center. I-59, 1 mi W of Toomsuba exit. SEASON: All yr; 1-day lmt. FACILITIES: Spaces for self-contained vehicles, drk wtr, food, toil, tbls, cga, phone. ACTIVITIES: Picnicking. MISC: Pets on leash.

VAIDEN

35/I-55 Truck Stop. I-55, exit 51; E on St Hwy 35. SEASON: All yr; 1-night lmt. FACILITIES: Spaces for self-contained vehicles, food, drk wtr, toil, gas, mechanic, 24-hr.

WATER VALLEY

Bynum Creek (COE; Enid Lake). 8-3/10 mi NW of Water Valley on St Hwy 315; 2-4/5 mi SW on paved road; 2-2/5 mi on gravel access road. SEASON: All yr; 14-day lmt. FACILITIES: 5 sites, tbls, toil, cga, drk wtr, f. ACTIVITIES: Picnicking; fishing. MISC: Pets on leash.

Water Valley Landing (COE; Enid Lake). S of Water Valley on St Hwy 7; 5-3/10 mi W on St Hwy 32; 3 mi NW. SEASON: 9/4-5/13, FREE; (rest of yr $1). FACILITIES: 14 sites, tbls, toil, cga, f, drk wtr. ACTIVITIES: Picnicking; fishing; swimming; boating,rl. MISC: Food/ice nearby. Pets on leash.

WEST

Edward's 76 Truck Stop. I-55, exit 164. SEASON: All yr; 1-night lmt. FACILITIES: Spaces for self-contained vehicles, drk wtr, toil, food, gas, 24-hr.

WIGGINS

Red Creek. 11 mi W of Wiggins on St Hwy 333. SEASON: All yr; 1-night lmt. FACILITIES: Spaces for self-contained vehicles. MISC: Pets on leash.

See page 7 for KEY TO ABBREVIATIONS.

MISSOURI

GENERAL STATE INFORMATION

Miscellaneous

Toll-Free Number for Travel Information:
1-800-325-0733 [from AR, IL, IN, IA, KS,
KY, MS, NB, OK, TN, WI]
1-800-392-0711 [within Missouri]
STATE CAPITOL: Jefferson City
STATE NICKNAME: Show Me State
STATE MOTTO: "The Welfare of the People
Shall be the Supreme Law"
STATE BIRD: Bluebird
STATE FLOWER: Hawthorn
STATE TREE: Dogwood

State Parks

Camping fees range from $3.00-5.00 per night. Pets are allowed in camping area if
kept on a leash. Further information: Missouri Division of Parks and Recreation;
PO Box 176; Jefferson City, MO 65102.

Rest Areas

Overnight stops are not permitted in Missouri Rest Areas.

State Forests

Camping is allowed in the the State Forests of Missouri, though there are no developed
facilities of any kind. Camping is strictly "primitive" on State Forest land. You
can get free maps of specific forests from: Forestry Division; Missouri Department
of Conservation; PO Box 180; Jefferson City, MO 65101.

Eleven Point National Scenic River (Mark Twain NF)

Eleven Point River is designated as a National Scenic River from Thomasville to St
Hwy 142 (45 miles). Float camps, campgrounds, visitor centers and access points are
being constructed as funds are made available. Plans call for a system of foot trails
through much of the Scenic River area. Float camps will be located at intervals along
the river. The camps will be located in areas where the mouth of a creek or backwater slough provides screening from the river. All units will be screened from the
river and will include tables, toilets, tent pads, fireplaces and signs to mark their
location. Upon arrival, check with the Ranger for current status on this project.
(Winona Ranger District; Winona, MO 65588; 314/325-4233. Doniphan Ranger District;
Doniphan, MO 63935; 314/996-2153.) Further information/map: Forest Supervisor; Mark
Twain NF; PO Box 937; Rolla, MO 65401.

Big Piney River

The Big Piney River, located in Texas and Phelps Counties, is about 100 miles long;
however, it is floatable during the normal recreation season (May-September) for about
77 miles. Early spring and periods of high water, one can float for about 83 miles.
Float fishing, free gravel bar camping, and canoeing are popular activities. There
are several access points located on the river and float trips can be made from a
few hours to a full week. Further information: Forest Supervisor; Clark NF; PO Box
937; Rolla, MO 65401.

Mark Twain NF Backcountry Camping

Camping or hiking is permitted anywhere on National Forest land in Missouri without
a special permit. Fires are allowed also, without a permit. However, the user is
considered responsible for any fires he lights, and any damage caused to public property as a result of the fire is considered the responsibility of the user. When backpacking or camping in undeveloped areas of the Forest, you are urged to inform the
District Ranger of that area of your whereabouts. Further information: Forest Supervisor; Mark Twain NF; PO Box 937; Rolla, MO 65401.

INFORMATION SOURCES

Maps

The following maps are available from Forsyth Travel Library (see order form in Appendix B):

State of Missouri [Up-to-date, showing all principal roads, points of interest, sports areas, parks, airports, mileage, etc. Full color.]

Completely indexed city maps, including all airports, lakes, rivers, etc., of: Kansas City; Overland Park; St. Louis; Sedalia.

State Information

Missouri Tourism Commission; PO Box 1055; Jefferson City, MO 65101.
Missouri Department of Conservation; 2901 North 10-Mile Drive; PO Box 180; Jefferson City, MO 65101.
Missouri Division of Parks and Recreation; PO Box 176; Jefferson City, MO 65102.

City Information

Branson Chamber of Commerce; Branson, MO.
Forsyth Chamber of Commerce; Forsyth, MO.
The Convention and Tourist Council of Greater Kansas City; 1212 Wyandotte; Kansas City, MO 64105.
Convention and Tourist Board of Greater St. Louis; 911 Locust Street; St. Louis, MO 63101.
St. Louis Council on World Affairs; Chase-Park Plaza Hotel; 212 North Kings Highway; St. Louis, MO 63108.

Miscellaneous

Ozark National Scenic Riverways; Box 490; Van Buren, MO 63965.
Missouri BLM [and MN/AR/LA/states east of Miss. River]; Eastern States Office; 7981 Eastern Avenue; Silver Spring, MD 20910.
Clark NF; PO Box 937; Rolla, MO 65401.
Mark Twain NF; PO Box 937; Rolla, MO 65401.
Corps of Engineers, Kansas City District; 700 Federal Building; Kansas City, MO 64106.
Corps of Engineers, Little Rock District; PO Box 867; Little Rock, AR 72203. [Has free campgrounds in Missouri.]

FREE CAMPGROUNDS

ALTON

*Barn Hollow (Mark Twain NF). 9 mi NE on St Hwy 19; 10-2/5 mi SE, BY BOAT, on river. SEASON: 4/15-10/30. FACILITIES: 6 tent sites; tbls, toil, cga; no drk wtr. ACTIVITIES: Picnicking; fishing; swimming; boating. MISC.: Elev 500 ft; 2 acres; scenic; pets. Eleven-Point River.

* Bliss Springs (Mark Twain NF). 9 mi NE of Alton on St Hwy 19; then 10.4 mi SE BY BOAT. Second travel route is the Eleven-Point river. SEASON: 5/1-10/30; 14-day lmt. FACILITIES: 2 tent sites, tbls, toil, cga, no drk wtr. ACTIVITIES: Picnicking; boating; fishing; swimming. MISC: Pets on leash.

* Boze Mill (Mark Twain NF). 5 mi N of Alton on St Hwy 19, then 4 mi NE on St Hwy 19, then 16-4/5 mi SE BY BOAT. SEASON: 4/15-10/30; 14-day lmt FACILITIES: 2 tent sites, tbls, toil, cga, no drk wtr, f. ACTIVITIES: Picnicking; fishing; boating; swimming MISC: Scenic. Eleven Point Scenic River. Pets; elev 500 ft; 2 acres.

*Greenbriar Float Camp (Mark Twain NF). 9 mi NE of Alton on St Hwy 19; 15 mi SE, BY BOAT. SEASON: 4/15-10/30. FACILITIES: 2 tent sites, tbls, toil, cga, no drk wtr, f, store, gas, ice. ACTIVITIES: Picnicking; fishing; boating,rld; swimming. MISC: Scenic. On Eleven Point River. Pets on leash. Elev 500 ft; 2 acres.

Greer Crossing (Mark Twain NF). 9 mi NE of Alton on St Hwy 19. SEASON: 4/15-11/15. FACILITIES: 19 sites (tr -22); tbls, toil, cga, f, no drk wtr. Store/gas/ice (2 mi). ACTIVITIES: Picnicking; fishing. Swimming/boating,l/hiking (1 mi). Boat rental (2 mi). MISC.: Elev 500 ft; 6 acres; pets; scenic. Eleven Point River.

* Horseshoe Bend Float Camp (Mark Twain NF). 5 mi N of Alton on St Hwy 19; 4 mi NE on St Hwy 19; 9-4/5 mi SE. BY BOAT. SEASON: 5/15-10/30; 14-day lmt. FACILITIES: 6 tent sites, tbls, toil, cga, f, no drk wtr ACTIVITIES: Picnicking; fishing; boating,d; swimming. MISC: Scenic. Eleven Point Scenic River. Pets. Elev 500 ft; 3 acres.

* Morgan Springs (Mark Twain NF). 15 mi SE of Alton on Hwy 160, then 7.3 mi S.by boat. SEASON: 4/15-10/30. FACILITIES: 2 tent sites, tbls, toil, cga, no drk wtr. ACTIVITIES: Picnicking; swimming; fishing; boating. MISC: Elev 500 ft; 2 acres; scenic. Eleven Point Scenic River. Pets.

* Stinking Pond (Mark Twain NF). 5 mi N of Alton on St Hwy 19, then 4 mi NE on St Hwy 19, the 5-3/5 mi SE. by BOAT. SEASON: 4/15-10/30; 14-day lmt. FACILITIES: 4 tent sites, tbls, toil, cga, no drk wtr. ACTIVITIES: Picnicking; boating; swimming; fishing. MISC: Elev 500 ft; 3 acres; scenic. Eleven Point Scenic River. Pets on leash.

*Whites Creek (Mark Twain NF). 5 mi N on St Hwy 19; 11-4/5 mi SE, BY BOAT, on river. SEASON: 4/15-10/30; 14-day lmt. FACILITIES: 4 tent sites; tbls, toil, cga, no drk wtr. ACTIVITIES: Picnicking; fishing; boating; swimming. MISC.: Elev 500 ft; 3 acres; scenic; pets. Eleven Point Scenic River.

BAKERSFIELD

Udall Park (COE; Norfork Lake). SW of Bakersfield on St Hwy 101 to Co Rd; 11 mi W to CG. SEASON: All yr; 14-day lmt. FACILITIES: 7 sites, tbls, toil, cga, drk wtr. ACTIVITIES: Picnicking; fishing; boating,rld; swimming. MISC: Pets on leash.

BERRYMAN

Berryman Camp (Mark Twain NF). 2 mi E of Berryman on St Hwy 8; 1-1/2 mi N on FS 2266. SEASON: 4/1-10/31. FACILITIES: 8 tent sites, tbls, toil, cga, no drk wtr. Store/gas/ice (2 mi). ACTIVITIES: Picnicking; hiking; horseback riding (1 mi). MISC:

Nature trails. Elev 100 ft; 5 acres; pets. Tr -22. Terminal camp for 24 mi hiking and riding trail.

Brazil Creek (Mark Twain NF). 2 mi E of Berryman on St Hwy 8; 4 mi NE on FS 2266; 3 mi NW on FS 2265; 1-1/2 mi NE on St Hwy W. SEASON: 4/1-10/31. FACILITIES: 8 sites, tbls, toil, cga. ACTIVITIES: Picnicking; hiking; horseback riding (1 mi). MISC: Elev 900 ft; 3 acres. Pets. Trailers less than 22 feet.

* Edward Beecher (Mark Twain NF). 2 mi E of Berryman on St Hwy 8; 1-1/2 mi NE on FS 2266; 1/10 mi W on FS. 2275; 5-1/2 mi NW on TRAIL. SEASON: 4/1-10/31. FACILITIES: 3 tent sites, tbls, toil, cga, no drk wtr. ACTIVITIES: Picnicking; hiking; horseback riding. MISC: Trail camp only. Pets; elev 900 ft; 3 acres.

* Harmon Springs (Mark Twain NF). 2 mi E of Berryman on Hwy 8, then 4 mi N on FS 2266, then 4 mi NW on FS 2265, then 10 mi N on TRAIL. SEASON: 4/1-10/31. FACILITIES: 3 tent sites, tbls, toil, cga, no drk wtr. ACTIVITIES: Picnicking; hiking; horseback riding (1 mi). MISC: Trail camp. Pets; elev 900 ft; 2 acres.

BETHANY

Van's Truck Stop. I-35 and St Hwy 136. SEASON: All yr; 1-night lmt. FACILITIES: Spaces for self-contained vehicles, drk wtr, food, gas, toil, mechanic, 24-hr.

BLUE EYE

Cow Creek (Mark Twain NF). 1 mi N of Blue Eye on St Hwy 13; 1-9/10 mi N on St Hwy 86; 2-1/10 mi N lmt FH181. SEASON: 4/1-9/15; 14-day lmt FACILITIES: 34 sites (no tr), tbls, toil, cga. Store/food/ice (4 mi). Laundry (5 mi). ACTIVITIES: Picnicking; hunting; fishing; swimming; boating,ld; waterskiing; hiking. MISC: Pets on leash.

Cow Creek (COE; Table Rock Lake). 5 mi N of Blue Eye. SEASON: All yr; 14-day lmt. FACILITIES: 39 sites, drk wtr. ACTIVITIES: Fishing; swimming; boating,rl; waterskiing. MISC: Pets on leash.

BOLIVAR

Bolivar (COE; Pomme de Terre Lake). 7 mi N of St Hwy 32 at Bolivar on Co Rds D/PP. SEASON: All yr; 14-day lmt. FACILITIES: 30 sites, tbls, toil, cga, dump, drk wtr. ACTIVITIES: Picnicking; fishing; swimming; boating,l. MISC: Pets on leash.

See page 7 for KEY TO ABBREVIATIONS.

BOONEVILLE

City Park. In Boonville. SEASON: All yr; 1-night lmt. FACILITIES: Spaces for self-contained vehicles, elec hkup. MISC: Park near the shelter for elec hookup. Pets on leash.

BOWLING GREEN

Jones Brothers Truck Stop. Jct US 54/61. SEASON: All yr; 1-night lmt. FACILITIES: Spaces for self-contained vehicles, drk wtr, toil, food, gas, mechanic, 24-hr.

BRANSON

Highway K (COE; Bull Shoals Lake). 1 mi S of Branson on US 65; 7 mi E on St Hwy 86; 4 mi S on Co Rd K. SEASON: All yr; 14-day lmt. FACILITIES: 20 sites, tbls, toil, cga, drk wtr. ACTIVITIES: Picnicking; fishing; boating,rld. MISC: Pets.

BRIAR

Compton (Mark Twain NF). 2 mi N of Briar on Co Rd C, then 4½ mi NE on FS 3144. SEASON: All yr; 14-day lmt. FACILITIES: 3 tent sites; toil, no drk wtr. ACTIVITIES: Fishing. MISC.: Pets.

BROOKFIELD

McCollum Car/Truck Plaza. Jct St Hwy 36 & Bus 36. SEASON: All yr; 14-day lmt. FACILITIES: Spaces for self-contained vehicles, food, drk wtr, toil, gas.

CANTON

Fenway Landing (COE; Miss. River PUA). 4-1/2 mi N of Canton on St Hwy 61; E on Co Rd over levee to campground. SEASON: All yr; 14-day lmt. FACILITIES: 20 sites, tbls, toil, cga, drk wtr. ACTIVITIES: Picnicking; fishing; swimming; boating,l. MISC: Pets on leash.

CEDAR CREEK

Woodard Park (COE; Bull Shoals Lake). 1-1/2 mi W of Cedar Creek on Co Rd KK; 6 mi SW to campground SEASON: All yr; 14-day lmt. FACILITIES: 6 sites, tbls, toil, cga, drk wtr. ACTIVITIES: Picnicking; fishing; boating,rl; hunting. MISC: Pets.

CHADWICK

Camp Ridge (Mark Twain NF). 1-1/2 mi S of Chadwick on Hwy 125; then 1 mi SW on Co Rd H. SEASON: All yr; 14-day lmt. FACILITIES: 8 sites (tr -22); tbls, toil, cga, no drk wtr. Store/gas/ice/food (3 mi). Laundry (4 mi). ACTIVITIES: Picnicking; fishing. MISC.: Pets; elev 1400 ft; 5 acres.

Cobb Ridge (Mark Twain NF). 1-1/5 mi S of Chadwick on St Hwy 125; 2½ mi SW on Co Rd H; ½ mi W on FS 171. SEASON: All yr; 14-day lmt. FACILITIES: 19 sites (tr -22); tbls, toil, cga, no drk wtr. Store/ice/food/gas (4 mi). Laundry (5 mi). ACTIVITIES: Picnicking. MISC.: Serves Chadwick Motorcycle area. Pets; elev 1400 ft; 10 acres.

CLINTON

Lee's Apco Auto/Truck Stop. 1 mi W of Clinton on St Hwy 7. SEASON: All yr; 1-day lmt. FACILITIES: Spaces for self-contained vehicles, drk wtr, toil, gas, food, LP gas, 24-hr.

CONCORDIA

The Good Old Days Truck Stop. Jct I-70 & St Hwy 23, at Concordia. SEASON: All yr; 1-night lmt. FACILITIES: Spaces for self-contained vehicles, drk wtr, food, gas, drk wtr, toil. 24-hr.

DONIPHAN

Buffalo Creek (Mark Twain NF). 16 mi W of Doniphan on US 160, then 2 mi N on FS 3145. SEASON: 5/15–10/30; 14-day lmt. FACILITIES: 3 sites (tr -22), tbls, toil, cga, well drk wtr. Store/gas/ice/food (3 mi). ACTIVITIES: Picnicking; fishing; swimming. MISC: Scenic; stream. Elev 600 ft; 2 acres. Pets on leash.

* **Compton Float Camp** (Mark Twain NF). 5 mi N of Doniphan on St Hwy Y; 1 mi W on FS 4359; 5 mi NW on River BY BOAT. SEASON: 5/15–10/30; 14-day lmt. FACILITIES: 3 tent sites, tbls, toil, cga, no drk wtr. ACTIVITIES: Picnicking; swimming; fishing; boating. MISC: Scenic. Current River. Pets on leash. Elev 500 ft; 2 acres.

EAGLEVILLE

Eagleville Truck Stop. I-35 & Rte "N", at Eagleville. SEASON: All yr; 1-night lmt. FACILITIES: Spaces for self-contained vehicles, toil, drk wtr, gas, food, mechanic, 24-hr.

ELDON

City Park. St Hwy 54 in Eldon. SEA-
SON: All yr; 1-night lmt. FACILI-
TIES: Spaces for self-contained vehic-
les. MISC: Pets on leash.

ELLINGTON

Webb Creek (COE; Clearwater Lake).
12 mi SE of Ellington on Co Rd H.
SEASON: All yr; 14-day lmt. FACILI-
TIES: 26 sites. ACTIVITIES: Fishing;
swimming; boating,rld; hunting; hiking. MISC: Pets on leash.

ELSINOR

Pinewoods (Mark Twain NF). 2 mi
W of Elsinor on US 60. SEASON: 4/15-
10/15; 14-day lmt. FACILITIES: 11
sites, drk wtr. Food/store/ice (1 mi)
ACTIVITIES: Picnicking; fishing;
boating,d. MISC: Pets on leash.

EMINENCE

Alley Spring (Ozark Natl Scenic
Riverway). 6 mi W of Eminence on
St Hwy 106. SEASON: LD-MD, FREE
($3 rest of yr); 14-day lmt. FACILI-
TIES: 197 sites, pull-thru spaces,
flush toil, tbls, cga, f ($1 per
bundle), showers, drk wtr, ice, food,
store. ACTIVITIES: Picnicking; fishing; swimming; boating,rl; horseback riding; canoeing/rental. MISC:
Phone; ranger station. Pets on leash.

Powder Mill (Ozark Natl Scenic Riverway).12 mi E of Eminence on St Hwy
106. SEASON: All yr; 14-day lmt. FA-
CILITIES: 27 sites, f ($), tbls, toil,
cga, drk wtr; store nearby. ACTIVI-
TIES: Picnicking; swimming; fishing;
boating,rl. MISC: Pets on leash.

Round Spring (Ozark Natl Scenic
Riverway). 13 mi N of Eminence on
St Hwy 19. SEASON: LD-MD, FREE ($3
rest of yr); 14-day lmt. FACILITIES:
54 reg. sites, 6 walk-ins, 3 group
sites, pull-thru sp; flush toil, showers, phone. ACTIVITIES: Picnicking;
swimming; fishing; boating,rl; canoe-
ing/rental. MISC: Store/ice/P.O.
nearby. Pets on leash.

FAUCETT

Farris Truck Stop. Jct I-29 & Hwy
"DD", at Faucett. SEASON: All yr;
1-night lmt. FACILITIES: Spaces for
self-contained vehicles, food, toil,
drk wtr, gas, 24-hr.

FLORISSANT

Tom's Mobile Service Stop (Truck
Stop). Jct I-270 & New Halls Ferry
Rd, at Florissant. SEASON: All yr;
1-night lmt. FACILITIES: Spaces for
self-contained vehicles, food, toil,
drk wtr, gas, 24-hr.

FORSYTH

River Run (COE; Bull Shoals Lake).
1/2 mi E of Forsyth on US 160 & 86;
S to campground. SEASON: All yr;
14-day lmt. FACILITIES: 20 sites,
tbls, toil, cga, drk wtr. ACTIVITIES:
Picnicking; fishing; boating,rl; hunting. MISC: Pets on leash.

FULTON

Trailer Parking Area. N of Fulton
on St Hwy 54. SEASON: All yr; 1-
night lmt. FACILITIES: Spaces for
self-contained vehicles. MISC: Pets.

GAINESVILLE

Spring Creek (COE; Bull Shoals Lake).
9 mi west of Gainesville on
US 160 to Isabella; 5 mi S on Co Rd
HH. SEASON: All yr; 14-day lmt. FA-
CILITIES: 16 sites, tbls, toil, cga,
drk wtr. ACTIVITIES: Picnicking;
fishing; boating,rl. MISC: Pets on
leash.

Tecumseh (COE; Norfork Lake). 11
mi E of Gainesville on US 160, at
Tecumseh. SEASON: All yr; 14-day lmt.
FACILITIES: 7 sites, tbls, toil, cga,
drk wtr. ACTIVITIES: Picnicking;
fishing; boating,rd. MISC: Pets.

GOLDEN

Kings River Park (COE; Table Rock
Lake). 2 mi N of Golden on Lake
Road M-27; 2 mi E on unpaved road
SEASON: All yr; 14-day lmt.
FACILITIES: 16 sites, tbls, toil, cga
drk wtr. ACTIVITIES: Picnicking;
fishing; swimming; boating,rl; hunt-
ing. MISC: Pets on leash.

GRANDIN

Cedar Creek (Mark Twain NF). 2 mi
S of Grandin on Hwy 21, then 2-1/5
mi W on St Hwy SHO, then 7/10 mi
S on FR 3141, then 3-4/5 mi SW by
TRAIL 3141. SEASON: 5/15-10/30; 14-
day lmt. FACILITIES: 2 tent sites,
tbls, toil, cga, no drk wtr. ACTIVI-
TIES: Picnicking; fishing; boating,
swimming; hiking. MISC: Current
River. Pets; elev 500 ft; 1 acre.

ISABELLA

Spring Creek Park (COE; Bull Shoals
Lake). 5 mi S of Isabella on Co Hwy

HH. SEASON: All yr; 14-day lmt. FA-CILITIES: 16 sites, tbls, toil, cga, drk wtr. ACTIVITIES: Picnicking; fishing; boating; swimming. MISC: Pets on leash.

LEBANON

B & D Truck Port (Truck Stop). I 44, exit 27, at Lebanon. SEASON: All yr; 1-night lmt. FACILITIES: Spaces for self-contained vehicles, food, gas, drk wtr, toil. LP gas, 24-hr, mechanic.

MARSTON

Mo-Tex Truck Stop. I-55, Marston exit, at Marston. SEASON: All yr; 1-night lmt. FACILITIES: Spaces for self-contained vehicles, food, gas, toil, drk wtr, mechanic, 24-hr.

MATTHEWS

Scotty's S & C Truck Plaza. I-55, St Hwy 80 exit, at Matthews. SEASON: All yr; 1-day lmt. FACILITIES: Spaces for self-contained vehicles, food, drk wtr, toil, gas, mechanic, 24-hrs.

MEXICO

Lake View Park. W Hwy 54, SE Fair-ground St, in Mexico. SEASON: All yr; 1-night lmt. FACILITIES: Spaces for self-contained vehicles. MISC: Pets on leash.

MONETT

H & W Oil Auto/Truck Stop. St Hwy 37 S in Monett. SEASON: All yr; 1-night lmt. FACILITIES: Spaces for self-contained vehicles, food, gas, drk wtr, toil, mechanic, 24-hr.

PATTONSBURG

Pattonsburg City Park. On US 69 be-tween Kansas City & Des Moines. SEA-SON: All yr; 1-night lmt. FACILI-TIES: Spaces for self-contained vehic-les, cga. MISC: Pets on leash.

PEVELY

I-55 Motor Truck Plaza. Jct of I-55 & St Hwy 2, at Pevely. SEASON: All yr; 1-nite lmt. FACILITIES: Spaces for self-contained vehicles, food, gas, toil, drk wtr, LP gas, 24-hr, mechanic.

PIEDMONT

Thurman Point (COE; Clearwater Lake). 7 mi SW of Piedmont on Co Rd H. SEASON: All yr; 14-day lmt. FACILITIES: 4 sites, tbls, toil, cga, drk wtr. ACTIVITIES: Picnicking; fishing; boating,rl; hunting; swim-ming. MISC: Pets on leash.

POPLAR BLUFF

Chaonia Campground (COE; Wappapel-lo Lake). 3 mi N of Poplar Bluff on St Hwy 67; 17 mi NE on St Hwy W. SEASON: All yr; 14-day lmt. FACILI-TIES: 12 sites (tr -25), tbls, toil, cga, f. Store/ice/food nearby. ACTIV-ITIES: Picnicking; fishing; swimming; boating,l; hunting; hiking. MISC: Pets on leash.

Old Greenville 29 mi N of Poplar Bluff on St Hwy 67. SEASON: All yr; 14-day lmt. FACILITIES: 12 sites (tr -20), tbls, toil, cga, no drk wtr. Store/ice nearby. ACTIVITIES: Pic-nicking; fishing; boating,rl. MISC: Wappapello lake. Pets on leash.

PROTEM

Buck Creek (COE; Bull Shoals Lake). 5 mi SE of Protem on St Hwy 125. SEASON: 5/15-9/15; 14-day lmt. FACILITIES: 33 sites, tbls, toil, cga, elec hkup; ice/laundry nearby. AC-TIVITIES: Picnicking; fishing; swim-ming; boating,rld. MISC: Pets.

RIDGEDALE

Cricket Creek (COE; Table Rock Lake). 6 mi SW of Ridgedale on Ark· Hwy 14. SEASON: 3/1-9/15; 14-day lmt. FACILITIES: 39 sites, tbls, toil, cga, food, store, drk wtr. ACTIVITIES: Picnicking; fishing; swimming; boat-ing,rld. MISC.: Pets.

ROLLA

Ozark Truck Plaza. 3 mi E of Rolla on I-44. SEASON: All yr; 1-nite lmt. FACILITIES: Spaces for self-contained vehicles, food, toil, drk wtr, gas, mechanic, 24-hr.

SALEM

Akers (Ozark Natl Scenic Riverway). 19 mi S of Salem on St Hwy 19; 6 mi W on Co Rd KK. SEASON: LD-MD, FREE ($3 rest of yr); 14-day lmt. FACILITIES: 81 sites + 5 group sites tbls, toil, cga, f ($), ice, store, no public phone. ACTIVITIES: Pic-nicking; fishing; swimming; boat-ing,rl; canoeing. MISC: Pets.

MISSOURI

Pulltite (Ozark Natl Scenic Riverway). 26 mi S of Salem on St Hwy 19; 4 mi W on Co Rd EE. SEASON: LD-MD, FREE; ($3 rest of yr); 14-day lmt. FACILITIES: 55 sites, tbls, toil, cga drk wtr, phone, pull-thru sp. ACTIVITIES: Picnicking; fishing; swimming; boating,rl; canoeing/rental. MISC: Pets on leash.

SHELL KNOB

Shell Knob (Mark Twain NF). 1 mi SE of Shell Knob on St Hwy 39; 1-3/10 mi SE on St Hwy YY. SEASON: 5/15-9/15. FACILITIES: 5 sites (tr -22), tbls, toil, cga, f, piped drk wtr. ACTIVITIES: Picnicking; hiking. Horseback riding and rental/fishing/swimming/waterskiing/boating,l (1 mi). Boat rental (3 mi). MISC.: Located on bluff overlooking Table Rock Lake Nature Trails. Pets; scenic; elev 1000 ft; 8 acres. Store/ice/laundry/gas (1 mi).

SPRINGFIELD

Overland Plaza Car/Truck Plaza. N of I-44 on Hwy "H", in Springfield. SEASON: All yr; 1-nite lmt. FACILITIES: Spaces for self-contained vehicles, food, drk wtr, toil, gas, 24-hr, mechanic.

STOCKTON

Cedar Ridge (COE; Stockton Lake). E of Stockton on St Hwy 32; S on St Hwy 245; N on Co Rd "RA". SEASON: 10/1-4/30, FREE ($3 rest of yr). FACILITIES: 35 sites, tbls, toil, cga, drk wtr, showers (water is shut off during winter). ACTIVITIES: Picnicking; fishing; swimming; boating,ld. MISC: Pets on leash.

Crabtree Cove (COE; Stockton Lake). 4 mi E of Stockton on St Hwy 32. SEASON: 10/1-4/30, FREE ($3 rest of yr). FACILITIES: 36 sites, tbls, toil, cga, drk wtr, showers. ACTIVITIES: Picnicking; swimming; fishing; boating,ld; golfing nearby. MISC: Water is shut off during winter. Pets.

Hawker Point (COE; Stockton Lake). 12 mi S and E of Stockton on St Hwy 39 and Co Rd "H". SEASON: 9/18-5/10, FREE ($3 rest of yr). FACILITIES: 35 sites, tbls, toil, cga, drk wtr, showers. ACTIVITIES: Picnicking; fishing; swimming; boating,ld. MISC: Water shut off during winter. Pets on leash.

Masters East (COE; Stockton Lake). SE of Stockton on St Hwy 32; S on Co Rd "RA" to Campground. SEASON:

9/18-5/10, FREE ($3 rest of yr). FACILITIES: 43 sites, tbls, toil, cga, drk wtr, showers. ACTIVITIES: Picnicking; fishing; swimming; boating, rld. MISC: Ice/food/store nearby Water is shut off during winter. Pets.

Mutton Creek (COE; Stockton Lake). 18 mi S and E of Stockton on St Hwy 39 and Co Rd "Y". SEASON: 9/18-5/10, FREE; ($3 rest of yr). FACILITIES: 40 sites, tbls, toil, cga, drk wtr, showers, food/laundry nearby, phone gas, oil. ACTIVITIES: Picnicking; fishing; swimming; boating,rld. MISC: Water shut off during winter.

UDALL

Udall Park (COE; Norfork Lake). 2 mi W of Udall on Hwy "O". SEASON: All yr; 14-day lmt. FACILITIES: 7 drk wtr. Picnicking; fishing; boating,rld; swimming. MISC: Pets.

VANBUREN

Big Spring (Ozark Natl Scenic Riverway). 4 mi S of VanBuren on St Hwy 103. SEASON: LD-MD, FREE ($3 rest of yr). FACILITIES: 195 sites, tbls, toil, cga, f ($), showers, drk wtr, phone, dining, lodge. ACTIVITIES: Picnicking; fishing; swimming; boating,rl. MISC.: Ranger station.

WILLOW SPRINGS

Noblett Lake (Sugar Hill; Mark Twain NF). 8 mi W of Willow Springs on Hwy 76, then 1-2/5 mi SW on Hwy 181, then 2-9/10 mi SE on Hwy AP, then 1 mi SW on FR 857. SEASON: 5/15-9/15; 14-day lmt. FACILITIES: 16 sites (tr -22); piped drk wtr, toil. ACTIVITIES: Picnicking; hiking; fishing; boating; swimming. MISC.: Pets.

WINONA

Gateway (Mark Twain NF). 5 mi W of Winona on US 60. SEASON: All yr. FACILITIES: 13 sites (tr -32); tbls, toil, cga, no drk wtr. Showers/ice/store/food/laundry/gas (5 mi). ACTIVITIES: Picnicking. MISC.: Elev 1000 ft; 15 acres; pets.

McCormack Lake (Mark Twain NF). 14 mi S of Winona on St Hwy 19; 2 mi SW on FS 3155. SEASON: 4/15-11/30. FACILITIES: 8 sites (tr -22); tbls, toil, cga, f, well drk wtr. ACTIVITIES: Picnicking; hiking; fishing; boating,d. Swimming (1 mi). MISC.: Elev 600 ft; 3 acres; pets. 1 mi from Eleven Point River.

See page 7 for KEY TO ABBREVIATIONS.
285

MONTANA

Miscellaneous

Toll-Free Number for Travel Information:
    1-800-548-3390 [from out of state]
Right Turns on Red: Permitted after full
    stop, unless otherwise posted.

STATE CAPITOL: Helena
STATE NICKNAME: Treasure State
STATE MOTTO: "Oro y Plata; Gold and Silver"
STATE BIRD: Western Meadowlark
STATE FLOWER: Bitterroot
STATE TREE: Ponderosa Pine

State Parks

Fees range from $2.00-3.00 per night. Pets are permitted. Any Montana resident who is 65 years of age or older may purchase a MONTANA STATE GOLDEN YEARS PASS for $1.00 which, when attached to his/her vehicle, allows the passengers of that vehicle to camp FREE in Montana state parks, recreation areas and fishing access sites. This pass is valid for the lifetime of the individual. For additional information on Montana's State Parks or the Golden Years Pass: Montana Department of Fish and Game; 1420 East Sixth Avenue; Helena, MT 59601.

Rest Areas

Overnight stops are not permitted in Montana's Rest Areas.

Department of Fish and Game

Get a detailed map plus additional information on State Parks, State Recreation Areas, and Fishing Access Sites from any of the following offices:

HEADQUARTERS: 1420 E. 6th Ave.; Helena, MT 59601; 449-3750.

REGIONAL OFFICES:
490 N. Meridian Rd.; Kalispell, MT 59901; 755-5505/6.
3309 Brooks; Missoula, MT 549-1496/0914.
Rt. 3, Box 274; Bozeman, MT 59715; 586-5419/5410.
Rt. 4, Box 243; Great Falls, MT 59401; 454-3441/2.
1125 Lake Elmo Drive; Billings, MT 59101; 252-4654/5.
Rt. 1 - 129; Glasgow, MT 59230; 228-9347/48.
Box 430; Miles City, MT 59301; 232-4265/4368.

Sun River Game Preserve (Lewis & Clark NF)

Located in the 1-million-acre Rocky Mountain Division of the Lewis and Clark NF portion of the Bob Marshall Wilderness. Big-game hunting area for antelope, Rocky Mountain elk, deer, black bear, and grouse. Bear country. Excellent fishing. Further information: Forest Supervisor; Lewis and Clark NF; PO Box 871;Great Falls, MT 59401.

Blackfoot River Floating and Camping

Hunting, fishing, floating, and free camping are available along the Blackfoot River. For a map that includes campsites, write to: Department of Fish and Game, Region 2; 3309 Brooks; Missoula, MT 59801. Ask for their free Blackfoot River Guide.

Montana Float Trips and Camping

In Montana you will find many rivers which are ideal for overnight camping. Montana's Department of Fish and Game put out an excellent free Floater's Guide which discusses many of the rivers, and hints for overnight camping/floating trips. Write to: Department of Fish and Game; Fish and Game Building; 1420 East Sixth Avenue; Helena, MT 59601.

INFORMATION SOURCES

Maps

The following maps are available from **Forsyth Travel Library** (see order form in Appendix B):

MONTANA

State of Montana [Up-to-date, showing all principal roads, points of interest, sports areas, parks, airports, mileage, etc. Full color.]

Gold Mining and Prospecting

Montana Bureau of Mines and Geology; Montana College of Mineral Science and Technology; Butte, MT 59701.

State Information

Montana Chamber of Commerce; PO Box 1730; Helena, MT 59601.
Montana Travel Promotion Unit; 1236 - 6th Avenue; Helena, MT 59601.
Advertising Unit; Montana Dept. of Highways; Garrett Bldg.; Helena, MT 59601.
Montana Division of Fish and Game; Fish and Game Building; 1420 East Sixth Avenue; Helena, MT 59601. 406/442-5468.
Bureau of Sport Fisheries and Wildlife; Missouri River Basin Studies; 711 Central Avenue; Billings, MT 59101. 245-6711, ext. 6269.

City Information

Butte Chamber of Commerce; 100 East Broadway; Butte, MT 59701.
Billings Chamber of Commerce; PO Box 2519; Billings, MT 59103.
Helena Chamber of Commerce; 201 East Lyndale Ave.; Helena, MT 59601.

National Forests

Forest Service; Northern Region; Division of Engineering; Ft. Missoula, MT 59801.
Beaverhead NF; Dillon, MT 59725.
Bitterroot NF; 316 North Third Street; Hamilton, MT 59840.
Custer NF; 2602 First Avenue North; Billings, MT 59101.
Deerlodge NF; PO Box 400; Federal Building; Butte, MT 59701.
Flathead NF; 290 North Main; PO Box 147; Kalispell, MT 59901.
Gallatin NF; PO Box 130; Bozeman, MT 59715.
Helena NF; Federal Building; Drawer 10014; 616 Helena Avenue; Helena, MT 59601.
Kootenai NF; PO Box AS; Libby, MT 59923.
Lewis and Clark NF; PO' Box 871; Great Falls, MT 59401.
Lolo NF; Building 24; Fort Missoula; Missoula, MT 59801.

Miscellaneous

Glacier National Park; West Glacier, MT 59936.
Bighorn Canyon National Recreation Area; Box 458; Fort Smithl, MT 59035.
Montana Bureau of Land Management; 316 North 26th Street; Billings, MT 59101.
Billings Area Office; Bureau of Indian Affairs; 316 North 26th Street; Billings, MT 59101.
Bureau of Reclamation; Regional Office; 316 North 26th Street; Billings, MT 59101.

BACKCOUNTRY AND WILDERNESS CAMPING

ABSAROKA PRIMITIVE AREA; Gallatin NF

Located along the Wyoming border. Yellowstone National Park is south of here. 64,000 acres; elevation ranges from 6,000-10,218 feet [most high plateau country]. Trout fishing. Fall hunting: elk, moose, mule deer, black bear, grizzlies. Further information: Forest Supervisor; Gallatin NF; Box 130; Bozeman, MT 59715.

ANACONDA-PINTLAR WILDERNESS; Bitterroot NF

Located in the Anaconda Range of the Rocky Mountains, the Wilderness encompasses 157,803 acres. Among the many hiking trails is a 45-mile trail along the crest of the Great Divide. Trout fishing. Hunting (moose, deer, black bear, elk). Further information: Forest Supervisor; Bitterroot NF; 316 North Third Street; Hamilton, MT 59840.

BEARTOOTH PRIMITIVE AREA; Custer NF

7½ mi N of Cooke City. 225,855 acres in rugged mountain country, south-central Montana, 80 mi SW of Billings. Elevation ranges from 5,900-12,799 feet. Although there are numerous trails, there is a large portion of the interior that has no trails. Trout fishing in 120-acre Goose Lake. Mountain climbing; camping; hiking. Very scenic: waterfalls, glaciers, bighorn sheep, moose, mountain goat, deer. WARNING: Bear country; do not visit this area alone. Also, subarctic climate and heavy winter snows; violent storms. Further information: Forest Supervisor; Custer NF; 2602 First Avenue North; Billings, MT 59103.

BOB MARSHALL WILDERNESS; Flathead NF

Big Prairie Ranger Station, within the Wilderness, is manned from early May to 11/15. Report to the Ranger Station where you are going in the Wilderness, how long you plan to stay, and where and when you plan to come out. This could help both you and the Ranger in case of unforeseen emergencies. On the edges of the Wilderness, there are three landing strips open to general use: Benchmark (on the SE edge); Schafer (in the Middle Fork Flathead River Valley); Meadow Creek (in the South Fork Flathead River Valley. For information about these landing fields, contact: Montana Aeronautics Commission; Helena Airport; Helena, MT 59601. This 950,000-acre Wilderness is larger than the state of Rhode Island. Rugged peaks, alpine lakes, mountain valleys, open meadows. Elevation ranges from 4,000-9,000 feet. The Continental Divide extends more than 60 miles through the Wilderness. ACTIVITIES: Big-game hunting (elk, grizzly, mule deer, white-tailed deer, black bear, mountain goats, bighorn sheep); fishing; horseback riding; ski touring; snowshoeing; mountain climbing; viewing geological formations (12-mile-long Chinese Wall). Locate your camp on a previously-used spot, or use a barren or rocky place where there will be little damage to vegetation. You can camp where you please, except for a few sites occupied by commercial outfitters and guides under special-use permits. These sites will be designated by signs indicating exclusive occupancy. Avoid camping at a heavily-used site. The summer range for three major elk herds. Spring/summer/fall range of Montana's largest herd of bighorn sheep. Further information: Forest Supervisor; Flathead NF; 290 North Main; Kalispell, MT 59901.

CABINET MOUNTAINS WILDERNESS; Kootenai NF

Located within both the Kootenai and Kaniksu NFs, this Wilderness covers 94,272 acres; elevation ranges from 3,000-8,712 feet. There are large fish in a few of the lakes, but due to short growing seasons and cold waters, pansize fish are predominate in most waters. Grizzly and black bear country. Trail access is extensive. Some trails are adequate for horse use. Unstable rock formations make technical climbing unsafe in most areas. Winter and spring: avalanche danger. Snowstorms may occur as late as June and as early as September. There are opportunities for cross-country skiing in some areas. Use trail registers. Locate your camps away from areas where other groups may also be seeking solitude. Where possible, use existing fire rings; use extreme caution with fire. Use only dead wood for your campsite. Many hikers have found that a modern backpacker's stove is most efficient. Even with fuel these stoves can be lighter than an ax. Huckleberries. Further information: Forest Supervisor; Kootenai NF; 418 Mineral Avenue; Box AS; Libby, MT 59923.

GATES OF THE MOUNTAINS WILDERNESS; Helena NF

Meriwether and Coulter Campgrounds are on the east side of the lake. Both campgrounds have tables, campfire/grill areas, toilets, and water. Meriwether Campground has a shelter and a large outdoor stove for group use. A resident guard is stationed at Meriwether through the summer months. There are boat docks at Meriwether; trails lead from there to the north and east into the Wilderness. No motorized vehicles or or equipment. No pets on trails. Water is scarce. Most of the area is limestone. Fall hunting: antelope, deer, elk, mountain goat, black or grizzly bear, gamebirds. 28,562 acres; on the Missouri River. 1200-foot-high Limestone Cliffs. Further information: Canyon Ferry Ranger Station; Helena NF; 2001 Poplar; Helena, MT 59601.

GLACIER NATIONAL PARK BACKCOUNTRY CAMPING

Backcountry overnight hikers must obtain a camping permit at the nearest Ranger Station, Visitor Center, Information Office, or Park Headquarters. Entrance fee into the National Park is $2.00 (or the Golden Eagle/Golden Age Passport**); however, there is no additional charge for hiking and camping in the backcountry. The Park is on US 2 and US 89, near US 91 and US 93. Buses connecting with transcontinental buslines at Great Falls and Missoula stop twice daily at West Glacier and East Glacier Park. A main transcontinental rail line serves the park. Both Great Falls and Kalispell have airline service. Evenings are cool, even throughout the summer. Be prepared for sudden thundershowers. The main summer travel season is 6/15-9/10. Pets are NOT allowed on trails or in the backcountry. Food left on tables or stored in tents and vehicles in open boxes or containers is an invitation for bears. Do not retire for the evening with food odors on your person or sleeping bag! Use caution around wildlife — do not feed, tease, tempt or disturb them. This is dangerous and illegal.

Glacier NP is located in the Rocky Mountains, containing nearly 1600 square miles. Numerous glaciers and lakes are among the higher peaks. Glacier forms the U.S. section of the Waterton Glacier International Peace Park, established in 1932. Waterton Lakes NP in Alberta forms the Canadian portion of the only park which crosses the international boundary.

Hunting is prohibited, as is the possession of any device designed to discharge missiles and capable of injuring or destroying animal life. No poisonous snakes in the

MONTANA

Park. Horseback travel is permitted. More than 700 miles of trails. Further information: Superintendent; Glacier NP; West Glacier, MT 59936.

JEWEL BASIN HIKING AREA; Flathead NF

Designated as a Special Interest Area, it encompasses 15,000 acres on the east side of the Flathead Valley in the Swan Range. Horses and motorized vehicles are prohibited. Located near the Bob Marshall Wilderness west of Hungry Horse Reservoir. 25 fishing lakes. In the high country; also bear country. Further information: District Ranger; Hungry Horse Ranger Station; Flathead NF; Hungry Horse, MT 59919.

MISSION MOUNTAINS PRIMITIVE AREA; Flathead NF

75,588 acres, with elevation ranging from 4,500-9,000 feet. Southern portion, the topography is generally rough and broken. The northern portion is more timbered and the terrain is not as steep and rugged. Grizzly and black bear, deer, mountain goats. Most of the fishing is confined to the lakes. Dense brush and windfalls along major streams make stream fishing difficult. The best time of the year to visit is 7/1-10/1. Snow-filled passes and high streams make earlier travel difficult and hazardous. High lakes do not open up until early or middle June. June is normally a wet month. July, August, early September are dry months. Daytime temperatures are in the 80's and 90's. Brief showers likely. Cool nights. More than 65 miles of Forest Service system trails. Little horseback use. Motorized vehicles and equipment are not permitted. Few of the trails can be called easy. No permit is necessary. Use existing camps and firespots where possible. Pack out all items that cannot be burned. Not campfire permit is required. No poisonous snakes in area. Sign and fill out all trail registers completely Further information: District Ranger; Flathead NF; Swan Lake Ranger Station; Bigfork, MT 59111.

SALMON RIVER BREAKS PRIMITIVE AREA; Bitterroot NF

Access to the Primitive Area is best from the end of Road No. 030 on the map (obtainable at the Ranger Station, free), at Corn Creek on the Salmon River below North Fork, Idaho, or the Nez Perce Rd from Magruder Ranger Station over Salmon Mountain to Elk City, Idaho. This road follows the northern boundary of the Salmon River Breaks Primitive Area. It is Road No. 468 on the Forest map, normally open by July 15. It is a slow road from the West Fork Ranger Station and a long way without service stations or other facilities, so have plenty of fuel and other needed supplies. This is a very scenic trip. It is possible to drive up West Fork over Horse Creek Pass to Shoup, Idaho. It is a mountain road passable to all types of vehicles, a slow road, and a long way between service stations. Generally it is open and in good condition by July 15th. District Ranger; Bitterroot NF; West Fork Ranger District; Darby, MT 59829.

SCAPEGOAT WILDERNESS; Helena NF

Located primarily in Helen NF, the Wilderness shares its 450,000 acres with Lolo and Lewis & Clark NFs. On the Continental Divide. Limestone cliffs; alpine meadows. Excellent fishing in numerous creeks and in Bighorn Lake. Further information: Forest Supervisor; Helena NF; 616 Helena Avenue; Federal Building; Drawer 10014; Helena, MT 59601.

SELWAY-BITTERROOT WILDERNESS; Bitterroot NF

No permit is required. No motorized equipment is permitted. The Montana portion of this million-acre wilderness is located in the heart of elk, big horn sheep, and black bear country. The innumerable blue alpine lakes provide excellent cutthroat, rainbow and brook trout fishing. Elevation ranges from 8,000-10,000 feet. It is accessible from roadends from St Hwy 93 and the Nez Perce Trail Road along the Selway River The quickest way to get into high country readily accessible to the Wilderness is to drive up the Lost Horse Road to Bear Creek Pass or Schumaker Campground. It is a short hike into Wilderness for any length of stay. Lost Horse Road is a narrow mountain road, slow, but used by all types of vehicles. It is usually open by late June. Further information: District Ranger; West Fork Ranger District; Bitterroot NF; Darby, MT 59829. OR, District Ranger; Darby Ranger District; Bitterroot NF; Darby, MT 59829. OR, District Ranger; Stevensville Ranger District; Bitterroot NF; Stevensville, MT 59870.

SPANISH PEAKS PRIMITIVE AREA; Gallatin NF

Located just west of the Gallatin River; 50,000 acres. Elevation ranges from 6,000-11,000 feet. Extremely rugged. More the 20 lakes. The largest band of mountain sheep in the area roam here. 50 miles of trails. Located 25 miles from Bozeman, Montana. Further information: Forest Supervisor; Gallatin NF; PO Box 130; Bozeman, MT 59715.

FREE CAMPGROUNDS

ALDER

Canyon (Beaverhead NF). 23-1/2 mi S of Alder on Co Hwy 357; 1-1/2 mi SE on FS 1001. **SEASON:** 5/1-11/15. **FACILITIES:** 3 sites (no tr); no drk wtr, tbls, toil, cga, f, stream. **ACTIVITIES:** Fishing; picnicking. **MISC.:** Elev 5900 ft; 1 acre; pets.

ANACONDA

Anaconda Sportsman's Park (Private). 2-1/2 mi S of Anaconda on St Hwy 274; from Divide, 25 mi W on St Hwy 43. **SEASON:** 5/15-10/31; 10-day lmt. **FACILITIES:** 30 sites, piped drk wtr, river, tbls, toil, cga, f, beach, bike trails. **ACTIVITIES:** Swimming; picnicking; fishing; hiking; rockhounding; biking. **MISC.:** Elev 4500 ft; pets on leash. Group camping.

Racetrack (Deerlodge NF). 3-1/10 mi E of Anaconda on US 10A; 6-3/5 mi N on St Hwy 48; 6-1/2 mi NW on 'Co Hwy; 1-1/2 mi NW on FS 169. **SEASON:** 6/15-11/15 14-day lmt. **FACILITIES:** 10 sites (tr - 22); tbls, toil, cga, f, no drk wtr. **ACTIVITIES:** Picnicking; fishing. **MISC.:** Elev 6000 ft; 5 acres; pets; stream; geological. 4 mi W to ghost town of Danielsville via very poor motor road unsuitable for passenger cars.

AUGUSTA

Bean Lake Fishing Access Site (Dept. of Fish and Game). 15 mi S of US 287 at Augusta, milepost 38, on Co Rd 434. **SEASON:** All year; 14-day lmt. **FACILITIES:** 50 sites; no drk wtr, tbls, toil, cga, f, snowmobile trails. **ACTIVITIES:** Ice skating; snowmobiling; swimming; picnicking; fishing; boating. **MISC.:** 17 acres; pets.

Benchmark (Lewis & Clark NF). 14 mi W of Augusta on Co Hwy 235; 15-1/2 mi SW on FS 235. **SEASON:** 6/1-9/15; 14-day lmt. **FACILITIES:** 34 sites (tr -22), well drk wtr, stream, tbls, toil, cga, f. **ACTIVITIES:** Hiking; picnicking; fishing. Horseback riding and rental (2 mi). **MISC.:** Elev 5200 ft; 19 acres; pets; stream. Trailhead into Scapegoat Wilderness.

Home Gulch (Lewis & Clark NF). 19-4/5 mi NW of Augusta on Co Hwy 1081; 1-7/10 mi W on FS 1082. **SEASON:** 5/15-9/15; 14-day lmt. **FACILITIES:** 15 sites (tr -16), well drk wtr, tbls, toil, cga. f. Store/gas (2 mi). **ACTIVITIES:** Fishing; picnicking. Horseback riding (1 mi). Boating,l (1 mi). **MISC.:** Elev 4400 ft; 6 acres; pets. Geological.

Mortimer (Lewis & Clark NF). 19-4/5 mi NW of Augusta on Co Hwy 1081; 3-9/10 mi W on FS 1082; 3 mi N on FS 8984. **SEASON:** 5/25-9/15; 14-day lmt. **FACILITIES:** 28 sites (tr -22), tbls, Toil, cga, no drk wtr. Food (1 mi). **ACTIVITIES:** Boating,ld; horseback riding; picnicking; fishing. **MISC.:** Elev 5300 ft; 8 acres; pets. Gibson Reservoir. Access to Bob Marshall Wilderness.

Pishkun Reservoir Fishing Access Site (Dept. of Fish and Game). N of Augusta milepost 46, on US 287; 12 mi NW on Co Rd. **SEASON:** 5/1-10/1; 14-day lmt. **FACILITIES:** Sites, no drk wtr, shelters, toil. **ACTIVITIES:** Fishing; boating; picnicking. **MISC.:** No pets.

South Fork (Lewis & Clark NF). 14 mi W of Augusta on Co Hwy 235; 16-1/2 mi SW on FS 235. **SEASON:** 6/1-9/15; 14-day lmt. **FAC:** 7 sites (tr -32); tbls, toil, cga, well drk wtr. **ACT:** Horseback riding/rentals; picnicking; fishing; hiking. **MISC.:** Elev 5200 ft; 9 acres; pets. Trailhead into Bob Marshall Wilderness. Stream.

Wood Lake (Lewis & Clark NF). 14 mi W of Augusta on Co Hwy 235; 9-3/5 mi SW on FS 235. **SEASON:** 6/1-9/15; 14-day lmt. **FACILITIES:** 7 sites (tr -22), tbls, toil, cga, f, well drk wtr. **ACTIVITIES:** Boating,l; picnicking; fishing. Horseback riding (1 mi). **MISC.:** Elev 5800 ft; 2 acres; pets.

BABB

St. Mary Lake (Glacier NP). 10 mi S of Babb on US 89. **SEASON:** 10/1-5/27, FREE (rest of yr, $3); 7-day lmt. **FACILITIES:** 156 sites (tr -26); flush toil, tbls, cga, dump, phone, food concession, store. **ACTIVITIES:** Horseback riding; boating; picnicking; fishing. **MISC.:** 13 acres; pets on leash.

BAKER

South Sandstone (SRA). W of Baker, milepost 680, on US 12; 7 mi S on Co Rd. **SEASON:** 5/1-10/1; 14-day lmt. **FACILITIES:** Sites; drk wtr, shelters, toil; tbls cga. **ACTIVITIES:** Boating; swimming; picnicking. **MISC.:** Pets.

BARRY'S LANDING

* **Medicine Creek Boat-In** (Bighorn Canyon NRA). 1 mi N of Barry's landing; access by BOAT. **SEASON:** 5/1-11/1; 30-day lmt. **FACILITIES:** 5 sites; tbls. **ACTIVITIES:** Swimming; picnicking; fishing. **MISC.:** Pets permitted.

BASIN

Basin Canyon (Deerlodge NF). 4 mi NW on FS 172 on dirt rd. **SEASON:** 6/1-9/15; 14-day lmt. **FACILITIES:** 3 sites (tr -32).

piped drk wtr, tbls, toil, cga, f. Store/
gas/ice/laundry/food (4 mi). ACTIVITIES:
Picnicking; fishing. Horseback riding
(1 mi). MISC.: Elev 5800 ft; 1 acre;
pets. Stream.

Ladysmith Campground (Deerlodge NF).
4 mi W on St Hwy 9; 3-2/5 mi W on FS
82. SEAS: 6/1-9/15; 14-day lmt. FACILI-
TIES: 5 sites (tr -16), well drk wtr,
tbls, toil, cga, f. ACTIVITIES: Horseback riding (1 mi); picnicking; fishing.
MISC.: Elev 5600 ft; 3 acres; pets.

Mormon Gulch (Deerlodge NF). 4 mi W
on St Hwy 91; 1 mi W on FS 82. SEA-
SON: 6/1-9/15; 14-day lmt. FACILITIES:
7 sites (tr -32), tbls, toil, cga, f,
piped drk wtr, stream. ACTIVITIES:
Horseback riding (1 mi); picnicking;
fishing. MISC.: Elev 5500 ft; 10 acres;
pets. Stream.

Shamrock (Deerlodge NF). 7-4/5 mi SW
of Basin on St Hwy 91. SEASON: 6/1-
9/15; 14-day lmt. FACILITIES: 7 sites
(tr -32), piped drk wtr, tbls, toil,
cga, f. ACTIVITIES: Horseback riding
(1 mi); picnicking; fishing. MISC.:
Elev 5500 ft; 8 acres; pets.

Whitehouse Campground (Deerlodge NF).
4 mi W of Basin on St Hwy 91; 7-1/10
mi W on FS 82. SEASON: 6/1-9/15; no
lmt. FACILITIES: 5 sites (no tr); no
drk wtr, stream, tbls, toil, cga, f.
ACTIVITIES: Horseback riding (1 mi);
picnicking; fishing. MISC.: Elev 6000
ft; 10 acres. Mountain meadow country.

BELGRADE

Blair's Self Service Truck Stop. I-90,
Belgrade exit, at Belgrade. SEASON:
All yr; 1-night lmt. FACILITIES: Spaces
for self-contained RVs; food, toil, drk
wtr, gas.

Belgrade (County Park). In Belgrade.
SEASON: All yr. FACILITIES: 4 sites;
tbls, toil, cga. ACTIVITIES: Picnicking.
MISC.: Pets on leash.

Lewis & Clark Town Park. Hwy 290 &
I-10, in town; gravel access rds. FAC-
ILITIES: No designated sites; tbls, toil,
playground. ACTIVITIES: Picnicking.

BIGFORK

Wayfarers State Recreation Area (SRA).
On St Hwy 35 at Bigfork milepost 31.
SEASON: 10/1-5/1, FREE (rest of year
$3.00); 14-day lmt. FACILITIES: 15
sites (tr -20), FLUSH TOIL, tbls, cga,
drk wtr, lake. ACTIVITIES: Swimming;
picnicking; fishing. MISC.: 43 acres.

BIG SKY

Buffalo Horn (Gallatin NF). 2-1/5 mi
E of Big Sky on St Hwy 191S; 12-1/10
mi S on US 191; 1-7/10 mi NE on FS
6907. SEASON: 7/1-9/15; 14-day lmt.
FACILITIES: 3 sites (tr -16); tbls,
toil, cga, f, no drk wtr. Store/gas/ice
food (3 mi). ACTIVITIES: Picnicking;
fishing. Horseback riding (2 mi).
MISC.: Elev 6800 ft; 3 acres; pets.
Scenic. Stream.

Cascade (Gallatin NF). 2-1/5 mi E of
Big Sky on St Hwy 191S; 1 mi N on
US 191; 3/10 mi S on FS 130. SEASON:
6/15-9/15; 14-day lmt. FACILITIES:
3 sites (no tr); tbls, toil, cga, f, no
drk wtr. Store/gas/food (4 mi). ACTIVI-
TIES: Picnicking; fishing. MISC.: Elev
5600 ft; 1 acre; pets. Scenic. 2-1/2
mi NE of Lava Lake.

McGill (Gallatin NF). 2-1/5 mi E of Big
Sky on St Hwy 191S; 6-3/5 mi S on US
191; 1/10 mi E on FS. SEASON: 6/15-9/15;
14-day lmt. FACILITIES: 6 sites (tr -16),
tbls, toil, cga, f, river. ACTIVITIES:
Fishing; picnicking. MISC.: Elev 6400
ft; pets. 10 mi N of Yellowstone National
Park.

BIG TIMBER

Bratten Fishing Access Site (Dept. of
Fish and Game). E of Big Timber, mile-
post 392, on I-90; 5 mi W on Frontage
Rd. SEASON: 5/1-10/1; 14-day lmt. FA-
CILITIES: Sites; toil, no drk wtr.
ACTIVITIES: Fishing; picnicking. MISC.:
Pack in and out.

Chippy Park (Gallatin NF). 25 mi S of
Big Timber on St Hwy 298; 9 mi S on
FS 212. SEASON: 6/15-10/15; 14-day lmt.
FACILITIES: 4 sites (tr -16), no drk
wtr, tbls, toil, cga, f, stream. ACTIVI-
TIES: Rockhounding; picnicking; fishing.
MISC.: Elev 5500 ft; 5 acres; pets.
Historic.

Culbertson Wayside. E edge of Big Timber. FACILITIES: 10 sites; tbls, toil.
ACTIVITIES: Fishing; picnicking.

Grey Bear Fishing Access Site (Dept. of
Fish and Game). 12 mi W of Big Timber,
milepost 360, on US 10; 1 mi NW on Co
Rd (gravel access rd). SEASON: 5/1-10/1.
14-day lmt. FACILITIES: 8 sites; no
drk wtr, river, beach, tbls, toil, cga,
trails. ACTIVITIES: Hunting; swimming;
picnicking; fishing; hiking; rockhounding. MISC.: Elev 4250 ft; small pets.
On Yellowstone River.

Halfmoon (Gallatin NF). 12 mi N of Big
Timber on St Hwy 19; 8 mi W on Co
Hwy 197; 2 mi W on FS 197. SEASON:
6/15-10/15; 14-day lmt. FACILITIES:
9 sites (no tr); tbls, toil, cga, f, well

drk wtr, stream. ACTIVITIES: Mountain climbing; picnicking; fishing. MISC.: Elev 6400 ft; 3 acres; pets. Crazy Mountain (only public access E side). Scenic.

Hells Canyon (Gallatin NF). 25 mi S of Big Timber on St Hwy 298; 14 mi S on FS 212. SEASON: 6/15-10/1; 14-day lmt. FACILITIES: 11 sites (tr -16), tbls, toil, cga, f, no drk wtr. ACTIVITIES: Rockhounding; picnicking; fishing MISC.: Elev 6000 ft; 5 acres. Scenic.

Indian Fort Fishing Acces Site (Dept. of Fish and Game). E of Big Timber milepost 392, on I-90; 1 mi N on Co Rd. SEASON: 5/1-10/1; 14-day lmt. FACILITIES: Sites, tbls, toil, cga, drk wtr. ACTIVITIES: Boating; picnicking; fishing.

West Boulder (Gallatin NF). 20 mi SW of Big Timber on St Hwy 298; 1 mi W on Co Hwy 35; 5-2/5 mi SW on FS 35. SEASON: 6/15-10/15; 14-day lmt. FACILITIES: 10 sites (no tr); well drk wtr, tbls, toil, cga, f. ACTIVITIES: Picnicking; fishing; hiking; mountain climbing. MISC.: Elev 5600 ft; 20 acres; pets; geological; stream; scenic. Jump off for the West Boulder backcountry and mountaineering in the Absaroka mountain range in the Absaroka-Beartooth Wilderness.

BILLINGS

BPC Service Corp. Husky (Truck Stop). I-90, exit 446; 2/5 mi E on City Center Rd in Billings. SEASON: All year; 1-night lmt. FACILITIES: Spaces for self-contained RVs; food, toil, drk wtr, gas. MISC.: Mechanic.

BOZEMAN

Blackmore (Gallatin NF). 8 mi S of Bozeman on Co Hwy 243; 9 mi SE on FS 62. SEASON: 6/15-9/15; 14-day lmt. FACILITIES: 3 sites, no tr; tbls, toil, cga, f. ACTIVITIES: Fishing; picnicking. MISC.: Elev 6600 ft.

* **Emerald Lake** (Gallatin NF). 8 mi S of Bozeman on Co Hwy 243; 11 mi SE on FS 62; 2-2/5 mi SE on FS 3163; 4-1/2 mi S on TRAIL 434. SEASON: 7/1-9/15. FACILITIES: 3 sites, no tr; toil. ACTIVITIES: Hiking; picnicking; fishing. MISC.: Elev 8000 ft.

Fairy Lake (Gallatin NF). 22 mi NE of Bozeman on St Hwy 293; 6 mi W on FS 74. (Access rd poor; tr not recommended). SEASON: 7/1-9/15; 14-day lmt. FACILITIES: 8 sites (no tr); tbls, toil, cga, f; no drk wtr. ACTIVITIES: Picnicking; fishing; hiking. MISC.: Elev 7600 ft; 2 acres; pets; geological. Limestone Peaks. Fairy Lake.

BRIDGER

Sage Creek (Custer NF). 3 mi S of Bridger on US 310; 22 mi SE on Co Hwy; 1/2 mi E on FS 50. SEASON: 6/15-9/15; 9-day lmt. FACILITIES: 12 sites (tr -32), piped drk wtr, tbls, toil, cga, f, stream. ACTIVITIES: Rockhounding; picnicking; fishing. MISC.: Elev 5600 ft; 17 acres. Pryor Mountains. Stream.

BROCKTON

Brockton Community Park (Fort Peck Indian Agency). 1/4 mi S of Brockton at Jct US 2 and St Hwy 404. SEASON: 5/1-9/15; no time lmt. FACILITIES: 4 sites (tr -15), tbls, cga, f. DUMP/store /bottled gas (1 mi). ACTIVITIES: Fishing; picnicking. MISC.: Pets.

BUTTE

Beaver Dam (Deerlodge NF). 7 mi W of Butte on I-90; 17-1/2 mi S on I-15; 5-1/2 mi W on FS 961. SEASON: 6/1-10/1. FACILITIES: 9 sites (tr -22); tbls, toil, cga, f, piped drk wtr. ACTIVITIES: Picnicking; hiking. Fishing (1 mi). MISC.: Elev 5800 ft; 6 acres; pets; stream. Nature Trails (1 mi).

Lowland (Deerlodge NF). 9 mi NE of Butte on I-15; 6-1/2 mi W on FS 442. SEASON: 6/10-10/10; no time lmt. FACILITIES: 7 sites (tr -22), well drk wtr, tbls, toil, cga, f. ACTIVITIES: Picnicking; fishing. MISC.: Elev 6400 ft; 5 acres. Pets.

CAMERON

Madison River (Beaverhead NF). 23-3/5 mi S of Cameron on St Hwy 287; 1/10 mi SW on Co Hwy 8381; 9/10 mi S on FS 8381B. SEASON: 6/15-9/15; 14-day lmt. FACILITIES: 10 sites (tr -32), well drk wtr, tbls, toil, cga, f, bike trails, river. Gas/Dump (2 mi). ACTIVITIES: Horseback riding; hiking; hunting; picnicking; fishing; rockhounding. MISC.: Elev 6000 ft; 4 acres; pets. Good trout fishing on adjacent Madison River.

West Fork (Beaverhead NF). 23-3/5 mi S of Cameron on St Hwy 287; 3/10 mi W on FS 8381. SEASON: 6/15-9/15; 14-day lmt. FACILITIES: 5 sites (tr -16), no drk wtr, stream, tbls, toil, cga, f, DUMP (1 mi); gas (2 mi). ACTIVITIES: Horsback riding; picnicking; fishing. MISC.: Elev 6000 ft; 2 acres. Campground is adjacent to good trout fishing on Madison River.

CHESTER

Tiber Reservoir Recreation Area (SRA).
10 mi S of Chester on St Hwy 223 and
unpaved road; 5 mi W. **SEASON:** 10/1–5/1
FREE; (rest of year, $2.00); 14-day lmt.
FACILITIES: 50 sites; drk wtr, tbls,
toil, cga. **ACTIVITIES:** Picnicking;
fishing; boating,l. **MISC.:** Pets.

CHINOOK

Chief Joseph State Monument. 16 mi S
of Chinook on Co Rd. **SEASON:** 5/1–10/1;
14-day lmt. **FACILITIES:** Unlimited tent
sites, 5 tr sites; tbls. **ACTIVITIES:** Picnicking. **MISC.:** Pets.

CHOTEAU

Arod Lake Fishing Access Site (Dept.
of Fish and Game). 1 mi E of Choteau
on Co Rd 221; 17 mi N on Co Rd 378.
SEASON: 5/1–10/1; 14-day lmt. **FACILI-
TIES:** sites, toil, tlbs. No drk wtr.
ACTIVITIES: Boating; picnicking; fishing
MISC.: Pets.

Cave Mountain (Lewis & Clark NF). 5-
1/2 mi N of Choteau on US 89; 22–4/5
mi W on Co Hwy 144.1; 1–1/2 mi W on
FS 144.2. **SEASON:** 4/1–9/15. **FACILITIES:**
14 sites (tr –16), well drk wtr, tbls,
toil, cga, f. **ACTIVITIES:** Picnicking; fishing; hiking. Horseback riding (1 mi). **MISC.:** Elev 5200 ft; 12
acres; pets. Take-off point for Bob
Marshall Wilderness via Route Creek
Pass.

Choteau Park (City Park). E on St
Hwy 221, off US 89 & 287 in town.
(Gravel Access Rds.). **SEASON:** 5/15–9/15;
3-day lmt. **FACILITIES:** 70 sites, FLUSH
TOIL, DUMP, playground, store/laundry/
bottled gas (1 mi). **ACTIVITIES:** Swim-
ming (1 mi); picnicking; fishing.
MISC.: Access to river.

City Park. Center of Choteau off Hwy.

Eureka Reservoir Fishing Access Site
(Dept. of Fish and Game). N of Choteau
milepost 345, on US 89; 4 mi W on Co
Rd. **SEASON:** 5/1–10/1; 14-day lmt. **FA-
CILITIES:** Sites, toil, no drk wtr, tbls.
ACTIVITIES: Fishing; picnicking; boat-
ing. **MISC.:** Pets.

Mill Falls (Lewis & Clark NF). 5–1/2
mi from Choteau on US 89; 18–4/5 mi
on Co Hwy 144; 6 mi S on Co Hwy 109;
3–1/2 mi W on FS 109. **SEASON:** 6/1–9/15;
14-day lmt. **FACILITIES:** 4 sites (tr
–16); tbls, toil, cga, f, no drk wtr.
ACTIVITIES: Picnicking; fishing.
Horseback riding/rental (1 mi).
MISC.: Elev 5600 ft;1 acre;pets;stream.

CIRCLE

Jaycees. In Circle. **SEASON:** All yr.
FACILITIES: 20 sites; piped drk wtr,

toil, playground, softball field. **ACTIV-
ITIES:** Rockhounding; hiking; swimming;
softball. **MISC.:** Water, toil quite a
distance from sites. Elev 2100 ft.

CLANCY

Park Lake (Helena NF). 1 mi N of
Clancy on Co Hwy 426; 5–1/2 mi W on
FS 4000; 2–1/10 mi SW on FS 426.1; 5
mi W on FS 4009. **SEASON:** 6/15–10/1;
15-day lmt. **FACILITIES:** 22 sites (tr
–32); tbls, toil, cga, f, no drk wtr.
ACTIVITIES: Picnicking; swimming;
fishing; boating,ld (no motors).
MISC.: Elev 6400 ft; 10 acres; pets.
Park Lake.

CLINTON

Bitterroot Flat (Lolo NF). 4–9/10 mi SE
of Clinton on I-90; 23 mi S on FS 102.
SEASON: 5/20–9/30. **FACILITIES:** 15
sites (tr –32); tbls, toil, cga, well
drk wtr, f. **ACTIVITIES:** Picnicking;
fishing. **MISC.:** Elev 4400 ft; 5 acres;
pets.

Dalles (Lolo NF). 4–9/10 mi SE of Clinton
on I-90; 14–3/5 mi S on FS 102. **SEASON:**
5/20–9/30. **FACILITIES:** 10 sites (tr
–32); tbls, toil, cga, f; no drk wtr.
Store/ice (3 mi). **ACTIVITIES:** Picnicking; fishing. **MISC.:** Elev 4400
ft; 3 acres; pets; stream.

Grizzly (Lolo NF). 4–9/10 mi SE of
Clinton on I-90; 10–3/5 mi S on FS 102;
1/2 mi SE on FS 88. **SEASON:** 5/20–9/30.
FACILITIES: 9 sites (tr –32); tbls,
toil, cga, f; no drk wtr. Ice/store
(2 mi). **ACTIVITIES:** Picnicking; fishing. **MISC.:** Elev 4200 ft; 6 acres;
pets; stream. 3 mi S of site of old
town of Quigley.

Harrys Flat (Lolo NF). 4–9/10 mi SE of
Clinton on I-90; 17–3/5 mi S on FS 102.
SEASON: 5/20–9/30. **FACILITIES:** 14
sites (tr –32); tbls, toil, cga, drk
wtr (piped). **ACTIVITIES:** Picnicking;
fishing. **MISC.:** Elev 4200 ft; 7 acres;
stream; pets.

Norton (Lolo NF). 4–9/10 mi SE of Clinton
on I-90; 10 mi S on FS 102. **SEASON:**
5/20–9/30. **FACILITIES:** 10 sites (no
tr); tbls, toil, cga, f, no drk wtr.
Store/ice (1 mi). **ACTIVITIES:** Picnicking; fishing. **MISC.:** Elev 4100
ft; 5 acres; pets; stream.

Siria (Lolo NF). 4–9/10 mi SE of Clinton
on I-90; 29–1/5 mi S on FS 102 (rough
rd). **SEASON:** 5/20–9/30. **FACILITIES:**
4 sites (tr –16); toil, cga, f, no drk
wtr. No tbls. **ACTIVITIES:** Picnicking; fishing. **MISC.:** Elev 4800 ft;
5 acres; pets; stream.

COAL BANKS LANDING

* **Hole-In-The-Wall Landing** (Missouri River Waterway). 21 mi E of Coal Banks Landing on Missouri River BY BOAT. SEASON: 5/1-9/30; 14-day lmt. FACILITIES: 5 tent sites, tbls. ACTIVITIES: Boating; picnicking. MISC.: Pets.

COLUMBIA FALLS

Tuchuck (Flathead NF). 53 mi N of Columbia Falls on FS 210; 10 mi W on FS 114. SEASON: 6/15-9/30; 14-day lmt. FACILITIES: 7 sites (tr -22), no drk wtr, tbls, toil, cga, f. ACTIVITIES: Fishing; picnicking. MISC.: Elev 4600 ft; 2 acres. Pets.

Upper Big Creek (Flathead NF). 22 mi N of Columbia Falls on FS 210. SEASON: 6/1-9/15; 14-day lmt. FACILITIES: 4 sites (tr -22), toil, cga, f. ACTIVITIES: Fishing; picnicking. MISC.: Elev 3300 ft. Across Flathead River from Glacier NP. Pets on leash.

COLUMBUS

Buffalo Jump Fishing Access Site (Dept. of Fish and Game). S on I-90 at Columbus, milepost 408, on Co Rd 307 to Absarokee; S on Co Rd 419 to milepost 21. SEASON: 5/1-10/1; 14-day lmt. FACILITIES: Sites; no drk wtr, tbls, toil, cga. ACTIVITIES: Fishing; picnicking. MISC.: Pets.

Castle Rock Fishing Access Site (Dept. S of I-90 at Columbus, milepost 408, on Co Rd 307 to Absarokee; 23 mi W on Co Rd 420. SEASON: 5/1-10/1; 14-day lmt. FACILITIES: Stes, drk wtr, toil, tbls. ACTIVITIES: Fishing; picnicking. MISC.: Pets.

Cliff Swallow Fishing Access Site (Dept. of Fish and Game). S of I-90 at Columbus, milepost 408, on Co Rd 307 to Absorokee; 10 mi W on Co Rd 420. SEASON: 5/1-10/1; 14-day lmt. FACILITIES: Sites, no 14-day lmt., toil. ACTIVITIES: Fishing; picnicking. MISC.: Pets.

Fireman's Point Fishing Access Site (Dept. of Fish and Game). S of I-90 at Columbus, milepost 408, on Co Rd 307, milepost 44; 1/2 mi W on Co Rd. SEASON: 5/1-10/1; 14-day lmt. FACILITIES: Sites, toil, no drk wtr. ACTIVITIES: Fishing; picnicking. MISC.: Pets.

Itch-Kep-Pe Fishing Access Site (Dept. of Fish and Game). 2 mi S of I-90 at Columbus, milepost 408, on Co Rd 307. SEASON: 5/1-10/1; 14-day lmt. FACILITIES: Sites, toil, drk wtr. ACTIVITIES: Boating; picnicking; fishing. MISC.: Pets.

Moraine Fishing Access Site (Dept. of Fish and Game). S of I-90 at Columbus, milepost 408, on Co Rd 307 to Absarokee; 24 mi W on Co Rd 420. SEASON: 5/1-10/1; 14-day lmt. FACILITIES: Sites; toil, drk wtr. ACTIVITIES: Fishing; picnicking. MISC.: Pets.

Rosebud Isle Fishing Access Site (Dept. of Fish and Game). S of I-90 at Columbus, milepost 408, on Co Rd 307 to Junction S of Absarokee; 3 mi SE on Co Rd 419 to Fishtall. SEASON: 5/1-10/1; 14-day lmt. FACILITIES: Sites, toil, no drk wtr. ACTIVITIES: Fishing; picnicking. MISC.: Pets.

White Bird Fishing Access Site (Dept. of Fish and Game). S of I-90 at Columbus, milepost 408, on Co Rd 307 to milepost 7. SEASON: 5/1-10/1; 14-day lmt. FACILITIES: Sites, toil, drk wtr. ACTIVITIES: Fishing; picnicking. MISC.: Pets.

CONDON

Fatty Creek (Flathead NF). 18 mi NW of Condon on St Hwy 209; 8 mi SE on FS 88. SEASON: 7/1-10/15. FACILITIES: 3 sites (tr -22), toil. ACTIVITIES: Fishing; picnicking. MISC.: Elev 5000 ft. 1 mi E of Mission Mountain Primitive Area. Pets on leash.

Holland Lake (Flathead NF). 8½ mi SE of Condon on St Hwy 209; 3 mi E on FS 44. SEASON: 6/1-9/15; 14-day lmt. FACILITIES: 46 sites (tr -22), tbls, toil, cga, f. dump. ACTIVITIES: Swimming; hunting; boating,rld; waterskiing; horseback riding; picnicking; fishing; hiking. MISC.: Elev 4000 ft; 24 acres. Pets. Lake, river, beach. Bob Marshall Wilderness (5 mi).

Lindbergh Lake (Flathead NF). 10 mi SE of Condon on St Hwy 83; 4 mi W on FS 79. SEASON: 5/26-9/15; 14-day lmt. FACILITIES: 4 sites (tr -22); tbls, toil, cga, no drk wtr. Food (1 mi). ACTIVITIES: Picnicking; boating,ld (rental, 1 mi); swimming; waterskiing; fishing. Horseback riding/rental (1 mi). MISC.: Elev 4200 ft; 3 acres; pets; scenic; stream. Mission Mountain Wilderness (4 mi).

Owl Creek (Flathead NF). 8-1/2 mi SE on St Hwy 83; 3 mi E on FS 44. SEASON: 7/1-11/15; 14-day lmt. FACILITIES: 6 sites (tr -22), tbls, toil, cga, f, piped drk wtr. Stock handling facilities available. Dump (1 mi). ACTIVITIES: Picnicking; hiking. Swimming/waterskiing/fishing/boating,rl/horseback riding & rental (1 mi). MISC.: Elev 4000 ft; 10 acres; pets; scenic; stream. Bob Marshall Wilderness (5 mi). Nature trails (1 mi).

See page 7 for KEY TO ABBREVIATIONS.

CONNER

Painted Rocks (SRA). 22-2/5 mi SW on St Hwy 473. SEASON: 5/15-10/30; 14-day lmt. FACILITIES: 28 sites, tbls, toil, cga, f, boat/l. ACTIVITIES: Rockhounding; hiking; boating; waterskiing; picnicking; fishing. MISC.: Elev 5000 ft. Small pets only. Reservoir water at pumps.

Slate Creek (NF). 19-3/10 mi SW of Conner on St Hwy 473. SEASON: 5/15-10/15; 10-day lmt. FACILITIES: 9 sites, tbls, toil, cga, f, boat/l, lake, river, beach ACTIVITIES: Boating; waterskiing; picnicking; fishing; hiking. MISC.: On Painted Rock Reservoir. Small pets on leash.

COOKE CITY

Chief Joseph (Gallatin NF). 4-4/5 mi E on US 212 [heavy trailers approach from West only]. SEASON: 7/1-9/10; 15-day lmt. FACILITIES: 5 sites (tr -22), well drk wtr, tbls, toil, cga, f. Gas/ice/food (1 mi). Store/dump/showers/laundry (5 mi). ACTIVITIES: Mountain climbing; picnicking. Fishing/horseback riding/rental (1 mi). Swimming/boating,rd (3 mi). MISC.: Elev 8000 ft; 5 acres; pets; scenic. NE entrance to Yellowstone National Park (10 mi).

Reef Creek. 14-2/5 mi SE of Cooke City on US 212; 12-2/5 mi SE on FS Rd 296. SEASON: 5/15-10/15; 14-day lmt. FACILITIES: 4 sites (tr -32), well drk wtr, tbls, toil, cga, f. ACTIVITIES: Horseback riding; picnicking. Fishing (5 mi). MISC.: Elev 6700 ft; 2 acres. Pets.

CRAIG

Craig Public Campground (SRA). I-15 at town interchange between I-15 and Missouri River [dirt access rds]. SEASON: 5/15-10/15; 14-day lmt. FACILITIES: 11 sites; tbls, toil, cga, f. ACTIVITIES:Hiking; rockhounding; boating,l; snow skiing; picnicking; fishing. MISC.: elev 3800 ft. Pets on leash.

Wolf Creek Canyon (SRA). I-15 at town interchange 3-3/5 mi N on Frontage Rd [dirt access rds]. SEASON: 5/15-10/15. FACILITIES: 5 sites, tbls, toil, cga, f, river, boat ramp. ACTIVITIES: Boating; rockhounding; snow skiing; hiking; picnicking; fishing. MISC.: Elev 3750 ft. Pets. Bike trails.

DARBY

Alta (Bitterroot NF). 4-1/10 mi S of Darby on US 93; 21-3/5 mi S on St Hwy 473; 6 mi S on Co Hwy 96. SEASON: 6/1-9/15; 10-day lmt. FACILITIES: 15 sites (tr -22), tbls, cga, f, toil, well drk wtr. ACTIVITIES: Picnicking; hunting;

hiking. Fishing (1 mi). Waterskiing (4 mi). MISC.: Elev 5000 ft; 6 acres; pets. On West Fork of Bitterroot River. Hughes Creek was site of early day placer gold mining. Near historical town of Alta & 1st Ranger Station in the United States.

Bear Creek Pass (Bitterroot NF). 7-3/10 mi N of Darby on US 93; 1-2/5 mi W on Co Hwy; 17 mi W on FS [dirt mountain rd to area]. SEASON: 7/15-9/15; 10-day lmt. FACILITIES: 7 sites (tr -22), no drk wtr; tbls, toil, cga. ACTIVITIES: Hunting; hiking; picnicking. Fishing (1 mi). Boating,ld (3 mi). MISC.: Elev 6200 ft; 2 acres; pets. At the head of Lost Horse Creek. Access point for Selway--Bitterroot Wilderness. Stream.

Boulder Creek Trail Takeoff (Bitterroot NF). 4-1/10 mi S of Darby on US 93; 12-9/10 mi SW on Co Hwy 473; 1 mi NW on 5631. SEASON: 6/1-9/15; 10-day lmt. FACILITIES: 11 sites (tr -22); tbls, toil, cga, f, no drk wtr. Showers/ice gas/food (5 mi). ACTIVITIES: Hunting; picnicking. Fishing (1 mi). Horseback riding (rental, 5 mi). MISC.: Elev 4400 ft; 8 acres. Selway Bitterroot Wildness takeoff (1/2 mi). Pets. Scenic.

Deep Creek (Bitterroot NF). 4-1/10 mi S of Darby on US 93; 14-2/5 mi SW on Co Hwy 473; 32-3/10 mi W on FS 468. SEASON: 6/15-11/26; 10-day lmt. FACILITIES: 3 sites (tr -16); no drk wtr; tbls, toil, cga,f. ACTIVITIES: Picnicking. Fishing (1 mi). MISC.: Elev 4200 ft; 2 acres. Stream. Pets.

Indian Creek (Bitterroot NF). 4-1/10 mi S of Darby on US 93; 14-2/5 mi SW on Co 473; 36-1/2 mi W on FS 6223; 5 mi N on FS 6223. SEASON: 6/15-11/26; 10-day lmt. FACILITIES: 8 sites (tr -16); no drk wtr; tbls, toil, cga, f. ACTIVITIES: Picnicking. MISC.: Elev 3600 ft; 2 acres. Artificial hatching channel for Spring Chinook Salmon located here. Pets.

Painted Rocks Reservoir (SRA). 3 mi S of Darby on US 93; 15 mi SW on Co Rd 473. SEASON: 5/1-10/1; 14-day lmt. FACILITIES: 10 sites (tr -25); tbls. ACTIVITIES: Swimming; picnicking; fishing; boating, l. MISC.: 262 acres. Pets.

Paradise (Bitterroot NF). 4-1/10 mi S of Darby on US 93; 14-2/5 mi SW on Co 473; 36-1/2 mi W on FS 468; 11-2/5 mi N on FS 6223. SEASON: 6/15-11/26; 10-day lmt. FACILITIES: 12 sites (tr -16); no drk wtr; tbls, toil, cga, f. ACTIVITIES: Picnicking. MISC.: Elev 3200 ft; 6 acres; pets. Scenic. Whitewater float trips down Selway River from here in June.

Rombo (Bitterroot NF). 4-1/10 mi S of Darby on US 93; 18 mi SW on Co Hwy 473. SEASON: 6/1-9/15: 10-day lmt. FACILITIES: 14 sites (tr -22); well drk wtr, tbls, toil, cga. ACT: Hunting; hiking; picnicking. Fishing (1 mi). MISC.: 4400 ft; 7 acres; pets. On W Fork of Bitterroot River. 3 air mi N of Painted Rocks Lake.

Schumaker (Bitterroot NF). 7-3/10 mi N of Darby on US 93; 1-2/5 mi W on Co Hwy 76; 16 mi W on FS 429; 2-2/5 mi N on FS 5605. SEASON: 7/15-9/15; 10-day lmt. FACILITIES: 5 sites (tr -22); no drk wtr; tbls, toil, cga, f. ACTIVITIES: Picnicking. Fishing (1 mi). Boating (1 mi). MISC.: Elev 6600 ft; 7 acres; pets. On Twin Lakes. Access to Selway-Bitterroot Wilderness (1 mi [unsurfaced rd]).

Slate Creek (Bitterroot NF). 4-1/10 mi S of Darby on US 93; 21-3/5 mi S on Co Hwy 473; 2 mi S on Co Hwy 96. SEASON: 6/1-9/15; 10-day lmt. FACILITIES: 9 sites (tr -22); tbls, toil, cga, f, well drk wtr. ACTIVITIES: Picnicking; fishing. Boating,ld/ waterskiing (1 mi). MISC.: Elev 4800 ft; 6 acres; pets; scenic. Adjacent to 700-acre Painted Rocks Lake on West Fork of Bitterroot River.

DAYTON

Lake Mary Ronan Recreaction Area (SRA). 7 mi NW of Dayton on US 93 (poor access rds). SEASON: 10/1-5/1, FREE (rest of yr, $3.00); 14-day lmt. FACILITIES: 20 sites (tr -20); tbls, f, drk wtr. ACTIVITIES: Boating,l; picnicking; fishing. MISC.: Elev 3200 ft; 76 acres; pets. Lake.

Lambeth (SRA). 7 mi NW of US 93 at Dayton, milepost 83. SEASON: 10/1-5/1 FREE (rest of yr, $2.00); 14-day lmt. FACILITIES: Sites; tbls, toil. ACTIVITIES: Boating; picnicking. MISC.: Pets.

DEER LODGE

Orofino (Deerlodge NF). 13 mi SE of Deer Lodge on FS 82 (Boulder Basin Rd) via Champion Pass. SEASON: 6/15-9/1; 10-day lmt. FACILITIES: 10 sites (tr -32); tbls, toil, cga, f, piped drk wtr. ACTIVITIES: Picnicking; hiking; horseback riding. MISC.: Elev 6600 ft; 3 acres; pets.

DILLON

Bannack State Park. On US 91, S of Dillon, milepost 57, 21 mi W on Co Rd 278. SEASON: 5/1-10/1; 14-day lmt. FAC-ILITIES: 10 sites (tr -20); tbls, toil, cga, f, drk wtr. ACTIVITIES: Picnicking. Fishing nearby. MISC.: 50 acres.

Clark Canyon Reservoir (SRA). 20 mi S of Dillon on I-15 (St Hwy 91). SEA-SON: 10/1-5/1, FREE (rest of yr, $2.00). 14-day lmt. FACILITIES: 30 sites (tr -25); drk wtr, tbls. ACTIVITIES: Boat-ing,l; swimming; picnicking; fishing. MISC.: Elev 5500 ft; 1200 acres; pets.

Glen Fishing Access Site (Dept. of Fish and Game). N of Dillon, milepost 85, on I-15; 6 mi S on Frontage Rd. SEA-SON: 5/1-10/1; 14-day lmt. FACILITIES: Sites, toil, no drk wtr. ACTIVITIES: Picnicking; fishing. MISC.: Pack in/out.

Grasshopper (Beaverhead NF). 4 mi S of Dillon on US 91; 27 mi NW on St Hwy 278; 11-1/2 mi N on Co Hwy 4843; 1/2 mi N on FS 4843. SEASON: 7/1-9/15; 14-day lmt. FACILITIES: 24 sites (tr -16); piped drk wtr, tbls, cga, toil, f. Showers/ice/gas/store (1 mi). ACTIVI-TIES: Picnicking. Horseback riding (1 mi). Fishing (3 mi). MISC.: Elev 7000 ft; 9 acres; pets. Near Elkhorn Hot Springs Resort.

Reservoir Lake (Beaverhead NF). 19 mi S of Dillon on US 91; 16-4/5 mi W on St Hwy 324; 10 mi NW on Co Hwy 1814; 5 mi N on FS 1813. SEASON: 7/1-9/15; 14-day lmt. FACILITIES: 19 sites (tr -16); tbls, toil, cga, f, well drk wtr. ACTIVITIES: Picnicking; swim-ming; fishing; boating,ld (no motors). MISC.: Elev 7000 ft; 11 acres; pets; 45-acre lake.

DIVIDE

Big Hole (County Campground). 25 mi W of Divide on I-15 at town on St Hwy 43 [dirt access rds]. SEASON: 5/15-10/30; 10-day lmt. FACILITIES: No designated sties; tbls, cga, f. ACTIVITIES: Rock-hounding; hiking; picnicking; fishing. MISC.: Elev 4500 ft. Pets on leash.

Fishtrap Creek. 25 mi W of Divide on I-15 at town on St Hwy 43 [dirt access rds]. SEASON: 5/15-10/30; 10-day lmt. FACILITIES: 22 sites; tbls, toil, cga, f. ACTIVITIES: Hiking; rockhounding; swimming; picnicking; fishing. MISC.: Elev 4700 ft. Pets on leash.

EAST GLACIER

Summit Campground (Helena NF). 10 mi SW of East Glacier on US 2. SEASON: 6/15-9/15. FACILITIES: 21 sites (tr -22); tbls, toil, cga, f. ACTIVITIES: Hiking; picnicking; fishing. MISC.: Elev 5200 ft; 1 acre. Small pets only. Adjacent to Glacier National Park. Bike trails.

EKALAKA

Ekalaka Park (Custer NF). 3-3/10 mi SE of Ekalaka on St Hwy 323; 4/5 mi W on Co Hwy; 5-1/10 mi S on FS 8131.

SEASON: 5/15-10/31. FACILITIES: 7 sites (tr -16); piped drk wtr, tbls, toil, cga, f. ACTIVITIES: Picnicking. MISC.: Elev 3800 ft; 5 acres; pets. Located in a cool hardwood draw.

Macnab Pond (Custer NF). 7 mi SE of Ekalaka on St Hwy 323; 2/5 mi E on Co Hwy. SEASON: 5/15-10/30. FACILITIES: 5 sites (tr -22); tbls, toil, cga, f, well drk wtr. ACTIVITIES: Picnicking; fishing (trout stocked pond). MISC.: Elev 3500 ft; 8 acres; pets. Lake.

Medicine Rocks (State Park). 11 mi N of Ekalaka, milepost 12, on Hwy 7; 1 mi W on Co Rd. SEASON: 5/1-10/1; 14-day lmt. FACILITIES: 20 sites (tr -25); tbls, toil, cga, drk wtr. MISC.: 320 acres. Pets.

ELMO

Elmo Recreation Area (SRA). N of Elmo, milepost 78, on US 93. SEASON: 10/1-5/1 FREE (rest of yr, $2.00); 14-day lmt. FACILITIES: Sites, drk wtr, shelters. ACTIVITIES: Swimming; picnicking. Boating.

ENNIS

᛫ **Ennis Fishing Access Site.** 5 mi SE of Ennis on US 287, milepost 48; BOAT ACCESS. SEASON: 10/1-5/1, FREE (rest of yr, $2.00). 14-day lmt. FACILITIES: 15 sites (tr -20); tbls, drk wtr. ACTIVITIES: Boating,l; picnicking; fishing. MISC.: 77 acres; pets.

Harrison Lake Fishing Access Site (Dept of Fish and Game). N of Ennis, milepost 75, on US 287; 5 mi E on Co Rd. SEASON: 5/1-10/1; 14-day lmt. FACILITIES: Sites, no drk wtr, toil. ACTIVITIES: Boating; picnicking; fishing. MISC.: Pets.

Jack Creek (Beaverhead NF). 3/5 mi SE of Ennis on St Hwy 287; 12 mi E on Co Hwy 166. SEASON: 6/15-9/15. FACILITIES: 6 sites (tr -32); well drk wtr, tbls, toil, cga, f. ACTIVITIES: Horseback riding; picnicking; fishing; hiking. MISC.: Elev 6000 ft; 2 acres; pets. Trailhead into Spanish Peaks Wilderness.

RUBY CREEK (BLM; West Madison Recreation Area). 17 mi S on US 287; turn right at W Madison Recreation Area sign to Madison River (MacAtee Bridge); turn left, drive 3 mi to Ruby Creek Campground. SEASON: 5/1-10/31. FACILITIES: 28 sites (tr-24); tbls, toil, cga, f, store. ACTIVITIES: Hunting; hiking; boating,l; picknicking; fishing. MISC.: Elev 5000 ft; 20 acres; pets. The Madison River runs thru the area.

Valley Garden Fishing Access Site (Dept of Fish and Game). W of Ennis, milepost 1, on US 287; 10 mi S on Co Rd. SEASON: 5/1-10/1; 14-day lmt. FACILITIES: Sites, drk wtr, toil. ACTIVITIES: Fishing; picnicking. MISC.: Pets. Pack in/out.

Varney Bridge Fishing Access Site (Dept of Fish and Game). W of Ennis, milepost 1, on US 287; 10 mi S on Co Rd. SEASON: 5/1-10/1; 14-day lmt. FACILITIES: Sites, toil, drk wtr. ACTIVITIES: Boating; picnicking; fishing. MISC.: Pets. Pack in/out.

South Madison Recreation Area. 26 mi S of Ennis on US 287; turn right at the South Madison Recreation Area sign, and proceed 1/4 mi to campground. SEASON: 5/1-10/31. FACILITIES: 44 sites (tr -24); tbls, toil, cga, f, store. ACTIVITIES: Hiking; hunting; float boating; mountain climbing; picnicking; fishing. MISC.: Elev 5700 ft; 80 acres; pets. Madison River runs through camping area. Excellent stream fishing.

EUREKA

Camp 32 (Kootenai NF). 7 mi W on FS 8562; 1½ mi S on FS 7182. SEASON: 6/1-10/15. FACILITIES: 4 sites (no tr); tbls, toil, cga, f, no drk wtr. ACTIVITIES: Picnicking; fishing. MISC.: Elev 2600 ft; 3 acres; pets; stream.

*****Gateway Boat Camp** (Kootenai NF). 1 mi N on St Hwy 93; 1½ mi W on St Hwy 37; 5½ mi NW on Co Hwy 3392; 1-4/5 mi N, BY BOAT. SEASON: 5/1-10/15; 14-day lmt. FACILITIES: 4 tent sites; tbls, toil, cga, f; no drk wtr. ACTIVITIES: Picnicking; fishing. Boating (1, 2 mi). MISC.: Elev 2500 ft; 3 acres; pets.

Glen Lake Fishing Acces Site (Dept. of Fish and Game). S of Eureka, milepost 174, on US 93; 6 mi E on Co Rd. SEASON: 5/1-10/1; 14-day lmt. FACILITIES: Sites, no drk wtr, toil. ACTIVITIES: Boating; swimming; picnicking; fishing. MISC.: Pets.

Sophie Lake Fishing Access Site (Dept. of Fish and Game). NW of Eureka, milepost 65, on St Hwy 37; 4 mi N on Co Rd. SEASON: 5/1-10/1; 14-day lmt. FACILITIES: Sites, toil, drk wtr. ACTIVITIES: Swimming; picnicking; fishing. MISC.: pets.

Tetrault Lake Fishing Access Site (Dept. of Fish and Game). NW of Eureka, milepost 65, on St Hwy 37; 3 mi N on Co

Rd. SEASON: 5/1-10/1; 14-day lmt.
FACILITIES: Sites, no drk wtr, toil.
ACTIVITIES: Boating; picnicking; fishing.
MISC.: Pets.

FORSYTH

East Rosebud (SRA). N from Main St
and Fifteenth Ave 1 mi. SEASON: 5/1-
10/1; 14-day lmt. FACILITIES: 20 sites,
tbls, toil, cga, f, drk wtr. ACTIVI-
TIES: Boating,l; hunting; hiking; picnicking; fishing; rockhounding. MISC.:
Elev 2390 ft. Small pets on leash. On
Yellowstone River.

Forsyth Spring (SRA). 1 mi W of
Forsyth on St Hwy 10. FACILITIES: 6
sites, piped drk wtr, tbls, toil, cga,
f. ACTIVITIES: Hiking; hunting; picnicking; fishing. MISC.: Elev 2390 ft.
Small pets on leash. Bike Trails.

West Rosebud (SRA). US 12 at Forsyth,
S side of bridge, milepost 270. SEASON:
5/1-9/30; 14-day lmt. FACILITIES: 15
sites (tr -25); tbls, toil, cga, f, playground. ACTIVITIES: Boating,l; hiking;
rockhounding; picnicking; fishing.
MISC.: 32 acres; small pets. On Yellowstone River. Bike trails.

FORT BENTON

Coal Banks Landing (SRA). N of Fort
Benton, milepost 67, on US 87; 8 mi
S on Co Rd. SEASON: 5/1-10/1; 14-day
lmt. FACILITIES: Sites, drk wtr, toil.
ACTIVITIES: Boating; picnicking.
MISC.: Pets.

FORTINE

Big Therriault Lake (Kootenai NF). 2-
4/5 mi NW of Fortine on US 93; 3-1/5
mi NE on Co Hwy 114; 10-3/5 mi NE on
FS 114; 13 mi W on FS 319. SEASON:
7/1-10/1; 14-day lmt. FACILITIES: 10
sites (tr -22); tbls, toil, cga, f, no
drk wtr. ACTIVITIES: Boating,l,d; picnicking; fishing; hiking. Horses (1 mi).
MISC.: Elev 5700 ft; 5 acres; pets.
Scenic. Therriault Lake (good fishing).
Trailhead into Ten Lakes Scenic Area
(1-1/2 mi).

Little Therriault Lake (Kootenai). 2-4/5
mi NW on US 93; 3-1/5 mi NE on Co Hwy
114; 10-3/5 mi NE on FS 114; 13-1/5 mi
W on FS 319. SEASON: 7/1-10/1; 14-day
lmt. FACILITIES: 6 sites (tr -22); tbls,
toil, cga, f, no drk wtr. ACTIVITIES:
Boating; horseback riding; picnicking;
fishing,d; hiking. MISC.: Elev 5800 ft;
1 acre; pets. Trailhead into Ten Lakes
Scenic Area (1 mi). Little Therriault
Lake. Scenic.

FORT PECK

Rock Creek Recreation Area (SRA). 35
mi S of Fort Peck on Hwy 24; 7 mi NW
[on E shore of Reservoir]. SEASON: 5/1-
10/1; 14-day lmt. FACILITIES: 40 sites;
drk wtr, tbls, toil, cga, f. ACTIVITIES:
Hiking; boating,l; swimming; picnicking;
fishing. MISC.: 235 acres. Shelters.

GALLATIN GATEWAY

Spanish Creek (Gallatin NF). 8-1/5 mi
S of Gallatin Gateway on US 191; 5-3/10
mi W on Co Hwy 982.1; 3-9/10 mi S on
FS 982.3. SEASON: 6/15-10/15; 14-day
lmt. FACILITIES: 6 sites (tr -16); well
drk wtr, toil, cga, f. ACTIVITIES: Hiking; picnicking; fishing. MISC.: Elev
6100 ft; 5 acres; pets. Stream. Spanish
Peaks Wilderness Area (1 mi S).

Spire Rock (Gallatin NF). 11-2/5 mi S
of Gallatin Gateway on US 191; 3-3/10
mi E on FS 1321. SEASON: 6/15-9/15; 14-
day lmt. FACILITIES: 17 sites (tr -16);
tbls, toil, cga, f, no drk wtr. Ice/gas/
food/store (4 mi). ACTIVITIES:
Picnicking; fishing. MISC.: Elev 5600
ft; 5 acres; pets. Spanish Peaks Wilderness Area (5 mi W). Stream.

Squaw Flats (Gallatin NF). 11-2/5 mi
S of Gallatin Gateway on US 191; 5-3/5
mi E on FS 132; 1/10 mi S on FS 3112.
SEASON: 6/15-9/15; 14-day lmt. FACILI-
TIES: 3 sites (tr -16); toil, cga, f,
no drk wtr. ACTIVITIES: Picnicking;
fishing. MISC.: Elev 5500 ft; 4 acres;
pets; stream. Rat Lake (2 mi).

GARDINER

Eagle Creek (Gallatin NF). 3 mi NE of
Gardiner on FS 493. SEASON: 6/15-9/15;
15-day lmt. FACILITIES: 4 sites (tr
-16), cga, f. ACTIVITIES: Picnicking.
MISC.: Elev 6200 ft; pets. 3 mi NE of
N entrance to Yellowstone NP.

Tom Miner (Gallatin NF). 16 mi NW of
Gardiner on US 89; 12 mi SW on Co Hwy
63; 3-1/2 mi SW on FS 63. SEASON:
5/15-11/30; 15-day lmt. FACILITIES:
12 sites (tr -22); tbls, toil, cga, f,
well drk wtr. ACTIVITIES: Horseback
riding; rockhounding; picnicking. Fishing (3 mi). MISC.: Elev 7300 ft; 5
acres; pets. Geological. Access road
may be closed to vehicles during wet
weather in spring, due to soft road-
bed. Stream.

See page 7 for KEY TO ABBREVIATIONS.

GARRISON

Welch's Truck Stop. I-12 and St Hwy 90, at Garrison. SEASON: All yr; 1-night lmt. FACILITIES: Spaces for self-contained RVs; toil, drk wtr, food, gas. MISC.: Mechanic.

GLASGOW

Fort Peck Dredge Cuts Fishing Access Site (Dept. of Fish and Game). S of Glasgow, milepost 58, on St Hwy 24; N on Co Rd 249 to milepost 5. SEASON: 5/1-10/1; 14-day lmt. FACILITIES: Sites, no drk wtr, toil, picnic, shelters. ACTIVITIES: Boating; picnicking; fishing. MISC.: Pets.

Husky Car/Truck Stop. W of Glasgow on St Hwy 2. SEASON: All yr; 1-night lmt. FACILITIES: Spaces for self-contained RVs; food, toil, drk wtr, gas. MISC.: Mechanic.

The Pines (Fort Pack Lake). 12 mi SE of Glasgow on St Hwy 24; 24 mi SW on gravel rd. SEASON: MD-LD; 14-day lmt. FACILITIES: 10 sites (tr -25); tbls, cga, f. ACTIVITIES: Boating,l; picnicking; fishing. MISC.: 701 acres.

GLEN

Dinner Station (Beaverhead NF). 6-1/2 mi S of Glen on US 91; 6-1/5 mi W on Co Hwy 981; 4-4/5 mi NW on FS 982; 1-7/10 mi W on FS 1922. SEASON: 6/15-9/15; 14-day lmt. FACILITIES: 7 sites (tr -16); tbls, toil, cga, f, well drk wtr. ACTIVITIES: Picnicking; mountain climbing. Fishing (3 mi). MISC.: Elev 7200 ft; 5 acres; pets; stream.

GLENDIVE

Glendive Husky Car/Truck Stop. I-94, Glendive exit, in Glendive. SEASON: All year; 1-night lmt. FACILITIES: Spaces for self-contained RVs; toil, drk wtr, gas, food. MISC.: Mechanic.

Intake Fishing Access Site (Dept. of Fish and Game). 16 mi N of Glendive, milepost 16, on St Hwy 16; 1-1/2 mi S on Co Rd (gravel rd). SEASON: 5/1-10/1; 14-day lmt. FACILITIES: 40 sites, drk wtr, toil, picnic shelters. ACTIVITIES: Swimming; hunting; hiking; picnicking; fishing; boating,l. MISC.: Pets.

Makoshika (State Park). 4 mi SE of I-94 in Glendive on paved Co Rd; follow signs [gravel access rds]. SEASON: 5/1-10/1; 14-day lmt. FACILITIES: 11 tent sites (no tr); tbls, toil, cga, f, no drk wtr. ACTIVITIES: Hiking; picnicking. MISC.: 800 acres. Pets on leash.

GREAT FALLS

Old Fort Park. 40 mi NE of Great Falls on St Hwy 87. SEASON: 5/1-9/30; 1-day lmt. FACILITIES: 8 sites, tbls, flush toil, swimming pool, playground. ACTIVITIES: Swimming; picnicking; boating,d. Fishing (1 mi). Golf (5 mi). MISC.: 7 acres. Prairie Land; access to river. Bottled gas/ice/f/laundry/store (1 mi).

Thain Creek (Lewis & Clark NF). 6 mi E of Great Falls on US 89; 13 mi E on St Hwy 228; 16 mi E on Co Hwy 121; 2 mi E on FS 8840. [Access rd too poor for tr.] SEASON: 5/20-10/15. FACILITIES: 13 sites (no tr), piped drk wtr, tbls, toil, cga, f. ACTIVITIES: Picnicking; fishing. MISC.: Elev 4600 ft; 16 acres; pets. Stream.

HAMILTON

Black Bear (Bitterroot NF). 3 mi S of Hamilton on US 93; 12-9/10 mi E on St Hwy 38. SEASON: 6/1-9/15; 10-day lmt. FACILITIES: 10 sites (tr -22); tbls, toil, cga, f, well drk wtr. ACTIVITIES: Hunting; hiking; picnicking. Fishing (1 mi). MISC.: Elev 4600 ft; 8 acres; pets. Skalkaho Falls (8-1/2 mi). Stream.

Bridgett Creek Park. 2 mi N of Hamilton on St Hwy 93. SEASON: All yr; 2-day lmt. FACILITIES: 15 sites (tr -22); tbls, cga, f. ACTIVITIES: Snowmobiling; picnicking; fishing. Golfing (5 mi). Snow skiing (within 25 mi). MISC.: 7 acres; pets. Mountainous terrain. Access to river.

Durland Park. 12 mi S of Hamilton on St Hwy 93. SEASON: 6/11-11/1; 2-day lmt. FACILITIES: 15 sites (tr -22); tbls, toil, cga, f, dump. ACTIVITIES: Hiking; picnicking; fishing; snowmobiling. Snow skiing (nearby). MISC.: 3 acres; pets. Mountainous terrain. Access to river.

Mill Creek Trail Takeoff (Bitterroot NF). 5 mi NW of Hamilton on Mill Creek. FACILITIES: Picnic and camping areas at undeveloped sites. MISC.: Access to Selway-Bitterrot Wilderness. Pets.

Painted Rocks (SRA). S of Hamilton on US 93; 23 mi SW on Co Hwy 473. SEASON: 5/1-10/1; 14-day lmt. FACILITIES: Sites, toil, drk wtr, picnic shelters. ACTIVITIES: Swimming; picnicking; boating. MISC.: Pets.

HARDIN

Afterbay (Bighorn Canyon NRA). 40 mi S of Hardin on Hwy 313. SEASON: All yr; 30-day lmt. FACILITIES: 35 sites (tr -20), tbls. Dump /bottled gas/ice/ laundry/store nearby . ACTIVITIES: Swimming; picnicking; boating,l d; fishing. MISC.: Pets.

See page 7 for KEY TO ABBREVIATIONS.

Bairs Truck Stop. I-90, City Center exit, in Hardin. SEASON: All year; 1-night lmt. FACILITIES: Spaces for self-contained RVs; toil, drk wtr, food, gas.

Big Horn Fishing Access Site (Dept. of Fish and Game). 29 mi S of I-90 at Hardin, milepost 497, on Co Rd 313. SEASON: 5/1-10/1; 14-day lmt. FACILITIES: Sites, toil, tbls. ACTIVITIES: Boating; picnicking; fishing. MISC.: Pets. Pack in and out.

Tow Leggins Fishing Access Site (Dept. of Fish and Game). S of I-90 at Hardin, milepost 497, on Co Rd 313, milepost 8. SEASON: 5/1-10/1; 14-day lmt. FACILITIES: Sites, no drk wtr, toil. ACTIVITIES: Fishing. MISC.: Pets.

HARLOWTON

Deadman's Basin Reservoir (SRA). 20 mi E of Harlowton, milepost 1200, on US 12; 3 mi N. SEASON: 10/1-5/1 FREE (rest of yr, $2.00). 14-day lmt. FACILITIES: 10 sites (tr -25); drk wtr, tbls. ACTIVITIES: Swimming; boating,l; picnicking; fishing. MISC.: 250 acres; pets.

Selkirk Fishing Access Site (Dept. of Fish and Game). W of Harlowton, milepost 80, on US 12. SEASON: 5/1-10/1; 14-day lmt. FACILITIES: Sites, toil, drk wtr. ACTIVITIES: Picnicking; fishing. MISC.: Pets.

Spring Creek (Lewis & Clark NF). 33 mi W of Harlowton on US 12; 4 mi N on FS 274. SEASON: 5/1-11/30. FACILITIES: 10 sites (tr -22); tbls, toil, cga, f, well drk wtr. ACTIVITIES: Hiking; picnicking; fishing. MISC.: Elev 5400 ft; 5 acres; pets. Stream.

HAVRE

Bear Paw Lake Fishing Access Site (Dept. of Fish and Game). 17 mi S of US 2 at Havre, milepost 382, on Co Rd 234. SEASON: 5/1-10/1; 14-day lmt. FACILITIES: Sites, drk wtr, toil, picnic shelters. ACTIVITIES: Boating; picnicking; fishing. MISC.: Pets.

HELENA

Black Sandy Beach (Mt. Power Company). Less than 10 mi NE of Helena on the W shore of the Hauser Dam Reservoir. SEASON: All yr; 14-day lmt. FACILITIES: Sites, tbls, cga, dump. ACTIVITIES: Boating; picnicking; fishing. MISC.: 2 natural boat ramps. Pets.

Cave Bay SRA. E of Helena, milepost 55, on US 287; 10 mi NE on Co Rd 284. SEASON: 10/1-5/1, FREE (rest of yr, $2.00); 14-day lmt. FACILITIES: Sites; toil, drk wtr. ACTIVITIES: Swimming; picnicking. MISC.: Pets.

* **Cemetery Island** (SRA). E of Helena on Canyon Ferry Reservoir. BOAT ACCESS ONLY. SEASON: 5/1-10/1; 14-day lmt. FACILITIES: Tent sites (no tr); toil. ACTIVITIES: Boating; picnicking. MISC.: Pets. Pack in/out.

Chinaman's Recreation Area (SRA). E of Helena, milepost 55, on US 287; 10 mi NE on Co Rd 284. SEASON: 10/1-5/1, FREE (rest of yr, $2.00); 14-day lmt. FACILITIES: Sites, toil, drk wtr. ACTIVITIES: Boating; picnicking; fishing; swimming. MISC.: Pets.

* **Coulter** (Helena NF). 2 mi NE of Helena on US 91; 15 mi N on US 15; 2-4/5 mi E on Co Hwy 17; 3-4/5 mi NE, BY BOAT [on lake]. SEASON: 6/1-9/30; 15-day lmt. FACILITIES: 7 tent sites, well drk wtr, tbls, toil, cga. ACTIVITIES: Boating; waterskiing; hiking; picnicking; fishing; sailing. MISC.: Elev 3600 ft; 2 acres; pets. Gates of the Mountains Wilderness. Limestone rock formation. Scenic. Nature trails. Gates of the Mountains Boat Club Landing (4 mi down river). Food (4 mi). No rd access.

Court Sheriff (SRA). E of Helena, milepost 55, on US 287; 9 mi NE on Co Hwy 284. SEASON: 10/1-5/1, FREE (rest of yr, $2.00); 14-day lmt. FACILITIES: Sites, toil, drk wtr, picnic shelters. ACTIVITIES: Swimming; picnicking. MISC.: Pets.

Crittenaon Recreation Area (SRA). E of Helena, milepost 55, on US 287; NE on Co Rd 284 to yacht basin, 4 mi S. SEASON: 5/1-10/1; 14-day lmt. FACILITIES: Sites, toil, picnic shelters, no drk wtr. ACTIVITIES: Swimming; picnicking. MISC.: Pets.

Hellgate Recreation Area (SRA). E of Helena, milepost 55, on US 287; 17 mi NE on Co Rd 284. SEASON: 10/1-5/1 FREE (rest of yr, $2.00); 14-day lmt. FACILITIES: Sites, toil, drk wtr, picnic shelters. ACTIVITIES: Boating; swimming; picnicking. MISC.: Pets.

Helena Reg. Reservoir Fishing Access Site (Dept. of Fish and Game). N of Helena on Montana Ave to Co Rd 280; 8 mi E. SEASON: 5/1-10/1; 14-day lmt. FACILITIES: Sites, toil, no drk wtr. ACTIVITIES: Picnicking; fishing. MISC.: Pets.

Holter Dam Reservoir Campground (Mt. Power Co.). Approx. 30 mi N of Helena near Wolf Creek. SEASON: All yr; 14-day lmt. FACILITIES: Sites; pumped well drk wtr, cga, toil, tbl, dump. ACTIVITIES: Boating; picnicking; fishing. MISC.: Pets on leash.

Husky Truck Stop. E of Helena on I-15. SEASON: All yr; 1-night lmt. FACILITIES: Spaces for self-contained RVs; drk wtr, toil, food, gas.

Kading (Helena NF). 22-3/10 mi W on St Hwy 12; 7-1/2 mi S on Co Hwy 00227; 4-4/5 mi S on FS 00227. SEASON: 6/20-10/15; 15-day lmt. FACILITIES: 13 sites (tr -22); tbls, toil, cga, f, piped drk wtr. ACTIVITIES: Berrypicking; picnicking; fishing; boating. MISC.: Elev 6100 ft; 10 acres; pets. Little Blackfoot River.

Missouri River-Wolf Creek (SP). 25 mi N of Helena on frontage rd, paralleling 1-15. SEASON: 5/1-9/30; 14-day lmt. FACILITIES: Unlimited sites, tbls. Ice/store/food/laundry nearby. ACTIVITIES: Boating,l; picnicking; fishing. MISC.: 28 acres; pets.

Moose Creek (Helena NF). 9-3/10 mi SW on US 12; 4-3/10 mi SW on Co Hwy F28. SEASON: 5/20-10/1; 15-day lmt. FACILITIES: 11 sites (tr -22); tbls, toil, cga, f, well drk wtr. ACTIVITIES: Picnicking. MISC.: Elev 5100 ft; 4 acres; pets. Ten Mile Canyon. Old mining community of Remini. Scenic. Stream.

Overlook (SRA). E of Helena, milepost 55, on US 287; NE on Co Rd 284 to Yacht Basin; 1 mi S. SEASON: 10/1-5/1, FREE (rest of yr, $2.00). 14-day lmt. FACILITIES: Sites, toil, no drk wtr. ACTIVITIES: Picnicking. MISC.: Pets.

Park Lake Fishing Access Site (Dept. of Fish and Game). S of Helena, milepost 182, on I-15; 12 mi W on Co Rd (forest service). SEASON: 10/1-5/1 FREE (rest of yr, $2.00). 14-day lmt. FACILITIES: Sites, toil, no drk wtr. ACTIVITIES: Picnicking; fishing. MISC.: Pets.

Pikes Gulch (Helena NF). 1 mi N of Helena on US 279; 18-4/5 mi NE on Co Hwy 23; 14-2/5 mi NE on FS 29. SEASON: 6/1-9/30; 15-day lmt. FACILITIES: 5 sites (tr -16); no drk wtr, tbls, toil, cga, f. ACTIVITIES: Picnicking. MISC.: Elev 6200 ft; 3 acres; pets. Scenic. Figure Eight Auto Tour. Stream.

Ponderosa (SRA). E of Helena, milepost 55, on US 287; 9 mi NE on Co Rd 284. SEASON: 10/1-5/1, FREE (rest of yr, $2.00). 14-day lmt. FACILITIES: Sites, toil, drk wtr. ACTIVITIES: Boating; swimming; picnicking. MISC.: Pets.

Porcupine (Helena NF). 12-1/2 mi W on US 12 [gravel access rds]. SEASON: 6/15-10/1; 15-day lmt. FACILITIES: 18 sites, not recommended for tr (tr -22); tabls, toil, cga, piped drk wtr. ACTIVITIES: Picnicking. MISC.: Elev 5400 ft; 7 acres; pets. Frontier Town. Sweeney Co. Ecology Trail. Stream.

Riverside (SRA). E of Helena, milepost 55, on US 287; NE on Co Rd 284 to Canyon Ferry Village; 1 mi NW on Co Rd. SEASON: 10/1-5/1. FREE (rest of yr, $2.00); 14-day lmt. FACILITIES: Sites, toil, drk wtr. ACTIVITIES: Boating; picnicking. MISC.: Pets.

Vigilante (Helena NF). 2 mi NE on US 91; 15 mi N on Co Hwy 23; 8-2/5 mi NE on FS 29. SEASON: 6/1-9/15: 15-day lmt. FACILITIES: 17 sites (tr -16); tbls, toil, cga, f, well drk wtr. ACTIVITIES: Hiking; picnicking. MISC.: Elev 4600 ft; 7 acres; pets. Scenic Overlook. Trout Creek Canyon. Scenic Figure Eight Auto Tour. Stream. 15 mi SE of Gates of the Mountain Wilderness.

White Earth (SRA). SE of Helena to Winston, milepost 64, on US 287; 5 mi E on Co Rd. SEASON: 10/1-5/1, FREE (rest of yr, $2.00); 14-day lmt. FACILITIES: Sites, toil, drk wtr. ACTIVITIES: Boating; picnicking. MISC.: Pets.

HOBSON

Ackley Lake (SRA). St Hwy 87 at Hobson; 1-1/2 mi Sw on St Hwy 239 to jct St Hwy 400; 3-1/2 mi W on St Hwy to gravel rd, right 1 mi, 1 mi left on unimproved road. FACILITIES: Open sites, no shade. Recommend small RVs. 10 sites (tr -18); toil, cga. ACTIVITIES: Swimming (beach); picnicking; fishing; hunting; boating,l. MISC.: Elev 4000 ft. Pets.

Hay Canyon (Lewis & Clark NF). 12 mi W on St Hwy 239; 11-4/5 mi SW on Co Hwy; 4-2/5 mi SW on FS 487. SEASON: 5/20-10/1. FACILITIES: 9 sites (tr -22); no drk wtr, tbls, toil, cga, f. ACTIVITIES: Fishing; picnicking. MISC.: Elev 5300 ft; 3 acres; pets. Stream.

Indian Hill (Lewis & Clark NF). 12 mi W of Hobson on St Hwy 239; 11-4/5 mi SW on Co Hwy; 3-1/10 mi SW on FS 487. SEASON: 5/20-10/1. FACILITIES: 7 sites (tr -22); tbls, toil, cga, f. Well drk wtr. ACTIVITIES: Picnicking; fishing. Horseback riding/rental. MISC.: Elev 5000 ft; 2 acres; pets.

HOLE-IN-THE-WALL LANDING

* **Slaughter River** (Missouri River Waterway). 14 mi SE of Hole-in-the-Wall Landing on Missouri River BY BOAT. SEASON: 5/1-9/30; 14-day lmt. FACILITIES: 5 tent sites; tbls. ACTIVITIES: Boating; picnicking. MISC.: 42 acres; pets.

HUNGRY HORSE

Doris Point Campground (Glacier NP). 10 mi W of US 2, W Glacier; 9 mi E of Hungry Horse [on W side of NP]. SEASON: June-September, FREE (Golden Eagle Passport** or entrance fee, $2.00 . FACILITIES: Tent sites; tbls, toil, cga, drk wtr. ACTIVITIES: Picnicking. MISC.: Pets.

* **Elk Island** (Flathead NP). 8 mi SE of Hungry Horse on FS 895; 10 mi SE BY

**See page 5.

BOAT. **SEASON:** 6/1-9/15; 14-day lmt. **FA-CILITIES:** 7 tent sites; no drk wtr, tbls, cga, f. **ACTIVITIES:** Swimming; picnicking; fishing; boating,ld. **MISC.:** 7 acres;

★ **Fire Island** (Flathead NF). 8 mi SE of Hungry Horse on FS 895; 4 mi SE, BY BOAT. **SEASON:** 6/1-9/15; 14-day lmt. **FACILITIES:** 4 tent sites; no drk wtr, toil, cga, f, tbls. **ACTIVITIES:** Swimming; picnicking; fishing; waterskiing; boating (1, 5 mi). **MISC.:** Elev 3600 ft; 2 acres; pets. On Hungry Horse Reservoir.

Handkerchief Lake (Flathead NF). 35 mi SE of Hungry Horse on FS 895; 2 mi NW on FS 897. **SEASON:** 6/1-9/15; 14-day lmt. **FACILITIES:** 9 sites (tr -22); tbls, toil, cga, f. **ACTIVITIES:** Boating,d; picnicking; fishing. **MISC.:** Elev 3800 ft; 4 acres; pets. Lake. Scenic. Jewel Basin Access 4 mi off reservoir.

Hungry Horse (Flathead NF). 5/10 mi W of Hungry Horse on US 2. **SEASON:** 6/1-9/15; 14-day lmt. **FACILITIES:** 27 sites (tr -22); tbls, toil, cga, f. Shower/ice/laundry/store (1 mi). **ACTIVITIES:** Hiking; hunting; rockhounding; picnicking; fishing. Swimming (3 mi). **MISC.:** Elev 3100 ft; 9 acres; pets. Bike Trails. Lake. River. Horseback riding. Glacier NP (10 mi N).

Lakeview (Flathead NF). 24 mi SE of Hungry Horse on FS 895. **SEASON:** 6/1-9/15; 14-day lmt. **FACILITIES:** 4 sites (tr -22); tbls, toil, cga, f, no drk wtr. **ACTIVITIES:** Picnicking; fishing. **MISC.:** Elev 3600 ft; 5 acres; pets. On Hungry Horse Reservoir.

Lid Creek (Flathead NF). 15 mi SE on FS 895. **SEASON:** 6/1-9/15; 14-day lmt. **FACILITIES:** 22 sites (tr -16); tbls, toil, cga, f, no drk wtr. **ACTIVITIES:** Picnicking; boating; swimming; fishing; waterskiing; berrypicking. **MISC.:** Elev 3600 ft; 10 acres; pets; scenic.

Lost Johnny Camp (Flathead NF). 8-1/2 mi SE of Hungry Horse on FS 895. **SEASON:** 6/1-9/15; 14-day lmt. **FACILITIES:** 4 sites (tr -22); no drk wtr; tbls, cga f, toil. **ACTIVITIES:** Boating,l; waterskiing; swimming; picnicking; fishing. **MISC.:** Elev 3600 ft; 2 acres; pets. On Hungry Horse Reservoir. Visitor Center (5 mi).

Lost Johnny Point (Flathead NF). 9 mi SE of Hungry Horse on FS 895. **SEASON:** 6/1-9/15; 14-day lmt. **FACILITIES:** 18 sites (tr -22); piped drk wtr; tbls, toil, cga, f. **ACTIVITIES:** Swimming; boating,ld; waterskiing; picnicking; fishing. **MISC.:** Elev 3600 ft; 6 acres; pets. On Hungry Horse Reservoir. Visitor Center (5 mi).

JACKSON

Miner Lake (Beaverhead NF). 18-3/5 mi S of Jackson on St Hwy 278; 6-4/5 mi W on Co Hwy 182; 3-1/5 mi W on FS 182. **SEASON:** 6/1-11/15. **FACILITIES:** 13 sites (tr -32); tbls, toil, cga, f, well drk wtr. **ACTIVITIES:** Boating,ld; picnicking; fishing. **MISC.:** Elev 7000 ft; 9 acres; pets. Lake.

North Van Houten (Beaverhead NF). 9/10 mi S of Jackson on St Hwy 278; 8-1/5 mi SW on Co Hwy 181; 2-1/2 mi SW on FS 181. **SEASON:** 6/1-11/1. **FACILITIES:** 3 sites (tr -32); well drk wtr, tbls, toil, cga, f. **ACTIVITIES:** Fishing; picnicking. **MISC.:** Elev 6800 ft; 1 acre; pets. Lake.

JORDAN

Hell Creek Recreation Area (SRA). 24 mi N of Jordan, milepost 213 at St Hwy 200, on Co Rd. **SEASON:** 10/1-5/1, FREE (rest of yr, $2); 14-day lmt. **FACILITIES:** 25 sites (tr -20); drk wtr, tbls, toil, shelter. **ACTIVITIES:** Boating,l; swimming; picnicking; fishing. **MISC.:** Elev 2800 ft; 113 acres; pets. Lake.

JUDITH LANDING

★ **Cow Island Landing** (Missouri River Waterway). 28 mi NE of Judith Landing on Missouri River BY BOAT. **SEASON:** 5/1-9/30; 14-day lmt. **FACILITIES:** 5 tent sites; tbls. **ACTIVITIES:** Boating; picnicking. **MISC.:** 21 acres; pets.

KALISPELL

Ashley Lake Recreation Area (SRA). 15 mi W of Kalispell, milepost 105, on US 2; 13 mi N on Co Rd. **SEASON:** 5/1-9/30; 14-day lmt. **FACILITIES:** 22 sites (tr -20); tbls, toil, cga, f. **ACTIVITIES:** Hiking; boating,ld; waterskiing; swimming; picnicking; fishing. **MISC.:** 31 acres; pets. Lake.

Bitterroot Lake Recreation Area (SRA). 15 mi SW of Kalispell, milepost 101, on US 2; 5 mi N on Marion Rd. **SEASON:** 10/1-5/1, FREE (rest of yr, $3); 14-day lmt. **FACILITIES:** 15 sites (tr -25); tbls, drk wtr, cga, f, shelters. **ACTIVITIES:** Boating,l; swimming; picnicking; fishing. **MISC.:** 30 acres; pets. Lake.

Kila Fishing Access Site (Dept. of Fish and Game). 8 mi W of Kalispell, milepost 112, on US 2; 1 mi S on Co Rd. **SEASON:** 5/1-10/1; 14-day lmt. **FACILITIES:** Sites, no drk wtr; toil. **ACTIVITIES:** Boating; picnicking; fishing. **MISC.:** Pets.

Logan Park Recreation Area (SRA). 45 mi W of Kalispell, milepost 77, on US 2. **SEASON:** 10/1-5/1, FREE (rest of yr, $3); 14-day lmt. **FACILITIES:** 25 sites

(tr -20); drk wtr, tbls, cga, f. ACTIVI-
TIES: Boating,ld; swimming; picnicking;
fishing. MISC.: Elev 3000 ft; 16 acres;
pets. Lake.

Sportsman's Bridge Fishing Access Site
(Dept. of Fish and Game). S of Kalispell,
milepost 104, on US 93; E on Co Rd 208
to milepost 6. SEASON: 5/1-10/1; 14-day
lmt. FACILITIES: Sites, toil, no drk wtr;
tbls. ACTIVITIES: Boating; picnicking;
fishing. MISC.: Pets.

West Shore (SP). 20 mi S of Kalispell,
milepost 93, on US 93. SEASON: 10/1-5/1
FREE (rest of yr, $3); 14-day lmt.
FACILITIES: 15 sites
(tr -20); drk wtr, tbls, cga, f. ACTIV-
ITIES: Swimming; boating,l; picnicking;
fishing. MISC.: 140 acres; pets.

Whitefish Lake (SP). W of Kalispell,
milepost 129, on US 93; 1 mi N. SEA-
SON: 10/1-5/1 . FREE (rest of yr, $3);
14-day lmt. FACILITIES: 15 sites (tr
-20); drk wtr, tbls, cga, f. ACTIVI-
TIES: Swimming; picnicking; fishing;
boating,l, (r nearby). MISC.: 15 acres;
pets.

LANDUSKY

Montana Gulch Campground (BLM). Drive
N on St Hwy 376 from its Jct with St
Hwy 191 approx. 4 ½ mi; turn right on
gravelled country toward Landusky for
approximately 3 mi; turn left at sign
to Mountain Gulch Campground on BLM
graded rd 1/5 mi. SEASON: 4/1-11/31.
FACILITIES: 8 sites (tr -24); no drk
wtr; tbls, cga, f. ACTIVITIES: Hiking;
mountain climbing; snowmobiling (winter); picnicking. MISC.: Elev 4100 ft;
20 acres; pets.

LAUREL

Bluewater Fishing Access Site (Dept.
of Fish and Game). S of Laurel, mile-
post 32, on US 310; 9 mi SE on Co Rds.
SEASON: 5/1-10/1; 14-day lmt. FACILI-
TIES: Sites; toil, tbls. ACTIVITIES:
Fishing; picnicking. MISC.: Pets.

Cooney State Recreation Area (SRA).
20 mi SW of Laurel on US 212 to Boyd;
9 mi W on Co Rd. SEASON: 10/1-5/1
FREE (rest of yr, $2); 14-day lmt.
FACILITIES: 30 sites (tr -20); tbls,
drk wtr. ACTIVITIES: Boating; swimming; picnicking; fishing. MISC.: Pets.

LEWISTOWN

Ackley Lake Fishing Access Site (Dept.
of Fish and Game). W of Lewistown,
milepost 58, on US 87; 5 mi W; 4 mi
SE on Co Rd. SEASON: 5/1-10/1; 14-day
lmt. FACILITIES: Sites; toil, no drk
wtr. ACTIVITIES: Boating; picnicking.
MISC.: Pets.

Crystal Lake (Lewis & Clark NF). 9
mi W of Lewistown on US 87; 16 mi S
on Co Hwy; 8 ½ mi S on FS 275. SEA-
SON: 6/15-9/15. FACILITIES: 28 sites
(tr -22); piped drk wtr, tbls, toil,
cga, f. ACTIVITIES: Picnicking; boating,d (l, 1 mi), no motors; fishing.
MISC.: Elev 6800 ft; 14 acres; pets.
Crystal Lake.

James Kipp (SRA). N of Lewistown, mile-
post 242, on US 191. SEASON: 10/1-5/1
FREE (rest of yr, $2); 14-day lmt.
FACILITIES: Sites, toil, drk wtr. ACTIV-
ITIES: Boating; picnicking. MISC.: Pets.

Snowy Mountain Jaycee Campground. W
end of Lewiston on St Hwy 87 (gravel
access rds). FACILITIES: 25 sites, toil,
tbls. ACTIVITIES: Picnicking. MISC.:
Pets on leash.

Upper Carter Pond Fishing Access Site
(Dept. of Fish and Game). N of Lewiston,
milepost 7, on US 191. SEASON: 5/1-10/1;
14-day lmt. FACILITIES: Sites, toil, no
drk wtr. ACTIVITIES: Boating; picnicking; fishing. MISC.: Pets.

LIBBY

Carrigan Campground (St. Regis Paper
Co). 12 mi N of Libby on Pipe Creek
Rd (oiled). SEASON: 6/1-9/15; 7-day lmt.
FACILITIES: 9 sites (tr -21); tbls, f,
cga. ACTIVITIES: Fishing; picnicking.
MISC.: 10 acres; pets. Mountainous ter-
rain. Access to river. Fishing streams
available.

Howard Lake (Kootenai NF). 12 mi S of
Libby on US 2; 11-3/5 mi S on FS 231
(low standard rd). SEASON: 6/1-9/15;
14-day lmt.. FACILITIES: 5 sites (tr -
16); tbls, toil, cga, f, well drk wtr.
ACTIVITIES: Boating,ld; picnicking; fishing. MISC.: Elev 4000; 2 acres; pets.
Beautiful lake; good fishing. Geological.
3 mi E of Cabinet Wilderness Area.

Lake Creek (Koontenai NF). 24-7/10 mi
S of Libby on US 2; 6-9/10 mi SW on
FS 231.4. SEASON: 6/1-9/15; 10-day lmt.
FACILITIES: 4 sites (tr -22); piped drk
wtr, tbls, toil, cga, f. ACTIVITIES:
Berry-picking (huckleberries); picnick-
ing; fishing. Horseback riding (2 mi).
MISC.: Elev 3400 ft; 9 acres; pets. Nice
stream. Scenic. Trailhead into Cabinet
Mountain wilderness.

Libby Creek Campground (St. Regis
Paper Co). 12 mi S of Libby on US 2.
SEASON: 5/15-9/15; 7-day lmt. FACILI-
TIES: 17 sites (tr -20); water hook-up,
tbls, toil, cga, f. ACTIVITIES: Hiking;
picnicking; fishing. MISC.: 20 acres;
pets. Mountainous terrain. Stream access.

Libby Volunteer Fireman Memorial Park
(City Park). W end of Libby on St
Hwy 2 (gravel access rds). SEASON:
5/15-10/15; 3-day lmt. FACILITIES: No
designated sites; tbls, toil, cga, f,
food. ACTIVITIES: Picnicking. MISC.:
Pets on leash.

Lion Springs Campground (St. Regis
Paper Co). SEASON: 6/1-9/15; 7-day lmt.
FACILITIES: 9 sites (tr -21); tbls, toil,
cga. ACTIVITIES: Fishing (access to
stream); picnicking. MISC.: Elev 2500
ft; 10 acres; pets. Pull-thru spaces.
Mountainous terrain.

Loon Lake (Koontenai NF). 3/5 mi N
of Libby on St Hwy 37; 17-9/10 mi N
on FS 68; 2-9/10 mi W on FS 471. SEA-
SON: 6/15-9/15; 14-day lmt. FACILITIES:
4 sites (tr -16); no drk wtr; tbls, toil,
cga, f. ACTIVITIES: Boating,l; picnicking; fishing. MISC.: Elev 3600 ft; 4
acres; pets. Lake.

McGillivray (Koontenai NF). 24-4/5 mi
NW of Libby on St Hwy 37. SEASON:
10/1-5/19 ,FREE (rest of yr, $2); 10-day
lmt. FACILITIES: 52 sites (tr -32);
tbls, flush toil, cga, f. Store/ice (3
mi). ACTIVITIES: Boating,rld; swimming ;
hiking; picnicking; fishing; water skiing. MISC.: Elev 2500 ft; 3 acres; pets .
Water shut down in Winter. Libby Dam
(6 mi) on paved rd.

Paul Bunyan (Koontenai NF). 11-3/10 mi
S of Libby on US 2. SEASON: 9/16-5/14
FREE (rest of yr, $2); 14-day lmt. FA-
CILITIES: 32 sites (tr -22); tbls, toil,
cga, f. ACTIVITIES: Hiking; picnicking;
fishing. MISC.: Elev 2700 ft; 22 acres;
pets. Water shut off (Winter). Near
Libby Creek early gold diggings. 6 mi
E ,Cabinet Wilderness Area. River.

Pleasant Valley (Koontenai NF). 31 mi
SE of Libby on US 2. SEASON: 9/16-5/14
FREE (rest of yr, $2); 10-day lmt. FA-
CILITIES: 18 sites (no tr); tbls, toil,
cga, f. ACTIVITIES: Hiking; boating,d;
picnicking. Fishing (5 mi). MISC.: Elev
3000 ft; 7 acres; pets. Water shut off
(Winter). On Fisher River. Self-guiding
nature trail.

Timberlane (Koontenai NF). 3/5 mi N of
Libby on St Hwy 37; 8-1/10 mi N on
FS 68. SEASON: 5/15-9/15; 14-day lmt.
FACILITIES: 11 sites (tr -22); tbls,
toil, cga, f, well drk wtr. ACTIVITIES:
Picnicking; fishing. MISC.: Elev 2700
ft; 8 acres; pets. Pipe Creek.

LINCOLN

Aspen Grove (Helena NF). 7-1/10 mi E
on St Hwy 200; 1/5 mi SE on FS 1040.
SEASON: 6/1-9/30; 10-day lmt. FACILI-
TIES: 19 sites (tr -22); well drk wtr,
tbls, toil, cga, f.   Food   (2

mi). ACTIVITIES: Hiking; hunting; picnicking; fishing. Horseback riding (rent,
5 mi). MISC.: Elev 4800 ft; 8 acres;
pets. Blackfoot River.

Cooper Creek (Helena NF). 6 ½ mi E of
Lincoln on St Hwy 200; 8-1/2 mi NW on
FS 330 (oiled rd). SEASON: 6/15-9/30;
10-day lmt. FACILITIES: 20 sites (tr -
22); tbls, toil, cga, f, well drk wtr.
ACTIVITIES: Berry-picking; picnicking;
fishing. MISC.: Elev 5300 ft; 3 acres;
pets. Stream. Copper Creek Corrals at
Indian Meadows (2 mi NE of Camp Trailhead into Scapegoat Wilderness). Snow-
bank Lake.

Hooper Recreation Area (SRA). Off St Hwy
20 at Lincoln. SEASON: 10/1-5/1, FREE
(rest of yr, $2). 14-day lmt. FACILI-
TIES: 15 sites (tr -25); tbls, f, drk wtr .
ACTIVITIES: Fishing; picnicking. Boating
(nearby). MISC.: 17 acres; pets.

Monture Fishing Access Site (Dept. of Fish
and Game). W of Lincoln, milepost 39,
on St Hwy 200. SEASON: 5/1-10/1; 14-day
lmt. FACILITIES: Sites, no drk wtr; toil.
ACTIVITIES: Fishing; picnicking. MISC.:
Pets.

Ninemile Prairie Fishing Access Site
(Dept. of Fish and Game). W of Lincoln,
milepost 26, on St Hwy 200; 4 mi W on
Co Rd. SEASON: 5/1-10/1; 14-day lmt.
FACILITIES: Sites; toil. ACTIVITIES:
Picnicking; fishing. MISC.: Pets. Pack
in; pack out.

River Junction Fishing Access Site (Dept
of Fish and Game). W of Lincoln, milepost 44, on St Hwy 200; 9 mi S on Co
Rd. SEASON: 5/1-10/1; 14-day lmt.
FACILITIES: Sites, toil, no drk wtr.
ACTIVITIES: Boating; picnicking; fishing. MISC.: Pets. Pack in; pack out.

LIVINGSTON

Big Creek (Gallatin NF). 32 mi SW of
Livingston on US 189; 4 mi W on Co
Hwy; 2 mi W on FS 361. SEASON: 6/1-
9/10; 14-day lmt. FACILITIES: 5 sites
(tr -16); tbls, toil, cga, f. ACTIVI-
TIES: Fishing; picnicking. MISC.: Elev
5800 ft; pets.

Dalley Lake Fishing Access Site (Dept
of Fish and Game). S of Livingston,
milepost 31, on US 89; 4 mi S across
river on Co Rd 540; 6 mi S on Co Rd.
SEASON: 5/1-10/1; 14-day lmt. FACILI-
TIES: Sites, toil, drk wtr. ACTIVITIES:
Boating; picnicking; fishing. MISC.:
Pets.

Loch Leven Fishing Access Site (Dept
of Fish and Game). S of Livingston,
milepost 44, on US 89; 2 mi E; 4 mi
S on Co Rd 540. SEASON: 5/1-10/1; 14-
day lmt. FACILITIES: Sites, toil, drk
wtr. ACTIVITIES: Boating; picnicking;
fishing. MISC.: Pets.

See page 7 for KEY TO ABBREVIATIONS.

Mallard's Rest Fishing Access Site (Dept of Fish and Game). S of Livingston, milepost 42, on US 89. SEASON: 5/1-10/1; 14-day lmt. FACILITIES: Sites, toil, drk wtr. ACTIVITIES: Boating; picnicking; fishing. MISC.: Pets. Pack in; pack out.

Sheep Mountain (SP). Leave I-90 at jct with US 89, E of Livingston; 1 mi N on US 89; 4-1/2 mi E on gravel Co Rd. SEASON: 14-day lmt. FACILITIES: 10 sites; no drk wtr, tbls, toil, cga, f. ACTIVITIES: Hiking; rockhounding; hunting; picnicking; fishing. MISC.: Elev 4300 ft; small pets on leash. On Yellowstone River (fishing access site). Bike trails.

LOGAN

Gray Cliff Fishing Access Site (Dept of Fish and Game). 15 mi S of I-90 at Logan, milepost 283, on Co Rds. SEASON: 5/1-10/1; 14-day lmt. FACILITIES: Sites, toil, no drk wtr. ACTIVITIES: Fishing; picnicking. MISC.: Pets.

LOLO

Chief Looking Glass (SRA). 3-1/5 mi S of Lolo on US 93; 1 mi E on Co Rd. SEASON: 5/15-10/30; 14-day lmt. FACILITIES: 20 sites, well drk wtr, tbls, toil, cga, f. ACTIVITIES: Hiking; hunting; picnicking; fishing. MISC.: Elev 3800 ft; small pets on leash. Bike Trails. On Bitterroot River.

Don Tripp's Truck Stop. In Lolo at jct of St Hwys 12/93. SEASON: All yr; 1-night lmt. FACILITIES: Spaces for self-contained RVs; drk wtr, toil, gas, food. MISC.: Mechanic.

White Sand (NF). 44-1/2 mi SW of Lolo on US 12; 2-1/5 mi E on FS 111. SEASON: 6/15-9/15; 10-day lmt. FACILITIES: 5 sites (tr -22); well drk wtr. Ice/laundry/store/gas/shower/food (2 mi). Tbls, toil, cga, f. ACTIVITIES: Berrypicking; picnicking; fishing. MISC.: Elev 3400 ft; 5 acres; pets. Scenic. Lochsa River. Lewis & Clark Trail.

LOVELL

Barry's Landing (Bighorn Canyon NRA). 3 mi E of Lovell on St Hwy 14A; 32 mi N (graded rd). SEASON: 5/1-11/1; 30-day lmt. FACILITIES: 30 sites (tr -16); tbls. ACTIVITIES: Boating,ld; ice skating; snowmobiling; swimming; picnicking; fishing.

MALTA

Camp Creek (BLM). 40 mi SW of Malta on US 191; 7 mi W on Co Rd (to Zortman). SEASON: 5/1-9/30. FACILITIES: 15 sites (tr -24); tbls, toil, cga, f. Ice/store

(within 1 mi). ACTIVITIES: Hunting; hiking; picnicking. MISC.: Elev 4000 ft; 15 acres; pets.

Nelson Reservoir (SRA). 15 mi NE of Malta on US 2, milepost 488, 5 mi NE on Co Rd (follow signs). SEASON: 5/1-10/1; 14-day lmt. FACILITIES: 5 sites (tr -35); tbls, toil, cga, well drk wtr. Store/ food (nearby). ACTIVITIES: Swimming; boating,l; picnicking; fishing. MISC.: 228 acres; pets. Lake.

MANHATTAN

Four Corners Fishing Access Site (Dept of Fish and Game). 3 mi E of I-90 at Manhattan, milepost 288, on Co Rd 346. SEASON: 5/1-10/1; 14-day lmt. FACILITIES: Sites, no drk wtr; toil. ACTIVITIES: Fishing; picnicking. MISC.: Pets. Pack in; pack out.

MARTIN CITY

Beaver Creek (Flathead NF). 55 mi SE of Martin City on FS 38; 10 mi E on FS 568. SEASON: 6/1-9/15; 14-day lmt. FACILITIES: 4 sites (tr -22); no drk wtr; tbls, toil, cga, f. ACTIVITIES: Fishing; picnicking. MISC.: Elev 4000 ft; 2 acres; pets.

Devils Corkscrew (Flathead NF). 35 mi SE of Martin City on FS 38. SEASON: 6/1-9/15; 14-day lmt. FACILITIES: 4 sites (tr -22); no drk wtr; tbls, toil, cga, f. ACTIVITIES: Boating,l; water skiing; swimming; picnicking; fishing; berrypicking. MISC.: Elev 3600 ft; 8 acres; pets. On Hungry Horse Reservoir.

*****Elk Island** (Flathead NF). 13 mi SE of Martin City on FS 38; 2 mi SE, BY BOAT. SEASON: 6/1-9/15; 14-day lmt. FACILITIES: 7 tent sites; tbls, toil, cga, no drk wtr. ACTIVITIES: Picnicking; fishing; swimming; waterskiing. Boating (l, 3 mi). MISC.: Elev 3600 ft; 7 acres; pets. Hungry Horse Reservoir.

Emery Bay (Flathead NF). 7 mi SE of Martin City on FS 38. SEASON: 6/1-9/15; 14-day lmt. FACILITIES: 9 sites (tr -22); tbls, toil, cga, f, piped drk wtr. ACTIVITIES: Boating,ld; water skiing; swimming; picnicking; fishing. MISC.: Elev 3600 ft; 4 acres; pets. On Hungry Horse Reservoir. Lake.

Murray Bay (Flathead NF). 22 mi SE of Martin City on FS 38. SEASON: 6/1-9/15; 14-day lmt. FACILITIES: 46 sites (tr -22); piped drk wtr, tbls, toil, cga, f. ACTIVITIES: Boating,ld; water skiing; swimming; picnicking; fishing. MISC.: Elev 3600 ft; 16 acres; pets. On Hungry Horse Reservoir.

See page 7 for KEY TO ABBREVIATIONS.

MONTANA

Peters Creek (Flathead NF). 42 mi SE of Martin City on FS 38. SEASON: 6/1-9/15; 14-day lmt. FACILITIES: 4 sites (tr -22); toil, cga, f. ACTIVITIES: Water skiing; picnicking; fishing. MISC.: Elev 3600 ft; pets. On Hungry Horse Reservoir.

Spotted Bear (Flathead NF). 55 mi SE of Martin City on FS 38. SEASON: 6/1-10/15; 14-day lmt. FACILITIES: 13 sites (tr -22); tbls, toil, cga, f, piped drk wtr; dump. Gas/food (1 mi). ACTIVITIES: Picnicking; fishing. Horseback.

MELROSE

Canyon Creek (Beaverhead NF). 1/5 mi S on US 91; 5 mi W on Co Hwy 1871; 5 mi W on FS 1872; 3-1/5 mi SW on FS 7401. SEASON: 7/1-9/15; 14-day lmt. FACILITIES: 3 sites (no tr); tbls, toil, cga, no drk wtr. ACTIVITIES: Picnicking; rockhounding; fishing. Horseback riding/rental (1 mi). MISC.: Elev 7400 ft; 2 acres; pets; stream.

Maidenrock Fishing Access Site (Dept of Fish and Game). 6 mi W and N of I-15 at Melrose, milepost 93, on Co Rd. SEASON: 5/1-10/1; 14-day lmt. FACILITIES: Sites, toil, drk wtr. ACTIVITIES: Fishing; picnicking. MISC.: Pets. Pack in; pack out.

MILES CITY

Branum Lake Fishing Access Site (Dept of Fish and Game). 1 mi N of I-94 at Miles City, milepost 135; 1 mi N on I-94 loop. SEASON: 5/1-10/1; 14-day lmt. FACILITIES: Sites, toil, no drk wtr. ACTIVITIES: Fishing; picnicking. MISC.: Pets.

Jack's Husky Super Truck Stop. I-94, E of Miles City. SEASON: All yr; 1-night lmt. FACILITIES: Spaces for self-contained RVs; drk wtr, toil, gas, food. MISC.: Mechanic.

MISSOULA

Beavertail Hill Recreation Area (SRA). 27 mi SE of Missoula, milepost 119, on I-90 to Beavertail exit. SEASON: 10/1-5/1, FREE (rest of yr, $3); 14-day lmt. FACILITIES: 15 sites, flush toil, tbls, drk wtr. ACTIVITIES: Fishing; picnicking. MISC.: 65 acres; pets.

Chief Looking Glass Fishing Access (Dept of Fish and Game). S of Missoula, milepost 77, on US 93; 2 mi E on Co Rd. SEASON: 5/1-10/1; 14-day lmt. FACILITIES: Sites, toil, drk wtr. ACTIVITIES: Picnicking; fishing. MISC.: Pets.

Clearwater Crossing Fishing Access Site (Dept. of Fish and Game). E of Missoula, milepost 31, on St Hwy 200. SEASON: 5/1-10/1; 14-day lmt. FACILITIES: Sites, toil, no drk wtr. ACTIVITIES: Picnicking; fishing. MISC.: Pets.

Frenchtown Pond Fishing Access Site (Dept. of Fish and Game). W of Missoula, milepost 91, on I-90; 1 mi W on frontage rd. SEASON: 10/1-5/1, FREE (rest of yr, $2); 14-day lmt. FACILITIES: Sites, toil, drk wtr. ACTIVITIES: Swimming; picnicking; fishing. MISC.: Pets.

Missoula Standard Truck Playa. Jct of I-90 and US 93 in Missoula. SEASON: All yr; 1-night lmt. FACILITIES: Spaces for self-contained RVs; toil, drk wtr, gas, food. MISC.: Mechanic.

Turah Fishing Access Site (Dept. of Fish and Game). E of Missoula, milepost 113, on I-90; 2 mi SE on Co Rd. SEASON: 10/1-5/1, FREE (rest of yr, $2); 14-day lmt. FACILITIES: Sites, drk wtr, toil. ACTIVITIES: Boating; picnicking; fishing. MISC.: Pets.

MONARCH

Logging Creek (Lewis & Clark NF). 3 mi N of Monarch on St Hwy 89; 5-7/10 mi W on Co Hwy 427; 6 mi SW on FS 253. SEASON: 6/1-10/15; 14-day lmt. FACILITIES: 29 sites (tr -22); tbls, toil, cga, f, well drk wtr. ACTIVITIES: Picnicking; fishing. MISC.: Elev 4600 ft; 8 acres; pets. Scenic. Access rds not suitable for large tr.

MONIDA

Upper Red Rock Lake (NWR). From I-15, Monida exit, 33 mi E. SEASON: 6/1-11/1. FACIL: 10 sites; tbls, f. ACTIVITIES: Boating,l; picnicking; fishing. MISC.: No dogs. No motor bikes.

NEIHART

Aspen (Lewis & Clark NF). 5 mi N on US 89 (gravel access rds). SEASON: 5/15-10/15; 14-day lmt. FACILITIES: 6 sites (tr -22); tbls, toil, cga, well drk wtr, gas, store, ice, food. ACTIVITIES: Picnicking; hunting; rockhounding; fishing. MISC.: Elev 5000 ft; 2 acres; pets; scenic. 5 mi S of Belt Creek Ranger Station.

Kings Hill (Lewis & Clark NF). 9 mi S of Neihart on St Hwy 89 (gravel access rds). SEASON: 7/1-9/15; 14-day lmt. FACILITIES: 15 sites (tr -22); tbls, toil, cga, f, piped drk wtr. ACTIVITIES: Hunting; rockhounding; hiking; picnicking; fishing; skiing. MISC.: Elev 7300 ft; 6 acres; pets. Showdown ski area. Porphyry Peak lookout. Bike Trails. Scenic.

Many Pines (Lewis & Clark NF). 3-1/2 mi SE of Neihart on St Hwy 89 (gravel access rds). SEASON: 6/15-10/15; 14-day lmt. FACILITIES: 23 sites (tr -22); tbls, toil, cga, piped drinking water, food, gas, store, ice. ACTIVITIES: Hunting; rockhounding; hiking; picnicking; fishing; skiing. MISC.: Elev 6000 ft; 15 acres; pets. Scenic. Showdown ski area. Memorial Falls. Bike Trails.

NORRIS

Red Mountain (BLM). 9 mi E of Norris on St Hwy 289; turn right at the Beartrap Canyon Recreation Area sign to Red Mountain campground. SEASON: 5/1-10/31. FACILITIES: 22 sites (tr -24); tbls, toil, cga, f, store. ACTIVITIES: Hunting; picnicking; fishing; hiking; rockhounding; float boating; mountain climbing. MISC.: Elev 4485 ft; 20 acres; small pets on leash. Madison River. Beartrap Primitive Area (3 mi S on BLM rds). Bike trails. CAUTION: High winds & lack of trees make tent inadvisable at times.

NOXON

Bull River Campground (Kootenai NF). 6 mi NW of Noxon on US 10A. SEASON: 9/16-6/14, FREE (rest of yr, $2); 14-day lmt. FACILITIES: 18 sites (tr -22); tbls, toil, cga. Showers/store/laundry (1 mi). ACTIVITIES: Hiking; water skiing; boating,ld; picnicking; fishing; swimming. MISC.: Elev 2200 ft; 13 acres; pets. Facilities shut off during Free Season. Bike trails. Lake. River. Beach. Access to Cabinet Gorge Reservoir. Next to Bull River, near Cabinet Mountains Wilderness.

NYE

Initial Creek (NF). 6 mi SW of Nye on St Hwy 420; 7 mi NW on FS 846. SEASON: 6/15-9/15; 9-day lmt. FACILITIES: 4 sites (no tr); toil, cga, f. ACTIVITIES: Rockhounding; picnicking; fishing. MISC.: Elev 6200 ft; pets. Trail access to lake plateau.

OLNEY

Stillwater State Forest. 8 mi N of Olney on US 93. SEASON: 6/1-10/31. FACILITIES: 5 tent sites (no tr); tbls. ACTIVITIES: Fishing; picnicking. MISC.: 4 acres; pets.

OVANDO

Big Nelson (Lolo NF). 8-3/10 mi E of Ovando on St Hwy 200; 11-1/5 mi NE on FS 500. SEASON: 6/15-9/15; 14-day lmt. FACILITIES: 6 sites (tr -32); tbls, toil, cga, f, no drk wtr. ACTIVITIES: Hiking;

picnicking; fishing; water skiing; boating,ld; sailing. Horseback riding (4 mi), (rental, 5 mi). MISC.: Elev 4200 ft; 3 acres; pets. Trails lead to Bob Marshall & Scapegoat Wilderness. On Coopers Lake. Scenic. Grocery/gas/ice (19 mi).

Monture (Lolo NF). 8-9/10 mi N on FS 77. SEASON: 6/15-9/30; 14-day lmt. FACILITIES: 5 sites (tr -22); no drk wtr; tbls, toil, cga, f. ACTIVITIES: Rockhounding; hiking; picnicking. Fishing (1 mi). Horseback riding (rental, 1 mi). MISC.: Elev 4200 ft; 3 acres; pets. Scenic. Nature Trails. Scapegoat Wilderness (8 mi by trail). Store/gas (9 mi). Bob Marshall Wilderness Area (13 mi by trail).

OTTER

Cow Creek (NF). 7-1/2 mi N of Otter on FS 51; 5 mi W on FS 95. SEASON: 6/1-9/15. FACILITIES: 5 sites (tr -32); piped drk wtr, tbls, toil, cga, f. ACTIVITIES: Picnicking; fishing (trout stocked pond). MISC.: Elev 3800 ft; 5 acres; pets; lake.

PARADISE

Cascade (Lolo NF). 2-1/2 mi SE of Paradise on US 200; 5-1/2 mi SW on St Hwy 461. SEASON: 5/15-10/31; 14-day lmt. FACILITIES: 12 sites (tr -32); tbls, toil, cga, f. Grocery/gas/ice (8 mi). ACTIVITIES: Hiking; rockhounding; picnicking; fishing. MISC.: Elev 2900 ft; 4 acres; small pets on leash. Adjacent Clark Fork River. Cascade Falls Nature Trail at campground. Bike trails.

PHILIPSBURG

Cable Mountain Campground (Deerlodge NF). 12-3/10 mi S of Philipsburg on St Hwy 10A; 3-1/10 mi N on FS 676; 3/10 mi S on FS 8617. SEASON: 6/15-9/15; 14-day lmt. FACILITIES: 11 sites (tr -22); tbls, toil, cga, f, well drk wtr. Store/gas/ice/food (3 mi). ACTIVITIES: Picnicking; rockhounding; fishing. Boating,rl (4 mi). MISC.: Elev 6500 ft; 5 acres; pets; historic; stream. Near Georgetown and Echo Lakes.

Copper Creek (Deerlodge NF). 6-1/5 mi S of Philipsburg on St Hwy 10A; 9-1/5 mi SW on St Hwy 38; 10 mi S on FS 80. SEASON: 6/15-9/15; 14-day lmt. FACILITIES: 7 sites (tr -32); tbls, toil, cga, f, well drk wtr. ACTIVITIES: Rockhounding; picnicking; fishing. MISC.: Elev 5900 ft; 2 acres; pets. Stream. Historic.

Crystal Creek (Deerlodge NF). 6-1/5 mi S of Philipsburg on St Hwy 10A; 24-1/2 mi SW on St Hwy 38. SEASON: 7/1-9/10; 14-day lmt. FACILITIES: 3 sites (tr -32); no drk wtr; tbls, toil, cga, f. ACTIVITIES: Rockhounding; picnicking. Fishing (2 mi). MISC.: Elev 7000 ft; 1 acre; pets. Historic. Stream.

East Fork Campground (Deerlodge NF). 6-1/5 mi S of Philipsburg on St Hwy 10A; 6 mi SW on St Hwy 38; 4-7/10 mi SE on FS 672; 1/2 mi S on FS 9349. SEASON: 6/1-9/15. FACILITIES: 7 sites (tr -32); well drk wtr, tbls, toil, cga, f. ACTIVITIES: Rockhounding; picnicking; fishing; swimming; waterskiing; boating,d. MISC.: Elev 6000 ft; 3 acres; pets. East Fork Reservoir. Jumpoff to Anaconda--Pintlar Wilderness Area.

Flint Creek (Deerlodge NF). 8 mi S of Philipsburg on St Hwy 10A; 3/10 mi SE on FS 1090 (21 mi W of Anaconda). SEASON: 5/15-9/15; 14-day lmt. FACILITIES: 10 sites (tr -32); no drk wtr; tbls, toil, cga, f.   Food   (5 mi). ACTIVITIES: Rockhounding; picnicking; fishing. Boating, (1, 4 mi). MISC.: Elev 5800 ft; 3 acres; pets. Historic. Stream.

Spillway (Deerlodge NF). 6-1/5 mi S of Philipsburg on St Hwy 10A; 6 mi SW on St Hwy 38; 5-1/10 mi SE on FS 672; 1 mi S on FS 5141. SEASON: 6/15-9/15; 14-day lmt. FACILITIES: 11 sites (tr -32), tbls, toil, cga, well drk wtr. ACTIVITIES: Picnicking; rockhounding; boating,d; swimming; waterskiing; fishing. MISC.: Elev 6400 ft; 3 acres; pets; historic; lake.

Squaw Rock Campground (Deerlodge NF). 14 mi W of Philipsburg on Co Hwy 348; 4-7/10 mi W on Co Hwy 102; 1/10 mi SW on FS 9346. SEASON: 6/1-9/20; 14-day lmt. FACILITIES: 10 sites (tr -32); tbls, toil, cga, f, well drk wtr. Store/ice (1 mi). ACTIVITIES: Rockhounding; picnicking; fishing. MISC.: Elev 5200 ft; 2 acres; pets. On Rock Creek. Historic. Very good fishing. Stream.

POLSON

Big Arm Recreation Area (SRA). 15 mi N of Polson, milepost 74, on US 93. SEASON: 10/1-5/1, FREE (rest of yr, $3); 14-day lmt. FACILITIES: 50 sites; flush toil, tbls, cga, f, drk wtr. ACTIVITIES: Swimming; picnicking; fishing; boating,l. MISC.: 65 acres; pets. Shelters.

Finley Point Recreation Area (SRA). 9 mi NE of Polson, milepost 6, on St Hwy 35; 4 mi W. SEASON: 10/1-5/1, FREE (rest of yr, $2); 14-day lmt. FACILITIES: 10 sites (tr -20); drk wtr, tbls, cga, f. ACTIVITIES: Swimming; picnicking; fishing; boating,ld. MISC.: Elev 3000 ft; 24 acres; pets.

Yellow Bay (SRA). 20 mi N of Polson, milepost 17, on St Hwy 35. SEASON: 10/1-5/1, FREE (rest of yr, $3); 14-day lmt.

FACILITIES: 15 sites (tr -20); flush toil, drk wtr, shelters, cga, f. ACTIVITIES: Swimming; boating,l; picnicking; fishing. MISC.: 15 acres; pets.

PONY

Potosi (Beaverhead NF). 3 mi SE of Pony on Co Hwy 1601; 5 mi SW on FS 1601. SEASON: 6/15-9/15. FACILITIES: 15 sites (tr -32); tbls, toil, cga, f, drk wtr. ACTIVITIES: Horseback riding; picnicking; fishing. MISC.: Elev 6200 ft; 3 acres; pets. Stream. Scenic South Willow Creek drainage.

POPLAR

JC REST STOP (Fort Peck Indian Agency). 1/4 mi W of Poplar on US 2; S to campground. SEASON: 5/1-9/15. FACILITIES: 10 sites; tbls. Dump/bottled gas/ice/ laundry, store (within 1 mi). ACTIVITIES: Swimming; boating,ld; picnicking; fishing. MISC.: 2 acres; pets.

Poplar Community Park (Fort Peck Indian Agency). 1/4 mi E of Poplar on US 2; N to campground. SEASON: 5/1-9/15. FACILITIES: 100 sites (tr -25); playground, tbls, cga, f. Dump/bottled gas/ice/laundry/store (within 1 mi). ACTIVITIES: Swimming; picnicking; fishing. MISC.: 25 acres; pets.

RED LODGE

Beaver Lodge Fishing Access Site (Dept of Fish and Game). 5 mi N of Red Lodge, milepost 76, on US 212; 1 mi E on Co Rd; 1-1/2 mi on Co Rd. SEASON: 5/1-10/1; 14-day lmt. FACILITIES: 5 sites, toil, no drk wtr; tbls, cga, f. ACTIVITIES: Swimming; rockhounding; hiking; picnicking; fishing. MISC.: Elev 5500 ft; small pets. River.

Bull Springs Fishing Access Site (Dept of Fish and Game). 5 mi N of Red Lodge, milepost 77, on US 212; 1 mi E on Co Rd. SEASON: 5/1-10/1; 14-day lmt. FACILITIES: 5 sites; tbls, toil, cga, f, no drk wtr. ACTIVITIES: Hiking; rockhounding; picnicking. MISC.: Elev 5550 ft; small pets. Rock Creek. River.

Cascade (Custer NF). 1-1/2 mi S of Red Lodge on US 212; 9-1/2 mi W on FS 71. SEASON: 6/15-9/15; 14-day lmt. FACILITIES: 30 sites (tr -32); tbls, toil, cga, f, well drk wtr. ACTIVITIES: Rockhounding; picnicking; fishing. MISC.: Elev 7600 ft; 12 acres; pets. Stream.

Horsethief Fishing Access Site (Dept of Fish and Game). 5 mi N of Red Lodge, milepost 76, on US 212; 1 mi S on Co Rd. SEASON: 5/1-10/1; 14-day lmt. FACILITIES: Sites, toil, cga, tbls, no drk wtr. ACTIVITIES: Rockhounding; hiking; picnicking; fishing. MISC.: Elev 5500 ft; small pets. Creek.

MK (Custer NF). 12 mi S of Red Lodge on US 212; 3–1/2 mi SW on FS 421. SEASON: 6/1–9/15; 9-day lmt. FACILITIES: 10 sites (tr –22); no drk wtr; tbls, toil, cga, f. ACTIVITIES: Rockhounding; picnicking; fishing. MISC.: Elev 7500 ft; 5 acres; pets. Scenic. Stream.

Palisades (Custer NF). 1–1/2 mi S of Red Lodge on US 212; 1 mi W on FS 71; 1-1/2 mi W on Co Hwy 3010; 1/2 mi NW on FS 3010. SEASON: 6/15–9/15; 9-day lmt. FACILITIES: 7 sites (tr –22); tbls, toil, cga, f, no drk wtr. Store/ice/gas/laundry/ dump/food (5 mi). ACTIVITIES: Rockhounding; picnicking; fishing. Horseback riding (rental, 5 mi). MISC.: Elev 6400 ft; 3 acres; pets. Stream.

Water Birch Fishing Access Site (Dept of Fish and Game). 6 mi N of Red Lodge (milepost 79) on US 212. SEASON: 5/1-10/1; 14-day lmt. FACILITIES: 20 sites, no drk wtr; tbls, toil, cga, f. ACTIVITIES: Hiking; rockhounding; picnicking; fishing. MISC.: Small pets. Bike Trails.

RICHEY

Kuester Lake (Municipal Park). 6 mi NE of Richey on St Hwy 200. SEASON: All year. FACILITIES: 10 sites; tbls, cga, f. ACTIVITIES: Swimming; picnicking; fishing; boating,ld. MISC.: 10 acres; pets. Lake.

Richey Community Park. On Hwy 200, SE corner of Richey. SEASON: All year. FACILITIES: 6 sites; flush toil, tbls, showers, playground. Laundry/store (1 mi). MISC.: Elev 2500 ft; 3 acres; pets. Prairie Land.

ROSCOE

East Rosebud Lake (Custer NF). 7 mi SW of Roscoe on Co Hwy 177; 6 mi SW on FS 177. SEASON: 6/15–9/15; 9-day lmt. FACILITIES: 12 sites (tr –16); tbls, toil, cga, f, piped drk wtr. ACTIVITIES: Boating,ld; hiking; water skiing; picnicking; fishing; mountain climbing; horseback riding & rental. mi). MISC.: Elev 6400 ft; 12 acres; pets. Scenic. Hiking and riding trail into Beartooth Primitive Area.

Jimmy Joe (Custer NF). 7 mi SW on Co Hwy 177; 3 mi SW on FS 177. SEASON: 6/15–9/15; 9-day lmt. FACILITIES: 10 sites (tr –32); no drk wtr; tbls, toil, cga, f. ACTIVITIES: Rockhounding; picnicking; fishing. Boating,l (4 mi). Horseback riding (rental, 4 mi). MISC.: Elev 5600 ft; 4 acres; pets. River.

ROUNDUP

Cow Bell Campground (Municipal Park). In Roundup, near fairgrounds; 1/2 mi E on East Second from intersection of Main St & Second. SEASON: All year. FACILITIES: 75 sites; tbls, cga, f, flush toil, playground. Dump/bottled gas/ice/laundry/store/swimming pool nearby. ACTIVITIES: Swimming; snow skiing; hunting; rockhounding; hiking; picnicking; fishing. Golf nearby. MISC.: Elev 3279; 11 acres; pets. River. Bike Trails. On Mussellshell River.

ST.MARY

St. Mary Lake (Glacier NP). 1 mi W of St. Mary Entrance to National Park. SEASON: Late September–June, FREE (rest of yr, $3); 7-day lmt. FACILITIES: 156 sites (tr –26); flush toil, tbls, piped drk wtr, food, store, bottled gas. ACTIVITIES: Hiking; picnicking; fishing. Swimming, horseback riding (nearby). MISC.: 13 acres; pets. Self-contained vehicles only; and water turned off during FREE Season. Golden Eagle Passport or $2 entrance fee .

SCOBEY

Whitetail Reservoir Fishing Access Site (Dept. of Fish and Game). E of Scobey, milepost 11, on St Hwy 5; N on Co Rd 511 to milepost 5. SEASON: 5/1-10/1; 14-day lmt. FACILITIES: Sites, no drk wtr, toil. ACTIVITIES: Boating; picnicking; fishing. MISC.: Pets. Pack in/out.

SEELEY LAKE

Harper Lake Fishing Access Site (Dept of Fish and Game). S of Seeley Lake, milepost 1, on Co Rd 209. SEASON: 5/1-10/1; 14-day lmt. FACILITIES: Sites, no drk wtr; toil. ACTIVITIES: Boating; picnicking; fishing. MISC.: Pets.

SHELBY

Bair's Truck Stop. Jct of I-15 an'/ US 12 in Shelby. SEASON: All yr; 1-night lmt. FACILITIES: Spaces for self-contained RVs; drk wtr, toil, food.

SHERIDAN

Branham Lakes (Beaverhead NF). 5-4/5 mi E of Sheridan on Co Hwy 1111; 5 mi E on FS 112; 3 mi N on FS 1110. SEASON: 7/15–9/15. FACILITIES: 3 sites (tr –22); tbls, toil, cga, no drk wtr. ACTIVITIES: Picnicking; fishing; boating (no motors; no boat launching facilities). MISC.: Elev 8800 ft; 3 acres; pets. Branham Lake.

Mill Creek Campground (Beaverhead NF). 5-4/5 mi E of Sheridan on Co Hwy 1111; 1-1/5 mi E on FS 1112. SEASON: 6/1-10/31; FACILITIES: 9 sites (tr –22); well drk wtr, tbls, toil, cga, f. ACTIVITIES:

Picnicking. **MISC.:** Elev 6400 ft; 5 acres; pets. Scenic area. Stream. Mountain Lakes (nearby). Reservations.

SIDNEY

Cartside Lake (County Park). 9 mi S of Sidney on St Hwy 16; 1 mi W on gravel rd (access rd poor). **SEASON:** All yr. **FACILITIES:** 108 sites (tr -15); tbls, toil, cga. Store (1 mi). **ACTIVITIES:** Hunting; hiking; rockhounding; picnicking; fishing; boating,l. **MISC.:** Elev 2041; lake; pets. Bike Trails.

Richland (County Campground). 5 mi NE of Sidney on St Hwy 200; 2 mi right on gravel rd. **FACILITIES:** 10 sites; well drk wtr, tbls, toil, cga, f. **ACTIVITIES:** Hiking; picnicking; fishing; hunting; softball. **MISC.:** Elev 2041 ft. Playground.

SLAUGHTER RIVER LANDING

* **Judith Landing** (Missouri River Waterway). 40 mi E of Slaughter River Landing on Missouri River BY BOAT. **SEASON:** 5/1-9/30; 14-day lmt. **FACILITIES:** 5 tent sites; tbls. **ACTIVITIES:** Boating; picnicking. **MISC.:** 6 acres; pets.

STANFORD

Dry Wolf (Lewis & Clark NF). 17-1/2 mi SW of Stanford on Co Hwy; 5-1/2 mi SW on FS 251. **SEASON:** 5/20-10/15. **FACILITIES:** 26 sites (tr -32); tbls, toil, cga, f, piped drk wtr, playground. **ACTIVITIES:** Hunting; hiking; picnicking; fishing. **MISC.:** Elev 5800 ft; 11 acres; pets. Bike Trails. Stream.

STEVENSVILLE

Burnt Fork Road (Bitterroot NF). 18 mi SE of Stevensville (on Burnt Fork Creek) [poor rd leads to it]. **FACILITIES:** No improved camping units. **ACTIVITIES:** Picnicking. **MISC.:** Access point for Burnt Fork Lake.

Gold Creek (Bitterroot NF). 3/5 mi S of Stevensville on Co Hwy 269; 10-2/5 mi SE on Co Hwy 372; 3-4/5 mi S on FS 312. **SEASON:** 6/1-9/15; 14-day lmt. **FACILITIES:** 3 sites (tr -22); no drk wtr; tbls, toil, cga, f. **ACTIVITIES:** Hiking; picnicking; fishing; hunting. **MISC.:** Elev 4800 ft; 3 acres; pets. Poor rd up Burnt Fork Creek.

STRYKER

North Dickey Lake (Kootenai NF). 4-7/10 mi NW of Stryker on US 93. **SEASON:** 10/1-5/31, FREE (rest of yr, $2); 10-day lmt. **FACILITIES:** 16 sites (tr -22); tbls, cga, piped drk wtr, toil. Gas/store/ice (2 mi). **ACTIVITIES:** Hiking; boating,ld; picnicking; fishing; water skiing; swimming. **MISC.:** Elev 3200 ft;

SULA

Crazy Creek (Bitterroot NF). 4-4/5 mi NW of Sula on US 93; 1 mi SW on Co Hwy 100; 3 mi SW on FS 370 (on Warm Springs Creek). **SEASON:** 6/1-11/30; 14-day lmt. **FACILITIES:** 14 sites (tr -22); tbls, toil, cga, f, well drk wtr. Laundry/showers/ice (3 mi). **ACTIVITIES:** Hiking; picnicking; fishing. Horseback riding (1 mi). Swimming (3 mi). **MISC.:** Elev 5000 ft; 9 acres; pets. Trailhead into Warm Springs Area. Upper loop open for hunter camps; lower loop closed to hunter camps.

East Fork Trail Takeoff (Bitterroot NF). 17 mi NE of Sula (on E Fork of the Bitterroot River). **SEASON:** 6/15-11/30. **FACILITIES:** No improved camping units except for stock unloading ramps; toil. **ACTIVITIES:** Horseback riding (corrals). **MISC.:** Access point for the Anaconda-Pintlar Wilderness.

Indian Trees (Bitterroot NF). 5-4/5 mi S of Sula on US 93; 1 mi SW on FS 729. **SEASON:** 6/15-9/30; 14-day lmt. **FACILITIES:** 18 sites (tr -22); tbls, toil, cga, f, piped drk wtr. **ACTIVITIES:** Hiking; picnicking. Fishing (1 mi). **MISC.:** Elev 5000 ft; 7 acres; small pets on leash. Stream.

Jennings (Bitterroot NF). 1/10 mi N of Sula on US 93; 4 mi NE on Co Hwy 472; 6-2/5 mi NE on FS FH80. **SEASON:** 6/15-11/30; 14-day lmt. **FACILITIES:** 4 sites (tr -22); well drk wtr, tbls, toil, cga, f. **ACTIVITIES:** Hunting; hiking; picnicking. Fishing (1 mi). **MISC.:** Elev 5000 ft; 1 acre; pets. On the E Fork of the Bitterroot River.

Martin Creek (Bitterroot NF). 1/10 mi N of Sula on US 93; 4 mi NE on Co Hwy 472; 12 mi NE on FS 80. **SEASON:** 6/1-11/30; 14-day lmt. **FACILITIES:** 7 sites (tr -32); tbls, toil, cga, f, well drk wtr. **ACTIVITIES:** Hunting; picnicking; hiking. Fishing (1 mi). **MISC.:** Elev 5400 ft; 3 acres; pets; scenic. On Moose & Martin Creeks.

SUPERIOR

Big Pine Fishing Access Site (Dept. of Fish and Game). S of Superior, milepost 66, on I-90; 5 mi NW on Co Rd. **SEASON:** 5/1-10/1; 14-day lmt. **FACILITIES:** Sites, toil, no drk wtr; tbls. **ACTIVITIES:** Picnicking; fishing. **MISC.:** Pets.

Forks Fishing Access Site (Dept. of Fish and Game). S of Superior, milepost 67, on I-90; 7 mi NW on Co Rd. **SEASON:** 5/1-10/1; 14-day lmt. **FACILITIES:** Sites, no drk wtr; toil. **ACTIVITIES:** Fishing; picnicking. **MISC.:** Pets.

Trout Creek (Lolo NF). 4-2/5 mi SE of Superior on St Hwy 269; 2-1/2 mi SW on FS 250. **SEASON:** 6/1-9/10; 14-day lmt. FACILITIES: 12 sites (tr -32); tbls, toil, cga, f, piped drk wtr. Gas/groceries (4 mi). ACTIVITIES: Fishing; picnicking. MISC.: Elev 3000 ft; 6 acres; pets. Stream.

SWAN LAKE

Cedar Creek (Swan River SF). 12 mi S of Swan Lake on US 209; 1 mi W on gravel rd at Cedar Creek. SEASON: 6/1-10/30. FACILITIES: 6 tent sites (no tr); tbls, toil, cga, f. ACTIVITIES: Fishing; picnicking. MISC.: 2 acres; pets.

Cilly Creek (Flathead NF). 6 mi S of Swan Lake on St Hwy 209; 1/2 mi W on FS. SEASON: 6/1-9/15. FACILITIES: 4 sites (tr -22); toil, cga, f. ACTIVITIES: Fishing; picnicking. MISC.: Elev 3100 ft; pets.

Point Pleasant (Swan River SF). 8 mi S of Swan Lake on Hwy 209 (Swan Valley Hwy). SEASON: 6/1-10/30. FACILITIES: 5 sites (tr -12); tbls, toil, cga, f. ACTIVITIES: Fishing; picnicking. MISC.: 5 acres; pets.

Soup Creek (Swan River SF). 6 mi S of Swan Lake on US 209; 4 mi E on Loop Rd (gravel rd). SEASON: 6/1-10/30. FACILITIES: 9 sites (tr -12); tbls, toil, cga. ACTIVITIES: Picnicking; fishing. MISC.: 5 acres; pets.

Swan Lake (Flathead NF). 1/2 mi NW of Swan Lake on St Hwy 209. SEASON: 6/1-9/15; 14-day lmt. FACILITIES: 6 sites (tr -22); tbls, toil, cga, f, piped drk wtr. Store/gas/showers/laundry/ice (1 mi). ACTIVITIES: Hiking; water skiing; boating,ld (r,1 mi); picnicking; fishing. Horseback riding (r, 1 mi). MISC.: Elev 3000 ft; 3 acres; pets. Lake. River. Bike Trails.

Swan Lake Annex (Flathead NF). 1/2 mi NW of Swan Lake on St Hwy 83. SEASON: 5/26-9/15; 14-day lmt. FACILITIES: 25 sites (tr -32); flush toil, cga, f, tbls, piped drk wtr. Store/ice/gas/showers/laundry (1 mi). Electricity in restrooms. ACTIVITIES: Picnicking; boating; swimming; fishing; waterskiing. Horseback riding (1 mi). MISC.: Elev 3000 ft; 2 acres; pets; stream.

TERRY

Highway 10 Picnic Area (Municipal Park). SEASON: All year. FACILITIES: 10 sites; tbls. ACTIVITIES: Picnicking. Fishing (1 mi). MISC.: 2 acres; pets.

Terry City Park. On US 10 at center of Terry. SEASON: 6/1-9/1. FACILITIES: 20 sites; flush toil, playground, tbls. Ice/dump/bottled gas/laundry/store (nearby). Swimming Pool (extra charge). ACTIVITIES: Picnicking; swimming. MISC.: 4 acres. Pets; river.

THOMPSON FALLS

Bend (Lolo NF). 5 mi E of Thompson Falls on St Hwy 200; 29-1/5 mi NE on FS 56. SEASON: 6/1-9/15; 14-day lmt. FACILITIES: 4 sites (tr -22); piped drk wtr, tbls, toil, cga. ACTIVITIES: Picnicking; fishing. MISC.: Elev 4000 ft; 2 acres; pets. 1/4 mi from Thompson River.

Clark Memorial (Lolo NF). 5 mi E of Thompson Falls on St Hwy 200; 5-2/5 mi NE on FS 56. SEASON: 6/1-9/30. FACILITIES: 5 sites (tr -16); tbls, toil, cga, food concession, store, gas, no drk wtr. ACTIVITIES: Picnicking; fishing. MISC.: Elev 2700 ft; 2 acres; pets. Thompson River.

Copper King (Lolo NF). 5 mi E on St Hwy 200; 4 mi NE on FS 56. SEASON: 6/1-9/30. FACILITIES: 5 sites (tr -16); no drk wtr; tbls, toil, cga, store, gas, food concession. ACTIVITIES: Picnicking; fishing. MISC.: Elev 2700 ft; 2 acres; pets. Thompson River.

Fishtrap Creek (Lolo NF). 5 mi E of Thompson Falls on St Hwy 200; 16 mi NE on FS 56; 9 mi NW on FS 516. SEASON: 6/1-9/30. FACILITIES: 4 sites (tr -22); well drk wtr, tbls, toil, cga. ACTIVITIES: Picnicking; fishing. MISC.: Elev 4200 ft; 2 acres; pets. Stream.

Fishtrap Lake (Lolo NF). 5 mi E of Thompson Falls on St Hwy 200; 13 mi NE on FS 56; 14-7/10 mi NW on FS 516; 1-4/5 mi W on FS 7593. SEASON: 5/15-9/15; 14-day lmt. FACILITIES: 9 sites (tr -32); well drk wtr, tbls, toil, cga. ACTIVITIES: Berry-picking; picnicking; fishing; rockhounding; water skiing. Boating (ld, 1/4 mi). MISC.: Elev 4200 ft; 5 acres; pets. Fishtrap Lake (1/4 mi).

Gold Rush (Lolo NF). 9 mi S of Thompson Falls on FS 352 (east fork of Dry Creek Rd). SEASON: 6/1-10/30. FACILITIES: 7 sites (tr -22); well drk wtr, tbls, toil, cga. ACTIVITIES: Picnicking. MISC.: Elev 3000 ft; 3 acres; pets. Stream.

Thompson Falls Recreation Area (SRA). 3 mi N of Thompson Falls on St Hwy 200; NW of Thompson Falls, milepost 50. SEASON: 10/1-5/1, FREE (rest of yr, $3); 14-day lmt. FACILITIES: 30 sites (tr -20); drk wtr, tbls, toil, cga, f. ACTIVITIES: Boating,l; picnicking; fishing. MISC.: 50 acres; pets. Shelters.

THREE FORKS

Cardwell Fishing Access Site (Dept. of Fish and Game). W of Three Forks, milepost 256, on I-90; 1 mi S across the river. SEASON: 5/1-10/1; 14-day lmt. FACILITIES: Sites; toil, no drk wtr, tbls.

MONTANA

ACTIVITIES: Picnicking; fishing; MISC.: Pets. Pack in/out.

Lewis and Clark Caverns (SP). W of Three Forks, milepost 271, on US 10. SEASON: 10/1-5/1, FREE (rest of yr, $3); 14-day lmt. FACILITIES: 40 sites; flush toil, cga, tbls, f, drk wtr, food. ACTIVITIES: Picnicking; fishing nearby. MISC.: 2770 acres; pets.

Missouri Headwaters State Park. I-90 at Three Forks, milepost 278, then 6 mi N on Co Rd 286. SEASON: 10/1-5/1 FREE (rest of yr, $2); 14-day lmt. FACILITIES: 10 sites (tr -35); drk wtr, tbls, cga, f. ACTIVITIES: Boating,ld; picnicking; fishing. MISC.: 516 acres; pets.

TOWNSEND

Deep Creek (Helena NF). 15-3/5 mi E on US 12. SEASON: 6/15-9/30. FACILITIES: 6 sites (no tr); tbls, toil, cga, f, no drk wtr. ACTIVITIES: Picnicking; fishing. MISC.: Elev 5000 ft; 3 acres; stream; pets.

Deep Dale Fishing Access Site (Dept. of Fish and Game). S of Townsend, milepost 82, on US 287. SEASON: 5/1-10/1; 14-day lmt. FACILITIES: Sites; no drk wtr; toil. ACTIVITIES: Boating; picnicking; fishing.

Indian Road (SRA). N of Townsend, milepost 75, on US 287 at bridge. SEASON: 10/1-5/1, FREE (rest of yr, $2); 14-day lmt. FACILITIES: Sites; drk wtr. ACTIVITIES: Boating; picnicking. MISC.: Pets.

Rotary Park. 1 mi N of Townsend (dirt access rds). FACILITIES: Tbls, toil. ACTIVITIES: Picnicking; fishing.

Silos (SRA). N of Townsend, milepost 70, on US 287. SEASON: 10/1-5/1, FREE; 14-day lmt. FACILITIES: Sites; drk wtr, shelters. ACTIVITIES: Boating; picnicking. MISC.: Pets.

Skidway (Helena NF). 23 mi E of Townsend on St Hwy 12; 2 mi S on FS 4042 (paved access rds). SEASON: 6/15-9/30; 15-day lmt. FACILITIES: 11 sites (tr -16); tbls, toil, cga, f, drk wtr (tank). ACTIVITIES: Picnicking; fishing. MISC.: Elev 6000 ft; 18 acres; pets.

TROY

Bad Medicine (Kootenai NF). 3 mi SE of Troy on US 2; 18-4/5 mi S on St Hwy 202 (Bull Lake Road); 1 mi W on FS 398; 1 mi N on FS 7170 (Last 2 mi on oiled rd.) SEASON: 5/20-9/30. FACILITIES: 7 sites (tr -22); tbls, toil, cga, f, piped drk wtr. Store/gas/ice/food (5 mi). ACTIVITIES: Picnicking; boating,l; fishing; hiking; waterskiing. MISC.: Elev 2200 ft; 8 acres; pets. Bull Lake. Ross Creek Cedars. Nature trails (4 mi).

Dorr Skeels (Kootenai NF). 3 mi SE of Troy on US 2; 13-1/2 mi S on St Hwy 202 (Bull Lake Rd); 4/5 mi W on FS 1117. SEASON: 5/1-9/15; 14-day lmt. FACILITIES: 6 sites (tr -22); no drk wtr; tbls, toil, cga, f. Store/gas/ice/food (1 mi). ACTIVITIES: Picnicking; boating,ld; waterskiing; fishing. MISC.: Elev 2200 ft; 2 acres; pets. Bull Lake.

Kilbrennen Lake (Kootenai NF). 2-7/10 mi NW of Troy on US 2; 9-4/5 mi NE on FS 2394. SEAS: 5/20-9/30. FACIL: 5 sites (tr - 22); tbls, toil, cga, f, no drk wtr. ACTIVITIES: Boating,rld; water skiing; picnicking; fishing. MISC.: Elev 2900 ft; 6 acres; pets. Beautiful lake. Good fishing.

Pete Creek (Kootenai NF). 10-1/5 mi NW on US 2; 6-1/5 mi NE on St Hwy 508; 19-3/5 mi NE on FS 92. SEASON: 6/1-9/30; 14-day lmt. FACILITIES: 10 sites (tr -22); tbls, toil, cga, f; no drk wtr. Store/gas/ice/food (3 mi). ACTIVITIES: Picnicking; fishing. Boating (3 mi). MISC.: Elev 3000 ft; 5 acres; pets. Yaak River. Good fishing. WAtch for logging trucks.

Spar Lake (Kootenai NF). 3 mi SE of Troy on US 2; 15-1/2 mi S on FS 384. SEASON: 5/20-9/30. FACILITIES: 8 sites (tr -22); tbls, toil, cga, piped drk wtr. ACTIVITIES: Boating,ld; picnicking; fishing; water skiing. MISC.: Elev 3100 ft; pets. Spar Lake. 5 acres.

Whitetail (Kootenai NF). 10-1/5 mi NW of Troy on US 2; 6-1/5 mi NE on St Hwy 508; 17 mi NE on FS 92. SEASON: 6/15-10/31; 14-day lmt. FACILITIES: 12 sites (tr -22); tbls, toil, cga, f, no drk wtr. Store/ice/gas/food (5 mi). ACTIVITIES: Picnicking; hiking; fishing; boating,d; berry-picking. MISC.: Elev 3000 ft; 8 acres; pets; nature trails; geological. Yaak River. Good fishing. River navigable short distance with small boat. Scenic. Watch for logging trucks.

Yaak (Kootenai NF). 7-1/2 mi NW of Troy on US 2. SEASON: 10/1-4/30 FREE (rest of yr, $2); 14-day lmt. FACILITIES: 43 sites (tr -22); tbls, toil, cga, f. ACTIVITIES: Hiking; picnicking; fishing; boating,d. MISC.: Elev 1800 ft; 17 acres; pets. Water shut off during free season. Yaak and Kootenai Rivers. Laundry/store/showers (5 mi).

Yaak Falls (Kootenai NF). 10 mi NW of Troy on US 2; 6-1/2 mi NE on St Hwy 508. SEASON: 5/20-9/30. FACILITIES: 7 sites (tr -22); no drk wtr; tbls, toil, cga, f. ACTIVITIES: Hiking; picnicking; fishing. MISC.: Elev 2500 ft; 3 acres.

MONTANA

TROUT CREEK

North Shore (Kootenai NF). 2-1/2 mi NW of Trout Creek on US 10A; 1/2 mi E on Co Rd. SEASON: 11/1-4/30, FREE (rest of yr, $2). FACILITIES: 12 sites (tr -32); tbls, toil, cga, f. ACTIVITIES: Swimming; picnicking; fishing; hiking; horseback riding; boating,ld. MISC.: Elev 2400 ft; 7 acres; pets. Water shut off during free season. On N shore of Noxon Rapids Reservoir. Near Cabinet Mountains Wilderness.

VIRGELLE

* **Coal Banks Landing** (Missouri River Waterway). 8 mi E of Virgelle on Missouri BY BOAT. SEASON: 5/1-9/30; 14-day lmt. FACILITIES: 5 tent sites; tbls. ACTIVITIES: Boating; picnicking. MISC.: Pets.

WEST GLACIER

Agpar (Glacier NP). 2 mi W of West Glacier near Park Headquarters. SEASON: Late September-June, FREE (rest of yr, $3); 7-day lmt. FACILITIES: 196 sites (tr -26); 10 group campsites; piped drk wtr, tbls, cga, f, flush toil, store, food. ACTIVITIES: Hiking; picnicking; fishing; boating,rl; water skiing. MISC.: Elev 3200 ft; 10 acres; pets. Water shut off and self-contained vehicles only during Free Season. Golden Eagle Passport**or $2 Entrance Fee.

Devil Creek (Flathead NF). 45 mi SE of West Glacier on US 2. SEASON: 6/1-9/15; 14-day lmt. FACILITIES: 13 sites (tr -22); piped drk wtr, tbls, toil, cga. Gas/food/ice (1 mi). ACTIVITIES: Picnicking; fishing. Horseback riding (r, 1 mi). MISC.: 5 acres; pets. Scenic. Accross Flathead River from Glacier Park. Elev 4600 ft.

WEST YELLOWSTONE

Cherry Creek (Gallatin NF). 7-1/2 mi W of West Yellowstone on US 191; 5-3/10 mi N on FS 167. SEASON: 6/1-9/15; 15-day lmt. FACILITIES: 5 sites (tr -32); no drk wtr; tbls, toil, cga, f. ACTIVITIES: Waterskiing; sailing; picnicking; fishing; boating. MISC.: Elev 6600 ft; 2 acres; pets; primitive. Excellent fishery. On the West shore of Hebgen Lake.

Cliff Point (Beaverhead NF). 12 mi N on US 191; 27 mi W on St Hwy 499; 3-1/2 mi S on St Hwy 237; 7 mi W on FS 5721. SEASON: 6/15-9/15; 14-day lmt. FACILITIES: 6 sites (tr -16); tbls, toil, cga, f, well drk wtr. ACTIVITIES: Hiking; picnicking; fishing; water skiing. Boating (rld, 1 mi). MISC.: Elev 6400 ft; 2 acres; pets. Botanical. Nature trails. Campground next to Cliff Lake. Good trout fishing.

Hilltop (Beaverhead NF). 12 mi N on US 191; 27 mi W on St Hwy 499; 28-7/10 mi S on St Hwy 287; 7-3/10 mi W on FS 5721. SEASON: 6/15-9/15. FACILITIES: 18 sites (tr -32); tbls, toil, cga, f, piped drk wtr. ACTIVITIES: Picnicking; horseback riding; sailing. Fishing/waterskiing/boating,rld (1 mi). MISC.: Elev 6400 ft; 8 acres; pets; scenic area; botanical. Campground is 1/2 mi from Wade & Cliff Lakes.

Red Canyon (Beaverhead NF). 8 mi N of West Yellowstone on US 191; 4-2/5 mi NW on US 287; 2-3/5 mi N on FS 681. SEASON: 6/1-10/1; 15-day lmt. FACILITIES: 3 sites (tr -22); toil, f. ACTIVITIES: Picnicking; rockhounding. MISC.: Elev 6700 ft; pets.

Rumbaugh (Beaverhead NF). 7-1/2 mi W of West Yellowstone on US 191; 6-2/5 mi N on FS 167. SEASON: 6/1-10/1; 15-day lmt. FACILITIES: 3 sites (tr -22); toil, cga, f. ACTIVITIES: Waterskiing; picnicking; fishing. MISC.: Elev 5600 ft; pets.

Rumbaugh Ridge (Beaverhead NF) 7-1/2 mi W of West Yellowstone on US 191; 7-1/5 mi N on FS 167. SEASON: 6/1-10/1; 15-day lmt. FACILITIES: 5 sites (tr -22); toil, f. ACTIVITIES: Water skiing; picnicking; fishing. MISC.: Elev 6600 ft; pets.

Spring Creek (Beaverhead NF). 7-1/2 mi W of West Yellowstone on US 191; 7-2/5 mi W on FS 167. SEASON: 6/1-10/1; 15-day lmt. FACILITIES: 3 sites (tr -22); toil, cga, f. ACTIVITIES: Water skiing; picnicking; fishing. MISC.: Elev 6600 ft; pets.

Wade Lake (Beaverhead NF). 12 mi N of West Yellowstone on US 191; 27 mi W on St Hwy 499; 3-1/2 mi S on St Hwy 287; 7 mi W on FS 5721. SEASON: 6/15-9/15; 14-day lmt. FACILITIES: 11 sites (tr -16); piped drk wtr, tbls, toil, cga, f. ACTIVITIES: Picnicking; fishing (good trout fishing on Wade Lake); water skiing; sailing. Boating,ld (r, 1 mi). Horseback riding (1 mi). MISC.: Elev 6200 ft; 5 acres; pets; Wade Lake.

WHITEFISH

Sylvia Lake (NF). 6 mi W of Whitefish on US 93; 35 mi W on FS 113; 4 mi S on FS 5380. SEASON: 6/1-9/15; 14-day lmt. FACILITIES: 3 sites (tr -22); no drk wtr; tbls, toil, cga. ACTIVITIES: Boating; picnicking; fishing. MISC.: Elev 4000; 1 acre; pets.

See page 7 for KEY TO ABBREVIATIONS.

313

WHITEHALL

Lewis and Clark Caverns (SP). 15 mi E of Whitehall on US 10. SEASON: 10/1–5/1, Free (rest of yr $3); 14-day lmt. FACILITIES: 40 sites; flush toil, tbls, cga, f, food, drk wtr. ACTIVITIES: Picnicking. Fishing nearby. MISC.: 2770 acres; pets.

Parrot Castel Fishing Access Site (Dept of Fish and Game). S of Whitehall, milepost 5, on St Hwy 28/; 3 mi E on Co Rd. SEASON: 5/1–10/1; 14-day lmt. FACILITIES: Sites, no drk wtr; toil. ACTIVITIES: Picnicking; fishing. MISC.: Pack in/out. Pets.

Pigeon Creek (Deerlodge NF). 15–3/5 mi W of Whitehall on St Hwy 10; 4–3/5 mi S on FS 668. SEASON: 6/1–9/15; 14-day lmt. FACILITIES: 6 sites (tr –16); well drk wtr, tbls, toil, cga, f. ACTIVITIES: Rockhounding; picnicking; fishing. MISC.: Elev 6000 ft; 7 acres; pets. Stream. Historic.

Toll Mountain (Deerlodge NF). 13 mi W of Whitehall on St Hwy 10; 1–1/2 mi N on FS 09315. SEASON: 6/1–9/15. FACILITIES: 10 sites (no tr); well drk wtr, tbls, toil, cga, f. ACTIVITIES: Picnicking; fishing; rockhounding. MISC.: Elev 6000 ft; 4 acres; pets; stream.

WHITE SULPHUR SPRINGS

Bair Reservoir (SP). 15 mi E of White Sulphur Springs on St Hwy 12 (dirt access rds). SEASON: 14-day lmt. FACILITIES: 10 sites, tbls, toil, cga, f. ACTIVITIES: Hiking; water skiing; snow skiing; boating,l; hunting; picnicking. MISC.: Elev 5400 ft. Pets on leash. Nature Trails. Bike Trails.

Grasshopper (Lewis & Clark NF). 7 mi E of White Sulphur Springs on US 12; 4–1/5 mi S on FS 211. SEASON: 6/15–9/15. FACILITIES: 11 sites (tr –22); tbls, toil, cga, f, well drk wtr. ACTIVITIES: Picnicking; fishing. MISC.: Elev 6000 ft; 8 acres; pets.

Jumping Creek (Lewis & Clark NF). 22 mi NE of White Sulphur Springs on US 89. SEASON: 6/15–10/15. FACILITIES: 10 sites (tr –22); well drk wtr, tbls, toil, cga, f, food concession. ACTIVITIES: Rockhounding; hiking; picnicking; fishing. MISC.: Elev 5700 ft; 10 acres; small pets on leash. River.

Moose Creek (Lewis & Clark NF). 18 mi N of White Sulphur Springs on US 89; 5–1/2 mi on FS 119; 3–1/5 mi N on FS 204. SEASON: 6/15–10/15. FACILITIES: 5 sites (tr –22); well drk wtr, tbls, toil, cga, f. ACTIVITIES: Fishing; picnicking. MISC.: Elev 6000 ft; 3 acres; pets. Stream.

North Fork Smith River Reservoir (SP). 11 mi E of White Sulphur Springs on St Hwy 12 (dirt access rds). SEASON: 14-day lmt. FACILITIES: 15 sites; tbls, toil, cga, f. ACTIVITIES: Boating,l; hiking; water skiing; picnicking; fishing. MISC.: Elev 5400 ft; pets on leash.

Richardson Creek (Lewis & Clark NF). 7 mi E of White Sulphur Springs on US 12; 48–7/10 mi S on FS 211. SEASON: 6/1–10/31; 14-day lmt. FACILITIES: 4 sites (tr –16); no drk wtr, toil, cga, no tbls. ACTIVITIES: Picnicking. MISC.: Elev 5900 ft; 3 acres; pets; stream.

Smith River Fishing Access Site (Dept. of Fish and Game). 13 mi NW of US 89 at White Sulphur Springs, milepost 126, on Co Rd 360; 6 mi N on Co Rd. SEASON: 5/1–10/1; 14-day lmt. FACILITIES: Sites, toil, no drk wtr. ACTIVITIES: Picnicking; fishing. MISC.: Pets.

WILBAUX

Rush Hall Fishing Access Site (Dept. of Fish and Game). S of Wibaux, milepost 52, on St Hwy 7; 3 mi W on Co Rd. SEASON: 5/1–10/1; 14-day lmt. FACILITIES: Sites, toil, no drk wtr. ACTIVITIES: Fishing; picnicking. MISC.: Pets.

WISDOM

Fishtrap Creek Fishing Access Site (Dept. of Fish and Game). N of Wisdom, milepost 49, on St Hwy 43. SEASON: 5/1–10/1; 14-day lmt. FACILITIES: Sites, toil, drk wtr. ACTIVITIES: Picnicking; fishing. MISC.: Pets. Pack in/out.

May Creek (Beaverhead NF). 17–1/5 mi W of Wisdom on St Hwy 43. SEASON: 11/1–5/30, FREE (Rest of yr, $2). FACILITIES: 12 sites (tr –32); piped drk wtr, tbls, toil, cga, f. ACTIVITIES: Rockhounding; hiking; picnicking; fishing. MISC.: Elev 6200 ft; 2 acres; pets. Water is off during free season. Open: Weather permitting.

Mussigbrod (Beaverhead NF). 1–1/10 mi W of Wisdom on St Hwy 43; 7 mi NW on Co Hwy; 8–1/10 mi W on Co Hwy; 2–4/5 mi NW on FS 573. SEASON: 6/1–11/1. FACILITIES: 4 sites (tr –22); no drk wtr; tbls, toil, cga, f. ACTIVITIES: Boating (no launch faciliites); water skiing; picnicking; fishing. MISC.: Elev 6500 ft; 3 acres; pets. Lake.

Twin Lakes Campground (Beaverhead NF). 6–4/5 mi S of Wisdom on St Hwy 278; 7–4/5 mi W on Co Hwy 1290; 4–4/5 mi S on FS 945; 5–4/5 mi SW on FS 183. SEASON: 6/15–11/1. FACILITIES: 14 sites (tr –32); well drk wtr, tbls, toil, cga, f. ACTIVITIES: boating,ld; water skiing; picnicking; fishing. MISC.: Elev 7200 ft; 13 acres; pets. Scenic. 75-acre lake.

See page 7 for KEY TO ABBREVIATIONS.

WISE RIVER

Little Joe (Beaverhead NF). 19-3/5 mi SW of Wise River on FS 484. SEASON: 6/15-9/30. FACILITIES: 4 sites (no tr); piped drk wtr, tbls, toil, cga, f. ACTIVITIES: Picnicking. Fishing/horseback riding (1 mi). MISC.: Elev 7000 ft; 2 acres; pets. River.

Lodgepole (Beaverhead NF). 12-9/10 mi SW of Wise River on FS 484. SEASON: 6/15-9/30. FACILITIES: 6 sites (tr -16); well drk wtr, tbls, toil, cga, f. ACTIVITIES: Picnicking; fishing (good stream fishing). Horseback riding (1 mi). MISC.: Elev 6400 ft; 2 acres; pets. Scenic Area. River.

Mono Creek (Beaverhead NF). 22-4/5 mi SW of Wise River on FS 484. SEASON: 6/15-9/30. FACILITIES: 5 sites (tr -16); toil, cga, tbls, well drk wtr. ACTIVITIES: Picnicking. Fishing/horseback riding (1 mi). MISC.: Elev 6800 ft; 2 acres; pets; stream. Jump off point for Torrey & Schulz Lakes.

Seymour (Beaverhead NF). 11-1/5 mi W of Wise River on St Hwy 43; 4 mi N on Co Hwy 274; 8 mi NW on FS 934. SEASON: 6/15-10/15. FACILITIES: 17 sites (tr - 16); tbls, toil, cga, f. ACTIVITIES: Picnicking; hunting; hiking. Fishing/ Horseback riding (1 mi). MISC.: Elev 6700 ft; 7 acres; pets. Well drk wtr. Stream. Trailhead into Anaconda-Pintlar Wilderness. Well drk wtr.

Willow Campground (Beaverhead NF). 13-2/5 mi SW of Wise River on FS 484. SEASON: 6/15-9/30. FACILITIES: 6 sites (tr -16); tbls, toil, cga, f, well drk wtr. ACTIVITIES: Picnicking; fishing. Horseback riding (1 mi). MISC.: Elev 6600 ft; 3 acres; pets. Scenic area on Wise River.

WOLF CREEK

Beartooth Recreation Area (SRA). 3 mi NE of I-15 at Wolf Creek on US 91; 5 mi S on Co Rd. SEASON: 10/1-5/1, FREE (rest of yr, $2); 14-day lmt. FACILITIES: 10 sites; drk wtr, tbls, toil, cga. ACTIVITIES: Picnicking; fishing. MISC.: Elev 3570 ft; 50 acres; pets.

WOLF POINT

Husky Car/Truck Stop. On St Hwy 2 at Wolf Point. SEASON: All yr; 1-night lmt. FACILITIES: Spaces for self-contained RVs; toil, drk wtr, food, gas.

Lewis & Clark Memorial Park (Municipal Park. 6 mi SE of Wolf Point on St Hwy 13. SEASON: MD-LD. FACILITIES: 75 sites; tbls, toil, cga, f, well drk wtr, playground. ACTIVITIES: Hiking; hunting; picnicking; fishing; rockhounding; horseback riding. MISC.: Elev 2238 ft; 40 acres; pets.

YELLOWTAIL DAM

* **Black Canyon Boat-In** (Bighorn Canyon NRA). 5 mi S of Yellowtail Dam; access BY BOAT. SEASON: 5/1-11/1; 30-day lmt. fFACILITIES: 6 tent sites; tbls. ACTIVITIES: Swimming; picnicking; fishing; boating,d. MISC.: Pets.

ZORTMAN

Camp Creek Campground (BLM). From St Hwy 191, take the gravelled Co Rd N towards Zortman for approximately 6-1/2 mi. At the road junction 1 mi SE of Zortman, continue N on the BLM graded rd 1 mi to the campground. SEASON: 4/1-11/30. FACILITIES: 9 sites; tbls, toil, cga. Store/ice/gas (1 mi). ACTIVITIES: Hiking; picnicking; fishing; snowmobiling. MISC.: Elev 4100 ft; 40 acres. Good stream and reservoir fishing. Pets.

NEBRASKA

GENERAL STATE INFORMATION

Miscellaneous

Toll-Free Number for Travel Information:
    1-800-228-4370 [outside of Nebraska]
    1-800-742-7595 [within Nebraska]
Right Turns on Red: Permitted after full
    stop; unless otherwise posted.
STATE CAPITOL: Lincoln
STATE NICKNAME: Cornhusker State
STATE MOTTO: "Equality Before The Law"
STATE BIRD: Western Meadow Lark
STATE FLOWER: Goldenrod
STATE TREE: Elm

See page 7 for KEY TO ABBREVIATIONS.

State Parks

State Park campgrounds charge a fee ranging from $2.00-4.00 per night. However the majority of their extensive State Recreation Areas are free (except for the entrance permit from 4/1-8/31). ENTRANCE PERMIT TO ALL STATE PARKS, MOST STATE RECREATION AREAS, AND TWO STATE WAYSIDE AREAS: Required from 4/1-8/31. State historical parks are exempt from permit requirements. Fees for the permits: Resident Annual, $7.50; Resident Daily, $1.50; Nonresident Annual, $12.50; Nonresident Daily, $2.00. Areas where the permit is required are posted at the entrance. Further information: Nebraska Game and Parks Commission; 2200 North 33rd Street; PO Box 30370; Lincoln, NB 68503.

Rest Areas

Overnight stops are permitted in Nebraska Rest Areas.

Nebraska Canoe Trails

There are several canoe trails in Nebraska, all of which offer camping facilities (mostly free). For an informative map which includes campgrounds and canoeing information, write to the Nebraska Game and Parks Commission; PO Box 30370; Lincoln, NB 68503. Ask for their free brochure NEBRASKA CANOE TRAILS.

Backpacking in Nebraska

There are multitudes of trails in all sections of Nebraska. A free booklet, BACKPACKING: TRAILS TO NEBRASKA'S GREAT OUTDOORS, gives detailed information on the trails and free camping opportunities. Further information: Nebraska Game and Parks Commission; PO Box 30370; Lincoln, NB 68503.

INFORMATION SOURCES

Maps

The following maps are available from **Forsyth Travel Library** (see order form in APPENDIX B):

State of Nebraska [Up-to-date, showing all principal roads, points of interest, sports areas, parks, airports, mileage, etc. Full color.]

Completely indexed city maps, including all airports, lakes, rivers, etc., of: **Kearney; Lincoln; North Platte; Omaha; Council Bluffs.**

State Information

Games and Parks Commission; 2200 North 33rd Street; PO Box 30370; Lincoln, NB 68503.
Division of Travel and Tourism; Nebraska Department of Economic Development; 301 Centennial Mall South; PO Box 94666, State Capitol; Lincoln, NB 68509.
Nebraska Game, Forestation, and Park Commission; State Capitol Building; Lincoln, NB 68509.

Miscellaneous

Omaha Chamber of Commerce; Farnam Building; Omaha, NB 68102.
Lincoln Chamber of Commerce; 200 Lincoln Building; Lincoln, NB 68508.
Nebraska Bureau of Land Management [plus Wyoming and Kansas]; 2515 Warren Avenue; PO Box 1828; Cheyenne, WY 82001.
Nebraska and Samuel R. McKelvie NF; The Game and Parks Commission; PO Box 30370; Lincoln, NB 68503.
Corps of Engineers, Kansas City District; 700 Federal Building; Kansas City, MO 64106. [Has free campgrounds in Nebraska.]
Corps of Engineers, Missouri River District; PO Box 103, Downtown Station; Omaha, NB 68101.
Corps of Engineers, Omaha District; 6014 U.S. Post Office and Court House; 215 North 17th Street; Omaha, NB 68102.

See page 7 for KEY TO ABBREVIATIONS.

NEBRASKA

FREE CAMPGROUNDS

AINSWORTH

* Calamus River Canoe Trail. 20 mi S of Ainsworth on St Hwy 7 to River BY BOAT. **SEASON:** 4/1–10/31. **FACILITIES:** Primitive undesignated sites; facilities limited in winter; no drk wtr. Begins at Moon Lake in Brown County, and covers a 50-mile stretch from St Hwy 7 to US 183. Several access points along the trail. 3 designated camping areas along the route. For map, write to Game & Parks Comm., PO Box 30370, Lincoln, NEB 68503.

Long Lake Recreation Area (SRA). 34 mi SW of Ainsworth on St Hwy 7 and Co Rd. **SEASON:** All yr; 14-day lmt. **FACILITIES:** Undesignated sites, tbls, toil, cga, drk wtr. **ACTIVITIES:** Picnicking; swimming; fishing; boating,l **MISC:** Entry permit.** Pets on leash.

ALBION

City Campground (City Park). Adjacent to City Park, at 11th and Fairview St., in Albion. **SEASON:** All yr; 14-day lmt. **FACILITIES:** Sites, flush toil, elec hkup, no drk wtr. **ACTIVITIES:** Swimming. **MISC:** Pets on leash.

Kiwanis Roadside Park (Kiwanis Club). 1/2 mi SE of jct St Hwys 39/14 in Albion. **SEASON:** All yr; 14-day lmt. **FACILITIES:** Sites, drk wtr, toil, elec hkup, playground. **MISC:** Pets.

ALEXANDRIA

Alexandria Lakes Rec. Area (SRA). 4 mi E of Alexandria on US 81, 136, or St Hwy 4. **SEASON:** All yr; 14-day lmt. **FACILITIES:** Undesignated sites; elec hookup ($), tbls, toil, cga, playground, drk wtr. **ACTIVITIES:** Picnicking; swimming; fishing; hunting; hiking; boating (nonpower or elec motor craft). **MISC:** Entrance permit**. Pets on leash.

ALMA

Methodist Cove (Harlan County Lake; COE). 3 mi E of A'ma on US 136; 1–1/2 mi S on Co Rd. **SEASON:** All yr; 14-day lmt. **FACILITIES:** 100 sites; tbls, toil, cga, drk wtr. **ACTIVITIES:** Picnicking; fishing; boating,l. **MISC:** Pets on leash.

North Cove (Harlan County Lake; COE). 5 mi E of Alma on US 136; 2–1/2 mi S on Co Rd. **SEASON:** All yr; 14-day lmt. **FACILITIES:** 30 sites, tbls, toil, cga, drk wtr. **ACTIVITIES:** Picnicking; fishing. **MISC:** Pets.

ARNOLD

Arnold Lake SRA. 1 mi S of Arnold on St Hwys 40 or 92. (On upper reaches of Loup River.) **SEASON:** All yr; 14-day lmt. **FACILITIES:** Undesignated sites; tbls, toil, cga, drk wtr, playground. Dump/ice/laundry/food/store nearby. **ACTIVITIES:** Picnicking; fishing; hunting; hiking; boating (nonpower or elec motor craft) **MISC.:** Entry permit**. Pets.

ATKINSON

Atkinson Lake Rec. Area (SRA). 1/2 mi W of Jct US 20; 1/2 mi S on St Hwy 11 (paved access rds). **SEASON:** All yr; 14-day lmt. **FACILITIES:** Undesignated sites; tbls, toil, cga, elec hkup ($), playground, drk wtr. **ACTIVITIES:** Picnicking; swimming; fishing; boating (nonpower or elec motor craft only); hunting. **MISC:** Sites need blocking. Entry permit**, Pets on leash.

AURORA

Streeter's Park (City Park). N side of Aurora on St Hwy 34. **SEASON:** All yr; 14-day lmt. **FACILITIES:** 20 sites (tr-27), tbls, toil, cga, drk wtr. **ACTIVITIES:** Picnicking; swimming (pool nearby). **MISC:** Pets on leash.

AYR

Crystal Lake Recreation Area (SRA). 1–1/2 mi N of Ayr on US 281. **SEASON:** All yr; 14-day lmt. **FACILITIES:** Undesignated sites; elec hkup ($), tbls, toil, cga, drk wtr. **ACTIVITIES:** Picnicking; fishing nearby; hunting; hiking; boating (nonpower or elec motor craft). **MISC:** Picnic shelters. Pets on leash.

BARTLETT

Bartlett Park (City Park). 2 blks W on St Hwy 281, in Bartlett. **SEASON:** All yr; 14-day lmt. **FACILITIES:** Spaces for self-contained vehicles; toil, drk wtr, cga. **ACTIVITIES:** Picnicking. **MISC:** Pets on leash.

Pibel Lake Rec. Area (SRA). 9 mi S and 1 mi E of Bartlett on US 281. **SEASON:** All yr; 14-day lmt. **FACILITIES:** Undesignated sites; tbls, toil, cga, drk wtr, playground. **ACTIVITIES:** Picnicking; fishing; boating,l (non-power or elec. motor craft only); hunting; hiking. **MISC:** Lake. Entry permit** Pets on leash.

BATTLE CREEK

Memorial Park (County Park). In Battle Creek. SEASON: 4/1-12/1. FACILITIES: Sites, tbls, toil, cga, playground. ACTIVITIES: Picnicking; fishing. MISC: River. Pets on leash.

BEATRICE

Big Indian Rec. Area (Natural Resources Dist.). 15 mi S & 3 mi E of Beatric. SEASON: All yr; 14-day lmt. FACILITIES: Sites, drk wtr. ACTIVITIES: Picnicking; boating,d; swimming; fishing; waterskiing; hiking. MISC: Pets on leash.

Rockford Site Rec. Area (SRA). 7 mi E of Beatrice; 2 mi S to campground. SEASON: All yr; 14-day lmt. FACILITIES: Undesignated sites; tbls, toil, cga, playground, drk wtr. ACTIVITIES: Picnicking; swimming; fishing; boating; hunting; hiking. MISC: Homestead Natl Monument nearby. Pets.

BEAVER CROSSING

Beaver Crossing Park (City Park). E Elk St and Martin Ave. in Beaver Crossing. SEASON: All yr; 14-day lmt. FACILITIES: Sites, elec hkup, flush toil, drk wtr, cga. ACTIVITIES: Swimming. MISC: Pets on leash.

BENNET

City Park. In Bennet. SEASON: All yr; 24-hrs. FACILITIES: Sites, tbls, toil, cga, playground. ACTIVITIES: Picnicking. MISC: Pets on leash.

BERWYN

Berwyn Park (City Park). On Main St. in Berwyn. SEASON: All yr; 14-day lmt. FACILITIES: Spaces for self-contained vehicles; wtr/elec hkups, drk wtr, cga. MISC: Pets on leash.

BIG SPRINGS

Woody's Truck Stop. I-80, exit 107 (south side) in Big Springs. SEASON: All yr; 1-night lmt. FACILITIES: Spaces. self-contained RVs, food, drk wtr, toil, gas, mechanic.

BLOOMFIELD

Bloomfield (City Park). E edge of Bloomfield on St Hwy 84. SEASON: All yr; 7-day lmt. FACILITIES: Spaces for self-contained vehicles; drk wtr, cga, elec hkup, flush toil. ACTIVITIES: Swimming. MISC: Pets on leash.

BLUE SPRINGS

Feit Memorial Park (City Park). N at W end of Blue River Bridge—Broad St., in Blue springs. SEASON: All yr. FACILITIES: Spaces for self-contained vehicles; drk wtr, toil, cga. ACTIVITIES: Swimming. MISC: Pets.

BRIDGEPORT

Bridgeport Rec · Area (SRA). SE on St Hwy 385 from US 26 in Bridgeport. SEASON: All yr; 14-day lmt. FACILITIES: Undesignated sites; tbls, toil, cga, drk wtr, dump, playground. ACTIVITIES: Picnicking; fishing; swimming; boating,ld; hunting, hiking. MISC: Pets on leash.

BROWNVILLE

Brownville Recreation Area (SRA). Near jct of US 136 and St Hwy 67 at Brownsville. SEASON: All yr; 14-day lmt. FACILITIES: Undesignated sites; tbls, toil, cga, drk wtr. ACTIVITIES: Picnicking; hunting; fishing; hiking; boating,l. MISC: On Missouri River. Site of historic "Meriweather Lewis." Pets on leash.

Indian Cave State Park. 9 mi S of Brownville on St Hwy 67; 4 mi E on St Hwy 64E. SEASON: All yr; 14-day lmt. FACILITIES: Sites, tbls, toil, cga, drk wtr. ACTIVITIES: Picnicking; fishing; hunting; hiking; horseback riding; playground. MISC: On Missouri River.

On the Nemaha-Richardson County line near Shubert, Nebraska.

The park encompasses 3,000 acres of land which includes 2386 acres of wooded area. The whole area is open for hiking. The park has pretty rugged terrain with a unique area of wooded bluffs overlooking the Mo. River. Indian Cave State Park is a very unique in that it is underdeveloped, has beautiful scenery and is relatively unchanged by civilization. There are 20 miles of backpacking trails, three water sources in the park, five round-up shelters for backpackers and hikers, numerous tent sites and primitive camping. The park is open year round, at no charge, with a fourteen day camping limit.

Indian Cave has several tent camping areas, a small R.V. campground with a capacity for 40-45 units, and many tent camping areas along the twenty miles of hiking trails for the backpack enthusiast.

See page 7 for KEY TO ABBREVIATIONS.

For people who own horses, there
is an area set up for them to camp
with their animals at the head of
a ten-mile horse trail.

BURCHARD

Burchard Lake (SRA). 3 mi E of
Burchard; then 1/2 mi N on St Hwy
65 or 4. SEASON: All yr; 14-day lmt.
FACILITIES: Undesignated sites; tbls,
toil, cga, drk wtr. ACTIVITIES: Picnicking; swimming; fishing; boating,1
MISC: Entry permit.** Pets on leash.

BURWELL

Burwell City Park (City Park). N
Burwell along Loup River. SEASON:
All yr; 14-day lmt. FACILITIES:
Spaces for self-contained vehicles;
elec hkup; toil, drk wtr, cga, store
ACTIVITIES: Swimming; fishing. MISC:
Pets on leash.

BUSHNELL

Lodgepole State Wayside Area. 4 mi
E of Bushnell on US 30. SEASON: All
yr; 1-day lmt. FACILITIES: 40 sites
tbls, toil, cga, drk wtr, playground
ACTIVITIES: Picnicking; fishing;
swimming; boating; hiking. MISC:
Highest point in Neb. is located
nearby. Pets on leash.

CAMBRIDGE

Cambridge City Park (City Park).
E edge of Cambridge on St Hwys 6/34
SEASON: All yr; 3-day lmt. FACILI-
TIES: Spaces for self-contained vehic-
les; wtr hkup; flush toil, drk wtr,
showers, cga, store. ACTIVITIES:
Fishing. MISC: Pets on leash.

Medicine Creek Reservoir Rec. Area
(SRA). 2 mi W of Cambridge on US
6; 7 mi N on US 34. SEASON: All yr;
14-day lmt. FACILITIES: Undesignated
sites; tbls, toil, cga, f, showers,
playground, drk wtr. Food/ice/store
nearby. ACTIVITIES: Picnicking;
fishing; swimming; boating,rld; hunting; hiking. MISC: Picnic shelters.
Entry permit.** Pets on leash.

CENTRAL CITY

Hord Lake Recreation Area (SRA).
1 mi S of Central City on US 30; 2
mi E on St Hwy 14 (paved access
rds). SEASON: All yr; 14-day lmt.
FACILITIES: Undesignated sites; tbls,
toil, cga, drk wtr. ACTIVITIES: Picnicking; fishing; swimming; playground; boating - nonpowered or elec
motor craft; hunting; hiking. MISC:
Sites need blocking. Entry permit.**
Pets on leash.

Lone Tree Wayside Area. 1 mi W of
Central City on S side of St Hwy 30.
SEASON: All yr; 1-nite lmt. FACILI-
TIES: Spaces for self-contained vehic-
les, tbls. ACTIVITIES: Picnicking.
MISC: Pets on leash.

CERESCO

Pioneer State Wayside Area. 3 mi N
of Ceresco on US 77. SEASON: All yr;
2-day lmt. FACILITIES: Undesignated
sites; tbls, toil, cga, playground,
drk wtr, shelters. ACTIVITIES: Picnicking; hiking. MISC: Pets.

CHADRON

**Nebraska National Forest, Pine Ridge
Division.** 7 mi S of Chadron on US
385. SEASON: All yr; 14-day lmt. FA-
CILITIES: Spaces for self-contained
vehicles, tbls, toil, cga, drk wtr.
ACTIVITIES: Picnicking; hiking.
MISC: Museum of Fur Trade nearby,
Pets on leash.

CHAMPION

Champion Lake (SRA). 1/2 mi W of
Champion on US 6 or St Hwy 106.
SEASON: All yr; 14-day lmt. FACILI-
TIES: Primitive sites, tbls, toil, cga
drk wtr. ACTIVITIES: Picnicking;
fishing; hunting; boating (nonpower
& elec motor craft only); hiking.
MISC: On Frenchman Creek. Entry
permit.** Pets on leash.

CHAPMAN

Chapman Rest Area. 1 mi E of Chapman on St Hwy 30. SEASON: All yr;
2-day lmt. FACILITIES: Sites (tr -
30), tbls, toil, cga. ACTIVITIES:
Picnicking. MISC: Pets on leash.

Longbridge Rec. Area. 1 mi E of
Chapman on St Hwy 30. SEASON: All
yr; 14-day lmt. FACILITIES: Spaces
for self-contained vehicles. MISC:
Pets on leash.

CHESTER

Chester City Park (City Park). 1
block W of jct of St Hwys 81/8 (on
St Hwy 8). SEASON: All yr; 14-day
lmt. FACILITIES: Sites, elec hkup,
flush toil, drk wtr, cga, store.
MISC: Pets on leash.

CLARKS

Mormon Trail Wayside Park. 1-1/2
mi S of Clarks on St Hwy 30; 3 mi
W via St Hwy 92. SEASON: All yr;
2-day lmt. FACILITIES: Undesignated
sites; tbls, toil, cga, drk wtr. AC-
TIVITIES: Picnicking; fishing; hiking. MISC: Pets on leash.

**See page 316.

CLARKSON

Wayside Rest Area. In Clarkson. SEASON: All yr; 1-nite lmt. FACILITIES: Spaces for self-contained vehicles; tbls, toil, cga. ACTIVITIES: Picnicking. MISC: Pets on leash.

COLERIDGE

Coleridge Park (City Park). NE corner of Town. SEASON: All yr; 1-nite lmt. FACILITIES: Spaces for self-contained vehicles, tbls, toil, cga, elec/wtr hkup, playground. ACTIVITIES: Picnicking; tennis; softball. MISC: Pets on leash.

COLUMBUS

Columbus Power House Park (Loup Power District). 1/2 mi E of city limits on US 30; 1-1/2 mi N on Co Rd. SEASON: All yr; 7-day lmt. FACILITIES: 6 sites; tbls, toil, cga, drk wtr. ACTIVITIES: Picnicking; fishing in the Loup Canal; playground. MISC: Adjacent to the Columbus Powerhouse (free tours available). Pets on leash.

Lake North (Loup Power District). 4 mi N of Jct of US 30 and 18th Ave in Columbus on 18th Ave (Monastery Rd) (paved access rds). SEASON: 5/1-11/1; 7-day lmt. FACILITIES: 100 sites; tbls, toil, cga, playground. ACTIVITIES: Picnicking; fishing; swimming; boating; waterskiing. MISC: Sites need blocking. More than 2 mi of beaches. Pets.

Loup Park (Loup Power District). 4 mi N of Columbus on 18th Ave; 1-1/2 mi W on Co Rd (paved access rds). SEASON: 5/1-11/1; 7-day lmt. FACILITIES: 120 sites; tbls, toil, cga, drk wtr, elec hkup. ACTIVITIES: Picnicking; fishing (particularly good on the western tip of Lake Babcock where the wtrs of the Loup Canal flow into it; & 1/4 mi E at Lake North). MISC: Located on the N & W shores of Lake Babcock. Playground. Pets on leash.

Trailrace Park (Loup Power District). 3 mi E of Columbus on 8th St Rd; 1-1/2 mi S on Co Rd. SEASON: 5/1-11/1; 7-day lmt. FACILITIES: 30 sites; tbls, toil, cga, drk wtr, playground. ACTIVITIES: Picnicking; fishing. MISC: Located where the Loup Canal pours its waters back into the Platte River. It is a spot of outstanding scenic beauty, heavily wooded with stately cottonwood trees. Electric area lights have been installed to illuminate the park areas at night.

COMSTOCK

Oak Grove (City Park). 1 mi W; 7 mi S of Comstock. SEASON: All yr; 14-day lmt. FACILITIES: Spaces for self-contained vehicles; toil, drk wtr, cga. ACTIVITIES: Fishing. MISC: Pets on leash.

City Park (City Park). 1/4 mi N of Diversion Dam in Comstock. SEASON: All yr; 14-day lmt. FACILITIES: Spaces for self-contained vehicles; toil, drk wtr, cga, store. ACTIVITIES: Fishing. MISC: Pets.

COZAD

Gallagher Canyon Recreation Area (SRA). 8 mi S of Cozad on St Hwy 21 on US 30. SEASON: All yr; 14-day lmt. FACILITIES: Undesignated sites; tbls, toil, cga, drk wtr, playground. ACTIVITIES: Picnicking; swimming; fishing; boating; hunting; hiking. MISC: Pets on leash.

CRAWFORD

City Park (City Park). In Crawford. (NOTE: When asking directions, this city park is not to be confused with Crawford City Park.) SEASON: All yr; 1-day lmt. FACILITIES: Spaces for self-contained vehicles; flush toil, drk wtr, cga. ACTIVITIES: Picnicking. MISC: Pets on leash.

Cochran State Wayside Area. 6 mi S of Crawford on St wy 2 (paved access rds). SEASON: All yr; 2-day lmt. FACILITIES: Undesignated sites; tbls, toil, cga, drk wtr. ACTIVITIES: Picnicking; hiking. MISC: Scenic. Pine Ridge Country. Pets on leash.

Toadstool Geologic Park Picnicground (Ogala Natl Grasslands). 20 mi N of Crawford on St Hwy 2; 1 mi W to campground. SEASON: All yr. FACILITIES: 6 sites; tbls, toil, cga, drk wtr. ACTIVITIES: Picnicking; hunting; hiking. MISC: Grasslands - 94,344 acres). Pets on leash.

CREIGHTON

Bruce Park (City Park). Main St. and Douglas Avenue in Creighton. SEASON: All yr; 14-day lmt. FACILITIES: Spaces for self-contained vehicles; elec hkup, flush toil, drk wtr, cga. ACTIVITIES: Swimming. MISC: Pets.

CROFTON

Bloomfield (Lewis and Clark Lake SRA). 8 mi N of Crofton; 8 mi W on Rec Rd E. SEASON: All yr; 14-day lmt. **FACILITIES:** Undesignated sites; tbls, toil, cga, drk wtr. **ACTIVITIES:** Picnicking; fishing; boating,1; playground; hiking; waterskiing; hunting. **MISC:** Lake; beach. Pets.

Crofton City Park (City Park). On St Hwy 12 in Crofton. **SEASON:** All yr; 14-day lmt. **FACILITIES:** Spaces for self-contained vehicles; wtr/swr hkup, flush toil, drk wtr, showers, cga, store. **ACTIVITIES:** Picnicking; swimming. **MISC:** Pets on leash.

Deep Water (Lewis & Clark Lake SRA). 8 mi N of Crofton; 1 mi W on Recreation Rd E. **SEASON:** All yr; 14-day lmt. **FACILITIES:** Spaces for self-contained vehicles; tbls, toil, cga, drk wtr. **ACTIVITIES:** Picnicking; fishing; hunting; hiking. **MISC:** Entry permit.** Pets on leash.

Lewis & Clark Lake (SRA). 15 mi N of Crofton on US 81 & St Hwy 121. **SEASON:** All yr; 14-day lmt. **FACILITIES:** Spaces for self-contained vehicles; tbls, toil, cga, drk wtr, shelters, tr. pads. **ACTIVITIES:** Picnicking; fishing; swimming; boating. **MISC:** 6 areas on Lewis & Clark Trail. Entry permit.** Pets on leash.

Miller Creek (Lewis & Clark Lake SRA). 6 mi N of Crofton, on St Hwy 98; 12 mi W; 1/2 mi S; 1 mi W to Campground. **SEASON:** All yr; 14-day lmt. **FACILITIES:** Undesignated sites; tbls, toil, cga, drk wtr. **ACTIVITIES:** Picnicking; fishing; boating,1; hunting; waterskiing. **MISC:** Pets on leash. Entry permit.**

South Shore (Lewis & Clark Lake SRA). 10 mi N of Crofton on St Hwy 121. **SEASON:** All yr; 14-day lmt. **FACILITIES:** Sites, tbls, toil, cga, drk wtr, playground. **ACTIVITIES:** Picnicking; fishing; hunting; boating,ld; hiking; waterskiing. **MISC:** Pets on leash. Entry permit.**

Weigand West (Lewis & Clark Lake SRA). 6 mi N of Crofton on St Hwy 98/121; 5 mi W to campground. **SEASON:** All yr; 14-day lmt. **FACILITIES:** 75 sites; tbls, toil, cga, drk wtr, bottled gas, gas, phone, dump, elec hkup, showers, food, store, playground. **ACT:** Picnicking; swimming; fishing; boating,rld; hunting; waterskiing; hiking. **MISC:** River; beach; nature trails. Entry permit.** Pets on leash.

CURTIS

Mill Park (City Park). 1/4 mi W of Curtis. **SEASON:** All yr; 14-day lmt.

FACILITIES: Spaces for self-contained vehicles; flush toil. **MISC:** Pets on leash.

DALTON

Railroad Park. W side of Dalton. **SEASON:** All yr; 5-day lmt. **FACILITIES:** 6 sites; tbls, toil, cga, playground. **ACTIVITIES:** Picnicking. **MISC:** Store. Pets on leash.

DECATUR

Blackbird Wayside Area. 2 mi NW of Decatur on US 73. **SEASON:** All yr; 2-day lmt. **FACILITIES:** Undesignated sites; tbls, toil, cga, drk wtr. **ACTIVITIES:** Picnicking; hiking. **MISC:** Overlooks Ms. River. Pets on leash.

DENTON

Conestoga Lake Rec. Area (Neb. Game & Parks Comm. SRA). 2 mi N of Denton **SEASON:** All yr; 14-day lmt. **FACILITIES:** Undesignated sites; tbls, toil, cga, drk wtr. **ACTIVITIES:** Picnicking; fishing (lgemouth, crappie, walleye, channel cat, bluegill, redear sunfish, bullhead); hunting (pheasant, quail, deer, cottontail, squirrel in season beginning Oct 1. No waterfowl hunting.); hiking; boating,ld. **MISC:** Picnic shelters. Entry permit.** Pets on leash.

Yankee Hill (Neb. Game & Pks. Comm.). 2-1/2 mi E, 1 mi S of Denton. **SEASON:** All yr; 14-day lmt. **FACILITIES:** Primitive sites. **ACTIVITIES:** Fishing (lgemouth bass, bluegill, bullhead, channel cat, walleye); hunting (pheasant, quail, deer, cottontail, squirrel, waterfowl in season). **MISC:** Dog training area. Pets on leash.

DESHLER

City Park (City Park). S part of Deshler, off 4th Street. **SEASON:** All yr; 2-day lmt. **FACILITIES:** Spaces for self-contained vehicles; wtr/elec hkup; flush toil, drk wtr, cga. **ACTIVITIES:** Picnicking. **MISC:** Pets.

EMERALD

Pawnee Lake Rec. Area (Neb. Game & Pks. Comm.). 2 mi W of Emerald on 3 mi N of US 6. **SEASON:** All yr; 14-day lmt. **FACILITIES:** Undesignated sites; tbls, toil, cga, drk wtr. **ACTIVITIES:** Picnicking; fishing; hunting; hiking; swimming; boating,ld. **MISC:** Dog training area. Green thumb area; picnic shelters; Blue Rock Area. Entry permit.** Pets on leash.

FAIRBURY

Crystal Springs (City Park). 1 mi S & 1 mi W of Fairbury. SEASON: All yr; 14-day lmt. FACILITIES: Sites, tbls, toil, cga, drk wtr. ACTIVITIES: Picnicking; swimming; fishing; boating,l; tennis. MISC: Pets on leash.

FAIRMONT

Crosstrails State Wayside Area. 1/2 mi SW of Fairmont on US 81. SEASON: All yr; 2-day lmt. FACILITIES: Undesignated sites; tbls, toil, cga, drk wtr, shelters. ACTIVITIES: Picnicking; hiking. MISC: Pets on leash.

FRANKLIN

Jaycee Park (Municipal Park). W edge of Franklin. SEASON: All yr; 14-day lmt. FACILITIES: Spaces for self-contained vehicles; toil, cga. MISC: Pets on leash.

GAVINS

South Shore (Lewis & Clark Lake SRA). 1/2 mi S of Gavins; 1/2 mi W to campground. SEASON: All yr; 14-day lmt. FACILITIES: Undesignated sites; tbls, toil, cga, drk wtr; playground. ACTIVITIES: Picnicking; fishing; boating,l; hunting. MISC: Pets.

GENOA

Headworks Park (Loup Power District). 6 mi W of Genoa on St Hwy 22. SEASON: All yr; 14-day lmt. FACILITIES: 25 sites; tbls, toil, cga, drk wtr, playground, elec hookup. ACTIVITIES: Picnicking; fishing (in small lake on the area or in the Loup Canal nearby). MISC: River. Pets allowed on leash. Adjacent to the entrace of the Loup Power District Headquarters, the beginning of the Loup Canal.

Pawnee Park (County Park). St Hwy 22 & 39, in Genoa. SEASON: All yr; 14-day lmt. FACILITIES: 8 sites; tbls, toil, cga, playground. ACTIVITIES: Picnicking; tennis; softball. MISC: Pets on leash.

GERING

Oregon Trail Park (City Park). 3 blks S, 2 blks W of jct St Hwys 71/92 SW corner of park, in Gering. SEASON: All yr; 14-day lmt. FACILITIES: Spaces for self-contained vehicles; elec hkup; flush toil, drk wtr, cga. ACTIVITIES: Swimming. MISC: Pets. on leash.

Wildcat Hills Rec. Area (SRA). 10 mi S of Gering on St Hwy 29. SEASON: All yr; 14-day lmt. FACILITIES: Undesignated sites; tbls, toil, cga, drk wtr, playground, shelters. ACTIVITIES: Picnicking; hiking; fishing. MISC: Sites need blocking; nature trails; game refuge with buffalo, elk. Entry permit.** Pets on leash.

GORDON

City of Gordon (Municipal Park). On St Hwy 20 near eastern city limits of Gordon (paved access roads). SEASON: All yr; 14-day lmt. FACILITIES: Spaces for self-contained vehicles; tbls, toil, cga, playground. ACTIVITIES: Picnicking. MISC: Pets.

GUIDE ROCK

Republican Valley Wayside Area. 2-1/2 mi W of Guide Rock; 1 mi N on US 136. SEASON: All yr; 2-day lmt. FACILITIES: Undesignated sites; tbls, toil, cga, drk wtr. ACTIVITIES: Picnicking; hiking. MISC: Willa Cather home nearby. Pets on leash.

HARRISON

Coffee Park. (Municipal Park). Sowbelly Canyon N of Harrison. SEASON: All yr; 14-day lmt. FACILITIES: Spaces for self-contained vehicles; toil, drk wtr, cga. ACTIVITIES: Picnicking. MISC: Pets on leash.

Gilbert-Baker (SRA). 4-1/2 mi N of US 20 in Harrison on Access road. SEASON: All yr; 14-day lmt. FACILITIES: Undesignated sites; tbls, toil, cga, drk wtr. ACTIVITIES: Picnicking; fishing; hunting. MISC: Pets.

HASTINGS

American Legion Memorial Wayside Area. 1/2 mi N of Hastings on US 281. (On N edge of town.) (paved access roads) SEASON: All yr; 2-day lmt. FACILITIES: Undesignated sites; tbls, toil, cga, drk wtr. ACTIVITIES: Picnicking; hiking. MISC: Sites need blocking. Pets on leash.

D.L.D. State Wayside Area. 5 mi E of Hastings on US 6. SEASON: All yr; 2-day lmt. FACILITIES: Undesignated sites; tbls, toil, cga, drk wtr, shelters. ACTIVITIES: Picnicking; hiking. MISC: On old Des Moines-Lincoln-Denver Line. Pets on leash.

Lake Hastings (Municipal Park). 1 mi N of Hastings. SEASON: All yr; 3-day lmt. FACILITIES: Spaces for self-contained vehicles; toil, drk wtr, cga. ACTIVITIES: Picnicking; fishing. MISC: Pets on leash.

Old Wayside Area. 8 mi E of Hastings on St Hwy 6. SEASON: All yr; 2-day lmt. FACILITIES: Undesignated sites; tbls, toil, cga. ACTIVITIES: Picnicking. MISC: Pets on leash.

HAY SPRINGS

Walgren Lake Recreation Area (SRA). 2-1/2 mi E of Hay Springs on St Hwy 20; 2 mi S on St Hwy 87. SEASON: All yr; 14-day lmt. FACILITIES: Undesignated sites; tbls, toil, cga, drk wtr. ACTIVITIES: Picnicking; fishing; hiking. MISC: Picnic shelters, playground, lake, Boating-nonpower or elec motor craft only. Pets on leash. Entry permit.**

HAYES CENTER

Hayes Center (SRA). 12 mi NE of St Hwy 25 in Hayes Center on Co Rd. SEASON: All yr; 14-day lmt. FACILITIES: Undesignated sites; tbls, toil, cga, playground. ACTIVITIES: Picnicking; fishing; swimming; hunting; boating,l. MISC: Pets.

HAZARD

Beaver Creek State Wayside Area. 1 mi W of Hazard and 1 mi N to campground. SEASON: All yr; 2-day lmt. FACILITIES: Undesignated sites; tbls, toil, cga, drk wtr. ACTIVITIES: Picnicking; fishing; playground; hiking; boating (nonpower craft only). MISC: Pets on leash.

HEMINGFORD

Box Butte Recreation Area (SRA). 9-1/2 mi N of Hemingford on St Hwy 2 (paved). SEASON: All yr; 14-day lmt. FACILITIES: Undesignated sites; tbls, toil, cga, drk wtr, picnic shelters. ACTIVITIES: Picnicking; swimming; fishing; boating,ld; hunting; hiking. MISC: Pets on leash.

HICKMAN

Kedgefield. 3 mi E, 1 mi S of Hickman SEASON: All yr; 14-day lmt. FACILITIES: Primitive sites; NO FACILITIES. ACTIVITIES: Fishing (lgemouth bass, bluegill, northern pike, walleye, channel cat, yellow perch); hunting (pheasant, quail, deer, cottontail, squirrel, waterfowl in season). MISC: Boating (non-powered). Pets.

Stagecoach Lake Recreation Area (SRA). SEASON: All yr; 14-day lmt.

FACILITIES: Undesignated sites (tr -35); tbls, toil, cga, drk wtr. ACTIVITIES: Picnicking; hiking; fishing; hunting. MISC: Pets on leash.

Wagon Train Lake Recreation Area (SRA) 2 mi E of Hickman. SEASON: All yr; 14-day lmt. FACILITIES: Undesignated sites; tbls, toil, cga, drk wtr. ACTIVITIES: Picnicking; fishing; swimming; boating,ld; waterskiing; hunting. MISC: Dog training area. Entry permit.** Pets on leash.

HOLDREGE

City Campground (Municipal Park). 202 S East Avenue in Holdrege. SEASON: All yr; 1-day lmt. FACILITIES: 10 sites; elec hkup; flush toil, drk wtr, cga. ACTIVITIES: Picnicking. MISC: Pets on leash.

HUMBOLDT

Humboldt City Park (Municipal Park). 1st and Long Branch in Humboldt. SEASON: All yr; 7-day lmt. FACILITIES: Sites, elec hkup, flush toil, no drk wtr, cga. ACTIVITIES: Swimming; fishing. MISC: Pets.

HUMPHREY

Humphrey City Park. On the S edge of Humphrey. SEASON: All yr; 1-nite lmt. FACILITIES: Sites, tbls, toil, cga, playground. ACTIVITIES: Picnicking; swimming; tennis. MISC: Pets on leash.

IMPERIAL

Champion Lake SRA. 7 mi W of Imperial on US 6. SEASON: All yr; 14-day lmt. FACILITIES: Undesignated sites; tbls, toil, cga, drk wtr. Food/ice/store nearby. ACTIVITIES: Picnicking; fishing; hunting. MISC: Pets.

Enders Reservoir Recreation Area (SRA). 5 mi E & 4-1/2 mi S of Imperial on St Hwy 61 or US 6. SEASON: All yr; 14-day lmt. FACILITIES: Undesignated sites; tbls, toil, cga, drk wtr. ACTIVITIES: Picnicking; hunting; swimming; fishing; boating,dl; hiking. MISC: Pets on leash. Entry permit.**

JACKSON

Beaver Dam State Wayside Area. 2 mi W of Jackson on US 20. SEASON: All yr; 2-day lmt. FACILITIES: Undesignated sites; tbls, toil, cga, drk wtr. ACTIVITIES: Picnicking; hiking. MISC: Near Ponca State Park. Picnic shelters. Pets on leash.

JOHNSTOWN

Long Lake (SRA). 20 mi SW of Johns-town on co rd. SEASON: All yr; 14-day lmt. FACILITIES: Primitive sites; tbls, toil, cga, drk wtr. ACTIVITIES: Picnicking; fishing; hunting; hiking. MISC: Pets on leash.

KIMBALL

Gotty Park (Municipal Park). On US 30 in city limits; E edge of Kimball. SEASON: All yr; 14-day lmt. FACILI-TIES: 10 sites (most sites are level); tbls, toil, cga, drk wtr. ACTIVITIES: Picnicking; horseshoes. MISC: Pets.

Lodgepole Wayside Area. 9 mi W of Kimball on US 30. SEASON: All yr; 2-day lmt. FACILITIES: Undesignated sites; tbls, toil, cga, drk wtr. AC-TIVITIES: Picnicking; fishing; fishing; swimming. MISC: Pets.

KRAMER

Olive Creek Lake Rec. Area (Neb. Game & Pks. Commission SRA). 1-1/2 mi SE of Kramer. SEASON: All yr; 14-day lmt. FACILITIES: Undesignated sites; tbls, toil, cga, drk wtr, playground ACTIVITIES: Picnicking; fishing; hunting; boating,ld. MISC: Pets.

Teal (Neb. Game & Pks. Comm.-SRA). 2-1/2 mi S of Kramer. SEASON: All yr; 14-day lmt. FACILITIES: Primi-tive sites; NO FACILITIES. ACTIVI-TIES: Fishing (black bullhead); hunting (pheasant, quail, wtrfowl, deer, cottontail, squirrel in season). MISC: Pets on leash.

LAUREL

Laurel City Park (Municipal Park). 4th and Pine in Laurel. SEASON: All yr; 14-day lmt. SEASON: Sites, elec/wtr hkup; flush toil, drk wtr, cga. ACTIVITIES: Fishing. MISC: Pets.

Laurel Lions Park (Lions Club). St Hwys 15/20, on the S edge of Laurel. SEASON: All yr; 14-day lmt. FACILI-TIES: Elec/wtr hkup; flush toil; drk wtr, cga. ACTIVITIES: Swimming. MISC: Pets on leash.

LEWELLEN

Ash Hollow Historical SP (SRA). 1/2 mi E & 3 mi S of Lewellen on US 26. SEASON: All yr; 14-day lmt. FACILI-TIES: Undesignated sites; tbls, toil, cga, drk wtr. ACTIVITIES: Picnick-ing; hiking. MISC: Historic area on Oregon Trail, cave, museum. Pets.

LONG PINE

Long Pine Recreation Area (SRA). 1 mi N of Long Pine on US 20. SEASON: All yr; 14-day lmt. FACILITIES: Un-designated sites; tbls, toil, cga, drk wtr. ACTIVITIES: Picnicking; fishing; swimming; hunting; hiking. MISC: Scenic canyons; on Long Pine Creek. Pets on leash.

LOUP CITY

Bowman Lake Recreation Area (SRA). 1/2 mi W of Loup City on St Hwy 92. SEASON: All yr; 14-day lmt. FACILI-TIES: Undesignated sites; tbls, toil, cga, drk wtr, playground. ACTIVI-TIES: Picnicking; swimming; fishing; hunting; hiking; boating-nonpower or elec motor craft. MISC: Pets.

Sherman Reservoir Recreation Area (SRA). 4 mi E of Loup City; 1 mi N on St Hwy 92. SEASON: All yr; 14-day lmt. FACILITIES: Undesignated sites; tbls, toil, cga, drk wtr, play-ground. ACTIVITIES: Picnicking; fishing; swimming; boating,rld; hunt-ing; hiking. MISC: Dump/store nearby. Entry permit.** Pets on leash.

LYONS

Lyons City Park. W edge of Lyons. SEASON: All yr; 14-day lmt. FACILI-TIES: 22 sites; tbls, toil, cga, dump, shower, elec/wtr hkup, playground. ACTIVITIES: Picnicking; tennis. MISC: Pets on leash.

MALCOLM

Branched Oak Lake (SRA). 3-1/2 mi N of Malcolm on US 34. SEASON: All yr; 14-day lmt. FACILITIES: Undesig-nated sites; tbls, toil, cga, drk wtr. ACTIVITIES: Picnicking; fishing; swimming; boating,rld; hunting; hik-ing. MISC: Entry permit.** Pets on leash. Dog training area.

MARTELL

Kildeer (Neb. Game & Pks. Comm.). 2-1/2 mi N of Martell. SEASON: All yr; 14-day lmt. FACILITIES: Primitive sites; NO FACILITIES. ACTIVITIES: Fishing (bullhead, lgemouth, bass, bluegill, walleye, channel cat); hunting (pheasant, quail, deer, cot-tontail, squirrel, waterfowl in sea-son). MISC: Non-powered boats. Pets on leash.

MCCOOK

Karrer Park (Municipal Park). At the E edge of McCook on St Hwy 6/34. SEASON: All yr; 2-day lmt.

FACILITIES: 8 sites (tr -30); tbls, toil, cga, dump, showers, wtr/elec/ swr hkup, drk wtr. Bottled gas/ice/ food/laundry/store nearby. ACTIVITIES: Picnicking; golf nearby. MISC: Near river. Pets on leash.

Red Willow Reservoir (State Area). 11 mi N of McCook on US 83. SEASON: All yr; 14-day lmt. FACILITIES: Undesignated sites; tbls, toil, cga, drk wtr. ACTIVITIES: Picnicking; swimming; fishing; boating,rld; hunting; hiking. MISC: Shelters; store/ice nearby; dump; showers; playground. Pets on leash. Historic George Norris home nearby. Entry permit.**

MCCOOL JUNCTION

Crosstrails (State Wayside Area). On St Hwy 81, W of McCool. SEASON: All yr; 2-day lmt. FACILITIES: Undesignated sites; tbls, toil, cga, drk wtr, playground. ACTIVITIES: Picnicking. MISC: Pets on leash.

MEADOW GROVE

Millstone State Wayside Area. 1 mi E of Meadow Grove on US 275. SEASON: All yr; 2-day lmt. FACILITIES: Undesignated sites; tbls, toil, cga, drk wtr, playground. ACTIVITIES: Picnicking (shelters); hiking. MISC: Interpretation of old millstones. Pets.

MEMPHIS

Memphis Lake State Recreation Area (SRA). 1/2 mi W of Memphis on St Hwy 63. SEASON: All yr; 14-day lmt. FACILITIES: Undesignated sites; tbls, toil, cga, drk wtr, dump, food.

MERRIMAN

Cottonwood Lake Rec. Area (SRA). 1/2 mi E of Merriman on US 20; 1/2 mi S on Park Rd (gravel access rd). SEASON: All yr; 14-day lmt. FACILITIES: Undesignated sites; tbls, toil, cga, drk wtr. ACTIVITIES: Picnicking; swimming; fishing; boating,ld; playground; hiking; hunting. MISC: Pets on leash. Most sites level. Entry permit.**

MILFORD

Blue River Wayside Area. Just Off US 6, S of Milford. SEASON: All yr; 2-day lmt. FACILITIES: Undesignated sites; tbls, toil, cga, drk wtr. ACTIVITIES: Picnicking; fishing; hiking; playground. MISC: Pets.

MITCHELL

Mitchell City Park (Municipal Park). In Mitchell. SEASON: All yr; 14-day lmt. FACILITIES: Spaces for self-contained vehicles; wtr/swer/elec hkups drk wtr, cga. ACTIVITIES: Swimming. MISC: Pets on leash.

MULLEN

* Dismal River Canoe Trail. 12 mi S of Mullen on St Hwy 97 to River (BY BOAT). SEASON: 4/1-10/31; limited facilities in winter. FACILITIES: 3 sites. 70-mile canoe trip between St Hwy 97 and Dunning. No drk wtr. U.S. 83 campsite has a hand pump 100 yards S of the river on the W side of the hwy. For map, write to Game & Parks Commission, PO Box 30370, Lincoln, NEB 68503.

NEBRASKA CITY

Riverview Marina Recreation Area (SRA). Located in town, on Mo. River. SEASON: All yr; 14-day lmt. FACILITIES: Undesignated sites; tbls, toil, cga, showers, drk wtr. Dump/bottled gas/ice/laundry/food/store nearby. ACTIVITIES: Picnicking; fishing; boating,l; hiking. MISC: Entry permit.** Pets on leash.

NELIGH

Riverside Park (Municipal Park). Located in the SE Part of Neligh on US 275. SEASON: All yr; 7-day lmt. FACILITIES: 20 sites; tbls, toil, cga, f, dump, btld gas, playground, drk wtr, store, ice. Laundry/food nearby. ACTIVITIES: Picnicking; fishing; tennis. MISC: Pets on leash.

NENZEL

Samuel R. McKelvic NF. 9 mi S of Nenzel. SEASON: All yr; 14-day lmt. FACILITIES: Sites, tbls, toil, cga. ACTIVITIES: Picnicking; fishing; hiking. MISC: Check at ranger station. Pets on leash.

Steer Creek (Samuel R. McKelvie NF). 19 mi S of Nenzel on St Hwy 97. SEASON: 5/30-9/15; 14-day lmt. FACILITIES: 23 sites (tr -22); tbls, toil, cga, f, drk wtr. ACTIVITIES: Picnicking; fishing. MISC: Pets. Elev 3000 ft; 10 acres.

NIOBRARA

Niobrara Municipal Campground (Municipal Park). 1/2 mi N of Niobrara. SEASON: SEASON: All yr; 14-day lmt.

FACILITIES: Spaces for self-contained vehicles. ACTIVITIES: Swimming; boating; fishing. MISC: Pets. on leash.

Santee Campground (Lewis & Clark Lake SRA). 4 mi E of Niobrara on St Hwy 12; 8 mi N on gravel rd. SEASON: All yr; 14-day lmt. FACILITIES: Undesignated sites; tbls, toil, cga, playground, drk wtr, store nearby. ACTIVITIES: Picnicking; fishing; boating,ld. MISC: Entry permit.** Pets on leash.

NORFOLK

Elkhorn Wayside. 1 mi N of Norfolk on US 81 (paved access rds). SEASON: All yr; 2-day lmt. FACILITIES: Undesignated sites; tbls, toil, cga, drk wtr, shelters. ACTIVITIES: Picnicking; hiking. MISC: Bottled gas/flush toil/showers/ice nearby. Game & Pks. Comm. District Office. Most sites are level. Pets on leash.

Ta-Ha-Zouka City Park. 1 mi S of Norfolk on US 81 (paved access rds). SEASON: All yr; 4-day lmt. FACILITIES: 12 sites; Spaces for self-contained vehicles; tbls, toil, cga, phone, playground, shower, dump. ACTIVITIES: Picnicking; fishing; softball. MISC: Pets on leash.

NORTH PLATTE

Cody Park (Municipal Park). On St Hwy 83 at the N city limits of North Platte. SEASON: All yr; 14-day lmt. FACILITIES: Sites, flush toil, cga. MISC: Pets on leash.

Lake Maloney State Recreation Area (SRA). 6 mi S of North Platte on US 83. SEASON: All yr; 14-day lmt. FACILITIES: Undesignated sites; tbls, toil, cga, drk wtr, playground, store nearby. ACTIVITIES: Picnicking; fishing; swimming; boating,dl; horseshoes; hunting; hiking. MISC: Buffalo Bill's ranch nearby; lake; river. Pets on leash.

OAKLAND

Oakland City Park (Municipal Park). SW edge of Oakland on St Hwy 32. SEASON: All yr; 5-day lmt. FACILITIES: Sites, wtr/elec hkup; flush toil drk wtr, cga. ACTIVITIES: Swimming. MISC: Pets on leash.

OCONTO

Pressey (SRA). 5 mi N of Oconto on St Hwy 21. SEASON: All yr; 14-day lmt. FACILITIES: Undesignated sites; tbls, toil, cga, elec hkup; playground. ACTIVITIES: Picnicking; fishing; swimming; hunting. MISC: Pets on leash.

ODESSA

Union Pacific State Wayside Area. 2 mi S of Odessa on access rd, at Odessa inter. (1-80). SEASON: All yr; 14-day lmt. FACILITIES: Undesignated sites; tbls, toil, cga, drk wtr. ACTIVITIES: Picnicking (shelters); fishing; hiking; boating (nonpowered) MISC.: Modern restrooms. Pets.

OGALLALA

Lake McConaughy (SRA). 12 mi N of Ogallala on St Hwy 61. (14 mi NW along shore) SEASON: All yr; 14-day lmt. FACILITIES: Undesignated sites; tbls, toil, cga, drk wtr, food. Store/ice nearby. ACTIVITIES: Picnicking; swimming; boating,rld; playground; hunting; hiking; fishing. MISC: Entry permit.** Pets on leash.

Ogallala Union 76 Truck Plaza. 103 Prospector Drive, in Ogallala. SEASON: All yr; 1-night lmt. FACILITIES: Spaces for self-contained vehicles; food, toil, drk wtr, gas.

O'NEILL

Carney Park (Municipal Park). In the south part of O'Neill on St Hwy 281; or as you come from the East or West on St Hwy 20, turn to the South at the stop light (only one in town) for 4 blocks, and as you cross the railroad tracks it is about a half block further on the west side of the road.

2-week lmt; seas: spring, summer & fall; electrical hkups and running water. Toil, dump station. sewr hkup drk wtr, cga.

Goose Lake (SRA). 22 mi S of O'Neill on US 281; 4 mi E to campground. SEASON: All yr; 14-day lmt. FACILITIES: Undesignated sites; tbls, toil, cga. ACTIVITIES: Picnicking; fishing; swimming; hunting. MISC: Pets.

Grove Lake (SRA). 29 mi E of O'Neill on St Hwy 20 to Royal, 2 mi N. SEASON: All yr; 14-day lmt. FACILITIES: Undesignated sites; tbls, toil, cga, playground. ACTIVITIES: Picnicking; swimming; fishing; boating,l. MISC: Pets on leash.

O'Neill City Campground. In O'Neill off US 20, 5 blks S (paved access rds). SEASON: All yr; 14-day lmt. FACILITIES: Spaces for self-contained vehicles; tbls, toil, cga. ACTIVITIES: Picnicking. MISC: Sites need blocking Pets on leash.

OSCEOLA

Osceola Park. US 81 and State Street, in Osceola. SEASON: All yr; 14-day lmt. FACILITIES: Spaces for self-contained vehicles;tbls, toil, cga. ACTIVITIES: Picnicking. MISC: Pets.

PARKS

Rock Creek Recreation Area. 4 mi N of Parks 1 mi W on US 34. SEASON: All yr; 14-day lmt. FACILITIES: Undesignated sites; tbls, toil, cga, drk wtr. ACTIVITIES: Picnicking; swimming; fishing; boating (nonpower); hunting. MISC: State fish hatchery nearby. Entry permit.** Pets.

PIERCE

Gilman Park (Municipal Park). North Mill St. in Pierce. SEASON: All yr; 14-day lmt. FACILITIES: Sites, tbls, toil, cga, drk wtr. ACTIVITIES: Picnicking; fishing; swimming; boating MISC: Pets on leash.

PILGER

Pilger City Park. SW corner of Pilger. SEASON: 4/15–10/15; 2-day lmt. FACILITIES: 3 sites; cga, toil, shower, phone, playground. ACTIVITIES: Swimming. MISC: Pets on leash.

PLATTSMOUTH

Memorial Park (Municipal Park). S 18th St, W of ball fields; in Plattsmouth. SEASON: All yr; 14-day lmt. FACILITIES: Sites, tbls, toil, cga. ACTIVITIES: Swimming; fishing. MISC: Pets.

PLEASANT DALE

Twin Lakes (Neb. Game & Pks. Comm.). 1/2 mi N; 1/2 mi W of Pleasant Dale Interchg. on I-80. SEASON: All yr; 14-day lmt. FACILITIES: Primitive sites. ACTIVITIES: Fishing (northern pike, walleye, lgemouth bass, bluegill, channel catfish); boating (nonpowered). No hunting. MISC: Pets on leash.

RAVENNA

Ravenna Lake Recreation Area (SRA). 1 mi SE of Ravenna on St Hwy 2. SEASON: All yr; 14-day lmt. FACILITIES: Undesignated sites; tbls, toil, cga, drk wtr, playground. Store/ice/laundry/food nearby. ACTIVITIES: Picnicking; fishing; swimming; boating,l (nonpower or elec motor craft only). MISC: Pets on leash. Entry permit.**

Ravenna Lion's Park (Lion's Club). 4 blocks E of Dairy Kreme, in Ravenna. SEASON: All yr; 5-day lmt. FACILITIES: Spaces for self-contained vehicles; tbls, toil, cga, drk wtr. ACTIVITIES: Picnicking. MISC: Pets on leash.

REPUBLICAN CITY

* **Republican River Canoe Trail.** 1/2 mi S of Republican City to dam (BY BOAT). SEASON: 7/1–9/31; facilities limited in winter. FACILITIES: Undesignated sites; no drk wtr. The best months are usually July & Aug. Up-to-date reports of releases from the dam may be obtained by phoning the Corps of Engineers Office at Republican City, 308/799-2105. Campsites are located near Franklin, Riverton, and Red Cloud. Potable water is not avail. on the sites. Red cloud campground also serves as a put-in or take-out point. For canoe trail map, write to Game & Parks Commission; PO Box 30370; Lincoln, NEB 68503.

REYNOLDS

Buckley Creek Recreation Area. 1 mi E and 3/4 mi N of Reynolds. SEASON: All yr; 14-day lmt. FACILITIES: Spaces for self-contained vehicles; tbls, toil, cga, drk wtr. ACTIVITIES: Picnicking; fishing. MISC: Pets.

ROYAL

Grove Lake (SRA). 2 mi N off US 20, in Royal (paved access rds). SEASON: All yr; 14-day lmt. FACILITIES: Sites; tbls, toil, cga. ACTIVITIES: Picnicking; fishing; hunting; boating,ld; hiking. MISC: Nature trails; lake. Pets on leash.

RUSHVILLE

Smith Lake (SRA). 23 mi S of Rushville on St Hwy 250. SEASON: All yr; 14-day lmt. FACILITIES: Undesignated sites; tbls, toil, cga, playground. ACTIVITIES: Picnicking; swimming; fishing; boating,l; hunting. MISC: Pets on leash.

ST. PAUL

North Loup Wayside Area. 4 mi N of St Paul on US 281. SEASON: All yr; 2-day lmt. FACILITIES: Undesignated sites; tbls, toil, cga, drk wtr. ACTIVITIES: Picnicking; fishing; hiking. MISC: River access. Pets.

See page 7 for KEY TO ABBREVIATIONS.

SCOTIA

Chalkmine State Wayside Area. 2 mi S of Scotia on St Hwy 11 (in Bluffs above the Loup River). SEASON: All yr; 14-day lmt. FACILITIES: Sites, tbls, toil, cga. ACTIVITIES: Picnicking; hiking. MISC: Site of former working mine. Explore one of the state's few shaft mines (daytime) days. Good place to cool off in the summer. The tunnels are 20 degrees cooler than the outside air. During winter, temp. in the mine is a constant 40 degrees. Take flashlights. Pets on leash.

SCOTTSBLUFF

Lake Minatare Rec. Area (SRA). 4 mi E of Scottsbluff on US 26; 4 mi N; 4 mi E to campground (paved access rds). SEASON: 1/15-9/30; facilities are limitied during winter; 14-day lmt. FACILITIES: Undesignated sites; tbls, toil, cga, food, store, drk wtr, dump, shelters. ACTIVITIES: Picnicking; fishing; swimming; boating,rld. MISC: Scotts Bluff Natl. Mon. nearby. Pets on leash.

SCRIBNER

Dead Timber Recreation Area (SRA). 4 mi N & 1-1/2 mi W of Scribner on US 275. SEASON: All yr; 14-day lmt. FACILITIES: Undesignated sites; tbls, toil, cga, drk wtr, playground; store nearby. ACTIVITIES: Picnicking; fishing; swimming; snowskiing; hiking; hunting; boating (nonpowered or elec motor craft). MISC: Native grass museum; shelters; nature trails. Pets on leash.

SEWARD

Blue Valley Wayside Area. 1/2 mi S of Seward on St Hwy 15. SEASON: All yr; 2-day lmt. FACILITIES: Undesignated sites; tbls, toil, cga, drk wtr. ACTIVITIES: Picnicking; fishing. MISC: Pets on leash.

SHELTON

War Axe State Wayside Area. 4 mi S of Shelton on access road. (At Shelton Interchange I-80) SEASON: All yr; 2-day lmt. FACILITIES: Undesignated sites; tbls, toil, cga, drk wtr. ACTIVITIES: Picnicking; fishing. MISC: Modern restrooms; picnic shelters; Pets on leash.

SHUBERT

Indian Cave State Park (SP). On the Nemaha-Richardson County Line near Shubert.

3000 acres including 2386 acres of wooded area. Several tent camping areas; a small RV CG with 40-45 sites; many tent camping areas along the 20 miles of hiking trails. All yr; 14-days. Water is located in three areas of the park. Picnic. Rugged terrain with a unique area of wooded bluffs overlooking the Mo River. Horseback riding (special camp for horse owners at the head of a 10-mile horse trail). Site of town site of St. Deroin, with schoolhouse and cemetery; log cabin.

SPENCER

★ Upper Mo. River Canal Trail. 10 mi N of Spencer on US 81; 3 on US 81/281 to Mo. River in SD. BY BOAT. SEASON: 4/1-10/31; facilities are limited in winter. FACILITIES: Undesignated sites; tbls, toil, cga. Begins below Fort Randall Dam, a few mi into SD, and ends at Niobrara, 40 mi downstream. Two campsites. For canoe trail map, write to Game & Parks Comm.;PO Box 30370; Lincoln NEB 68503.

SPRAGUE

Bluestem Lake State Rec. Area (SRA). 2-1/2 mi W of Sprague on St Hwy 33. SEASON: All yr; 14-day lmt. FACILITIES: Undesignated sites; tbls, toil, cga, drk wtr. ACTIVITIES: Picnicking; fishing; hunting; boating; hiking. MISC: Pets on leash. Entry permit.**

STAPLETON

Stapleton Park (Municipal park). 1-1/2 blocks W of Main St. on St Hwy 92 or 3rd st in Stapleton. SEASON: All yr; 14-day lmt. FACILITIES: Sites, tbls, toil, cga, drk wtr. ACTIVITIES: Picnicking; fishing. MISC: Pets.

STROMSBURG

Buckley Park (Municipal Park). Located on the S edge of Stromsburg on US 81. SEASON: All yr; 2-day lmt. FACILITIES: 20 sites; tbls, toil, cga, dump, f, showers, playground. Food/ice/laundry/store nearby. ACTIVITIES: Picnicking; swimming; tennis; softball. MISC:Pets:elec:Donations.

STUART

Stuart Community Park. 6 blocks N of Stuart on St Hwy 20. SEASON: All yr. FACILITIES: 15 sites; tbls, toil, cga, dump, showers. Btld gas/ice/food/laundry/store nearby. ACTIVITIES: Picnicking; swimming; horseback riding; fishing. MISC: Pets.

THEDFORD

Thedford Park (City Park). From Jct of St Hwys 2 and 83; 1 mi W on St Hwy 2. SEASON: All yr; 5-day lmt. FACILITIES: 25 Spaces for self-contained vehicles; tbls, toil, cga, elec/wtr hkups, air cond., playground. Dump/gas/ice/food/store nearby. ACTIVITIES: Picnicking. MISC: Snowmobile trails. Pets on leash.

TILDEN

Tilden City Park (Municipal Park). Jct of & Hwy 276 and 2nd St., in Tilden. SEASON: All yr; 14-day lmt. FACILITIES: Spaces for self-contained vehicles; tbls, toil, cga, drk wtr, store. ACTIVITIES: Picnicking. MISC: Pets on leash.

TRENTON

Little Nemaha State Wayside Area. Near St Hwy 2 in Trenton. SEASON: All yr; 14-day lmt. FACILITIES: Undesignated sites; tbls, toil, cga, drk wtr. ACTIVITIES: Picnicking; fishing; swimming; boating,rld. MISC: Pets on leash. Entry permit.**

UNADILLA

Swanson Lake Area (SRA). 2 mi W of Unadilla on US 34. SEASON: All yr; 14-day lmt. FACILITIES: Undesignated sites; tbls, toil, cga. Ice/store nearby. ACTIVITIES: Picnicking; hiking. MISC: Adjoins Unadilla Community Park. Pets on leash.

VALENTINE

City Park (Municipal Park). 1 mi N of Valentine on St Hwy 20 (follow Main St N toward the pine-covered hills and down into the valley). SEASON: All yr; 14-day lmt. FACILITIES: Sites, tbls, toil, cga, showers. MISC: A natural park on the banks of the Minnechaduza Creek. ACTIVITIES: Picnicking; fishing.

Merritt Reservoir State Rec. Area (SRA) 25 mi SW of Valentine on paved road. SEASON: All yr; 14-day lmt. FACILITIES: Sites, tbls, toil, cga, drk wtr, shelters. ACTIVITIES: Picnicking; hunting; fishing; boating, rld; hiking. MISC: Wildlife refuges.

VERDON

Verdon Lake State Rec. Area (SRA). 1/2 mi W of Verdon on US 73. SEASON: All yr; 14-day lmt. FACILITIES: undesignated sites; tbls, toil, cga, drk wtr, playground. ACTIVITIES: Picnicking; fishing. Swimming nearby. Hunting; hiking; boating (nonpowered or elec motor craft). MISC: Pets on leash. Entry permit.**

WAYNE

Henry Victor Meml. Park (Municipal park). From the jct of St Hwys 15/35 1 mi S on St Hwy 15 in Wayne. SEASON: All yr; 3-day lmt. FACILITIES: 12 sites; tbls, toil, cga, dump, drk wtr. Store/gas/ice/laundry nearby. ACTIVITIES: Picnicking. MISC: Pets.

Lions Park (Lions Club). 1-1/2 mi E of Wayne on St Hwy 35 at Airport. SEASON: All yr; 14-day lmt. FACILITIES: 12 sites; tbls, toil, cga, phone drk wtr. ACTIVITIES: Picnicking. MISC: Pets on leash.

WEST POINT

City Park (Municipal Park). In West Point. SEASON: All yr; 14-day lmt. FACILITIES: Sites, tbls, toil, cga, drk wtr. ACTIVITIES: Picnicking. MISC: Pets on leash.

* **Elkhorn River Canoe Trail.** 1/2 mi W of West Point to river on St Hwy 32 BY BOAT. SEASON: 4/1-10/31. FACILITIES: Limited in winter. MISC.: The greatest stream flow generally occurs from March thru early July. However, there is often enough water for canoeing in Sept. and Oct. as well. 3 overnight camps are located along the 75-mile stretch from West Point to near the Douglas-Sarpy county line at Dead Timber State Recreation Area, one near Winslow, and one near US 30 in SE Dodge County.

WILBER

Legion Post 101. 1/2 mi S of Wilber. SEASON: All yr; 14-day lmt. FACILITIES: Sites, elec hkup, toil. MISC: Pets on leash.

WILLIS

Beaver Dam State Wayside Area. 1/2 mi NW of Jct of St Hwy 12 & US 20. SEASON: All yr; 14-day lmt. FACILITIES: Sites, tbls, toil, cga, drk wtr. ACTIVITIES: Picnicking; fishing. MISC: Pets on leash.

WISNER

Wisner City Park (Municipal Park). S on corner of First Natl & Citizens Bank, cross rr, 1 blk S; in Wisner. SEASON: All yr; 14-day lmt. FACILITIES: Sites, tbls, toil, cga, drk wtr. ACTIVITIES: Picnicking. MISC: Pets ·

WOOD LAKE

Wood Lake City Park (Municipal Park). 3 blocks N of St Hwy 20 on Main St. and 1 block E in Wood Lake. SEASON: All yr; 14-day lmt. FACILITIES: Site; tbls, toil, cga, drk wtr. ACTIVITIES: Picnicking. MISC: Pets on leash.

**See page 316.

NEVADA

GENERAL STATE INFORMATION

Miscellaneous

Toll-Free Number for Travel Information:
  1-800-634-6333 [from outside of NV]
Right Turns on Red: Permitted after full stop,
  unless otherwise posted.
STATE CAPITOL: Carson City
STATE NICKNAME: Silver State
STATE MOTTO: "All For Our Country"
STATE FLOWER: Sagebrush
STATE TREE: Single-leaf Pinon

State Parks

Annual Permit for day use and camping: $30.00. Individual fees: Camping, $4.00;
Day Use, $4.00. Free Senior Citizen Permit: For Nevada residents 60 years or older.
Good for all uses including group reservations if the group consists of all senior citizens. Proof of age and residency is required prior to issuance. Pets permitted if
kept on a leash. Further information: Division of State Parks; Department of Conservation and Natural Resources; Capitol Complex; Carson City, NV 89710.

Rest Areas

Overnight stops are permitted in Nevada Rest Areas unless otherwise posted.

Hoover Wilderness

Part of the Hoover is administered by Inyo NF, headquartered at Bishop, California.
The Toiyabe portion is within the Bridgeport District, which is headquartered at
Bridgeport, California. No fee. For the Toiyabe portion, the required permit is
available at the Bridgeport Ranger Station. Maps and other information are available at Bridgeport, as well as at the Forest Supervisors' offices in Bishop, California,
and Reno, Nevada. Further information: Toiyabe NF; 111 North Virginia Street, Room
601; Reno, NV 89501.

Jarbridge Wilderness

64,830 acres; rugged mountainous region, with the Columbia River Plateau on the north
and the Great Basin Desert on the south. The Jarbidge Mountains have 8 peaks that
exceed 10,000 feet in elevation. HUNTING: Some of the largest mule deer trophy heads
ever taken in the State of Nevada have come from here. ENTRANCE: The head of the
west fork of the Jarbidge River or Hummingbird Spring near the Pole Creek Ranger
Station are the best. Further information: Forest Supervisor; Humboldt, NF; 976
Mountain City Highway; Elko, NV 89801.

Ruby Mountains Scenic Area

40,720 acres, from Overland Lake on the south to Verdi Peak on the north; including
11,000-foot Ruby Dome. Lamoille Canyon is 25 mi SE of Elko (major recreational canyon
in the area). A series of trails (Ruby Crest, Kleckner, Smith Creek, Overland) provide interesting routes for hikers and horsemen. Plenty of room to camp. Picnic
area. HUNTING: Deer, sage grouse, mountain lion, bobcat, beaver, Himalayan snow
partridge, ruffed grouse, chuckar partridge, Rocky Mountain goats. FISHING: Pansize trout in most streams and lakes. Further information: Ruby Mountains Ranger
District; Humboldt NF; Wells, NV 89835.

INFORMATION SOURCES

Maps

The following maps are available from **Forsyth Travel Library** (see order form in Appendix B):

  State of Nevada [Up-to-date, showing all principal roads,
  points of interest, sports areas, parks, airports, mileage,
  etc. Full color.]

  Completely indexed city maps, including all airports, lakes,
  rivers, etc., of: **Las Vegas; Reno.**

NEVADA

Gold Mining and Prospecting

Nevada Bureau of Mines; University of Nevada; Reno, NV 89507.

State Information

Division of State Parks; Department of Conservation and Natural Resources; 201 South Fall Street; Nye Building; Capitol Complex; Carson City, NV 89710.
Tourism-Travel Division; Department of Economic Development; State Capitol Building; Carson City, NV 89701.
Department of Fish and Game; Box 10678; Reno, NV 89510.

City Information

Carson City Chamber of Commerce; 1191 South Carson Street; Carson City, NV 89701.
Las Vegas Chamber of Commerce; 2301 East Sahara Avenue; Las Vegas, NV 89105.
North Las Vegas Chamber of Commerce; 1023 East Lake Mead; North Las Vegas,NV 89030.

Miscellaneous

Nevada Bureau of Land Management; Federal Building, Room 3008; 300 Booth Street; PO Box 12000; Reno, NV 89520.
Refuge Manager; Sheldon National Wildlife Refuge; Sheldon-Hart Mountain Complex; Box 111; Lakeview, OR 97630.
Refuge Manager; Stillwater NWR; PO Box 1236; Fallon, NV 89406.
Humboldt National Forest; 976 Mountain City Highway; Elko, NV 89801.
Toiyabe National Forest; 111 North Virginia Street, Room 601; Reno, NV 89501.

FREE CAMPGROUNDS

AUSTIN

Big Creek (Toiyabe NF). 1 mi W of Austin on US 50; 11 mi S on FS 20012. SEASON: 5/1-10/15; 14-day lmt. FACILITIES: 6 sites (tr -16); tbls, toil, cga, f, piped drk wtr. ACTIVITIES: Mountain climbing; hunting; picnicking; fishing (trout). Horseback riding (1 mi). MISC.: Elev 6700 ft; 3 acres; pets. Big Creek is adjacent. No off-season camping.

Hickison Petroglyph Recreation Site (BLM). 24 mi E of Austin on US 50. [Gravel access rds.] In Central Nevada. SEASON: All yr; 14-day lmt. FACILITIES: 21 sites (tr -18); tbls, toil, cga, no drk wtr. The nearest gas station and general store are 14 miles W of the campground. ACTIVITIES: Hunting (sage grouse, chukar, deer, mountain lion); hiking; picnicking. No fishing. MISC.: Elev 6500 ft; 40 acres; picnic shelters; pets. Most sites are level pull-through spaces. Petroglyphs in the area.

Kingston (Toiyabe NF). 12 mi E of Austin on US 50; 16 mi S on St Hwy 8A; 6 mi NW on FS 20012. [Improved gravel rds.] SEAS: 5/15-10/15; 14-day lmt. FAC: 12 sites (tr -22); tbls, toil, cga, no drk wtr. ACT: Mtn climbing; picnicking; fishing (trout); hunting. Horseback riding (1 mi). Swimming and non-power boating (2 mi). MISC.: Elev 7000 ft; 12 acres; pets; stream; pets. Adjacent to fish and game reservoirs. No off-season camping. Food (3 mi).

BAKER

Baker Creek (Humboldt NF). 5 mi W of Baker on St Hwy 74; 3 mi S on FS 10590. SEASON: 5/15-10/15; 16-day lmt. FACILITIES: 17 sites (tr -16); tbls, toil, cga, f, drk wtr. Food/visitor center (4 mi). ACTIVITIES: Hunting; picnicking; fishing; hiking. Horseback riding (1 mi). MISC.: Elev 8000 ft; 30 acres; pets; scenic. Baker Creek. Lehman Caves National Monument (3 mi). Wheeler Park Scenic Area.

CARSON CITY

Rest Area. South end of town; 1 block S of Carson Mall Shopping Center. SEASON: All yr; 1-night lmt. FACILITIES: 15 small spaces; tbls, toil, cga, food. Wash basins with electric hand dryers. ACTIVITIES: Picnicking. MISC.: Pets.

DENIO

Sheldon Antelope Refuge (NWR). 27 mi W of Denio on St Hwy 140; 3 mi on gravel road. [NOTE: Denio is located on the Nevada-Oregon border, 87 mi N and slightly W of Winnemucca, Nevada.] SEASON: Season of use for all the camps, except Virgin Valley, is dependent on weather conditions and resultant road conditions. From May-October most are usually accessible. Virgin Valley Camp is available all year. FACILITIES: Camping is restricted to the **18 designated campgrounds** shown on the map that can be obtained from the Sheldon Antelope Refuge; PO Box 111; Lakeview,

See page 7 for KEY TO ABBREVIATIONS.

331

OR 97630; or from Refuge Headquarters.
(Tr -25). All camps, with the exception
of Virgin Valley Camp, are primitive.
There are no facilities and the water,
available at most, is limited to natural
spring water. At Virgin Valley Camp,
there are restroom facilities and water.
ACTIVITIES: Hunting [All wildlife is
protected except those species authorized
to be taken during special hunting seasons. Migratory bird hunting is prohibited.]; rockhounding [Rockhounds
are permitted to collect rock specimens
not to exceed 7 pounds per person.
Digging and blasting are prohibited.].
MISC.: Campfires are permitted during
times of low fire hazard. Inquire at
Refuge sub-headquarters for current
regulations. Pets are permitted on leash.

ELKO

Jack Creek (Humboldt NF). 27 mi NW
of Elko on St Hwy 51; 33 mi NW on St
Hwy 11; 1-4/5 mi NE on FS 473. SEASON:
6/16-11/15; 16-day lmt. FACILITIES: 9
sites (tr -22); tbls, toil, cga, f, no
drk wtr. ACTIVITIES: Hunting; picnicking; fishing. Horseback riding (1 mi).
MISC.: Elev 6500 ft; 4 acres; pets.
Jack Creek.

Jerry's Amoco Service Truck Stop. 909
Avenue F, at the junction of US 93/50/56
in Elko. SEASON: All yr; 1-night lmt.
FACILITIES: Spaces for self-contained
RVs; toil, drk wtr, LP gas, mechanic.

ELY

Cherry Creek (Humboldt NF). 24 mi S
of Ely on US 6; 43 mi S on St Hwy 38;
32 mi W on FS 10410. SEASON: 6/1-9/30.
FACILITIES: 4 sites (tr -16); tbls, toil,
cga, f, no drk wtr. ACTIVITIES: Hunting;
picnicking; fishing. Horseback riding
(1 mi). MISC.: Elev 6700 ft; 1 acre;
pets. Cherry Creek.

Currant Creek (Humboldt NF). 45 mi SW
of Ely on US 6. SEASON: 6/1-10/20. FACI-
LITIES: 6 sites (tr -16); tbls, toil, cga,
f, piped drk wtr. ACTIVITIES: Fishing;
picnicking. Horseback riding (1 mi).
MISC.: Elev 6200 ft; 2 acres. Currant
Creek. Pets permitted if kept on leash.

White River Recreation Area (Humboldt
NF). 37 mi SW of Ely on US 6; 8 mi W
on FS 10405. SEASON: 6/1-10/20; 16-day
lmt. FACILITIES: 4 sites (tr -16); tbls,
toil, cga, f, piped drk wtr. ACTIVITIES:
Hunting; picnicking; fishing. Horseback
riding (1 mi). MISC.: Elev 7000 ft; 8
acres; pets. White River.

GABBS

Columbine Camp (NF). 2 mi N of Gabbs
on St Hwy 23; 6 mi NE on Co Hwy 20057;
17 mi NE on 20057; 9 mi E on St Hwy
21. SEASON: 6/1-9/30. FACILITIES: 4

sites (tr -16); toil, cga, f. ACTIVITIES:
Hiking; fishing. MISC.: Elev 7000 ft;pets.

GARRISON

Snake Creek (Humboldt NF). 1½ mi NW
of Garrison on St Hwy 21; 1 mi NW on
St Hwy 73; 12 mi SW on FS 10448. SEASON:
5/15-10/15; 16-day lmt. FACILITIES: 8
sites (tr -22); tbls, toil, cga, f, no
drk wtr. ACTIVITIES: Hunting; picnicking; fishing. Horseback riding (1 mi).
MISC.: Elev 8000 ft; 10 acres; pets;
scenic. Snake Creek. Wheeler Park Scenic Area.

HAWTHORNE

Alum Creek (Toiyabe NF). 6-1/5 mi SW
of Hawthorne on St Hwy 31; 4½ mi SW
on FS 20109. SEASON: 5/1-10/30; 14-day
lmt. FACILITIES: 13 sites (tr -22); tbls,
toil, cga, f, piped drk wtr. ACTIVITIES:
Hiking; hunting; rockhounding; picnicking. MISC.: Elev 6400 ft; 20 acres; pets.
Nature trails. No off-season camping.
Walker Lake (14 mi).

Tamarack Point Recreation Site (BLM).
18 mi N of Hawthorne on US 95. (The
Western shore of Walker Lake.) SEASON:
All yr; 14-day lmt. FACILITIES: 10 sites
(tr -20); tbls, toil, cga. Drinking
water is available at Sportsman's Beach,
2 mi S. Water is piped to Marack Point
but because of its high mineral content,
it is not fit for human consumption.
ACTIVITIES: Boating,l; picnicking; fishing (cutthroat trout, all year); swimming; hiking; horseback riding; sailing; waterskiing; rockhounding; photography; hunting (upland game birds,
mule deer, non-game wildlife, bighorn
sheep in the Wassuk Range, pelicans).
MISC.: Elev 4500 ft; 90 acres; pets.
Walker Lake has a surface area of
38,000 acres, a maximum depth of 126
feet, and is 15 miles long. The Gillis
Range is E of the lake, and the Wassuk
Range, with Mt. Grant (11,239 feet),
is west.

JARBIDGE

Jarbidge Campground (Humboldt NF).
1-1/10 mi S of Jarbidge on FS 10062.
SEASON: 6/1-10/31; 16-day lmt. FACILI-
TIES: 5 sites (tr -16); tbls, toil, cga,
f, piped drk wtr. ACTIVITIES: Hunting;
picnicking; fishing; hiking. MISC.:
Elev 6300 ft; 2 acres; pets; stream.
Food/gas/horseback riding (1 mi). Near
Jarbidge Wilderness.

Pine Creek (Humboldt NF). 3 mi S of
Jarbidge on FS 10062. SEASON:6/15-10/31;
16-day lmt. FACILITIES: 7 sites (tr
-16); tbls, toil, cga, f, piped drk wtr.
Food/gas (3 mi). ACTIVITIES: Hunting;
picnicking; fishing; hiking. Horseback
riding (1 mi). MISC.: Elev 6600 ft; 2
acres; pets. Pine Creek. Near Jarbidge
Wilderness.

See page 7 for KEY TO ABBREVIATIONS.

LAS VEGAS

Cold Creek Recreation Site (BLM). 31½ mi NW of Las Vegas on US 95; 13½ mi W on paved Co Rd; 3/5 mi W on dirt road; ¼ mi S on dirt road. SEASON: 3/1-11/30; 14-day lmt. FACILITIES: 6 sites (tr -16); tbls, toil, cga, no drk wtr. ACTIVITIES: Fishing (in season, for small brown trout); picnicking. No hunting. MISC.: Elev 6000 ft; 160 acres; pets permitted if kept on a leash.

Fletcher View (Toiyabe NF). 15 mi NW of Las Vegas on US 95; 18 mi W on St Hwy 39. SEASON: 5/1-10/15; 5-day lmt. FACILITIES: 12 sites (tr -22); tbls, toil, cga, drk wtr. ACT: Hiking; rockhounding; picnicking. MISC.: Elev 7200 ft; 6 acres; pets; paved sites.

Las Vegas Auto/Truck Plaza. 4 mi S of Las Vegas on I-15, Blue Diamond exit. SEASON: All yr; 1-night lmt. FACILITIES: Spaces for self-contained RVs; food, toil, drk wtr, LP gas, dump, mechanic.

Willow Springs Recreation Site (BLM). 14 mi W of Las Vegas on Charleston Boulevard; 4 mi NW on Red Rock Scenic Drive. SEASON: All yr; 14-day lmt. FACILITIES: 19 sites (tr -16); tbls, toil, cga, no drk wtr. ACTIVITIES: Hiking; mountain climbing; horseback riding; bicycling; nature study; rockhounding; hunting [A county ordinance prohibits shooting within the Red Rock Canyon Recreation Lands below 5,000 feet elevation. Above 5,000 feet, hunting is allowed.]; no fishing. MISC.: Elev 4500 ft; 190 acres; pets. Part of the 62,000-acre Red Rock Canyon Recreation Lands. Multicolored sandstone bluffs rising more than 3,000 feet above the valley floor and extending nearly 20 miles.

Willow Creek Recreation Site (BLM). 31½ mi NW of Las Vegas on US 95; 13½ m W on paved Co Rd; 3-3/10 mi W on dir road. SEASON: 3/1-11/30; 14-day lmt. FACILITIES: 7 sites (tr -16); tbls, toil, cga, no drk wtr. ACTIVITIES: Picnicking; horseback riding; fishing [allowed; although not plentiful, small brown trout can be caught in the nearby stream]. Hunting is not allowed. MISC.: Elev 6000 ft; 640 acres; pets. Willow Creek.

McGILL

Berry Creek (Humboldt NF). 5 mi N of McGill on US 93; 10½ mi SE on Co Hwy 23; 5½ mi SE on FS 10424. SEASON: 5/15-10/15; 16-day lmt. FACILITIES: 4 sites (tr -22); tbls, toil, cga, f, piped drk wtr. ACTIVITIES: Fishing; picnicking. Horseback riding (1 mi). MISC.: Elev 8200 ft; 2 acres; stream. Pets on leash.

East Creek (Humboldt NF). 5 mi N of McGill on St Hwy 93; 4 mi E on Co Hwy 23; 1 mi NE on FS 10427; 3½ mi E on

FS 10564. SEASON: 5/1-10/15. FACILITIES: 4 sites; tbls, toil, cga, f, no drk wtr. ACTIVITIES: Fishing; picnicking. Horseback riding (1 mi). MISC.: Elev 7400 ft; 8 acres; stream. Pets on leash.

Timber Creek (Humboldt NF). 5 mi N of McGill on US 93; 8½ mi SE on Co Hwy 23; 4 mi SE on FS 10425. SEAS: 5/15-10/15; 14-day lmt. FAC: 15 sites (tr -16); tbls, toil, cga, drk wtr. ACT: Picnicking; hunting; fishing. MISC.: Elev 8200 ft; pets. Timber Creek.

OVERTON

Overton Beach (Lake Mead NRA). 10 mi S of Overton on St Hwy 169. SEASON: All yr; 30-day lmt. FACILITIES: Undesignated sites; tbls, toil, cga, drk wtr. Store/food/ice nearby. ACTIVITIES: Boating,rl (marina); picnicking. Swimming/fishing nearby. MISC.: Pets on leash.

PARADISE VALLEY

Lye Creek (Humboldt NF). 8 mi N of Paradise Valley on St Hwy 8B; 9-4/5 mi N on FS 10084; 1½ mi W on FS 10087. [16 mi N of Paradise Valley Ranger Station.] SEASON: 7/1-10/31; 16-day lmt. FACILITIES: 6 sites (tr -16); tbls, toil, cga, f, piped drk wtr. ACTIVITIES: Hunting; picnicking. Horseback riding (1 mi). Fishing (4 mi). MISC.: Elev 7400 ft; 6 acres; pets. Lye Creek.

SPARKS

Sierra Sid's 76 Truck Stop. I-80 and McCarran Blvd. junction, at Sparks. SEASON: All yr; 1-night lmt. FACILITIES: Spaces for self-contained RVs; food, toil, drk wtr, LP gas, dump, mechanic.

TONOPAH

Peavine Creek (Toiyabe NF). 6 mi E of Tonopah on US 6; 38 mi N on St Hwy 8A; 7 mi W on Co Rd 20020; 3 mi NW on FS 20. SEASON: 5/1-10/30; 16-day lmt. FACILITIES: 8 sites (tr -32); tbls, toil, cga, f, piped drk wtr. ACTIVITIES: Rockhounding; picnicking;fishing (trout); hunting. Horseback riding (1 mi). MISC.: Elev 6700 ft; 6 acres; pets. Peavine Creek. No off-season camping.

Pine Creek (Toiyabe NF). 6 mi E of Tonopah on US 6; 15 mi NE on St Hwy 8A; 56 mi NE on Co Hwy 82; 2½ mi W on FS 20009. SEASON: 5/1-10/15; 16-day lmt. FACILITIES: 24 sites (tr -32); tbls, toil, cga, f, piped drk wtr. ACTIVITIES: Horseback riding; picnicking; fishing (trout); hunting; rockhounding. MISC.: Elev 7600 ft; 2 acres; pets. Pine Creek is adjacent. No off-season camping.

Saulsbury Wash (Toiyabe NF). 30 mi E of Tonopah on US 6. SEASON: All yr. FACILITIES: 12 sites (tr -32); tbls, toil, cga, well drk wtr. ACTIVITIES: Rockhounding; picnicking. MISC.: Elev 5800.

See page 7 for KEY TO ABBREVIATIONS.

VERDI

Crystal Peak (Toiyabe NF). 8–2/5 mi NW of Verdi on FS 20002 (Henness Pass Road); 1/10 mi SW on FS 20008. SEASON: 6/10–10/15; 14-day lmt. FACILITIES: 21 sites (tr –16); tbls, toil, cga, f, piped drk wtr. ACTIVITIES: Hiking; picnicking; horseback riding. MISC.: Elev 6700 ft; 12 acres; nature trails; pets. No off-season camping is allowed.

Dog Valley (Toiyabe NF). 6–3/10 mi NW of Verdi on FS 10002 (Henness Pass Road); 4/5 mi W on FS 10030. SEASON: 6/10–10/15; 14-day lmt. FACILITIES: 10 sites (tr –16); tbls, toil, cga, f, piped drk wtr. ACTIVITIES: Hiking; horseback riding; picnicking. MISC.: Elev 6300 ft; 5 acres; pets;nature trails. No off-season camping.

Moe's Station (Toiyabe NF). 3–2/5 mi NW of Verdi on FS 10002 (Henness Pass Road). SEASON: 5/15–10/15; 14-day lmt. FACILITIES: 7 sites; tbls, toil, cga, f. Store (4 mi). ACTIVITIES: Picnicking. Swimming/fishing (4 mi). MISC.: Elev 5900 ft; pets. South Branch Creek and Truckee River (4 mi).

WELLINGTON

Desert Creek (Toiyabe NF). 5 mi SE of Wellington on St Hwy 22; 6–1/5 mi S on FS 20027. SEASON: 5/1–10/30; 14-day lmt. FACILITIES: 13 sites (tr –22); tbls, toil, cga, f, no drk wtr. ACTIVITIES: Hunting; picnicking; fishing. MISC.: Elev 6300 ft; 3 acres; pets. Desert Creek. No off-season camping is allowed.

WELLS

Four-Way Service Truck Stop. At the junction of I-80 and US 93, at Wells. SEASON: All yr; 1-night lmt. FACILITIES: Spaces for self-contained RVs; food, toil, drk wtr, LP gas, mechanic.

WINNEMUCCA

Forty-Niner 76 Truck/Auto Plaza. W of Winnemucca on I-80. SEASON: All yr; 1-night lmt. FACILITIES: Spaces for self-contained RVs; food, toil, drk wtr, LP gas, dump, mechanic.

NEW HAMPSHIRE

GENERAL STATE INFORMATION

Miscellaneous

Toll-Free Number for Travel Information:
   1-800-258-3608 [calling from CT, ME, MA,
          eastern NY; RI; VT]
Right Turns on Red: Permitted after
   full stop, unless otherwise posted.
STATE CAPITOL: Concord
STATE NICKNAME: Granite State
STATE MOTTO: "Live Free Or Die"
STATE BIRD: Purple Finch
STATE FLOWER: Purple Lilac
STATE TREE: White Birch

State Parks

Overnight camping fees range from $4.00–6 00. Pets are permitted on leash in the parks, but not in the water or on the beach. Further information: Division of Parks and Recreation; Department of Resources and Economic Development; PO Box 856; State House Annex; Concord, NH 03301.

Rest Areas

Overnight stops are not permitted in New Hampshire Rest Areas.

Canoeing/Camping Along the Connecticut River

There are a number of sites along the river privately and municipally owned. However, on other land along the river, you can usually camp providing you obtain permission from the owner. Most owners have no objections if you take good care of your camping area. The dam site superintendents are good sources of information on where to camp, as they live in the area, know the property owners, and know which sites canoeists have been able to use for FREE. Ask the Vermont Division of Recreation and Department of Water Resources (Agency of Environmental Conservation; Montpelier, VT 05602) for a free copy of CANOEING ON THE CONNECTICUT RIVER.

See page 7 for KEY TO ABBREVIATIONS.

Backcountry Camping in the White Mountain National Forest

A free fire permit is required for open fires. No camping or open fires allowed above the treeline. Limit your group size to 8 people. Protect the trees and ground cover holding the soil in place. No bough beds, no trenching around tents, and no building of lean-tos or any wood construction of any kind. Further information: The Appalachian Mountain Club; 5 Joy Street; Boston, MA; or, White Mountain NF; Federal Building; 719 Main Street; PO Box 638; Laconia, NH 03246.

The Appalachian Trail

More than 2000 miles long, the Appalachian Trail (from Maine to Georgia) is the longest continuous marked trail in the world.

CAMPING: More than 200 open-front shelters/lean-tos are spaced approximately 10 miles apart on the Trail (one-day intervals). As they are occupied on a first-come first-served basis, carry a tent in case the shelters are full. Potable spring water is usually available at each site, but should be purified by tablets or boiling. And always "pack it in, pack it out".

PERMITS: No permit is required to hike the Trail. However, camping permits must be obtained for overnight stays in Shenandoah NP (Luray, VA 22835) and Great Smokey Mountains NP (Gatlinburg, TN 37733). These are free of charge and available from the ranger stations or by mail. A free camping permit must be obtained for overnight stays in White Mountain National Forest Restricted Use Area (PO Box 638; Laconia, NH 03246).

APPALACHIAN TRAIL CONFERENCE: A private, nonprofit, national organization which represents citizen's interest in the Appalachian Trail. They offer detailed guidebooks and maps for sale, as well as the A.T. Data Book which gives the location and distances between shelters and certain post offices, supply points, water sources, lodging and meals. Further information: A.T.C.; PO Box 236; Harpers Ferry, WV 25425.

INFORMATION SOURCES

Maps

A detailed, up-to-date map of the State of New Hampshire is available from Forsyth Travel Library (see order form in Appendix B).

State Information

Department of Resources and Economic Development; Division of Parks and Recreation; PO Box 856; State House Annex; Concord, NH 03301.
Fish and Game Department; 34 Bridge Street; Concord, NH 03301.
North Conway and Concord; White Mountains Region Association; Lancaster, NH 03584.
Appalachian Mountain Club; Pinkham Notch; Gorham, NH 03581.
Appalachian Mountain Club; Northern NE Regional Office; Gorham, NH 03581.
White Mountains News Bureau; PO Box 176; North Woodstock, NH 03262.

City Information

Concord Chamber of Commerce; 116 North Main Street; Concord, NH 03301.
Laconia Chamber of Commerce; 9 Veterans Square; Laconia, NH 03246.
Manchester Chamber of Commerce; 57 Market Street; Manchester, NH 03101.

National Forests

White Mountain NF; Federal Building; 719 Main Street; PO Box 638; Laconia, NH 03246.

FREE CAMPGROUNDS

BARTLETT

* Carrigain Tower (White Mountain NF). 3-4/5 mi N of Bartlett on US 302; 2-1/10 mi SW on FS FH34; 5 mi NW on TRAIL 273. SEASON: 5/15-10/30; 7-day lmt. FACILITIES: 1 tent site; no drk wtr; toil, f, no tbls. ACTIVITIES: Hiking.

* Desolation Shelter AMC (White Mountain NF). 4 mi NW of Bartlett on US 302; 2-1/10 mi SW on FS 34; 1-7/10 mi NE on TRAIL 273; 6-1/2 mi NE on TRAIL 274. SEASON: 6/1-9/30. FACILITIES: 1 tent site; no drk wtr; toil, cga, f, no tbls. ACTIVITIES: Mountain climbing; hiking. MISC.: Elev 2100 ft; 1 acre; pets. Scenic.

See page 7 for KEY TO ABBREVIATIONS.

* **Dry River Shelter** (White Mountain NF). 9-2/5 mi N of Bartlett on US 302; 5 mi N on TRAIL 83. SEASON: 5/15-10/30; 7-day lmt. FACILITIES: 1 tent site; no drk wtr; cga, f, no tbls. ACTIVITIES: Mountain climbing; fishing; hiking. MISC.: Elev 2500 ft; 1 acre; pets.

* **Dry River Shelter 3** (White Mountain NF). 9-2/5 mi N of Bartlett on US 302; 7-1/10 mi N on TRAIL 83. SEASON: 5/15-10/30; 7-day lmt. FAC: 1 tent site; no drk wtr; toil, cga, no tbls. ACT: Fishing; mtn climbing; hiking. MISC.: Elev 3100 ft; 1 acre; pets.

* **Mount Langdom Shelter** (White Mountain NF). 1/10 mi N of Bartlett on US 302; 3/5 mi N on Co Rd TR; 3-7/10 mi N on TRAIL 60092. SEASON: 5/15-10/30; 7-day lmt. FACILITIES: 1 tent site; no drk wtr; toil, cga, f, no tbls. ACTIVITIES: Mountain climbing; hiking. MISC.: Elev 1800 ft; 1 acre; pets.

* **Resolution Shelter AMC** (White Mountain NF). 6-3/5 mi N of Bartlett on US 302; 3-9/10 mi NE on TRAIL 70. SEASON: 5/15-10/30. FACILITIES: 1 tent site; no drk wtr; toil, cga, f, no tbls. ACTIVITIES: Mountain climbing; hiking. MISC.: Elev 2900 ft; 1 acre; pets.

* **Sawyer Pond Shelter** (White Mountain NF). 3-4/5 mi N of Bartlett on US 302; 3-1/10 mi SW on FS FH34; 1-4/5 mi E on TRAIL 271. SEASON: 5/15-10/30; 7-day lmt. FACILITIES: 1 tent site; no drk wtr; toil, no tbl. ACTIVITIES: Hiking; fishing; boating (no motors). MISC.: Elev 1900 ft; 1 acre; pets.

CAMPTON

* **Black Mountain Pond Shelter SLA** (White Mountain NF). 4 mi E of Campton on St Hwy 49; 5-3/10 mi SE on Co Hwy TR; 1-7/10 mi NE on TRAIL 293; 2-2/5 mi N on TRAIL 501. SEASON: 6/1-9/30. FACILITIES: 1 tent site; no drk wtr; toil, cga, f, no tbls. ACTIVITIES: Mountain climbing; hiking; fishing. MISC.: Elev 2300 ft; 1 acre; pets. Scenic.

CHOCORUA

* **Camp Penacook** (White Mountain NF). 4-9/10 mi N of Chocorua on St Hwy 16; 3-1/10 mi NW on TRAIL 324. SEASON: 5/15-10/30; 2-day lmt. FACILITIES: 1 tent site; no drk wtr; toil, cga, f, no tbls. ACTIVITIES: Mountain climbing; hiking. MISC.: Elev 2700 ft; 1 acre; pets.

* **Jim Liberty Cabin** (White Mountain NF). 1-3/5 mi N of Chocorua on St Hwy 16; 3-7/10 mi W on Co Hwy TR; 4 mi N on TRAIL 319. SEASON: All year; 2-day lmt. FACILITIES: 1 tent site; no drk wtr; toil, cga, f, tbls. ACTIVITIES: Mountain climbing; hiking. MISC.: Elev 2900 ft; 1 acre; pets.

CONWAY

* **Passaconaway Lodge WODC** (White Mountain NF). 1/2 mi S of Conway on St Hwy 112; 4-1/10 mi S on TRAIL 288; 1-4/5 mi W on TRAIL 304. SEASON: 5/15-10/30. FACILITIES: 1 tent site; no drk wtr; toil, cga, f, no tbls. ACTIVITIES: Mountain climbing; hiking. MISC.: Elev 3400 ft; 1 acre; pets.

FRANCONIA

* **Coppermine Shelter** (White Mountain NF). 3-2/5 mi S of Franconia on St Hwy 116; 2-2/5 mi SE on TRAIL 498. SEASON: 5/30-10/15; 7-day lmt. FACILITIES: 1 tent site; no drk wtr; toil, cga, no tbls. ACTIVITIES: Mountain climbing; hiking. Fishing (1 mi). MISC.: Elev 2100 ft; 1 acre; pets. Stream.

* **Kinsman Cabin** (White Mountain NF). 4-3/10 mi S of Franconia on St Hwy 116; 1-1/2 mi SE on TRAIL 491. SEASON: 5/30-10/15; 7-day lmt. FACILITIES: 1 tent site; no drk wtr; toil, cga, f, no tbls. ACTIVITIES: Mountain climbing; hiking. Fishing (1 mi). MISC.: Elev 1900 ft; 1 acre; pets. Stream.

GLEN

* **Mountain Pond Cabin** (White Mountain NF). 1-1/2 mi S of Glen on US 302; 3/5 mi E on St Hwy 16A; 6-1/10 mi NE on FS 17; 1-1/10 mi NE on TRAIL 184. SEASON: All year; 7-day lmt. FACILITIES: 1 tent site; no drk wtr; toil, cga, f, tbls. ACTIVITIES: Hiking; picnicking; fishing; boating (no motors). MISC.: Elev 1500 ft; 1 acre; pets. Lake.

* **Mountain Pond Shelter** (White Mountain NF). 1-1/2 mi S of Glen on US 302; 3/5 mi E on St Hwy 16A; 6-1/10 mi NE on FS 17; 9/10 mi E on TRAIL 184. SEASON: 5/15-10/30; 7-day lmt. FACILITIES: 1 tent site; no drk wtr; toil, cga, f, no tbls. ACTIVITIES: Hiking; fishing; sailing; boating (no motors). MISC.: Elev 1500 ft; 1 acre; pets. Lake.

* **Rocky Branch Shelter 1** (White Mountain NF). 4/5 mi N of Glen on US 302; 1-1/10 mi NW on Co Rd TR; 3-3/10 mi NW on TRAIL 85. SEASON: 5/15-10/30; 7-day lmt. FACILITIES: 1 tent site; no drk wtr; toil, cga, f, no tbls. ACTIVITIES: Hiking; fishing. MISC.: Elev 1400 ft; 3 acres; pets. Stream.

* **Rocky Branch Shelter 2** (White Mountain NF). 4/5 mi N of Glen on US 302; 1-1/10 mi NW on Co Rd TR; 7-1/2 mi NW on TRAIL 85. SEASON: 5/15-10/30; 7-day lmt. FACILITIES: 1 tent site; no drk wtr; toil, cga, f, no tbls. ACTIVITIES: Fishing; mountain climbing; hiking. MISC.: Elev 2800 ft; 1 acre; pets. Stream.

See page 7 for KEY TO ABBREVIATIONS.

GLENCLIFF

* **Oliverian** (White Mountain NF). 2-3/10 mi NW on St Hwy 25. SEASON: 5/15-10/16; 14-day lmt. FACILITIES: 13 sites (tr - 22); well drk wtr. Store/ice (5 mi). ACTIVITIES: Mountain climbing; hiking; fishing; boating,ld. MISC.: 3 acres; pets. Lake. Scenic. Adjacent to Oliverian Impoundment.

* **Wachipauka Shelter DOC** (White Mountain NF). 1-2/5 mi W of Glen Cliff on St Hwy 25; 1-2/5 mi W on TRAIL 465; 4/5 mi N on TRAIL 466. SEASON: 6/1-9/30. FACILITIES: 1 tent site; no drk wtr; toil, cga, f, no tbls. ACTIVITIES: Mountain climbing; hiking. Boating/fishing (1 mi). MISC.: Elev 2200 ft; 1 acre; pets. Scenic.

GORHAM

* **Blue Book Shelter** (White Mountain NF). 12 mi E of Gorham on US 2; 3 mi S on St Hwy 113; 5-1/2 mi SW on FS 12; 2-3/10 mi S on TRAIL 167. SEASON: 6/1-10/15; 5-day lmt. FACILITIES: 1 tent site; no drk wtr; toil, cga, f, no tbls. ACTIVITIES: Mountain climbing; hiking. Fishing (2 mi). MISC.: Elev 1800 ft; 1 acre; pets.

* **Crag Camp RMC** (White Mountain NF). 6 mi W of Gorham on US 2; 3 mi N on TRAIL 26. SEASON: All year. FACILITIES: 1 tent site; tbls, toil, cga. ACTIVITIES: Mountain climbing; hiking; picnicking; fishing. MISC.: Elev 4300 ft; 1 acre; pets. Scenic. Mountain cabin for hikers.

* **Gray Knob** (White Mountain NF). 6 mi W of Gorham on US 2; 3 mi N on TRAIL 26. SEASON: All year. FACILITIES: 1 tent site; tbls, toil. ACTIVITIES: Mountain climbing; hiking; picnicking; fishing. MISC.: Elev 4500 ft; 1 acre; pets. Scenic. Site operated by the city. Mountain cabin for hikers.

* **Hermit Lake** (White Mountain NF). 10 mi S of Gorham on St Hwy 16; 2-2/5 mi W on TRAIL 66. SEASON: All year. FACILITIES: 8 tent sites; flush toil, no drk wtr. ACTIVITIES: Picnicking; hiking; fishing.

* **IMP Shelter AMC** (White Mountain NF). 2 mi S of Gorham on St Hwy 16; 3 mi SE on TRAIL 511. SEASON: All year. FACILITIES: tent site; no drk wtr; toil, cga, f, no tbls. ACTIVITIES: Mountain climbing; hiking; fishing. MISC.: Elev 3300 ft; 1 acre; pets. Scenic. Stream. On Appalachian Trail. Mountain shelter for hikers.

* **Perch RMC** (White Mountain NF). 9 mi W of Gorham on US 2; 3 mi NE on TRAIL 31. SEASON: All year. FACILITIES: 1 tent site; no drk wtr; toil, cga, f, no tbls. ACTIVITIES: Mountain climbing; hiking;

fishing. MISC.: Elev 4300 ft; 1 acre; pets. Site operated by quasi-public agency. Mountain shelter for hikers.

* **Rattle River Shelter** (White Mountain NF). 4 mi E of Gorham on US 2; 1-3/5 mi S on TRAIL 155. SEASON: All year. FACILITIES: tent site; no drk wtr; toil, cga, f, no tbls. ACTIVITIES: Mountain climbing; hiking; fishing. MISC.: Elev 1400 ft; 1 acre; pets. Hiking shelter on Appalachian Trail. Scenic.

* **Spruce Brook Shelter** (White Mountain NF). 12 mi E of Gorham on US 2; 3 mi S on St Hwy 113; 5-1/2 mi SW on FS FH12; 3-2/5 mi SW on TRAIL 165. SEASON: 6/1-10/15; 5-day lmt. FACILITIES: 1 tent site; no drk wtr; toil, cga, f, no tbls. ACTIVITIES: Mountain climbing; hiking; fishing. MISC.: Elev 1600 ft; 1 acre; pets. Stream.

JACKSON

* **Black Mountain Cabin** (White Mountain NF). 3-7/10 mi N of Jackson on St Hwy 16B; 2 mi E on TRAIL 218. SEASON: All year; 7-day lmt. FACILITIES: 1 tent site; no drk wtr; toil, cga, f, tbls. ACTIVITIES: Mountain climbing; hiking; picnicking. MISC.: Elev 2500 ft; 1 acre; pets.

* **Doublehead Cabin J** (White Mountain NF). 1-9/10 mi NE of Jackson St Hwy 16B; 3/5 mi S on Co Hwy TR; 1-4/5 mi E on TRAIL 202. SEASON: All year; 7-day lmt. FACILITIES: 1 tent site; no drk wtr; tbls, toil, cga, f. ACTIVITIES: Mountain climbing; hiking; picnicking. MISC.: Elev 3000 ft; 1 acre; pets.

* **Isolation Shelter AMC** (White Mountain NF). 5-7/10 mi N of Jackson on St Hwy 16; 3-3/10 mi W on TRAIL 85; 2-1/2 mi N on TRAIL 84. SEASON: 5/15-10/30. FACILITIES: tent site; no drk wtr; toil, cga, f, no tbls. ACTIVITIES: Mountain climbing; hiking. MISC.: Elev 3800 ft; 1 acre; pets.

* **Perkins Notch Shelter** (White Mountain NF). 4-1/5 mi N of Jackson on St Hwy 16B; 1-1/2 mi NE on Co Rd; 2-7/10 mi NE on TRAIL 214; 1-1/5 mi E on TRAIL 165. SEASON: 6/1-10/15; 5-day lmt. FACILITIES: 1 tent site; no drk wtr; toil, cga, f, no tbls. ACTIVITIES: Mountain climbing; hiking; fishing. MISC.: Elev 2600 ft; 1 acre; pets.

LANCASTER

* **Cabot Cabin** (White Mountain NF). 2 mi SE of Lancaster on St Hwy 50; 5-2/5 mi E on Co Hwy 61; 2-1/5 mi E on TRAIL 132; 1-3/10 mi NE on TRAIL 133. SEASON: All year. FACILITIES: 2 tent sites; no drk wtr; toil, tbls. ACTIVITIES: Mountain climbing; hiking. Fishing (2 mi). MISC.: Elev 4100 ft; 1 acre; pets. For hikers only; ORV restricted.

See page 7 for KEY TO ABBREVIATIONS.

LINCOLN

* **Franconia Brook Shelter** (White Mountain NF). 4-7/10 mi E of Lincoln on Kancamagus Hwy; 2-7/10 mi N on Wilderness TRAIL. SEASON: 6/1-9/30. FACILITIES: 32 tent sites; no drk wtr; no tbls, toil, cga, f. ACTIVITIES: Mountain climbing; hiking; picnicking. MISC.: 1 acre; pets. Scenic.

* **13 Falls Shelter** (White Mountain NF). 4-7/10 mi E on Kancamagus Hwy; 2-4/5 mi N on TR 383; 5 mi N on TRAIL 379. SEASON: 6/1-9/30. FACILITIES: 12 tent sites; no drk wtr; no tbls, toil, cga. ACTIVITIES: Mountain climbing; hiking; picnicking. MISC.: 1 acre; pets. Scenic.

NORTH SANDWISH

* **Flat Mountain Pond Shelter** (White Mountain NF). 2-4/5 mi N of North Sandwich on Co TR 113; 4-1/5 mi N on TRAIL 291. SEASON: 5/15-10/30; 7-day lmt. FACILITIES: 1 tent site; no drk wtr; toil, cga, f, no tbls. ACTIVITIES: Hiking; fishing; boating (no motors). MISC.: Elev 2400 ft; 1 acre; pets. Lake.

NORTH WOODSTOCK

* **Kinsman Pond Shelter AMC** (White Mountain NF). 6-1/10 mi N of North Woodstock on US 3; 4-3/10 mi NW on TRAIL 488. SEASON: 6/1-9/30. FACILITIES: 1 tent site; no drk wtr; toil, cga, f, no tbls. ACTIVITIES: Mountain climbing; hiking. MISC.: Elev 3800 ft; 1 acre; pets. Lake. Scenic.

PITTSBURG

Lake Francis (SRA). Just off Route 3 in Pittsburg, on Connecticut River.

RUMNEY

* **Three Ponds Shelter** (White Mountain NF). 7 mi N of Rumney on Co Hwy TR; 2-1/5 mi N on Three Ponds Trail. SEASON: 6/1-9/30. FACILITIES: 1 tent site; no drk wtr; toil, cga, f, no tbls. ACTIVITIES: Mountain climbing; hiking; fishing. MISC.: Elev 1700 ft; 1 acre; pets. Scenic.

TWIN MOUNTAIN

* **Garfield Ridge Shelter** (White Mountain NF). 5-1/2 mi W of Twin Mountain on US 3; 1-1/0 mi S on FS 92; 4-3/5 mi S on TRAIL 412; 3/10 mi E on TRAIL 414. SEASON: 5/30-10/15. FACILITIES: 7 tent sites; piped drk wtr. ACTIVITIES: Mountain climbing; hiking. MISC.: 3 acres; pets. Close to Appalachian Trail on Mt. Garfield.

WONALANCET

* **Old Shag Camp CMC** (White Mountain NF). 9/10 mi E of Wonalancet on Co Hwy TR113; 1-2/5 mi N on TRAIL 312. SEASON: 5/15-10/30. FACILITIES: 1 tent site; no drk wtr; toil, cga, f, no tbls. ACTIVITIES: Mountain climbing; hiking. MISC.: Elev 2900 ft; 1 acre; pets.

NEW JERSEY

GENERAL STATE INFORMATION

Miscellaneous

Toll-Free Number for Travel Information about the Atlantic City area:
1-800-257-8631 [calling outside of NJ]
1-800-582-7065 [calling within NJ]
Right Turns on Red: Permitted after full stop, unless posted otherwise.
STATE CAPITOL: Trenton
STATE NICKNAME: Garden State
STATE MOTTO: "Liberty and Prosperity"
STATE BIRD: Eastern Goldfinch
STATE FLOWER: Purple Violet
STATE TREE: Red Oak

State Parks

Overnight camping fees range from $4.00-5.00. No pets are allowed. Further information: Bureau of Parks; PO Box 1420; Trenton, NJ 08625.

Rest Areas

Overnight stops are not permitted in New Jersey Rest Areas.

See page 7 for KEY TO ABBREVIATIONS.

Canoeing/Camping along the Delaware River

A set of 10 maps (OUTDOOR RECREATION MAPS OF THE DELAWARE RIVER) which describe the river in detail (200 miles, from Hancock, NY, to Trenton, NJ), including campsites, can be obtained for $1.00/set from: Delaware River Basin Commission; PO Box 360; Trenton, NJ 08603.

The Appalachian Trail

More than 2000 miles long, the Appalachian Trail (from Maine to Georgia) is the longest continuous marked trail in the world.

CAMPING: More than 200 open-front shelters/lean-tos are spaced approximately 10 miles apart on the Trail (one-day intervals). As they are occupied on a first-come first-served basis, carry a tent in case the shelters are full. Potable spring water is usually available at each site, but should be purified by tablets or boiling. And always "pack it in, pack it out".

PERMITS: No permit is required to hike the Trail. However, camping permits must be obtained for overnight stays in Shenandoah NP (Luray, VA 22835) and Great Smokey Mountains NP (Gatlinburg, TN 37733). These are free of charge and available from the ranger stations or by mail. A free camping permit must be obtained for overnight stays in White Mountain National Forest Restricted Use Area (PO Box 638; Laconia, NH 03246).

APPALACHIAN TRAIL CONFERENCE: A private, nonprofit, national organization which represents citizen's interest in the Appalachian Trail. They offer detailed guidebooks and maps for sale, as well as the A.T. Data Book which gives the location and distances between shelters and certain post offices, supply points, water sources, lodging and meals. For more information on this organization, write to them at: PO Box 236; Harpers Ferry, WV 25425.

INFORMATION SOURCES

Maps

A detailed, up-to-date map of the **State of New Jersey** is available from **Forsyth Travel Library** (see order form in Appendix B).

State Information

New Jersey State Promotion; Department of Labor and Industry; PO Box 400; Trenton, NJ 08625.
Division of Fish, Game and Shellfisheries; Department of Environmental Protection; PO Box 1809; Labor and Industry Building; Trenton, NJ 08625.

New Jersey Department of Transportation; 1035 Parkway Avenue; Trenton, NJ 08618. Bureau of Parks; PO Box 1420; Trenton, NJ 08625.

City Information

Englewood Chamber of Commerce; 49 North Dean Street; Englewood, NJ 07631.
Fort Lee Chamber of Commerce; 175A North Marginal Road; Fort Lee, NJ 07024.
Hackensack Chamber of Commerce; 140 Main Street; Hackensack, NJ 07601.
Jersey City Chamber of Commerce; 911 Bergen Avenue; Jersey City, NJ 07306.
Newark Chamber of Commerce; 50 Park Place; Newark, NJ 07102.
Princeton Chamber of Commerce; 44 Nassau Street; PO Box 486; Princeton, NJ 08540.

FREE CAMPGROUNDS

BLOOMSBURY

Garden State Truck Plaza. I-78, Bloomsbury exit. **SEASON:** All yr; 1-night lmt. **FACILITIES:** Spaces for self-contained RVs; food, toil, drk wtr, dump, gas, mechanic.

CLINTON

Johnny's Truck Stop. I-78, Jutland-Norton exit, at Clinton. **SEASON:** All yr; 1-night lmt. **FACILITIES:** Spaces for self-contained RVs; food, toil, drk wtr, gas, mechanic.

See page 7 for KEY TO ABBREVIATIONS.

COLUMBIA

Truck Stops of America. I-80 at St Hwy 94, in Columbia. SEASON: All yr; 1-night lmt. FACILITIES: Spaces for self-contained RVs; toil, drk wtr, gas, mechanic.

DEEPWATER

Bridgeview Truck Plaza. I-295 S, Deepwater exit., at Deepwater. SEASON: All yr; 1-night lmt. FACILITIES: Spaces for self-contained RVs; food, toil, drk wtr, gas.

MAHWAH

Truck Stops of America. New York Thruway I-87, Suffern exit, on St Hwy 17. SEASON: All yr; 1-night lmt. FACILITIES: Spaces for self-contained RVs; toil, drk wtr, mechanic, gas.

MAYWOOD

Maywood Auto Repair (24-hour Truck Stop). 14 East Pleasant Avenue in Maywood. SEASON: All yr; 1-night lmt. FACILITIES: Spaces for self-contained RVs; toil, drk wtr, gas, mechanic.

PAULSBORO

76 Travelers Plaza (24-hour Truck Stop). I-295, Mt. Royal Exit, at Paulsboro. SEASON: All yr; 1-night lmt. FACILITIES: Spaces for self-contained RVs; food, toil, drk wtr, mechanic, gas.

PEMBERTON

Drayton Sales and Service (24-hour Truck Stop). South Pemberton Road, in Pemberton. SEASON: All yr; 1-night lmt. FACILITIES: Self-contained spaces for RVs. Toil, drk wtr, gas, mechanic.

NOTICE TO CAMPERS

As you can see, New Jersey doesn't have much in the way of free campgrounds. That is why we included these specific truck stops. In addition to these truck stops, read page 5 for additional places to camp for free.

READ THIS!

All information relative to each campground and state is currently accurate to the best of the publisher's knowledge. However, non-fee status and facilities are subject to change.

If any inaccuracies in this directory are discovered, or you know of any additional FREE campgrounds, please contact: VMPI; Box 1289; Clearwater, FL 33517.

INFORMATION ON HOW TO PURCHASE ADDITIONAL COPIES OF THIS BOOK AS WELL AS QUANTITY DISCOUNT INFORMATION IS ALSO AVAILABLE AT THIS ADDRESS.

NEW MEXICO

GENERAL STATE INFORMATION

Miscellaneous

Toll-Free Number for Travel Information:
   1-800-545-9877/2040 [calling
       outside of New Mexico]
   1-800-432-4269 [within New Mexico]
Right Turns on Red: Permitted after
   full stop, unless otherwise posted.
STATE CAPITOL: Santa Fe
STATE NICKNAME: Land of Enchantment
STATE MOTTO: "It Grows As It Goes"
STATE BIRD: Roadrunner
STATE FLOWER: Yucca
STATE TREE: Pinon

State Parks

Overnight camping fee is $2.00 plus $1.00 for electricity. Pets on leash are permitted. Further information: State Parks and Recreation Commission; PO Box 1147; Santa Fe, NM 87501.

Rest Areas

Overnight stops are permitted in New Mexico Rest Areas.

See page 7 for KEY TO ABBREVIATIONS.

BACKCOUNTRY AND WILDERNESS CAMPING

BANDELIER NATIONAL MONUMENT (Backcountry Camping)

Most of Bandelier's 29,661 acres are open to backcountry camping all year.   Areas closed to camping in the backcountry are as follows:
1. Tsankawi Section
2. 75 feet from any spring
3. 50 feet from either side of any stream
4. Frijoles Canyon from the Rio Grande to 2 mi above Ceremonial Cave
5. Within ½ mile of Painted Cave
6. Within ½ mile of the Shrine of the Stone Lions
7. Within any cave or archeological site

For your safety, free permits are required prior to travel into the backcountry. These may be obtained at the Visitor Center in Frijoles Canyon, 7 days a week from 8:00-5:00. Please register in and out at trailheads. ENTRANCE FEE: One single-visit entrance fee will be charged regardless of the number of days visitors stay within a given area. By car, $1.00; by foot, 50¢. On the day the entrance fee is paid, visitors may also leave and re-enter the area without payment of an additional entrance fee. Further information: Superintendent; Bandelier National Monument; Los Alamos, NM 87544.

BLACK RANGE PRIMITIVE AREA; Gila NF

This 169,356-acre area is located just east of the Gila Primitive Area, created to preserve the wild and natural state of these rugged mountains, the forest, and a rocky canyon. Further information: Superintendent; Gila NF; 2601 North Silver Street; Silver City, NM 88061.

CARLSBAD CAVERNS NATIONAL PARK (Backpacking)

Entrance fee is $3.00 per car, or annual Golden Eagle or Golden Age Passports**. Register at the Visitor Center, where complete information is available. The park is rugged, with steep trails and sheer cliffs leading off many ridge tops. Taking shortcuts or cliff climbing is dangerous and can lead to serious accidents. Have adequate maps with you to avoid becoming lost. Wear good hiking shoes to protect you from the elements. Rattlesnakes are native to the area. Topographic maps are available at the Visitor Center. Free open-fire permit available at Visitor Center. No overnight camping along any of the roads in the park. Individual campgrounds are not designated, but camping is permitted along any of the hiking trails west of Lowe Ranch. All litter and trash must be packed out. Water is not available and must be packed in. No pets allowed in backcountry. Further information: Superintendent; Carlsbad Caverns NP; 3225 National Parks Highway; Carlsbad, NM 88220.

CHACO CANYON NATIONAL MONUMENT (Backcountry Camping)

Located in northwestern New Mexico. From the north, turn off St Hwy 44 at Blanco Trading Post and follow St Hwy 57 for 23 mi to the N entrance of the monument. The visitor center is 7 mi beyond this entrance. From the south, turn north on St Hwy 57 from I-40 at Thoreau and go 44 mi on paved road. A marked turnoff begins a 20-mile stretch of St Hwy 57 leading to the south entrance. The visitor center is 1½ mi ahead. Inquire locally or call the monument (505/786-5384) about dirt road conditions during stormy weather. Pick up backcountry permit, map and information from the visitor center. Pets are not allowed on trails. Further information: Superintendent; Chaco Canyon NM; Star Route 4; Box 6500; Bloomfield, NM 87413.

CIBOLA NATIONAL FOREST (Backcountry Camping)

No permits are necessary. If you are backpacking, there are no regulations governing the size of groups or length of stay in the back areas of the Districts. Most areas are quite dry, and existing streams and springs are not perennial; plan to carry water for drinking and camping in backcountry.

The Cibola NF has two classified Wilderness areas: Sandia Wilderness Area (just E of Albuquerque in the Sandia Mountains; 30,900 acres); Manzano Wilderness Area (30 mi SE of Albuquerque in the Manzano Mountains; 37,000 acres). There are many other areas that offer solitude and enjoyable backpacking opportunities, particularly the Crest trails within the Magdalena, Mountainair, and Sandia Ranger Districts.

The mountainous backcountry is rugged and isolated and there are no camping facilities in these wild-like areas. It is recommended that you consult the local District Ranger before planning an extended trip.

Further information: Forest Supervisor; Cibola NF; 10308 Candelaria, NE; Albuquerque, NM 87112 [505/766-2185].

NEW MEXICO

GILA PRIMITIVE AREA; Gila NF

Around the edges of Gila Wilderness are 11 separated areas totaling another 130,637. Once a part of the Wilderness, the Primitive Area was separated from it during WWII. Fishing, hiking, horseback riding, camping. No backcountry permit is required. Further information: Forest Supervisor; Gila NF; 2601 North Silver Street; Silver City, NM 88061.

GILA WILDERNESS; Gila NF

The 433,690-acre roadless Gila Wilderness offers outstanding scenery (canyons, springs, rivers, streams) as well as solitude (some sections of its 2,578 miles of trails are rarely visited by man; one can hike for weeks without seeing another person). The highest mountains in the National Forest are here. Elevations range from 4,800-10,890 feet. Fishing, hiking, horseback riding, camping. No permit is required. Further information: Forest Supervisor; Gila NF; 2601 North Silver Street; Silver City, NM 88061.

GUADALUPE MOUNTAINS NATIONAL PARK (Backcountry Camping)

63 miles of rocky and rugged trails, often steep. High timber, canyon and desert country. Plan to carry all your own water and to camp in designated backcountry sites. No fires or pets in backcountry. Obtain permits and information at the Information Station (55 mi SW of Carlsbad on US 62-180). Topographical maps and hikers guides are available. Further information: Superintendent; Guadalupe NP; 3225 National Parks Highway; Carlsbad, NM 88220.

PECOS WILDERNESS; Carson NF

Part of the famous 167,000-acre Pecos Wilderness is contained within Carson NF. It is accessible only by hiking or by horseback. Hunting, fishing. A Wilderness Permit is mandatory all year. The Ranger who issues your permit will advise you on current conditions at your intended destination. Pets on leash are permitted. Further information: Forest Supervisor; Carson NF; Forest Service Building; PO Box 558; Taos, NM 87571.

PECOS WILDERNESS; Santa Fe NF

A large portion of the 167,000-acre Pecos Wilderness is located in Santa Fe NF, with its high peaks, lakes, alpine meadows and above-timberline tundra. Plenty of opportunity for solitude here. Hunting, fishing, hiking, horseback riding, mountain climbing, camping; skiing in winter. Pets allowed on leash. Free permit required. Further information: Forest Supervisor; Santa Fe NF; Federal Building; PO Box 1689; Santa Fe, NM 87501.

SAN PEDRO PARKS WILDERNESS; Santa Fe NF

The 41,000-acre Wilderness is located in the Jemez Division of Santa Fe National Forest. The high plateau averages 10,000 feet in elevation. The Wilderness is located between the towns of Cuba and Coyote. Hunting, fishing, hiking, horseback riding; skiing and snowmobiling in winter; mountain climbing, camping. Pets permitted if kept on a leash. Free permit is required. Further information: Forest Supervisor; Santa Fe NF; Federal Building; PO Box 1689; Santa Fe, NM 87501.

WHEELER PEAK WILDERNESS; Carson NF

The 6000-acre Wilderness is accessible only by hiking or by horseback. Hunting, fishing, camping. A free Wilderness Permit is mandatory all year. The Ranger who issues your permit will advise you on current conditions at your intended destination. Permits are available from Questa Ranger Station (1 mi E of Questa on St Hwy 38) and from Taos Ranger Station (Armory Street; Taos, NM). A permit may be obtained up to 10 days before your proposed trip. Pets allowed on leash. Further information: Forest Supervisor; Carson NF; Forest Service Building; PO Box 558; Taos, NM 87571.

WHITE MOUNTAINS WILDERNESS (and Backcountry Camping in Lincoln NF)

There are numerous hiking trails, and solitude is easy to find. Carry water with you as it is not always accessible. Sometimes during fire season (5/15-7/3) open campfires are restricted to designated campgrounds. The rains normally start July 4th and open fires are permitted from then on. Check at ranger stations for free undeveloped camp areas. Pets on leash. However, they should be kept inside at night when the bears come into the campgrounds and camping areas. Further information: Forest Supervisor; Lincoln NF; Federal Building; 11th and New York Streets; Alamogordo, NM 88310.

NEW MEXICO

INFORMATION SOURCES

Maps

The following maps are available from **Forsyth Travel Library** (see order form in Appendix B):

> **State of New Mexico** [Up-to-date, showing all principal roads, points of interest, sports areas, parks, airports, mileage, etc. Full color.]

> Completely indexed city maps, including all airports, lakes, rivers, etc., of: **Alamogordo; Albuquerque; Gallup; Las Cruces; Los Alamos; Roswell; Silver City; White Rock.**

Gold Mining and Prospecting

New Mexico State Bureau of Mines and Mineral Resources; New Mexico Institute of Mining and Technology; Socorro, NM 87801.

State Information

Tourist Division; New Mexico Department of Development; 113 Washington Avenue; Santa Fe, NM 87503.

State Parks and Recreation Commission; 141 East DeVargas; PO Box 1147; Santa Fe, NM 87501.

U.S. Bureau of Sport Fisheries and Wildlife; 500 Gold Avenue, SW; Albuquerque, NM 87102.

Department of Game and Fish; Villagra Building; Santa Fe, NM 87503.

City Information

Albuquerque Chamber of Commerce; 401 - 2nd Street NW; Albuquerque, NM 87102.
Carlsbad Chamber of Commerce; PO Box 910; Carlsbad, NM 88220.
Deming Chamber of Commerce; 109 East Pine; PO Box 8; Deming, NM 88030.
Gallup Chamber of Commerce; PO Box 1395; Gallup, NM 87301.
Las Cruces Chamber of Commerce; PO Box 519; Las Cruces, NM 88001.

National Forests

Carson NF; Forest Service Building; PO Box 558; Taos, NM 87571.
Cibola NF; 10308 Candelaria Road NE; Albuquerque, NM 87112.
Gila NF; 2610 North Silver Street; Silver City, NM 88061.
Lincoln NF; Federal Building; 11th and New York Streets; Alamogordo, NM 88310.
Santa Fe NF; Federal Building; PO Box 1689; Santa Fe, NM 87501.

Miscellaneous

Gila Cliff Dwellings NM; Route 11, Box 100; Silver City, NM 88061.
Chaco Canyon NM; Star Route 4, Box 6500; Bloomfield, NM 87431.
El Morro NM; Ramah, NM 87321.
Carlsbad Caverns NP; 3225 National Parks Highway; Carlsbad, NM 88220.
Guadalupe Mountains NP; c/o Carlsbad Caverns NP; 3225 National Parks Highway; Carlsbad, NM 88220.
New Mexico BLM; U.S. P.O. and Federal Building; PO Box 1449; Santa Fe, NM 87501.
Albuquerque Area Office; Bureau of Indian Affairs; PO Box 8327; Albuquerque,NM 87108.
Corps of Engineers, Albuquerque District; PO Box 1580; Albuquerque, NM 87103.

FREE CAMPGROUNDS

ABIQUIU

Riana Area Campground (COE; Abiquiu Dam). 7 mi W of Abiquiu on US 84; 2 mi S on St Hwy 96. **SEASON:** All yr; 14-day lmt. **FACILITIES:** 10 sites (tr -33); flush toil, tbls, cga, food, f. **ACTIVITIES:** Boating,l; waterskiing; hunting (waterfowl); swimming; picnicking; fishing. **MISC.:** Elev 6140 ft. Pinon-juniper woodland with grassland, mesas & canyons. Scenic Trail. Ghost Ranch Museum (nearby), Summer drk wtr.

ALBUQUERQUE

Galisteo Dam (COE). 35 mi N on I-25; US 85 to access rd; 5 mi E on access rd. **SEASON:** All yr; 14-day lmt. **FACILITIES:** Sites; tbls, cga; toil (at overlook). **ACTIVITIES:** Picnicking. **MISC.:** Elev 5500 ft. Semi-arid, rolling hills, canyons and mesas. The reservoir is dry except when used for flood control; thus, water recreation is very limited.

See page 7 for KEY TO ABBREVIATIONS.

Jemez Canyon Dam (COE). 14 mi N of Albuquerque on I-25; 5 mi W on St Hwy 44 to access rd; 6 mi N on access rd. SEASON: All yr; 14-day lmt. FACILITIES: Sites; tbls, toil, cga, f. ACTIVITIES: Picnicking. MISC.: Elev 5140 ft; pets. Not much shade. Semi-arid, rolling hills, canyons and mesas. drk wtr.

BELEN

John F. Kennedy (Cibola NF). 5 mi SE of Belen on St Hwy 6; 20 mi NE on Co Hwy 68. SEASON: 3/1-10/31; 14-day lmt. FACILITIES: 18 sites (tr -22); well drk wtr, tbls, toil, cga, f. ACTIVITIES: Hiking; picnicking. MISC.: Elev 6800 ft; 10 acres; pets. Nature trails. Campground is on the West boundary of the Manzano Wilderness.

BLOOMFIELD

Angel Peak Recreation Site (BLM). 13 mi SE of Bloomfield on St Hwy 44 in NW New Mexico. SEASON: All yr (weather permitting). FACILITIES: 16 sites; no drk wtr; tbls, toil, cga, shelters. ACTIVITIES: Hiking; rockhounding; picnicking. MISC.: Elev 6400 ft; 200 acres.

Gallo Campground (Chaco Canyon NM). 27 mi S of Bloomfield on St Hwy 44; 29 mi S on St Hwy 57 to N entrance of the monument. The visitor center is 7 mi beyond this entrance. The campground is located 1 mi from the visitor center. [NOTE: Call the monument (505-786-5384) about dirt road conditions during stormy weather.] SEASON: All yr; 14-day lmt. FACILITIES: 36 sites (tr -30); flush toil, drk wtr, tbls, cga. No hookups; no f. ACTIVITIES: Picnicking; hiking. MISC.: 8 acres. Pets are allowed in campground but not on trails. A group campsite is available. Some years there is a $2 charge; some years it is FREE. It depends upon the availability of personnel to collect fees (which is not frequent).

CANJILON

Canjilon Creek (Carson NF). 8-1/2 mi NE of Canjilon on FS 559; 1-3/10 mi N on FS 130 (primitive rd). SEASON: 6/1-9/15; 14-day lmt. FACILITIES: 4 sites (no tr); no drk wtr; tbls, toil, cga, f. ACTIVITIES: Picnicking; fishing. MISC.: Elev 9300 ft; 2 acres; pets. Scenic.

CARLSBAD

Pine Springs Canyon Campground (Guadalupe Mountains NP). Frijole Information Station is located 55 mi SW of Carlsbad on US 62-180. The campground is located 1-1/2 mi W of the Information Station. FACILITIES: 20 sites for self-contained RVs; tbls, toil, cga. ACTIVITIES: Hiking; picnicking. MISC.: Pets allowed in campground. There is no entrance fee to this NP.

CEBOLLA

Trout Lakes (Carson NF). 1 mi S of Cebolla on US 84; 9-1/2 mi NE on FS 125 (primitive rd). SEASON: 5/20-9/15; 14-day lmt. FACILITIES: 5 sites (tr -16); no drk wtr; tbls, toil, cga. ACTIVITIES: Picnicking; fishing. MISC.: Elev 9300 ft; 4 acres; pets; scenic. Not recommended for trailers over 16 because of primitive road.

CHAMIZAL

Trampas Canyon (Carson NF). 2 mi S of Chamizal on St Hwy 76; 1 mi SE on FS 22072; 6-1/2 mi SE on FS 22072. SEASON: 5/26-9/10; 14-day lmt. FACILITIES: 4 sites (tr -16); no drk wtr; flush toil, cga. ACTIVITIES: Hiking; picnicking. MISC.: Elev 9000 ft; 2 acres; pets. Gateway to Pecos Wilderness. Nature trails.

CLAYTON

Airport Park. 1 mi from center of Clayton. SEASON: All yr.

CLOUDCROFT

Sleepy Grass (Lincoln NF). 2-1/10 mi E on US 82; 31 miles NE of White Sands National Monument. SEASON: 4/15-12/15; 14-day lmt. FACILITIES: 55 sites (tr -22); tbls, toil, cga, piped drk wtr. Store/gas/ice/laundry/food/dump (2 mi). ACTIVITIES: Picnicking; berry-picking; hiking. Horseback riding (2 mi). MISC.: Elev 8700 ft; 59 acres; scenic; pets.

CORDOVA

Borrego Mesa (Santa Fe NF). 9/10 mi SE of Cordova on FS 440; 5-3/5 mi E on FS 306; 1/5 mi S on FS 437. SEASON: 5/1-10/31; 14-day lmt. FACILITIES: 8 sites (tr -32); no drk wtr; tbls, toil, cga. ACTIVITIES: Picnicking; hiking. Fishing (1 mi). MISC.: Elev 8700 ft; 3 acres; pets. Jump-off to Pecos Wilderness.

CORONA

Red Cloud (Cibola NF). 9-1/2 mi SW of Corona on US 54; 1-1/5 mi W on FS 161; 6-1/5 mi NW on FS 99. SEASON: 4/1-10/31; 14-day lmt. FACILITIES: 9 sites (tr -32); no drk wtr; tbls, toil, cga, f. ACTIVITIES: Picnicking. MISC.: Elev 7600 ft; 2 acres; pets. Primitive forest environment. Rudimentary improvements.

See page 7 for KEY TO ABBREVIATIONS.

COWLES

Cowles (Santa Fe NF). 1/5 mi W of Cowles on FS 121. SEASON: 5/1-10/31; 14-day lmt. FACILITIES: 3 sites (tr -16); toil, cga. ACTIVITIES: Hiking; picnicking; fishing. MISC.: Elev 8200 ft; pets. Wilderness access.

Iron Gate (Santa Fe NF). 1-1/5 mi S of Cowles on St Hwy 63; 4-1/5 mi NE on FS 223 (fair weather rd only). SEASON: 5/1-10/31; 14-day lmt. FACILITIES: 15 sites (tr -16). Ice/food/store (5 mi). ACTIVITIES: Hiking; picnicking; fishing. MISC.: Elev 9400 ft; 8 acres; pets. Pecos Wilderness jump off.

Winsor Creek (Santa Fe NF). 1 mi W of Cowles on FS 121. SEASON: 5/1-10/31; 14-day lmt. FACILITIES: 6 sites (tr -16). Ice/food/store (1 mi). ACTIVITIES: Hiking; picnicking; fishing. MISC.: Elev 8400 ft; 5 acres; pets. Wilderness access.

COYOTE

Rio Puerco (Santa Fe NF). 4-4/5 mi W on St Hwy 96; 9-3/5 mi S on FS 103. SEASON: 5/1-10/31; 14-day lmt. FACILITIES: 5 tent sites (no tr); no drk wtr; tbls, toil, cga, f. ACTIVITIES: Fishing; picnicking. MISC.: Elev 8200 ft; 2 acres; pets.

CUBA

Clear Creek (Santa Fe NF). 11-2/5 mi E of Cuba on St Hwy 126. SEASON: 5/1-10/31; 14-day lmt. FACILITIES: 5 sites (tr -16); no drk wtr; tbls, toil, cga, f. ACTIVITIES: Picnicking; fishing. MISC.: Elev 8500 ft; 2 acres; pets. Stream.

Rio Las Vacas (Santa Fe NF). 12-7/10 mi E of Cuba on St Hwy 126. SEASON: 5/1-10/31; 14-day lmt. FACILITIES: 5 sites (tr -16); no drk wtr, tbls, toil, cga, f. ACTIVITIES: Fishing; picnicking. MISC.: Elev 8200 ft; 2 acres; pets. Stream.

EL RITO

El Rito (Carlson NF). 5-2/5 mi NW of El Rito on St Hwy 110. SEASON: 4/15-10/15; 14-day lmt. FACILITIES: 7 sites (tr -22); no drk wtr; f. ACTIVITIES: Picnicking; fishing. MISC.: Elev 7600 ft; 5 acres; pets.

ESPANOLA

Echo Amphitheater Park. 45 mi NW of Espanola on St Hwy 84. SEASON: All yr. FACILITIES: Combination sites.

DATIL

Datil Well Campground (BLM). 1/4 mi W of US 60 near Datil in western New Mexico. SEASON: All yr (weather permitting); 7-day lmt. FACILITIES: 22 sites; drk wtr, tbls, toil, cga, recreation hall, ice. Store/food (nearby). ACTIVITIES: Picnicking. MISC.: Elev 7000; 640 acres. Interpretive Display.

DEMING

Ledbetter's Supermarket (Private). 501 N. Gold. [505/546-9413] I-10, exit 82A or 82B, then 1 block N of I-10 on St Hwy 180. This friendly oasis welcomes self-contained travelers year round to use their parking lot for the night. Free lighted overnight parking in their parking lot (in after 7:00 PM, out by 9:00 PM, PLEASE). Store is open Monday-Saturday, 8-8. Self service gasoline. Full meat market featuring only USDA Choice Iowa Corn Fed Beef.

ESPANOLA

Borrego Mesa (Santa Fe NF). 20 mi E of Espanola. Take State Hwy 76 from Espanola to Chimayo; St Hwy 4 toward Santa Cruz Lake; E on FS 306. There are 10 mi of unsurfaced rd to the campground from this intersection. Very muddy if wet. SEAS: 5/1-10/31; 14-day lmt. FAC: 8 sites (tr -32); no drk wtr. ACTIVITIES: Hiking; picnicking; fishing. MISC.: Elev 8400; 3 acres; pets. Located in Ponderosa pine, Douglas fir, and White fir trees. Stream in canyon (1/2 mi; steep access); campground on mesa. Pecos Wilderness boundary is approximately 4-3/10 mi from campground by good trail.

Riana Area Campground (COE; Abiquiu Dam). 30 mi NW of Espanola on US 84; 2 mi W on St Hwy 96. SEASON: All yr; 14-day lmt. FACILITIES: 10 sites (tr -33); flush toil, f. ACTIVITIES: Hiking; picnicking; fishing; boating,l; water-skiing; hunting (waterfowl); swimming. MISC.: Pinon-juniper woodland with grassland, mesas & canyons. Ghost Ranch Museum nearby. Scenic Trail. Drk Wtr in Summer.

Santa Cruz Lake Recreation Area (BLM). 13 mi E of Espanola on St Hwys 4/76 (23 mi NE of Pojoaque near Rio Chiquito and Cundiyo in north central NM). SEASON: 4/1-11/30; 14-day lmt. FACILITIES: 25 sites; tbls, toil, cga, shelters, drk wtr, food, store, ice, f. ACTIVITIES: Hiking; picnicking; fishing. Boating,rd (fee to put a boat on lake as charged by the private water users). MISC.: Extensive trails. Pay phone avilable in Summer.

EUNICE

Stephen Park (Municipal Park). 4 mi W of Eunice on St Hwy 176. SEASON:

All yr. FACILITIES: 15 sites; flush toil, drk wtr, sheltered picnic units, electric, water. ACTIVITIES: Tennis; picnicking; fishing. Baseball fields; croquet courts; horseshoes. Golf (nearby).

GALLUP

El Morro Campground (El Morrow Natl Monument). 58 mi SE of Gallup on St Hwys 32/53 to Visitor Center; the campgd is just off to the left as you drive up to Visitor Ctr off St Hwy 53, and is marked by the National Park symbols of a tent and two people. SEASON: All yr (closed only when the snow accumulation is too deep). FACILITIES: 9 sites; tbls, toil, cga, drk wtr (available except for the freezing Winter months; water may be obtained at the Visitor Center when it is off at the campground). ACTIVITIES: Picnicking. MISC.: During the Summer months, the Park offers campfire talks (Friday, Saturday, Sunday, & holidays). These take place at the campfire ring, located in the center of the nine campsites.

GLEN RIO

Glen Rio Rest Area. State line near New Mexico border on I-40 (40 mi from Tucumcari) [paved access rds]. SEASON: All yr; 1-day lmt. FACILITIES: 25 sites (pull-thru spaces); tbls, toil, cga, dump, phone. ACTIVITIES: Picnicking (picnic shelters with cooking facilities). MISC.: Pets.

GRANTS

El Morro Campground (El Morro National Monument). 43 mi W of Grants on St Hwy 53 to Visitor Center. SEASON: All yr (closed only when the snow accumulation is too deep). FACILITIES: 9 sites; tbls, toil, cga, drk wtr (available except for the freezing Winter months; water may be obtained at the Visitor Center when it is off at the campground). ACTIVITIES: Picnicking. MISC.: During the Summer months, the Park offers campfire talks (Friday, Saturday, Sunday, & holidays). These take place at the campfire ring (located in the center of the nine campsites.

Lobo Canyon (Cibola NF). 8-3/5 mi NE of Grants on St Hwy 547; 1-1/2 mi SE on FS 193. SEASON: 4/1-10/31; 10-day lmt. FACILITIES: 4 sites (no tr); no drk wtr; tbls, toil, cga. ACTIVITIES: Hiking; picnicking. MISC.: Elev 7400 ft; 4 acres; pets. Nature trails (4 mi).

HILLSBORO

Wrights Cabin (Gila NF). 18-7/10 mi W of Hillsboro on St Hwy 90. SEASON:

4/1-11/30. FACILITIES: 7 sites (tr -22); no drk wtr; tbls, toil, cga, f. ACTIVITIES: Hiking; picnicking; fishing. Horseback riding (1 mi). MISC.: Elev 7500 ft; 2 acres; pets. Nature Trails. On Scenic route between interstate 25 and US 180. Stream.

JEMEZ SPRINGS

Banco Bonito (Santa Fe NF). 14-3/10 mi NE of Jemez Springs on St Hwy 4; 1-1/5 mi S on FS 133. SEASON: 5/20-10/31; 7-day lmt. FACILITIES: 4 sites (tr -16); tbls, toil, cga, f. ACTIVITIES: Fishing; picnicking. MISC.: Elev 7900 ft; pets.

Horseshoe Springs (Santa Fe NF). 9-1/10 mi NE of Jemez Springs on St Hwy 4; 4/5 mi N on St Hwy 126; 1 mi W on Co Hwy 2. SEASON: 5/1-10/31. FACILITIES: 3 sites (tr -16); piped drk wtr, tbls, toil, cga, f. Food (1 mi). ACTIVITIES: Picnicking; hiking. Fishing (1 mi). MISC.: Elev 7800 ft; 3 acres; pets. Scenic. Nature trails.

Jemez Falls (Santa Fe NF). 14-3/10 mi NE on St Hwy 4; 1-1/5 mi S on FS 133. SEASON: 5/1-10/31; 7-day lmt. FACILITIES: 4 sites (tr -16); no drk wtr; tbls, toil, cga, f. Food (4 mi). ACTIVITIES: Picnicking; hiking; fishing. MISC.: Elev 7900 ft; 2 acres; pets; scenic.

Seven Springs (Santa Fe NF). 9-1/10 mi NE of Jemez Springs on St Hwy 4; 9-7/10 mi NW on St Hwy 126; 1-3/5 mi E on FS 314. SEASON: 5/1-10/31; 14-day lmt. FACILITIES: 7 sites (tr -16); tbls, toil, cga, f, piped drk wtr. ACTIVITIES: Boating,d (1, 5 mi); picnicking; fishing. MISC.: Elev 8000 ft; 3 acres; pets. State Fish Hatchery (2 mi).

LAS CRUCES

Aguirre Spring (BLM). 5 mi S of US 70 and 17 mi E of Las Cruces. SEASON: All yr; 7-day lmt. FACILITIES: 35 sites (tr -22); no drk wtr; tbls, toil, cga, shelters. ACTIVITIES: Hiking; picnicking. MISC.: The area has interpretive trails and facilities.

LAS VEGAS

Ev Long (Santa Fe NF). 16-1/5 mi NW of Las Vegas on St Hwy 65; 1/10 mi SW on FS 156. SEASON: 5/1-10/31. FACILITIES: 11 sites (tr -16); well drk wtr, tbls, toil, cga. Store/gas (1 mi). ACTIVITIES: Picnicking; fishing. Horseback riding (r, 4 mi). MISC.: Elev 7500 ft; 5 acres; pets.

LOS ALAMOS

Las Conchas (Santa Fe NF). 18-3/10 mi SW of Los Alamos on St Hwy 4. SEASON:

5/1-10/31; 14-day lmt. FACILITIES: 6
sites (no tr); flush toil, cga, tbls, no
drk wtr. ACTIVITIES: Picnicking; fishing.
MISC.: Elev 8400 ft; 2 acres; pets.
Geological.

LOVINGTON

Avenue D Park (City Park). St Hwy 82
on Ave D at 11th St. SEASON: All year.
FACILITIES: Self-contained RV sites;
drk wtr, tbls, toil, cga, dump, shower.
ACTIVITIES: Picnicking. MISC.: Elev
3900 ft; pets. Shade.

Chaparral Park (City Park). 2 mi SE
of truck bypass St Hwy 82. SEASON:
All year. FACILITIES: 15 self-contained
sites; tbls, toil, cga, phones. ACTIVI-
TIES: Picnicking; fishing. MISC.: Elev
3900 ft; pets. Lake.

City Park. US 82 in Lovington. SEA-
SON: All year. FACILITIES: Combin-
ation sites. ACTIVITIES: Picnicking.
MISC.: Pets.

MAGDALENA

Bear Trap (Cibola NF). 12 mi W of
Magdalena on US 60; 15 mi SW on St
Hwy 52; 1/10 mi E on FS 328. SEASON:
5/1-10/31; 14-day lmt. FACILITIES: 4
sites (tr -22); tbls, toil, cga, f. AC-
TIVITIES: Picnicking. MISC.: Elev 8500
ft; 3 acres; pets. Primitive improvements.

Water Canyon (Cibola NF). 11 mi SE
on US 60; 5 mi SW on FS 235. SEA-
SON: 3/15-11/15; 14-day lmt. FACILI-
TIES: 4 sites (tr -22); tbls, toil, cga,
well drk wtr. ACTIVITIES: Picnicking; berry-picking. MISC.: Elev 6800
ft; 8 acres; scenic; pets. At the base
of the Magdalena Mountains. Site of
early day mining activity.

MAYHILL

James Canyon Campground (Lincoln NF).
2 mi NW of Mayhill on US 82. SEASON:
All year; 14-day lmt. FACILITIES: 5
sites (tr -16); no drk wtr; tbls, toil,
cga. Store/gas/ice/food (2 mi). ACTIVI-
TIES: Picnicking; fishing. MISC.: Elev
6800 ft; 4 acres; pets. Botanical. 16
mi SE of Cloudcroft views of 1951 Allen
Canyon Burn.

MIMBRES

Lower Black Canyon (Gila NF). 29-3/5
mi N of Mimbres on St Hwy 61; 3/5 mi
W on Co Hwy 6150C. SEASON: 4/1-11/30;
14-day lmt. FACILITIES: 3 sites (tr
-22); no drk wtr; tbls, toil, cga. AC-
TIVITIES: Hiking; picnicking. Fishing
(1 mi). Horseback riding (1 mi).
MISC.: Elev 6900 ft; 2 acres; pets.
Scenic.

Sapillo Group (Gila NF). 9-4/5 mi NW
of Mimbres on St Hwy 61; 6-3/5 mi W
on St Hwy 35; 1/2 mi S on FS 606. SEA-
SON: All year. FACILITIES: 8 sites; no
drk wtr; no tbls, toil, cga. Store/gas/
ice/dump (4 mi). ACTIVITIES: Hiking;
horseback riding (1 mi); fishing (2 mi);
boating (1, 3 mi; r, 4 mi). MISC.: Elev
6100 ft; 5 acres; pets. Scenic.

MOGOLLON

Gilita (Gila NF). 19-2/5 mi E of Mogollon
on St Hwy 78. SEASON: 4/1-11/15; 14-day
lmt. FACILITIES: 6 sites (tr -22); no
drk wtr. ACTIVITIES: Hiking; horseback
riding; picnicking. Fishing (1 mi).
MISC.: Elev 8100 ft; 2 acres; pets. Near
edge of Gila Wilderness.

MONTICELLO

Luna Park (Cibola NF). 4-2/5 mi NE
of Monticello on FS 139; 4-3/5 mi N on
FS 225. SEASON: 4/1-11/15; 14-day lmt.
FACILITIES: 3 sites (tr -22); tbls, toil,
cga. ACTIVITIES: Picnicking. MISC.:
Elev 7400 ft; 1 acre; pets. Primitive improvements.

Springtime (Cibola NF). 4-2/5 mi NE of
Monticello on FS 139; 11 mi N on FS 225.
SEASON: 4/15-11/15; 14-day lmt. FACILI-
TIES: 6 sites (no tr); piped drk wtr,
tbls, toil, cga, f. ACTIVITIES: Picnick-
ing. MISC.: Elev 7400 ft; 3 acres; pets.
Dog shelters. Isolated. Trailers must
park at entrance.

PECOS

Cow Creek (Santa Fe NF). 8 mi NE of
Pecos on FS 86; 2-3/10 mi NW on FS
322. SEASON: 5/1-10/31; 14-day lmt.
FACILITIES: 5 sites (no tr); no drk
wtr; tbls, toil, cga. ACTIVITIES: Fishing; picnicking. Horseback riding (r,
1 mi). MISC.: Elev 8300 ft; 5 acres;
pets. Stream.

Cowles (Santa Fe NF). 20 mi N of Pecos
on St Hwy 63; 1/5 mi W on FS 121.
SEASON: 5/1-10/31; 14-day lmt. FACILI-
TIES: 3 sites (tr -16); no drk wtr;
tbls, toil, cga. ACTIVITIES: Hiking;
picnicking; fishing. Horseback riding
(r, 1 mi). MISC.: Elev 8200 ft; 3 acres;
pets. Scenic. Pecos Wilderness jump-off.

Holy Ghost (Santa Fe NF). 13-3/10 mi
N of Pecos on St Hwy 63; 2-3/10 mi NW
on FS 122. SEASON: 5/1-10/31; 14-day
lmt. FACILITIES: 21 sites (tr -16);
tbls, toil, cga, no drk wtr. Store/gas/
ice (3 mi). ACTIVITIES: Hiking; picnicking; fishing. Horseback riding (r,
3 mi). MISC.: Elev 8100 ft; 20 acres;
pets. Pecos Wilderness jump-off. Scenic.

Iron Gate (Santa Fe NF). 18-4/5 mi N
of Pecos on St Hwy 63; 4-1/5 mi NE on
FS 223. SEASON: 5/1-10/31; 14-day lmt.
FACILITIES: 15 sites (tr -16); tank drk
wtr, tbls, toil, cga. ACTIVITIES: Hiking; picnicking; fishing. Horseback
riding (r, 5 mi). MISC.: Elev 9400 ft;
8 acres; pets. Pecos Wilderness jump-
off.

Manzanares (Santa Fe NF). 11-3/10 mi
NE of Pecos on FS 86. SEASON: 5/1-10/31;
14-day lmt. FACILITIES: 3 sites (no
tr); no drk wtr; tbls, toil, cga. AC-
TIVITIES: Picnicking. Fishing (2 mi).
MISC.: Elev 8600 ft; 1 acre; pets.

Winsor Creek (Santa Fe NF). 20 mi N
of Pecos on St Hwy 63; 1 mi W on FS
121. SEASON: 5/1-10/31; 14-day lmt.
FACILITIES: 6 sites (tr -16); piped drk
wtr, tbls, toil, cga. ACTIVITIES: Hiking; picnicking; fishing. Horseback
riding (r, 1 mi). MISC.: Elev 8400 ft;
5 acres; pets. Pecos Wilderness jumpoff.

QUESTA

Cabresto Lake (Carson NF). 6 mi NE
of Questa on FS 134; 2 mi NE on FS
134A. SEASON: 5/1-10/31; 14-day lmt.
FACILITIES: 10 sites (tr -16); no drk
wtr; tbls, toil, cga. ACTIVITIES: Boating (no motors in lake); picnicking;
fishing. MISC.: Elev 9500 ft; 3 acres;
pets.

Cebolla Mesa (Carson NF). 4-9/10 mi
W of Questa on St Hwy 3; 3-2/5 mi W
on FS 29. SEASON: 4/1-10/31; 14-day
lmt. FACILITIES: 5 sites (tr -32); no
drk wtr; tbls, toil, cga. ACTIVITIES:
Picnicking; fishing. MISC.: Elev 7300
ft; 2 acres; pets.

Rio Grande Wild River Area (BLM).
There are six campgrounds within this
area which can be reached by going
3 mi N of Questa on St Hwy 3; and
then 1/5 mi NW past Cerro, on St Hwy
378. The 47 cumulative sites are technically open all year; however, the
area receives heavy snow from November
-March;(14-day lmt). There is a Visitor
Center and Administrative Site. Primitive;
pack-in camping is available by
descending into the canyon; shelter
areas are available. Information/Map:
Bureau Land Management; PO Box 1449;
Santa Fe, New Mexico 87501.

Big Arsenic Spring Campground (Rio
Grande Wild River). FACILITIES: Toil,
tbls, shelters. ACTIVITIES: Hunting;
picnicking; fishing; floating; hiking;
white water boating.

Chiflo Campground (Rio Grande Wild
River). FACILITIES: Shelters, tbls,
toil, cga. ACTIVITIES: Hunting; picnicking; fishing; hiking; floating;
white water boating.

El Aguaje Campground (Rio Grande Wild
River). FACILITIES: Shelters, tbls, toil,
cga. ACTIVITIES: Hiking; hunting; picnicking; fishing; floating; white water
boating.

La Junta Campground (Rio Grande Wild
River). FACILITIES: Shelters; tbls, toil,
cga. ACTIVITIES: Hunting; picnicking;
fishing; hiking; floating; white water
boating.

Little Arsenic Spring Campground (Rio
Grande Wild River). FACILITIES: Shelters,
tbls, toil, cga. ACTIVITIES: Hunting;
picnicking; fishing; hiking; floating;
white water boating.

Sheep Crossing Campground (Rio Grande
Wild River). FACILITIES: Shelters, tbls,
toil, cga. ACTIVITIES: Hunting; hiking;
picnicking; fishing; floating; white
water boating.

RED RIVER

Elephant Rock (Carson NF). 2-4/5 mi W
of Red River on St Hwy 38. SEASON: 5/1-
10/15; 14-day lmt. FACILITIES: 22 sites
(tr -16); flush toil, no drk wtr; cga,
tbls. Dump (1 mi). Showers/ice/food/store
/laundry/gas (3 mi). ACTIVITIES: Picnicking; fishing. Horseback riding (r,
3 mi). MISC.: Elev 8300 ft; 2 acres;
pets. Stream.

Goose Lake (Carson NF). 3/10 mi SE of
Red River on St Hwy 38; 3/10 mi SW on
FS 58; 8 mi SW on FS 486. SEASON: 6/1-
10/31; 14-day lmt. FACILITIES: 4 sites
(no tr); no drk wtr; tbls, toil, cga.
ACTIVITIES: Fishing; picnicking. MISC.:
Elev 12700 ft; 1 acre; pets. Lake. Jeep
road access.

Junebug (Carson NF). 2-1/5 mi W of Red
River on St Hwy 38. SEASON: 5/1-10/31;
14-day lmt. FACILITIES: 14 sites (tr -22);
no drk wtr; tbls, toil, cga. Showers/ice/
food/store/gas (2 mi). ACTIVITIES: Fishing; picnicking. Horseback riding (r,
2 mi). MISC.: Elev 8500 ft; 5 acres;
pets. Stream.

RESERVE

Ben Lilly (Gila NF). 5 mi S of Reserve
on St Hwy 435; 28-1/2 mi SE on FS 6141;
12-1/2 mi SW on St Hwy 78; 1 mi W on
FS 6507. SEASON: 4/1-11/25. FACILITIES:
6 sites (tr -16); no drk wtr; tbls, toil,
cga. ACT: Picnicking; fishing. Horseback riding (1 mi). MISC.: Elev 8100
ft; 2 acres; pets. This site is at
Northern edge of Gila Wilderness.

Gilita (Gila NF). 5 mi S of Reserve on St Hwy 435; 28-1/2 mi SE on FS 6141; 11-1/2 mi SW on St Hwy 78. **SEASON:** 4/1-11/25. **FACILITIES:** 6 sites (tr -16); no drk wtr; tbls, toil, cga. **ACTIVITIES:** Hiking; picnicking. Horseback riding/fishing (1 mi). **MISC.:** Elev 8100 ft; 2 acres; pets. Near the edge of Gila Wilderness.

Pueblo Park (Gila NF). 8 mi SW of Reserve on St Hwy 12; 4 mi SW on US 180; 6 mi SW on FS 1285. **SEASON:** 4/1-11/30; 14-day lmt. **FACILITIES:** 6 sites (tr -16); no drk wtr; tbls, toil, cga. **ACTIVITIES:** Hiking; picnicking; rockhounding. **MISC.:** Elev 7000 ft; 7 acres; pets. Scenic. Nature Trails.

Willow Creek (Gila NF). 5 mi S of Reserve on St Hwy 435; 28-1/2 mi SE on FS 6141; 12-1/2 mi SW on St Hwy 78. **SEASON:** 4/1-11/25. **FACILITIES:** 6 sites (tr -16); no drk wtr; tbls, toil, cga. **ACTIVITIES:** Hiking; picnicking; fishing. Horseback riding (1 mi). **MISC.:** Elev 8000 ft; 2 acres; pets. Site at northern edge of Gila Wilderness.

RODARTE

Hodges (NF). 3 mi E of Rodarte on St Hwy 73; 3 mi S on FS 2116; 1/2 mi S on FS 2702. **SEASON:** 5/26-9/10; 14-day lmt. **FACILITIES:** 4 sites; no drk wtr; tbls, toil, cga, f. Food/laundry/ice (3 mi). **ACTIVITIES:** Picnicking; fishing. **MISC.:** Elev 8200 ft; 12 acres; pets.

ROSWELL

Two Rivers Dam (COE). 14 mi W of Roswell on US 70/380 to access road; 7 mi S on access rd. **SEASON:** All year; 14-day lmt. **FACILITIES:** Combination sites; toil (at overlook), picnic sites. **ACTIVITIES:** Picnicking. **MISC.:** Elev 3950; pets. The reservoir is dry except when used for flood control;drk wtr.

ROY

Mills Canyon (Cibola NF). 10 mi NW of Roy on St Hwy 39; 9 mi W on FS 600 (primitve access rd). **SEASON:** 5/15-9/15; 14-day lmt. **FACILITIES:** 8 sites (no tr); no drk wtr, tbls, toil, cga. **ACTIVITIES:** Picnicking. Fishing (1 mi). **MISC.:** Elev 5600 ft; 3 acres; pets.

RUIDOSO

Cedar Creek Campground (Lincoln NF). 1-1/5 mi N of Ruidoso on St Hwy 37; 3/5 mi NW on FS 88. **SEASON:** 4/1-10/31; 14-day lmt. **FACILITIES:** 36 sites (tr -16); well drk wtr, tbls, toil, cga. Store/gas/ice/food (2 mi). Laundry/dump (2 mi). **ACTIVITIES:** Picnicking. Swimming/horseback riding (r,4 mi). **MISC.:** Elev 6900 ft; 11 acres; pets. Scenic.

Monjeau Campground (Lincoln NF). 5 mi N of Ruidoso on St Hwy 37; 5 mi NW on FS 117. **SEASON:** 5/15-9/15. **FACILITIES:** 4 sites (tr -16); tbls, toil, cga. Store/gas (5 mi). **ACTIVITIES:** Picnicking; hiking. **MISC.:** Elev 9500 ft; 2 acres; pets. Crest Trail nearby. Panoramic view. No drk wtr.

Oak Grove Campground (Lincoln NF). 5 mi N of Ruidoso on St Hwy 37; 4 mi W on FS 127. **SEASON:** 5/15-10/31; 14-day lmt. **FACILITIES:** 29 sites (tr -16); no drk wtr, cga, tbls. **ACTIVITIES:** Picnicking. Fishing (3 mi). **MISC.:** Elev 9000 ft; 6 acres; pets. Scenic. Quiet mountain setting.

Skyline Campground (Lincoln NF). 5 mi N of Ruidoso on St Hwy 37; 4 mi NW on FS 117. **SEASON:** 5/15-9/15; 14-day lmt. **FACILITIES:** 17 sites (tr -16); no drk wtr, tbls, toil, cga, f. Storage (4 mi). **ACTIVITIES:** Picnicking. **MISC.:** Elev 9000 ft; 4 acres; pets. Panoramic views of Eagle Creek Drainage.

SAN LORENZO

Iron Creek (Gila NF). 15-1/2 mi NE of San Lorenzo on St Hwy 90. **SEASON:** 4/1-11/30. **FACILITIES:** 15 sites (tr -22). **ACTIVITIES:** Hiking; picnicking. **MISC.:** Elev 7300 ft; 7 acres; pets. Nature trails. On scenic route between I-25 and US 180.

SANTA FE

Aspen Basin (Santa Fe NF). From Santa Fe, 1/5 mi N on St Hwy 22; 16 mi NE on St Hwy 475. **SEASON:** 5/15-10/31; 14-day lmt. **FACILITIES:** 14 sites (tr -16); no drk wtr; tbls, toil, cga. **ACTIVITIES:** Hiking; picnicking. **MISC.:** Elev 10,300 ft; 5 acres; pets. Scenic. Stream. Pegono Wilderness jump-off.

Big Tesuque (Santa Fe NF). 1/5 mi N of Santa Fe on St Hwy 22; 12-1/10 mi NE on St Hwy 475. **SEASON:** 5/15-10/31; 14-day lmt. **FACILITIES:** 5 sites (no tr); no drk wtr; tbls, toil, cga. **ACTIVITIES:** Picnicking. Horseback riding (r, 5 mi). **MISC.:** Elev 9700 ft; 4 acres; pets. Scenic.

SANTA ROSA

James Wallace Memorial Park. 1 mi from Santa Rosa on I-40. **SEASON:** All year. **FACILITIES:** Combination sites; toil, shelters. **ACTIVITIES:** Picnicking.

SILVER CITY

Cherry Creek (Gila NF). 13-1/5 mi NW of Silver City on St Hwy 15. **SEASON:** 4/1-11/30. **FACILITIES:** 12 sites (tr -22); well drk wtr, tbls, toil, cga. Ice/food/store/gas (5 mi). **ACTIVITIES:** Picnicking. **MISC.:** Elev 7400 ft; 6 acres; pets. Stream.

See page 7 for KEY TO ABBREVIATIONS.

Divide (Gila NF). 28 mi SW of Silver City on St Hwy 90. SEASON: All year. FACILITIES: 4 sites (tr -22); no drk wtr; tbls, toil, cga. ACTIVITIES: Picnicking. Horseback riding (r, 1 mi). MISC.: Elev 6200 ft; 2 acres; pets.

Forks Campground (Gila Cliff Dwellings NM). 44 mi N of Silver City on St Hwy 15; located near the main Gila Bridge. [NOTE: St Hwy 15 is a 2-lane blacktop which was only recently a rough winding trail. The trip through this mountainous terrain takes about 2 hrs because of the road's condition, trailers more than 20' are recommended to use St Hwy 35 thru the scenic Mimbres Valley instead of St Hwy 15. This is reached from St Hwy 61, N from San Lorenzo, which is 19 mi E of Silver City on St Hwy 90.] SEASON: All year (except during flood conditions). FACILITIES: 5 primitive sites; no drk wtr. Ice/food/store (5 mi). ACTIVITIES: Hiking; picnicking. Fishing (nearby). MISC.: View the Cliff Dwellings nearby (100-400 A.D.).

Grapevine Campground (Gila Cliff Dwellings NM). 44 mi N of Silver City on St Hwy 15; located at main Gila Bridge. [NOTE: St Hwy 15 is a 2-lane blacktop which was only recently a rough winding trail. The trip through this mountainous terrain takes about 2 hours. Because of the rd's condition, trailers more than 20' are recommended to use St Hwy 35 through the scenic Mimbres Valley instead of St Hwy 15. This is reached from St Hwy 61, north from San Lorenzo, which is 19 mi E of Silver City on St Hwy 90.] SEASON: All year (except during flood conditions). FACILITIES: 5 primitive sites; toil, no drk wtr. Store/ice/food (5 mi). ACTIVITIES: Hiking; picnicking. Fishing nearby. MISC.: View the Cliff Dwellings nearby (100-400 A.D.).

Picnic Springs (Gila NF). 29 mi SW of Silver City on St Hwy 90. SEASON: All year. FACILITIES: 4 sites (tr -22); toil. ACTIVITIES: Picnicking. MISC.: Elev 5700 ft; pets.

Scorpion (Gila Cliff Dwellings NM). 44 mi N of Silver City on St Hwy 15. [Note: St Hwy 15 is a 2-lane blacktop which was only recently a rough winding trail. The trip through this mountainous terrain takes about 2 hrs. Because of the road's condition, trailers more than 20' are recommended to use St Hwy 35 through the scenic Mimbres Valley instead of St Hwy 15. This is reached from St Hwy 61, north from San Lorenzo, which is 19 mi E of Silver City on St Hwy 90.] SEASON: All year (except during flood conditions). FACILITIES: 10 sites (tr -22); flush toil, dump, tbls, toil, cga. Water (available at tr. dump site; except during Winter months).

Store/food/ice/gas (5 mi). ACTIVITIES: Picnicking; hiking. Fishing (1 mi). Horseback riding (1 mi) and rental (5 mi). MISC.: Elev 5700 ft; 5 acres; pets. One of the 22 access areas to Gila NF Wilderness and Primitive Areas. View the Cliff Dwellings nearby (100-400 A.D.).

TAJIQUE

Tajique (Cibola NF). 2-3/5 mi NW of Tajique on FS 55. SEASON: 4/1-10/31; 14-day lmt. FACILITIES: 5 sites (tr -22); tbls, toil, cga, f. Store/ice/gas (3 mi). ACTIVITIES: Hiking; picnicking. MISC.: Elev 6800 ft; 2 acres; pets. Nature Trails. No drk wtr.

TAOS

Capulin (Carson NF). 7 mi SE of Taos on US 64. SEASON: 5/1-10/31; 14-day lmt. FACILITIES: 9 sites (tr -16); no drk wtr; tbls, flush toil, cga, f. Food/store/gas (1 mi). ACTIVITIES: Picnicking; fishing. MISC.: Elev 8000 ft; 6 acres; pets. Stream.

Cuchilla (Carson NF). 4 mi NW of Taos on St Hwy 3; 5 mi N on St Hwy 150; 4 mi NE on St Hwy 230. SEASON: 5/1-10/31; 14-day lmt. FACILITIES: 3 sites (tr -16); no drk wtr; tbls, toil, cga, f. Gas (3 mi). Store (4 mi). ACTIVITIES: Picnicking; fishing. MISC.: Elev 7800 ft; 1 acre; pets.

El Nogal (Carson NF). 2-9/10 mi SE of Taos on US 64. SEASON: 4/1-10/31; 14-day lmt. FACILITIES: 8 sites (tr -16); flush toil, no drk wtr; cga, f, tbls. Showers/store/ice/food/gas (3 mi). ACTIVITIES: Hiking; picnicking; fishing. Horseback riding (r, 3 mi). MISC.: Elev 7200 ft; 2 acres; pets. Visitor Center (3 mi). Historic. Nature Trails. Stream. Trailhead for south boundary and Devi Saders Trails.

La Sombra (Carson NF). 7-1/2 mi SE of Taos on US 64. SEASON: 4/30-9/30; 14-day lmt. FACILITIES: 13 sites (tr -16); flush toil, cga, f, no drk wtr. Store/food (1 mi). ACTIVITIES: Horseback riding; picnicking; fishing. MISC.: Elev 7800 ft; 3 acres; pets.

La Vinateria (Carson NF). 3-3/10 mi SE of Taos on US 64. SEASON: 4/30-9/30; 14-day lmt. FACILITIES: 8 sites (tr -16); flush toil. Showers/ice/store/food (3 mi). ACTIVITIES: Horseback riding; picnicking; fishing. MISC.: Elev 7300 ft; 3 acres; pets.

Las Petacas (Carson NF). 4-3/10 mi SE of Taos on US 64. SEASON: 4/? 10/31; 14-day lmt. FACILITIES: 7 sites (tr -16); no drk wtr; tbls, toil, cga, f. Showers/ice/laundry (4 mi). Store/food/gas (3 mi). ACTIVITIES: Picnicking; fishing.

Horseback riding (r, 4 mi). MISC.: Elev 7400 ft; 2 acres; pets. Historic. Visitor Center (4 mi).

Leroux (Carson NF). 4 mi NW of Taos on St Hwy 3; 5 mi N on St Hwy 150; 10-2/5 mi NE on St Hwy 230. SEASON: 5/1-10/31; 14-day lmt. FACILITIES: 4 sites (tr -16); no drk wtr; tbls, toil, cga. ACTIVITIES: Picnicking; fishing. MISC.: Elev 9200 ft; 3 acres; pets. Stream.

Lower Hondo (Carson NF). 4 mi NW of Taos on St Hwy 3; 5 mi N on St Hwy 150; 3-1/5 mi NE on St Hwy 230. SEASON: 5/1-10/31; 14-day lmt. FACILITIES: 5 sites (tr -16); no drk wtr; tbls, toil, cga. Gas (2 mi). Store (3 mi). ACTIVITIES: Picnicking; fishing. MISC.: Elev 7700 ft; 1 acre; pets. Stream.

Twining (Carson NF). 4 mi NW of Taos on St Hwy 3; 5 mi N on St Hwy 150; 10-7/10 mi NE on St Hwy 230. SEASON: 5/1-10/31; 14-day lmt. FACILITIES: 4 sites (tr -16); no drk wtr; tbls, toil, cga. ACTIVITIES: Picnicking; fishing. MISC.: Elev 9300 ft; 3 acres; pets. Stream.

Upper Cuchilla (Carson NF). 4 mi NW of Taos on St Hwy 3; 5 mi N on St Hwy 150; 4-2/5 mi NE of Taos on St Hwy 230. SEASON: 5/1-10/31; 14-day lmt. FACILITIES: 3 sites (tr -16); no drk wtr; tbls, toil, cga. Gas (4 mi). Store (5 mi). ACTIVITIES: Picnicking; fishing. MISC.: Elev 8000 ft; 1 acre; pets. Stream.

TATUM

City Park. Off St Hwy 380 in Tatum. SEASON: All year. FACILITIES: Combination sites. ACTIVITIES: Picnicking.

THOREAU

Ojo Redondo (Cibola NF). 24-1/2 mi SE on FS 178; 3-1/5 mi E on FS 480. SEASON: 5/1-9/1; 14-day lmt. FACILITIES: 20 sites (tr -22); no drk wtr; tbls, toil, cga, f. ACTIVITIES: Picnicking. MISC.: Elev 8900 ft; 10 acres; pets. Isolated site.

THREE RIVERS

Three Rivers Campground (Lincoln NF). 15 mi E of Three Rivers on FS 408. SEASON: All year; 14-day lmt. FACILITIES: 6 sites (tr -16); no drk wtr; tbls, toil, cga, f. ACTIVITIES: Hiking; mountain climbing; picnicking. Fishing (1 mi). MISC.: Elev 6400 ft; 10 acres; pets. Good cool weather campground. Trailhead into White Mountain Wilderness. Scenic.

Three Rivers Petroglyph Site (BLM). 5 mi E of Three Rivers, off St Hwy 54 on a gravel country road. SEASON: All year. FACILITIES: 6 sites; tbls, toil, cga, picnic shelters, drk wtr (available at the picnic sites). ACTIVITIES: Hiking; picnicking. MISC.: 120 acres. The area has extensive interpretive displays. See carvings made with stone tools (900 - 1400 A.D.). The site contains more than 500 petroglyphs. Although Rattlesnakes are not common in this area, stay on the trail, don't sit on rocks, and be alert.

TIJERAS

Cedro Peak (Cibola NF). 5-1/2 mi SE of Tijeras on St Hwy 10; 1-1/2 mi NE on FS 252. SEASON: 3/1-11/30; 14-day lmt. FACILITIES: 50 sites (no tr); no drk wtr; toil, cga, no tbls. ACTIVITIES: Horseback riding (r, 3 mi). MISC.: Elev 6500 ft; 10 acres; pets. Reservations advisable. For youth group overnight camping. Minimum sanitation. No developed units. Group use only.

TORREON

Capillo Peak (Cibola NF). 6-1/2 mi SW of Torreon on St Hwy 10; 8-1/2 mi NW on FS 245. SEASON: 5/1-9/30; 14-day lmt. FACILITIES: 7 sites (tr -16); tbls, toil, cga, f, no drk wtr. ACTIVITIES: Hiking; picnicking. MISC.: Pets. Located on east boundary of Manzano Wilderness. Capillo Lo Rough Mountain Road (1/2 mi). No motors.

New Canyon (Cibola NF). 6-1/2 mi SW of Torreon on St Hwy 10; 5 mi W on FS 245. SEASON: 4/1-10/31; 14-day lmt. FACILITIES: 5 sites (tr -22); piped drk wtr; tbls, toil, cga, f. ACTIVITIES: Picnicking. MISC.: Elev 7800 ft; 2 acres; pets.

TRES PIEDRAS

Hopewell Lake (Carson NF). 22 mi W of Tres Piedras on US 64; 1/10 mi W on FS 91B. SEASON: 5/1-9/15; 14-day lmt. FACILITIES: 6 sites, no drk wtr; tbls, toil, cga. ACTIVITIES: Boating (16 ft or smaller); picnicking; fishing. MISC.: Elev 9000 ft; 10 acres; pets. Scenic. 13 acre Hopewell Lake.

Laguna Larga (Carson NF). 10 mi N of Tres Piedras on US 285; 11-1/2 mi NW on FS 87; 3-2/5 mi NE on FS 78. SEASON: 5/15-10/30; 14-day lmt. FACILITIES: 8 sites (tr -22); no drk wtr; tbls, toil, cga. ACTIVITIES: Boating (lake small: advise 16 ft boat or smaller); picnicking; fishing. MISC.: Elev 9000 ft; 10 acres; pets. Road is in poor condition during rainy season.

Lagunitas (Carson NF). 10 mi N of Tres Piedras on US 285; 26 mi NW on FS 87; 4/5 mi NW on FS 87B. SEASON: 5/25-9/15; 14-day lmt. FACILITIES: 12 sites (tr -16); piped drk wtr, tbls, toil, cga.

See page 7 for KEY TO ABBREVIATIONS.

ACTIVITIES: Picnicking; fishing. MISC.: Elev 10,400 ft; 5 acres; pets. Scenic. Road poor during rainy season.

TULAROSA

City Park. Behind Police Station. SEASON: All year; 1-night lmt. FACILITIES: Self-contained sites.

VADITO

Agua Piedra (Carson NF). 3 mi E of Cadito on St Hwy 75; 7 mi E on St Hwy 3. SEASON: 5/1-9/30; ; 14-day lmt. FACILITIES: 10 sites (tr -22); flush toil, no drk wtr; cga, f, tbls. Store/ice/food/gas (1 mi). ACTIVITIES: Hiking; picnicking; fishing. MISC.: Elev 8100 ft; 6 acres; pets.

Angostura (Carson NF). 3 mi E of Vadito on St Hwy 75; 11 mi E on St Hwy 3. SEASON: 5/1-9/30; 14-day lmt. FACILITIES: 11 sites (tr -16); flush

toil, no drk wtr, cga, f, tbls. Store/ice/gas (3 mi). Food (5 mi). ACTIVITIES: Picnicking; fishing. MISC.: Elev 9200 ft; 10 acres; pets. Stream.

La Junta Canyon (Carson NF). 3 mi E of Vadito on St Hwy 75; 8-1/2 mi E on St Hwy 3; 3-1/2 mi N on FS 2761. SEASON: 5/26-9/10; 14-day lmt. FACILITIES: 5 sites (tr -16); no drk wtr; f. ACTIVITIES: Picnicking; fishing. MISC.: Elev 9200 ft; 4 acres; pets. Store/food/ice (5 mi).

Upper La Junta (Carson NF). 3 mi E of Vadito on St Hwy 75; 8-1/2 mi E on St Hwy 3; 4 mi N on FS 2761. SEASON: 5/1-9/30; 14-day lmt. FACILITIES: 8 sites (tr -16); no drk wtr; tbls, toil, cga, f. Store/gas/food/ice (5 mi). ACTIVITIES: Hiking; picnicking; fishing. MISC.: Elev 9400 ft; 8 acres; pets.

NEW YORK

GENERAL STATE INFORMATION

Miscellaneous

Toll-Free Number for Travel Information:
    1-800-833-3456 [calling outside of NY]
    1-800-342-3717 [calling within NY]
Right Turns on Red: Permitted after
    full stop, unless otherwise posted.
STATE CAPITOL: Albany
STATE NICKNAME: Empire State
STATE MOTTO: "Excelsior, Ever Upward"
STATE BIRD: Eastern Bluebird
STATE FLOWER: Rose
STATE TREE: Sugar Maple

State Parks and State Forest Preserves

Although camping fees range from $3.50 to $5.00 per night, disabled New York residents eligible for the Access Pass (see below) may camp free of charge in both State Parks and State Forest Preserve areas. PETS: Allowed everywhere EXCEPT Long Island, Palisades and Taconic State Park Regions, on the Lake George Islands, or in the State Forest day-use areas. Where they are allowed, proof of a currently effective rabies inoculation is required for dogs. FURTHER INFORMATION: Office of Parks and Recreation; South Mall; Albany, NY 12223; OR, New York State Department of Environmental Conservation (DEC); Division of Lands and Forests; 50 Wolf Road; Albany, NY 12201.

Access Pass for New York Disabled Residents

It provides permanently disabled New York residents free use of parks, historic sites, and recreation facilities operated by the New York State Office of Parks and Recreation and the Department of Environmental Conservation. It covers all services including camping.

To qualify, the New York resident must have one of the following permanent disabilities: Amputee (loss of any part of arm or leg, excluding extremities of hands and feet); Blind (vision of not more than 20/200); Disabled Veteran (any veteran of the wars of the U.S. who has at any time been awarded by the Federal Government an allowance towards the purchase of an automobile or is eligible for such an award); Non-ambulatory (unable to move about without wheelchair, crutches or other device of a similar nature; suffered severe permanent damage to or has a severely limiting condition of the pulmonary or cardio-vascular system; permanent neuro-muscular dysfunction which severely limits mobilityi). Further information: New York State Department of Environmental Conservation; 50 Wolf Road; Albany, NY 12201.

NEW YORK

Rest Areas

Overnight parking in rest areas is permitted for genuine emergencies only (not encouraged).

Primitive Camping on Forest Preserve Lands

Backpackers may camp anywhere, not otherwise posted, on State Reforestation Areas. Regulations vary on Forest Preserve lands but generally camping is permitted except above 4000 feet altitude. It is best to check with the local Forest Ranger before entering an area. It is in the camper's best interest to register with the local Ranger before backpacking on any State lands. Further information: New York State Department of Environmental Conservation; Division of Lands and Forests; 50 Wolf Road; Albany, NY 12201.

The Department of Environmental Conservation is responsible for the administration of 2.6 million acres of State-owned land located within the Forest Preserve Park Region. A minute portion of this area is utilized as developed campgrounds. At all these developed sites there is a service fee. Camping is permitted free of charge on other State lands with minor exceptions. Since the State lands are mixed with private holdings, specific directions are difficult to convey. Most road maps of the State show the Preserve boundaries. Specific land ownership patterns are shown on the County Maps. These maps are available from the Department for 50¢ each.

Outside the Preserve Region, this Department administers almost 700,000 acres of State Reforestation areas. Again, with minor exceptions, these areas are open to camping. These areas are shown on the County Maps also.

Trails in New York State

The Department of Environmental Conservation offers a number of brochures detailing trails throughout the State. These free brochures include maps, general information, and specifics on trail campsites. Write to them and indicate which area of the state you will be traveling in. Further information: New York State Department of Environmental Conservation; Division of Lands and Forests; 50 Wolf Road; Albany, NY 12201.

Mount Marcy Trails and Camping

Mount Marcy is the highest peak in the Adirondacks and in New York State, with an elevation of 5344. There are several well-marked trails which converge at or near the mountain's peak. A free booklet entitled TRAILS TO MARCY includes a map and locates lean-tos (with toilet and fireplace) along the trails. During peak season, carry a light plastic fly for shelter in case all lean-tos are filled. For information: New York State Department of Environmental Conservation; Division of Lands and Forests; 50 Wolf Road; Albany, NY 12201.

Catskill Trails

This vast forest area has been cut by a network of trails which reaches most of the major mountain peaks. Trails are maintained in passable condition year round. They are clearly marked. Camping, picnicking, hunting, fishing, hiking. Pets are permitted. Registration booths are available at important trail access points and junctions. Please sign in before embarking on your hike. For a free, detailed booklet that describes and locates hiking trails and lean-tos (which have a fireplace and toilet), write to: New York State Department of Environmental Conservation; 21 South Putt Corners Road; New Paltz, NY 12561 [914/255-5453; ext. 79].

Appalachian Trail

More than 2000 miles long, the Appalachian Trail (from Maine to Georgia) is the longest continuous marked trail in the world.

CAMPING: More than 200 open-front shelters/lean-tos are spaced approximately 10 miles apart on the Trail (one-day intervals). As they are occupied on a first-come first-served basis, carry a tent in case the shelters are full. Potable spring water is usually available at each site, but should be purified by tablets or boiling. And always "pack it in, pack it out".

PERMITS: No permit is required to hike the Trail. However, camping permits must be obtained for overnight stays in Shenandoah NP (Luray, VA 22835) and Great Smokey Mountains NP (Gatlinburg, TN 37733). These are free of charge and available from the ranger stations or by mail. A free camping permit must be obtained for overnight stays in White Mountain National Forest Restricted Use Area (PO Box 638; Laconia, NH 03246).

NEW YORK

APPALACHIAN TRAIL CONFERENCE: A private, nonprofit, national organization which represents citizen's interest in the Appalachian Trail. They offer detailed guidebooks and maps for sale, as well as the A.T. Data Book which gives the location and distances between shelters and certain post offices, supply points, water sources, lodging and meals. For more information on this organization, write to them at: PO Box 236; Harpers Ferry, WV 25425.

Canoeing and Camping along the Delaware River

A set of 10 maps (OUTDOOR RECREATION MAPS OF THE DELAWARE RIVER) which describe the river in detail (200 miles, from Hancock, NY, to Trenton, NJ), including camp-sites, can be obtained for $1.00/set from: Delaware River Basin Commission; PO Box 360; Trenton, NJ 08603.

Adirondack Canoe Routes

A brochure/map is available free of charge which describes the network of canoe routes in the Adirondack region, as well as canoe camping information. Write to: New York State Department of Environmental Conservation; Division of Lands and Forests; 50 Wolf Road; Albany, NY 12201.

INFORMATION SOURCES

Maps

The following maps are available from **Forsyth Travel Library** (see order form in Appendix B):

> State of New York [Up-to-date, showing all principal roads, points of interest, sports areas, parks, airports, mileage, etc. Full color.]

> Completely indexed city maps, including all airports, lakes, rivers, etc., of numerous cities in New York.

State Information

Travel Bureau; New York State Department of Commerce; 99 Washington Avenue; Albany, NY 12210.
Chamber of Commerce of the State of New York; 65 Liberty Street; New York, NY.
Division of Fish and Wildlife; Department of Environmental Conservation; 50 Wolf Road; Albany, NY 12233.
Commerce and Industry Association of New York; 99 Church Street; New York, NY.
Department of Commerce and Industrial Development; 415 Madison Avenue; New York, NY.
Department of Commerce and Public Events; 521 Fifth Avenue; New York, NY.
The New York State Travel Center; 6 East 48th Street; New York, NY.

City Information

Buffalo Area Chamber of Commerce; 238 Main Street; Buffalo, NY 14202.
Buffalo Convention and Tourist Bureau; 155 Franklin Street; Buffalo, NY 14202.
Lake Placid Chamber of Commerce; Olympic Arena; Lake Placid, NY 12946.
New York City Junior Chamber of Commerce; 1 Liberty; New York, NY.
New York Convention and Visitors Bureau; 90 East 42nd Street; New York, NY.
Niagara Falls Area Chamber of Commerce; 45 Falls Street; Niagara Falls, NY 14303.
Niagara Falls Convention and Visitors Bureau; 45 Falls Street; Niagara Falls, NY 14303.
Syracuse Chamber of Commerce; 351 South Warren Street; Syracuse, NY 13202.
Rochester Chamber of Commerce; 55 St. Paul Street; Rochester, NY 14604.

Department of Environmental Conservation Regional Headquarters

Region 1: SUNY, Building 40; Stony Brook, NY 11790 [516/751-7900].
Region 2: 2 World Trade Center; New York, NY 10047 [212/488-2755].
Region 3: 21 South Putt Corners Road; New Paltz, NY 12561 [914/255-5453].
Region 4: 50 Wolf Road; Albany, NY 12233 [518/457-5861].
Region 5: Ray Brook, NY 12977 [518/891-1370].
Region 6: 317 Washington Street; Watertown, NY 13601 [315/782-0100].
Region 7: 7481 Henry Clay Blvd.; Liverpool, NY 13088 [315/473-8301].
Region 8: PO Box 57; Avon, NY 14414 [716/226-2466].
Region 9: 584 Delaware Avenue; Buffalo, NY 14202 [716/842-5824].

NEW YORK

State Park and Recreation Commission

Office of Parks and Recreation; South Mall; Albany, NY 12223.
New York State Parks and Recreation; State Park and Recreation Commission for City of New York; 1700 Broadway; New York, NY 10019.

REGIONAL OFFICES:

Allegany State Park and Recreation Commission; Salamanca, NY 14779.
Central New York Park and Recreation Commission; Jamesville, NY 13078.
Finger Lakes State Park and Recreation Commission; Trumansburg, NY 14886.
Genesee State Park and Recreation Commission; Castile, NY 14427.
Long Island State Park and Recreation Commission; Babylon, NY 11702.
Niagara Frontier State Park and Recreation Commission; Niagara Falls, NY 14303.
Palisades Interstate Park Commission; Bear Mountain, NY 10911.
Saratoga-Capital District State Park and Recreation Commission; Saratoga Springs, NY 12866.
Taconic State Park and Recreation Commission; Staatsburg, NY 12580.
Thousand Islands State Park and Recreation Commission; Alexandria Bay, NY 13607.

FREE CAMPGROUNDS

CRANBERRY LAKE

Cranberry Lake Region Trails. Approximately 1½ mi from Cranberry Lake on the Lone Pine Road.

Under the jursidiction of New York State Department of Environmental Conservation, Cranberry Lake is the northern gateway to the Five Ponds Wilderness Area. It covers an area of 11 square miles and has a 55-mile shoreline (of which over 40 are State owned). This is one of the largest remote areas remaining in the State. Trout fishing.

Over 50 miles of well-maintained hiking trails and 13 Adirondack lean-tos (open camps). Normally a pit toil, tbls, and cga are provided, and potable water is available.

CANOE TRIP: The Oswegatchie River provides a canoe trip of approximately 20 mi upstream from the lake. There are 5 lean-tos located adjacent to the river.....one at Griffin Rapids, approximately 5 mi from Inlet; one at Cage Lake Spring hole; two at High Falls; and one on the N shore of Inlet to Cranberry Lake one mi below the Ranger School. Parking space and boat launching is available at Inlet free of charge.

For a free detailed map, write to the NYS Dept. of Environmental Conservation; 30 Court Street; PO Box 109; Canton, NY 13617.

EDWARDS

Huckleberry Lake. Approximately 5 mi W of Edwards. The following hiking trails offer campsites for backpackers. Fishing for bass in Huckleberry Lake is very good. Hiking/camping is permitted all year, but winter snows might make the trails impassable. 3-day lmt. Additional info: New York State Dept. of Environmental Conservation; 30 Court Street; PO Box 109; Canton, NY 13617.

Huckleberry Lake to Talcville. The trail is approximately 1 mi long. It is marked by round yellow trail markers. Good fishing in Huckleberry Lake (bass). A beaver pond can be seen on the E side of the trail. Lean-to, tbls, toil, cga, drk wtr are available at Huckleberry Lake.

Moon Lake to Huckleberry Lake. The trail is approximately 1½ mi long. It is marked by yellow trail markers posted on trees along the trail. There are blueberries all along the trail. A beaver pond can be seen on the trail. Lean-to, tbls, toil, cga, drk wtr are available at Moon Lake and at Huckleberry Lake.

Moon Lake to Talcville. The trail is approximately 2 mi Long. It is marked by round red trail markers. Blueberries can be found all along this trail. Lean-to, tbls, toil, cga, drk wtr is available at Moon Lake.

Pond Road to Wolf Lake. The trail is approximately 3½ mi long. One mi into the trail there is a stone bridge. 2½ mi into the trail there is a bridge made up of logs. At this locations there is also a beaver dam. If you look hard enough you will find blueberries all along the trail. The trail is marked by round yellow trail markers nailed to trees; other markers include orange arrows painted on rock clearings. Lean-to, tbls, toil, cga, drk wtr are available at Wolf Lake.

Wolf Lake to Moon Lake. The trail is approximately ½ mi long, from Wolf Lake to Moon Lake. The trail is marked by round red trail markers. All along the trail there are blueberries. At Moon Lake the berries are much bigger than those along the trail. Lean-to, tbls, toil, cga, drk wtr are available at Wolf Lake and at Moon Lake.

FULTONVILLE

Truck Stops of America. New York State Thruway, exit 28, at Fultonville. SEASON: All yr; 1-night lmt. FACILITIES: Spaces for self-contained RVs; food, toil, drk wtr, LP gas.

HUNTINGTON

West Hills (County Park). Go S on State Route 110 from Main Street (in town); right on Walt Whitman Rd; right on West Hills Rd; left on Reservoir Rd. [Information: 516/421-4655.] SEASON: 7-day lmt. FACILITIES: 6 sites; tbls, toil, cga. ACTIVITIES: Horseback riding and rental; hiking; picnicking. MISC.: Nature trails. Pets on leash. Group camping; mainly caters to youth groups.

MAYBROOK

Truck Stops of America. Exit 5 off I-84 (on Neelytown Rd), at Maybrook. SEASON: All yr; 1-night lmt. FACILITIES: Spaces for self-contained RVs; food, toil, drk wtr, gas, mechanic.

NEWBURGH

Walden Thruway Service Truck Stop. New York State Thruway, Milepost 103N, at Newburgh. SEASON: All yr; 1-night lmt. FACILITIES: Spaces for self-contained RVs; food, toil, drk wtr, gas, mechanic.

PATCHOGUE

Watch Hill (Fire Island National Seashore). You can reach this campground by commercial ferry (which is $4.00 round trip) or by private boat. To arrive at the Patchogue Sandspit for the commercial ferry, go S on Ocean Avenue from the Long Island Expressway, Sunrise Highway or Montauk Highway. At the very end of Ocean Avenue, make a right onto Maiden Lane, a right on Cedar Avenue, and a quick left turn on Brightwood St. which runs into the Sandspit. [Ferry information: 516/475-1665.] 20-minute trip. Phone reservation necessary one month in advance 516/597-6633. SEASON: 5/1-10/9; 5-day lmt per season.

FACILITIES: 37 sites; tbls, flush toil, cga, showers, drk wtr. MARINA: Concession operated, 5/13-10/15, 9-9, 516/597-6644, 158 slips, coin-operated pump out, water, partial electricity. VISITOR CENTER: 6/24-9/4, 516/597-6455, information, exhibits, interpretive publications, first

aid. Change rooms on beach. Dog walk area. ACTIVITIES: Swimming; fishing; boating,d (marina); hiking. Daily, 6/24-9/4: walks, talks, evening programs, special events; check bulletin board for schedule. MISC.: No motorized vehicles. Pets are allowed if kept on a leash. LIFEGUARDS (swimming beach): 6/25-9/4, 10-5; weekends, 5/27-6/24 and 9/9-10/1. CONCESSION: 5/13-10/15, 516/597-6644; snack bar, groceries, souvenirs, pay phone. Sunday-Thursday, 8-5:45; Friday, Saturday, holidays, 8am-10pm. Nature trails.

ROCHESTER

Signal Truckstop. 3 mi off I-90, exit 46, on St Hwys 15A/252, at Rochester. SEASON: All yr; 1-night lmt. FACILITIES: Spaces for self-contained RVs; food, toil, drk wtr, LP gas, mechanic.

SAVONA

Sanford Lake Day Use Area. 3 mi N of Savona on St Hwy 226; turn left on Round Lake Road; go approximately 1 mi; road into area is on the left. SEASON: 5/1-12/1. FACILITIES: 10 primitive sites for tents and smaller RVs; tbls, toil, cga, no water. ACTIVITIES: Fishing; swimming; picnicking. MISC.: Located on 50-acre Sanford Lake. Free permit from local Forest Ranger required when camping more than 4 days. Pets.

SYRACUSE

Warner's Thruway Service. New York State Thruway, Milepost 292 (West Warner Service Area), at Syracuse. SEASON: All yr; 1-night lmt. FACILITIES: Spaces for self-contained RVs; food, toil, drk wtr, mechanic.

WATKINS GLEN

*Interloken Trail Shelter (Green Mountain NF). 4 mi NE of Watkins Glen on St Hwy 79; 1 mi N on Co Hwy 4; 1-1/5 mi NE on FS 3; 3/10 mi E on TRAIL. SEASON: 5/1-12/10; 14-day lmt. FACILITIES: 2 tent sites; tbls, toil, cga, f, no drk wtr. Store/gas (2 mi). Food/ice/laundry (3 mi). ACTIVITIES: Hiking; picnicking; berry-picking. Fishing (1 mi). MISC.: Elev 1700 ft; 1 acre; pets on leash.

Sugar Hill Recreation Area. 7 mi W of Watkins Glen on Co Rds 28 and 23; turn left on Co Rd 21; go approximately 1 mi and turn right on Tower Hill Rd. Entrance is on left, ½ mi at top of hill. SEASON: 5/1-11/1. FACILITIES: 20 primitive sites; tbls, toil, cga, state-approved water. ACTIVITIES: Hiking; horseback riding. Hunting (during season; available on 10,000 acres of adjacent State land). Picnicking. MISC.: Horse and hiking trails. Remote lean-tos on trails. Fire tower area. Pets allowed on leash.

NORTH CAROLINA

Miscellaneous

Toll-Free Number for Travel Information:
  1-800-238-1000
Right Turns on Red: Permitted after
  full stop, unless otherwise posted.
STATE CAPITOL: Raleigh
STATE NICKNAME: Tarheel State
STATE MOTTO: "To Be Rather
               Than To Seem"
STATE BIRD: Cardinal
STATE FLOWER: Dogwood
STATE TREE: Pine

State Parks

Fees for camping range from $2.00-4.50 per night. Pets are permitted if kept on a leash. Further information: Division of State Parks; North Carolina Department of Natural and Economic Resources; PO Box 27687; Raleigh, NC 27602.

Rest Areas

Overnight stops are not permitted in North Carolina Rest Areas.

Cherokee Indian Reservation (Great Smoky Mountain NP and Blue Ridge Parkway)

Located at the southern entrance of both the great Smoky Mountain NP and the Blue Ridge Parkway, the reservation, with over 56,000 acres, is the home of 8,000 Eastern Cherokees. There are no free campgrounds in this area, and fish and game regulations are different from the rest of the state. For more information on the area itself, write: Cherokee Tribal; Travel and Promotion; PO Box 465; Cherokee, NC 28719 [Toll free out-of-state; in North Carolina only: 1-800-222-1611. Local: 497-9195.] For fish and game regulations, write: Fish and Game Management Enterprise of the Easatern Band of Cherokee Indians; PO Box 302; Cherokee, NC 28719 [Toll free out-of-state: 1-800-438-1601. Local: 704/497-5201.]

Camping in North Carolina National Forests (General Information)

Forest trails, wilderness areas, landings, etc., are open all year. Linville Gorge and Shining Rock Wilderness require entrance permits. Group size in all wilderness areas is limited to 10 persons. Primitive camping is allowed anywhere in the National Forests unless otherwise posted. Permits are not needed for primitive camping. However, permits are required for entrance to Linville Gorge and Shining Rock .Wilderness, and can be obtained at the District Ranger stations that administer these areas. HUNTING AND FISHING are allowed under State of North Carolina regulations. Licenses consist of: State License, Game Lands Permit, and Big Game or Trout Stamp, depending on sport. A "Sportsman License" satisfies all license requirements. Off-road vehicles are permitted on roads and trails unless otherwise posted. Vehicle drivers must be licensed. Vehicles and operators must conform to all State laws. CAMPFIRES: A permit is not needed for a campfire. However, you are responsible for your fire and any wildfire that results from a spreading campfire. Remember, have your fire "dead out".

The Appalachian Trail

More than 2000 miles long, the Appalachian Trail (from Maine to Georgia) is the longest continuous marked trail in the world.

CAMPING: More than 200 open-front shelters/lean-tos are spaced approximately 10 miles apart on the Trail (one-day intervals). As they are occupied on a first-come first-served basis, carry a tent in case the shelters are full. Potable spring water is usually available at each site, but should be purified by tablets or boiling. And always "pack it in, pack it out".

PERMITS: No permit is required to hike the Trail. However, camping permits must be obtained for overnight stays in Shenandoah NP (Luray, VA 22835) and Great Smoky Mountains NP (Gatlinburg, TN 37733). These are free of charge and available from

The Appalachian Trail (cont.)

the ranger stations or by mail. A free camping permit must be obtained for overnight stays in White Mountain National Forest Restricted Use Area (PO Box 638; Laconia, NH 03246).

APPALACHIAN TRAIL CONFERENCE: A private, nonprofit, national organization which represents citizen's interest in the Appalachian Trail. They offer detailed guidebooks and maps for sale, as well as the A.T. Data Book which gives the location and distances between shelters and certain post offices, supply points, water sources, lodgings and meals. For more information on this organization, write to them at: PO Box 236; Harpers Ferry, WV 25425.

BACKCOUNTRY AND WILDERNESS CAMPING

Bob's Creek Pocket Wilderness (Bowater Southern Paper Corporation). A 500-acre wilderness area with two trails, one 8 miles and a shorter loop of 3½ miles. It is an outstanding scenic and natural area with a number of waterfalls, interesting rock formations, and huge, old-growth hemlock trees. Bob's Creek was the first trail in North Carolina to become a National Recreation Trail. Halfway around the trail is a BACKPACK CAMPING AREA located near a mountain stream.

Cheoah Bald Wilderness (Nantahala NF). 19,000 acres; located in Nantahala NF, just east of the Joyce Kilmer Forest. Cheoah Bald has an elevation of 5,062 feet. 12 panoramic miles of the the Appalachian Trail pass through the Wilderness. Very scenic, with deep canyons, abundant virgin timber, numerous waterfalls, extensive hiking trails.

Joyce Kilmer Wilderness Area (Nantahala NF). Located SW of the Great Smoky Mountains NP. 32,500 acres of rugged terrain, waterfalls, 10,000 acres of virgin timber. The 3,840-acre Joyce Kilmer Memorial Forest is located within the Wilderness. Hunting, fishing, hiking, and camping. The Wilderness lies on either side of the Tennessee-North Carolina state line.

Linville Gorge Wilderness (Pisgah NF). There are no restrictions as to where people may camp; however, visitors should use existing fire rings, and whenever possible, small hiking stoves. Food taken into the Gorge must be in disposable containers that can be burned. Free entrance permits may be obtained at the District Ranger's office located in the basement of the Library Building at the corner of West Court and Logan Streets; Marion, NC; Monday through Friday, 8:00 to noon and 12:30 to 4:30. Permits may also be obtained by mail (Grandfather Ranger District; Pisgah NF; PO Box 519; Marion, NC 28752) or by telephone (704/652-4841). CAUTION: Native snakes include the poisonous copperhead and timber rattler.

Shining Rock Wilderness (Pisgah NF). 478,000 acres in NW North Carolina. Hunting (wild turkey, boar, black bear, deer); fishing; hiking; wilderness camping; canoe camping. In June there is a rhododendron festival on top of the mountain. Obtain a free permit from the District Ranger (Toecane Ranger District; PO Box 128; Burnsville, NC 28714 [704/682-6146]).

Smoky Mountains National Park; Backcountry Camping. Free backcountry permits may be obtained at any visitor center or Ranger Station. Party size limit is eight persons. Permits for shelters must be requested in person, not more than 24 hours prior to departure on trail. Permits other than for shelters may be issued on arrival in park or by mail/phone no more than 30 days in advance of start of trip. Use of these campsites is limited to three consecutive nights per site. Winter camping is available. No pets, bicycles, or motorized equipment on trails. Build fires at designated sites only. When camped, food must be kept in a trail shelter having bear exclosure fencing, or must be suspended at least 10 feet above the ground and 4 feet from any post, tree truck, or limb. Horses are permitted in park; prohibited on trails designated as hiker trails only, on maintained portions of park roadways and in developed campgrounds and picnic areas. Further information and permits: Great Smoky Mountains NP; Gatlinburg, TN 37738; ATTN: Backcountry Office.

Snowbird Creek Wilderness (Nantahala NF). 15,000 acres. The trails follow former logging roads throughout the Wilderness and its mountains. Trout fishing. A free Snowbird Area Trail Map is available from the US Forest Service; Nantahala NF; PO Box 2750; Asheville, NC 28802.

NORTH CAROLINA

Whiteside Mountain (Nantahala NF). Whiteside Mountain, located between Highland and Cashiers, NC, is a unique part of the Nantahala NF. Spectacular view from a high ridge top. The road is closed to motorized vehicles; foot traffic only is permitted. Visitors hike all or part of the 2-mile loop trail that goes to the top and back. The Whiteside Mountain Trail is designated a National Recreation Trail and is a component of the National Trail System. The north ridge trail (formerly Co Rd 1522) and the south ridge trail are strictly for hiking. Motorized vehicles are prohibited on these areas in order to protect the landscape, the soil, and the vegetation. CAMPING: Primitive-style camping is allowed in this area on Forest Service land. No camping facilities are provided. Do not cut live trees for firewood or any other use. Campers may use dead or down wood for fires. Collection of plants or wildlife is prohibited.

INFORMATION SOURCES

Maps

The following maps are available from **Forsyth Travel Library** (see order form in Appendix B):

> **State of North Carolina** [Up-to-date, showing all principal roads, points of interest, sports areas, parks, airports, mileage, etc. Full color.]

> Completely indexed city maps, including all airports, lakes, rivers, etc., of numerous cities in North Carolina.

Tennessee Valley Authority

TVA designated campgrounds are no longer free. However, unimproved TVA lands may be used for informal camping. No fees or permits are required. These areas are shown on recreation maps of individual TVA lakes. For map, contact: TVA; Knoxville, TN 37902.

State Information

Division of State Parks; North Carolina Department of Natural and Economic Resources; PO Box 27687; Raleigh, NC 27602.
Travel and Promotion Division; North Carolina Department of Natural and Economic Resources; PO Box 27687; Raleigh, NC 27602.
Wildlife Resources Commission; 512 North Salisbury; Raleigh, NC 27602.

Miscellaneous

Charlotte Chamber of Commerce; PO Box 1867; Charlotte, NC 28233.
Blue Ridge Parkway; PO Box 7606; Asheville, NC 28807.
Cape Hatteras National Seashore; Route 1, Box 675; Manteo, NC 27954.
Corps of Engineers, Wilmington District; PO Box 1890; Wilmington, NC 28401.
Mattamuskeet NWR; New Holland, NC 27885.
National Forests in North Carolina; PO Box 2750; Asheville, NC 28802.

FREE CAMPGROUNDS

ASHEVILLE

Crabtree Meadows (Blue Ridge Parkway, NRA). 45 mi NE of Asheville on Blue Ridge Parkway, milepost 339.5. (Information and Parkway Maps: 700 Northwestern Bank Building; Ashville, NC 28801.) SEASON: 11/1-4/30, FREE, (rest of yr, $3). FACILITIES: 93 sites (tr -30); drk wtr, cga, flush toil, tbls, telephone, gas station, ice, food, store, concession. [During FREE SEASON no facilities other than chemical toilets.] ACTIVITIES: Picnicking; hiking. MISC.: Elev 3750; 253 acres; pets.

Mt. Pisgah (Blue Ridge Parkway, NRA). 26 mi SW of Asheville on Blue Ridge Parkway; milepost 408.6. (Information and Parkway Maps: 700 Northwestern Bank Building; Asheville, NC 28801.) SEASON: 11/1-4/30, FREE, (rest of yr, $3); 14-day lmt. FACILITIES: 140 sites (tr -30); dump, flush toil, cga, f, tbls, telephone, food concession, store, drk wtr, ice, gas station. (No facilities other than chemical toils are provided during the Winter) ACTIVITIES: Picnicking; hiking. MISC.: Elev 5000 ft; 690 acres; pets.

See page 7 for KEY TO ABBREVIATIONS.

359

BLOWING ROCK

Julian Price Memorial Park (Blue Ridge Parkway, NRA). 5 mi W of Blowing Rock on Blue Ridge Parkway to milepost 297.1. (Information & Parkway Maps: 700 Northwestern Bank Building; Asheville, NC 28801) SEASON: 11/1-4/30, FREE, (rest of yr, $3); 14-day lmt. FACILITIES: 197 sites (tr -30); tbls, cga, f, flush toil, drk wtr, dump . Store nearby. ACTIVITIES: Picnicking; hiking; fishing; boating,l. MISC.: Elev 3400 ft; 3900 acres; pets. Lake. (During the Winter: no facilities other than chemical toil.)

BULLOCK

Grassy Creek Public Use Area (COE; John H. Kerr Lake). Approximately 5 mi NW of Bullock on St Hwy 1443. SEASON: 4/1-10/30; 14-day lmt. FACILITIES: 10 sites (tr -32); tbls, picnic shelter. ACTIVITIES: Picnicking; fishing; waterskiing; swimming; boating,l. MISC.: Pets.

EDGEMONT

Mortimer (Pisgah NF). 2 mi NW of Edgemont on St Hwy 90 (Wilson Creek Rd). SEASON: All year. FACILITIES: 16 sites (no tr); tbls, toil, cga, f, piped drk wtr, gas, store. ACTIVITIES: Picnicking; fishing; swimming; hiking; mountain climbing. MISC.: Elev 1600 ft; 3 acres; pets. Scenic. On a beautiful mountain stream.

ELM CITY

Truckland Truck Stop. 1 mi S of Elm City on St Hwy 301 North. SEASON: All year; 1-night lmt. FACILITIES: Spaces for self-contained RVs; toil, drk wtr, gas, food.

FONTANA

✱**Cable Gap Shelter** (Nantahala NF). 4-7/10 mi NE of Fontana on St Hwy 28; 1-1/2 mi W on St Hwy 1242; 1 mi N on TRAIL 12A. SEASON: All yr. FACILITIES: 1 site (no tr); flush toil, cga. Store/gas/ice (3 mi). Shower (4 mi). ACTIVITIES: Picnicking; hiking. Fishing/swimming/ boating/waterskiing/horseback riding (5 mi). MISC.: Elev 2800 ft; 1 acre; pets. Primitive campground with trail shelter. Overlooks Fontana Lake. Both rd & trail access.

FRANKLIN

Deep Gap (Nantahala NF). 18-9/10 mi SW of Franklin on US 64; 4-1/2 mi S on FS 711. SEASON: 5/24-10/15; 14-day lmt. FACILITIES: 4 sites (no tr); no drk wtr; tbls, toil, cga, f. ACTIVITIES: Picnicking; fishing; berry-picking; hiking.

MISC.: Elev 4400 ft; 2 acres; pets. Adjacent to Appalachian Trail. Scenic.

HAYESVILLE

Bob Allison (NF). 8-4/5 mi NE of Hayesville on St Hwy 1307; 4-1/2 mi N on FS 440. SEASON: All year. FACILITIES: 12 sites (no tr); piped drk wtr, tbls, toil, cga, f. ACTIVITIES: Picnicking; fishing. MISC.: Elev 3000 ft; 2 acres; pets. Trout fishing in Tuni Creek. 3 mi S of Nantahala Lake. Road not recommended for trailers. Stream. Scenic.

Fires Creek Hunter (NF). 5-7/10 mi NW of Hayesville on St Hwy 1300; 1-1/10 mi N on St Hwy 1344. SEASON: All year; 14-day lmt. FACILITIES: 2 sites (no tr); no drk wtr; toil, no tbls. Store/gas (2 mi). ACTIVITIES: Hiking; berry-picking; fishing. MISC.: Elev 1800 ft; 9 acres; pets. Scenic. Nature Trails.

Lynn Cove (NF). 5-7/10 mi NW of Hayesville on St Hwy 1300; 1-1/10 mi N on St Hwy 1344. SEASON: 5/27-9/5; 14-day lmt. FACILITIES: 2 sites (no tr); toil. ACTIVITIES: Hiking. Fishing/hunting (at Fires Creek Wildlife Management Area). MISC.: Elev 1800 ft; pets.

HIGHLANDS

Ammons Branch (NF). 4-9/10 mi SE of Highlands on FS 1603; 1-1/5 mi SE on FS 1100. SEASON: All year; 14-day lmt. FACILITIES: 3 sites (no tr); no drk wtr; tbls, toil, cga, f. ACTIVITIES: Picnicking. Fishing (1 mi). MISC.: Elev 2600 ft; 2 acres; pets.

Blue Valley (NF). 6-1/5 S of Highlands on St Hwy 28; 2-1/10 mi W on St Hwy 1618. SEASON: All year; 14-day lmt. FACILITIES: 4 sites (no tr); no drk wtr; no tbls, toil. ACTIVITIES: Rock-hounding; fishing. MISC.: Elev 2700 ft; 3 acres; pets; stream.

East Fork (NF). 2½ mi S on St Hwy 28; 1 mi W on St Hwy 1618. SEASON: All year. FACILITIES: 6 sites (no tr); tbls, toil, cga, piped drk wtr. ACTIVITIES: Picnicking. MISC.: Elev 2600 ft; 3 acres; pets.

HOT SPRINGS

Rocky Bluff (Pisgah NF). 3 mi S of Hot Springs on St Hwy 209. SEASON: 4/2-12/15; 14-day lmt. FACILITIES: 32 sites (tr -22); flush toil, cga, f, tbls, piped drk wtr. Food store/gas (3 mi). ACTIVITIES: Picnicking; hiking; fishing. Boating (r, 3 mi). Mountain climbing and tubing. MISC.: Elev 1900 ft; 5 acres; pets. Wooded area along mountain stream. Inner tube floating--Spring Creek, white Water, French Broad River.

JONAS RIDGE

Chestnut Mountain (Pisgah NF). 10 mi SE of Jonas Ridge on St Hwy 181; 4 mi NE on FS 38; 4 mi NW on FS 38A. SEASON: All year; 14-day lmt. FACILITIES: 3 sites (no tr); no drk wtr; tbls, toil, cga, f. ACTIVITIES: Picnicking; hiking; fishing; hunting. MISC.: Elev 2800 ft; 9 acres; pets. Stream. Hunter camp. Nature trails.

Fox Camp (Pisgah NF). 12 mi SE of Jonas Ridge on St Hwy 181. SEASON: 4/1-10/31; 14-day lmt. FACILITIES: 3 sites (no tr); no drk wtr; no tbls, toils, cga, f. ACTIVITIES: Hiking; hunting; fishing; swimming. MISC.: Elev 2000 ft; 5 acres; pets. Hunter Camp. Nature Trails.

Greentown (Pisgah NF). 20 mi SE of Jonas Ridge on St Hwy 181; 4 mi NE on FS 38; 5 mi NW on FS 38A. SEASON: 4/1-10/31; 14-day lmt. FACILITIES: 2 sites (no tr); tbls. ACTIVITIES: Picnicking; fishing; hunting; hiking. MISC.: Elev 2200 ft; 5 acres; pets. Nature Trails. Hunter Camp.

Kawana (Pisgah NF). 4-1/2 mi NE of Jonas Ridge on FS 464. SEASON: All year; 14-day lmt. FACILITIES: 2 sites (tr -22); no drk wtr; no tbls, toil, cga. ACTIVITIES: Hiking; fishing; hunting. MISC.: Elev 3000 ft; 6 acres; pets. Nature trails. Hunter camp.

LAUREL SPRINGS

Doughton Park (Blue Ridge Parkway, NRA). On Blue Ridge Parkway at Milepost 241.1, 11 mi S of Laurel Springs (from US 21). [Information & Parkway Map; 700 Northwestern Bank Bldg., Asheville, NC 28801.] SEASON: 11/1-4/30, FREE, (rest of yr, $3). FACILITIES: tbls, flush toil, gas station, telephone, f. Ice/food concession nearby. ACTIVITIES: Picnicking; hiking; fishing. MISC.: Elev 3600 ft; 6430 acres; pets. No facilities other than chemical toilets are provided during the Winter.

LENOIR

Boone Fork (Pisgah NF). 7 mi NW of Lenoir on St Hwy 90; 4-7/10 mi NW on St Hwy 1368; 2 mi NE on FS 2055. SEASON: 4/1-10/31; 14-day lmt. FACILITIES: 35 sites (tr -22); tbls, toil, cga, f, well drk wtr. ACTIVITIES: Picnicking; hiking. MISC.: Elev 1300 ft; 10 acres; pets. In wooded setting on mountain stream. Scenic. 18 mi S of Blue Ridge Parkway milepost 293. Gas/store/ice (5 mi).

MARION

Linville Falls (Blue Ridge Parkway, NRA). 23 mi W of Marion on US 211; milepost 316.3. [Information & Parkway Map: 700 Northwestern Bank Building, Asheville, NC 28801.] SEASON: 11/1-4/30, FREE, (rest of yr, $3); 14-day lmt. FACILITIES: 75 sites (tr -30); tbls, flush toil, cga, f. Ice/food concession /store nearby. ACTIVITIES: Picnicking; hiking; fishing. MISC.: Elev 3000 ft; 996 acres; pets. No facilities other than chemical toil are provided during Winter.

MEBANE

Red Horse Auto/Truck Service. I-85, exit 152 (Trollingwood Road). SEASON: All year; 1-night lmt. FACILITIES: Spaces for self-contained RVs, toil, drk wtr, gas, food, dump. MISC.: 24-hr. Mechanic.

OLD FORT

Curtis Creek (NF). 1-7/10 mi E of Old Fort on US 70; 3 mi N on St Hwy 1227; 1-7/10 mi N on FS 482. SEASON: 4/1-10/31; 14-day lmt. FACILITIES: 6 sites (tr -22); well drk wtr, toil, no tbls. ACTIVITIES: Hiking. Fishing (1 mi). MISC.: Elev 2000 ft; 1 acre; pets; scenic.

OXFORD

Grassy Creek (COE; John H. Kerr Project). 10 mi NW of Oxford on US 15 to Bullock; 5 mi NW. SEASON: 4/1-10/30; 14-day lmt. FACILITIES: 10 sites (tr -32); flush toil, tbls, cga. ACTIVITIES: Picnicking; hiking; fishing; swimming; boating,l. MISC.: Pets.

ROBBINSVILLE

Chestnut Flat (Nantahala NF). 1-1/10 mi N of Robbinsville on US 129; 3-1/2 mi SW on St Hwy 1116; 2-1/10 mi S on St Hwy 1127; 6-3/5 mi SW on St Hwy 1115. SEASON: All year; 14-day lmt. FACILITIES: 2 sites (tr -16); no drk wtr; tbls, toil, cga, f. ACTIVITIES: Picnicking; fishing; swimming. MISC.: Elev 2300 ft; 1 acre; pets. On Big Snowbird Creek.

Deerlick (Nantahala NF). 1-1/10 mi N on US 129; 3-1/2 mi SW on St Hwy 1116; 2-1/10 mi S on St Hwy 1127; 8-4/5 mi SW on St Hwy 1115. SEASON: All year; 14-day lmt. FACILITIES: 2 sites (tr -16); no drk wtr; tbls, toil, cga, f. ACTIVITIES: Picnicking; fishing; boating,l. MISC.: Elev 2500 ft; 1 acre; pets. On Big Snowbird Creek.

Junction (Nantahala NF). 1-1/10 mi N on US 129; 3-1/2 mi SW on St Hwy 1116; 2-1/10 mi NW on St Hwy 1127; 9-9/10 mi SW on St Hwy 1115. SEASON: All year; 14-day lmt. FACILITIES: 2 sites (tr -22); no drk wtr, tbls, toil, cga, f. ACTIVITIES: Picnicking; hiking; swimming; fishing. MISC.: Elev 2700 ft; 2 acres; pets. Nature Trails. On Big Snowbird Creek.

Santeetlah Hunt Shelter (Nantahala NF). 1-3/10 mi NW of Robbinsville on US 129; 3 mi W on St Hwy 1116; 8-2/5 mi W on St Hwy 1127; 2-7/10 mi SW on FS 81. SEASON: All year; 14-day lmt. FACILITIES: 1 site (no tr); piped drk wtr, tbls, toil, cga, f. ACTIVITIES: Picnicking; fishing. MISC.: Elev 2400 ft; 1 acre; pets. On Big Santeetlah Creek.

Wilson Cabin (Nantahala NF). 1-1/10 mi N of Robbinsville on US 129; 3-1/2 mi SW on St Hwy 1116; 2-1/10 mi S on St Hwy 1127; 7-7/10 mi SW on St Hwy 1115. SEASON: All year; 14-day lmt. FACILITIES: 2 sites (tr -16); no drk wtr; tbls, toil, cga, f. ACTIVITIES: Picnicking; fishing; swimming. MISC.: Elev 2400 ft; 1 acre; pets. Stream.

SANFORD

Kelly's K-P Truck Stop. Junction of St Hwys 1/15/501/421/87. SEASON: All year; 1-night lmt. FACILITIES: Spaces for self-contained RVs; toil, drk wtr, gas, food. MISC.: 24-hr. Mechanic.

STERLING

* **Big Creek** (Great Smoky Mountains NP). 1 mi W of Sterling on St Hwy 32 or 284; BY FOOT in Great Smoky Mountains NP. SEASON: 4/15-10/31; 7-day lmt. FACILITIES: 9 tent sites; toil. Store/ice nearby. ACTIVITIES: Hiking; picnicking; fishing. Pets okay (but not on trails). No entrance fee into this National Park.

SWANSBORO

Cedar Point (Croatan NF). 3-3/10 mi SE of Swansboro on St Hwy 24; 4/5 mi NE on St Hwy 58; 1/2 mi NW on Co Hwy 1114; 7/10 mi SW on FS 153A. SEASON: All year; 14-day lmt. FACILITIES: 43 sites (tr -22); tbls, toil, cga, f, piped drk wtr. Store/ice/gas (2 mi). Food/dump (4 mi). ACTIVITIES: Picnicking; fishing; hiking. Boating,rld (4 mi); waterskiing (4 mi). Swimming (5 mi). MISC.: 20 acres; pets. On Pettifords Bay, 8 mi from Atlantic Ocean near Bogue Sound free ferry & high rise bridge. Heavily wooded with large pines and hardwoods. Wildlife viewing trail nearby. Oystering. Elev 100 ft.

TAPOCO

Indian Grave Branch (NF). 1-1/5 mi SE of Tapoco on St Hwy 129; 2 mi SW on FS 445. SEASON: All year; 14-day lmt. FACILITIES: 1 site (no tr); no drk wtr, no tbls, toil, cga, f. Food/gas/store/showers (3 mi). ACTIVITIES: Fishing; hiking. MISC.: Elev 2000 ft; 1 acre; pets. Primitive shelter on low standard road.

TOWNSVILLE

Ivy Hill (COE; John H. Kerr Lake); 7 mi NW of Townsville on St Hwy 39 and St Hwy 825 [located at the dead end of St Hwy 825, approximately 2 mi NE of Island Creek Dam and Pumping Station]. SEASON: 4/1-10/30; 14-day lmt. FACILITIES: 25 sites (tr -32); tbls, dump; picnic area and shelter. ACTIVITIES: Picnicking; fishing; swimming; boating,l. MISC.: Pets.

TROY

Uwharrie Hunt Camp (Uwharrie NF). 9 mi NW of Troy on St Hwy 109; 2/5 mi on St Hwy 1153. SEASON: All year; 14-day lmt. FACILITIES: 2 tent sites; well drk wtr; tbls, toil, cga, f. Ice (1 mi). ACTIVITIES: Picnicking; hiking. Horseback riding (1 mi). Swimming (4 mi). Boating,l, (4 mi). Water skiing (4 mi). MISC.: Elev 400 ft; 2 acres; pets. Nature trails. Store/gas (1 mi).

WAYNESVILLE

Cataloochee (Great Smoky Mountains NP). 20 mi NW of Waynesville on St Hwy 294 in Great Smoky Mountains National Park. SEASON: 4/15-10/31; 7-day lmt. FACILITIES: 23 sites; toil. ACTIVITIES: Fishing; hiking; swimming. MISC.: No entrance fee to NP. Pets are allowed, but not on the trails.

Sunburst (Pisgah NF). 7 mi E of Waynesville on US 276; 6 mi S on St Hwy 215. SEASON: 4/1-12/10. FACILITIES: 14 sites (tr -22); tbls, flush toil, cga, piped drk wtr. ACTIVITIES: Hiking; picnicking; fishing; berry-picking. MISC.: Elev 3000 ft; 2 acres; pets; scenic. Forested site near mountain stream. Adjacent to Shining Rock Wilderness Area.

WILKESBORO

Bandit's Roost Park No. 2 (COE; West Kerr Scott Dam and Lake). 5 mi W of Wilkesboro. SEASON: LD weekend to MD. FREE ($3 rest of yr). FACILITIES: Sites; tbls, flush toil, cga, f, drk wtr, laundry, playground, basketball courts, showers. ACTIVITIES: Boating,rld; swimming; picnicking; fishing. Waterskiing in designated area from center of reservoir to within 100 feet of the N shore. Floating signs indicate upstream and downstream limits. **MISC.:** Marina with fuel, oil, fishing bait, tackle, is nearby. Pets on leash.

Marley's Ford (COE; West Kerr Scott Dam and Lake). 8-4/5 mi W of Wilkesboro on St Hwy 268. [Gravel access rds.] **SEASON:** All yr; 14-day lmt. **FACILITIES:** 11 sites (tr -22); tbls, toil, cga, f. Dump nearby. Drk wtr; playground. **ACTIVITIES:** Hiking; basketball; picnicking; fishing. Swimming nearby.

MISC.: Marina with fuel, oil, fishing **Warrior Creek Park** (COE; West Kerr Scott Dam and Lake). 5 mi W of Wilkesboro. **SEASON:** LD weekend to MD, FREE ($3 rest of yr). **FACILITIES:** Sites; tbls, flush toil, cga, f, drk wtr. **ACTIVITIES:** Basketball; boating, rld; swimming; picnicking; fishing. Waterskiing in designated area from center of reservoir to within 100 feet of the north shore. Floating signs indicate upstream and downstream limits. **MISC.:** Laundry; playground; pets. Marina with fuel, oil, fishing bait, tackle, nearby.

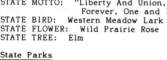

NORTH DAKOTA

GENERAL STATE INFORMATION

Miscellaneous

Toll-Free Number for Travel Information:
   1-800-437-2077 [calling outside of ND]
   1-800-472-2100 [calling within ND]
Right Turns on Red: Permitted after
   full stop, unless otherwise posted.
STATE CAPITOL: Bismarck
STATE NICKNAME: Flickertail State
STATE MOTTO: "Liberty And Union, Now And
        Forever, One and Inseparable"
STATE BIRD: Western Meadow Lark
STATE FLOWER: Wild Prairie Rose
STATE TREE: Elm

State Parks

Camping fees range from $3.00-5.00 per night, plus an entrance fee. Pets are permitted if kept on leash. Further information: North Dakota Parks and Recreation; RR #3, Box 139; Mandan, ND 58554.

Rest Areas

Overnight stops are not permitted in North Dakota Rest Areas.

Theodore Roosevelt National Memorial Park (Backcountry Camping)

An entrance fee of $2.00/vehicle is charged from mid-June to Labor Day (or use a Golden Eagle or Golden Age Passport**). Wilderness and trailside camping is available by permit which may be obtained from the ranger stations located in both the North and South Units. There is no charge for this permit. The Little Missouri is canoeable from mid-April to mid-June, depending on the spring thaw and the amount of moisture accumulated in the winter snow. Further information: Theodore Roosevelt National Memorial Park; Medora, ND 58645.

Little Missouri National Grasslands (Custer NF)

The Medora Ranger District contains 524,685 acres of National Grasslands, intermingled with approximately 723,354 acres of private and state land. Camping is allowed on any of the public lands where appropriate. A contact with the nearest rancher to the area you wish to use is a local custom, and a courtesy that may make your trip more pleasant. He often will aid in providing limits on locations of water, history of the area, and points of interest. There are numerous attractive campsites throughout the Grasslands, but the supply of available firewood is limited. For this reason it is recommended that your cooking be done on liquid or gas-fueled campstoves. However, safe open fires are permitted on the Grasslands, except during extreme fire danger. As a courtesy, please pick up all litter and carry your non-combustible trash with you until you can properly dispose of it in a suitable waste receptacle.

NORTH DAKOTA

Some campsites to avoid include: (1) Low spots and drainage-ways that have a hazard potential from flash floods; and also may be cold sites, as cold damp air flows downhill at night. (2) Sites right beside water developments on which livestock and game depend for water. Your disturbance may keep them from water, and they may keep you from sleep. (3) Sites beneath overhanging banks, rocks, or trees with bad branches. The Badlands country is unstable and these situations present hazards.

Temperatures, precipitation, and road conditions may vary widely throughout the camping season, and lack of adequate sources of drinking water and food make advanced preparations advisable. Only the main roads are graveled or have scoria on them, and a short rain may quickly make a clay or dirt road impassable. Local conditions should be checked before depending on access, and changes should be anticipated. Plan to have an adequate supply of water and food for your camping trip, and don't forget adequate wind protection and a first aid kit.

Shooting of prairie dogs is allowed on the Grasslands, except inside of campgrounds and the Theodore Roosevelt National Memorial Park. Prairie dog towns are located on both Federal and privately-owned land, and contact with the Forest Service and local ranchers is recommended. Consider if your backstop is adequate to control ricochets. The best time to hunt is in the spring, and no license is needed to hunt. For additional hunting information: North Dakota Game and Fish Department; 2121 Lovett Avenue; Bismarck, ND 58501.

MAPS: Free North Dakota Highway Map shows travel routes, towns, and points of interest (State Travel Division; Highway Building; Bismarck, ND 58501). Maps of the Little Missouri National Grasslands are available at the Medora Ranger District (1409 West Villard; Dickinson, ND 58601), and at the Watford Ranger District (Star Route 2, Box 26; Watford City, ND 58854). 50¢ per map.

Little Missouri River Float Trips

By canoe, the 120-mile trip between the South and North Units of Theodore Roosevelt National Memorial Park requires about four days of travel time. To continue from Long X Bridge on Route 85 to Lost Bridge on Route 22 takes an additional two days. There are numerous attractive campsites in the cottonwood groves along the river, but the supply of available firewood is severely limited. For this reason, and because much of the land bordering the water is in private ownership, it is recommended that all cooking be done on campstoves. As a courtesy, please pick up all litter and carry your non-combustible trash with you until you can properly dispose of it in a suitable waste receptacle. If you plan to camp in the park at locations other than the designated campgrounds, you must get a permit, which a ranger will issue to you free of charge. On years when the river rises high enough to occupy the flood plain, a thick deposit of mud limits campsites to higher terraces adjacent to the banks in early spring. After the channel is ice free early in the season, it is common to have large heaps of mud covered ice slabs lining the shores. This condition can also increase difficulty of campsite selection. Further information: Medora Ranger District; 1409 West Villard; Dickinson, ND 58601.

INFORMATION SOURCES

Maps

The following maps are available from **Forsyth Travel Library** (see order form in Appendix B):

> **State of North Dakota** [Up-to-date, showing all principal roads, points of interest, sports areas, parks, airports, mileage, etc. Full color.]

> Completely indexed city maps, including all airports, lakes, rivers, etc., of: **Fargo; Morehead.**

State Information

North Dakota Parks and Recreation Department; RR #2, Box 139; Mandan, ND 58554. North Dakota Travel Department; Highway Department Building; State Capitol Grounds; Bismarck, ND 58501.
Game and Fish Department; 2121 Lovett Avenue; Bismarck, ND 58501.

City Information

Bismarck Chamber of Commerce; 412 North 6th Street; Bismarck, ND 58501.
Fargo Chamber of Commerce; PO Box 2443; Fargo, ND 58102.
Wahpeton Chamber of Commerce; 418 Dakota Avenue; Wahpeton, ND 58075.
West Fargo Chamber of Commerce; PO Box 555; West Fargo, ND 58078.

NORTH DAKOTA

National Wildlife Refuges

North Dakota Wildlife Refuges; Federal Building; Bismarck, ND 58501.
Audubon NWR; Coleharbor, ND 58531.
Des Lacs NWR; Kenmare, ND.
J. Clark Salyer NWR; Upham, ND 58789.
Lostwood NWR; Lostwood, ND 58754.
Slade NWR; Kidder County, ND.
Sullys Hill National Game Preserve;
   Fort Totten, ND.
Tewaukon NWR; Sargent County, ND.

Miscellaneous

Theodore Roosevelt National Memorial Park; Medora, ND 58645.
North Dakota [plus Montana and South Dakota] Bureau of Land Management; 222 North 32nd Street; PO Box 30157; Billings, MT 69107.
Medora Ranger District; Custer NF; 1409 West Villard; Dickinson, ND 58601.
Corps of Engineers, St. Paul District; 1135 US P.O. and Custom House; St. Paul, MN 55101. [Has free campgrounds in ND.]
Corps of Engineers; Downstream Public Use Area; Riverdale, ND 58565.

FREE CAMPGROUNDS

ALEXANDER

City Park (Municipal Park). On St Hwy 85 in Alexander. SEASON: All yr; 1-nite lmt. FACILITIES: 4 sites, tbls, toil, cga, playground. ACTIVITIES: Picnicking. MISC: Policed. Pets.

Sather Lake (Custer NF). 16 mi SW of Alexander on St Hwy 68. SEASON: 5/1-11/15; 10-day lmt. FACILITIES: 8 sites (tr -32); tbls, toil, cga, no drk wtr. ACTIVITIES: Picnicking; fishing; swimming; boating,d. MISC.: Elev 2500 ft; 30 acres; pets. Lake stocked with Rainbow Trout.

AMIDON

Burning Coal Vein (Custer NF). 2 mi W of Amidon on US 85; 12 mi NW on Co Rd 742; 1-2/5 mi E on FS 772. SEASON: 5/1-11/1. FACILITIES: 5 sites (tr -22), tbls, toil, cga, no drk wtr, f. ACTIVITIES: Picnicking; hiking; berry-picking. Swimming/fishing/boating (2 mi). MISC: Burning Coal Vein & Columnar Juniper Tree area nearby scenic. Elev 2600 ft; 2 acres; pets.

ANAMOOSE

City Park (Municipal park). 3 blks N of US 52/St Hwy 14 jct on Main St., in Anamoose. SEASON: All yr; 2-day lmt. FACILITIES: 14 sites, tbls, toil, cga,, drk wtr, sewer/elec hookups. ACTIVITIES: Picnicking. MISC: Pets on leash.

ANETA

Aneta Campground. (City Park). 1/2 mi N of Aneta on St Hwy 32; 1/2 mi W on co rd. SEASON: 5/15-9/15. FACILITIES: 10 sites, tbls, toil, cga. Store/food/ice nearby. ACTIVITIES: Picnicking; swimming. MISC: Pets.

ASHLEY

Lake Hoskins Park (Municipal Park). 3 mi W of Ashley on St Hwy 11; 1 mi N. SEASON: 5/1-10/31. FACILITIES: Undesignated sites; tbls, toil, cga, no drk wtr; f, elec hkup. ACTIVITIES: Picnicking; fishing; swimming; boating,ld; golfing nearby. MISC: Pets on leash.

BALTA

Balta Recreation Area (Municipal Park). 1 mi S of Balta. SEASON: All yr; 1-nite lmt. FACILITIES: 25 sites, tbls, toil, cga. ACTIVITIES: Picnicking; fishing; swimming. MISC: Pets.

BARNEY

Barney City Park (Municipal Park). N of St Hwy 13, in Barney. SEASON: 5/1-10/31. FACILITIES: Undesignated sites; tbls, toil, cga, drk wtr, elec hkup. Food nearby. ACTIVITIES: Picnicking. MISC: Pets on leash.

BELCOURT

Belcourt Lake (Indian Tribal Council). 1 mi N of Belcourt. SEASON: All yr. FACILITIES: Undesignated sites; tbls, toil, cga, drk wtr. ACTIVITIES: Picnicking; swimming; fishing; boating,l. MISC: Pets on leash.

Broken Arrow Resort (Indian Tribal Council). 7 mi N of Belcourt; 1-1/2 mi W to campground. SEASON: 5/15-9/30. FACILITIES: 10 sites (tr -25); tbls, toil, cga, drk wtr. ACTIVITIES: Picnicking; fishing; swimming; boating,l. MISC: Pets on leash.

Camp Waupun (Indian Tribal Council) 3 mi N of Belcourt. SEASON: 5/15-9/30 FACILITIES: 10 sites (tr -25); tbls, toil, cga, drk wtr. **ACTIVITIES:** Picnicking; fishing; swimming; boating,d. **MISC:** Pets on leash.

Jarvis Lake Access (Indian Tribal Council). 7 mi N of Belcourt; 5 mi W to campground. **FACILITIES:** 5 sites tbls; toil, cga, drk wtr. **ACTIVITIES:** Picnicking; fishing; boating,l. **MISC:** Reservations accepted. Pets on leash.

Lake Gordon (Indian Tribal Council). 6 mi N and 1 mi W of Belcourt. **SEASON:** All yr. **FACILITIES:** Undesignated sites; tbls, toil, cga, drk wtr. **ACTIVITIES:** Picnicking; swimming; fishing; boating,l. **MISC:** Pets.

Wheaton Lake Area (Indian Tribal Council). 7 mi N of Belcourt; 2 mi W to campground. **SEASON:** 5/15-9/30. **FACILITIES:** 10 sites (no tr); tbls, toil, cga, drk wtr. **ACTIVITIES:** Picnicking; fishing; boating,l; swimming nearby. **MISC:** Pets on leash.

BELLFIELD

Belfield Tourist Park (Municipal Park). Inquire locally for directions. **SEASON:** All yr. **FACILITIES:** 11 sites; tbls, toil, cga, drk wtr. **ACTIVITIES:** Picnicking. **MISC:** Pets on leash.

BEULAH

Beulah Bay (Municipal Park). 16 mi N of Beulah. **SEASON:** 5/15-9/15; 14-day lmt. **FACILITIES:** Undesignated sites; tbls, toil, cga, drk wtr, shelters, store. **ACTIVITIES:** Picnicking; swimming; fishing; boating,ld. **MISC:** Pets on leash.

City Park (Municipal Park). 1/4 mi S of Beulah. **SEASON:** All yr. **FACILITIES:** Undesignated sites; tbls, toil, cga, drk wtr. **ACTIVITIES:** Picnicking. **MISC:** Pets on leash.

BISMARCK

Top's Truck Stop. 24 mi E of Bismarck on I-94 and US 83 South. **SEASON:** All yr; 1-nite lmt. **FACILITIES:** Spaces for self-contained vehicles; food, toil, drk wtr, gas, 24-hrs.

BOTTINEAU

Bottineau City Park (Municipal Park). E end of First Street, in Bottineau. **SEASON:** All yr. **FACILITIES:** 24 sites; tbls, toil, cga, showers, drk wtr. **ACTIVITIES:** Picnicking. **MISC:** Pets.

Dalen Recreation Area (Turtle Mtn. SF). Inquire locally for directions. **SEASON:** All yr. **FACILITIES:** Undesignated sites (primitive camping); tbls,

toil, cga. **ACTIVITIES:** Picnicking. **MISC:** Pets on leash.

Pelican Sandy Lake Rec. Area (Homan SF). 10 mi N of Bottineau on Co Rd; 6 mi E on St Hwy 43. **SEASON:** All yr. **FACILITIES:** Undesignated sites; tbls, toil, cga, drk wtr. **ACTIVITIES:** Picnicking; swimming; fishing; boating,ld; snow skiing nearby. **MISC:** Pets on leash.

Strawberry Lake Rec. Area (Turtle Mtn. SF). 9-1/2 mi N of Jct St Hwys 14/5; 2-1/2 mi E on St Hwy 43. **SEASON:** All yr. **FACILITIES:** 30 sites (tr -28); tbls, toil, cga, drk wtr. **ACTIVITIES:** Picnicking, fishing, boating,rld; snowskiing nearby. snowmobiling. **MISC:** Pets.

Twisted Oaks Rec. Area (Turtle Mtn. SF). 9-1/2 mi N of jct St Hwys 14/5; 1-1/2 mi E on St Hwy 43. **SEASON:** All yr. **FACILITIES:** 15 sites; tbls, toil, cga, drk wtr. **ACTIVITIES:** Picnicking. **MISC:** Pets on leash.

BOWBELLS

City Park (Municipal Park). Inquire locally for directions. **SEASON:** All yr. **FACILITIES:** 6 sites; tbls, toil, cga, showers, elec hkup. **ACTIVITIES:** Picnicking; swimming. **MISC:** Pets.

BOWDON

Bowdon City Park (City Park). 1/2 mi N of St Hwy 200 in Bowdon. **SEASON:** All yr. **FACILITIES:** 6 sites (tr -26); tbls, toil, cga, elec hkup ($). Food/store/ice/laundry nearby. **ACTIVITIES:** Picnicking. **MISC:** Pets.

BOWMAN

Haley Recreation Area (Municipal Park). Approx. 20 mi SE of Bowman. **SEASON:** All yr. **FACILITIES:** Undesignated sites; tbls, toil, cga, drk wtr. **ACTIVITIES:** Picnicking; fishing; swimming. **MISC:** Pets on leash.

CANDO

City Park (Municipal Park). Inquire locally for directions. **SEASON:** All yr. **FACILITIES:** 4 sites; tbls, toil, cga, drk wtr. **ACTIVITIES:** Picnicking. **MISC:** Pets on leash.

CARBURY

Dalen Rec. Area (Turtle Mtn. SF). 7-3/4 mi N of Carbury on St Hwy 14; 4 mi E to campground. **SEASON:** All yr. **FACILITIES:** 10 sites; tbls, toil, cga, drk wtr. **ACTIVITIES:** Picnicking; snowmobiling. **MISC:** Pets.

CARSON

City Park (Municipal Park). Inquire locally for directions. SEASON: All yr. FACILITIES: Undesignated sites; tbls, toil, cga, drk wtr. ACTIVITIES: Picnicking. MISC: Pets on leash.

CENTER

City Park. (Municipal Park). E edge of Center. SEASON: All yr. FACILITIES: Undesignated sites; tbls, toil, cga, drk wtr. ACTIVITIES: Picnicking. MISC: Pets on leash.

CROSBY

Long Creek Park (Municipal Park). 4-1/2 mi N of Crosby. FACILITIES: Undesignated sites; tbls, toil, cga, drk wtr. SEASON: 6/1-9/30. ACTIVITIES: Picnicking; swimming. Golfing nearby. MISC: Pets on leash.

CRYSTAL

City Park (Municipal Park). Inquire locally for directions. SEASON: All yr. FACILITIES: Undesignated sites; tbls, toil, cga, showers, drk wtr. ACTIVITIES: Picnicking. MISC: Pets.

DAWSON

Lee Pettibone Meml. Park (Municipal Park). Off I-94 in SE edge of Dawson. SEASON: All yr. FACILITIES: Undesignated sites; tbls, toil, cga, drk wtr. ACTIVITIES: Picnicking. MISC: Pets.

DEVILS LAKE

Armour's Truck Stop. E of Devil's Lake on US 2. SEASON: All yr; 1-nite lmt. FACILITIES: Spaces for self-contained vehicles; food, toil, drk wtr, gas. mechanic.

DICKINSON

Patterson Lake (Bureau of Reclamation). 3 mi E of Dickinson on US 10/I-95; 1 mi S (Paved access rds). SEASON: 5/1-10/31; 3-day lmt. FACILITIES: Undesignated sites; tbls, toil, cga, drk wtr. ACTIVITIES: Picnicking; swimming; fishing; boating,ld; golfing nearby; hunting; hiking. MISC: Lake; beach; shelter. Pets.

DRAYTON

Schumacher Park (Municipal Park). Inquire locally for directions. SEASON: All yr. FACILITIES: Undesignated sites; tbls, toil, cga, drk wtr. ACTIVITIES: Picnicking; swimming. MISC: Pets on leash.

EDGELEY

Kulm–Edgeley Dam. 5 mi W; 2 mi S; 1/2 mi W of Edgeley. SEASON: All yr. FACILITIES: Undesignated sites; tbls, toil, cga, drk wtr. ACTIVITIES: Picnicking; swimming; fishing; boating. MISC: Pets on leash.

ELGIN

Sheep Creek Dam. At Jct of St Hwys 49/21, 4 mi S and 1/2 mi W of Elgin. SEASON: All yr. FACILITIES: 10 sites tbls, toil, cga, drk wtr. ACTIVITIES: Picnicking; swimming; fishing. MISC: Pets on leash.

ELLENDALE

Ellendale Public Park (Municipal Park). Inquire locally for directions. SEASON: All yr. FACILITIES: 3 sites; tbls, toil, cga, drk wtr. ACTIVITIES: Picnicking; swimming. MISC: Pets.

EMMET

Douglas Creek (COE; Lake Sakakawea). 2 mi W of Emmet on St Hwy 37; 7 mi S on gravel road. SEASON: All yr; 14-day lmt. FACILITIES: Undesignated sites; tbls, toil, cga, drk wtr. ACTIVITIES: Picnicking; swimming; fishing; boating,l. MISC: Pets.

ENDERLIN

Little Yellowstone Park. 15 mi W of Enderlin. SEASON: All yr. FACILITIES: Undesignated sites; tbls, toil, cga, drk wtr. ACTIVITIES: Picnicking. MISC: Pets on leash.

Patrick Pierce Park (Municipal Park). Inquire locally for directions. SEASON: All yr. FACILITIES: 20 sites; tbls, toil, cga, drk wtr. ACTIVITIES: Picnicking; fishing; boating. MISC: Pets on leash.

ESMOND

Buffalo Lake Park (Municipal Park). 5 mi W and 2 mi S of Esmond. SEASON: All yr. FACILITIES: Undesignated sites; tbls, toil, cga, drk wtr. ACTIVITIES: Picnicking; swimming; fishing; boating. MISC: Pets.

FESSENDEN

Fessenden City Park (Municipal Park). In town; inquire locally. SEASON: All yr. FACILITIES: 15 sites; tbls, toil, cga, shower, elec hkup. ACTIVITIES: Picnicking; swimming. MISC: Pets on leash.

See page 7 for KEY TO ABBREVIATIONS.

FLASHER

City Park (Municipal Park). Inquire locally for directions. SEASON: All yr. FACILITIES: Undesignated sites; tbls, toil, cga, no drk wtr. ACTIVITIES: Picnicking. MISC: Pets.

FORDVILLE

Fordville Park (Municipal Park). Inquire locally for directions. SEASON: All yr. FACILITIES: Undesignated sites; tbls, toil, cga. ACTIVITIES: Picnicking; swimming; fishing; boating. MISC: Pets on leash.

FOREST RIVER

Forest River City Park (Municipal Park). Inquire locally for directions. SEASON: All yr. FACILITIES: 20 sites; tbls, toil, cga, drk wtr. ACTIVITIES: Picnicking; swimming. MISC: Pets.

FORMAN

Silver Lake Recreation Area (Municipal Park). 5 mi E of Forman on St Hwy 11; 2 mi S to Rutland; 3 mi W; 1-1/2 mi S to CG. SEASON: 6/1-9/10. FACILITIES: Undesignated sites; tbls, toil, cga. ACTIVITIES: Picnicking; swimming; fishing; boating,l. MISC: Pets on leash.

GARRISON

Totten Trail Park (COE; Lake Sakakawea). 8 mi SE of Garrison (gravel access road). SEASON: All yr; 14-day lmt. FACILITIES: 13 sites; tbls, toil, cga, well drk wtr. ACTIVITIES: Picnicking; swimming; fishing; boating,ld. MISC: Pets on leash.

GASCOYNE

Gascoyne Lake (City Park). 1/4 mi W of Gascoyne on US 12; 1/4 mi N. SEASON: All yr. FACILITIES: 10 sites; tbls, toil, cga. ACTIVITIES: Picnicking; fishing; swimming; boating,l. MISC: Pets on leash.

GLEN ULLIN

Memorial Park (Municipal Park). 1/2 mi W on Old St Hwy 10. SEASON: All yr. FACILITIES: 40 sites; tbls, toil, cga, drk wtr. ACTIVITIES: Picnicking. MISC: Pets on leash.

GOODRICH

City Park (Municipal Park). Inquire locally for directions. SEASON: All yr. FACILITIES: 30 sites; tbls, toil, cga, drk wtr. ACTIVITIES: Picnicking. MISC: Pets on leash.

GRAFTON

City Park (Municipal Park). Inquire locally for directions. SEASON: All yr. FACILITIES: Undesignated sites; tbls, toil, cga, drk wtr. ACTIVITIES: Picnicking. MISC: Pets on leash.

GRAND FORKS

Thorsgard's Big Sioux Truck Stop. Jct of I-29 and St Hwy 2 W of Grand Forks. SEASON: All yr; 1-nite lmt. FACILITIES: Spaces for self-contained vehicles; food, gas, drk wtr, toil.

GRASSY BUTTE

Summit (Custer NF). 10 mi N of Grassy Butte on US 85. SEASON: 6/1-10/31. FACILITIES: 5 sites (tr -32); tbls, toil, cga, no drk wtr. ACTIVITIES: Rockhounding; picnicking. MISC.: Elev 2500 ft; 1 acre; pets. 4 mi south of N Unit of Theodore Roosevelt National Memorial Park.

GRENORA

Sunset Park (Municipal Park). Take St Hwy 50 to Main St; travel 2 blocks to the park, in Grenora. SEASON: 4/1-10/31; 3-day lmt. FACILITIES: 50 sites (tr -24); tbls, flush toil, cga, drk wtr, f, playground, electric/water hookups. MISC.: Pets allowed if on a leash.

HAGUE

Roadside Park (Municipal Park). Inquire locally for directions. SEASON: All year. FACILITIES: 30 sites; tbls, toil, cga, dump, playground. ACTIVITIES: Picnicking. MISC.: Policed. Pets on leash.

HALLIDAY

Charging Eagle Bay (COE; Lake Sakakawea [managed by Halliday Park Board]). 14 mi N of Halliday on St Hwy 8; 4 mi W and 4½ mi NW to campground. SEASON: 4/1-10/31. FACILITIES: Undesignated sites; tbls, toil, cga, f, dump, well drk wtr, showers, store, electric hookup. ACTIVITIES: Swimming; picnicking; fishing; boating,rl (fuel and storage facilities). MISC.: Pets.

Red Butte Bay (COE; Lake Sakakawea). 14 mi N and 5 mi E of Halliday. SEASON: All year. FACILITIES: Undesignated sites; tbls, toil, cga, no drk wtr. ACTIVITIES: Boating,l; picnicking; fishing. MISC.: Pets permitted on leash.

Twin Buttes Recreation Area (Three Affiliated Tribes). 15 mi N on St Hwy 8; 6 mi E of Twin Buttes School. SEASON: 5/1-9/30; 14-day lmt. FACILITIES: 200 sites (tr -32); tbls, toil, cga, f, drk wtr. ACTIVITIES: Boating,l; picnicking; fishing. Swimming nearby. MISC.: Pets.

See page 7 for KEY TO ABBREVIATIONS.

HAMPDEN

Hampden Park (Municipal Park). Inquire locally for directions. SEASON: All year. FACILITIES: 10 sites; tbls, toil, cga, 1 electric hookup, playground. ACTIVITIES: Picnicking. MISC.: Policed. Pets.

HANKINSON

City Park (Municipal Park). Inquire locally for directions. SEASON: All year. FACILITIES: 30 sites; tbls, toil, cga, drk wtr, playground, electric hookup. ACTIVITIES: Picnicking. MISC.: Policed. Pets permitted if kept on a leash.

HANNAFORD

Hannaford Park (Municipal Park). Inquire locally for directions. SEASON: All year. FACILITIES: 15 sites; tbls, toil, cga, dump, drk wtr, playground. MISC.: Pets. Policed.

HARVEY

West Side Park (Municipal Park). Inquire locally for directions. SEASON: All year. FACILITIES: 24 sites; tbls, toil, cga, showers, drk wtr, electric hookups, playground. MISC.: Policed. Pets on leash.

HAZELTON

Hazelton (COE; Oahe Lake). 12 mi W of Hazelton on gravel road. SEASON: All year; 14-day lmt. FACILITIES: 30 sites (tr -24); tbls, toil, cga, f, drk wtr. ACTIVITIES: Boating,ld; picnicking; fishing. MISC.: Pets on leash.

HAZEN

Riverside Park (Municipal Park). ½ mi S of Hazen. SEASON: All year. FACILITIES: 24 sites; tbls, toil, cga, drk wtr, playground. ACTIVITIES: Picnicking. MISC.: Policed. Pets permitted on leash.

HILLSBORO

Woodland Park (Municipal Park). Inquire locally for directions. SEASON: All year. FACILITIES: 10 sites; tbls, flush toil, cga, dump, 2 electric hookups, drk wtr, playground. ACTIVITIES: Swimming; picnicking; fishing. MISC.: Pets. Policed.

HOOPLE

City Park (Municipal Park). Inquire locally for directions. SEASON: All year. FACILITIES: Undesignated sites; tbls, cga, playground. ACTIVITIES: Picnicking; swimming. MISC.: Pets. Policed.

HOPE

Hope Rest Area. W of Hope on St Hwy 38. SEASON: 5/1-10/31. FACILITIES: 25 sites; tbls, toil, cga, drk wtr, dump.

Store/food/ice/laundry nearby. ACTIVITIES: Picnicking. Golf nearby. MISC.: Pets permitted if kept on a leash.

JAMESTOWN

Parkhurst, Pipestem Lake (COE; Lake Sakakawea). 4 mi N of Jamestown on St Hwy 281; 1 mi W on gravel road to campground. SEASON: LD-MD, 14-day lmt. FACILITIES: 16 sites (tr -24); tbls, toil, cga, f, drk wtr. ACTIVITIES: Swimming; picnicking; fishing; boating,ld. Golf nearby. MISC.: Pets. Store.

KILDEER

City Park (Municipal Park). 2 mi N of junction of St Hwys 200/22 (gravel access roads). SEASON: All year. FACILITIES: Undesignated sites; tbls, toil, cga, drk wtr, playground. ACTIVITIES: Picnicking. MISC.: Pets on a leash.

Little Missouri Bay State Park. 18 mi N of Kildeer on St Hwy 22; 15 mi E on Co Rd. SEASON: All yr; 14-day lmt. FACILITIES: 25 sites; tbls, toil, cga, f, drk wtr. ACTIVITIES: Snowmobiling; horseback riding; picnicking; fishing. MISC.: Snowmobile trails; pets.

KINDRED

Kindred Mill State Park (Municipal Pk). 1 mi S of Kindred on St Hwy 46; gravel road on the E side of the river. SEASON: 5/15-10/1. FACILITIES: 24 sites; tbls, toil, cga, dump, drk wtr, electric hookup, f. Store/food/laundry nearby. ACTIVITIES: Fishing; picnicking; boating,d. MISC.: River; pets on leash.

KULM

City Park (Municipal Park). Inquire locally for directions. SEASON: All year. FACILITIES: Undesignated sites; tbls, flush toil, cga, drk wtr, playground. ACTIVITIES: Swimming; picnicking. MISC.: Pets on leash. Policed.

LA MOURE

La Moure Dam Site (Municipal Park). ½ mi W of LaMoure on St Hwy 13. SEASON: 5/1-10/1; tbls, toil, cga, drk wtr. Store/food/ice/laundry nearby. ACTIVITIES: Swimming; boating,d; picnicking; fishing. Golf nearby. MISC.: Pets. Policed.

LANGDON

City Park (Municipal Park). Inquire locally for directions. SEASON: All year. FACILITIES: 10 sites; tbls, flush toil, cga, drk wtr, electric hookups, showers, playground. ACTIVITIES: Swimming; picnicking. MISC.: Pets on leash. Policed.

See page 7 for KEY TO ABBREVIATIONS.

LEEDS

Memorial Park (Municipal Park). Inquire locally for directions. SEASON: All year. FACILITIES: 12 sites; tbls, flush toil, cga, electric hookups, drk wtr, playground. ACTIVITIES: Swimming; picnicking. MISC.: Pets on leash.

LINTON

Beaver Creek Public Use Area (COE; Oahe Lake). 16 mi W of Linton. SEASON: All yr; 14-day lmt. FACILITIES: Undesignated sites (tr -30); tbls, flush toil, cga, f, showers, drk wtr, picnic shelters, playground. ACTIVITIES: Boating,ld; picnicking; fishing; swimming. MISC.: Pets.

Seeman Park (Municipal Park). 1 mi E of US 83 on St Hwy 13; ¼ mi S to campground. SEASON: 5/1-12/31. FACILITIES: 35 sites; tbls, flush toil, cga, drk wtr, f, electric hookup ($), showers, playground. ACTIVITIES: Fishing; picnicking. MISC.: River; pets; policed.

LISBON

Sandager Park (Municipal Park). Inquire locally for directions. SEASON: All year. FACILITIES: 15 sites; tbls, toil, cga, dump, drk wtr, electric hookups, electric hookups, playground. ACTIVITIES: Swimming; boating; picnicking. MISC.: Pets on leash. Policed.

MADDOCK

City Park (Municipal Park). 2 blocks E of St Hwy 30, on Maddock's main st. SEASON: 6/15-9/15. FACILITIES: 6 tent sites; tbls, flush toil, cga, laundry, playground. ACTIVITIES: Picnicking. Golf nearby. MISC.: Policed; pets; drk wtr.

MAKOTI

City Park (Municipal Park). 1 mi S of St Hwy 23 in Makoti. SEASON: 6/1-9/30; 7 sites (tr -20); tbls, flush toil, cga, f, drk wtr, playground. Store/food nearby. ACTIVITIES: Swimming (pool $); picnicking. MISC.: Pets on leash.

MANDAREE

Lost Bridge Picnic Area (Indian Tribal Council). 10 mi S of Mandaree on St Hwy 22. SEASON: 5/1-9/30; 14-day lmt. FACILITIES: 25 sites (tr -32); tbls, toil, cga, f, drk wtr. ACTIVITIES: Swimming; picnicking; fishing; boating,l. MISC.: Pets on leash.

MARMARTH

Marmarth City Park (City Park). 7 mi E of the MT/ND State Line on US 12. [On Little Missouri River.] SEASON: 5/1-10/30; 1-day lmt. FACILITIES: 10 sites (tr -20); tbls, flush toil, cga, f, playground. Store/food/laundry nearby. ACTIVITIES: Picnicking. Fishing/swimming nearby. MISC.: Pets on leash.

MAYVILLE

Island Park (Municipal Park). Inquire locally for directions. SEASON: All year. FACILITIES: Undesignated sites; tbls, toil, cga, drk wtr. ACTIVITIES: Fishing; picnicking. MISC.: Pets. Policed.

MEDORA

Buffalo Gap (Custer NF). 7 mi W on I-94; I/10 mi N on Co Hwy 7263; 9/10 mi W on FS 726A. SEASON: 5/25-9/8; 10-day lmt. FACILITIES: 37 sites (tr -22); piped drk wtr, tbls, toil, cga, f. ACTIVITIES: Picnicking; berrypicking; hiking. Fishing (1 mi). MISC.: Elev 2600 ft; 4 acres; scenic; pets. 8 mi W of Theodore Roosevelt National Memorial Park. A Grasslands experience campsite.

Sully's Creek State Park. 2½ mi S of Medora on East River Road. SEASON: 5/15-9/15; 14-day lmt. FACILITIES: 150 sites; tbls, toil, cga, f, drk wtr. ACTIVITIES: Horseback riding; picnicking. MISC.: Policed. Pets on leash.

MICHIGAN

City Park (Municipal Park). Inquire locally for directions. SEASON: All year. FACILITIES: 9 sites; tbls, flush toil, cga, dump, sewer hookup, playground. ACTIVITIES: Picnicking. MISC.: Pets.

MINOT

City Park (Municipal Park). Inquire locally for directions. SEASON: All year. FACILITIES: 12 sites; tbls, toil, cga, 4 electric hookups, drk wtr. ACTIVITIES: Swimming; picnicking. MISC.:Pets;policed.

Schatz Crossroads Truck Stop. 1 mi E of Minot on St Hwy 2/52 bypass. SEASON: All yr; 1-night lmt. FACILITIES: Spaces for self-contained RVs; food, toil, drk wtr, mechanic.

MOHALL

Mouse River Memorial Park (Municipal Park). Inquire locally for directions. SEASON: All year. FACILITIES: Undesignated sites; tbls, toil, cga, drk wtr, electric hookups. ACTIVITIES: Swimming; picnicking; fishing; boating,d. MISC.: Pets on leash. Policed.

MUNICH

City of Munich Park (City Park). On St Hwy 20, S edge of Munich. SEASON: 6/1-10/31; 7-day lmt. FACILITIES: 10 sites; tbls, flush toil, cga, drk wtr, playground. Store/food/bottled gas nearby. ACTIVITIES: Picnicking. MISC.: Pets.

NAPOLEON

Napoleon Park (Municipal Park). Inquire locally about directions. SEASON: All

See page 7 for KEY TO ABBREVIATIONS.

year. FACILITIES: 4 sites; tbls, flush toil, cga, drk wtr, 2 electrick hookups, playground. ACTIVITIES: Picnicking. MISC.: Pets on leash.

NEW LEIPZIG

Sheep Creek Dam Campground (Municipal Park). 2 mi S of jct of St Hwys 21/49 at New Leipzig, on St Hwy 49; E on access rd to campground. SEASON: 6/1-9/15; 3-day lmt. FACILITIES: 12 sites (tr -25); tbls, toil, cga, f, drk wtr, electric hookup, playground. ACTIVITIES: Boating,l; picnicking; fishing. Golf nearby. MISC.: Near lake. Pets on leash.

NEW ROCKFORD

Kiwanis Park. In New Rockford on St Hwy 281 at jct with St Hwy 15. [Gravel access roads.] SEASON: All year. FACILITIES: 7 sites; tbls, toil, cga, electric hookup. ACTIVITIES: Picnicking. MISC.: Pets allowed if kept on a leash.

North Riverside Park (Municipal Park). North of jct of St Hwy 15 and US 281, in New Rockford. [Gravel access roads.] SEASON: All year. FACILITIES: 20 sites; tbls, toil, cga, drk wtr. ACTIVITIES: Boating; picnicking; fishing. MISC.: Pets on leash. Policed.

Peoples Park (Municipal Park). South of New Rockford. SEASON: All year. FACILITIES: 40 sites; tbls, flush toil, cga, drk wtr. MISC.: Pets. Policed.

South Riverside Park (Municipal Park). North of jct of St Hwy 15 and US 281. [Gravel access roads.] SEASON: All year. FACILITIES: Undesignated sites; tbls, flush toil, cga, drk wtr, playground. ACTIVITIES: Swimming; picnicking; fishing; tennis; boating. MISC.: Pets on leash. Policed.

NEW SALEM

North Park (Municipal Park). ½ mi N of New Salem. SEASON: All yr; 7-day lmt. FACILITIES: 45 sites; tbls, flush toil, cga, drk wtr, 1 electric hookup, f. Store/ice/food/laundry/dump/bottled gas nearby. ACTIVITIES: Picnicking. Golf nearby. MISC.: Pets on leash.

NEW TOWN

Bear Den Recreation Area (Indian Tribal Council). West of New Town on St Hwy 23 to jct with St Hwy 22; 12 mi S on St Hwy 22. SEASON: 5/1-9/30; 14-day lmt. FACILITIES: 20 sites (tr -32); tbls, cga, f. ACTIVITIES: Boating,l; fishing; picnicking. Swimming nearby. MISC.: Pets on leash.

New Town Recreation Area (Municipal Park). East of New Town on St Hwy

23. SEASON: All year. FACILITIES: 20 sites; tbls, flush toil, cga, drk wtr, 2 electric hookups, showers, playground. ACTIVITIES: Boating; swimming; picnicking; fishing. MISC.: Pets. Policed.

OAKES

City Park (Municipal Park). Inquire locally for directions. SEASON: All year. FACILITIES: 15 sites; tbls, toil, cga, dump, playground, drk wtr. ACTIVITIES: Picnicking. MISC.: Policed. Pets.

Hockenberry Park (Municipal Park). On St Hwy 1, the N edge of Oakes. SEASON: MD-LD. FACILITIES: 10 sites (tr -16), tbls, toil, cga, f, electric hookup, playground, drk wtr. Store/food/laundry nearby. ACTIVITIES: Picnicking. Golf nearby. MISC.: Reservations accepted. Pets.

PARK RIVER

Park River City Park. In Park River. SEASON: 5/31-LD. FACILITIES: 20 sites; tbls, flush toil, cga, f, dump, showers, playground, drk wtr. ACTIVITIES: Swimming; picnicking; fishing; boating,ld. Golf nearby. MISC.: Lake; pets. Reservations accepted.

PARSHALL

Deepwater Creek (COE; Sakakawea Lake). 14 mi S of Parshall. SEASON: All yr; 14-day lmt. FACILITIES: Sites; tbls, toil, cga, well drk wtr, picnic shelters. ACTIVITIES: Boating,ld; picnicking; fishing. MISC.: Pets on leash.

PEMBINA

Pembina Park (Municipal Park). ½ mi E of I-29 on Pembina. SEASON: All year. FACILITIES: Undesignated sites; tbls, toil, cga, dump, electric hookups, drk wtr, playground. ACTIVITIES: Boating; picnicking; fishing. MISC.: Pets; policed.

PORTLAND

Park District (Municipal Park). Inquire locally for directions. SEASON: 4/11-10/31. FACILITIES: 7 sites; tbls, flush toil, cga, f, playground, drk wtr. ACTIVITIES: Picnicking. Golf nearby. MISC.:Pets;river.

RIVERDALE

Wolf Creek (COE; Lake Sakakawea). 6 mi N of Riverdale. SEASON: All yr; 14-day lmt. FACILITIES: Sites; tbls, toil, cga, no drk wtr. ACTIVITIES: Swimming; picnicking; fishing; boating,l. MISC.: Pets allowed if kept on a leash.

ROCK LAKE

City Park (Municipal Park). Inquire locally for directions. SEASON: All year.

FACILITIES: 8 sites; tbls, toil, cga, dump, drk wtr, playground. ACTIVITIES: Picnicking. MISC.: Pets. Policed.

ROLLAS

City Park. Inquire locally for directions. SEASON: All year. FACILITIES: 4 sites; cga, drk wtr, dump, playground. ACTIVITIES: Swimming; picnicking. MISC.: Pets.

RUGBY

Rugby Fairgrounds (Municipal Park). US 2, in Rugby. SEASON: All year. FACILITIES: 25 sites; tbls, flush toil, cga, drk wtr, playground. ACTIVITIES: Picnicking. MISC.: Policed. Pets.

SHEYENNE

Hendrickson Park (Municipal Park). 1½ mi W of Sheyenne. SEASON: All year. FACILITIES: 22 sites; tbls, toil, cga, drk wtr, electric hookups, playground. ACTIVITIES: Playground. MISC.: Pets.

Sheyenne Municipal Park (Municipal Park). Inquire locally for directions. SEASON: All year. FACILITIES: 30 sites; toil, cga, dump, electric hookup, playground. MISC.: Policed. Pets on leash.

STANLEY

Stanley Park (Municipal Park). On US 2, across from the courthouse, in the N edge of Stanley. SEASON: 5/1-11/15; 5-day lmt. FACILITIES: 20 sites (tr -18); tbls, flush toil, cga, f, dump, electric/water hookup, drk wtr, playground. Store/ice/food/laundry nearby. Showers. ACTIVITIES: Picnicking. Fishing/swimming/golf nearby. MISC.: Pets on leash. Lake. Policed.

STEELE

Steele Park (Municipal Park). 3 mi W of Steele on old US 10; S of I-94 Interchange. SEASON: 5/1-10/1. FACILITIES: Undesignated sites; tbls, toil, cga,dump, drk wtr, playground. ACTIVITIES: Picnicking. Golf nearby. MISC.: Policed.

STRASBURG

Lawrence Welk Park (Municipal Park). Inquire locally for directions. SEASON: All year. FACILITIES: Undesignated sites; tbls, flush toil, cga, dump, drk wtr, playground. ACTIVITIES: Swimming; picnicking. MISC.: Policed. Pets.

SYKESTON

Lake Hiawatha (Municipal Park). 1 mi N of Sykeston. [On Lake Hiawatha.] SEASON: All year. FACILITIES: 5 sites; tbls, toil, cga, drk wtr, f, playground. Store/ice/food/laundry/dump nearby. ACTIVITIES: Swimming; picnicking; fishing; tennis. MISC.: Lake; pets. Policed.

TIOGA

City Park (Municipal Park). 3 mi N of US 2 on St Hwy 40, in Tioga. [On NE edge of town.] SEASON: MD-LD; 3-day lmt. FACILITIES: Undesignated sites; tbls, flush toil, cga, f, drk wtr, playground, showers, dump. Store/ice/food/laundry nearby. Electric hookup. ACTIVITIES: Swimming; picnicking. Fishing/golf nearby. MISC.: Lake; policed; pets.

TOWER CITY

Tower Truck Stop. Exit 74, off I-94, at Tower City. SEASON: All yr; 1-night lmt. FACILITIES: Spaces for self-contained RVs; food, toil, drk wtr, mechanic, gas.

TOWNER

City Park (Municipal Park). Inquire locally for directions. SEASON: All year. FACILITIES: 15 sites; tbls, toil, cga, drk wtr, dump, playground. ACTIVITIES: Picnicking. MISC.: Policed. Pets on leash.

Towner Recreation Area (Mouse River SF). 2 mi N of Towner on paved county road. SEASON: All year. FACILITIES: Undesignated sites; tbls, toil, cga, f, dump, drk wtr, playground. ACTIVITIES: Fishing; picnicking. Golf nearby. MISC.:Pets.

Vagabond Recreation Area (Mouse River SF). 10 mi N of Towner on paved county road. SEASON: All year. FACILITIES: Undesignated sites; tbls, toil, cga, f, drk wtr. ACTIVITIES: Snowmobiling; picnicking; fishing. MISC.: Pets on leash.

UNDERWOOD

City Park (Municipal Park). Inquire locally for directions. SEASON: All year. FACILITIES: Undesignated sites; tbls, toil, cga, dump, drk wtr, playground. ACTIVITIES: Picnicking. MISC.: Pets on leash. Policed.

UPHAM

City Park (Municipal Park). Inquire locally for directions. SEASON: All year. FACILITIES: 20 sites; tbls, toil, cga, dump, drk wtr, playground. ACTIVITIES: Picnicking. MISC.: Policed. Pets on leash.

VALLEY CITY

Baldhill Dam and Reservoir (COE; St. Paul District). As county highways in this area are unmarked, campers should ask at the visitor center (11 mi NW of Valley City on Co Hwy 17) for directions to the four camping areas. SEASON: 5/15-11/30; 14-day lmt. FACILITIES: 30 sites are FREE [100 are $2] (tr -32]; tbls, toil, cga, f, drk wtr, playground, visitor center, food. ACTIVITIES: Swimming; picnicking; fishing; boating.l. MISC.: Pets on leash.

VELVA

Velva Park (Municipal Park). Inquire locally for directions. SEASON: All year. FACILITIES: Undesignated sites; tbls, toil, cga, drk wtr, playground, 3 electric hookups. ACTIVITIES: Swimming; picnicking; fishing. MISC.: Pets;policed.

WAHPETON

Chahinkapa Park (Municipal Park). 2nd Street North and 8th Avenue, in Wahpeton. SEASON: 5/1–9/30; 3-day lmt. FACILITIES: 30 sites (tr -30); tbls, flush toil, cga, f, dump, playground, electric/water hookups, showers. Store/ice/food/bottled gas nearby. ACTIVITIES: Boating,l; picnicking; fishing; tennis; swimming. Golf nearby. MISC.: Pets on leash. River. Policed.

WALHALLA

Riverside Park (Municipal Park). Inquire locally for directions. SEASON: All year. FACILITIES: 50 sites; tbls, flush toil, cga, 10 electric hookups, drk wtr, playground. ACTIVITIES: Swimming; picnicking. MISC.: Policed. Pets on leash.

State Historical Park (Municipal Park). Inquire locally for directions. SEASON: All year. FACILITIES: 10 sites; tbls, flush toil, cga, drk wtr. ACTIVITIES: Picnicking. MISC.: Policed. Pets.

WASHBURN

Riverside Park (Municipal Park). West of Washburn. SEASON: All year. FACILITIES: 4 sites; tbls, toil, cga. drk wtr, playground. ACTIVITIES: Swimming; picnicking; fishing. MISC.: Policed; pets.

WATFORD CITY

Tobacco Garden Bay (COE; Lake Sakakawea [managed by COE.). 2 mi E of Watford City on St Hwy 23; 27 mi NE on gravel road. SEASON: All yr; 14-day lmt. FACILITIES: 50 sites (tr -24); tbls, flush toil, cga, f, playground, well drk wtr, electric hookups, showers. ACTIVITIES: Picnicking; swimming; fishing; boating,ld (fuel). MISC.: Pets. Policed.

Watford City Park (City Park). ½ mi E of Watford City on St Hwy 23. SEASON: 5/1–10/1. FACILITIES: Undesignated sites; tbls, flush toil, cga, dump, 8 electric hookups, drk wtr, showers, playground, phone. Store/ice/laundry/food nearby. ACTIVITIES: Fishing; picnicking. Golf nearby. MISC.: Policed. Pets on leash.

WILLISTON

Eddie B's Skelly Truck Stop. 4 mi W of Williston on St Hwys 2/85. SEASON: All yr; 1-night lmt. FACILITIES: Undesignated spaces for RVs; food, toil, drk wtr, gas, mechanic.

WIMBLEDON

Victory Park (Municipal Park). Inquire locally for directions. SEASON: All year. FACILITIES: 12 sites; tbls, flush toil, cga, drk wtr, playground, sewage hookup, dump, 6 electric hookups. ACTIVITIES: Picnicking. MISC.: Policed; pets.

WILTON

City Park. Inquire locally for directions. SEASON: All year. FACILITIES: Undesignated sites; tbls, toil, cga, dump, drk wtr, playground. ACTIVITIES: Picnicking. MISC.: Policed. Pets allowed on leash.

ZAP

City Park. Inquire locally for directions. SEASON: All year. FACILITIES: 5 sites; tbls, toil, cga, drk wtr, 2 electric hookups, dump, playground. ACTIVITIES: Picnicking. MISC.: Pets on leash.

OHIO

GENERAL STATE INFORMATION

Miscellaneous

Toll-Free Number for Travel Information:
    1-800-848-1300 [outside of Ohio]
    1-800-282-1085 [within Ohio]
Right Turns on Red: Permitted after
    full stop, unless otherwise posted.
STATE CAPITOL: Columbus
STATE NICKNAME: Buckeye State
STATE MOTTO: "With God all things are possible"
STATE BIRD: Cardinal
STATE FLOWER: Scarlet Carnation
STATE TREE: Buckeye

See page 7 for KEY TO ABBREVIATIONS.

State Parks

Camping fees range from $2.00–14.00 per night.   14–day limit; all year.   No pets are allowed.   Further information: Ohio Department of Natural Resources; Division of Parks and Recreation; Fountain Square; Columbus, Ohio 43224.

GOLDEN BUCKEYE CARD: Available to Ohio residents 65 and older.   Contact your local senior citizens agency or Ohio Commission on Aging (50 W. Broad St.; 9th Floor; Columbus, OH 43215; 614/466-3583).   Permanently and totally disabled veterans are also entitled to the same discounts offered to senior citizens.   Contact: Veterans Administration Regional Office; Veterans Benefit Counsellor; Federal Office Building; 1240 East Ninth Street; Cleveland, OH 44199 (1-800-362-9024).   50% camping reduction, Sunday nights through Thursday nights, year round.

Any Ohio veteran who has a disability that has been determined by the VA to be permanently and totally disabling, and who receives a pension or compensation from the VA, and who has an honorable discharge from the US armed forces, may camp FREE. Disabled veterans who have received a special set of Ohio license plates under Section 4503.101 of the Ohio Revised Code may also camp free.

Rest Areas

Overnight stops are not permitted in Ohio Rest Areas.

Ohio Power Recreation Land

35,000 acres of lakes and forests, with picnic tables, fire rings for cooking, drinking water, sanitary facilities, free firewood, hundreds of tent and RV sites; 320 lakes and ponds stocked with hundreds of thousands of fish (large–mouth bass, bluegill, muskie), requires an Ohio fishing license.   Everything is FREE.   The Recreation Land is located in the counties of Morgan, Muskingum, and Noble.....22 miles from Zanesville, 25 miles from Cambridge, 8 miles from McConnelsville, 8 miles from Caldwell, 28 miles from Marietta.   Get a free camping permit, plus a detailed map, from any Ohio Power Company office; or write to Ohio Power Company (PO Box 328; McConnelsville, Ohio 43756); or Publication Center (Department of Natural Resources; Fountain Square; Building C; Columbus, OH 43224).

Burr Oak Backpack Trail

A 29–mile loop trail, which winds its way around the shores of Burr Oak Reservoir. Camping is free in all primitive areas.   Pets are not permitted on the trails or in the primitive campgrounds.   Further information and free map: Ohio Department of Natural Resources; Division of Parks and Recreation; Fountain Square, Building C; Columbus, OH 43224.

Shawnee Wilderness Area

There is an extensive backpacking trail system within the nearly 8,000 acres of wilderness.   All walk-in camps have drinking water, fire circles, and toilet facilities. A free permit can be obtained up to 24 hours in advance of your trip.   Pets are not allowed on the trails.   Watch for poisonous snakes.   Further information: Forest Supervisor; Shawnee SF; Ohio Department of Natural Resources; Division of Forestry; Fountain Square; Columbus, OH 43224.

Bear Lake Horsemen's Camp (Shawnee SF)

Shawnee State Forest has more than 70 miles of bridle trails, most of which are directly accessible from the horsemen's campground.   The free campground has 58 campsites; 110 horse stalls; toilet facilities; drinking water; water for the horses.   Further information and free map: Forest Supervisor; Shawnee SF; Ohio Department of Natural Resources; Division of Forestry; Fountain Square; Columbus, OH 43224.

Zaleski Backpack Trail (Zaleski State Forest)

This extensive trail includes areas of historical interest as well as scenic.   A free permit can be obtained up to 24 hours before entering the trail.   Pets are not allowed in the backpack campgrounds.   Watch for poisonous snakes.   You may camp only in the designated campgrounds as shown on their free map.   Further information and free map: Forest Supervisor; Zaleski SF; Ohio Department of Natural Resources; Division of Forestry; Fountain Square; Columbus, OH 43224.

See page 7 for KEY TO ABBREVIATIONS.

INFORMATION SOURCES

Maps

The following maps are available from **Forsyth Travel Library** (see order form in Appendix B):

> **State of Ohio** [Up-to-date, showing all principal roads, points of interest, sports areas, parks, airports, mileage, etc. Full color.]

> Completely indexed city maps, including all airports, lakes, rivers, etc., of numerous cities in Ohio.

State Information

Division of Parks and Recreation; Ohio Department of Natural Resources; Fountain Square; Columbus, OH 43224.
Division of Forestry; Ohio Department of Natural Resources; Fountain Square; Columbus, OH 43224.
Travel and Tourist Bureau; Ohio Department of Economic Development; 25th Floor; State Office Tower; PO Box 1001; Columbus, OH 43216.
Ohio Turnpike Commission; Berea, OH 44017. [Ask for "Travel Trailer Parks" brochure.]
Ohio Department of Highway Safety; 240 Parsons Avenue; Columbus, Ohio 43205.
Ohio Historical Society; Ohio Historical Center; I-71 and 17th Avenue; Columbus, OH 43211.
Lake Erie Tourist Information Center; 1018 Ramada Street; Sandusky, OH 44870. [For information on North-Central Ohio and Lake Erie Islands.]
Great Lakes Historical Society; 480 Main Street; Vermilion, OH 44089.
Buckeye Tourist Council; 853 Wheeling Avenue; Box 307; Cambridge, OH 43725.
Tecumseh Tourist Council; RR #2; West Liberty, OH 43357.

City Information

Akron Area Chamber of Commerce; Convention and Visitors Bureau; 200 Delaware Building; Akron, OH 44308.
Cleveland Convention and Visitors Bureau; 511 Terminal Tower; Cleveland, OH 44113.
Greater Cleveland Growth Association; 690 Union Commerce Building; East 9th and Euclid Streets; Cleveland, OH 44115.
Convention and Visitors Bureau; 200 West Fifth Street; Cincinnati, OH 45202.
The Greater Cincinnati Chamber of Commerce; 120 West Fifth Street; Cincinnati,OH 45202.
Columbus Area Chamber of Commerce; 50 West Broad Street; Columbus, OH 43216.
Dayton Area Chamber of Commerce; Sheraton-Dayton Hotel; Dayton, OH 45402.
Toledo Convention and Visitors Bureau; 218 Huron Street; Toledo, OH 43604.

Corps of Engineers

U.S. Army Engineer Division, Ohio River; PO Box 1159; Cincinnati, OH 45201.

Department of Natural Resources

Ohio Department of Natural Resources; Fountain Square; Columbus, OH 43224.
Division of Parks and Recreation   [camping information]
Division of Natural Areas and Preserves
Publications Division
Division of Wildlife   [free Wildlife Area Maps]
Division of Forestry   [State Forest information]

FREE CAMPGROUNDS

ADELPHI

Tar Hollow (SP). 10 mi S of Adelphi on St Hwy 327. SEASON: All yr; 14-day lmt. FACILITIES: 20 tent sites and 20 walk-in sites; picnic shelter, toil. ACTIVITIES: Hunting; picnicking; fishing; hiking; swimming; scuba diving. Horseback riding in adjacent State Forest area. MISC.: NO PETS.

AMHERST

Middle Ridge Plaza (Turnpike Commission). On I-808, W to milepost 140. SEASON: All yr; 1-night lmt. FACILITIES: 10 spaces for self-contained RVs (tr -30); tbls, flush toil, dump, food, drk wtr, phone, gas. ACTIVITIES: Picnicking. MISC.: Open 4:00 p.m. to 10:00 a.m. Stone-surfaced parking area especially designated for use by travel trailers. Pet exercise area.

See page 7 for KEY TO ABBREVIATIONS.

Vermilion Valley Plaza (Turnpike Commission). On I-80, E to milepost 138. SEASON: All yr; 1-night lmt. Open 4:00 p.m. to 10:00 a.m. FACILITIES: 10 spaces for self-contained RVs; tbls, flush toil, dump, food, phone, drk wtr, gas. ACTIVITIES: Picnicking. MISC.: Stone-surfaced parking area especially designated for use by travel trailers. Pet exercise area.

ANDOVER

*Pymatuning (SP). 2 mi E of Andover on US 85. SEASON: All yr; 14-day lmt. FACILITIES: Walk-in tent sites; picnic shelters. Food nearby. Drk wtr at boat rental. Toil; playground. ACTIVITIES: Boating,rld; picnicking; fishing; hiking; hunting; swimming. MISC.: Dump at State Park. Seasonal naturalist. Beach concession. NO PETS.

CALDWELL

*Wolf Run (SP). The park is located near Caldwell, ½ mi E of the Belle Valley interchange of I-77, at the jct of St Hwy 821. The entrance to the office and camping areas is on Bond Ridge Road off St Hwy 215. The swimming beach and boat launch area entrance is of St Hwy 215. The free campground here is a FLY-IN camping area located on the N side of the lake. The area is within walking distance of the 4,700-foot runway at Noble County Airport. SEASON: All yr; 14-day lmt. FACILITIES: 20 FLY-IN tent sites; picnic shelters; tbls, toil, cga, public telephone. ACTIVITIES: Hunting; picnicking; fishing; hiking; swimming; scuba diving. Boating,ld (nearby). Sledding, cross-country skiing, ice skating/fishing in winter. MISC.: Seasonal naturalist in park. NO PETS.

CHILLICOTHE

*Scioto Trail (SP). 9 mi S of Chillicothe on US 23; 3 mi on St Hwy 372. SEASON: All yr; 14-day lmt. FACILITIES: 50 walk-in tent sites; picnic shelters, toil. Drk wtr is in Class "B" camp area, nearby. ACTIVITIES: Hunting; hiking; picnicking; fishing; swimming; scuba diving. Horseback riding in adjacent State Forest area. MISC.: NO PETS.

DEERFIELD

German Church (COE). On Berlin Lake, near Deerfield. SEASON: May-September; 14-day lmt. FACILITIES: 30 sites; tbls, toil, cga, drk wtr. ACTIVITIES: picknicking; fishing. MISC: 18 acres; pets.

DEFIANCE

*Independence Dam (SP). 3 mi E of Defiance on St Hwy 24. SEASON: All yr; 14-day lmt. FACILITIES: 10 walk-in tent sites; picnic shelters, toil, well water. ACTIVITIES: Boating,ld; picnicking; fishing; hunting; hiking. Sledding and ice skating in winter. MISC.: NO PETS.

GLOUSTER

Burr Oak (SP). 2 mi N of Glouster on St Hwy 13. SEASON: All yr; 14-day lmt. FACILITIES: 30 sites (no tr); picnic shelters, toil, playground. Drk wtr near boat launch. Food nearby. ACTIVITIES: Horseback riding; picnicking; fishing; boating,rld; hunting; hiking; swimming; scuba diving. MISC.: Seasonal naturalist program. Beach concession. NO PETS.

LOUDONVILLE

*Mohican (SP). 2 mi S of Loudonville on St Hwys 3/97. It lies entirely within the 4,091-acre Mohican-Memorial State Forest. Free WALK-IN camp area is located in the S park area of St Hwy 97. SEASON: All yr; 14-day lmt. FACILITIES: 40 walk-in tent sites; picnic shelters. ACTIVITIES: Canoeing; picnicking; fishing; hunting; hiking; horseback riding; boating,r. Skiing, sledding, skating in winter. MISC.: Seasonal naturalist program. Food nearby. River. NO PETS.

MANTUA

Brady's Leap Plaza (Turnpike Commission). On I-80, E to milepost 196. SEASON: All yr; 1-night lmt. Open 4:00 p.m. to 10:00 a.m. FACILITIES: 10 spaces for self-contained RVs (tr -30); tbls, flush toil, dump, food, drk wtr, gas, phone. ACTIVITIES: Picnicking. MISC.: Stone-surfaced parking area especially designated for use by travel trailers. Pet exercise area.

McCONNELSVILLE

Parksite #A (Ohio Power Company). Approximately 10½ mi NE of McConnelsville on St Hwy 78; approximately ½ mi N on St Hwy 284; approximately 2-1/3 mi NE on St Hwy 83; entrance on right side of road. SEASON: All yr; 14-day lmt. FACILITIES: Sites; toil, drk wtr, shelter house, parking area. ACTIVITIES: Boating; picnicking; fishing; hiking; hunting; trapping. No swimming or scuba diving. MISC.: No Pets. Get your FREE camping permit by stopping in at any Ohio Power Company office; or write Ohio Power Co.; PO Box 328; McConnelsville, OH [ask for map].

Parksite #C (Ohio Power Company). Approximately 10½ mi NE of McConnelsville on St Hwy 78; approximately 2½ mi N on St Hwy 284; 3/10 mi NE on unpaved all-weather road. SEASON: All yr; 14-day lmt. FACILITIES: Sites; tbls, drk wtr, shelter house, f, cga. ACTIVITIES: Boating; picnicking; fishing; hiking; hunting; trapping. No swimming or scuba diving. MISC.: Registration. Get FREE camping permit at any Ohio Power Company office; or write Ohio Power Co.; PO Box 328; McConnelsville, OH 43756 [ask for map]. Pets allowed if on leash.

Parksite #D (Ohio Power Company). Approximately 10¼ mi NE of McConnelsville on St Hwy 78; approximately ½ mi N on St Hwy 284; approximately 3½ mi NE on St Hwy 83; 4/5 mi S on Haul Road. SEASON: All yr; 14-day lmt. FACILITIES: Sites; toil, shelter house, drk wtr. ACTIVITIES: Boating; picnicking; fishing; hiking; hunting; trapping. No swimming or scuba diving. MISC.: Registration. Get FREE camping permit at any Ohio Power Company office; or write Ohio Power Co.; PO Box 328; McConnelsville, OH 43756 [ask for map]. Pets on leash.

Parksite #F (Ohio Power Company). Approximately 10 mi NE of McConnelsville on St Hwy 78 on left side of road. SEASON: All yr; 14-day lmt. FACILITIES: Sites; tbls, toil, cga, shelter house, information center, parking area, f, drk wtr. ACTIVITIES: Boating; picnicking; fishing; hiking; hunting; trapping. No swimming or scuba diving. MISC.: Pets on leash. Get your FREE camping permit by stopping in at any Ohio Power Company office; or write to Ohio Power Co.; PO Box 328; McConnelsville, OH 43756 [ask for map].

Parksite #G (Ohio Power Company). Approximately 10¼ mi NE of McConnelsville on St Hwy 78; approximately ½ mi N on St Hwy 284. SEASON: All yr; 14-day lmt. FACILITIES: Sites; tbls, toil, cga, drk wtr, parking area, f. ACTIVITIES: Boating; picnicking; fishing; hiking; hunting; trapping. No swimming or scuba diving. MISC.: Pets on leash. Get your FREE camping permit by stopping in at any Ohio Power Company office; or write to Ohio Power Co.; PO Box 328; McConnelsville, OH 43756 [ask for map].

Parksite #L (Ohio Power Company). Approximately 10¼ mi NE of McConnelsville on St Hwy 78; approximately ½ mi N on St Hwy 284; approximately ½ mi NE on St Hwy 83; approximately 1-1/10 mi SE on unpaved all-weather road. SEASON: All yr; 14-day lmt. FACILITIES: Sites; tbls, toil, cga, f, drk wtr. ACTIVITIES: Boating; picnicking; fishing; hiking; hunting; trapping. No swimming or MISC.: Pets on leash. Registration. Get FREE camping permit at any Ohio Power Company office; or write Ohio Power Co.; PO Box 328; McConnelsville, OH 43756 [ask for map].

Parksite #N (Ohio Power Company). Approximately 10¼ mi NE of McConnelsville on St Hwy 78; approximately ½

mi N on St Hwy 284; approximately 4 mi NE on St Hwy 83; approximately 1¼ mi S on Co Rd 27. SEASON: All yr; 14-day lmt. FACILITIES: Sites; toil, cga, f, parking area. ACTIVITIES: Hiking; picnicking; fishing; boating; trapping; hunting. No swimming or scuba diving. MISC.: Pets on leash. Get FREE camping permit at any Ohio Power Company office; or write Ohio Power Co.; PO Box 328; McConnelsville, OH 43756 [ask for map].

Parksite #Q (Ohio Power Company). Approximately 10¼ mi NE of McConnelsville on St Hwy 78; approximately ½ mi N on St Hwy 284; approximately 3½ mi NE on St Hwy 83; approximately 3/4 mi NW on Haul Road. SEASON: All yr; 14-day lmt. FACILITIES: Sites; toil, drk wtr, f. ACTIVITIES: Boating; fishing; hiking; hunting; trapping. No swimming or scuba diving. MISC.: Pets on leash. Get FREE camping permit at any Ohio Power Company office; or write Ohio Power Co.; PO Box 328; McConnelsville, OH 43756 [ask for map].

Parksite #B (Ohio Power Company). Approximately 1-3/4 mi SW of Reinersville on St Hwy 78; approximately ½ mi N on paved all-weather road. SEASON: All yr; 14-day lmt. FACILITIES: Sites; toil, f, drk wtr. ACTIVITIES: Fishing; boating; hiking; hunting; trapping. No swimming or scuba diving. MISC.: Get FREE camping permit at any Ohio Power Company office; or write Ohio Power Co.; PO Box 328; McConnelsville, OH 43756 [ask for map]. Pets allowed if kept on a leash.

Parksite #H (Ohio Power Company). Approximately 2 mi SW of Reinersville on St Hwy 78; approximately 3¼ mi N on winding Haul Road (parallel to railroad tracks). SEASON: All yr; 14-day lmt. FACILITIES: Sites; toil, drk wtr, parking area, f. ACTIVITIES: Fishing; boating; hiking; hunting; trapping. MISC.: Registration. Get FREE camping permit at any Ohio Power Company office; or write Ohio Power Co.; PO Box 328; McConnelsville, OH 43756 [ask for map].

Parksite #R (Ohio Power Company). Approximately 2 mi SW of Reinersville on St Hwy 78; approximately ½ mi NE on haul rd; approximately ½ mi N on haul rd which turns into unpaved all-weather road. SEASON: All yr; 14-day lmt. FACILITIES: Sites; drk wtr, toil, f, cga. ACTIVITIES: Fishing; boating; hiking; hunting; trapping. No swimming or scuba diving. MISC.: Get FREE camping permit at any Ohio Power Company office; or write Ohio Power Co.; PO Box 328; McConnelsville, OH 43756 [ask for map]. Pets.

WELLINGTON

Findley (SP). 2 mi S of Wellington on St Hwy 58. SEASON: All yr; 14-day lmt.

FACILITIES: 50 walk-in tent sites; picnic shelter, toil, playground. Drk wtr at check-in. Dump at SP. Food nearby. ACTIVITIES: Tennis; swimming; picnicking; fishing; boating,rl; hunting; hiking; scuba diving. MISC.: Seasonal naturalist program. Adjacent to a state wildlife area. NO PETS ALLOWED.

WEST UNITY

Indian Meadow Plaza (Turnpike Commission). On I-80; W to milepost 21. SEASON: All yr; 1-night lmt. FACILITIES: 8 spaces for self-contained RVs (tr -30); tbls, flush toil, dump, food, phone, drk wtr, gas. ACTIVITIES: Picnicking. MISC.: Open 4:00 p.m. to 10:00 a.m. Stone-surfaced parking area. Pet exercise area.

ZANESVILLE

*Blue Rock Campground #1 (SP). 15 mi S of Zanesville on SR 60. The main entrance is on Cutler Lake Rd (Co Rd 45); 6 mi SE of SR 60. Signs mark the road to the park. The park office is located off Park Road 3, opposite the beach area. The free WALK-IN camp area is off Cutler Lake Road (Co Rd 45) SE of the lake. A ½-mi trail leads to the camp area. SEASON: All yr; 14-day lmt. FACILITIES: Tent sites; picnic shelter, toil. No drk wtr at campsites. ACTIVITIES: Boating,rl; picnicking; fishing; hiking; swimming; scuba diving. Hunting and horseback riding in adjacent state forest area. Ice boating/skating/fishing in winter. MISC.: Seasonal naturalist program. Beach concession. NO PETS ALLOWED.

*Blue Rock Campground #2 (SP). 15 mi S of Zanesville on SR 60. The main entrance is on Cutler Lake Road (Co Rd 45); 6 mi SE of SR 60. Signs mark the road to the park. The park office is located off Park Road 3, opposite the beach area. The free WALK-IN camp area is near the firetower, off Twp. Rd. 452. SEASON: All yr; 14-day lmt. FACILITIES: Tent sites; toil, drk wtr. ACTIVITIES: Boating,rl; fishing; picnicking; swimming; scuba diving. Ice boating/skating/fishing in winter. Horseback riding and hunting in adjacent SF area. Hiking. MISC.: Picnic shelters. Seasonal naturalist program. Beach concession. NO PETS ALLOWED.

OKLAHOMA

GENERAL STATE INFORMATION

Miscellaneous

Toll-Free Number for Travel Information: 1-800-522-8565 [calling within OK]
Right Turns on Red: Permitted after full stop, unless otherwise posted.
STATE CAPITOL: Oklahoma City
STATE NICKNAME: Sooner State
STATE MOTTO: "Labor Conquers All Things"
STATE BIRD: Scissor-tailed Flycatcher
STATE FLOWER: Mistletoe
STATE TREE: Redbud

State Parks

Basic camping (no hookups) is free in all non-assigned areas in Oklahoma's state parks and recreation areas. Hookups in non-assigned areas are $3.50-4.50. Hookups in assigned areas are $5.50-6.50. Tent sites in assigned areas are $2.00 per night. Tent sites in non-assigned areas are free.

SENIOR CITIZENS DISCOUNTS: In non-assigned areas the regular $3.50 rate is reduced to $1.75. The $4.50 rate is reduced to $2.25. In assigned areas, the regular $5.50 rate is $2.75 and the regular $6.50 rate is $3.25. Senior citizens get assigned tent site rates of $1.00, half of the regular $2.00 price. Further information: Oklahoma Department of Tourism and Recreation; 504 Will Rogers Building; Oklahoma City, OK 73105.

Rest Areas

Overnight stops in self-contained vehicles are permitted.

See page 7 for KEY TO ABBREVIATIONS.

OKLAHOMA

Wichita Mountains Wildlife Refuge (Backpacking)

The Charons Garden Wilderness Area has been designated for backpacking within the Wichita Mountains Wildlife Refuge. A free permit must be picked up in person at the Refuge Headquarters. Maximum length of stay is 3 days. Open fires are prohibited. Use backpackers stove. Pets are not encouraged. Further information: Refuge Manager; Route 2, Box 448; Indiahoma, OK 73552.

Oklahoma Backpacking Trails

Backpackers are free to select their campsites along the trails   Water is generally abundant along the Ouachita Trails, particularly during October-May. Stream water should be boiled or purified prior to drinking. Further information: Oklahoma Tourism and Recreation Department; 500 Will Rogers Building; Oklahoma City, OK 73105. Ask for their free OKLAHOMA TRAILS GUIDE.

INFORMATION SOURCES

Maps

The following maps are available from **Forsyth Travel Library** (see order form in Appendix B):

> **State of Oklahoma** [Up-to-date, showing all principal roads, points of interest, sports areas, parks, airports, mileage, etc. Full color.]
>
> Completely indexed city maps, including all airports, lakes, rivers, etc., of: **Oklahoma City; Tulsa.**

State Information

Division of Tourism Promotion; Tourism and Recreation Department; 500 Will Rogers Building; Oklahoma City, OK 73105.
Travel Information Center; 215 NE 28th; Oklahoma City, OK 73105.
Department of Wildlife Conservation; 1801 North Lincoln; PO Box 53465; Oklahoma City, OK 73105.
Eastern Oklahoma Development District; PO Box 1367; Muskogee, OK 74401.
Grand Lake O'The Cherokees; Grand Lake Association; Route 2, Box 95-A; Grove, OK 74344.

Miscellaneous

Oklahoma City Chamber of Commerce; 200 Skirvin Tower, Oklahoma City, OK 73101.
Tulsa Chamber of Commerce; 616 South Boston Avenue; Tulsa, OK 74119.
Corps of Engineers, Tulsa District; PO Box 61; Tulsa, OK 74102.
Oklahoma [plus New Mexico and Texas] Bureau of Land Management; US P.O. and Federal Building; PO Box 1449; Santa Fe, NM 87501.
Salt Plains National Wildlife Refuge; Route 1, Box 76; Jet, OK 73749.
Wichita Mountains National Wildlife Refuge; Box 448; Cache, OK 73527.
Tishomingo National Wildlife Refuge; PO Box 248; Tishomingo, OK 73460.
Bureau of Indian Affairs; Easteran Oklahoma Development District; PO Box 1367; Muskogee, OK 74401.
Bureau of Indian Affairs; Anadarko Area Office; PO Box 368; Anadarko, OK 73005.

FREE CAMPGROUNDS

ANADARKO

Randlett (City Park). St Hwy 62 to W edge of Anadarko. **SEASON:** All year. **FACILITIES:** 35 sites for self-contained RVs; tbls, toil, cga, f, drk wtr, playground. **ACTIVITIES:** Swimming; picnicking; fishing; softball. **MISC.:** River; pets.   Lighted and patrolled at night. Electricity.

ARKOMA

Arkoma Park (COE; W.D. Mayo Dam) East of US 271 to St Hwy 9A; N to SW corner of Arkoma. **SEASON:** All yr; 14-day lmt. **FACILITIES:** 14 sites; tbls, toil, cga, dump, drk wtr. Ice/food/laundry nearby. **ACTIVITIES:** Fishing; picnicking. **MISC.:** Pets on leash.

See page 7 for KEY TO ABBREVIATIONS.

BROKEN ARROW

Bluff View (COE; Chouteau and Newt Graham). 12 mi E of Broken Arrow on 71st Street; 1 mi N on Co Rd. SEASON: All yr; 14-day lmt. FACILITIES:26 sites; tbls, toil, cga, drk wtr, bottled gas. ACTIVITIES: Boating,ld; picnicking; fishing. MISC.: Pets on leash.

BROWN

Kansas Creek (COE; Lake Texoma, Denison Dam). 4 mi W of Brown on St Hwy 199. SEAS: All yr; 14-day lmt. FAC: 3 sites; tbls, toil, cga, drk wtr. ACTIVITIES: Hunting; picnicking; fishing (sunfish, bass, catfish, striped bass); waterskiing. Tennis/golf/horseback riding nearby. MISC.: Heated fishing dock; pets.

CANTON

Blaine Park (COE; Canton Lake). 1 mi W of Canton on St Hwy 51; 5 mi NE on St Hwy 58A. SEASON: All yr; 14-day lmt. FACILITIES: 20 sites; tbls, flush toil, cga, drk wtr, ice, food, store. ACTIVITIES: Boating,ld; hunting; picnicking; fishing (walleye); swimming. Golf nearby. Rodeo each fall. MISC.: Pets on leash. Air strip.

Dam Site Recreation Area (COE; Canton Lake). 1 mi W of Canton on St Hwy 51; 5 mi NE on St Hwy 58A. SEASON: All yr; 14-day lmt. FACILITIES: 40 sites; tbls, flush toil, cga, drk wtr, ice, food. Store nearby. ACTIVITIES: Swimming; picnicking; fishing (walleye); hunting; boating,rld; horseback riding/rental; tennis; softball; hiking. Golf nearby. Rodeo each fall, nearby. MISC.: Lake; air strip; pets.

Primitive (COE; Canton Lake). 1 mi W of Canton on St Hwy 51; 1½ mi N on St Hwy 58A. SEASON: All yr; 14-day lmt. FACILITIES: 15 sites for self-contained RVs. ACTIVITIES: Swimming; fishing (walleye); horseback riding; hunting. Golf nearby. Rodeo each fall, nearby. MISC.: Air strip nearby; pets on leash.

CARTWRIGHT

Willafa Woods (COE; Lake Texoma, Denison Dam). 4 mi N of Cartwright. SEASON: Free from 9/12 to 5/27 (rest of year $3.00). 14-day lmt. FACILITIES:15 sites; tbls, toil, cga, drk wtr. ACTIVITIES: Fishing (sunfish, bass, catfish), hunting; waterskiing; boating,rl; picnicking. Tennis/golf/horseback riding nearby. MISC.: Heated fishing dock; pets.

CATOOSA

Rogers Point (COE; Chouteau & Newt Graham). 4 mi E of Catoosa on US 66. SEASON: All yr; 14-day lmt. FACILITIES: 23 sites; tbls, toil, cga, drk wtr. ACTIVITIES: Boating,ld; picnicking; fishing. MISC.: Pets allowed if kept on a leash.

CHECOTAH

Holiday Cove (COE; Eufaula Lake). 6 mi W of Checotah on I-40; 1 mi S to campground. SEASON: 3/1-11/1; 14-day lmt. FACILITIES: 15 sites; tbls, toil, cga, drk wtr. Store/ice nearby. ACTIVITIES: Boating,l; picnicking; fishing; hiking; waterskiing. MISC.: Pets; lake; beach. Near Prague's Kolache Festival.

CHEROKEE

Great Salt Plains (COE; Great Salt Plains Lake). 18 mi E of Cherokee on St Hwys 8/11; 8 mi N on jct St Hwy 38A. SEASON: All yr; 14-day lmt. FACILITIES: 20 sites; tbls, toil, cga, drk wtr, showers, dump, electric hookup, food. Store/ice nearby. ACTIVITIES: Hunting; hiking; waterskiing; swimming; boating,l; picnicking; fishing; selenite crystal hunting for rockhounds. MISC.: Pets allowed on leash.

CHOUTEAU

Chouteau Bend (COE; Eufaula Lake). 3 mi E of Chouteau on St Hwy 33. SEASON: All yr; 14-day lmt. FACILITIES: 38 sites (tr -30); tbls, toil, cga, drk wtr, f, food, store. ACTIVITIES: Swimming; boating,rld; picnicking; fishing. MISC.: Pets on leash. Lake.

Mazie Landing (COE; Fort Gibson Lake). 3 mi S of Chouteau on US 69; 3 mi E on paved road to campground. SEASON: All yr; 14-day lmt. FACILITIES: 5 sites (tr -30); tbls, toil, cga, f, drk wtr, food. ACTIVITIES: Hiking; hunting; swimming; waterskiing; picnicking; fishing; boating,l. Golf/horseback riding/stagecoach rides nearby. MISC.: Lake; pets. Air strip is nearby.

CLEVELAND

Osage Point (COE; Keystone Lake). 2 mi NE of Cleveland on St Hwy 99; 4 mi E on Co Rd. SEASON: All yr; 14-day lmt. FACILITIES: 18 sites; tbls, flush toil, cga, drk wtr, dump, showers. Store/ice/food nearby. ACTIVITIES: Swimming; picnicking; fishing; boating,l; sailing; waterskiing; hiking. MISC.: Lake;beach;pets.

COLBERT

Sunset Camp (COE; Lake Texoma, Denison Dam). 4 mi W of Colbert on St Hwy 75A to Cartwright; 2 mi N to campground. SEASON: All yr; 14-day lmt. FACILITIES: 19 sites; tbls, flush toil, cga, drk wtr. ACTIVITIES: Swimming; picnicking; fishing (sunfish, bass, catfish); hunting; waterskiing; boating,l. Golf/tennis/horseback riding nearby. MISC.: Lake; beach; pets. Heated fishing dock.

See page 7 for KEY TO ABBREVIATIONS.

COPAN

Caney Bend (COE; Hulah Lake). 13 mi W of Copan on St Hwy 10. SEASON: All yr; 14-day lmt. FACILITIES: 7 sites; tbls, toil, cga, drk wtr. ACTIVITIES: Swimming; picnicking; fishing; boating,rl; hunting; waterskiing. MISC.: Store/food nearby. Lake. Pets on leash.

Dam Site (COE; Hulah Lake). 12 mi W of Copan on St Hwy 10. SEASON: All yr; 14-day lmt. FACILITIES: 7 sites; tbls, toil, cga, drk wtr, dump. Store/food nearby. ACTIVITIES: Boating,l; picnicking; fishing (catfish); hunting; waterskiing. MISC.: Lake. Pets on leash.

Skull Creek (COE; Hulah Lake). 10 mi W on St Hwy 10 ; 5 mi N to campground SEASON: Free. 9/14-4/31 (rest of yr. $3); 14-day lmt. FACILITIES: 20 sites; tbls. toil, cga. drk wtr. ACTIVITIES: Boating,l; picnicking; fishing; hunting; waterskiing. MISC: Lake. pets.

DISNEY

Cherokee #2 (SRA). E of Disney city limits on St Hwy 28. SEASON: All yr; 14-day lmt. FACILITIES: 16 sites (tr -20); tbls, toil, cga, drk wtr, electric hookup; showers; playground. ACTIVITIES: Swimming; hiking; waterskiing; picnicking; fishing; boating,l. MISC.: Lake; beach. Pets allowed on leash.

Cherokee #3 (SRA). 1 mi E of Disney on E end of Dam. SEASON: All yr; 14-day lmt. FACILITIES: 30 sites; tbls, toil, cga, electric hookup, showers, playground. ACTIVITIES: Boating,l; waterskiing; swimming; picnicking; fishing. MISC.: Lake. Pets allowed if on leash.

EL RENO

Lake El Reno City Park. At W edge of El Reno on US 66; S on Country Club Road; 1st rd after the clubhouse, turn W to campground. SEASON: All yr; 14-day lmt. FACILITIES: 15 sites; tbls, toil, cga, playground. ACTIVITIES: Swimming; picnicking; fishing; boating,l; softball. MISC.: Lake; pets.

ELK CITY

Ackley Park (Municipal Park). On the W side of Elk City on St Hwy 66. SEASON: All year. FACILITIES: 25 sites; tbls, flush toil, cga, dump, showers, drk wtr. Store/food/laundry/bottled gas nearby. ACTIVITIES: Tennis; picnicking. Golf nearby. MISC.: Pets.

ENID

Munn Park (Municipal Park). On St Hwy 81, in the 800-block of N Van Buren St, in Enid. Use east-side exit of north overpass. SEASON: All year. FACILITIES: 50 sites (tr -24); tbls, toil, cga, drk wtr. ACTIVITIES: Picnicking. MISC.: Pets.

ERICK

East Bound. I-40 Rest Area. 2 mi E of St Hwy 30 on I-40. [8 mi E of Texas state line.] SEASON: All yr; 1-night lmt. FACILITIES: Spaces for self-contained RVs; tbls, toil, cga, drk wtr, dump, phone. ACTIVITIES:Picnicking. MISC.:Pets.

West Bound I-40 Rest Area. 2 mi E of St Hwy 30 on I-40. SEASON: All yr; 1-night lmt. FACILITIES: Spaces for self-contained RVs; tbls, toil, cga, dump, phone. ACTIVITIES:Picnicking. MISC.:Pets.

EUFAULA

Cardinal Point (COE; Eufaula Lake). 14 mi S of Eufaula on US 69. SEASON: 3/1-11/1; 14-day lmt. FACILITIES: 10 sites; tbls, toil, cga, drk wtr. ACTIVITIES: Hiking; picnicking; fishing; boating,l; waterskiing (nearby). MISC.: Lake; pets. Prague's Kolache Festival is nearby.

Eufaula Cove North (Municipal Park). In Eufaula on McKinley Avenue. SEASON: All yr; 14-day lmt. FACILITIES: Sites; tbls, toil, cga, f, store, showers. ACTIVITIES: Boating,l; picnicking; fishing. MISC.: Pets on leash. Lake.

Gaines Creek (COE; Eufaula Lake). 4 mi S of Eufaula on US 69; 1½ mi NE on St Hwy 9a; 3 mi S to campground. SEASON: 3/1-11/1; 14-day lmt. FACILITIES: 12 sites; tbls, toil, cga, drk wtr. ACTIVITIES: Hiking; boating,l; picnicking; fishing; waterskiing. MISC.: Lake; pets. Prague's Kolache Festival is nearby.

Mill Creek Bay (COE; Eufaula Lake). 6 mi W on St Hwy 9; approximately 2 mi S to campground. SEASON: Free 9/12-5/27 (rest of yr, $3); 14-day lmt. FACILITIES: 10 sites; tbls, toil, cga, drk wtr. ACTIVITIES: Boating,l; picnicking; fishing; hiking; waterskiing. MISC.: Lake; pets. Prague's Kolache Festival.

Oak Ridge (COE; Eufaula Lake). 5 mi S on US 69; 3/10 mi E on SR 9A. SEASON: Free 9/12-5/27 (rest of yr. $3); FACILITIES: 10 sites; tbls, toil, cga, no drk wtr. ACTIVITIES: Hiking; picnicking; fishing; boating,l; waterskiing. MISC.: Lake; pets. (Prague's Kolache).

West Crowder Point (COE; Eufaula Lake). 12 mi S of Eufaula on US 69. SEASON: All yr; 14-day lmt. FACILITIES: 5 sites; tbls, toil, cga, drk wtr. ACTIVITIES: Hiking; waterskiing; boating,l; picnicking; fishing. MISC.: Lake; pets. Prague's Kolache Festival is nearby.

FORT GIBSON

Ft. Gibson Park (COE; Webbers Falls Dam). Cross the County Bridge near Ft. Gibson to the campground. SEASON: All yr; 14-day lmt. FACILITIES: 9 sites; tbls, toil, cga, drk wtr. Store/ice/

food/laundry nearby. ACTIVITIES: Hunting; picnicking; fishing; boating,ld. MISC.: Pets. Tsa-La-Gi Cherokee Indian Village is located nearby.

Mallard Bay (COE; Fort Gibson Lake). ½ mi W of Dam on St Hwy 251-A; 2 mi E to the campground. SEASON: All yr; 14-day lmt. FACILITIES: Undesignated sites; tbls, toil, cga, drk wtr, f. ACTIVITIES: Hunting; hiking; waterskiing; swimming; boating,l; picnicking; fishing. Golf/horseback riding/stagecoach rides nearby. MISC.: Lake; pets. Air strip nearby.

Wolf Creek Park Fort Supply Lake (COE; Ft. Gibson Lake). 7/10 mi S of Ft. Gibson on US 270; 1 mi E to campground. SEASON: All yr; 14-day lmt. FACILITIES: 14 sites; tbls, toil, cga. ACTIVITIES: Hunting; hiking; picnicking; fishing; waterskiing. Golf/horseback riding/stagecoach rides nearby. MISC.: Lake; pets. Air strip nearby.

FOYIL

Clermont Parks #1 and #2 (COE; Oologah Lake). 2 mi W of Foyil; 3 mi N; 2 mi W; 2 mi SW to the campgrounds. SEASON: Free from, 9/12 to 5/20. Rest of the year $3.00 charge. .FACILITIES:25 sites; tbls, toil, cga, drk wtr, dump, f. ACTIVITIES: Swimming; picnicking; fishing; boating,l; hunting; waterskiing. MISC.: Pets; lake.

GORE

Dam Site (COE; Tenkiller Ferry). 7 mi NE of Gore on St Hwy 100. SEASON: All yr; 14-day lmt. FACILITIES: 10 sites (tr -30); tbls, flush toil, cga, drk wtr, f. ACTIVITIES: Hunting; hiking; waterskiing; scuba diving; boating,l; picnicking; fishing. Float trips nearby. MISC.: Lake. Pets on leash.

HINTON

Red Rock Canyon. ½ mi S of Hinton on US 8. SEASON: All year. FACILITIES: 200 sites; f, electric/sewer hookups, playground. ACTIVITIES: Swimming; hiking. MISC.: Pets on leash.

HULBERT

Hulbert Landing (COE; Fort Gibson Lake). 2 mi W of Hulbert on blacktop road. SEASON: All yr; 14-day lmt. FACILITIES: 9 sites (tr -30); tbls, toil, cga, f, drk wtr. ACTIVITIES: Hiking; hunting; waterskiing; boating,l; picnicking; fishing. Golf/horseback riding/stagecoach ride nearby. MISC.: Lake. Pets on leash.

JET

Jet Recreation Area (Salt Plains NWR). 3 mi N of Jet on St Hwy 38. SEASON: 4/15-10/15; 7-day lmt. FACILITIES: 20 sites (tr -20), tbls, toil, cga, f, drk wtr. ACTIVITIES: Hiking; waterskiing; boating,l; swimming; picnicking; fishing. MISC.: Pets on leash. No off-road vehicles. The Salt Plains are a perfectly flat expanse of mud, completely devoid of vegetation.

KELLYVILLE

Sunset Bay (COE: Heyburn Lake). 6 mi W on Co Rd. SEASON: Free, 9/10-5/9(rest of year $3); 14-day lmt. FACILITIES: Undesignated sites; tbls, toil, cga, f, drk wtr. ACTIVITIES: Boating,ld; swimming; picnicking; fishing. MISC.: Pets.

LOCUST GROVE

Earbob Ferry (COE; Fort Gibson Lake). 3 mi S of Locust Grove on St Hwy 82; 7 mi SW on paved rd to campground. SEASON: All yr; 14-day lmt. FACILITIES: 5 sites (tr -30); tbls, toil, cga, drk wtr, f, food. ACTIVITIES: Boating,rld; picnicking; fishing; waterskiing; hiking; hunting. Golf/horseback riding/stagecoach rides nearby. MISC.: Lake; Pets. Air strip nearby.

LONGDALE

Fairview (COE; Canton Lake). 2 mi W of Longdale on Co Rd; 1 mi N; 1 mi W on dirt rd. SEASON: All yr; 14-day lmt. FACILITIES: 12 sites; tbls, toil, cga, drk wtr. ACTIVITIES: Swimming; picnicking; fishing (walleye); hunting. Golf nearby. Rodeo nearby each fall. MISC.: Pets. Air strip nearby.

Longdale (COE; Canton Lake). 2 mi W of Longdale on Co Hwy. SEASON:9/12-4/31; 14-day lmt. FACILITIES: 30 sites; tbls, toil, cga, drk wtr. ACTIVITIES: Hunting; picnicking; fishing (walleye); boating,ld. Rodeo nearby, each fall. MISC.: Pets on leash. Air strip nearby.

MADILL

Alberta Creek (COE; Lake Texoma, Denison Dam). 15 mi SE of Madill on US 70 and 70A. SEASON: All yr; 14-day lmt. FACILITIES: 14 sites; tbls, flush toil, cga, drk wtr, electric/water/sewer hookups, store. ACTIVITIES: Hunting; boating,rld; picnicking; fishing (sunfish, bass, catfish). Tennis, golf, and horseback riding are nearby. MISC.: Pets on leash. Heated fishing dock.

Arrowhead Point (COE; Lake Texoma, Denison Dam). 15 mi S of Madill. SEASON: All yr; 14-day lmt. FACILITIES: 18 sites; tbls, toil, cga, drk wtr, electric hookup. Food nearby. ACTIVITIES: Hunting; waterskiing; picnicking; fishing (sunfish, bass, catfish); boating,rl. Tennis, golf, horseback riding nearby. MISC.: Pets; heated fishing dock; lake.

See page 7 for KEY TO ABBREVIATIONS.

Briar Creek (COE; Lake Texoma, Denison Dam). 13 mi SW of Madill on St Hwy 99; 1½ mi W to campground. SEASON: All yr; 14-day lmt. FACILITIES: 10 sites; tbls, toil, cga, drk wtr, store. ACTIVITIES: Boating,rl; picnicking; fishing (sunfish, bass, catfish); hunting; waterskiing. Tennis, golf, horseback riding nearby. MISC.: Pets; lake. Heated fishing dock.

Cumberland Cove (COE; Lake Texoma, Denison Dam). 12 mi SE of Madill on St Hwy 199; 2 mi S on paved road. SEASON: 9/12-5/27; day lmt. FACILITIES: 11 sites; tbls, flush toil, cga, drk wtr. Store/food nearby. ACTIVITIES: Boating,1; picnicking; fishing (sunfish, bass, catfish); hunting; waterskiing. Tennis, golf, horseback riding nearby. MISC.: Pets; lake. Heated fishing dock nearby.

Lebanon (COE; Lake Texoma, Denison Dam). 13 mi SW of Madill on St Hwy 99C. SEASON: 9/12-5/27; 14-day lmt. FACILITIES: 18 sites; tbls, toil, cga, drk wtr. Food nearby. ACTIVITIES: Hunting; picnicking; fishing (sunfish, bass, catfish); boating,rl; waterskiing. Golf, tennis, horseback riding nearby. MISC.: Pets on leash. Heated fishing dock is nearby.

Roads End (COE; Lake Texoma, Denison Dam). 13 mi SE of Madill on US 70/70A. SEASON:9/12-5/27; 14-day lmt. FACILITIES: 18 sites; tbls, flush toil, cga, drk wtr. ACTIVITIES: Boating,rl; picnicking; fishing (sunfish, bass, catfish); hunting; waterskiing. Tennis, golf, horseback riding are nearby. MISC.: Pets on leash. Heated fishing dock is nearby.

Soldier Creek (COE; Lake Texoma, Denison Dam). 12 mi E of Madill on US 70 and St Hwy 708. SEASON: All yr; 14-day lmt. FACILITIES: 19 sites; tbls, flush toil, cga, drk wtr, electric/water/sewer hookups, food. Store/ice nearby. ACTIVITIES: Boating,rld; picnicking; fishing (sunfish, bass, catfish); hunting; waterskiing. Tennis, golf, horseback riding nearby. MISC.: Pets. Heated fishing dock nearby.

MANNFORD

Old Mannford Ramp (COE; Keystone Lake). 4 mi W of Mannford on US 51; 2 mi N on St Hwy 48; 1 mi E on Co Rd. SEASON: All yr; 14-day lmt. FACILITIES: 29 sites; tbls, toil, cga, drk wtr. Store/ice nearby. ACTIVITIES: Swimming; picnicking; fishing (striped bass); boating,l; sailing; waterskiing; hiking. MISC.: Pets; lake; beach.

Sandy Park (COE; Keystone Lake). 3 mi N of Mannford on Co Hwy; 3 mi E on gravel Co Rd. SEASON: All yr; 14-day lmt. FACILITIES: Undesignated sites; tbls, toil, cga, drk wtr. ACTIVITIES: Swimming; picnicking; fishing (striped bass); sailing; waterskiing; hiking. MISC.: Pets on leash. Lake.

MARIETTA

Hickory Creek (COE; Lake Texoma, Denison Dam). 7 mi E of Marietta on St Hwy 32; ¼ mi S of Bridge. SEASON: All yr; 14-day lmt. FACILITIES: tbls, toil, cga, drk wtr, food. ACTIVITIES: Boating,rl; picnicking; fishing (sunfish, bass, catfish); hunting; waterskiing. Golf, tennis, horseback riding are nearby. MISC.: Pets on leash. Heated fishing dock is nearby. Lake,

McALESTER

Elm Point (COE; Eufaula Lake). 11 mi NE of McAlester on St Hwy 31. SEASON: 9/12-5/27; day lmt. FACILITIES: 7 sites; tbls, toil, cga, drk wtr. ACTIVITIES: Swimming; picnicking; fishing; boating,l; hiking; waterskiing. MISC.: Pets. Lake. Near Prague's Kolache Festival.

Hickory Point (COE; Eufaula Lake). 10 mi E of McAlester on paved rd to campground. SEASON:9/12-5/27; 14-day lmt. FACILITIES: 10 sites; tbls, toil, cga, drk wtr. ACTIVITIES: Swimming; picnicking; fishing; hiking; waterskiing; boating,l. MISC.: Lake; pets. Prague's Kolache Festival is nearby.

MUSE

Billy Creek (Ouachita NF). 2 mi E of Muse on St Hwy 63; 3 mi N on FS 22. SEASON: All yr; 14-day lmt. FACILITIES: 14 sites (tr -22); tbls, toil, cga, drk wtr, f. Store/ice nearby. ACTIVITIES: Hiking; rockhounding; hunting; picnicking; fishing. MISC.: Elev 800 ft;3 acres; stream; pets. 5 mi S of Talimena Scenic Drive.

MUSKOGEE

Hopewell Park (COE; Webbers Fall Dam). 4½ mi E of Muskogee Turnpike on paved rd; ½ mi S on gravel rd to campground. SEASON: All yr; 14-day lmt. FACILITIES: 17 sites; tbls, flush toil, cga, drk wtr, dump. ACTIVITIES: Boating,ld; picnicking. MISC.: Pets on leash. Showers.

Tullahassee Loop (COE; Chouteau & Newt Graham). 7 mi N of Muskogee on US 69; 2½ mi W on Chouteau L & D rd. SEASON: All yr; 14-day lmt. FACILITIES: 8 sites; tbls, toil, cga, drk wtr. ACTIVITIES: Swimming; boating,l; picnicking; fishing. MISC.: Pets on leash.

NOWATA

Big Creek Cove (COE; Oologah Lake). 5 mi E of Nowata on St Hwy 60; 2½ mi N to campground. SEASON: All yr; 14-day lmt. FACILITIES: 7 sites; tbls, toil, cga, f, drk wtr. ACTIVITIES: Hunting; waterskiing; boating,l; picnicking; fishing; swimming. MISC.: Lake. Pets.

See page 7 for KEY TO ABBREVIATIONS.

OOLOGAH

Verdigris River Park (COE;Oologah Lake). 2 mi SE of Oologah on St Hwy 88. SEASON: All yr; 14-day lmt. FACILITIES: 7 sites; tbls, toil, cga, f, drk wtr. Store/ice/food/dump nearby. ACTIVITIES: Hunting; waterskiing; picnicking; fishing. Swimming nearby. MISC.: Lake. Pets.

PLATTER

Platter Flats (COE; Lake Texoma, Denison Dam). 1 mi N of Platter. SEASON: All yr; 14-day lmt. FACILITIES: 17 sites; tbls, flush toil, cga, drk wtr. ACTIVITIES: Hunting; boating,l; picnicking; fishing (sunfish, bass, catfish); waterskiing. Tennis, golf, horseback riding are nearby. MISC.: Pets on leash. Heated fishing dock is nearby. 9/10-5/27

SALLISAW

East Bound I-40 Rest Area. 3 mi E of Sallisaw at Milepost 314. SEASON: All yr; 1-night lmt. FACILITIES: Spaces for self-contained RVs; tbls, toil, cga, dump. MISC.: Pets on a leash.

Sallisaw (SRA). 3 mi W of Sallisaw on US 64. SEASON: All yr; 14-day lmt. FACILITIES: 30 sites; tbls, flush toil, cga, drk wtr, showers, playground. ACTIVITIES: Swimming; boating,l; picnicking; fishing. MISC.: Pets on leash.

West Bound I-40 Rest Area. 5 mi E of Sallisaw at Milepost 316. SEASON: All yr; 1-night lmt. FACILITIES: Spaces for self-contained RVs; toil, dump, phone. MISC.: Pets allowed on a leash.

SAND SPRINGS

Appalachia Bay (COE; Keystone Lake). 12 mi W of Sand Springs on US 64; 1¼ mi SW on Co Rd. SEASON:9/12-5/20 14-day lmt. FACILITIES: 20 sites; tbls, toil, cga, drk wtr. Store/ice/food nearby. ACTIVITIES: Swimming; picnicking; fishing (striped bass); sailing; boating,ld; waterskiing; hiking. MISC.: Pets on leash. Lake.

Cimarron (COE; Keystone Lake). 19 mi W of Sand Springs on St Hwy 64; 1 mi S on Co Rd. SEASON: All yr; 14-day lmt. FACILITIES: Undesignated sites; tbls, toil, cga, drk wtr. ACTIVITIES: Swimming; picnicking; fishing (striped bass); hiking; sailing; waterskiing. MISC.: Lake; beach. Pets on leash.

Keystone Ramp (COE; Keystone Lake). 11 mi W of Sand Springs on US 51; 1¼ mi N on Co Rd. SEASON: All yr; 14-day lmt. FACILITIES: 13 sites; tbls, toil, cga, drk wtr. Store/ice/food nearby. ACTIVITIES: Swimming; picnicking; fishing (striped bass); boating,l; sailing; waterskiing; hiking. MISC.: Lake; beach. Pets allowed if on a leash.

SEMINOLE

East Bound I-40 Rest Area. 3 mi W of Seminole exit on I-40. SEASON: All Yr; 1-night lmt. FACILITIES: Spaces for self-contained RVs; tbls, toil, cga, dump, phone, playground. ACTIVITIES: Picnicking. MICS.: Pets

SHAWNEE

West Bound I-40 Rest Area. 14 mi E of Shawnee on I-40. SEASON: All yr; 1-night lmt. FACILITIES: Spaces for self-contained RVs; tbls, toil, cga, dump, phone, playground. ACTIVITIES: Picnicking. MISC.: Pets on leash.

SULPHUR

Arbuckle Public Hunting Area (SRA). 1 mi W of Sulphur on St Hwy 7; 3 mi S on Point Road. SEASON: All yr; 1-night lmt. FACILITIES: Primitive sites. ACTIVITIES: Fishing; hunting. MISC.: Lake. Pets allowed if kept on a leash.

TAHLEQUAH

Carters Landing (COE; Tenkiller Ferry). 11 mi S of Tahlequah on St Hwy 82. SEASON: All yr; 14-day lmt. SEASON: All yr; 14-day lmt. FACILITIES: 31 sites (tr -30); tbls, toil, cga, f, store, ice, food, drk wtr. ACTIVITIES: Swimming; picnicking; fishing; boating,rld. MISC.: Pets permitted on leash.

Elk Creek (COE; Tenkiller Ferry). 17 mi SE of Tahlequah on St Hwy 82. SEASON: 9/13-4/31; 14-day lmt. FACILITIES: 35 sites (tr -30); tbls, toil, cga, f, drk wtr, dump, store, food, ice. ACTIVITIES: Swimming; picnicking; fishing; boating,rld. MISC.: Pets on leash.

Sisemore Landing (COE; Tenkiller Ferry). 15 mi S of Tahlequah on St Hwy 82. SEASON:9/16-5/27; 14-day lmt. FACILITIES: 32 sites (tr -30); tbls, toil, cga, f, drk wtr. ACTIVITIES: Swimming; picnicking; fishing; boating,l. MISC.: Pets on leash.

Standing Rock (COE; Tenkiller Ferry). 20 mi SE of Tahlequah on St Hwy 82. SEASON:9/16-5/27; 14-day lmt. FACILITIES: 15 sites (tr -30); tbls, toil, cga, f, drk wtr. ACTIVITIES: Boating,l; picnicking; fishing. MISC.: Pets on leash.

TALALA

Sunnyside Ramp (COE; Oologah Lake). 3¼ mi E of Talala on Co Rd. SEASON: 9/12-5/27;14-day lmt. FACILITIES: 8 sites; tbls, toil, cga, f, drk wtr, store, ice. ACTIVITIES: Picnicking; boating,l; fishing. MISC.: Pets.

See page 7 for KEY TO ABBREVIATIONS.

OKLAHOMA

TISHOMINGO

Blue River Public Hunting and Fishing Area (SRA). 3 mi E of Tishomingo on St Hwy 78; 8 mi N to campground. SEASON: All year. FACILITIES: Sites (tr -20); tbls, toil, cga. ACTIVITIES: Hunting; picnicking; fishing. MISC.: Pets on leash. River.

Butcher Pen (COE; Lake Texoma, Denison Dam). 11 mi SE of Tishomingo on St Hwys 78/22. SEASON: All yr; 14-day lmt. FACILITIES: 11 sites; tbls, flush toil, cga, drk wtr. ACTIVITIES: Hunting; picnicking; fishing (sunfish, bass, catfish); boating,rl; waterskiing. Tennis, golf, horseback riding are nearby. MISC.: Lake; pets. Heated fishing dock.

Pennington Creek (COE; Lake Texoma, Denison Dam). On the west side of Tishomingo; S and E ¼ mi on St Hwy 99. SEASON: All yr; 14-day lmt. FACILITIES: 9 sites; tbls, flush toil, cga, drk wtr. Store/ice/food/laundry nearby. ACTIVITIES: Boating,rl; picnicking; fishing; hunting; waterskiing. Tennis, golf, horseback riding are nearby. MISC.: Pets on leash. Heated fishing dock.

TONKAWA

Ray See Park (City Park). 500 South Main Street, in Tonkawa. SEASON: All yr; 3-day lmt. FACILITIES: 10 sites; tbls, toil, cga, dump, phone, playground. ACTIVITIES: Swimming; picnicking. MISC.: Electric hookup. Pets.

VALLIANT

Pine Creek Cove (COE; Pine Creek Lake). 7 mi N of Valliant to COE office. SEASON: All yr; 14-day lmt. FACILITIES: 8 sites (tr -20); tbls, toil, cga, f, drk wtr. Store nearby. ACTIVITIES: Swimming; picnicking; fishing; boating,l. MISC.: Pets on leash.

WAGONER

Long Bay Landing (COE; Fort Gibson Lake). 4 mi E of Wagoner on St Hwy 51; 1 mi N on Co Rd; 1 mi W on Co Rd. SEASON: All yr; 14-day lmt. FACILITIES: 15 sites (tr -30); tbls, toil, cga, dump, drk wtr. Electric/water hookups. ACTIVITIES: Swimming; boating,rld; picnicking; fishing; hunting; hiking; waterskiing. Golf, horseback riding, stagecoach rides are nearby. MISC.: Lake; pets; air strip.

Snug Harbor (COE; Fort Gibson Lake). 3 mi N of Wagoner on St Hwy 69; 3½ mi E. SEASON: All yr; 14-day lmt. FACILITIES: Undesignated sites (no trailers); tbls, toil, cga, drk wtr. ACTIVITIES: Hiking; hunting; waterskiing; picnicking. Golf, horseback riding, stagecoach rides nearby. MISC.: Lake; pets; air strip.

WATONGA

Roman Nose. On U.S. 8A, near St Hwy 281. SEASON: All year. FACILITIES: 11 sites; sewer hookup. ACTIVITIES: Swimming; boating,r; golf. MISC.: Pets.

WISTER

Wister. 2 mi S of Wister off St Hwy 270. SEASON: All yr; 14-day lmt. FACILITIES: 135 sites; tbls, toil, cga, cold shower, store, food, playground, electric and water hookups. ACTIVITIES: Boating,rl; waterskiing; picnicking; fishing. MISC.: Pets allowed if kept on a leash.

OREGON

GENERAL STATE INFORMATION

Miscellaneous

Toll-Free Number for Travel Information: 1-800-452-5687 [calling within Oregon]
Right Turns on Red: Permitted after full stop, unless otherwise posted.
STATE CAPITOL: Salem
STATE NICKNAME: Beaver State
STATE MOTTO: "The Union"
STATE BIRD: Western Meadow Lark
STATE FLOWER: Oregon Grape
STATE TREE: Douglas Fir

State Parks

Overnight camping fees range from $3.00–6.00; plus an additional $2.00 daily surcharge for all out-of-state campers. Pets are permitted if kept on a leash. Further information: Parks and Recreation Branch; Department of Transportation; 525 Trade Street, SE; Salem, OR 97310.

See page 7 for KEY TO ABBREVIATIONS.

OREGON

Rest Areas

"Camping" is not allowed in rest areas. As a safety promotion measure, vehicles are allowed to park in the rest areas, but for no longer than 14 hours in any single 24-hour period.

Pacific Crest National Scenic Trail

For a current FREE map and information on the 2500-mile trail which traverses Washington, Oregon, and California, write: Pacific Northwest Region; Regional Forester; PO Box 3623; Portland, OR 97208.

Crater Lake National Park

Park Roads: St Hwy 62, from W and S, is open all year, and the park road to the lake is open throughout the winter, weather permitting. The road from Rim Village to the north entrance opens about June 1st. The entire 33-mile Rim Drive opens about July 4th. The north entrance road and Rim Drive are closed by snow in late fall. The Park averages 50 feet of snowfall annually.

Fishing: Fishing is limited as fish are not native to Crater Lake. No fishing license is required in the National Park.

Entrance Fees: Entrance fees to the park are $2.00 per car. These fees are covered by holders of the Golden Eagle Passport, and the Golden Age Passport.**

Pacific Crest Trail: Bisects the park from north to south. Excellent backpacking trail. Backcountry permits are required, obtainable at park headquarters.

Winter: No gas is available in the Park during the winter months; and no campgrounds are open during that time.

Pets: Pets are permitted on leash, but not allowed in buildings or on trails WITH THE EXCEPTION OF the Pacific Crest Trail only when the backcountry camper is traveling THROUGH the National Park. The traveler must enter and exit on Pacific Crest Trail. Pets are not permitted on any of the spur or access trails to or from the Pacific Crest Trail. CAUTION: Be sure your pet does not venture over the rim wall, where there is loose pumice soil and a 1,000-foot drop.

WILDERNESS AND BACKCOUNTRY CAMPING

Crater Lake NP

All camping in the backcountry is FREE. (However, the NP entrance fee applies; see above section on Crater Lake NP.)
Backcountry use permits are required for all backcountry overnight stays (camping anywhere outside a developed drive-in campground). These permits can be obtained from one of the designated public information stations or by going to a self-registration box. Camping with fires is permitted   Dead and down wood may be used for firewood. Cutting or damaging living or standing vegetation is prohibited. All non-burnable materials must be carried out of the backcountry and deposited in proper receptacles.

PROHIBITED: Pets, firearms, bicycles, motorized vehicles, hunting.

Further information: Superintendent; Crater Lake NP; Box 7; Crater Lake, OR 97604.

Crooked River Backcountry   (Ochoco NF)

Grassland area located in central Oregon, at the western end of Blue Mountains. HUNTING: Mule deer, pronghorn antelope (Big Summit Prairie; spring, summer, fall); Rocky Mountain elk, pheasant, valley quail, ruffed grouse, chukar partridge.   FISHING: Best is in Crooked River below Prineville Dam (rainbow trout). Hiking; camping. Further information: Forest Supervisor; Ochoco NF; PO Box 490; Prineville, OR 97754.

Deschutes NF Wilderness Areas: Mt. Jefferson; Mt. Washington; Three Sisters; and Diamond Peak

Parts of the above wilderness areas are located in Deschutes NF. All motorized equipment is prohibited from being used in these areas: motor vehicles, snowmobiles, seaplanes, power saws, motor boats, for example. The NF has 400 miles of trails, some for hiking and some for horse travel (watch for signs). SPORTS: Cross-country skiing, snowshoeing; numerous lakes and rivers for boating and swimming; mountain climbing. FISHING: One of the most popular fishing areas in the Pacific NW Region. There are 150 lakes and reservoirs in the NF which have trout and salmon. There are also 235 miles of fishable streams and rivers. HUNTING: Mule deer (can be seen in summer and fall); black-tailed deer and Roosevelt elk spend the summer at higher elevations of the NF, returning to the Willamette Valley during the winter. A few pronghorned antelope summer along the eastern edge of the Forest. ENDANGERED BIRDS: About 12 pairs of bald eagles nest near the Cascade Lakes Highway. American osprey, greater sandhill crane, and prairie falcon. FISHING AND HUNTING for waterfowl and deer are permitted on the Management Area during the regular seasons, but no hunting is allowed from 4/1-9/30, the osprey's nesting season.

Entry into all wilderness areas requires a free permit obtainable at a ranger station; self-registration at trailheads. Further information: Forest, Supervisor; Deschutes NF; 211 NE Revere; Bend OR 97701.

Eagle Cap Wilderness (Wallowa-Whitman NF)

293,735 acres; located in the Wallowa Mountains of NE Oregon. The world's entire population of the rare Wallowa Gray-crowned rosy finch nests only in selected areas of this Wilderness. Good trout fishing. The most popular period of use is July and August; however, September is very enjoyable. Elk and mule deer hunting. Free permits are available at the Forest Service offices. Further information: Forest Supervisor; Wallowa-Whitman NF; PO Box 907; Baker, OR 97814.

Gearhart Mountain Wilderness (Fremont NF)

1,194,000 acres; on the east slope of the Cascade Range, in south central Oregon. Gearhart Mountain (8,364 feet in elevation; volcanic mountain). Rocky Mountain mule deer range here during summer and fall. HUNT: Mountain lion, wildcat, coyote, black bear, mule deer, blue grouse. EXCELLENT FISHING in Sprague River and the Chewaucan River (trout; dry fly-fishing). WATERFOWL HUNTING: Goose Lake, on the California-Oregon border. FURTHER INFORMATION: Forest Supervisor; Fremont NF; PO Box 551; Lakeview, OR 97630.

Hells Canyon - Seven Devils Scenic Area (Wallowa-Whitman NF)

The 130,000-acre Area lies astride 26 miles of the Snake River Canyon on the Idaho-Oregon border. The largest, formally-designated scenic area in the contiguous 48 states, it is in 2 states (33,000 acres in Oregon and 97,000 acres in Idaho) and extends into 3 National Forests (36,000 acres in Nezperce NF; 61,000 acres in Payette NF; and 33,000 acres in Wallowa-Whiteman NF). The Snake River has cut the deepest gorge in North America. Multipurpose roads and a trail system permit all types of Forest recreation: hunting, boating, fishing, hiking, camping, sightseeing. HUNTING: Elk, mule deer, mountain goat, white-tailed deer, bear, cougar, bobcat, grouse, chukar, Hungarian partridge, wild turkey, quail. Further information: Hells Canyon-Seven Devils Area; Joseph Ranger District; Wallowa-Whitman NF; Joseph, OR 97846. CAUTION: Watch for rattlesnakes. Boating the Snake River requires experience and special equipment. Snowmobiling in winter.

Kalmiopsis Wilderness (Siskiyou NF)

76,900 acres; in the Siskiyou Mountains. There are still a few old shelters and cabins left over from gold-rush days. Trails are steep and rocky. Hunting: Roosevelt elk, mountain lions, deer, black bear, quail. Plenty of fishing opportunities. Further information: Forest Supervisor; PO Box 440; Grants Pass, OR 97526.

Mount Hood National Forest Wildernesses

MOUNT HOOD WILDERNESS: 14,160 acres. Mount Hood (11,245 feet) is Oregon's highest mountain. Hunting, fishing, hiking, camping. Further information: District Ranger; Zigzag District; Mount Hood NF; Zigzag, OR 97073.

GREAT GORGE AREA and EAGLE ROADLESS AREA: 52,000 acres. Hunting, fishing, camping, hiking. Further information: District Ranger; Columbia Gorge District; Mount Hood NF; Route 3, Box 44-A; Troutdale, OR 97060.

WARM SPRINGS RESERVATION: 300,000 acres. Adjacent to the National Forest's eastern boundary. Fantastic fishing area; but overnight camping is generally not permitted. Further information: Forest Supervisor; Mount Hood NF: 2440 SE 195th Avenue; Portland, OR 97230. Also available from this address are FREE special area maps of: Bagley Hot Springs; Dalles Watershed; Bull of the Woods; Rock Lakes Basin. Plus additional camping information.

Mount Jefferson Wilderness (Willamette NF)

99,600 acres in three National Forests: Deschutes, Mount Hood, and Willamette NFs. In volcanic plateau country. Mount Jefferson (10,495 feet); has 5 major glaciers. More than 160 miles of trails (36 miles of Pacific Crest Trail). Fishing in alpine lakes. Popular mountain climbing area. Further information: Forest Supervisor; Post Office Building; Eugene, OR 97401.

OREGON

Mount Washington Wilderness   (Willamette NF)

46,655 acres.   Mount Washington (7802 feet) is popular with mountain climbers.   28 lakes for fishing.   HUNTING: Mule deer, black-tailed deer, mountain lions, black bear, snowshoe rabbit.   Further information: District Ranger; Willamette NF; McKenzie Ranger Station; McKenzie Bridge, OR 97401.

Mountain Lakes Wilderness   (Winema NF)

23,071 acres; in the southern part of the National Forest.   Alpine lakes with timbered shorelines; high mountain peaks.   Good fishing.   Campsites along shoreline.   Hunting: ducks, geese, deer.   Further information: Forest Supervisor; PO Box 1390; Klamath Falls, OR 97601.

Sky Lakes Wilderness Area   (Rogue River NF)

Elevation ranges from 3800 feet (Middle Fork Canyon of Rogue River) to 9497 feet (Mount McLoughlin).   35 miles of the Pacific Crest Trail winds its way through this area.   Excellent Hunting: Roosevelt elk, deer, mountain lions, black bear, ducks, geese, doves, grouse, quail.   Fishing: Rogue River was made famous as a top fishing area by Zane Grey (steelhead and salmon).   Further information: Forest Supervisor; Rogue River NF); PO Box 520; Medford, OR 97501.

Strawberry Wilderness   (Malheur NF)

Big game hunting for deer and elk.   5 glacial lakes open year round for fishing. 33,000-acre wilderness; Strawberry Mountain (9044 feet).   About 100 miles of trails within the area; open by the middle of July and remain so until about November 1st. At the most-used campsites, some simple sanitary facilities are provided.   Free permits are available at Forest offices in John Day, Prairie City, and Burns.   Further information: Forest Supervisor; Malheur NF; John Day, OR 97845.

Umpqua National Forest Wilderness

Excellent fishing; hiking; camping; deer and elk hunting.   Historic Bohemia Mining District.   Further information: Forest Supervisor; Umpqua NF; PO Box 1008; Roseburg, OR 97470.

Wenaha Backcountry   (Umatilla NF)

111,200 acres; on the crest of northern Blue Mountains.   More than 900 miles of trails. Watch for rattlesnakes.   Whitetail deer (on the banks of the Wenaha River, in the fall).   Hunting: Elk and mule deer, Rocky Mountain sheep, wild turkey.   Fishing; hiking; camping.   Further information: Forest Supervisor; Umatilla NF; 2517 SW Hailey; Pendleton, OR 97801.

INFORMATION SOURCES

Maps

The following maps are available from **Forsyth Travel Library** (see order form in Appendix B):

> **State of Oregon** [Up-to-date, showing all principal roads, points of interest, sports areas, parks, airports, mileage, etc.   Full color.]
>
> Completely indexed city maps, including all airports, lakes, rivers, etc., of: **Ashland; Coos Bay; Klamath Falls; North Bend; Portland.**

Gold Mining and Prospecting

Oregon State Department of Geology and Mineral Industries; 1069 State Office Building; Portland, OR 97201.

State Information

Parks and Recreation Branch; Department of Transportation; 525 Trade Street, SE; Salem, OR 97310.
Travel Information Section; Department of Transportation; State Transportation Building; Salem, OR 97310.
Fish and Wildlife Department; PO Box 3503; Portland, OR 97208.

City Information

Oregon City Chamber of Commerce; 703 John Adams Street; Oregon City, OR 97045.
Portland Chamber of Commerce; 824 SW 5th Avenue; Portland, OR 97204.
Salem Chamber of Commerce; PO Box 231; Salem, OR 97308.

OREGON

National Forests

Deschutes NF; 211 NE Revere; Bend, OR 97701.
Fremont NF; PO Box 551; Lakeview, OR 97630.
Malheur NF; John Day, OR 97845.
Mount Hood NF; 2440 SE 195 Avenue; Portland, OR 97233.
Ochoco NF; PO Box 490; Prineville, OR 97754.
Rogue River NF; PO Box 520; Medford, OR 97501.
Siskiyou NF; PO Box 440; Grants Pass, OR 97526.
Siuslaw NF; Reedsport, OR 97467.
Umatilla NF; 2517 SW Hailey; Pendleton, OR 97801.
Umpqua NF; PO Box 1008; Roseburg, OR 97470.
Wallowa-Whitman NFs; Federal Building; PO Box
    907; Baker, OR 97814.
Willamette NF; Post Office Building; Eugene, OR 97401.
Winema NF; PO Box 1390; Klamath Falls, OR 97601.

Miscellaneous

Oregon [and Washington] BLM; PO Box 2965; Portland, OR 97208.
Sheldon-Hart Mountain NWR Complex; Box 111; Lakeview, OR 97630.
Bureau of Indian Affairs; PO Box 3785; Portland, OR 97208.
Corps of Engineers; PO Box 2946; Portland, OR 97208.
Crater Lake NP; Box 7; Crater Lake, OR 97604.

FREE CAMPGROUNDS

AGNESS

*Brushy Bar (Siskiyou NF). 5-9/10 mi N
of Agness on Co Hwy 375; 8 mi NE on
Trail 1160. SEASON: 3/1-9/30; 14-day
lmt. FACILITIES: 8 tent sites; tbls,
toil, cga, f, drk wtr. ACTIVITIES:
Fishing; swimming; picnicking; boating. MISC.: Elev 300 ft; scenic; pets.

ALBANY

Santiam River Rest Area. 8 mi N of
Albany on I-5. SEASON: All yr. FACILI-
TIES: drk wtr. ACTIVITIES: Fishing.
MISC.: Stream. Pets permitted on leash.

ALSEA

Slide (NF). 15-1/2 mi E of Alsea on
St Hwy 34. SEASON: All yr; 10-day lmt.
FACILITIES: 6 sites (tr -16); tbls, toil,
cga. ACTIVITIES: Fishing; swimming;
picnicking. MISC.: Elev 100 ft. 15½ mi
from Pacific Ocean. Pets.

APPLEGATE

Thompson (NF). 16 mi W of Applegate
on St Hwy 238; 10 mi S on Co Hwy; 2
mi S on FS 3900. SEASON: 5/1-10/30;
14-day lmt. FACILITIES: Tent sites (no
trailers); tbls, toil, cga, f. ACTIVI-
TIES: Picnicking. MISC.: Elev 3000 ft.
Pets permitted if kept on leash.

ARLINGTON

Boardman Rest Area. 22 mi E of Arlington on I-80N. SEASON: All yr. FACILI-
TIES: drk wtr. MISC.: Pets permitted.

Mt. Ashland (Klamath NF). 12-1/10
mi SE on I-5; 1-1/10 mi W on Co Hwy
993; 9-1/10 mi W on Co Hwy 1151; 4-
8/10 mi W on FS 40S01. SEASON: 6/1-
10/15. FACILITIES: 6 sites (tr -16);
tbls, toil, cga, no drk wtr. ACTIVI-
TIES: Picnicking; mountain climbing;
hiking. Ski bowl (1/2 mi). MISC.:
Elev 6600 ft; 1 acre; geological interest. 1½ mi, Mt. Ashland summit via
rough road. Pets.

North Fork (Rogue River NF). 25 mi
NE of Ashland on Co Hwy; 7-7/10 mi
N on FS 3706. SEASON: 5/20-9/30; 14-
day lmt. FACILITIES: 7 sites (tr -16);
tbls, toil, cga, f, no drk wtr.
Store/ice (3 mi). ACTIVITIES: Picnicking; fishing; boating,rld. Swimming (3 mi). MISC.: Elev 4500 ft;
2 acres; pets.

Siskiyou Rest Area. 6 mi SE of Ashland
on I-5. SEASON: All yr. FACILITIES: drk
wtr; info center. MISC.: Scenic view;
pets permitted if kept on a leash.

Surveyor (BLM). 20 mi E of Ashland on
Dead Indian Rd; 10 mi E on Keno Rd.
SEASON: 6/1-10/31; 14-day lmt. FACILI-
TIES: 9 sites (tr -20); tbls, toil, cga,
f, drk wtr. ACTIVITIES: Berry-picking;
hiking; picnicking; fishing. MISC.: Elev
5160 ft; 5 acres; scenic. Pets permitted.

Wrangle (Rogue River NF). 11 mi SE of
Ashland on US 15; 10 mi W on FS 4059;
10 mi SW on FS 392. SEASON: 7/1-10/30;
14-day lmt. FACILITIES: 3 tent sites (no
tr); tbls, toil, cga, no drk wtr. ACT:
Picnicking; hiking; horse riding. MISC.:
Elev 6400 ft; 2 acres. Historical community kitchen built by CCC. High
mountain scenery-Mt. Lassen. Pets.

See page 7 for KEY TO ABBREVIATIONS.

AZALEA

Devils Flat (Umpqua NF). 18–1/5 mi E of Azalea on Co 36. SEASON: 5/15–10/30; 14–day lmt. FACILITIES: 6 sites (tr –16); tbls, toil, cga, no drk wtr. ACTIVITIES: Picnicking; hiking. MISC.: Elev 2100 ft; 2 acres. Pets permitted on leash.

BAKER

Baker Valley Rest Area. 10 mi N of Baker on I-80N. SEASON: All yr. FACILI-TIES: drk wtr. MISC.: Pets permitted.

Dooley Mountain Rest Area. 13 mi S of Baker on St Hwy 7. SEASON: All yr. FA-CILITIES: drk wtr. MISC.: Scenic view. Pets permitted if kept on a leash.

Union Creek (Wallow Whitman NF). 9 mi S on St Hwy SH7; 8 mi W on St Hwy SH 220 (paved access rds). SEASON: 4/20–10/31; 10–day lmt. FACILITIES: 57 sites (tr –22); tbls, flush toil, cga, f, piped drk wtr, elec/wtr/dump hook-ups. ACTIVITIES: Picnicking; fishing; swim-ming; hunting; boating,ld; waterskiing; hiking; horseshoes. MISC.: Elev 4120 ft; 32 acres; beach; fish cleaning station. $2.00. Free after elk season (11/1–4/19); water & fac. shut off. Pets.

Weatherby Rest Area. 30 mi S of Baker on I-80N. SEASON: All yr. FACILITIES: drk wtr. MISC.: Pets permitted on leash.

BATES

Deerhorn (Malheur NF). 4–2/5 mi NW on FS 5930. SEASON: 6/1–11/1. FACILI-TIES: 2 sites (tr –22); toil. ACTIVI-TIES: Fishing. MISC.: Elev 3800 ft. Pets permitted if kept on a leash.

Dixie Camp (Malheur NF). 1 mi SE of Bates on St Hwy 36; 5½ mi SW on US 26; 5 mi N on FS 1220. SEASON: 6/1–10/30. 14–day lmt. FACILITIES: 7 sites (tr –22); tbls, toil, cga. ACTIVITIES: Picnicking; fishing. MISC.: Elev 5000 ft; 10 acres. Pets permitted if on leash.

Looney Springs (Malheur NF). 8 mi E of Bates on Co Hwy S390; 1 mi S on St Hwy 36; 1 mi E on US 26; 11½ mi S on FS 1129. SEASON: 6/15–10/15. FA-CILITIES: 5 tent sites (no trailers); toil, cga. ACTIVITIES: Picnicking; fish-ing. MISC.: Elev 6400 ft. Insufficient space & inadequate access for trailers. Pets permitted if kept on a leash.

Middle Fork (Malheur NF). 6 mi NW of Bates on FS S930. SEASON: 6/15–10/20. FACILITIES: 8 sites (tr –22); tbls, toil, cga, no drk wtr. ACTIVITIES: Picnick-ing; fishing; rockhounding. MISC.: Elev 4200 ft; 3 acres. Adjacent to middle fork John Day River. Pets permitted.

BEAVER

Rocky Bend (Siuslaw NF). 1 mi NE of Beaver on US 101; 15–3/5 mi E on Co Hwy 542. SEASON: 4/15–10/15; 10–day lmt. FACILITIES: 7 sites (tr –16); tbls, toil, cga, no drk wtr. ACTIVITIES: Pic-nicking; fishing; swimming. MISC.: On the Nestucca River. Pets permitted. Elev 600 ft; 2 acres.

BEND

Benham Falls (Deschutes NF). 11–7/10 mi S of Bend on US 97; 3–4/5 mi W on FS 1831. SEASON: 6/1–10/15; 14–day lmt. FACILITIES: 5 sites (no trailers); tbls, toil, cga, no drk wtr. ACTIVITIES: Pic-nicking; fishing. MISC.: Elev 4100 ft; 5 acres. On Deschutes River. Pets.

Big River (Deschutes NF). 18 mi S of Bend on US 97; 1½ mi W on Co Hwy E-36; 5–3/10 mi SW on FS 2114. SEASON: 6/1–10/15; 14–day lmt. FACILITIES: 17 sites (tr –22); tbls, toil, cga, no drk wtr. ACTIVITIES: Boating (l, 1 mi); picnicking; fishing. MISC.: Elev 4200 ft; 5 acres. Deschutes River. Pets.

Brothers Oasis Rest Area. 43 mi SE of Bend on US 20. SEASON: All yr. FACILI-TIES: drk wtr. MISC.: Pets permitted.

Bull Bend (Deschutes NF). 28 mi S of Bend on US 97; 4 mi W on Co Hwy 1032; 3½ mi NW on FS 204; 2 mi S on FS 205. SEASON: 6/1–10/15; 14–day lmt. FACILI-TIES: 3 sites (no tr); tbls, toil, cga, no drk wtr. ACTIVITIES: Picnicking; fishing. MISC.: Elev 4400 ft; 8 acres; river; pets.

Cow Meadow (Deschutes NF). 41–9/10 mi SW of Bend on FS 46; 1 mi E on FS 2019. SEASON: 5/1–10/15; 14–day lmt. FACILI-TIES: 17 sites (tr –22); tbls, toil, cga, no drk wtr. ACTIVITIES: Picnicking; fishing; boating,d. MISC.: Elev 4500 ft; 8 acres. On Deschutes River, N end of Crane Prairie Reservoir. Pets permitted.

Crane Prairie (Deschutes NF). 26 mi S of Bend on US 97; 1–3/10 mi W on Co Hwy E-36; 20 mi W on FS 204; 6–1/10 mi W on FS 204. SEASON: 5/1–9/30; 14–day lmt. FACILITIES: 32 sites (tr –22); tbls, toil, cga, well drk wtr. ACTIV-ITIES: Picnicking; fishing; boating (rl, 1 mi). Store/gas/ice (1 mi). MISC.: Elev 4400 ft; 10 acres. On Crane Prairie Reservoir. Pets permitted.

Cultus Lake N. Unit (Deschutes NF). 43 mi SW of Bend on FS 46; 2½ mi NW on FS 2025. SEASON: 5/1–9/30; 14–day lmt. FACILITIES: 30 sites (tr –22); tbls, cga, no drk wtr. Store (2 mi). ACTIVI-TIES: Swimming; picnicking; fishing; boating,rld; waterskiing; hiking. MISC.: Elev 4700 ft; 15 acres; lake. Pets.

See page 7 for KEY TO ABBREVIATIONS.

OREGON

Deschutes Bridge (Deschutes NF). 37–9/10 mi SW of Bend on FS 46. **SEASON:** 6/20–10/15; 14–day lmt. **FACILITIES:** 32 sites (tr –22); tbls, toil, cga, no drk wtr. Store/ice (1 mi). **ACTIVITIES:** Picnicking; fishing. **MISC.:** Elev 4600 ft; 11 acres. On Deschutes River. Pets.

Devils Lake (Deschutes NF). 26–7/10 mi W of Bend on FS 46. **SEASON:** 6/15–9/30; 14–day lmt. **FACILITIES:** 9 sites (tr –22); tbls, toil, cga, no drk wtr. **ACTIVITIES:** Picnicking; fishing; boating,d (no motors); swimming; mountain climbing. **MISC.:** Elev 5500 ft; 4 acres; lake; pets.

Dillon Falls (Deschutes NF). 7 mi S on FS 46; 4½ mi on FS 1808; 1–3/10 mi E on FS 1831. **SEASON:** 6/1–10/1; 14–day lmt. **FACILITIES:** 7 sites (tr –32); tbls, toil, cga, no drk wtr. **ACTIVITIES:** Picnicking; fishing; boating. **MISC.:** Elev 4000 ft; 1 acre; scenic; pets. On Deschutes River.

Fall Creek Trail MDO (Deschutes NF). 25 mi W of Bend on FS 46. **SEASON:** 5/30–9/30; 14–day lmt. **FACILITIES:** 2 tent sites (no trailers); tbls, toil, cga, no drk wtr. **ACTIVITIES:** Picnicking; horseback riding. Fishing/boating (1 mi). **MISC.:** Elev 6200 ft; 1 acre. Trailhead into Three Sisters Wilderness. Pets permitted if kept on a leash.

Fall River (Deschutes NF). 18 mi S of Bend on US 97; 1½ mi W on Co Hwy E–36; 14½ mi SW on FS 2114. **SEASON:** 6/1–10/15; 14–day lmt. **FACILITIES:** 12 sites (tr –22); tbls, toil, cga, no drk wtr. **ACTIVITIES:** Picnicking; fishing. **MISC.:** Elev 4000 ft; 4 acres; Fall River; pets.

Green Lakes Trail Camp (Deschutes NF). 25 mi W of Bend on FS 46; ½ mi N on FS. **SEASON:** 5/30–9/30; 14–day lmt. **FACILITIES:** 1 tent site (no trailers); toil. **ACTIVITIES:** Hiking. **MISC.:** Elev 6200 ft. Trailhead into Three Sisters Wilderness. Pets permitted on leash.

Irish & Taylor MDO (Deschutes NF). 43 mi S of Bend on FS 46; 4/5 mi W on FS 2025; 2–3/10 mi SW on FS 2022; 9–3/10 mi W on FS 2049. **SEASON:** 6/30–9/30; 14–day lmt. **FACILITIES:** 3 sites (no tr); toil, no tbls, no drk wtr. **ACTIVITIES:** Picnicking; fishing; boating (no motors). **MISC.:** Elev 5700 ft; 4 acres. 5½ mi W of Little Culters Lake via primitive road. Pets.

Island Meadow Trail Camp (Deschutes NF). 30½ mi W on FS 46; ½ mi on FS 1853. **SEASON:** 5/30–10/15. **FACILITIES:** 1 tent site (no trailers); toil. **ACTIVITIES:** Hiking. **MISC.:** Elev 5000 ft. Trailhead to Three Sisters Wilderness. Pets permitted if kept on a leash.

Lava Island (Deschutes NF). 6½ mi SW of Bend on FS 46; 1–7/10 mi SE on FS 1831. **SEASON:** 6/20–10/15; 14–day lmt. **FACILITIES:** 2 sites (tr –16); toil, no tbls, no drk wtr. **ACTIVITIES:** Picnicking; fishing; boating. **MISC.:** Elev 3900 ft; 2 acres. On Deschutes River. Geological interest. Pets.

Little Cultus (Deschutes NF). 43 mi SW of Bend on FS 46; ½ mi NW on FS 2025; 1–9/10 mi SW on FS 2022; 1–1/10 mi W on FS 2049. **SEASON:** 5/30–9/30; 14–day lmt. **FACILITIES:** 10 sites (tr –22); tbls, toil, cga, no drk wtr. **ACTIVITIES:** Boating; swimming; picnicking; fishing. **MISC.:** Elev 4800 ft; 9 acres; lake. Pets.

Little Fawn (Deschutes NF). 30 mi W of Bend on FS 46; 2–1/10 mi SE on FS 46; 1/10 mi SW on FS 1853. **SEASON:** 5/30–9/30; 14–day lmt. **FACILITIES:** 4 sites (tr –22); tbls, toil, cga. **ACTIVITIES:** Swimming; picnicking; fishing; boating,l. **MISC.:** Elev 4900 ft; Elk Lake. Pets permitted if kept on a leash.

Little Lava Lake (Deschutes NF). 35–9/10 mi SW of Bend on FS 46; 1 mi E on FS 1927. **SEASON:** 6/1–9/30; 14–day lmt. **FACILITIES:** 11 sites (tr –22); tbls, toil, cga, no drk wtr. Store/gas/ice (1 mi). **ACTIVITIES:** Picnicking; fishing; boating (rld, 1 mi). **MISC.:** Elev 4800 ft; 3 acres; pets. Little Lava Lake.

Mallard Marsh (Deschutes NF). 33 mi W of Bend on FS 46; 1–9/10 mi N on FS 1822. **SEASON:** 5/30–9/30; 14–day lmt. **FACILITIES:** 17 sites (tr –22); tbls, toil, cga, well drk wtr. Store/gas/ice (4 mi). **ACTIVITIES:** Picnicking; fishing; boating (l, 1 mi). Horseback riding (1 mi). **MISC.:** Elev 4900 ft; 15 acres. On Hosmer Lake. Pets.

Meadow (Deschutes NF). 5–1/10 mi SW of Bend on FS 46; 9/10 mi SE on FS 1827. **SEASON:** 4/20–10/15; 14–day lmt. **FACILITIES:** 13 sites (tr –22); toil, cga. **ACTIVITIES:** Fishing. **MISC.:** Elev 4000 ft; On the Deschutes River. Pets.

Mile (Deschutes NF). 36–1/5 mi SW of Bend on FS 46; 1/5 mi E on FS 1945. **SEASON:** 5/30–9/30; 14–day lmt. **FACILITIES:** 8 sites (tr –22); tbls, toil, cga, no drk wtr. **ACTIVITIES:** Picnicking; fishing. **MISC.:** Elev 4700 ft; 3 acres. On Upper Deschutes River. Pets.

North Twin Lake (Deschutes NF). 18 mi S of Bend on US 97; 1½ mi W on Co Hwy E–36; 15 mi SW on FS 204; 1/5 mi S on FS 216. **SEASON:** 6/1–9/30; 14–day lmt. **FACILITIES:** 9 sites (tr –22); tbls, toil, cga, no drk wtr. Store/gas/ice/ (2 mi). **ACTIVITIES:** Picnicking; fishing; swimming. Boating (r, 2 mi), no motors. **MISC.:** Elev 4300 ft; 8 acres; pets. North Twin Lake.

Pringle Falls (Deschutes NF). 26 mi S of Ben on US 97; 9 mi W on FS 204; 1 mi N on FS 218. SEASON: 6/1-10/15; 14-day lmt. FACILITIES: 12 sites (tr -22); tbls, toil, cga, no drk wtr. ACTIVITIES: Picnicking; fishing. MISC.: Elev 4300 ft; 6 acres. On Deschutes River. Pets permitted if kept on leash.

Quinn Meadow Horse Camp (Deschutes NF). 30 mi W of Bend on FS 46; 3/10 mi E on FS 1832. SEASON: 7/1-9/30; 5-day lmt. FACILITIES: 22 sites (tr -16); tbls, toil, cga, f, no drk wtr. Store/ice (1 mi). ACTIVITIES: Picnicking; horseback riding; fishing; hiking. MISC.: Elev 5100 ft; 5 acres. RESERVATIONS REQUIRED. Pets.

Reservoir (Deschutes NF). 57½ mi SW of Bend on FS 46; 2 mi E on FS 217. SEASON: 5/1-10/31; 14-day lmt. FACILITIES: 28 sites (tr -22); tbls, toil, cga, no drk wtr. ACTIVITIES: Boating; picnicking; fishing. MISC.: Elev 4400 ft; 10 acres. On S shore of Wickiup Reservoir. Pets permitted on leash.

Rock Creek (Deschutes NF). 46-3/5 mi SW of Bend on FS 46; ½ mi E on FS 2024. SEASON: 5/15-10/15; 14-day lmt. FACILITIES: 34 sites (tr -22); tbls, toil, cga, well drk wtr. ACTIVITIES: Boating,d; picnicking; fishing; hiking. MISC.: Elev 4400 ft; 13 acres. On Crane Prairie Reservoir. Nature trails (3 mi). Pets permitted if kept on a leash.

Sand Springs (Deschutes NF). 20 mi E of Bend on US 20; 18-3/5 mi SE on FS 2043. SEASON: 5/15-10/30. FACILITIES: 7 sites (tr -22); toil, no tbls, no drk wtr. ACTIVITIES: Picnicking. MISC.: Elev 5100 ft; 3 acres; pets.

Sheep Bridge (Deschutes NF). 28 mi S on US 97; 19½ mi NW on FS 204; 3/5 mi S on FS 216; 7/10 mi W on FS 216B. SEASON: 5/1-10/15; 14-day lmt. FACILITIES: 18 sites (tr -22); tbls, toil, cga, well drk wtr. Dump (3 mi). Store/gas/ice (2 mi). ACTIVITIES: Picnicking; fishing. Boating,rl (1 mi). MISC.: Elev 4400 ft; 20 acres. On Deschutes River. Channel of Wickiup Reservoir. Pets.

Slough (Deschutes NF). 6¼ mi SW of Bend on FS 46; 2-1/10 mi S on FS 1808; 1-9/10 mi SE on FS 1831. SEASON: 6/1-10/15; 14-day lmt. FACILITIES: 5 sites (tr -16); tbls, toil, cga, no drk wtr. ACTIVITIES: Picnicking; fishing; horseback riding; rental (5 mi). MISC.: Elev 4000 ft; 3 acres. On Deschutes River. Pets.

Soda Creek (Deschutes NF). 24-9/10 mi W of Bend on FS 46; 1/10 mi SW on FS 1823. SEASON: 5/30-10/15; 14-day lmt. FACILITIES: 12 sites (tr -22); tbls, toil, cga, no drk wtr. ACTIVITIES: Picnicking; fishing; mtn climbing; boating 1 mi (no motors). MISC.: Elev 5400 ft; 1 acre. On Sparks Lake; scenic. Pets

South (Deschutes NF). 33 mi W of Bend on FS 46; 1-1/5 mi N on FS 1822. SEASON: 5/30-9/30; 14-day lmt. FACILITIES: 23 sites (tr -22); tbls, toil, cga, no drk wtr. Store/gas/ice (4 mi). ACTIVITIES: Picnicking; fishing; boating,l; rental (4 mi); Horseback riding (4 mi). MISC.: Elev 4900 ft; 11 acres. On Hosmer Lake. Pets permitted if kept on leash.

Swamp Wells Horse Camp (Deschutes NF). 1¼ mi S on US 97; 6 mi E on FS 1821; 5½ mi S on FS 1915; 3-1/5 mi SE on FS 1924. SEASON: 4/1-11/30; 14-day lmt. FACILITIES: 7 sites (tr -22); tbls, toil, cga, no drk wtr. ACTIVITIES: Picnicking; hiking. Horseback riding (1 mi). MISC.: Elev 5400 ft; 15 acres; pets; scenic. Centrally located on Trail 61 between Horse Butte and Paulina.

* **Todd Lake** (Deschutes NF). 22 mi W of Bend on FS 46; 4/5 mi NE on FS 15341; 3/10 mi NW on TRAIL. SEASON: 5/30-10/15; 14-day lmt. FACILITIES: 4 tent sites (no trailers); tbls, toil, cga, no drk wtr. ACTIVITIES: Hiking; picnicking; fishing; mountain climbing; boating (no motors). Horseback riding (1 mi). MISC.: Elev 6200 ft; 10 acres; pets; scenic. Todd Lake.

Tumalo Falls (Deschutes NF). 10½ mi W of Bend on Co Hwy 698; 2-1/10 mi W on FS 1828. SEASON: 5/1-9/30; 14-day lmt. FACILITIES: 4 tent sites (no trailers); tbls, toil, cga, no drk wtr. ACTIVITIES: Picnicking; fishing. MISC.: Elev 5000 ft; 3 acres; stream; scenic. Pets permitted if kept on a leash.

Tumalo Rest Area. 5 mi NW of Bend on US 20. SEASON: All yr. FACILITIES: toil. ACTIVITIES: Fishing. MISC.: Stream. Pets permitted if kept on leash.

* **West Cultus** (Deschutes NF). 43 mi SW of Bend on FS 46; 1-9/10 mi NW on FS 2025; 2-7/10 mi W BY BOAT. SEASON: 6/1-9/30; 7-day lmt. FACILITIES: 15 tent sites (no trailers); tbls, toil, cga, piped drk wtr. Store/gas/ice (3 mi). ACTIVITIES: Picnicking; fishing; water-skiing; sailing; swimming; boating (rl, 3 mi). MISC.: Elev 4700 ft; 4 acres. On Cultus Lake. Pets.

Wickiup Butte (Deschutes NF). 3 mi NW of Bend on US 97; 12 mi W on FS 204; 3-9/10 mi SW on FS 210; 3-3/10 mi SE on FS 217.3. SEASON: 5/1-10/31; 14-day lmt. FACILITIES: 6 sites (tr -22); tbls, toil, cga, no drk wtr. ACTIVITIES: Picnicking; fishing; boating,l (1 mi). MISC.: Elev 4400 ft; 11 acres . On E shore Wickiup Reservoir. Pets permitted.

BLUE RIVER

Dutch Oven (Willamette NF). 5 mi E of Blue River on US 126; 17 mi S on FS 163. SEASON: 5/1-10/31; 10-day lmt. FACILITIES: 6 tent sites (no trailers); tbls, toil, cga, f, no drk wtr. ACTIVITIES: Picnicking; fishing; hunting. MISC.: Elev 2200 ft; 1 acre; river; pets.

Frissell Crossing (Willamette NF). 5 mi E of Blue River on US 126; 23 mi S on FS 163. SEASON: 5/1-10/31; 10-day lmt. FACILITIES: 13 sites (tr -16); tbls, toil, cga, f, no drk wtr. ACTIVITIES: Hiking; hunting; picnicking; fishing. MISC.: Elev 2600 ft; 2 acres; river. Pets.

Homestead (Willamette NF). 5 mi E of Blue River on US 126; 19 mi S on FS 163. SEASON: 5/1-10/31; 10-day lmt. FACILITIES: 4 tent sites (no trailers); tbls, toil, cga, f, no drk wtr. ACTIVITIES: Picnicking; fishing. MISC.: Elev 2200 ft; 3 acres. Pets permitted if kept on a leash.

Roaring River (Willamette NF). 5 mi E of Blue River on Hwy 126; 23½ mi S on FS 163. SEASON: 5/1-10/31; 10-day lmt. FACILITIES: 5 tent sites (no trailers); tbls, toil, cga, f, no drk wtr. ACTIVITIES: Picnicking; fishing. MISC.: Elev 2600 ft; 3 acres; river. Pets permitted.

Slide Creek (Willamette NF). 5 mi E of Blue River on US 126; 11-3/5 mi S on FS 163; 1½ mi N on FS 1663. SEASON: 5/1-10/31; 10-day lmt. FACILITIES: 8 tent sites (no trailers); tbls, toil, cga, f, piped drk wtr. ACTIVITIES: Swimming; picnicking; fishing; boating,ld; sailing; waterskiing. MISC.: Elev 1700 ft; 5 acres; lake. Pets permitted if on leash.

Twin Springs (Willamette NF). 5 mi E of Blue River on US 126; 21 mi S on FS 163. SEASON: 5/1-10/31; 10-day lmt. FACILITIES: 3 tent sites (no trailers); tbls, toil, cga, f, no drk wtr. ACTIVITIES: Picnicking; fishing; hunting. MISC.: Elev 2400 ft; 2 acres; river. Pets permitted if kept on a leash.

BLY

Corral Creek (Fremont NF). 1-2/5 mi SE of Bly on Hwy 140; ½ mi N on Co K1257; 14-3/5 mi E on FS 348; ½ mi NW on FS 3621. SEASON: 6/15-10/15; 14-day lmt. FACILITIES: 5 tent sites (no trailers); tbls, toil, cga, no drk wtr. ACTIVITIES: Hunting; picnicking; fishing. MISC.: Elev 6000 ft; 3 acres; stream. A remote site. Within 2 mi Gearhart Mt. Pets.

Cronin Spring (Fremont NF). 29 mi SE of Bly on FS 375; 1-2/5 mi SW on FS 4003. SEASON: 6/15-10/31. FACILITIES: 5 sites (tr -16); toil. ACT: Hunting.

MISC.: Elev 5500 ft; lake. A hunter camp and only used in season. Good graveled rd to sites. In a remote area. Pets permitted if kept on a leash.

Gerber Reservoir (BLM). 18 mi S of Bly off St Hwy 140. SEASON: 5/15-10/1; 14-day lmt. FACILITIES: 50 sites; toil, cga. ACTIVITIES: Fishing; swimming; hunting; boating,l; hiking. MISC.: Elev 4800 ft; lake. Pets permitted on leash.

Lofton Reservoir (Fremont NF). 12-9/10 mi SE of Bly on Hwy 140; 7-1/10 mi S on FS 3715; 1-3/10 mi NE on FS 3715A. SEASON: 6/1-10/30; 14-day lmt. FACILITIES: 17 sites; tbls, toil, cga, well drk wtr. ACTIVITIES: Hunting; boating,ld (no motors); good fishing. MISC.: Elev 6200 ft; 8 acres. Gravel road, 2 mi steep grades. Pets permitted.

Mitchell Rec. Area & Mon. 1 mi E of Bly on Co Rd; 12 mi E of its jct with St Hwy 66. SEASON: All yr. MISC.: Pets.

Sprague River (Fremont NF). 4-1/5 mi SE of Bly on St Hwy 140; 1-1/10 mi N on FS 3731. SEASON: 5/1-10/30; 7-day lmt. FACILITIES: 16 sites (tr -16); tbls, toil, cga, well drk wtr. Store (5 mi). ACTIVITIES: Fishing; hunting; picnicking. MISC.: Elev 4400 ft; 7 acres; stream. Pets permitted on leash.

BONANZA

Gerber Reservoir (BLM). 9 mi E of Bonanza to Lorella; 11 mi NE on Gerber Rd (gravel). SEASON: 4/15-10/15; 14-day lmt. FACILITIES: 50 sites (tr -30); tbls, toil, cga, f, pull-thru spaces. ACTIVITIES: Swimming; picnicking; fishing; boating,ld; hiking. MISC.: elev 4800 ft; 25 acres; scenic view. Pets.

BROOKINGS

Brookings Safety Rest Area. 2 mi N of Brookings on US 101. SEASON: All yr. FACILITIES: Info center; drk wtr. MISC.: Scenic view. Pets permitted.

BROTHERS

Pine Mountain (Deschutes NF). 10 mi W on US 20; 4-1/10 mi S on FS 2012. SEASON: 5/15-10/30. FACILITIES: 4 sites (tr -22); tbls, toil, cga, store, gas, food. No drk wtr. ACTIVITIES: Picnicking. MISC.: Elev 6200 ft; 2 acres; pets. 1/4 mi S of Pine Mountain Observatory.

BURNS

Blue Spring (Malheur NF). 27-1/5 mi NW of Burns on FS 1911; 2 mi W on FS 1843; 3-9/10 mi N on FS 1935. SEASON: 7/1-10/20. FACILITIES: 3 sites (tr -16); toil, cga. MISC.: Elev 5000 ft; 1 acre. Pets.

Buchanan Springs Rest Area. 24 mi E of Burns on US 20. SEASON: All yr. FACILITIES: Drk wtr. MISC.: Pets permitted.

Buck Springs (Malheur NF). 26½ mi W of Burns on US 20; 14-9/10 mi N on Co Hwy; 1-2/5 mi N on FS 1842; 7-2/5 mi N on FS 2034. SEAS: 6/15-10/31. FAC: 6 sites (tr -22); toil, cga, f. ACTIVITIES: Fishing. MISC.: Elev 5600 ft; pets permitted if kept on a leash.

Delintment Lake (Malheur NF). 7 mi W of Burns on Co Hwy R1911; 7-3/10 mi NW on FS 1911; 30-3/5 mi NW on FS 1810. SEASON: 4/20-10/31. FACILITIES: 16 sites (tr -32); tbls, toil, cga, f. ACTIVITIES: Swimming; picnicking; fishing; boating,l. MISC.: Elev 5600 ft; pets permitted if kept on a leash.

Idlewild (Malheur NF). 17 mi N of Burns on US 395. SEASON: 6/1-10/31; 14-day lmt. FACILITIES: 17 tent sites; 8 tr sites (tr -32); tbls, toil, cga, piped drk wtr. ACTIVITIES: Hunting; picnicking; fishing. MISC.: Elev 5000 ft; 18 acres. Pets permitted if kept on a leash.

Joaquin Miller (Malheur NF). 19-1/5 mi N of Burns on US 395. FACILITIES: 17 tent sites; 8 tr sites (tr -32); tbls, toil, cga, f, piped drk wtr. SEASON: 6/1-10/31; 14-day lmt. ACTIVITIES: Hunting; picnicking; fishing; rockhounding. MISC.: Elev 5000 ft; 14 acres Pets permitted if kept on a leash.

Rock Springs (Malheur NF). 33-2/5 mi N of Burns on US 395; 4½ mi E on FS 1836. SEASON: 7/1-10/31; 14-day lmt. FACILITIES: 2 sites (tr -32); tbls, toil, cga, f, drk wtr. ACTIVITIES: Picnicking. MISC.: Elev 5200 ft; 7 acres. Pets.

Sage Hen Rest Area. 16 mi W of Burns on US 20. SEASON: All yr. FACILITIES: Drk wtr. MISC.: Pets permitted.

Tamarack Spring (Malheur NF). 33-2/5 mi N of Burns on US 395; 4-1/5 mi E on FS 1836; 2-3/5 mi N on FS 178. SEASON: 7/1-10/31; 14-day lmt. FACILITIES: 2 sites (tr -32); toil. MISC.: Elev 5600 ft; 1 acre. Pets permitted if kept on a leash.

Yellowjacket (Malheur NF). 30 mi NW of Burns on FS 1911; 2½ mi E on FS 1912; 1 mi S on FS 197. SEASON: 4/25-10/30; 14-day lmt. FACILITIES: 22 sites (tr -22); tbls, flush toil, cga. ACTIVITIES: Hunting; picnicking; fishing; boating,d. MISC.: Elev 4800 ft; 10 acres. Adjacent to Yellow Jacket Reservoir. Pets permitted if kept on a leash.

BURNS JUNCTION

Crooked Creek Springs Rest Area. 5 mi E of Burns Junction on US 95. SEASON:

All yr. FACILITIES: Drk wtr. MISC.: Scenic view; historic ; pets permitted.

BUTTE FALLS

Blue Rock Saddle MDH (Rogue River NF). 10 mi SE of Butte Falls on Co Hwy 356; 10 mi SE on FS 3520; 5-1/5 mi S on FS 3414. SEASON: 7/1-9/30. FACILITIES: 1 site (no tr); tbls, toil, cga, f, no drk wtr. ACTIVITIES: Picnicking. MISC.: Elev 6200 ft; 1 acre; pets.

Fourbit Ford (Rogue River NF). 9-3/10 mi SE of Butte Falls on Co Hwy; 1-1/5 mi NE on FS 3317. SEASON: 5/1-11/1; 14-day lmt. FACILITIES: 7 sites (no tr); tbls, toil, cga, well drk wtr. Store/gas/ice/food/showers (5 mi). ACTIVITIES: Picnicking; fishing. Horseback riding (3 mi). Boating, rld; waterskiing (5 mi). MISC.: Elev 3200 ft; 4 acres; pets.

Gypsy Spring (Rogue River NF). 9-3/10 mi SE of Butte Falls on Co Hwy; 9½ mi NE on FS 3317; 4-2/5 mi S on FS 3414; 3/10 mi S on FS 3414F. SEASON: 7/1-10/1. FACILITIES: 2 tent sites (no trailers); toil, cga, f. MISC.: Elev 5600 ft. Pets.

Parker Meadows (Rogue River NF). 4/5 mi E of Butte Falls on Co; 1-3/10 mi NE on Co; 12-7/10 mi NE of FS 3520; 1-2/5 mi N on FS 3317. SEASON: 6/1-10/15. FACILITIES: 6 sites (tr -16); tbls, toil, cga, f. ACTIVITIES: Picnicking; horseback riding. Fishing (1 mi). MISC.: Elev 5000 ft; 6 acres; pets; no drk wtr.

Snowshoe (Rogue River NF). 9-3/10 mi SE on Butte Falls on Co; 4-4/5 mi NE on FS 3317. SEASON: 6/15-10/15. FACILITIES: 6 tent sites (no trailers); tbls, toil, cga, f, well drk wtr. ACTIVITIES: Picnicking. Horseback riding (1 mi). Fishing (3 mi). MISC.: Elev 4000 ft; 3 acres; pets.

COQUILLE

Bear Creek (BLM). 26 mi SE of Coquille on St Hwy 42. SEASON: All yr; 14-day lmt. FACILITIES: 10 sites (tr -16); tbls, toil, cga, f. ACTIVITIES: Picnicking; fishing; swimming; hiking. MISC.: Elev 700 ft; 26 acres. Pets permitted.

CAMAS VALLEY

Bear Creek (BLM). 8 mi SW of Camas Valley on St Hwy 42. SEASON: All yr; 14-day lmt. FACILITIES: 17 sites (tr -16); tbls, toil, cga, f, drk wtr. ACTIVITIES: Berry-picking; picnicking; fishing; swimming; hiking. MISC.: Elev 700 ft; 26 acres. Pets permitted if kept on a leash.

See page 7 for KEY TO ABBREVIATIONS.

CAMP SHERMAN

Abbot Creek (Deschutes NF). 8 mi NW of Camp Sherman on FS 1153. SEASON: 6/1-9/30; 14-day lmt. FACILITIES: 7 sites (tr -16); tbls, toil, cga; no drk wtr. ACTIVITIES: Picnicking; fishing. MISC.: Elev 3100 ft; 2 acres; pets. Abbot Creek.

Candle Creek (Deschutes NF). 10 mi N of Camp Sherman on FS 113; 2 mi N on FS 1210. SEASON: 5/1-10/1; 14-day lmt. FACILITIES: 5 sites (tr -16); tbls, toil, cga, no drk wtr. ACTIVITIES: Picnicking; fishing. MISC.: Elev 2800 ft; 1 acre. Pets permitted if kept on leash.

Jack Creek (Deschutes NF). 4 mi N of Camp Sherman on FS 1153; 3 mi NW on FS 1211. SEASON: 5/1-10/1; 14-day lmt. FACILITIES: 5 sites (tr -16); tbls, toil, cga, no drk wtr. ACTIVITIES: Picnicking; fishing; hiking. MISC.: Elev 3100 ft; 3 acres; stream. Pets.

Lower Canyon Creek (Deschutes NF). 5 mi N of Camp Sherman on FS 1138. SEASON: 4/30-9/30; 14-day lmt. FACILITIES: 5 sites (tr -16); tbls, toil, cga, no drk wtr. Store/gas/ice/food/laundry (5 mi). ACTIVITIES: Picnicking; fishing. Horseback riding/rental (5 mi). MISC.: Elev 2900 ft; 2 acres; pets. Lower Canyon Creek.

Riverside (Deschutes NF). 2 mi S of Camp Sherman on FS 113. SEASON: 5/1-9/30; 7-day lmt. FACILITIES: 7 sites (tr -22); tbls, toil, cga, no drk wtr. Store/shower/gas/ice/laundry (2 mi). ACTIVITIES: Rockhounding; picnicking; fishing. MISC.: Elev 3000 ft; 3 acres; river. Pets permitted if kept on a leash.

Sheep Springs Horse Camp (Deschutes NF) 3/5 mi W of Camp Sherman on FS 1317; 3½ mi N on FS 1153; ½ mi SW on FS 1138; 3 mi NW on FS 1226. SEASON: 4/1-10/20; 14-day lmt. FACILITIES: 9 sites (tr -16); tbls, toil, cga, f, no drk wtr. ACTIVITIES: Horseback riding; picnicking; fishing. MISC.: Elev 3200 ft; 5 acres. Pets. RESERVATIONS REQUIRED.

The Burn (Deschutes NF). 5 mi N of Camp Sherman on FS 113. SEASON: 5/1-10/1; 14-day lmt. FACILITIES: 4 sites (tr -22); toil. ACTIVITIES: Fishing. MISC.: Elev 2800 ft. Pets permitted on leash.

CANYON CITY

Windfall (NF). 15-1/10 mi SE of Canyon City on US 395; 1 mi NW on FS 1542. SEASON: 5/10-11/1. FACILITIES: 2 sites (tr -16); tbls, toil, cga. ACTIVITIES: Picnicking. MISC.: Elev 5200 ft. Pets.

CARLTON

Alder Glen (BLM). 21 mi W of Carlton on Nestucca Access Rd (off US 101; 18 mi NE of Alder Glen). SEASON: 6/1-10/31; 14-day lmt. FACILITIES: 8 sites (tr -24); tbls, toil, cga. ACTIVITIES: Hunting; picnicking; fishing; swimming. MISC.: Elev 800 ft; 4 acres; pets.

Dovre (BLM; Salem Dist.). 14 mi W of Carlton on Nestucca Access rd. SEASON: All yr; 7-day lmt. FACILITIES: 5 sites (tr -24); tbls, toil, cga. ACTIVITIES: Swimming; picnicking; fishing. MISC.: Pets on leash.

Fan Creek (BLM, Salem Dist.). 16 mi W of Carlton on Nestucca access rd. SEASON: All yr; 7-day lmt. FACILITIES: 8 sites (tr -24); tbls, toil, cga. ACTIVITIES: Swimming; picnicking; fishing. MISC.: Primitive. Pets on leash.

CASCADE LOCKS

Herman Creek (NF). 3-3/5 mi NE of Cascade Locks on US 30; 1/5 mi E on Co Hwy; 1-3/5 mi S on FS N22 (rough rd). SEASON: 4/1-10/31. FACILITIES: 4 tent sites (no trailers); toil, cga, f, spg drk wtr. ACTIVITIES: Fishing; hiking. MISC.: Elev 1000 ft; pets permitted if kept on a leash.

★ **Seven One Half Mile** (Mt Hood NF). 2½ mi SW of Cascade Locks on I-80; ½ mi S on FS N24; 7 mi SE on TRAIL 440. SEASON: 3/1-12/31; 14-day lmt. FACILITIES: 15 tent sites (no trailers); tbls, toil, cga, f, no drk wtr. ACTIVITIES: Swimming; hiking; picnicking; fishing. MISC.: Elev 1500 ft; 4 acres; stream; nature trls; scenic. Parking available at Eagle Creek trailhead. Pets.

CASCADE SUMMIT

★ **Pebble Bay** (Deschutes NF). 1-7/10 mi SE of Cascade Summit BY BOAT on lake. SEASON: 6/15-10/31; 14-day lmt. FACILITIES: 2 tent sites; tbls, toil, cga, f, no drk wtr. Store/gas (2 mi). ACTIVITIES: Berry-picking; swimming; picnicking; fishing. Boating,rl (2 mi); waterskiing. MISC.: Elev 4800 ft; 2 acres; at SW end of Odell Lake. Pets permitted if kept on a leash. Access to camp by BOAT ONLY.

CAVE JUNCTION

Bolan Lake (Siskiyou NF). ½ mi S of Cave Junction on Hwy 199; 8 mi SE on Co 12; 14 mi SE on Co 4007; 6 mi E on FS R408. SEASON: 7/1-11/1; 14-day lmt. FACILITIES: 12 sites (tr -16); tbls, toil, cga, f, no drk wtr. ACTIVITIES: Swimming; picnicking; fishing;

boating,ld. **MISC.**: Elev 5400 ft; 3 acres; scenic; lake. Pets permitted if kept on a leash.

Tannen Lake (Siskiyou NF). ½ mi S of Cave Junction on St Hwy 199; 8 mi SE on Co Hwy 12; 14 mi SE on Co Hwy 4007; 9 mi E on FS R408. **SEASON**: 7/1-10/1; 14-day lmt. **FACILITIES**: 3 tent sites (no trailers); tbls, toil, cga, f, no drk wtr. **ACTIVITIES**: Swimming; picnicking; fishing. **MISC.**: Elev 5200 ft; 1 acre; lake; scenic. Pets permitted.

CHEMULT

Beaver Marsh Rest Area. 3 mi S of Chemult on US 97. **SEASON**: All yr. **FACILITIES**: Drk wtr. **MISC.**: Pets permitted.

Bed Pan Spring (Winema NF). 5 mi S of Chemult on US 97; 16-1/5 mi SE on FS 286; 1 mi E on FS 286F. **SEASON**: 6/1-10/31. **FACILITIES**: 3 sites (tr -22); toil, cga, f. **MISC.**: Elev 4600 ft. Pets

Boundary Spring (Winema NF). 24¼ mi S of Chemult on US 97; 23½ mi NE on Co Hwy 676; 5½ mi SE on FS 29071; 2-1/10 mi E on FS R2971. **SEASON**: 6/1-10/31 **FACILITIES**: 3 sites (tr -22); toil, f. **MISC.**: Elev 6000 ft. Pets permitted.

Cabin Spring (Winema NF). 5 mi S of Chemult on US 97; 6-3/10 mi E on FS 286; 7-4/5 mi NE on FS 2653; 1-3/10 mi N on FS 2627. **SEASON**: 6/1-10/31. **FACILITIES**: 3 sites (tr -22); toil, f. **MISC.**: Elev 5400 ft. Pets permitted if kept on a leash.

Corral Springs (Winema NF). 2-7/10 mi N of Chemult on US 97; 1-9/10 mi W on FS 2652A. **SEASON**: 5/15-10/31; 14-day lmt. **FACILITIES**: 5 sites (tr -22); tbls, toil, cga, f, no drk wtr. Store/ice/snacks (5 mi). **ACTIVITIES**: Picnicking; swimming pool (5 mi). **MISC.**: Elev 4900 ft; 2 acres. Good access from US 97. MOSQUITOES ABOUND. Pets. Historic.

Deer Scaffold (Winema NF). 5 mi S of Chemult on US 97; 15-2/5 mi SE on FS 286; 3-3/10 mi E on FS 2976; 1 mi NE on FS 29760. **SEASON**: 6/1-10/31. **FACILITIES**: 3 sites (tr -16); toil, f. **MISC.**: Elev 4600 ft; pets permitted if kept on a leash.

Halfway Spring (Winema NF). 4-1/5 mi N of Chemult on US 97; 4 mi E on FS 265; 3½ mi S on FS 2782. **SEASON**: 6/1-10/31. **FACILITIES**: 3 sites (tr -22); toil, cga, f. **MISC.**: Elev 5400 ft. Pets.

Indian Spring (Winema NF). 5 mi S of Chemult on US 97; 10 mi SE on FS 286; 6 mi E on FS R283; 2 mi SE on FS 283A. **SEASON**: 7/1-10/31. **FACILITIES**: 5 sites (tr -22); toil, cga, f, no drk wtr. **MISC.**: Elev 4800 ft; 2 acres. Pets.

Irving Creek Spring (Winema NF). 24½ mi S of Chemult on US 97; 22-1/10 mi NE on Co Hwy 676; 7½ mi SE on FS 3037. **SEASON**: 6/1-10/31. **FACILITIES**: 6 sites (tr -22); toil, cga, f. **ACTIVITIES**: Fishing (2 mi). **MISC.**: Elev 4600 ft; 1 acre. Pets permitted if kept on a leash.

Jackson Creek (Winema NF). 24½ mi S of Chemult on US 97; 22-1/10 mi NE on Co 676; 5-3/10 mi SE on FS 3037. **SEASON**: 5/1-11/15; 14-day lmt. **FACILITIES**: 12 sites (tr -22); tbls, toil, cga, f, no drk wtr. **ACTIVITIES**: Picnicking; fishing. **MISC.**: Elev 4600 ft; 3 acres; pets. 10 mi SE of Yamsay Mt. Crater.

Scott Creek (Winema NF). 13 mi S of Chemult on US 97; 10-3/5 mi SW on Hwy 232; 1-9/10 mi W on FS 2992. **SEASON**: 6/1-10/31. **FACILITIES**: 6 sites (tr -22); tbls, toil, cga, f, no drk wtr. Store/ice/snack bar (5 mi). **ACTIVITIES**: Picnicking; fishing. **MISC.**: Elev 4800 ft; 2 acres. Pets permitted if on leash.

Walker Rim Spring (Winema NF). 4-2/5 mi N of Chemult on US 97; 1-7/10 mi SE on FS 265. **SEASON**: 6/1-10/31. **FACILITIES**: 4 sites (tr -22); toil, cga, f. **MISC.**: Pets permitted if on leash.

CHILOQUIN

Corral Springs (Winema NF). 20 mi N of Chiloquin on US 97; 13 mi E on Co Hwy 676; 2 mi SE on FS 3150. **SEASON**: 7/1-10/31. **FACILITIES**: 3 sites (tr -32); toil, f. **MISC.**: Elev 4600 ft; pets.

Dice Crane Springs (Winema NF). 12½ mi N of Chiloquin on US 97; 5½ mi E on Co Hwy 4210; 4-1/5 mi NE on FS 3143G. **SEASON**: 9/15-10/31. **FACILITIES**: 6 sites (tr -32); toil, f, no drk wtr. **MISC.**: Elev 4600 ft; 1 acre. Site used mostly during deer season. Pets.

Head of the River (Winema NF). 5 mi NE of Chiloquin on Co 858; 27 mi NE on Co 600; 1 mi N on FS 3037. **SEASON**: 6/15-10/31; 14-day lmt. **FACILITIES**: 6 sites (tr -32); tbls, toil, cga, f, no drk wtr. **ACTIVITIES**: Fishing. **MISC.**: Elev 4400 ft; 2 acres. Pets.

Lamms Camp (Winema NF). 20 mi N of Chiloquin on US 97; 13 mi E on Co Hwy 676. **SEASON**: 9/15-10/31. **FACILITIES**: 6 sites (tr -32); tbls, toil, cga, f, no drk wtr. **ACTIVITIES**: Hunting; fishing. **MISC.**: Elev 4500 ft; 1 acre. Pets permitted if kept on a leash. 2 mi, Klamath Wildlife Refuge.

Spring Creek (Winema NF). 8 mi N of Chiloquin on US 97; 3-3/5 mi W on FS 3302. **SEASON**: 6/1-10/31; 14-day lmt. **FACILITIES**: 24 sites (tr -32); tbls, toil,

cga, f, no drk wtr. ACTIVITIES: Picnicking; fishing. MISC.: Elev 4200
ft; 7 acres; pets; scenic. 6½ mi from
Collier Memorial State Park.

CLATSKANIE

City Park Center of town. SEASON: All
yr. MISC.: Pets permitted if on leash.

COQUILLE

Laverne (County). 18 mi NE of Coquille
off Oregon Rt 42. SEASON: All yr. FACIL-
ITIES: 45 sites tbls, toil, cga, f. AC-
TIVITIES: Fishing; picnicking. MISC.:
Pets permitted on a leash.

Park Creek (BLM; Coos Bay Dist.). 24
mi E of Coquille on Middle Cove Rd.
SEASON: May-Nov. 14-day lmt. FACILITIES:
12 sites; dump, tbls, toil, cga, drk wtr.
ACTIVITIES: Picnicking; fishing; hunting; berry-picking. MISC.: Elev 500 ft;
6 acres. Pets permitted if kept on leash.

COTTAGE GROVE

Mosby Creek (County). 5 mi SE of
Cottage Grove off I-5. SEASON: All yr.
FACILITIES: 5 sites; tbls, toil, cga.
ACTIVITIES: Fishing; swimming. MISC.:
Pets permitted if kept on a leash.

Sharps Creek (BLM). 18 mi E of Cottage
Grove exit (off I-5) on Row River Co.;
4 mi S on Sharps Creek Co. SEASON: All
yr. FACILITIES: 10 sites (tr -20); tbls,
toil, cga, f, drk wtr. ACTIVITIES: Hunting; swimming; picnicking; fishing; hiking. MISC.: Elev 1200 ft; 10 acres;
stream; scenic. Pets permitted on leash.

Primitive Park (COE). Approx. 7 mi
E of Cottage Grove on Co Rd 2700
(London Road). Follow signs to Pine
Meadow CG once you arrive at the
lake. Primitive area is approx. 1/4
mi S of Pine Meadow . SEASON: All yr.
FACILITIES: 15 graveled designated
camping pads; toil, tbls, cga. ACTIVI-
TIES: Nearby: Swimming, boating,l,
picnicking. MISC.: 14-day lmt. Pets.

COVE

Moss Spring (Wallowa Whitman NF). 1½
mi SE of Cove on Co 602; 6½ mi E on
FS 6220. SEASON: 7/1-9/15; 10-day lmt.
FACILITIES: 6 sites (tr -22); tbls, toil,
cga, no drk wtr. ACTIVITIES: Fishing
(2 mi). MISC.: Elev 5400 ft; 4 acres;
horse loading ramp available. Pets.

CRATER LAKE

Lost Creek Campground (Crater Lake
NP). Approximately 3 miles SE on Branch
Rd off the main Rim Drive (follow signs

toward "The Pinnacles"). SEASON: 7/1-
9/1 (depending on the weather); 14-
day lmt. FACILITIES: Toil, cga, running wtr. ACTIVITIES: Hiking; fishing
(no fishing license required in Crater
Lake NP); but NO hunting. MISC.: Elev
5972 ft. Pets allowed on leash. Store
at Rim Village; gas near Park Headquarters. The Grayback Motor Nature
Road begins here.

CRESCENT

Boundary Spring (Deschutes NF). 2-7/10
mi SW of Crescent on US 97; 5-3/5 mi
SE on FS 257. SEASON: 7/1-10/15; 14-
day lmt. (used mostly during hunting
season) FACILITIES: 6 sites (tr -16);
tbls, toil, cga, f. ACTIVITIES: Hunting; picnicking. MISC.: Elev 4400 ft;
0 acres. No fires. Reservations advisable. At base of Walker Rim. Pets.

Crescent Creek (Deschutes NF). 8-1/5
mi W on Co Hwy 1351. [At Co. Rd.
crossing.] SEASON: 5/1-10/31; 14-day
lmt. FACILITIES: 7 sites (tr -22);
tbls, toil, cga, f, no drk wtr. ACTI-
VITIES: Picnicking; fishing. MISC.:
Elev 4500 ft; 3 acres. On Crescent
Creek. Pets.

Lava Flow (Deschutes NF). 9 mi W of
Crescent on Co 1351; 9 mi N on FS 2221.
SEASON: 5/20-10/31; 14-day lmt. FACILI-
TIES: 12 sites (tr -22); tbls, toil, cga,
f, no drk wtr. ACTIVITIES: Rockhound-
ing; picnicking; excellent fishing; boat-
ing. MISC.: Elev 4400 ft; 1 acre. On
E shore of Davis Lake. Pets permitted.

Little Deschutes (Deschutes NF). 10 mi
S of Crescent on US 97; 4-1/10 mi NW
on Hwy 58; 1/10 mi W on Co 2570. SEA-
SON: 5/1-10/31; 14-day lmt. FACILITIES:
5 sites (tr -22); tbls, toil, cga, f, well
drk wtr. ACTIVITIES: Picnicking; fishing. MISC.: Elev 4700 ft; 5 acres. On
Little Deschutes River. Pets permitted
if kept on a leash. Store/ice (1 mi).

North Davis Creek (Deschutes NF). 9 mi
W of Crescent on Co 1451; 12-3/5 mi N
on FS 46. SEASON: 5/1-10/31; 14-day lmt.
FACILITIES: 15 sites (tr -22); tbls, toil,
cga, f, no drk wtr. ACTIVITIES: Picnicking; fishing; boating,ld. MISC.:
Elev 4400 ft; 13 acres. Located between
Two Springs at W end of Wickiup Reservoir. Pets permitted if kept on leash.

Reservoir (Deschutes NF). 9 mi W of
Crescent on Co Hwy 1351; 12-3/5 mi N
on FS 2221; 1½ mi E on FS 217. SEASON:
5/1-10/31; 21-day lmt. FACILITIES: 10
sites (tr -22); tbls, toil, cga, f, no
drk wtr. ACTIVITIES: Fishing; picnicking. MISC.: Elev 4400 ft; 1 acre. On
S shore of Wickiup Reservoir. Pets.

See page 7 for KEY TO ABBREVIATIONS.

Round Swamp (Deschutes NF). 9 mi W of Crescent on Co Hwy 1351; 12-3/5 mi N on FS 2221; 4½ mi E on FS 217. SEASON: 5/1-10/31; 14-day lmt. FACILITIES: 4 sites (tr -22); tbls, toil, cga, f, no drk wtr. ACTIVITIES: Boating; picnicking; fishing. MISC.: elev 4400 ft; 20 acres. On S shore Wickiup Reservoir. Pets permitted if kept on a leash.

Wickiup Butte (Deschutes NF). 9 mi W of Crescent on Co Hwy 1351; 12-3/5 mi N on FS 2221; 10 mi E on FS 217. SEASON: 5/1-10/31; 14-day lmt. FACILITIES: 5 sites (tr -22); tbls, toil, cga, f, no drk wtr. ACTIVITIES: Boating,l; picnicking; fishing. MISC.: Elev 4400 ft; 11 acres. On E shore Wickiup Reservoir. Pets permitted if kept on a leash.

CRESCENT LAKE

Contorta Point (Deschutes NF). 2-1/10 mi SW on St Hwy 209; 5-3/5 mi SW on FS 244.1; 3-1/5 mi E on FS 244.1; 1 mi NW on FS 244F. SEASON: 6/1-10/31; 14-day lmt. FACILITIES: 6 sites (tr -22); tbls, toil, cga, f, no drk wtr. ACTIVITIES: Picnicking; swimming; waterskiing; fishing; sailing; boating (l, 1 mi). MISC.: Elev 4800 ft; 12 acres; river; pets. At south end of Crescent Lake.

Summit Lake (Deschutes NF). 2-1/10 mi SW on St Hwy 208; 5-1/5 mi SW on FS 244.1; 6-7/10 mi on FS 211. SEASON: 7/1-10/31; 14-day lmt. FACILITIES: 3 sites (tr -22); tbls, toil, cga, f, no drk wtr. ACTIVITIES: Picnicking; swimming; fishing; boating; mtn climbing; hiking. MISC.: Elev 5600 ft; 3 acres; pets. Access to pct trail (200 yards). On north shore of Summit Lake. Diamond Peak Wilderness (1 mi).

*****Whitefish Horse Camp** (Deschutes NF). 2-1/10 mi SW on St Hwy 209; 4½ mi SW on FS 2441. SEASON: 6/1-10/31. FACILITIES: Undesignated tent sites; no facilities. Store/gas/laundry/food (5 mi). ACTIVITIES: Picnicking; horseback riding; hiking. Swimming (1 mi). Waterskiing/fishing/boating,l (2 mi). Boat rental (5 mi). MISC.: Elev 4800 ft; 30 acres; pets. At west end of Crescent Lake.

CULP CREEK

Lund Park (Umpqua NF). 5 mi SE on FS 2149; 6-3/10 mi E on Co Hwy 36. SEASON: 5/25-9/15; 14-day lmt. FACILITIES: 4 sites (tr -16); tbls, toil, cga, no drk wtr. Store/gas (4 mi). ACTIVITIES: Picnicking; berry-picking; swimming; fishing. MISC.: Elev 1200 ft; 6 acres; steam; pets.

Rujada (Umpqua NF). 4-3/10 mi E on Co Hwy 202; 2 mi NE on FS 2143; 1/10 mi S on FS 2148. SEASON: 5/25-9/15; 14-day lmt. FACILITIES: 10 sites (tr -22); tbls, toil, cga, electricity in restrooms, piped drk wtr. Store/gas (3 mi). ACTIVITIES: Picnicking; berry-picking; swimming; fishing. MISC.: Elev 1200 ft; 9 acres; stream; pets.

CULVER

Monty (Deschutes NF). 20 mi W of Culver on Co Hwy; 10 mi NW on FS 113. SEASON: 5/1-10/1; 14-day lmt. FACILITIES: 45 sites (tr -22); tbls, toil, cga, f, piped drk wtr. ACTIVITIES: Picnicking; fishing. Boating,ld (3 mi). Swimming/waterskiing (5 mi). MISC.: Elev 2000 ft; 10 acres; pets.

Perry South (Deschutes NF). 20 mi W of Culver on Co Hwy 1; 5 mi NW of FS 113. SEASON: 5/1-10/1; 14-day lmt. FACILITIES: 68 sites (tr -22); tbls, toil, cga, piped drk wtr. ACTIVITIES: Swimming; picnicking; fishing; boating,l; waterskiing. MISC.: Elev 2000 ft; 21 acres; pets. On Metolius Arm, Lake Billy Chinook & near Cove State Park. Geological interest.

DALE

Olive Lake (Umatilla NF). 1 mi NE on US 395; 3/5 mi SE on FS 55; 26-3/10 mi SE on FS 10; 3/10 mi SW on FS 10480. SEASON: 6/15-11/15; 10-day lmt. FACILITIES: 4 tent sites (no trailers); tbls, toil, cga, f, piped drk wtr. ACTIVITIES: Picnicking; fishing. Horseback riding/swimming/boating,l (1 mi). Berry-picking. MISC.: Elev 6000 ft; 11 acres. Area not fully developed. Scenic. Adjacent to Olive Lake (160 acre lake). Pets.

DETROIT

Breitenbush (Willamette NF). 9-4/5 mi NE of Detroit on FS R546. SEASON: 5/1-10/31; 10-day lmt. FACILITIES: 31 sites (tr -16); tbls, toil, cga, no drk wtr. Store (1 mi). ACTIVITIES: Fishing; picnicking; Swimming (1 mi). MISC.: 14 acres; pets. Breitenbush Hot Springs Resort (1 mi).

Cleator Bend (Willamette NF). 9-3/5 mi NE of Detroit on FR R546. SEASON: 4/15-10/31. FACILITIES: 8 sites (tr -16); tbls, toil, cga, no drk wtr. Store (1 mi). ACTIVITIES: Fishing; picnicking. Swimming (1 mi). MISC.: Elev 2200 ft; 2 acres; river. 1 mi to Breitenbush Hot Springs Resort. Pets permitted.

Elk Lake (Willamette NF). 4-3/5 mi
NE on FS RS46; 7-1/10 mi N on FS 4696;
9½ mi NW on FS 2209; 3/5 mi SW on
FS 430. SEASON: 7/1-9/15; 10-day lmt.
FACILITIES: 13 sites (tr -16); tbls,
toil, cga, no drk wtr. ACTIVITIES:
Picnicking; swimming; fishing; boating,l; hunting; berry-picking. MISC.:
Elev 4000 ft; 10 acres; pets; 63-acre
lake. Last 2½ mi of road is low standard. Boat launch low standard.

* **Piety Island** (Willamette NF). 1-1/10
mi SW of Detroit BY BOAT. SEASON: 6/1-
9/15; 10-day lmt. FACILITIES: 12 tent
site; tbls, toil, cga, no drk wtr.
Store/gas/ice/showers (1 mi). ACTIVI-
TIES: Swimming; picnicking; fishing;
waterskiing; sailing. Boating,rl (1 mi).
MISC.: Elev 1600 ft; 2 acres; Detroit
Lake. Pets permitted if kept on leash.

Upper Arm (Willamette NF). 1-1/10 mi
NE of Detroit on FR RS46. SEASON: 4/15-
10/31; 10-day lmt. FACILITIES: 5 sites
(tr -16); tbls, toil, cga, no drk wtr.
Store/ice/toil/gas/food/laundry (1
mi). ACTIVITIES: Swimming; picnicking;
fishing; sailing. Boating,rl (1 mi).
Waterskiing (4 mi). MISC.: Elev 1600
ft; 2 acres. On Breitenbush Arm of Detroit Lake. Pets permitted on leash.

DISSTON

Cedar Creek (Umpqua NF). 4-1/5 mi SE
of Disston on FR 2149. SEASON: 5/25-
9/15; 14-day lmt. FACILITIES: 8 sites
(tr -16); tbls, toil, cga, no drk wtr.
Store (4 mi). ACTIVITIES: Swimming;
picnicking; fishing. MISC.: Elev 1600
ft; 5 acres; stream. Pets permitted if
kept on a leash.

Lundpark (Umpqua NF). 7-1/5 mi SE
of Disston on FS 2149. SEASON: 5/25-
9/15; 14-day lmt. FACILITIES: 4 sites
(tr -16); tbls, toil, cga. ACTIVITIES:
Picnicking; fishing. MISC.: Pets.

DRAIN

Gunther-Smith River (BLM; Roseburg
Dist.). 2 mi N of Drain on I-5 ; 10
mi NW on Smith River Co Rd. SEASON:
5/1-10/31; 14-day lmt. FACILITIES: 8
sites (tr -22); tbls, toil, cga, f. AC-
TIVITIES: Picnicking; hunting; hiking;
fishing. MISC.: Elev 750 ft; 10 acres.
Pets; scenic.

DUFUR

City Park. In town on US 197. SEASON:
All yr. MISC.: Pets permitted if kept
on a leash.

Eight Mile Crossing (Mt. Hood NF). 12
mi SW of Dufur on Co 1; 4-3/10 mi W
on FR 44; 3/5 mi N on FR 105 (rough
road). SEASON: 6/1-10/31; 10-day lmt.

FACILITIES: 14 sites (tr -16); tbls, toil,
cga, no drk wtr. ACTIVITIES: Hunting;
picnicking; fishing. Horseback riding
(5 mi). MISC.: Elev 4200 ft; 4 acres;
stream. Pets permitted if kept on leash.

Fifteen Mile (Mt. Hood NF). 2 mi S of
Dufur on St Hwy 197; 14 mi W on Co Hwy
118; 9 mi W on FS 205. SEASON: 6/1-
10/31. FACILITIES: 4 sites (tr -16);
tbls, toil, cga. ACTIVITIES: Picnicking;
horseback riding (5 mi). MISC.: Elev
4600 ft; 1 acre; stream; pets permitted.

Knebal Springs (Mt. Hood NF). 12 mi SW
of Dufur on Co Hwy 1; 4-3/10 mi SW on
FS 44; 4 mi NW on FS 105; 1 mi SW on
FS 16. SEASON: 6/1-10/31; 10-day lmt.
FACILITIES: 4 sites (tr -22); tbls, toil,
cga, f, no drk wtr. ACTIVITIES: Horseback riding; picnicking. MISC.: Elev
4000 ft; 1 acre. Pets okay on leash.

Lower Crossing (Mt. Hood NF). 12 mi SW
of Dufur on Co Hwy 1; 4 mi W on FS
44; 1 mi N on FS 167. SEASON: 6/1-10/31;
10-day lmt. FACILITIES: 2 sites (tr
-16); tbls, toil, cga. ACTIVITIES: Hunting; picnicking; fishing. Horseback riding (5 mi). MISC.: Elev 3800 ft; 5
acres; stream; pets. No drk wtr.

Pebble Ford (Mt. Hood NF). 12 mi SW of
Dufur on Co Hwy 1; 5 mi W on FS 44;
½ mi S on FS 21C. SEASON: 6/1-10/31;
10-day lmt. FACILITIES: 3 sites (tr -16);
tbls, toil, cga, no drk wtr. ACTIVITIES:
Hunting; Picnicking. Horseback riding
(5 mi). MISC.: Elev 4000 ft; 1 acre;
stream. Pets permitted if kept on leash.

EDDYVILLE

Big Elk (Stuslaw NF). 10 mi E of Eddyville on Hwy 20; 7½ mi S on Co 547; 1-
1/10 mi W on Co 538. SEASON: 5/25-12/1;
10-day lmt. FACILITIES: 12 sites (tr -
16); tbls, toil, cga, piped drk wtr. AC-
TIVITIES: Swimming; picnicking; fishing.
MISC.: Elev 200 ft;2 acres;pets;stream.

ELGIN

Black Mountain (Umatilla NF). 13-3/5
mi NW on St Hwy 204; 14-3/5 mi SW
on FS 31; 8-4/5 mi W on FS 3128; 3/10
mi SW on FS 3135. SEASON: 6/1-11/30;
10-day lmt. FACILITIES: 5 sites (no
tr); tbls, toil, cga, f, piped drk wtr.
ACTIVITIES: Picnicking; berry-picking.
Horseback riding (1 mi). MISC.: Elev
5100 ft; 3 acres; pets; scenic. Pack
out your own garbage.

Ford Spring (Umatilla NF). 14½ mi NW
of Elgin on St Hwy S204; 2½ mi W on
FS N31. SEASON: 6/1-11/30; 10-day lmt.
FACILITIES: 3 tent sites (no trailers);
toil, cga, f. MISC.: Elev 4900 ft; pets.

See page 7 for KEY TO ABBREVIATIONS.

Larger Spring (Umatilla NF). 24-3/5 mi NW on St Hwy 204; 10 mi NE on FS 64; 5-3/5 mi SE on FS 63; 1-9/10 mi W on FS 6306. SEASON: 7/1-11/1. FACILITIES: 5 sites (tr -16); tbls, toil, cga, f, no drk wtr. ACTIVITIES: Picnicking; berry-picking. Fishing/swimming/horseback riding (1 mi). MISC.: Elev 5000 ft; 6 acres; pets.

Mosier Spring (Umatilla NF). 21-2/5 mi N of Elgin on Co Hwy; 7-9/10 mi N on FS N53; 12-1/5 mi NE on FS N50. SEASON: 7/1-11/25. FACILITIES: 4 sites (tr -22); tbls, toil, cga, f. ACTIVITIES: Picnicking. MISC.: Elev 4700 ft; pets permitted if kept on a leash.

Ruckel (Umatilla NF). 14-3/5 mi on St Hwy 204; 11-7/10 mi SW on FS N31. SEASON: 6/1-11/30; 10-day lmt. FACILITIES: 4 tent sites (no trailers); cga. MISC.: Elev 4200 ft. Pets permitted if on leash.

Timothy Spring (Umatilla NF). 21-2/5 mi N on Co; 7-9/10 mi N on FR N53; 1-7/10 mi N on fR N50; 6-3/5 mi W on FR N534. SEASON: 7/1-10/15. FACILITIES: 8 sites (tr -22); tbls, toil, cga, f, no drk wtr. ACTIVITIES: Picnicking. Horseback riding (1 mi); Fishing (3 mi). MISC.: Elev 4600 ft; 5 acres. Pets.

Wallowa River Rest Area. 16 mi E of Elgin on St Hwy 82. SEASON: All yr. FACILITIES: Drk wtr. MISC.: Stream scenic view. Pets permitted on leash.

Woodland (Umatilla NF). 16 mi NW of Elgin on Hwy S204. SEASON: 6/1-11/30; 10-day lmt. FACILITIES: 6 sites (tr -22); tbls, toil, cga; no drk wtr. Dump (4 mi). ACTIVITIES: Picnicking; berry-picking. Horseback riding (1 mi). MISC.: Elev 5000 ft; 1 acre; pets; scenic. Must pack out garbage.

ENTERPRISE

Buckhorn (Wallowa Whitman NF). 3 mi S of Enterprise on Hwy 82; 5-1/5 mi NE on Co 772; 25-4/5 mi NE on Co 798; 9-3/5 mi NE on FS N436. SEASON: 6/1-11/30; 10-day lmt. FACILITIES: 6 sites (tr -22); tbls, toil, cga, f. ACTIVITIES: Picnicking. MISC.: Elev 5200 ft; 4 acres; pets. Piped drk wtr.

Coyote (Wallowa Whitman NF). 3 mi E of Enterprise on Hwy 82; 21-3/5 mi N on Co 799; 19 mi N on FR N436. SEASON: 5/15-12/1; 10-day lmt. FACILITIES: 21 sites (tr -22); tbls, toil, cga, f. ACTIVITIES: Picnicking. MISC.: Elev 4800 ft; 6 acres; pets. Piped drk wtr.

Dougherty (Wallowa Whitman NF). 15 mi N of Enterprise on Hwy 3; 12 mi NE on FS N201; 10 mi E on FS 431; 10 mi NE on FR N437. SEASON: 6/1-12/1; 14-day lmt. FACILITIES: 10 sites (tr -22); tbls,

toil, cga, no drk wtr. ACTIVITIES: Picnicking. MISC.: Elev 4900 ft; 6 acres. Pets; scenic.

Kirkland (Wallowa Whitman NF). 3 mi E of Enterprise on St Hwy 82; 21-3/5 mi N on Co Hwy 799; 18 mi N on FS N436; 2 mi W on FS N520. SEASON: 6/1-12/1; 10-day lmt. FACILITIES: 4 sites (tr -22); toil, cga, f. MISC.: Elev 5000 ft; pets permitted if kept on a leash.

Vigne (Wallowa Whitman NF). 3 mi E of Enterprise on Hwy 82; 21-3/5 mi N on Co 799; 6½ mi N on FR N436; 11 mi E on FR N431. SEASON: 4/15-11/30; 10-day lmt. FACILITIES: 12 sites (tr -22); tbls, toil, cga, f. ACTIVITIES: Fishing; picnicking. MISC.: Elev 3000 ft; 4 acres. Pets. Well drk wtr.

ESTACADA

* **Alder Flat** (Mt Hood NF). 25-4/5 mi SE of Estacada on Hwy 224; 7/10 mi W on Trl 574. SEASON: 4/21-11/1; 14-day lmt. FACILITIES: 6 tent sites; tbls, no drk wtr. ACTIVITIES: Picnicking; fishing. MISC.: Elev 1300 ft; 4 acres; pets.

* **Bagby Hot Springs** (Mt Hood NF). 26-7/10 mi SE of Estacada on St Hwy 244; 3-7/10 mi S on FS S46; 3-2/5 mi S on FS S63; 6-3/10 mi SW on FS S70; 1¼ mi on Trail 544. SEASON: All year; 14-day lmt. FACILITIES: 8 tent sites (no trailers); tbls, toil, cga, f, drk wtr. ACTIVITIES: Rockhounding; picnicking; fishing. Horseback riding (1 mi). MISC.: Elev 2200 ft; 9 acres. Pets. Bath house on site.

Camp Ten (Mt. Hood NF). 27 mi SE of Estacada on Hwy 224; 21-4/5 mi S on FS 46; 8-1/5 mi SE on FS 806; 6-1/10 mi S on FS 42. SEASON: 5/28-9/15; 14-day lmt. FACILITIES: 8 sites (tr -16); tbls, toil, cga, no drk wtr. ACTIVITIES: Picnicking; fishing; sailing; boating,rl (1 mi) (no motors). MISC.: Elev 5000 ft; 3 acres; lake; scenic. Pets permitted if kept on a leash.

Cripple Creek (Mt. Hood NF). 22 mi SE of Estacada on St Hwy 224. SEASON: 4/15-10/31; 14-day lmt. FACILITIES: 6 sites (tr -16); toil, cga, f. ACTIVITIES: Rockhounding; fishing. MISC.: Elev 1000 ft. Pets permitted on leash.

* **East Twin Lake** (Mt. Hood NF). 26-7/10 mi SE on St Hwy 224; 3-7/10 mi S on FS S46; 1/2 mi S on FS S63; 8 mi SW on FS S708; 3½ mi on FS S739; 10 mi on TRAILS 549, 558, 573. SEASON: 7/1-10/30. FACILITIES: 1 tent site; tbls, toil, cga, f, no drk wtr. ACTIVITIES: Picnicking; fishing; rockhounding. Horseback riding (1 mi). MISC.: Elev 4100 ft; 20 acres; scenic; pets.

Frazier Fork (Mt. Hood NF). 27 mi SE of Estacada on Hwy 224; 7½ mi E on FS S57; 7 mi NE on FS S58; 2-1/5 mi NE on FS S457; 4-1/5 mi W in FS S456 (primitive gravel road). SEASON: 7/1-10/15; 14-day lmt. FACILITIES: 8 tent sites (no trailers); tbls, toil, cga, no drk wtr. ACTIVITIES: Hunting; berry-picking; picnicking; fishing. Horseback riding (1 mi). MISC.: Elev 4700 ft; 2 acres. Pets permitted if kept on leash.

Hambone Springs (Mt. Hood NF). 7 mi SE of Estacada on St Hwy 224; 7-9/10 mi SE on FS S403; 17-1/5 mi SE on FS S469 (long rough road). SEASON: 7/1-10/15; 14-day lmt. FACILITIES: 3 tent sites (no trailers); tbls, toil, cga, no drk wtr. ACTIVITIES: Berry-picking; hiking; picnicking. Horseback riding (1 mi). MISC.: Elev 4200 ft; 2 acres; scenic. Pets.

Hideaway Lake (Mt. Hood NF). 27 mi SE of Estacada on Hwy 224; 7½ mi E on FS S57; 3 mi N on FS S58; 5-3/10 mi NW on FS S596. SEASON: 5/28-11/1; 14-day lmt. FACILITIES: 9 sites (tr -16); tbls, toil, cga, piped drk wtr. ACTIVITIES: Picnicking; swimming; fishing; boating (no motors). Horseback riding (1 mi). MISC.: Elev 4500 ft; 3 acres; lake; scenic. Pets permitted if kept on leash.

Highrock Spring (Mt. Hood NF). 27 mi SE of Estacada on St Hwy 224; 7½ mi E on FS S57; 9 mi NE on FS S58; 1½ mi NW on FS 3457. SEASON: 6/15-11/1; 14-day lmt. FACILITIES: 7 sites (no trailers); tbls, toil, cga, f, piped drk wtr. ACTIVITIES: Hunting; picnicking. MISC.: Elev 4400 ft; 1 acre; pets; scenic.

Horseshoe Lake (Mt. Hood NF). 27 mi SE of Estacada on St Hwy 224; 21-4/5 mi S on FS S46; 8-1/5 mi SE on FS S806; 8-3/10 mi S on FS S42 (rough rd). SEASON: 5/28-9/15; 10-day lmt. FACILITIES: 4 tent sites (no trailers); tbls, toil, cga, f, no drk wtr. ACTIVITIES: Hunting; picnicking; fishing; hiking. Boating,rl (3 mi), no motors. Horseback riding (1 mi). Berry-picking. MISC.: Elev 5200 ft; lake; pets.

Kingfisher (Mt. Hood NF). 26½ mi SE of Estacada on St Hwy 224; 3½ mi S on FS S46; 3 mi S on FS S63; 2 mi SW on FS S70. SEASON: 4/15-10/15; 14-day lmt. FACILITIES: 21 sites (tr -16); tbls, toil, cga. ACTIVITIES: Picnicking; fishing. MISC.: 1 acre. Pets.

Lake Harriet. 30 mi SE on St Hwy 224; 6 mi E on Service Rd. SEASON: 5/1-10/1; 7-day lmt. FACILITIES: 6 sites (tr -20); tbls. ACTIVITIES: Picnicking; fishing; boating,l. MISC.: 3 acres. Pets permitted if kept on leash.

* Lake Lenore (Mt. Hood NF). 26-7/10 mi SE of Estacada on St Hwy 224; 3-7/10 mi S on FS S46; 5-2/5 mi S on FS S63; 2-9/10 mi SW on FS S708; 2 mi on FS 708A; 6 mi on TRAIL 553. SEASON: 7/1-10/30. FACILITIES: Hiking; picnicking; fishing. Horseback riding (1 mi). MISC.: Elev 4800 ft; 10 acres; lake; pets.

Lookout Springs (Mt. Hood NF). 7 mi SE of Estacada on Hwy 224; 7-9/10 mi SE on FS S403; 5-1/10 mi NE on FS S469. SEASON: 7/1-10/15; 14-day lmt. FACILITIES: 10 tent sites (no trailers); tbls, toil, cga, piped drk wtr. ACTIVITIES: Picnicking; hunting; berry-picking. Horseback riding (1 mi). Fishing (3 mi). MISC.: Elev 4000 ft; 2 acres. Pets permitted if kept on a leash.

Lower Lake (Mt. Hood NF). 27 mi SE of Estacada on Hwy 224; 21-4/5 mi S on FS S46; 8-1/5 mi SE on FS S806; 4½ mi S on FS 42. SEASON: 5/28-9/15; 14-day lmt. FACILITIES: 8 tent sites (no trailers); tbls, toil, cga, f, no drk wtr. Store/gas (1 mi). ACTIVITIES: Picnicking; berry-picking; horseback riding; Boating,rl/fishing (1 mi). MISC.: Elev 4600 ft; 2 acres. Pets.

North Fork Crossing (Mt. Hood NF). 7 mi SE of Estacada on Us 224; 8 mi SE on FS S403; ½ mi NW on FS S457. SEASON: 4/15-10/15; 14-day lmt. FACILITIES: 9 tent sites (no trailers); tbls, toil, cga, f, no drk wtr. ACTIVITIES: Hunting; fishing; picnicking. MISC.: Elev 2000 ft; 3 acres; stream. Pets. On banks of clear, swift, mtn stream.

Olallie Meadows (Mt. Hood NF). 27 mi SE of Estacada on Hwy 224; 21-4/5 mi S on FS S46; 8-1/5 mi SE on FS S806; 1-2/5 mi S on FS S42. SEASON: 5/28-9/15; 14-day lmt. FACILITIES: 7 tent sites (no trailers); tbls, toil, cga, f, no drk wtr. Store/gas (4 mi). ACTIVITIES: Berry-picking; picnicking; boating,rld (4 mi); fishing (1 mi). MISC.: Elev 4500 ft; 1 acre; spring. Pets.

*Pansy Lake (Mt. Hood NF). 26-7/10 mi SE on St Hwy 224; 3-7/10 mi S on FS S46; 5-2/5 mi S on FS S63; 3½ mi S on FS 739; 1 mi on TRAILS 549,558. SEASON: 7/1-1/30. FACILITIES: 3 tent sites; tbls, toil, cga, no drk wtr. ACTIVITIES: Picnicking; fishing. Horseback riding (1 mi). MISC.: Elev 4000 ft; 12 acres; pets; scenic.

Pegleg Falls (Mt. Hood NF). 26½ mi SE of Estacada on Hwy 224; 3½ mi S on FS S46; 3 mi S on FS S63; 6 mi SW on FS S70. SEASON: 4/15-10/1; 14-day lmt. FACILITIES: 20 sites (tr -16); tbls, toil, cga, well drk wtr. ACTIVITIES: Rockhounding; hiking; picnicking; fishing. MISC.: Elev 2000 ft; 8 acres; stream. 13 walk-in units. Horseback riding (1 mi). Pets permitted on leash.

Paul Dennis (Mt. Hood NF). 27 mi SE of Estacada on Hwy 224; 21-4/5 mi S on FS 46; 8-1/5 mi SE on FS 806; 6-3/10 mi S on FS 42. SEASON: 5/28-9/15; 10-day lmt. FACILITIES: 14 tent sites (no trailers); tbls, toil, cga, f, store, gas. ACTIVITIES: Boating,rld: (no motors); horseback riding; picnicking; fishing; sailing. MISC.: Elev 5000 ft; 4 acres. Pets permitted if kept on a leash.

Raab (Mt. Hood NF). 27 mi SE on St Hwy 224; 4 mi SE on S46; 10 mi SE on S63. SEASON: 4/21-9/15; 14-day lmt. FACILITIES: 27 sites (tr -22); tbls, toil, cga, no drk wtr. ACTIVITIES: Picnicking; fishing; rockhounding. MISC.: Elev 1500 ft; 10 acres; river; pets; scenic.

River Ford (Mt. Hood NF). 27 mi SE of Estacada on Hwy 224; 3½ mi S on FS S46. SEASON: 4/21-12/1; 14-day lmt.. FACILITIES: 10 sites (tr -16); tbls, toil, cga, f, no drk wtr. ACTIVITIES: Rockhounding; picnicking; fishing. MISC.: elev 1500 ft; 3 acres; river. Pets.

Round Lake (Mt. Hood NF). 27 mi SE of Estacada on Hwy 224; 3-3/5 mi S on FS 46; 12-2/5 mi SE on FS 63; 6-7/10 mi SE on FS 760. SEASON: 5/28-10/15; 10-day lmt. FACILITIES: 6 tent sites (no trailers); tbls, toil, cga, f, no drk wtr. ACTIVITIES: Picnicking; fishing. MISC.: Elev 3200 ft; 2 acres; lake. Pets.

Scout Camp (Mt. Hood NF). 27 mi SE of Estacada on St Hwy 224; 21-4/5 mi On FS 46; 8-1/5 mi SE on FS 806; 6-3/10 mi S on FS 42. SEASON: 6/20-9/15; 14-day lmt. FACILITIES: 10 tent sites (no trailers); toil, cga, f. ACTIVITIES: Fishing; boating,rl. MISC.: Elev 5000 ft; pets permitted if kept on leash.

Shellrock Creek (Mt. Hood NF). 27 mi SE of Estacada on Hwy 224; 7½ mi E on FS S57; 2/5 mi N on FS S58. SEASON: 4/15-11/15; 14-day lmt. FACILITIES: 5 tent sites (no trailers); tbls, toil, cga, f, no drk wtr. ACTIVITIES: Rockhounding; picnicking; fishing; hunting. MISC.: Elev 2300 ft; 1 acre; stream. Pets.

Shining Lake (Mt. Hood NF). 27 mi SE of Estacada on St Hwy 224; 7½ mi E on FS S57; 7 mi NE on FS S58; 2-1/5 mi NE on FS S457. SEASON: 7/1-10/1; 14-day lmt. FACILITIES: 3 sites (no tr); tbls, toil, cga, no drk wtr. ACTIVITIES: Picnicking; fishing; berry-picking. Horseback riding (1 mi). MISC.: Elev 4200 ft; pets; scenic.

*****Silver King Lake** (Mt. Hood NF). 26-7/10 mi SE on St Hwy 224; 3-7/10 mi S on FS S46; 3-2/5 mi S on FS S63; 6-3/10 mi S on FS S70; take TRAIL

544 then 520, 7½ mi. SEASON: 7/1-10/30. FACILITIES: 1 tent site; tbls, cga, f, no drk wtr. ACTIVITIES: Picnicking; fishing; rockhounding; hiking. Horseback riding (1 mi). MISC.: Elev 4100 ft;6 acres;scenic;pets.

Summit Lake (Mt. Hood NF). 27 mi SE of Estacada on St Hwy 224; 5-3/10 mi E on FS S57; 7-3/10 mi SE on FS S601; 1 mi SE on FS S601D (rough rd). SEASON: 5/30-10/1; 14-day lmt. FACILITIES: 6 tent sites (no trailers); tbls, toil, cga, f, no drk wtr. ACTIVITIES: Swimming; picnicking; fishing; boating (no motors). Horseback riding (1 mi). MISC.: Elev 4000 ft; 3 acres; lake. Pets permitted if kept on a leash.

Twin Springs (Mt. Hood NF). 7 mi SE of Estacada on Hwy 224; 7-9/10 mi SE on FS S403; 10-9/10 mi SE on FS S469. SEASON: 7/1-10/15; 14-day lmt. FACILITIES: 8 tent sites (no trailers); tbls, toil, cga, no drk wtr. ACTIVITIES: Picnicking; berry-picking. Horseback riding (2 mi). Fishing (4 mi). MISC.: Elev 4200 ft; 3 acres. Pets.

EUGENE

Eugene Blue Star Memorial Rest Area. 4 mi N of Eugene on US 99W. SEASON: All yr. FACILITIES: Drk wtr. MISC.: Pets permitted if kept on a leash.

Gettings Creek Rest Area. 30 mi S of Eugene on I-5. SEASON: All yr. FACILITIES: Drk wtr. MISC.: Pets.

Oakgrove Rest Area. 14 mi N of Eugene on I-5. SEASON: All yr. FACILITIES: Drk wtr. MISC.: Pets permitted.

FLORENCE

Carter Lake East (Siuslaw NF). 8-3/5 mi S of Florence on US 101. SEASON: 1/1-12/31; 10-day lmt. FACILITIES: 11 sites (tr -16); tbls, toil, cga. Store/ice/snack bar (2 mi). ACTIVITIES: Swimming; picnicking; fishing; horseback riding; hiking; boating,ld (rental 2 mi). MISC.: Elev 100 ft; 2 acres; sand dunes. Adjacent to Carter Lake. Pets permitted.

Carter Lake West (Siuslaw NF). 8½ mi S of Florence on US 101. SEASON: 6/15-9/15; 10-day lmt. FACILITIES: 22 sites (tr -22); tbls, flush toil. Store (3 mi). ACTIVITIES: Swimming; picnicking; fishing; boating,rld; horseback riding. MISC.: Elev 100 ft; 6 acres. Pets.

Driftwood (Siuslaw NF). 7 mi S on US 101; 1-3/5 mi W on FS 1080. SEASON: All yr; 10-day lmt. FACILITIES: 13 sites (tr -22); tbls, toil, cga, piped drk wtr. Store/gas/ice/food (2 mi). ACTIVITIES: Picnicking; hiking;

See page 7 for KEY TO ABBREVIATIONS.

fishing; berry-picking. Boating,rld/
waterskiing (2 mi). Horseback riding/
rental (3 mi). **MISC.**: Elev 100 ft;
2 acres; scenic; pets.

Lodgepole (Siuslaw NF). 7 mi S on
US 101; 1 mi W on FS 1070. SEAS: All
yr; 10-day lmt. FAC: 3 sites (tr
-22); tbls, toil, cga, piped drk wtr.
Store/gas/ice/food (2 mi). ACTIVITIES:
Swimming; picnicking; fishing; hiking;
berry-picking. Boating,rld/waterskiing
(2 mi). Horseback riding/rental (3 mi).
MISC.: Elev 100 ft; 1 acre; scenic. Pets.

North Fork Siuslaw (Siuslaw NF). 1 mi
E of Florence on Hwy 36; 13½ mi NE
on Co Rd 5070; 1/2 mi E on FS 715.
SEASON: All yr; 10-day lmt. FACILI-
TIES: 5 sites (no tr); tbls, toil, cga,
no drk wtr. ACTIVITIES: Picnicking;
fishing. **MISC.**: Elev 100 ft; 11 acres;
river; pets.

Tyee (Siuslaw NF). 6 mi S on US 101;
1/10 mi SE on FS 1068. SEASON: All
yr; 10-day lmt. FACILITIES: 13 sites
(tr -22); tbls, toil, cga, piped drk
wtr. Store/ice/gas/food (1 mi). AC-
TIVITIES: Picnicking; swimming; fishing; boating,rld; berry-picking; hiking. Horseback riding (2 mi).
MISC.: Elev 100 ft; 5 acres; pets;
scenic. Siltcoos Lake (1 mi). In
Oregon Dunes National Recreation Area.

FT. KLAMATH

Seven Mile Marsh (Winema NF). 5-9/10
mi W on Co Rd 1419; 1-2/5 mi W on
TR32; 1/2 mi S on TR334A. SEASON:
6/15-10/1. FACILITIES: 8 sites (no
tr); tbls, toil, cga, f, no drk wtr.
ACTIVITIES: Picnicking; horseback
riding; hiking. Swimming/fishing (5
mi). **MISC.**: Elev 5500 ft; 3 acres;
pets; scenic. Trailhead for Oregon
Skyline. Trail and access to Sky-
lakes Limited Area.

Seven Mile Marsh (Winema NF). 4-1/5
mi W on Co 1419; 1/10 mi W on TR32;
1/2 mi S on TR334A. SEASON: 6/1-10/31.
FACILITIES: 8 tent sites (no trailers);
tbls, toil, cga, f, no drk wtr. ACTIVI-
TIES: Picnicking; horseback riding;
hiking; fishing (5 mi). **MISC.**: Elev
5500 ft; 3 acres. Trailhead for Oregon
Skyline. Trail & access to Skylakes
Limited Area. Pets.

FT. ROCK

Cabin Lake (Deschutes NF). 9-4/5 mi
N of Ft. Rock on FS 1821. SEASON: 5/15-
10/30; 14-day lmt. FACILITIES: 14 sites
(tr -32); tbls, toil, cga. ACTIVITIES:
Hunting; picnicking; bird watching.
MISC.: Elev 4500 ft; 5 acres. Deer
hunting camps. Good place to get away
from it all. Pets. Piped drk wtr.

China Hat (Deschutes NF). 22-7/10 mi
N of Ft. Rock on FS 1821. SEASON: 5/1-
10/30; 14-day lmt. FACILITIES: 14 sites
(tr -32); tbls, toil, cga, piped drk wtr.
ACTIVITIES: Picnicking; hunting; horseback riding. **MISC.**: Elev 5100 ft; 6
acres. Deer hunting camps. Pets.

FOX

Beech Creek (Malheur NF). 6 mi S of
Fox on US 395. SEASON: 6/1-11/1; 14-
day lmt. FACILITIES: 8 sites (tr -16);
tbls, toil, cga, piped drk wtr. ACTIVI-
TIES: Picnicking; fishing. **MISC.**: Elev
4500 ft; 3 acres; stream. Pets.

FRENCHGLEN

Blitzen Crossing (BLM; Burns Dist.). 10
mi S of Frenchglen on Hwy 205; 15 mi
E on Steens Mtn Rd. SEASON: 7/1-10/31;
14-day lmt. FACILITIES: 5 sites (tr
-24); tbls, toil, cga, f, no drk wtr.
ACTIVITIES: Picnicking. Fishing (1 mi).
MISC.: Elev 7200 ft; 2 acres. Pets.

Fish Lake (BLM; Burns Dist.). Off Hwy
205; 16 mi E on Steens Mtn Rd (gravel). SEASON: 7/1-10/31; 14-day lmt.
FACILITIES: 20 sites (tr -24); tbls,
toil, cga, f. ACTIVITIES: Swimming;
picnicking; fishing; boating,rld. **MISC.**:
Elev 7200 ft; 20 acres. Pets permitted.

Jackman Park (BLM; Burns Dist.). Off
Hwy 205; 20 mi E on Steens Mtn Rd.
SEASON: 7/1-10/31; 14-day lmt. FACILI-
TIES: 5 sites (tr -24); tbls, toil, cga,
f. ACTIVITIES: Picnicking. Fishing (1
mi). **MISC.**: Elev 7200 ft; 3 acres. Pets.

Page Springs (BLM; Burns Dist.). 3 mi
E of Frenchglen on Steens Mtn Rd
(gravel). SEASON: 4/1-10/31; 14-day
lmt. FACILITIES: 16 sites (tr -24);
tbls, toil, cga, drk wtr (must be
boiled). ACTIVITIES: Picnicking; fishing; hunting; hiking. **MISC.**: Elev 4200
ft; 5 acres; river; geological interest.
Pets permitted if kept on a leash.

GARDINER

Elbow Lake (Siuslaw NF). 5-7/10 mi NW
of Gardiner on US 101. SEASON: All yr.
FACILITIES: 11 sites (tr -22); tbls,
ing; fishing; boating,l. **MISC.**: Elev
100 ft; 2 acres. This site owned & operated by Crown Zellerbach Corp. Pets.

GLENDALE

Tucker Flat (BLM; Medford Dist.). 20 mi
W of Glendale on Cow Cr. Rd; 5 mi W
on Mule Cr. Rd; 14 mi SW on Marial Rd.
SEASON: 5/1-10/31; 14-day lmt. FACILI-
TIES: 10 prim. tent sites (no trailers);
tbls, f. ACTIVITIES: (Nearby) swimming; fishing. **MISC.**: 5 acres. Pets.

GLIDE

Coolwater (Umpqua NF). 13-1/10 mi SE of Glide on Co 17; 2-9/10 mi E on FS 272. SEASON: 5/5-10/31; 14-day lmt. FACILITIES: 7 sites (tr -16); tbls, toil, cga, well drk wtr. ACTIVITIES: Swimming; picnicking; fishing. MISC.: Elev 1300 ft; 6 acres; river. Pets permitted.

Hemlock Lake (Umpqua NF). 13-1/10 mi E of Glide on Co 17; 18-3/10 mi E on FS 272; ½ mi S on FS 272J. SEASON: 6/14-10/31; 14-day lmt. FACILITIES: 15 sites (tr -22); tbls, toil, cga, no drk wtr. ACT: Swimming; picnicking; fishing; boating (1, 2 mi), no motors; berries; hiking. MISC.: Elev 4400 ft; 5 acres; lake. Yellow Jacket Glade Loop Trail, 5 mi long; adjacent to site. Pets.

Lake in the Woods (Umpqua NF). 13-1/10 mi E of Glide on Co 17; 14 mi E on FS 272. SEASON: 6/4-10/31; 14-day lmt. FACILITIES: 11 sites (tr -16); tbls, flush toil, cga, piped drk wtr. ACTIVITIES: Berry-picking; picnicking; fishing; boating,d; swimming. MISC.: Elev 3000 ft; 6 acres; lake. Old trail cabin on site; ½ mi to Hemlock Falls; 7/10 mi to Trail to Yakso Falls. Pets.

Lower Twin Lakes (Umpqua NF). 13-1/10 mi E of Glide on Co 17; 15-4/5 mi E on FS 272; 8½ mi E on FS 2715; 4-3/5 mi NE on FS 2796; 2 mi NE on Old Trail 1500. SEASON: 6/24-10/31. FACILITIES: 6 tent sites (no trailers); tbls, toil, cga, no drk wtr. ACTIVITIES: Picnicking; fishing; swimming; boating,d; horseback riding (1 mi). MISC.: Elev 5000 ft; 2 acres. Old trail shelter on site. Pets.

Wolf Creek (Umpqua NF). 12-2/5 mi SE of Glide on Co 17. SEASON: 5/5-10/31; 14-day lmt. FACILITIES: 8 sites (tr -22); tbls, toil, cga, piped drk wtr; electricity in restrooms. Store/gas/ice (5 mi). ACTIVITIES: Swimming; picnicking; fishing; hiking. MISC.: Elev 1100 ft; 3 acres; river; pets.

GOLD BEACH

Elko (Siskiyou NF). 1-3/5 mi S of Gold Beach on US 101; 6-1/10 mi SE on Co Hwy 635; 9-9/10 mi SE on FS 368; ½ mi E on FS 368B. SEASON: 6/15-10/30; 14-day lmt. FACILITIES: 3 tent sites (no trailers); tbls, toil, cga, f, no drk wtr. ACTIVITIES: Picnicking. MISC.: Elev 3000 ft; 2 acres; pets.

Huntley Park (Maintained by US Plywood). 7 mi off St Hwy 101 on S bank of Rogue River Rd. SEASON: All yr. FACILITIES: 52 sites; tbls, toil, cga, f, pump drk wtr. ACTIVITIES: Picnicking; fishing.

MISC.: Park has beautiful setting on river among Myrtlewood trees. Pets permitted if kept on a leash. Gates locked 10 pm to 6 am.

Jetty. S side of harbor of Rogue River. SEASON: All yr. MISC.: Pets permitted.

Lobster Creek (Siskiyou NF). 4-1/5 mi NE of Gold Beach on Co Hwy 375; 5-3/5 mi NE on FS 333. FACILITIES: 5 sites; piped drk wtr, flush toil, elec in restrooms, cga, tbls. ACTIVITIES: Rockhounding; picnicking; fishing; boating,l. Swimming/fishing/waterskiing (1 mi). MISC.: Elev 100 ft; 4 acres; pets; scenic. SEASON: All year.

Ophir Rest Area. 9 mi N of Gold Beach on US 101. SEASON: All yr. FACILITIES: Drk wtr. MISC.: Pets permitted.

Quosatana (Siskiyou NF). 4-1/5 mi NE of Gold Beach on Co 595; 10 mi NE on FS 333. SEASON: 4/1-10/31; 14-day lmt. FACILITIES: 24 sites (tr -32); tbls, toil, cga, f, drk wtr. ACTIVITIES: Swimming; picnicking; fishing; boating,ld. MISC.: Elev 100 ft; 6 acres. Pets.

Wildhorse (Siskiyou NF). 1-3/5 mi S of gold Beach on US 101; 6-1/10 mi SE on Co Hwy 635; 16½ mi NE on FS 368; 4-3/5 mi NE on FS 357. SEASON: 6/15-10/31; 14-day lmt. FACILITIES: 3 tent sites (no trailers); tbls, toil, cga, f, piped drk wtr. ACTIVITIES: Picnicking. MISC.: Elev 3600 ft; 2 acres; pets.

GOLD HILL

Elderberry Flat (BLM). 15 mi N of Gold Hill, off I-5. SEASON: 4/1-10/1; 14-day lmt. FACILITIES: 10 sites; toil, cga, no drk wtr. ACTIVITIES: Fishing; hunting; picnicking; berry-picking. MISC.: Elev 1990 ft. Pets.

GOV'T. CAMP

Alpine (Mt. Hood NF). 4/5 mi of Gov't Camp E on US 26; 4-3/5 mi NE on Hwy 50. SEASON: 7/1-9/1; 14-day lmt. FACILITIES: 10 sites (tr -22); tbls, toil, cga, f, piped drk wtr. ACTIVITIES: Picnicking. MISC.: Elev 5400 ft; 4 acres. Snack bar (1 mi). 1 mi below Timberline Lopdge on new rd. Pets.

Barlow Creek (Mt. Hood NF). 2 mi E of Gov't Camp on US 26; 4½ mi N on Hwy 35; 4-1/5 mi SE on FS S30. SEASON: 5/1-10/1; 14-day lmt. FACILITIES: 5 tent sites (tr -16); tbls, toil, cga, f, no drk wtr. ACTIVITIES: Picnicking; hunting; fishing. Horseback riding/hiking (1 mi). MISC.: Elev 3100 ft; 3 acres. Pets permitted.

See page 7 for KEY TO ABBREVIATIONS.

Barlow Crossing (Mt. Hood NF). 2 mi E of Gov't. Camp on US 26; 4½ mi N on St Hwy 35; 5-1/5 mi SE on FS S30 (dirt rd). SEASON: 5/1-10/1; 14-day lmt. FAC: 4 sites (tr -16); tbls, toil, cga, f, no drk wtr. ACTIVITIES: Picnicking; fishing. Horseback riding (1 mi). Hiking (2 mi). MISC.: Elev 3100 ft; 2 acres; stream. Pets permitted.

Devils Half Acre (Mt. Hood NF). 2 mi E of Gov't. Camp on US 26; 4½ mi N on St Hwy 35; 1 mi E on FS S30 (dirt rd). SEASON: 5/1-10/1; 14-day lmt. FACILITIES: 4 tent sites; tbls, toil, cga, f, no drk wtr. ACTIVITIES: Picnicking; horseback riding/hiking (1 mi). MISC.: Elev 3600 ft; 1 acre; stream. Nature trails (1 mi). Pets.

Fir Tree (Mt. Hood NF). 1 mi E of Gov't. Camp on US 26; 5-1/10 mi SW on FS S32 (long rough road). SEASON: 6/15-9/30; 14-day lmt. FACILITIES: 5 tent sites; tbls, toil, cga, f, piped drk wtr. ACTIVITIES: Picnickinng; hunting; berry-picking. Swimming/fishing (1 mi). MISC.: Elev 4500 ft; 5 acres. Excellent huckleberry area. Pets. Trailhead to Veda Lake.

Frog Lake (Mt. Hood NF). 7½ mi SE of Gov't. Camp on US 26; 1 mi SE on FS S458. SEASON: 5/15-10/1; 14-day lmt. FACILITIES: 18 sites (tr -16); tbls, toil, cga, f, well drk wtr. Store/gas (4 mi). ACTIVITIES: Picnicking; swimming; fishing; boating (l, 1 mi) (no motors). Horseback riding/hiking (1 mi). MISC.: Elev 3800 ft; 9 acres. Pets permitted.

Gone Creek (Mt. Hood NF). 15 mi SE of Gov't. Camp on US 26; 8 mi S on FS S42; 3½ mi W on FS S57. SEASON: 5/1-10/1; 14-day lmt. FACILITIES: 76 tent sites; tbls, toil, cga, f, piped drk wtr. ACTIVITIES: Hiking; boating,d. Swimming/fishing (1 mi). MISC.: Elev 3200 ft; 14 acres. Pets permitted if kept on a leash.

Grindstone (Mt. Hood NF). 2 mi E of Gov't. Camp on US 26; 4½ mi N on St Hwy 35; 3 mi SE on FS S30 (dirt road). SEASON: 5/1-10/1; 14-day lmt. FACILITIES: 3 sites (tr -16); tbls, toil, cga, f, no drk wtr. ACTIVITIES: Picnicking; fishing; hunting. Hiking (3 mi). MISC.: Elev 3400 ft; 1 acre. Pets.

Hood View (Mt. Hood NF). 15 mi SE of Gov't. Camp on US 26; 8 mi S on FS S42; 4 mi W on FS S57. SEASON: 6/1-10/1; 14-day lmt. FACILITIES: 46 sites (tr -16); tbls, toil, cga, f, piped drk wtr. ACTIVITIES: Picnicking; hiking; swimming; fishing. Horseback riding (1 mi). MISC.: Elev 3200 ft; 11 acres. Pets permitted.

Hood View Forest Camp. 26 mi SE of Gov't. Camp on US 26 & Skyline Rd, on Timothy Lake. SEASON: 6/1-9/1; 7-day lmt. FACILITIES: 46 sites (tr -20); tbls, toil, cga. ACTIVITIES: Fishing; swimming; boating,ld. MISC.: 12 acres. Pets.

Kinzel Lake (Mt. Hood NF). 1 mi E of Gov't. Camp on US 26; 10-3/5 mi SW on FS S32. SEASON: 6/15-9/30; 14-day lmt. FAC: 5 sites (no tr); tbls, toil, cga, f, no drk wtr. ACTIVITIES: Swimming; picnicking; berry-picking. MISC.: Elev 4400 ft; 5 acres. In excellent huckleberry area. Pets.

Linney Creek (Mt. Hood NF). 15 mi SE of Gov't. Camp on US 26; 4 mi S on FS S42; 11-7/10 mi SW on FS S457; 4-3/10 mi N on FS S457U. SEASON: 5/1-10/1; 14-day lmt. FACILITIES: 4 tent sites (no trailers); tbls, toil, cga, f, no drk wtr. ACTIVITIES: Picnicking; fishing. Horseback riding/hiking (1 mi). MISC.: Elev 2800 ft; 2 acres; stream. Pets permitted if kept on a leash.

Meditation Point (Mt. Hood NF). 15 mi SE on US 26; 8 mi S on FS S42; 6 mi W on S57. SEASON: 6/1-10/1; 14-day lmt. FACILITIES: 3 sites (no tr); tbls, toil, cga, f, no drk wtr. ACTIVITIES: Picnicking; fishing; swimming; boating; hiking. Horseback riding (1 mi). MISC.: Elev 3200 ft; 1 acre; pets. Site privately operated.

Nanitch (Mt. Hood NF). 4/5 mi E on US 26; 1 mi NE on FS S31. SEASON: 6/1-9/30; 14-day lmt. FACILITIES: 5 sites (tr -16); tbls, toil, cga, f. ACTIVITIES: Picnicking. MISC.: Elev 4400 ft; Along old rd to Timberline Lodge. Pets.

Oak Grove Camp (Mt. Hood NF). 15 mi SE of Gov't. Camp on US 26; 7 mi S on FS S42. SEASON: 5/1-10/1; 14-day lmt. FACILITIES: 9 sites (tr -16); tbls, toil, cga, f, no drk wtr. Visitor ctr. (1 mi). ACTIVITIES: Picnicking; fishing. Boating,l/swimming (2 mi). MISC.: Elev 3400 ft; 3 acres. Pets.

Phlox Point (Mt. Hood NF). 4/5 mi E of Gov't. Camp on US 26; 5 mi NE on St Hwy 50; 3/5 mi W on FS S31. SEASON: 6/15-9/30; 14-day lmt. FACILITIES: 4 tent sites (no trailers); tbls, toil, cga, f. ACTIVITIES: Picnicking. MISC.: Elev 5600 ft. 1 mi below Timberline Lodge on old hwy. Pets permitted.

*Veda Lake (Mt. Hood NF). 2 mi S on FS S32; 3 mi W on FS12; 1 mi N on TRAIL 673. SEASON: 7/1-9/1. FACILITIES: 2 tent sites; tbls, f, food, ACTIVITIES: Picnicking; swimming; fishing. MISC.: Elev 4200 ft; 1 acre; pets.

See page 7 for KEY TO ABBREVIATIONS.

White River Station (Mt. Hood NF). 2 mi E of Gov't. Camp on US 26; 4½ mi N on St Hwy 35; 7 mi NE on FS S30. SEASON: 5/1-10/1; 14-day lmt. FACILITIES: 5 sites (tr -16); tbls, toil, cga, no drk wtr. ACT: Picnicking; fishing. Horseback riding (1 mi). Hiking (3 mi). MISC.: Elev 2800 ft; 1 acre; river; pets.

GRANTS PASS

Big Pine (Siskiyou NF). 3-2/5 mi N of Grants Pass on US 5; 12-2/5 mi NW on Co 2-6; 12-4/5 mi SW on FS 355. SEASON: 5/31-9/15; 14-day lmt. FACILITIES: 14 sites (tr -22); tbls, toil, cga, f. ACTIVITIES: Picnicking; fishing. MISC.: Elev 2400 ft; 15 acres. 12½ mi SW of Rogue River. Outstanding Ponderosa Pine stand adjacent to site. Pets; botanical.

Cow Creek Rest Area. 24 mi N of Grants Pass on I-5. SEASON: All yr. FACILITIES: Drk wtr. MISC.: Pets permitted if kept on a leash.

Monzanita Rest Area. 4 mi N of Grants Pass on I-5. SEASON: All yr. FACILITIES: Drk wtr. MISC.: Pets permitted if kept on a leash.

HAINES

Anthony Lake (Wallowa Whitman NF). 17 mi NW of Haines on St Hwy SH 411; 1 mi W on FS S73. SEASON: 10/1-6/30, FREE; ($1.00 rest of yr). FACILITIES: 37 sites (tr -22); tbls, toil, cga, f, piped drk wtr. ACTIVITIES: Picnicking; fishing; swimming; hunting; boating,rld (no motors); mtn climbing; hiking. MISC.: Elev 7100 ft; 12 acres. 10-day lmt. Water shut off during FREE season. Pets permitted if kept on a leash.

Grande Ronde Lake (Wallowa Whitman NF). 17 mi NW of Haines on St Hwy SH 411; 8¼ mi W on FS S73; ½ mi NW on FS S438; 1/5 mi W on FS S438B. SEASON: 10/1-6/30, FREE; ($1.00 rest of yr); 10-day lmt. FACILITIES: 10 sites (tr -16); tbls, toil, cga, f, piped drk wtr. Store/ice (2 mi). ACTIVITIES: Picnicking; fishing; swimming; boating,rld (no motors); hiking. MISC.: Elev 7200 ft; 3 acres. Adjacent to small 10-acre lake, cool in summer. Water shut off during FREE season. Pets.

Mud Lake (Wallowa Whitman NF). 17 mi NW of Haines on St Hwy SH 411; 7-3/10 mi W on FS S73. SEASON: 10/1-6/30, FREE ($1.00 rest of yr); 10-day lmt. FACILITIES: 14 sites (tr -16); tbls, toil, cga, piped drk wtr. Store/ice (1 mi). ACT: Swimming; picnicking; fishing; boating,rld; hiking. MISC.: Elev 7100 ft; 4 acres; pets. Adjacent to small lake, cool in summer. Water shut off during FREE season.

HALFWAY

Fish Lake (Wallowa Whitman NF). 5 mi N on Co Rd 733; 18-3/5 mi N on FS 66. SEASON: 7/1-9/15; 10-day lmt. FACILITIES: 21 sites (tr -22); tbls, toil, cga, f, piped drk wtr. ACTIVITIES: Picnicking; swimming; fishing; boating,d. MISC.: Elev 6600 ft; 12 acres; stream; pets; scenic.

Lake Fork (Wallowa Whitman NF). 10 mi E of Halfway on Hwy 86; 8-3/10 mi N on FS 39; 2/5 mi W on FS 39. SEASON: 6/1-10/31; 10-day lmt. FACILITIES: 8 sites (tr -22); tbls, toil, cga, f. ACTIVITIES: Picnicking; fishing. MISC.: Elev 3200 ft; 3 acres. Pets.

McBride (Wallowa Whitman NF). 5 mi NW on St Hwy 442; 2¼ mi W on FS 7710; 2-1/10 mi W on FS 77. SEASON: 6/1-10/31; 10-day lmt. FACILITIES: 5 sites (tr -16); tbls, toil, cga, no drk wtr. ACTIVITIES: Picnicking. MISC.: Elev 4800 ft; 2 acres; pets; scenic.

Twin Lakes (Wallowa Whitman NF). 10 mi E on US 86; 13 mi N on FS 39; 20 mi W on FS 66. SEASON: 7/1-9/15. FACILITIES: 7 sites (tr -22); tbls, toil, cga, f, no drk wtr. ACTIVITIES: Swimming; picnicking; fishing; rockhounding; horseback riding. MISC.: Elev 6500 ft; 6 acres; lake; scenic; nature trails (hiking). Pets.

HEBO

Castle Rock (Siuslaw NF). 4-7/10 mi SE of Hebo on St Hwy 22. SEASON: All year; 10-day lmt. FACILITIES: 4 sites (tr -16); tbls, toil, cga, f, well drk wtr. ACTIVITIES: Picnicking; fishing. MISC.: Elev 200 ft; 1 acre; river; pets.

Hebo Lake (Siuslaw NF). 1/10 mi NE of Hebo on US 101; 3/10 mi SE on Hwy 22; 4½ mi E on FS 430. SEASON: 4/15-10/15; 10-day lmt. FACILITIES: 10 sites (tr -16); tbls, toil, cga, f. Store/ice/food/gas/snack bar (5 mi). ACTIVITIES: Swimming; picnicking; fishing; boating,d. MISC.: Elev 1600 ft; 10 acres. Pets. Hebo Lake.

Mount Hebo (Siuslaw NF). 1/10 mi N of Hebo on US 101; 3/10 mi SE on St Hwy 22; 9-3/5 mi E on FS 430; 1/10 mi E on FS 430C. SEASON: 5/15-11/15; 10-day lmt. FACILITIES: 4 tent sites (no trailers); tbls, toil, cga, no drk wtr. ACTIVITIES: Picnicking; berry-picking. Fishing/boating (2 mi). MISC.: Elev 3000 ft; 1 acre; historic; pets.

South Lake (Siuslaw NF). 1/10 mi N of Hebo onn US 101; 3/10 mi SE on St Hwy 22; 11-4/5 mi E on FS 430; 2/5 mi S on FS 434. SEASON: 5/15-10/15; 10-day lmt. FACILITIES: 3 tent sites (no trailers); tbls, toil, cga, no drk wtr. ACTIVITIES: Picnicking; boating (no motors). MISC.: Elev 2200 ft; 1 acre; lake; pets.

HINES

Buck Springs (Ochoco NF). 24½ mi W of Hines on US 20; 12-3/5 mi N on Co Ru 1938; 7 mi N on FS 1938; 9/10 mi NW on FS 2034. SEASON: 6/15-10/31. FACILITIES: 8 sites (tr -22); tbls, toil, cga, f, piped drk wtr. ACTIVITIES: Picnicking. MISC.: Elev 5600 ft; 4 acres; pets.

Delintment Lake (Ochoco NF); 1 mi S of Hines on US 20; 25 mi NW on FS 19; 17 mi NW on FS 1834; 6 mi W on FS 1972. SEASON: 4/20-10/31. FACILITIES: 16 sites (tr -32); tbls, toil, cga, f, well drk wtr. ACTIVITIES: Swimming; boating,ld; picnicking; fishing. MISC.: 11 acres; lake; scenic; pets; elev 5600 ft.

Emigrant Creek (Ochoco NF). 1 mi S of Hines on US 20; 25 mi NW on FS 19; 10 mi W on FS 1843; 2/5 mi W on FS 2087. SEASON: 5/15-10/31. FACILITIES: 5 sites (tr -32); tbls, toil, cga, f, piped drk wtr. ACTIVITIES: Picnicking; fishing. MISC.: Elev 5100 ft; 3 acres. Pets permitted if kept on a leash.

Falls (Ochoco NF). 1 mi S of Hines on US 20; 25 mi NW on FS 19; 8½ mi W on FS 1843; 2/5 mi NW on FS 1843C. SEASON: 5/15-10/31. FACILITIES: 4 sites (tr -32); tbls, toil, cga, f, no drk wtr. ACTIVITIES: Picnicking; fishing. MISC.: Stream. Pets permitted. Scenic.

Howard Camp (Ochoco NF). 1 mi S of Hines on US 20; 25 mi NW on FS 19; 17 mi NW on FS 1843; 5 mi N on FS 1972. SEASON: 6/15-10/31. FACILITIES: 4 sites (tr -32); tbls, toil, cga, f. ACTIVITIES: Picnicking. MISC.: Elev 5200 ft. Pets.

HOOD RIVER

Kingsley (Mt. Hood NF). 4 mi N of Hood River on Hwy 281; 3½ mi W on Co; 6 mi W on FS N20. SEASON: 6/1-9/15. FACILITIES: 8 sites (no trailers); tbls, toil, cga, no drk wtr. ACTIVITIES: Swimming; picnicking; fishing; boating,d. MISC.: Elev 2800 ft; 5 acres; river. Adjacent to county irrigation reservoir. Pets permitted if on leash.

Routson Park (Municipal Park). 23 mi S of Hood River on St Hwy 35. SEASON: 6/1-11/1. FACILITIES: 25 sites (tr -30); tbls, flush toil, cga, f, drk wtr. ACTIVITIES: Picnicking; fishing. MISC.: Mailing address: 918 18th St, Hood River 97031. Pets permitted if on leash.

HUNTINGTON

Spring Rec. Site (BLM;Baker Dist). 3½ mi NE of Huntington on Snake River Rd (gravel). SEASON: 5/1-10/1 (limited during winter). FACILITIES: 14 sites (tr -30); tbls, toil, cga. ACTIVITIES: Picnicking; swimming; fishing; boating,l. MISC.: Pets permitted if kept on leash.

IDANHA

Lost Lake (Willamette NF). 26-9/10 mi SE of Idanha on Hwy 22; 1-3/5 mi E on US 20. SEASON: 4/1-10/31; 10-day lmt. FACILITIES: 20 sites (tr -22); tbls, toil, cga, f, no drk wtr. Store/gas/visitor center (2 mi). ACTIVITIES: Swimming; picnicking; fishing; boating,rl. MISC.: Elev 4000 ft; 6 acres; lake; scenic. No trolling with motor boats; no fishing after July 31; speed limits for boats; special fishing season (see State Regulations). Pets permitted.

White Water (Willamette NF). 7 mi E of Idanha on Hwy 22; ½ mi N on FR 102b. SEASON: 5/1-10/15; 10-day lmt. FACILITIES: 5 tent sites (no trailers); tbls, toil, cga, no drk wtr. Store (5 mi). ACTIVITIES: Picnicking; fishing (1 mi). MISC.: Elev 2400 ft; 7 acres. Pets.

IDLEYLD PARK

Apple Creek (Umpqua NF). 22½ mi E of Idleyld on Hwy 138. SEASON: 1/1-12/31; 14-day lmt. FACILITIES: 8 sites (tr -22); tbls, toil, cga, no drk wtr. Store/ice/showers/laundry/gas (3 mi). Snack bar (5 mi). ACTIVITIES: Picnicking; fishing. Swimming (5 mi). MISC.: Elev 1200 ft; 6 acres; pets. On the North Umpqua River.

Boulder Flat (Umpqua NF). 31-4/5 mi E of Idleyld Park on Hwy 138. SEASON: 5/15-12/1; 14-day lmt. FACILITIES: 11 sites (tr -22); tbls, toil, cga, no drk wtr. Store/gas/ice (5 mi). ACTIVITIES: Picnicking; fishing. MISC.: Elev 1600 ft; 4 acres; pets. On North Umpqua River.

Bunker Hill (Umpqua NF). 42-2/5 mi E of Idleyld Park on St Hwy 138; 5-2/5 mi N on FS 2610; ½ mi SE on FS 268. SEASON: 4/15-10/31. FACILITIES: 4 tent sites (tr -16); tbls, toil, cga, no drk wtr. Store/gas/ice/showers/laundry/ food (1 mi). ACTIVITIES: Picnicking; fishing; swimming; waterskiing; boating (1,2mi; r,1mi). MISC.: Elev 4200 ft; 1 acre; pets. Located on Lemolo Lake.

Canton Creek (Umpqua NF). 18 mi E of Idleyld Park on St Hwy 138; 2/5 mi NE on FS 232. SEASON: 5/15-10/31; 10-day lmt. FACILITIES: 8 sites (no tr); tbls, toil, cga, piped drk

wtr. Store/gas/ice/food (1 mi).
ACTIVITIES: Picnicking. Fishing
(1 mi). **MISC.:** Elev 1200 ft; 3
acres; pets. On Steamboat Creek;
stream closed to all fishing. Shelter
with 3 tables on site.

Clearwater Falls (Umpqua NF). 46-1/5
mi E of Idleyld on Hwy 138; 3/10 mi E
on FS 2735A. **SEASON:** 6/1-10/31;
14-day lmt. **FACILITIES:** 8 sites (tr
-16); tbls, toil, cga, no drk wtr. **AC-
TIVITIES:** Picnicking; fishing. **MISC.:**
Elev 4200 ft; 1 acre. Pets permitted.

East Lemolo (Umpqua NF). 49-2/5 mi
E of Idleyld on Hwy 138; 3-1/5 mi N
on FS 2610; 2-3/10 mi NE on FS 2666.
SEASON: 4/15-9/30. **FACILITIES:**
6 sites (tr -22); tbls, toil, cga,
no drk wtr. Store/showers/ice/gas/
laundry/food (4 mi). **ACTIVITIES:**
Picnicking; swimming; fishing; waterskiing. Boating,rl (4 mi). **MISC.:**
Elev 4200 ft; 3 acres; pets. Minimum
development fishing camp.

Inlet (Umpqua NF). 49-2/5 mi E of
Idleyld Park on Hwy 138; 3-1/5 mi N
on FS 2610; 2-7/10 mi NE on FS 2666.
SEASON: 4/15-9/30; 14-day lmt. **FACILI-
TIES:** 13 sites (tr -22); tbls, toil, cga,
no drk wtr. Store/gas/showers/ice/snack
bar/laundry/dump (4 mi). **ACTIVITIES:**
Picnicking. Swimming/fishing/boating,rl/
waterskiing. (2 mi). **MISC.:** Elev 4200
ft; 5 acres; river. Located at Lemolo
Lake. Pets permitted if kept on a leash.

Island (Umpqua NF). 19 mi E of Idleyld
on Hwy 138. **SEASON:** 1/1-12/31; 14-day
lmt. **FACILITIES:** 7 sites (tr -22); tbls,
toil, cga, no drk wtr. Store/gas/ice/
snacks/showers (1 mi). **ACTIVITIES:** Picnicking; fishing. Swimming (1 mi).
MISC.: Elev 1200 ft; 2 acres; river. On
the N. Umpqua River. Pets permitted.

N. Crater Trailhead (Umpqua NF). 58-1/10
mi E of Idleyld Park on st Hwy 138; ½
mi N on FS 2900. **SEASON:** 6/1-10/31; 14-
day lmt. **FACILITIES:** 5 tent sites (no
trailers); tbls, toil, cga. **ACTIVITIES:**
Picnicking; horseback riding; mtn climbing. **MISC.:** Elev 5800 ft; 5 acres. Geological interest. Loading ramp & horse
tr parking. Pets. No drk wtr.

Scaredman Creek (BLM; Roseburg Dist.).
39½ mi NE of Idelyld Park on Hwy 138
to Steamboat; 3 mi N on Canton Cr. Rd.
SEASON: 5/1-10/31; 14-day lmt. **FACILI-
TIES:** 10 sites (tr -18); tbls, toil, cga.
ACTIVITIES: Swimming; picnicking.
MISC.: 10 acres. Motor bikes prohibit-
ed. Pets permitted if kept on a leash.

Steamboat Falls (Umpqua NF). 18 mi
NE of Idleyld Park on Hwy 138; 5½ mi
NE on FS 232; 3/5 mi SE on FS 2432.

SEASON: 6/1-12/1; 14-day lmt. **FACILI-
TIES:** 13 sites (tr -22); tbls, toil, cga,
no drk wtr. **ACTIVITIES:** Picnicking;
swimming. **MISC.:** Elev 1400 ft; 4 acres.
On Steamboat Creek, stream closed to
all fishing. Pets.

Thielsen (Umpqua NF). 50-1/10 mi E
of Idleyld Park on St Hwy 138. **SEASON:**
6/1-10/31. **FACILITIES:** 3 sites (no
tr); tbls, toil, cga, no drk wtr.
ACTIVITIES: Picnicking. Fishing
(1 mi). **MISC.:** Elev 4400 ft; 1 acre;
pets; stream.

Thielson View (Umpqua NF). 54-3/10
mi E of Idleyld Park on Hwy 138; 3-
1/10 mi W on FS 271. **SEASON:** 5/25-
9/30; 14-day lmt. **FACILITIES:** 63 sites
(tr -32); tbls, toil, cga, piped drk
wtr. Store/gas/snacks/ice/showers/dump
laundry/visitor center (3 mi). **ACTIVI-
TIES:** Picnicking; fishing; swimming;
sailing; boating,l (rental, 3 mi).
Horseback riding/rental; hiking (3 mi).
MISC.: Elev 5200 ft; 23 acres. On Diamond Lake, 15 mi N of Crater Lake.
Pets permitted if kept on a leash.

Toketee Lake (Umpqua NF). 35-1/5 mi
E of Idleyld Park on Hwy 138; 1-2/5
mi NE on FS 268. **SEASON:** 4/15-10/31;
14-day lmt. **FACILITIES:** 33 sites (tr
-22); tbls, toil, cga, no drk wtr. **AC-
TIVITIES:** Boating,ld; waterskiing; picnicking; fisning. Swimming (1 mi).
MISC.: Elev 2400 ft; 6 acres. Pets. River.

Umpqua Hot Spring (Umpqua NF). 35-
1/5 mi E of Idleyld Park on St Hwy
138; 6-7/10 mi NE on FS 268; 2 mi S
on FS 2687. **SEAS:** 5/1-9/30; 14-day
lmt. **FAC:** 2 sites (no tr); toil.
ACTIVITIES: Picnicking. Fishing (1 mi).
MISC.: Elev 3000 ft; 1 acre. Trailhead
for hot mineral spring bathing. Pets.

Whitehorse Falls (Umpqua NF). 42-2/5
mi E of Idleyld on Hwy 138. **SEASON:**
6/1-10/31; 14-day lmt. **FACILITIES:** 9
sites (tr -16); tbls, toil, cga, no drk
wtr. **ACTIVITIES:** Picnicking; fishing.
MISC.: Elev 3800 ft; 4 acres. Pets.

IMNAHA

Sacajaewa (Wallowa Whitman NF). 17-1/5
mi SE of Imnaha on FS N163; 5-3/10 mi
E on FS N38; 1-3/5 mi E on FS S114.
SEASON: 7/1-11/30; 10-day lmt. **FACILI-
TIES:** 8 sites (tr -22); tbls, toil, cga,
f, piped drk wtr. **ACTIVITIES:** Picnicking; fishing. **MISC.:** Elev 6800
ft; 3 acres; scenic; pets.

JOHN DAY
Canyon Meadows (Malheur NF). 10 mi
S of John Day on US 395; 9 mi SE on
FS 1541; 5 mi NE on FS 1520. **SEASON:**
5/15-10/30; 14-day lmt. **FACILITIES:** 19
sites (tr -16); tbls, toil, cga, f, piped

drk wtr. **ACTIVITIES:** Picnicking; boating,ld (no motors); fishing. **MISC.:** Elev 5100 ft; 19 acres; lake; pets. Reservoir water level very low after August.

Ray Cole (Malheur NF). 10 mi **S** of John Day on US 395; 3 mi SE on FS 1541; 1 mi N on FS 1519. **SEASON:** 5/1-11/20; 14-day lmt. **FACILITIES:** 4 sites (tr -22); tbls, toil, cga, no drk wtr. **ACTIVITIES:** Picnicking. **MISC.:** Elev 4300 ft; 1 acre; pets.

Vance Creek Rest Area. 11 mi S of John Day on US 395. **SEASON:** All yr. **FACILITIES:** Drk wtr. **MISC.:** Pets.

Wickiup (Malheur NF). 10 mi S of John Day on US 395; 8 mi SE on FS 1541. **SEASON:** 5/20-11/1; 14-day lmt. **FACILITIES:** 9 sites (tr -16); tbls, toil, cga, f, piped drk wtr. **ACTIVITIES:** Picnicking; fishing. **MISC.:** Elev 4300 ft; 4 acres; stream. Pets. 9 acres.

JORDAN VALLEY

Antelope Reservoir (BLM-Salem Dist). From US 95 W of Jordan Valley, 1-1/4 mi S on dirt rd; follow signs. **SEASON:** 4/15-11/15; 14-day lmt. **FACILITIES:** Sites (tr -30); tbls, toil, cga, drk wtr (must be boiled). **ACTIVITIES:** Picnicking; swimming; fishing; boating,l. **MISC.:** 80 acres; pets permitted.

Community Park. US 95, N side of town. **SEASON:** All yr. **MISC.:** Pets permitted.

Cow Lakes (BLM;Vale Dist). 7-4/5 mi W of Jordan Valley on US 95; 12 mi NW on Cow Lakes Rd (gravel). **SEASON:** 4/1-12/1; 14-day lmt. **FACILITIES:** 10 sites (tr -30); tbls, toil, cga, drk wtr. **ACTIVITIES:** Hiking; picnicking; fishing; swimming; hunting; boating,l. **MISC.:** Elev 4340 ft; 10 acres; geological interest. Pets.

JOSEPH

Falls Creek (Wallowa Whitman NF). 1/10 mi N of Joseph on St Hwy 82; 1-9/10 mi W on Co Hwy 774; 4 mi SW on FS S218; ½ mi SW on FS S218B. **SEASON:** 6/1-10/15; 10-day lmt. **FACILITIES:** 17 sites (tr -32); tbls, toil, cga, no drk wtr. **ACTIVITIES:** Horseback riding; picnicking; fishing. **MISC.:** Elev 5000 ft; 7 acres. Trailhead into Eagle Cap Wilderness. Pets permitted if on leash.

Hurricane Creek (Wallowa Whitman NF). 1/10 mi N of Joseph on St Hwy 82; 1-9/10 mi W on Co Hwy 774; 3/10 mi SW on FS S218A. **SEASON:** 6/1-10/15; 10-day lmt. **FACILITIES:** 4 sites (tr -16); tbls, toil, cga. **ACTIVITIES:** Picnicking; fishing. **MISC.:** Elev 4800 ft. Pets.

Lick Creek (Wallowa Whitman NF). 1/10 mi N of Joseph on Hwy 82; 9 mi E on Hwy 350; 15-4/5 mi S on FS S393. **SEASON:** 7/1-11/15; 10-day lmt. **FACILITIES:** 12 sites (tr -32); tbls, toil, cga, f. Piped drk wtr. **ACTIVITIES:** Picnicking; fishing; berry-picking. **MISC.:** Elev 5400 ft; 4 acres; pets.

JUNTURA

Chuckar Park (BLM,Vale Dist). From Juntura on US 20, 6 mi NW on Co Rd. **SEASON:** 4/1-12/1; 14-day lmt. **FACILITIES:** 19 sites (tr -30); tbls, toil, cga, drk wtr. **ACTIVITIES:** Picnicking; fishing; hunting; rockhounding. **MISC.:** Elev 3100 ft; 10 acres. Pets. Geological interest.

KENO

Keno Res/Rec. Area. ½ mi W of Keno on St Hwy 66 to sign, 1 mi N. **SEASON:** 4/1-11/30; 14-day lmt. **FACILITIES:** 20 sites; tbls, flush toil, showers. Store (1 mi). **ACTIVITIES:** Swimming; picnicking; fishing; boating,ld. **MISC.:** 17 acres.

Surveyor (BLM, Medford Dist). 20 mi E of Keno on Dead Indian Rd; 10 mi E on Keno Rd. **SEASON:** 6/1-11/1; 14-day lmt. **FACILITIES:** 8 sites (tr -20); tbls, toil, cga, f, no drk wtr. **ACTIVITIES:** Picnicking; fishing. **MISC.:** 5 acres. Pets.

Topsy (BLM, Medford Dist). 6 mi W of Keno on Hwy 66; 1 mi S on Topsy Co. **SEASON:** 4/1-10/31; 14-day lmt. **FACILITIES:** 12 tent sites (no trailers); tbls, toil, cga, f, no drk wtr. **ACTIVITIES:** Swimming; picnicking; fishing; boating,l. **MISC.:** 4 acres; pets.

KIMBERLY

Lone Pine (BLM;Burns Dist). From Kimberly off Hwy 19; 1-3/4 mi NE on paved Co Rd. **SEASON:** All yr. **FACILITIES:** 4 sites (tr -24); tbls. **ACTIVITIES:** Picnicking; fishing. **MISC.:** 4 acres. Pets.

KLAMATH FALLS

Cold Springs (Winema NF). 27½ mi NW of Klamath Falls on St Hwy 140; 8½ mi N of FS 3561. **SEASON:** 6/1-10/1. **FACILITIES:** 2 tent sites (no trailers); tbls, toil, cga, f, no drk wtr. **ACTIVITIES:** Picnicking. Horseback riding (1 mi); Fishing (5 mi). **MISC.:** Elev 5800 ft; 1 acre. Trailhead for Oregon Skyline Trail & access to Skylakes Limited Area. Pets; scenic.

Fourmile Lake (Winema NF). 33-1/10 mi NW of Klamath Falls on Hwy 140; 5½ mi N on FS 3661. **SEASON:** 6/1-10/1; 14-day lmt. **FACILITIES:** 21 sites (tr -22); tbls, toil, cga, f, well drk **wtr.** ACTIVITIES: Picnicking; fisning; **swimming**; horseback riding; boating,rld; hiking. MISC.: Elev 5800 ft; 14 acres; lake. Trailhead for Oregon Skyline. Trail & access to Sky-lakes Limited Area. Pets.

Hagelstein Park (County Park). 9 mi N of Klamath Falls on Hwy 97. SEASON: 4/1-11/30; 14-day lmt. FACILITIES: 20 sites; tbls, flush toil, cga. ACTIVI-TIES: Swimming; picnicking; fishing; boating,l; waterskiing; hiking. MISC.: 3 acres. Pets permitted.

Odessa (Winema NF). 21½ mi NW of Klamath Falls on St Hwy 140; 9/10 mi NE on FS 3639. SEASON: 5/15-10/31. FA-CILITIES: 5 sites (tr -22); tbls, toil, cga, f, no drk wtr. Store/gas/dump/ice (4 mi). ACTIVITIES: Picnicking; fish-ing; boating,l (r, 2 mi). Waterski-ing (3 mi). MISC.: Elev 4100 ft; 1 acre; stream; pets. Mosquitos; access to upper Klamath Lake.

Spruce (Winema NF). 33 mi NW of Kla-math Falls on St Hwy 140; 3/10 mi S on FS 3658. SEASON: 6/1-10/31; 14-day lmt. FACILITIES: 8 sites; toil, cga, f. MISC.: Elev 5000 ft. Pets permitted.

Stevenson Park 11 mi E of Klamath Falls on Rte 140. SEASON: All yr. MISC.: Pets permitted if kept on a leash.

Topsy (BLM). 20 mi SW of Klamath Falls, off St Hwy 66. SEASON: 4/15-10/1; 14-day lmt. FACILITIES: 12 sites, toil, cga. ACTIVITIES: Hiking; fishing; swim..ing; hunting; boating. MISC.: Elev 3800 ft; pets permitted if kept on a leash.

LA GRANDE

Bikini Beach (Wallowa Whitman NF). 9-1/10 mi NW of La Grande on US 180N; 12-9/10 mi SW on St Hwy 244; 4½ mi S on FS 51. SEASON: 5/20-11/20; 14-day lmt. FACILITIES: 5 sites (tr -22); tbls, toil, cga, f, no drk wtr. Store/ice/gas/dump (1 mi). ACTIVITIES: Pic-nicking; fishing. Horseback riding (1 mi). MISC.: Elev 3700 ft; 1 acre; scenic; pets.

Daniel Spring (Wallowa Whitman NF). 17 mi NW of La Grande on I-80; 11 mi E on FS N31. SEASON: 6/1-11/30; 10-day lmt. FACILITIES: 3 tent sites (no trail-ers); toil, f. MISC.: Elev 4200 ft. Pets.

Grandview (Wallowa Whitman NF). 20 mi W on US 180N; 20 mi N on Co Hwy 31; 3-1/5 mi S on FS 3120. SEASON: 7/10-11/10; 10-day lmt. FACILITIES: 4 sites (tr -22); tbls, toil, cga, f, piped drk wtr. ACTI-VITIES: Picnicking; berry-picking; horseback riding. MISC.: Elev 6000 ft; 1 acre; scenic; pets.

River (Wallowa Whitman NF). 8-1/10 mi NW of La Grande on US 80; 12-3/5 mi SW on Hwy 244; 10-9/10 mi S on FS 5125. FACILITIES: 6 sites (tr -22); tbls. toil, cga, f, well drk wtr. ACTIVITIES: Picnicking; berry-picking; fishing; horseback riding. MISC.: Elev 3800 ft; 6 acres; pets; scenic.

Sherwood Forest (Wallowa Whitman NF). 9-1/10 mi NW of La Grande on US 180N; 12-9/10 mi SW on St Hwy 244; 6½ mi S on FS 51. SEASON: 5/20-11/20; 14-day lmt. FACILITIES: 5 sites (tr -22); tbls, toil, cga, f, no drk wtr. ACTIVITIES: Picnicking; fishing. Horseback riding (1 mi). MISC.: Elev 3800 ft; 1 acre; scenic. Pets permitted if kept on leash.

Woodly (Wallowa Whitman NF). 9-1/10 mi NW of La Grande on US 180N; 12-9/10 mi SW on St Hwy 244; 16 mi S on FS 51. SEASON: 5/20-11/20; 14-day lmt. FACILITIES: 7 sites (tr -22); tbls, toil, cga, piped drk wtr. ACTIVITIES: Pic-nicking; fishing; rockhounding. Hiking. Horseback riding (1 mi). MISC.: Elev 4500 ft; 2 acres; pets.

LAKE CREEK

Willow Prairie (Rogue River NF). 16-1/5 mi E of Lake Creek on Hwy 140; 1-3/10 mi N on FS 356. SEASON: 5/15-10/15. FACILITIES: 9 sites (tr -16); tbls, toil, cga, f, piped drk wtr. Store/ice/food (5 mi). ACTIVITIES: Picnicking. Boating,rl/fishing (5 mi). MISC.: Elev 4400 ft; 6 acres; pets.

LAKEVIEW

Alkali Lake Rest Area. 61 mi N of Lakeview on US 395. SEASON: All yr. FACILITIES: Drk wtr. MISC.: Pets per-mitted if kept on a leash.

Can Spring (Fremont NF). 5-2/5 mi N of Lakeview on US 395; 6½ mi E on St Hwy 140; 12-3/5 mi N on Fs 3615; 9 mi NE on FS 3720. SEASON: 7/1-10/30. FACILITIES: 8 sites (tr -22); tbls, toil, cga. ACTIVITIES: Picnicking; fishing; hunting. MISC.: Elev 5500 ft; 5 acres. Good gravel roads to site. Pets.

Cinder Hill (Fremont NF). 5 mi W of Lakeview on Hwy 140; 7 mi S on Co W60; 13 mi W on FS 4017. SEASON: 5/15-10/30; 14-day lmt. FACILITIES: 5 sites (tr -16); tbls, toil, cga, piped drk wtr. ACTIVITIES: Picnicking; swim-ming; fishing. Boating l (1 mi), r (2 mi). MISC.: Elev 5100 ft; 2 acres. At Dog Lake. Pets.

Cottonwood Meadows (Fremont NF). 20 mi W on St Hwy 140; 5 mi NE on FS 387. SEASON: 6/15-10/30; 14-day lmt.

FACILITIES: 26 sites (tr -32); tbls, toil, cga, piped drk wtr. **ACTIVITIES:** Swimming; picnicking; fishing; boating (no motors). **MISC.:** Elev 6200 ft; 7 acres. Popular site on reservoir. 5 mi forest rd surfaced, 2 lane. lake. Pets.

Cox Fork (Fremont NF). 8½ mi N of Lakeview on US 395; 9 mi NW on FS 3628. **SEASON:** 5/15-10/30. **FACILITIES:** 6 sites (tr -22); tbls, toil, cga, no drk wtr. **ACTIVITIES:** Picnicking; fishing. **MISC.:** 5 acres. Pets permitted if kept on leash.

Deep Creek (Fremont NF). 5-2/5 mi N of Lakeview on US 395; 6½ mi E on Hwy 140; 16-1/10 mi S on FS 391. **SEASON:** 6/15-10/30; 14-day lmt. **FACILITIES:** 9 tent sites (no trailers); tbls, toil, cga, no drk wtr. **ACTIVITIES:** Hunting; picnicking; fishing. A remote site along a good fishing stream. Good gravel roads to area. Elev 5600 ft; 3 acre;pets.

Dicks Creek No 1 (Fremont NF). 16½ mi N of Lakeview on US 395; 3 mi NW on FS 3627. **SEASON:** 7/1-10/30. **FACILITIES:** 1 sites (tr -16); f. **ACTIVITIES:** Fishing. **MISC.:** Elev 5300 ft; pets.

Dismal Creek (Fremont NF). 5 mi N of Lakeview on US 395; 6½ mi E on St Hwy 140; 21 mi SE on FS 391. **SEASON:** 5/15-10/30. **FACILITIES:** 6 sites (tr -16); tbls, toil, cga, f, no drk wtr. **ACTIVITIES:** Picnicking; fishing. **MISC.:** Elev 5700 ft; 5 acres. Pets.

Dog Lake (Fremont NF). 5 mi W of Lakeview on Hwy 140; 7 mi S on Co W60; 13 mi W on FS 4017. **SEASON:** 5/15-10/30; 14-day lmt. **FACILITIES:** 13 sites (tr -16); tbls, toil, cga, piped drk wtr. **ACTIVITIES:** Hunting; picnicking; fishing. **MISC.:** Elev 5100 ft; 4 acres. Popular as an all-yr fishing spot, good gravel rds within forest. Lake. Pets.

Fawn Creek (Fremont NF). 8 mi N of Lakeview on US 395; 5 mi NW on FS 3628. **SEASON:** 6/1-10/31. **FACILITIES:** 6 sites (tr -16); toil, f. **ACTIVITIES:** Hunting; fishing. **MISC.:** Elev 5100 ft; A hunting & fishing camp, good blacktop & gravel rds to site. Pets permitted.

First Swale (Fremont NF). 5 mi N of Lakeview on US 395; 8½ mi E on US 140; 20 mi N on FS 3615; 5½ mi NE on FS 3720. **SEASON:** 6/1-10/30. **FACILITIES:** 6 sites (tr -16); f. **ACTIVITIES:** Fishing. **MISC.:** Elev 6300 ft. Pets.

Horseshoe Meadow (Fremont NF). 7 mi W of Lakeview on US 140; 8½ mi SW on Co Hwy 1-11; 2 mi W on FS 120; 3-4/5 mi W on FS 401. **SEASON:** 5/15-10/30. **FACILITIES:** 6 sites (tr -32); toil, f. **MISC.:** Elev 5800 ft. Primitive dirt road to site. Pets.

Loveless Creek Camp (Fremont NF). 11½ mi N of Lakeview on US 395; 5½ mi NE on FS 3744; 1-1/5 mi N on FS 3624; 1/10 mi NE on FS. **SEASON:** 6/15-10/30. **FACILITIES:** 1 tent site (no trailers), toil, f. **ACTIVITIES:** Swimming; fishing. **MISC.:** Elev 6700 ft. Pets permitted.

Middle Fork Crooked Creek. (4-4/5 mi N of Lakeview on US 395; 7-4/5 mi SE on St Hwy 140; 10 mi NE on FS 3615. **SEASON:** 6/1-10/30. **FACILITIES:** 5 sites (tr -16); toil, f. **ACTIVITIES:** Fishing. **MISC.:** Elev 7300 ft. Good gravel surface rds to site; located along N. Warner Auto Tour. Pets.

Mud Creek (Fremont NF). 5-2/5 mi N of Lakeview on US 395; 6½ mi E on Hwy 140; 6-1/10 mi N on FS 3615. **SEASON:** 6/15-10/30; 14-day lmt. **FACILITIES:** 6 sites (tr -16); tbls, toil, cga, piped drk wtr. **ACTIVITIES:** Hunting; picnicking; fishing. **MISC.:** Elev 6600 ft; 6 acres; stream. A remote area; good fishing; scenic drive; good gravel rds to area. Pets.

Mud Spring (Fremont NF). 7 mi W of Lakeview on St Hwy 140; 8 mi S on FS N30; 1-1/5 mi W on Co Hwy 565; 1-1/5 mi NW on FS 401. **SEASON:** 6/1-10/30. **FACILITIES:** 6 sites (tr -22); toil, f. **MISC.:** Elev 5500 ft. Receives hunter use in season only; surfaced rds to within 1-1/5 mi of site. Pets permitted if kept on a leash.

Siesta Spring (Fremont NF). 8 mi NE of Lakeview on US 395; 1 mi NE on FS 3744; 1 mi NE on FS 3721. **SEASON:** 6/1-10/31. **FACILITIES:** Sites (tr -16); tbls, toil, cga, f. **ACTIVITIES:** Picnicking; fishing; hunting. **MISC.:** Elev 5000 ft. A good hunting & fishing camp; last mi of rd unsurfaced. Pets permitted.

State Line (Fremont NF). 5 mi W of Lakeview on St Hwy 140; 7 mi S on Co Hwy W70; 22-7/10 mi SW on FS 4017; 7/10 mi S on FS 418. **SEASON:** 6/1-10/30. **FACILITIES:** 6 sites (tr -22); toil, cga. **ACTIVITIES:** Hunting. **MISC.:** Elev 5300 ft. A hunter Camp only; good gravel rds to within 1 mi of site. Pets.

Stud Spring (Fremont NF). 4-3/5 mi W of Lakeview on st Hwy 140; 10-2/5 mi SW on Co Hwy W60; 11 mi W on FS 4017; 1-4/5 mi W on FS 375. **SEASON:** 5/1-10/31. **FACILITIES:** 7 sites (tr -16); tbls, toil, cga, f. **ACTIVITIES:** Hunting. **MISC.:** Elev 5400 ft; A hunter camp used in season; blacktop & gravel rds to site. Pets permitted if kept on a leash.

Twin Springs (Fremont NF). 5 mi N of Lakeview on US 395; 6½ mi E on US 140; 4 mi S on US 391; 2 mi E on FS 395. **SEASON:** 5/15-10/30. **FACILITIES:** 3 sites (tr -16); toil, f. **MISC.:** Elev 6400 ft. Pets permitted if kept on a leash.

See page 7 for KEY TO ABBREVIATIONS.

Vee Lake (Fremont NF). 5 mi N of Lakeview on US 395; 8½ mi E on St Hwy 140; 15 mi N on FS 3615; 7½ mi NE on FS 3616. SEASON: 7/15–10/30. FACILITIES: 7 sites (tr -22); f, no drk wtr. ACTIVITIES: Fishing; swimming; boating,d. MISC.: Elev 6100 ft; 5 acres. Pets.

Vernon Spring (Fremont NF). 4–4/5 mi N of Lakeview on US 395; 6–4/5 mi SE on St Hwy 140; 8 mi S on FS 391; 2/5 mi NE on FS 391A. SEASON: 6/1–10/30. FACILITIES: 5 sites (tr -16); tbls, toil, cga, f. ACTIVITIES: Hunting. MISC.: Elev 6000 ft. A hunting & fishing camp; good gravel & blacktop rds most of the site. Pets permitted if kept on a leash.

Willow Creek (Fremont NF). 5–2/5 mi N of Lakeveiw on US 395; 6½ mi E on Hwy 140; 10–1/10 mi S on FS 391. SEASON: 6/15–10/30; 14-day lmt. FACILITIES: 10 sites (tr -22); tbls, toil, cga, well drk wtr. ACTIVITIES: Picnicking; fishing. MISC.: Elev 5800 ft; 5 acres. A remote, restful, quiet spot; fishing streams nearby; good gravel roads to area. Pets permitted if kept on leash.

Woodchopper Spring (Fremont NF). 17–4/5 mi N of Lakeview on US 395; 9/10 mi NW on FS 3630. SEASON: 5/1–10/31. FACILITIES: 5 sites (tr -16); toil, f. ACTIVITIES: Hunting; fishing. MISC.: Elev 5000 Ft. A hunting & fishing camp; last part of rd is rough & unsurfaced. Pets.

LA PINE

Chief Paulina Horse Camp (Deschutes NF). 5 mi N on US 97; 15 mi E on Co Hwy 2129. SEASON: 5/25–10/30; 14-day lmt. FACILITIES: 13 sites (tr -32); tbls, cga, no toil. Store/gas/ice/dump/food (2 mi). Laundry/showers (3 mi). ACTIVITIES: Picnicking; boating (r, 2 mi); horseback riding; swimming; fishing; hiking. MISC.: Elev 6300 ft; 30 acres; pets. Inside Newberry Crater 2 mi E of Ent. Station. RESERVATIONS REQUIRED.

Irish & Taylor Meadow (Deschutes NF). 2–2/5 mi NE of La Pine on US 97; 19–7/10 mi W on FS 204; 6–1/5 mi N on Co Hwy 46; 7/10 mi NW on FS 2025. SEASON: 5/30–9/30; 14-day lmt. FACILITIES: 3 tent sites (no trailers); toil. ACTIVITIES: Fishing. MISC.: Elev 5700 ft. 5½ mi W of Little Cultus Lake via primitive road. Pets permitted.

McKay Crossing (Deschutes NF). 5 mi N of La Pine on US 97; 3 mi SE on Co 2129; 2–1/10 mi E on FS 2045. SEASON: 6/1–10/30; 14-day lmt. FACILITIES: 10 sites (tr -22); tbls, toil, cga, no drk wtr. ACTIVITIES: Horseback riding; picnicking; fishing. MISC.: Elev 4400 ft; 2 acres. Pets. On Paulina Creek.

*****Paulina Point** (Deschutes NF). 5 mi N of La Pine on US 97; 13–1/10 mi E on Co Hwy 2129; 1 mi NE on TRAIL. SEASON: All yr. FACILITIES: 1 site; tbls, toil, cga, no drk wtr. Store/gas/ice SON: 5/15–10/30; 14-day lmt. FACILITIES: 1 tent site; toil, cga, no drk wtr, no tbls. Store/gas/ice/food (1 mi). Shower/laundry (5 mi). ACTIVITIES: Picnicking; hiking; boating (rl, 1 mi). Horseback riding (1 mi). MISC.: Elev 6300 ft; 3 acres; pets. South shore Paulina Lake in Newberry Crater.

Prairie (Deschutes NF). 5 mi N of La Pine on US 97; 3 mi SE on Co 2129. SEASON: 5/25–10/30; 14-day lmt. FACILITIES: 14 sites (tr -32); tbls, toil, cga, well drk wtr. Store/gas/ice (5 mi). ACTIVITIES: Picnicking; fishing. MISC.: Elev 4400 ft; 6 acres. Near Paulina Creek. Pets permitted if kept on a leash.

Rosland (Deschutes NF). On little Deschutes River, 1 mi W of Wickiup Jct. 3 mi NE of LaPine on US 97; 2 mi W on Co Hwy 1032. SEASON: 4/20–10/31; 14-day lmt. FACILITIES: 9 sites (tr -22); tbls, toil, cga, f, no drk wtr. Store/gas/ice (2 mi). Laundry/food (3 mi). ACTIVITIES: Picnicking; swimming; fishing; hiking. MISC.: Elev 4200 ft; 15 acres; pets.

South La Pine Rest Area. 6 mi S of La Pine on US 97. SEASON: All yr. FACILITIES: Drk wtr. MISC.: Pets permitted

Summit Station Rest Area. 28 mi SE of La Pine on St Hwy 31. MISC.: Pets.

*****Warm Springs** (Deschutes NF). 5 mi N on US 97; 13–1/10 mi E on Co Hwy 2129; 1–2/5 mi N, BY BOAT. SEASON: 5/15–10/30; 14-day lmt. FACILITIES: 4 tent sites; toil, cga, no drk wtr. Store/gas/ice/food (1 mi). Showers/laundry (5 mi). ACTIVITIES: Picnicking; hiking; fishing; boating (rl, 1 mi). Horseback riding (3 mi). MISC.: Elev 6300 ft; 3 acres; pets; scenic.

Wickiup Butte (Deschutes NF). 3 mi NW of LaPine on US 97; 12 mi W on FS 204; 3–9/10 mi SW on FS 210; 3–3/10 mi SE on FS 217.3. SEASON: 5/1–10/31; 14-day lmt. FACILITIES: 6 sites (tr -22); tbls, toil, cga, no drk wtr. ACTIVITIES: Boating,l; picnicking; fishing. MISC.: Elev 4400 ft; 11 acres; lake. On East shore Wickiup Reservoir. Pets permitted if kept on a leash.

LONG CREEK

Carter Rest Area 3 mi S of Long Creek on US 395. SEASON: All yr. FACILITIES: Drk wtr. MISC.: Pets permitted on leash.

See page 7 for KEY TO ABBREVIATIONS.

Middle Fork John Day River Rest Area.
13 mi N of Long Creek on US 395. SEA-
SON: All yr. MISC.: Scenic view;
stream. Pets permitted if kept on leash.

LOSTINE

Shady (Wallowa Whitman NF). 7 mi S
of Lostine on Co Hwy 551; 10-1/10 mi
S on FS S202. SEASON: 6/15-11/1; 10-
day lmt. FACILITIES: 16 sites (tr -16);
tbls, toil, cga, f, no drk wtr. ACTIVI-
TIES: Swimming; picnicking; fishing.
Horseback riding (2 mi). MISC.: Elev
5400 ft; 7 acres; river. Pets permitted.

Two Pan (Wallowa Whitman NF). 7 mi
S of Lostine on Co Hwy 551; 10-4/5 mi
S of FS S202. SEASON: 6/15-11/1;
10-day lmt. FACILITIES: 9 sites
(tr -16); tbls, toil, cga, f, no
drk wtr. ACTIVITIES: Picnicking;
swimming; berry-picking; fishing.
Horseback riding (2 mi). MISC.:
Elev 5600 ft; 3 acres; river; pets.

Williamson (Wallowa Whitman NF). 7
mi S of Lostine on Co Hwy 551; 4 mi
S on FS S202. SEASON: 6/15-11/1; 10-
day lmt. FACILITIES: 10 sites (tr -16);
tbls, toil, cga, f, no drk wtr. ACTIVI-
TIES: Swimming; picnicking; fishing.
Horseback riding (4 mi). MISC.: Elev
5000 ft; 4 acres; river. Pets permitted.

LOWELL

Big Pool (Willamette NF). 1-4/5 mi N
of Lowell on Co 6220; 9-9/10 mi E on
Co 6240; 1-7/10 mi E on FS 181. SEA-
SON: 5/1-9/15; 10-day lmt. FACILITIES:
5 tent sites (no trailers); tbls, toil,
cga, f, piped drk wtr. ACTIVITIES:
Swimming; picnicking; fishing; hunting.
MISC.: Elev 1000 ft; 1 acre. Pets.

Bedrock (Willamette NF). 1-4/5 mi N
of Lowell on Co 6220; 9-9/10 mi E on
Co 6240; 4-4/5 mi E on Fs 181. SEASON:
5/1-9/15; 10-day lmt. FAC: 18 sites
(tr -22); tbls, toil, cga, piped drk
wtr. ACT: Picnicking; swimming;
fishing; hunting. MISC.: Elev 1100
ft; 13 acres; stream; pets. North
from Lowell to Unity Junction; E
from Unity Junction.

Puma (Willamette NF). 1-4/5 mi N of
Lowell on Co 6220; 9-9/10 mi E on Co
6240; 6½ mi E on FS 181. SEASON: 5/1-
9/15; 10-day lmt. FACILITIES: 10 sites
(tr -16); tbls, toil, cga, f, piped drk
wtr. ACTIVITIES: Swimming; picnicking;
fishing. Hiking (3 mi). ACTIVITIES: Elev
1100 ft; 6 acres; stream. N from Lowell
to Unity Jct., E from Unity Jct. Pets.

Winberry (Willamette NF). 1-4/5 mi N
of Lowell on Co 6220; 2/5 mi E on Co
6240; 5-4/5 mi SE on Co 62450; 3½ mi
SE on FS 191. SEASON: 1/1-12/31; 10-day
lmt. FACILITIES: 6 sites (tr -16); tbls,
toil, cga, f, no drk wtr. ACTIVITIES:
Hunting; picnicking; fishing. MISC.:
Elev 1100 ft; 5 acres; stream. N. from
Lowell to Unity Jct, turn rt at Log Scale
Station then drive E. Pets permitted.

MADRAS

Cow Canyon Rest Area. 21 mi N of Madras
on US 97. SEASON: All yr. FACILITIES:
Drk wtr. MISC.: Scenic view. Pets permitted if kept on a leash.

Haystack Lake (Ochoco NF). 9-3/10 mi
S of Madras on US 07; 3-3/10 mi SE on
Co CR6; N on FS 1275. SEASON: 5/15-9/15
14-day lmt. FACILITIES: 24 sites (tr -
22); tbls, flush toil, cga, f. ACTIVI-
TIES: Swimming; picnicking; fishing;
boating,ld. MISC.: Pets.

MAPLETON

Turner Creek (BLM;Eugene Dist.). 6-7/10
mi E of Mapleton on St Hwy 126. SEASON:
All yr. FACILITIES: 10 sites (tr -20);
tbls, f. ACTIVITIES: Picnicking. MISC.:
6 acres. Pets permitted if kept on leash.

MAUPIN

Clear Creek (Mt. Hood NF). 25 mi W of
Maupin on Hwy 216; 3 mi N on FS S401.
SEASON: 5/1-10/1; 14-day lmt. FACILI-
TIES: 6 sites (tr -16); tbls, toil, cga,
f, no drk wtr. ACTIVITIES: Picnicking;
fishing. Horseback riding/hiking (1
mi). MISC.: Elev 3000 ft; 2 acres;
stream. Pets permitted if kept on leash.

Keeps Mill (Mt. Hood NF). 24 mi W of
Maupin on St Hwy 216; 3 mi N on FS
S483. SEASON: 5/1-10/1; 14-day lmt.
FACILITIES: 4 tent sites (no trailers);
tbls, toil, cga, f, no drk wtr. ACTIVI-
TIES: Picnicking; fishing. Horseback
riding/niking (1 mi). MISC.: Elev 2600
ft; 1 acre; river. Pets.

McCubbins Gulch (Mt. Hood NF) 24½ mi
NW of Maupin on St Hwy 216; 1 mi E
on FS S508. SEASON: 5/1-10/1; 14-day
lmt. FACILITIES: 5 sites (tr -16); tbls,
toil, cga, f, no drk wtr. ACTIVITIES:
Picnicking; fishing. MISC.: Elev 3000
ft; 10 acres; stream. Minimum development. Pets permitted if kept on leash.

McKENZIE BRIDGE

Alder Springs (Willamette NF). 4-3/10
mi E of McKenzie Bridge on Hwy 126;
8-1/5 mi E on Hwy 242. SEASON: 6/1-
10/31; 10-day lmt. FACILITIES: 7 tent
sites (no trailers); tbls, toil, cga, f.
ACTIVITIES: Picnicking; fishing. MISC.:
Elev 3600 ft; 2 acres. Trail to Linton
Lake. Scenic; pets. No drk wtr.

See page 7 for KEY TO ABBREVIATIONS.

413

Clear Lake (Willamette NF). 14-3/5 mi NE on St Hwy 126; 1/10 mi E on FS 1449. **SEASON:** 5/15-10/31; 10-day lmt. **FACILITIES:** 28 sites (no tr); tbls, toil, cga, f, electricity in restrooms, piped drk wtr, store, food. **ACTIVITIES:** Picnicking; fishing; boatin,rl (no motors); sailing. **MISC.:** Elev 3600 ft; 25 acres; lake; scenic; pets. Headwaters of McKenzie River, day use site only.

Fish Lake (Willamette NF). 22-2/5 mi NE of McKenzie Bridge on Hwy 126; 1/10 mi W on FS 1374. **SEASON:** 4/1-11/30; 10-day lmt. **FACILITIES:** 7 sites (tr -22); tbls, toil, cga, f, piped drk wtr. Store/ice/sncaks/gas/groceries (3 mi). **ACTIVITIES:** Hunting; picnicking; fishing; Swimming. Boating,1; rental (3 mi) (no motors). **MISC.:** Elev 3200 ft; 1 acre; lake; scenic; geological interest. Lake recedes in summer because of porous lava substrata. Pets permitted if kept on a leash. Special fish season; see State Regulations.

Frog (Willamette NF). 3-2/5 mi E of McKenzie Bridge on St Hwy 126; 13-3/5 mi NE on St Hwy 242; 3/10 mi E on FS 1634. **SEASON:** 7/1-10/31; 10-day lmt. **FACILITIES:** 4 sites (tr -22); tbls, toil, cga, f, no drk wtr. **ACTIVITIES:** Hiking; hunting; picnicking; mtn climbing. **MISC.:** Elev 4900 ft; 2 acres; stream; scenic. Trailhead, Obsidian Trail to Pacific Crest Trail. Pets.

* **Hand Lake MDF** (Willamette NF). 2-1/5 mi NE of McKenzie Bridge on St Hwy 126; 15-1/10 mi E on St Hwy 242; ¼ mi N on TRAIL 3513. **SEASON:** 7/1-10/31; 10-day lmt. **FACILITIES:** 3 tent sites (no trailers); toil, f. **ACTIVITIES:** Fishing; boating (no motors). Horseback riding (1 mi). **MISC.:** Elev 4800 ft; 1 acre; lake; scenic. Adjacent to lava fields. Pets.

* **Lakes End** (Willamette NF). 13-1/5 mi NW of McKenzie Bridge on Hwy 126; 3-3/10 mi NW on FS 1477; 1-4/5 mi N, BY BOAT 4903. **SEASON:** 4/1-10/31; 10-day lmt. **FACILITIES:** 17 sites; tbls, toil, cga, f, no drk wtr. **ACTIVITIES:** Picnicking; fishing; boating. **MISC.:** Elev 3000 ft; 9 acres; lake; scenic. On Smith Reservoir; accessible by boat only (10 mph boating speed). Pets permitted.

Limberlost (Willamette NF). 4-3/10 mi E of McKenzie Bridge on Hwy 126; ½ mi E on Hwy 242. **SEASON:** 4/1-11/30; 10-day lmt. **FACILITIES:** 12 tent sites (no trailers); tbls, toil, cga, no drk wtr. **ACTIVITIES:** Picnicking; fishing. **MISC.:** Elev 1800 ft; 3 acres; stream; scenic. On Lost Creek. Pets.

Olallie (Willamette NF). 11-1/10 mi NE of McKenzie Bridge on Hwy 126. **SEASON:** 4/1-12/31; 10-day lmt. **FACILITIES:** 19 sites (tr -22); tbls, toil, cga, f, no drk wtr. **ACTIVITIES:** Picnicking; fishing; boating,ld (3 mi). **MISC.:** Elev 2000 ft; 8 acres; stream; scenic. CG at Confluence of McKenzie River & Olallie Creek. Pets permitted if kept on a leash.

Scott Lake (Willamette NF). 3-2/5 mi E of McKenzie Bridge on Hwy 126; 14-3/5 mi NE on Hwy 242; 2/5 mi SW on FS 1532. **SEASON:** 7/1-10/31; 10-day lmt. **FACILITIES:** 20 sites (no trailers); tbls, toil, cga, f, no drk wtr. **ACTIVITIES:** picnicking; fishing; swimming; boating (no motors); hunting; hiking. **MISC.:** Elev 4800 ft; 1 acre; lake. Scott Lake closed to angling from motor driven crafts. Pets permitted if kept on leasn.

MEDFORD

Suncrest Rest Area. 7 mi SE of Medford on I-5. **SEASON:** All yr. **FACILITIES:** Drk wtr. **MISC.:** Pets permitted if kept on a leash.

MEDICAL SPRINGS

Eagle Creek (Wallowa Whitman NF). 5¼ mi SE of Medical Springs on FS S66; 10-1/5 mi E on FS S679; 8-9/10 mi SE on FS S550. **SEASON:** 6/15-9/30; 10-day lmt. **FACILITIES:** 12 sites (tr -22); tbls, toil, cga, f. **ACTIVITIES:** Picnicking; fishing. **MISC.:** Elev 3400 ft; 4 acres. Pets permitted if kept on leash.

Kettle Creek (Wallowa Whitman NF). 5¼ mi SE of Medical Springs on FS S66; 10-1/5 mi E on FS S679; 6-7/10 mi SE on FS S550; 5-9/10 mi NE on FS S611. **SEASON:** 6/15-9/30; 10-day lmt. **FACILITIES:** 12 tent sites (no trailers); tbls, toil, cga, f. **ACTIVITIES:** Fishing; picnicking. **MISC.:** Elev 4600 ft; 4 acres. Campers Only. Pets permitted.

Tamarack (Wallowa Whitman NF). 5¼ mi SE on FS 6700; 10-1/8 mi E on FS 6700; 3/10 mi E on FS 7700. **SEASON:** 6/15-9/30; 10-day lmt. **FACILITIES:** 10 sites (tr -22); tbls, toil, cga, f. Store/snacks/ice (5 mi). Piped drk wtr. **ACTIVITIES:** Picnicking; fishing. Horseback riding and rental (5 mi). **MISC.:** Elev 4600 ft; 4 acres; pets; scenic.

Two Color (Wallowa Whitman NF). 5¼ mi SE on FS 6700; 10-1/5 mi E on FS 6700; 1-1/5 mi NE on FS 7755. **SEASON:** 6/15-9/30; 10-day lmt. **FACILITIES:** 14 sites (tr -22); tbls, toil, cga, f, piped drk wtr. Store/food/ice/gas (3 mi). **ACTIVITIES:** Picnicking; fishing. Horseback riding and rental (3 mi). **MISC.:** Elev 4800 ft; 4 acres; pets; stream; scenic.

See page 7 for KEY TO ABBREVIATIONS.

MEHAMAN

Shady Cove (Willamette NF). 9/10 mi E on St Hwy 22; 15-3/10 mi E on Co Rd 967; 1-1/10 mi E on FS S80; 2-1/10 mi E on FS S81. SEASON: 5/1-9/15; 10-day lmt. FACILITIES: 9 sites (tr -16); tbls, toil, cga, no drk wtr. ACTIVITIES: Picnicking; fishing; rockhounding. MISC.: Elev 1400 ft; 4 acres; pets; scenic. On Little N Santiam River.

MILTON-FREEWATER

Bone Spring (Umatilla NF). 9-1/5 mi S on St Hwy 11; 17½ mi E on St Hwy 204; 16-3/10 mi E on FS 64; 1/10 mi NE on FS 360. SEASON: 7/1-10/15. FACILITIES: 13 sites (tr -22); tbls, toil, cga, f, no drk wtr. ACTIVITIES: Picnicking; fishing. MISC.: elev 5600 ft; 2 acres; scenic. Pets. Pack out your own garbage.

MITCHELL

Cottonwood (NF). 10 mi E of Mitchell on St Hwy 25; 6-9/10 mi S on FS 1240; 6-1/10 mi SE on FS 127; 2/5 mi S on FS 127W. SEASON: 6/15-10/20. FACILITIES: 1 site (tr -22); toil, cga, f, no drk

Derr (NF). 10 mi E of Mitchell on US 26; 6-9/10 mi S on FS 1240; 1-3/10 mi SE on FS 127; 2/5 mi S on 127K. SEASON: 7/1-10/30. FACILITIES: 6 sites (tr -22); toil, cga, f. ACTIVITIES: Picnicking. MISC.: Elev 5900 ft; pets.

Scotts (NF). 2/5 mi E of Mitchell on US 26; 7 mi SE on Co Hwy 123; 6-1/5 mi SW on FS 1222. SEASON: 6/15-10/15. FACILITIES: 3 sites (tr -22); toil, cga, f. MISC.: Elev 5800 ft; pets permitted.

Wildwood (NF). 9-9/10 mi W of Mitchell on US 26; 5-9/10 mi S on Co Hwy 123; 1-3/5 mi SW on FS 1204. SEASON: 6/15-9/15. FACILITIES: 7 sites (tr -22); toil, cga, f. ACTIVITIES: Rocknounding. MISC.: Elev 4900 ft; pets permitted if kept on a leash.

MOUNT VERNON

Magone Lake (Malheur NF). 9 mi N of Mount Vernon on US 395; 8 mi NE on FS 1036; 2 mi N on FS 1219. SEASON: 5/15-11/1; 14-day lmt. FACILITIES: 25 sites (tr -16); tbls, toil, cga, f, piped drk wtr. ACTIVITIES: Swimming; picnicking; fishing; boating,ld; hiking. MISC.: Elev 5100 ft; 14 acres; lake. Pets. Adjacent to Magone Lake and geological area.

Rock Springs (Malheur NF). 10-3/5 mi NE of Mount Vernon on US 395; 8-1/10 mi E on FS 1036. SEASON: 7/15-11/1. FACILITIES: 2 sites (tr -22); toil. MISC.: Elev 4200 ft. Pets permitted if kept on a leash.

NESKOWIN

Neskowin Creek (Siuslaw NF). 1½ mi SE of Neskowin on US 101; 4-7/10 mi SE on Co 592; 1/10 mi W on FS S6440. SEASON: 4/15-10/15; 10-day lmt. FACILITIES: 12 sites (tr -16); tbls, toil, cga, f, no drk wtr. Store/snacks/ice (5 mi). ACTIVITIES: Picnicking; fishing. MISC.: Elev 400 ft; 5 acres. Pets.

NORTH BEND

Bluebill Lake (Siuslaw NF). 2½ mi N of North Bend on US 101; 4/5 mi W on Co Hwy; 2-3/10 mi NW on FS 2431. SEASON: 6/1-11/1; 10-day lmt. FACILITIES: 18 sites (tr -22); tbls, flush toil, cga, f. Store/gas/ice (4 mi). ACTIVITIES: Boating,l,d; picnicking; fishing; biking. MISC.: 2 acres. Pets permitted.

Spinreel (Siuslaw NF). 8 mi NW of North Bend on US 101; 1 mi NW on Co Rd. SEASON: 1/1-12/31; 10-day lmt. FACILITIES: 25 sites (tr -22); tbls, toil, cga, f, no drk wtr. Store/gas/ice/showers/laundry (1 mi). ACTIVITIES: Picnicking; fishing. Swimming/waterskiing/boating,rl (1 mi). MISC.: Elev 100 ft; 10 acres. 2 mi from Ten Mile Lake. Pets permitted if kept on a leash.

O'BRIEN

Sourdough (Siskiyou NF). 4 mi SW of O'Brien on Co Hwy 5550; 24 mi SW on FS 4014. SEASON: 6/1-11/1; 14-day lmt. FACILITIES: 3 tent sites (no trailers); tbls, toil, cga, no drk wtr. ACTIVITIES: Swimming; picnicking; fishing. MISC.: Elev 1000 ft; 1 acre; stream scenic. Pets permitted if kept on a leash.

OAKRIDGE

Blair Lake (Willamette NF). 1 mi E of Oakridge on Co 149; 8 mi NE on FS 2042 2-4/5 mi E on FS 2002; 6-1/10 mi NE on FS 2004. SEASON: 6/1-10/15; 10-day lmt. FACILITIES: 5 tent sites (no trailers); tbls, toil, cga, f, well drk wtr. ACTIVITIES: Hiking; hunting; picnicking; fishing; berry-picking; boating,d (no motors). Horseback riding (1 mi). MISC.: Elev 4800 ft; 3 acres; pets. Blair Lake closed to fishing from motor-driven craft.

See page 7 for KEY TO ABBREVIATIONS.

Campers Flat (Willamette NF). 2-1/5 mi SE of Oakridge on St Hwy 58; ½ mi SE on Co Hwy 360; 20 mi S on FS 211. SEASON: 1/1-12/31; 10-day lmt. FACILITIES: 5 sites (tr -16); tbls, toil, cga, f, well drk wtr. ACTIVITIES: Picnicking; fisning. MISC.: Elev 2000 ft; 2 acres; river. Pets.

Ferrin (Willamette NF). 2-1/10 mi W of Oakridge on Hwy 58. SEASON: 4/15-11/20; 10-day lmt. FACILITIES: 7 sites (tr -16); tbls, toil, cga, no drk wtr. Store/ice/gas/snacks (1 mi). Laundry/dump (3 mi). ACTIVITIES: Hunting; picnicking; fishing. MISC.: Elev 1200 ft; 3 acres; river. Pets.

Harralson Horse Camp (Willamette NF). 23-1/10 mi SE of Oakridge on St Hwy 58; 12-1/5 mi NE on Fs 204; 1-1/5 mi NW on FS 2170; 1/10 mi on FS. SEASON: 7/1-10/15. FACILITIES: 5 sites (tr -16); tbls, toil, cga, dump, no drk wtr. ACTIVITIES: Picnicking; horseback riding; fishing; boating,l; hiking; sailing. MISC.: Elev 5500 ft; 3 acres; scenic; pets.

Indigo Springs (Willamette NF). 2-1/5 mi SE of Oakridge on St Hwy 58; ½ mi SE on Co Hwy 360; 28-4/5 mi SE on FS 211. SEASON: 1/1-12/31; 10-day lmt. FACILITIES: 3 sites (no trailers); tbls, toil, cga, f, no drk wtr. ACTIVITIES: Hunting; picnicking. Fishing (1 mi). MISC.: Elev 2800 ft; 3 acres; stream. Pets permitted if kept on a leash.

Noisy Creek (Willamette NF). 2-1/5 mi SE of Oakridge on St Hwy 58; ½ mi SE on Co Hwy 360; 25-4/5 mi SE on FS 211; 2/5 mi SE on FS 2402. SEASON: All year; 10-day lmt. FACILITIES: 4 tent sites (no trailers); tbls, toil, cga, no drk wtr. ACTIVITIES: Picnicking. Fishing (1 mi). MISC.: Elev 2500 ft; 3 acres; stream. Interior rd part of old Oregon Central Military Wagon Rd. Pets.

❋ **Rhodendron Island** (Willamette NF). 23-1/10 mi SE of Oakridge on St Hwy 58; 6-1/5 mi NE on FS 204; 2-1/5 mi NW on FS 204D; 1-3/5 mi NW, BY BOAT. (access by boat only from Wala Campground). SEASON: 7/1-10/15; 10-day lmt. FACILITIES: 3 tent sites, tbls, toil, cga, no drk wtr. ACTIVITIES: Picnicking; boating; sailing. MISC.: Elev 5400 ft; 2 acres; scenic. Pets.

Sacandaga (Willamette NF). 2-1/5 mi SE of Oakridge on Hwy 58; ½ mi SE on Co 360; 24-7/10 mi SE on FS 211. SEASON: 4/15-11/15; 10-day lmt. FACILITIES: 18 sites (tr -16); tbls, toil, cga, f, piped drk wtr. ACTIVITIES: Picnicking; fishing; hunting. MISC.: Elev 2400 ft; 8 acres; river. Pets.

Secret (Willamette NF). 2-1/5 mi SE on Hwy 58; ½ mi SE on Co 360; 18-3/10 mi S on FS 211. SEASON: 1/1-12/31; 10-day lmt. FACILITIES: 6 tent sites (no trailers); tbls, toil, cga, f. ACTIVITIES: Picnicking; fishing. MISC.: Elev 2000 ft; 5 acres; river. Pets permitted.

Salmon Creek Falls (Willamette NF). 1 mi E of Oakridge on Co 149; 3-7/10 mi NE on FS 2042. SEASON: 4/15-10/31; 10-day lmt. FACILITIES: 12 sites (tr -16); tbls, toil, cga, no drk wtr. Store/gas/ice/laundry/snacks/dump (5 mi). ACTIVITIES: Picnicking; fishing. MISC.: Elev 1500 ft; 9 acres; stream. Pets.

Salt Creek Falls Willamette NF). 20-7/10 mi SE of Oakridge on Hwy 58. SEASON: 5/15-10/31; 10-day lmt. FACILITIES: 5 sites (tr -16); tbls, toil, cga, no drk wtr. ACTIVITIES: Hunting; hiking; picnicking; fishing. MISC.: Elev 4000 ft; 7 acres. Second highest waterfall in Ore. (286 ft). Pets.

Salt Creek Rest Area. 19 mi SE of Oakridge on St Hwy 58. SEASON: All yr. FACILITIES: Drk wtr. MISC.: Scenic view; water falls. Pets permitted.

Taylor Burn (Willamette NF). 23-1/10 mi NE of Oakridge on Hwy 58; 12-1/5 mi NE on FS 204; ½ mi NW on FS 2170; 6-4/5 mi NW on FS 2170A. SEASON: 7/1-10/15; 10-day lmt. FACILITIES: 15 sites (tr -16); tbls, toil, cga, piped drk wtr. ACTIVITIES: Horseback riding; picnicking; fishing; hunting; hiking. MISC.: Elev 5200 ft; 6 acres. Trail access to Erma Bells & other high country lakes. Pets permitted if kept on a leash.

Timpanogas Lake (Willamette NF). 2-1/5 mi SE of Oakridge on Hwy 58; ½ mi SE on Co 360; 38-2/5 mi SE on FS 211; 3 mi S on FS 250. SEASON: 6/15-10/15; 10-day lmt. FACILITIES: 10 sites (tr -16); tbls, toil, cga, f, well drk wtr. ACTIVITIES: Swimming; picnicking; fishing; boating,d (no motors); hunting; hiking. MISC.: Elev 5200 ft; 9 acres; lake. Pets.

ONTARIO

Ontario Rest Area. I-80N at Ontario. SEASON: All yr. FACILITIES: Drk wtr; info center. MISC.: Pets permitted if kept on a leash.

Snake River Slides Rest Area. 24 mi N of Ontario on US 30N. SEASON: All yr. FACILITIES: Drk wtr. MISC.: Pets.

NEWPORT

Otter Crest Rest Area. 10 mi N of Newport, on US 101. SEASON: All yr. FACILITIES: Drk wtr. MISC.: Scenic view. Pets permitted if kept on a leash.

ONBOW

* Dove Creek (Wallowa Whitman NF). 8 mi N of Onbow on Co Rd 210; 6-2/5 mi N on TRAIL 1890. SEASON: 4/1-11/30; 10-day lmt. FACILITIES: 4 tent sites; tbls, toil, cga, drk wtr. ACTIVITIES: Hiking; picnicking; fishing; boating; swimming. MISC.: Elev 1900 ft; 1 acre; scenic. Pets.

*Kirby Creek (Wallowa Whitman NF). 8 mi N on Co Hwy 210; 6-2/5 mi N on TRAIL 1890. SEASON: 4/1-11/30; 10-day lmt. FACILITIES: 4 sites (no tr); tbls, toil, cga, f, no drk wtr. ACTIVITIES: Picnicking; swimming; fishing; boating; waterskiing. MISC.: Elev 1700 ft; 1 acre; scenic; pets.

* Leep Creek (Wallowa Whitman NF). 8 mi N of Onbow on Co Hwy 210; 4-7/10 mi N on TRAIL 1890. SEAS: 4/1-11/30; 10-day lmt. FAC: 3 tent sites; tbls, toil, no drk wtr. ACT: Swimming; picnicking; fishing; boating; waterskiing. MISC.: Elev 1700 ft; 1 acre; lake. Pets permitted if kept on a leash.

* Lynch Creek (Wallowa Whitman NF). 8 mi N of Onbow on Co Hwy 210; 7-3/10 mi NE on TRAIL 1890. SEASON: 4/1-11/30; 10-day lmt. FACILITIES: 3 tent sites (no trailers); tbls, toil, cga, f, no drk wtr. ACTIVITIES: Swimming; picnicking; fishing; boating. MISC.: Elev 1700 ft; 1 acre; lake; scenic. Pets.

PACIFIC CITY

Sand Beach (Siuslaw NF). 1/5 mi W of Pacific City on Co Hwy; 8-2/5 mi N on Co Hwy; 1 mi W on Co Hwy; 1-4/5 mi SW on FS 3001. SEASON: All yr; 10-day lmt. FACILITIES: 101 sites (tr -22); tbls, toil, cga. Shower (3 mi). ACTIVITIES: Swimming; picnicking; fishing; boating,d. MISC.: Elev 100 ft; 2 acres. Pacific Ocean 3/10 mi W. Dunebuggy Area. Pets permitted if kept on leash.

PAISLEY

Campbell Lake (Fremont NF). 1 mi W of Paisley on Co 422; 22-7/10 mi W on FS 331; 3 mi S on FS 2823; 3-2/5 mi W on FS 3403. SEASON: 6/15-9/30; 14-day lmt. FACILITIES: 21 sites (tr -16); tbls, toil, cga, well drk wtr. ACTIVITIES: Picnicking; fishing; boating,d (no motors); hunting; swimming. MISC.: Elev 7200 ft; 4 acres. Remote natural, high mtn lake, fishing good, gravel surfaced rd 3/4 distance, poor, unsurfaced 1/4 distance. 1 mi to Deadhorse Lake. Pets permitted if kept on leash.

Deadhorse Creek (Fremont NF). 1 mi W of Paisley on Co Hwy 422; 1 mi W on Co Hwy 422; 22-7/10 mi W on FS 331; 3 mi S on Co Hwy 2823; 4-2/5 mi S on FS 3403. SEASON: 6/15-9/30; 14-day lmt. FAC: 10 sites (tr -16); tbls,toil,cga. well drk wtr. ACTIVITIES: Boating; picnicking; fishing. MISC.: Elev 7400 ft; 1 acre. Very little development, good fishing. Pets permitted if kept on leash.

Deadhorse Lake (Fremont NF). 1 mi W of Paisley on Co 422; 22-7/10 mi W on FS 331; 3 mi S on FS 2823; 4-2/5 mi S on FS 3403. SEASON: 7/1-9/15; 14-day lmt. FACILITIES: 14 sites (tr -16); tbls, toil, cga, well drk wtr. ACTIVITIES: Hunting; picnicking; fishing; boating (no motors). MISC.: Elev 7400 ft; 9 acres. 1 mi to Campbell Lake. Remote natural, high mtn lake; fishing good; gravel surfaced rd. Pets permitted.

Hanan Springs (Fremont NF). 1 mi W of Paisley on Co Hwy 422; 4-3/5 mi W on FS 331; 2-1/10 mi S on FS 336. SEASON: 6/1-10/30. FACILITIES: 6 tent sites (no trailers); toil, no drk wtr. MISC.: Elev 5500 ft; 1 acre. A hunter camp only; remote. Pets permitted if kept on leash.

Happy Camp (Fremont NF). 1 mi S of Paisley on Co 422; 20-3/10 mi S on FS 330; 2-2/5 mi S on FS 2823; 1 mi W on FS 3675. SEASON: 6/1-10/30; 14-day lmt. FACILITIES: 9 sites, tbls, toil, cga, piped drk wtr. ACTIVITIES: Hunting; picnicking; fishing. MISC.: Elev 5200 ft; 10 acres; pets; good road. Popular fishing site on Dairy Creek.

Lee Thomas (Fremont NF). 1 mi W of Paisley on Co 422; 26-9/10 mi W on FS 331. SEASON: 6/15-10/30; 14-day lmt. FACILITIES: 7 sites (tr -16); tbls, toil, cga, well drk wtr. ACTIVITIES: Hunting; picnicking; fishing. MISC.: Elev 6200 ft; 3 acres. Remote area popular fishing spot; good & fair rds. Pets permitted.

Marsters Springs (Fremont NF). 1 mi W of Paisley on Co 422; 7-1/10 mi S on FS 331. SEASON: 5/15-11/15; 14-day lmt. FACILITIES: 10 sites (tr -22); tbls, toil, cga, well drk wtr. ACTIVITIES: Hunting; picnicking; fishing. MISC.: Elev 4700 ft; 4 acres; river; stream. Newly constructed CG on river; good fishing; good graveled road. Pets permitted if kept on a leash.

Sandhill Crossing (Fremont NF). 1 mi W of Paisley on Co Hwy 42; 29-1/5 mi W on FS 331. SEASON: 6/15-10/30; 14-day lmt. FACILITIES: 5 sites (tr -16); tbls, toil, cga, no drk wtr. ACTIVITIES: Picnicking; fishing. MISC.: Elev 6100 ft; 2 acres; river. Remote area. Good fishing spot. Good & fair roads. Pets permitted if kept on a leash.

See page 7 for KEY TO ABBREVIATIONS.

PARKDALE

Cloud Cap Saddle (Mt. Hood NF). 8 mi S of Parksdale on Co Rd 428; 11-7/10 mi W on FS S12. SEASON: 7/1-9/15. FACILITIES: 3 tent sites; toil, cga, f, tbls. ACTIVITIES: Hiking; picnicking; mtn climbing. MISC.: Elev 6000 ft; 1 acre. Starting point for climbing Mt. Hood on Timberline Trail. Pets permitted.

Cloud Cap Parking (Mt. Hood NF). 8 mi S of Parkdale on Co Hwy 482; 12 mi W on FS S12. SEASON: 7/1-9/15; 14-day lmt. FACILITIES: 3 tent sites (no trailers); tbls, toil, cga, f, no drk wtr. ACTIVITIES: Picnicking; mtn climbing; hiking. MISC.: Elev 6000 ft; 2 acres. Photography potential; geological interest. Pets.

Gibson Prairie Horse Camp (Mt. Hood NF). 2 mi NE on Co Hwy 428; 3 mi N on St Hwy 35; 15 mi SE on FS N107. SEASON: 5/15-10/15; 14-day lmt. FACILITIES: 3 sites (tr -16); toil, cga. ACTIVITIES: Camp is designated for visitors with horses. MISC.: Elev 3900 ft; 4 acres; pets.

Hood River Meadows (Mt. Hood NF). 2½ mi SE of Parkdale on Co 281; 16½ mi S on Hwy 35. SEASON: 6/15-9/15; 14-day lmt. FACILITIES: 6 sites, tbls, toil, cga, no drk wtr. ACTIVITIES: Picnicking; hiking. MISC.: Elev 4400 ft; 2 acres; stream. Near ski area. Trailhead to Mt. Hood Wilderness. Pets.

Indian Springs (Mt. Hood NF). 6 mi N of Parkdale on St Hwy 281; 6 mi SW on Co Hwy; 5 mi W on Fs N13; 8 mi NW on FS N18. SEASON: 7/1-9/15. FACILITIES: 4 sites (no tr); tbls, toil, cga, f, no drk wtr. ACTIVITIES: Picnicking; berry-picking. MISC.: Elev 4200 ft; 1 acre. Skyline Trail passes thru site. Pets.

Polallie (Mt. Hood NF). 2½ mi SE of Parkdale on Co 281; 7 mi S on Hwy 35. SEASON: 5/15-10/15. FACILITIES: 10 sites (tr -16); tbls, toil, cga, f. ACTIVITIES: Picnicking; fishing. MISC.: Elev 3000 ft; 3 acres. Pets permitted.

Rainy Lake (Mt. Hood NF). 6 mi N of Parkdale on Hwy 281; 10 mi W on FS N205. SEASON: 6/15-9/15. FACILITIES: 5 tent sites (no trailers); tbls, toil, cga, no drk wtr. ACTIVITIES: Swimming; picnicking; fishing; berry-picking. Boating (5 mi). MISC.: Elev 4100 ft; 3 acres. Secluded high elevation area. Lake 1/4 mi from campground. Pets. per-

Robinhood (Mt. Hood NF). 2½ mi SE of Parkdale on Co 281; 12½ mi S on Hwy 35. SEASON: 6/1-10/15. FACILITIES: 43 sites (tr -16); tbls, toil, cga, f. ACTIVITIES: Swimming; picnicking; fishing; boating,d. MISC.: Elev 3600 ft; 6 acres. Good fishing. Pets.

Sherwood (Mt. Hood NF). 2½ mi SE of Parkdale on Co 281; 8½ mi S on Hwy 35. SEASON: 6/1-10/15. FACILITIES: 33 sites (tr -16); tbls, toil, cga, f. ACTIVITIES: Swimming; picnicking; fishing. MISC.: Elev 3000 ft; 4 acres. Easy access. Pets.

Tilly Jane (Mt. Hood NF). 8 mi S of Parkdale on Co 428; 11 mi W on FS S12. SEASON: 7/1-9/15. FACILITIES: 14 sites (tr -16), tbls, toil, cga, f. ACTIVITIES: Picnicking; mtn climbing. MISC.: Elev 5600 ft; 9 acres; stream; geological interest. Starting point for climbing Mt. Hood. Pets. No drk wtr.

Wahtum Lake (Mt. Hood NF). 6 mi W of Parkdale on Hwy 281; 5 mi SW on Co; 5 mi W on FS N13; 8 mi NW on FS N18. SEASON: 6/15-9/15. FACILITIES: 5 sites (tr -16); tbls, toil, cga, f, no drk wtr. ACTIVITIES: Berry-picking; picnicking; fishing. MISC.: Elev 3900 ft; 1 acre. Located on rd 1/4 mi from Wahtum Lake. Pets.

Wahtum Lakeside (Mt. Hood NF). 6 mi N of Parkdale on Hwy 281; 5 mi SW on Co; 5 mi W on FS N13; 8 mi NW on FS N18. SEASON: 6/15-9/15; 14-day lmt. FACILITIES: 8 sites (no trailers); tbls, toil, cga, f, no drk wtr. ACTIVITIES: Swimming; picnicking; fishing; boating. MISC.: Elev 3700 ft; 1 acre; pets.

PAULINA

Big Springs (Ochoco NF). 3½ mi E of Paulina on Co Hwy 112; 6½ mi N on Co Hwy 113; 2 mi N on FS 142; 1 mi N on FS 154. SEASON: 6/1-10/30. FACILITIES: 5 sites (no tr); tbls, toil, cga, piped drk wtr. ACTIVITIES: Picnicking; fishing; horseback riding. MISC.: Elev 5000 ft; 8 acres; pets.

Frazier (Ochoco NF). 3½ mi E on Co Hwy 112; 2-1/5 mi N on Co Hwy 113; 10 mi E on Co Hwy 135; 6-3/10 mi E on FS 158; 1-1/10 mi NE on FS 1548. SEASON: 5/15-10/30; 30-day lmt. FACILITIES: 10 sites (tr -22); tbls, toil, cga, f, no drk wtr. ACTIVITIES: Picnicking. Horseback riding (1 mi). MISC.: Elev 5000 ft; 7 acres. Pets.

Mud Spring (Ochoco NF). 4 mi E of Paulina on Co Hwy 112; 2-1/5 mi N on Co Hwy 113; 10-1/5 mi E on Co Hwy

135; 4-1/5 mi E on FS 158; 6 mi N on FS 127. **SEASON:** 6/1-10/20; 20-day lmt. **FACILITIES:** 3 sites (tr -22); tbls, toil, cga, f, no drk wtr. **ACTIVITIES:** Picnicking. Horseback riding (1 mi). Fishing (5 mi). **MISC.:** Elev 5000 ft; 4 acres. Pets permitted if kept on leash.

Sugar Creek (Ochoco NF). 3½ mi E on Co Hwy 112; 6½ mi N on Co Hwy 113; 4/5 mi N on FS 142; 1 mi E on FS 158. **SEASON:** 4/15-10/20. **FACILITIES:** 4 sites (tr -22); tbls, toil, cga, f, no drk wtr. **ACTIVITIES:** Picnicking. Fishing/horseback riding (1 mi). **MISC.:** Elev 4000 ft; 2 acres; stream. Pets.

Twin Spring (Ochoco NF). 3½ mi E of Paulina on Co Hwy 112; 6-3/5 mi N of Co Hwy 113; 16½ mi N on FS 142; 1-9/10 mi N on FS 1412. **SEASON:** 5/1-10/30. **FACILITIES:** 2 sites (tr -22); tbls, toil, cga. **ACTIVITIES:** Picnicking. **MISC.:** Elev 4500 ft. Pets.

Wolf Creek (Ochoco NF). 3½ mi E of Paulina on Co 112; 6-3/5 mi N on Co 113; 1-3/5 mi N on FS 142; 1/5 mi N on FS 154. **SEASON:** 4/15-10/20. **FACILITIES:** 17 sites (tr -22); tbls, toil, cga, f, no drk wtr. **ACTIVITIES:** Picnicking. Horseback riding/fishing (1 mi). **MISC.:** Elev 4100 ft; 3 acres; stream. Pets permitted.

PENDLETON

Deadman's Pass 20 mi SE of Pendleton on I-80N. **SEASON:** All yr. **FACILITIES:** Drk wtr. **MISC.:** Pets permitted if kept on a leash.

Stanfield Rest Area 22 mi W of Pendleton on I-80N. **SEASON:** All yr. **FACILITIES:** Drk wtr. **MISC.:** Pets permitted if kept on a leash.

Umatilla Forks (Umatilla NF). 32 mi E of Pendleton on Co Hwy N32. 3/5 mi SE on FS N32. **SEASON:** 4/20-11/30; 10-day lmt. **FACILITIES:** 24 sites (tr -22); tbls, toil, cga, piped drk wtr. **ACTIVITIES:** Picnicking. Fishing/horseback riding (1 mi). Nature trails (1 mi). **MISC.:** Elev 2300 ft; 5 acres. No garbage service. Scenic; river; pets; pack out garbage.

Mary's Peak (Siuslaw NF). 1 mi W on St Hwy 20; 9-1/10 mi SW on St Hwy 34; 9-1/5 mi NW on FS 3010. **SEASON:** 5/1-10/31. **FACILITIES:** 12 sites (no tr); tbls, toil, cga, piped drk wtr. **ACTIVITIES:** Picnicking; hiking. **MISC.:** Elev 3600 ft; 30 acres; pets; scenic.

PLUSH

Hart Mountain Nat'l Antelope Refuge (NWR). 65 mi NE of Lakeview via St Hwy 395 N; then St Hwy 140 E to Co Hwy 3A

Rd 313 to Plush; 26 mi NE on dirt rd to Refuge Headquarters. Ask for current map.

The refuge is usually accessible from May through October, although extreme weather conditions may shorten the period of accessibility. Many of the outlying areas within the Refuge are accessible only with four-wheel-drive vehicles, even during the summer months.

The Hot Springs Campground, located 3 mi S of Refuge Hdqtrs, is the only CG open year round. Three additional campgrounds, Guano Creek, Deer Creek, and Robinson Draw are designated as overflow areas and are available only during the fall hunting seasons. Although open all year, the Hot Springs CG is often inaccessible during the winter and early spring due to snow accumulation or muddy road conditions. THERE IS NO CAMPING FEE AT ANY OF THE CAMPGROUNDS.

CGs are primitive, with pit toilets only. Water must be carried from natural springs nearby. There are no individually designated campsites, but rather an open-camping system. CGs accommodate travel trailers as well as tents. Being primitive sites, there are, of course, no trailer hookups. Nor are there facilities on the Refuge for dumping trailer storage tanks. The nearest telephone is located at the Hart Mountain store in Plush.

Hiking in the remote parts of the refuge is gaining popularity. OVERNIGHT WILDERNESS CAMPING is allowed by special permit obtained at Refuge Headquarters.

Campfires are permitted during times of low fire hazard. Inquire at Refuge Hdqtrs for current regulations.

The possession of firearms in the field is permitted only during authorized refuge hunting seasons and only by those with the required permit.

Rockhounds are permitted to collect rock specimens not to exceed 7 pounds per person. Digging and blasting are prohibited. The removal of Indian artifacts is prohibited.

PORT ORFORD

Butler Bar (Siskiyou NF). 3 mi N of Port Orford on US 101; 7-2/5 mi SE on Co 208; 11-1/5 mi SE on FS 325. **SEASON:** 5/15-9/30; 14-day lmt. **FACILITIES:** 11 sites (tr -16); tbls, toil, cga, f, piped drk wtr. **ACTIVITIES:** Swimming; picnicking; fishing; berry-picking. **MISC.:** Elev 600 ft; 4 acres; river. 11 mi W of Elk River Fish Hatchery. Pets.

See page 7 for KEY TO ABBREVIATIONS.

McGribble (Siskiyou NF). 3 mi N of Port Orford on US 101; 7-2/5 mi SE on Co 208; 2-4/5 mi SE on FS 325; 1 mi S on FS 3302. SEASON: 5/15-9/30; 14-day lmt. FACILITIES: 5 tent sites (no trailers); tbls, toil, cga, piped drk wtr. ACTIVITIES: Picnicking. Fishing (1 mi). Swimming (2 mi). MISC.: Elev 800 ft: 2 acres; beach; pets. 10 mi NE of Humbog Mountain State Park.

Panther Creek (Siskiyou NF). 3 mi N of Port Orford on US 101; 7-2/5 mi SE on Co Hwy 208; 9-9/10 mi SE on FS 325. SEASON: 5/15-10/1; 14-day lmt. FACILITIES: 4 tent sites (no trailers); toil, cga, f. ACTIVITIES: Fishing; swimming. MISC.: Elev 600 ft. Pets.

Sixes River (BLM; Coos Bay Dist.). 4-2/5 mi N of Port Orford on US 101; 11 mi E on Sixes River Rd (gravel). SEASON: 6/1-10/31; 14-day lmt. FACILITIES: 19 sites (tr -16); tbls, toil, cga, dump, drk wtr, f. ACTIVITIES: Swimming; picnicking; fishing; hunting; hiking; berry-picking. MISC.: Elev 400 ft; 20 acres. Pets permitted if kept on a leash.

PORTLAND

Baldock Rest Area. 14 mi S of Portland on I-5. SEASON: All yr. FACILITIES: Drk wtr. MISC.: Nature study. Pets permitted if kept on a leash.

Gone Creek Forest Camp. 26 mi SE of Portland on US 26 & Skyline Rd; on Timothy Lake. SEASON: 6/1-9/1; 7-day lmt. FACILITIES: 50 sites (tr -20); tbls, toil, cga, drk wtr. ACTIVITIES: Swimming; fishing; boating,ld. MISC.: Pets.

Lake Harriet. 30 mi SE of Portland on Hwy 224; 6 mi E on Service Rd. SEASON: 5/1-10/1; 7-day lmt. FACILITIES: 6 sites (tr -20); tbls, toil, cga, drk wtr. ACTIVITIES: Picnicking; fishing; boating,l. MISC.: Pets.

Oxbow (Co. Pk.). Off US 26; 20 mi SE. SEASON: All yr. FACILITIES: 86 sites; tbls, toil, cga, f. ACTIVITIES: Picnicking; fishing; hiking; boating,l. MISC.: Scenic view. Pets permitted if kept on a leash.

POWERS

Boundary (Siskiyou NF). 4-1/5 mi SE of Powers on Co 90; 1/10 mi S on FS 333. SEASON: 5/30-9/30; 14-day lmt. FACILITIES: 5 tent sites (no trailers); tbls, f, no drk wtr. ACTIVITIES: Picnicking; fishing. MISC.: Pets permitted. Elev 300 ft; 1 acre; stream.

China Flat Rec. Area. 13 mi S of Powers. SEASON: All yr. FACILITIES: 20 sites. MISC.: Pets permitted if kept on leash.

Daphne Grove (Siskiyou NF). 4-1/5 mi SE of Powers on Co 90; 10-2/5 mi S on FS 333. SEASON: 5/30-9/30; 14-day lmt. FACILITIES: 13 tent sites (no trailers); tbls, toil, cga, f, piped drk wtr. ACTIVITIES: Swimming; picnicking; fishing; hiking; berry-picking. MISC.: Elev 800 ft; 6 acres; river; nature trails. Pets permitted if kept on a leash.

Myrtle Grove (Siskiyou NF). 4-1/5 mi SE of Powers on Co 90; 4½ mi S on FS 333. SEASON: 5/30-9/30; 14-day lmt. FACILITIES: 4 sites; tbls, toil, cga, f, no drk wtr. ACTIVITIES: Swimming; picnicking; fishing. MISC.: Elev 600 ft; 2 acres. Pets. River.

Rock Creek (Siskiyou NF). 4-1/5 mi SE of Powers on Co Hwy 90; 13 mi S on FS 333; 1-3/10 mi Sw on FS 3301. SEASON: 5/30-9/30; 14-day lmt. FACILITIES: 4 tent sites (no trailers); tbls, toil, cga, f, no drk wtr. ACTIVITIES: Swimming; picnicking; fishing; berry-picking; hiking. MISC.: Elev 1200 ft; 2 acres; stream; nature trails. Pets.

Squaw Lake (Siskiyou NF). 4-1/5 mi SE of Powers on Co 90; 12-3/5 mi S on FS 333; 4-3/5 mi SE on FS 321; 1 mi E on FS 3342. SEASON: 5/30-9/30; 14-day lmt. FACILITIES: 5 tent sites (no tr); tbls, toil, cga, no drk wtr. ACTIVITIES: Picnicking; fishing. MISC.: Elev 2200 ft; 2 acres; pets. Stream.

PRAIRIE CITY

Crescent (Malheur NF). 8-3/10 mi SE of Prairie City on Co Hwy 62; 8½ mi S on FS 1427. SEASON: 5/15-11/10; 14-day lmt. FACILITIES: 4 sites (tr -14); toil, cga, f, no drk wtr. ACTIVITIES: Fishing. MISC.: Elev 5200 ft; 2 acres. Pets.

Dixie Camp (Malheur NF). US 26; 8 mi E of town; 21 mi W John Day. SEASON: All yr; 10-day lmt. FACILITIES: 11 sites; tbls, toil, cga, f. ACTIVITIES: Picnicking; hiking. MISC.: Elev 4400 ft. Nature trails. Restful, shaded; needs leveling. Pets permitted if kept on leash.

Elk Creek (Malheur NF). 8-3/10 mi SE of Prairie City on Co Hwy 14; 16 mi S on FS 130; 1-3/10 mi S on FS 16. SEASON: 6/15-10/15. FACILITIES: 3 sites (tr -32); toil, cga, no drk wtr. ACTIVITIES: Fishing. MISC.: Elev 5100 ft; 1 acre. Adjacent to N fork Malheur River. Pets.

Indian Springs (Malheur NF). 1-1/10 mi W on St Hwy 26. FACILITIES: 7 sites (tr -16); tbls, toil, cga, piped drk wtr, store, gas, ice, showers, laundry, dump, food, visitor center, electricity in restrooms. ACTIVITIES: Picnicking; hiking. MISC.: Elev 4300 ft; 12 acres; pets.

Little Crane (Malheur NF). 8-3/10 mi SE of Prairie City on Co Hwy 14; 16 mi S on FS 13; 5-7/10 mi S on FS 16. SEASON: 6/1-11/10; 14-day lmt. FACILITIES: 5 sites (tr -16); tbls, toil, cga, no drk wtr. ACTIVITIES: Picnicking; fishing. MISC.· Elev 5600 ft; 1 acre; pets.

McNaughton Spring (Malheur NF). 6-3/5 mi S on Prairie City on Co Hwy 60; 1-4/5 mi S on FS 1428. SEASON: 6/1-10/15. FACILITIES: 4 sites (tr -22); tbls, toil, cga, f, no drk wtr. ACTIVITIES: Fishing. MISC.: Elev 4900 ft; 1 acre; pets.

North Fork Malheur (Malheur NF). 8-3/10 mi SE of Prairie City on Co 14; 16 mi SE on FS 13; 2 mi S on FS 16; 2-7/10 mi S on FS 13010. SEASON: 5/15-10/15. FACILITIES: 5 sites (tr -32); tbls, toil, cga, f, no drk wtr. ACTIVITIES: Picnicking; fishing. MISC.: Elev 4900 ft; 2 acres. On N fork Malheur River. Pets permitted if kept on leash.

Slide Creek (Malheur NF). 61-3/5 mi S on Co Hwy 60; 2-1/10 mi S on FS 1428. SEASON: 6/1-11/10. FACILITIES: 1 site (tr -22); tbls, toil, cga, no drk wtr. ACTIVITIES: Picnicking; fishing; horseback riding. MISC.: Elev 4900 ft; 1 acre; pets.

Strawberry (Malheur NF). 6-3/5 mi S of Prairie City on Co 60; 4-2/5 mi S on FS 1428. SEASON: 6/1-10/15; 14-day lmt. FACILITIES: 11 sites (tr -22); tbls, toil, cga, f. ACTIVITIES: Picnicking; fishing (1 mi). MISC.: Elev 5700 ft; 2 acres. End of rd at Strawberry Mtn Wilderness. Pets.

Trout Farm (Malheur NF). 8-3/10 mi SE of Prairie City on Co 14; 6-9/10 mi S on FS 14. SEASON: 5/1-11/10; 7-day lmt. FACILITIES: 8 sites (tr -16); tbls, toil, cga, f, piped drk wtr. ACTIVITIES: Picnicking; fishing. MISC.: Elev 4900 ft; 3 acres. Not designed for tr use; small fishing pond nearby. Pets.

PRINEVILLE

Antelope Reservoir (Ochoco NF). 29 mi SE of Prineville on Hwy 380; 9 mi S on FS 1729; 1-3/10 mi S on FS 1729G. SEASON: 4/23-10/23. FACILITIES: 24 sites (tr -32); tbls, toil, cga, f, no drk wtr. ACTIVITIES: Picnicking; fishing; boating;ld; swimming. MISC.: Elev 4600 ft; 20 acres; lake; beach. Access by walking for 25 yds from parking area for trailers under 32'. Pets permitted if kept on a leash.

Bandit Springs Rest Area. 29 mi NE of Prineville on US 26. SEASON: All yr.

FACILITIES: Drk wtr. MISC.: Scenic view. Pets permitted if kept on leash.

Canyon Creek (Ococho NF). 16-7/10 mi E of Prineville on US 26; 8¼ mi NE on Co Hwy 123; 2-4/5 mi SE on FS 142; 9/10 mi SE on FS 142K. SEASON: 6/15-10/15. FACILITIES: 5 sites (tr -22); toil, cga, f. MISC.: Elev 4400 ft. Pets.

Cayuse (Ococho NF). 9-1/5 mi E of Prineville on US 26; 10-9/10 mi N of FS 1331; 1-3/5 mi NW on FS 133; 2/5 mi N on FS 133G. SEASON: 6/17-10/18. FACILITIES: 3 sites (tr -32); tbls, toil, cga, f, no drk wtr. ACTIVITIES: Picnicking; rockhounding. Fishing (2 mi). Horseback riding (1 mi). MISC.: Elev 4100 ft; 5 acres; pets.

Cougar (Ochoco NF). 26 mi NE of Prineville on US 26; 1/10 mi S on FS 1356. SEASON: 5/1-10/15. FACILITIES: 6 sites (tr -22); tbls, toil, cga, f, no drk wtr. ACTIVITIES: Picnicking; fishing; rockhounding. MISC.: Elev 4000 ft; 1 acre. Pets permitted if kept on a leash.

Deep Creek (Ochoco NF). 16-7/10 mi E of Prineville on US 26; 8½ mi NE on Co 123; 23-3/5 mi SE on FS 142; 1/10 mi S on FS 142g. SEASON: 6/15-10/15. FACILITIES: 6 sites (tr -22); tbls, toil, cga, f, piped drk wtr. ACTIVITIES: Picnicking; fishing. MISC.: Elev 4200 ft; 2 acres. Pets, River.

Drake Creek (Ochoco NF). 34 mi SE of Prineville on US 380; 4-3/10 mi SE on FS 1728. SEASON: 6/17-10/18. FACILITIES: 4 sites (tr -32); tbls, toil, cga, f, piped drk wtr. ACTIVITIES: Picnicking; fishing; rockhounding. MISC.: Elev 4500 ft; 1 acre; pets.

Ochoco (Ochoco NF). 16-7/10 mi E of Prineville on US 26; 8-3/10 mi NE on Co Hwy 123; 1/10 mi N on FS 1332. SEASON: 5/15-10/15. FACILITIES: 5 sites (tr -22); toil, cga, f. ACTIVITIES: Fishing; rockhounding. MISC.: Elev 4000 ft. Pets permitted if kept on a leash.

Ochoco Divide (Ochoco NF). 30-4/5 mi NE of Prineville on US 26; 1/10 mi SE on FS 1207. SEASON: 10/16-5/14, FREE (weather permitting); ($2.00 rest of yr). FACILITIES: 28 sites (tr -22); tbls, toil, cga, f. ACTIVITIES: Picnicking; rockhounding. Fishing (2 mi). MISC.: Elev 4700 ft; 5 acres. Water shut off during free season. Pets.

Walton Lake (Ochoco NF). 16-7/10 mi E of Prineville on US 26; 8½ mi NE on Co Hwy 123; 6-1/5 mi NE on FS 1222. SEASON: 10/16-5/14, FREE (weather permitting); ($2.00 rest of yr). FACILITIES: 23 sites (tr -22); tbls, toil, cga. ACTIVITIES: Picnicking; rockhounding. MISC.: Elev 5000 ft; 6 acres. Pets.

See page 7 for KEY TO ABBREVIATIONS.

White Rock (Ochoco NF). 9-1/5 mi E of Prineville on US 26; 8½ mi N on FS 1224; 4½ mi E on FS 1334; 1-3/10 mi N on FS 1333. SEASON: 6/17-10/18. FACILITIES: 6 sites (tr -22); toil, cga, f. ACTIVITIES: Rockhounding. MISC.: Elev 5400 ft. Pets permitted.

Wildcat (Ochoco NF). 9-1/5 mi E of Prineville on US 26; 10-9/10 mi NE of FS 1331. SEASON: 4/23-10/23. FACILITIES: 17 sites (tr -32); tbls, toil, cga, f, drk wtr. ACTIVITIES: Rockhounding; picnicking. Fishing (1 mi). MISC.: Elev 3700 ft; 11 acres. Pets.

Wiley Flat (Ochoco NF). 34 mi SE of Prineville on US 380; 9-4/5 mi S on FS 1728; 1 mi W on FS 1728B. SEASON: 6/17-10/18. FACILITIES: 5 sites (tr -32); tbls, toil, cga, f, drk wtr. ACTIVITIES: Picnicking. Fishing (2 mi). Horseback riding (1 mi). MISC.: Elev 5000 ft; 3 acres; Pets.

PROSPECT

Huckleberry City (Rogue River NF). 17-2/5 mi E of Prospect on Hwy 62; 4-1/10 mi S on FS 311. SEASON: 6/25-10/15; 14-day lmt. FACILITIES: 15 sites (tr -22); tbls, toil, cga, f, drk wtr. ACTIVITIES: Picnicking; fishing. MISC.: Elev 5400 ft; 10 acres. 21 mi W of Crater Lake Nat'l Park. Pets. a leash.

Huckleberry Gap (Rogue River NF). 6 mi E of Prospect on St Hwy 62; 2 mi N on FS 318; 9 mi N on FS 3017. SEASON: 6/15-11/15; 14-day lmt. FACILITIES: 5 tent sites (no trailers); tbls, toil, cga, f, no drk wtr. ACTIVITIES: Picnicking; horseback riding. MISC.: Elev 5700 ft; 2 acres. Pets permitted if kept on leash.

Imnaha (Rogue River NF). 2-7/10 mi SE of Prospect on Co Hwy; 8 mi SE on FS 3317. SEASON: 5/15-10/15. FACILITIES: 4 tent sites (no trailers); tbls, toil, cga, f, no drk wtr. ACTIVITIES: Fishing; picnicking. MISC.: Elev 3800 ft; 2 acres. Pets permitted if kept on leash.

Lake West (Rogue River NF). 12 mi NE of Prospect on St Hwy 62; 12 mi N on St Hwy 230; 1 mi E on FS 2964; 7 mi E on FS 281. SEASON: 6/1-10/30; 14-day lmt. FACILITIES: 3 tent sites (no trailers); toil, cga, f. ACTIVITIES: Fishing. MISC.: Elev 5300 ft. Pets.

Mill Creek (Rogue River NF). 2 mi N of Prospect on Hwy 62; 1 mi E on FS 3247. SEASON: 5/1-10/20; 14-day lmt. FACILITIES: 8 sites (tr -22); tbls, toil, cga, f, no drk wtr. Store/gas/ice/snacks (3 mi). ACTIVITIES: Picnicking; fishing. MISC.: Elev 2800 ft; 2 acres. Pets permitted if kept on a leash.

Natural Bridge (Rogue River NF). 9-9/10 mi N of Prospect on Hwy 62; 1 mi W on FS 3106. SEASON: 6/1-10/20; 14-day lmt. FACILITIES: 21 sites (tr -22); tbls, toil, cga, no drk wtr. Store/ice/gas/snack bar (2 mi). ACTIVITIES: Picnicking; fishing. MISC.: Elev 3200 ft; 4 acres; river. 25 mi W on Crater Lake Nat'l Park. Pets. Visitor Center.

National Creek (Rogue River NF). SEASON: 6/1-11/1; 14-day lmt. FACILITIES: 4 sites (tr -16); toil, cga, f. ACTIVITIES: Fishing. MISC.: Elev 3800 ft. Pets permitted if kept on a leash.

River Bridge (Rogue River NF). 4 mi N of Prospect on Hwy 62; 1 mi W on FS 3103. SEASON: 5/1-10/20; 14-day lmt. FACILITIES: 6 sites (tr -22); tbls, toil, cga, f, no drk wtr. ACTIVITIES: Picnicking; fishing. MISC.: Elev 2900 ft; 2 acres; river. Pets.

Whiskey Creek (Rogue River NF). 19½ mi NE of Prospect on St Hwy 62; 1 mi E on FS 3162. SEASON: 6/15-10/20. FACILITIES: 5 sites (no tr); tbls, toil, cga, no drk wtr. ACTIVITIES: Picnicking. Fishing (3 mi). MISC.: Elev 4700 ft; 1 acre; pets. 12 mi W of Crater Lake National Park. Scenic.

REEDSPORT

Driftwood (Siuslaw NF). 12 mi N of Reedsport on US 101. Take exit, follow signs. SEASON: All yr. FACILITIES: 5 sites but area will hold up to 185 dispersed campers, mainly used by ORV's; toil, piped drk wtr. ACTIVITIES: Picnicking. MISC.: In Ore. Dunes NRA. Pets.

Eel Creek (Siuslaw NF). 12-1/10 mi SW of Reedsport on US 101. SEASON: All yr; 10-day lmt. FACILITIES: 85 sites (tr -22); tbls, flush toil, cga, f. Store/ice (1 mi). ACTIVITIES: Picnicking; boating, rld; hiking. Fishing/swimming (1 mi). MISC.: Elev 100 ft; 22 acres. 1 mi from Eel Lake. Sand dunes. Pets.

Lodgepole (Siuslaw NF). 12 mi N of Reedsport on US 101. Take Lodgepole CG exit. SEASON: All yr. FACILITIES: toil, piped drk wtr. MISC.: In Ore. Dunes NRA. Pets permitted if kept on a leash.

Noel Ranch (Siuslaw NF). 1-2/5 mi N on US 101; 8½ mi NE on Co 48. SEASON: All yr. 10-day lmt. FACILITIES: 5 sites (tr -16); tbls, toil, cga, no drk wtr. ACTIVITIES: Picnicking; fishing; boating. MISC.: Elev 100 ft; 3 acres; pets. On Smith River.

Smith River Falls (BLM; Coos Bay Dist.). 28 mi NE of Reessport on Smith Riv Rd, off US 101. SEASON: All yr; 14-day lmt. FAC: 8 sites; tbls, toil, cga, dump, no

See page 7 for KEY TO ABBREVIATIONS.

drk wtr. **ACTIVITIES:** Picnicking; berry-picking. Swimming/fishing (1 mi). **MISC.:** Elev 100 ft; 2 acres. Pets permitted if kept on a leash.

Umpqua River Rest Area. 13 mi E of Reedsport on St Hwy 38. **SEASON:** all yr. **MISC.:** Stream; scenic view. Pets.

RHODODENDRON

Barlow (NF). 7-9/10 mi E of Rhododendron on US 26; 2 mi E on St Hwy Old 26. **SEASON:** 6/1-9/30; 14-day lmt. **FACILITIES:** 4 sites (tr -16); tbls, toil, cga, f. **ACTIVITIES:** Picnicking; fishing. **MISC.:** Elev 3000 ft. Next to Kiwanis Camp. Pets.

Devils Meadow (NF). 1½ mi SE of Rhododendron on US 26; 6-4/5 mi NE on FS S24. **SEASON:** 6/13-9/30; 14-day lmt. **FACILITIES:** 3 tent sites (no trailers); tbls, toil, cga, f. **ACTIVITIES:** Picnicking; hiking. **MISC.:** Elev 3800 ft. Trailhead for Burnt & Cast lakes & Zig Zag Mtn. Pets.

Twin Bridges (NF). 7-9/10 mi E on US 26; 1-3/10 mi E on St Hwy Old 26. **SEASON:** 6/1-9/30; 14-day lmt. **FACILITIES:** 4 tent sites (no trailers); tbls, toil, cga, f. **ACTIVITIES:** Picnicking; fishing. **MISC.:** Elev 2800 ft. Trailhead for Paradise Park trail. Pets permitted.

RICHLAND

Copperfield Trailer Park (Private). Approx. 20 mi N of Richland on St Hwy 86. **SEASON:** All yr; 7-day lmt. **FACILITIES:** 100 sites (tr -25); tbls, flush toil. **ACTIVITIES:** Picnicking; fishing. **MISC.:** 6 acres; sewer/elec/wtr hookups Pets permitted if kept on a leash.

Eagle Forks (Wallowa Whitman NF). 8-1/10 mi NW of Richmond on Co 833; 2-7/10 mi N on FS 7735. **SEASON:** 6/1-10/31; 10-day lmt. **FACILITIES:** 7 sites (tr -16); tbls, toil, cga, f. Piped drk wtr. **ACTIVITIES:** Picnicking; fishing. **MISC.:** Elev 4000 ft; 3 acres; scenic; pets; stream.

RILEY

Chickahominy Reservoir (BLM; Burns Dist.) 6 mi W of Riley on US 20. **SEASON:** All yr; 14-day lmt. **FACILITIES:** primitive sites (tr -24); tbls, toil, cga, f. **ACTIVITIES:** Picnicking; fishing; boating,l; ice skating. **MISC.:** 200 acres. Pets.

ROSEBURG

Cabin Creek Rest Area. 18 mi N of Roseburg on I-5. **SEASON:** All yr. **FACILITIES:** Drk wtr. **MISC.:** Pets permitted if kept on a leash.

Scaredman Creek (BLM; Roseburg Dist.). 39½ mi NE of Roseburg on St Hwy 138 to Steamboat; 3 mi N on Canton Creek Rd. **SEASON:** 5/1-10/31; 14-day lmt. **FACILITIES:** 10 sites (tr -18); tbls, toil, cga, f, drk wtr. **ACTIVITIES:** Picnicking; swimming; hiking. **MISC.:** 10 acres. No motorbikes. Pets.

South Umpqua Rest Area. 13 mi S of Roseburg on I-5. **SEASON:** All yr. **FACILITIES:** Drk wtr. **MISC.:** Pets permitted.

RUFUS

LePage Park (COE; Lake Umatilla). 4 mi E of Rufus on I-84 at the John Day River Recreation Area Interchange, located at the mouth of the John Day River. **SEASON:** All yr; 14-day lmt. **FACILITIES:** 10-15 sites; toil; nearby are restrooms with hot showers (open April-Oct.), cga, tbls w/picnic shelters, drk wtr. **ACTIVITIES:** Boating,ld; swimming area and beach located between the day use and overnight camping area. Fishing. Hiking. Upland game bird and deer hunting on nearby public lands; closed to waterfowl hunting. Waterskiing.

* **PHILIPPI Park** (COE; Lake Umatilla). 4 mi E of Rufus on I-84 at the John Day River Recreation Area Interchange, located at the mouth of the John Day River then BY BOAT 3-½ mi upstream from LePage park along the east bank of the John Day River, or BY FOOT. **SEASON:** All yr; 14-day lmt. **FACILITIES:** Restrooms with hot showers, bar-b-ques and tables. Restrooms open Apr-Oct. Good fishing in John Day River. Hunting for upland game birds and deer. Closed to waterfowl hunting. Grassy tenting and play area. Float-circled swim bay with diving platform, large dock, ski float. Waterskiing; drk wtr.

ST. HELENS

Columbia Rest Area. 3 mi N of St. Helens on US 30. **SEASON:** All yr. **FACILITIES:** Drk wtr, cga. **MISC.:** Pets permitted if kept on a leash.

SALEM

Gervais Blue Star Memorial Rest Area. 10 mi N of Salem on US 99E. **SEASON:** All yr. **FACILITIES:** Drk wtr. **MISC.:** Scenic view; historical. Pets permitted if kept on a leash.

SANDY

Coffman (Mt. Hood NF). 2½ mi SE on US 26; 5-3/5 mi SE on Co Hwy; 7-4/5 mi SE on FS S35; 3 mi SE on TRAIL 761. **SEASON:** 6/15-9/30; 14-day lmt.

See page 7 for KEY TO ABBREVIATIONS.

FACILITIES: 1 tent site; tbls, toil, cga, f, no drk wtr. ACTIVITIES: Picnicking; horseback riding. MISC.: Elev 4000 ft; 1 acre; pets. Minimal developed site with shelter; Road S35 gated during summer.

* Eagle Creek South. 7 mi SE of Sandy on Co; 3 mi E on TRL 501. SEASON: 3/1-12/1. FACILITIES: 6 tent sites (no trailers); tbls, toil, cga, f, no drk wtr. ACTIVITIES: Picnicking; fishing. MISC.: Elev 2200 ft; 1 acre; stream. Pets permitted if kept on a leash.

SELMA

Deer Creek (BLM; Medford Dist.). 6 mi E of Selma on Deer Creek Rd. SEASON: 5/1-10/31; 14-day lmt. FACILITIES: 16 sites (tr -20); tbls, toil, cga, f. ACTIVITIES: Picnicking; fishing. MISC.: Elev 1484 ft; 10 acres; scenic view. Pets permitted if kept on a leash.

Lake Selmac (Co Pk). US 199; 2-7/10 mi E of town. SEASON: All yr. FACILITIES: 34 sites (tr -16); tbls, toil, cga, wtr hookup. ACTIVITIES: Swimming; picnicking; fishing; boating,rld; horseback riding,r; hiking; softball. MISC.: Elev 1400 ft; lake; nature trails. Pets.

Store Gulch (NF). 2 mi W of Selma on Co Hwy 5070; 8 mi W on FS 3504. SEASON: All year; 14-day lmt. FACILITIES: 4 tent sites (no trailers); tbls, toil, cga, piped drk wtr. ACTIVITIES: Picnicking; fishing; swimming. MISC.: Elev 1200 ft; 2 acres; scenic; river. Pets permitted if kept on a leash.

SENECA

Big Creek (Malheur NF). 20½ mi E of Seneca on FS 16; ½ mi N on FS 162E. SEASON: 5/15-11/10; 14-day lmt. FACILITIES: 14 sites (tr -22); tbls, toil, cga, f, well drk wtr. ACTIVITIES: Picnicking; fishing. MISC.: Elev 5100 ft; 4 acres; stream. On edge of Logan Valley. Pets.

Murray (Malheur NF). 19 mi E of Seneca on FS 16; 2 mi N on FS 1513. SEASON: 5/15-11/10; 14-day lmt. FACILITIES: 4 sites (tr -16); tbls, toil, cga, no drk wtr. ACTIVITIES: Picnicking; fishing. MISC.: Elev 5200 ft; 1 acre. Strawberry Mtn Wilderness within 5 mi. Pets.

Parish Cabin (Malheur NF). 12 mi E of Seneca on FS 162. SEASON: 5/15-11/20; 14-day lmt. FACILITIES: 20 sites (tr -22); tbls, toil, cga, piped drk wtr. ACTIVITIES: Picnicking; fishing. MISC.: Elev 4900 ft; 10 acres; pets.

Starr (Malheur NF). 9-1/10 mi N of Seneca on US 395. SEASON: 5/10-11/1; 14-day lmt. FACILITIES: 14 sites (tr -

16); tbls, toil, cga, f, piped drk wtr. ACTIVITIES: Picnicking. Fishing (5 mi). MISC.: Elev 5100 ft; 7 acres. Pets.

SILVER LAKE

East Bay (Fremont NF). ½ mi W of Silver Lake on Hwy 31; 13-1/5 mi S on FS 2823; 1½ mi W on FS 2823D. SEASON: 5/15-10/30; 14-day lmt. FACILITIES: 19 tent sites (no trailers); tbls, toil, cga, f, well drk wtr. ACTIVITIES: Swimming; picnicking; fishing; boating,l; hunting. MISC.: Elev 5000 ft; 6 acres; lake. Pets.

Silver Creek Marsh (Fremont NF). 1 mi W of Silver Lake on Hwy 31; 9-7/10 mi S on FS 288; 1/5 mi SW on FS 2919. SEASON: 5/15-10/30; 14-day lmt. FACILITIES: 5 tent sites (no trailers); tbls, toil, cga, f. ACTIVITIES: Picnicking; fishing. MISC.: Elev 5000 ft; 5 acres. Good rds; good camping; overflow area for Thompson Reservoir. Well drk wtr.

Thompson Reservoir (Fremont NF). 1 mi W of Silver Lake on Hwy 31; 13-7/10 mi S on FS 288; 1-1/10 mi E on FS 3024. SEASON: 5/15-10/30; 14-day lmt. FACILITIES: 22 sites (tr -22); tbls, toil, cga, f, well drk wtr. ACTIVITIES: Hunting; picnicking; fishing; swimming; boating,l. MISC.: Elev 5000 ft; 8 acres; lake; river. Excellent fishing. Pets. Good boat ramp. Good roads.

SISTERS

Black Pine Spring (Deschutes NF). 9 mi S on FS 1534. SEASON: 6/1-10/1; 14-day lmt. FACILITIES: 4 sites (tr -16); toil, cga, f, no drk wtr. ACTIVITIES: Picnicking. MISC.: Elev 4300 ft; 2 acres; pets.

Cold Spring (Deschutes NF). 5 mi W of Sisters on St Hwy 242. SEASON: 3/1-10/1; 14-day lmt. FACILITIES: 22 sites (tr -22); tbls, toil, cga, no drk wtr. Store/gas/ice/dump/showers/food (5 mi). ACTIVITIES: Picnicking. MISC.: Elev 3400 ft; 12 acres. Pets. Stream.

Driftwood (Deschutes NF). 17 mi S of Sisters on FS 1534; 1 mi S on FS 1795. SEASON: 6/15-9/15; 7-day lmt. FACILITIES: 16 sites (tr -16); tbls, toil, cga, f, store, ice, no drk wtr. ACTIVITIES: Swimming; picnicking; fishing; boating (rl, 1 mi), no motors. MISC.: Elev 6400 ft; 3 acres; pets; lake.

Graham Corral (Deschutes NF). 4½ mi NW of Sisters on US 20; 1 mi SW on FS 1424; 1 mi NW on FS 1375; 1 mi W on FS 1445. SEASON: 4/1-11/1; 14-day lmt. FACILITIES: 10 sites (tr -16); tbls, toil, cga, piped drk wtr. ACTIVITIES: Horseback riding/rental; picnicking. MISC.: Elev 3400 ft; 1 acre; pets.

Huckleberry Lake (Deschutes NF). 13-2/5 mi W of Sisters on St Hwy 242; ¼ mi SE on FS 150. SEASON: 7/15-10/31; 10-day lmt. FACILITIES: 3 tent sites (no trailers); f. MISC.: Elev 5100 ft. Very rough road into CG; lake unsatisfactory for fishing. Pets permitted. if kept on a leash.

Lava Camp Lake (Deschutes NF). 17 mi W of Sisters on Hwy 242; 1 mi SE on FS 1550. SEASON: 6/1-9/1; 14-day lmt. FACILITIES: 12 sites (tr -22); tbls, toil, cga, no drk wtr. ACT: Swimming; picnicking; fishing. MISC.: Elev 5200 ft; 7 acres; lake; geological interest. Pets permitted if kept on leash.

Round Lake (Deschutes NF). 12 mi NW of Sisters on Hwy 20; 5 mi NW on FS 1319. SEASON: 5/1-10/1; 14-day lmt. FACILITIES: 5 tent sites (no trailers); tbls, toil, cga, no drk wtr. ACTIVITIES: Swimming; picnicking; fishing; boating (no motors); horseback riding. MISC.: Elev 4200 ft; 1 acre; lake. Pets.

Suttle Lake (Deschutes NF). 14 mi NW of Sisters on St Hwy 20. SEASON: 5/1-10/1. FACILITIES: 7 tent sites (no trailers); tbls, toil, cga, piped drk wtr. Store/ice (3 mi). Gas (1 mi). ACTIVITIES: Picnicking; fishing; swimming; boating,rl/waterskiing (1 mi). Horseback riding (3 mi). MISC.: Elev 3400 ft; 6 acres; lake. Pets permitted.

Three Creek Lake (Deschutes NF). 17 mi S of Sisters on FS 1534; 1 mi S on FS 1745. SEASON: 6/15-9/15; 7-day lmt. FACILITIES: 10 sites (tr -16); tbls, toil, cga, no drk wtr. Store/ice/food (3 mi). ACTIVITIES: Swimming; picnicking; fishing. Boating,rl (3 mi). Horseback riding (1 mi). MISC.: Elev 6300 ft; 12 acres. Pets permitted if kept on a leash.

Three Creek Meadow (Deschutes NF). 17 mi S of Sisters on Co Hwy 1534. SEASON: 6/15-9/15; 14-day lmt. FACILITIES: 10 sites (tr -16); tbls, toil, cga, f, no drk wtr. Store/ice/gas (3 mi). ACTIVITIES: Picnicking. Boating/swimming/fishing (3 mi). MISC.: Elev 6300 ft; 12 acres; stream. Pets permitted.

Whispering Pine (Deschutes NF). 6 mi W of Sisters on St Hwy 242; 5 mi S on FS 1535. SEASON: 5/30-9/30; 14-day lmt. FACILITIES: 8 sites (tr -22); tbls, toil, cga. ACTIVITIES: Picnicking; fishing; horseback riding. MISC.: Elev 4400 ft; 3 acres; pets.

SPRAY

Bull Prairie (Umatilla NF). 13 mi NE on St Hwy 207; 3 mi NE on FS 2039; 1/2 mi SE on FS 30. SEASON: 5/1-11/30; 10-day lmt. FACILITIES: 21 sites (tr -32); tbls, toil, cga, f, piped drk wtr. ACTIVITIES: Picnicking. Fishing/swimming/boating,ld,no motors (1 mi). MISC.: Elev 4900 ft; 7 acres; pets. On lake shore.

Fairview (Umatilla NF). 12 mi NE on St Hwy 207; 1/2 mi W on FS 400. SEASON: 5/1-11/30. FACILITIES: 5 sites (tr -16); tbls, toil, cga, f, piped drk wtr. ACTIVITIES: Picnicking. Fishing/swimming/boating,ld (4 mi). MISC.: Elev 4100 ft; 7 acres; pets. 4 mi from Bull Prairie Area.

SPRINGFIELD

Finn Rock Rest Area 8 mi E of Springfield on St Hwy 126. SEASON: All yr. ACTIVITIES: Boating,l; fishing. MISC.: Stream. Pets permitted if kept on leash.

Little Falls Creek Rec. Area (Private). 15 mi SE at end of Little Fall Creek Rd. SEASON: All yr. FACILITIES: tbls, toil, cga. ACTIVITIES: Swimming; fishing; horseshoes; playing field. MISC.: Pets permitted if kept on a leash.

STAYTON

Elkhorn Valley (BLM). 17-20 E of Stayton, off St Hwy 22. SEASON: All yr; 7-day lmt. FACILITIES: 16 sites (tr -16); toil, drk wtr. ACTIVITIES: Picnicking; fishing; swimming; hiking. MISC.: Elev 1000 ft. Pets.

SUMPTER

Blue Springs (Wallowa Whitman NF). 3 mi NW of Sumpter on Hwy SH220; 5½ mi SW on FS 73. SEASON: 5/30-11/20; 10-day lmt. FACILITIES: 6 sites (tr -16); tbls, toil, cga, no drk wtr. Store/snacks/ice (5 mi). ACTIVITIES: Picnicking. Fishing (3 mi). MISC.: Elev 5600 ft; 2 acres. Must haul water approx. 1 mi. Pets permitted if kept on a leash.

Deer Creek Campground (Wallowa Whitman NF). 3 mi E of Sumpter on Hwy S220. 3 mi N on FS 6530. SEASON: 5/10-10/30; 10-day lmt. FACILITIES: 8 sites (tr -16); tbls, toil, cga, f, dump, no drk wtr. ACTIVITIES: Swimming; picnicking; fishing; boating,l; waterskiing. MISC.: Elev 4600 ft; 2 acres; stream. Secluded;low use. Pets.

McCully Forks (Wallowa Whitman NF). 3 mi NW of Sumpter on Hwy SH220. SEASON: 5/30-10/30; 10-day lmt. FACILITIES: 7 sites (tr -16); tbls, toil, cga, no drk wtr. Store/ice/snacks (3 mi). ACTIVITIES: Picnicking; fishing. MISC.: Elev 4600 ft; 2 acres; pets; historic. Cool in summer; small stream on site.

hiking. MISC.: Elev 250 ft; 10 acres; scenic view. Pets.

See page 7 for KEY TO ABBREVIATIONS.

425

SUTHERLIN

Tyee (BLM;Roseburg Dist.). 12 mi NW of Sutherline on Hwy 138 & Co 57 (Bullock Rd). SEASON: 5/1-10/31; 14-day lmt. FACILITIES: 11 sites (tr -18); tbls, toil, cga, f, drk wtr. Store (1 mi). ACTIVITIES: Swimming; picnicking; fishing;

SWEET HOME

Lost Prairie (Willamette NF). 39-1/5 mi E of Sweet Home on US 20. SEASON: 6/15-11/15; 10-day lmt. FACILITIES: 10 sites (tr -22); tbls, toil, cga. ACTIVITIES: Picnicking. MISC.: Elev 3300 ft; 7 acres. Pets permitted if kept on a leash.

Yukwah (Willamette NF). 19-3/10 mi E on Highway 20. SEASON: All yr ; 10-day lmt. FACILITIES: 23 sites (tr -22); tbls, toil, cga, well drk wtr. Store/gas/cafe/snack bar (4 mi). ACTIVITIES: Picnicking; fishing; hiking. MISC.: Elev 1300 ft; 15 acres. Yukwah nature trail around campground. Pets. Swimming.

TAFT

North Creek (Siuslaw NF). 3-1/10 mi S of Taft on US 101; 5-1/10 mi SE on Hwy 229; 5-3/10 mi N on FS 727. SEASON: 4/14-10/15; 10-day lmt. FACILITIES: 11 tent sites (no trailers); tbls, toil, cga, f, no drk wtr. ACTIVITIES: Swimming; picnicking; fishing. MISC.: Elev 400 ft; 3 acres. Pets permitted if kept on leash.

Schooner Creek (Siuslaw NF). 1 mi S of Taft on US 101; 6-4/5 mi NE on Co 106; 1 mi S on FS S7000. SEASON: 4/15-10/15; 10-day lmt. FACILITIES: 5 tent sites (no trailers); tbls, toil, cga, f, well drk wtr. ACTIVITIES: Picnicking; fishing. MISC.: Elev 200 ft; 4 acres; stream. Pets permitted if kept on a leash.

TILLAMOOK

Farmer Creek Rest Area. 17 mi S of Tillamook on US 101. SEASON: All yr. ACTIVITIES: Boating,l; fishing. MISC.: Stream. Pets permitted if kept on a leash.

Fern Rock Rest Area. 28 mi NE of Tillamook on St Hwy 6. SEASON: All yr. FACILITIES: Drk wtr. MISC.: Stream. Pets.

Tillamook River Rest Area. 5 mi S of Tillamook on US 101. SEASON: All yr. FACILITIES: Drk wtr. ACTIVITIES: Fishing. MISC.: Stream; nature study. Pets.

Wilson River Rest Area. 23 mi E of Tillamook off St Hwy 6. ACTIVITIES: Fishing; swimming. SEASON: All yr. MISC.: Pets permitted if kept on leash.

TILLER

Beaver Swamp Trail Head (Umpqua NF). 3/10 mi SE on St Hwy 227; 6-1/5 mi NE on Co Hwy 46; 20-2/5 mi NE on FS 284; 1-7/10 mi SE on FS 2830; 4-2/5 mi NE on FS 2840. SEASON: 4/20-

10/30. FACILITIES: 1 site (tr -16); tbls, toil, cga, f, no drk wtr. ACTIVITIES: Picnicking; hiking. Fishing/swimming/boating (2 mi). MISC.: Elev 4000 ft; 1 acre; scenic; pets. 2 mi on Trail 1572 to Fish Lake; hikers only.

TILLER

Boulder Creek (Umpqua NF). 3/10 mi SE of Tiller on St Hwy 227; 6-1/5 mi NE on Co Hwy 46; 7-7/10 mi NE on FS 284. SEASON: 5/20-10/31; 14-day lmt. FACILITIES: 8 sites (tr -16); tbls, toil, cga, well drk wtr. ACTIVITIES: Picnicking; fishing; swimming. MISC.: Elev 1400 ft. Pets. 3 acres.

*Buckeye Lake (Umpqua NF). 3/10 mi SE on St Hwy 227; 6-1/5 mi NE on Co Hwy 46; 20-2/5 mi NE on FS 284; 5-3/10 mi SE on FS 2830; 1½ mi SE on TRAIL 1575 or ¼ mi SE on TRAIL 1578. SEASON: 4/20-10/30. FACILITIES: 1 tent site; tbls, toil, cga, no drk wtr. ACTIVITIES: Picnicking; fishing; swimming; boating (no motors). Horseback riding (1 mi). MISC.: Elev 4200 ft; 2 acres; scenic; lake; pets.

Buckhead Mtn (Umpqua NF). 6 mi NE of Tiller on Co Hwy 46; 17-7/10 mi NE on FS 284; 4 mi N on FS 276; 5½ mi N on FS 2814. SEASON: 6/1-9/15; 14-day lmt. FACILITIES: 5 sites (tr -16); toil, cga. MISC.: Elev 5100 ft. Pets.

Camp Comfort (Umpqua NF). 3/10 mi SE of Tiller on St Hwy 227; 6-1/5 mi NE on Co Hwy 46; 17-9/10 mi NE on FS 284; 2 mi NE on FS 2739. SEASON: 5/20-10/31; 14-day lmt. FACILITIES: 6 sites (tr -16); tbls, toil, cga. ACTIVITIES: Picnicking; swimming; fishing; hiking. MISC.: Elev 2000 ft; 3 acres; pets. One open front shelter avail.

* Cliff Lake (Umpqua NF). 3/10 mi SE of Tiller on St Hwy 227; 6-1/5 mi NE on Co Hwy 46; 20-2/5 mi NE on FS 284; 1½ mi SE on TRAIL 1575; 4/5 mi SE on TRAIL 1578. SEASON: 4/20-10/30. FACILITIES: 4 tent sites; tbls, toil, cga, f, no drk wtr. ACTIVITIES: Picnicking; fishing; swimming; hiking; boating (no motors). Horseback riding (1 mi). MISC.: Elev 4400 ft; 2 acres; nature trails; scenic; pets.

Cover (Umpqua NF). 3/10 mi E of Tiller on Hwy 227; 5 mi NW on Co 46; 13 mi E on FS 293. SEASON: 5/15-10/30; 14-day lmt. FACILITIES: 6 sites (tr -16); tbls, toil, cga, no drk wtr. ACTIVITIES: Swimming; picnicking; fishing. MISC.: Elev 1700 ft; 3 acres. Pets permitted.

*Cripple Camp (Umpqua NF). 3/10 mi SE of Tiller on St Hwy 227; 5 mi NE on Co Hwy 46; 22 mi E on FS 293; 6-7/10 mi E on FS 2933; 7/10 mi NE on TRAIL 1435. SEASON: 6/15-10/30. FACILITIES: 1 tent site; tbls, toil, cga, f, no drk wtr. ACTIVITIES: Picnicking; hiking. Horseback riding/fishing (1 mi). MISC.: Elev 5000 ft; 1 acre; pets.

Dumont Creek (Umpqua NF). 3/10 mi SE of Tiller on Hwy 227; 6-1/5 mi NE on Co 46; 5-2/5 mi NE on FS 284. SEASON: 5/20-10/31; 14-day lmt. FACILITIES: 6 sites (tr -16); tbls, toil, cga, no drk wtr. ACTIVITIES: Swimming; picnicking; fishing. MISC.: Elev 1300 ft; 2 acres. Pets; stream.

Fish Lake Trail Head (Umpqua NF). 3/10 mi SE on St Hwy 227; 6-1/5 mi NE on Co Hwy 46; 20-2/5 mi NE on FS 284; 1-7/10 mi SE on FS 2830; 3/10 mi NE on FS 2840. SEASON: 4/20-10/30. FACILITIES: 2 sites (tr -16); tbls, toil, cga, f, no drk wtr. ACTIVITIES: Picnicking; hiking; fishing. Boating/swimming (4 mi). Horseback riding (1 mi). MISC.: Elev 3000 ft; 2 acres, stream; scenic; pets. 4 mi on Trail 1570 to Fish Lake.

Huckleberry Lake (Umpqua NF). 3/10 mi E of Tiller on St Hwy 227; 5 mi NE on Co Hwy 46; 9-3/5 mi E on FS 293; 15 mi SE on FS 2923. SEASON: 6/15-10/30; 14-day lmt. FACILITIES: 3 tent sites (no trailers); toil, cga. MISC.: Elev 5200 ft. Pets permitted if kept on a leash.

Neal Springs (Umpqua NF). 3/10 mi E of Tiller on Hwy 227; 5 mi NE on Co 46; 9-3/5 mi E on FS 293; 15-1/5 mi SE on FS 2923. SEASON: 6/15-10/30; 14-day lmt. FACILITIES: 7 sites (no tr); tbls, toil, cga. ACTIVITIES: Picnicking. MISC.: Elev 5200 ft; 3 acres; pets.

Threehorn (Umpqua NF). 12-7/10 mi SE of Tiller on Hwy 227. SEASON: 5/15-10/30; 14-day lmt. FACILITIES: 6 sites (tr -22); tbls, toil, cga, no drk wtr. ACTIVITIES: Picnicking. MISC.: Elev 2600 ft; 7 acres. Pets permitted.

TYGH VALLEY

Bonney Crossing (Mt. Hood NF). 6 mi NW of Tygh Valley on Co Hwy 226; 1 mi W on FS 408; 2 mi NW on FS 466; 1-2/5 mi N on FS 3010 (rough rd). SEASON: 4/15-11/24. FACILITIES: 8 tent sites (no trailers); tbls, toil, cga, no drk wtr. ACTIVITIES: Boating; picnicking; hunting. Horseback riding (5 mi). MISC.: Elev 2200 ft; 1 acre; stream; pets.

UKIAH

Bear Wallow Creek (Umatilla NF). 11 mi E of Ukiah on St Hwy 244. SEASON: 5/15-11/30; 10-day lmt. FACILITIES: 9 sites (tr -22); tbls, toil, cga, f, piped drk wtr. ACTIVITIES: Picnicking; fishing (1 mi). MISC.: Elev 3900 ft; 4 acres. Pets permitted if kept on a leash.

Big Creek (Umatilla NF). 22-9/10 mi SE of Ukiah on FS S522. SEASON: 6/1-11/30. FACILITIES: 4 sites (tr -16); toil. MISC.: Elev 5200 ft. Pets.

Drift Fence (Umatilla NF). 7-7/10 mi S on Ukiah on FS S522. SEASON: 6/1-11/30. FACILITIES: 6 sites (tr -22); cga, f, toil. ACTIVITIES: Hunting. MISC.: Elev 4300 ft. Popular camp for big game hunters. Pets permitted if kept on leash.

Divide Well (Umatilla NF). 1-1/10 mi W of Ukiah on Hwy 244; 7/10 mi N onn US 395; 16-7/10 mi W on FS S518; 8-3/10 mi SE on FS S415. SEASON: 6/15-11/30; FACILITIES: 5 sites (tr -22); f, no drk wtr. MISC.: 4 acres. Pets.

Four Corners (Umatilla NF). 20½ mi E of Ukiah on St Hwy 244. SEASON: 5/15-11/30; 10-day lmt. FACILITIES: 6 sites (tr -30); tbls, toil, cga, f, no drk wtr. Store (4 mi). ACTIVITIES: Picnicking. Fishing (1 mi). Swimming (4 mi). MISC.: Elev 4300 ft; 8 acres. Lehman Hot Springs Resort (4 mi). Pets permitted.

Frazier (Umatilla NF). 18-1/10 mi E on Hwy 244; 1/2 mi S on FS S226; 2/10 mi E on FS 20. SEASON: 5/15-11/30; 10-day lmt. FACILITIES: 29 sites (tr -32); tbls, toil, cga, no drk wtr. Store (1 mi). Showers (2 mi). ACTIVITIES: Picnicking; horseback riding. Fishing (1 mi). Swimming (2 mi). MISC.: Elev 4300 ft; 10 acres; scenic; pets. Swimming & therapeutic pools, motels & cabins. A popular camp for big game hunters.

Frazier CR Meadows (Umatilla NF). 18-1/10 mi E of Ukiah on St Hwy 244; 5½ mi SE on FS S534. SEASON: 6/15-11-30. FACILITIES: 3 tent sites (no trailers); toil, f. ACTIVITIES: Hunting. MISC.: Elev 5400 ft. Remote hunter camp. Pets.

Hunter Spring (Umatilla NF). 12 mi E of Ukiah on St Hwy 244; 7½ mi S on FS S20; 1 mi NW on FS S535. SEASON: 6/1-11/30. FACILITIES: 3 sites (no trailers); toil. ACTIVITIES: Hunting. MISC.: Elev 4500 ft. Remote Hunter camp. Pets permitted if kept on leash.

Lane Creek (Umatilla NF). 10½ mi E of Ukiah on Hwy 244. SEASON: 5/15-11/30; 10-day lmt. FACILITIES: 10 sites (tr -32); tbls, toil, cga, f, no drk wtr. **ACTIVITIES:** Horseback riding; picnicking; fishing (1 mi). **MISC.:** Elev 3800 ft; 6 acres. A popular camp for big game hunters. Pets permitted.

N.F. John Day (Umatilla NF). 38½ mi SE of Ukiah on FS 52. **SEASON:** 6/15-11/15; 10-day lmt. **FACILITIES:** 7 sites (tr -22); tbls, toil, cga, f, no drk wtr. **ACTIVITIES:** Horseback riding; picnicking; fishing (1 mi). **MISC.:** Elev 5200 ft; 3 acres. Not fully developed; 8 mi to Granite. Pets.

Wapitii (Umatilla NF). 18-1//10 mi E of Ukiah on St Hwy 244; 65 mi SE on FS S534. **SEASON:** 6/15-11/30. **FACILITIES:** 3 tent sites (no trailers); toil, f. **ACTIVIT?ES:** Hunting. **MISC.:** Elev 5500 ft. Remote hunter camp. Pets.

UNION

North Catherine Trailhead (Wallowa Whitman NF). 10 mi SE of Union on Co Rd 203; 4 mi E on FS 7700; 3½ mi NE on FS 7785. **SEAS:** 6/15-10/30; 10-day lmt. **FACILITIES:** 5 sites (tr -22); tbls, toil, cga, no drk wtr. **ACTIVITIES:** Hiking; picnicking; fishing; boating; waterskiing. **MISC.:** Elev 4400 ft; 3 acres; stream. Pets permitted if kept on leash.

UNITY

Dad's Camp (Wallowa Whitman NF). 1½ mi N on Co Hwy 507. **SEASON:** 6/1-9/15; 10-day lmt. **FACILITIES:** 2 sites (tr -16); tbls, toil, cga, f, no drk wtr. **ACTIVITIES:** Picnicking; berry-picking. **MISC.:** Elev 4000 ft; 3 acres; stream; pets.

Mammoth Springs (Wallowa Whitman NF). 1½ mi SW on St Hwy 6005. **SEASON:** 6/1-9/15; 10-day lmt. **FACILITIES:** 3 sites (tr -16); tbls, toil, cga, f, no drk wtr. **ACTIVITIES:** Picnicking. **MISC.:** Elev 4400 ft; 4 acres; stream; pets.

Oregon (Wallowa Whitman NF). 10½ mi NW of Unity on US 26. **SEASON:** 10/2-5/31, FREE ($1.00 rest of yr); 10-day lmt. **FACILITIES:** 8 sites (no trailers); tbls, toil, cga, no drk wtr. **ACTIVITIES:** Hiking; picnicking; fishing. **MISC.:** Elev 5000 ft; 4 acres. Water shut off during FREE season. Pets.

South Fork (Wallowa Whitman NF). 5½ mi SW of Unity on Co Hwy 1300; 1 mi SW on FS 1159. **SEASON:** 6/1-9/15; 10-day lmt. **FACILITIES:** 17 sites (tr -16); tbls, toil, cga, f, piped drk wtr. **ACTIVITIES:** Berry-picking; picnicking; fishing. **MISC.:** Elev 4800 ft; 8 acres; stream. Pets permitted if kept on a leash.

Stevens Creek (Wallowa Whitman NF). 7 mi SW on Co Hwy 6005. **SEASON:** 6/1-9/15; 10-day lmt. **FACILITIES:** 3 sites (tr -16); tbls, toil, cga, f, no drk wtr. **ACTIVITIES:** Picnicking; berry-picking. **MISC.:** Elev 4400 ft; 3 acres; stream; pets.

Wetmore (Wallowa Whitman NF). 8-1/5 mi NW of Unity on US 26. **SEASON:** 10/2-5/31, FREE ($1.00 rest of yr); 10-day lmt. **FACILITIES:** 13 sites (no trailers); tbls, toil, cga, f, piped drk wtr. **ACTIVITIES:** Rockhounding; picnicking; fishing; waterskiing; hiking. **MISC.:** Elev 4400 ft. Handicap trail to Yellow Pine CG. Water shut off during FREE season. Pets permitted if kept on leash.

Yellow Pine (Wallowa Whitman NF). 9-1/5 mi NW of Unity on US 26. **SEASON:** 10/2-5/31, FREE ($1.00 rest of yr). **FACILITIES:** 21 sites (no trailers); tbls, toil, cga, f. **ACTIVITIES:** Hiking; picnicking; fishing. **MISC.:** Elev 4400 ft; 1 acre; nature trails. Water shut off during FREE season. Pets.

VALE

City Park. US 20 S part of town. **SEASON:** All yr. **MISC.:** Pets permitted if kept on a leash.

Twin Springs (BLM; Dist.). 1 mi E. of 80 N.; 20; 28 mi S on gravel road. **SEASON:** 4/1-11/1; 14-day lmt. **FACILITIES:** 3 sites (tr -20); tbls, toil, cga, f, dump, drk wtr. **ACTIVITIES:** Hiking; picnicking; fishing; hunting. **MISC.:** Elev 3240 ft; 160 acres; stream; lake; creek. Pets.

VERONICA

Scaponia (BLM; Salem Dist.). 7 mi NE of Veronica on St Hwy 47. **SEASON:** All yr. **FACILITIES:** 7 sites; cga, drk wtr. **ACTIVITIES:** Hiking; picnicking; fishing; hunting. **MISC.:** Elev 600 ft; scenic. Pets permitted if kept on a leash.

VIDA

Gate Creek Park. 1½ mi N of St Hwy 126. **SEASON:** All yr. **FACILITIES:** 2 sites; toil, drk wtr. **ACTIVITIES:** Fishing.

WALDPORT

Canal Creek (Suislaw NF). 7 mi E of Waldport on Hwy 34; 4-1/10 mi S on FS 3462. **SEASON:** All yr. **FACILITIES:** 12 sites (tr -22); tbls, toil, cga, well drk wtr. Snack bar (4 mi). **ACTIVITIES:** Boating;rld; picnicking; fishing. **MISC.:** Elev 200 ft; 8 acres; stream. First 2 mi of rd 3462 narrow & winding not recommended for trailers. Pets.

Maples (Siuslaw NF). 20-3/5 mi E on Waldport on Hwy 34; 3 mi S on Co Hwy

33; 1-2/10 mi W on Co Hwy 32. SEA-
SON: 5/25-12/1; 10-day lmt. FACILI-
TIES: 7 sites (tr -16); tbls, toil, cga,
no drk wtr. ACTIVITIES: Picnicking;
swimming; fishing. MISC.: Elev 200
ft; 2 acres; river; pets.

Slide (Siuslaw NF). 15½ mi E of Waldport on Hwy 34. SEASON: 5/25-12/1; 10-
day lmt. FACILITIES: 8 sites (tr -16);
tbls, toil, cga. Store/ice/gas (5 mi).
ACTIVITIES: Swimming; picnicking; fishing; boating,1 (2 mi). MISC.: Elev 100
ft; 4 acres; pets; no drk wtr.   15½
road miles from Pacific Ocean.

WALLA WALLA

Squaw Spring (Umatilla NF). 2 mi E of
Walla Walla on US 12; 16 mi E on Co
Hwy; 12-7/10 mi E on FS 55; 5-1/10 mi
S on FS 64.   SEASON: 7/1-11/15. FACIL-
ITIES: 10 sites (tr -22); tbls, toil, cga,
f, no drk wtr. ACTIVITIES: Picnicking;
horseback riding. MISC.: Elev 5000 ft;
3 acres; scenic. Pets. Pack out garbage.

WALLOWA

Boundary (Wallowa Whitman NF). 5 mi
S of Co Hwy 515; 1-9/10 mi S on FS
S163.   SEASON: 6/15-11/1; 10-day lmt.
FACILITIES: 12 sites (tr -16); tbls, toil,
cga, f, no drk wtr. ACTIVITIES: Swim-
ming; picnicking; fishing; berry-picking.
MISC.: Elev 3600 ft; 4 acres; stream.
Pets permitted if kept on a leash.

Summit Spring (Wallowa Whitman NF).
4 mi NE of Wallowa on Co Hwy 786; 7-
1/5 mi N on Co Hwy 762; 1-3/5 mi NE
on FS N430. SEASON: 5/15-11/30; 10-day
lmt. FACILITIES: 7 sites (tr -16); toil,
cga, f. MISC.: Elev 4600 ft. Pets.

WAMIC

Badger Lake (Mt. Hood NF). 6 mi SW of
Wamic on Co Hwy 226; 11 mi SW on FS
408; 10 mi NW on FS 339; 5 mi NW on
FS 340. SEASON: 7/1-10/31; 10-day lmt.
FACILITIES: 4 tent sites (no trailers);
tbls, toil, cga, f, no drk wtr. ACTIVI-
TIES: Swimming; picnicking; fishing;
boating,1 (no motors). Horseback riding
(5 mi); berry-picking. MISC.: Elev 4400
ft; 1 acre; lake. Pets.

Bonney Crossing (Mt. Hood NF). 6 mi NW
of Wamic on Co Hwy 226; 1 mi W on FS
408; 2 mi NW on FS 466; 1-2/5 mi N on
FS 3010. SEASON: 4/15-11/10. FACILITIES:
8 sites (no trailers); tbls, toil, cga,
f, no drk wtr. ACTIVITIES: Boating;
picnicking; fishing. Horseback riding
(5 mi). MISC.: Elev 2200 ft; 1 acre;
stream. Pets permitted if kept on leash.

Bonney Meadows (Mt. Hood NF). 6 mi SW
of Wamic on Co Hwy 226; 14-7/10 mi SW
on FS 408; 5-9/10 mi N on FS 338. SEA-
SON: 7/1-10/31; 10-day lmt. FACILITIES:

4 sites (tr -22); tbls, toil, cga, f, no
drk wtr. ACTIVITIES: Berry-picking;
picnicking; fishing. Horseback riding
(5 mi). MISC.: Elev 4800 ft; 1 acre;
stream. Pets permitted if kept on leash.

* Boulder Lake (Mt. Hood NF). 6 mi SW
of Wamic on Co Hwy 226; 12-1/5 mi SW
on FS 408; 5-7/10 mi N on FS 446; ½
mi W on TRAIL 463. SEASON: 6/15-10/31;
14-day lmt. FACILITIES: 4 tent sites;
tbls, toil, cga, f, no drk wtr. ACTIVI-
TIES: Swimming; picnicking; fishing;
boating (no motors). MISC.: Elev 4600
ft; 2 acres, lake. Pets.

Forest Creek (Mt. Hood NF). 6 mi SW
of Wamic on Co Hwy 226; 12-3/5 mi SW
on FS 408; 1 mi SE on FS 415; 1/5 mi
S on FS 30. SEASON: 6/1-10/31; 10-day
lmt. FACILITIES: 5 sites (tr -22); tbls,
toil, cga, f, no drk wtr. ACTIVITIES:
Picnicking; fishing. MISC.: Elev 3000
ft; 2 acres; stream; historical interest;
horseback riding (5 mi). Pets permitted.

Jean Lake (Mt. Hood NF). 6 mi SW of
Wamic on Co Hwy 226; 10½ mi SW on
FS 408; 10-3/10 mi NW on FS 339; 2 mi
NE on FS 21. SEASON: 7/1-10/31; 14-day
lmt. FACILITIES: 3 tent sites (no trailers); toil, cga, f, no drk wtr. ACTIVI-
TIES: Swimming; picnicking; fishing;
boating,1 (no motors). MISC.: Elev 4800
ft; 2 acres; lake. Pets permitted.

Post Camp (Mt. Hood NF). 6 mi SW of
Wamic on Co Hwy 226; 11 mi SW on
FS 408; 2 mi NW on FS 339; 7/10 mi
W on FS 468. SEASON: 6/1-10/31. FACIL-
ITIES: 3 sites (tr -22); tbls, toil, cga,
f, no drk wtr. ACTIVITIES: Picnicking;
fishing. Horseback riding (5 mi).
MISC.: Elev 4000 ft; 1 acre. Pets.

WESTFIR

Kiahanie (Willamette NF). 19-3/10 mi
NE of Westfir on FS 196. SEASON: 4/15-
11/20; 10-day lmt. FACILITIES: 21 sites
(tr -16); tbls, toil, cga, piped drk
wtr. ACTIVITIES: Picnicking; fishing.
MISC.: Elev 2200 ft; 15 acres; river.
Pets permitted if kept on a leash.

Skookum Creek (Willamette NF). 31-2/5
mi NE on FS 196; 3-7/10 mi SE on FS
163. SEASON: 5/15-10/15; 10-day lmt.
FACILITIES: 8 sites (tr -16); tbls, toil,
cga, well drk wtr. ACTIVITIES: Picnicking; horseback riding. Swimming/fishing
(2 mi). MISC.: Elev 4500 ft; 2 acres.
Begin trail access to Erma Bell & other
high country lakes. Pets.

WEST LINN

Willamette Falls Rest Area. I-205 at West
Linn. SEASON: All yr. FACILITIES: Drk
wtr. MISC.: Stream, water falls, scenic
view. Pets permitted if kept on a leash.

See page 7 for KEY TO ABBREVIATIONS.

WESTON

Dusty Spring (Umatilla NF). 17½ mi E on Hwy 204; 2-3/5 mi E on FS 64; 7½ mi NE on FS 6403. SEASON: 7/1-10/15. FACILITIES: 5 sites (tr -16); tbls, toil, cga, f, no drk wtr. ACTIVITIES: Picnicking; berry-picking. Horseback riding (1 mi). Fishing (4 mi). MISC.: Elev 5600 ft; 3 acres; pets; scenic.

Mottet (Umatilla NF). 17½ mi E on Hwy 204; 2-1/10 mi E on FS 64; 4/5 mi NE on FS 20; 9-1/12 mi NE on FS 6403. SEASON: 7/1-10/15. FACILITIES: 9 sites (tr -22); tbls, toil, cga, f, no drk wtr. ACTIVITIES: Picnicking; berry-picking. Fishing and horseback riding (1 mi). MISC.: Elev 5200 ft; 4 acres; stream; pets; scenic. Pack out garbage.

Target Meadows (Umatilla NF). 17½ mi E on Hwy 204; 3/10 mi E on FS N50; 2-1/5 mi N on FS N41. SEASON: 6/15-11/25; 10-day lmt. FACILITIES: 14 sites (tr -22); tbls, toil, cga, f, piped drk wtr. Store/gas/food (5 mi). Dump (3 mi). ACTIVITIES: Picnicking; fishing; berry-picking. Horseback riding (1 mi). MISC.: Elev 5000 ft; 2 acres; pets; historic. Pack out garbage.

Woodward (Umatilla NF). 17½ mi E of Weston on Hwy 204. SEASON: 6/1-10/15; 10-day lmt. FACILITIES: 26 sites (tr -22); tbls, toil, cga, f. ACTIVITIES: Picnicking; horseback riding. Fishing (1 mi). MISC.: Elev 5100 ft; 15 acres. Pets; piped drk wtr; berry-picking.

WHITE CITY

North Fork (Rogue River NF). 28-1/10 mi NE on Co Hwy 140; 1 mi S on FS 3706. SEASON: 5/20-9/30; 14-day lmt. FACILITIES: 7 sites (tr -16); tbls, toil, cga, no drk wtr. Store/ice/gas (3 mi). ACTIVITIES: Picnicking; fishing; boating,rld. Swimming (3 mi). MISC.: Elev 4500 ft; 2 acres; pets.

WOLF CREEK (Co Pk).. From I-5 take town exit, on Main St. SEASON: All yr. FACILITIES: 10 sites; tbls, toil, cga. ACTIVITIES: Picnicking; rockhounding; hiking. MISC.: Pets.

YACHATS

Big Creek (NF). 10-7/10 mi S of Yachats on US 101; 6-2/5 mi E on FS 57. SEASON: All yr. FACILITIES: 4 sites (tr -16); tbls, toil, cga, no drk wtr. ACTIVITIES: Picnicking; fishing. MISC.: Elev 500 ft; 1 acre. Cape Perpetua scenic area 14 mi NW; Rd 1658 narrow & winding. Pets.

Tenmile Creek (NF). 7 mi S of Yachats on US 101; 5-3/5 mi E on FS 56. SEASON: All yr. FACILITIES: 4 sites (tr -16); tbls, toil, cga, no drk wtr. ACTIVITIES: Picnicking; fishing. MISC.: Elev 400 ft; Cape Perpetua scenic area 10 mi NW; Road 56 narrow & winding. Pets. 2 acres.

ZIGZAG

* **Burnt Lake** (Mt. Hood NF). 4 mi NE of Zigzag on Co; 4 mi NE on FS S25; 3 mi S on TRAIL 727. SEASON: 7/1-11/1. FACILITIES: 12 tent sites; f, no drk wtr. ACTIVITIES: Swimming; fishing. MISC.: 2 acres. Pets.

* **Cast Lake** (Mt. Hood NF). 2 mi E of Zigzag on US 26; 5 mi N on FS 27; 3 mi NE on TRAIL 727; 1 mi W on TRAIL 767. SEASON: All yr. FACILITIES: 7 sites; f, no drk wtr. ACTIVITIES: Horseback riding; fishing. MISC.: 1 acre; pets.

* **Goat Creek** (Mt. Hood NF). 6 mi S of Zigzag on FS S38; 4 mi E on TRAIL 742. SEASON: 5/1-11/1. FACILITIES: 7 sites; f, no drk wtr. ACTIVITIES: Fishing. MISC.: 1 acre. Pets.

Riley (Mt. Hood NF). 4-4/5 mi NE of Zigzag on Co N12; 1-1/5 mi E on FS S25; 1/10 mi SE on FS S250. SEASON: 5/1-9/30; 14-day lmt. FACILITIES: 11 sites (tr -22); tbls, toil, cga, f, piped drk wtr. ACTIVITIES: Horseback riding; picnicking; fishing. MISC.: Elev 2100 ft; 8 acres; stream. Horse unloading & horse bars provided. Pets.

* **Rolling Rifle** (Mt. Hood NF). 1/5 mi W of Zigzag on US 26; 4-9/10 mi S on FS S38; 1-4/5 mi E on TRAIL 742. SEASON: 5/15-9/30; 14-day lmt. FACILITIES: 10 tent sites; tbls, toil, cga, f, no drk wtr. ACTIVITIES: Hiking; picnicking; fishing. MISC.: Elev 2000 ft; 1 acre. Min. developed site along Salmon River Trail. Pets permitted if kept on a leash.

* **Rushing Water** (Mt. Hood NF). 4 mi NE of Zigzag on Co; 3 mi NE on FS S25; 2 mi NE on TRL 797; 1 mi S on Trail 2000. SEASON: 5/1-11/1. FACILITIES: 7 tent sites; tbls, toil, cga, no drk wtr. MISC.: Elev 3400 ft;1 acre;stream;pets. ACTIVITIES: Picnicking; fishing.

* **Yocum Ridge** (Mt. Hood NF). 4 mi NE of Zigzag on Co; 3 mi NE on FS S25; 2 mi NE on TRAIL 797; 3 mi E on TRAIL 771. SEASON: 7/1-10/1. FACILITIES: 5 tent sites; f, no drk wtr. MISC.: 2 acres. Pets permitted if kept on a leash.

See page 7 for KEY TO ABBREVIATIONS.

PENNSYLVANIA

GENERAL STATE INFORMATION

Miscellaneous

Right Turns on Red: Permitted after
   full stop, unless otherwise posted.
STATE CAPITOL: Harrisburg
STATE NICKNAME: Keystone State
STATE MOTTO: Virtue, Libery, and Independence
STATE BIRD: Ruffed Grouse
STATE FLOWER: Mountain Laurel
STATE TREE: Eastern Hemlock

State Parks

Overnight camping fees range from $2.00-3.00 per night. No pets in overnight or swimming areas; okay in day use areas. Further information: Commonwealth of Pennsylvania; Department of Environmental Resources; PO Box 1467; Harrisburg, PA 17120.

Rest Areas

Overnight stops are not permitted in Pennsylvania Rest Areas.

The Appalachian Trail

More than 2000 miles long, the Appalachian Trail (from Maine to Georgia) is the longest continuous marked trail in the world.

CAMPING: More than 200 open-front shelters/lean-tos are spaced approximately 10 miles apart on the Trail (one-day intervals). As they are occupied on a first-come first-served basis, carry a tent in case the shelters are full. Potable spring water is usually available at each site, but should be purified by tablets or boiling. And always "pack it in, pack it out".

PERMITS: No permit is required to hike the Trail. However, camping permits must be obtained for overnight stays in Shenandoah NP (Luray, VA 22835) and Great Smoky Mountains NP (Gatlinburg, TN 37733). These are free of charge and available from the ranger stations or by mail. A free camping permit must be obtained for overnight stays in White Mountain National Forest Restricted Use Area (PO Box 638; Laconia, NH 03246).

APPALACHIAN TRAIL CONFERENCE: A private, nonprofit, national organization which represents citizen's interest in the Appalachian Trail. They offer detailed guidebooks and maps for sale, as well as the A.T. Data Book which gives the location and distances between shelters and certain post offices, supply points, water sources, lodging and meals. For more information on this organization, write to them at: PO kBox 236; Harpers Ferry, WV 25425.

Tiadaghton State Forest Camping

Temporary camping is permitted on the Tiadaghton State Forest provided campers possess a free camping permit. Camping permits may be obtained from the District Office (423 East Central Avenue; South Williamsport, PA; 717/326-3576) or at the Forest Foreman's headquarters at Little Bear Creek, Ranchtown, Ross Village and Pump Station. Backpackers need not secure a permit if they sign the trail registers located on maintained hiking trails.

Two types of camping will be recognized: (1) Backpack camping, utilizing a tent and other gear transported on the trail by use of a backpack; (2) Family Unit Camping, utilizing a large tent, tent trailer, camping van, trailer or mobile camper. No more than 3 family units may camp at one location. Family camping units will be limited to a stay of 7 days. Backpackers are limited to one night at any one site without a·permit; a permit must be obtained to camp for a longer period. Further information: Forest Supervisor; Tiadaghton SF; 423 East Central Avenue; South Williamsport, PA.

Backpack Camping Along The Quehanna Trail

A free camping permit is required. The route of the Quehanna Trail is marked with orange paint blazes placed on trees every 150-200 feet along the trail route. Two

PENNSYLVANIA

Backpack Camping Along The Quehanna Trail (cont.)

blazes, one over the other, indicate a change in trail direction. Connector trails are marked in a similar manner with blue paint. 2-night limit per campsite. The Quehanna Trail passes near numerous springs and small runs. These sources of water are not tested for contamination. It is recommended that you boil or treat your drinking water. Camping is NOT permitted on State Game lands. Free permits and further information: District Forester; Moshannon SF; Box 34, 1229 South Second Street; Clearfield, PA 16840; 814/765-5361. OR, District Forester; Elk SF; RD #1, Route 155, Box 327; Emporium, PA 15834; 814/483-3354.

Susquehannock Trail System "STS"

Backpack in the beautiful Allegheny Mountains. Travel through unspoiled forests, over mountains 2500 feet high, through meadows and along streams, in areas inhabited only by the whitetail deer, black bear and wild turkey. Enjoy nature at its best on the 85-mile Susquehannock Trail System. Trail entrances are located at the Northern Gateway, U.S. Route 6, on Denton Hill or Southern Gateway, on Route 144 in Cross Fork. For further information and list of publications: Potter County Recreation, Inc.; PO Box 245; Coudersport, PA 16915.

Backcountry Camping in Allegheny NF

Six "boat-access" primitive type campgrounds are located on the Allegheny Reservoir. Camping within the NF is not permitted on the shores and within 1500 feet of the timberline around Allegheny and Tionesta Reservoirs, except in areas developed or designated for such use. In addition, no camping will be allowed within 1500 feet of the Allegheny Reservoir Scenic Drive and the main access roads into Jakes Rock, Rimrock, and Old State Road Recreation Areas. A similar 1500-foot camping restriction applies to either side of the main channel of Kinzua Creek from Red Bridge upstream to Mead Run. Campfire permits are not required. Further information: Forest Supervisor; Allegheny NF; PO Box 847; Warren, PA 16365.

INFORMATION SOURCES

Maps

Detailed, up-to-date maps are available from **Forsyth Travel Library** (see order form in Appendix B) for the **State of Pennsylvania** and numerous Pennsylvania cities.

State Information

Bureau of Travel Development; Pennsylvania Department of Commerce; 431 South Office Building; Harrisburg, PA 17120.
Department of Environmental Resources; PO Box 1467; Harrisburg, PA 17101. [Information on State Parks and State Forests.]
Fish Commission; PO Box 1673; Harrisburg, PA 17120.
Game Commission; PO Box 1567; Harrisburg, PA 17120.

Miscellaneous

Philadelphia Chamber of Commerce; 121 S. Broad St.; Philadelphia, PA 19107.
Chamber of Commerce of Greater Pittsburgh; Chamber of Commerce Building; Pittsburgh, PA 15219.
Allegheny NF; PO Box 847; Warren, PA 16365.
Corps of Engineers, Pittsburgh District; Federal Building; 1000 Liberty Avenue; Pittsburgh, PA 15222.
Corps of Engineers, Baltimore District; PO Box 1715; Baltimore, MD 21203. [Free campgrounds in Pennsylvania.]

FREE CAMPGROUNDS

BRADFORD

* Old State Road (Allegheny NF). 2-3/10 mi S of Bradford on US 219; 6-2/5 mi SW on St Hwy 770; 7-7/10 mi W on St Hwy 59; 2-3/10 mi W on Co TRAIL. **SEASON:** 4/1-10/31. **FACILITIES:** 28 sites (no tr); well drk wtr; tbls, toil, cga,f. Showers/ice/food (5 mi). **ACTIVITIES:** Picnicking; fishing; hiking; sailing; water skiing. Boating,d, (r 1, 5 mi). Swimming (lifeguard, 5 mi). **MISC.:** Elev 1400 ft; 8 acres; pets. Scenic. Allegheny Reservoir.

ENTRIKEN

* Peninsula Boat-to-Shore Campground (COE: Raystown Lake). Approximately 2-4/5 mi W of Entriken on St Hwy 26; approx. 2 mi SE on LR 31025 to Shy Beaver Boat Launch. Campground can be reached BY BOAT or HIKING, and is located between Markers 23 and 24 on the lake. 3 mi S, BY BOAT from Shy Beaver Boat Launch. HIKE IN access may be gained from the Terrace Mountain Trail which runs from Weaver's

Bridge North to Trough Creek State park. At Beaver Boat Launch: parking area, toil, no drk wtr, boat launch. At Campground: 29 campsites; toil, drk wtr, tbls cga, f. Pets. Open April 1st-mid/December, weather permitting.

* **Putt's Boat-to-Shore Campground** (COE; Raystown Lake). Approximately 2-4/5 mi W of Entriken on St Hwy 26; approximately 2 mi SE on LR 31025 to Shy Beaver Boat Launch. Campground is located at Marker 26 on the lake. BOAT access. HIKE IN access may also be gained from the Terrace Mountain Trail. This camp is approximately 2-1/2 mi N from Weaver Falls Boat Launch and 6-1/2 mi S from Tatman Run Boat Launch At Shy Beaver Boat Launch: parking area, toil, drk wtr, boat launch. At campground: 12 sites; toil, drk wtr, cga, tbls. April 1-mid/December (weather permitting). Pets.

Rothrock Campground (COE; Raystown Lake). Located off St Hwy 994 approximately 5 mi E of St Hwy 26 at Entriken. SEASON: 4/1-mid/May & mid/Sept.-Dec. (weather permitting) FREE; [Mid/May-mid/Sept.,$4]. FACILITIES: Six camps with the total of 200 sites. Tbls, toil, drk wtr, dump, cga, f. MISC.: Pets.

HAWLEY

*Bruce Lake State Forest Natural Area. 12 mi S of Hawley on St Hwy 390; 5 mi to the Natural Area which is adjacent to Promised Land State Park. SEASON: All year; 14-day lmt. FACILITIES: 10 tent sites; tbls, toil, drk wtr. ACTIVITIES: Picnicking; fishing; snowmobiling (Winter). MISC.: 2300 acres; pets. Accessible only by means of a 2-3 mile foot trail; and only a limited number of camping permits are issued at the Promised Land State Park Office. The sites are near a natural glacial lake formation.

ERIE

Hammermill Paper Company Recreation Area. There are no specifically identified campsites or any developed facilities for providing water, restroom accomodations, picnic tables or fireplaces. However, a self-contained camping unit is welcome to utilize any suitable site on the 170,000 acres of hardwood forest land in northwestern Pennsylvania and southwestern New York owned by Hammermill Paper Company. Write to them at PO Box 14400, Erie, PA 16533, to obtain their Sportsmans Maps. SEASON: All Year. ACTIVITIES: Picnicking; hiking; fishing; hunting. MISC.: Pets.

HESSTON

Seven-Points Campground (COE: Raystown Lake). 3 mi E of St Hwy 26 at Hesston. SEASON: 4/1-mid/May & mid/Sept.-mid/Dec, FREE. [Mid/May-mid/Sept $4]. FACILITIES: 5 camps, total of 162 sites. Tbls, tiol, cga, f, drk wtr, dump. ACTIVITIES: Picnicking. MISC.: Adjacent is a large day-use area with a boat launch, 400-slip marina, boat rentals, beach, food, bath house, Concrete-bottomed swimming area.

Susquehannock Campground (COE; Raystown Lake). 7-1/2 mi E/NE on St Hwy 26 at Hesston and 3-1/2 mi NE of the Administration Building; at marker 7. (Along the western lakeshore 7 mi above the dam, 2 mi downlake of Seven Points.) SEASON: MD to mid/September. FACILITIES: 62 sites; toil, tbls,cga, f. ACTIVITIES: Picnicking; swimming. MISC.: An exclusive beach. No drk wtr. Pets. Dump at nearby Seven Points Campground.

HUNTINGDON

Branch Campground (COE; Raystown Lake). 4 mi off St Hwy 22 at Huntington on TR 434, 4 mi downstream of the breast of Raystown Dam on the Raystown Branch of the Juniata River. (3 mi below Dam.) SEASON: 4/1-mid/May and mid/September to December, FREE;(mid/May to mid/September, $3). FACILITIES: 29 sites; toil, tbls, no drk wtr. ACTIVITIES: Picnicking; fishing; boating; canoeing; swimming. MISC.: Pets.

KANE

Big Rock Overflow (Allegheny NF). 8 mi NW of Kane on St Hwy 321. SEASON: 5/24-9/5; 14-day lmt. FACILITIES: 25 sites (tr -22); no drk wtr, no tbls, toil. Ice/food/store (1 mi). Showers (3 mi). ACTIVITIES: Boating,d (r 1, 1 mi). Fishing (1 mi). Swimming (lifeguard, 3 mi). Water skiing (4 mi). MISC.: Elev 1400 ft; 4 acres; pets.

Galbos (City Park). On St Hwy 321. SEASON: All year. FACILITIES: 3 sites. ACTIVITIES: Picnicking. MISC.: Elev 2100 ft.

MARKLESBURG

*Nancy's Boat-to-Shore Campground (COE; Raystown Lake). Located at Marker 16 on the lake. 3 mi BY BOAT from James Creek Boat Launch which is located approximately 4/5 mi W of Marklesburg on St Hwy 26; approximately 4/5 mi S/SE to launch. SEASON: 4/1 to mid/Dec. (weather permitting). FACILITIES: 34 sites; toil, drk wtr, tbls, cga. ACTIVITIES: Picnicking; boating. MISC.: Pets.

MILLVILLE

*Fisherman's Camp (Allegheny Power System). Located at its Millville Project on the Shenandoah River. Located on an island in the river and is only accessible BY BOAT. SEASON: All year; 14-day lmt. MISC.: No facilities. Pets.

NEW BETHLEHEM

Mahoning Creek Lake (COE; Mahoning Creek Lake). 6 mi S of New Bethlehem on St Hwy 66 & paved access rds to campground. SEASON: All year; 14-day lmt. FACILITIES: 10 sites (tr -20); tbls, toil, cga, f. ACTIVITIES: Picnicking; boating,l. Fishing/swimming nearby. MISC: Pets.

Sportsman's Area (COE; Mahoning Creek Lake). 6 mi S of New Bethlehem on St Hwy 66 and paved rds to campground. SEASON: 4/1-12/1; 14-day lmt. FACILITIES: 12 sites (tr -20); tbls, toil, cga, f. ACTIVITIES: Picnicking; fishing; boating,l. Swimming nearby. MISC.: Pets.

NORTH EAST

Pennsylvania Tourist Information Center. On I-90 at New York/Pennsylvania state line. SEASON: All year; 1-day lmt. FACILITIES: Sites. MISC: Pets.

ROCKWOOD

Laurel Ridge State Park. The 15,425 acre park stretches along the Laurel Mountain from the picturesque Youghiogheny River to Ohiopyle to the Conemaugh Gorge near Johnstown. This large park spans Cambria, Fayette, Somerset and Westmoreland Counties. [Information: Laurel Ridge State Park, Department of Environmental Resources, RD 3, Rockwood, PA 15557; phone 412/455-3744.] LAUREL HIGHLANDS HIKING TRAIL. SEASON: All year; 14-day lmt, in park, but only one night at a hiking shelter. ACTIVITIES: Picnicking; fishing; hiking; hunting. MISC.: No pets at a shelter. Major 70-mi hiking/backpacking trail. The trail is blazed approximately every 100 ft with 2x5 yellow blazes. Side trails are marked with blue blazes. Mileage monuments are found every mile. Large wooden signs mark trail access points at every major highway crossing. Six 30-car parking areas provide starting points and water. Every 8-10 miles along the trail, one of 8 overnight shelter areas are located. Each area contains 5 adirondack-type shelters with fireplaces, 2 latrines, a water supply and spaces for 30 tents. A Hiker's Guide to the Laurel Highlands Trails is available from the Pennsylvania Chapter of the Sierra Club, PO Box 7404, Pittsburg, PA 15213.

SALTSBURG

Loyalhanna Lake (COE; Bush Lake). 4 mi S of Saltsburg. SEASON: 5/15-9/15; 14-day lmt. FACILITIES: 32 sites (tr-20); toil, tbls, cga; no drk wtr. Store /ice nearby. ACTIVITIES: Picnicking; fishing; boating,l. MISC.: Pets.

SHARPSVILLE

Mercer Recreation Area (COE; Shenango River Lake). Take exit I-N off I-80 in Pennsylvania. The exit sign will

SHARPSVILLE (cont.)

Mercer Recreation Area (cont.) say "Sharon, Farrell". The sign will also say PA 60. Exit onto PA 60 North. Go approximately 1/4 mi and exit on PA 18 North. Go approximately 1/4 mi and exit on PA 18 North. Take PA 18 North approximately 9 mi until you cross the lake. At the N end of the Causeway, immediately after you cross the lake, make a right turn off PA 18 onto East Lake Drive. Proceed on East Lake Drive approximately 1-3/4 mi; the entrance will be a dirt road on your right. The area itself sets back off the road along the lake; but is visible from the road. [The Area is approximately 9 mi N of I-80 and approximately 5 mi from the Pennsylvania/Ohio border.] SEASON: MD-LD (No free camping at the project off-season.); 14-day lmt. FACILITIES: 30 sites; flush toil, running water, tbls, cga. ACTIVITIES: Picnicking; fishing; boating; water skiing; sailing; canoeing; hiking. MISC.: Pets. Kidd's Mills Covered Bridge nearby.

TIONESTA

City Park. (in town. SEASON: All year; 1-day lmt. FACILITIES: Sites.

★ **Glassner Run** (COE; Tionesta Lake). On Tionesta Lake, near Tionesta. Boat access. SEASON: April-November. FACILITIES: 12 sites; no drk wtr; toil, tbls, cga. ACTIVITIES: Picnicking; fishing; boating. MISC.: Pets. 14-day lmt.

★ **Kellettville Recreation Area** (COE; Tionesta Lake). On Tionesta Lake, near Tionesta. SEASON: All year; 14-day lmt. FACILITIES: 24 sites (tr-20). Drk wtr, tiol, dump, 6 walk-in primative sites. Food/store nearby. ACTIVITIES: Fishing, boating,l; swimming. MISC.: Pets.

★ **Lackey Flats** (COE; Tionesta Lake). On Tionesta Lake, near Tionesta. Boat access. SEASON: April-November. FACILITIES: 28 sites; no drk wtr; tbls, toil, cga. ACTIVITIES: Picnicking; fishing; boating. 14-day lmt.

★ **Upper Tionesta Boat Access** (Allegheny NF). 1 mi S of Tionesta on St Hwy 36; 3 mi E, BY BOAT. SEASON: 5/30-9/2; 14-day lmt. FACILITIES: 20 tent sites; toil, tbls, cga, f. Grocery/gas/ice/laundry/food (1 mi). ACTIVITIES: Picnicking; fishing; water skiing; sailing; boating (l, 1 mi). MISC.: Elev 1100 ft; 16 acres; pets. Access by boat only. 2nd travel route signed to Tionesta Reservoir.

WARREN

* **Handsome Lake** (Allegheny NF). 2 mi SE of Warren on US 6; 10 mi E on St Hwy 59; 9 mi N, BY BOAT. SEASON: 4/1-10/31; 14-day lmt. FACILITIES: 10 tent sites; tbls, toil, cga, f, well drk wtr. Showers/food/gas (5 mi). ACTIVITIES: Picnicking; fishing; water skiing; sailing; boating,d r, (1, 1 mi). Swimming (lifeguard, 5 mi). MISC.: Elev 1400 ft; 7 acres; pets. This campground is accessible only by boat on Allegheny Reservoir.

* **Hooks Brook** (Allegheny NF). 2 mi SE of Warren on US 6; 10 mi E on St Hwy 59; 7-4/5 mi N, BY BOAT. SEASON: 4/1-10/31; 14-day lmt. FACILITIES: 20 tent sites; toil, tbls, cga, well drk wtr. ACTIVITIES: Picnicking; fishing; water skiing; boating,d (1, 2 mi). MISC.: Elev 1300 ft; 10 acres; pets. Campground is accessible only by boat on Allegheny Reservoir.

* **Hopewell** (Allegheny NF). 2 mi SE of Warren on US 6; 10 mi E on St Hwy 59; 4 mi N, BY BOAT. SEASON: 4/1-10/31; 14-day lmt. FACILITIES: 8 tent sites; tbls, toil, cga, f, well drk wtr. ACTIVITIES: Picnicking; fishing; waterskiing; sailing; boating,rld. Swimming (lifeguard, 4 mi). MISC.: Elev 1400 ft; 5 acres; pets. Campground in accessible by boat on Allegheny Reservoir. Visitor Center (4 mi).

* **Morrison** (Allegheny NF). 2 mi SE of Warren on US 6; 10 mi E on St Hwy 59; 4-1/10 mi SE, BY BOAT. SEASON: 4/1-11/30; 14-day lmt. FACILITIES: 32 tent sites; tbls, toil, cga, f, piped drk wtr. Showers/dump (3 mi). Food/gas/ Visitor Center (4 mi). ACTIVITIES: Picnicking; fishing; sailing; water skiing. Boating,d (1, 1 mi; r, 4 mi). Swimming (lifeguard, 3 mi). MISC.: Elev 1300 ft; 20 acres; pets. Campground acaessible only by boat on Allegheny

* **Pine Grove** (Allegheny NF). 2 mi SE on US 6; 10 mi E on St Hwy 59;

1 mi N on Co Hwy. SEASON: 4/1-10/31; 14-day lmt. FACILITIES: 15 sites (no tr); tbls, toil, cga, f, well drk wtr. Food/gas/showers (2 mi). ACTIVITIES: Picnicking; fishing; skiing; sailing. Boating, rld/swimming (2 mi). MISC.: Elev 1400 ft; 20 acres; lake; pets. Campground accessible only by boat on Allegheny Reservoir.

WILCOX

East Branch Camping Area (COE; East Branch Lake). 6 mi from Wilcox on Legislative Route 24013 to main entrance of dam. Follow signs. SEASON: LD-MD, FREE (rest of yr, $2). FACILITIES: 41 sites; tbls, cga, drk wtr, flush toil, dump. ACTIVITIES: Picnicking; hiking. MISC.: 9 acres; pets.

East Branch Over Flow Area (COE; East Branch Lake). 6 mi from Wilcox on Legislative Route 24013 to main entrance of dam. Follow signs. Located on the right side of main entrance to the lake. SEASON: All year; 14-day lmt. FACILITIES: 15 sites; toil, drk wtr, tbls, dump are located at the nearby East Branch Camping Area.

A PICNIC AREA is located on the hilltop above the right abutment of the dam on approximately 3 acres of forested land. Facilities include paved parking spaces for 102 vehicles, a public sanitary shelter, 24 picnic tbls, 10 grills and an overlook area.

BOAT LAUNCHING AREA: Located on the right bank of the lake approximately 1500 ft upstream from the dam. The facilities include a parking area for 38 car-trailers and 50 cars, 2 turnarounds, a single-laned concrete launching ramp and a vault-type comfort station. Drk wtr. Hiking. ACTIVITIES: Boating; hiking; fishing; hunting; water skiing; bird-watching; picnicking.

READ THIS!

See page 7 for KEY TO ABBREVIATIONS.

RHODE ISLAND

Miscellaneous

Toll-Free Number for Travel Information:
   1-800-556-2484/5 [out-of-state calls]
Right Turns on Red: Permitted after
   full stop, unless otherwise posted.
STATE CAPITOL: Providence
STATE NICKNAME: Little Rhody
STATE MOTTO: "Hope"
STATE BIRD: Rhode Island Red
STATE FLOWER: Violet
STATE TREE: Red Maple

State Parks

Overnight camping fees are $4 to $9 per night. Pets are NOT permitted in Rhode Island State Parks.   Further information: Department of Environmental Management; Division of Parks and Recreation; Veterans' Memorial Building; 83 Park Street; Providence, RI 02903 [277-2632].

Rest Areas

Overnight stops are not permitted in Rhode Island Rest Areas.

The Appalachian Trail

More than 2000 miles long, the Appalachian Trail (from Maine to Georgia) is the longest continuous marked trail in the world.

CAMPING: More than 200 open-front shelters/lean-tos are spaced approximately 10 miles apart on the Trail (one-day intervals).   As they are occupied on a first-come first-served basis, carry a tent in case the shelters are full.   Potable spring water is usually available at each site, but should be purified by tablets or boiling.   And always "pack it in, pack it out".

PERMITS: No permit is required to hike the Trail.   However, camping permits must be obtained for overnight stays in Shenandoah NP (Luray, VA 22835) and Great Smoky Mountains NP (Gatlinburg, TN 37733).   These are free of charge and available from the ranger stations or by mail.   A free camping permit must be obtained for overnight stays in White Mountain National Forest Restricted Use Area (PO Box 638; Laconia, NH 03246).

APPALACHIAN TRAIL CONFERENCE: A private, nonprofit, national organization which represents citizen's interest in the Appalachian Trail.   They offer detailed guidebooks and maps for sale, as well as the AT Data Book which gives the location and distances between shelters and certain post offices, supply points, water sources, lodging and meals.   For more information on this organization, write to them at: PO Box 236; Harpers Ferry, WV 25425.

INFORMATION SOURCES

Maps

The following maps are available from **Forsyth Travel Library** (see order form in Appendix B):

> State of Rhode Island [Up-to-date, showing all principal roads,
> points of interest, sports areas, parks, airports, mileage,
> etc. Full color.]

> Completely indexed city map, including all airports, lakes,
> rivers, etc., of **Providence**.

State Information

Department of Environmental Management; Division of Parks and Recreation; Veterans' Memorial Building; 83 Park Street; Providence, RI 02903.

RHODE ISLAND

State Information (cont.)

Rhode Island Development Council; Information Division; Roger Williams Building; Providence, RI 02908.

Rhode Island Turnpike and Bridge Authority; PO Box 437; Jamestown, RI 02835.

Tourism Promotion Division; Department of Economic Development; 1 Weybosset Hill; Providence, RI 02903.

Division of Fish and Wildlife; Washington County Government Center; Tower Hill Road; Wakefield, RI 02879.

City Information

Preservation Society of Newport County; 35 Touro Street; Newport, RI 02840.

Greater Providence Chamber of Commerce; 10 Dorrance Street; Providence, RI 02903.

FREE CAMPGROUNDS

CHARLESTOWN

*Canoe Campsite (Burlingame Management Area). On the shore of the Pawcatuck River, near Charlestown. [Accessible BY CANOE.] SEASON: All year; 14-day lmt. [3/15-5/15, no open fires, 10:00-5:00.] FACILITIES: 2 sites, cga. ACTIVITIES: Canoeing. MISC.: No permit is required. Pets allowed if on leash.

RICHMOND

*Canoe Campsite (Carolina Management Area). On the shore of the Pawtucket River, near Richmond. SEASON: All year; 14-day lmt. [3/15-5/15, no open fires, 10:00-5:00.] FACILITIES: 2 tent sites; toil, cga, f. ACTIVITIES: Canoeing. MISC.: No permit is required. Pets.

READ THIS!

All information relative to each campground and state is currently accurate to the best of the publisher's knowledge. However, non-fee status and facilities are subject to change.

If any inaccuracies in this directory are discovered, or you know of any additional FREE campgrounds, please contact: VMPI; Box 1289; Clearwater, FL 33517.

INFORMATION ON HOW TO PURCHASE ADDITIONAL COPIES OF THIS BOOK AS WELL AS QUANTITY DISCOUNT INFORMATION IS ALSO AVAILABLE AT THIS ADDRESS.

See page 7 for KEY TO ABBREVIATIONS.

SOUTH CAROLINA

GENERAL STATE INFORMATION

Miscellaneous

Right Turns on Red: Permitted after
full stop, unless otherwise posted.
STATE CAPITOL: Columbia
STATE NICKNAME: Palmetto State
STATE MOTTO: "While I Breathe, I Hope"
STATE BIRD: Carolina Wren
STATE FLOWER: Yellow Jessamine
STATE TREE: Palmetto Palm

State Parks

Overnight camping fees range from $6.00–$11.00 per night. Pets are permitted if kept
on a leash. Further information: South Carolina Division of State Parks; Box 71, Room
30; Columbia, SC 29202 [803/758-3622].

Rest Areas

Overnight stops are not permitted in South Carolina Rest Areas.

South Carolina Game Management Area Program

Approximately 1¼ million acres are made available to the public. The program's lands
assure both sportsmen and non-hunters of vast areas open to public use and enjoyment.
Only hunters are required to pay a use fee through the purchase of a Game Management Area Permit. The many campgrounds and scenic spots offer year-round recreation
and relaxation. Non-hunters may enjoy these lands with NO CHARGE provided they
observe the Game Management Area Regulations and use caution during the scheduled
hunting season. Further information/maps: South Carolina Wildlife and Marine Resources Department; PO Box 167; Dutch Plaza; Building D; Columbia, SC 29202 [758-
6291].

Santee Cooper

All of the areas which are listed under "Primitive Camping Areas" on their map/bro-
chure are free. The islands which are shown as primitive camping areas range in
size from 100–415 acres in size and are easily accessible by boat. The North Dike,
Sandy Beach, Halls Woods, Santee River, and Trezevant's provide excellent outdoor
activities and can be reached by boat or car. The upper Santee Swamp is located
on the upper reaches of Lake Marion, beginning at the confluence of the Wateree and
Congaree Rivers. The total acreage of the swamp is 16,700 acres. Although the majority of the areas within the swamp can be reached via small boat, there are several
high bluffs along the river which are accessible by car. Further information and
free map/brochure "Camping Guide to Santee Cooper County": Santee Cooper; South
Carolina Public Service Authority; 223 North Live Oak Drive; Moncks Corner, SC 29461.

State Forests

Free primitive camping, accessible by car or by foot, is allowed at both Manchester
State Forest and Sand Hills State Forest. For further information: South Carolina State
Commission of Forestry; Box 21707; Columbia, SC 29221.

SUMTER NATIONAL FOREST

Hiking/Camping Along The Andrew Pickens Ranger District Trails

Camping is permitted only in designated areas except within the Chattooga River Corridor (an area approximately ¼ mile wide on each side of the River) and the Ellicott
Rock Wilderness. In these areas campers may select their own site provided the site
is at least 50 feet from the trail, 50 feet from the River or any tributary stream,
¼ mile from the road, and at least 200 yards from any other occupied site. Designated camping sites are marked on the ground with signs showing the distance and
direction from the trail. Further information: District Ranger; Andrew Pickens Ranger
District; Star Route; Walhalla, SC 29691 [Hwy 28, 7 mi N of Walhalla].

SOUTH CAROLINA

Hiking/Camping Along The Turkey Creek Trail

Primitive camping is available at Key Bridge Hunt Camp throughout the year. This facility offers water, toilets, and garbage containers. Camping in the general forest area requires a special written permit from the District Ranger. Water available along the trail is not safe to drink. The water system at Key Bridge Hunt Camp is tested monthly. Plan your water needs before entering trail. Further information: District Ranger; Edgefield Ranger District; 321 Bacon Street; PO Box 30; Edgefield, SC 29824.

Horseback Riding/Hiking/Camping on the Buncombe Trail

Camping is available at Brick House Campground open during the late spring, summer, autumn and early winter seasons. This 23-unit campsite has corrals along one side for the convenience of the horseback riders. Camping in the general forest area requires a special written permit from the District Ranger. Further information: District Ranger; Enoree Ranger District; 3218 College Street; PO Box 376; Newberry, SC 29108.

Horseback Riding/Hiking/Camping on the Long Cane Trail

Full facility camping and picnicking are available at Parson's Mountain Recreation Area during the summer and early autumn seasons. Individuals and small groups must keep their horses in the provided corral area. Large horseriding groups are requested to contact the District Ranger for permission to use Fell Hunt Camp. Camping in the general forest area requires a special written permit from the District Ranger. Further information: District Ranger; Room 201, Federal Building; PO Box 3168; Greenwood, SC 29646.

Floating/Camping Along the Tyger River

Overnight camping within the National Forest requires a permit from the District Ranger stationed in Union, SC. Due to the amount of private land along the river, care must be taken to insure that your campsite is located on National Forest land. Fires are permitted, and users are urged to be careful. Further information: District Ranger; Tyger Ranger District; Duncan By-pass Hwy 176; PO Drawer 10; Union, SC 29379.

INFORMATION SOURCES

Maps

The following maps are available from **Forsyth Travel Library** (see order form in Appendix B):

> State of S. Carolina [Up-to-date, showing all principal roads, points of interest, sports areas, parks, airports, mileage, etc. Full color.]

> Completely indexed city maps, including all airports, lakes, rivers, etc., of: **Anderson; Charleston; Clemson; Columbia; Greenville; Myrtle Beach and Beach Area; Rock Hill; Spartanburg; Sumter.**

Gold Mining and Prospecting

South Carolina Division of Geology; State Development Board; PO Box 927; Columbia, SC 29200.

State Information

Division of Travel and Tourism; South Carolina Department of Parks, Recreation, and Tourism; Edgar A. Brown Building; 1205 Pendleton Street; Box 71; Columbia,SC 29202.
Division of State Parks; Department of Parks, Recreation and Tourism; PO Box 1358; Columbia, SC 29202.
South Carolina State Commission of Forestry; Box 21707; Columbia, SC 29221.
South Carolina Wildlife and Marine Resources Department; PO Box 167; Dutch Plaza, Building D; Columbia, SC 29202.
Pendleton District Historical and Recreation Commission; PO Box 234; Pendleton, SC 29670. [Information on Anderson, Oconee, and Pickens Counties.]

City Information

Charleston Trident Chamber of Commerce; Municipal Marina; PO Box 975; Charleston, SC 29402.

Miscellaneous

Francis Marion NF; 1801 Assembly Street; Columbia, SC 29201.
Sumpter NF; 1801 Assembly Street; Columbia, SC 29201.
Corps of Engineers; Clark Hill Project; Clark Hill, SC 29821.
Cape Romain NWR; Route 1, Box 191; Awendaw, SC 29429.

FREE CAMPGROUNDS

ABBEVILLE

Fell Hunt (Francis Marion Sumter NF). 8 mi SE of Abbeville on St Hwy 33; 1½ mi NE on St Hwy 47. SEASON: 10/1-12/31. FACILITIES: 40 sites (tr -32); toil, cga, f, well drk wtr. No tables. Store/gas (2 mi). ACTIVITIES: Berry-picking; hunting. Fishing (3 mi). MISC.: Elev 600 ft; 40 acres; historic; pets.

ANDERSON

River (COE; Hartwell Lake). 5 mi N of Hartwell, GA, on US 29, between Hartwell, GA, and Anderson, SC. SEASON: 10/1-4/1, FREE ($2 rest of yr); 14-day lmt. FACILITIES: 15 sites (tr -30); tbls, flush toil, cga, drk wtr. Dump nearby. ACTIVITIES: Fishing; picnicking. MISC.: Pets on leash.

Watsadler's (COE; Hartwell Lake). 4 mi E of Hartwell, GA, on US 29; between Hartwell, GA, and Anderson, SC. SEASON: 10/1-4/1, FREE ($3 rest of yr); 14-day lmt. FACILITIES: 37 sites (tr -30); tbls, flush toil, cga, dump, showers, drk wtr. ACTIVITIES: Swimming; boating,l; picnicking; fishing. MISC.: Pets,

AWENDAW

Halfway Creek (Francis Marion Sumter NF). 1/5 mi SW of Awendaw on US 17; 4-7/10 mi NW on St Hwy 1032; 3/10 mi SW on FS 200. SEASON: All year. FACILITIES: 30 sites (tr -16); ACTIVITIES: Hiking. MISC.: Elev 100 ft; 4 acres; pets. Primitive camp for swamp fox trail.

CARLISLE

Whiteoak Hunt (Francis Marion Sumter NF). 1/5 mi SE of Carlisle on St Hwy 215; 3-3/5 mi SW on St Hwy 72. SEASON: 10/1-1/31. FACILITIES: 12 sites (tr -16); tbls, toil, cga, no drk wtr. Store/gas (4 mi). ACTIVITIES: Hunting; picnicking. Fishing (2 mi). MISC.: Elev 500 ft; 5 acres; pets.

CHESTER

Leeds (Francis Marion Sumter NF). 12-1/10 mi SW of Chester on St Hwy 72; 2-1/10 mi N on St Hwy 25; 3-3/5 mi N on St Hwy 49; 3/10 mi NW on St Hwy 574. SEASON: 10/1-1/31; 14-day lmt. FACILITIES: 12 sites (tr -22); tbls, toil, cga, f, piped drk wtr. ACTIVITIES: Picnicking. MISC.: Elev 500 ft; 12 acres; pets.

Woods Ferry (Francis Marion Sumter NF). 12-1/10 mi SW of Chester on St Hwy 72; 2-1/10 mi N on St Hwy 25; 3-3/5 mi N on St Hwy 49; 3-3/5 mi NW on St Hwy 574. SEASON: 4/15-10/15; 14-day lmt. FACILITIES: 38 sites (tr -22); tbls, toil, cga, f, piped drk wtr, showers. ACTIVITIES: Waterskiing; boating,ld; picnicking; fishing. MISC.: Elev 300 ft; 25 acres; river; pets. Electricity in restrooms.

CLEMSON

Locust Point (COE; Hartwell Lake). Located on the banks of the Seneca River near the Highway 37 bridge between Seneca and Clemson. SEASON: 4/1-9/30; 14-day lmt. FACILITIES: Primitive sites. ACTIVITIES: Horseback riding; hiking. MISC.: Mainly by equestrians, but not limited to groups with horses. Pets.

CLINTON

Tip Top Hunt (Francis Marion Sumter NF). 7 mi E of Clinton on St Hwy 72. SEASON: 10/1-1/31; 14-day lmt. FACILITIES: 40 sites (tr -22); toil, cga, f, well drk wtr. No tables. Store/ice/food/gas (5 mi). ACTIVITIES: Berry-picking; hunting; picnicking. MISC.: Elev 600 ft; 10 acres; pets on leash.

GREENWOOD

Midway Hunt (Francis Marion Sumter NF). 6-4/5 mi W of Greenwood on St Hwy 72; ¼ mi S on Co Hwy. SEASON: 10/1-12/31; 14-day lmt. FACILITIES: 25 sites (tr -32); well drk wtr, toil, f, store, gas, ice. No tables. ACTIVITIES: Hiking; hunting. Nature trails (1 mi). Waterskiing (2 mi). MISC.: 4 acres. Pets allowed if on a leash.

JACKSON

Crackerneck Hunt (Francis Marion Sumter NF). 7 mi SE of Jackson on St Hwy 125; 1 mi NW on Co Hwy 5; 4 mi SW on Co Rd; 4 mi SE on FS 805. SEASON: 10/1-12/31; 14-day lmt. FACILITIES: 5 sites (tr -16); tbls, toil, cga, no drk wtr. ACTIVITIES: Hunting; hiking; horseback riding; picnicking. MISC.: Elev 100 ft; 2 acres; lake; pets on leash.

JAMESTOWN

Guilliard Lake (Francis Marion Sumter NF). 3-4/5 mi SE of Jamestown on St

Hwy 45; 1-3/5 mi NE on FS 150; 1-1/5 mi N on FS 150G. SEASON: All yr; 14-day lmt. FACILITIES: 6 sites (tr -22); tbls, toil, cga, f, well drk wtr. ACTIVITIES: Boating,d; picnicking; fishing. MISC.: Elev 100 ft; 2 acres; pets.

LOCKHART

Poolus-Loop Hunt (Francis Marion Sumter NF). 5 mi SE of Lockhart on St Hwy 9; 7/10 mi W on Co Hwy 49; 3-1/10 mi W on FS 301; ½ mi N on FS. SEASON: 10/1-1/31. FACILITIES: 20 sites (tr - 16); toil. No drk wtr. Store/ice/gas (4 mi). ACTIVITIES: Hunting; hiking. Fishing (1 mi). MISC.: Elev 400 ft; 4 acres; pets. Area serves as a primitive hunt camp only.

McCLELLANVILLE

Buck Hall (Francis Marion Sumter NF). 3/5 mi N of McClellanville on St Hwy 9; 7 mi SW on US 17; 1/5 mi SE on FS 236. SEAS: All yr; 14-day lmt. FAC: 15 sites (tr -22); tbls, toil, cga, drk wtr. Store/ice/gas (4 mi). ACTIVITIES: Boating,ld; picnicking; fishing. MISC.: Elev 100 ft; 5 acres; river; pets. Located on the Intracoastal Waterway.

Elmwood (Francis Marion Sumter NF). 3/5 mi N of McClellanville on St Hwy 9; 6 mi NE on US 17; 1-9/10 mi NW on St Hwy 857; 1-3/5 mi W on FS 204. SEASON: 11/1-4/30; 14-day lmt. FACILITIES: 20 sites (tr -22); toil, piped drk wtr. No tables. ACTIVITIES: Hiking; hunting. MISC.: Elev 100 ft; 5 acres; pets.

Honey Hill (Francis Marion Sumter NF). 3/10 mi N of McClellanville on St Hwy 9; 3/5 mi NW on St Hwy 1189; 8-2/5 mi N on St Hwy 45. SEASON: All yr; 14-day lmt. FACILITIES: 9 sites (tr -22); tbls, toil, cga, well drk wtr. Store/gas (2 mi). ACTIVITIES: Picnicking. MISC.: Elev 100 ft; 3 acres; pets on leash.

McCORMICK

Morrows Bridge Hunt (Francis Marion Sumter NF). 2-3/10 mi NW of McCormick on St Hwy 28; 4/5 mi SW on Co Hwy 39. SEASON: 10/1-12/31; 14-day lmt. FACILITIES: 25 sites (tr -32); toil, f, well drk wtr, store, gas. No tables. ACTIVITIES: Hunting. Swimming/fishing/boating,d (1 mi). MISC.: Elev 400 ft;4 acres; pets on leash.

MONCKS CORNER

Bonneau (Francis Marion Sumter NF). 8-1/10 mi N of Moncks Corner on US 52. SEASON: All yr; 14-day lmt. FACILITIES: 13 sites (tr -22); tbls, toil, cga, drk wtr. Store/ice/laundry (1 mi). ACTIVITIES: Picnicking. MISC.: Elev 100 ft; 5 acres; pets.

NEWBERRY

Long Lane Hunt (Francis Marion Sumter NF). 9 mi N of Newberry on St Hwy 121; 9/10 mi W on St Hwy 81. SEASON: 10/1-1/1; 14-day lmt. FACILITIES: 20 sites (tr -22); toil, well drk wtr, store, gas. No tables. ACTIVITIES: Hunting; hiking. Fishing (2 mi). MISC.: Elev 500 ft; 8 acres; pets. With reservations, will open outside of normal use season.

Willow Oak Hunt (Francis Marion & Sumter NF). 10 mi N on St Hwy 121; 3-4/5 mi SW on US 176; 3/10 mi N on FS 387; 1-7/10 mi NE on FS 386. SEASON: 10/1-1/1; 14-day lmt. FACILITIES: 20 sites (tr -22); toil, well drk wtr, no tbls. ACTIVITIES: Picnicking; berry-picking; fishing. MISC.: Elev 400 ft; 2 acres; pets.

NEW ELLENTON

Talatha (Francis Marion Sumter NF). 4 mi S of New Ellenton on St Hwy 19; 1 mi SW on FS SRR-1. SEASON:10/1-12/31; 14-day lmt. FACILITIES: 8 sites (tr -16); tbls, toil, cga, f, well drk wtr. Gas/ice (2 mi). Store/food/laundry (5 mi). ACTIVITIES: Picnicking. MISC.: Elev 400 ft; 10 acres; pets on leash.

NORTH AUGUSTA

Fork (Francis Marion Sumter NF). 6-3/10 mi NW of North Augusta on St Hwy 230; 3-4/5 mi W on St Hwy 53. SEASON: 4/4-6/5; 14-day lmt. FACILITIES: 5 sites (tr -22); toil, cga, well drk wtr. No tables. ACTIVITIES: Picnicking. MISC.: Elev 400 ft; 5 acres; pets on leash.

PARKSVILLE

Parksville Wayside (COE; Clark Hill Lake). ½ mi SE of Parksville on US 221. SEASON: 11/1-2/28, FREE ($4 rest of yr); 14-day lmt. FACILITIES: 8 sites (tr -30); tbls, flush toil, cga, drk wtr. ACTIVITIES: Swimming; picnicking; fishing; boating,l. MISC.: Pets on leash.

SALEM

Cherokee Hunt Camp (Francis Marion Sumter NF). 5-1/10 mi W of Salem on St Hwy 11; 4 mi NW on St Hwy 375; 1 mi S on Co Hwy. SEASON: 10/15-12/15. ACTIVITIES: Hunting; picnicking; fishing. FACILITIES: 5 sites (no tr); toil, f, well drk wtr. No tables. Store/ice/gas (5 mi). MISC.: Elev 1100 ft; 5 acres; pets on leash.

SENECA

Locust Point (COE; Hartwell Lake). Located on the banks of the Seneca River near the Highway 37 bridge between Seneca and Clemson. SEASON: 4/1-9/30; 14-day lmt. FACILITIES: Primitive sites. ACTIVITIES: Hiking; horseback riding. MISC.: Mainly used by equestrians, but not limited to groups with horses. Pets.

See page 7 for KEY TO ABBREVIATIONS.

TOWNVILLE

Apple Island (COE; Hartwell Lake). From jct of St Hwy 24 and Co Rd 86; 1½ mi S to campground. SEASON: 4/1-9/30; 14-day lmt. FACILITIES: 30 sites (tr -30); tbls, toil, cga, drk wtr. ACTIVITIES: Swimming; boating,l; picnicking; fishing. MISC.: Pets on leash.

UNION

Beatty's Bridge Hunt Camp (Francis Marion Sumter NF). 9 mi S of Union on US 176; 1/5 mi E on St Hwy 278. SEASON: 10/1-1/2. FACILITIES: 10 sites (tr -16); toil, f. No tables. ACTIVITIES: Hunting; hiking. Boating/fishing (1 mi). MISC.: Elev 500 ft; 2 acres; pets. Area serves as a primitive hunt camp only.

Fair Forest Hunt (Francis Marion Sumter NF). 1/5 mi W of Union on St Hwy 49; 1 mi S on US 176; 6 mi SW on Co Hwy 16. SEASON: 10/1-1/31. FACILITIES: 8 sites (tr -16); toil, piped drk wtr. No tables. Store/ice/gas (5 mi). ACTIVITIES: Hunting; hiking. Fishing (2 mi). MISC.: Historic; pets. Area serves as a primitive hunt camp only. Elev 500 ft; 4 acres.

Hickory Nut Hunt Camp (Francis Marion Sumter NF). 10-3/5 mi S of Union on St Hwy 16; ½ mi E on St Hwy 136. SEASON: 10/1-1/2. FACILITIES: 10 sites (tr -16); toil, f. No tables. ACTIVITIES: Hunting; hiking. Fishing (2 mi). Boating (3 mi). MISC.: Elev 500 ft; 3 acres; pets; historic. Nature trails (2 mi). Area serves as a primitive hunt camp only.

Sedalia Hunt (Francis Marion Sumter NF). 11 mi SW of Union on St Hwy 49; 1-9/10 mi SE on Co Hwy 18; 3/10 mi NE on Co Hwy. SEASON: 10/1-1/31. FACILITIES: 13 sites (tr -16); toil, well drk wtr. No tables. Store/ice/gas (2 mi). ACTIVITIES: Hunting; hiking. Fishing (2 mi). MISC.: Elev 600 ft; 8 acres; pets. Area serves as a primitive hunt camp only.

Sedalia Tower Hunt Camp (Francis Marion Sumter NF). 9 mi S of Union on St Hwy 16; 3 mi W on St Hwy 63; 1 mi N on St Hwy 79. SEASON: 10/1-1/2. FACILITIES: 20 sites (tr -16); toil, f. No tables. ACTIVITIES: Hunting; hiking. Boating/fishing (2 mi). MISC.: Elev 500 ft; 2 acres; pets; historic. Area serves as a primitive hunt camp only.

WALHALLA

*Burrells Ford** (Francis Marion Sumter NF). 8-9/10 mi NW of Walhalla on St Hwy 28; 9-3/5 mi N on St Hwy 107; 2-3/5 mi W on FS 708; 1/5 mi S on TRAIL 708B. SEASON: All yr; 14-day lmt. FACILITIES: 9 tent sites; tbls, toil, cga, well drk wtr. ACTIVITIES: Hiking; picnicking; fishing. MISC.: Elev 2000 ft; 5 acres; pets; scenic. On the Chattooga River.

Cassidy Bridge Hunt Camp (Francis Marion Sumter NF). 5½ mi NW of Walhalla on St Hwy 28; 4½ mi SW on St Hwy 290; 4/5 mi W on St Hwy 193. SEASON: 10/11-12/8. FACILITIES: 5 sites (no tr); toil, f, well drk wtr. No tables. Store/ice/gas (5 mi). ACTIVITIES: Hunting; hiking; fishing. MISC.: Elev 1200 ft; 5 acres; pets; river. Open to organized groups via reservation year round.

WESTMINSTER

Pine Mountain Hunt Camp (Francis Marion Sumter NF). 7 mi W of Westminster on US 76; 5 mi SW on St Hwy 90; 3 mi N on Co Hwy; 4/5 mi SW on FS 752. SEASON: 10/15-12/15. FACILITIES: 5 sites (no tr); toil, f, well drk wtr. No tbls. ACTIVITIES: Hunting; fishing; hiking. MISC.: Elev 1500 ft; 5 acres; pets.

Tabor (COE; Hartwell Lake). Take St Hwy 123 SW from Westminster. SEASON: All yr; 14-day lmt. FACILITIES: Primitive sites; tbls, toil, cga, drk wtr. ACTIVITIES: Boating,l; picnicking. MISC.: Pets on leash.

WHITMIRE

Brick House (Francis Marion Sumter NF). 6-1/5 mi SW of Whitmire on St Hwy 66; 3/10 mi S on FS 358. SEASON: 4/1-12/31; 14-day lmt. FACILITIES: 23 sites (tr -22); tbls, toil, cga, f, well drk wtr. Store (1 mi). Ice (2 mi). ACTIVITIES: Horseback riding; hiking; picnicking. MISC.: Elev 500 ft; 12 acres; pets. Terminal point on riding trail.

Collins Creek Hunt (Francis Marion Sumter NF). 3-1/5 mi NE of Whitmire on St Hwy 121; 4-1/5 mi SE on St Hwy 45; 3/5 mi SW on FS FH393. SEAS: 10/1-1/1; 14-day lmt. FACILITIES: 40 sites (tr -22); toil, well drk wtr, store, gas. No tbls. ACTIVITIES: Hunting; hiking. MISC.: Elev 400 ft; 8 acres; pets. With reservations will open outside of normal use.

Ridge Road Hunt Camp (Francis Marion Sumter NF). 5 mi W of Whitmire on St Hwy 72; 1½ mi N on FS 355. SEASON: 10/1-1/2. FACILITIES: 10 sites (tr -16); toil, f. No tables. ACTIVITIES: Hunting; hiking. MISC.: Elev 500 ft; 2 acres; pets. Area serves as a primitive hunt camp only.

Scenic Area Hunt (Francis Marion Sumter NF). 3-1/5 mi NE of Whitmire on St Hwy 121; 7-1/5 mi SE on St Hwy 45; 1-1/10 mi N on St Hwy 54; 1-9/10 mi E on Co Rd. SEASON: 10/1-1/1; 14-day lmt. FACILITIES: 25 sites (tr -22); toil, well drk wtr, store, gas. No tables. ACTIVITIES: Berry-picking; hunting; hiking. Fishing/swimming (1 mi). MISC.: Elev 400 ft; 6 acres; pets; botanical. With reservations open outside of normal use season.

See page 7 for KEY TO ABBREVIATIONS.

WILLINGTON

Leroy's Ferry (COE; Clark Hill Lake). From jct of St Hwys 81/821, 3 mi NE; 3½ mi W on access rd (between Calhoun Falls and McCormick). **SEASON:** All yr; 14-day lmt. **FACILITIES:** 10 sites (tr -30); toil. No tbls or drk wtr. **ACTIVITIES:** Swimming; boating,l; picnicking; fishing. **MISC.:** Pets on leash.

WINNSBORO

Rocky Branch Hunt (Francis Marion Sumter NF). 14 mi W of Winnsboro on St Hwy 34; 1-3/10 mi N on St Hwy 215; 2-2/5 mi SW on FS 412. **SEAS:** 10/1-1/1; 14-day lmt. **FACILITIES:** 20 sites (tr -22); drk wtr, toil. No tables. Store/gas (4 mi). **ACTIVITIES:** Berry-picking; hunting. **MISC.:** Elev 500 ft; 2 acres; pets.

SOUTH DAKOTA

GENERAL STATE INFORMATION

Miscellaneous

Toll-Free Number for Travel Information:
   1-800-843-1930 [calling outside of SD]
STATE CAPITOL: Pierre
STATE NICKNAME: Sunset State
STATE MOTTO: "Under God, The People Rule"
STATE BIRD: Ring Neck Pheasant
STATE FLOWER: Pasque
STATE TREE: Black Hills Spruce

State Parks

Overnight camping fees range from $3.00-4.00. Pets are permitted if kept on a leash. Further information: Division of Parks and Recreation; South Dakota Department of Wildlife, Parks and Forestry; Sigurd Anderson Building; Pierre, SD 57501.

Rest Areas

Overnight stops are not permitted in South Dakota Rest Areas.

INFORMATION SOURCES

Maps

A detailed, up-to-date map of the **State of South Dakota** is available from **Forsyth Travel Library** (see order form in Appendix B).

Gold Mining and Prospecting

South Dakota State Geological Survey; Science Center; University of South Dakota; Vermillion, SD 57069.

State Information

Travel Division; Department of Tourism and Economic Development; State Office Building No. 2; Pierre, SD 57501.
Division of Parks and Recreation; South Dakota Department of Wildlife, Parks and Forestry; Sigurd Anderson Building; Pierre, SD 57501.
Department of Game, Fish and Parks; Anderson Building; Pierre, SD 57501.

Miscellaneous

Black Hills NF; PO Box 792; Custer, SD 57730.
Wind Cave NP; Hot Springs, SD 57747.
Badlands National Monument; Box 6; Interior,SD 57750.
South Dakota [plus Montana and North Dakota] Bureau of Land Management; 222 North 32nd Street; PO Box 30157; Billings, MT 69107.
Aberdeen Area Office; Bureau of Indian Affairs; 820 South Main Street; Aberdeen, SD 57401.

See page 7 for KEY TO ABBREVIATIONS.

FREE CAMPGROUNDS

ALCESTER

Alcester Campground. 8 mi E of Alcester on I-25; 4 mi S on St Hwy 46 between Sioux Falls, SD, and Sioux City, Iowa. SEASON: All year. FACILITIES: 6 sites; toil, electric/water hookups. ACTIVITIES: Swimming and golf nearby. MISC.: Pets.

BELLE FOURCHE

Center of the Nation. 26 mi N of Belle Fourche on St Hwy 85. SEASON: All yr· 14-day lmt. FACILITIES: Sites; tbls, toil, cga, drk wtr, dump. ACTIVITIES: Picnicking. MISC.: Pets on leash.

Orman Dam. 10 mi E of Belle Fourche on St Hwy 212. SEASON: All yr; 14-day lmt. FACILITIES: Sites; tbls, toil. ACTIVITIES: Boating,d; swimming; fishing. MISC.: Pets allowed if on leash.

BONESTEEL

South Scalp (COE; Lake Francis Case). 4 mi S of Bonesteel on US 18; 11 mi NE on Co Rd. SEASON: 5/19-9/4; 14-day lmt. FACILITIES: 25 sites (tr -24); tbls, cga, f. ACTIVITIES: Boating,l; picnick-MISC.: Pets on leash.

Whetstone Bay (COE; Lake Francis Case). 8 mi N of Bonesteel on gravel road. SEASON: 5/21-9/5; 14-day lmt. FACILITIES: 10 spaces for self-contained RVs; tbls, toil, cga, drk wtr. ACTIVITIES: Swimming; picnicking; fishing; boating,ld. MISC.: Pets allowed on leash.

BROOKINGS

Sexauer's Park (City Park). ¼ mi W and N on US 14. [In W Brookings.] SEASON: 5/15-10/15; 3-day lmt. FACILITIES: 3 sites with electric hookups and additional tent (tr -20); tbls, toil, cga, f, drk wtr. Store/food/laundry/dump nearby. ACTIVITIES: Picnicking. Swimming nearby. MISC.: Pets on leash.

BUFFALO

Picnic Spring (Custer NF). 26 mi NE of Buffalo on US 85; 4-1/10 mi W on Co Hwy 7330; 2 mi S on Co Rd; 1-3/5 mi W on FS 114. SEASON: 5/15-10/31. FACILITIES: 9 sites (tr -22); tbls, toil, cga, f, piped drk wtr. ACTIVITIES: Picnicking; hiking. MISC.: Elev 3300 ft; 3 acres; pets. In the scenic north cave hills.

Reva Gap (Custer NF). 1 mi S of Buffalo on US 85; 19 mi E on St Hwy 20. SEASON: 5/15-10/31. FACILITIES: 4 sites (tr -22); tbls, toil, cga, f, no drk wtr. Store/gas (4 mi). ACTIVITIES: Picnicking. MISC.: Close by are the colorful "Castles" rock formations. Elev 3600 ft; 13 acres. Pets.

BURKE

Burke City Park (City Park). 300 feet off the N side of US 18/47, in Burke. SEASON: All yr; 7-day lmt. FACILITIES: 8 sites; tbls, flush toil, dump, playground, electric/water/sewer hookups. Store/ice/food/laundry nearby. ACTIVITIES: Horseback riding; picnicking. Swimming/fishing/golf nearby. MISC.:Pets;lake.

Burke Lake (State Recreation Area). 1 mi E of Burke on US 18. SEASON: 5/1-9/30 (limited facilities during winter); 5-day lmt. FACILITIES: 15 sites; tbls, toil, cga, f, drk wtr, playground. Ice/store/food nearby. ACTIVITIES: Hiking; hunting; swimming; picnicking; fishing; boating,ld. MISC.: Nature trails; lake; beach. Pets allowed if kept on leash.

CAMP CROOK

Lantis Spring (Custer NF). 3 mi W of Camp Crook on St Hwy 20; 11 mi NW on FS 117. SEASON: 5/15-10/31. FACILITIES: 5 sites (tr -16); tbls, toil, cga, f, piped drk wtr. ACTIVITIES: Picnicking. MISC.: Elev 3900 ft; 6 acres; pets. Nearby is Tripoint fire lookout tower.

Wickham Gulch (Custer NF). 3 mi W of Camp Crook on St Hwy 20; 1-4/5 mi N on FS 117; 1-2/5 mi NW on FS 3049. SEASON: 6/1-9/30. FACILITIES: 3 sites (tr -16); tbls, toil, cga, f. ACTIVITIES: Picnicking. MISC.: Elev 3400 ft; pets. In the long pines of Southeastern S.D.

CARTHAGE

Lake Carthage Lakeside Use Area. ¼ mi NE of Carthage. SEASON: All yr; 5-day lmt. FACILITIES: No developed campsites, but camping is allowed; tbls, toil, cga, shelters, drk wtr. ACTIVITIES: Swimming; picnicking;fishing;boating,ld. MISC.:Pets.

CHAMBERLAIN

American Creek Recreation Area (COE; Lake Francis Case). N of Chamberlain on St Hwy 47. SEASON: 9/6-5/20, FREE ($3 rest of yr). FACILITIES: 50 sites (tr -24); tbls, flush toil, cga, f, drk wtr. [Water is shut off during free season.] Store/ice/food/laundry nearby. ACTIVITIES: Boating,rld; picnicking; fishing; swimming. MISC.: Showers; pets.

West Chamberlain (COE; Lake Francis Case). 1½ mi W of Chamberlain on US 16; 2 mi N on paved rd. SEASON: 9/6-5/20, FREE ($3 rest of yr); 14-day lmt. FACILITIES: 40 sites (tr -24); tbls, flush toil, cga, showers, drk wtr; dump. Electric hookup ($). Laundry nearby. ACTIVITIES: Fishing; picnicking. MISC.: Water is shut off during free season.

See page 7 for KEY TO ABBREVIATIONS.

CLEAR LAKE

Cochrane Lake (SRA). 10 mi E of Clear Lake off St Hwy 22. FACILITIES: 15 sites; tbls, toil, cga, drk wtr. ACTIVITIES: Swimming; picnicking; fishing. MISC.: Pets allowed if kept on leash.

CUSTER

Bismarck Lake (Black Hills NF). 4 mi E of Custer on US 16A. SEASON: 9/16-5/31, FREE ($3 rest of yr); 10-day lmt. [During free season, water is shut off, and only one loop is open.] FACILITIES: 23 sites (tr -22); tbls, toil, cga, piped drk wtr. Showers/food (1 mi). Store/gas/ice/laundry/dump (4 mi). ACTIVITIES: Boating; picnicking; fishing. Swimming/waterskiing (1 mi). Horseback riding/rental (2 mi). MISC.: Lifeguard (1 mi). Scenic; lake; pets on leash. Elev 5300 ft; 4 acres.

Comanche Park (Black Hills NF). 6½ mi W of Custer on US 16. SEASON: 9/16-5/31, FREE ($3 rest of yr); 10-day lmt. FACILITIES: 27 sites (tr -22); tbls, toil, cga, piped drk wtr. [Water is shut off during free season.] Store/gas/ice/food/laundry (5 mi). ACTIVITIES: Picnicking. MISC.: Elev 5100 ft; 8 acres; pets. 6 mi E of Jewel Cave Natl Mon.

DEADWOOD

Roubaix Lake (Black Hills NF). 1½ mi SW of Deadwood on I-85; 14 mi S on US 385; 1 mi W on FS 255. SEASON: 10/2-5/31, FREE ($3 rest of yr); 10-day lmt. [One loop open, and water shut off, free seas.] ACT: Swimming; picnicking; fishing; boating. FACILITIES: 44 sites (tr -22), tbls, toil, cga, piped drk wtr. Store/ice/food/gas (5 mi). MISC.: Elev 4700 ft; 27 acres; lake; pets.

Strawberry Hill (Black Hills NF). 1½ mi SW of Deadwood on US 85; 3½ mi S on US 385. SEASON: 6/1-10/1; 10-day lmt. FACILITIES: 8 sites (tr -22); tbls, toil, cga, piped drk wtr. Store/ice/laundry/gas/showers (1 mi). Food (4 mi). ACTIVITIES: Fishing; picnicking. MISC.: Elev 5700 ft; 4 acres; lake. Pets on leash.

DeSMET

City Park. ½ mi E of DeSmet. SEASON: All year. FACILITIES: Sites. MISC.:Pets.

EAGLE BUTTE

Foster Bay (COE; Lake Oahe). 3 mi W of Eagle Butte on US 212; 22 mi S on St Hwy 63. SEASON: All yr; 14-day lmt. FACILITIES: 20 sites (tr -24); tbls, toil, cga, drk wtr. ACTIVITIES: Swimming; picnicking; fishing; boating,l. MISC.: Pets on leash.

ELLENDALE

City Park. In Ellendale. Inquire locally for directions. SEASON: All year. FACILITIES: Sites. MISC.: Pets.

FAIRBURN

French Creek Campground (Buffalo Gap National Grasslands). 10½ mi E of Fairburn on US 79. SEASON: 5/30-9/15. FACILITIES: 7 sites; tbls, toil, cga, drk wtr. ACTIVITIES: Picnicking. MISC.: Pets.

FAITH

City Park. 4 blocks S of US 212 on Main Street, in Faith. SEASON: All year. FACILITIES: 6 sites with electric hookups, 30 tent sites (tr -25); tbls, flush toil, cga, picnic shelters, f, dump, drk wtr. Store/ice/food/laundry. ACTIVITIES: Picnicking. Swimming nearby. MISC.: Pets.

Durkee Lake City Park (City Park). 3 mi S of Faith on St Hwy 73. SEASON: All year. FACILITIES: 10 sites; tbls, toil, cga, dump, f, drk wtr. ACTIVITIES: Swimming; picnicking; fishing; boating,l. Golf nearby. MISC.: Lake. Pets on leash.

FAULKTON

Lake Faulkton Lakeside Use Area. 1½ mi W of Faulkton on US 12. SEASON: All yr; 5-day lmt. FACILITIES: No developed campsites, but camping is allowed. Tbls, toil, cga, drk wtr, shelters. ACTIVITIES: Boating,ld; picnicking; fishing. MISC.: Pets on leash.

FORTH PIERRE

Lake Oaha Park. Near Ft. Pierre on Lake Oaha. SEASON: All year. FACILITIES: Sites. MISC.: Pets.

FORT THOMPSON

North Shore Park (COE; Lake Sharpe). 2 mi W of Ft. Thompson on St Hwy 47 and access road. SEASON: All yr; 14-day lmt. FACILITIES: 38 sites (tr -24); tbls, toil, cga, drk wtr, f. Dump nearby. ACTIVITIES: Waterskiing; swimming; boating,ld; picnicking; fishing. MISC.: Lake; beach. Pets on leash.

Old Ft. Thompson (COE; Lake Sharpe). 2 mi W of Ft. Thompson on St Hwy 47W. SEASON: 9/6-5/20, FREE ($2 rest of yr); 14-day lmt. FACILITIES: 54 sites (tr -24); tbls, flush toil, cga, f, drk wtr, dump. Store/food/laundry nearby. [Water is shut off during free season.] ACTIVITIES: Boating,l; picnicking; fishing. Swimming nearby. MISC.: Pets. Lake Sharpe. Waterskiing.

Tailrace Marina (COE; Lake Sharpe). 2½ mi SW of Ft. Thompson on St Hwy 47W, below the dam. SEASON: 9/6–5/20, FREE ($3 rest of yr); 14-day lmt. FACILITIES: 150 sites (tr -24); tbls, flush toil, cga, f, showers, drk wtr, electric hookup ($). MISC.: Water is shut off during free season. Pets. ACTIVITIES: Fishing; picnicking; boating,ld.

Tailrace Right Bank (COE; Lake Sharpe). 3 mi SW of Ft. Thompson on St Hwy 47W, below the dam. SEASON: 9/6–5/20, FREE ($3 rest of yr). FACILITIES: 12 sites (tr -24); tbls, flush toil, drk wtr. ACTIVITIES: Boating,ld; picnicking; fishing. MISC.: Dump nearby. Water is shut off during free season. Pets.

GETTYSBURG

Forest City (COE; Lake Oahe). 17 mi W of Gettysburg on US 212, on W side of Lake Oahe. SEASON: All yr; 14-day lmt. FACILITIES: 7 sites (tr -24); tbls, toil, cga, no drk wtr, f. ACTIVITIES: Boating,ld; picnicking; fishing. MISC.: Pets allowed on leash.

City Park. 5 blocks S of St Hwy 212 in Gettysburg. SEASON: 5/1–10/1. FACILITIES: 10 sites; tbls, flush toil, cga, showers, drk wtr, electric hookup ($). ACTIVITIES: Swimming; picnicking. Golf nearby. MISC.: Store/food/dump nearby. Pets.

West Whitlocks Bay (COE; Lake Oahe). 12 mi W of Gettysburg on US 212; 10 mi W on gravel road to campground. SEASON: All yr; 14-day lmt. FACILITIES: 20 sites (tr -30); tbls, toil, cga, f, drk wtr. Store/ice nearby. ACTIVITIES: Boating,ld; picnicking; fishing. MISC.: Pets on leash.

GROTON

Amsden Dam Lakeside Use Area. 6 mi E of Groton on US 12; 7 mi S; 1 mi E; 1 mi N to campground. SEASON: All yr; 5-day lmt. FACILITIES: No developed campsites, but camping is allowed. Tbls, toil, cga. ACTIVITIES: Swimming; picnicking; fishing; boating,l. MISC.: Pets.

City Park. On Main Street in Groton. SEASON: All year. FACILITIES: Sites; 4 electric hookups; tbls, flush toil, cga, dump, drk wtr, sewer hookup. ACTIVITIES: Picnicking. MISC.: Donations welcome, but not required. Pets on leash.

HERREID

Herreid City Park. S of Herreid on St Hwy 83. SEASON: All year. FACILITIES: 10 sites; tbls, flush toil, cga, picnic shelters. ACTIVITIES: Picnicking. MISC.: Pets on leash.

HIGHMORE

City Park. In the center of Highmore on US 14. SEASON: All year. FACILITIES: Sites. MISC.: Pets on leash.

HILL CITY

Bear Gulch (Black Hills NF). 12-3/5 mi NE of Hill City on US 385; 4 mi W on FS 251; 3-1/5 mi N on FS 253. SEASON: 6/1–9/5; 10-day lmt. FACILITIES: 8 sites (tr -22); tbls, toil, cga, no drk wtr. ACTIVITIES: Boating (rl at nearby Pactola Campground); picnicking; fishing. Waterskiing (1 mil). MISC.: Elev 4600 ft; 1 acre; pets. On the S shore of Pactola Lake.

Dutchman (Black Hills NF). 12 mi NW of Hill City on US 385; 4 mi W on Co Hwy 110; 1-1/5 mi N on FS 371. SEASON: 10/2–5/31, FREE ($3 rest of yr); 10-day lmt. FACILITIES: 45 sites (tr --22); tbls, toil, cga, piped drk wtr,f. Store/gas/food (4 mi). ACTIVITIES: Picnicking. Boating (l, 1 mi; r, 4 mi). Fishing (1 mi). MISC.: Elev 6100 ft; 18 acres; pets. On S side of Deerfield Lake. One loop open and water shut off during free season.

Newton Lake (Black Hills NF). 4 mi NW of Hill City on Co Hwy 17. SEASON: 6/1–10/1; 10-day lmt. FACILITIES: Sites (tr-24); tbls, toil, cga, f. ACTIVITIES: Fishing (trout); picnicking. MISC.: Lake. Pets on leash.

Pactola (Black Hills NF). 12-3/5 mi NE of Hill City on US 385; 2 mi N on FS 258. SEASON: 9/6–5/31, FREE ($3 rest of yr); 5-day lmt. FACILITIES: 56 sites (tr -22); tbls, toil, cga, piped drk wtr. Store/ice/laundry/food (1 mi). Gas (5 mi). ACTIVITIES: Boating,l; picnicking; fishing; waterskiing. MISC.: Elev 4700 ft; 55 acres; pets. Visitor Center (1 mi). One loop open and water shut off during free season. On the south shore of Pactola Lake.

Sheridan Southside (Black Hills NF). 6½ mi NE of Hill City on US 385. SEASON: 9/6–5/31, FREE ($2 rest of yr); 5-day lmt. FACILITIES: 106 sites (tr -22); tbls, toil, cga, piped drk wtr. Showers (1 mi). Store/ice/gas/food (2 mi). ACTIVITIES: Waterskiing; picnicking; fishing. Boating (l, 1 mi; r, 2 mi). Swimming (1 mi). MISC.: Elev 4600 ft; 35 acres; scenic; pets. On the south side of Sheridan Lake. 2 loops open and water shut off during free season.

Whitetail (Black Hills NF). 12 mi NW of Hill City on Co Hwy 17; 5 mi W on Co Hwy 110; 1 mi NW on FS 421. SEASON: 10/2–5/31, FREE ($3 rest of yr); 10-day lmt. FACILITIES: 17 sites (tr -22); tbls, toil, cga, f, piped drk wtr. ACTIVITIES: Fishing; picnicking. Boating (r, 2 mi; l, 4 mi). MISC.: Elev 6100 ft; 5 acres; pets. One loop open and water shut off during free season. On the south shore of Deerfield Lake.

Willow Creek (Black Hills NF). 3 mi
S of Hill City on US 16; 3 mi E on St
Hwy 244. SEASON: 6/1-9/30; 10-day lmt.
FACILITIES: 10 sites (tr -22); tbls,
toil, cga, f, no drk wtr. Store/ice/
food/showers/laundry (1 mi). ACTIVI-
TIES: Picnicking. Horseback riding
(rental, 1 mi). MISC.: Elev 5000 ft;
5 acres; pets. Willow Creek.

HOT SPRINGS

Cold Brook Reservoir (State Recreation
Area). 1 mi NW of Hot Springs on US
385. SEASON: 5/1-9/30 (limited facilities
during winter months); 5-day lmt. FACIL-
ITIES: 5 sites; tbls, toil, cga, f, drk
wtr. ACTIVITIES: Boating,rld; picnicking;
fishing. MISC.: Pets on leash.

South Shore Area (COE; Cottonwood Springs
Lake). 4 mi W of Hot Springs on US 18;
1 mi N on gravel rd. SEASON: 4/15-10/15;
14-day lmt. FACILITIES: 18 sites (tr -
-30); tbls, flush toil, cga, drk wtr.
ACTIVITIES: Picnicking. Golf nearby.
MISC.: Pets permitted if kept on leash.

HURON

Lake Byron Lakeside Use Area. 18 mi
N of Huron on St Hwy 37. SEASON: All
yr; 5-day lmt. FACILITIES: No developed
campsites, but camping is allowed. ACTI-
VITIES: Swimming; picnicking; fishing;
boating,ld. FACILITIES: Shelters, tbls,
toil, cga, drk wtr. MISC.: Pets on leash.

INTERIOR

Cedar Pass (Badlands NM). 2 mi NE of
Interior on St Hwy 40A. SEASON: 10/1-
5/1, FREE ($3 rest of yr); 14-day lmt.
FACILITIES: 140 sites (tr -20); tbls,
toil, cga, dump, drk wtr. Ice/food nearby. ACTIVITIES: Picnicking. MISC.:
Pets permitted if kept on a leash.

Sage Creek Primitive (Badlands NM). 12
mi W of Pinnacles Ranger Station (on
US 16A) on Sage Creek Road. SEASON:
10/1-5/1, FREE ($3 rest of yr); 14-day
lmt. FACILITIES: Undesignated sites (tr
-20); no tbls or drk wtr; toil, cga.
MISC.: Pets on leash.

KENNEBEC

Cedar Creek (COE; Lake Sharpe). 12 mi
N of Kennebec on gravel rd; 6 mi NW
to campground. SEASON: 5/21-9/5; 14-day
lmt. FACILITIES: 10 sites (tr -24); tbls,
toil, cga, f, drk wtr. ACTIVITIES: Boating,l; picnicking; fishing. MISC.: Pets.

Iron Nation Area (COE; Lake Sharpe).
13 mi W of Kennebec; 9 mi E on Indian
Bureau Rd. SEASON: All yr; 14-day lmt.
FACILITIES: 30 sites (tr -24); tbls, toil,
cga, f, drk wtr. ACTIVITIES: Boating,ld; picnicking; fishing. MISC.: Pets.

LAKE ANDES

Pease Creek (COE; Lake Francis Case).
9 mi W of Lake Andes on St Hwy 50;
1 mi S and 1 mi W on gravel rd. SEA-
SON: All yr; 14-day lmt. FACILITIES:
25 sites (tr -24); tbls, toil, cga, drk
wtr. ACTIVITIES: Boating,ld; picnicking;
fishing. MISC.: Pets on leash.

LAKE CITY

Clear Lake Lakeside Use Area. 4 mi
E of Lake City off St Hwy 10. SEASON:
All yr; 5-day lmt. FACILITIES: No developed campsites, but camping is allowed. ACTIVITIES: Boating,ld; swimming; picnicking; fishing. MISC.: Pets.

LAKE PRESTON

City Park. East of Lake Preston on
US 14. SEASON: All year. MISC.: Pets.

LEAD

Hanna (Black Hills NF). 8 mi SW of
Lead on US 85; 2-1/5 mi S on FS 17.
SEASON: 6/1-10/1; 10-day lmt. FACILI-
TIES: 7 sites (tr -22); tbls, toil, cga,
well drk wtr. Store/gas (2 mi). ACTIV-
ITIES: Hiking; picnicking. MISC.:
Elev 5600 ft; 3 acres; nature trails;
stream. Pets on leash. Fishing.

LEOLA

Leola City Park. North of Leola at Leola
Dam. SEASON: All year. FACILITIES:
20 sites; limited electric hookups, tbls,
toil, cga, well drk wtr. ACTIVITIES:
Boating,l; picnicking. MISC.: Pets.

LEMMON

Llewellyn Johns Memorial (State Recreation Area). 1 mi W of Lemmon on US
12; 10 mi S on St Hwy 73; W to campground. SEASON: 5/1-9/30 (limited facilities during winter); 5-day lmt.
FACILITIES: 10 sites; tbls, toil, cga,
f, drk wtr. ACTIVITIES: Fishing; picnicking. MISC.: Pets on leash.

MENNO

City Park. On US 18, in Menno. SEA-
SON: All year. FACILITIES: Sites.
MISC.: Pets on leash.

MILLER

Lake Louise (SRA). 6 mi N of Miller
on St Hwy 45; 7 mi W to campground.
[Paved access rds.] FACILITIES: 30
sites; toil, electric hookup. ACTIVITIES:
Boating,l; hiking. MISC.: Pets.

Miller City Park. On 7th Street, W of
St Hwy 14, in Miller. SEASON: All year.
FACILITIES: 12 sites with electric hookups; tbls, flush toil, cga, drk wtr,
dump. ACTIVITIES: Picnicking. MISC.:
Pets. Tenters allowed in the more primitive area.

See page 7 for KEY TO ABBREVIATIONS.

NEMO

Boxelder Forks (Black Hills NF). 2 mi W of Nemo on FS 140. SEASON: 10/2-5/31, FREE ($2 rest of yr); 10-day lmt. FACILITIES: 15 sites (tr -22); tbls, toil, cga, well drk wtr. [Water is shut off during free season.] Store/food/ice/gas (2 mi). ACTIVITIES: Hiking; hunting; picnicking; fishing. Horseback riding/rental (2 mi). MISC.: Elev 4700 ft; 2 acres; stream. Pets on leash.

NEWCASTLE

Moon (NF). 10 mi SE of Newcastle on US 16; 15 mi N on FS 117. SEASON: 6/1-11/30; 10-day lmt. FACILITIES: 3 sites (tr -22); tbls, toil, cga, no drk wtr. ACTIVITIES: Picnicking. MISC.: Elev 6400 ft; 1 acre; pets on leash.

NOON SOCKET

Twin Lakes Recreation Area (State Recreation Area). 9 mi SW of Noon Socket on Co Rd. SEASON: 5/1-9/30; 5-day lmt. FACILITIES: 6 sites; tbls, toil, cga, f, drk wtr. ACTIVITIES: Swimming; picnicking; fishing; boating,l. MISC.: Pets.

ONIDA

Little Bend (COE; Lake Oahe). 30 mi W of Onida on gravel rd. SEASON: All yr; 14-day lmt. FACILITIES: 30 sites (tr -24); tbls, toil, cga, drk wtr. ACTIVITIES: Fishing; swimming; boating,l; picnicking. MISC.: Pets allowed on leash.

PARKSTON

Parkston State Park. 8 mi W of Parkston on St Hwy 44. FACILITIES: Sites; toil. MISC.: Pets on leash.

PICKSTOWN

North Point (COE; Lake Francis Case). 1 mi N of Pickstown on US 18/281; 1 mi W on paved rd to campground. FACILITIES: 70 sites (tr -24); tbls, flush toil, cga, f, drk wtr, showers, dump. SEASON: 9/6-5/24 FREE ($3 rest of yr); 14-day lmt. ACTIVITIES: Boating,l; picnicking; fishing; swimming. Golf nearby. MISC.: Water shut off during free season. Pets.

Randall Creek (COE; Lake Francis Case). 1 mi S of Pickstown on US 18, below the dam. SEASON: 5/21-9/5, FREE ($3 rest of yr); 14-day lmt. FACILITIES: 134 sites (tr -24); tbls, flush toil, cga, f, electric hookup ($), showers, drk wtr. Store/food/laundry/dump nearby. [Water is shut off during free season.] ACTIVITIES: Boating,ld; picnicking; fishing. Golf nearby. MISC.: Pets.

PIERPONT

Pierpont Lake (City Park). 2 mi S of Pierpont at Lake Pierpont on St Hwy 27. SEASON: All year. FACILITIES: 50 sites; tbls, toil, cga, drk wtr, dump. ACTIVITIES: Picnicking. MISC.: Pets.

PIERRE

City Park. West of Pierre on US 14. SEASON: All year. FACILITIES: Sites.

Cow Spring Creek (COE; Lake Oahe). 19 mi W of Pierre on gravel rd. SEASON: 5/19-9/4; 14-day lmt. FACILITIES: 31 sites (tr -24); tbls, toil, cga, f, no drk wtr. ACTIVITIES: Boating,ld; picnicking; fishing; hiking; rockhounding. MISC.: Lake Oahe. Pets on leash.

De Grey Area (COE; Lake Sharpe). 20 mi E of Pierre on St Hwy 34; 1 mi S to campground. SEASON: All yr; 14-day lmt. FACILITIES: 38 sites (tr -24); tbls, toil, cga, f, drk wtr. ACTIVITIES: Boating,ld; picnicking; fishing. MISC.: Pets.

Griffin Park (City Park). In Pierre on Missouri Avenue, between Crow Street and Washington Avenue; near St Hwy 34; SW of St. Mary's Hospital. [Information: Chamber of Commerce; 605/224-7361.] SEASON: All yr; 3-day lmt. FACILITIES: 25 sites; tbls, flush toil, cga, drk wtr, some electric hookups, ball field, picnic shelters. ACTIVITIES: Summer band concerts; tennis; swimming. Picnicking. MISC.: Beach; pets. Boat marina nearby.

West Bend (COE; Lake Sharpe). 25 mi E of Pierre on St Hwy 34; 9 mi S on gravel rd to campground. SEASON: All yr; 14-day lmt. FACILITIES: 30 sites (tr -24); tbls, toil, cga, f, drk wtr. ACTIVITIES: Boating,ld; picnicking; fishing. MISC.: Pets on leash.

PLATTE

Snake Creek (COE; Lake Francis Case). 18 mi W of Platte on St Hwy 44. SEASON: 5/21-9/5; 14-day lmt. FACILITIES: 40 sites (tr -24); tbls, toil, cga, drk wtr. Food nearby. ACTIVITIES: Picnicking; boating,rld; fishing. MISC.: Pets.

PRINGLE

Rifle Pit (Black Hills NF). 5 mi E of,f Pringle on US 385. SEASON: 6/1-9/15; 10-day lmt. FACILITIES: 25 sites (tr -22); tbls, toil, cga, no drk wtr. Food (2 mi). Store/gas (5 mi). ACTIVITIES: Berry-picking; picnicking. MISC.: Elev 4800 ft; 11 acres; geological; pets. Visitor Center (2 mi). 2 mi N of Wind Cave National Park.

RAPID CITY

Highway Rest Area. 15 mi W of Rapid City on westbound side near milepost 41. [Paved access rds.] SEASON: All yr; 1-night lmt. FACILITIES: 20 spaces for self-contained RVs; tbls, toil, cga, shelters, phone, dump. ACTIVITIES: Picnicking. MISC.: Elev 3500 ft. Pets on leash.

See page 7 for KEY TO ABBREVIATIONS.

Mt. Perrin (Black Hills NF). 16-7/10 mi W of Rapid City on St Hwy 40. FACILITIES: 6 sites; 10-day lmt. ACTIVITIES: Boating,ld; picnicking. FACILITIES: No drk wtr. Tbls, toil, cga. Store/ice/food (2 mi). MISC.: Fishing (2 mi). Pets.

REDFIELD

City Park. ¼ mi W of Redfield on St Hwy 212. SEASON: All yr. FACILITIES: 20 sites; 15 electric hookups; tbls, toil, cga, drk wtr, picnic shelter. ACTIVITIES: Picnicking. MISC.: Pets on leash.

ROCHFORD

Black Fox (Black Hills NF). 8 mi W of Rochford on FS 231. SEASON: 6/1-10/1; 10-day lmt. FACILITIES: 9 sites (tr -22); tbls, toil, cga, f, well drk wtr. ACTIVITIES: Fishing; picnicking. MISC.: Elev 5800 ft; 1 acre; stream. Pets on leash.

Castle Peak (Black Hills NF). 3½ mi SW of Rochford on FS 17; 1 mi S on FS 187; 3 mi E on FS 181. SEASON: 6/1-10/1; 10-day lmt. FACILITIES: 9 sites (tr -16); tbls, toil, cga, f, well drk wtr. ACTIVITIES: Fishing; picnicking. MISC.: Elev 5300 ft; 2 acres; stream; pets on leash.

Custer Trail (Black Hills NF). 8½ mi SW of Rochford on Co Hwy 17; 1 mi SW on Co Hwy 188; 1½ mi SE on FS 417. SEASON: 6/1-10/1; 10-day lmt. FACILITIES: 8 sites (tr -22); tbls, toil, cga, f, well drk wtr. Store/gas (4 mi). ACTIVITIES: Boating,ld; picnicking; fishing. MISC.: Elev 5900 ft; 5 acres; pets. north shore of Deerfield Lake.

ROSCOE

Roscoe City Park (City Park). 6 blocks N of US 12 on Main Street; 2 blocks E on 3rd Avenue, in Roscoe. SEASON: 5/1-10/1. FACILITIES: 4 sites with electric hookup (additional tent sites); tbls, flush toil, cga, picnic shelter, f, drk wtr. Store/ice/food nearby. ACTIVITIES: Picnicking. Golf nearby. MISC.: Pets permitted if kept on a leash.

SELBY

Swan Creek (COE; Lake Oahe). 10 mi S of Selby on US 83; 12 mi W on Spur 20. SEASON: All yr; 14-day lmt. FACILITIES: 19 sites (tr -24); tbls, toil, cga, no drk wtr. ACTIVITIES: Boating,ld; picnicking; fishing. MISC.: Pets.

SPEARFISH

Timon (Black Hills NF). 1 mi E of Spearfish on US 14A; 13 mi S on US 14; 4 mi SW on FS 222. SEASON: 6/1-10/1; 10-day lmt. FACILITIES: 6 sites (tr -22); tbls, toil, cga, piped drk wtr. Food/gas (4 mi). ACTIVITIES: Hiking; picnicking. Fishing (2 mi). MISC.: Pets on leash; stream; nature trails.

Rod and Gun (Black Hills NF). 1 mi E of Spearfish on US 14A; 13 mi S on US 14; 2½ mi SW on FS 222. SEASON: 6/1-10/1; 10-day lmt. FACILITIES: 7 sites (no tr); tbls, toil, cga, well drk wtr. Food/gas (2 mi). ACTIVITIES: Fishing; picnicking. MISC.: Elev 5500 ft; 1 acre; stream. Pets on leash.

SPRINGFIELD

Sand Creek Lakeside Use Area. 2 mi N and 3 mi E of Springfield. SEASON: All yr; 5-day lmt. FACILITIES: No developed campsites, but camping is allowed; tbls, toil, cga, drk wtr, shelters. ACTIVITIES: Boating,ld; picnicking; fishing. MISC.: Pets allowed on leash.

Springfield Recreation Area (State Recreation Area; Lewis and Clark Lake). 1 mi E of Springfield on St Hwy 52. SEASON: 5/1-9/30 (limited facilities during winter); 5-day lmt. FACILITIES: 21 sites (tr -35); electric hookup, tbls, flush toil, cga, f, showers, phone. Store/ice/laundry/food nearby. ACTIVITIES: Swimming; picnicking; fishing; hiking; boating,ld. MISC.: Nature trails; lake; beach; pets.

Terrace Park (City Park). 4 blocks S of St Hwy 37 in Springfield. SEASON: All year. FACILITIES: Tent sites; tbls, toil, cga, shelters. ACTIVITIES: Picnicking. MISC.: Pets permitted if on leash.

Westside City Park (City Park). 4 blocks W of Springfield off St Hwy 37. SEASON: All year. FACILITIES: Numerous tent sites; tbls, flush toil, cga, picnic shelters. ACTIVITIES: Swimming (pool). MISC.: Pets permitted if on a leash.

STICKNEY

Roadside Park (City Park). Across St Hwy 281 from town. SEASON: All year. FACILITIES: Sites; tbls, toil, cga, electric hookup, drk wtr. Showers in summer. ACTIVITIES: Picnicking. MISC.: Pets.

TABOR

Tabor Lakeside Use Area. 6 mi S of Tabor on St Hwys 50/52. SEASON: All yr; 5-day lmt. FACILITIES: No developed campsites, but camping is allowed; tbls, toil, cga, shelters. ACTIVITIES: Picnicking. MISC.: Pets allowed if kept on leash.

TYNDALL

Tyndall City Park. NW corner of town, in Tyndall. SEASON: All yr; 7-day lmt. FACILITIES: Sites; tbls, toil, cga, shower, playground. ACTIVITIES: Tennis; softball; swimming; picnicking; fishing. MISC.: Pets allowed if kept on leash.

VERMILLION

Clay County (State Recreation Area). 3 mi SW of Vermillion on St Hwy 50 and Co Rd. FACILITIES: 5/1–9/30 (limited facilities during winter); 5-day lmt. FACILITIES: 8 sites; tbls, toil, cga, drk wtr, food. ACTIVITIES: Boating,ld; hiking; picnicking; fishing. MISC.: Pets.

Lions' Park (City Park). On West Cherry Street/St Hwy 50, on W side of Vermillion. SEASON: 5/1–11/1; 1-night lmt. FACILITIES: 15 sites with water hookups; tbls, flush toil, cga, f. Store/ice/food/laundry/food nearby. ACTIVITIES: Tennis; softball; picnicking. Swimming/fishing/golf nearby. MISC.: Pets on leash.

WAUBAY

Blue Dog Lake Campgrounds (City Park). Two campgrounds ½ mi apart on the south side of Blue Dog Lake. SEASON: All year. FACILITIES: Sites; some electric hookups; toil, cga, pumped water. ACTIVITIES: Boating,ld. MISC.: Pets.

WESSINGTON SPRINGS

City Park. One block N of St Hwy 34 in Wessington Springs. SEASON: All yr; 3-night lmt. FACILITIES: 20 sites; tbls, toil, cga, drk wtr; 2 electric hookups. Flush toil at swimming pool ½ block further north. ACTIVITIES: Swimming; picnicking. MISC.: Pets on leash.

WHITE

Lake Hendricks Lakeside Use Area. 14 mi E of White on St Hwy 30. SEASON: All yr; 5-day lmt. FACILITIES: No developed campsites, but camping is allowed; tbls, toil, cga, drk wtr. ACTIVITIES: Boating,ld; picnicking; fishing. MISC.: Pets on leash.

WHITE RIVER

White River City Park. 4 blocks E of St Hwy 83 on Co Rd at S edge of White River. SEASON: All year. FACILITIES: 8 sites; tbls with sun shades, toil, cga, drk wtr, dump. ACTIVITIES: Picnicking. MISC.: Pets on leash.

WOONSOCKET

Twin Lakes Lakeside Use Area. 7 mi SW of Woonsocket on St Hwy 12. SEASON: All yr; 5-day lmt. FACILITIES: 6 sites; tbls, toil, cga, picnic shelters, drk wtr. ACTIVITIES: Boating; swimming; picnicking; fishing. MISC.: Pets.

YANKTON

Lesterville Lakeside Use Area. 14 mi W, 3 mi S of Yankton on St Hwy 50. SEASON: All yr; 5-day lmt. FACILITIES: No developed campsites, but camping is allowed; tbls, toil, cga. ACTIVITIES: Fishing; picnicking. MISC.: Pets.

TENNESSEE

GENERAL STATE INFORMATION

Miscellaneous

Right Turns on Red: Permitted after full stop, unless otherwise posted.
STATE CAPITOL: Nashville
STATE NICKNAME: Volunteer State
STATE MOTTO: "America At Its Best"
STATE BIRD: Mockingbird
STATE FLOWER: Iris
STATE TREE: Tulip Poplar

State Parks

Overnight camping fees, $2.00–$6.00. Pets are permitted if kept on a leash. Further information: Tennessee Tourist Development; 505 Fesslers Lane; Nashville, TN 37210.

Rest Areas

Overnight stops are not permitted in Tennessee Rest Areas.

Tennessee Valley Authority

TVA designated campgrounds are no longer free. However, unimproved TVA lands may be used for informal camping. These areas are shown on recreation maps of individual TVA lakes. No fees or permits are required. Further information: TVA; Knoxville, TN 37902.

See page 7 for KEY TO ABBREVIATIONS.

TENNESSEE

Bowaters Trails

Bowater Southern Paper Corporation has several networks of trails and free primitive camping facilities in Tennessee. In addition to their trails, they maintain a free Pocket Wilderness program. For information and a free brochure/map on Bowaters multiple-use facilities (including hunting and fishing, as well as camping), contact the Public Relations Department at either Bowater Carolina Corporation, Catawba, SC 29704; or Bowater Southern Paper Corporation; Calhoun, TN 37309.

Backcountry Camping in Smoky Mountains NP

Free backcountry permits may be obtained at any visitor center or Ranger Station. Party size limit is 8 persons. Permits for shelters must be requested in person, not more than 24 hours prior to departure on the trail. Permits other than for shelters may be issued on arrival in the park or by mail/phone no more than 30 days in advance of start of trip. Use of these campsites is limited to 3 consecutive nights per site. Winter camping is available. No pets, bicycles or motorized equipment on trails. Build fires at designated sites only. When camped, food must be kept in a trail shelter having bear exclosure fencing, or must be suspended at least 10 feet above the ground and 4 feet from any post, tree trunk or limb. Horses are permitted in Park; prohibited on trails designated as hiker trails only, on maintained portions of Park roadways, and in developed campgrounds and picnic areas. Further information and permits: Superintendent; Great Smoky Mountains NP; Gatlinburg, TN 37738; ATTN: Backcountry Office.

Backcountry Camping in Cherokee NF

Backcountry camping is allowed almost anywhere within the Forest. Since Gee Creek Wilderness is such a small area, they are not encouraging camping within the area. The Bald River Gorge area is not yet a wilderness. It has been recommended by the President to Congress for designation as wilderness. As yet, a management plan has not been prepared for the Bald River area, but due to the small size, it is anticipated that camping will not be recommended. Currently, no backcountry camping permits are required. Further information: Forest Supervisor; Cherokee NF; PO Box 400; Cleveland, TN 37311.

The Appalachian Trail

More than 2000 miles long, the Appalachian Trail (from Maine to Georgia) is the longest continuous marked trail in the world.

CAMPING: More than 200 open-front shelters/lean-tos are spaced approximately 10 miles apart on the Trail (one-day intervals). As they are occupied on a first-come first-served basis, carry a tent in case the shelters are full. Potable spring water is usually available at each site, but should be purified by tablets or boiling. And always "pack it in, pack it out".

PERMITS: No permit is required to hike the Trail. However, camping permits must be obtained for overnight stays in Shenandoah NP (Luray, VA 22835) and Great Smoky Mountains NP (Gatlinburg, TN 37733). These are free of charge and available from the ranger stations or by mail. A free camping permit must be obtained for overnight stays in White Mountain National Forest Restricted Use Area (PO Box 638; Laconia, NH 03246).

APPALACHIAN TRAIL CONFERENCE: A private, nonprofit, national organization which represents citizen's interest in the Appalachian Trail. They offer detailed guidebooks and maps for sale, as well as the A.T. Data Book which gives the location and distances between shelters and certain post offices, supply points, water sources, lodging and meals. For more information on this organization, write to them at: PO Box 236; Harpers Ferry, WV 25425.

INFORMATION SOURCES

Maps

The following maps are available from **Forsyth Travel Library** (see order form in Appendix B):

> State of Tennessee [Up-to-date, showing all principal roads, points of interest, sports areas, parks, airports, mileage, etc. Full color.]
>
> Completely indexed city maps, including all airports, lakes, rivers, etc., of: Chattanooga; Johnson City; Kingsport; Knoxville; Memphis; Nashville.

See page 7 for KEY TO ABBREVIATIONS.

TENNESSEE

State Information

Division of Tourism Development; Department of Economic and Community Development; Andrew Jackson State Office Building; Room 1021; Nashville, TN 37219.
Tennessee Tourist Development; 505 Fesslers Lane; Nashville, TN 37120.
Division of State Parks; 2611 West End Avenue; Nashville, TN 37203.
Tennessee Wildlife Resources Agency; Ellington Agricultural Center; PO Box 40747; Nashville, TN 37204.
Natchez Trace Parkway; RR #1; NT 143; Tupelo, MS 38801.

City Information

Chattanooga Chamber of Commerce; 819 Broad Street; Chattanooga, TN 37402.
Chattanooga Convention and Visitors Bureau; Memorial Auditorium; Chattanooga, TN 37403.
Greater Knoxville Chamber of Commerce; 705 Gay Street, SW; Knoxville, TN 37902.
Knoxville Tourist Bureau; 811 Henley Street, SW; Knoxville, TN 37902.
Memphis Area Chamber of Commerce; PO Box 224; Memphis, TN 38101.
Nashville Chamber of Commerce; 161 Fourth Avenue North; Nashville, TN 37219.

Miscellaneous

Cherokee NF; 2321 NW Ocoee Street; PO Box 400; Cleveland, TN 37311.
Great Smoky Mountains NP; Gatlinburg, TN 37738.
Tennessee NWR; Box 849; Paris, TN 38242.
Corps of Engineers, Nashville District; PO Box 1070; Nashville, TN 37202.
Corps of Engineers, Memphis District; 668 Clifford David Federal Building; Memphis, TN 38103.

FREE CAMPGROUNDS

ALLONS

Willow Grove (COE; Dale Hollow Lake). ⅓ mi N of Allons on St Hwy 52; 15 mi NE on Willow Grove Rd. Signs posted on highway. SEASON: 9/1-3/31, FREE ($3.50 rest of yr); 14-day lmt. FACILITIES: 87 sites; tbls, flush toil, cga, dump, showers, water hookups, amphitheater. Store/food nearby. ACTIVITIES: Boating,rld; swimming; picnicking; fishing; hunting. MISC.: Pets on leash.

BYRDSTOWN

Cove Creek (COE; Dale Hollow Lake). 2 mi SW of Byrdstown on St Hwy 42; 3 mi SE. [Follow posted signs to campground.] SEASON: All yr; 14-day lmt. FACILITIES: 12 sites; tbls, toil, cga, drk wtr. Laundry nearby. ACTIVITIES: Boating,l; picnicking; fishing; hunting. MISC.: Pets on leash.

Obey River (COE; Dale Hollow Lake). 6 mi SW of Byrdstown on St Hwy 42. SEASON: 9/1-3/31, FREE ($3.50 rest of yr). FACILITIES: 161 sites; tbls, flush toil, cga, dump, showers, drk wtr. Store/food nearby. Amphitheater. ACTIVITIES: Boating,rld; swimming; picnicking; fishing. MISC.: Pets on leash.

CARTHAGE

*Bearwaller Gap Hiking Trail (COE; Cordell Hull Lake). Take I-40 to the Carthage exit and take St Hwy 53 to Carthage. From Carthage, take St Hwy 85 to Defeated, TN, and follow the signs to the Defeated Creek Recreation Area. Camping is permitted only at the two designated primitive campsites along the trail. No permit or special permission is required to camp on the trail; however, you should register in and out at the trail entrances. [Information: COE Resource Manager; Route 1, Box 62; Carthage, TN 37030; 615/735-2244.]

Defeated Creek Campground (COE; Cordell Hull Lake). Take I-40 to Carthage-Gordonsville exit; then N on St Hwy 53 through South Carthage and across the Cumberland River; go through Carthage. 5 mi N of Carthage on St Hwy 85. Follow signs. SEASON: 9/15-4/1, FREE ($3 rest of yr); 14-day lmt. FACIL: 120 sites; electric/water hookups; tbls, flush toil, cga, dump, drk wtr. During free season, one loop of the campground containing 15 sites remains open all winter. ACTIVITIES: Hiking; tennis; basketball; volleyball; swimming; picnicking; fishing; boating,l. Campfire centers with special programs on weekends from May-September. MISC.: Full service marina; sand beaches; bicycle trail; 6-mi hiking trail; pets.

CELINA

Dale Hollow Dam (COE; Dale Hollow Lake). 3 mi W of Celina on St Hwy 53. Follow signs on St Hwy 53 to entrance of Dam area. SEASON: 9/1-3/31, FREE ($3.50 rest of yr); 14-day lmt. FACILITIES: 76 sites; electric hookup, tbls, flush toil, water hookup, drk wtr. Store/laundry nearby. ACTIVITIES: Boating,l; picnicking; fishing; hiking. MISC.: Pets.

*First Island (COE; Dale Hollow Lake).
9 mi from Celina on St Hwy 53; SE on
paved road to Holly Creek dock. Access
BY BOAT. SEASON: All yr; 14-day lmt.
FACILITIES: 12 tent sites; tbls, toil,
cga, no drk wtr. ACTIVITIES: Hunting;
picnicking; fishing. MISC.: Pets.

Pleasant Grove Park (COE; Dale Hollow
Lake). 4 mi E of Celina on St Hwy 53;
1½ mi SE to campground. [Follow signs.]
SEASON: All yr; 14-day lmt. FACILITIES:
20 sites; tbls, flush toil, cga, drk wtr.
Store/food nearby. ACTIVITIES: Swimming;
boating,l; picnicking; fishing; hunting;
hiking. MISC.: Pets on leash.

CLEVELAND

Sylco (Cherokee NF). 12½ mi E of Cleveland on US 64; 3 mi SE on Co Hwy 75;
7-2/5 mi SE on FS 55. SEASON: All yr;
14-day lmt. FACILITIES: 12 sites (tr
-22); tbls, toil, cga, well drk wtr. ACTI-
VITIES: Hiking; picnicking. Fishing
(3 mi). MISC.: Nature trails (1 mi).
Elev 1200 ft; 4 acres. Pets on leash.

Thunder Rock (Cherokee NF). 28½ mi E
of Cleveland on US 64; 1/5 mi S on FS
45. SEASON: All yr; 14-day lmt. FACILI-
TIES: 6 sites (tr -22); tbls, toil, cga,
piped drk wtr. ACTIVITIES: Picnicking. MISC.: Elev 1200 ft; 2 acres;
river; pets.

COPPERHILL

Tumbling Creek (Cherokee NF). 1-4/5
mi NW of Copperhill on St Hwy 68; 4-
9/10 mi W on Co Rd 5496; 2-1/10 mi
N on FS 221. SEASON: All year; 14-day
lmt. FACILITIES: 8 sites (tr -22); tbls,
toil, cga, piped drk wtr. Store/ice/gas
(5 mi). ACTIVITIES: Fishing; picnicking. MISC.: Elev 1400 ft; 3 acres;
stream. Pets on leash.

CUMBERLAND CITY

Guises Creek Recreation Area (COE; Lake
Barkley). 3 mi E of Cumberland City
on St Hwy 149. FACILITIES: 20 sites;
tbls, toil, cga, no drk wtr. ACTIVITIES:
Boating,l; picnicking; fishing. SEASON:
All yr; 14-day lmt. MISC.: Lake; beach;
pets on leash.

River Bend Recreation Area (COE; Lake
Barkley). 3 mi N of Cumberland City.
SEASON: All yr; 14-day lmt. FACILITIES:
15 sites; tbls, toil, cga, no drk wtr.
ACTIVITIES: Boating,l; picnicking; fish-
ing; waterskiing. MISC.: Lake; beach.
Pets on leash.

DAMASCUS

Backbone Rock (Cherokee NF). 5 mi SW
of Damascus on St Hwy 133. SEASON:
All yr; 14-day lmt. FACILITIES: 13 sites
(tr -16); tbls, toil, cga, f, piped drk
wtr. Store/ice/food/gas/laundry (5 mi).

ACTIVITIES: Hiking; picnicking; fishing.
MISC.: Elev 2200 ft; 5 acres; geological;
pets; nature trails; stream.

DOVER

Blue Creek Recreation Area (COE; Lake
Barkley). 5 mi N of Dover on St Hwy
20; W to access road, to campground.
SEASON: All yr; 14-day lmt. FACILITIES:
20 sites; tbls, toil, cga, no drk wtr.
ACTIVITIES: Boating,l; waterskiing;
picnicking; fishing. MISC.: Lake; pets.

Bumpus Mills Recreation Area (COE; Lake
Barkley). 7 mi E of Dover on US 79;
5 mi N on St Hwy 120; 6 mi W to campground. SEASON: 4/1-11/30; 14-day lmt.
FACILITIES: 33 sites; tbls, flush toil,
cga, drk wtr, showers. Store/food nearby. ACTIVITIES: Hiking; waterskiing;
boating,l; picnicking; fishing. MISC.:
Nature trails; pets; lake.

Hickman Creek Recreation Area (COE;
Lake Barkley). 4 mi NW of Dover; N on
US 79. SEASON: 4/1-11/30; 14-day lmt.
FACILITIES: 17 sites; tbls, toil, cga,
drk wtr. ACTIVITIES: Boating,l; picnick-
ing; fishing. MISC.: Pets on leash.

Lick Creek Recreation Area (COE; Lake
Barkley). 2 mi E of Dover on St Hwy
79. SEASON: All yr; 14-day lmt. FACILI-
TIES: 18 sites; tbls, toil, cga, no drk
wtr. ACTIVITIES: Waterskiing; boating,l;
picnicking; fishing. MISC.: Lake; pets.

ELIZABETHTON

Low Gap (NF). 18 mi NE of Elizabethton
on St Hwy 91; 7 mi W on FS 56. SEASON:
All year. FACILITIES: 4 sites (tr -16);
tbls, toil, cga, f, piped drk wtr. ACTIV-
ITIES: Picnicking. MISC.: Elev 4000 ft;
1 acre; pets. On Holston Mountain.

ETOWAH

Lost Creek (Cherokee NF). 7 mi S of Etowah on US 411; 6 mi SE on St Hwy 30;
7 mi E on FS 103. SEASON: All yr; 14-
day lmt. FACILITIES: 12 sites (tr -16);
tbls, toil, cga, f, well drk wtr. ACTIVI-
TIES: Picnicking; fishing. MISC.: Elev
1000 ft; 5 acres; pets; scenic. 10 mi
from scenic Hiwassee River.

GORDONSVILLE

Buffalo Valley Recreation Area (COE; Center Hill Lake). 10 mi SE of Gordonsville
on St Hwy 141 to Center Hill Dam Site;
then just below the Dam on St Hwy 141.
SEASON: April-November; 14-day lmt. FA-
CILITIES: 3 sites; tbls, toil, cga, drk
wtr. ACTIVITIES: Boating,l; hiking; hunting. MISC.: Self-guiding interpretive
nature trail approximately ¼ mi in
length. Pets on leash.

Center Hill Recreation Area (COE; Center Hill Lake). 10 mi SE of Gordonsville on St Hwy 141, at the Center Hill Dam Site. SEASON: April–November; 14-day lmt. FACILITIES: 14 sites; tbls, flush toil, cga, drk wtr, small picnic shelter. ACTIVITIES: Boating,l; picnicking; fishing; hunting. MISC.: Pets on leash.

Long Branch Recreation Area (COE; Center Hill Lake). 10 mi SE of Gordonsville on St Hwy 141 to Center Hill Dam Site; then beyond Buffalo Valley Recreation Area below Center Hill Dam on St Hwy 141. SEASON: April–November; 14-day lmt. FACILITIES: 9 sites; tbls, toil, cga, no drk wtr. ACTIVITIES: Boating,l; picnicking; fishing (trout). MISC.: Pets.

GRANVILLE

*Cordell Hull Lake Horseback Riding Trails (COE; Cordell Hull Lake). Take I-40 to the Carthage exit and stay on St Hwy 53 to Granville. The trail entrance is beside the road just past Granville. [Information: COE Resource Manager; Route 1, Box 62; Carthage, TN 37030.] Primitive camping and picnicking are encouraged along the trails.

Granville Recreation Area (COE; Cordell Hull Lake). 2 mi S of Granville on St Hwy 53. SEASON: 4/1–11/1; 14-day lmt. FACILITIES: 75 sites; tbls, flush toil, cga, showers, dump, drk wtr. ACTIVITIES: Boating,l; picnicking; fishing. MISC.: Pets on leash.

Indian Creek Campground (COE; Cordell Hull Lake). Just off St Hwy 53 near Granville. SEASON: 4/1–9/15. FACILITIES: Sites; 2 large bath houses. ACTIVITIES: Swimming; boating,l. MISC.: Pets;beach. Gate attendant on duty for assistance.

GREENVILLE

Old Forge (Cherokee NF). 9 mi E of Greenville on St Hwy 107; 3 mi S on FS FH94; 3 mi SW on FS 331. SEASON: 5/1–10/31; 14-day lmt. FACILITIES: 9 sites; tbls, toil, cga, f, well drk wtr. ACTIVITIES: Swimming; picnicking; fishing; horseback riding (loading ramp, trail, and stalls are available). MISC.: Elev 2000 ft; 5 acres; stream; pets.

HAMPTON

Dennis Cove (Cherokee NF). 1 mi E of Hampton on US 321; 7 mi SE on FS 50. SEASON: 4/14–11/27, 14-day lmt. FACILITIES: 18 sites (tr –16); tbls, toil, cga, f, drk wtr. ACTIVITIES: Swimming; picnicking; fishing. MISC.: Elev 2600 ft; 2 acres; pets. Within Laurel Fork Wildlife Management Area.

HOHENWALD

Meriwether Lewis Campground [was "Little Swan"] (Natchez Trace Parkway). Near St Hwy 20. SEASON: All yr; 15-day lmt. FACILITIES: 32 sites; tbls, toil, cga, drk wtr. ACTIVITIES: Picnicking. MISC.: The site of Grinder's Inn, where Lewis died of gunshot wounds. A monument in the park guards his remains. Pets.

LEXINGTON

Crazy Doe [Beech Lake] (Beach River Watershed, State Area). Lexington exit, off I-40; 6 mi S on St Hwy 22; 2 mi W to campground. SEASON: All year. FACILITIES: 22 sites; tbls, toil, cga, f, drk wtr. ACTIVITIES: Swimming; picnicking; fishing; boating,d. Golf nearby. MISC.: Pets on leash.

LIVINGSTON

Lillydale (COE; Dale Hollow Lake). 19 mi NE of Livingston on St Hwy 52 and Willow Grove Road. [Signs posted on highway.] SEASON: 9/1–3/31, FREE ($3.50 rest of yr). FACILITIES: 92 sites; tbls, flush toil, cga, showers, amphitheater, water hookups. Store nearby. ACTIVITIES: Hunting; swimming; boating,l; picnicking; fishing. MISC.: Pets on leash.

MARYVILLE

Chilhowee Lake. A small lake (1600 acres) located about 20 mi S of Maryville. There are 3 public boat launching areas. US 129 borders the lake on one side and privately owned land on the other. No campgrounds, but the public uses highway right-of-way on the lake bank for short-term camping. Fishing (small and large mouth bass, rainbow trout and bream).

NASHVILLE

Shutes Branch Recreation Area (COE; Old Hickory Lake). [8 mi NE of Nashville on US 70; N on Saundersville Rd.] Exit from I-40 at Exit 221, Old Hickory Blvd. Proceed on Old Hickory Blvd., turn right (E) on US 70N. After 2 mi turn left (N) on Andrew Jackson Parkway; 3 mi on the Parkway to campground. SEAS: All yr; 14-day lmt. FAC: 84 sites; tbls, flush toil, cga, showers, dump. ACTIVITIES: Hunting; boating,l; picnicking; fishing. MISC.: Store nearby.

NEWPORT

Houston Valley (Cherokee NF). 13 mi E of Newport on US 25; 5 mi NE on St Hwy 107. SEASON: 4/15–9/30; 14-day lmt. FACILITIES: 10 sites (tr –22); tbls, flush toil, cga, f, drk wtr. ACTIVITIES: Picnicking. Fishing (1 mi). MISC.:Pets.

Round Mountain (Cherokee NF). 7 mi SE of Newport on US 25; 13 mi SE on St Hwy 107. SEASON: 4/15–9/30; 14-day lmt. FACILITIES: 16 sites (tr –16); tbls, toil, cga, f, drk wtr. MISC.: Elev 3500 ft; 6 acres. Pets on leash.

See page 7 for KEY TO ABBREVIATIONS.

SHADY VALLEY

Fagall Branch (NF). 6 mi NE of Shady Valley on St Hwy 133. SEASON:9/30–12/31; 14-day lmt. FACILITIES: 4 sites (tr –16); toil, cga, f. ACTIVITIES: Fishing. MISC.: Pets.

SMITHVILLE

Cove Hollow Recreation Area (COE; Center Hill Lake). 14 mi NE of Smithville on US 70. [Located on the Dale Ridge Road of DeKalb County some 4 mi from Center Hill Dam.] SEASON: 4/1–11/1; 14-day lmt. FACILITIES: 25 sites; tbls, flush toil, cga, drk wtr. Food nearby. ACTIVITIES: Boating,l; picnicking; fishing; hunting. MISC.: Located adjacent to Cove Hollow Boat Dock. Pets allowed if on a leash.

Floating Mill Park (COE; Center Hill Lake). 14 mi NE of Smithville (5 mi S of I–40), just off St Hwy 56. SEASON: September to mid-May, FREE ($3 rest of yr); 14-day lmt. [December, January, February, limited facilities.] FACILITIES: 120 sites; tbls, flush toil, cga, dump, drk wtr, showers. ACTIVITIES: Boating,rld; picnicking; fishing; swimming; hiking; hunting. MISC.: Concrete and sand beaches; pets; nature trail.

Holmes Creek Recreation Area (COE; Center Hill Lake). Approximately 9 mi NW of Smithville on Hurricane Ridge Road. SEASON: September to mid-May, FREE ($2 rest of yr); 14-day lmt. [Decembere, January, February, limited facilities.] FACILITIES: 150 sites; tbls, flush toil, cga, showers, drk wtr. ACTIVITIES: Hunting; picnicking; fishing; swimming; boating,l. MISC.: Pets on leash.

Hurricane Bridge Recreation Area (Center Hill Lake; COE). 8 mi N of Smithville off St Hwy 56, at Hurrican Bridge which crosses Center Hill Lake. SEASON: 4/1–11/1; 14-day lmt. FACILITIES: 39 sites; tbls, flush toil, cga, drk wtr. ACTIVITIES: Hunting; picnicking; fishing; boating,l; hiking. MISC.: Pets on leash.

Johnson Chapel Recreation Area (COE; Center Hill Lake). 10 mi E of Smithville just off St Hwy 70. SEASON: 4/1–11/1; 14-day lmt. FACILITIES: 22 sites (tr –22); tbls, flush toil, cga, drk wtr, store. ACTIVITIES: Boating,l; picnicking; fishing; hiking; hunting. MISC.: Pets.

Ragland Bottom Recreation Area (COE; Center Hill Lake). 6 mi E of Smithville off St Hwy 70. SEASON: September to mid-May, FREE ($3 rest of yr); 14-day lmt. [December, January, February, limited facilities.] FACILITIES: 78 sites; tbls, flush toil, cga, dump, showers, picnic shelter. ACTIVITIES: Hiking; swimming; boating,rld; picnicking; fishing. MISC.: Pets; 1-mi nature trail. Beautiful flowering dogwood trees in the spring. This area also has 33 sites only for picnicking, equipped with a tbl/cga.

SPRING CITY

Newby Branch Forest Camp (Bowater Southern Paper Corporation). An isolated relatively primitive campsite near Spring City; the upper terminus of the Piney River Trail. BY FOOT. SEASON: All year. FACILITIES: Tent pads; tbls, toil, cga, hand pump. ACTIVITIES: Hiking; picnicking. MISC.: Pets on a leash.

Piney River Tree Farm (Bowaters Southern Paper Corporation). On Walden's Ridge, just W of the city. It offers: 2 picnic areas (Piney River and Flat Rock) located near the Shut-In Gap Rd bridge across Piney River; Twin Rocks Nature Trail, which adjoins Piney River Picnic Area; Stinging Fork Pocket Wilderness, for rugged hiking; and Newby Branch Forest Camp (relatively primitive with no electricity or running water; pump, tbls, toil, cga). Use of camp is on a first-come first-served basis; if possible, in advance contact Hiwassee Land Company; PO Box 537; Spring City, TN 37381. For brochure that includes helpful map to this and other Bowaters locations, write: PR Dept.; Bowaters Southern Paper Corp.; Calhoun,TN 37309; 615/336–2211. Pets permitted on leash.

TELLICO PLAINS

Holly Flats (Cherokee NF). 4–9/10 mi SE of Tellico Plains on Co Hwy 165; 13–3/10 mi SE on FS FH210; 5 mi W on FS 126. SEASON: 3/1–12/18; 14-day lmt. FACILITIES: 17 sites (tr –22); tbls, toil, cga, well drk wtr. ACTIVITIES: Hiking; picnicking; fishing. MISC.: Elev 1800 ft; 6 acres; pets. In Tellico Wildlife Management Area on Bald River. Hiking trail down Bald River to Tellico River (5 mi).

Jake Best (Cherokee NF). 4 mi E of Tellico Plains on Co Hwy 165; NE on FS 35. SEASON: All year. FACILITIES: 7 sites (no tr); tbls, toil, cga, well drk wtr. ACTIVITIES: Swimming; picnicking; fishing (trout); hunting. MISC.: Stream; pets on leash.Elev 1000 ft; 2 acres.

Limestone Cove (Cherokee NF). 5 mi E of Unicoi on St Hwy 107. SEASON: 4/14–10/16; 14-day lmt. FACILITIES: 18 sites (tr –22); tbls, toil, cga, f, piped drk wtr. Store/gas (2 mi). Ice/food (5 mi). ACTIVITIES: Fishing; picnicking. MISC.: Elev 2400 ft; 6 acres; stream; pets.

WALTERHILL

Fall Creek (COE; J. Percy Priest Reservoir). 1 mi N of Walterhill on US 231; 9 mi NW to campground. SEASON: All yr; 14-day lmt. FACILITIES: 37 sites; tbls, toil, cga, no drk wtr. ACTIVITIES: Fishing; picnicking; boating,l. MISC.: Pets.

See page 7 for KEY TO ABBREVIATIONS.

TEXAS

GENERAL STATE INFORMATION

Miscellaneous

Right Turns on Red: Permitted after full
stop, unless otherwise posted.

STATE CAPITOL: Austin
STATE NICKNAME: Lone Star State
STATE MOTTO: "Friendship"
STATE BIRD: Mockingbird
STATE FLOWER: Bluebonnet
STATE TREE: Pecan

State Parks

The fee is $3.00 per night for camping in Texas State Parks. Pets are permitted on
a leash.   Further information: Parks and Wildlife Department; John H. Reagan Building; Austin, TX 78701.

Rest Areas

Overnight stops are not permitted in Texas Rest Areas.

INFORMATION SOURCES

Maps

The following maps are available from **Forsyth Travel Library** (see order form in Appendix B):

> **State of Texas** [Up-to-date, showing all principal roads,
> points of interest, sports areas, parks, airports, mileage,
> etc.   Full color.]

> Completely indexed city maps, including all airports, lakes,
> rivers, etc., of 18 different Texas cities, itemized in Appen-
> dix B.

Gold Mining and Prospecting

Texas Bureau of Economic Geology; University of Texas; Austin, TX 78712.

State Information

State Department of Highways and Public Transportation; Travel and Information Divi-
    sion; PO Box 5064; Austin, TX 78763.   [Ask for their free book entitled TEXAS: LAND
    OF CONTRASTS.]
Texas Tourist Development Agency; Box 12008, Capitol Station; Austin, TX 78711.
East Texas Chamber of Commerce; Box 1592; Longview, TX 75601.
Parks and Wildlife Department; John H. Reagan Building; Austin, TX 78701.

City Information

Dallas Chamber of Commerce; Fidelity Union Tower Building; Dallas, TX 75201.
El Paso Chamber of Commerce; 820 North Mesa; PO Box 682; El Paso, TX 79944.
Forth Worth Chamber of Commerce, Convention and Visitors Bureau; 700 Throckmorton
    Street; Fort Worth, TX 76102.
Houston Chamber of Commerce; 1006 Main Street; Houston, TX 77002.
San Antonio Convention and Visitors Bureau; 602 HemisFair Plaza Way; PO Box 2277;
    San Antonio, TX 78206.

National Forests

Angelina NF; PO Box 969; Lufkin, TX 75901.
Davy Crockett NF; PO Box 969; Lufkin, TX 75901.
Sabine NF; PO Box 969; Lufkin, TX 75901.
Sam Houston NF; PO Box 969; Lufkin, TX 75901.

Corps of Engineers

U.S. Army Engineer District, Fort Worth; PO Box 17300; Fort Worth, TX 76102.
U.S. Army Engineer District, Galveston; PO Box 1229; Galveston, TX 77553.
U.S. Army Engineer District, New Orleans; PO Box 60267; New Orleans, LA 70160.
    [All of their free campgrounds are in Texas.]
U.S. Army Engineer Division, Southwestern; 1200 Main Street; Dallas, TX 75202.

TEXAS

Miscellaneous

Texas Bureau of Land Management; U.S.P.O. and Federal Building; PO Box 1449; Santa Fe, NM 87501. [Includes New Mexico and Oklahoma.]
Amistad NRA; PO Box 1463; Del Rio, TX 78840.
Lake Meredith NRA; PO Box 1438; Fritch, TX 79036.
Padre Island National Seashore; 9405 South Padre Island Drive; Corpus Christi, TX 78418.
Aransas NWR; Box 100; Austwell, TX 77950.
Muleshoe NWR; Box 549; Muleshoe, TX 79347.

FREE CAMPGROUNDS

ALPINE

State Rest Area. 16 mi NW of Alpine on St Hwy 118. SEASON: All yr. FACILITIES: 4 spaces for self-contained RVs; tbls, cga. ACTIVITIES: Picnicking. MISC.: Elev 4500 ft. Pets permitted.

AMARILLO

Bates Canyon (Lake Meredith Rec. Area). 36 mi NE of Amarillo on St Hwy 136; 5 mi N on Alibates Road. SEASON: All yr; 14-day lmt. FACILITIES: Undesignated sites; tbls, toil, cga, no drk wtr. ACTIVITIES: Picnicking; fishing; boating,ld. MISC.: Pets.

Rosita Flats (Lake Meredith Rec. Area). N of Amarillo on US 87/287 to Canadian River Bridge; E on dirt road SEASON: All yr; 14-day lmt. FACILITIES: Prim. undesignated sites; toil, no tbls. MISC.: Pets permitted if kept on leash.

ANAHUAC

Fort Anahuac Park (Co. Park). 1 mi S of Anahuac on South Main Street. SEASON: All yr; 2-day lmt. FACILITIES: 10 sites; elec/wtr hkup, flush toil, tbls. Store/food/ice/laundry (nearby). ACTIVITIES: Swimming; picnicking; fishing; boating,l; playground. Golf (nearby). MISC.: Reservation Required. On Trinity Bay. Pets.

White Memorial Park (Municipal Park). From I-10, 200 yards S on St Hwy 61, in Anahuac. SEASON: All yr; 2-day lmt FACILITIES: 20 sites; tbls, flush toil, Store/food/laundry (nearby). ACTIVITIES: Swimming; picnicking; fishing; boating,ld. Golf (nearby). MISC.: Pets.

ANDREWS

Andrews Prairie Dog Town (Municipal Park). In Andrews on Broadway, W of US 385 between 6th & 7th Streets. SEASON: All yr; 3-day lmt. FACILITIES: 11 sites (tr -30); elec/wtr/sewer hkups, pull-thru spaces, flush toil, showers, phone. Store/food/laundry/ice (nearby). ACTIVITIES: Tennis; softball; picnicking; fishing. Swimming/golf (nearby). MISC.: Lake; rec. hall. Pets permitted.

City Park. In Andrews on St Hwy 115/176; 7 blks W from US 385. SEASON: All yr; 3-day lmt. FACILITIES: 11 sites; tbls, toil, cga. ACTIVITIES: Swimming; picnicking; fishing; golfing. MISC.: Pets.

ARLINGTON

Randol Mill Park (City Park). On Randol Mill Road. SEASON: All yr; 2-day lmt. FACILITIES: tbls, toil. ACTIVITIES: Swimming; picnicking; hiking. MISC.: Pets.

ARTHUR CITY

Forest Point (COE; Pay Mayse Lake). Approx. 7 mi W of Arthur City on Co Rd 197; 1½ mi S. SEASON: All yr; 14-day lmt. FACILITIES: 24 sites; tbls, toil, cga, drk wtr. ACTIVITIES: Swimming; picnicking; fishing; boating,l. MISC.: Pets.

ATLANTA

Armstrong Creek (COE; Wright Patman Dam & Lake). From intersection of US Hwy 59 & St Hwy 96; 7-2/5 mi NW on St Hwy 96; 1-2/5 mi S on St Hwy 96; NW to Campground. SEASON: All yr (limited facilities in winter); 14-day lmt. FACILITIES: 10 sites; tbls, toil, cga, drk wtr. ACTIVITIES: Picnicking; fishing; swimming in designated areas; hunting in the undeveloped areas during hunting season. MISC.: No firearms in developed public use areas. Pets.

Jackson Creek Rec. Area (COE; Wright Patman Dam & Lake). 12 mi NW of Atlanta on St Hwy 77 & Co Road. SEASON: All yr; 14-day lmt. FACILITIES: 10 sites; tbls, toil, cga, drk wtr. ACTIVITIES: Hunting; picnicking; fishing; boating,l. MISC.: On Lake Texarkana. Pets permitted if kept on leash.

Mill Creek Rec. Area (COE; Wright Patman Dam & Lake). 8 mi N of Atlanta on US 59 to local rd; 2 mi W (on Lake Texarkana). SEASON: All yr; 14-day lmt. FACILITIES: sites, tbls, toil, cga, drk wtr. ACTIVITIES: Picnicking; fishing. MISC.: Pets.

Over Cup (COE; Wright Patman Dam & Lake). 1 mi SW of Atlanta on US 59 to St Hwy 77; 11 mi NW to St Hwy 8; 3 mi N to local rd; 6 mi W. SEASON: MD - LD; 14-day lmt. FACILITIES: Sites, tbls, toil, cga, drk wtr. ACTIVI-TIES: Hunting; picnicking; fishing; boating,r. MISC.: On Lake Texarkana. Pets permitted if kept on leash.

Sawmill Hill Rec. Area (COE; Wright Patman Dam & Lake). From intersection of US Hwy 59 and St Hwy 96, 7-4/5 mi N on US Hwy 59; SW to campground. SEASON: MD - LD (limited facilities in winter); 14-day lmt. FACILITIES: 14 sites; tbls, toil, cga, drk wtr. AC-TIVITIES: Swimming (in designated areas); hunting in the undeveloped areas during hunting season; picnick-ing; fishing. MISC.: No firearms in developed public use areas. Pets.

Sherman Landing Rec. Area (COE; Wright Patman Dam & Lake). 10 mi N on US 59 to Co Rd; 7/10 mi NW. SEASON: MD - LD; 14-day lmt. FACILITIES: Sites, tbls, toil, cga, drk wtr. ACTIVI-TIES: Hunting; picnicking; fishing; boating,rl. MISC.: Pets permitted.

South Abutment Rec. Area (COE; Wright Patman Dam & Lake). 12 mi N of Atlan-ta on US 59; 3 mi W on Co Hwy. SEA-SON: MD-LD; 14-day lmt. FACILITIES: Sites, tbls, toil, cga, drk wtr. ACTIVI-TIES: Swimming; picnicking; fishing; boating,rl. MISC.: Lake. Pets permitted.

Thomas Lake Rec. Area (COE; Wright Patman Dam & Lake). 1 mi SW on US 59; 19 mi SW on St Hwy 77; 3 mi N on St Hwy 994; 3 mi NE on Co Hwy. SEA-SON: MD-LD; 14-day lmt. FACILITIES: Sites, tbls, toil, cga, drk wtr. ACTIVI-TIES: Hunting; picnicking; fishing; boating,l. MISC.: Pets.

AUSTIN

Cedar Point Park (COE). 1 mi E of Austin on St Hwy 29; 16 mi NE on St Hwy 2241; 6 mi NE on Co Hwy (on Lake Buchanan). SEASON: MD-LD; 14-day lmt. 120 sites; tbls, toil, cga, drk wtr. AC-TIVITIES: Swimming; picnicking; fish-ing; boating,r. MISC.: Pets permitted.

LCRA Mansfield Dam Rec. Area (Co. Park). On RR 620 at N end of Mans-field Dam. SEASON: All yr; 7-day lmt. FACILITIES: 40 sites; tbls, toil, cga. ACTIVITIES: Hiking; picnicking; fish-ing; boating,ld; waterskiing. MISC.: Bike trails. Pets permitted if kept on leash.

AVINGER

Cedar Springs Park (COE; Lake O'The Pines). 14 mi SW of Avinger on St Hwy 155. SEASON: MD-LD (limited facility during winter); 14-day lmt. FACILI-TIES: 26 sites; tbls, toil, cga. Store (nearby). ACTIVITIES: Picnicking; swimming; fishing; boating,l. MISC.: Pets permitted if kept on leash.

Mims Chapel (COE; Lake O'The Pines). 9 mi SW of Avinger on St Hwy 155; 3-1/2 mi SE on St Hwy 729. SEASON: MD-LD (Limited facilities during win-ter); 14-day lmt. FACILITIES: 9 sites; tbls, toil, cga, drk wtr. ACTIVITIES: Boating,l; picnicking; fishing; swim-ming in designated areas; hunting in the undeveloped areas during hunt-ing season. MISC.: No firearms in de-veloped public use areas. Pets.

Oak Valley Park (COE; Lake O'The Pines). 9 mi SW of Avinger on St Hwy 155; 1-2/5 mi SE on St Hwy 729 to access rd. SEASON: MD-LD (limited facilities during winter); 14-day lmt. FACILITIES: 16 sites; tbls, toil, cga, drk wtr. ACTIVITIES: Boat-ing,l; picnicking; fishing; swimming in designated swimming areas; hunting in the undeveloped areas during hunt-ing season. MISC.: No firearms in de-veloped public use areas. Pets.

BALLINGER

City Park. In town. SEASON: All yr; 1-day lmt. FACILITIES: 5 sites; tbls, toil, cga. ACTIVITIES: Swimming; pic-nicking; fishing; boating,r. MISC.: Pets permitted if kept on leash.

BANDERA

State Roadside Park. 2-4/5 mi N of Bandera on St Hwy 16. SEASON: All yr; 1-day lmt. FACILITIES: 12 self-con-tained sites; tbls, toil, cga, ACTIVI-TIES: Swimming; picnicking; fishing; hunting; hiking. MISC.: Bike trails. Pets permitted if kept on leash.

BARDWELL

Love Park (COE; Bardwell Lake). NE of Bardwell on St Hwy 34; across Brad-well Lake. SEASON: All yr; 14-day lmt. FACILITIES: Undesignated sites; tbls, toil, cga. ACTIVITIES: Boating,l; pic-nicking; fishing. MISC.: Pets permitted.

BELTON

Belton Lakeview Park (COE; Belton Lake). 9 mi NW of Belton on St Hwy 2271. SEASON: All yr; 14-day lmt. FA-CILITIES: 8 sites; tbls, toil, cga, phone. Ice/gas (nearby). ACTIVITIES: Hiking; picnicking; fishing; boating,rl; swimming; waterskiing. MISC.: Bike trails; lake. Pets.

See page 7 for KEY TO ABBREVIATIONS.

Bluff Park (COE; Stillhouse Hollow Lake). 5 mi SW of Belton on US 190 & FM 1670. SEASON: All yr; 14-day lmt. FACILITIES: Undesignated sites; toil. ACTIVITIES: Fishing. MISC.: Pets.

Cedar Gt Park (COE; Stillhouse Hollow Lake). 5 mi SW of Belton on US 190 & FM 2410. SEASON: All yr; 14-day lmt. FACILITIES: Undesignated sites; toil, no drk wtr. ACTIVITIES: Fishing; boating, MISC.: Pets.

Iron Bridge Park (COE). 14 mi N of Belton on St Hwy 317; 5 mi W; 1 mi SW on Co Hwy (on Lake Belton). SEASON: All yr; 14-day lmt. FACILITIES: 10 sites; tbls, toil, cga, drk wtr. ACTIVITIES: Swimming; picnicking; fishing; boating,rl. MISC.: Pets permitted.

Rogers Park (COE; Belton Lake). 8 mi NW of Belton on St Hwys 317/2483. SEASON: All yr; 14-day lmt. FACILITIES: 13 sites; tbls, toil, cga, drk wtr. Store/ice (nearby). ACTIVITIES: Boating,rl; picnicking; fishing. Swimming (nearby). MISC.: Pets.

Stillhouse Park (COE; Stillhouse Hollow Lake). 5 mi W of Belton on US 190; 2 mi S on paved rd. SEASON: All yr; 14-day lmt. FACILITIES: 31 sites; tbls, toil, cga, f, drk wtr. ACTIVITIES: Swimming; picnicking; fishing; boating,rld. MISC.: Pets.

West Cliff Park Area (COE; Belton Lake). 5 mi N of Belton on St Hwy 2271. SEASON: All yr; 14-day lmt. FACILITIES: 5 sites; tbls, toil, cga, drk wtr. ACTIVITIES: Swimming; picnicking; fishing; boating,rl. Store/ice (nearby). MISC.: Pets.

BENBROOK

Dutch Branch (COE; Benbrook Lake). 1 mi S of Benbrook on US 377. SEASON: All yr; 14-day lmt. FACILITIES: Undesignated sites; tbls, toil, cga, drk wtr. Store/food/ice (nearby). ACTIVITIES: Boating,l; picnicking; fishing; swimming (nearby). MISC.: Pets.

Longhorn (COE; Benbrook Lake). 2 mi SE of Benbrook on Co Hwy 1043. SEASON: All yr; 14-day lmt. FACILITIES: Undesignated sites; tbls, toil, cga, drk wtr. ACTIVITIES: Boating,l; picnicking; fishing. Golf (nearby). MISC.: Pets.

Rocky Creek (COE; Benbrook Lake). 4 mi E of Benbrook on Co Hwy 1043; 1 mi S on Old Granbury; 3½ mi SW on Co Rd. SEASON: All yr; 14-day lmt.

FACILITIES: Undesignated sites; tbls, toil, cga, drk wtr. Store/food/laundry/ice (nearby). ACTIVITIES: Boating,l; picnicking; fishing; swimming. MISC: Pets permitted if kept on leash.

BIG LAKE

Big Lake (City Park). Main Street in Big Lake. SEASON: All yr. FACILITIES: 35 sites; tbls, toil, cga. ACTIVITIES: Swimming; picnicking; fishing; softball. MISC.: Pets.

BIG SPRING

Tourist Camp (Municipal Park). 2 mi S of Big Spring on US 87. SEASON: All yr. FACILITIES: Spaces for self-contained RVs. MISC.: Pets permitted if kept on leash.

Comanche Trail (City Park). 2½ mi S on US 87. SEASON: All yr; 1-day lmt. FACILITIES: 13 sites; tbls, toil, cga. ACTIVITIES: Hiking; picnicking; fishing; softball. MISC.: Pets permitted.

Spencer Reservoir Public Area (City Park). 1 mi W of Big Spring on Lu Loop 229; 1 mi N on Co Hwy (at Spencer Reservoir). SEASON: All yr; 7-day lmt. FACILITIES: Sites, tbls, toil, cga. ACTIVITIES: Swimming; picnicking; fishing; boating,rl. MISC.: Pets permitted if kept on leash.

Moss Creek Lake (City Park). 6 mi S of I-20 on Moss Creek Lake Road, 5 mi E of Big Spring. SEASON: All yr. FACILITIES: 13 sites; tbls, toil, cga, store, elec hkup, food, ice. ACTIVITIES: Hiking; picnicking; fishing; boating,ld. MISC.: Pets permitted.

BLUM

Noland River Park (COE; Whitney Lake). 4 mi SW of Blum on St Hwy 933 and Co Roads. SEASON: All yr; 14-day lmt. FACILITIES: 7 sites; tbls, toil, cga, drk wtr. ACTIVITIES: Swimming; boating,l; picnicking; fishing. MISC.: Pets.

BORGER

Huber Park (City Park). At S city lmts of Borger on St Hwy 207. SEASON: All yr; 3-day lmt. FACILITIES: Sites, tbls, toil, cga. ACTIVITIES: Golf; Swimming; picnicking; fishing; hunting; boating,r; horseback riding/rental. MISC.: Pets.

BOWIE

Pelham Park (Municipal Park). In Bowie take St Hwy 81 exit off US 287. SEASON: All yr. FACILITIES: 50 sites; tbls, toil, cga, drk wtr, elec/wtr hkups. Store/food/ice/laundry/bottled gas (nearby). ACTIVITIES: Golf; tennis (nearby), Picnicking. MISC.: Pets.

Selma Park (City Park). 3 mi SW of Bowie on St Hwy 59 (on Omon Carter Lake). SEASON: All yr. FACILITIES: Sites, tbls, toil, cga. ACTIVITIES: Boating,r; picnicking; fishing. MISC.: Pets permitted if kept on leash.

BRACKETTVILLE

Rest Area. 7 mi W of Brackettville on St Hwy 90. SEASON: All yr; 1-nite lmt. FACILITIES: 4 self-contained sites; tbls, toil, cga. ACTIVITIES: Picnicking. MISC.: Pets.

Rest Area 6 mi S of Bracketville. SEASON: All yr; 1-nite lmt. FACILITIES: Spaces for self-contained vehicles; tbls, toil, cga. ACTIVITIES: Picnicking. MISC.: Pets.

BRIDGEPORT

Wise County Park (Co. Park). 4 mi W of Bridgeport on St Hwy 1658. 1 mi N on Co Rd (on Lake Bridgeport). SEASON: All yr; 7-day lmt. FACILITIES: Sites, tbls, toil, cga. ACTIVITIES: Swimming; picnicking; fishing. MISC.: Pets.

BRONTE

Coke (Co. Park). 4/5 mi E of Bronte on Co Rd (on Old City Lake). SEASON: All yr. FACILITIES: 28 sites; tbls, toil, cga. ACTIVITIES: Swimming; picnicking; fishing; hunting; boating,r; golfing. MISC.: Pets.

BURNET

Burnet (Co. Park). 3 mi W of Burnett on St Hwy 29; 11 mi N on RR 2341. SEASON: All yr; 14-day lmt. FACILITIES: 10 sites; tbls, toil, cga, store, gas, phone. ACTIVITIES: Swimming; picnicking; fishing; boating,l; waterskiing. MISC.: Pets.

CARRIZO SPRINGS

Midway Park (Municipal Park). 4 mi N of Carrizo Springs on US 83; 1 mi E on dirt rd. FACILITIES: 10 sites; tbls, toil, cga. ACTIVITIES: Picnicking; swimming; fishing; boating,l; golf nearby. MISC.: Pets.

CHILDRESS

City Park In Childress. SEASON: All yr. FACILITIES: 45 sites; tbls, toil, cga, cold showers, elec hkup, food. ACTIVITIES: Swimming; picnicking; fishing; tennis; softball; trampolines. MISC.: River. Pets.

CLIFTON

Cedron Creek Park (COE). 9 mi NE of Clifton on St Hwy 219; 1 mi E on St Hwy 22; 9 mi N on St Hwy 56; 4 mi E on Co Rd. SEASON: All yr; 14-day lmt. FACILITIES: 8 sites; tbls, toil, cga. ACTIVITIES: Swimming; picnicking; fishing; boating,rl. MISC.: On Lake Whitney. Pets.

COLEMAN

Friendship Park (COE; Hords Creek Lake). 8 mi W of Coleman on St Hwy 53. SEASON: All yr; 14-day lmt. FACILITIES: 5 sites; tbls, toil, cga, drk wtr. ACTIVITIES: Hiking; picnicking; fishing; swimming; boating,l. MISC.: Elev 2150; 295 acres. Hords Creek Lake. Pets permitted if kept on leash.

Press Morris (City Park). 14 mi N of Coleman on US 283; 2 mi W on Co Rd 1274. SEASON: All yr; 10-day lmt. FACILITIES: 56 sites; tbls, toil, cga. ACTIVITIES: Swimming; picnicking; fishing; boating,ld; hiking; waterskiing. MISC.: Bike trails; lake. Pets permitted.

COLORADO CITY

Fisher (City Park). 9 mi S of US 80 on St Hwy 208; follow signs 3 mi W. SEASON: All yr. FACILITIES: 26 sites; tbls, toil, cga, ice, food, store, gas, showers (cold). ACTIVITIES: Swimming; picnicking; fishing; boating,rld; hiking. MISC.: Bike trails. Pets permitted.

Ruddick Park (Municipal Park). 1 mi From Colorado City Business District on St Hwy 208 & US 80. SEASON: All yr. FACILITIES: 50 sites, elec/wtr hkup Ice/food/store/laundry nearby. ACTIVITIES: Swimming ($); picnicking. MISC.: Pets.

COMANCHE

High Point Park (COE). 11 mi NE of Comanche on US 67/377; 5 mi W on St Hwy 1476 (on Proctor Reservoir). SEASON: All yr. FACILITIES: Sites, tbls, toil, cga. ACTIVITIES: Swimming; picnicking; fishing; boating,rl. MISC.: Pets permitted if kept on leash.

Sowell Creek Park (COE). 11 mi NE of Comanche on US 67/377; 2 mi W on St Hwy 1476; 3/10 mi S on Co Rd (on Proctor Reservoir). SEASON: All yr. FACILITIES: Sites, toil. ACTIVITIES: Fishing; swimming; boating,r. MISC.: Pets permitted if kept on leash.

COMSTOCK

Rest Area. 12 mi W of Comstock on St Hwy 90. SEASON: All yr; 1-nite lmt. FACILITIES: 12 self-contained sites; tbls, toil, cga. ACTIVITIES: Picnicking. MISC.: Pets.

CORPUS CHRISTI

Padre Island National Seashore. Padre Island is E and S of Corpus Christi. There is only one entrance: St Hwy

358 (South Padre Island Drive). As you leave the city this becomes Park Road 22. After crossing the John F. Kennedy Causeway, turn S into the Seashore. Headquarters is at 9405 South Padre Island Dr., Corpus Christi 78418.

Camping is permitted on the beach on the seaward side of the sand dunes only. Camping is not permitted on or in the dunes or in the grasslands. NORTH BEACH: A mile-long stretch of open beach at the N end of the seashore is provided with chemical toil and trash receptacles. SOUTH BEACH: About 5 mi of beach are open to primitive camping. Chemical toil and trash receptacles. LITTLE SHELL & BIG SHELL BEACHES: Camping is permitted, but you will need a 4-wheel drive vehicle to reach these rugged areas. Camping is not permitted on the designated swimming beach at Malaquite Beach. SEASON: All yr; 14-day lmt. Fishing; swimming; water is available at Malaquite Beach CG and Ranger Station. Cold water showers are available at the concession facility at Malaquite Beach FREE. Nature trail. Beachcombing. Scuba diving and snorkeling. Hiking, hunting, pets (not on posted beaches). Don't camp in grassy areas-rattlesnakes. No entrance fee to Seashore.

CRANE

Crane County Campground (Co. Park). 1/2 mi N of Crane on US 385; 1/2 mi W on Co Rd. SEASON: All yr. FACILITIES: 6 sites; flush toil, showers, elec/wtr hkup. Store/food/ice/laundry/bottled gas nearby; drk wtr. ACTIVITIES: Picnicking; golf nearby. MISC.: Pets.

CROCKETT

Mission Tejas. 21 mi NE of Crockett on st Hwy 21; NW on Park Rd 44. SEASON: All yr. FACILITIES: Sites, tbls, toil, cga. ACTIVITIES: Picnicking; fishing. MISC.: Replica of Mission. Pets.

CRYSTAL CITY

Crystal City Park. On US 83 at S city limits of Crystal City. SEASON: All yr. FACILITIES: Undesignated sites, tbls, cga. ACTIVITIES: Picnicking. MISC.: Must check in with police chief. Pets.

CUERO

Cuero (City Park). On US 87 at E city limits of Cuero. SEASON: All yr. FACILITIES: 22 sites; tbls, toil, cga. ACTIVITIES: Picnicking; swimming; golf; tennis; hiking. MISC.: Pets permitted.

Guadalupe River (City Park). 3 mi S of Cuero on Us 183 & US 77. SEASON: All yr; 3-day lmt. FACILITIES: 10 sites. ACTIVITIES: Hunting; fishing; swimming; hiking. MISC.: Bike trails. Pets permitted if kept on leash.

DAINGERFIELD

Lone Star Park (COE; Lake O'The Pines). 8 mi S of Daingerfield on US 259. SEASON: MD-LD; 14-day lmt. FACILITIES: 7 sites; tbls, toil, cga, drk wtr. ACTIVITIES: Picnicking; fishing; boating,l. MISC.: Limited facilities during winter. Pets permitted.

DALHART

Rita Blanca Lake Camp (Co. Park). 2 mi S of Dalhart on St Hwy 281 (On Rita Blanca Lake). SEASON: All yr. FACILITIES: 7 sites; tbls, toil, cga. ACTIVITIES: Picnicking; fishing. MISC.: Pets permitted.

DEL RIO

Amistad Recreation Area (NRA). The Nat'l Park Service headquarters building is located 3 mi N of Del Rio on US 90 W. The bldg is open, M-F, 8-5, all yr; 9-6 wkends (Nov-Mar, 8-5). You may camp anywhere along the shoreline below the maximum flood pool level. ACTIVITIES: Boating; fishing; swimming; scuba diving; waterskiing; hunting. MISC.: Interpretive programs are held at various times and places; schedules available at headquarters.

Governor's Landing (Amistad Natl Rec. Area). 9 mi E of Del Rio on Us 90 to Amistad Dam; N on dirt rd. SEASON: All yr; 14-day lmt. FACILITIES: 17 sites (tr -28); no drk wtr. ACTIVITIES: Fishing; swimming; boating,d; waterskiing; hunting. MISC.: Pets.

North Highway 277 (Amistad Natl Rec. Area). 9 mi N of Del Rio on US 277. SEASON: All yr; 14-day lmt. FACILITIES: 8 sites (tr -28); flush toil, tbls, no drk wtr. ACTIVITIES: Picnicking; fishing; swimming; boating,l; waterskiing; hunting. MISC.: Pets.

Rest Area 12 mi S of Del Rio on St Hwy 227. SEASON: All yr; 1-night lmt. FACILITIES: 12 self-contained sites; tbls, toil, cga. ACTIVITIES: Picnicking. MISC.: Pets permitted if kept on leash.

San Pedro Flats (Amistad Natl Rec. Area). 6 mi W of Del Rio on US 90 to Spur 454; N on dirt road. SEASON: All yr; 14-day lmt. FACILITIES: 18 sites (tr -28); tbls, toil, cga, no drk wtr. Store/ice nearby. ACTIVITIES: Hunting; picnicking; fishing; swimming; boating,d; waterskiing. MISC.: Pets.

South, Highway 277 (Amistad Natl Rec. Area). 7 mi N of Del Rio on US 277. SEASON: All yr; 14-day lmt. FACILITIES: 4 sites (tr -28), no drk wtr. ACTIVITIES: Fishing; boating,ld; swimming nearby. MISC.: Pets permitted.

Spur 406 (Amistad Natl Rec. Area). 20 mi W of Del Rio on US 9; 4 mi S on Spur 406. SEASON: All yr; 14-day lmt. FACILITIES: 12 sites (tr -28), flush toil, no drk wtr. ACTIVITIES: Fishing; swimming; boating,l; waterskiing; hunting. MISC.: Pets.

DENISON

Forest Point Park (COE; Lake Texoma-Denison Dam). 14 mi N. on US 271; 6 mi W on St Hwy 197; 1 mi S on Co Rd. (On Pat May SE Reservoir). SEASON: All yr; 14-day lmt. FACILITIES: Sites, tbls, toil, cga, drk wtr. ACTIVITIES: Boating; picnicking; fishing. MISC.:Pets

Island View (COE; Lake Texoma-Denison Dam). 13 mi NW of Denison on St Hwy 120. SEASON: All yr; 14-day lmt. FACILITIES: Undesignated sites, tbls, toil, cga, drk wtr. ACTIVITIES: Boating,l; picnicking; fishing. MISC.: Pets.

Paradise Cove Camp (COE; Lake Texoma-Denison Dam). 13 mi W of Denison on St Hwy 120; 1 mi N of Flowing Wells CG (On Lake Texoma). SEASON: All yr; 14-day lmt. FACILITIES: 7 sites; tbls, toil, cga, elec/wtr/swr hkups; food nearby. ACTIVITIES: Boating,rld; swimming; picnicking. MISC.: Pets permitted.

DENTON

Cottonwood Park (COE; Lake Texoma-Denison Dam). 11 mi E of Denton on I-35 & St Hwy 24; 6 mi S on St Hwy 720; 7/10 mi on Co rd. SEASON: All yr; 14-day lmt. FACILITIES: 14 sites, tbls, toil, cga, drk wtr. ACTIVITIES: Swimming; picnicking; fishing; boating,rld. MISC.: On Garja Little Elm Reservoir. Pets.

Hickory Creek Park (COE; Lewisville). 10 mi SE of Denton on US 77 (On Garza Little Elm Reservoir. SEASON: All yr; 14-day lmt. FACILITIES: 7 sites; tbls, toil, cga. Store nearby. ACTIVITIES: Swimming; boating,l; picnicking; fishing; hiking. MISC.: Pets permitted.

Sycamore Bend (COE; Lewisville). 6 mi SE of Denton on US 77; 2 mi SW on Co Rd. SEASON: All yr; 14-day lmt. FACILITIES: 7 sites; tbls, toil, cga, drk wtr. ACTIVITIES: Swimming; boating,l; picnicking; fishing. MISC.: Pets.

DENVER

Yoakum (Co. Park). 6 mi N of Denver City on St Hwy 214. SEASON: All yr. FACILITIES: 25 sites; tbls, toil, cga, drk wtr, shower, elec hkup, dump. ACTIVITIES: Picnicking; fishing. MISC.: Pets permitted if kept on leash.

DOUGLASSVILLE

Jackson Creek (COE; Wright Patman Dam & Lake). From Intersection of US Hwy 59 & St Hwy 77, 7-9/10 mi NW on St Hwy 77; 1-4/5 mi N on Farm Market 279; 3-1/2 mi NW to area. FACILITIES: 10 sites; tbls, toil, cga, drk wtr. ACTIVITIES: Boating,l; picnicking; fishing; swimming in designated swim areas; hunting in the undeveloped areas during hunting season. MISC.: No firearms in developed public use areas. Pets permitted if kept on leash.

Overcup (COE; Wright Patman Dam & Lake). SEASON: MD-LD (limited facilities in winter); 14-day lmt. FACILITIES: 13 sites; tbls, toil, cga, drk wtr. ACTIVITIES: Picnicking; fishing; swimming in designated swim areas; hunting in the undeveloped areas during hunting season. MISC.: No firearms in developed public use areas. Pets permitted if kept on leash.

Thomas Lake (COE; Lake O'The Pines). 8 mi W of Douglassville on St Hwy 77; 6 mi N on Co Rd & access roads. SEASON: MD-LD; (limited facilities in winter); 14-day lmt. FACILITIES: 16 sites; tbls, toil, cga, drk wtr. ACTIVITIES: Boating,l; picnicking; fishing. MISC.: Pets permitted if kept on leash.

DUMAS

City Park In Dumas. SEASON: All yr. FACILITIES: 24 sites; toil, elec/wtr hkup, dump. MISC.: Pets permitted.

Pioneer Park (City Park). On 14th Street in Dumas. SEASON: All yr. FACILITIES: Sites, tbls, toil, cga. ACTIVITIES: Picnicking; fishing; swimming. MISC.: Pets permitted if kept on leash.

Plum Creek (Lake Meredith Rec. Area). Approximately 19 mi on St Hwy 152 from Dumas; 3 mi on St Hwy 1319 to St Hwy 1913 which you follow to the marked Plum Creek Road. SEASON: All yr; 14-day lmt. FACILITIES: 15 sites; toil, no drk wtr, tbls. ACTIVITIES: Hunting; picnicking; fishing; boating,ld; waterskiing; bank fishing. MISC.: Pets permitted if kept on leash. Shallow-water launching ramp.

Texoma Park (City Park). 500 W First Street in Dumas. SEASON: All yr. FACILITIES: Sites, tbls, toil. ACTIVITIES: Picnicking; swimming. MISC.: Bicycle trails. Pets permitted if kept on leash.

EAGLE PASS

Rest Area. 18 mi N of Eagle Pass on St Hwy 277. SEASON: All yr; 1-night lmt. FACILITIES: 12 self-contained sites; tbls, toil, cga. ACTIVITIES: Picnicking. MISC.: Pets permitted.

EDNA

Bemmet Park (Co. Park). 4 mi SW of Edna on US 59; 10 mi SE on St Hwy 234; 3 mi SW on St Hwy 616; 4/5 mi NW on Co Rd; 2/5 mi SW; 4/5 mi NW; 1/10 mi SW to CG. SEASON: All yr; 14-day lmt. FACILITIES: 10 sites; tbls, toil, cga. ACTIVITIES: Swimming; picnicking; fishing; hiking; boating,r. MISC.: Nature trails. Pets permitted.

EL PASO

El Paso Auto-Truck Stop. 19 mi E of El Paso on I-10 at Horizon turnoff. SEASON: All yr; 1-night lmt. FACILITIES: Spaces for self-contained RVs, tbls, toil, cga, drk wtr, gas, dump, ice, food, phone. MISC.: Pets.

McBride Canyon (Lake Meredith Rec. Area). 6 mi on St Hwy 136 from Fritch to Alibates Rd; 3 mi on Alibates Rd to jct and take left-hand fork to the CG. SEASON: All yr; 14-day lmt. FACILITIES: 10 sites; tbls, toil, cga, no drk wtr. ACTIVITIES: Hunting; picnicking; fishing; waterskiing. MISC.: Pets permitted if kept on leash.

Sanford-Yake (Lake Meredith Rec. Area). 1 mi E of Fritch on St Hwy 136; 4 mi N on St Hwy 687; W to CG. SEASON: All yr; 14-day lmt. FACILITIES: 53 sites (some with shade shelters); tbls, flush toil, cga, drk wtr. Store/food/ice nearby. ACTIVITIES: Picnicking; boating; waterskiing; hunting; fishing. MISC.: Deep-water launching ramp and courtesy dock; dryland boat storage. Pets.

EMORY

Rains (Co. Park). 11 mi W of Emory on St Hwy 35; 1 mi S on Co Rd (On Lake Tawakoni). SEASON: All yr; 14-day lmt. FACILITIES: 30 sites; toil. ACTIVITIES: Fishing; swimming; boating,r. MISC.: Pets.

ENNIS

Little Mustang (COE; Bardwell Lake). 2 mi W of Ennis on Co Rd. SEASON: All yr; 14-day lmt. FACILITIES: Undesignated sites; tbls, toil, cga, drk wtr. ACTIVITIES: Boating,l; picnicking; fishing. MISC.: Pets permitted.

ETOILE

Ralph McAlister (COE; Sam Rayburn Lake). 6 mi E of Etoile on St Hwy 103. SEASON: All yr; 14-day lmt. FACILITIES: Undesignated primitive sites; tbls, toil, cga, no drk wtr. Ice nearby. ACTIVITIES: Swimming; picnicking; fishing; boating,l. MISC.: Pets.

FORT WORTH

Cottonwood (COE; Lewisville). 32 mi NE of Fort Worth on St Hwy 121. SEASON: All yr; 14-day lmt. FACILITIES: 7 sites; tbls, toil, cga, drk wtr. ACTIVITIES: Swimming; picnicking; fishing. MISC.: Store nearby. Pets permitted if kept on leash.

Eastvale (COE; Lewisville). 32 mi NE of Ft. Worth on St Hwy 121. SEASON: All yr; 14-day lmt. FACILITIES: 5 sites; tbls, toil, cga, drk wtr. ACTIVITIES: Swimming; picnicking; fishing; boating,l. MISC.: Store nearby. Pets.

Lake Granbury and DeCordova Bend Dam (Brazos River Authority). The lake is SW of Ft. Worth on St Hwy 377. There are 2 free CGs on the lake. One is N of US 377 on FM51. The other is SE of US 377, by the dam (call 817/766-1441 for details).

Rocky Point (COE; Grapevine Lake). 23 mi NE of Fort Worth on St Hwy 121. SEASON: All yr; 14-day lmt. FACILITIES: Undesignated sites; tbls, toil, cga, drk wtr. ACTIVITIES: Boating,l; picnicking; fishing. MISC.: Pets.

FRISCO

Frisco Park (City Park). 7 mi W of Frisco on St Hwy 720 (On Garga Little Elm Reservoir). SEASON: All yr. FACILITIES: Sites, tbls, toil, cga, food. ACTIVITIES: Swimming; hunting; picnicking; fishing; boating,rl. MISC.: Pets.

FRITCH

Cedar Canyon (Lake Meredith Rec. Area). 6 mi NE of Fritch and 3 mi W of Sanford. Proceed on the marked county roads from either Fritch or Sanford. SEASON: All yr; 14-day lmt. FACILITIES: Semi-developed with random camping, toil, no drk wtr, deep-water launching ramp, courtesy dock, opportunity for camping varies with the fluctuating lake level. ACTIVITIES: Boating; waterskiing; hunting. MISC.: Pets permitted if kept on leash.

Fritch Fortress (Lake Meredith Rec. Area) E of Fritch on Eagle Blvd; N on Co Rd to CG. SEASON: All yr; 14-day lmt. FACILITIES: Undesignated sites; flush toil, tbls (with shelters), drk wtr. ACTIVITIES: Picnicking; fishing; boating,ld; waterskiing; hunting. MISC.: Deep-water launching ramp and courtesy dock. Pets permitted.

Harbor Bay (Lake Meredith Rec. Area). Turn off St Hwy 136 at the SW outskirts of Fritch on to the Harbor Bay

See page 7 for KEY TO ABBREVIATIONS.

(Double Diamond) access road. **SEASON:** All yr; 14-day lmt. **FACILITIES:** Semi-developed with random camping; toil, no drk wtr. **ACTIVITIES:** Waterskiing; hunting; fishing. **MISC.:** Opportunity for camping varies with the fluctuating lake level. Pets.

Rock Ledge Park (COE; Grapevine Lake). 2 mi N of Grapevine on St Hwy 121. **SEASON:** All yr; 14-day lmt. **FA-CILITIES:** Undesignated sites; tbls, toil, cga, drk wtr. Store/food/laundry/ice nearby. **ACTIVITIES:** Swimming; picnicking; fishing; boating,rl. **MISC.:** On Lake Grapevine. Pets permitted.

Silver Lake Park (COE; Grapevine Lake). 2 mi N of Grapevine on St Hwy 121. (On Lake Grapevine.) **SEASON:** All yr; 14-day lmt. **FACILITIES:** 25 sites; tbls, toil, cga, drk wtr. Store nearby. **ACTIVITIES:** Boating,l; picnicking; fishing. **MISC.:** Pets.

Twin Coves Park (COE; Grapevine Lake). 2 mi NE of Grapevine on St Hwy 121; 2 mi N on Co Rd; 2 mi N on St Hwy 2499; 1 mi W on Co Rd; ½ mi N on Co Rd; 1 mi W on Co Rd. **SEASON:** All yr; 14-day lmt. **FACILITIES:** Sites, tbls, toil, cga, drk wtr. **ACTIVITIES:** Boating,rl; picnicking; fishing. **MISC.:** Pets permitted.

GATESVILLE

Rest Area. 4 mi E of Gatesville on US 84. **SEASON:** All yr; 1-nite lmt. **FACILITIES:** Spaces for self-contained RVs. **MISC.:** Pets permitted if kept on leash.

GEORGE WEST

Texas State Park & Wildlife Refuge. 3 mi E of George West (at the beginning of large overpass). **SEASON:** All yr. **FACILITIES:** 20 sites. **ACTIVITIES:** Fishing; swimming. **MISC.:** Pets.

GONZALES

Independence Park (City Park). 1 mi S of Gonzales on US 183. **SEASON:** All yr. **FACILITIES:** 60 sites; tbls, toil, cga. **ACTIVITIES:** Swimming; picnicking; fishing; boating,l; golf; tennis; softball; hiking. **MISC.:** Pets permitted.

GRAHAM

Fort Belknap Park (Co. Park). 10 mi W of Graham on St Hwy 61. **SEASON:** All yr; 1-nite lmt. **FACILITIES:** Sites, tbls, toil, cga. **ACTIVITIES:** Picnicking. **MISC.:** Pets.

Kindley Park (City Park). 7 mi NW of Graham on St Hwy 24 (at Lake Graham Bridge). On Lake Graham. **SEASON:** All yr. **FACILITIES:** 22 sites; tbls, toil, cga. **ACTIVITIES:** Swimming; picnicking; fishing; boating,r. **MISC.:** Pets.

Lake Graham (City Park). 5 mi NW of Graham on St Hwy 24 (on Lake Graham). **SEASON:** All yr; 15-day lmt. **FACILI-TIES:** Sites, tbls, toil, cga. **ACTIVI-TIES:** Swimming; picnicking; fishing; boating,r. **MISC.:** Pets permitted.

GRANBURY

DeCordova Park (SRA). 6 mi from US 377 on Co Rd 208 to Acton; 3 mi on Co Rd 1190 to Park. **SEASON:** All yr; 2-day lmt. **FACILITIES:** Undesignated sites; toil. **ACTIVITIES:** Swimming; boating,l; waterskiing; hiking. **MISC.:** Bike trails. Pets permitted if kept on leash.

GRAPEVINE

Marshall Creek Park (COE; Grapevine Lake). 6 mi NW of Grapevine on St Hwy 114; 2 mi N on Co Rd. **SEASON:** All yr; 14-day lmt. **FACILITIES:** 40 sites; tbls, toil, cga, drk wtr. **ACTIVITIES:** Swimming; picnicking; fishing; boating,l. **MISC.:** On Lake Grapevine. Pets.

Meadowmere Park (Grapevine Lake COE). 5 mi NW of Grapevine on St Hwy 114 and Co Rd. **SEASON:** All yr; 14-day lmt. **FACILITIES:** 26 sites; tbls, toil, cga, drk wtr, ice, food. **ACTIVITIES:** Swimming; picnicking; fishing; boating,rl. **MISC.:** On Lake Grapevine. Pets.

Murrell Park (Grapevine Lake). 4 mi N of Grapevine on St Hwy 121 and Co Rd. **SEASON:** All yr; 14-day lmt. **FACIL-ITIES:** 25 sites; tbls, toil, cga, drk wtr, ice, food, store. **ACTIVITIES:** Swimming; picnicking; fishing; boating,l. **MISC.:** On Lake Grapevine. Pets.

Oak Grove Park (COE; Grapevine Lake). 2 mi NW of Grapevine on Co Rd. **SEA-SON:** All yr; 14-day lmt. **FACILITIES:** 110 sites; tbls, toil, cga, drk wtr, ice. Store/food/btld gas nearby. **ACTIVITIES:** Boating,rl; picnicking; fishing. **MISC.:** Pets permitted if kept on leash.

GROOM

Lake McClellan (NF). 21 mi E of Groom on I-40; 2 mi N on Co Rd 13438. **SEA-SON:** 4/15-9/15; 14-day lmt. **FACILI-TIES:** 10 sites (tr -16); flush toil, tbls, cga, drk wtr, store, gas. **AC-TIVITIES:** Boating,rld; picnicking; fishing; waterskiing. **MISC.:** Elev 3500 ft; 12 acres. Pets permitted.

HALLETTSVILLE

Hallettsville (City Park). Off US 77 in Hallettsville; follow signs. **SEASON:** All yr; 3-day lmt. **FACILITIES:** All undesignated sites; tbls, toil, cga, phone, showers (cold). **ACTIVITIES:** Golf; tennis; picnicking. **MISC.:** Pets.

HASKELL

City Park. On US 277, in Haskell. **SEA-SON:** All yr. **FACILITIES:** Sites for self-contained vehicles. **MISC.:** Pets.

HEMPHILL

Lakeview Rec. Area (Sabine NF). 9-1/5 mi SE of Hamphill on St Hwy 87; 4-4/5 mi NE on St Hwy 2928; 4-1/5 mi SE on FS 120 (in pine-hardwood forest) on the shore of Toledo Bend Reservoir. SEASON: 3/1-10/1; 14-day lmt. FACILITIES: 10 sites (tr -16); tbls, flush toil, cga, f, piped drk wtr. Store/food/ice/gas (4 mi). ACTIVITIES: Picnicking; fishing; sailing; boating,ld; rental (4 mi). MISC.: Elev 200 ft; 4 acres; primitive boat ramp; lake. Pets permitted.

HONDO

City Park. 40 mi W of San Antonio. SEASON: All yr. FACILITIES: Sites for self-contained vehicles. MISC.: Pets.

HOUSTON

Alexander Deussen Park (Co. Park). 7 mi E of Houston on I-10; 11 mi N on S Lake Houston Parkway. (On Lake Houston.) SEASON: All yr. FACILITIES: 75 sites, tbls, toil, cga, store. ACTIVITIES: Swimming; picnicking; fishing; boating,r; hiking. MISC.: Nature trails; bike trails. Pets permitted.

Bear Creek (Co. Park). 3 mi N of Houston off I-10; turn right at Clay Rd (Pk. sign); 7/10 mi to entrance. SEASON: All yr; 14-day lmt. FACILITIES: 105 sites, tbls, toil, cga, shower, dump, elec hkup ($). ACTIVITIES: Picnicking; hiking. Golf nearby. MISC.: Bike trails. Pets permitted.

IRA

Lake J.B. Thomas (City Pk.). 10 mi W of Ira on Co Rd 1606; follow signs to park. SEASON: All yr. FACILITIES: 42 sites, tbls, toil, cga, dump. ACTIVITIES: Picnicking; fishing. MISC.: Pets.

JASPER

Bluff View (COE; Town Bluff Dam). 15 mi W of Jasper on US 190; 9 mi S on St Hwy 92. SEASON: All yr; 14-day lmt. FACILITIES: Undesignated sites; tbls, flush toil, cga, drk wtr, ice, food, store. ACTIVITIES: Picnicking; fishing. MISC.: Pets permitted.

Boggy Creek (COE). 11 mi S of Jasper on St Hwy 147; 8 mi W on St Hwy 103; 6 mi E on Etorle St Hwy 103. SEASON: all yr; 14-day lmt. FACILITIES: Sites, tbls, toil, cga, drk wtr. ACTIVITIES: Swimming; picnicking; fishing; boating,rl. MISC.: On Sam Rayburn Reservoir. Pets permitted if kept on leash.

Campers Cove (COE; Town Bluff Dam). 15 mi W of Jasper on US 190 and St Hwy 92. SEASON: All yr; 14-day lmt. FACILITIES: 25 sites, tbls, toil, cga, drk wtr, elec ($). Store/food/ice/laundry nearby. MISC.: Pets permitted.

East End (COE; Town Bluff Dam). Ask for directions at Hdqtrs office (located within Town Bluff Dam-Steinhagen Lake Area). SEASON: All yr; 14-day lmt. FACILITIES: 6 sites; tbls, toil, cga, drk wtr. Store/ice nearby. ACTIVITIES: Swimming; picnicking; fishing; boating,l. MISC.: Pets.

Ebenezer Park (COE; Sam Rayburn Lake). 15 mi NW of Jasper on St Hwy 63; 4 mi N on FM 255; 1 mi N on entrance rd. SEASON: All yr; 14-day lmt. FACILITIES: 17 sites (tr -30); tbls, toil, cga, drk wtr. ACTIVITIES: Swimming; picnicking; fishing; boating,l. MISC.: Pets.

Jasper Co. Park (COE; Town Bluff Dam). 11 mi W of Jasper on US 190 (On Steinhagen Lake). SEASON: All yr; 14-day lmt. FACILITIES: Undesignated sites; tbls, toil, cga, drk wtr, ice, food, store. ACTIVITIES: Swimming; picnicking; fishing; boating,l. MISC.: Pets permitted if kept on leash.

Monterey (COE; Sam Rayburn Lake). 32 mi NW of Jasper on St Hwy 63 to Zavalla; 5 mi N to CG. SEASON: All yr; 14-day lmt. FACILITIES: Undesignated sites; tbls, toil, cga, drk wtr. ACTIVITIES: Swimming; picnicking; fishing; boating,l. MISC.: Pets.

JEFFERSON

Copeland Creek (COE; Lake O'The Pines). From intersection of US Hwy 59 and St Hwy 49, 3-3/10 mi NW on St Hwy 49, then 3-3/10 mi W on Farm Market 729; 8-9/10 mi SW on Farm Market 726 to CG. SEASON: MD-LD (limited facilities in winter); 14-day lmt. FACILITIES: 10 sites; tbls, toil, cga, f, drk wtr. ACTIVITIES: Boating,l; picnicking; fishing; swimming in designated areas; hunting in the undeveloped areas during hunting season. MISC.: No firearms in developed public use areas. Pets.

Hwy 155 Park (COE; Lake O'The Pines). 16 mi NW of Jefferson on St Hwy 49 to Avinger; 14 mi SW on St Hwy 155; 1 mi SE on Co Rd. SEASON: All yr; 14-day lmt. FACILITIES: Sites; tbls, toil, cga, drk wtr. ACTIVITIES: Swimming; picnicking; fishing; boating,l. MISC.: On Lake O'The Pines. Historical site. Pets permitted if kept on leash.

Hurricane Creek (COE; Lake O'The Pines). From intersection of US Hwy 59 and St Hwy 49; 3-3/10 mi NW on St Hwy 49; 5-4/5 mi W along Farm Market 729. SEASON: MD-LD (limited facilities during winter); 14-day lmt. FACILITIES: 13 sites; tbls, toil, cga, drk wtr. ACTIVITIES: Swimming; picnicking; fishing; hunting in the undeveloped areas during hunting season. MISC.: No firearms in developed public use areas. Pets permitted if kept on leash.

Mims Chapel (COE; Lake O'The Pines). 3 mi NW of Jefferson on St Hwy 49; 13 mi W on St Hwy 729; 6 mi S on Co Rd 120. SEASON: All yr; 14-day lmt. FACILITIES: Sites, tbls, toil, cga, drk wtr. ACTIVITIES: Swimming; picnicking; fishing; boating,rl. MISC.: On Lake O'The Pines. Pets.

Overlook Park (COE; Lake O'The Pines). NW of Jefferson on St Hwy 49 (On Lake O'The Pines). SEASON: All yr; 14-day lmt. FACILITIES: Sites, tbls, toil, cga drk wtr. ACTIVITIES: Boating,rl; picnicking; fishing. MISC.: Pets permitted.

LAKE DALLAS

Arrowhead Park (Lewisville; COE). 1 mi S of Lake Dallas on US 77. SEASON: All yr; 14-day lmt. FACILITIES: 12 sites; tbls, toil, cga, drk wtr, wtr

Arrowhead Park (cont.) hkup; elec ($). Store/food/ice nearby. ACTIVITIES: Swimming; picnicking; fishing; boating,l. MISC.: Pets permitted.

Copperas Branch Park (COE; Lewisville). 2 mi S of Lake Dallas on US 77. SEASON: All yr; 14-day lmt. FACILITIES: 24 sites; tbls, toil, cga, drk wtr, elec ($). water hkup. ACTIVITIES: Swimming; picnicking; fishing; boating,rl. MISC.: Pets permitted.

Westlake Park (COE; Lewisville). 2 mi SE of Lake Dallas. SEASON: All yr; 14-day lmt. FACILITIES: 7 sites; tbls, toil, cga, drk wtr. Store nearby. ACTIVITIES: Swimming; picnicking; fishing; boating,l. MISC.: Pets.

LAMESA

Forest Park (City Park). 1/2 mi S of US 180 on St Hwy 137. SEASON: All yr. FACILITIES: 40 sites; tbls, toil, cga, drk wtr. ACTIVITIES: Picnicking; softball. MISC.: Pets permitted.

LEVELLAND

Levelland-Hockley CS (Municipal Park). 1 mi S of Levelland on US 385. SEASON: All yr; 5-day lmt. FACILITIES: 24 sites; tbls, toil, cga, drk wtr, elec/wtr hkup. ACTIVITIES: Boating,d picnicking; fishing. MISC.: Pets.

LEWISVILLE

Arrowhead Park (COE; Lewisville). 6 mi E of Lewisville on I-35 E at N end of bridge (On Garza Little Elm Reservoir). SEASON: All yr; 14-day lmt. FACILITIES: 24 sites; tbls, toil, cga, drk wtr. ACTIVITIES: Swimming; picnicking; fishing; boating,rl. MISC.: Pets permitted if kept on leash.

Big Sandy Park (COE; Lewisville). 10 mi N of Lewisville on I-35. SEASON: All yr; 14-day lmt. FACILITIES: Undesignated sites; tbls, flush toil, cga, drk wtr. Store nearby. ACTIVITIES: Swimming; picnicking; fishing; boating rl. MISC.: Pets.

Copperos Brand Park (COE; Lewisville). 5 mi N of Lewisville on I-35 E; W at S end of bridge (On Garja Little Elm Reservoir). SEASON: All yr; 14-day lmt. FACILITIES: 48 sites; tbls, toil, cga, drk wtr. ACTIVITIES: Swimming; picnicking; fishing; boating,rl. MISC.: Pets permitted if kept on leash.

East Hill Park (COE; Lewisville). 7 mi NE of Lewisville on St Hwys 121/423 on Garza Little Elm Reservoir. SEASON: All yr; 14-day lmt. FACILITIES: 10 sites; tbls, toil, cga, drk wtr, elec ($). ACTIVITIES: Swimming; picnicking; fishing; boating,rl. MISC.: Pets.

Hackberry Park (COE; Lewisville). 6 mi E of Lewisville on St Hwy 121; 5 mi N on St Rd 423; 3 mi W on Co Rd. SEASON: All yr; 14-day lmt. FACILITIES: 8 sites; tbls, toil, cga, drk wtr. ACTIVITIES: Swimming; picnicking; fishing; boating,rl. MISC.: On Garza Little Elm Reservoir. Pets.

Lewisville Lake (COE; Lewisville). 1 mi N of Lewisville on St Rd 407 to Lake Park Road; 1/2 mi E to CG. SEASON: All yr; 14-day lmt. FACILITIES: 55 sites; tbls, toil, cga, drk wtr. Store/food/ice nearby. ACTIVITIES: Swimming; picnicking; fishing; boating,l. Golf nearby. MISC.: On Garza Little Elm Reservoir. Pets.

Pilot Knoll Park (COE; Lewisville). 3 mi N of Lewisville on I-35 E; 4 mi W on St Hwy 407; 3 mi N on Co Rd. SEASON: All yr; 14-day lmt. FACILITIES: 12 sites; tbls, toil, cga, drk wtr. ACTIVITIES: Swimming; picnicking; fishing; boating,l. MISC.: On Garza Little Elm Reservoir. Pets.

Stewart's Creek Park (COE; Lewisville). 6 mi E on St Hwy 121; 2 mi N on St Hwy 423; 2 mi W on Co. Rd. SEASON: All yr; 14-day lmt. FACILITIES: 10 sites; tbls, toil, cga, drk wtr. ACTIVITIES: swimming; picnicking; fishing; boating,rl. MISC.: On Garza Little Elm Reservoir. Pets permitted.

Sycamore Bend Park (COE; Lewisville). 7 mi N of Lewisville on I-35 E; 1 mi W on Tuberville Rd; 1 mi S on co rd (On Garza Little Elm Reservoir). SEASON: All yr; 14-day lmt. FACILITIES: 14 sites; tbls, toil, cga, drk wtr. ACTIVITIES: Swimming; picnicking; fishing; boating,rl. MISC.: Pets.

West Lake Park (COE; Lewisville). SEASON: All yr; 14-day lmt. FACILITIES: 14 sites; tbls, toil, cga, drk wtr. ACTIVITIES: Swimming; picnicking; fishing; boating,rl. MISC.: On Garza Little Elm Reservoir. Pets.

Willow Grose Park (COE; Lewisville 7 mi N of Lewisville on I-35; 1 mi E on Tubeville Rd. (On Gaza Little Elm Reservoir.) SEASON: All yr; 14-day lmt. FACILITIES: Sites, tbls, toil, cga, drk wtr. ACTIVITIES: Picnicking; fishing. MISC.: Pets permitted.

Wynnewood Park (COE; Lewisville). 6 mi E of Lewisville on St Hwy 121; 4 mi N on St Rd 423; 3 mi W on Co Rd. SEASON: All yr; 14-day lmt. FACILITIES: 12 sites; tbls, toil, cga, drk wtr. ACTIVITIES: Swimming; picnicking; fishing; boating,l. MISC.: On Garza Little Elm Reservoir. Pets.

LITTLEFIELD CS (Municipal Park). On US 385 in Littlefield. SEASON: All yr; 7-day lmt. FACILITIES: 8 self-contained sites; flush toil, tbls, cga, elec/wtr/sewer hkup, drk wtr. Store/food/laundry/ice/btld gas nearby. ACTIVITIES: Picnicking; fishing; golf nearby. MISC.: Pets.

Travelers (City Park). On US 385 on S side of Littlefield. SEASON: All yr. FACILITIES: 8 sites; tbls, toil, cga. ACTIVITIES: Picicking. MISC.: Pets.

LONE STAR

Lone Star Park (COE; Lake O' The Pines). 1 mi S of Lone Star on US Hwy 259; 1 mi S on Corps access rd. SEASON: All yr; 14-day lmt. FACILITIES: 7 prim. sites; tbls, toil, cga, drk wtr. ACTIVITIES: Picnicking; fishing; hunting in the undeveloped areas during hunting season; swimming in designated swimming areas. MISC.: No firearms in developed public use areas. Pets.

LUFKIN

Ellen Trout Lake Park (City Park). N of Lufkin on Kurth Drive (US 69); 1 mi N on Lake Street. (On Ellen Trout Lake.) SEASON: All yr. FACILITIES: Sites, tbls, toil, cga. ACTIVITIES: Boating,rl; picnicking; fishing. MISC.: Pets permitted if kept on leash.

Etoile (COE; Sam Rayburn Lake). 15 mi E of Lufkin on St Hwy 103. SEASON: All yr; 14-day lmt. FACILITIES: Undesignated primitive sites; tbls, toil, cga, no drk wtr. ACTIVITIES: Swimming; picnicking; fishing; boating,l. MISC.: Pets permitted if kept on leash.

Marion Ferry (COE; Sam Rayburn Lake). 11 mi E of Lufkin on St Hwy 103; 2 mi N on Co Rd 1669. SEASON: All yr; 14-day lmt. FACILITIES: Undesignated primitive sites; tbls, toil, cga, no drk wtr. ACTIVITIES: Swimming; picnicking; fishing; boating,l. MISC.: On Sam Rayburn Reservoir. Pets.

MADISON

Wilson Shoals Park (Co. Park). 11 mi NE of Madison on St Hwy 21; 8 mi S on St Rd 242; 3 mi E on co rd. SEASON: All yr; 60-day lmt. FACILITIES: Sites, tbls, toil, cga, drk wtr. Store. ACTIVITIES: Swimming; picnicking; fishing; boating,r. MISC.: On Trinity River. Pets permitted.

MAUD

Berry Farm (COE; Wright Patman Dam & Lake). From US Hwy 67 & St Hwy 8, 1-1/10 mi S on St Hwy 8; 3-9/10 mi SE on Farm Market 2624; 2-1/2 mi S. SEASON: MD-LD (limited facilities in winter); 14-day lmt. FACILITIES: 11 sites; tbls, toil, cga, drk wtr. ACTIVITIES: Picnicking; fishing; swimming in designated swimming areas; hunting in the undeveloped areas during hunting season. MISC.: No firearms in developed public use areas. Pets.

Herron Creek (COE; Wright Patman Dam & Lake). From US Hwy 67 and St Hwy 8, 2-1/5 mi S on St Hwy 8; then E & S to area. SEASON: MD-LD (limited facilities in winter); 14-day lmt. FACILITIES: 14 sites; tbls, toil, cga, drk wtr. ACTIVITIES: Boating,l; picnicking; fishing; swimming in designated swimming areas; hunting in the undeveloped areas during hunting season. MISC.: No firearms in developed public use areas. Pets.

Malden Lake (Wright Patman Dam & Lake). From intersection of US Hwy 67 & St Hwy 8, 4-4/5 mi S on St Hwy 8 to area. SEASON: MD-LD (limited facilities in winter); 14-day lmt. FACILITIES: 12 sites; tbls, toil, cga, drk wtr. ACTIVITIES: Picnicking; fishing; swimming in designated swimming a areas; hunting in the undeveloped areas during hunting season. MISC.: No firearms in developed public use areas. Pets.

MCCAMEY

Santa Fe Park (Municipal Park). From jct St Hwy 385 & US 67, 1 blk E (on edge of McCamey). SEASON: All yr; 3-day lmt. FACILITIES: 6 self-contained spaces; flush toil, tbls, cga, drk wtr, elec/wtr hkup. Store/food/ice/btld gas/laundry nearby. ACTIVITIES: Picnicking; golf nearby. MISC.: Mountainous area. Pets.

See page 7 for KEY TO ABBREVIATIONS.

MCGREGOR

Midway (COE; Waco Lake). 8 mi NE of McGregor on US 84; 2 mi NW to CG. SEASON: All yr; 14-day lmt. FACILITIES: Undesignated sites; tbls, toil, cga, drk wtr, store, ice, food. ACTIVITIES: Swimming; picnicking; fishing; boating,l. MISC.: Pets permitted.

MCKINNEY

Frisco Park (COE; Lewisville). 20 mi SW of McKinney on St Hwy 720. SEASON: All yr; 14-day lmt. FACILITIES: 6 sites; tbls, toil, cga, drk wtr. Store/food nearby. ACTIVITIES: Swimming; picnicking; fishing; boating,rl. MISC.: Pets.

MENARD

City Park. In Menard. SEASON: All yr. FACILITIES: Sites for self-contained vehicles; tbls, cga, f. ACTIVITIES: Picnicking. MISC.: Pets permitted.

MIDLAND

Rest Area. S of Midland on I-20 at mileage marker 142. SEASON: All yr; 1-nite lmt. FACILITIES: 40 self-contained sites; tbls, toil, cga, phone. ACTIVITIES: Picnicking. MISC.: Pets.

MINEOLA

Lake Hawkins (Co. Park). 14 mi E of Mineola on US 80; 1 mi N on Lake Hawkins Rd (On Lake Hawkins). SEASON: All yr; 30-day lmt. FACILITIES: Sites; tbls, toil, cga, dump. ACTIVITIES: Picnicking; fishing; swimming; boating,r; hiking. MISC.: Bike trails. Pets.

MORGAN

Kimball Bend Park (COE; Whitney Lake). 10 mi NE of Morgan on St Hwy 174 (On Lake Whitney). SEASON: All yr; 14-day lmt. FACILITIES: 6 sites; tbls, toil, cga, drk wtr. Food/laundry nearby. ACTIVITIES: Swimming; picnicking; fishing; boating,rl. MISC.: Pets permitted.

Morgan Lakeside Park (COE; Whitney Lake). 6 mi E of Morgan on St Hwy 56. (On Lake Whitney.) SEASON: All yr; 14-day lmt. FACILITIES: 5 sites; tbls, toil, cga, drk wtr. ACTIVITIES: swimming; picnicking; fishing; boating, rl. MISC.: Pets.

Plowmann Creek (COE; Whitney Lake). 7 mi NE of Morgan on St Hwy 174; 2 mi S on St Hwy 56; 5 mi S on co rd; 1 mi E on co rd. SEASON: All yr; 14-day lmt. FACILITIES: 3 sites; tbls, toil, cga, drk wtr. ACTIVITIES: Swimming; picnicking; fishing; boating,rl. MISC.: Pets permitted if kept on leash.

Steele Creek Park (COE; Whitney Lake). 7 mi E of Morgan on St Hwy 927; 1 mi S on St Hwy 56; 2 mi S on co rd. SEASON: All yr; 14-day lmt. FACILITIES: 7 sites; tbls, toil, cga, drk wtr. ACTIVITIES: Swimming; picnicking; fishing; boating,rl. MISC.: Pets.

MULESHOE

Muleshoe NWR. 20 mi S of Muleshoe on St Hwy 214. (Refuge headquarters can be reached by traveling W for 2-1/4 mi on a gravel rd from St Hwy 214. Visitors register here. Overnight campsites are in the recreation area. Tbls, toil, cga. No hunting or boating. One of a chain of refuges in the Central Flyway; a wintering area for migratory waterfowl.

NAPLES

Thomas Lake (COE; Wright Patman Dam & Lake). From St Hwy 8 and St Hwy 77, 8 mi W on St Hwy 77, then 3-1/5 mi N on Farm Market 994; 2 mi NE on farm Market 1766 to area. SEASON: All yr; 14-day lmt. FACILITIES: 16 sites; tbls, toil, cga, drk wtr. ACTIVITIES: Picnicking; fishing; swimming in designated swimming areas; hunting in the undeveloped areas during hunting season. MISC.: No firearms in developed public use areas. Pets.

NEW BRAUNFELS

Comal (COE; Canyon Lake). 6 mi W of New Braunfels on St Hwy 46; 8 mi N on Co Rd 2722; 2 mi NW on Co Rd 2673; 2 mi N on Co Rd to CG. SEASON: All yr; 14-day lmt. FACILITIES: Undesignated sites; tbls, toil, cga, drk wtr. Store/food/ice/phone nearby. ACTIVITIES: Swimming; picnicking; fishing; boating,ld; hiking; waterskiing. MISC.: Lake. Pets permitted.

North (COE; Canyon Lake). NW of New Braunfels on St Hwy 306. SEASON: All yr; 14-day lmt. FACILITIES: Undesignated sites; tbls, toil, cga, drk wtr. Store/ice/food nearby. ACTIVITIES: Boating,l; picnicking; fishing. MISC.: Pets permitted if kept on leash.

NEW WAVERLY

Kelly Pond (Davy Crockett NF). 11 mi W of New Waverly on St Hwy 1375; 2/5 mi S on FS 204; 3/5 mi W on FS 271. SEASON: All yr; 14-day lmt. FACILITIES: 8 sites; flush toil, cga, tbls, well drk wtr. ACTIVITIES: Picnicking; fishing; hiking. MISC.: Primitive camping area; heavily used by off-road vehicle enthusiasts in a pine-hardwood forest. Elev 300 ft; 6 acres; pets.

NOCONA

East Park (City Park). 5 mi N of
Nocona on St Hwy 103; 3 mi E on St
Hwy 2634; 2 mi NE on St Hwy 2953; 1/2
mi S on co rd to CG. SEASON: All yr;
15-day lmt. FACILITIES: Sites, tbls,
toil, cga. ACTIVITIES: Swimming; picnicking; fishing; boating,r; horseback
riding/rental. MISC.: On Lake Nocona.
Pets permitted if kept on leash.

Jaycee Park (City Park). 5 mi N of
Nocona on St Hwy 103; 3 mi on St Hwy
1634. (On Lake Nocona.) SEASON: All
yr; 15-day lmt. FACILITIES: Sites,
tbls, toil, cga. ACTIVITIES: Swimming;
picnicking; fishing; boating,r. MISC.:
Pets permitted if kept on leash.

Joe Benton Park (City Park). 5 mi N
of Nocona on St Hwy 103; 3 mi E on
St Hwy 2634; 2 mi NE on St Hwy 2953.
SEASON: All yr; 15-day lmt. FACILI-
TIES: Sites, tbls, toil, cga. ACTIVI-
TIES: Swimming; picnicking; fishing;
boating,r. MISC.: On Lake Nocona. Pets.

ORANGE GROVE

Lipentitlan 4 mi E of Orange Grove on
St Hwy 624; 2 mi NE on St Hwy 70; 8
mi NE on co rd; 1 mi NE on co rd; 1-
1/2 NE on co rd to CG. SEASON: All
yr. FACILITIES: Primitive sites; tbls.
ACTIVITIES: Picnicking. MISC.: Pets.

ORE CITY

Cedar Springs (COE; Lake O'The Pines).
1 mi E of Ore City on Farm Market
155 from jct of Farm Market 155 and
US Hwy 259, then 1 mi SE on recreation
access rd. SEASON: All yr; 14-day lmt.
FACILITIES: 26 sites; tbls, toil, cga,
drk wtr. ACTIVITIES: Picnicking; fishing. Buoyed swimming beach provided;
hunting in the undeveloped areas during hunting season. MISC.: No firearms in developed public use areas.
Pets permitted if kept on leash.

Pine Hill (COE; Lake O'The Pines).
From intersection of US Hwy 259 and
Farm Market 450, 2 mi E along Farm
Market 450; then 2 mi NE to CG. SEA-
SON: MD-LD (limited facilities during
winter); 14-day lmt. FACILITIES: 32
sites; tbls, toil, cga, drk wtr. ACTIV-
ITIES: Boating,l; picnicking; fishing;
a buoyed swimming beach is provided; hunting in the undeveloped
areas during hunting season. MISC.:
No firearms in developed public use
areas. Pets.

PINE SPRINGS

Pine Springs Canyon CG (Guadalupe
Mtns NP). Frijole Information Station
is located on US 62-180, one mi E of
Pine Springs. The campground is located 1-1/2 mi W of the Information
Station. FACILITIES: 20 sites for self-
contained vehicles; toil; tbls, cga.

ACTIVITIES: Picnicking; hiking.
MISC.: There is no entrance fee to
this National Park. Pets.

PLAINVIEW

Broadway City Park. SE First St & Broadway, in Plainview. SEASON: All yr;
3-day lmt. FACILITIES: Sites, tbls,
toil, elec hkup. ACTIVITIES: Picnicking; softball. MISC.: Rec. hall. Pets.

POINT

Skypoint Park (Sabine River Authority).
1-1/5 mi E of jct FM 35/513 in Point
on FM35; S on Oil Road to CG. SEASON:
All yr. FACILITIES: Sites, tbls, toil,
cga. ACTIVITIES: Boating,l; picnicking;
swimming. MISC.: Pets permitted.

PORT LAVACA

Indianola (COE). 4 mi W of Port Lavaca
on St Hwy 238; 9 mi SE on St Hwy 316.
(On Gulf of Mexico.) SEASON: All yr.
FACILITIES: Sites, tbls, toil, cga. AC-
TIVITIES: Swimming; picnicking; fish-
ing; boating,r. MISC.: Pets permitted.

PROCTOR

Copperas Creek Park (COE; Proctor
Lake). 9 mi NE of Proctor on US 67/377.
SEASON: All yr. FACILITIES: Sites,
tbls, toil, cga, drk wtr, elec hkup.
ACTIVITIES: Swimming; picnicking; fish-
ing; hunting; boating,l; waterskiing.
MISC.: Lake. Pets.

High Point (COE; Proctor Lake). 5 mi
NW of Proctor on Co Rds. SEASON: All
yr; 14-day lmt. FACILITIES: 10 sites
(tr -20); tbls, toil, cga, drk wtr.
Store/ice/food nearby. ACTIVITIES:
Swimming; picnicking; fishing; boating,rl. MISC.: Pets permitted.

Promontory Park (COE; Proctor Lake).
9 mi NE of Proctor on US 67/377. SEA-
SON: All yr. FACILITIES: Sites, tbls,
toil, cga, drk wtr. ACTIVITIES: Hunting; picnicking; fishing; swimming;
boating,l; waterskiing. MISC.: Lake;
Pets permitted if kept on leash.

QUINLAN

Arm Point Park (Sabine River
Authority). 1/2 mi W of Tawakoni
Causeway; 1 mi S to CG. SEASON: All
yr. FACILITIES: Sites, tbls, toil, cga
ACTIVITIES: Picnicking; boating,l;
swimming. MISC.: Pets.

Sowell Creek (COE; Proctor Lake). 1
mi W of Proctor on US 67/377 at Co
Rd 1476. SEASON: All yr; 14-day lmt.
FACILITIES: 40 sites; tbls, toil, cga,
drk wtr, elec hkup. ACTIVITIES:
Swimming; picnicking; fishing; boating,rl; waterskiing. MISC.: Lake. Pets.

QUITMAN

Lake Holbrook (Co. Park). 2 mi W of Quitman on US 80; 1 mi W on Old US 80; 3/10 mi N on Co Rd. (On Lake Holbrook.) SEASON: All yr; 30-day lmt. FACILITIES: Sites, tbls, toil, cga, store, dump. ACTIVITIES: Swimming; picnicking; fishing; boating,r; hiking MISC.: Bike trails. Pets.

Lake Quitman (Co. Pk.). 4 mi N of Quitman on St Hwy 2966; E on Co Rd. (On Lake Quitman.) SEASON: All yr ; 30-day lmt. FACILITIES: Sites, tbls, toil, cga, store. ACTIVITIES: Swimming; picnicking; fishing; boating,r; hiking. MISC.: Bike trails. Pets permitted.

RIO VISTA

Chisholm Trail Park (COE; Whitney Lake). 12 mi SW of Rio Vista on St Hwy 174. SEASON: All yr; 14-day lmt. FACILITIES: 3 sites; tbls, toil, cga, drk wtr. Store/food nearby. ACTIVITIES: Swimming; picnicking; fishing; boating,l. MISC.: Pets permitted.

RIVIERA

Kickug (Co. Pk.). 5 mi S of Riviera on Loop 428; 10 mi S on US 77; 6 mi E on St Hwy 771; 1 mi N on St Hwy 1546; 2 mi E on St Hwy 628; 3/10 mi E on Co Rd to CG. SEASON: All yr. FACILITIES: Sites, tbls, toil, cga, dump. ACTIVITIES: Picnicking; fishing; swimming. MISC.: Pets.

ROBERT LEE

Coke Co. Park (Co. Park). 1 blk N on St Hwy 158 on St Hwy 208; 3 blks E on Austin St. in Robert Lee. SEASON: All yr; 3-day lmt. FACILITIES: 30 sites; toil, cga, elec/wtr hkup, store. ACTIVITIES: Swimming; picnicking; fishing; boating,r; golf; tennis; hiking. MISC.: Rec. hall; bike trails. Pets.

Point Creek (City Park). 5 mi W of Robert Lee on St Hwy 158. SEASON: All yr. FACILITIES: Undesignated sites; tbls, toil, cga. ACTIVITIES: Swimming; picnicking; fishing; boating,ld; waterskiing; biking. MISC.: Lake. Pets.

RUSK

Jimm Hogg State Historic Park. 2 mi NE of Rusk on US 84; S on Park Rd to CG. SEASON: 5/1-9/15; 14-day lmt. FACILITIES: Sites, tbls, toil, cga. ACTIVITIES: Picnicking. MISC.: Pets.

Robert Lee Park. In Robert Lee; St Hwy 208/158; 4 blks N of blinker light on Mtn Creek Lake. SEASON: All yr. FACILITIES: 14 sites; tbls, toil, cga, dump, store, laundry. ACTIVITIES: Swimming; picnicking; fishing; hunting; golfing; hiking. MISC.: Bike trails. Pets permitted if kept on leash.

SAN ANGELO

Dry Creek (COE; San Angelo Lake). 5 mi NW of San Angelo on US 87; 1 mi S on St Hwy 2288. (On N Concho Lake.) SEASON: All yr; 14-day lmt. FACILITIES: 5 sites; tbls, toil, cga, drk wtr. ACTIVITIES: Swimming; picnicking; fishing. MISC.: Lake. Pets permitted.

Grandview Park (COE; O.C. Fisher Lake). 6 mi NW of San Angelo on St Hwy 2288. SEASON: All yr; 14-day lmt. FACILITIES: 10 sites; tbls, toil, cga, drk wtr. ACTIVITIES: Picnicking. MISC.: Pets.

Highland Range Park (COE; O.C. Fisher Lake). 3 mi SW of San Angelo on US 67; 2 mi W on I-853; 2 mi N on N Conche Lake. SEAS: All yr; 14-day lmt. FACILITIES: 10 sites; tbls, toil, cga, drk wtr. ACTIVITIES: Swimming; picnicking; fishing. MISC.: Lake; trails. Pets permitted.

SAN ANTONIO

Rest Area. E of San Antonio on I-10 at mileage marker 591. SEASON: All yr; 1-nite lmt. FACILITIES: 10 self-contained sites; tbls, toil, cga, dump. ACTIVITIES: Picnicking. MISC.: Pets.

Rest Area. 12 mi N of Loop 410 on I-35 at mileage marker 179. SEASON: All yr; 1-nite lmt. FACILITIES: 10 self-contained sites; tbls, cga, phone. ACTIVITIES: Picnicking. MISC.: Pets.

Laguna Atascosa NWR. 8 mi from San Antonio on St Hwy 345; 6 mi E on St Hwy 106; 7 mi E on co rd; 2 mi N on co rd. SEASON: All yr; 3-day lmt. FACILITIES: Sites, tbls, toil, cga. ACTIVITIES: Boating,r; picnicking; fishing. MISC.: Pets.

SANFORD

Bugbee (Lake Meredith Rec. Area). Take St Hwy 687 from Sanford across Sanford Dam to the Bugbee Road; proceed on Bugbee Rd to CG. SEASON: All yr; 14-day lmt. FACILITIES: Semi-developed with random camping, toil, no drk wtr. ACTIVITIES: Hunting; waterskiing; fishing. MISC.: Nestled within a narrow canyon; road access is difficult. Opportunity for camping varies with the fluctuating lake level. Pets permitted if kept on leash.

SANTO

Rest Area. I-20 at mile marker 390 (paved access rds). SEASON: All yr; 1-nite lmt. FACILITIES: Undesignated sites; tbls, toil, cga, dump. ACTIVITIES: Picnicking. MISC.: Pets permitted.

See page 7 for KEY TO ABBREVIATIONS.

SHERMAN

Big Mineral Camp (COE). 14 mi W of Sherman on US 82; 10 mi N on St Hwy 901; 2 mi E on co rd (On Lake Jehoma). SEASON: All yr; 14-day lmt. FACILITIES: Sites, tbls, toil, cga, drk wtr. ACTIVITIES: Swimming; picnicking; fishing; boating,r. MISC.: Pets permitted.

Cedar Bayou Resort (COE). 18 mi W of Sherman on US 82 to Whitesboro; 13 mi N on US 377; N on co rd to CG. SEASON: All yr; 14-day lmt. FACILITIES: Sites. tbls. toil, cga, drk wtr. ACTIVITIES: Swimming; picnicking; fishing; boating,rl. MISC.: On Lake Texoma. Pets permitted if kept on leash.

Rock Creek Camp (COE). 18 mi W of Sherman on US 82 (to Whitesboro); 11 mi N on US 377; 6 mi W on St Hwy 901; 1 mi E on co rd to CG. (On Lake Texoma.) SEASON: All yr; 14-day lmt. FACILITIES: Sites, tbls, toil, cga, drk wtr. ACTIVITIES: Swimming; picnicking; fishing; boating,rl. MISC.: Pets.

SHINER

Green Dickson (City Park). On US 90A at the W edge of Shiner; follow signs 1/2 mi N to CG. SEASON: All yr; 1-day lmt. FACILITIES: 20 sites; tbls, toil, cga. ACTIVITIES: Hiking; picnicking; fishing; golfing; tennis; softball. MISC.: Pets.

SPRING BRANCH

Knibble St Hwy Park. 1 mi N of Spring Branch on US 281. SEASON: All yr; 1-nite lmt. FACILITIES: Sites for self-contained vehicles. MISC.: Pets permitted if kept on leash.

STINNET

Stinnet City Park. On Broadway St, 1 blk W of St Hwy 136/207, in Stinnet. SEASON: All yr. FACILITIES: Sites for self contained vehicles. MISC.: Pets.

SWEETWATER

Newman City Park. N of Sweetwater on Co Rd 419. SEASON: All yr. FACILITIES: 300 sites; tbls, toil, cga. ACTIVITIES: Swimming; picnicking; fishing; golfing; tennis; hiking; biking. MISC.: Pets.

TEMPLE

Cedar Ridge Park (COE). 8 mi NW of Temple on St Hwy 36; 3 mi S on co rd to CG (on Lake Belton). SEASON: All yr; 14-day lmt. FACILITIES: 20 sites; tbls, toil, cga, drk wtr. ACTIVITIES: Swimming; picnicking; fishing; boating,rl. MISC.: Pets.

Iron Bridge (COE; Belton Lake). 16 mi NE of Temple on St Hwy 36/2409; 4 mi W on St Hwy 2601. SEASON: All yr; 14-day lmt. FACILITIES: 5 sites; tbls, toil, cga, drk wtr, store. ACTIVITIES: Boating,l; picnicking; fishing. MISC.: Pets.

Leona Park (COE; Belton Lake). 12 mi NW of Temple on St Hwy 36 at Leon River on Lake Belton. SEASON: All yr; 14-day lmt. FACILITIES: Undesignated sites; tbls, toil, cga, drk wtr. ACTIVITIES: Swimming; picnicking; fishing; boating,rl. MISC.: Pets permitted.

McGregor Park (COE; Belton Lake). 10 mi NW of Temple on St Hwy 36; 2 mi SW on co rd to CG (On Lake Belton). SEASON: All yr; 14-day lmt. FACILITIES: Un-designated sites; tbls, toil, cga, drk wtr. Store/ice nearby. ACTIVITIES: Swimming; picnicking; fishing; boating,rl. MISC.: Pets.

Owl Creek Park (COE; Belton Lake). 13 mi NW of Temple on St Hwy 36; 1 mi W on co rd; 1 mi S on co rd to CG. FACILITIES: 14 primitive sites; tbls, toil, cga, drk wtr. ACTIVITIES: Swimming; picnicking; fishing; boating,rl. MISC.: Pets permitted.

White Flint Park (COE; Belton Lake). 14 mi NW of Temple on St Hwy 36, on Lake Belton. SEASON: All yr; 14-day lmt. FACILITIES: 10 primitive sites; tbls, toil, cga, drk wtr. ACTIVITIES: Swimming; picnicking; fishing; boating,rl. MISC.: Pets.

Winkler Park (COE; Belton Lake). 12 mi NW of Temple on St Hwy 36; 2 mi N to CG (On Lake Belton). SEASON: All yr; 14-day lmt. FACILITIES: 10 primitive sites; tbls, toil, cga, drk wtr. ACTIVITIES: Swimming; picnicking; fishing; boating,rl. MISC.: Pets.

TEXARKANA

Clear Spring Rec. Area (COE). 10 mi SW of Texarkana on US 67; 1 mi S on co rd; 5 mi E (on Lake Texarkana). SEASON: All yr; 14-day lmt. FACILITIES: Sites, tbls, toil, cga, drk wtr. ACTIVITIES: Swimming; picnicking; fishing; hunting; boating,rl. MISC.: Pets.

North Abutment Rec. Area (COE). 9 mi W of Texarkana on US 59; 1 mi N on St Hwy 2148; 1 mi W on co rd (on Lake Texarkana). SEASON: All yr; 14-day lmt. FACILITIES: Sites, tbls, toil, cga drk wtr. ACTIVITIES: Swimming; picnicking; fishing; hunting; boating,rl. MISC.: Pets permitted if kept on leash.

See page 7 for KEY TO ABBREVIATIONS.

Oak Grove Rec. Area (COE). 10 mi SW of Texarkana on US 59; 1 mi SW on co rd (On Lake Texarkana). SEASON: All yr; 14-day lmt. FACILITIES: Sites, tbls, toil, cga, drk wtr. ACTIVITIES: Hunting; picnicking; fishing. MISC.: Pets permitted if kept on leash.

Overlook Rec. Area (COE). 12 mi SW of Texarkana on US 59 (On Lake Texarkana). SEASON: All yr. FACILITIES: Sites, tbls, toil, cga, drk wtr. ACTIVITIES: Picnicking; fishing. MISC.: Pets permitted if kept on leash.

VICTORIA

Higgins. 9 mi W of Victoria on St Hwy 59. SEASON: All yr. FACILITIES: 6 sites; tbls, toil, cga, drk wtr. ACTIVITIES: Hiking; picnicking; fishing. MISC.: Pets permitted if kept on leash.

WACO

Ham Creek (COE; Whitney Lake). 29 mi NW of Waco on st Hwy 6 and Co Hwy 56. SEASON: All yr; 14-day lmt. FACILITIES: Undesignated sites; tbls, toil, cga, drk wtr. ACTIVITIES: Swimming; picnicking; fishing; boating,l. MISC.: Pets permitted if kept on leash.

Koehne Park (COE; Waco Lake). 2 mi NW of Waco on FM 1637; 1-1/2 mi S on paved road (on Lake Waco). FACILITIES: Undesignated sites; tbls, toil, cga, drk wtr, store, ice nearby. SEASON: All yr; 14-day lmt. ACTIVITIES: Swimming; picnicking; fishing; boating,rl. MISC.: Pets.

Riverside (COE; Whitney Lake). 29 mi NW of Waco on St Hwy 6 and Co Hwy 56. SEASON: All yr; 14-day lmt. FACILITIES: Undesignated sites; tbls, toil, cga, drk wtr. ACTIVITIES: Boating,l; picnicking; fishing. MISC.: Pets.

Soldiers Bluff (COE; Whitney Lake). 19 mi NW of Waco on St Hwy 6 and Co Rd 56. SEASON: All yr; 14-day lmt. FACILITIES: Undesignated sites; tbls, toil, cga, drk wtr, food/ice nearby. ACTIVITIES: Swimming; picnicking; fishing. MISC.: Pets.

WHITESBORO

Cedar Bayou (COE; Lake Texoma-Denison Dam). 13 mi N of Whitesboro on US 377. SEASON: All yr; 14-day lmt. FACILITIES: 12 sites; tbls, toil, cga, drk wtr, elec/wtr/swr hkups. ACTIVITIES: Boating,rld; picnicking; fishing MISC.: Pets permitted.

Paw Paw Point (COE; Lake Texoma-Denison Dam). 16 mi N of Whitesboro on US 377 and access roads. SEASON: All yr; 14-day lmt. FACILITIES: Undesignated sites; tbls, toil, cga, drk

wtr. ACTIVITIES: Boating,l; picnicking; fishing. MISC.: 1 mi S of Rock Creek. Pets.

Rock Creek (COE; Lake Texoma-Denison Dam). 15 mi NW of Whitesboro on US 377 & access roads. SEASON: All yr; 14-day lmt. FACILITIES: 20 sites; flush toil, tbls, cga, drk wtr, sewer/wtr/elec hookups. ACTIVITIES: Boating,l; picnicking; fishing. MISC.: Pets.

WHITNEY

Cedar Creek Park (COE; Whitney Lake). 5 mi N of Whitney on St Hwy 933; 2 mi SW on St Hwy 2604; 8 mi SE on co rd. SEASON: All yr; 14-day lmt. FACILITIES: 6 sites; tbls, toil, cga, drk wtr. Store/food nearby. ACTIVITIES: Swimming; picnicking; fishing; boating,rl. MISC.: Pets.

McCown Valley Park (COE; Whitney Lake). 5 mi W of Whitney on Co Rds. SEASON: All yr; 14-day lmt. FACILITIES: 7 sites; tbls, toil, cga, elec/wtr hookups, drk wtr, store/ice nearby. ACTIVITIES: Swimming; boating,dl; waterskiing; picnicking; fishing. MISC.: Pets permitted if kept on leash.

Noland River Park (COE; Whitney Lake). 14 mi N of Whitney on St Hwy 933 (to Blum); 1 mi N on St Hwy 933; 3 mi W on St Hwy 174; 3 mi S on Co Rd to CG SEASON: All yr; 14-day lmt. FACILITIES: 9 sites, tbls, toil, cga, drk wtr ACTIVITIES: Swimming; picnicking; fishing; boating,rl. MISC.: Pets permitted.

Old Fort Park (COE; Whitney Lake). 5 mi N of Whitney on St Hwy 933; 2 mi SW on St Hwy 2604; 5 mi W on co rd. (On Lake Whitney.) SEASON: All yr; 14-day lmt. FACILITIES: 5 sites; tbls, toil, cga, drk wtr. Food nearby. ACTIVITIES: Swimming; picnicking; fishing; boating,rl. MISC.: Pets permitted.

Walling Bend Park (COE; Whitney Lake). 1 mi SE of Whitney on St Hwy 933; 10 mi SW on St Hwy 22; 1 mi N on St Hwy 56; 2 mi E on St Hwy 2841 (on Lake Whitney). SEASON: All yr; 14-day lmt. FACILITIES: 8 sites; tbls, toil, cga, drk wtr, store/ice nearby. ACTIVITIES: Swimming; picnicking; fishing; boating,rl. MISC.: Pets.

WILLS POINT

Van Zandt County Park (Sabine River Authority). 1-1/2 mi W of Spillway CG; on the N side of Iron Bridge Dam. SEASON: All yr; 14-day lmt. FACILITIES: 32 sties; tbls, toil, cga, dump. ACTIVITIES: Swimming; picnicking; fishing; boating,rl. MISC.: Pets permitted.

YOAKUM

Yoakum (City Park). On N edge of Yoakum; from US 77 follow signs to pk. SEASON: All yr; 2-day lmt. FACILITIES: 40 sites; tbls, toil, cga, phone. ACTIVITIES: Swimming; picnicking; golfing. MISC.: Rec. hall. Pets permitted if kept on leash.

ZAVALLA

Bouton Lake (Angelina NF). 8 mi SE of Zavalla on St Hwy 63; 7 mi S on FS 303. SEASON: All yr; 14-day lmt. FACILITIES: 7 sites (tr -22); tbls, toil, cga, f, piped drk wtr. ACTIVITIES: Boating (no motors); picnicking; fishing. MISC.: 7-acre lake in old river channel bordered by river-bottom hardwoods. Elev 200 ft; pets.

Cassells-Boykin Park (COE; Sam Rayburn Lake). 7 mi NE of Zavalla on St Hwy 147 (paved access roads). SEASON: All yr; 14-day lmt. FACILITIES: 10 sites; tbls, toil, cga, drk wtr. Store/ice/food nearby. ACTIVITIES: Swimming; picnicking; fishing; boating,rl; waterskiing. MISC.: Lake. Pets.

UTAH

GENERAL STATE INFORMATION

Miscellaneous

Right Turns on Red: Permitted after full stop, unless otherwise posted.
STATE CAPITOL: Salt Lake City
STATE NICKNAME: Beehive State
STATE MOTTO: "Industry"
STATE BIRD: Seagulll
STATE FLOWER: Sego Lily
STATE TREE: Blue Spruce

State Parks

Overnight camping fees range from $2.00-5.00; plus a $1.00 entrance fee. Pets are permitted if kept on a leash. Further information: State of Utah; Division of Parks and Recreation; 1596 West North Temple; Salt Lake City, Utah 84116.

Rest Areas

No overnight stopping on Interstate rest areas.

Camping Along the Rivers of Southeastern Utah

Although campsites are available along the rivers, heavy use threatens some popular sites. To minimize the impact on any one site, please seek an area that is not heavily used. Whenever possible, set up camp on beaches or sandbars. This reduces damage to fragile vegetation and soils caused by foot traffic, and allows high water to remove evidence of your camp. Locate shelters so water drains away naturally. Further information: BLM; 136 East South Temple; Salt Lake City, Utah 84111.

High Uintas Primitive and Related Areas

Located in Ashley and Wasatch National Forests. The Uintas Mountains have outstanding wilderness qualities and are geologically unique in that they constitute the highest mountain range in Utah, and the most prominent east-west range in the U.S. Elevations vary from 800-13,528 feet. Some fall hunting for moose, elk, and deer. Trout fishing throughout the area. Black bear are common. Backpacking/camping is available throughout the entire area. Information such as trail, campsite, and fishing conditions, and areas for maximum solitude, can best be obtained from the District Office having responsibility for the area in which you expect to travel:

Duchesne Ranger District; Hwy 40; Duchesne, UT 84021
Vernal Ranger District; 650 N. Vernal Ave.; Vernal, UT 84078
Kamas Ranger District; Kamas, UT 84036
Evanston Ranger District; Federal Building; Evanston, WY 82930
Roosevelt Ranger District; 150 S. 2nd East; Roosevelt, UT 84066
Flaming Gorge Ranger District; Dutch John, UT 84046
Mountain View Ranger District; Mountain View, WY

No permit is necessary.

Backcountry Camping in Fishlake and Manti Lasal National Forests

Camping and hiking are allowed anywhere in the backcountry of the Forests. No permits are necessary. Further information: Forest Supervisor; Fishlake NF; 170 North Main Street; Richfield, UT 84701. Forest Supervisor; Manti Lasal NF; 350 East Main Street; Price, UT 84501.

INFORMATION SOURCES

Maps

A detailed, up-to-date map of the **State of Utah** is available from **Forsyth Travel Library** (see order form in Appendix B).

Gold Mining and Prospecting

Utah Geological and Mineralogical Survey; 103 Civil Engineering Building; University of Utah; Salt Lake City, UT 84102

State Information

Utah Travel Council; Council Hall; Capitol Hill; Salt Lake City, UT 84114.
Division of Parks and Recreation; State of Utah; 1596 West North Temple; Salt Lake City, UT 84116.
Division of Wildlife Resources; Department of Natural Resources; 1596 West North Temple; Salt Lake City, UT 84116.

City Information

Brigham City Chamber of Commerce; PO Box 458; Brigham City, UT 84302.
Moab Chamber of Commerce; 805 N. Main; Moab, UT 84532.
Provo Chamber of Commerce; 10 E. 300 North; Provo, UT 84601.
Salt Lake City Chamber of Commerce; 19 East 2nd South; Salt Lake City, UT 84116.

National Forests

Ashley NF; 437 E. Main St.; Vernal, UT 84078.
Dixie NF; 500 S. Main St.; Cedar City, UT 84720.
Fishlake NF; 170 N. Main St.; Richfield, UT 84701.
Manti Lasal NF; 350 E. Main St.; Price, UT 84501.
Uinta NF; Box 1428; Provo, UT 84601.
Wasatch NF; 125 State St.; Salt Lake City, UT 84111.

Miscellaneous

Cedar Breaks NM; Box 749; Cedar City, UT 84720.
Natural Bridges NM; c/o Canyonlands NP; Moab, UT 84532.
Arches NP; c/o Canyonlands NP; Moab, UT 84532.
Bryce Canyon NP; Bryce Canyon, UT 84717.
Canyonlands NP; Moab, UT 84532.
Capitol Reef NP; Torrey, UT 84775.
Zion NP; Springdale, UT 84767.
Utah BLM; Univ. Club Bldg; 136 E. South Temple; Salt Lake City, UT 84111.
Bear River Migratory Bird Refuge; PO Box 459; Brigham City, UT 84302.

FREE CAMPGROUNDS

ALTONAH

Bridge (Ashley NF). 12 mi NW of Altonah on Co Hwy 10119; 2-3/5 mi N on FS 10119. SEASON: 5/25-9/10; 14-day lmt. FACILITIES: 5 sites (tr -22); tbls, toil, cga, piped drk wtr. Food (1 mi). ACTIVITIES: Picnicking; fishing. Horseback riding/rental (1 mi). MISC.: Elev 7700 ft; 2 acres; river. Pets.

Reservoir (Ashley NF). 12 mi NW of Altonah on Co Hwy 10119; 5-2/5 mi N on FS 10119. SEASON: 5/25-9/10; 14-day lmt. FACILITIES: 5 sites (tr -22); tbls, toil, cga, well drk wtr. Food (1 mi). ACTIVITIES: Picnicking; fishing. Horseback riding/rental (1 mi). MISC.: Elev 7900 ft; 3 acres; lake. Pets permitted if kept on a leash.

Riverview (Ashley NF). 12 mi NW of Altonah on Co Hwy 10119; 6½ mi N on FS 10119. SEASON: 5/25-9/10; 14-day lmt. FACILITIES: 19 sites (tr -22); tbls, toil, cga, piped drk wtr. Food (2 mi). ACTIVITIES: Picnicking; fishing; hunting. Horseback riding/rental (2 mi). MISC.: Elev 8000 ft; 7 acres; river. Pets permitted if kept on leash.

BEAVER

Mahogany Cove (Fishlake NF). 11 mi E of Beaver on St Hwy 153. SEASON: 6/1-10/30; 14-day lmt. FACILITIES: 10 sites (tr -22); tbls, toil, cga, f, drk wtr. ACTIVITIES: Picnicking. Fishing (2 mi). Hunting. MISC.: Elev 7700 ft; 7 acres. Near Beaver Canyon. Pets.

BICKNELL

Sunglow (Fishlake NF). 7/10 mi SE of Bicknell on Co Hwy 24; 1-3/10 mi NE on FS 1431. SEASON: 5/1-11/1; 5-day lmt. FACILITIES: 2 sites (tr -16); tbls, toil, cga, f, piped drk wtr. ACTIVITIES: Hiking; picnicking; fishing; rockhounding. Horseback riding (1 mi). MISC.: Elev 7500 ft; 12 acres; stream; nature trails. Store/gas/ice/food (2 mi). Pets permitted if kept on a leash.

BLANDING

* **Grand Gulch Primitive Area** (BLM). Obtain a permit from the rangers at Kane Gulch Ranger Station (Star Route; Blanding 84511; Mobile Phone JL7-1192) or the San Juan Resource Area office in Monticello (Box 7, Blanding 84535; 801-587-2201) before entering the Canyon.

No motorized vehicles. No camping within 100 ft of a water source. 2-night limit per campsite. Drk wtr isn't avail. at the Kane Gulch Ranger Station. Use water purification tablets on all water. During July, Aug, and Sept. there is a danger of flash floods from thunderstorms. If you are in the Gulch when it rains, stay out of stream channel. Never camp in a stream channel any time of the year. Be careful of quicksand pockets in the stream channel after the water recedes. Watch for scorpions, black widow spiders, and rattlesnakes.

Hite Marina (Glen Canyon NRA). 60 mi W of Blanding on St Hwy 95. SEASON: All yr. FACILITIES: 6 sites (tr -20); tbls, toil, cga, boat san. stat. at marina. Store/food (nearby). ACTIVITIES: Swimming; fishing; boating,lr; picnicking. MISC.: Pets permitted if kept on leash.

Hovenweep Natl Mon. 16 mi S of Blanding on St Hwy 163; 24 mi E on St Hwy 262 and graded road. SEASON: All yr. FACILITIES: 31 sites (tr -20); flush toil. MISC.: 505 acres; pets permitted.

Natural Bridges NM. 38 mi W of Blanding via St Hwys 95/275 (good paved roads). 13 sites; tbls; cga; toil; drk wtr at visitor center; approx. 1/4 mi from CG; campfire circle with Ranger-lead slide programs from MD-9/15, 190 yds from CG. Open all year; but there is a $1 entrance fee to the national monument from approx. mid-May to Mid-Oct. They honor Golden Eagle/Age passports.** Pets are allowed; but not on trails.

Red Bluff Campground (Manti-Lasal NF). 7-9/10 mi N of Blanding on Co Hwy 50095; 7-1/10 mi N on FS 50079. SEASON: 5/20-10/25; 14-day lmt. FACILITIES: 5 sites (tr -16); tbls, toil, cga, f, no drk wtr. ACTIVITIES: Picnicking; Horseback riding (1 mi). Pets.

BRIGHAM CITY

Bear River Bird Refuge (NWR). 15 mi W of Brigham City on Co blacktop rd. SEASON: 3/15-12/31. FACILITIES: no desig sites, flush toil. ACTIVITIES: Fishing. MISC.: 5 acres. Pets.

CEDAR CITY

Deer Haven (Dixie NF). 15 mi SE of Cedar City on St Hwy 14; 4 mi S on Co Hwy. SEASON: 6/1-10/30; 14-day lmt. FACILITIES: 20 sites (no tr); tbls, toil, cga, f, piped drk wtr. ACTIVITIES: Picnicking. MISC.: Elev 8900 ft; 15 acres. Pets permitted if kept on a leash. GROUP AREA: reservations req.

CLEVELAND

San Rafael (BLM). 25 mi SE of Cleveland on Co Rd. SEASON: 4/1-10/31; 14-day lmt. FACILITIES: 8 sites (tr -30); tbls, toil, cga, drk wtr. ACTIVITIES: Picnicking. MISC.: Pets permitted.

DUCHESNE

Moon Lake Overflow (Ashley NF). 14 mi N of Duchesne on St Hwy 87; 12 mi N on St Hwy 134; 5-3/10 mi NW on Co Hwy 10131. SEASON: 7/1-8/31; 3-day lmt. FACILITIES: 25 sites (tr -22); tbls, toil, cga, f, piped drk wtr. Store/food/gas (1 mi). ACTIVITIES: Swimming; picnicking; fishing; boating,rld. Horseback riding/rental (1 mi) MISC.: Elev 8100 ft; 20 acres; lake. Trail to Wilderness nearby. Pets.

DUTCH JOHN

Arch Dam Overflow (Ashley NF). 2 ½ mi SW of Dutch John on St Hwy 260; 3/10 mi E on FS 10190. SEASON: 5/25-9/5; 14-day lmt. FACILITIES: 200 sites (tr -32); tbls, toil, cga, f, piped drk wtr. Store/gas/ice/laundry/food (2 mi). ACTIVITIES: Fishing/horseback riding/ visitor center (1 mi). Boating,rld/water skiing (2 mi). Rockhounding. MISC.: Elev 6200 ft; 25 acres. Near Green River. Pets permitted if kept on leash.

See page 7 for KEY TO ABBREVIATIONS.

Gooseneck Boating Camp (Ashley NF).
5 mi SW of Dutch John on st Hwy 260;
1-3/10 mi NW on FS 10183; 1/10 mi N
on FS 10391; 8¼ mi W, BY BOAT. SEASON:

5/25-9/5; 14-day lmt. FACILITIES: 6
sites (no trailers); tbls, toil, cga,
piped drk wtr. ACTIVITIES: Hunting;
picnicking; fishing; swimming; sailing;
waterskiing; boating,d. MISC.: Elev 6100
ft; 3 acres; lake. Flaming Gorge nearby.
Pets permitted if kept on a leash.

* **Jarvies Canyon Boating Camp** (Ashley
NF). 5 mi SW of Dutch John on St Hwy
260; 1-3/10 mi NW on FS 10183; 1/10 mi
N on FS 10391; 5 mi NW BY BOAT. SEA-
SON: 5/25-9/5; 14-day lmt. FACILITIES:
8 tent sites; tbls, toil, cga. Store/food/
gas/dump (5 mi). ACTIVITIES: Swimming;
picnicking; fishing; hunting; sailing;
boating,d. MISC.: Elev 6100 ft; 5 acres.
Flaming Gorge nearby. Pets.

Little Hole (Ashley NF). 7 mi SE of
Dutch John on FS 10075. SEASON: 5/20-
9/15; 14-day lmt. FACILITIES: 17 sites
(tr -22); tbls, toil, cga, f, no drk wtr.
ACTIVITIES: Hunting; picnicking; fishing; boating,ld; hiking. MISC.: Elev
5600 ft; 14 acres; scenic; Green River.
Float boating on Green River. Pets.

EDEN

North Arm (Wasatch NF). 2 mi W of Eden
on St Hwy 162. SEASON: 5/25-9/15; 7-day
lmt. FACILITIES: 13 sites (tr -22). AC-
TIVITIES: Fishing; boating,ld. Swimming
(2 mi). MISC.: Elev 5000 ft; 6 acres.
Pets permitted if kept on a leash.

ENTERPRISE

Pine Park (Dixie NF). 17 mi W of Enterprise on St Hwy 120; 5½ mi SW on FS
001. SEASON: 5/20-10/31. FACILITIES: 11
tent sites; tbls, toil, cga, f.
ACTIVITIES: Hunting; picnicking; fishing; hiking. Horseback riding (1 mi).
MISC.: Elev 6200 ft; 10 acres; scenic
rock formations. Pets permitted.

ESCALANTE

Blue Spruce (Dixie NF). 17 mi N of Escalante on FS 153. SEASON: 6/15-9/15. FA-
CILITIES: 6 sites (tr -16); tbls, toil,
cga, f, drk wtr. ACTIVITIES: Picnicking; fishing. MISC.: Elev 8500 ft; 3
acres. Hell Backbone Loop Road. Pets.

* **Camping/Hiking the Escalante River**
(BLM). Maps and exact info can be obtained from the BLM office on the west
edge of Escalante (801)826-4368 or from
the BLM office at 320 N. First, in Knab,
Escalante 84741.

Good camping spots abound and firewood is common. Springs are fairly
common, but sterilize all drking and
dish water. Suggested season is mid-
April thru Oct. Winters are cold with
ice; summers are hot with thunderstorms.

FARMINGTON

Bountiful Peak (Wasatch NF). ½ mi N
of Farmington on Co Hwy; 8-4/5 mi E
on FS. SEASON: 6/15-9/7; 14-day lmt.
FACILITIES: 44 tent sites; reservations
accepted, drk wtr. ACTIVITIES: Hunting.
Fishing (1 mi). MISC.: 14 acres; Elev
7500 ft. Rte is a narrow, winding,
steep canyon road. Pets.

Sunset (Wasatch NF). 4 mi NE of
Farmington on FS FH007. SEASON: 5/1-
10/15. FACILITIES: 32 tent sites (no
trailers); tbls, toil, cga, piped drk
wtr. ACTIVITIES: Picnicking; mtn
climbing; hunting. Fishing/horseback
riding (1 mi). MISC.: Elev 6500 ft; 3
acres. Pets permitted if kept on leash.

FERRON

Ferron Canyon (Manti-Lasal NF). 5-3/10
mi W of Ferron on Co Hwy; 3-1/5 mi
NW on FS 50022. SEASON: 4/15-9/10; 14-
day lmt. FACILITIES: 4 sites (tr -22);
tbls, toil, cga, f, drk wtr. ACTIVI-
TIES: Hunting;ʼ picnicking; fishing.
MISC.: Elev 7000 ft; stream. Pets.

FOUNTAIN GREEN

Maple Canyon (Manti Lasal NF). 6½ mi
S of Fountain Green on St Hwy 30; 3-
1/2 mi W on St Hwy 116. SEASON: 5/15-
9/30; 14-day lmt. FACILITIES: 12 sites
(tr -16); tbls, toil, cga. ACTIVITIES:
Picnicking; fishing. MISC.: Elev 6800
ft; 1 acre. Interesting geological formations near this site. Pets permitted.

GRANTVILLE

Intake (Wasatch NF). 1/5 mi W of
Grantsville on US 40; 4-7/10 mi S on Co
Hwy 138; 3½ mi SW on Co Hwy 45; 1½
mi SW on FS 80171. SEASON: 5/1-10/1;
14-day lmt. FACILITIES: 4 sites (no
trailers); tbls, toil, cga, f, no drk wtr.
ACTIVITIES: Hunting; picnicking; fishing; rockhounding. MISC.: Elev 7200 ft;
3 acres; archaeological. Pets permitted.

Loop (Wasatch NF). 1/5 mi W on Us 40;
4-7/10 mi S on 138; 3½ mi SW on Co Hwy
45; 3-4/5 mi SW on FS 80171. SEASON:
6/1-9/15; 14-day lmt. FACILITIES: 5
sites (tr -16); tbls, toil, cga, no drk
wtr. ACTIVITIES: Rockhounding; hunting;
picnicking; fishing. Horseback riding
(1 mi). MISC.: Elev 7800 ft; 5 acres;
stream; archeological interest. Pets.

Lower Narrows (Wasatch NF). 1/5 mi W of Grantsville on US 40; 4-7/10 mi S on Co Hwy; 3½ mi SW in Co Hwy; 2-2/5 mi SW on FS 80171. SEASON: 5/15-9/15; 14-day lmt. FACILITIES: 6 tent sites (no trailers); tbls, toil, cga, drk wtr. ACTIVITIES: Hunting; picnicking; fishing; rockhounding. MISC.: Elev 7600 ft; 3 acres; stream. Pets.

GREENWICH

Lower Box Creek Reservoir. 1 mi N of Greenwich on St Hwy 62; 8 mi NW on FS 40069. SEASON: 6/1-9/30; 14-day lmt. FACILITIES: 1 site: (tr -16); toil, f. ACTIVITIES: Fishing. MISC.: Elev 8400 ft. Pets permitted if kept on a leash.

HANKSVILLE

Lonesome Beaver Campground (BLM). 23 mi S of Hanksville on rough mtn rd. SEASON: 6/1-10/31; 14-day lmt. FACILITIES: 5 sites (tr -30); tbls, toil, cga, drk wtr. ACTIVITIES: Picnicking. MISC.: 5 acres. Pets permitted if kept on leash.

Starr Springs (BLM). 50 mi SW of Hanksville on US 276. SEASON: 4/1-10/31; 14-day lmt. FACILITIES: 12 sites (tr -30); tbls, toil, cga, drk wtr. ACTIVITIES: Picnicking. MISC.: 10 acres; pets.

HANNA

Miners Gulch (Ashley NF). 20-2/5 mi NE of Hanna on FS 10134. SEASON: 5/25-9/10; 14-day lmt. FACILITIES: 6 sites (tr -22); tbls, toil, cga, f, no drk wtr. ACTIVITIES: Picnicking; fishing. Horseback riding (1 mi); rental (5 mi). MISC.: Elev 7500 ft; 25 acres. Pets.

South Fork (Ashley NF). 15-4/5 mi NE of Hanna on FS 10134. SEASON: 5/25-9/10; 14-day lmt. FACILITIES: 5 sites (tr -16); tbls, toil, cga, f, no drk wtr. ACTIVITIES: Picnicking; fishing. Horseback riding/rental (1 mi). MISC.: Elev 8000 ft; 15 acres. Pets permitted.

Upper Stillwater (Ashley NF). 15 mi NE of Hanna on FS 10134. SEASON: 5/25-9/10; 14-day lmt. FACILITIES: 12 sites (tr -16); tbls, toil, cga, f, no drk wtr. ACTIVITIES: Picnicking; fishing; hunting; hiking. Horseback riding (1 mi). MISC.: Elev 8000 ft; 20 acres. Trail to wilderness nearby. Pets.

Yellow Pine Flat (Ashley NF). 19-2/5 mi NE of Hanna on FS 10134. SEASON: 5/25-9/10; 14-day lmt. FACILITIES: 10 sites (tr -16); tbls, toil, cga, f, no drk wtr. ACTIVITIES: Hunting; picnicking; fishing. Horseback riding (1 mi); rental (4 mi). MISC.: Elev 7600 ft; 15 acres; stream. Pets.

HEBER

State Area. 1-15 at Orem to St Hwy 189N, thru Provo Canyon to Heber. SEASON: All yr. ACTIVITIES: Fishing; hiking; rockhounding; biking; snow skiing. MISC.: Pets permitted if kept on leash.

HUNTSVILLE

Anderson Cove B (Wasatch NF). 2½ mi SW of Huntsville on St Hwy 39. SEASON: 5/15-9/30. FACILITIES: 2 sites; toil, no tbls, no drk wtr. Store (2 mi). Gas/ice/food (1 mi). ACTIVITIES: Fishing; boating,rl; waterski; sailing. MISC.: Elev 5000 ft; 10 acre, pets.

Hawthorne (Wasatch NF). 7½ mi E of Huntsville on St Hwy 39. SEASON: 5/15-9/15; 3-day lmt. FACILITIES: 10 sites (tr -22); tbls, toil, cga, piped drk wtr. Food (1 mi). ACTIVITIES: Picnicking; fishing. Horseback riding (1 mi). MISC.: Elev 5300 ft; 3 acres. Pets.

Hobble (Wasatch NF). 6 mi E of Huntsville on St Hwy 39. SEASON: 5/15-9/30; 7-day lmt. FACILITIES: 8 sites (tr -22); tbls, toil, cga, no drk wtr. ACTIVITIES: Picnicking. Fishing/horseback riding (1 mi). MISC.: Elev 5200 ft; 3 acres. Food/gas (3 mi). Pets permitted.

Jefferson Hunt (Wasatch NF). 2 mi S of Huntsville on St Hwy 39. SEASON: 5/15-9/30; 7-day lmt. FACILITIES: 29 sites (tr -22); Ice/food (1 mi); Store (1 mi). ACTIVITIES: Fishing; swimming; boating,rld; horseback riding; rockhounding. MISC.: Elev 5000 ft; 9 acres; stream. Pets permitted if kept on leash.

The Maples (Wasatch NF). 10 mi SW of Huntsville on St Hwy 226; 2 mi NW on FS 20122. SEASON: 6/1-9/15; 7-day lmt. FACILITIES: 25 sites (tr -16); tbls, toil, cga, no drk wtr. ACTIVITIES: Picnicking; mtn climbing. Horseback riding (1 mi). MISC.: Elev 6200 ft; 20 acres. Pets permitted if kept on a leash.

South Arm (Wasatch NF). 2 mi S of Huntsville on St Hwy 39. SEASON: 6/1-9/15; 7-day lmt. FACILITIES: 19 sites (tr -16); Store (2 mi); Ice/food (1 mi). ACTIVITIES: Fishing; swimming; boating,rld. MISC.: Elev 5000 ft; 8 acres. Lake. Pets permitted if kept on leash.

Wild Cat (Wasatch NF). 11 mi SW of Huntsville on St Hwy 39. SEASON: 6/1-9/30; 7-day lmt. FACILITIES: 8 tent sites (no trailers). ACTIVITIES: Fishing (1 mi). MISC.: Elev 6200 ft; 5 acres. Pets permitted if kept on a leash.

JUNCTION

La Beron Lake (Fishlake NF). 1/10 mi N of Junction on US 89; 14 mi W on St

Hwy 153; 3½ mi SW on FS 40137. SEA-
SON: 6/1-9/15. FACILITIES: 1 site (tr
-22); tbls, toil, cga, f, no drk wtr.
ACTIVITIES: Swimming; picnicking; fishing. Horseback riding (1 mi).
MISC.: Elev 9800 ft; 5 acres; scenic;
lake. Pets permitted if on a leash.

City Creek (Fishlake NF). 1/10 mi N
on US 89; 5-3/10 mi NW on St Hwy
153; 1 mi NE on FS 40131. SEASON:
5/21-10/30; 16-day lmt. FACILITIES:
5 sites (tr -16); tbls, toil, cga,
piped drk wtr. ACTIVITIES: Picnicking; hiking; fishing; hunting. Horseback riding (1 mi). MISC.: Elev
7600 ft; 3 acres; stream; pets.

KAMAS

* Highline Trailhead Packer (Wasatch NF).
34 mi E of Kamas on St Hwy 150; HIKER.
SEASON: 7/1-9/7; 14-day lmt. FACILI-
fishing. Boating,rld (2 mi). Horseback riding (1 mi) and rental (3
mi). MISC.: Elev 10,200 ft; 4 acres;
pets; mangers; tie racks; water
troughs; unload ramps for horses.

Yellow Pine (Wasatch NF). 6 mi E of
Kamas on St Hwy 150. SEASON: 6/1-9/10;
14-day lmt. FACILITIES: 33 sites (tr -
16); tbls, toil, cga, f, piped drk wtr.
Food (4 mi). Gas (5 mi). ACTIVITIES:
Picnicking. Fishing/horseback riding (1
mi). MISC.: Elev 7200 ft; 11 acres. Pets.

KANAB

* Paria Canyon Primitive Area (BLM). Your
free permit can be obtained from the
Kanab District Office (320 N. 1st East;
Kanab 84741; 801/644-2672); they will
also supply you with map/info.

This is a hike-in area only. Caution:
the most hazardous period for flash
floods is during July, Aug. & Sept.
Always camp away from the stream.
Water is available all through the
canyon; but should be treated.

KOOSHAREM

Upper Box Creek Reservoir (NF). 5 mi
S of Koosharem on St Hwy 62; 1¼ mi W
on Co Hwy 40069; 7 mi NW on FS 40069.
SEASON: 6/1-9/30; 14-day lmt. FACILI-
TIES: 1 site (tr -16); toil, f. ACTIVI-
TIES: Fishing. MISC.: Elev 9000 ft. Pets.

LA POINT

Paradise Park (Ashley NF). 16½ mi NW
of La Point on Co Hwy 121; 8-4/5 mi NW
on FS 104 (poor access rd). SEASON:
6/15-9/10. FACILITIES: 15 sites (tr -22);
tbls, toil, cga, no drk wtr. ACTIV:
Picnicking; fishing; hunting; hiking.
Horseback riding (1 mi). MISC.: Elev
10,000 ft; 8 acres; lake; stream. Trail
to High Uintas Wilderness nearby. Pets.

LOA

Elkhorn (Fishlake NF). 12½ mi NE of
Loa on St Hwy 72; 7½ mi SE on FS 2062.
SEASON: 6/15-10/30; 5-day lmt. FACILI-
TIES: 5 sites (tr -16); tbls, toil, cga,
f, piped drk wtr. ACTIVITIES: Hunting;
picnicking; fishing (1 mi). MISC.: Elev
9300 ft; 5 acres; scenic view; stream.
Pets permitted if kept on a leash.

Forsyth Reservoir (Fishlake NF). 12
mi NE of Loa on St Hwy 72. SEASON:
6/1-10/1; 5-day lmt. FACILITIES: 3
sites (tr -16); tbls, toil, cga. ACTIVI-
TIES: Picnicking; swimming; fishing;
hunting; waterskiing. MISC.: Elev 7400
ft. Pets permitted if kept on a leash.

Johnson Reservoir (Fishlake NF). 13
mi NW of Loa on St Hwy 24; 10 mi NE
on St Hwy 25; 7 mi NE on FS 40640;
1 mi E on FS 40013. SEASON: 6/1-10/15;
16-day lmt. FACILITIES: 2 sites (tr
-16); toil. ACTIVITIES: Fishing; waterskiing. MISC.: Elev 8600 ft. Pets.

LOGAN

Twin Bridges (Wasatch NF). 16-1/2 mi
E of Logan on US 89; 1/5 mi S on FS.
SEASON: 6/1-9/10; 5-day lmt. FACILI-
TIES: 6 tent sites; tbls, toil, cga, no
drk wtr. ACTIVITIES: Picnicking; fishing. Horseback riding (1 mi). Hiking
(5 mi). MISC.: Elev 5600 ft; 4 acres;
river; poor access. Pets permitted.

MANILA

Browne Lake (Ashley NF). 14 mi S of
Manila on St Hwy 44; 3 mi W on FS
10218; ½ mi W on FS 10364; 3 mi W on
FS 10221. SEASON: 5/25-9/5; 14-day lmt.
FACILITIES: 8 tent sites (no trailers);
tbls, toil, cga, f, piped drk wtr. AC-
TIVITIES: Boating,d; picnicking; fishing; hunting. MISC.: Elev 8200 ft; 4
acres; stream; lake; scenic. Pets.

Deep Creek (Ashley NF). 14 mi S of
Manila on St Hwy 44; 3 mi W on FS
10218; 4½ mi SE on FS 10539. SEASON:
5/25-9/5; 14-day lmt. FACILITIES: 17
sites (tr -22); tbls, toil, cga, f, piped
drk wtr. ACTIVITIES: Hiking; picnicking; fishing; hunting. MISC.: Elev 7800
ft; 8 acres; stream. Pets permitted.

Henrys Fork (Ashley NF). 3 mi NE of
Manila on St Hwy 43; 1 mi NE on St Hwy
530; 3/10 mi SE on FS 60015. SEASON:
5/1-9/15; 14-day lmt. FACILITIES: 9
sites (tr -22); tbls. Store/showers/ice
(4 mi). ACTIVITIES: Fishing; boating,rld. MISC.: Elev 7000 ft; 7 acres.
Pets permitted if kept on a leash.

* Hideout (Ashley NF). 7-1/5 mi SE of
Manila on St Hwy 44; ½ mi NE on FS
10092; 3 mi E BY BOAT. SEASON: 5/25-
9/5; 14-day lmt. FACILITIES: 19 tent
sites; tbls, toil, cga, f, piped drk wtr.

ACTIVITIES: Swimming; picnicking; fishing; boating,ld; sailing. MISC.: Elev 6100 ft; 8 acres. Boat camp on Flaming George Lake. Pets permitted.

Kingfisher Island (Ashley NF). 7-1/5 mi S of Manila on St Hwy 44; 2-3/10 mi NE BY BOAT; ½ mi NE on FS 10092. SEASON: 5/25-9/5; 14-day lmt. FACILITIES: 5 tent sites; tbls, toil, cga, f, no drk wtr. ACTIVITIES: Boating,ld; picnicking; fishing. Swimming (1 mi). MISC.: Elev 6100 ft; 3 acres; lake. Within Flaming George NRA Boat Camp. Pets.

Spirit Lake (Ashley NF). 14 mi S of Manila on St Hwy 44; 3 mi W on FS 10218; 1/2 mi W on FS 10364; 14 mi W on FS 10221 (dirt access rds). SEASON: 6/25-9/5; 14-day lmt. FACILITIES: 24 sites (tr -22); tbls, toil, cga, f, piped drk wtr. Store/food/ice/gas (1 mi). ACTIVITIES: Hunting; hiking; rockhounding. Boating,rl/horseback riding (1 mi). MISC.: Elev 10,000 ft; 11 acres; lake. Scenic. Trail to Wilderness Area nearby. Pets permitted if kept on a leash.

Squaw Hollow (Ashley NF). 2-4/5 mi NE of Manila on St Hwy 43; 12-7/10 mi N on St Hwy 530; 2½ mi E on FS 60004. SEASON: 5/1-9/15. FACILITIES: 12 sites (tr -22); tbls. ACTIVITIES: Fishing; boating,ld; horseback riding. MISC.: Elev 9000 ft; 1 acre. Pets permitted.

MANTI

City Park. 2½ blocks W of Main St. SEASON: All yr. MISC.: Pets permitted if kept on leash.

MANTUA

Willard Basin (NF). 4 mi S of Mantua on FS 84; 12 mi W on FS 841. SEASON: 6/30-9/15; 7-day lmt. FACILITIES: 4 sites (no trailers); tbls, toil, cga, piped drk wtr. ACTIVITIES: Picnicking. Horseback riding (1 mi). MISC.: Elev 9000 ft; 3 acres. Pets permitted.

MENDON

Maple Bench (Wasatch NF). 1 mi S of Mendon on St Hwy 23; 1 mi SW on Co Hwy; 2 mi SW on Co Hwy 86. SEASON: 6/15-9/10. FACILITIES: 6 tent sites (no trailers); tbls, toil, cga, no drk wtr. ACTIVITIES: Picnicking; Horseback riding (1 mi). MISC.: Elev 6000 ft; 3 acres. Pets.

MOAB

Arches NP. 5 mi N of Moab on US 163 to Park Entrance; 18 mi NE of Visitor Center. SEASON: 11/1-3/1; FREE ($3 rest of yr, CG; $1 entrance). Water shut off during FREE season. FACILITIES: 54 sites (tr -20); tbls, toil, cga, pull-thru sp, drk wtr. ACTIVITIES: Picnicking; hiking. MISC.: Pets.

* **Arches NP Backcountry Camping.** 5 mi N of Moab on US 163 to Visitor Center. $1 entrance fee into park from Mar-Oct. Backcountry hikers should inform park rangers about trip plans. Once in the backcountry, stay away from washes and other areas prone to flash floods. Don't camp in washes.

Lions Club Park (City Park). On St Hwy 163 at Colo River Bridge in Moab. SEASON: All yr. FACILITIES: 30 sites; tbls, toil, cga. ACTIVITIES: Picnicking. MISC.: Pets permitted if kept on leash.

Lions Club CG & Park. 3 mi from Moab at jct of US 163 & St Hwy 128 (on Cole River). SEASON: All yr. FACILITIES: 30 sites; tbls, toil, cga, phone. ACTIVITIES: Hiking; rockhounding; picnicking; fishing. MISC.: Elev 4000 ft; nature trails. Near Arches Natl Mon & Canyonland. Pets.

Moose Park (BLM). 10 mi from Moab on St Hwy 128. SEASON: All yr. FACILITIES: 10 self-contained sites; tbls, toil, cga. ACTIVITIES: Picnicking; fishing; swimming; hunting; hiking; bike trails; rockhounding. MISC.: Elev 4000 ft. Pets permitted if kept on leash.

Squaw Flat (Canyonlands NP). 40 mi S of Moab on US 163; 45 mi W on St Hwy 211 (paved rds). SEASON: 10/1-5/1, FREE ($2 rest of yr.). FACILITIES: 27 sites (tr -20); tbls, toil, cga, drk wtr is avail. at the Ranger Station about 3 mi from the CG. ACTIVITIES: Picnicking. MISC.: Pets.

Willow Flat CG (Canyonlands NP). 12 mi N of Moab on US 163; 33 mi SW on St Hwy 313; 7 mi on dirt entrance road to Island in the Sky Ranger Station. (The campground is about 8 mi beyond the Ranger Station.) SEASON: All yr. FACILITIES: 8 prim sites (tr -20); tbls, toil, cga, no drk wtr. ACTIVITIES: Picnicking. MISC.: Park Rangers give campfire programs each evening during the summer. Pets.

MONTICELLO

Dalton Springs. 5 mi W of Monticello on FS 501005. SEASON: 5/20-10/25; 14-day lmt. FACILITIES: 13 sites (tr -22); tbls, toil, cga, f, piped drk wtr. Ice/food/store/showers/gas (5 mi). ACTIVITIES: Hunting; picnicking. Horseback riding (1 mi). Fishing (4 mi). MISC.: Elev 8200 ft; 5 acres; scenic. Pets.

Hatch Point CG (BLM; Canyon Rims Complex). 22 mi N of Monticello on US 163; 23 mi NW on BLM rd. SEASON: 4/1-10/31; 14-day lmt. FACILITIES: 10 sites (tr -30); tbls, toil, cga, drk wtr. ACTIVITIES: Picnicking; fishing. MISC.: 8 acres. Pets.

NEPHI

Cottonwood (Uinta NF). 6 mi E of Nephi on St Hwy 11; 6 mi N on FS 015. SEASON: 5/15-10/31; 10-day lmt. FACILITIES: 8 sites (tr -16); tbls, toil, cga, f, piped drk wtr. ACTIVITIES: Hunting; picnicking; fishing. Horseback riding (1 mi). MISC.: Elev 6400 ft; 9 acres; stream. Located near Mt. Nebo. Site not recommended for tourist use. Pets.

PARA GONAH

Red Creek Reservoir (NF). 7 mi SE of Para Gonah on FS 78. SEASON: 6/15-9/15. FACILITIES: 1 site (tr -22); tbls, toil, cga. ACTIVITIES: Picnicking; Horseback riding (1 mi). MISC.: Elev 7700 ft; 1 acre. Pets permitted. tbls, toil, cga, no drk wtr. ACTIVITIES: Picnicking. Horseback riding (1 mi). MISC.: Elev 7700 ft; 1 acre; pets. Red Creek Reservoir.

PLEASANT GROVE

Summit (NF). 5½ mi N of Pleasant Grove on St Hwy 146; 10-4/5 mi E on St Hwy 92; 1/10 mi W on FS 144. SEASON: 6/1-9/30; 16-day lmt. FACILITIES: 2 sites (tr -16); tbls, toil, cga, f, no drk wtr. ACTIVITIES: Picnicking; fishing. Horseback riding (1 mi). MISC.: Elev 8000 ft; 3 acres; scenic. Road restricts larger trailers. Not recommended for tourist use. Pets.

PROVO

Rock Canyon (Uinta NF). 6 mi N of Provo on St Hwy 189; 11 mi S on FS 027. SEASON: 6/1-10/15. FACILITIES: 8 tent sites; drk wtr. ACTIVITIES: Hunting. MISC.: Elev 6800 ft; 42 acres. Pets permitted if kept on leash.

RICHMOND

High Creek (NF). 2 mi NE of Richmond on St Hwy 91; 4 mi E on Co Hwy; 2 mi E on FS 20048. SEASON: 6/15-9/15; 5-day lmt. FACILITIES: 3 sites (tr -16); tbls, toil, cga, piped drk wtr. ACTIVITIES: Picnicking; fishing. Horseback riding (1 mi). MISC.: Elev 5000 ft; 3 acres; pets.

Richmond City Park. In Richmond. SEASON: All yr. FACILITIES: 1-day lmt. MISC.: Pets permitted if kept on leash.

ST GEORGE

City Park. In town. SEASON: All yr. MISC.: Pets permitted if kept on leash.

ROOSEVELT

Wandin (Ashley NF). 9½ mi N of Roosevelt on St Hwy 121; 12 mi NW on Co Hwy; 4 mi NW on FS 10118. SEASON: 5/25-9/10; 14-day lmt. FACILITIES: 7 sites (tr -22); tbls, toil, cga, f, piped drk wtr. ACTIVITIES: Hunting; picnicking; fishing. Horseback riding/rental (1 mi). MISC.: Elev 7700 ft; 5 acres; river. Pets.

ST GEORGE

Oak Grove (Dixie NF). 16 mi NE of St George on US 15; 8 mi NW on FS 032. SEASON: 5/20-10/31. FACILITIES: 6 sites (tr -16); tbls, toil, cga, f, piped drk wtr. ACTIVITIES: Hunting; picnicking; fishing. Horseback riding (1 mi). MISC.: Elev 6800 ft; 11 acres. Pine Valley Mtns nearby. Pets permitted.

SALINA

Gooseberry (NF). 7½ mi SE of Salina on St Hwy 70; 4 mi S on Co Hwy; 5½ mi SE on FS 40025. SEASON: 5/21-11/7; 16-day lmt. FACILITIES: 4 sites (tr -22); tbls, toil, cga, f, piped drk wtr ACTIVITIES: Picnicking; fishing. Horseback riding (1 mi). MISC.: Elev 7800 ft; 10 acres. Pets.

Rest Area. 28 mi E of Salina on I-70 on river. SEASON: All yr. MISC.: On river; shade sites; good pull-off on 107-mi stretch of "no facilities" between Salina and Green River. Pets permitted.

SALT LAKE CITY

Brighton (Wasatch NF). 6-4/5 mi SE of Salt Lake City on US 40; 1-3/10 mi S on US 415; 6-3/10 mi S on Co Hwy 71; 13-9/10 mi E on St Hwy 152. SEASON: 6/1-9/15. FACILITIES: 8 sites (no trailers); tbls, toil, cga, piped drk wtr. Store/food (1 mi). ACTIVITIES: Picnicking. Fishing/horseback riding (1 mi). MISC.: Elev 8800 ft; 7 acres. Pets permitted.

SANTA CLARA

Gunlock Lake (City Park). 20 mi NW of St George on Old Hwy 91 right up Santa Clara Road. SEASON: All yr. FACILITIES: Prim. sites. ACTIVITIES: Hiking; fishing; boating,1; waterskiing. MISC.: Elev 3800 ft. Pets.

SCOFIELD

Fish Creek (Manti Lasal NF). 3-4/5 mi N of Scofield on FS 50008; 1½ mi W on FS 50123. SEASON: 6/15-9/10; 9-day lmt. FACILITIES: 5 tent sites (no trailers); tbls, toil, cga, drk wtr. ACTIVITIES: Hunting; picnicking; fishing. Horseback riding (1 mi). Boating/waterskiing (3 mi). MISC.: 2 acres; stream. Near Scofield Reserv. Resort. Access requires pickup or 4-wheel drive vehicles; elev 7000 ft; pets.

See page 7 for KEY TO ABBREVIATIONS.

SEVIER

Castle Rock (Fishlake NF). 6-1/10 mi SW of Sevier on St Hwy 4; 1-7/10 mi S on FS 40113. SEASON: 5/1-10/30; 16-day lmt. FACILITIES: 10 sites (tr - 22); tbls, flush toil, cga, f, well drk wtr. ACTIVITIES: Picnicking; fishing. Horseback riding (1 mi). MISC.: Elev 6200 ft; 9 acres; scenic; stream. Pets.

SMITHFIELD

Smithfield Canyon (Wasatch NF). 5 mi NE on Co Hwy. SEASON: 5/15-10/1; 5-day lmt. FAC: 8 sites (tr -16),tbls, toil, cga, piped drk wtr. Store/gas/ice/ laundry/food (5 mi). ACTIVI-TIES: Picnicking; fishing. Horseback riding (1 mi). MISC.: Elev 5200 ft; 3 acres. Pets permitted if kept on leash.

SPANISH FORK

Hawthorne (Uinta NF). 3-1/5 mi E of Spanish Fork on St Hwy 147; 9 mi SE on US 50; 14-7/10 mi NE on FS 1. SEA-SON: 6/1-10/31; 10-day lmt. FACILITIES: 5 sites (tr -16); tbls, toil, cga, piped drk wtr. ACTIVITIES: Hunting; picnicking; fishing. Horseback riding (1 mi). MISC.: Elev 6000 ft; 1 acre; stream. Last 9 mi not recommended for autos or trailers. Pets.

Three Forks (Uinta NF). 3-1/5 mi E of Spanish Fork on St Hwy 147; 9 mi SE on US 50; 10-3/10 mi NE on FS 70029. SEASON: 6/1-10/31; 16-day lmt. FACILITIES: 6 tent sites; tbls, toil, cga, f, drk wtr. ACTIVITIES: Hunting; picnicking; fishing. Horseback riding (1 mi). MISC.: Elev 5600 ft; 3 acres; stream. Pets. Last 4 mi road to site not recommended for trailers.

SPRINGDALE

* **Backcountry Camping** (Zion NP). Free backcountry permit and specific information is available at the visitor center, 1/2 mi NE of Springdale.

Pets are not allowed on trails or in the backcountry. Boil/purify all water. Water is ltd; take one gallon per person per day with you. During the summer, canyon temperatures can exceed 100 degrees. Plateau temperatures will run some 20 degrees cooler. Much of the backcountry is covered with snow from Dec-Mar.

SPRINGVILLE

Birch (NF). 6-7/10 mi E of Springville on St Hwy 79; 2-4/5 mi E on FS 70058. SEASON: 5/15-10/31; 10-day lmt. FACILITIES: 3 sites (no trailer); tbls, toil, cga, f, no drk wtr. ACTIVITIES: Mtn climbing; picnicking; fishing. Horseback riding (1 mi). MISC.: Elev 5600 ft; 2 acres; stream. Pets

TEASDALE

Blind Lake (Dixie NF). 7 mi SE of Teasdale on St Hwy 117; 6 mi S on TRAIL 3119. SEASON: 5/25-9/15. FACILITIES: 1 tent site; tbls, toil, cga, no drk wtr. ACTIVITIES: Picnicking; fishing; hiking. Horseback riding (1 mi). MISC.: Elev 10,300; 51 acres; lake. Pets permitted if kept on leash.

Lower Bowns Reservoir (Dixie NF). 22 mi SE of Teasdale on St Hwy 117; 4 mi E on FS 181. SEASON: 5/25-10/15. FACILITIES: 1 site; tbls, toil, cga, no drk wtr. ACTIVITIES: Boating;picnicking; fishing. Horseback riding (1 mi). MISC.: Elev 7400 ft; 68 acres; lake. Pets permitted if kept on leash.

TORREY

* **Backcountry Camping** (Capitol Reef NP). 12 mi E of Torrey on St Hwy 24 to Visitor Center.

Obtain free permit, map and info from the visitor center or any park ranger. Spring and fall are ideal times for backcountry hiking and camping, because of the mild temperatures. Insects can be a problem in June and July. Flash floods occur from July-Sept. Don't camp in the bottoms of drainages.

Cedar Mesa CG (Capitol Reef NP). 12 mi E of Torrey on St Hwy 24 to Visitor Center; 34-4/5 mi S on Notom Rd to CG. SEASON: All yr; 14-day lmt. FACILITIES: 4 sites; tbls, toil, no drk wtr. ACTIVITIES: Picnicking. MISC.: Pets permitted if kept on leash.

VERNON

Little Valley (Uinta NF). 1 mi SE of Vernon on St Hwy 36; 5 mi S on Co Rd; 4 mi SE on FS 80052; 1/2 mi W on FS 80006. SEASON: 5/1-10/31; 10-day lmt. FACILITIES: 6 sites (tr -16); tbls, toil, cga, f, piped drk wtr. ACTIVITIES: Rockhounding; picnicking; fishing. Horseback riding (1 mi). MISC.: Elev 7000 ft; 2 acres; stream. Pets permitted if kept on leash.

Kaler Hollow (NF). 20 mi N of Vernon on St Hwy 44; 11½ mi NW on FS 018. SEASON: 6/1-9/10. FACILITIES: 4 sites (tr -22); tbls, toil, cga, f, no drk wtr. ACTIVITIES: Picnicking; Horseback riding (1 mi). Fishing/boating waterskiing (4 mi). MISC.: Elev 8900 ft; 2 acres; stream; pets.

Oaks Park (Ashley NF). 20 mi N of Vernon on St Hwy 44; 14 mi NW on FS 018; 1 mi N on FS 024. SEASON: 6/1-10/15. FACILITIES: 13 sites (tr -22); tbls, toil, cga, f, well drk wtr. ACTIVITIES: Boating,d; picnicking; fishing; hunting. Horseback riding (1 mi) MISC.: Elev 9200 ft; 7 acres; stream; lake. Oaks Park Reservoir. Pets.

See page 7 for KEY TO ABBREVIATIONS.

Simpson Springs (BLM). 25 mi W of Vernon on graveled co rd. SEASON: 2/15-11/1; 14-day lmt. FACILITIES: 14 sites (tr -30); tbls, toil, cga, no drk wtr. ACTIVITIES: Picnicking; fishing. MISC.: 40 acres. Pets.

VIRGIN

Lava Point Primitive CG (Zion NP). The CG is approx 35 mi (the last 2 mi are gravel roads) from the park's S entrance on St Hwy 9, just E of Virgin. Take the Kolob Reservoir Road N approx 20 mi (the last mile is gravel), turn right when you reach the Lava Point Road, then continue 1-1/2 mi to reach the CG.

5 sites; no drk wtr; late May - late Oct., depending upon snow conditions; 14-day lmt. The area is inaccessible by vehicle during the winter.

Hiking. Pets okay, but not on trails or in bldgs.

There is a $2 park entrance fee; but the Golden Eagle Passport is accepted. ** If you don't have one, it can be purchased at park entrance for $10 allowing unltd entrance into the national parks for a full yr.

WOODRUFF

Birch Creek (BLM) 10 mi W of Woodruff on US 39. SEASON: 6/1-11/1; 14-day lmt. FACILITIES: 5 sites, tbls, toil, cga, no drk wtr. ACTIVITIES: Picnicking. MISC.: Pets permitted if kept on leash. Fishing.

WHITEROCKS

Pole Creek Lake (Ashley NF). 8 mi N of Whiterocks on Co Hwy; 13½ mi NW on FS 10117. SEASON: 6/15-9/10; 14-day lmt. FACILITIES: 18 sites (tr -22), tbls, toil, cga, f, no drk wtr. ACTIVITIES: Hunting; picnicking; fishing. Horseback riding (1 mi). MISC.: Elev 10,200 ft; 6 acres; stream; lake. Pets.

VERMONT

GENERAL STATE INFORMATION

Miscellaneous

Right Turns on Red: Permitted after full stop, unless otherwise posted.
STATE CAPITOL: Montpelier
STATE NICKNAME: Green Mountain State
STATE MOTTO: "Freedom and Unity"
STATE BIRD: Hermit Thrush
STATE FLOWER: Red Clover
STATE TREE: Sugar Maple

State Parks

Overnight camping fees range from $4.00-7.00. Pets are permitted if kept on a leash; but not in beach and picnic areas. Further information: State of Vermont; Department of Forests, Parks, and Recreation; Montpelier, VT 05602.

Rest Areas

Overnight stops are not permitted in Vermont Rest Areas.

Canoeing and Camping Along The Connecticut River

There are a number of sites along the river privately and municipally owned. However, on other land along the river, you can usually camp providing you obtain permission from the owner. Most owners have no objections if you take good care of your camping area. The dam site superintendents are good sources of information on where to camp, as they live in the area, know the property owners, and know which sites canoeists have been able to use FOR FREE. Further information: Vermont Division of Recreation and Department of Water Resources; Agency of Environmental Conservation; Montpelier, VT 05602. Ask for a free copy of CANOEING ON THE CONNECTICUT RIVER.

Camping on State Lands

Primitive camping is allowed for small groups on the Victory State Forest; large groups of eleven or more individuals require a permit. Primitive camping is not generally allowed on any of the Wildlife Management Areas, except during the 16-day deer season in November. At that time selected Wildlife Management Areas open to camping

See page 7 for KEY TO ABBREVIATIONS.

to facilitate hunter access. The Wildlife Management Areas open to camping during the deer season vary from year to year. A list of these selected Areas can be obtained from the Information and Education Section of the Fish and Game Department each Fall. Further information: Department of Fish and Game; Agency of Environmental Conservation; Montpelier, VT 05602.

Bristol Cliffs Wilderness (Green Mountain NF)

This Wilderness offers the visitors spectacular views of the Champlain Valley over the steep talus slopes on its west face. Two small ponds sit high on the ridge near its center, and primitive Vermont woodland covers most of its 3740 acres. The Bristol Cliffs Wilderness has no developed campsites or trail shelters. There is no trail system nor are there developed parking facilities. Permits are no longer required. Further information: Forest Supervisor; Green Mountain NF; Federal Building; 151 West Street; Rutland, VT 05701.

Lye Brook Wilderness (Green Mountain NF)

The Lye Brook Wilderness contains 14,300 acres of primitive Vermont woodland, with no developed campsites or other services. The Swezey Shelter and Swezey camp, two trail shelters along the Long-Appalachian Trail, are located near the northern boundary. Two shelters are also located along the Long-Appalachian Trail at Bourn Pond. In cooperation with the Forest Service, the Green Mountain Club provides caretakers at the Bourn Pond shelters during the summer season. These uniformed volunteers are available to assist you, and a modest fee is charged for overnight camping here. All these shelters in the Wilderness are heavily used and often occupied. Assume they are occupied and be prepared to spend the night either in your tent or out under the stars. Permits are no longer required. Further information: Forest Supervisor; Green Mountain NF; Federal Building; 151 West Street; Rutland, VT 05701.

Green Mountain Club

Membership is open to all who enjoy the out-of-doors and have a special interest and pride in the mountains of Vermont. Further information: The Green Mountain Club, Inc.; PO Box 889; Montpelier, VT 05602.

The Appalachian Trail

More than 2000 miles long, the Appalachian Trail (from Maine to Georgia) is the longest continuous marked trail in the world.

CAMPING: More than 200 open-front shelters/lean-tos are spaced approximately 10 miles apart on the Trail (one-day intervals). As they are occupied on a first-come first-served basis, carry a tent in case the shelters are full. Potable spring water is usually available at each site, but should be purified by tablets or boiling. And always, "pack it in, pack it out".

PERMITS: No permit is required to hike the Trail. However, camping permits must be obtained for overnight stays in Shenandoah NP (Luray, VA 22835) and Great Smoky Mountains NP (Gatlinburg, TN 37733). These are free of charge and available from the ranger stations or by mail. A free camping permit must be obtained for overnight stays in White Mountain National Forest Restricted Use Area (PO Box 638; Laconia, NH 03246).

APPALACHIAN TRAIL CONFERENCE: A private, nonprofit, national organization which represents citizen's interest in the Appalachian Trail. They offer detailed guidebooks and maps for sale, as well as the A.T. Data Book which gives the location and distances between shelters and certain post offices, supply points, water sources, lodging and meals. For more information on this organization, write to them at: PO Box 236; Harpers Ferry, WV 25425.

INFORMATION SOURCES

Maps

The following maps are available from **Forsyth Travel Library** (see order form in Appendix B):

> State of Vermont [Up-to-date, showing all principal roads, points of interest, sports areas, parks, airports, mileage, etc. Full color.]
>
> Completely indexed city map, including all airports, lakes, rivers, etc., of Burlington.

State Information

Information/Travel Division; Agency of Development and Community Affairs; 61 Elm Street; Montpelier, VT 05602.
Vermont Information Center; Rockefeller Center; New York, NY 11020.
Department of Forests, Parks, and Recreation; State of Vermont; Montpelier, VT 05602.
Fish and Game Department; 5 Court Street; Montpelier, VT 05602.

City Information

Central Vermont Chamber of Commerce; PO Box 336; Montpelier, VT 05602.
The Stowe Area Association; Stowe, VT 05672.

Miscellaneous

Green Mountain NF; Federal Building; 151 West Street; Rutland, VT 05701.
Upper Connecticut River Office; Corps of Engineers; North Springfield Lake; 98 Reservoir Road; Springfield, VT 05156.

FREE CAMPGROUNDS

ARLINGTON

* **Bourn Pond North – Long Trail Shelter** (Green Mountain NF). 10–2/5 mi E of Arlington on FS 6; 2–7/10 mi N on TRAIL 7; 7/10 mi N on TRAIL 111; 3/10 mi N on TRAIL 1. SEASON: 5/1–10/31; 2-day lmt. FACILITIES: 2 tent sites; trail shelter that will accomodate 8 people; no drk wtr; tbls, toil, cga, f. ACTIVITIES: Mountain climbing; hiking; picnicking; swimming; fishing. MISC.: Elev 2500 ft; 1 acre; pets. Lake.

* **Bourn Pond South – Long Trail Shelter** (Green Mountain NF). 10–2/5 mi E of Arlington on FS 6; 2–7/10 mi N on TRAIL 7; 7/10 mi N on TRAIL 111. SEASON: 5/1–10/31; 2-day lmt. FACILITIES: 2 tent sites; trail shelter that will accomodate 8 people; no drk wtr; toil, cga, f, no tbls. ACTIVITIES: Mountain climbing; hiking; swimming; fishing. MISC.: Elev 2500 ft; 1 acre; pets. Lake. Scenic.

* **Caughnawaga Trail Shelter** (Green Mountain NF). 7–3/10 mi E of Arlington on Co Hwy TR3; 5–1/15 mi S on TRAIL 1. SEASON: 5/1–11/30; 2-day lmt. FACILITIES: 2 tent sites; 5-person shelter, no drk wtr; tbls, toil, cga, f. ACTIVITIES: Hiking; picnicking. MISC.: Elev 2800 ft; 1 acre;pets. Stream. Scenic.

* **Kid Gore Trail Shelter** (Green Mountain NF). 7–7310 mi E of Arlington on Co Hwy TR3; 5–1/5 mi S on TRAIL 1. SEASON: 5/1–11/30; 2-day lmt. FACILITIES: 2 tent sites; trail shelter that will accomodate 8 people;, no drk wtr; tbls, toil, cga, f. ACTIVITIES: Hiking; picnicking. MISC.: Elev 2800 ft; 1 acre; pets. Stream. Scenic.

* **Story Spring – Long Trail Shelter** (Green Mountain NF). 10–2/5 mi E of Arlington on FS 6; 4/5 mi S on TRAIL 1. SEASON: 5/1–10/31; 2-day lmt. FACILITIES: 2 tent sites; trail shelter that will accomodate 8 people; no drk wtr; tbls, toil, cga, f. ACTIVITIES: Mountain climbing; hiking; picnicking. Fishing (2 mi). MISC.: Elev 3000 ft; 1 acre; pets. Stream.

BENNINGTON

* **Congdon Camp** (Green Mountain NF). 2 mi E of Bennington on St Hwy 9; 3 mi S on TRAIL 1. SEASON: 5/1–10/31; 2-day lmt. FACILITIES: 2 tent sites; no drk wtr; tbls, toil, cga, f. Gas/food (4 mi). Ice/showers/laundry (5 mi). ACTIVITIES: Hiking; picnicking. MISC.: Elev 2100 ft; 1 acre; pets. Scenic. Stream.

* **Glastenbury Trail Shelter** (Green Mountain NF). 3–3/10 mi E of Bennington on St hwy 9; 8–1/2 mi N on TRAIL 1. SEASON: 5/1–11/30; 2-day lmt. FACILITIES: 2 tent sites; 6-person trail shelter; no drk wtr; tbls, toil, cga, f. ACTIVITIES: Hiking; picnicking. MISC.: Elev 3700 ft; 1 acre; pets. Stream. Scenic.

BRANDON

* **Sunrise Camp – Long Trail Shelter** (Green Mountain NF). 7–1/2 mi E of Brandon on St Hwy 73; 1 mi S on TRAIL 51. SEASON: 5/1–10/31. FACILITIES: 2 tent sites; no drk wtr; tbls, toil, cga, f. ACTIVITIES: Hiking; picnicking. MISC.: Elev 2600 ft; 1 acre; pets. Scenic. Fishing (2 mi).

BRISTOL

* **Emily Proctor – Long Trail Shelter** (Green Mountain NF). 1–3/5 mi E of Bristol on St Hwy 116; 4–1/2 mi SE on FS 54; 3–1/2 mi SE on TRAIL 55. SEASON: 5/1–10/31; 2-day lmt. FACILITIES: 2 tent sites; tbls, toil, cga, f. ACTIVITIES: Mountain climbing;

VERMONT

hiking; picnicking. Fishing (4 mi).
MISC.: Elev 2400 ft; 1 acre; pets.
Stream. Scenic.

DANBY

* **Big Branch Long – Trail Shelter**
(Green Mountain NF). 3/5 mi E
of Danby on FS 1; 2-2/5 mi NE on
FS 10; 1-1/5 mi SE on TRAIL 1.
SEASON: 5/1-10/31; 2-day lmt. **FACILI-
TIES:** 2 tent sites; trail shelter
that will accomodate 8 people; no
drk wtr; tbls, toil, cga, f. Store/gas/ice/
food (5 mi). **ACTIVITIES:** Mountain
climbing; hiking; fishing. Picnicking (3 mi). **MISC.:** Elev 1400 ft;
1 acre; pets; stream.

* **Little Rock Pond – Long Trail Shelter**
(Green Mountain NF). 3/5 mi E of Danby
on FS 1; 2-2/5 mi NE on FS 10; 2-1/5
mi N on TRAIL 1. **SEASON:** 5/1-10/31;
2-day lmt. **FACILITIES:** 2 tent sites;
trail shelter that will accomodate 8
people; no drk wtr; tbls, toil, cga,
f. **ACTIVITIES:** Mountain climbing; hiking; boating; picnicking; fishing.
MISC.: Elev 1800 ft; 1 acre; pets.
MISC.: Lake.

* **Lost Pond – Long Trail Shelter** (Green
Mountain NF). 3/5 mi E of Danby on
FS 1; 2-2/5 mi NE on FS 10; 2-4/5 mi
on TRAIL 1. **SEASON:** 5/1-10/31; 2-day
lmt. **FACILITIES:** 2 tent sites; trail
shelter that will accomodate 8 people;no
drk wtr; tbls, toil, cga, f. **ACTIVITIES:**
Mountain climbing; hiking. Fishing
(2 mi). **MISC.:** Elev 2200 ft; 1 acre;
pets. Stream.

* **Lula Tye – Long Trail Sheleter** (Green
Mountain NF). 7/10 mi E of Danby on
Co Hwy 1; 2-3/10 mi E on FS 10; 2
mi N on TRAIL 1. **SEASON:** 5/1-10/31;
2-day lmt. **FACILITIES:** 2 tent sites;
no drk wtr; tbls, toil, cga, f. **ACTIVI-
TIES:** Hiking; picnicking; fishing; swimming. **MISC.:** Elev 2500 ft; 1 acre;
pets. Scenic. Store/gas/ice/food (5 mi).

* **Old Joe – Long Trail Shelter** (Green
Mountain NF). 3/5 mi E of Danby on
FS 1; 2-2/5 mi NE on FS 10; 2-1/5 mi
SE on TRAIL 1. **SEASON:** 5/1-10/31;
2-day lmt. **FACILITIES:** 2 tent sites;
trail shelter that will accomodate 8
people; no drk wtr; tbls, toil, cga,
f. **ACTIVITIES:** Mountain climbing; hiking; fishing; picnicking. **MISC.:** Elev
1600 ft; 1 acre; pets. Stream.

FORESTDALE

* **Keewaydin Camps** (Green Mountain NF).
6 mi N of Forestdale on St Hwy 53;
1/2 mi E, BY TRAIL. **SEASON:** 5/1-10/31;
14-day lmt. **FACILITIES:** 2 tent sites;
no drk wtr; tbls, toil, cga, f. Store/gas/

ice/showers/food (2 mi). **ACTIVITIES:**
Hiking; picnicking. Fishing (1 mi).
Boating,r/swimming/water skiing (2
mi). **MISC.:** Elev 1000 ft; 1 acre; pets.
Scenic. Stream.

* **Silver Lake Campground** (Green Mountain
NF). 5-1/5 mi N of Forestdale on
St Hwy 53; 1-7/10 mi SE on TRAIL
127. **SEASON:** 5/1-10/31; 14-day lmt.
FACILITIES: 7 tent sites; well drk
wtr, tbls, toil, cga, f. Food (3
mi). Store/gas/ice/showers/laundry
(5 mi). **ACTIVITIES:** Hiking; picnicking;
berry-picking. Swimming/fishing
(1 mi). Boating,rl/water skiing (3
mi). **MISC.:** Elev 1300 ft; 7 acres;
pets. Lake. Scenic. Closed to motorized
vehicles except snowmobiles.

JAMAICA

* **Winhall Brook Camping Area** (COE;
New England Division). Located at
Ball Mountain Lake in Jamaica. The
campground is 2-1/2 mi S of South
Londonderry, Vermont, off St Route
100. **SEASON:** Mid/May-mid/October (includes
four holidays plus the peak of the
foliage season in Vermont). **FACILITIES:**
50 sites; flush toil, showers. **ACTIVITIES:**
Hiking; picnicking; fishing; snowmobiling.
MISC.: Off-season camping is prohibited.
Interpretive programs are held in
the camping area. White-water canoeing
events are held during one weekend
in May and one in October. Pets.

MANCHESTER

* **Bromley Lodge – Long Trail Shelter**
(Green Mountain NF). 6 mi NE of
Manchester on St Hwy 11; 7/10 mi
N on TRAIL 1. **SEASON:** 5/1-10/31;
2-day lmt. **FACILITIES:** 2 tent sites;
trail shelter that will accomodate
8 people; no drk wtr; tbls, toil,
cga, f. **ACTIVITIES:** Mountain climbing;
hiking; picnicking. Fishing (5 mi).
MISC.: Elev 2000 ft; 1 acre; pets.
Stream.

* **Douglas Trail Shelter** (Green Mountain
NF). 2 mi E on St Hwy 11; 2-1/5
mi SE on Co Hwy TR30; 2-7/10 mi S
on TRAIL 1. **SEASON:** 5/1-11/30; 2-
day lmt. **FACILITIES:** 2 tent sites;
a 10-person shelter; no drk wtr;
tbls, toil, cga, f. **ACTIVITIES:**
Picnicking; hiking. Fishing (1 mi).
MISC.: Elev 2000 ft; 1 acre; pets;
scenic.

* **Swezy Camp Trail Shelter** (Green
Mountain NF). 2 mi E of Manchester
on St Hwy 11; 2-1/5 mi SE on Co
Hwy TR30; 2-7/10 mi S on TRAIL
1. **SEAS:** 5/1-11/30; 2-day lmt. **FACIL-
ITIES:** 2 tent sites; 4 person trail
shelter; no drk wtr; no tbls, toil,
f. **ACTIVITIES:** Hiking. Fishing (1 mi).
MISC.: Elev 2300 ft; 1 acre; pets.
Stream. Scenic.

VERMONT

PERU

* **Griffith Lake – Long Trail Shelter** (Green Mountain NF). 1-3/5 mi N of Peru on FS 3; 2-1/5 mi W on FS 21; 4-3/5 mi N on TRAIL 1. **SEASON:** 5/1-10/31; 2-day lmt. **FACILITIES:** 2 tent sites; trail shelter that will accomodate 8 people; tlbs, toil, cga, f. **ACTIVITIES:** Mountain climbing; hiking; picnicking; swimming; fishing. **MISC.:** Elev 2600 ft; 1 acre; pets. Stream.

* **Mad Tom – Long Trail Shelter** (Green Mountain NF). 1-3/5 mi N of Peru on FS 3; 2-1/5 mi W on FS 21; 1/10 mi N on TRAIL 1. **SEASON:** 5/1-10/31; 2-day lmt. **FACILITIES:** 2 tent sites; trail shelter that will accomodate 8 people; no drk wtr; tbls, toil, cga, f. **ACTIVITIES:** Mountain climbing; hiking; picnicking. Boating (1, 4 mi). Swimming/fishing (5 mi). **MISC.:** Elev 2400 ft; 1 acre; pets. Stream.

* **Peru Peak – Long Trail Shelter** (Green Mountain NF). 1-3/5 mi N of Peru on FS 3; 2-1/5 mi W on FS 21; 3-9/10 mi N on TRAIL 1. **SEASON:** 5/1-10/31; 2-day lmt. **FACILITIES:** 2 tent sites; trail shelter that will accomodate 8 people. no drk wtr; tbls, toil, cga, f. **ACTIVITIES:** Mountain climbing; hiking; picnicking; fishing. **MISC.:** Elev 2000 ft; 1 acre; pets. Stream.

RIPTON

* **Boyce – Long Trail Shelter** (Green Mountain NF). 5-2/5 mi E of Ripton on St Hwy 125; 3-1/5 mi N on TRAIL 1. **SEASON:** 5/1-10/31; 2-day lmt. **FACILITIES:** 2 tent sites; no drk wtr; tbls, toil, cga, f. **ACTIVITIES:** Hiking; picnicking. Fishing (2 mi). **MISC.:** Elev 3000 ft; 1 acre; pets. Scenic.

* **Skyline Lodge – Shelter** (Green Mountain NF). 5-2/5 mi E of Ripton on St Hwy 125; 5-1/5 mi N on TRAIL 55. **SEASON:** 5/1-10/31; 2-day lmt. **FACILITIES:** 2 tent sites; no drk wtr; tbls, toil, cga, f. **ACTIVITIES:** Mountain climbing; hiking; picnicking. Fishing (3 mi). **MISC.:** Elev 3400 ft; 1 acre; pets. Stream. Scenic. There is a $1 charge for use of the shelter.

* **Sucker Brook – Long Trail Shelter** (Green Mountain NF). 5-2/5 mi E of Ripton on St Hwy 125; 4-2/5 mi S on TRAIL 1. **SEASON:** 5/1-10/31; 2-day lmt. **FACILITIES:** 2 tent sites; no drk wtr; tbls, toil, cga, f. **ACTIVITIES:** Mountain climbing; hiking; picnicking. Boating,1/swimming/fishing (2 mi). **MISC.:** Elev 2400 ft; 1 acre; pets. Stream. Scenic.

WALLINGFORD

* **Greenwall – Long Trail Shelter** (Green Mountain NF). 3-2/5 mi E of Wallingford on St Hwy 140; 1-4/5 mi S on TRAIL 1. **SEASON:** 5/1-10/31; 2-day lmt. **FACILITIES:** 2 tent sites; trail shelter that will accomodate 8 people; no drk wtr; tbls, toil, cga, f. **ACTIVITIES:** Mountain climbing; hiking; picnicking. Fishing (1 mi). **MISC.:** Elev 2400 ft; 1 acre; pets.

WARREN

* **Battell – Long Trail Shelter** (Green Mountain NF). 4-1/2 mi SW of Warren on FS 34; 2 mi N on TRAIL 31. **SEASON:** 5/1-10/31. **FACILITIES:** 2 tent sites; no drk wtr, tbls, toil, cga, f. **ACTIVITIES:** Mountain climbing; hiking; picnicking. Fishing (3 mi). **MISC.:** Elev 3300 ft; 1 acre; pets. Scenic.

* **Cooley Glen – Long Trail Shelter** (Green Mountain NF). 4-3/5 mi W of Warren on St Hwy TR3-2; 4-7/10 mi S on TRAIL 1. **SEASON:** 5/1-10/31. ent **FACILITIES:** 2 tent sites; no drk wtr; ga, tbls, toil, cga, f. **ACTIVITIES:** ng; Mountain climbing; hiking; picnick-i). ing. Fishing (3 mi). **MISC.:** Elev:ts. 3200 ft; 1 acre; pets; stream; scenic.

* **Emily Proctor – Long Trail Shelter** (Green Mountain NF). 4-3/5 mi W of Warren on St Hwy TR3-2; 10-3/10 mi SE on TRAIL 1. **SEASON:** 5/1-10/31; 2-day lmt. **FACILITIES:** 2 tent sites; no drk wtr; tbls, toil, cga, f. **ACTIVITIES:** Mountain climbing; hiking; picnicking. Fishing (3 mi). **MISC.:** Elev 3500 ft; 1 acre; pets. Stream. Scenic.

READ THIS!

All information relative to each campground and state is currently accurate to the best of the publisher's knowledge. However, non-fee status and facilities are subject to change.

If any inaccuracies in this directory are discovered, or you know of any additional FREE campgrounds, please contact: VMPI; Box 1289; Clearwater, FL 33517.

INFORMATION ON HOW TO PURCHASE ADDITIONAL COPIES OF THIS BOOK AS WELL AS QUANTITY DISCOUNT INFORMATION IS ALSO AVAILABLE AT THIS ADDRESS.

VIRGINIA

GENERAL STATE INFORMATION

Miscellaneous

Right Turns on Red: Permitted after
   full stop, unless otherwise posted.
STATE CAPITOL: Richmond
STATE NICKNAME: Old Dominion
STATE MOTTO: "Thus Always to Tyrants"
STATE BIRD: Cardinal
STATE FLOWER: American Dogwood Blossom
STATE TREE: American Dogwood

State Parks

Overnight camping fees range from $3.00-4.00.   Pets are allowed if kept on a leash.
Further information: Department of Conservation and Economic Development; Division
of Parks; 1201 State Office Building; Capitol Square; Richmond, VA 23219.

Rest Areas

Overnight stops are permitted in certain designated areas.

Assateague Island National Seashore

No regular campgrounds exist in the Virginia section of the seashore.   Only one hike-
in campsite (see Chinoteague).   During certain hours, bikers and hikers can have
Wildlife Drive to themselves.   BOATING: Public boat ramp at Chincoteague Memorial
Park; boat rentals in Chincoteague.   OVERSAND VEHICLES: Obtain a beach access permit
for oversand travel, and stay on marked oversand vehicle routes.   CHINCOTEAGUE NWR:
No camping; no pets permitted.

Arrive from Chincoteague, VA, onto the widest part of the island.   Paved road leads
3 miles through south end of NWR before it comes to the beach.

Hunting; fishing; clam-digging; hiking.   PETS: Prohibited in Assateague State Park,
the NWR, the Virginia section of the National Seashore, and in the hike-in and canoe-
in campsites.   Permitted in the rest of the Maryland section if on leash (10 feet or
less).

Further information and map: Superintendent; Assateague Island National Seashore;
Route 2, Box 294; Berlin, MD 21811.   OR, Virginia District Ranger; Assateague Island
National Seashore; PO Box 38; Chincoteague, VA 23336.

Jefferson National Forest Backcountry Camping

There are two basic kinds of trails in the National Forest: foot and all-purpose.
Some trails, such as the Appalachian Scenic Trail, the Cascades National Recreation
Trail, and the Mount Rogers National Recreation Trail, are limited to foot travel.
Horses are not allowed in campgrounds, but they may use all trails not specifically
prohibited to them.   Off-road-vehicles may do the same, but must be tagged and licensed according to state law.   Some roads and trails may be closed at various times
to protect the Forest resources.

Camping is permitted Forest-wide except where specifically prohibited.   Persons are
responsible for their fires, however, and are asked to carry out all trash and garbage.   The National Forests belong to and are the responsibility of all citizens.   The
Forest Service maintains many campgrounds throughout the Forest to serve all types
of users.   Further information: Forest Supervisor; Jefferson NF; 210 Franklin Road,
SW; Caller Service 2900; Roanoke, VA 24001.

George Washington National Forest Trails

The National Forest offers free brochures and maps on its NUMEROUS hiking/camping
trails.   Further information and maps: Forest Supervisor; George Washington NF; 210
Federal Building; PO Box 233; Harrisonburg, VA 22801.

Backcountry Camping in Shenandoah NP

Pick up your free backcountry permit (during daylight hours only) at a ranger station
at one of the two park visitor centers, or at park headquarters.   Ranger stations
are located at Front Royal at the northern end of the park; Matthews Arm, Thornton
Gap and Big Meadows; and at Simmons Gap and Rockfish Gap in the southern part
of the park.   PARK HEADQUARTERS is 4 miles west of Thornton Gap on US 211.   You
may get your permit ahead of time by writing to: Superintendent; Shenandoah NP;
Luray, VA 22835 (Attention: Backcountry Permit).   Tell him the dates you will be in

VIRGINIA

the park, the number in your party, the location and dates of each overnight camp, and your name/address. If you are going to fish, purchase a 5-day Virginia license at a park concession facility. Fishing season: April to mid-October.

Six locked cabins are located in backcountry areas of the Park. These cabins will accommodate as many as 12 persons, and are fully equipped except for food. Reservations must be made with the Potomac Appalachian Trail Club; 1718 "N" Street, NW; Washington, DC 20036 [NOT FREE].

No person shall backcountry camp more than 2 consecutive nights at a single location; i.e., that particular campsite and the surrounding area within a 250-yard radius of that campsite. DOGS are prohibited on certain trails which are posted by appropriate signs. Dogs must be kept on leash AT ALL TIMES.

There is a $2.00 park entrance fee, or the Golden Eagle or Gold Age Passport.**

The Appalachian Trail

More than 2000 miles long, the Appalachian Trail (from Maine to Georgia) is the longest continuous marked trail in the world.

CAMPING: More than 200 open-front shelters/lean-tos are spaced approximately 10 miles apart on the Trail (one-day intervals). As they are occupied on a first-come first-served basis, carry a tent in case the shelters are full. Potable spring water is usually available at each site, but should be purified by tablets or boiling. And always "pack it in, pack it out".

PERMITS: No permit is required to hike the Trail. However, camping permits must be obtained for overnight stays in Shenandoah NF (Luray, VA 22835) and Great Smoky Mountains NP (Gatlinburg, TN 37733). These are free of charge and available from the ranger stations or by mail. A free camping permit must be obtained for overnight stays in White Mountain National Forest Restricted Use Area (PO Box 638; Laconia, NH 03246).

APPALACHIAN TRAIL CONFERENCE: A private, nonprofit, national organization which represents citizen's interest in the Appalachian Trail. They offer detailed guidebooks and maps for sale, as well as the A.T. Data Book which gives the location and distances between shelters and certain post offices, supply points, water sources, lodging and meals. For more information on this organization, write to them at: PO Box 236; Harpers Ferry, WV 25425.

INFORMATION SOURCES

Tennessee Valley Authority

TVA designated campgrounds are no longer free. However, unimproved TVA lands may be used for informal camping. No fees or permits are required. These areas are shown on recreation maps of individual TVA lakes. Further information: TVA; Knoxville, TN 37902.

Maps

The following maps are available from **Forsyth Travel Library** (see order form in Appendix B):

See page 5.

State of Virginia [Up-to-date, showing all principal roads, points of interest, sports areas, parks, airports, mileage, etc. Full color.]

Completely indexed city maps, including all airports, lakes, rivers, etc., of: Bristol; Charlottesville; Danville; Lynchburg; Norfolk; Hampton Roads; Newport News; Portsmouth; Richmond; Roanoke; Salem.

State Information

Department of Conservation and Economic Development; Virginia State Travel Service; 6 North 6th Street; Richmond, VA 23219.
Division of Parks; Department of Conservation and Economic Development; 1201 State Office Building; Capitol Square; Richmond, VA 23219.
Department of Agriculture and Commerce; 203 North Governor Street; Richmond, VA 23219.
Commission of Game and Inland Fisheries; PO Box 11104; Richmond, VA 23230.
Department of Highways and Transportation; 1221 East Broad Street; Richmond, VA 23219.
Virginia State Chamber of Commerce; 611 East Franklin Street; Richmond, VA 23219.

VIRGINIA

City Information

Norfolk Convention and Visitors Bureau; 269 Boush Street; Norfolk, VA 23510.
Richmond Chamber of Commerce; 616 East Franklin Street; Richmond, VA 23219.
Williamsburg-James City County Chamber of Commerce; PO Drawer HQ; Williamsburg, VA 23185.
Colonial Williamsburg, Inc.; Williamsburg, VA 23185.

Miscellaneous

Jefferson NF; 3517 Brandon Avenue, SW; Roanoke, VA 24018.
George Washington NF; 210 Federal Building; Harrisonburg, VA 22801.
Shenandoah NP; Luray, VA 22835.
Prince William Forest Park; Triangle, VA 22172.
Chincoteague NWR; PO Box 62; Chincoteague, VA 23336.
Corps of Engineers, Norfolk District; 803 Front Street; Norfolk, VA 23510.

FREE CAMPGROUNDS

BENTONVILLE

* **Hazard Mill Canoe Camp** NF). 14 mi S of Bentonville on St Hwy 340; 3-3/10 mi NW on St Hwy 675; 7-1/2 mi NE on St Hwy 684; 13 mi NE, BY BOAT. SEASON: All year; 14-day lmt. FACILITIES: 10 tent sites; no drk wtr; tbls, toil, cga, f. Store/ice (4 mi). Gas (5 mi). ACTIVITIES: Picnicking; fishing; boating,d (1, 1 mi). MISC.: Elev 600 ft; 2 acres; pets. Access by river only for canoe campers.

BLAND

Walnut Flats (Jefferson NF). 12 mi NE of Bland on St Hwy 42; 1 mi NW on St Hwy 606; 3-1/2 mi NE on FS 201. SEASON: All year; 14-day lmt. FACILITIES: 4 sites (tr -22); well drk wtr, tbls, toil, cga, f. Store/gas (3 mi). ACTIVITIES: Picnicking; fishing. MISC.: Elev 2600 ft; 1 acre; pets.

BUCHANAN

Cold Springs Sportsman Shelter (Jefferson NF). 2-1/10 mi NE of Buchanan on I-81; 8-1/2 mi SE on St Hwy 614; 3-9/10 mi SE on FS 59. SEASON: 14-day lmt. FACILITIES: 1 site (no tr); cga, f. ACTIVITIES: Fishing; hunting. MISC.: Elev 1500 ft; pets.

* **Colon Hollow Sportsman Shelter** (Jefferson NF). 2-1/10 mi NE of Buchanan on I-81; 2-9/10 mi SE on St Hwy 614; 2-2/5 mi E on FS FH59; 1/10 mi E on TRAIL 14. SEASON: All year; 14-day lmt. FACILITIES: 1 tent site; no drk wtr; tbls, toil, cga, f. Dump (1 mi). Store/gas (3 mi). Ice/showers/laundry (5 mi). ACTIVITIES: Picnicking; hiking; hunting. Fishing (1 mi). Swimming (lifeguard, 5 mi). MISC.: Elev 1100 ft; 1 acre; pets. Scenic.

* **Cove Creek Sportsman Shelter** (Jefferson NF). 2-1/10 mi NE of Buchanan on

I-81; 4-1/5 mi SE on St Hwy 614; 1/10 mi Se on TRAIL 25. SEASON: All year; 14-day lmt. FACILITIES: 1 tent site; toil, tbls, cga. Gas/ice (2 mi). Laundry (5 mi). ACTIVITIES: Picnicking; fishing. Swimming (lifeguard, 5 mi). MISC.: Elev 1000; 1 acre; pets. Showers (5 mi).

North Creek (Jefferson NF). 2-1/10 mi NE of Buchanan on I-81; 2-9/10 mi SE on St Hwy 614; 2-2/5 mi E on FS 59. SEASON: 5/1-11/30; 14-day lmt. FACILITIES: 16 sites (tr -22); well drk wtr, tbls, toil, cga, f. Ice/store (3 mi). Showers (5 mi). ACTIVITIES: Picnicking; hiking; fishing (stocked trout stream). Swimming (lifeguard 5 mi). MISC.: Elev 1100 ft; 5 acres; pets. Nature trails. Stream.

CHINCOTEAGUE

* **Hike-In Campsite #3** (Assateague Island National Seashore). This site is located 13-1/2 mi S of Site #2 (in MD) and 2-1/2 mi S of the Virginia Ranger Station After passing the 2nd vehicle dune crossing and beach marker #8, turn W to a double barrier dune. A hiking symbol sign will point out the barricaded double dune within which all camping must be done. Reservations are required, but they will not be accepted prior to 30 days before the camping date. 2-night lmt per site from LD-6/15; 1-night lmt, 6/15-LD. Maximum occupancy—20 campers per site. April-October weekends are often booked to capacity. FACILITIES: Toil, tbls, trash can, tent sites, picnic, no wtr. MISC.: Insect repellent is a necessity, particularly at night from 5/15 to the first killing frost. CAUTION: This trail can be unexpectedly rugged even for the most experienced hiker. Do no touch/feel wild ponies. Snakes in this area are harmless. All camping should be within the section of double

See page 7 for KEY TO ABBREVIATIONS.

dunes that is established by barricades. Do not camp on sand dunes or sleep on beach. No camping in the refuge. Pets are permitted in any hike-in sites, in any of the Chincoteague NWR, or in the VA portion of the National Seashore. RESERVATIONS and REGISTRATION OF SITE: Advance reservations may be made by writing: Assateague Island National Seashore; VA District Ranger; PO Box 38; Chincoteague, VA 23336; or call 804/336-6577. ACTIVITIES: Fishing; clamming; crabbing (alone shore, except where prohibited by signs). Swimming (in designated areas). Hiking. No firearms except in designated areas during hunting season.

DAYTON

Hone Quarry (George Washington NF). 11 mi NW of Dayton on St Hwy 257. SEASON: 4/1-12/1; 14-day lmt. FACILITIES: 10 sites (tr -22); tbls, toil, cga, f, well drk wtr. Gas/store/ice (3 mi). ACTIVITIES: Picnicking; fishing. MISC.: Elev 2000 ft; 4 acres; pets. Secluded quiet retreat under the shadow of the Sheandoah Mountain Range. Stream.

FERRUM

Ryans Branch (COE; Philpott Lake). 7 mi SW of Ferrum on Co Hwy 623 [between Fairystone SP and Ferrum, on St Hwy 623 near the Patrick/Franklin County line]. SEASON: 5/6-9/6; 14-day lmt. Camp closed during Winter months. FACILITIES: 13 sites (tr -32); drk wtr, tbls, toil, cga, Store nearby. ACTIVITIES: Picnicking; hunting; hiking; fishing.

MARION

Raccoon Branch Campground (NF). 2 mi SW on St Hwy 16; 12 mi S of Marion (paved access rds). SEASON: 5/1-11/30. FACILITIES: 16 sites (tr -22); tbls, toil, cga, f. ACTIVITIES: Picnicking; fishing; hiking. MISC.: Elev 2300 ft; pets. Nature trails. Cold Showers.

MARTINSVILLE

Philpott Lake (COE; Philpott Lake). 11 mi NW & W of Martinsville on St Hwy 57; 2 mi N on park rd 904.

*Deer Island (Philpott Lake). 2 mi from dam, BY BOAT. (Ask directions locally.) SEASON: All year; 14-day lmt. FACILITIES: 29 tent sites; drk wtr, tbls, toil, cga, f. Store/ice nearby. ACTIVITIES: Picnicking; fishing; swimming; boating,d. MISC.: Pets.

* Mize Point (Philpott Lake). 1/2 mi from dam, BY BOAT. (Ask directions locally.)

SEASON: All year; 14-day lmt. FACILITIES: 12 tent sites; drk wtr, tbls, toil, cga, f. Store/food nearby. ACTIVITIES: Picnicking; fishing; swimming; boating,d. MISC.: Pets.

MIDDLESBORO

Martins Fork Backcountry Campground (Cumberland Gap NHP). 4 mi E of Middlesboro on US 25; 2 mi N on US 58 & Park Road. SEASON: All year; 14-day lmt. FACILITIES: 6 sites (no tr); tbls, toil, cga, f. Drk wtr must be boiled. ACTIVITIES: Picnicking. MISC.: Reservations accepted.

NEW CASTLE

The Pines (Jefferson NF). 5 mi NE of New Castle on St Hwy 615; 4-9/10 mi W on St Hwy 611; 5-1/2 mi NE on St Hwy 617. SEASON: All year; 14-day lmt. FACILITIES: 17 sites (tr -16); tbls, toil, cga, f, well drk wtr. ACTIVITIES: Picnicking; fishing. MISC.: Elev 1900 ft; 4 acres; pets. Stream.

NORTH BRIDGE STATION

Hopper Creek (Jefferson NF). 3/10 mi E of North Bridge Station on St Hwy 130; 5-1/10 mi S on St Hwy 759. SEASON: All year; 14-day lmt. FACILITIES: 10 sites (no tr); well drk wtr; tbls, toil, cga, f. Store/gas/ice/food (3 mi). ACTIVITIES: Picnicking. Fishing (2 mi). Swimming (lifeguard 3 mi). MISC.: Elev 1100 ft; 5 acres; pets. Reservations required. Designed to accomodate church groups, Boy Scouts, etc. Not designed for travel trailers.

PAINT BANK

Steel Bridge (Jefferson NF). 1/10 mi N of Paint Bank on St Hwy 311; 3-1/2 mi NE on St Hwy 18. SEASON: All year; 14-day lmt. FACILITIES: 10 sites (tr -16); well drk wtr, tbls, toil, cga, f. Store/gas (4 mi). ACTIVITIES: Picnicking; fishing; swimming. MISC.: Elev 1900 ft; 2 acres; pets. Stream.

POUND

Laurel Fork Campground (COE; North Fork of Pound Lake). 9-1/2 mi W of Pound on St Hwy 671. SEASON: All year; 14-day lmt. FACILITIES: 8 sites (no tr); drk wtr, tbls, toil, cga, f. ACTIVITIES: Picnicking; hiking. MISC.: Pets.

PRINUM

Chapawamsic (Prince William Forest Park). Exit from I-95; 3 mi on St Hwy 619W. SEASON: 4/1-10/31; 7-day lmt. Reservation required. FACILITIES: 24 sites (no tr); no drk wtr, tbls, toil, cga, f. ACTIVITIES: Picnicking; hiking. MISC.: Pets.

RICHMOND

Hanover Wayside Park. 7 mi N on US 301. SEASON: All year; 1-night lmt. FACILITIES: Combination sites.

RILEYVILLE

*****High Cliff Canoe Camp** (George Washington NF). 8 mi S of Rileyville on St Hwy 340; 3-3/10 mi NW on St Hwy 675; 7-1/2 mi NE on St Hwy 684; 2 mi E, BY BOAT. SEASON: All year; 14-day lmt. FACILITIES: 10 tent sites; no drk wtr; tbls, toil, cga, f. Food (3 mi). Store/ice/gas (1 mi). ACTIVITIES: Picnicking; fishing. Horseback riding (1 mi). Boating,ld (rental 5 mi). MISC.: Elev 800 ft; 2 acres; pets. Scenic. Access by river only.

SPEEDWELL

Comers Rock (Jefferson NF). 5-2/5 mi SW of Speedwell on US 21; 4 mi W on FS 57. SEASON: All year; 14-day lmt. FACILITIES: 9 sites (tr -16); well drk wtr, tbls, toil, cga, f. Store/gas (4 mi). ACTIVITIES: Picnicking; hiking; fishing (trout at Hale Lake; 1-1/2 mi W of Campground). MISC.: Elev 4000 ft; 3 acres; pets. Nature trail. Check state regulations on licenses.

STAUNTON

North River (George Washington NF). 20 mi W of Staunton on US 250; 3 mi N on St Hwy 715; 1 mi NE on FS 95; 1 mi SW on FS 95B. SEASON: 4/1-12/1; 14-day lmt. FACILITIES: 10 sites (tr -22); piped drk wtr, tbls, toil, cga. ACTIVITIES: Picnicking; hiking; hunting; fishing. Swimming (lifeguard 3 mi). Boating (l d, 3 mi). MISC.: Elev 2000; 3 acres; pets. Scenic. In heart of Shenandoah Mountains.

TROUTDALE

Fox Creek Trailhead (Jefferson NF). 1/2 mi N of Troutdale on St Hwy 16; 3-1/2 mi W on St Hwy 603. SEASON: All year. FACILITIES: 15 sites (tr - 22); no drk wtr, no tbls, toil, cga, f. Showers/dump (2 mi). Store/gas/ice/ food (4 mi). ACTIVITIES: Hiking; fishing. Horseback riding (rental 1 mi). MISC.: Elev 3600 ft; 5 acres; pets. Scenic. Visitor Center. Serves Virginia Highlands equestrian trail.

WAKEFIELD

Union Camp (Union Camp Corporation). 4-acre site on Airfield Millpond near Wakefield, VA. Just off Hwy 628; 4 mi S of Wakefield. FACILITIES: Sites; toil, cga, tbls, well drk wtr. ACTIVI-TIES: Picnicking.

WARM SPRINGS

Blowing Springs (George Washington NF). 9 mi W of Warm Springs on St Hwy 39. SEASON: 4/1-12/1; 14-day lmt. FACILITIES: 12 sites (tr -22); well drk wtr, tbls, toil, cga, f, dump. Store/gas/ice (3 mi). ACTIVITIES: Picnicking; fishing; swimming; rockhounding. MISC.: Elev 1800 ft; 3 acres; pets. Mountain spring produces gusts of cool underground air. Scenic. Will accomodate trailers.

Hidden Valley (George Washington NF). 1-2/5 mi W on St Hwy 39; 1 mi N on St Hwy 621; 1-4/5 mi N on FS 2410. SEASON: All year; 14-day lmt. FACILITIES: 30 sites; well drk wtr, tbls, toil, cga, dump. Store/gas/ice (4 mi). ACTIVITIES: Picnicking; fishing. MISC.: Elev 1800 ft; 16 acres; pets; river; historic.

WASHINGTON

GENERAL STATE INFORMATION

Miscellaneous

Toll-Free Number for Travel Information:
 1-800-238-8000
Right Turns on Red: Permitted after
 full stop, unless otherwise posted.
STATE CAPITOL: Olympia
STATE NICKNAME: Evergreen State
STATE BIRD: Willow Goldfinch
STATE FLOWER: Rhododendron
STATE TREE: Western Hemlock

WASHINGTON

State Parks

Overnight camping fees range from $3.50-5.50. Pets are permitted if kept on a leash. Further information: Washington State Parks and Recreation Commission; 7150 Cleanwater Lane; PO Box 1128; Olympia, WA 98504.

Rest Areas

Overnight stops are not permitted in Washington Rest Areas.

Boise Cascade Corporation

Boise Cascade owns about 2 million acres of timberlands in Washington, Minnesota, California, Oregon, and Idaho, and with Boise Southern Company in Louisiana. Hunting (deer, elk, bird); fishing (salmon, trout, whitefish, walleye, northern pike, bass or pan fish, depending on the area); horseback riding; canoeing; snowmobiling in winter. For information on specific campgrounds, see "Cle Elum", "Yakima", "Goldendale", "Naches". Further information: Boise Cascade Corporation; PO Box 51; Yakima, WA 98901.

Pacific Crest National Scenic Trail

For a current FREE map and information on the 2500-mile trail which traverses Washington, Oregon, and California, write: Pacific Northwest Region; Regional Forester; PO Box 3623; Portland, OR 97208.

Sportman's Map

Send for a free map which was prepared cooperatively by Boise Cascade Corporation, Crown Zellerbach, Department of Game, Department of Natural Resources, Longview Fibre Company, International Paper Company, and Weyerhaeuser Company, which provides comprehensive information about one of Washington's leading outdoor recreation areas. Free map: Public Information Director; Washington Forest Protection Association; 1411 Fourth Avenue Building; Suite 1220; Seattle, WA 98101.

Lake Chelan National Recreation Area   (North Cascades NP)

No National Park entrance fee. Lake Chelan is 55 miles long and 1-2 miles wide for most of its length; only the northerly 5 miles and about 2,000 acres are within Lake Chelan NRA.

20 camping areas (ask Park Ranger for map and detailed directions); fishing for trout (a Washington State fishing license is required); mountain climbing. The waters are very cold; even in August, water activities are mainly confined to boating and fishing. Hunting is allowed in the NRA (but not in the Park proper of which it is a part). No pets are allowed.

Five campgrounds (Bridge Creek; Dolly Varden; Harlequin; High Bridge; Cottonwood) are located along the Stehekin Valley Road which is serviced by the Stehekin Shuttle Bus System. There is no outside road access into the Stehekin Valley. Daily boat service from Stehekin to Chelan is maintained from 5/15-9/30. From 10/1-5/14, the boats go on Sunday, Monday, Wednesday, and Friday.

Further information and map: Superintendent; Lake Chelan NRA; North Cascades NP; 800 State Street; Sedro Woolley, WA 98284.

Ross Lake National Recreation Area

No National Park entrance fee. Vehicular access to Ross Lake is from the north only through Canada to Hozomeen. Hozomeen is reached via the 40-mile rough gravel road (Silver-Skagit Road) west of Hope, B.C., which branches south from St Hwy #1. This road is hard on vehicles and caution should be used. 122 camping sites are provided; however, the campground fills rapidly on Friday evenings during the summer weekends. Visitors should contact the Marblemount Ranger Station before leaving on weekends to determine if camping sites are still available at Hozomeen, as overflow camping is not permitted. Phone number for the Ranger Station is 206/873-4590.

Pets are not allowed. Drinking water is piped and treated. There are no trailer hookups, dump stations, or flush toilets available. Boat launching ramps are provided. Visitors are requested to follow a pack-it-out policy with all litter and refuse.

Access to Ross Lake from the south is limited to trail and water routes. The Diablo Lake Trail, which begins near the Diablo Lake Resort, goes to Ross Dam (3½ mi). From the dam, people may continue via boat or trail to specific sites along Ross Lake. The Ross Lake Resort has small rental boats and provides water taxi service at reasonable rates. The resort should be contacted in advance to insure the availability of boats and to determine charges for water taxi transportation. Those wishing to transport small crafts, canoes, kayaks, etc., to Ross Lake can launch them at Colonial Creek Campground and proceed on Diablo Lake to Ross Dam. At the dam, the craft and gear must be portaged over the dam on a mile-long jeep road or arrangements can be made with the Ross Lake Resort to transport the items by truck. Although more difficult, canoes may also be portaged to and from the lake via Ross Dam Trail. An alternate method of reaching Ross Lake is to ride the Seattle City Light tugboat that leaves twice a day for Ross Dam from Diablo Dam (8:30 a.m./3:30 p.m.). Only personal gear can be carried. Gasoline or other flammable liquids may not be transported on the tug. The charge is $3.00 per person round trip, $2.50 if less than 12 years of age, and no charge under 3 years of age. The tug leaves Ross Dam on the return trip to Diablo Dam at 9:00 a.m./4:10 p.m. Be a few minutes early, as the boats are committed to a definite schedule. Schedules and charge subject to change.

15 boat-access camping areas are located on Ross Lake, many of which have docking facilities; others have none and are usable by visitors with small crafts such as kayaks and canoes. No treated drinking water is provided. Pit toilets and tables are provided. Pets are not allowed in Big Beaver or Little Beaver Campgrounds. Ross Lake may not be at full pool during the entire use season, and with low water, boating hazards are abundant. Watch for brush, rocks, stumps and snags at or just below the water surface. Obstruction buoys on the lake mark only rock projects near the water surface. Be constantly on the lookout for hazards, especially floating debris.

The weather is normally warm and sometimes quite hot during the summer with temperatures frequently in the high 90's. Even with the high temperatures, the lake water is very cold. Waterskiing and swim aren't recommended. Warm fall days with cool nights can be quite pleasant. Strong winds and whitecaps occur frequently and without warning. Parties in small crafts, canoes, etc., are advised to follow close to the shorelines and to carry adequate food in case they are forced to spend an extra night in the area.

7 major trails lead outward from Ross Lake into the backcountry. The east side of Ross Lake may be reached from the North Cascades Highway by trail at Panther Creek, approximately 8 miles from Colonial Creek Campground. An alternate trail access to Ross Dam from St Hwy 20 is found 4-1/5 mi E of Colonial Creek Campground, just west of the Happy Creek area.

Further information: Superintendent; Ross Lake National Recreation Area; North Cascades NP; 800 State Street; Sedro Woolley, WA 98284.

BACKCOUNTRY AND WILDERNESS CAMPING

Glacier Peak Wilderness (Mt. Baker-Snoqualmie and Wenatchee NFs)

464,240 acres. Glacier Peak, the fourth highest mountain in Washington, is 10,436 feet high. Ice fields; numerous trails including the Cascade Crest Trail; trout fishing; mountain climbing; hunting (black bear, Rocky Mountain goat, deer, grouse). Wilderness Permits are required for overnight stays and can be obtained free of charge at the Darrington Ranger Station. Further information: Forest Supervisor;Mount Baker-Snoqualmie NF; Federal Office Building; 915 Second Ave., Room 110; Seattle, WA 98174.

Goat Rocks Wilderness (Gifford Pinchot NF)

82,680 acres, located in the Cascades, with elevations ranging from Glacier Lake's 3000 feet to Mount Curtis Gilbert's 8201 feet. Mountain goats roam the area in bands. 95 miles of trails, including the Cascade Crest Trail. Big-game hunting (black bear, Rocky Mountain goat, blacktail deer, elk). Free Wilderness Permit is required; obtained by mail or in person at a District Ranger's office or in the Forest headquarters in Vancouver. During the winter, enter via White Pass Chairlift and ski cross-country to Hogback Mountain. Snowshoeing. 85 miles of trail provide unlimited horseback riding. 82,680 acres in SW Washington between Mt. Rainier and Mt. Adams. Yakima Indian Reservation borders the Goat Rocks area on the SE side, but is closed to the general public. Further information: Forest Supervisor; Gifford Pinchot NF; PO Box 449; Vancouver, WA 98660.

Mount Adams Wilderness (Gifford Pinchot NF)

32,400 acres. Mount Adams is 12,307 feet high, second only to Mt. Ranier in height in the State of Washington. Rugged area. Numerous trails, including Round-the-Mountain Trail and the Cascade Crest Trail. Poor fishing. Good big-game hunting (black bear, Rocky Mountain goat, blacktail deer). Wilderness Permit is required; obtained by mail or in person at a District Ranger's office or in the Forest headquarters in Vancouver [free]. Further information: District Ranger; Mt. Adams Ranger District; Gifford Pinchot NF; Trout Lake, WA 98650.

Mount Margaret Backcountry (Gifford Pinchot NF)

Network of trails; scenic alpine setting; trout lakes. Herd of Roosevelt elk ranges here in the summer. Elevations range from 3500-5898 feet (Mount Margaret). Further information: Forest Supervisor; Gifford Pinchot NF; PO Box 449; Vancouver, WA 98660.

Mount Rainier NP Backcountry Camping

Entrance fee to the National Park is $2.00 or the Golden Eagle, or Golden Age, Passport.** Free permits for overnight backpacking can be obtained at visitors centers, ranger stations, or by mail. Mountain climbing; fishing; hiking; camping. No pets on trails. Watch for bears. Stay off glaciers; they contain deep, hidden crevasses. Further information: Superintendent; Mount Rainier NP; Tahoma Woods, Star Route; Ashford, WA 98304.

North Cascades NP Backcountry Camping

Free permits may be obtained at Ranger Stations. There is no entrance fee for this National Park. No hunting or trapping. Bears are commonly seen in backcountry areas. Pets are prohibited in the backcountry. Mountain climbing. Further information: Superintendent; North Cascades NP; 800 State Street; Sedro Woolley, WA 98284.

Olympic NF and NP Backcountry

Free Wilderness Permits are required. You may obtain one in person at a ranger station, or by mail from the Forest Supervisor. These are required for trail or beach camping. Trout fishing; hunting (black bear, Roosevelt elk, dee'). Mt. Olympus (7954 feet). Hundreds of miles of trails. Forest Supervisor; Olympic NF; PO Box 2288; Olympia, WA 98507. OR, Park Superintendent; Olympic NP; 600 East Park Avenue; Port Angeles, WA 98362.

Pasayton Wilderness (Okanogan NF)

505,514 acres; located in Okanogan and Mt. Baker-Snoqualmie National Forests, and along the boundary of Ross Lake NRA (in North Cascades NP). Hundreds of miles of trails, including the Cascades Crest Trail. Jack Mountain (9070 feet) is the Wilderness' highest point. Area is accessible from July-October ('irst snowfall). Good trout fishing in alpine lakes. September hunting for goats and buck deer. Wilderness Permits are required. These are free and can be obtained in person at ranger stations or by mail from the Forest Supervisor. Further information: Forest Supervisor; Okanogan NF; Okanogan, WA 98840.

INFORMATION SOURCES

Maps

The following maps are available from **Forsyth Travel Library** (see order form in Appendix B):

> **State of Washington** [Up-to-date, showing all principal roads, points of interest, sports areas, parks, airports, mileage, etc. Full color.]

> Completely indexed city maps, including all airports, lakes, rivers, etc., of: **Bellingham; Federal Way; Seattle; Spokane; Tacoma.**

Gold Mining and Prospecting

Washington Division of Mines and Geology; Department of Conservation; 335 General Administration Building; Olympia, WA 98501.

State Information

Travel Development Division; Department of Commerce and Economic Development; 101 General Administration Building; Olympia, WA 98504.
Public Information Director; Washington Forest Protection Association; 1411 Fourth Avenue Building; Suite 1220; Seattle, WA 98101.
Washington State Parks and Recreation Commission; 7150 Cleanwater Lane; PO Box 1128; Olympia, WA 98504.
Department of Game; 600 North Capitol Way; Olympia, WA 98504.
Department of Fisheries; 115 General Administration Building; Olympia, WA 98504.
Public Information Office; Department of Natural Resources; Public Lands Building; Olympia, WA 98504.
Washington State Patrol; General Administration Building; Olympia, WA 98504.
National Parks and Forests; Combined Information Service; Pacific NW Region; 915 - 2nd Avenue; Room 110; Seattle, WA 98174.

WASHINGTON

City Information

Port Angeles Chamber of Commerce; 1217 East First Street; Department "P";Port Angeles, WA 98362.
Seattle Convention and Visitors Bureau; 215 Columbia Street; Seattle, WA 98104.
Spokane Chambe of Commerce; 1020 West Riverside Avenue; Spokane, WA 99201.
Tacoma Chamber of Commerce; Winthrop Hotel; Tacoma, WA 98401.

National Forests

Colville NF; PO Box 950; Okanogan, WA 98840.
Gifford Pinchot NF; PO Box 449; Vancouver, WA 98660.
Mount Baker NF; 1601 Second Avenue Building; Seattle, WA 98101.
Okanogan NF; PO Box 950; Okanogan, WA 98840.
Olympic NF; PO Box 2288; Olympia, WA 98507.
Snoqualmie NF; 1601 Second Avenue Building; Seattle, WA 98101.
Wenatchee NF; 301 Yakima Street; PO Box 811; Wenatchee, WA 98801.

Corps of Engineers

COE, Seattle District; 1519 Alaskan Way South; PO Box C-3755; Seattle, WA 98134.
COE; Walla Walla District; Building 602, City-County Airport; Walla Walla, WA 99362.

Miscellaneous

Mount Rainier NP; Longmire, WA 98387.
North Cascades NP; Sedro Woolley, WA 98284.
Olympic NP; 600 East Park Avenue; Port Angeles, WA 98362.
Coulee Dam NRA; Box 37; Coulee Dam, WA 99116.
Lake Chelan NRA; c/o North Cascades NP; Sedro Woolley, WA 98284.
Ross Lake NRA; c/o North Cascadaes NP; Sedro Woolley, WA 98284.
Washington [and Oregon] BLM; 729 NE Oregon Street; PO Box 2965; Portland, OR 97208.
Columbia NWR; PO Drawer F; Othello, WA 99344.

FREE CAMPGROUNDS

AMANDA PARK

July Creek (North Cascades NP). 2 mi NW of Amanda Park on US 101; 2 mi NE. [Gravel access rds.] SEASON: All yr; 14-day lmt. FACILITIES: 31 sites (tr -21); tbls, flush toil, cga, dump. ACTIVITIES: Swimming; picnicking; fishing.

AMBOY

Canyon Creek (Gifford Pinchot NF). 3 mi E of Amboy on St Hwy 503; 3 mi E on Co Hwy; 12-3/10 mi SE on FS N56. SEASON: 5/1-10/15; 14-day lmt. FACILITIES: 8 sites (tr -16); tbls, toil, cga, f, no drk wtr. ACTIVITIES: Hiking; picnicking; fishing. Horseback riding (5 mi). MISC.: Elev 1200 ft; 8 acres; pets; stream.

Jakes Creek (Gifford Pinchot NF). 3 mi E of Amboy on St Hwy 503; 3 mi E on Co Hwy; 14-3/5 mi SE on FS N56. SEASON: 5/1-10/15; 14-day lmt. FACILITIES: 2 sites (no tr); toil, f. ACTIVITIES: fishing. MISC.: Elev 1400 ft;pets.

ARLINGTON

Arlington Fish Camp. E of Arlington on Burke St; turn left on Talcott Rd; cross bridge; campground is on the right. SEASON: 14-day lmt. FACILITIES: Undesignated spaces for self-contained units (room for 10 RVs); tbls, toil, cga.

ACTIVITIES: Hunting; picnicking; fishing (steelhead). MISC.: Stillaguamish River.

ASOTIN

Seven Sisters Spring (Umatilla NF). 24 mi SW of Asotin on Co Hwy 105; 4 mi SW on FS N812; 1 mi E on FS N 800. SEASON: 6/15-11/15; 10-day lmt. FACILITIES: 3 sites (no tr); toil; f. ACTIVITIES: Picnicking. MISC.: 1 mi E of Wenotchee guard station, accessible via Cloverland Rd and Anatone. Pets.

Wickiup (Umatilla NF). 24 mi SW of Asotin on Co Hwy 105; 7 mi SW on FS 4300. SEASON: 6/15-10/15; 10 day lmt. FACILITIES: 9 sites (tr -16); piped drk wtr, tbls, toil, cga, f. ACTIVITIES: Berry-picking; picnicking; fishing (5 mi); horseback riding (1 mi). MISC.: 3 mi W of Wenatchee Guard Station.Pets.

BARSTOW

Elbow Lake (Colville NF). 12 mi N of Barstow on Co Hwy 815; 10 mi E on FS 402. SEASON: 6/1-9/30; 14-day lmt. FACILITIES: 4 sites (tr -16); well drinking wtr, tbls, toil, cga. ACTIVITIES: Picnicking. Fishing (1 mi). MISC.: Elev 3000; lake; pets.

Snag Cove (Coulee Dam NRA). 7 mi SE of Barstow. FACILITIES: 4 sites; tbls, toil, cga. ACTIVITIES: Fishing; boating; picnicking. MISC.: pets.

See page 7 for KEY TO ABBREVIATIONS.

BOYDS

Davis Lake (Colville NF). 1/2 mi N of Boyds on US 395; 8 mi NW on FS 9500. SEASON: 6/1-10/15; 14-day lmt. FACILI-TIES: 4 sites (tr -16); tbls, toil, cga, no drk wtr. ACTIVITIES: Boating,l; picnicking; fishing. MISC.: Elev 4600 ft; lake; pets.

BRADY

Swinging Bridge Park (Weyerhaeuser Co). 10 mi N of Brady and US Hwy 12 [on W Fork of Satsop River]. FACILITIES: 30 sites; cga, playground, no drk wtr. ACTIVITIES: Fishing. MISC.: Rustic swinging bridge to far side of river.

BREMERTON

Tahuya Multiple Use Area (Department of Natural Resources). The Tahuya Peninsula, located on the SW corner of the Kitsap Peninsula, contains a multitude of lakes, creeks and rivers. The Hood Canal forms its southern and western boundaries.

Composed of 33,000 acres of state-owned lands managed by the Dept. of Natural Resources (DNR), the area is intermingled with private ownerships. The public is urged to observe NO TRES-PASS signs and private ownership rights in this area.

ROUTES AND APPROACHES: Lying in the center of the Puget Sound Basin, the Tahuya Multiple Use Area (MUA) is within 1-1/2 hrs from Seattle and Tacoma. Belfair, the nearest community at the edge of the MUA is only 1-1/4 hr by ferry and 20 mi of good highway from downtown Seattle; less than an hour via the famed Narrows Bridge, from Tacoma. Coming from Tacoma a left turn at Purdy on St Hwy 302 followed by a right turn 6 mi S will take you through the community of Allyn to Belfair. En route to Belfair on St Hwy 302 a left turn S to the Longbranch Peninsula will take you to the Robert F. Kennedy Camp and Picnic area (see "Long-branch"), a DNR park with protected saltwater frontage open to the public. Access roads from the S and E into the interior of the Tahuya Peninsula are, for the most part, graded and kept in good condition.

The 11 DNR recreational sites offer-ing 61 camp units, 20 picnic units and 13 miles of trails, are well signed and easily found. Additional info and/or MUA map: Public Affairs Office, DNR, Public Lands Bldg., Olympia, WA 98504; or S. Puget Sound Area Office, 28329 SE 448 St., Enumclaw, WA 98022; or call toll free 1-800-562-6010.

CLIMATE: Daily summer tempatures range from the 70's during the day to the 50's at night. During the Win-ter the daily temperatures span from the 40's during the day to the 30's at night. Rainy season begins in mid-Oct. and reaches its peak in Dec. and Jan. Snowfall is usually light and the depth staying on the ground rarely ex-ceeds 3-6 inches.

HORSES: There are horse facilities at both Tahuya River Horse Camp and Green Mountain Horse Camp. The 13 mile Tahuya all purpose trail system is for horsemen, hikers and off-road vehicles.

FISHING: 14 public accesses to fishing waters are provided by the Game Dept. Many of the 68 lakes in the MUA have been stocked with fish--rain-bowtrout, steelhead and sea run cut-throat.

HUNTING: Bear, deer and game birds can be hunted during the seasons set by the State Game Dept.

There are a number of interpretive signs to tell the story of each area. Look for these legend or story boards throughout the southern portion of the MUA--at Camp Spillman, Tahuya Horse Camp and Howell Lake.

RECREATION (misc): The adjacent tidelands of Hood Canal--a 68 mile arm of inland sea--provides opportunities for crabbing, oystering, clamming, fish-ing for salmon and rockfish, boating and other water activities.

Aldrich Lake (Tahuya MUA; DNR). 21 mi SW of Bremerton on Aldrich Lake on Tahuya Peninsula. FACILITIES: 4 sites; Drk Wtr, tbls, toil, cga. ACTIVITIES: Boating,l; picnicking; fishing.

Bald Point Vista (Tahuya MUA; DNR). 25 mi SW of Bremerton on southwesterly ridge of Tahuya Peninsula. FACILITIES: 5 sites; tbls, toil, cga, no drk wtr. ACTIVITIES: Picnicking. MISC.: Vista.

Camp Spillman (Tahuya MUA; DNR). 13 mi SW of Bremerton on Tahuya River. FACILITIES: 5 sites; Drk Wtr, tbls, toil, cga, group shelter. ACTIVITIES: Hiking, picnicking; fishing.

Green Mountain Horse Camp (Tahuya MUA; DNR). 5 mi SW of Bremerton on Green Mountain. FACILITIES: 9 sites; Drk Wtr, tbls, toil, cga, horse facilities. ACTIVI-TIES: Picnicking; hiking; horseback rid-ing.

Howell Lake (Tahuya MUA; DNR). 17 mi SW of Bremerton on Howell Lake on Tahuya Peninsula. FACILITIES: 6 sites; Drk wtr, tbls, toil, cga. ACTIVITIES: Boating,l; picnicking; fishing; hiking.

Tahuya River Horse Camp (Tahuya MUA; DNR) 13 mi SW of Bremerton on Tahuya River. FACILITIES: 8 sites; Drk wtr, tbls, toil, cga, horse facilities. ACTIVI-TIES: Hiking; picnicking; fishing; horse-back riding.

See page 7 for KEY TO ABBREVIATIONS.

Toonerville (Tahuya MUA; DNR). 9 mi SW of Bremerton on Tahuya Peninsula. FACILITIES: 4 sites; tbls, toil, cga, drk wtr, ACCOMODATES THE HANDICAPPED. ACTIVITIES: Picnicking; hiking.

Twin Lakes (Tahuya MUA, DNR). 14 mi SW of Bremerton on Twin Lakes. FACILITIES: 6 sites; tbls, toil, cga, drk wtr. ACTIVITIES: Boating,l; picnicking; fishing.

BREWSTER

Brewster City Park. Take Brewster Exit from St Hwy 97; drive directly through town to 6th St. SW; just before bridge. Watch for "City Park" sign; campground is 2 blocks further, on the right. FACILITIES: Undesignated spaces for self-contained units (room for 6 RV's on gravel parking area). Playground, tbls, toil, cga, water, community kitchen. ACTIVITIES: Picnicking.

BRINNON

Collins (Olympic NF). 2 mi S of Brinnon on US 101; 4-4/5 mi W on FS 2515 (Duckabush Rec. Area), which starts 3/10 mi N of Duckabush River Bridge. [Narrow, gravel access.] SEASON:5/1-10/28; 14-day lmt. FACILITIES: 14 sites (tr -16); tbls, toil, cga, f, no drk wtr. ACTIVITIES: Hiking; picnicking; fishing; hunting; berrypicking (July). MISC.: Elev 200 ft; pets; nature trails. Pack out litter. Adjacent to Duckabush River.

Elkhorn (Olympic NF). 1 mi N of Brinnon along Hood Canal; 10 mi W on FS 261 (Dosewallips Rec. Area). [Campground on left.] SEASON: 5/1-10/28; 14-day lmt. [Not gated during Winter]. FACILITIES: 18 sites (tr -22); tbls, toil, cga, f, no drk wtr. ACTIVITIES: Hiking; picnicking; fishing; hunting; mountain climbing. MISC.: Elev 600 ft; 8 acres; pets. No trash pickup. (Pack litter out). Enchanted Valley Trailhead (4 mi); extremely scenic. Lake Constance Trailhead (2 mi W). Tunnel Creek Trailhead nearby. Nature trails. Paved and well maintained gravel access rds. Watch out for logging trucks (Mon-Fri).

Steelhead (Olympic NF). 1 mi N of Brinnon on US 101 (where it follows Hood Canal); 8-1/2 mi W on FS 261 (Dosewallips Rec. Area). [Campground is on left.] SEASON: 5/1-10/28; 14-day lmt. [Not gated during Winter.] FACILITIES: 7 sites (no tr); tbls, toil, cga, no drk wtr. ACTIVITIES: Hunting, picnicking; fishing; hiking; mountain climbing; berrypicking (salmon berries). MISC.: Elev 600 ft; 2 acres; pets. No trash pickup (pack litter out). Adjacent to Tunnel Creek Trail. Adjacent to Dosewallips River. Tunnel Creek Trailhead

(1-1/2 mi). Enchanted Valley Trailhead (6 mi W); very scenic. Paved and well maintained single-lane gravel access. Watch out for logging trucks (Mon-Fri).

CARSON

Crest (Gifford Pinchot NF). 4-9/10 mi NW of Carson on Co Hwy 135; 1 mi NW on Co Hwy 139; 10-1/5 mi NW on FS 605; 2-2/5 mi on FS 60. SEASON: 6/15-9/30; 14-day lmt. FACILITIES: 3 sites (tr -16); tbls, toil, cga, f, no drk wtr. ACTIVITIES: Hiking; picnicking; horseback riding. MISC.: Elev 3500 ft; 2 acres; pets. Trailhead for Cascade Crest Trail.

*****Falls Creek Horse Camp** (Gifford NF Pinchot). 9 mi W on Co Hwy 135; 1¼ mi E on FS 405; 12¼ mi N on FS 605. SEASON: 6/15-9/30; 14-day lmt. FACILITIES: 3 sites (tr -16); tbls, toil, cga, f, no drk wtr. ACTIVITIES: Picnicking; berry-picking; fishing; horseback riding. MISC.: Elev 3500 ft; 2 acres; stream; pets. Trailhead for Indian Haven Area and Indian Race Track. Historical.

Little Soda Springs (Gifford Pinchot NF). 13 mi NW of Carson on Co Hwy 135; 9/10 mi S on FS N511. SEASON: 5/15-10/1; 14-day lmt. FACILITIES: 5 sites (no tr); tbls, toil, cga, f, well drk wtr. ACTIVITIES: Hiking; picnicking; fishing. MISC.: Elev 1100 ft; 1 acre; pets. Sodamineral water available on site. Nature trails (4 mi); historic hiking.

Panther Creek (Gifford Pinchot NF). 4-1/2 mi NW of Carson on Co Hwy 135; 3 mi N on Co Hwy N605. SEASON: 5/15-10/15 14-day lmt. FACILITIES: 22 sites (tr -22); tbls, toil, cga, no drk wtr (stream), f. Gas (3 mi). ACTIVITIES: Hiking; picnicking; fishing. Horseback riding (1 mi). Swimming (4 mi). MISC.: Elev 1000 ft; 3 acres; pets. Pacific Crest Trail

CHELAN

Antilon Lake (Wenatchee NF). 5-4/5 mi NW of Chelan on Hwy 150; 5-1/5 mi N on Co Hwy 10; 2-9/10 mi N on FS 3001. SEASON: 4/15-11/15; 14-day lmt. FACILITIES: 3 sites (no tr); tbls, toil, cga, no drk wtr, f. FACILITIES: Boating; picnicking; fishing. MISC.: Elev 2300 ft; 1 acre; pets.

***Big Creek** (Wenatchee NF). 27 mi NW of Chelan BY BOAT. SEASON: 5/1-10/31; 14-day lmt. FACILITIES: 3 tent sites (no tr); no drk wtr; tbls, toil, cga. ACTIVITIES: Swimming; picnicking; fishing; boating; sailing; water skiing. MISC.: Elev 1100 ft; 1 acre; pets. Shelter on site. Boat launches available to Twenty-five Mile Creek.

Chelan Rest Area. 7 mi N of Chelan on St Hwy 97. FACILITIES: Spaces for self-contained units (W side of road); 2 RV's (E side of road). NO OTHER FACILITIES. ACTIVITIES: Hunting; hiking; fishing.

See page 7 for KEY TO ABBREVIATIONS.

* **Corral Creek** (Wenatchee NF). 27-3/5 mi NW of Chelan BY BOAT. SEASON: 5/1-10/31 14-day lmt. FACILITIES: 2 tent sites (no tr); tbls, toil, cga, f. no drk wtr. ACTIVITIES: Picnicking; boating; fishing; swimming; waterskiing; sailing. MISC.: Elev 1100 ft; 1 acre; pets. Boat launches available to Twenty-Five Mile Creek.

* **Deer Point** (Wenatchee NF). 21-7/10 mi NW of Chelan BY BOAT. SEASON: 5/1-10/31; 14-day lmt. FACILITIES: 2 tent sites; tbls, toil, cga, no drk wtr; f, lake. ACTIVITIES: Swimming; picnicking; fishing; boating; water skiing; sailing. MISC.: Elev 1100 ft; 2 acres; pets. Boat launches available to Twenty-five Mile Creek.

* **Domke Falls** (Wenatchee NF). 37-1/2 mi NW of Chelan BY BOAT. SEASON: 5/1-10/31; 14-day lmt. FACILITIES: 1 tent site (no tr); no drk wtr; tbls, toil, cga, f. ACTIVITIES: Boating; picnicking; fishing; swimming; water skiing; sailing. MISC.: Elev 1100 ft; 1 acre; pets. Boat launches available to Twenty-five Mile Creek.

* **DOMKE LAKE** (Wenatchee NF). 40 mi NW of Chelan BY BOAT; 3 mi S, BY BOAT on 1280. Alternate Route, 35 mi BY AIR. SEASON: 5/1-10/31; 14-day lmt. FACILITIES: 6 tent sites; tbls, toil, cga, f. ACTIVITIES: Swimming; picnicking; fishing; boating. MISC.: Elev 2200 ft; 1 acre; pets. Showers/ice/gas/food/store (3 mi). Domke Lake. No dr wtr.

* **Elephant Rock** (Wenatchee NF). 43 mi NW of Chelan BY BOAT. SEASON: 5/1-10/31; 14-day lmt. FACILITIES: 1 tent site; no drk wtr; tbls, toil, cga, f. ACTIVITIES: Swimming; picnicking; fishing; water skiing; boating; sailing. MISC.: Boat launches available to Twenty-five Mile Creek. Pets.

* **Graham Harbor Creek** (Wenatchee NF). 31 mi NW of Chelan BY BOAT. SEASON: 5/1-10/31; 14-day lmt. FACILITIES: 4 tent sites; no drk wtr; tbls, toil, cga, f. ACTIVITIES: Boating; picnicking; fishing; water skiing; sailing. MISC.: Elev 1100 ft; 4 acres; pets. Shelter on site. Boat launches available to Twenty-five Mile Creek.

Grouse Mountain (Wenatchee NF). 3-1/10 mi NW of Chelan on US 97; 16 mi NW on Co Hwy 10; 8 mi W on FS 298. SEASON: 6/15-11/15; 14-day lmt. FACILITIES: 4 sites (tr -16); tbls, toil, cga, f, piped drk wtr. ACTIVITIES: Picnicking. MISC.: Elev 4500 ft; 1 acre; pets.

HandySpring (Wenatchee NF).3-1/10 mi W of Chelan on US 97; 16 mi NW on Co Hwy 10; 14-1/2 mi W on FS 298; 7/10 mi S on FS 298A. SEASON: 7/1-10/31; 14-day lmt. FACILITIES: 1 site (no tr); piped drk wtr, tbls, toil, cga, f. ACTIVITIES: Picnicking. MISC.: Elev 6000 ft; 1 acre; pets.

* **Hatchery** (Wenatchee NF). 40 mi NW of Chelan BY BOAT; 3 mi S on Trail 1280; 1 mi SE, BY BOAT. SEASON: 6/1-10/31; 14-day lmt. FACILITIES: 2 tent sites; ice/gas/showers/food (4 mi); no drk wtr; tbls, toil, cga, f. ACTIVITIES: Swimming; picnicking; fishing; boating (rental 1 mi). MISC.: Elev 2200 ft; 1 acre; pets. Stream. Alternate route, 35 mi BY AIR.

* **Holden** (Wenatchee NF). 41-1/5 mi NW of Chelan BY BOAT; 11-1/0 mi W on FS 3100. SEASON: 6/15-9/30; 14-day lmt. FACILITIES: 2 tent sites; no drk wtr; tbls, toil, cga, f. Store/showers/food (1 mi). ACTIVITIES: Hiking; picnicking; fishing; mountain climbing. MISC.: Elev 3200 ft; 1 acre; pets. Stream. Entry to Glacier Peak Wilderness.

Junior Point (Wenatchee NF). 3-1/10 mi W of Chelan on US 97; 16 mi NW on Co Hwy 10; 14-3/10 mi W on FS 298. SEASON: 7/15-9/30; 14-day lmt. FACILITIES: 5 sites (no tr); tank drk wtr, tbls, toil, cga, f. ACTIVITIES: Picnicking. MISC.: Elev 6600 ft; 1 acre; pets.

* **Lucerne** (Wenatchee NF). 41-1/5 mi NW of Chelan BY BOAT. SEASON: 5/1-10/31, 14-day lmt. FACILITIES: 2 tent sites; no drk wtr; lake, toil. ACTIVITIES: Boating; water skiing; sailing; swimming fishing. MISC.: Elev 1100 ft; 1 acre; pets. Boat launches available to Twenty-five Mile Creek.

* **Mitchell Creek** (Wenatchee NF). 14-9/10 mi NW of Chelan BY BOAT. SEASON: 5/1-10/31, 14-day lmt. FACILITIES: 4 tent sites; no drk wtr; stream, tbls, toil, cga, f. Store/gas/ice/showers (2 mi). ACTIVITIES: Picnicking; fishing; water skiing; sailing; boating (1, 4 mi). MISC.: Elev 1100 ft; 6 acres; pets. Picnic shelters on site. Boat launches available to Twenty-five Mile Creek.

* **Prince Creek** (Wenatchee NF). 35-1/5 mi NW of Chelan BY BOAT. SEASON: 5/1-11/15 14-day lmt. FACILITIES: 5 tent sites; tbls, toil, cga, f, no drk wtr. ACTIVITIES: Swimming; boating,d; waterskiing; sailing. MISC.: Elev 1100 ft; 2 acres; pets. Prince Creek. Boat launches available to Twenty-Five Mile Creek.

* **Refrigerator Harbor** (Wenatchee NF). 41 mi NW of Chelan BY BOAT. SEASON: 5/1-10/31; 14-day lmt. FACILITIES: 4 tent sites; no drk wtr; tbls, toil, cga, f. Store/gas/showers/food (1 mi). ACTIVITIES: Sailing; picnicking; boating (r, 1 mi). MISC.: Elev 1100 ft; 1 acre; pets. Lake. Boat launches available to Twenty-five Mile Creek.

South Navarre (Wenatchee NF). 2-1/5 mi NW of Chelan on St Hwy 150; 38-1/2 mi NW on FS 3007. SEASON: 7/1-10/31; 14-day lmt. FACILITIES: 4 sites (no tr); no drk wtr; tbls, toil, cga, f. ACTIVITIES: Hiking; picnicking. MISC.: Elev 6000; 1 acre; pets.

See page 7 for KEY TO ABBREVIATIONS.

CHESAW

Beth Lake (Okanogan NF). 7-1/2 mi SE of Chesaw on Co Hwy 9480. SEASON: 5/1-10/30. FACILITIES: 17 sites (tr - 32); tbls, toil, cga, f, piped drk wtr. ACTIVITIES: Swimming; picnicking; fishing; hiking; boating,dl. MISC.: Elev 2900 ft; 9 acres; pets. Nature trails. Beth Lake.

CHEWELAH

Chewelah City Park. North edge of Chewelah, by Chewelah Creek; 50 mi N of Spokane on US 395. SEASON: All year; 1-day lmt for tent (to avoid damage to grass); 3-day lmt for RV's. FACILITIES: 50 sites; electric hookup, tbls, flush toil, cga, playground. Ice/gas/laundry nearby. ACTIVITIES: Picnicking. MISC.: Pets.

CLARKSTON

Silcott Road Camp. 6-3/5 mi W of Clarkston on St Hwy 12; N on Silcott Rd; cross bridge [on Snake River]. SEASON: All year, 14-day lmt. FACILITIES: 30 sites. ACTIVITIES: Boating,dl; fishing; swimming. MISC.: No shade. Park on graded gravel lot.

CLE ELUM

Baker (Wenatchee NF). 4 mi SE of Cle Elum on US 10; 12 mi NE on US 97. SEASON: 4/15-11/30; 14-day lmt. FACILITIES: 3 sites (no tr); toil, cga. ACTIVITIES: Fishing. MISC.: Elev 2600 ft; pets.

Beverly (Wenatchee NF). 4 mi SE of Cle Elum on US 10; 4-1/5 mi NE on US 97; 13 mi N on Co Hwy 107; 4 mi NW on FS 232. SEASON: 6/1-11/15; 14-day lmt. FACILITIES: 16 sites (tr -22); tbls, toil, cga, no drk wtr. ACTIVITIES: Fishing; picnicking. Horseback riding (1 mi). MISC.: Elev 3200 ft; 5 acres; pets. River.

Buck Meadows (Wenatchee NF). 12 mi SE of Cle Elum on I-90; 5 mi S on Co Hwy 9123; 6 mi W on FS 1902; 8 mi S on FS 1905. SEASON: 6/1-11/15; 14-day lmt. FACILITIES: 5 sites (tr -16); no drk wtr (stream); tbls, toil, cga. ACTIVITIES: Horseback riding (1 mi); picnicking; fishing. MISC.: Elev 4200 ft; 1 acre; pets.

Cle Elum River (Wenatchee NF). 11-1/5 mi NW of Cle Elum on St Hwy 903; 7 mi NW on Co Hwy 903. [There are 2 entrances; 2nd is in better condition]. SEASON: 5/15-11/15; 14-day lmt. FACILITIES: 23 sites (tr -22); tbls, toil, cga, no drk wtr (river). ACTIVITIES: Hiking; hunting; picnicking; fishing; berry-picking; swimming; horseback riding. Boating (d, 1 mi; l, 5 mi). MISC.: Elev 2200 ft; 5 acres; pets.

De Roux (Wenatchee NF). 4 mi SE of Cle Elum on US 10; 4-1/5 mi NE on US 97; 13 mi N on Co Hwy 107; 8 mi NW on FS 232. SEASON: 6/1-10/31; 14-day lmt. FACILITIES: 4 sites (no tr); no drk wtr (stream); tbls, toil, cga. ACTIVITIES: Mountain climbing; picnicking; fishing; hiking. MISC.: Elev 3800 ft; 2 acres; pets. Scenic.

Dickey Creek Campground (Boise Cascade Corp). 7 mi E of Cle Elum on US 97; Teansway Valley Rd NW to jct with Middle Fork; 3 mi N. SEASON: 5/1-11-1; 14-day lmt. FACILITIES: Undesignated sites; drk wtr, tbls, toil, cga. ACTIVITIES: Hunting; picnicking; fishing; hiking. MISC.: 5 acres. On N Fork of Teanaway River near mouth of Dickey Creek. Lower sites may be subject to flooding in Spring. Snowmobiling (Winter).

Eldorado (Wenatchee NF). 7 mi E of Cle Elum on US 97; 13 mi N on Co Hwy 107; 7 mi NW on FS 232. SEASON: 6/1-10/31; 14-day lmt. FACILITIES: 2 sites; tbls, toil, cga. ACTIVITIES: Fishing.

Esmerelda (Wenatchee NF). 7 mi E of Cle Elum on US 97; 13 mi N on Co Hwy 107; 9 mi NW on FS 232. SEASON: 6/1-10/30; 14-day lmt. FACILITIES: 3 sites (tr -16); no drk wtr; tbls, toil, cga. ACTIVITIES: Mountain climbing; picnicking; fishing. MISC.: Elev 4200 ft; 1 acre; pets. Scenic. Stream.

Fish Lake (Wenatchee NF). 11-1/5 mi NW of Cle Elum on St Hwy 903; 10-7/10 mi NW on Co Hwy 903; 11 mi NE on FS 2405. SEASON: 7/1-10/1; 14-day lmt. FACILITIES: 10 sites (no tr); tbls, toil, cga. ACTIVITIES: Berry-picking; picnicking; fishing; boating (1 mi). MISC.: Elev 3400 ft; 2 acres; pets. Scenic. No drk wtr. Stream.

Haney (Wenatchee NF). 22 mi NE of Cle Elum on US 97; 4 mi S on FS 2107; 6 mi E on FS 2100. SEASON: 6/15-10/31; 14-day lmt. FACILITIES: Sites (tr -16); tbls, toil, cga. ACTIVITIES: Fishing; picnicking. MISC.: Pets.

Owhi (Wenatchee NF). 11-1/5 mi NW of Cle Elum on St Hwy 903; 9-7/10 mi NW on Co Rd 903; 4-9/10 mi NW on FS 228; 1/5 mi N on FS 235. SEASON: 6/15-10/15; 14-day lmt. FACILITIES: 22 sites (no tr); no drk wtr; lake, tbls, toil, cga, f. ACTIVITIES: Swimming; picnicking; fishing; hiking; berry-picking; boating (no motors on lake). MISC.: Elev 2800; 15 acres; pets. Trailhead to Cascade Crest Trailand. Alpine Lakes Wilderness.

Park (Wenatchee NF). 4 mi SE of Cle Elum on US 10; 16-1/2 mi NE on US 97; 1 mi on FS 2208. SEASON: 4/15-11/30; 14-day lmt. FACILITIES: 3 sites (no tr); no drk wtr; tbls, toil, cga. Store/gas/food/showers/laundry (4 mi). ACTIVITIES: Picnicking; horseback riding. MISC.: Elev 3000 ft; 2 acres; pets; stream.

See page 7 for KEY TO ABBREVIATIONS.

Quartz Mountain (Wenatchee NF). 12 mi SE on US I-90; 5 mi S on Co Hwy 9123; 6 mi W on FS 1902; 19 mi S on FS 1905. **SEASON:** 6/15-10/15; 14-day lmt. **FACILITIES:** 3 sites (tr -16); tbls, toil, cga, piped drk wtr. **ACTIVITIES:** Picnicking. Horseback riding (1 mi). **MISC.:** Elev 6100 ft; 1 acre; scenic; pets.

Red Mountain (Wenatchee NF). 11-1/5 mi NW of Cle Elum on St Hwy 903; 8-3/10 mi NW on Co Hwy 903. **SEASON:** 5/15-11/15; 14-day lmt. **FACILITIES:** 15 sites (tr -16). No drk wtr; tbls, toil, cga. **ACTIVITIES:** Berry-picking; fishing; picnicking. Horseback riding (2 mi). Swimming/boating/water skiing (3 mi). **MISC.:** 2200 ft; 2 acres; pets; river.

Red Top (Wenatchee NF). 18 mi NE of Cle Elum on US 97; 3 mi NW on FS 2106; 6 mi W on FS 2106B. **SEASON:** 6/1-10/15; 14-day lmt. **FACILITIES:** 3 sites; no drk wtr; tbls, toil, cga. **ACTIVITIES:** Picnicking; rockhounding. Horseback riding (1 mi). **MISC.:** Elev 5100 ft; 3 acres; pets. Scenic.

Scatter Creek (Wenatchee NF). 11-1/5 mi NW of Cle Elum on St Hwy 903; 11 mi NW on Co Hwy 903; 10-9/10 mi N on FS 2405. **SEASON:** 6/15-10/15; 14-day lmt. **FACILITIES:** 12 sites (tr -32); no drk water; tbls, toil, cga. **ACTIVITIES:** Boating; picnicking; fishing. **MISC.:** Elev 3300; 2 acres; pets. River.

South Fork Meadow (Wenatchee NF). 12 mi SE of Cle Elum on I-90; 5 mi S on Co Hwy 9123; 11 mi W on FS 1902. **SEASON:** 5/15-11/15; 14-day lmt. **FACILITIES:** 4 sites (tr -16); piped drk wtr; tbls, toil, cga. **ACTIVITIES:** Picnicking; fishing. Horseback riding (1 mi). **MISC.:** Elev 3500 ft; 1 acre; pets.

Stafford (Wenatchee NF). 8 mi E of Cle Elum on US 97; 13 mi N on Co Hwy 107; 1 mi N on FS 232; 1-1/2 mi NE on FS 2226. **SEASON:** 6/1-11/30; 14-day lmt. **FACILITIES:** 10 sites (tr -16), tbls, toil, cga, no drk wtr. **ACTIVITIES:** Horseback riding; picnicking; fishing. **MISC.:** Elev 2800 ft; 7 acres; pets.

Tamarack Spring (Wenatchee NF). 15 mi SE of Cle Elum on I-90; 4/5 mi S on Co Hwy 3M; 5-3/5 mi NW on Co Hwy 51; 4-3/5 mi on FS 1902; 6-2/5 mi SW on FS 1904. **SEASON:** 6/1-11/30; 14-day lmt. **FACILITIES:** 2 sites (no tr); tbls, toil, cga, piped drk wtr. **ACTIVITIES:** Picnicking. **MISC.:** Elev 4700 ft; 2 acres; pets.

Taneum (Wenatchee NF). 15 mi SE of Cle Elum on I-90; 4/5 mi S on Co Hwy 3M; 5-3/5 mi NW on Co Hwy 51; 4-1/5 mi NW on FS 1902. **SEASON:** 5/1-11/30; 14-day lmt. **FACILITIES:** 13 sites (tr -22); tbls, toil, cga, piped drk wtr, f. **ACTIVITIES:** Picnicking; fishing.

MISC.: Elev 2400 ft; 8 acres; pets.

Taneum Lake Trail (Wenatchee NF). 72 mi SE of Cle Elum on US 190; 5 mi S on Co Hwy 9123; 6 mi W on FS 1902; 15 mi S on FS 1905. **SEASON:** 6/1-10/31; 14-day lmt. **FACILITIES:** 2 sites (tr -16); tbls, toil, cga. **ACTIVITIES:** Fishing; picnicking. **MISC.:** Pets.

Taneum Jct (Wenatchee NF). 12 mi SE of Cle Elum on US 190; 5 mi on Co Hwy 9123; 7 mi W on FS 1902. **SEASON:** 5/1-11/30; 14-day lmt. **FACILITIES:** 3 sites (tr -16); tbls, toil, cga. **ACTIVITIES:** Fishing. **MISC.:** Pets.

Teanaway (Boise Cascade Corp.). 6-2/5 mi E of Cle Elum on St Hwy 970; 7-1/10 mi NW on Teanaway River Road; left on West Fork Teanaway River Road for 7/10 mi where road brances in three directions; take left branch, pass Bible Rock Camp, and continue to campground. **SEASON:** 5/1-11/1; 14-day lmt. **FACILITIES:** 175 sites; no drk wtr; tbls, toil, cga. **ACTIVITIES:** Hunting; picnicking; fishing; hiking; swimming (1/2 mi stream frontage for swimming). **MISC.:** 35 acres. On Teanaway River. Snowmobiling in Winter.

Tucquala Meadows (Wenatchee NF). 11-1/5 mi NW of Cle Elum on St Hwy 903; 10-7/10 mi NW on Co Hwy 903; 12-9/10 mi NE on FS 2405. **SEASON:** 7/1-10/1. **FAC:** 9 sites (tr -16); tbls, toil, cga, f, no drk wtr. **ACTIVITIES:** Mountain climbing; picnicking; fishing (2 mi); boating (1 mi); hiking. **MISC.:** Elev 3400 ft; 2 acres; pets. Scenic. Trailhead to Cascade Crest Trail & Alpine Lakes Wilderness. Stream.

Twenty-nine Pines (Boise Cascade Corp.). 7 mi E of Cle Elum on US 970; Teanaway Valley Rd NW to jct with Middle Fork; 6 mi N. **SEASON:** 5/1-11/1; 14-day lmt. **FACILITIES:** 130 sites; tbls, toil, cga, drk wtr. **ACTIVITIES:** Hunting; picnicking; fishing; hiking; swimming. **MISC.:** 20 acres; pets. Stream frontage nearby on Teanaway River. Snowmobiling (Winter).

COLVILLE

Little Twin Lakes (Colville NF). 12 ½ mi E of Colville on St Hwy 294; 1 ½ mi N on Co Hwy 633; 4½ mi N on FS 617. **SEASON:** 5/1-10/31. **FACILITIES:** 4 sites (tr -16); tbls, toil, cga, f, **ACTIVITIES:** Boating, r; picnicking; fishing. **MISC.:** 3800 ft; pets. Lake.

Twin Lakes (Colville NF). 12-1/2 mi E of Colville on St Hwy 294; 1-1/2 mi N on Co Hwy 633; 4-1/2 mi N on FS 617. **SEASON:** 5/15-9/15; 14-day lmt. **FACILITIES:** 16 sites (tr -16); tbls, toil, cga, f, well drk wtr. **ACTIVITIES:** Swimming; picnicking; fishing. Boating, ld (r, 2 mi). **MISC.:** Elev 3800 ft; 16 acres; pets; lake.

See page 7 for KEY TO ABBREVIATIONS.

CONCONULLY

Alder (Okanogan NF). 1-4/5 mi NW of Conconully on Co Rd 2361; 2-4/5 mi NW on FS 391. SEASON: 4/15-10/30. FACIL-ITIES: 4 sites (tr -22); tbls, toil, cga, f, no drk wtr. Store/gas/ice/showers/laundry/dump/food (5 mi). ACTIVITIES: Picnicking; fishing. Boating (r,l,d, 5 mi). Swimming (lifeguard, 5 mi). Water skiing (5 mi). MISC.: Elev 3200 ft; 2 acres; pets. Stream. Historic.

Cottonwood (Okanogan NF). 1-4/5 mi N of Conconully on Co Hwy 2361; 3/10 mi N on FS 391. SEASON: 4/15-10/30. FACILITIES: 5 sites (tr -22); tbls, cga, f. Showers/ice/laundry/store (2 mi). ACTIVITIES: Horseback riding; picnicking; fishing; boating. Swimming (2 mi). MISC.: Elev 2700 ft; 2 acres; pets. Artesian well.

Kerr (Okanogan NF). 1-4/5 mi NW of Conconully on Co Hwy 2361; 2 mi NW on FS 391. SEASON: 4/15-10/30; no time lmt. FACILITIES: 12 sites (tr -22); tbls, toil, cga, f, no drk wtr. Showers/ice/laundry/store/gas/dump/food (4 mi). ACTIVITIES: Hiking; picnicking; fishing. Swimming/water skiing (4 mi). Boating (r,l,d, 4 mi). MISC.: Elev 3100 ft; 3 acres; pets. Historic.

Kootenai (Okanogan NF). 3-9/10 mi NE of Conconully on Co Hwy 4015. SEASON: 4/15-10/30. FACILITIES: 2 sites (no tr); no drk wtr; tbls, toil, cga, f. Store/gas/laundry (4 mi). ACTIVITIES: Hiking; picnicking; fishing; water skiing. Boating (r, 4 mi). Horseback riding (4 mi). Swimming (lifeguard, 4 mi). MISC.: Elev 2400 ft; 1 acre; scenic;lake;pets.

Oriole (Okanogan NF). 1-4/5 mi NW of Conconully on Co Hwy 2361; 7/10 mi NW on FS 391; 2/5 mi NW on FS 362. SEASON: 4/15-10/30; no time lmt. FACILITIES: 8 sites (tr -22); tbls, toil, cga, well drk wtr, f. Showers/ice/food/laundry/store/gas/dump (3 mi). ACTIVITIES: Hiking; picnicking; fishing. Swimming (lifeguard 3 mi). Water skiing (3 mi). Boating (r,l,d, 3 mi). Horseback riding (3 mi). MISC.: Elev 2900 ft; 1 acre; pets.

Roger Lake (Okanogan NF). 2-3/10 mi SW of Conconully on Co Hwy 2017; 21-1/5 mi NW on FS 364; 1-3/5 mi NE on FS 370. SEASON: 7/1-9/30. FACILITIES: 1 site (tr -16); no drk wtr (lake); tbls, toil, cga, f. ACTIVITIES: Boating; picnicking; fishing. MISC.: Elev 6000 ft; 1 acre; pets. Scenic.

Salmon Meadows (Okanogan NF). 1-4/5 mi NW of Conconully on Co Hwy 2361; 6-9/10 mi NW on FS 391. SEASON: 6/1-10/30. FAC: 14 sites (tr -22); piped drk wtr, tbls, toil, cga, f, stream, trails. ACTIVITIES: Hiking; picnicking; horseback riding (1 mi). MISC.: Elev 4500 ft; 6 acres; pets. Scenic.

State Road Cabin (Okanogan NF). 2-3/10 mi SW of Conconully on Co Hwy 2017; 9/10 mi SW on FS 364; 3-1/2 mi SW on FS 352. SEASON: 6/1-10/30. FACILITIES: 2 sites (tr -16); no drk wtr; stream, tbls, toil, cga, f. ACTIVITIES: Picnicking; fishing (1 mi); horseback riding (1 mi). MISC.: Elev 3400 ft; 1 acre; pets.

Sugarloaf (Okanogan NF). 4-1/2 mi NE of Conconully on Co Hwy 4051. SEASON: 4/15-10/30; no time lmt. FACILITIES: 5 sites (tr -22); tbls, toil, cga, f, well drk wtr. Showers/ice/laundry/store/gas/food (5 mi). ACTIVITIES: Picnicking; fishing; horseback riding. Swimming (life guard, 5 mi). Boating (r,l,d, 5 mi). MISC.: Elev 2400 ft; 2 acres; pets. Lake.

Tiffany Spring (Okanogan NF). 1-4/5 mi SW of Conconully on Co Hwy 2017; 21-1/5 mi NW on FS 364; 7-1/2 mi NE on FS 370. SEASON: 7/1-9/30. FACIL-ITIES: 3 sites (tr -16); no drk wtr; tbls, toil, cga, f. ACTIVITIES: Picnicking; fishing (1 mi); horseback riding (1 mi). MISC.: Elev 6800 ft; 1 acre; pets. Scenic.

Tiffany Meadows (Okanogan NF). 1-4/5 mi SW of Conconully on Co Hwy 2017; 21-1/5 mi NW on FS 364; 6-2/5 mi NE on FS 370. SEAS: 7/1-9/30. FAC:2 sites (tr -16); no drk wtr; tbls, toil, cga, f. ACTIVITIES: Mountain climbing; picnicking; fishing; horseback riding (1 mi). MISC.: Elev 6200 ft; 1 acre; pets. Scenic.

Wagon Camp (Okanogan NF). 1-4/5 mi SW of Conconully on Co Hwy 2017; 5-9/10 mi NW on FS 364; 1-3/5 mi NW on FS 3619. SEASON: 7/1-9/30. FACILITIES: 3 sites (no tr); no drk wtr; tbls, toil, cga, f. ACTIVITIES: Picnicking; fishing; horseback riding (1 mi). MISC.: Elev 3900 ft; 1 acre; pets.

CONCRETE

Baker Lake (Mt. Baker-Snoqualmie NF). 16 mi N of Concrete on Co Hwy 25, on Baker Lake. SEASON: 4/20-10/20; 14-day lmt. FACILITIES: 16 secluded sites (tr -22); tbls, cga, f, toil, no drk wtr. Showers/store (1 mi). ACTIVITIES: Mountain climbing; picnicking; fishing; hiking; swimming; boating,rld. MISC.: Elev 700 ft; 7 acres; pets. On the shore of Baker Lake (5 mi E of Mt. Baker). Baker Hot Springs (1 mi N) [open free of charge to public].

Boulder Creek (Mt. Baker-Snoqualmie NF). 14 mi N of Concrete on Co Hwy 25. SEA-SON:4/20-10/20; 14-day lmt. FACILITIES: 10 sites (tr -16); no drk wtr; stream, tbls, toil, cga, f. Showers/store/food (3 mi). ACTIVITIES: Picnicking. Fishing/swimming/water skiing (2 mi). Boating (l,d, 2 mi); r, 3 mi). MISC.: Elev 1100 ft; 4 acres; pets. 5 mi SW of Mt. Baker.

See page 7 for KEY TO ABBREVIATIONS.

501

Depression Lake (Mt. Baker-Snoqualmie NF). 9-3/5 mi N of Concrete on Co Hwy 25; 2-1/0 mi NE on FS 394; 1-3/10 mi E on FS 3720; 1/2 mi N on FS 3720A. SEASON: 4/20-10/30; 14-day lmt. FACILITIES: 3 sites (tr -16); no drk wtr; tbls, toil, cga, f. Dump (1 mi). ACTIVITIES: Fishing; picnicking; hiking. Boating (l,d, 2 mi) [no motors allowed on lake]. Swimming/water skiing (3 mi). MISC.: Elev 700 ft; 3 acres; pets. Baker Lake (2 mi). Nature Trails (2 mi).

Finney Creek Shelter (Mt. Baker-Snoqualmie NF). 11 mi SE of Concrete on Co Hwy 353; 5 mi SW on FS 353. SEASON: 5/15-10/30; 10-day lmt. FACILITIES: 2 sites no tr ; tbls, toil, cga, f. ACTIVITIES: Fishing; picnicking. MISC.: Elev 800;

Griners (Mt. Baker-Snoqualmie NF). 23 mi N of Concrete on Co Hwy 25; 1/2 mi N on FS 382. SEASON: 5/20-10/15; 14-day lmt. FACILITIES: 1 site (tr -16); no drk wtr; stream, no tbl; toil, cga, f. ACTIVITIES: Fishing, picnicking boating (l,d, 3 mi); waterskiing (3 mi); hiking. MISC.: Elev 800 ft; 1 acre ; pets. Trailhead to the N Cascade Primitive Area. Scenic.

Lower Park Creek (Mt. Baker-Snoqualmie). 17 mi N of Concrete on Co Hwy 25. SEASON: 4/20-10/20; 14-day lmt. FACILITIES: 2 sites (tr -16); no drk wtr; tbls, toil, cga, f. ACTIVITIES: Fishing; picnicking. Boating (r,l,d, 1 mi). Waterskiing (1 mi). MISC.: Elev 800 ft; 2 acres; pets. Store/shower/gas (1 mi).

Lower Sandy Creek (Mt. Baker-Snoqualmie). 9-3/5 mi N of Concrete on Co Hwy 25; 4-7/10 mi N on FS 394; 9/10 mi E on FS 3719; 9/10 mi SE on FS 3719A. SEASON: 5/20-9/15; 14-day lmt. FACILITIES:4 sites (tr -22); no drk wtr; lake no tbls, toil, cga, f. ACTIVITIES: Hiking; picnicking; fishing; boating (l, 5 mi); waterskiing. MISC.: Elev 700 ft; 5 acres; pets. Nature trails (3 mi). On Baker Lake.

* Maple Grove (Mt. Baker-Snoqualmie NF). 12 mi N of Concrete on Co Hwy 25; 2 mi E on FS 373; 1 mi N, BY BOAT. SEASON:5/1-10/31; 14-day lmt. FACILITIES: 6 tent sites; tbls, toil, cga, f. ACTIVITIES: Swimming; picnicking; fishing; boating,d (l, 1 mi, r, 3 mi). MISC.: Elev 700 ft; 4 acres; pets. On the E shore of Baker Lake in view of Mt. Baker. No drk wtr; stream. Showers/gas store/food (3 mi).

Martin Lake (Mt. Baker-Snoqualmie NF). 16-3/10 mi N of Concrete on Co Hwy 25; 9-3/10 mi N on FS 385. SEASON: 6/15-10/1. FACILITIES: 2 sites (no tr); toil, cga, f. ACTIVITIES: Fishing; picnicking. MISC.: Elev 3700 ft; pets.

Morovits (Mt. Baker-Snoqualmie NF). 17 mi N of Concrete on Co Hwy 25; 1

mi NW on FS 3816. SEASON: 5/20-9/30; 14-day lmt. FACILITIES: 2 sites (tr -16); no drk wtr; stream, tbls, toil, cga, f. Store/food/gas/showers (1 mi). ACTIVITIES: Picnicking. Fishing (1 mi). Boating (rl, 1 mi). Waterskiing (1 mi). MISC.: Elev 900 ft; 3 acares; pets. 5 mi E of Mt. Baker.

Panorama Point (Mt. Baker-Snoqualmie NF). 16 mi N of Concrete on Co Hwy 25 [on shore of Baker Lake]. SEASON: 4/20-10/20; 14-day lmt. FACILITIES: 16 sites (tr -22); no drk wtr; lake, tbls, toil, cga, f. Store/gas/shower/food (1 mi). ACTIVITIES: Waterskiing; sailing; fishing; picnicking. Boating,l (r, 1 mi). MISC.: Elev 700 ft; 7 acres; pets. 5 mi E of Mt. Baker.

Park Creek (Mt. Baker-Snoqualmie NF). 17 mi N of Concrete on Co Hwy 25. SEASON:5/15-10/20; 14-day lmt. FACILITIES: 12 sites (tr -16); tbls, toil, cga, f, no drk wtr. Shower/gas/store (1 mi). ACTIVITIES: Picnicking. Fishing/swimming (1 mi). Boating (r,l,d, 1 mi). MISC.: Elev 800 ft; 7 acres; pets. Baker Lake (1 mi).

Shannon Creek (Mt. Baker-Snoqualmie NF). 9-3/5 mi N of Concrete on Co Hwy FH 25; 12-1/5 mi N on FS 394; 1 mi SE on FS 3830. SEASON: 4/20-10/30; 14-day lmt. FACILITIES: 20 sites (tr -22); tbls, toil, cga, f. Shower/store/gas/food (5 mi). ACTIVITIES: Hiking; swimming; picnicking; berry-picking. Boating,l d, (r, 5 mi). MISC.: Elev 800 ft; 13 acres; pets. Located on Baker Lake. Shannon Creek. Baker Hot Springs (3-3/10 mi S; no charge for public use). No drk wtr.

COOK

Oklahoma (Gifford Pinchot NF). 14-2/5 mi N of Cook on Co Hwy 3087. SEASON: 5/15-10/15; 14-day lmt. FACILITIES: 21 sites (tr -22); tbls, toil, cga, f, well drk wtr, stream. ACTIVITIES: Swimming; picnicking; fishing. MISC.: Elev 1700 ft; 12 acres; pets.

COUGAR

Kalama Spring (Gifford Pinchot NF). 1 mi W of Cougar on Co Hwy 16; 12-1/5 mi N on FS N818. SEASON: 6/15-11/15; 14-day lmt. FACILITIES: 18 sites (tr -16); tbls, toil, cga, f, no drk wtr; stream. ACTIVITIES: Picnicking; fishing. MISC.: Elev 2800 ft; 7 acres; pets.

COULEE CITY

Banks Lake Fish Camp. 11-4/5 mi N of Coulee City on St Hwy 155 (6-1/2 mi S of Grand Coulee Dam); on the E shore of Banks Lake. FACILITIES: No designated sites; room for 20 RVs on large,flat gravel area (no size lmt); tbls, toil, cga. ACTIVITIES: Boating,l; hunting; picnicking. MISC.: Beach.

Geological interest (unusual rock formations in the area).

CRESTON

Hawk Creek (Coulee Dam NRA). 14 mi
NE of Creston on paved rd. SEASON:
All year; 14-day lmt. FACILITIES: 6
sites (tr -16); tbls, toil, cga, no drk
wtr. ACTIVITIES: Boating,ld; fishing;
picnicking. MISC.: Pets.

CURLEW

Deer Creek Summit (Colville NF). 11-1/2
mi E of Curlew on Co Hwy 602. SEASON:
6/1-10/31; 14-day lmt. FACILITIES: 4
sites (tr -16); no drk wtr; tbls, toil,
cga, f. ACTIVITIES: Berry - picking;
picnicking. MISC.: Elev 4600; 2 acres;
pets.

DARRINGTON

Bedal (Mt. Baker-Snoqualmie NF). 1-
3/10 mi NE of Darrington on Co Hwy
17-7/10 mi SE on FS 322. SEASON: 5/15-
10/31; 10-day lmt. FACILITIES: 15 sites
(tr -22); tbls, toil, cga, no drk wtr;
river. ACTIVITIES: Picnicking; fishing.
MISC.: Elev 1300 ft; 6 acres; pets.

Buck Creek (Mt. Baker-Snoqualmie NF).
7-7/10 mi N of Darrington on Co Hwy;
15-1/5 mi SE on FS 345 (located just
past bridge); beside Buck Creek. SEA-
SON:4/30-10/31; 10-day lmt. FACILITIES:
49 sites (tr -22); tbls, toil, cga, no
drk wtr; stream. ACTIVITIES: Hunting;
Picnicking; fishing; hiking; rockhounding. MISC.: Elev 1200 ft; 17 acres;
pets. Huckleberry Mountain Trailhead
nearby. Scenic. Sheltered community.

Chokwich (Mt. Baker-Snoqualmie NF).
1-3/10 mi NE of Darrington on Co Hwy;
19-1/2 mi SE of FS 322. SEASON: 5/15-
9/30; 10-day lmt. FACILITIES: 11 sites
(tr -22); tbls, toil, cga, no drk wtr;
river. ACTIVITIES: Fishing; picnicking.
MISC.: Elev 1500 ft; 4 acres; pets.

Clear Creek (Mt. Baker-Snoqualmie NF).
2-3/10 mi SE of Darrington on Co Hwy;
1/5 mi SE on FS 3205 (on Sauk River
where it meets Clear Creek). SEASON:
4/30-10/31; 10-day lmt. FACILITIES: 10
secluded sites (tr -22); tbls, toil, cga,
f, no drk wtr; river. ACTIVITIES: Hunting; hiking; picnicking; fishing. MISC.:
Elev 600 ft; 4 acres; pets. No trash pickup (pack litter out). Scenic. Frog Lake
Trailhead.   Store/ice/laundry/gas/food
(3 mi).

Crystal Creek (Mt. Baker-Snoqualmie NF).
1-3/10 mi NE of Darrington on Co Hwy;
10-3/10 mi SE on FS 322; 5-3/10 mi E
on FS 314. SEASON: 4/30-10/31; 10-day
lmt. FACILITIES: 1 site (tr -22); no drk
wtr; river, tbls, cga, f. ACTIVITIES:
Picnicking; fishing. MISC.: Elev 1700
ft; 1 acre; pets.

Downey Creek (Mt. Baker-Snoqualmie NF).
7-7/10 mi N of Darrington on Co Hwy;
20-4/5 mi SE on FS 345. SEASON: 5/30-
10/31; 10-day lmt. FACILITIES: 12 sites
(tr -16); tbls, toil, cga, f, no drk wtr.
ACTIVITIES: Hiking; picnicking; fishing.
MISC.: Elev 1400 ft; 4 acres; pets. Trail
head   to   Glacier Peak Wilderness   via
Downey Creek.

French Creek (Mt. Baker-Snoqualmie NF).
8-1/10 mi W of Darrington on St Hwy 530
4/5 mi S on FS 320. SEASON: 4/30-10/31;
10-day lmt. FACILITIES: 30 sites (tr -
22); tbls, toil, cga, f, no drk wtr;
stream. ACTIVITIES: Picnicking; fishing
(2 mi). MISC.: Elev 700 ft; 12 acres;
pets. Store/gas (3 mi).

* Goat Lake (Mt. Baker-Snoqualmie NF).
1-3/10 mi N of Darrington on Co Hwy;
20-4/5 mi S on FS FH 322; 3-9/10 mi SE
on FS FH309; 2-1/2 mi SE on TRAIL 647.
SEASON: 6/15-10/1. FACILITIES: 10 tent
sites; no drk wtr; lake, tbls, toil. ACT-
IVITIES: Mountain climbing; picnicking;
fishing; swimming. MISC.: Elev 2200;
5 acres; pets.

Hyakchuck (Mt. Baker-Snoqualmie NF).
1-3/10 mi NE of Darrington on Co Hwy;
3-3/5 mi SE on FS 322. SEASON: 5/30-
10/31; 10-day lmt. FACILITIES: 2 sites
(tr -16); no drk wtr, stream, tbls, toil,
cga, f. ACTIVITIES: Picnicking; fishing
(1 mi). MISC.: Elev 600 ft; 3 acres;
pets. Store/gas/ice/laundry (5 mi).

Owl Creek (Mt. Baker-Snoqualmie NF).
1-3/10 mi NE of Darrington on Co Hwy;
10-3/10 mi SE on FS 322; 10-1/0 mi E
on FS 314. SEASON: 5/30-10-31; 10-day
lmt. FACILITIES: 5 sites (tr - 22); no
drk wtr; stream, tbls, toil, cga, f.
ACTIVITIES: Hiking; picnicking; fishing
horseback riding; parking; pack and
saddle stock unloading facilities.
MISC.: Elev 1800 ft; 2 acres; pets.
Geological. Trailhead to Glacier Peak
Wilderness.

Sloan Creek (Mt. Baker-Snoqualmie NF).
1-3/10 mi NE of Darrington on Co Hwy;
17-3/10 mi on FS 322; 6-3/10 mi SE
on FS 308. SEASON: 6/1-10/31; 10-day
lmt. FACILITIES: 7 sites (tr - 16);
tbls, toil, cga, no drk wtr. ACTIVI-
TIES: Picnicking; fishing. MISC.: Elev
2200 ft; 3 acres; pets. Trailhead to
Glacier Peak Wildnerness.

South Fork (Mt. Baker-Snoqualmie NF).
1-3/10 mi NE of Darrington on Co Hwy;
19-7/10 mi SE on FS 322. SEASON: 5/15-
10/31; 10-day lmt. FACILITIES: 8 sites
(tr -22); tbls, toil, cga, no drk wtr,
river. ACTIVITIES: Picnicking; fishing
MISC.: Elev 1500 ft; 2 acres; pets.

Sulphur Creek (Mt. Baker-Snoqualmie
NF). 7-7/10 mi E of Darrington on Co
Hwy; 22-1/2 mi SE on FS 345. SEASON:
5/30-10/31;   10-day   lmt.   FACILITIES:
28 sites (tr -16); tbls, toil, cga, f,

no drk wtr; stream. ACTIVITIES: Hiking picnicking; fishing. MISC.: Elev 1500 ft; 3 acres; pets. Sulphur Creek Trailhead.

Texas Wand (Mt. Baker-Snoqualmie NF). 6-1/5 mi N on Co Hwy; 6 mi NW on FS 3334. SEASON: 5/30-10/31; 10-day lmt. FACILITIES: 3 sites (no tr); tbls, toil, cga, f, no drk wtr. ACTIVITIES: Picnicking; fishing. MISC.:

Twin Peaks (Mt. Baker-Snoqualmie NF). 1-3/10 mi NE of Darrington on Co Hwy; 20 mi SE on FS 322. SEASON: 5/15-10/31; 10-day lmt. FACILITIES: 4 sites (tr -16); no drk wtr; river, tbls, toil, cga. ACTIVITIES: Picnicking; fishing. MISC.: Elev 1600 ft; 1 acre ; pets.

Tyee Pool (Mt. Baker-Snoqualmie NF). 1-3/10 mi NE of Darrington on Co Hwy; 20-2/5 mi SE on FS 322. SEASON: 5/30-10/31; 10-day lmt. FACILITIES: 2 sites (tr - 16); no drk wtr; river, tbls, toil, cga. ACTIVITIES: Fishing; picnicking. MISC.: Elev 1700 ft; 1 acre; pets.

Whitechuck (Mt. Baker-Snoqualmie NF). 1-3/10 mi NE of Darrington on Co Hwy; 10-1/10 mi SE on FS 322. SEASON: 4/30-10/31; 10-day lmt. FACILITIES: 12 sites (tr -16); tbls, toil, cga, f, no drk wtr. ACTIVITIES: Picnicking; boating,d; fishing. MISC.: Elev 900 ft; 4 acres; pets. Kayak whitewater boating. River.

DAYTON

Goodman (Umatilla NF). 14 mi SE of Dayton; on Co Hwy 118; 11 mi S on FS 46. SEASON: 6/15-10/15; 10-day lmt. FACILITIES: 7 sites (tr -16); piped drk wtr, tbls, toil, cga, f. ACTIVITIES: Hiking; picnicking; fishing (4 mi); berry-picking; horseback riding (1 mi). MISC.: Elev 5600 ft; 9 acres; pets. Good view of Winaha Wilderness. Accessible via E Touchet Rd or Kendall Skyline Rd. Scenic.

Goose Corral (Umatilla NF). 14 mi SE of Dayton on Co Hwy 118; 9 mi S on FS N910; 3 mi NE on FS N817. SEASON: 6/15-10/15; 10-day lmt. FACILITIES: 3 sites (no tr), tbls, toil, cga, f. ACTIVITIES: Hunting; horseback riding (rental). MISC.: Elev 5600 ft; pets. Packerguide service during hunting season. Godman Rd. Station (3 mi E).

Stockade Spring (Umatilla NF). 14 mi SE of Dayton on Co Hwy 118; 2 mi S on FS N910. SEASON: 6/15-11/15; 10-day lmt. FACILITIES: 2 sites (no tr); tbls, toil, cga, f. ACTIVITIES: Picnicking. MISC.: Elev 4600 ft; pets. Godman Guard Station (8 mi S).

Teepee (Umatilla NF). 14 mi SE of Dayton on Co Hwy 118; 11 mi S on FS 46.

5 mi NE on FS 4608 SEASON: 7/1-10/15; 10-day lmt. FACILITIES: 7 sites (tr -22); no drk wtr; tbls, toil, cga, f. ACTIVITIES: Picnicking; berry-picking; horseback riding (1 mi); fishing (3 mi). MISC.: Elev 5700 ft; 3 acres; pets. 6 mi E of Godman Guard Station.

DELPHI

Fall Creek (Capitol Forest Multiple Use Area; DNR). 5 mi W of Delphi entrance to Capitol Forest on Fall Creek. FACILITIES: 10 sites; drk wtr, horse facilities, toil, cga; facilities accomodate the handicapped. ACTIVITIES: Fishing; picnicking. ADDITIONAL INFORMATION: See "Littlerock" entry for overview information on Capitol Forest Multiple Use Area. Further information and a map can be obtained from Public Affairs Office, Dept. of Natural Resources, Public Lands Bldg., Olympia, WA 98504; or Central Area Office, PO Box 1004, Chehalis, WA 98532; or call toll free: 1-800-562-6010.

DOLE

Cold Creek (Yacolt Multiple Use Area; DNR). 2 mi S of Dole on Cold Creek. FACILITIES: 6 sites; picnic area, tbls, toil, cga, drk wtr, trails, group picnic shelter. ADDITIONAL INFORMATION: See "Washougal" heading for an overview of Yacolt MUA. For maps and further information, write Public Affairs Office, Dept. of Natural Resources, Public Lands Bldg, Olympia, WA 98504, or SW Area Office, Box 798, Castle Rock WA 98611 or call toll free 1-800-562-6010.

ELBE

Alder Roadside Park (Tacoma City Light). Approximately 2 mi NW of Elbe on St Hwy 7 (on Alder Lake). FACILITIES: Camp sites; tbls, cga, boat,l. ACTIVITIES: Picnicking; boating.

ELDON

Hamma Hamma (Olympic NF). 1-7/10 mi N of Eldon on US 101; 6-1/2 mi W on FS 249; Adjacent to Hamma Hamma River. SEASON: 5/1-10/28; 14-day lmt. FACILITIES: 12 sites (tr -22); tbls, toil, cga, f, well drk wtr, nature trails, river. ACTIVITIES: Hiking; picnicking; fishing; mountain climbing. MISC.: Elev 600 ft; 5 acres; pets. 2-1/2 mi W to Lena Lakes Trailhead. [Is gated during Winter.]

Lena Creek (Olympic NF). 1-7/10 mi N of Eldon on US 101; 9 mi W on FS 249 at the confluence of Lena Creek and the Hamma Hamma River. SEASON: 5/1-10/28; 14-day lmt. FACILITIES: 14 sites (tr -22); tbls, toil, cga, f, well drk wtr, nature trails. ACTIVITIES: Hiking; picnicking; fishing; mountain climbing. MISC.: Elev 700 ft; 7 acres; pets. Adjacent to Lena Lakes Trail.

ELLENSBURG

Lion Rock Spring (Wenatchee NF). 12-2/5 mi N on Co Hwy 179; 97 mi N on FS 2008; 4/5 mi W on FS 2008E. SEASON: 6/15-10/15; 14-day lmt. FACILITIES: 3 sites (no tr); no drk wtr; tbls, toil, cga. ACTIVITIES: Picnicking. MISC.: Elev 6300 ft; 1 acre; pets. Scenic.

ENTIAT

Big Hill (Wenatchee NF). 1-2/5 mi SW of Entiat on US 97; 25-1/5 mi NW on Co Hwy 371; 4-1/5 mi NW on FS 317; 7-9/10 mi N on FS 298; 1-1/2 mi N on FS 298A. SEASON: 7/15-9/30; 14-day lmt. FACILITIES: 1 site (no tr); no drk wtr; tbls, toil, cga, f. ACTIVITIES: Picnicking; horseback riding (1 mi). MISC.: Elev 6800 ft; 1 acre; pets. Shelter on site.

Cottonwood (Wenatchee NF). 1-2/5 mi SW of Entiat on US 97; 25-1/5 mi NW on Co Hwy 371; 12-7/10 mi NW on FS 317. SEASON: 6/15-10/15; 14-day lmt. FACILITIES: 26 sites (tr -22); tbls, toil, cga, f, horse corral (available at site). ACTIVITIES: Horseback riding; picnicking; fishing; berry- picking. MISC.: Elev 3100 ft; 9 acres; pets. Piped drk wtr. River. Departure point for Glacier Peak Wilderness.

Fox Creek (Wenatchee NF). 1-2/5 mi SW of Entiat on US 97; 25-1/5 mi on Co Hwy 371; 1-4/5 mi NW on FS 317. SEASON: 5/15-10/15; 14-day lmt. FACILITIES: 9 sites (tr -16); tbls, toil, cga, f, no drk wtr; river. ACTIVITIES: Picnicking; fishing. MISC.: Elev 2300 ft; 3 acres; pets. Campground vegetation burned by fire, Summer, 1970.

Half Way Spring (Wenatchee NF). 1-2/5 mi SW of Entiat on US 97; 25-1/5 mi NW on Co Hwy 371; 4-1/5 mi NW on FS 317; 3-9/10 mi N on FS 298. SEASON: 6/15-10/15; 14-day lmt. FACILITIES: 5 sites (tr -22); tbls, toil, cga, f, no drk wtr. MISC.: Elev 5000 ft; 3 acres; pets.

Lake Creek (Wenatchee NF). 1-2/5 mi SW of Entiat on US 97; 25-1/5 mi NW on Co Hwy 371; 3 mi NW on FS 317. SEASON: 5/15-10/15; 14-day lmt. FACILITIES: 12 sites (tr -16); tbls, toil, cga, f, no drk wtr; stream, horse corral (available at site). ACTIVITIES: Horseback riding; picnicking; fishing. MISC.: Elev 2400 ft; 6 acres; pets. Vegetation burned by fire, Summer, 1970.

Mad Lake (Wenatchee NF). 1-/25 mi SW of Entiat on US 97; 10 mi NW on Co Hwy 371; 2/15 mi NW on FS 2710; 9 mi SW on FS 2615. SEASON: 7/15-9/30; 14-day lmt. FACILITIES: 3 sites (no tr); tbls, toil, cga, f. ACTIVITIES: Picnicking; fishing. MISC.: Pets.

North Fork (Wenatchee NF). 1-2/5 mi SW of Entiat on US 97; 25-1/5 mi NW on Co Hwy 371; 8-3/10 mi NW on FS 317. SEASON: 6/15-10/15; 14-day lmt. FACILITIES: 8 sites (tr -22); tbls, toil, cga, f, no drk wtr; river. ACTIVITIES: Picnicking; fishing. MISC.: Elev 2700 ft; 3 acres; pets.

Pine Flat (Wenatchee NF). 1-2/5 mi SW of Entiat on US 97; 10 mi NW on Co Hwy 371; 3-7/10 mi NW on FS 2710. SEASON: 5/1-10/31; 14-day lmt. FACILITIES: 9 sites (tr -22); toil, cga, f, no drk wtr; river. ACTIVITIES: Horseback riding; picnicking; fishing. MISC.: Elev 1900 ft; 9 acres; pets. Ice/store/gas/food (4 mi).

Shady Pass (Wenatchee NF). 1-2/5 mi SW of Entiat on US 97; 25-1/5 mi NW on Co Hwy 371; 4-1/5 mi NW on FS 317; 7-9/10 mi N on FS 298. SEASON: 7/1-9/30; 14-day lmt. FACILITIES: 1 site (tr -22); toil, cga, f. ACTIVITIES: Picnicking. MISC.: Elev 5400 ft; pets.

Silver Falls (Wenatchee NF). 1-2/5 mi SW of Entiat on US 97; 25-1/5 mi NW on Co Hwy 371; 5-1/5 mi NW on FS 317. SEASON: 6/1-10/15; 14-day lmt. FACILITIES: 34 sites (tr -22); tbls, toil, cga, f, piped drk wtr, stream. ACTIVITIES: Fishing, picnicking, hiking. MISC.: Elev 2400 ft; 26 acres; pets.

Spruce Grove (Wenatchee NF). 1-2/5 mi SW of Entiat on US 97; 25-1/5 mi NW on Co Hwy 371; 9-4/5 mi NW on FS 317. SEASON: 6/15-10/15; 14-day lmt. FACILITIES: 2 sites (no tr); no drk wtr, tbls, toil, cga, f. ACTIVITIES: Fishing; picnicking. MISC.: Elev 2900 ft; 2 acres; pets.

Three Creek (Wenatchee NF). 1-2/5 mi SW of Entiat on US 97; 25-1/5 mi NW on Co Hwy 371; 10-1/2 mi NW on FS 317. FACILITIES: 3 sites (no tr); no drk wtr, tbls, toil, cga, f. MISC.: Elev 2900 ft; 2 acres; pets. SEASON: 6/15-10/15; 14-day lmt.

ENUMCLAW

Corral Pass (Mt. Baker-Snoqualmie NF). 31 mi SE of Enumclaw on US 410; 6-1/10 mi E on FS 185. SEASON: 7/1-10/30; 14-day lmt. FACILITIES: 12 sites (no tr); tbls, toil, cga, f, no drk wtr; stream. ACTIVITIES: Hiking; picnicking; fishing (1 mi); berry-picking. MISC.: Elev 5700 ft; 12 acres; pets. Scenic. Located in Alpine setting, within easy hike to mountain reserve.

* **Echo Lake** (Mt. Baker-Snoqualmie NF). 32-1/10 mi SE of Enumclaw on US 410; 6-7/10 mi E on FS 185; 5-1/5 mi NE on TRAIL 1176. SEASON: 7/1-9/15; 14-day lmt. FACILITIES: 6 tent sites; no drk wtr; lake, no tbls, toil, cga, f. ACTIVITIES: Fishing; hiking. MISC.: Elev 3800 ft; 5 acres; pets. Trail shelter.

See page 7 for KEY TO ABBREVIATIONS.

★ **Government Meadow** (Mt. Baker–Snoqualmie NF). 18-7/10 mi SE of Enumclaw on US 410; 8-1/10 mi E on FS 197; 6-3/10 mi SE on TRAIL 1175. SEASON: 7/1-10/30. FACILITIES: 2 tent sites; no drk wtr; stream, cga,f, no tbls. ACTIVITIES: Hiking; fishing (5 mi); horseback riding (1 mi). MISC.: Elev 4900 ft; 2 acres; pets. On Pacific Crest National Scenic Trail; shelter.

Greenwater River Park (Weyerhauser Co). 24 mi E of Enumclaw off St Hwy 410 [on Greenwater River]. SEASON: All year;no time lmt. FACILITIES: 30 sites (tr -22); drk wtr, tbls, cga, toil. ACTIVITIES: Hiking. MISC.: 50 acres. Stream. Mountainous terrain. Pull-thru spaces.

Twin Camp (Wenatchee NF). 20 mi E of Enumclaw on US 410; 7-3/10 mi E on FS 197; 3 mi NE on FS 1917. SEASON: 7/1-10/30; 14-day lmt. FACILITIES: 3 sites (no tr); no drk wtr; tbls, toil, cga, f. ACTIVITIES: Hiking; berry-picking; horseback riding (1 mi). MISC.: Elev 3700 ft; 5 acres; pets. 3 mi S of Kelley Butte Lodge. 5 mi W of Pacific Crest Trail & Windy Gap.

White River (Mt. Rainier NP). 27 mi SE of Enumclaw on St Hwy 410; 5 mi W of White River Entrance (NE corner of Park) —very narrow, twisting entrance road. SEASON: 10/16-6/30, FREE (rest of yr, $3 + NP entrance fee); 14-day lmt. FACILITIES: 117 sites (tr -20); tbls, FLUSH toil, cga, river, amphitheater. ACTIVITIES: Picnicking; hiking; fishing (no license required in Park). MISC.: Elev 4400 ft; pets.

EVANS

North Gorge (Coulee Dam NRA). 20 mi N of Evans on St Hwy 25. SEASON: All year; 14-day lmt. FACILITIES: 9 sites; tbls, toil, cga. ACTIVITIES: Picnicking; fishing; boating,ld.

EVERETT

Smokey Point (SRA). 12 mi N of Everett on I-5. FACILITIES: Toils, wash basins with hot wtr & soap, electric hand dryers, phone, tbls. ACTIVITIES: Picnicking. MISC.: Random parking. Pets.

FORKS

Ashenbrenner Campground & Picnic Area (Olympic NP). 25 mi S of Forks on US 101 to NP entrance, then continue on US 101 for an additional 5-3/10 mi to campground (paved road). SEASON: 3/15 -11/1; 14-day lmt. [Closed in Winter; but then Kalaloch Campground is free and open for camping.] FACILITIES: Parking area with undetermined number of sites (no size lmt); tbls, toil, cga. ACTIVITIES: Hiking; fishing and clamming in season (no license required in NP)—check with ranger about season lmts and tides; picnicking; beachcombing for driftwood and shells. MISC.:

Elev less than 100 ft. Overlooking Pacific Ocean. Ranger Station—3-4/5 mi N: information and backcountry use permits all year. Kalaloch Beach Resort (2-7/10 mi N)-gas/grocery/food.

HOH Campground (Olympic NP). 14 mi S of Forks; turn N at Hoh River Bridge & go 1-4/5 mi; then 17-9/10 mi E on paved rd along Hoh River, which is open all year. Paved, but narrow and winding roads. Watch for logging trucks. SEASON: LD-6/30, FREE (rest of yr, $5). No NP entrance fee. 14-day lmt. FACILITIES: 95 sites (tr -21); FLUSH toil, tbls, dump. ACTIVITIES: Picnicking; fishing (no license required in Park); hiking. MISC.: Elev 578 ft; pets. Two nature trails and Hoh River Trail. Roosevelt Elk in vicinity of trails. Hoh River Trail (18 mi) leads to climb of Mt. Olympus [the highest peak in the Olympic Range]. RANGER STATION—information and backcountry use permits all year. From the park boundary to the end, this road passes thru one of the finest examples of RAIN FOREST.

Kalaloch Campground (Olympic NP). 25 mi S of Forks on US 101 to NP entrance, then continue on US 101 for an additional 8-3/5 mi to campground (paved road: open all year). SEASON: LD-6/30, FREE (rest of yr, $5). No NP entrance fee. 14-day lmt. FACILITIES: 179 sites (tr -21); tbls, FLUSH toil, cga. ACTIVITIES: Hiking; picnicking; fishing (no license required in NP); beachcombing for driftwood and shells; clamming in season (check with ranger about seasons, lmts, and tides). MISC.: Elev less than 100 ft. 9 short trails lead from hwy to beaches. RANGER STATION (1/2 mi) information and backcountry use permits all year. Campground overlooks Pacific Ocean. Kalaloch Beach Resort (3 mi S); gas/grocery/food.

Klahanie (Olympic NF). 1-7/10 mi NW of Forks on US 101; 5-2/5 Mi E on FS 300. Adjacent to Calawah River. SEASON: 5/15-11/10; 14-day lmt. FACILITIES: 13 sites (tr -22); tbls, toil, cga, f, no drk wtr. ACTIVITIES: Swimming; hunting picnicking. MISC.: Elev 300 ft; 27 acres; pets. Tent pads at 6 sites. Scenic. Excellent example of Olympic Rain Forest at this site.

Minnie Peterson (Olympic NP & DNR). 14 mi S of Forks on US 101; 4-7/10 mi E on Hoh Rain Forest Road. SEASON: All year; 14-day lmt. (No NP entrance fee). FACILITIES: 6 sites (tr -22); well drk wtr, tbls, toil, cga. ACTIVITIES: Hunting; picnicking; fishing (no license required in park). MISC.: Food/gas/ice.

Mora (Olympic NP). 2 mi N of Forks on US 101; 12 mi W (road to campground paved but narrower than US 101; open all year). 1-2/10 mi N of Forks on St

Hwy 101; 3-1/10 mi W at La Push sign; Area sign; left at next La Push sign; 4-4/5 mi to "Y" at store & take right fork; 3-1/5 mi to Mora. SEAS: LD-6/30, FREE (rest of yr, $5). No NP entrance fee. 14-day lmt. FAC: 91 sites (tr -21); DUMP, tbls, FLUSH toil, cga. ACTIVITIES: Hiking; picnicking; fishing (no license required in park) [salmon]; observation of sea and bird life. MISC.: Elev sea level. Food/ice/gas (3-1/5 mi E). Boat launch at Public Fishing Access (3 mi E). Rialto Beach; day use only (2 mi W). Can hike to Lake Ozette on the North Wilderness Beach (18-1/2 mi); but check with Ranger regarding tide tables, as some portions can be crossed only at low tide.

Spruce Creek (Olympic NP & DNR). 14 mi S of Forks on US 101; 9-3/5 mi E on Hoh Rain Forest Road (located on stream). SEASON: All year; 14-day lmt. FACILITIES: 5 sites (tr -22); tbls, toil, cga, no drk wtr. ACTIVITIES: Hunting; picnicking; fishing (no license required in park).

Tumbling Rapids Park (Rayonier Development of ITT). 11-1/2 mi N of Forks on St Hwy 101 (on Soleduck River). SEASON: 5/1-11/15; 10-day lmt. FACILITIES: 10 sites (tr -24); tbls, cga, f, FLUSH toil, community kitchen with electric outlets/stove/lights/running wtr. ACTIVITIES: Hunting; hiking; picnicking. MISC.: 6 acres. Near Soleduck Hot Springs. Mountainous terrain. No motor bikes. Stream.

FORT SPOKANE

★ Detillon (Coulee Dam NRA). 6 mi NE of Fort Spokane BY BOAT. SEASON: All year; 14-day lmt. FACILITIES: 8 sites (no tr); tbls, toil, cga. ACTIVITIES: Swimming; picnicking; fishing; boating,d.

GLACIER

Bridge (Mt. Baker-Snoqualmie NF). 1 mi E of Glacier on St Hwy 542; 4-1/5 mi E on FS 3907. SEASON: 5/15-10/1; 10-day lmt. FACILITIES: 12 sites (tr -16); tbls, toil, cga, f, store, food concession, gas, visitor center, no drk wtr, river. ACTIVITIES: Hiking; picnicking; fishing. MISC.: Elev 1300 ft; 3 acres; pets.

Canyon Creek (Mt. Baker-Snoqualmie NF). 2 mi NE of Glacier on St Hwy 542; 7-1/10 mi N on FS FH400. SEASON: 6/1-9/30; 10-day lmt. FACILITIES: 6 sites (tr -16); tbls, toil, cga, f, no drk wtr. ACTIVITIES: Hiking; picnicking; fishing. MISC.: Elev 2200 ft; 2 acres; pets.

Excelsior (Mt. Baker-Snoqualmie NF). 6-1/2 mi E of Glacier on St Hwy 542.

SEASON: 5/15-10/1; 10-day lmt. FACILITIES: 13 sites no tr ; tbls, toil, cga, f, no drk wtr, river. ACTIVITIES: Fishing; picnicking. MISC.: Elev 1300 ft; 4 acres; pets. Botanical. 2-3/5 mi W of N fork of Nooksack Natural Area.

★ Galena Chain Lake (Mt.Baker-Snoqualmie NF). 22 mi E of Glacier on St Hwy 642; 2-1/0 mi NW on TRAIL 687; 3-3/5 mi NW on TRAIL 682. SEASON: 7/1-10/1. FACILITIES: 3 tent sites; no drk wtr, no tbls, lake, cga, f. ACTIVITIES: Fishing. MISC.: Elev 4800 ft; 16 acres; pets. Scenic.

Hannegan (Mt. Baker-Snoqualmie NF). 12-2/5 mi E of Glacier on St Hwy 542; 4 mi E on FS FH402. SEASON: 6/1-10/15; 10-day lmt. FACILITIES: 6 sites (tr -16); tbls, toil, cga, f, no drk wtr, stream. ACTIVITIES: Hiking; picnicking; fishing; mountain climbing. MISC.: Elev 3100 ft; 3 acres; pets. Entrance to North Cascade Primitive Area.

★Kulshan Cabin (Mt. Baker-Snoqualmie NF). 1 mi E on St Hwy 542; 8 mi S on FS 3904; 2 mi E on TRAIL 677. SEASON: 6/15-9/15. FACILITIES: 4 tent sites; tbls, toil, cga, f, no drk wtr. ACTIVITIES: Picnicking; mountain climbing; rockhounding. MISC.: Elev 4800 ft; 1 acre; stream; pets. Site operated by quasi-public agency. Starting point for climbing Mt. Baker.

Twin Lakes (Mt. Baker-Snoqualmie NF). 12-3/10 mi E of Glacier on St Hwy 542; 4 mi N on FS FH401; 2-1/2 mi NE on TRAIL 672. SEASON: 8/1-9/30; 10-day lmt. FACILITIES: 10 sites (no tr); no drk wtr, lake, tbls, toil, cga. ACTIVITIES: Hiking; picnicking; fishing. MISC.: Elev 5100 ft; 5 acres; pets. Winchester Mt. Lookout (1 mi N).

GOLDENDALE

Lower Bowman Creek. 12 mi N of Goldendale on Cedar Valley Rd, then 1-1/2 mi W; 1/2 mi S. SEASON: 5/1-11/1; 14-day lmt. FACILITIES: 10 sites; tbls, toil, cga. ACTIVITIES: Hiking; picnicking; fishing.

Three Creeks. 9 mi N of Goldendale on US 97 [on a creek]. SEASON: 5/1-11/1; 14-day lmt. FACILITIES: 20 sites (tr -16); tbls, toil, cga, stream frontage. ACTIVITIES: Hiking; picnicking; fishing; hunting.

Upper Bowman Creek. On Cedar Valley Rd, 14-1/2 mi N of Goldendale. FACILITIES: Stream frontage; tbls, toil, cga.

GRAND COULEE

Spring Canyon (Coulee Dam NRA). 3 mi E of Grand Coulee on St Hwy 174; turn left at NRA sign and travel 1-3/10 mi

See page 7 for KEY TO ABBREVIATIONS.

on paved road. [On Roosevelt Lake].
SEASON: LD-MD, FREE (rest of yr, $5).
FACILITIES: 100 sites (tr -26); DUMP,
FLUSH toil, food concession, sandy
beach, changing rooms, playground,
cga, tbls. ACTIVITIES: Swimming; water
skiing; hunting; picnicking; fishing;
hiking; boating,ld. MISC.: Pets on leash.

GRANITE FALLS

Beaver Bar (Mt. Baker-Snoqualmie NF).
24-3/10 mi E of Granite Falls on Co
Hwy FH7. SEASON: 5/15-10/31; 10-day
lmt. FACILITIES: 3 sites (tr -16); no
drk wtr, stream, tbls, toil, cga, f.
ACTIVITIES: Boating; swimming; picnicking; fishing. MISC.: Elev 1600 ft;
2 acres; pets. Geological.

Beaver Creek (Mt. Baker-Snoqualmie
NF). 24-1/5 mi E of Granite Falls on
Co Hwy FH7. SEASON: 5/15-9/30; 10-day
lmt. FACILITIES: 8 sites (tr -16); tbls,
toil, cga, no drk wtr, river. ACTIVI-
TIES: Picnicking; fishing. MISC.: Elev
1600 ft; 2 acres; pets.

Boardman (Mt. Baker-Snoqualmie NF).
16-3/5 mi E of Granite Falls on Co Hwy
FH7. SEASON: 4/1-10/30; 10-day lmt.
FACILITIES: 7 sites (tr -16); tbls, toil,
cga, no drk wtr, river. ACTIVITIES:
Picnicking; fishing. MISC.: Elev 1500
ft; 2 acres; pets.

Board Man Lake (Mt. Baker-Snoqualmie
NF). 15 mi E on Co Hwy FH7; 4 mi
S on FS 3015; 1/2 mi S on TRAIL 704.
SEASON: 6/1-10/31; 10-day lmt. FACI-
LITIES: 8 tent sites; tbls, toil, cga.
ACTIVITIES: Picnicking; fishing.
MISC.: Elev 3100 ft;3 acres;lake;pets.

Canyon Lake (Mt. Baker-Snoqualmie NF)
7 mi E of Granite Falls on Co Hwy 7;
1-4/5 mi N on FS 320; 1-4/5 mi E on
FS 318; 6-3/5 mi E on FS 3032. SEASON:
6/15-10/1. FACILITIES: 3 sites (no tr);
tbls, toil, cga. ACTIVITIES: Picnicking.
MISC.: Elev 2700 ft; pets.

Coal Creek (Mt. Baker-Snoqualmie NF).
23-2/5 mi E of Granite Falls on Co Hwy
FH7. SEASON: 5/15-10/31; 10-day lmt.
FACILITIES: 5 sites (tr -32); tbls, toil,
cga, no drk wtr, river. ACTIVITIES:
Picnicking; mountain climbing; swimming; fishing. MISC.: Elev 1600 ft;
2 acres; pets; scenic.

Coal Creek Bar (Mt. Baker— Snoqualmie
NF). 23-4/5 mi E of Granite Falls on
Co Hwy FH7. SEASON: 5/15-9/30; 10-day
lmt. FACILITIES: 9 sites (tr -16); no
drk wtr; river, tbls, toil, cga, f,
nature trails. ACTIVITIES: Hiking; boating; picnicking; fishing; swimming.
MISC.: Elev 1600 ft; 3 acres; pets. Geological.

Coal Lake (Mt. Baker-Snoqualmie NF).
25-1/2 mi E of Granite Falls on Co Hwy
FH7; 4-2/5 mi N on FS 3006. SEASON:
6/1-10/1; 10-day lmt. FACILITIES: 5
sites (no tr); no drk wtr; tbls, toil,
cga. ACTIVITIES: Picnicking; fishing.
MISC.: Elev 2800 ft; 2 acres; pets.

Dicksperry (Mt. Baker-Snoqualmie NF).
21-1/10 mi E of Granite Falls on Co Hwy
FH7. SEASON: 5/15-10/15; 10-day lmt.
FACILITIES: 9 sites; no drk wtr; river,
tbls, toil, cga, nature trails. ACTIVI-
TIES: Hiking; swimming; picnicking;
fishing; boating. MISC.: Elev 1400 ft;
1 acre; pets. Geological.

Esswine (Mt. Baker-Snoqualmie NF). 16-
1/5 mi E of Granite Falls on Co Hwy FH7.
SEASON: 5/1-10/30; 10-day lmt. FACILI-
TIES: 5 sites; no drk wtr; river, tbls,
toil, cga, f, store, gas, ice, visitor
center, food. ACTIVITIES: Boating;
swimming; picnicking; fishing. MISC.:
Elev 1200 ft; 2 acres; pets.

Haps Hill (Mt. Baker-Snoqualmie NF).
30-1/2 mi E of Granite Falls on Co Hwy
FH7; 2-1/2 mi S on Co Rd. SEASON: 6/15-
10/31; 10-day lmt. FACILITIES: 7 sites
(no tr); no drk wtr, river, tbls, toil,
cga, f. ACTIVITIES: Swimming; picnicking; fishing. MISC.: Elev 2500 ft;
3 acres; pets.

Hemple Creek (Mt. Baker-Snoqualmie NF).
12-4/5 mi E of Granite Falls on Co Hwy
FH7. SEASON: 4/1-11/15; 10-day lmt. FACIL-
ITIES: 3 sites (tr -32); piped drk wtr,
tbls, toil, cga, river. ACTIVITIES: Picnicking; fishing. MISC.: Elev 1000 ft;
4 acres; pets. Store/food/ice (4 mi). Gas
(5 mi).

Marten Creek (Mt. Baker-Snoqualmie NF).
20-3/5 mi E of Granite Falls on Co Hwy
FH7. SEAS: 5/15-9/30; 10-day lmt. FAC:5
sites; no drk wtr; river, tbls, toil,
cga, f. ACTIVITIES: Boating; swimming;
picnicking; fishing. MISC.: Elev 1400
ft; 1 acre; pets. Geological.

Monte Cristo (Mt. Baker-Snoqualmie NF).
30-3/10 mi E of Granite Falls on Co
Hwy FH7;4-1/10 mi SE on FS 2963. SEA-
SON: 6/15-10/31; 10-day lmt. FACILI-
TIES: 3 sites (no tr); no drk wtr;
stream, tbls, toil, cga. ACTIVITIES:
Mountain climbing; picnicking; fishing.
MISC.: Elev 2800 ft; 2 acres; pets,
Scenic.

Old Trail (Mt. Baker-Snoqualmie NF).
30-1/2 mi E on Co Hwy FH7. SEASON:
5/15-10/31; 10-day lmt. FACILITIES:
1 site (no tr); tbls, toil, cga, f, no
drk wtr. ACTIVITIES: Picnicking;
fishing; swimming. MISC.: Elev 1500
ft; 1 acre; river; pets.

Perry Creek (Mt. Baker-Snoqualmie NF).
26-1/10 mi E of Granite Falls on Co

Hwy FH7. **SEASON:** 5/15-10/31. **FACILI-TIES:** 8 sites (tr -16); no drk wtr; stream, tbls, cga. **ACTIVITIES:** Picnicking; fishing. **MISC.:** Elev 1800 ft; 3 acres; pets.

Red Bridge (Mt. Baker-Snoqualmie NF). 17-7/10 mi E of Granite Falls on Co Hwy FH7 by Stillaguamish River. **SEASON:** 5/15-9/30; 10-day lmt. **FACILITIES:** 11 sites (tr -32); no drk wtr, river, tbls, toil, cga. **ACTIVITIES:** Hiking; picnicking; fishing. **MISC.:** Elev 1300 ft; 6 acres; pets.

River Bar (Mt. Baker-Snoqualmie NF). 17-7/10 mi E of Granite Falls on Co FH7. **SEASON:** 3/15-11/15; 10-day lmt. **FACILITIES:** 6 sites (tr -32); tbls, toil, cga, no drk wtr; river. **ACTIVITIES:** Picnicking; fishing. **MISC.:** Elev 1300 ft; 1 acre; pets.

Road Camp (Mt. Baker-Snoqualmie NF). 16-2/5 mi E of Granite Falls on Co Hwy FH7. **SEASON:** 5/1-10/1. **FACILITIES:** 3 sites (tr -22). **MISC.:** Pets.

Sauk River (Mt. Baker-Snoqualmie NF). 30-1/10 mi E of Granite Falls on Co Hwy FH7; 4 mi S on Co Rd. **SEASON:** 6/15-10/31; 10-day lmt. **FACILITIES:** 4 sites (no tr); no drk wtr; river, tbls, toil, cga, f. **ACTIVITIES:** Swimming; fishing; picnicking. **MISC.:** Elev 2600 ft; 1 acre; pets.

Silvertop (Mt. Baker-Snoqualmie NF). 30-1/2 mi E of Granite Falls on Co Rd FH7; 2-7/10 mi S on Co Rd. **SEASON:** 6/15-10/31; 10-day lmt. **FACILITIES:** 5 sites (no tr); no drk wtr, stream; tbls, toil, cga, f. **ACTIVITIES:** Picnicking; swimming; fishing. **MISC.:** Elev 2500 ft; 1 acre; pets.

South Fork Canyon Crossing (Mt. Baker-Snoqualmie NF). 6-1/2 mi E of Granite Falls on Co Hwy FH7; 8-2/5 mi N on FS 320. **SEASON:** 5/1-10/15; no time lmt. **FACILITIES:** 5 sites (no tr);` no drk wtr, stream, cga, f, toil. **ACTIVITIES:** Picnicking. **MISC.:** Elev 1600 ft; 2 acres; pets. Stream.

Sunnyside (Mt. Baker-Snoqualmie NF). 17-1/10 mi E of Granite Falls on Co Hwy 7. **SEASON:** 5/1-10/15; 10-day lmt. **FACILITIES:** 7 sites (tr -32); toil, cga. **ACTIVITIES:** Fishing; picnicking. **MISC.:** Elev 1300 ft.

Twin Bridges (Mt. Baker-Snoqualmie NF). 30-3/10 mi E of Granite Falls on Co Hwy 7; 1-1/10 mi S on FS 2963. **SEASON:** 6/15-11/15; 10-day lmt. **FACILITIES:** 1 site (tr -32); no drk wtr; river, tbls, toil, cga. **ACTIVITIES:** Fishing; picnicking. **MISC.:** Elev 2400 ft; 1 acre; pets. Scenic. Food (5 mi).

White Deer (Mt. Baker-Snoqualmie NF). 30-1/2 mi E of Granite Falls on Co Rd FH7; 3 mi N on FS 322. **SEASON:** 5/30-10/31; 10-day lmt. **FACILITIES:** 8 sites (no tr); no drk wtr; tbls, toil, cga, f. **ACTIVITIES:** Swimming; picnicking; fishing. **MISC.:** Elev 1800 ft; 2 acres; pets.

GREENBANK

Rhododendron Park (Dept. of Natural Resources). 9-1/10 mi N of Greenbank to Jct of St Hwy 525 and 20; watch for "Rhododendron Park" sign and then follow narrow entrance road which isn't labeled. On Whidby Island. [Narrow, rough, access.] **FACILITIES:** 6 sites (pull-thru spaces); tbls, toil, cga, drk wtr. **ACTIVITIES:** Picnicking. **MISC.:** Scenic.

HOQUIAM

Graves Creek (Olympic NP). 39 mi N of Hoquiam; 18-3/5 mi on Quinault River Valley Road (S Shore Lake Quinault Rd), 1st 7 mi are paved; then gravel road (gravel portion may be closed in Winter by snow); narrow road. **SEASON:** All yr; 14-day lmt. **FAC:** 45 sites (tr -21); tbls, toil, cga, trails. **ACTIVITIES:** Fishing (no license required in NP); boating; swimming; picnicking; hiking; **MISC.:** Elev 540 ft. No NP entrance fee. Road passes through town of Quinault and US Forest Service Lake Quinault Rec. Area; road winds up valley to a dense stand of RAIN FOREST that begins beyond point where Quinault River branches.

* **July Creek Campground** (Olympic NP). 41 mi N of Hoquiam on US 101; 3-9/10 mi on paved rd. **SEASON:** Open all year 14-day lmt. **FACILITIES:** Walk-in only; no tr, toil, cga. **ACTIVITIES:** Hiking; fishing (Washington State license and Indian Reservation Fishing Permit required). **MISC.:** Elev 200 ft. No NP entrance fee. RAIN FOREST beyond upper level of Lake Quinault. 1-9/10 mi—Quinault Ranger Station, information and backcountry permits.

North Fork Campground (Olympic NP). 41 mi N of Hoquiam on US 101; 18-1/5 mi on paved and gravel road (paved first 8 mi; closed in Winter by snow; not suitable for tr). **SEASON:** 4/15-10/15 14-day lmt. Closed Winter. **FACILITIES:** Sites (no tr); toil, cga. **ACTIVITIES:** Hiking; fishing (Washington State license and Indian Reservation Fishing Permit required). **MISC.:** No entrance permit for NP. RAIN FOREST beyond upper level of Lake Quinault.

HOODSPORT

Big Creek (Olympic NF). 8 mi W on Co Hwy 9420; 1/2 mi S on FS 245. **SEASON:** 5/1-10/28; 14-day lmt. **FACILITIES:** 43 sites (tr -22); tbls, toil, cga, no drk wtr; store on site. **ACTIVITIES:** Picnicking; fishing; boating;

swimming; skiing. **MISC.** Elev 700 ft; 30 acres; pets.

Lilliwaup (Olympic NF; Dept. of Natural Resources). St Hwy 101 from Hoodsport; 9-1/5 mi W on Lake Cushman Rec. Area Rd (Paved); turn right at end of road and go 1-9/10 mi to campground (gravel road, well-maintained). SEASON: 10-day lmt. FACILITIES: 6 sites (tr -16); tbls, toil, cga. ACTIVITIES: Mountain climbing; hiking; hunting; picnicking; fishing. MISC.: Trailheads to Mt. Washington and Mt. Ellinor nearby. (Beside Lilliwaup Creek). Additional information and map: Public Affairs Office, DNR, Public Lands Building; Olympia, WA 98504; Toll free in Washington 1-800-562-6010.

Staircase (Olympic NP). Start at US 101 at Hoodsport on Hood Canal; 16 mi NW on River Road (paved 9 mi, then gravel; closed by snow at times in Winter; suitable for small trailers). SEASON: LD-6/30, FREE (rest of yr, $3). No NP entrance fee. 14-day lmt. FACILITIES: 63 sites (tr -16); tbls, FLUSH toil. ACTIVITIES: Fishing (no license required in NP); hiking; mushroom gathering; picnicking. MISC.: Elev 890 ft. By the Skokomish River (1 mi upriver are the Staircase Rapids). Three trails begin at campground: North Fork Skokomish Trail; Shady Lane Trail; Four Stream Trail, which passes the Staircase Rapids.

HUMPTULIPS

Campbell Tree Grove (Olympic NF). 4 mi NE of Humptulips on US 101; 8 mi NE on FS 220 (Promised Land Rec. Area, to A & M's Logging Camp); 4 mi N on FS 2302; 9-1/2 mi NE on FS 23021. SEASON: 5/15-11/20; 14-day lmt. FACILITIES: 6 sites (tr -22); tbls, toil, cga, f, piped drk wtr. ACTIVITIES: Berrypicking; hiking; picnicking; fishing (in river). MISC.: Elev 1100 ft; 14 acres; pets.

Promised Land Park. 2-9/10 mi N of Humptulips on St Hwy 101. [Watch for "Rest Stop" signs]. Located by Stevens Creek. SEASON: 4/1-11/15; 14-day lmt. FACILITIES: 15 sites (tr -24); FLUSH toil, tbls, cga, community kitchen with running wtr/large stove, f, electric hookups. ACTIVITIES: Hunting; hiking; picnicking; fishing. MISC.: No Motorbikes. Mountainous terrain.

HUNTERS

Gifford (Coulee Dam NRA). Approx. 12 mi N of Hunters on St Hwy 25; on Roosevelt Lake. SEASON: All year; 14-day lmt. FACILITIES: 8 sites (tr-16); tbls, cga, toil. ACTIVITIES: Swimming; boating,ld; hunting; hiking; picnicking; fishing. MISC.: Scenic. Sandy beach. Floating raft.

Hunters Park (Coulee Dam NRA). 2 mi W of Hunters on access rd. SEASON: 5/15-10/15; 14-day lmt. FACILITIES: 36 sites (tr -26); FLUSH toil, cga, tbls. ACTIVITIES: Swimming; picnicking; fishing; boating,ld.

INDEX

San Juan (Mt. Baker-Snoqualmie NF). 14 mi NE of Index on Co Hwy 290 (Index Road). [On the banks of Skykomish river.] SEASON: 5/15-10/1; 14-day lmt. Closed in Winter. FACILITIES: 12 sites (no tr); tbls, toil, cga, f, no drk wtr. ACTIVITIES: Berrypicking (salmon & wild raspberries); hunting; hiking; picnicking; fishing. MISC.: Elev 1500 ft; 5 acres; pets. Watch for deer.

Troublesome Creek (Mt. Baker-Snoqualmi NF). 12 mi NE of Index on Co Hwy 290. (Index Rd.) [On N. Fork of Skykomish River.] SEASON: 5/15-10/1; 14-day lmt. Closed in Winter. FACILITIES: 22 sites (tr -22); tbls, toil, cga, f, no drk wtr, river. ACTIVITIES: Hunting; hiking; picnicking; fishing. MISC.: Elev 1300 ft; 15 acres; pets. Watch for deer. Trailhead to Troublesome Creek Interpretive Trail.

IONE

Ione (Colville NF). 1 mi S of Ione on St Hwy 31; 3/10 mi E on Co Hwy 303; 2 mi N on Co Hwy 306; 1-4/5 mi W on FS 1724. SEASON: 5/15-9/15; 14-day lmt. FACILITIES: 23 sites (tr -22); tbls, toil, cga, piped drk wtr. Ice/laundry/store/gas/dump (4 mi). ACTIVITIES: Berry-picking; swimming; boating,ld; picnicking; fishing; water skiing. MISC.: Elev 2100 ft; 10 acres; pets.

KAHLOTUS

Windust. 7/10 mi SW of Kahlotus on Spokane Ave; 8-1/5 mi S at Lower Monumental Dam Sign (3 mi past dam). FACILITIES: 20 sites, FLUSH toil, tbls, cga. ACTIVITIES: Boating,ld; hunting; picnicking; fishing; swimming; MISC.: Playground.

KETTLE FALLS

Bradbury Beach (Coulee Dam NRA). 4/5 mi from Kettle Falls on US 395; 8 mi S on St Hwy 25 (campground is on right). SEASON: 14-day lmt. FACILITIES: 5 tent sites; no drk wtr; tbls, toil, cga, changing facilities. ACTIVITIES: Swimming; hunting; picnicking; fishing; boating,l; waterskiing. MISC.: Pets.

Canyon Creek (Colville NF). 3½ mi NW on US 395; 11 mi W on St Hwy 20; 1/5 mi S on FS 2000. SEASON: 5/15-10/15; 14-day lmt. FACILITIES: 12 sites (tr

-32); tbls, toil, cga, f, well drk wtr. ACTIVITIES: Picnicking; hiking; fishing. MISC.: Elev 2200 ft; 5 acres; pets. Interpretive Center nearby.

Cloverleaf Camp. 4/5 mi W of Kettle Falls; 23 mi S on St Hwy 25 [On Roosevelt Lake]. FACILITIES: 8 shaded sites for tents; parking area for tr; boat,l; well drk wtr; tbls, toil, cga; changing house. ACTIVITIES: Boating; waterskiing; picnicking; fishing; hunting. MISC.: Sanay beach; sheltered bay which is roped off for swimming (floating raft).

Colville River. 4/5 mi W of Kettle Falls on US 395; 3-7/10 mi S on St Hwy 25. Access road is unmarked; watch on the right for gravel road located just before the white guard rail. [Rough, narrow, steep, but short (approx. 200 yards) access road.] FACILITIES: Undesignated sites; room for 10 RVs. No facilities. ACTIVITIES: Hunting; fishing (in Roosevelt Lake). MISC.: Large area amidst a grove of evergreens.

Evans (Coulee Dam NRA). 8 mi N of Kettle Falls on St Hwy 25; on Roosevelt Lake. SEASON: LD-5/31, FREE (rest of yr, $3). 14-day lmt. FACILITIES: 67 sites (tr -26); FLUSH toil, tbls, cga. ACTIVITIES: Hunting; swimming; picnicking; fishing; waterskiing; boating,l. MISC.: Wild strawberries.

Kamloops (Coulee Dam NRA). 7 mi W of Kettle Falls and N on US 395 [where Kettle River enters Roosevelt Lake]. SEASON: All year; 14-day lmt. FACILITIES: 6 sites (no tr); no drk wtr; tbls, toil, cga. ACTIVITIES: Swimming; hunting; picnicking; fishing; boating,d. MISC.: CAUTION: Deep Water. Raft.

Kettle Falls (Coulee Dam NRA). 2 mi W of Kettle Falls on US 395; left at NRA sign for 1-7/10 mi (by Roosevelt Lake) to campground. SEASON: LD-MD FREE (rest of yr, $3); 14-day lmt. FACILITIES: 74 sites (tr -26); dump, flush toil, tbls, cga, f, playground, food concession. ACTIVITIES: Hunting; picnicking; fishing; boating,ld; water skiing; hiking; berry-picking (wild strawberries). MISC.: Nature trail.

Kettle River (Coulee Dam NRA). 13 mi NW of Kettle Falls on US 395. FACILITIES: 3 sites; 14-day lmt., no drk wtr; tbls, toil, cga. ACTIVITIES: Fishing; picnicking. MISC.: Pets.

Marcus Island (Coulee Dam NRA) 4 mi N of Kettle Falls on St Hwy 25. SEASON: All year, 14-day lmt. FACILITIES: 8 sites (tr - 20); tbls, toil, cga. ACTIVITIES: Swimming; picnicking; fishing. MISC.: Store nearby. Pets.

Northeast Lake Ellen (Colville NF). 3-1/2 mi NW of Kettle Falls on US 395; 4 mi S on St Hwy 20; 4½ mi SW on Co Hwy 2014; 5½ mi SW on FS 2014. SEASON: 5/15-10/15;14-day lmt. FACILITIES: 11 sites (tr -22); tbls, toil, cga, lake, well drk wtr, f. ACTIVITIES: Fishing; picnicking; boating,ld; MISC.: Elev 2400 ft; 4 acres; pets.

Trout Lake (Colville NF). 3-1/2 mi NW of Kettle Falls on US 395; 5-1/2 mi W on St Hwy 20; 5 mi NW on FS 2000. SEASON: 6/1-10/15; 14-day lmt. FACILITIES: 4 sites (tr -16); piped drk wtr; lake; tbls, toil , cga, f. ACTIVITIES: Berry-picking; picnicking; fishing; boating,ld. MISC.: Elev 3000 ft; 3 acres; pets.

LEAVENWORTH

Alpine Meadow (Wenatchee NF). 15-9/10 mi NW of Leavenworth on US 2; 4 mi N on St Hwy 207; 1 mi E on Co Hwy 22; 19-1/2 mi NW on FS 311. SEASON: 6/15-10/15;14-day lmt. FAC: 4 sites (no tr); no drk wtr; tbls, toil, cga, lake. ACTIVITIES: Fishing; picnicking; berry-picking. MISC.: Elev 2700 ft; 1 acre; pets.

Atkinson Flat (Wenatchee NF). 15-9/10 mi NW of Leavenworth on US 2; 4 mi N on St Hwy 207; 1 mi E on Co Hwy 22; 15 mi NW on FS 311. SEASON: 6/15-10/15; 14-day lmt. FACILITIES: 4 sites (tr -22); no drk wtr; river, tbls, toil, cga, f. ACTIVITIES: Mountain climbing; picnicking; fishing. MISC.: Elev 2500 ft; 1 acre; pets.

Blue Pool (Wenatchee NF). 15 mi NW of Leavenworth on US 1; 4 mi N on St Hwy 207; 1-1/5 mi NE on Co Hwy 22; 16 mi N on FS 311. SEASON: 6/15-10/15; 14-day lmt. FACILITIES: 2 sites (tr -16); no drk wtr; river, tbls, toil, cga, f. ACTIVITIES: Fishing; picnicking. MISC.: Elev 2500 ft; 1 acre; pets.

Bonanza (Wenatchee NF). 4-1/2 mi SE on US 2; 13-1/10 mi S on US 97. SEASON: 4/15-11/30; 14-day lmt. FACILITIES: 5 sites (tr -16); tbls, toil, cga, well drk wtr. ACTIVITIES: Picnicking. Horseback riding (1 mi). MISC.: Elev 3000 ft; 2 acres; pets.

Bridge Creek (Wenatchee NF). 1/2 mi SW on US 2; 2-9/10 mi S on Co Hwy 71; 5-2/5 mi W on FS 2451 (Icicle Creek Rd). SEAS: 5/1-10/31 [closed in Winter]; 14-day lmt. FACILITIES: 3 sites (tr -22); no drk wtr; Bridge Creek, tbls, toil, cga, f, no garbarge pickup (pack litter out). ACTIVITIES: Mountain climbing; picnicking; fishing; hiking. MISC.: Elev 1900 ft; 3 acres; pets. NOTE: campers OK; not enough room for tr. to turn around. Trailhead to Alpine Lakes Wilderness (5 mi E at "Snow Creek Trail" sign).

Chatter Creek (Wenatchee NF). 1/2 mi SW of Leavenworth on US 2; 2-9/10 mi S on Co Hwy 71; 12-3/10 mi NW on FS 2451. SEASON: 5/1-10/31; 14-day lmt. FACILITIES: 12 sites (tr -22); tbls, toil, cga, f, no drk wtr; stream. ACTIVITIES: Fishing; picnicking. MISC.: Elev 2800 ft; 23 acres; pets.

Chiwaukum Creek (Wenatchee NF). 10-3/10 mi NW of Leavenworth on US 2; 1-1/2 mi W on FS 265. SEASON: 5/1-10/31; 14-day lmt. FACILITIES: 7 sites (tr – 22); tbls, toil, cga, f, no drk wtr; horse corral on site. ACTIVITIES: Picnicking; horseback riding; fishing. MISC.: Elev 2400 ft; 2 acres; pets.

Deep Creek (Wenatchee NF). 3/10 mi E on US 1; 17½ mi N on St Hwy 209; 2-1/5 mi N on FS 2476. SEASON: 5/1-10/31. FACILITIES: 3 sites; tbls, toil, cga, f, no drk wtr. ACTIVITIES: Fishing; picnicking. MISC.: Elev 2200 ft; 1 acre; pets.

Deer Camp (Wenatchee NF). 3/10 mi E of Leavenworth on US 2; 14-1/2 mi N on St Hwy 209; 3 mi NE on Co Hwy 22; 1-1/2 mi N on FS 2746; 2 mi NE on FS 2722. SEASON: 5/1-10/1; 14-day lmt. FACILITIES: 3 sites (no tr); no drk wtr; tbls, toil, cga, f. ACTIVITIES: Picnicking. MISC.: Elev 4000 ft; 1 acres; pets.

Eightmile (Wenatchee NF). 1/2 mi SW of Leavenworth on US 2; 2-9/10 mi S on Co Hwy 71; 4-1/5 mi W on FS 2451 (Icicle Creek Rd). [Rd closed in Winter by snow.] SEASON: 5/1-10/31; 14-day lmt. FACILITIES: 8 sites (tr –22); tbls, toil, cga, f, horse corral on site, no trash pickup (pack litter out), no drk wtr, Icicle Creek. ACTIVITIES: Mountain climbing; hunting; hiking; picnicking; fishing; berrypicking (also Oregon grapes); horseback riding. MISC.: Elev 1800 ft; 5 acres; pets. Horse rental (5 mi). Trailhead to Alpine Lakes Wilderness Area (3 mi E at Snow Creek Trail sign).

Finner (Wenatchee NF). 15-9/10 mi NW of Leavenworth on St Hwy 207; 1 mi E on Co Hwy 22; 11 mi NW on FS 311. SEASON: 6/15-10/15; 14-day lmt. FACILITIES: 3 sites (tr –32); piped drk wtr, tbls, toil, cga, f, stream. ACTIVITIES: Hiking; picnicking; fishing; mountain climbing. MISC.: Elev 2500 ft; 1 acre; pets. Schaeffer Lake. Basalt Ridge Trailhead.

Fish Pond (Wenatchee NF). 15-9/10 mi NW of Leavenworth on US 2; 4/5 mi NE on St Hwy 207. SEASON: 5/1-10/31; 14-day lmt. FACILITIES: 3 sites (no tr); no drk wtr, tbls, toil, cga, f. Food/gas (1 mi). Store/laundry/lifeguard/boat,1 (4 mi). ACTIVITIES: Boating/swimming (4mi); picnicking; fishing. MISC.: Elev 1800 ft; 1 acre; pets.

Goose Creek (Wenatchee NF). 3/10 mi E of Leavenworth on US 2; 17-1/2 mi N on St Hwy 209; 3-1/5 mi N on FS 2746. SEASON: 6/1-10/15; 14-day lmt. FACILITIES:

4 sites (tr –31); no drk wtr; stream, tbls, toil, cga, f. ACTIVITIES: Fishing; picnicking. MISC.: Elev 2200 ft; 2 acres; pets.

Grasshopper Meadows (Wenatchee NF). 15-9/10 mi NW of Leavenworth on US 2; 8-2/5 mi N on St Hwy 207; 9/10 mi NW on Co Hwy 22; 7-9/10 mi on FS 293. SEASON: 6/1-10/15; 14-day lmt. FACILITIES: 4 sites (no tr); no drk wtr; river, tbls, toil, cga, f. ACTIVITIES: Berrypicking; picnicking; fishing. MISC.: Elev 2000 ft; 2 acres; pets.

Grouse Creek (Wenatchee NF). 15-9/20 mi NW of Leavenworth on US 2; 4 mi N on St Hwy 207; 1 mi E on Co Hwy 22; 7 mi N on FS 311. SEASON: 6/1-10/15; 14-day lmt. FACILITIES: 4 sites (no tr); no drk wtr; tbls, toil, cga, f. ACTIVITIES: Fishing; picnicking. MISC.: Elev 2400 ft; 3 acres; pets.

Ida Creek (Wenatchee NF). 1/2 mi SW of Leavenworth on US 2; 2-9/10 mi S on Co Hwy 71; 10-1/5 mi NW on FS 2451 (Icicle Creek Rd). SEASON: 5/1-10/31; 14-day lmt. FACILITIES: 4 sites (tr –22); no drk wtr; stream, tbls, toil, cga, f, no trash pickup (pack litter out). ACTIVITIES: Hiking; picnicking; fishing. MISC.: Elev 1900 ft; 4 acres; pets.

Johnny Creek (Wenatchee NF). 1/2 mi SW of Leavenworth on US 2; 2-9/10 mi S on Co Hwy 71; 8-1/10 mi NW on FS 2451 (Icicle Creek Rd) to campground sign. [Road closed in Winter by snow.] SEASON: 5/1-10/31; 14-day lmt. FACILITIES: 14 sites (tr –22); well drk wtr, tbls, toil, cga, f, stream; no trash pick up (pack litter out). ACTIVITIES: Hunting; mountain climbing; hiking; picnicking; fishing; berrypicking. MISC.: Pets. Elev 2300 ft; 7 acres.

Lake Creek (Wenatchee NF). 15-9/10 NW of Leavenworth on US 2; 8-2/5 mi N on ST Hwy 207; 1-1/2 mi W on Co Hwy 22; 9-4/5 mi W on FS 283. SEASON: 5/1-10/31; 14-day lmt. FACILITIES: 8 sites (tr –32); no drk wtr; stream, tbls, toil, cga, f. ACTIVITIES: Berrypicking; picnicking; fishing. MISC.: Elev 2300 ft; 8 acres; pets.

* **Lake Julius** (Wenatchee NF). 20-9/10 mi NW of Leavenworth on US 2; 1-1/5 mi SE on FS 2734; 6-4/5 mi SW on TRAIL 1584. SEASON: 7/1-10/15; 14-day lmt. FACILITIES: 2 sites (no tr); tbls, toil, cga, f. ACTIVITIES: Picnicking; fishing. MISC.: Elev 4400 ft; pets. Lakeshore closed to horses within 200 ft.

Lake Wenatchee Ranger Station (Wenatchee NF). 15-9/10 mi NW of Leavenworth on US 2; 3-9/10 mi N on St Hwy 207. SEASON: 5/1-10/31; 14-day lmt. FACILITIES: 8 sites (no tr); tbls, toil, cga, f, piped drk wtr. Store/gas/food

See page 7 for KEY TO ABBREVIATIONS.

(1 mi). Ice (5 mi). ACTIVITIES: Hiking; mountain climbing; swimming; fishing; picnicking; boating,d (r,l, 1 mi); water skiing. MISC.: Elev 1900 ft; 4 acres; pets. Dirty Face L.O. Trail head.

Little Wenatchee Ford (Wenatchee NF). 15-9/10 mi NW of Leavenworth on US 2; 8-2/5 mi N on St Hwy 207; 1-1/2 mi W on Co Hwy 22; 14-7/10 mi NW on FS 283. SEASON: 6/15-9/15; 14-day lmt. FACILITIES: 3 sites (no tr); o drk wtr, tbls, toil, cga, f. ACTIVITIES: Hiking; berrypicking; picnicking; fishing. MISC.: Elev 2900 ft; 1 acre; pets. Departure at Little Wenatchee Ford to Cascade Crest Trail & Glacier Park Wilderness.

Maple Creek (Wenatchee NF). 15-9/10 mi NW of Leavenworth on US 2; 4 mi N on St Hwy 207; 1 mi E on Co Hwy 22; 19 mi NW on FS 311. SEASON: 6/15-10/15; 14-day lmt. FACILITIES: 7 sites (tr -22); no drk wtr; stream, tbls, toil, cga, f. ACTIVITIES: Hiking; picnicking; fishing. MISC.: Elev 2600 ft; 3 acres; pets. Entrance to Glacier Park Wilderness via Little Giant Trail.

Meadow Creek (Wenatchee NF). 15-9/10 mi NW of Leavenworth on US 2; 4 mi NE on St Hwy 207; 1 mi E on Co Hwy 22; 2-2/5 mi NE on FS 311; 2-1/0 mi NW on FS 2815. SEASON: 5/1-10/31; 14-day lmt. FACILITIES: 3 sites no tr; no drk wtr; river, tbls, toil, cga, f. Store/food/gas (5 mi). ACTIVITIES: Fishing; picnicking. MISC.: Elev 2300 ft; 1 acre; pets.

Napeequa (Wenatchee NF). 15-9/10 mi NW on US 2; 8-2/5 mi N on St Hwy 207; 9/10 mi NW on Co Hwy 22; 5-9/10 mi NW on FS 293. SEAS: 5/15-10/31; 14-day lmt. FAC: 5 sites (tr -32); no drk wtr; tbls, toil, cga. ACTIVITIES: Hiking; berrypicking; picnicking; fishing. MISC.: Elev 2000 ft; 2 acres; pets. Entrance to Glacier Peak Wilderness; Twin Lakes Trail.

Nineteen Mile (Wenatchee NF). 15-9/10 mi NW of Leavenworth on US 2; 4 mi N on St Hwy 207; 1 mi E on Co Hwy 22; 18 mi NW on FS 311. SEASON: 6/15-10/15; 14-day lmt. FACILITIES: 3 sites (tr -22); no drk wtr; river, tbls, toil, cga, f. ACTIVITIES: Fishing; picnicking. MISC.: Elev 2600 ft; 2 acres; pets.

Phelps Creek (Wenatchee NF). 15-9/10 mi NW on US 2; 4 mi N on St Hwy 207; 1 mi E on Co Hwy 22; 21 mi NW on FS 311. SEASON: 6/15-10/15; 14-day lmt. FACILITIES: 7 sites (no tr); no drk wtr; river, tbls, toil, cga, f; horse unloading ramp, corral, & parking area available . ACTIVITIES: Mountain climbing; picnicking; fishing; horseback riding.

MISC.: Elev 2800 ft; 4 acres; pets. Entrance to Glacier Peak Wilderness.

Riverside (Wenatchee NF). 15-9/10 mi NW of Leavenworth on US 2; 8-2/5 mi on St Hwy 207; 1-1/5 mi W on Co Hwy 22; 5-9/10 mi W on FS 283. SEASON: 5/1-10/31; 14-day lmt. FACILITIES: 6 sites (tr -32); no drk wtr; river, tbls, toil, cga, f. ACTIVITIES: Berrypicking; picnicking; fishing. MISC.: Elev 2000 ft; 2 acres; pets.

Rock Creek (Wenatchee NF). 15-9/10 mi NW of Leavenworth on US 2; 4 mi N on St Hwy 207; 1 mi E on Co Hwy 22; 13 mi NW on FS 311. SEASON: 6/15-10/15; 14-day lmt. FACILITIES: 4 sites (tr -22); no drk wtr; stream, tbls, toil, cga, f. ACTIVITIES: Hiking; picnicking; fishing. MISC.: Elev 2500 ft; 1 acre; pets.

Rock Island (Wenatchee NF). 1/2 mi SW of Leavenworth on US 2; 2-9/10 mi S on Co Hwy 71; 13-7/10 mi NW on FS 2451. SEASON: 5/1-10/31; 14-day lmt. FACILITIES: 18 sites (tr -22); no drk wtr; stream, tbls, toil, cga, f. ACTIVITIES: Berrypicking; picnicking; fishing. MISC.: Elev 2900 ft; 5 acres; pets.

Schaefer Creek (Wenatchee NF). 15-9/10 mi NW on US 2; 4 mi N on St Hwy 207; 1 mi N on Co Hwy 22; 14 mi NW on FS 311. SEASON: 6/15-10/15; 14-day lmt. FACILITIES: 3 sites (no tr); no drk wtr; river, tbls, toil, cga, f. ACTIVITIES: Fishing; picnicking. MISC.: Elev 2600 ft; 1 acre; pets.

Scotty (Wenatchee NF). 4-1/2 mi SE of Leavenworth on US 2; 11-9/10 mi S on US 97; 1-1/5 mi SW on FS 2208; 4/5 mi SE on FS 223. SEASON: 5/1-11/15; 14-day lmt. FACILITIES: 5 sites no tr; toil, cga. ACTIVITIES: Fishing; picnicking. MISC.: Elev 2800 ft; pets.

Soda Springs (Wenatchee NF). 15-9/10 mi NW of Leavenworth on US 2; 8-2/5 mi N on St Hwy 207; 1-1/2 mi W on Co Hwy 22; 7-1/5 mi W on FS 283. SEASON: 5/1-10/31; 14-day lmt. FACILITIES: 5 sites (no tr); no drk wtr; stream, tbls, toil, cga, f. ACTIVITIES: Hiking; picnicking; fishing; berrypicking. MISC.: Elev 2000 ft; 2 acres; pets. Nature trails. Soda Spring on site.

Theseus Creek (Wenatchee NF). 15 mi NW of Leavenworth on US 2; 9 mi NW on St Hwy 207; 6 mi W on FS 283; 4-1/2 mi W on FS 2713. SEASON: 5/15-10/31; 14-day lmt. FACILITIES: 2 sites (tr -16); no drk wtr; river, tbls, toil, cga, f. ACTIVITIES: Fishing; picnicking. MISC.: Elev 2300 ft; 1 acre; pets.

Top Lake (Wenatchee NF). 15-9/10 mi NW of Leavenworth on US 2; 8-2/5 mi NW on St Hwy 207; 1-1/2 mi W on Co

Hwy 22; 2-9/10 mi W on FS 283. SEA-SON: 7/15-9/30; 14-day lmt. FACILITIES: 2 sites (no tr); cga, f. ACTIVITIES: Fishing; picnicking. MISC.: Elev 5500 ft; pets. Located near Cascade Crest Trail. Closed to horses within 200 ft of lake shore.

Tronsen (Wenatchee NF). 4-1/2 mi SE of Leavenworth on US 2; 18-1/10 mi S on US 97 (Swauk Pass Hwy) [1-1/2 mi N of the Summit]. SEASON: 5/15-10/30; 14-day lmt [closed off-season]. FACIL-ITIES: 17 shaded sites (tr -22); no drk wtr; stream, tbls, toil, cga, f, horse (1 mi). ACTIVITIES: Hunting; hiking; picnicking; fishing; rockhounding. MISC.: Elev 3900 ft; 17 acres; pets. Small creek flows through campground.

Whitepine (Wenatchee NF). 24-9/10 mi NW of Leavenworth on US 2; 1/2 mi W on FS 266. SEASON: 5/1-10/31; 14-day lmt. FACILITIES: 4 sites (tr -22); no drk wtr; stream, tbls, toil, cga, f. Store/gas (1 mi). ACTIVITIES: Berry-picking; picnicking; fishing. Horseback riding (1 mi). MISC.: Elev 1900 ft; 2 acres; pets.

White River Falls (Wenatchee NF). 15-9/10 mi NW of Leavenworth on US 2; 8-2/5 mi N on St Hwy 207; 9/10 mi NW on Co Hwy 22; 9 mi NW on FS 293. SEASON: 6/1-10/15; 14-day lmt. FACILITIES: 5 sites (no tr); no drk wtr; river, tbls, toil, cga, f. ACTIVITIES: Berrypicking; picnicking; fishing; hiking. MISC.: Elev 2100 ft; 2 acres; pets. Entrance to Glacier Park Wilderness.

LITTLEROCK

Capitol Forest Multiple Use Area (DNR). Lies 15 W of Olympia not far from the southernmost waters of Puget Sound. It encompasses slightly more than 70,000 acres of forested hills and valleys under the stewardship of the Washington State Department of National Resources. Bounded on the N by St Hwy 410, on the E by the Black River, and on the S and western edges by the Chehalis River, Capitol Fores is part of the Black Hills.

Capitol Forest MUA offers many and varied outdoor experiences ranging from hiking to trailbike riding, from camping on sparkling streams to climbing the highest peaks which reach more than 2,000 ft.

HUNTING: The Washington State Game Department estimates there are about 2300 deer in Capitol Forest with perhaps 2800 during the fawn season. Some 500 deer are taken each hunting season. Special bow and arrow hunting seasons are established for either sex deer in Capitol Peak Unit 667 by the Game Dept. Grouse and pigeons also can be hunted during season.

FISHING: Some of the beaver ponds have been stocked with fish by the State Game Department in cooperation with the DNR. Some fishing is also to be enjoyed in the creeks and streams of Capitol Forest.

CLIMATE: A temperate zone. With the Pacific Ocean only 60 mi to the W, the coastal mountains lift and cool moist air from the ocean causing fairly heavy precipitation during the Winter months. Summers are generally warm and dry as high pressures move in from the Pacific coast. High tempera-tures are rare and nights are usually cool.

ROUTES AND APPROACHES: Capitol Forest can be reached easily from I-5 at any one of several exits. Coming from Seattle and the north, take the S. Tumwater-Black Lake exit and travel west to Littlerock where signs will direct you to Capitol Forest. From the West, watch for the county road to Malone and Porter off St Hwy 410, or take St Hwy 8 at Elma to Oakville and Littlerock. From the South, turn at the Maytown exit off St Hwy 5 about 8 mi S of Olymipa. St Hwy 101 leads you through the interchange at Capitol Lake and Tumwater—again take the S Tum-water-Black Lake exit to Littlerock.

ADDITIONAL INFORMATION AND MAP: Public Affairs Office, Dept. of Natural Resources, Public Lands Bldg, Olympia, WAS 98504, or Central Area Office, P. O. Box 1004, Chehalis, WA 98532 or call toll free: 1-800-562-6010.

Hollywood (Capitol Forest MUA; DNR). 6 mi NW of Littlerock on Waddell Creek in Capitol Forest. 5 sites; drk wtr, tbls, toil, cga, off-road facilities, trails. ACTIVITIES: Hiking; picnicking; fishing.

Margaret McKenny (Capitol Forest MUA; DNR). 3 mi NW of Littlerock along Wad-dell Creek Road in Capitol Forest. 11 sites; tbls, toil, cga, horse facilities, drk wtr, trails, ATV trails; facilities to accomodate handicapped. ACTIVI-TIES: Horseback riding; picnicking; fishing.

Sherman Valley "Y" (Capitol Forest MUA, DNR). 9 mi W of Littlerock along Cedar Creek in Capitol Forest. 11 sites; drk wtr, cga, toil, trails. ACTIVITIES: Hik-ing; picnicking; fishing.

LONGVIEW

County Line Park. 12-3/5 mi W of Long-view on St Hwy 4 to Cowlitz/Wahkiakum county line. SEASON: All year. FACILI-TIES: 24 sites; FLUSH toil, tbl, cga. ACTIVITIES: Picnicking; fishing (salmon). MISC.: On Columbia River; sandy beach. Park on paved parking area.

See page 7 for KEY TO ABBREVIATIONS.

LOOMIS

Okanogan Multiple Use Area (DNR). Most of it lies in the more mountainous portion of Okanogan County in north central Washington State. Encompassing 177,000 acres, the Okanogan MUA is composed of 2 acres--the Loomis state land ownership block in the northern portion and the Loup Loup block in the southern --separated by about 2 miles. Conconully State Park on Conconully Lake is located in that space in between.

Bounded on the W by the Okanogan NF and the Pasayten Wilderness Area, by Canada which forms the northern border, with various state, federal and private lands which lie to the E.

Today's modern US Hwy 97 follows the old Caribou Trail along the length of the Okanogan River--a north/south trail used since ancient times by early day Indians, fur trappers, gold miners and settlers. Good county and state roads afford excellent access to this rather remote part of Washington.

ROUTES AND APPROACHES: US Hwy 97 from Canada S, or N from Wenatchee. A number of cross state routes include St Hwy 30 from Republic, Colville and Spokane; St Hwy 17 from Grand Coulee via the upper end of the Big Bend area and Bridgeport to Brewster, where you connect with US 97; and the new North Cross State Hwy 20 which brings you from northern Puget Sound during the summer months. This pass is closed during the Winter months due to avalanche danger. Sherman Pass, E of Republic on St Hwy 30 is a year-round pass although it is the highest such hwy pass in the state at 5,575 feet in elevation.

CLIMATE: Temperatures can decrease 3 degrees with each 1,000 ft of elev gain. At the base elev of 1,000 ft, summer daytime highs reach the upper 80's, cooling at night to the 50's. Average Winter daytime tempatures range from the freezing level with night time readings some 10 degrees colder. Extreme temperatures in mid-Summer can range over 100 degrees in the valleys and below zero during mid-winter. Snow begins to accumulate on the higher ridges in November and remains until the following June. Even in the lowest valleys up to 24" of snow remains on the ground from mid-December to February.

HORSEBACK RIDING AND HIKING TRAILS: There are facilities for horses at Cold Springs Camp.

HUNTING: Very popular mule deer hunting area. Major deer migration routes to and from the Sinlahekin Valley Winter range mean great numbers of deer. During the general hunting season in October and November there is a high demand for recreational facilities. (Non-hunters, take note.)

FISHING: Chopaka Lake features catch and release fly fishing with barbless hook only for Atlantic salmon. It attracts serious, experienced fishermen from all over the Pacific NW. Leader Lake has trout fishing and is periodically restocked by the Washington State Game Department. Conconully Lake, Rock Lake and Leader Lake offer good fishing.

ALL TERRAIN VEHICLES: Roads in this MUA are open to ATV use unless posted closed. All vehicles must stay on established routes and cross-country travel is prohibited.

SNOWMOBILING: Snowmobiles may use all roads and trails unless posted closed. The DNR now maintains 20 mi of snowmobile trails and marks an additional 20 miles in the northern block of the MUA out of Loomis on the Toat's Coulee Road.

ADDITIONAL INFORMATION AND MAPS: Public Affairs Office, Dept. of Natural Resources, Public Lands Bldg., Olympia WA 98504; or Northeast Area Office, Box 190, Colville, WA 99114; or call toll free: 1-800-562-6010.

Chopaka Lake (Okanogan MUA; DNR). 5 mi NW of Loomis on bank of Chopaka Lake. FACILITIES: 15 sites; drk wtr. accommodations for handicapped, cga, toil. ACTIVITIES: Fishing; boating (hand boat launch).

Cold Springs (Okanogan MUA; DNR). 14 mi NW of Loomis. FACILITIES: 12 sites; no drk wtr; toil, cga.

North Fork Nine Mile (Okanogan MUA). 8 mi NW of Loomis along Toats-Coulee Creek. FACILITIES: 13 sites; drk wtr; accommodations for handicapped; cga, toil. ACTIVITIES: Fishing; picnicking.

Toats Junction (Okanogan MUA; DNR). 9 mi W of Loomis off Toats-Coulee Creek. FACILITIES: 9 sites; no drk wtr; game racks, toil, trails, cga, tbls, picnic area. ACTIVITIES: Hiking; picnicking.

Daisy (Okanogan NF). 2-1/10 mi N of Loomis on Co Hwy 9425; 1 mi NW on Co Hwy 390; 14-3/10 mi W on FS 390. SEASON: 7/1-9/30. FACILITIES: 2 sites (tr -16); no drk wtr; stream, tbls, toil, cga, f. ACTIVITIES: Picnicking; fishing (2 mi). MISC.: Elev 4800 ft; 1 acre; pets.

Fourteen Mile (Okanogan NF). 2-1/10 mi NW of Loomis on Co Hwy 9425; 1 mi SW on Co Hwy 390; 7-1/10 mi NW on FS 390; 4-3/5 mi NW on Co Hwy T1100. SEASON: 7/1-10/15, no time lmt. FACILITIES: 8 sites (tr -16); tbls, toil, cga, f, no drk wtr; stream. ACTIVITIES: Hiking; picnicking; fishing. Horseback riding

(1 mi). MISC.: Elev 4700 ft; 2 acres; pets. Scenic.

Iron Gate (Okanogan NF). 2-1/10 mi NW of Loomis on Co Hwy 9425; 1 mi SW on Co Hwy 390; 14 mi NW on FS 390; 6 mi NW on FS 3938. SEASON: 7/1-9/30. FACILITIES: 3 sites (no tr); no drk wtr; tbls, toil, cga; nature trails (1 mi). ACTIVITIES: Hiking; picnicking. MISC.: Elev 6200 ft; 1 acre; pets. Historical.

Long Swamp (Okanogan NF). 2-1/0 mi N of Loomis on Co Hwy 9425; 1 mi N on Co Hwy 390; 20-1/2 mi W on FS 390. SEASON: 7/1-9/30. FACILITIES: 2 sites (tr -16); no drk wtr; stream, tbls, toil, cga. ACTIVITIES: Picnicking; fishing (5 mi). MISC.: Elev 5500 ft; 1 acre; pets.

MARBLEMOUNT

* Big Beaver (North Cascade NP). 22 mi NE of Marblemount on St Hwy 20; 10 mi by TRAIL AND BOAT. SEASON: 6/1-11/1; 14-day lmt. FACILITIES: 7 tent sites; tbls, toil, cga. ACTIVITIES: Picnicking; fishing; swimming; boating,d.

* Cat Island (North Cascades NP). 22 mi NE of Marblemount on St Hwy 20; 17 mi N by TRAIL & BOAT. SEASON: 6/1-11/1; 14-day lmt. FACILITIES: 7 tent sites; tbls, toil, cga. ACTIVITIES: Picnicking; fishing; swimming; boating, d.

Goodell Creek (see under Newhalen). 14 mi E of Marblemount on St Hwy 20.

* Green Point (North Cascade NP). 22 mi NE of Marblemount on St Hwy 20; 8 mi N, BY BOAT AND TRAIL. SEASON: 6/1-11/1; 14-day lmt. FACILITIES: 10 tent sites. ACTIVITIES: Swimming; fishing; boating, d.

* Lightning Creek (North Cascade NP). 22 mi NE of Marblemount on St Hwy 20; 17 mi N, BY BOAT AND TRAILS. SEASON: 6/1-11/1; 14-day lmt. FACILITIES: 6 tent sites; tbls, toil, cga. f. ACTIVITIES: Swimming; boating; picnicking; fishing. MISC.: 2 acres.

* Little Beaver (North Cascades NP). 22 mi NE of Marblemount on St Hwy 20; 20 mi N, BY BOAT AND TRAIL. SEASON: 6/1-11/1; 14-day lmt. FACILITIES: 7 tent sites; tbls, toil cga. ACTIVITIES: Swimming; picnicking; boating,d; fishing. MISC.: 1 acre.

Marble Creek (Mt. Baker-Snoqualmie NF). 8 mi E of Marblemount on Co Hwy 3528. SEASON: 4/15-11/15; 14-day lmt. FACILITIES: 27 sites (tr -16); tbls, toil, cga, f, no drk wtr; river. ACTIVITIES: Mountain climbing; hunting; hiking; picnicking; fishing. MISC.: Elev 900 ft; 40 acres; pets. Geological. Scenic. [Adjacent to Cascade River].

6/10 mi of access road is narrow and winding. Co-sponsored by Seattle City Light.

Mineral Park (Mt. Baker-Snoqualmie NF; co-sponsored by Seattle City Light). 15 Mi E of Marblemount on Co Hwy 3528 (Cascade River Road); campground is on the right. [1/4 mi further on the right across the bridge is a smaller section of the same campground.] SEASONS: 4/15-11/15; 14-day lmt. FACILITIES: 19 sites (tr -16); tbls, toil, cga, f, no drk wtr. ACTIVITIES: Picnicking; hunting; hiking; mountain climbing; fishing. MISC.: Elev 1400 ft; 7 acres; pets; scenic. Narrow and winding road.

MAYFIELD

Winston Creek (Department of Natural Resources). 2 mi E of Mayfield on St Hwy 12; 5 mi S on Winston Creek Rd [portions of rd are rough]. SEASON: All year; 14-day lmt. FACILITIES: 10 sites (tr -16); no drk wtr; tbls, toil, cga, creek. ACTIVITIES: Hiking; picnicking. MISC.: On Winston Creek. Additional information and map: Public Affairs Office, DNR, Public Lands Bldg, Olympia, WA 98504, or call toll free (in Washington) 1-800-562-6010.

McKENNA

Bald Hill Lake Park. 16 mi SE of McKenna on Bald Hill Rd.

METALINE FALLS

Crescent Lake (Colville NF). 11 mi N of Metaline Falls on St Hwy 31. SEASON: 6/1-9/15; 14-day lmt. FACILITIES: 13 sites (tr -32); tbls, toil, cga, well drk wtr. ACTIVITIES: Hiking; fishing; picnicking; boating,d. MISC.: Elev 2600 ft; 4 acres; pets. Crescent Lake.

Millpond (Colville NF). 1-1/2 mi E on St Hwy 31; 3-1/2 mi E on Co Hwy 302; on Sullivan Lake. SEASON: 5/15-10/1; 14-day lmt. FACILITIES: 10 sites (tr -22); tbls, toil, cga, well drk wtr. Showers/ice/laundry/store/gas/food (5 mi). ACTIVITIES: Hunting; hiking; picnicking; fishing. Boating,d (1 mi). Swimming (1 mi). MISC.: Elev 2400 ft; 3 acres; pets. Stream.

Sullivan Road # 1 (Colville NF). 1-1/2 mi E of Metaline Falls on St Hwy 31; 5-1/2 mi E on Co Hwy 302. SEASON: 6/1-9/15; 14-day lmt. FACILITIES: 2 sites (tr -22); tbls, toil, cga, f, stream. ACTIVITIES: Fishing; picnicking. MISC.: Elev 2700 ft; pets.

Sullivan Road # 2 (Colville NF). 1-1/2 mi E of Metaline Falls on St Hwy 31; 6-4/5 mi E on Co Hwy 302. SEASON: 6/1-9/15; 14-day lmt. FACILITIES: 2 sites (tr -22); tbls, toil, cga. ACTIVITIES:

Picnicking; fishing. MISC.: Elev 2700 ft; pets; stream.

MONTESANO

*Chetwoot (Olympic NF). 12 mi N of Montesano on Co Hwy 58; 21 mi N on FS 220; 2-1/2 mi N on FS 234; 1/2 mi E on TRAIL 878. [HIKE IN OR FLOAT IN ONLY.] SEASON: 5/15-11/10; 14-day lmt. FACILITIES: 8 tent sites; no drk wtr; lake, tbls, toil, cga, nature trails, visitor center. ACTIVITIES: Hiking; waterskiing; boating; picnicking; fishing; swimming. MISC.: Elev 1000 ft; pets.

*Tenas (Olympic NF). 12 mi N on Co Hwy 58; 20 mi N on FS 220; 2 mi N on FS 22022; 1/2 mi W on TRAIL 878. SEASON: 5/15-10/30; 14-day lmt. FACILITIES: 8 tent sites; toil, no drk wtr. ACTIVITIES: Picnicking; hiking; fishing; swimming; waterskiing; boating,l. MISC.: Elev 800 ft; 2 acres; lake; visitor center; pets. Hike-in or float-in only.

Wynoochee Falls (Olympic NF). 18-1/2 mi N of Montesano on Co Hwy 141; 26-7/10 mi N on FS 220; 10 mi NE on FS 2312. [Heavy construction and logging traffic enroute to site.] SEASON: 5/15-11/10: 14-day lmt. FACILITIES: 18 sites (no tr); well drk wtr, tbls, toil, cga, f. ACTIVITIES: Picnicking; swimming; fishing. Horseback riding (1 mi). MISC.: Elev 1000 ft; pets.

MORTON

Alder Camp (Department of Natural Resources). 13-4/5 mi N of Morton on St Hwy 7; 4 mi W on Pleasant Valley Rd [campground is on right]; by Alder Lake. SEASON: All year; 14-day lmt. FACILITIES: 11 sites (tr -22); well drk wtr, tbls, toil, cga. ACTIVITIES: Hiking; hunting; swimming; picnicking; fishing; boating,l. MISC.: Near Mt. Rainier NP. Watch for logging trucks.

Alder Lake Public Recreation Access. 15-9/10 mi N of Morton on St Hwy 7; 1-7/10 mi W on St Hwy 706. (Campground on left at Public Rec. Access sign.) SEASON: All year; 14-day lmt. FACILITIES: 10 sites (tr -16); tbls, toil, cga. ACTIVITIES: Swimming; boating,l; fishing; picnicking; water skiing. MISC.: On Alder Lake; near Mt Rainier NP. Scenic.

Indian Hole. 4-1/5 mi NW of Morton on St Hwy 508 [on Tilton River, near Mt. Ranier NP]. SEASON: 6/1-9/15. FACILITIES: 20 sites (tr -30); tbls, toil, cga, river. ACTIVITIES: Hiking; swimming; picnicking; fishing.

MOSSYROCK

Mossyrock Park (Tacoma City Light). 3 mi E of Mossyrock on Viewpoint Rd [campground in on right]; on Davison Riffe Lake (located halfway between Tacoma and Portland, 17 mi E of I-5 and US 12). SEASON: All year; 14-day lmt. FACILITIES: 22 sites; tbls. ACTIVITIES: Boating,l; swimming; fishing; picnicking.

MOUNT VERNON

Koma Kulshan Campground (Puget Sound P & L Co.). Take I-5 N from Mount Vernon to Burlington Exit; 26 mi E on St Hwy 20 to the Baker Lake Road intersection; turn left and proceed N for 16 mi to sign, "Baker Lake Recreation Area"; turn right and proceed for 1 mi to campground on left. [Located on Baker Lake in Whatcom County, WA] FACILITIES: 40 sites; water and sewer hookups; cga, tbls; FLUSH toil; Visitor Information Center.

Lion's Park (City Park). In the town of Mt. Vernon. If traveling N on I-5 take the City Center exit, #226; turn left; cross RR tracks; on Third, turn right and continue until reaching to the other side of the overpass; turn right on Freeway Drive, campground is on the left. If traveling S on I-5, take E. College Way exit, #227; turn right at traffic light and travel 1/2 block; left on Freeway Drive for 4/5 mi to campground on right. FACILITIES: Undesignated sites; enough room for 15 RVs; wtr, toil, tbls, community kitchens. ACTIVITIES: Fishing (steelhead); picnicking. MISC.: Campground overlooks Skagit River. Located in busy commercial area.

Naches

American Forks (Wenatchee NF). 4-3/10 mi W of Naches on St Hwy 12; 27-4/5 mi NW on St Hwy 410; 1/5 mi SW on FS 174. SEASON: 6/15-9/15; 14-day lmt. FACILITIES: 13 sites (tr -22); well drk wtr, tbls, toil, cga, f. ACTIVITIES: Picnicking; fishing. Horseback riding 91 mi). MISC.: Elev 2800 ft; 15 acres; pets.

Bumping Crossing (Wenatchee NF). 4-3/10 mi W of Naches on St Hwy 12; 27-4/5 mi NW on St Hwy 410. SEASON: 5/15-11/15 14-day lmt. FACILITIES: 7 sites (tr -16); tbls, toil, cga, f, no drk wtr. Store/ gas/food/ice (1 mi). ACTIVITIES: Picnicking; fishing; sailing. Swimming (1 mi). Boating (d, 1 mi; l, 2mi; r, 3 mi). MISC.: Elev 3200 ft; 3 acres; pets.

Bumping Dam (Wenatchee NF). 4-3/10 mi W of Naches on St Hwy 12; 27-4/5 mi

---

NW on St Hwy 410; 10-4/5 mi SW on FS 174; 3/5 mi N on FS 1602. SEASON: 5/15-9/15; 14-day lmt. FACILITIES: 31 sites (tr -16); tbls, toil, cga, f, no drk wtr; river. Store (1 mi). Ice/gas (3 mi). ACTIVITIES: Picnicking; fishing. Horseback riding (2 mi). Boating,rld (1 mi). MISC.: Elev 3400 ft; 8 acres; pets.

Cedar Springs (Wenatchee NF). 4-3/10 mi W of Naches on St Hwy 12; 27-4/5 mi NW on St Hwy 410; 1/2 mi SW on FS 174. SEASON: 6/15-11/15; 14-day lmt. FACILITIES: 18 sites (tr -16); tbls, toil, cga, f, no drk wtr. ACTIVITIES: Picnicking; fishing. Horseback riding (1 mi). MISC.: Elev. 2800 ft; 5 acres; pets. River.

Clear Lake (Wenatchee NF). 32-2/5 mi W of Naches on St Hwy 12; 2/5 mi S on Fs 143; 7/10 mi S on FS 1312. SEASON: 5/1-10/31; 14-day lmt. FACILITIES: 72 sites (tr -22); tbls, toil, cga, f, no drk wtr. Store/gas (3 mi). ACTIVITIES: Picnicking; fishing. Horseback riding (2 mi). Boating (1, 1 mi; r, 3 mi). MISC.: Elev 3100 ft; 33 acres; pets.

Clear Lake Boat Landing (Wenatchee NF). 32-2/5 mi W of Naches on St Hwy 12; 2/5 mi S on FS 143; 1-2/5 mi S on FS 1312. SEASON: 5/1-10/31; 1-day lmt. FACILITIES:10 sites (no tr); no drk wtr; lake, tbls, toil, cga. ACTIVITIES: Fishing; picnicking; boating,ld (r, 3 mi). Horseback riding (2 mi). MISC.: Elev 3100 ft; 2 acres; pets.

Clover Springs (Wenatchee NF). 16 mi NW of Naches on St Hwy 410; 1-1/5 mi S on Co Hwy 1555; 18-1/2 mi NW on FS 161. SEASON: 7/15-10/15; 14-day lmt. FACILITIES: 8 sites (tr -16); cga, f. MISC.: Elev 6300 ft; pets.

Crane Park (Wenatchee NF). 23 mi W of Naches on St Hwy 12; 2-9/10 mi S on FS 143; 1 mi W on FS 1382. SEASON: 4/15-10/31; 14-day lmt. FACILITIES: 6 sites (no tr); no drk wtr; lake, tbls, toil, cga, f. Store/gas (5 mi). ACTIVITIES: Picnicking; fishing; swimming; water skiing. Boating (1, 1 mi). Horseback riding (1 mi). MISC.: Elev 3000 ft; 3 acres; pets.

Crow Creek (Wenatchee NF). 4-3/10 mi W of Naches on St Hwy 12; 24-1/2 mi NW on St Hwy 410; 2-7/10 mi NW on FS 197; 2/5 mi W on FS 182. SEASON: 6/15-11/15; 14-day lmt. FACILITIES: 16 sites (tr -16); no drk wtr; river, tbls, toil, cga, f. ACTIVITIES: Fishing; picnicking, horseback riding (1 mi). MISC.: Elev 2900 ft; 8 acres; pets.

Deep Creek (Wenatchee NF). 4-3/10 mi W of Naches on St Hwy 12; 27-4/5 mi NW on St Hwy 410; 13-3/10 mi SW on FS 174; 7 mi SW on FS 162. SEASON:

7/15-10/15; 14-day lmt. FACILITIES: 6 sites (tr -16); no drk wtr; stream, tbls, toil, cga, f. ACTIVITIES: Picnicking; hiking; fishing (1 mi); horseback riding (1 mi). MISC.: Elev 4300 ft; 5 acres; pets. Scenic. Trailhead into Cougar Lake area.

East Point (Wenatchee NF). 23 mi W of Naches on St Hwy 12; 2-9/10 mi S on FS 143; 1-1/2 mi W on FS 1382. SEASON: 4/15-10/31; 14-day lmt. FACILITIES: 6 sites (no tr); no drk wtr; lake, tbls, toil, cga, f. ACTIVITIES: Boating; picnicking; fishing; swimming; horseback riding (2 mi); waterskiing. MISC.: Elev 3000, 3 acres; pets.

Granite Lake (Wenatchee NF). 4-3/10 mi W of Naches on St Hwy 12; 27-4/5 mi NW on St Hwy 410; 13-9/10 mi SW on FS 174;3-7/10 mi SW on FS 163.SEAS: 7/15-10/15; 14-day lmt. FACILITIES: 8 sites (tr -16); tbls, toil, cga, f, no drk wtr. ACTIVITIES: Boating,d; picnicking; swimming; fishing. MISC.: Elev 5000 ft; 4 acres; pets. Scenic area.

Grey Creek (Wenatchee NF). 23 mi W of Naches on St Hwy 12; 4-1/2 mi S on FS 143; 5-7/10 mi SW on FS 133. SEASON: 6/1-10/31; 14-day lmt. FACILITIES: 5 sites (tr -16); tbls, toil, cga, f, no drk wtr. ACTIVITIES: Picnicking; fishing. Horseback riding (1 mi). MISC.: Elev 4000 ft; 3 acres; pets.

Halfway Flat (Wenatchee NF). 4-3/10 mi W of Naches on St Hwy 12; 21 mi NW on St Hwy 410; 2-9/10 mi NW on FS 175. SEASON: 6/15-11/15; 14-day lmt. FACILITIES: 12 sites (tr -16); tbls, toil, cga, f, no drk wtr. Ice/store/gas/food (4 mi). ACTIVITIES: Picnicking; fishing. Horseback riding (91 mi). MISC.: Elev 2500 ft; 5 acres; pets.

Hanging Tree (Boise Cascade Corp.). 4 mi NW of Naches on St Hwy 12; 8 mi N on St Hwy 410; 1-2/5 mi left on dirt rd at Eagle Rock Store; take left branch of fork & go 1-1/0 mi; right on FS 150, then right again on narrow dirt rd to campground. SEASON: All year; 14-day lmt. FACILITIES: 10 tent sites; drk wtr, tbls, toil, cga. ACTIVITIES: Fishing; picnicking. MISC.: 3 acres; pets. On Rattlesnake Creek. No trailers.

Little Naches (Wenatchee NF). 4-3/10 mi W of Naches on St Hwy 12; 24-3/10 mi NW on St Hwy 410; 1/10 mi NW on FS 197. SEASON: 5/15-11/15; 14-day lmt. FACILITIES: 17 sites (tr -16); no drk wtr; tbls, toil, cga, f. Ice/store/food (4 mi). ACTIVITIES: Picnicking; fishing. Horseback riding (1 mi). MISC.: Elev 2500 ft; 4 acres; pets. 24 mi to Mt. Ranier NP.

Lonesome Cove (Wenatchee NF). 23 mi W of Naches on St Hwy 12; 2-9/10 mi S on FS 143; 2 mi SW on FS 1382.

SEASON: 4/15-10/31; 14-day lmt. FACILI-TIES: 5 sites (no tr); no drk wtr; lake, tbls, toil, cga, f. ACTIVITIES: Water-skiing; picnicking; fishing. MISC.: Elev 3000 ft; 3 acres; pets.

Longmire Meadow (Wenatchee NF). 4-3/10 mi W of Naches on St Hwy 12; 24-3/10 mi NW on St Hwy 410; 4-1/0 mi NW on FS 197. SEASON: 5/15-11/15; 14-day lmt. FACILITIES: 13 sites (tr -16); no drk wtr; tbls, toil, cga, f. ACTIVITIES: Picnicking; fishing. Horseback riding (1 mi). MISC.: Elev 2800 ft; 7 acres; pets. Historic. River.

Lost Lake (Wenatchee NF). 23 mi W of Naches on St Hwy 12; 1/5 mi S on FS 143; 4-3/5 mi SE on FS 1402. SEASON: 6/1-10/31; 14-day lmt. FACILITIES: 5 sites (no tr); no drk wtr; tbls, toil, cga, f. ACTIVITIES: Swimming; fishing; picnicking; boating,d. Horseback riding (1 mi). MISC.: Elev 3500 ft; 3 acres;. pets. Lake.

Naches River. 4 mi NW of Naches on St Hwy 12; 4 mi N on St Hwy 410 [camp ground on left] on Naches River. SEA-SON: All year; 14-day lmt. FACILITIES: 30 sites (tr -32); tbls, toil, cga. ACT-IVITIES: Hunting (elk); picnicking; fishing.

Nile Creek (Wenatchee NF). 16 mi NW of Naches on St Hwy 410; 1-1/5 mi S on Co Hwy 1555; 3-/15 mi NW on FS 161. SEASON: 6/15-11/15; 14-day lmt. FACIL-ITIES: 2 sites (tr -16); toil, cga, f. ACTIVITIES: Fishing; picnicking. MISC.: Elev 2500 ft; pets.

Pine Needle (Wenatchee NF). 4-3/10 mi W of Naches on St Hwy 12; 30-1/10 mi NW on St Hwy 410. SEASON: 6/15-9/15; 14-day lmt. FACILITIES: 6 tent sites (no tr); no drk wtr; tbls, toil, cga, f. ACTIVITIES: Picnicking; fishing. Horseback riding (1 mi). MISC.: Elev 3000 ft; 2 acres; pets. River.

Pleasant Valley (Wenatchee NF). 4-3/10 mi W of Naches on St Hwy 12;' 36-1/10 mi NW on St Hwy 410. SEASON: 7/15-11/15; 14-day lmt. FACILITIES: 14 sites (tr -22); tbls, toil, cga, f, no drk wtr. ACTIVITIES: Picnicking; fishing. Horseback riding (1 mi). MISC.: Elev ' 3300 ft; 23 acres; pets. River.

Section 3 Lake (Wenatchee NF). 32-2/5 mi W of Naches on St Hwy 12; 5-1/2 mi S on FS 143; 5-7/10 mi S on FS 1311 4 mi SW on FS 1314. SEASON: 7/1-10/31; 14-day lmt. FACILITIES: 3 sites (no tr); no drk wtr; tbls, toil, cga, f. ACTIVITIES: Horseback riding (1 mi); picnicking; fishing. MISC.: Elev 6000 ft; 3 acres; pets.

Soda Springs (Wenatchee NF). 4-3/10 mi W of Naches on St Hwy 12; 27-4/5 mi NW on St Hwy 410; 4-4/5 mi SW on

FS 174. SEASON: 6/15-11/15; 14-day lmt. FACILITIES: 26 sites (tr -16); well drk wtr, tbls, toil, cga, f. Ice/store/gas/food (4 mi). ACT: Picnicking; fishing. Horseback riding (1 mi). MISC.: Elev 3100 ft; 15 acres; pets. Geological. Natural mineral springs. River.

South Fork (Wenatchee NF). 23 mi W of Naches on St Hwy 12; 4 mi S on FS 143; 1/2 mi S on FS 1326. SEASON: 4/15-10/31; 14-day lmt. FACILITIES: 12 sites (tr -16); tbls, toil, cga, f, no drk wtr. ACTIVITIES: Picnicking; fishing; water skiing; horseback riding. Boating,d (1, 3 mi). MISC.: Elev 3000 ft; 7 acres; pets. River.

South Fork Bay (Wenatchee NF). 23 mi W of Naches on St Hwy 12; 4 mi S on FS 143; 1/10 mi S on FS 1326. SEASON: 4/15-10/31; 14-day lmt. FACILITIES: 5 sites (tr -16); tbls, toil, cga, f, no drk wtr. ACTIVITIES: Waterskiing; fish-ing; picnicking; horseback riding. Boat-ing,d (1, 3 mi). MISC.: Elev 2900 ft; 3 acres; pets. River.

Benton Creek Campsite 15 mi W of Natches on US 410 to Bald Mountain Rd; 3 mi NE to camp. FACILITIES: Spring wtr, tbls, cga. ACTIVITIES: Picnicking.

NEW HALEM

Goodell Creek (Ross Lake NRA, N Cas-cades NP; co-sponsored by Seattle City Light). 1/2 mi SW of New Halem on St Hwy 20. SEASON: 10/1-3/31, FREE (rest of yr, $1). No NP entrance fee. FACILI-TIES: 26 sites; tbls, toil, cga, piped drk wtr. ACTIVITIES: Boating; hiking; hunting; picnicking; fishing. MISC.: Elev 500 ft; Diablo Lake. Free Season open until rds closed by snow; wtr shut-off.

NEWPORT

Albeni Cove (COE; Albeni Falls Project). Albeni Falls Dam is located in Idaho, near the Washington State border. 3 mi E of Newport, WA, S of the dam, via US Hwys 2 and 195. SEASON: 5/25-9/16; 14-day lmt. FACILITIES: 13 sites (tr -20); FLUSH toil, change house, drk wtr, cga,f. ACTIVITIES: Swimming (floating dive platform); boating,ld; waterskiing; picnicking; fishing. MISC.: Elev 2080 ft; forested area; pets on leash. For Maps and Additional Information: Con-tact Dept. of the Army; Seattle Dist. COE; 1519 Alaskan Way S; PO Box C-3755; Seattle, WA 98124; or Box 310, Newport, WA 99156 [208/437-3133].

NORTH BEND

Denny Creek (Mt. Baker-Snoqualmie NF). 17 mi SE of North Bend on I-90; 2-1/5 mi NE on FS 2219 [near the summit of Snoqualmi Pass]. SEASON: 5/1-10/15; 10-day lmt. FACILITIES: 31 sites (tr

See page 7 for KEY TO ABBREVIATIONS.

-22); well drk wtr, tbls, toil, cga, f. Gas/food (3 mi). ACTIVITIES: Hiking; picnicking; fishing; hunting. Horseback riding (1 mi). MISC.: Elev 2200 ft; 15 acres; pets. Scenic. Nature trails.

Dingford Jct (Wenatchee NF). 3-9/10 mi SE of North Bend on I-90; 14-4/5 mi NE on FS 2445; 6-1/10 mi SE on FS 241. SEASON: 5/15-11/30; 14-day lmt. FACIL-ITIES: 3 sites. (no tr); cga, f, toil. ACTIVITIES: Fishing; picnicking. MISC.: Elev 1200 ft; pets.

Taylor River (Mt. Baker-Snoqualmie NF) 3-9/10 mi SE of North Bend on I-90; 14-4/5 mi NE on FS 2445; 1-3/10 mi SE on FS 241; 1/2 mi W on FS 2444. SEA-SON: 5/15-10/15; 14-day lmt. FACILI-TIES: 20 sites (no tr); no drk wtr; stream, tbls, toil, cga, f. ACTIVITIES: Mountain climbing; picnicking; fishing. MISC.: Elev 1000 ft; 10 acres; pets. Scenic.

OAK HARBOR

Partridge Beach Campground (Dept. of Natural Resources). 6 mi SW of Oak Harbor on St Hwy 20; when you reach a subtle "Y" in the road, bear W-right-and go 9/10 mi W on Libby Road to "Partridge Beach" sign; 4 mi left on Valley Dr; turn left at "Y" and travel 1-1/10 mi to campground. FACILITIES: 12 sites (tr -16); 6 drive-in sites, 6 walk-in sites. No drk wtr, tbls, toil, cga. ACTIVITIES: Hiking; beachcombing; picnicking. MISC.: 14-day lmt.

OAKVILLE

North Creek (Capitol Forest MUA; DNR). 6 mi NE on Cedar Crk Rd in Capitol Forest. FACILITIES: 5 sites; drk wtr, tbls, toil, cga, trails. ACTIVITIES: Hiking; pic-nicking; fishing. ADDITIONAL INFORM-ATION: See "Littlerock" entry for over-view information on Capitol Forest MUA. Further info and a map can be obtained from Public Affairs Office, Dept. of Natural Resources, Public Lands Bldg., Olympia, WA 98504, or Central Area Office, P.O. Box 1004, Chehalis, WA 98532, or call toll free 1-800-562-6010.

OKANOGAN

Leader Lake (Okanogan Multiple Use Area; DNR). 9 mi W of Okanogan off Loup-Loup Hwy on bank of Leader Lake. FACILI-TIES: 8 sites; no drk wtr, river, tbls, toil, cga, hand boat launch. ACTIVI-TIES: Boating; picnicking; fishing. ADDITIONAL INFO/MAPS: Public Affairs Office, Dept. of Natural Resources, Pub-lic Lands Bldg., Olympia, WA 98504; or NE Area Office, Box 190, Colville, WA 99114. Or call toll free: 1-800-562-6010.

Rock Creek (Okanogan Multiple Use Area; DNR). 11 mi NW of Okanogan on Loup Creek. FACILITIES: 9 sites; drk wtr, trails, toil, cga. ADDITIONAL INFO/ MAPS: Public Affairs Office, Dept. of Natural Resources, Public Lands Bldg., Olympia, WA 98504, or NE Area Office, Box 190, Colville, WA 99114. Or call toll free: 1-800-562-6010.

Rock Lakes (Okanogan MUA; DNR). 18 mi NW of Okanogan on Rock Lakes near Buck Mountain. FACILITIES: 6 sites; no drk wtr, trail, toil, cga; accomodations for handicapped. ACTIVITIES: Hiking; picnicking; fishing. ADDITIOANL INFO/ MAP: Public Affairs Office, Dept. of Nat-ural Resources, Public Lands Bldg., Olympia , WA 98504; or NE Area Office, Box 190, Colville, WA 99114. Or call toll free 1-800-562-6010.

OLYMPIA

Swinging Bridge Campground. Take St Hwy 101 exit (Aberdeen) off I-5 at Olympia, and travel 6 mi, then W on St Hwy 12 until the Brady exit, take the exit and travel N 3-1/3 mi following signs to Swinger Bridge and Schafer Park; then turn W at junction for 5-4/5 into the campground. [Blacktop rd which narrows near campground entrance]. SEASON: All year; 5-day lmt. FACILI-TIES: 30 sites; tbls, toil, cga, play-ground, shelter with cook stove. ACTIV-ITIES: Fishing (steelhead); picnicking. MISC.: Satsop River.

ORIENT

Pierre Lake (Colville NF). 3-4/5 mi E on Co Hwy 1510L; 3-1/5 mi N on Co Hwy 1500. SEASON: 5/1-10/15; 14-day lmt. FACILITIES: 15 sites (tr -32); tbls, toil, cga, f, well drk wtr. Store/gas/ice/food (1 mi). ACTIVI-TIES: Picnicking; fishing; swimming; waterskiing; boating,l (r, 1 mi). MISC.: Elev 2000 ft;8 acres;lake;pets.

Summit Lake (Colville NF). 3-4/5 mi E of Orient on Co Hwy 1510; 5 mi N on Co Hwy 1500; 3 mi N on FS 1206. SEA-SON: 6/1-10/15; 14-day lmt. FACILITIES: 5 sites (no tr); well drk wtr;lake, tbls, toil, cga, f. ACTIVITIES: Boating,ld; picnicking; fishing. MISC.: Elev 3600 ft; 2 acres; pets.

OZETTE

* Erickson's Bay (Olympia NP). 1/2 mi S of Ozette; acess BY BOAT only. SEA-SON: All year; 14-day lmt. FACILI-TIES: 15 tent sites; tbls.

PACKWOOD

Dog Lake (Wenatchee NF). 22-1/5 mi NE of Packwood on St Hwy 12. SEASON: 6/1-10/31; 14-day lmt. FACILITIES: 9 sites (tr -16); tbls, toil, cga, f, no drk wtr. Laundry/store/gas/food (3

See page 7 for KEY TO ABBREVIATIONS.

mi). **ACTIVITIES:** Mountain climbing; boating,ld; hunting; hiking; picnicking; rockhounding; fishing. Horseback riding (1 mi). **MISC.:** Elev 4300 ft; 3 acres; pets. Lake. Near Goat Rocks Wilderness and Mt. Rainier. No trash pickup (pack litter out).

HATCHERY R.V. CAMP (Gifford Pinchot NF). 7-1/10 mi NE of Packwood on US 12; 4/5 mi W on FS 1407. SEASON: 5/25-9/5; 14-day lmt. FACILITIES: 30 sites (tr -22); tbls, toil, cga, f, no drk wtr. Store/gas/ice/laundry (3 mi). ACTIVITIES: Fishing; picnicking. MISC.: Elev 1400 ft; 14 acres; pets. Mt. Rainier NP (4 mi N). River.

Ohanapecosh (Mt. Ranier NP). 7-1/2 mi NE of Packwood on US 12; 3-1/2 mi N on St Hwy 123. (SE corner of Park.) SEASON: 11/1-MD, FREE (rest of yr, $5 + NP entrance fee); 14-day lmt. FACILITIES: 232 sites (tr -30); tbls, dump, flush toil, cga, f, amphitheater. ACTIVITIES: Hiking; fishing (fly fishing only; artificial flies required; no license required in Park); picnicking; hiking. MISC.: The Grove of the Patriarchs (1000-year-old forest) nearby. Ohanapecosh River. Silver Falls.

Soda Springs (Gifford Pinchot NF). 8-9/10 mi NE of Packwood on US 12; 5-1/2 mi W on FS 1400. SEASON: 6/15-9/5; 14-day lmt. FACILITIES: 8 sites (no tr); no drk wtr; stream, tbls, toil, cga, f. ACTIVITIES: Hiking; picnicking; fishing. Horseback riding (1 mi). MISC.: Elev 3200 ft; 4 acres; pets. Trailhead to Cougar Lakes. Summit Area. Geological.

Summit Creek (Gifford Pinchot NF). 8-9/10 mi NE of Packwood on US 12; 2-1/10 mi N on FS 1400. SEASON: 6/15-9/5; 14-day lmt. FACILITIES: 7 sites no tr; no drk wtr; stream, tbls, toil, cga, f. ACTIVITIES: Picnicking; fishing. Horseback riding (2 mi). MISC.: Elev 2400 ft; 2 acres; pets.

Walupt Lake Horse (Gifford Pinchot NF). 2-7/10 mi SW of Packwood on US 12; 16-2/5 mi SE on FS 1302; 3-1/2 mi E on FS 1114. SEASON: 6/15-9/5; 14-day lmt. FACILITIES: 6 sites (tr -16); tbls, toil, cga, f, no drk wtr, stream. ACTIVITIES: Boating,d (1 mi); swimming/fishing (1 mi); picnicking. MISC.: Elev 3900 ft; 2 acres; pets.

White Pass Lake (Wenatchee NF). 20-9/10 mi NE of Packwood on St Hwy 12; 3/10 mi N on FS 1310. SEASON: 6/1-10/31; 14-day lmt. FACILITIES: 16 sites (tr -16); tbls, toil, cga, f, no drk wtr. Store/laundry/gas/food (1 mi). ACTIVITIES: Swimming; picnicking; fishing; horseback riding (1 mi). Boating,ld (r, 3 mi). MISC.: Elev 4500 ft; 6 acres; pets. Lake.

PALOUSE

Palouse Lions Club Camp Area. On St Hwy 27 at S edge of town (gravel access rd). NO FEE; donation only. 20 sites (tr -30). Pets on leash.

PASCO

Fishhook Park (Ice Harbor Project-Lower Monumental). 5 mi SE of Pasco on US 395; 15 mi E on St Hwy 124; 4 mi N on Page Road [on Lake Sacajawea]. SEASON: 11/16-4/30, FREE (rest of yr, $3); 14-day lmt. FACILITIES: 41 sites (tr -45). 8 pull-thru sites , paved sites; tbls, toil, cga, FLUSH TOIL, SHOWERS, drk wtr, DUMP, playground, handicapped facilities, public phone, change house. ACTIVITIES: Waterskiing; boating,l; picnicking; fishing; swimming. (Hunting prohibited.) MISC.: Elev 450 ft; 46 acres; pets on leash. Local park address: P.O.Box 2427, Tri-Cities, WA 99302; phone 509/547-7781.

Madame Dorion (COE; McNary Project). 18 mi S of Pasco on St Hwy 12; 1/5 mi N of jct of St Hwy 12 and 730 [on Lake Wallula]. SEASON: ALL YEAR; 14-day lmt. FACILITIES: No designated sites (large enough for approx. 15 self-contained units); RV & tent sites [5 pull-thru spaces]; tbls, toil, cga, drk wtr. ACTIVITIES: Fishing; picnicking. MISC.: Elev 350 ft; 29 acres; pets on leash. NO hunting. NO horses. Gently sloping riverbank area; semi-open with sagebrush-willow community.

Windust Park (COE; Ice Harbor-Lower Monumental Project). 30 mi NE of Pasco on Pasco-Kahiotus Rd; 5-1/5 mi S and E on Burr Canyon Rd [on Lake Sacajawea]. SEASON: ALL YEAR. FACILITIES: No designated sites (room for approx. 10 self-contained units; both RV and tent sites), FLUSH toil, tbls, toil, cga, drk wtr, playground, handicapped facilities, boat/l, pool. ACTIVITIES: Swimming; boating,l; picnicking. MISC.: Elev 450 ft; 53-1/2 acres; pets on leash. Hunting prohibited. Gently sloped, semi-open, grassy park along lakeshore (fishing). 14-day lmt. Local park address: P.O.Box 2427, Tri Cities, WA 99302; phone: 509/547-7781.

PATEROS

Pateros City Center Park. Pateros is 19 mi N of Chelan on St Hwy 97. Entering Pateros from S, cross the bridge, turn right; park is beyond the Shell station, across from a grocery store. FACILITIES: No designated sites; enough paved area for 18 RVs; FLUSH TOIL, sheltered tbls with wtr and electric. ACTIVITIES: Boating,d; picnicking; hunting; fishing; waterskiing; rockhounding. MISC.: By Columbia River. No Shade.

See page 7 for KEY TO ABBREVIATIONS.

WASHINGTON

POMEROY

Alder Thicket (Umatilla NF). 9-1/0 mi S of Pomeroy on ST Hwy 128; 7-7/10 mi S on Co Hwy 107; 3-3/10 mi S on FS 40. SEASON: 6/15-10/15; 10-day lmt. FACILITIES: 6 sites (tr -16); no drk wtr; tbls, toil, cga, f, horse (1 mi). ACTIVITIES: Berrypicking; picnicking; horseback riding. MISC.: Elev 5100 ft; 2 acres; pets. 5 mi N of Clearwater guard station.

Big Springs (Umatilla NF). 14-4/5 mi SE of Pomeroy on St Hwy 128; 3-2/5 mi S on Co Hwy 191; 5-1/0 mi SW on FS 42000. SEASON: 6/15-10/15; 10-day lmt. FACILITIES: 6 sites (tr -16); tbls, toil, cga, f, piped drk wtr, horse (1 mi). ACTIVITIES: Berrypicking; picnicking; fishing; horseback riding. MISC.: Elev 5300 ft; 7 acres; pets. 4 mi NE of Clearwater Guard Station.

Cabin Saddle (Umatilla NF). 9-1/0 mi S of Pomeroy on St Hwy 128; 7-7/10 mi S on Co Hwy 107; 18-2/5 mi SE on FSN. 911. SEASON: 6/15-11/15; 10-day lmt. FACILITIES: 3 sites (no tr); toil, cga. ACTIVITIES: Picnicking. MISC.: Elev 5500 ft; pets.

Forest Boundary (Umatilla NF). 9-1/10 mi S of Pomeroy on St Hwy 128; 7-7/10 mi S on Co Hwy 107; 1/10 mi S FS 40 SEASON: 5/15-10/15; 10-day lmt. FACILITIES: 5 sites (tr -32); no drk wtr; tbls, toil, cga, f. ACTIVITIES: Berrypicking; picnicking. Horseback riding (1 mi). MISC.: Elev 4400 ft; 2 acres; pets.

Goverment Spring (Umatilla NF). 9-1/10 mi S of Pomeroy on St Hwy 128; 7-7/10 mi S on Co Hwy 107; 2 mi S on FS N911. SEASON: 6/15-10/15; 10-day lmt. FACILITIES: 2 sites (no tr); tbls, toil, cga, f. ACTIVITIES: Picnicking. MISC.: Elev 4600 ft; pets. 6 mi N of Clearwater Guard Station near Rose Springs.

Misery Springs (Umatilla NF). 9-1/10 mi S of Pomeroy on St Hwy 128; 7-7/10 mi SE on Co Hwy 107; 16-1/5 mi SE on FS 40; 1/2 mi S on FS 4030. SEASON: 7/1-10/15; 10-day lmt. FACILITIES: 4 sites (tr -16); no drk wtr; tbls, toil, cga, f. ACTIVITIES: Berrypicking; picnicking; fishing (5 mi). MISC.: Elev 6000 ft; 7 acres; pets. Scenic. Located immediately S of Mount Misery Rd. Jct. 9 mi S of Clearwater Guard Station. Wenaha Wilderness Viewpoint.

Misery Junction (Umatilla NF). 9-1/10 mi S of Pomeroy on St Hwy 128; 7-7/10 mi S on Co Hwy 107; 16-2/5 mi SE on FS N911. SEASON: 6/15-11/15; 10-day lmt. FACILITIES: 2 sites (no tr); tbls, toil, cga, f. ACTIVITIES: Picnicking. MISC.: Elev 6000 ft; pets.

Panjab (Umatilla NF). 17 mi SW of Pomeroy on Co Hwy 101; 12-1/10 mi SW on FS 47; 1/5 mi S on FS 47130. SEASON: 5/15-10/15; 10-day lmt. FACILITIES: 6 sites (tr -16); no drk wtr; river, tbls, toil, cga, f. ACTIVITIES: Horseback riding/fishing (1 mi); picnicking. MISC.: Elev 3000 ft; 2 acres; pets. Site also accessible via Co Rd from Dayton.

Pataha (Umatilla NF). 10-3/5 mi S of Pomeroy on St Hwy 128; 5 mi S on Co Hwy 185; 3/10 mi S on FS 4016; 1-3/10 mi W on FS 20. SEASON: 5/15-10/15; 10-day lmt. FACILITIES: 7 sites (tr -16); no drk wtr; tbls, toil, cga, f. ACTIVITIES: Picnicking. Horseback riding and fishing (1 mi). MISC.: Elev 4200 ft; 5 acres; pets.

Spruce Spring (Umatilla NF). 9-1/10 mi S of Pomeroy on St Hwy 128; 7-7/10 mi S on Co Hwy 107; 10-9/10 mi SE on FS 40000. SEASON: 6/15-10/15; 10-day lmt. FACILITIES: 4 sites (tr -15); tbls, toil, cga, f, piped drk wtr. ACTIVITIES: Picnicking; fishing (5 mi). MISC.: Elev 5700 ft; 5 acres; pets. 2 mi S Teal Spring Camp.

Teal Spring (Umatilla NF). 9-1/10 mi S of Pomeroy on St Hwy 128; 7-7/10 mi S on Co Hwy 107; 8-4/5 mi S on FS 40; 3/10 mi S on FS 200. SEASON: 6/15-10/15; 10-day lmt. FACILITIES: 8 sites (tr-16); piped drk wtr, tbls, toil, cga, f. ACTIVITIES: Berrypicking; picnicking. Fishing (3 mi); horseback riding (1 mi). MISC.: Elev 5600 ft; 7 acres; pets. View of Tucannon River watershed and high country. 2 mi S of Clearwater Guard Station.

Tucannon (Umatilla NF). 17 mi SW of Pomeroy on Co Hwy 101; 8-1/10 mi SW on FS 47000; 1/5 mi S on FS 160. SEASON: 4/30-10/15; 10-day lmt. FACILITIES: 15 sites (tr -16); piped drk wtr, river tbls, toil, cga, f. ACTIVITIES: Picnicking; fishing/horseback riding (1 mi). MISC.: Elev 1600 ft; 11 acres; pets.

PORT ANGELES

Altaire Campground (Olympic NP). 9 mi W of Port Angeles on US 101; 4-1/5 mi S along Elwha River on Elwha River Valley Road. [Paved road follows Elwha River; suitable for small travel trailers; portions of road closed by snow in Winter.] SEASON: 10/1-5/31, FREE (rest of yr, $3). No NP entrance fee. 14-day lmt. FACILITIES: 29 sites (tr -21); flush toil, cga. ACTIVITIES: Fishing (no license required in park); hiking; picnicking. MISC.: Elev 450 ft. Mountain goats and elk can sometimes be seen on rocks across the river in late Winter and early Spring.

Bouldger Creek (Olympic NP). 9 mi W of Port Angeles on US 101; 11-7/10 mi SW along Elwha River (gravel access rds), on Elwha River Valley Road; at end of road. SEASON: 6/15-9/30; 14-day lmt. (no park entrance fee). FACILITIES: 50 sites (no tr); FLUSH TOIL, tbls, toil, cga. **ACTIVITIES:** Hiking; picnicking; fishing (no license required in park). **MISC.:** Elev 2060 ft; pets on leash. Closed by snow in Winter. Mountain goats and sometimes elk may be seen on rocks across river in late Winter.

Deer Park (Olympic NP). 6 mi E of Port Angeles on US 101; 18 mi S (gravel access rds). **SEASON:** 6/15-9/30; 14-day lmt. **FACILITIES:** 10 sites (no tr); tbls, toil, cga. **ACTIVITIES:** Picnicking. **MISC.:** Elev 5400 ft; pets. Views of Strait of Juan de Fuca, inner Olympic Mountains & Mt. Baker. Alpine Wildflower display in Summer. No park entrance fee.

Elwha (Olympic NP). 9 mi W of Port Angeles; 3 mi S along Elwha River on Elwha River Valley Road [paved rd]; suitable for sm. tr.; part of rd closed in Winter. **SEASON:** 10/1-5/31, FREE (rest of yr, $3), No NP entrance fee. 14-day lmt. **FACILITIES:** 41 sites (tr -21); FLUSH TOIL, tbls, cga. **ACTIVITIES:** Hiking; picnicking; fishing (no license required in park). **MISC.:** Elev 390 ft; Mountain goats and elk can sometimes be seen on the rocks across the river in late Winter and early Spring.

Fairholm (Olympic NP). 17-9/10 mi W of Port Angeles on US 101 (Lake Crescent Rd); 10-7/10 mi on North Shore Road; 1/10 mi to campground and Fairholm Ranger Station. Roads are steep. **SEASON:** LD-6/30, FREE (rest of yr, $5). No NP entrance fee. 14-day lmt. **FACILITIES:** 87 sites (tr -21); FLUSH toil, tbls, cga. **ACTIVITIES:** Boating,ld; picnicking; fishing (no license required in park); hiking. **MISC.:** Elev 580 ft. Lake Crescent is nestled between Locate next to Lake Crescent. Lake Crescent is nestled between high, forested peaks, and is the largest lake in the NP.

Heart O'The Hills (Olympic NP). Start at US 101 at Race St, 4/5 mi inside eastern city limits of Port Angeles; then 5-2/5 mi S on Hurrican Ridge Road [paved road; often closed by snow in Winter]. **SEASON:** LD-6/30, FREE (rest of yr, $5). No NP entrance fee. 14-day lmt. **FACILITIES:** 105 sites (tr -21); FLUSH TOIL, tbls, cga, piped drk wtr, **ACTIVITIES:** Hiking; picnicking. **MISC.:** Elev 1807 ft. Trail starting in campground leads to Mt. Angeles (6400 ft).

Lyre River (Dept. of Natural Resources) 4 mi W of Port Angeles on St Hwy 101 to jct with St Hwy 112; 14-7/10 mi N on St Hwy 112 to campground sign, turn right and go 1/2 mi to the fork in the road; take the left fork (gravel rd) to campground. **FACILITIES:** 9 sites (tr -22); tbls, toil, cga,drk wtr. **ACTIVITIES:** Picnicking; hiking. **MISC.:** On the Lyre River; secluded sites. **ADDITIONAL INFO/MAP:** Public Affairs Office, DNR, Public Lands Bldg., Olympia WA 98504 [or call toll free 1-800-562-6010].

Soleduck Campground (Olympic NP). 30 mi W of Port Angeles on US 101; 12-4/5 mi SE on Soleduck River Valley Road (paved, fairly narrow in spots, suitable for tr, closed by snow in Winter). **SEASON:** 10/1-5/31, FREE (rest of yr, $3). No NP entrance fee. 14-day lmt. **FACILITIES:** 84 sites (tr -21); FLUSH TOIL, DUMP, tbls, cga. **ACTIVITIES:** Swimming; hiking; picnicking; fishing (no license required in park). **MISC.:** Elev 1680 ft. At the end of the road (1-2/5 mi), trails begin which lead to Soleduck Falls (9/10 mi), Seven Lakes Basin and other high country of exceptional beauty.

PORTER

Porter Creek (Capitol Forest MUA; DNR). 5 mi NE of Porter on Porter Creek Rd in Capitol Forest. **FACILITIES:** 10 sites; drk wtr, tbls, toil, cga, horse facilities, trails. **ACTIVITIES:** Hiking; picnicking; fishing. **ADDITIONAL INFORMATION:** See "Littlerock" entry for overview info on Capitol Forest MUA. Further info/map can be obtained from Public Affairs Office, Dept. of Natural Resources, Public Lands Bldg., Olympia, WA 98504, or Central Area Office, P.O.Box 1004, Chehalis, WA 98532; or call toll free 1-800-562-6010

PULLMAN

Military Hill. E of Pullman on Grand Ave.; 100 yd N on Stadium Way to fork in rd; 1/2 mi on Hall. **FACILITIES:** 10 sites; tbls, cga, playground, tennis court, community kitchen with electric outlet, gravel parking. **ACTIVITIES:** Tennis; fishing; picnicking. **MISC.:** On Snake River. Washington State University nearby. University of Idaho in Moscow less than 10 mi.

QUEETS

Queets (Olympic NP). 5 mi E of Queets on US 101; 13-1/2 mi NE on gravel rd along Queets River (open all yr; not suitable for tr.). **SEASON:** 6/1-LD; 14-day lmt. **FACILITIES:** 26 sites (no tr); tbls, toil, cga. **ACTIVITIES:** Fishing (no license required in park); picnicking. **MISC.:** Elev 290 ft; pets. Roosevelt elk often seen in abandoned homestead fields Rain Forest. Queets Campground Trail. Queets Ranger Station (1-1/2 mi) info and backcountry use permits Summer & Fall; closed Winter. No NP entrance fee.

QUILCENE

Big Quilcene (Olympic NF). 2 mi SW of Quilcene on US 101; 3-1/2 mi S on Co Hwy 78; 1 mi SW on FS 2812; 1/2 mi W on FS 2740. **SEASON:** 5/1-10/1. **FACILITIES:** 3 sites. (no tr); cga, toil, tbls. **ACTIVITIES:** Picnicking. **MISC.:** Elev 1400 ft; pets.

Dosewallips (Olympic NP). 9 mi S of Quilcene at Brinnon on Hood Canal on

US 101; 15-2/5 mi W along Dosewallips River on rd that is narrow & paved 6 mi and gravel 9 mi (closed by snow in Winter); upper end of rd is steep--not suitable for tr. SEASON: 6/1-9/30; 14-day lmt. FACILITIES: 33 sites (no tr); FLUSH TOIL, cga, tbls showers. ACTIVITIES: Fishing (no license required in park); picnicking. MISC.: Elev 1640 ft. No NP entrance fee. Dosewallips Ranger Station (1/10 mi); info and backcountry se permits summer only.

Spencer Creek. 6-4/5 mi S of Quilcene on St Hwy 101; 5 mi N of Dosewallips River bridge at Brinnon. [No campground sign; turn in at large pull-out area on the W side of rd (across the road from country maintenance depot fence) and follow dirt rd to campground]. FACILITIES: 13 sites (tr -22); toil, no drk wtr. ACTIVITIES: Hunting; berry-picking (huckleberries, grapes, salmon berries); picnicking. Fishing nearby. MISC.: Mt. Walker Lookout (2 mi N) overlooking mountains and Hood Canal.

RANDLE

Adams Fork (Gifford Pinchot NF). 3-1/0 mi S of Randle on Co Hwy; 15-7/10 mi SE on FS 123; 4-7/10 mi SE on FS 1302; 1/5 mi E on FS 101. SEASON: 6/1-9/30; 14-day lmt. FACILITIES: 23 sites (tr - 16); tbls, toil, cga, f, well drk wtr. ACTIVITIES: Berry-picking; picnicking; fishing; horseback riding. MISC.: Elev 2600 ft; 8 acres; pets. Cat Creek Guard Station (2 mi) on Forest Rd 1302. Stream.

Blue Lake Creek (Gifford Pinchot NF). 3-1/10 mi S of Randle on Co Hwy; 13-1/5 mi SE on FS 123. SEASON: 5/15-9/15; 14-day lmt. FACILITIES: 11 sites (tr -22); tbls, cga, toil, piped drk wtr, ACTIVITIES: Berry-picking; picnicking; fishing; horseback riding. MISC.: Elev 1900 ft; 3 acres; pets. Stream.

Cat Creek (Gifford Pinchot NF). 3-1/10 mi S of Randle on Co Hwy; 15-7/10 mi SE on FS 123; 6-1/10 mi SE on FS 1302. SEASON: 6/1-10/31; 14-day lmt. FACILITIES: 3 sites (tr -16); no drk wtr; tbls, toil, cga, f. ACTIVITIES: Picnicking; fishing; berry-picking. Horseback riding (1 mi). MISC.: elev 3000 ft; 1 acre; pets. Cat Creek Guard Station (3/5 mi).

Council Lake (Gifford Pinchot NF). 3-1/0 mi S of Randle on Co Hwy; 31-1/10 mi SE on FS 123; 3/10 mi N on FS N925. SEASON: 7/1-9/15; 14-day lmt. FACILITIES: 11 sites (tr -16); tbls, toil, cga, f, no drk wtr. ACTIVITIES: Boating,d; picnicking; fishing; hiking; berrypicking. Horseback riding (1 mi). MISC.: Elev 4300 ft; 2 acres; pets. Council Bluff (1-7/10 mi W). Excellent view. Mt. Adams Wilderness (2 mi).

Horseshoe Lake (Gifford Pinchot NF). 3-1/10 mi S of Randle on Co Hwy; 15-7/10 mi SE on FS 123; 4-7/10 mi SE on FS 1302; 12-4/5 mi E on FS 101. SEASON: 7/1-9/15; 14-day lmt. FACILITIES: 8 sites (tr -16); tbls, toil, cga, no drk wtr; f. ACTIVITIES: Boating,d; picnicking; fishing; berry-picking. Horse riding (1 mi). MISC.: Elev 4200 ft; 3 acres; pets. 2 mi NW of Mt. Adams.

Keenes Horse Camp (Gifford Pinchot NF). 3-1/10 mi SE of Randle on Co Hwy; 15-7/10 mi SE on FS 123; 4-7/10 mi SE on FS 1302; 12-2/5 mi E on FS 101. SEASON: 7/1-9/15; 14-day lmt. FACILITIES: 15 sites (tr -16); no drk wtr; stream, tbls, toil, cga, f. ACTIVITIES: Mountain climbing; horseback riding; picnicking; fishing. MISC.: Elev 4300 ft; 5 acres; pets. Scenic. 2-2/5 mi NW of Mt Adams Wilderness.

Killen Creek (Gifford Pinchot NF). 3-1/10 mi S on Co Hwy; 15-7/10 mi S on FS 123; 4-7/10 mi SE on FS 1302; 13-2/5 mi E on FS 101. SEASON: 7/1-9/15; 14-day lmt. FAC:8 sites (tr -16);tbls,toil,cga,no drk wtr. ACTIVITIES: Mountain climbing; hiking;picnicking; fishing. Horseback riding (1 mi). MISC.: Elev 4400 ft; 4 acres; pets. Trailhead for climbing N face Mt Adams. Stream.

Midway Meadows (Umatilla NF). 3-1/10 mi S of Randle on Co Hwy; 15-7/10 mi SE on FS 123; 4-7/10 mi SE on FS 1302; 9 mi E on FS 101. SEASON: 7/1-9/15. FACILITIES: 4 sites (no tr); tbls, toil, cga, f. ACTIVITIES: Fishing; picnicking MISC.: Elev 4400 ft; pets. 2 mi W of Yakima Indian Reservation, Cascade Crest Trail.

North Fork (Gifford Pinchot NF). 3-1/10 mi S of Randle on Co Hwy; 8-7/10 mi SE on FS 123. SEASON: 5/15-9/30; 14-day lmt. FACILITIES: 42 sites (tr -16); tbls, toil, cga, f. ACTIVITIES: Horseback riding; picnicking; fishing. MISC.: Elev 1500 ft; 13 acres; pets. N fork Cispus River divides campground.

Olallie Lake (Gifford Pinchot NF). 3-1/10 mi S of Randle on Co Hwy; 28-9/10 mi SE on FS 123, 4/5 mi N on FS 101; 3/5 mi N on FS 1007. SEASON: 7/1-9/15; 14-day lmt. FACILITIES: 6 sites (tr -16); no drk wtr; lake, tbls, toil, cga, f. ACTIVITIES: Boating (no motors); picnicking; fishing. Horseback riding (1 mi). Berrypicking. MISC.: Elev 3700 ft; 3 acres; pets. Scenic. Excellent view of Mt. Adams.

Pole Patch (Gifford Pinchot NF). 2 mi S on Co Hwy; 20-3/10 mi S on FS 125; 2-4/5 mi E on FS 112; 6-1/10 mi N on FS 113. SEASON: 7/1-9/15; 14-day lmt. FACILITIES: 12 sites (tr -16); no drk wtr; stream, tbls, toil, cga, f . ACTIVITIES: Berrypicking; picnicking; fishing; horseback riding.

See page 7 for KEY TO ABBREVIATIONS.

MISC.: Elev 4400 ft; 10 acres; pets. Excellent viewpoint of 3 snowcapped mountains (1 mi).

Ryan Lake (Gifford Pinchot NF). 2 mi S of Randle on Co Hwy; 6-4/5 mi SW on FS 125; 12-3/5 mi SW on FS 115; 1/5 mi on FS 1203. SEASON: 6/1-9/15; 14-day lmt. FACILITIES: 4 sites., (no tr); no drk wtr; lake, tbls, toil, cga, f. ACTIVITIES: Hiking; picnicking; fishing; horseback riding. MISC.: Elev 3200 ft; 1 acre; pets. Botanical. Trailhead for Green River, Mt. Margaret.

Spring Creek (Gifford Pinchot NF). 3-1/10 mi S of Randle on Co Hwy; 15-7/10 mi SE on FS 123; 4-7/10 mi on FS 1302; 12-1/10 mi E on FS 101. SEASON: 7/1-9/15. FACILITIES: 3 sites (no tr); tbls, toil, cga, f. ACTIVITIES: Fishing; picnicking. MISC.: Elev 4000 ft; pets. Mount Adams Wilderness (2 mi SE).

Takhlakh (Gifford Pinchot NF). 3-1/10 mi S on Co Hwy; 28-9/10 mi SE on FS 123; 1-3/5 mi N on FS 101. SEASON: 7/1-9/15; 14-day lmt. FACILITIES: 41 sites (tr -22); tbls, toil, cga, f, piped drk wtr, lake. ACTIVITIES: Mountain climbing; boating,ld; picnicking; fishing. Horseback riding (1 mi). MISC.: Elev 4500 ft; 21 acres; pets. Scenic. Excellent view of Mt Adams. Unusual rock pile (across lake 1 mi E).

Wobbly Lake (Gifford Pinchot NF). 3-1/10 mi S of Randle on Co Hwy; 8-2/5 mi SE on FS 123; 8-3/10 mi E on FS 1111; 2-7/10 mi on FS 1124. SEASON: 6/15-9/15; 14-day lmt. FACILITIES: 3 sites (no tr); toil, cga, f. ACTIVITIES: Fishing; picnicking. MISC.: Elev 3400 ft; pets.

REPUBLIC

Ferry Lake (Colville NF). 7 mi S of Republic on St Hwy 21; 6 mi SW on FS 5300; 1 mi N on FS 1488. SEASON: 6/1-9/30 14-day lmt. FACILITIES: 9 sites (tr -22); tbls, toil, cga, f, well drk wtr. ACTIVITIES: Boating,ld; picnicking; fishing. Horseback riding/swimming (1 mi). MISC.: Elev 3300 ft; 4 acres; pets.

Haag Cove (Coulee Dam NRA). 25 mi E of Republic on St Hwy 30; 5 mi S on Co Hwy. SEASON: All year; 14-day lmt. FACILITIES: 11 sites (tr -26); tbls, toil, cga. ACTIVITIES: Boating,d; swimming; picnicking; fishing.

Kettle Range (Colville NF). 1/2 mi E of Republic on St Hwy 21; 18 mi E on St Hwy 30. SEASON: 6/15-9/30; 14-day lmt. FACILITIES: 9 sites (tr -22); Well drk wtr; tbls, toil, cga, f, nature trails. ACTIVITIES: Hiking; picnicking; horseback riding. MISC.: Elev 5400 ft; 3 acres; pets.

Long Lake (Colville). 7 mi S of Republic on St Hwy 21; 8 mi SW on FS 5300; 1-1/2 mi S on FS 1487. SEASON: 5/15-10/15; 14-day lmt. FACILITIES: 12 sites (tr -22); tbls, toil, cga, f. boat/d. Boat/l (1 mi); Well drk wtr. ACTIVITIES: Swimming/horseback riding (1 mi). Picnicking; fishing (fly fishing only); berrypicking. MISC.: Elev 3200 ft; 4 acres; pets. Long Lake.

Swan Lake (Colville NF). 7 mi S of Republic on St Hwy 21; 8 mi SW on FS 353. SEASON: 5/15-10/15; 14-day lmt. FACILITIES: 25 sites (tr -32); tbls, toil, cga, f, boat 1/d, piped drk wtr. Swan Lake. ACTIVITIES: Boating, picnicking; fishing; horseback riding; berrypicking. MISC.: Elev 3600 ft; 6 acres; pets.

Ten Mile (Colville NF). 10 mi S of Republic on St Hwy 21. SEASON: 5/15-10/15; 14-day lmt. FACILITIES: 9 sites (tr -16); tbls, toil, cga, f, stream. ACTIVITIES: Horseback riding; picnicking; fishing. MISC.: Elev 2200 ft; 4 acres; pets.

RIVERSIDE

Crawfish Lake (Okanogan NF). 17-7/10 mi E of Riverside on Co Hwy 9320; 1-7/10 mi S on FS 3612; 2/5 mi SE on FS 3525. SEASON: 5/1-10/30; 14-day lmt. FACILITIES: 22 sites (tr -32); no drk wtr; tbls, toil, cga, f, Crawfish Lake, boat/l/d ACTIVITIES: Boating, waterskiing; picnicking; fishing. MISC.: Elev 4500 ft; 9 acres; pets. Balance Rock Spring (drk wtr, 1 mi).

SAPPHO

Bear Creek (Dept. of Natural Resources). 1-9/10 mi E of Sappho along St Hwy 101 on the HOH River Rd. FACILITIES: 6 sites (tr -26); well drk wtr, tbls, toil, cga, trails. Food (nearby). ACTIVITIES: Hiking; hunting; picnicking; fishing. MISC.: By Soleduck River. ADDITIONAL INFO/MAP: Public Affairs Office, DNR, Public Lands Bldg., Olympia, WA 98504; or call toll free 1-800-562-6010.

SEQUIM

Dungeness Forks (Olympic NF). 4 mi SE of Sequim on US 101; 4-1/2 mi S on Co Hwy 9537; 3 mi SW on FS 2958. [At the junction of the Dungeness & Greywolf Rivers.] SEASON: 5/1-10/1; 14-day lmt. FACILITIES: 9 sites (no tr); tbls, toil, cga, f, picnic shelter, drk wtr (from centrally located well). ACTIVITIES: Hiking; hunting; picnicking; fishing. MISC.: Elev 1000 ft; 6 acres; pets. Geological.

East Crossing (Olympic NF). 3 mi SE of Sequim on US 101; 8 mi S on Co Hwy 9537; 3 mi S on FS 295. Paved & gravel access (narrow, winding & steep, but in good condition). SEASON: 5/1-10/1; 14-day lmt. FACILITIES: 9 secluded sites (tr -16); tbls, toil, cga, well drk wtr. ACTIVITIES: Hiking; hunting; picnicking; fishing. MISC.: Elev 1200 ft; 7 acres; pets. Gold Creek Trailhead (1 mi S on FS 295). Gray Wolf Trailhead nearby. Along Dungeness River. Scenic.

Slab (Olympic NF). 2 mi W of Sequim on US 101; 2-1/2 mi S on Co Hwy; 6 mi SW on FS 2926. SEASON: 5/1-10/1; 14-day lmt. FACILITIES: 3 sites (no tr); no drk wtr, stream, tbls, toil, cga, f. Horse/nature trails (1 mi). ACTIVITIES: Horseback riding; hiking; picnicking. MISC.: Elev 2600 ft; 1 acre, pets. Greywolf Trailhead to Olympic NP. Scenic.

SHELTON

Brown Creek (Olympic NF). 7-1/2 mi N of Shelton on US 101; to the Purdy Creek Intersection; 5-3/10 mi NW on Co Hwy 242; 8-7/10 mi N on FS 226 and cross the South Fork Skokomish Bridge; 1/2 mi E on FS 2286. SEASON: 5/15-11/10; 14-day lmt. FACILITIES: 16 sites (tr -22); tbls, toil, cga, f, well drk wtr. ACTIVITIES: Picnicking; swimming; fishing. Horseback riding (1 mi). MISC.: Elev 600 ft; 6 acres; pets.

Shelton Rest Stop. 2 mi N of Shelton on St Hwy 101. FACILITIES: Sites; overnite parking is permitted here; drk wtr, tbls, toil, cga, tennis courts. ACTIVITIES: Tennis; picnicking.

SKYKOMISH

Beckler River (Mt. Baker-Snoqualmie NF). 1 mi E of Skykomish on US 2; 1 mi N on FS 280 (Becker Rd). SEASON: 5/15-11/1; 14-day lmt. FACILITIES: 21 sites (tr -22); tbls, toil, cga, f, no drk wtr, stream . Store/ice/gas/food (2 mi). ACTIVITIES: Hunting; hiking; picnicking; fishing. MISC.: Elev 900 ft; 12 acres; pets.

Foss River (Mt. Baker-Snoqualmie NF). 2 mi E of Skykomish on US 2; 4-1/2 mi S on FS 2622. SEASON: 5/15-10/1; 14-day lmt. FACILITIES: 4 sites (tr -16); no drk wtr; river, tbls, toil, cga, f. ACTIVITIES: Hiking; picnicking; fishing. Horseback riding (1 mi). MISC.: Elev 1400 ft; 4 acres; pets. 2 mi N of Alpine Lakes Wilderness Boundary.

Miller River (Mt. Baker-Snoqualmie NF). 2-1/2 mi W of Skykomish on US 2; 3-1/2 mi S on FS 2516 (Miller River Rd); adjacent to Miller River. SEASON: 5/15-10/1; 14-day lmt. FACILITIES: 12 sites (tr -22); well drk wtr, tbls, toil, cga, f. ACTIVITIES: Hiking; hunting; swimming; picnicking; fishing. MISC.: Elev 1100 ft; 10 acres; pets. 6 mi N of Alpine Lakes Wilderness Boundary.

Money Creek (Mt. Baker-Snoqualmie NF). 2-1/2 mi W of Skykomish on US 2; 4-3/5 mi S on Money Creek Rd (Old Cascade Hwy); turn right, cross bridge, watch for campground on both sides of road. SEASON: 5/1-11/1; 14-day lmt. FACILITIES: 17 secluded sites (tr -22); tbls, toil, cga, f. Store/ice (3 mi). ACTIVITIES: Swimming; picnicking; fishing; hunting; hiking. MISC.: Elev 900 ft; 13 acres; pets. On Skykomish River. Located high in the Cascade Range. Nearby-NE, Johnson Ridge Trailhead, from Beckler River Rd.

Tye Canyon (Wenatchee NF). 6 mi E of Skykomish on US 2; 2 mi E on FS 2607. SEASON: 6/1-10/1; 14-day lmt. FACILITIES: 2 sites (no tr); cga, f. ACTIVITIES: Fishing; picnicking. MISC.: Elev 2200 ft.

SPRINGDALE

Long Lake (Dept. of Natural Resources). (near Spokane.) 13-3/5 mi S of Springdale on St Hwy 231; turn E at DNR sign on River Rd and go 4-4/5 mi; turn rt to campgd sign on left. FAC.: 12 sites tr -32); tbls, toil, cga. ACTIVITIES: Hunting; boating, waterskiing; hiking; picnicking; fishing. MISC.: Long Lake is nearby.

STEHEKIN

Bridge Creek (Lake Chelan NRA; N Cascade NP). 16 mi NW of Stehekin on unpaved Co Rd. SEASON: 6/15-11/1; 14-day lmt. FACILITIES: 7 sites (no tr); tbls, toil, cga, f, stream. ACTIVITIES: Fishing; picnicking.

Harlequin (Lake Chelen NRA; N Cascades NP). 5 mi NW of Stehekin on unpaved rd. SEASON: 5/1-11/30; 14-day lmt. FACILITIES: 7 sites (no tr); stream, tbls, toil, cga, f. ACTIVITIES: Fishing; picnicking. MISC.: 3 acres.

Weaver Point (Lake Chelen NRA; N Cascades NP). SEASON: 6/1-11/30; 14-day lmt. FACILITIES: 22 sites (no tr); tbls, toil, cga, f. boat/l. Store/ice (nearby). ACTIVITIES: Fishing; picnicking. MISC.: 3 acres.

Olney Park (Weyerhaeuser Co. in cooperation with State Dept. of Natural Resources). 6 mi N of Sultan on Sultan Basin Rd (gravel access rds). [On Olney Creek.] FACILITIES: 8 sites (tr -35); no drk wtr; toil. ACTIVITIES: Hunting; picnicking; fishing; hiking. MISC.: 14-day lmt. Pets on leash.

SULTAN

Sultan Sportsman Club Rec. Area. 6 mi N of Sultan on Sultan Basin Rd (gravel access rds). No designated sites. River. ACTIVITIES: Fishing; hunting; picnicking. MISC.: DUMP.

See page 7 for KEY TO ABBREVIATIONS.

SUMA

Sumas Lions Club Park. At South edge of Suma, at the E edge of the bridge. **FACILITIES:** 8 shaded sites; drk wtr, FLUSH TOIL, cga, tbls, small creek. **ACTIVITIES:** Picnicking.

TACOMA

Alder Roadside Park (Tacoma City Light). 30 mi S of Tacoma on St Hwy 7, overlooking Alder Lake. The park is located on lakeshore dr. **FAC:** Sites, tbls, boat/l. **ACTIVITIES:** Boating; picnicking; fishing; waterskiing. **MISC.:** Boat rentals and tackle available near the dam. [Information: Community Services Office, Tacoma City Light 206/383-2471, ext 159].

Bear Gulch (Tacoma City Light). Located at the head of Lake Cushman, which is on the Olympic Peninsula near Hood Canal. **SEASON:** All year; 14-day lmt. **FACILITIES:** Numerous sites, trails, boat/l (nearby). **ACTIVITIES:** Swimming; boating; picnicking; fishing. **MISC.:** 18-hole golf course/horse stable for rides and pack trips (nearby). [Info: Community Services Office, Tacoma City Light, 206/383-2471, ext. 159].

TENINO

Deschutes River Camp (Weyerhaeuser Co.). 3 mi E of Tenino on St Hwy 507; 2 mi left on McIntosh Lake Rd. (Campground is on right). **FACILITIES:** 20 sites; tbls, toil, cga, f, community kitchen. **ACTIVITIES:** Hunting; picnicking; fishing. **MISC.:** On Deschutes River.

THUNDER ARM

Colonial Creek (Ross Lake NRA; N Cascades NP, co-sponsored by Seattle City Light). On St Hwy 20; on Diablo Lake at Thunder Arm. **SEASON:** 10/2-4/14, FREE. No NP entrance fee (rest of yr, $2.00). 14-day lmt. **FACILITIES:** 162 sites; FLUSH TOIL, piped drk wtr, tbls, cga, f, boat ramp, fish cleaning station. **ACTIVITIES:** Boating,l; picnicking; fishing; hiking; hunting. **MISC.:** Elev 1200 ft; pets on leash. FREE SEASON: wtr shut off; open until rds closed by snow.

TIGER

West Branch Leclerc Creek (Colville NF). 6 mi E of Tiger on Co Hwy 2; 10 mi SE on FS 307. **SEASON:** 6/1-9/15; 14-day lmt. **FACILITIES:** 8 sites (tr -22); tbls, toil, cga, no drk wtr; stream. **ACTIVITIES:** Horseback riding; berrypicking; picnicking; fishing. **MISC.:** Elev 2400 ft; 4 acres; pets.

TONASKET

Aeneas Spring (Okanogan NF). 12-3/5 mi E of Tonasket on St Hwy 30; 9-1/5 mi SE on Co Hwy 164; 4-1/2 mi SE on

FS 3612. **SEASON:** 5/15-10/30. **FACILITIES:** 3 sites (tr -32); no drk wtr, stream, tbls, toil, cga. **ACTIVITIES:** Fishing; picnicking. **MISC.:** Elev 3600 ft; 4 acres; pets.

Beaver Lake (Okanogan NF). 20-1/10 mi E of Tanasket on St Hwy 30; 11 mi NE on FS 396. **SEASON:** 5/15-10/15; 14-day lmt. **FACILITIES:** 11 sites (tr -22); tbls, toil, cga, boat/l/d, well drk wtr, nature trails. **ACTIVITIES:** Hiking; fishing; swimming; boating. **MISC.:** Elev 3000 ft; 4 acres; pets. Beaver Lake.

Lyman Lake (Okanogan NF). 12-3/5 mi E on St Hwy 30; 13 mi SE on Co Hwy 9455; 2-2/5 mi S on FS 357; 1/5 mi NW on FS 358. **SEASON:** 5/15-10/30. **FACILITIES:** 6 sites (tr -32); no drk wtr; lake, tbls, toil, cga. **ACTIVITIES:** Swimming; picnicking; fishing. **MISC.:** Elev 2900 ft; 4 acres; pets.

Palmer Lake. In Tonasket on St Hwy 97, turn W on 3rd and ride across Okanogan River Bridge; 17 mi N and W on Many Lakes Recreational Area Road to Loomis; campground is 8-1/5 mi N on North shore of Palmer Lake. **SEASON:** 5/15-10/15; 14-day lmt. **FACILITIES:** 7 shaded, lakeside sites (tr -22); tbls, toil, cga. **ACTIVITIES:** Boating; picnicking; fishing; hunting; rockhounding. **MISC.:** Watch for rattlesnakes.

Split Rock. In Tonasket on St Hwy 97, turn W on 3rd and drive across Okanogan River Bridge; 17 mi N and W on Many Lakes Recreation Area Road to Loomis. Campground is 4-1/5 mi N of Tonasket, by Palmer Lake. **SEASON:** 5/15-10/15; 14-day lmt. **FACILITIES:** Undesignated sites on large gravel parking area (enough room for 12 RVs); sandy beach, tbls, toil, cga. **ACTIVITIES:** Hunting; picnicking; fishing; rockhounding; swimming; boating,l; waterskiing. **MISC.:** Watch for rattlesnakes.

Tonasket City Park. In town, watch for "Overnight Camping" signs. 72-hour lmt. **FACILITIES:** undesignated sites, enough room for 12 RVs; drk wtr, tbls, toil, community kitchen with coin operated elec stoves/outlets, swimming pool. **ACTIVITIES:** Swimming; picnicking; fishing. **MISC.:** Many Lakes Recreational area nearby. All conveniences within walking distance.

Upper Beaver Lake (Okanogan NF). 20-1/10 mi E of Tonasket on St Hwy 30; 11 mi NE on FS 396; 3-3/10 mi NW on FS 3945. **SEASON:** 5/1-10/30. **FACILITIES:** 4 sites (tr -16); well drk wtr, lake, tbls, toil, cga. **ACTIVITIES:** Boating,l; swimming; picnicking; fishing. **MISC.:** Elev 3000 ft; 5 acres; pets.

West Fork San Poil (Okanogan NF). 12-3/5 mi E of Tonasket on St Hwy 30; 29-3/5 mi SE on Co Hwy 9455; 3-1/5 mi SE on FS 359. SEASON: 5/1–10/30; no time lmt. FACILITIES: 8 sites (tr –32); tbls, toil, cga, no drk wtr, stream. ACTIVI-TIES: Fishing; picnicking. MISC.: Elev 2300 ft; 6 acres; pets.

Whitestone Lake (Fish and Game Dept. Public Access). In Tonasket on St Hwy 97; turn W on 3rd & drive across Okano-gan River Bridge, then 10–9/10 mi N on Many Lakes Recreational Area Rd to the first fishing area with large paved parking area on Whitestone Lake. (There are other parking areas like this on the Lake; but this in the only one that allows overnight parking.) FACILITIES: Undesignated sites, room for 15 Rvs; toil. boat/r. ACTIVITIES: Boating, picnicking; fishing. MISC.: 3–day lmt.

TOUTLE

*****Bear Cove** (Gifford Pinchot NF). 34–4/5 mi E of Toutle on St Hwy 504; 1 mi E on FS N929, 1 mi N on Spirit Lake, BY BOAT. SEASON: 6/15–10/15; 14–day lmt. FACILITIES: 11 sites, no tr; tbls, toil, cga, f, no drk wtr. Store/ice/gas/ food (2 mi). ACTIVITIES: Picnicking; boating,d (rental, 1 mi); waterskiing; fishing; sailing. MISC.: Elev 3200 ft; 4 acres; pets; scenic; lake. Visi-tor Center (1 mi).

***** Cedar Creek** (Gifford Pinchot NF). 34–4/5 mi E of Toutle on St Hwy 504; 1–1/2 mi N on TRAIL 1 [on E shore of Spirit Lake]. SEASON: 6/15–10/15; 14–day lmt. FACILITIES: 12 sites, no tr; tbls, toil, cga, f, no drk wtr. Store/ice/food (2 mi). ACTIVITIES: Picnicking; fish-ing; swimming; waterskiing; sailing; boating (l, 1 mi). Hiking. MISC.: Elev 3200 ft; 2 acres; pets; lake; scenic. Visitor Center (1 mi).

*****Donnybrook** (Gifford Pinchot NF). 34–4/5 mi E of Toutle on St Hwy 504; 1 mi N on TRAIL 1. BOAT & TRAIL access only. [On Spirit Lake]. SEASON: 6/15–10/15; 14–day lmt. FACILITIES: 12 sites, tbls, toil, cga, no drk wtr. Store/ ice/food (2 mi). Gas (4 mi). ACTIV-ITIES: Picnicking; fishing; swimming; waterskiing; sailing; boating (l, 1 mi; r, 2 mi); hiking. MISC.: Elev 3200 ft; 2 acres; pets; scenic. Visi-tor Center and nature trails (1 mi).

Studebaker Horse (Gifford Pinchot NF). 31 mi E of Toutle on St Hwy S504; 1/2 mi E on FS N903. SEASON: 5/1–11/20; 14–day lmt. FACILITIES: 54 sites (tr –22); no drk wtr; tbls, toil, cga, f. Store/gas (4 mi). ACTIVITIES: Horseback riding; hiking; picnicking. Swimming/ fishing/boating,r,l (5 mi). Waterskiing (5 mi). MISC.: Elev 2600 ft; 6 acres; pets. SCENIC. Within 5 mi of Mt. St. Helens and Spirit Lake.

***** Timberline** (Gifford Pinchot NF). 38–1/5

mi E of Toutle on St Hwy 504; 1/10 mi E on TRAIL 24DA. SEASON: 6/15–10/30; 14–day lmt. FACILITIES: 38 sites; tbls, toil, cga, f, piped drk wtr. Store/ice/ visitor center (4 mi). ACTIVITIES: Mountain climbing; picnicking; hiking. Fishing/waterskiing/boating (4 mi); boating,r (4 mi); boating,l (5 mi). MISC.: Elev 4200 ft; 14 acres; pets. Large parking lot for self-contained RVs. Camp for climbers of Mt. St. Helens (short trail in). Scenic.

TROUT LAKE

Chain of Lakes (Gifford Pinchot NF). 25 mi S of Trout Lake on FS N84; 31–2/5 mi NE on FS 123. SEASON: 7/1–9/15. FACILITIES: 2 sites (no tr); tbls, toil, cga, f. ACTIVITIES: Fishing; picnicking. MISC.: Elev 4300 ft; pets.

Cold Springs (Gifford Pinchot NF). 1/5 mi SE of Trout Lake on St Hwy 141; 1–9/10 mi N on Co Hwy 17; 2–7/10 mi N on FS N80; 8–7/10 mi N on FS N 81 [at Trailhead on Mt. Adams]. SEASON: 7/1–9/30; 14–day lmt. FACILITIES: 8 sites (no tr); no drk wtr; tbls, toil, cga, f. ACTIVITIES: Mountain climbing; hiking; picnicking; horseback riding. MISC.: Elev 5700 ft; 3 acres; pets.

Cold Springs Indian (Gifford Pinchot NF). 5–1/2 mi SW of Trout Lake on St Hwy 141; 15–1/5 mi NW on FS 123; 9/10 mi NE on FS 123]. SEASON: 6/15–9/30; 14–day lmt. FACILITIES: 9 sites (tr –16); tbls, toil, cga, f, no drk wtr. ACTIVITIES: Berry-picking; picnicking; horseback riding. MISC.: Elev 4200 ft; 1 acre; pets. Reserved for Indian use only.

Goose Lake (Gifford Pinchot NF). 5–1/2 mi SW of Trout Lake on St Hwy 141; 2–1/2 mi W on FS 123; 5–1/5 mi SW on FS N60. SEASON: 6/15–9/30; 14–day lmt. FACILITIES: 29 sites (tr –16); no drk wtr; tbls, toil, cga, f. ACTIVITIES: Horseback riding; picnicking; fishing; swimming; berry-picking; boating,l,d. MISC.: Elev 3200 ft; 7 acres; pets.

Ice Cave (Gifford Pinchot NF). 5–1/2 mi SW of Trout Lake on St Hwy 141; 9/10 mi W on FS 123; 1/5 mi S on FS N601. SEASON: 6/1–10/31; 14–day lmt. FACILI-TIES: 8 sites (tr –16); tbls, toil, cga, f, no drk wtr. ACTIVITIES: Berry-pick-ing; picnicking. MISC.: Elev 2800 ft; 4 acres; pets. Geological. Small lava cave and visual display.

Lewis River (Gifford Pinchot NF). 1–2/5 mi W of Trout Lake on St Hwy 141; 2–3/10 mi NW on FS N88; 7–1/5 mi N on FS N819; 5–1/10 mi W on FS N87. SEASON: 6/15–9/30; 14–day lmt. FACILITIES: 5 sites (no tr); tbls, toil, cga, f, no drk wtr. ACTIVITIES: Horseback riding; pic-nicking; fishing; swimming. MISC.: Elev 1500 ft; 2 acres; pets. Scenic.

See page 7 for KEY TO ABBREVIATIONS.

Little Goose (Gifford Pinchot NF). 5-1/2 mi SW of Trout Lake on St Hwy 141; 10-1/10 mi NW on FS 123. SEASON: 6/1-10/31; 14-day lmt. FACILITIES: 27 sites (tr - 16); tbls, toil, cga, f, piped drk wtr. ACTIVITIES: Berry-picking; picnicking. Fishing/horseback riding (1 mi). MISC.: Elev 4000 ft; 15 acres; pets.

Little Goose Horse (Gifford Pinchot NF). 5-1/2 mi SW of Trout Lake on St Hwy 141; 10-1/10 mi NW on FS 123. SEASON: 6/1-10/31; 14-day lmt. FACILITIES: 6 sites (tr -16); piped drk wtr, tbls, toil, cga, f. ACTIVITIES: Hiking; picnicking; berry-picking. Fishing (1 mi). MISC.: Elev 4000 ft; 3 acres; pets. Trailhead for access to Indian Heaven. Roadless area which is very scenic in the Fall.

Meadow Creek Indian (Gifford Pinchot NF). 5-1/2 mi SW of Trout Lake on St Hwy 141;14-3/10 mi NW on FS 123. SEAS:6/15-9/30; 14-day lmt. FACILITIES: 8 sites (tr -16); tbls, toil, cga, f, no drk wtr, stream. ACTIVITIES: Berrypicking; horseback riding; picnicking; fishing. MISC.: Elev 4100 ft; 2 acres; pets. Reserved for Indian use only.

Morrison Creek (Gifford Pinchot NF). 1/5 mi SE on St Hwy 151; 1-9/10 mi N on Co Hwy 17; 2-7/10 mi N on FS N80; 6-1/10 mi N on FS N81. SEASON: 7/1-9/30; 14-day lmt. FACILITIES: 12 sites (no tr); no drk wtr, stream, tbls, toil, cga, f. ACTIVITIES: Mountain climbing; picnicking; horseback riding (1 mi). MISC.: Elev 4600 ft; 3 acres; pets.

Morrison Creek Horse (Gifford Pinchot NF). 1/5 mi SE of Trout Lake on St Hwy 141; 1-9/10 mi N on Co Hwy 17; 2-7/10 mi N on FS N80; 6 mi N on FS N81. SEASON: 7/1-9/30; 14-day lmt. FACILITIES: 5 sites (tr -16); no drk wtr; stream, tbls, toil, cga, f. ACTIVITIES: Mountain climbing; picnicking; horseback riding. MISC.: Elev 4600 ft; 3 acres. Historic. Pets.

Saddle (Gifford Pinchot NF). 5-1/2 mi SW of Trout Lake on St Hwy 141; 18-3/10 mi NW on FS 123; 1-3/10 mi N on FS N705. SEASON: 6/15-9/30; 14-day lmt. FACILITIES: 12 sites (tr -16); no drk wtr; tbls, toil, cga, f. ACTIVITIES: Berrypicking; horseback riding; picnicking. MISC.: Elev 4200 ft; 5 acres; pets.

Smokey Creek (Gifford Pinchot NF). 5-1/2 mi SW of Trout Lake on St Hwy 141; 8-4/5 mi NW on FS 123. SEASON: 6/15-10/31; 14-day lmt. FACILITIES: 3 sites (no tr); toil, cga, f.

South (Gifford Pinchot NF). 5-1/2 mi SW of Trout Lake on St Hwy 141; 18-3/10 mi NW on FS 123; 3/10 mi E on FS N705. SEASON: 6/15-9/30; 14-day lmt. FACILITIES: 9 sites (tr -16); well drk wtr, tbls, toil, cga, f. ACTIVITIES:

Berrypicking; horseback riding; picnicking. MISC.: Elev 4000 ft; 2 acres; pets.

Surprise Lakes Indian (Gifford Pinchot NF). 5½ mi SW on St Hwy 141; 16-3/10 mi NW on FS 123. SEASON: 6/15-9/30; 14-day lmt. FACILITIES: 9 sites (tr -16); tbls, toil, cga, f, no drk wtr. ACTIVITIES: Picnicking; berry-picking; fishing; horseback riding. MISC.: Elev 4100 ft; 10 acres; scenic; pets. RESERVED FOR INDIAN USE ONLY.

Timberline (Gifford Pinchot NF). 1/5 mi SE of Trout Lake on Co Hwy 17; 2-7/10 mi N on FS N80; 10-1/10 mi N on FS N81. SEASON: 7/1-9/30; 14-day lmt. FACILITIES: 3 sites (no tr); toil, cga, f. ACTIVITIES: Picnicking. MISC.: Elev 6300 ft; pets. 1 mi S of Mt. Adams Wilderness.

Twin Falls (Gifford Pinchot NF). 1-2/5 mi W of Trout Lake on St Hwy 141; 16-3/10 mi NW on FS N88; 5-1/5 mi N on FS 123. SEASON: 7/1-9/30; 14-day lmt. FACILITIES: 7 sites (tr -16); no drk wtr, river, tbls, toil, cga, f. ACTIVITIES: Horseback riding; picnicking; fishing. MISC.: Elev 2700 ft; 4 acres; pets.

TWISP

Black Pine Lake (Okanogan NF). 2 mi E of Twisp on St Hwy 20; 9-3/10 mi S on St Hwy 153; 12 mi NW on FS 3202. SEASON: 5/15-11/15; no time lmt. FACILITIES: 26 sites (tr -22); tbls, toil, cga, f, boat/d. ACTIVITIES: Boating; picnicking; fishing. MISC.: Elev 4200 ft; 2 acres; pets.

Crate Creek (Okanogan NF). 2 mi E of Twisp on St Hwy 20; 12-1/5 mi S on St Hwy 153; 1/10 mi W on Co Hwy 1029; 5-4/5 mi W on FS 3201. SEASON: 5/15-10/15. FACILITIES: 2 sites (no tr); no drk wtr; stream, tbls, toil, cga, f. ACTIVITIES: Picnicking. MISC.: Elev 2800 ft; 2 acres; pets.

Foggy Dew (Okanogan NF). 2-1/5 mi E of Twisp on St Hwy 20; 11-7/10 mi S on St Hwy 153; 3 mi SW on Co Rd 1029; 4-1/10 mi W on FS 3201. SEASON: 5/15-10/15; 14-day lmt. FACILITIES: 15 sites (no tr); piped drk wtr, stream, tbls, toil, cga, f. ACTIVITIES: Picnicking; fishing. MISC.: Elev 2400 ft; 10 acres; pets.

Hidden (Okanogan NF). 12-1/2 mi E of Twisp on St Hwy 20; 7/10 mi N on FS 3621. SEASON: 5/15-10/15; 14-day lmt. FACILITIES: 3 sites (tr -16); piped drk wtr, tbls, toil, cga, f. ACTIVITIES: Picnicking. MISC.: Elev 3500 ft; 1 acre; pets.

J R (Okanogan NF). 12-1/10 mi E of Twisp on St Hwy 20; 1/5 mi N on FS 3325. SEASON: 5/15-11/15; no time lmt. FACILITIES: 5 sites (no tr); piped drk wtr, tbls, toil, cga, f. **ACTIVITIES:** Picnic l - ing. **MISC.:** Elev 3900 ft; 3 acres; pets.

Lyda (Okanogan NF). 13 mi E of Twisp on St Hwy 20; 3-2/5 mi N on FS 3523. **SEASON:** 6/1-10/15; 14-day lmt. **FACILI- TIES:** 2 sites (no tr); no drk wtr; stream, tbls, toil, cga, f. **ACTIVITIES:** Picnicking. **MISC.:** Elev 4300 ft; 1 acre pets.

Mystery (Okanogan NF). 10-4/5 mi W on Co Hwy 9114; 7-3/10 mi NW on FS 349. **SEASON:** 5/15-10/15; 14-day lmt. **FACILITIES:** 5 sites (tr -16); no drk wtr; river, tbls, toil, cga, f. **ACTIVI- TIES:** Fishing; picnicking. **MISC.:** Elev 2800 ft; 1 acre; pets.

Poplar (Okanogan NF). 10-4/5 mi W of Twisp on Co Hwy 9114 (Twisp River Rd); 9-2/5 mi NW on FS 349. **SEASON:** 5/15- 11/15; no time lmt. **FACILITIES:** 17 shaded sites (tr -22); tbls, toil, cga, f, community kitchen; no trash pickup (pack litter out). **ACTIVITIES:** Hunting; mountain climbing; picnicking; fishing; hiking. **MISC.:** Elev 2900 ft; 4 acres; pets. By Twisp River.

Roads End (Okanogan NF). 10-4/5 mi W of Twisp on Co Hwy 9114; 14-2/5 mi NW on FS 349. **SEASON:** 6/1-9/30; 14-day lmt. **FACILITIES:** 4 sites (no tr); no drk wtr; river, tbls, toil, cga, f. **ACT- IVITIES:** Picnicking; fishing. **MISC.:** Elev 3600 ft; 2 acres; pets. Gilbert Historical Site (1 mi E).

South Creek (Okanogan NF). 10-4/5 mi W of Twisp on Co Hwy 9114; 11-3/10 mi NW on FS 349. **SEASON:** 6/1-10/15; 14-day lmt. **FACILITIES:** 5 sites (no tr); no drk wtr; river, tbls, toil, cga, f. **ACTIVITIES:** Picnicking; fishing. **MISC.:** Elev 3100 ft; 2 acres; pets.

USK

Browns Lake (Colville NF). 6-1/2 mi NE of Usk on FS 305; 3 mi N on FS 309. **SEASON:** 5/25-10/10; 14-day lmt. **FACILI- TIES:** 16 sites (tr -22); tbls, toil, cga, f, boat/l/d, piped drk wtr. **ACTIVITIES:** Boating; berrypicking; picnicking; fish - ing. **MISC.:** Elev 3400 ft; 22 acres; pets. Browns Lake.

Panhandle (Colville NF). 3/10 mi E of Usk on Co Hwy CH091; 16-1/5 mi N on Co Hwy CH007. **SEASON:** 5/1-10/25; 14-day lmt. **FACILITIES:** 11 sites (tr -22); tbls, toil, cga, f, boat/l/d (20-ft concrete ramp), piped drk wtr. **ACTIVITIES:** Boat- ing; waterskiing; picnicking; fishing. **MISC.:** Elev 2000 ft; 9 acres; pets. Box Canyon Reservoir.

South Skookum Lake (Colville NF). 7-1/2 mi NE of Usk on FS 305. **SEASON:** 5/20- 10/15; 14-day lmt. **FACILITIES:** 13 sites (tr -22); tbls, toil, cga, f, no drk wtr; lake, boat/l/d. **ACTIVITIES:** Boating; picnicking; fishing; berrypicking. **MISC.:** Elev 3600 ft; 20 acres; pets.

VANCOUVER

Beaver Bay Camp (Pacific P & L). 26 mi N of Vancouver on I-5; then approx. 30-1/2 mi E on Woodland on St Hwy 503; on Lewis River. **SEASON:** December-March, FREE (rest of yr, $2.00). **FACILITIES:** 63 sites; drk wtr, shower, tbls, toil, cga, boat/l, DUMP. **ACTIVITIES:** Boating; swimming; picnicking.

Cougar Camp (Pacific P & L). 26 mi N of Vancouver on I-5; then approx. 29 mi E of Woodland on St Hwy 503; on Lewis River. **SEASON:** LD-MD FREE, (rest of year $2.00). **FACILITIES:** 45 sites; drk wtr, boat/l, tbls, toil, cga. **ACTIVITIES:** Swimming; boating; picnicking.

Saddle Dam Park (Pacific P & L). 26 mi N of Vancouver on I-5 to Woodland; then 22 mi E on St Hwy 503; 5 mi S to campground. **SEASON:** April-November. **FACILITIES:** 14 sites; drk wtr, SHOWER, dump, tbls, toil, cga. **ACTIVITIES:** Picnicking; swimming; boating,l. **MISC.:** On Lewis River.

WALLA WALLA

Squaw Spring (Umatilla NF). From Walla Walla 2 mi E on US 12; 16 mi E on Co Hwy; 12-7/10 mi E on FS N62; 5-1/10 mi S on FS N910. **SEASON:** 7/1-11/5; no time lmt. **FACILITIES:** 10 sites (tr -22) tbls, toil, cga, f, no drk wtr. **ACTIVI- TIES:** Horseback riding; picnicking. **MISC.:** Elev 5000 ft; 3 acres; pets.

WASHOUGAL

Yacolt Multiple Use Area; DNR. There are more than 79,020 acres of DNR-man- aged state-owned lands in the Yacolt MUA which has, as a next door neigh- bor, the Gifford Pinchot NF. Located just E of Vancouver, Washington and I-5, S of the Lewis River and the Cas- cade peaks of St. Helens and Adams, W of the Wind River drainage, and N of the Columbia River. It is easily ac- cessible from all directions. However, because of the rather unpredictable climate of the southern portion of Wash- ington in which the Yacolt MUA is lo- cated, this region is for the sturdier type of recreationists.

ROUTES AND APPROACHES: Good black- top roads lead into the interior of the Yacolt area from all directions. From Vancouver take St Hwy 503 N through Battleground to Yacold and Amboy and on to Canyon Creek. By following Can- yon Creek you can eventually come out over US Forest Service roads into the Winder River Country and down to the Columbia River about 60 miles E of Van- couver. From I-5 you can turn at Wood- land, follow St Hwy 503 up the N side of the North Fork on the Lewis River, or the Clark County Road 16 up the S side of the North Fork of the Lewis River, into the Yacolt MUA. Go S from

Amboy and Yacolt to Co Rd 12, which follows the East fork of the Lewis River. Go E along Co Rd 12 to Dole Valley Bridge and cross the bridge to the S and into the Yacolt MUA. The signing is good. There are seasonally maintained, primitive surfaced roads leading N from the Columbia River off St Hwy 14 but they are not recommended for passenger car travel.

RECREATION: HORSEBACK RIDING. Most of the trails within the MUA are all-purpose trails for both foot and horse traffic. At Rock Creek Camp and Picnic Area there are horse stations, manure boxes and loading ramp. HIKING. The re-located Pacific Crest Trail will traverse through the Three Corner Rock area of the Yacolt MUA.

ALL TERRAIN VEHICLE: The Jones Creek Trailbike Trail is a 12-1/2 mi system of trailbike trails. In addition there is a 1/2 mi minibike trail, located adjacent to Jones Creek ATV camp.

FISHING: Lakes, streams and rivers are stocked by the Department of Game for the public's fishing pleasure. Rainbow and cutthroat trout, plus runs of Silver, Chinook and Jack salmon are found in the rivers and streams. The Washougal River is closed to fishing from Salmon Falls upstream.

HUNTING: Deer, bear, bird.

CLIMATE: Midsummer tempatures are in the upper 70's in the daytime and 50's at night—occasionally they will go to 90 or more than 100 degrees during July and August. During the Winter there can be ice storms when the famed Columbia River Gorge "silver thaw" occurs. East winds can blow at 60-70 mph from the last week of July thru the first week in November. The weatherman's advice is: be prepared for anything when you come to the Yacolt country.

FOR MAPS AND ADDITIONAL INFO: Public Affairs Office, Dept. of Natural Resources, Public Lands Bldg, Olympia WA 98504 or Southeast Area Office, Box 798, Castle Rock, WA 98611; or call toll free 1-800-562-6010.

Dougan (Yacolt MUA; DNR). 15 mi NE of Washougal out Washougal River Valley. FACILITIES: 7 sites; drk wtr, trails, tbls, toil, cga. Accomodates the handicapped. ACTIVITIES: Hiking; picnicking.

Jones Creek (Yacolt MUA; DNR). 9 mi NE of Washougal on Jones Creek. FACILITIES: 8 sites; tbls, toil, cga, drk wtr, trails, off-road facilities (ATV-oriented shelter). ACTIVITIES: Hiking; picnicking.

WILBUR

Keller Ferry (Coulee Dam NRA). 14 mi N of Wilbur on St Hwy 21. SEASON: All year; 14-day lmt. FACILITIES: 22 sites

(tr -16); flush toil, cga, tbls. ACTIVITIES: Boating,ld; picnicking; fishing; swimming.

WINTHROP

Andrews Creek (Okanogan NF). 6-3/5 mi N of Winthrop on Co Hwy 1213; 16-9/10 mi N on FS 392. SEASON: 6/1-10/1. FACILITIES: 1 site (tr -16); no drk wtr; stream, tbls, toil, cga. ACTIVITIES: Horseback riding; hiking; picnicking. MISC.: Elev 3000 ft; 1 acre; pets.

Ballard (Okanogan NF). 13-1/5 mi NW of Winthrop on St Hwy 20; 6-9/10 mi NW on Co Hwy 1163; 2-1/10 mi NW on FS 374 (well-maintained gravel rd). SEASON: 6/1-10/15; 14-day lmt. FACILITIES: 7 sites (tr -22); well drk wtr, tbls, toil, cga. ACTIVITIES: Hunting; hiking; picnicking; fishing. MISC.: Elev 2600 ft; 1 acre; pets. Scenic. [On W fork of the Methow River.] Easy access to Slate Peak Lookout—highest point in Washington (more than 7000 ft) reachable by motorized vehicle.

Buck Lake (Okanogan NF). 6-3/5 mi N of Winthrop on Co Hwy 1213; 2-4/5 mi N on FS 392; 3/5 mi NW on FS 383; 2-3/10 mi NW on FS 3626. SEAS: 5/15-10/15. FAC: 4 sites (tr -16); piped drk wtr, tbls, toil, cga. ACTIVITIES: Picnicking; fishing; boating. MISC.: Elev 3200 ft; 2 acres; pets; lake.

Camp 4 (Okanogan NF). 6-3/5 mi N of Winthrop on Co Hwy 1213; 11-3/10 mi NE on FS 392. SEASON: 6/1-10/15; no time lmt. FACILITIES: 5 sites (tr -16); no drk wtr; river, tbls, toil, cga. ACTIVITIES: Picnicking; fishing. MISC.: Elev 2400 ft; 3 acres; pets.

Chancellor (Okanogan NF). 13-1/5 mi NW of Winthrop on St Hwy 20; 6-9/10 mi NW on Co Hwy 1163; 21-7/10 mi NW on FS 374. SEASON: 7/1-10/1; no time lmt. FACILITIES: 6 sites, (no tr); no drk wtr; stream, tbls, toil, cga. ACTIVITIES: Fishing; picnicking; berrypicking (huckleberries). MISC.: Elev 4800 ft; 2 acres; pets. Historic. Near old mining towns.

Chewack (Okanogan NF). 3/10 mi W of Winthrop on St Hwy 20; 6-3/5 mi N on Co Hwy 1213; 8-3/5 mi NE on FS 392 [on Chewack River]. SEASON: 6/1-10/15. FACILITIES: Large, open, undeveloped area with undesignated number of sites; no drk wtr; river, tbls, toil, cga; no trash pickup (pack litter out). ACTIVITIES: Hunting; picnicking; fishing; hiking. MISC.: Elev 2200 ft; 2 acres; pets. Watch for rattlesnakes.

Chewack River Fish Camp (Okanogan NF). 3/10 mi W of Winthrop on St Hwy 20; turn right and drive 9-3/5 mi on FS 1213 at jct of FS 383 and 392; take FS 392 4/5 mi to campground which is on the right [on Chewack River]. SEASON: 14-day lmt. FACILITIES: 16 sites; tbls, toil, cga; no trash pickup (pack litter). MISC.: Pasayten Wilderness nearby. Watch for rattlesnakes.

Falls Creek (Okanogan NF). 6-3/5 mi N of Winthrop on Co Hwy 1213; 5-3/10 mi N on FS 392. SEASON: 5/15-10/15; no time lmt. FACILITIES: 7 sites (tr -16); tbls, toil, cga, well drk wtr. ACTIVITIES: Hunting; hiking; picnicking; fishing. MISC.: Elev 2300 ft; 5 acres; pets. Beautiful falls. Near Pasayten Wilderness Watch for rattlesnakes.

Flat (Okanogan NF). 6-3/5 mi N of Winthrop on Co Hwy 1213; 2-4/5 mi N on 2 mi NW on FS 383 [on Eightmile Creek]. SEASON: 6/1-10/15. FACILITIES: 9 sites (tr -16); tbls, toil, cga, well drk wtr. ACTIVITIES: Picnicking; hiking; hunting; backpacking; fishing; berry-picking. MISC.: Elev 2600 ft; 3 acres; pets. Near Pasayten Wilderness Area.

Gate Creek (Okanogan NF). 13-1/5 mi NW of Winthrop on St Hwy 20; 4-1/2 mi NW on Co Hwy 1163. SEASON: 5/1-10/15; 14-day lmt. FACILITIES: 4 sites (tr -22); well drk wtr, tbls, toil, cga. ACTIVITIES: Picnicking; fishing. MISC.: Elev 2800 ft; 2 acres; pets.

Harts Pass (Okanogan NF). 13-1/5 mi NW of Winthrop on St Hwy 20; 6-9/10 mi NW on Co Hwy 1163; 12-1/2 mi NW on FS 374. SEASON: 7/1-10/1; 14-day lmt. FACILITIES: 5 sites (no tr); no drk wtr; tbls, toil, cga. ACTIVITIES: Horseback riding; mountain climbing; picnicking. MISC.: Elev 6200 ft; 2 acres; pets. Near viewpoint of Cascade Crest. Scenic.

Honeymoon (Okanogan NF). 6-3/5 mi N of Winthrop on Co Hwy 1213; 2-4/5 mi N on FS 392; 8-9/10 mi NW on FS 383. SEASON: 6/1-10/15; no time lmt. FACILITIES: 6 sites (tr -16); no drk wtr; stream, tbls, toil, cga. ACTIVITIES: Picnicking; fishing. MISC.: Elev 3300 ft; 2 acres; pets.

Lake Creek (Okanogan NF). 6-3/5 mi N of Winthrop on Co Hwy 1213; 14-1/2 mi N on FS 392. SEASON: 6/1-10/15. FACILITIES: 3 sites (tr -16); no drk wtr; tbls, toil, cga. ACTIVITIES: Fishing; picnicking. MISC.: Elev 2800 ft; 2 acres; pets.

Lake Creek Corral (Okanogan NF). 6-3/5 mi N of Winthrop on Co Hwy 1213; 14-1/2 mi N on FS 392; 2-2/5 mi NW on FS 3801. SEASON: 6/1-10/1. FACILITIES: 1 site (no tr); no drk wtr; stream cga; toil. ACTIVITIES: Horseback riding; hiking; picnicking; fishing. MISC.: Elev 3200 ft; 1 acre; pets. Trailhead into Pasayten Wilderness.

Meadows (Okanogan NF). 13-1/5 mi NW of Winthrop on St Hwy 20; 6-9/10 mi NW

on Co Hwy 1163; 12-1/2 mi NW on FS 374; 1 mi S on FS 3739. SEASON: 7/1-10/1; 14-day lmt. FAC: 14 sites (no tr); no drk wtr; tbls, toil, cga. ACT: Hiking; horseback riding; rockhounding. MISC.: Elev 6200 ft; 10 acres; pets. Botanical. Scenic Trail; pine meadows. Access to Pacific National Scenic Trail.

Memorial (Okanogan NF). 6-3/5 mi N of Winthrop on Co Hwy 1213; 1 mi N on FS 392. SEASON: 5/1-10/15; 10-day lmt. FACILITIES: 2 sites (tr -16); well drk wtr, tbls, toil, cga, river. ACTIVITIES: Fishing; picnicking. MISC.: Elev 2000 ft; 1 acre; pets.

Nice (Okanogan NF). 6-3/5 mi N of Winthrop on Co Hwy 1213; 2-4/5 mi N on FS 392; 3-1/5 mi NW on FS 383. SEASON: 6/1-10/15. FACILITIES: 3 sites (tr -16); well drk wtr, tbls, toil, cga. ACTIVITIES: Fishing; picnicking. MISC.: Elev 2700 ft; 2 acres; pets.

River Bend (Okanogan NF). 13-1/5 mi NW of Winthrop on St Hwy 20; 6-9/10 mi NW on Co Hwy 1163; 2-1/2 mi NW on FS 374; 1/2 mi W on FS 3700. [Winding, narrow rd not advisable for tr.] SEASON: 6/1-10/15; 14-day lmt. FACILITIES: 5 sites (tr -22); tbls, toil, cga, well drk wtr. ACTIVITIES: Berrypicking (Oregon grapes and wild strawberries); picnicking; fishing. MISC.: Elev 2700 ft; 3 acres; pets. Historic.

Robinson Creek (Okanogan NF). 13-1/5 mi NW of Winthrop on St Hwy 20; 6-3/5 mi W on Co Hwy 1163; 2 mi W on FS 374. SEASON: 6/1-10/15; 14-day lmt. FACILITIES: 4 sites (tr -16); no drk wtr; stream, tbls, toil, cga. ACTIVITIES: Hiking; picnicking; fishing; horseback riding. MISC.: Elev 2400 ft; 10 acres; pets. Trailhead to Pasayten Wilderness.

Ruffed Grouse (Okanogan NF). 6-3/5 mi W of Winthrop on Co Hwy 1213; 2-4/5 mi N on FS 293; 7-4/5 mi NW on FS 383. SEASON: 6/1-10/15. FACILITIES: 4 sites (tr -16); well drk wtr, stream, tbls, toil, cga. ACTIVITIES: Fishing; picnicking. MISC.: Elev 3200 ft; 2 acres; pets.

Thirtymile (Okanogan NF). 6-3/5 mi N of Winthrop on Co Hwy 1213; 22-7/10 mi NE on FS 392. SEASON: 6/1-10/1; no time lmt. FACILITIES: 10 sites (tr -16); tbls, toil, cga, no drk wtr. ACTIVITIES: Picnicking; fishing. MISC.: Elev 3600 ft; 7 acres; pets; stream.

WOODLAND

Beaver Bay Camp (Pacific P & L). Approx. 30-1/2 mi E of Woodland on St Hwy 503, on Lewis River. [Woodland is located 26 mi N of Vancouver, WA on I-5.] SEASON: Dec.-March, FREE, (rest of yr, $2.00). FACILITIES: 63 sites; drk wtr, tbls, toil, cga, shower, dump, ACTIVITIES: Swimming; boating,1; picnicking.

See page 7 for KEY TO ABBREVIATIONS.

Cougar Camp (Pacific P & L). Approx. 29 mi E of Woodland on St Hwy 503, on Lewis River. [Woodland is located 26 mi N of Vancouver, WA, on I-5.] SEASON: LD-MD, FREE (rest of yr, $2). FACILITIES: 45 sites; drk wtr, tbls, toil, cga, shower. ACTIVITIES: Swiming; boating,l.

Saddle Dam Park (Pacific P & L). 22 mi E of Woodland on St Hwy 503; then 5 mi S to campground. [Woodland is located 26 mi N of Vancouver, WA on I-5.] SEASON: April-November. FACILITIES: 14 sites; drk wtr, shower, toil, dump. ACTIVITIES: Swimming; boating

YAKIMA

Ahtanum Multiple Use Area (DNR). On a clear day, from the top of Darland Mountain in the heart of the Ahtanum MUA, you can literally see forever. The second highest spot in the state accessible by car is atop Darland Mountain at 6,981 ft in elevation. The roads are quite good for the most part with the use of caution needed on the more narrow roads. A 360 degree panoramic view takes in much of the Yakima Valley and the vast Columbia Basin to° the east; the Coastal Range off toward the Pacific Ocean; Mount Jefferson (central Ore), Mount Hood (northern Ore), and the southern Washington peaks of Mount St. Helens and Mount Adams, the Goat Rocks, Mount Rainier, with the Stuart Range and Glacier Peak to the North. You don t have to be the sturdy hiker type to reach this vista point on 6,981 ft Darland Mountain. You can drive there. In fact, it's the 2nd highest point in Washington to which you can drive.

ROUTES AND APPROACHES: 35 mi W of Yakima via an asphalt surfaced county road. Located on the eastern slopes of Washington's central Cascades.

CLIMATE: Winter can arrive with the first snowfall in October and deep snow can remain in the upper reaches from November 1st until July. It is zero minus during the Winter but get warm in mid-Summer. Snow depths average 42" at the DNR Ahtanum headquarters with 5-8 feet at Tree Phones Camp and drifts which reach 18-20 feet at the summit of Darland Mountain. It is always wise to prepare for cool nights during the summer with warm clothing, sleeping bags and rain protection.

HORSEBACK RIDING: At Snow Cabin Camp there are horse camp units with stanchions and manure boxes furnished. Antanum Trail is an all-purpose trail about 4-3/4 mi long connecting Dead Horse Flat to Divide Ridge. Tree Phones Camp has been a horse camp for many years and when reconstructed it will still have facilities in 4 of the camps for horses, plus 14 camp units, 3 picnic units and a snowmobile shelter.

HUNTING: Chukars, ruffed grouse, ring-necked pheasant, and quail, in the lower timberlands and valleys. Waterfowl —wood ducks, mallards and teal nest, along Ahtanum Creek. Rocky Mountain elk, permissible along Divide Ridge from Darland Mountain to Dome Peak and throughout the Cowiche Block of state land.

FISHING: Rainbow, cuthroat trout and whitefish. The trout are stocked by the Washington State Game Dept. in Ahtanum Creek and in some of the larger lakes.

NOTE: The State of Washington Fish and Game Laws do apply except where the Yakima Indians manage big game and fish on the Yakima Indian Reservation.

TERRAIN VEHICLES: Trails and roads in this MUA are open to ATV unless posted closed. All vehicles must stay on established routes and cross-country is prohibited. Snowmobiles may use all roads and trails unless posted closed. Ahtanum Meadows is a popular camp for all terrain vehicle owners. It has a play and meeting area with camping and day use units for ATV people.

SNOWMOBILING: Popular in the Ahtanum during the Winter when the snow is deep, and it can get several feet deep in the Ahtanum Meadows which is close to the county road and has winter-time parking. Tree Phones Camp on the Middle Fork of Ahtanum Creek has a snowmobile shelter.

ADDITIONAL INFORMATION AND MAPS: Write Public Affairs Office, Department of Natural Resources, Public Lands Bldg Olympia, WA 98504 or Southeast Area Office, 713 E. Bowers Rd., Ellensburg, WA 98926; or call toll free 1-800-562-6010.

Ahtanum (Ahtanum MUA; DNR). 30 mi W of Yakima at the jct of North and Middle Fork Ahtanum Creeks. FACILITIES: 11 sites; drk wtr, toil, cga. ACTIVITIES: Fishing; picnicking.

Ahtanum Meadows (Ahtanum MUA; DNR). 29-1/2 mi W of Yakima at the jct of North and Middle Fork Ahtanum Creek. FACILITIES: 11 sites; tbls, toil, cga, picnic area. ACTIVITIES: Picnicking.

Clover Flats (Ahtanum MUA; DNR). 38 mi W of Yakima along the Middle Fork Ahtanum Road. FACILITIES: 9 sites; drk wtr, cga, toil. ACTIVITIES: Hiking; picnicking.

Green Lake (Ahtanum MUA; DNR). 42 mi W of Yakima on Green Lake. FACILITIES: 6 sites; toil, cga. ACTIVITIES: Fishing; picnicking.

See page 7 for KEY TO ABBREVIATIONS.

North Fork (Ahtanum MUA; DNR). 32 mi W of Yakima on North Fork of Ahtanum Creek. FACILITIES: 13 sites; no drk wtr; tbls, toil, cga, trails. ACTIVITIES: Hiking; picnicking.

Snow Cabin (Ahtanum MUA; DNR). 37 mi W of Yakima along North Fork Ahtanum Creek. FACILITIES: 8 sites; tbls, toil, cga, horse facilities. ACTIVITIES: Picnicking; fishing; horseback riding.

Tree Phone (Ahtanum MUA; DNR). 36 mi W of Yakima on Middle Fork of Ahtanum Creek. FACILITIES: 12 sites; horse facilities, group shelter, toil, cga. ACTIVITIES: Horseback riding; picnicking.

Benton Creek, SEASON: 5/1–11/1 14-day lmt. FACILITIES: Undesignated number of sites; spring water, tbls, cga. ACTIVITIES: Hunting; picnicking; fishing. MISC.: ATVs restricted to established rds.

Wenas Campground and Bird Sanctuaary (Boise Cascade Corp.). 28 mi NW of Yakima on Wenas Valley Rd to end payment, then 2 mi N on gravel [on north fork of Wenas Creek]. SEASON: All year; 14-day lmt. FACILITIES: 200 sites (tr no lmt); drk wtr, tbls, toil, cga. ACTIVITIES: Birdwatching (more than 85 species of birds); hunting; picnicking; hiking; snowmobiling; berrypicking. MISC.: 30 acres. No motorbikes.

WEST VIRGINIA

GENERAL STATE INFORMATION

Miscellaneous

Toll-Free Number for Travel Information: 1-800-624-9110
Right Turns on Red: Permitted after full stop, unless otherwise posted.
STATE CAPITOL: Charleston
STATE NICKNAME: Mountain State
STATE BIRD: Cardinal
STATE FLOWER: Rosebay Rhododendron
STATE TREE: Sugar Maple

State Parks

Overnight camping fees range from $2.00–5.00. Pets are permitted if kept on a leash. Further information: West Virginia Department of Natural Resources; State Capitol; Charleston, WV 25305.

Rest Areas

Overnight stops are not permitted in West Virginia Rest Areas.

INFORMATION SOURCES

Maps

The following maps are available from **Forsyth Travel Library** (see order form in Appendix B):

State of West Virginia [Up-to-date, showing all principal roads, points of interest, sports areas, parks, airports, mileage, etc. Full color.]

Completely indexed city maps, including all airports, lakes, rivers, etc., of: Charleston; Huntington; Parkersburg; **Wheeling.**

State Information

Travel Development Division; West Virginia Department of Commerce; 1900 Washington Street, East; Charleston, WV 25305.
West Virginia Department of Natural Resources; State Capitol; Charleston, WV 25305.

For emergency assistance or to report a rural area accident, phone 1-800-642-9061. Ask for the State Police.

See page 7 for KEY TO ABBREVIATIONS.

WEST VIRGINIA

Miscellaneous

Charleston Chamber of Commerce; 914 Quarrier Street; PO Box 471; Charleston,WV 25322.
Nine-Valley Travel Council; PO Box 45; Charleston, WV 25301.
Monongahela NF; USDA Building; Sycamore Street; Box 1231; Elkins, WV 26241.
Corps of Engineers, Huntington District; PO Box 2127; Huntington, WV 25721.
Harpers Ferry National Historical Park; Harpers Ferry, WV 25425.

FREE CAMPGROUNDS

BARTOW

Island (Monongahela NF). 3 mi NE of Bartow on US 250; 2-7/10 mi NE on St Hwy 28; 1/5 mi NW on FS 36. SEASON: 4/15-11/30. FACILITIES: 4 sites (tr - 16); tbls, toil, cga, f, no drk wtr. Gas/food (2 mi). Store/ice (5 mi). ACTIVITIES: Fishing; picnicking. MISC.: Elev 3000 ft; 6 acres; pets; stream.

Laurel Fork (Monongahela NF). 3 mi NE of US 250; 1-9/10 mi NE on St Hwy 28; 18-2/5 mi N on FS 14; 1-3/5 mi SE on FS 423. SEASON: 4/15-11/30; 14-day lmt. FACILITIES: 6 sites (tr -16); tbls, toil, cga, well drk wtr. ACTIVITIES: Picnicking; fishing. MISC.: Elev 3100 ft;4 acres;pets;stream.

BOWDEN

Bear Heaven (Monongahela NF). 2-3/10 mi E of Bowden on US 33; 2-9/10 mi NW on FS 91. SEASON: 4/1-11/30; 14-day lmt. FACILITIES: 7 sites (tr -22); tbls, toil, cga, well drk wtr. Store/food/gas (3 mi). ACTIVITIES: Mountain climbing; hiking; picnicking. Fishing (5 mi). MISC.: Elev 3600 ft; 2 acres; scenic; pets on leash.

Stuart (Monongahela NF). 3-9/10 mi W of Bowden on US 33; ½ mi NW on St Hwy 6. SEASON: All year. FACILITIES: 10 sites (no tr); tbls, toil, cga, well drk wtr. Store/gas/food (1 mi). ACTIVITIES: Hiking; picnicking. Swimming/fishing (1 mi). MISC.: Elev 2200 ft; 3 acres. Pets allowed if kept on a leash.

BRANDYWINE

Camp Run (George Washington NF). 4 mi N of Brandywine on US 33; 10 mi N on St Hwy 3; 2 mi E on Co Hwy 3. [Rough access rd.] SEASON: 4/1-12/1; 14-day lmt. FACILITIES: 9 sites (no tr); tbls, toil, cga, well drk wtr. Store/gas (3 mi). ACTIVITIES: Picnicking. Boating,d [no motor boats] (1 mi). Fishing (1 mi). MISC.: Elev 1500 ft; 3 acres; pets; stream. Nearby lake is stocked for fishing. Good area for scout troops.

COWEN

Beechy Run (NF). 2 mi E of Cowen on St Hwy 20; 7 mi SE on St Hwy 46; 4 mi SE on FS 86; 1 mi SE on FS 108. SEASON: 5/1-12/31; 14-day lmt. FACILITIES: 1 site (no tr); f, cga. MISC.: Elev 2500 ft. Pets permitted if on a leash.

Middlefork (NF). 2 mi E of Cowen on St Hwy 20; 7 mi SE on ST Hwy 46; 4 mi SE on FS 86. SEASON: 5/1-11/1; 14-day lmt. FACILITIES: 4 sites (tr -32); toil, f, cga. MISC.: Elev 2500 ft; pets.

FROST

Bird Run (Monongahela NF). 1½ mi E of Frost on St Hwy 84. SEASON: 3/1-12/1. FACILITIES: 22 sites (tr -32); tbls, toil, cga, f, well drk wtr. Store/gas (2 mi). ACTIVITIES: Fishing; picnicking. MISC.: Elev 2700 ft; 7 acres; pets; stream.

GLADY

Laurel Fork (Monongahela NF). 4-4/5 mi SE of Glady on FS 1; 3/10 mi S on FS 14; 1½ mi SE on FS 1. SEASON: 4/15-11/30; 14-day lmt. FACILITIES: 6 sites (tr -16); tbls, toil, cga, f, well drk wtr. ACTIVITIES: Mountain climbing; picnicking; fishing. MISC.: Elev 3100 ft; 4 acres; stream; pets.

MILL POINT

South Fork Gate (NF). 8-7/10 mi NW of Mill Point on St Hwy 39; 2½ mi NW on FS 102. SEASON: 5/1-11/1. FACILITIES: 2 sites (tr -22); toil, cga. ACTIVITIES:. Picnicking. MISC.: Adjacent to Cranberry Glades Botanical Area. Elev 3300 ft;pets.

MINNEHAHA SPRINGS

Pocahontas (Monongahela NF). 3 mi SE of Minnehaha Springs on St Hwy 39; 2¼ mi S on St Hwy 92. SEASON: 3/1-12/1; 14-day lmt. FACILITIES: 19 sites (tr -32); tbls, toil, cga, f, well drk wtr. ACTIVITIES: Fishing; picnicking. MISC.: Elev 2400 ft; 6 acres; stream; pets.

ONEGO

Seneca (Monongahela NF). 2 mi NW of Onego on US 33; 7/10 mi SW on St Hwy 7. SEASON: 4/1-11/15. FACILITIES: 6 sites (tr -22); tbls, toil, cga, well drk wtr.

See page 7 for KEY TO ABBREVIATIONS.

ACTIVITIES: Mountain climbing; picnicking; fishing. MISC.: Elev 2100 ft;3 acres; pets; store; gas; scenic; stream. Seneca Rocks 5 mi E within Spruce Knob Seneca Rocks National Recreation Area.

RICHWOOD

Big Rock (Monongahela NF). 6-1/5 mi N of Richwood on FS 76. SEASON: 3/15-12/1; 14-day lmt. FACILITIES: 5 sites (tr -16); tbls, toil, cga, well drk wtr. ACTIVITIES: Berry-picking; picnicking; fishing. MISC.: Elev 2200 ft; 1 acre; river; pets.

Iron Bridge (Monongahela NF). 2 mi N of Richwood on St Hwy 7; 3 mi N on FS 761. SEASON: 5/1-11/1; 14-day lmt. FACILITIES: 3 sites (no tr); toil, cga. ACTIVITIES: Picnicking. MISC.: Elev 2200 ft; pets. Along Cranberry River.

Summit Lake (Monongahela NF). 9-9/10 mi E of Richwood on St Hwy 39. SEASON: 3/1-11/1; 14-day lmt. FACILITIES: 17 sites (tr -22); tbls, toil, cga, well drk wtr. ACTIVITIES: Boating,d (no motor boats); picnicking; fishing. MISC.: Elev 3500 ft; 15 acres; lake; pets.

RIVERTON

*Udy Springs (Monongahela NF). 2½ mi S of Riverton on US 33; 2-3/5 mi W on Co Hwy 4; 10-1/5 mi S on FS 112; 3 mi N on TRAIL 515. SEASON: 5/1-10/15. FACILITIES: 6 tent sites; toil, cga, f, well drk wtr, no tbls. ACTIVITIES: Picnicking; fishing; mountain climbing; hiking. MISC.: Elev 3500 ft; 2 acres; pets; scenic; stream. Nature Trails (5 mi). Within Spruce Knob Seneca Rocks National Recreation Area.

SAINT ALBANS

St. Albans Roadside Park. On St Hwy 60, near St. Albans. SEASON: All yr; 1-night lmt.

SUTTON

Bee Run Trailer Park (COE;Sutton Lake). 4 mi N of Sutton on US 19; 1 mi right on Co Hwy 15; 1 mi right at first boat launching area to camping area on left. SEASON: 5/1-9/30; 14-day lmt. FACILITIES: 21 sites (tr -30); tbls, toil, cga, no drk wtr. Store/ice/food nearby. ACTIVITIES: Boating,rl; picnicking. Swimming/fishing nearby. MISC.: Elev 1000 ft; 2 acres; pets on leash.

Brocks Run (COE; Sutton Lake). 4 mi N of Sutton on US 19 to Co Rd 15; 7½ mi right to Neville Rd; 2 mi right. [Rough narrow access road.] SEASON: All yr; 14-day lmt. FACILITIES: 22 sites (tr -19); tbls, toil, cga, no drk wtr. Store nearby. ACTIVITIES: Swimming; picnicking; fishing (excellent); boating,l. MISC.: Elev 1000 ft; 12 acres; lake; very scenic; pets on leash.

WARDENSVILLE

Hawk (George Washington NF). 5-3/5 mi NE of Wardensville on St Hwy 55; 2-9/10 mi NE on FS 502; 1-1/10 mi W on FS 347. SEASON: All yr; 14-day lmt. FACILITIES: 15 sites (tr -22); tbls, toil, cga, f, well drk wtr. ACTIVITIES: Mountain climbing; picnicking. Horseback riding (1 mi). MISC.: Elev 1200 ft; 6 acres; pets. Quiet isolated woodland campground.

WISCONSIN

GENERAL STATE INFORMATION

Miscellaneous

Toll-Free Number for Travel Information:
    1-800-356-9508 [calling from IL, IO, MI, MN]
    1-800-362-9566 [calling within WI]
Right Turns on Red: Permitted after
    full stop, unless otherwise posted.
STATE CAPITOL: Madison
STATE NICKNAME: Badger State
STATE BIRD: Robin
STATE FLOWER: Butterfly Violet
STATE TREE: Sugar Maple

State Parks

Overnight camping fees range from $2.00-4.00. Pets are allowed if kept on a leash. Further information: Bureau of Parks and Recreation; Department of Natural Resources; Box 7921; Madison, WI 53707.

See page 7 for KEY TO ABBREVIATIONS.

WISCONSIN

Rest Areas

Overnight stopping is not permitted in Wisconsin Rest Areas.

Backpacking in the Nicolet NF

You do not need a permit to camp in Nicolet NF. Pack it in, pack it out. Drinking water is available only at the developed campgrounds and day use areas. The water in the streams and flowages within the Forest has not been tested for drinking. Further information: Forest Supervisor; Nicolet NF; Federal Building; 68 South Stevens; Rhinelander, WI 54501.

CHEQUAMEGON NATIONAL FOREST

Flambeau Trails

The Flambeau Trail System passes through varying types of forest cover; both conifers and hardwoods. Approximately 100 miles in length, it crosses several streams, creeks and the South Fork of the Flambeau River. There are several small lakes and ponds adjacent to the trail system. There are two parking lots for the trail system and three rustic campgrounds (Fishtrap, Smith Rapids, Sailor Lake). Other rustic campgrounds, boat landings, picnic areas and swimming beaches are available within a 30 minute drive of the trail parking lots, or within walking distance from specific points on the trail. These campgrounds provide drinking water, sanitation facilities and fireplaces. Drinking water is not available at Fishtrap Campground. Further information: District Ranger; Park Falls Ranger District; City Hall Building;Park Falls, WI 54552.

Rainbow Lake Wilderness

6,583 acres of hiking; camping; cross-country skiing; fishing; canoeing. Six miles of the North Country Trail crosses the area. 15 undeveloped lakes which are 5 acres or larger, and nine smaller ponds; no streams. No permit is necessary. Further information: District Ranger; Washburn, WI 54891.

Ice Age Trail

A National Recreation Trail; approximately 40 miles long and available for year-round use. Developed campsites and drinking water near the trail are available on the Mondeaux Flowage. Camping is also allowed at Jerry Lake and Lake Eleven and at least 50 feet back from other portions of the trail. There are many access points on the trail for those who wish to hike only for short distances. Developed parking facilities are available at the Mondeaux Flowage and off FS 571 at Jerry Lake. Further information: District Ranger; Medford Ranger District; Medford, WI 54451.

North Country Trail

This 60-mile scenic trail traverses the northern half of the Chequamegon National Forest. Camping is permitted along the trail at locations other than Adirondack shelters or developed campgrounds. Campsites should be kept at least 50 feet away from the trail or water's edge in order to protect natural features that presently exist. Proper handling of garbage and sanitation is expected. The North Country Trail passes through the recently established Rainbow Lake Wilderness. This Wilderness Area of some 6,600 acres is located northwest of Drummond, WI. A Wilderness Area Registration Permit is required for entrance. For the convenience of the daily using public, self-registration stations have been located at all entrance points into the Wilderness. However, those desiring to camp overnight in the Wilderness must obtain a camping permit. These must be obtained in advance of entrance into the Wilderness. Camping permits are available by writing or calling the office of the District Forest Ranger; U.S. Forest Service; Washburn, WI 54891 [1-715-373-2667].

INFORMATION SOURCES

Maps

The following maps are available from **Forsyth Travel Library** (see order form in Appendix B):

> **State of Wisconsin** [Up-to-date, showing all principal roads, points of interest, sports areas, parks, airports, mileage, etc. Full color.]

> Completely indexed city maps, including all airports, lakes, rivers, etc., of: **Green Bay; Madison; Milwaukee; Oshkosh.**

State Information

Bureau of Vacation and Travel Services; Department of Natural Resources; PO Box 450; Madison, WI 53701.
Bureau of Parks and Recreation; Department of Natural Resources; Box 7921; Madison, Wisc 53707.
Wisconsin Division of Tourism; PO Box 177; Madison, WI 53701.
Game and Fish Commission; Department of Natural Resources; Box 450; Madison, WI 53701.

Miscellaneous

Frederic Area Community Association; Frederic, WI 54837.
Milwaukee Convention and Visitors Bureau; 828 North Broadway; Milwaukee, WI 53202.
St. Croix National Scenic Riverway; PO Box 708; St. Croix Falls, WI 54024.
Nicolet NF; Federal Building; Rhinelander, WI 54501.
Chequamegon NF; Federal Building; Park Falls, WI 54552.
Upper Mississippi River Wildlife and Fish Refuge; PO Box 415; Room 208, P.O. Building; LaCrosse, WI 54601.
Trempealeau NWR; Upper Mississippi River Wild Life Refuge; District Refuge Manager; Route 1, Box 308; Trempealeau, WI 54661.
Upper Mississippi River Wild Life and Fish Refuge; District Refuge Manager; PO Box 27; Cassville, WI 53806.
Apostle Islands National Lakeshore; 1972 Centennial Drive; Route #1, Box 152; Bayfield, WI 54814.
Corps of Engineers, St. Paul District; 1135 US P.O. and Custom House; St. Paul, MN 55101.

FREE CAMPGROUNDS

ABBOTSFORD

Red Arrow (City Park). ½ mi W of Abbotsford at the jct of St Hwys 13/29. SEASON: All year. FACILITIES: 10 sites; flush toil, store,playground. MISC.:Pets.

ALMA

Modena Rod and Gun Club Park. 13 mi N of Alma on St Hwy 37. [On Buffalo River.] SEASON: All year. FACILITIES: 4 sites;toil, electric hookup. MISC.:Pets.

Rieck's Lake. 2 mi N of Alma on St Hwy 35. FACILITIES: 20 sites; toil, f, playground, electric hookup. ACTIVITIES: Boating,d. SEASON: April-November. MISC.: Rieck's Lake; Mississippi River; pets allowed if kept on a leash.

AMBERG

Campsite #2 (Wisconsin Michigan Power Company). 6-9/10 mi E of Amberg on Co Rd "K"; ½ mi N; 2 mi E; 1-1/5 mi NE to campground on Menominee River. SEASON: All year (probably not plowed out in winter). FACILITIES: Primitive sites; tbls, toil, cga, no drk wtr. ACTIVITIES: Hunting in season (whitetail deer, ruffed grouse); picnicking; fishing. Ice fishing and cross-country skiing in winter. MISC.: Pets on leash.

Campsite #32 (Wisconsin Michigan Power Company). 6-9/10 mi E on Co Rd "K"; ½ mi N on Co Rd; 2 mi E on Co Rd; 1-9/10 mi S on Co Rd to campground. SEASON: All year (probably not plowed out in winter). FACILITIES: Primitive sites; tbls, toil, cga, no drk wtr. ACTIVITIES: Hunting in season (whitetail deer, ruffed grouse); picnicking; fishing;boating,l. Ice fishing and cross-country skiing in winter. MISC.: On Menominee River. Pets on leash.

AUGUSTA

Coon Fork Lake (Eau Claire County Park). 1 mi E of Augusta on 12 on Coon Fork Road; 4 mi to dam; campground on Coon Fork Lake. [Information: 715/286-2639.] SEASON: May-October. FACILITIES: 81 sites; toil, cga, f. ACTIVITIES: Boating,l; swimming. MISC.: Playground. Pets on leash.

AURORA

Campsite #24 (Wisconsin Michigan Power Company). 7-3/10 mi W on Co Rd "N"; 1-7/10 mi N on Co Rd; 2½ mi W on Co Rd; 1 mi N on Co Rd to campground. SEASON: All year (probably not plowed out in winter). FACILITIES: Primitive sites; no drk wtr; tbls, toil, cga. ACTIVITIES: Hunting in season (whitetail deer, ruffed grouse); picnicking; boating,l. Ice fishing and cross-country skiing, winter. MISC.: Pets. On Pine River.

BALSOM LAKE

Balsam Lake Village Campground (Polk County Park). In the village of Balsom Lake. [Information: 715-485-3252.] FACILITIES: 15 sites; flush toil, cga, f, electric hookup, store, playground. Kitchen facilities and diningroom for campers' use. ACTIVITIES: Boating,l; swimming. SEASON: All year. MISC.: Donations asked, but not demanded. Showers. Pets on leash.

BAY CITY

Bay City Park (Pierce County). In Bay City, on Lake Pepin. [Information: 715-594-3131.] SEASON: May-October. FACILITIES: 10 sites; toil, cga, f, store, playground. ACTIVITIES: Boating,rld; swimming. MISC.: Pets on leash.

BAYFIELD

Apostle Islands National Seashore. Maps, information and camping permit (free) can be obtained at the main office: 1972 Centennial Drive; Rural Route; Bayfield, WI 54814.

Primitive camping is allowed on the islands and mainland. A free backcountry use permit is required. All year. Boat access is by boat through the Apostle Islands Outfitters, Inc. [Bayfield, WI 54814] (they don't allow pets), unless visitors have their own boat. Canoeing is not recommended because of the sudden storms which can arise. Winter access is on foot (cross-country skiing, snowshoeing, etc.) and ice conditions should be checked through the Park personnel before venturing out. Drinking water is dipped from Lake Superior. Boiling the water for at least 5 minutes will assure its safe use.

The Apostle Islands are 22 islands in Lake Superior which range in size from 3 to more than 14,000 acres. 20 are included in Apostle Islands National Lakeshore. Hiking, boating, swimming, fishing.

3 mi N of Bayfield is the Red Cliff Indian Reservation, the home of approximately 600 Chippewa Indians. The Red Cliff Cultural Center is open all year.

BENNETT

Lyman Lake Park (County Park). 8 mi W of Bennett on St Hwy L. SEASON: 5/1-11/30. FACILITIES: Sites; toil, cga, f, store. ACTIVITIES: Boating,d. MISC.: Pets on leash.

BLANCHARDVILLE

McKellar Memorial City Park (Lafayette County Park). In the village of Blanchardville on St Hwy 78 (30 mi S of Madison, Pecatonica River). [Paved access rds.] SEASON: All year. FACILITIES: 25 sites; tbls, flush toil, cga, electric hookup, showers, store, playground. ACTIVITIES: Boating,l; swimming; picnicking; fishing; softball; hiking; horseshoes; hunting. MISC.:Pets.

CASSVILLE

Bertom Lake (COE; Mississippi River Public Use Area). 3½ mi S of Cassville on St Hwy 133; 2 mi W on Co Rd to campground. SEASON: All yr; 14-day lmt. FACILITIES: 10 sites; tbls, toil,

cga, drk wtr. Store/ice nearby. ACTIVITIES: Swimming; picnicking; fishing; boating,rl;horseback riding. MISC.:Pets.

Upper Mississippi River Wild Life and Fish Refuge. Maps of the Refuge (Pools 10 and 11) and additional information is available at the Refuge Office, above the Badger State Bank, in Cassville [608-725-5198].

There are no designated campsites on the Refuge and all campsites are primitive. All year, 14-day limit at or within 100 yards of any site. Persons engaged in hunting may camp only on sites readily visible from the main navigation channel of the Mississippi River or on designated developed campsites (run at a fee by other sources). No

Upper Miss. River Refuge (cont.) person engaged in hunting may camp within areas closed to hunting. Trappers may not camp on the Refuge. Stinging nettles and poison ivy are very dense during the camping season and limit camping to bare dredge spoil beaches along the main river channel. Boating (excursion trips and boat rentals at marinas, landings or municipal boatyards along the river). Fishing. Thousands of visitors use the sandbars and beaches along the main channel for picnicking and swimming. No specific facilities.

CHETEK

Rest Area. 5 mi S of Chetek on US 53 south. SEASON: All year; 1-night lmt. ACTIVITIES: Spaces for self-contained RVs; tbls, toil, cga, dump, phone. ACTIVITIES: Picnicking. MISC.: Pets.

CHIPPEWA FALLS

Irvine Park (City Park). North part of Chippewa Falls on St Hwy 53. SEASON: 4/20-10/20. FACILITIES: 55 sites; tbls, flush toil, cga, f, playground, store. Phone. ACTIVITIES: Boating,r; swimming; picnicking; hiking; tennis. Golf nearby. MISC.: Duncan Creek; Glen Lock Flowage; pets. Donations. Zoo nearby. Donations.

COLUMBUS

Astico Park (County Park). 3 mi E of Columbus off St Hwy 16. SEASON: 4/15-10/15. FACILITIES: Sites; toil, cga, f, playground, tbls. Flowing well. ACTIVITIES: Boating; picnicking. MISC.: Pets; park ranger in attendance at all times. Over 1500 feet of frontage on the meandering Crawfish River.

CORNUCOPIA

Siskiwit Lake (City Park). 10 mi S of Cornucopia on Hwy "C". SEASON: May-November. FACILITIES: 10 sites; toil, cga, f, playground. ACTIVITIES: Boating,r; swimming. MISC.: On Siskiwit Lake. Beach. Pets on leash.

See page 7 for KEY TO ABBREVIATIONS.

DARLINGTON

Darlington Riverside Park (City Park).
In the city of Darlington, on the N edge
of town, on St Hwy 23. SEASON: All yr.
FACILITIES: 10 sites; tbls, cga. ACTIVI-
TIES: Boating,l; fishing. MISC.: On the
Pecatonia River. Playground; pets.

DURAND

Durand City Park. In the city of Durand
on the Chippewa River. SEASON: 5/1-9/10.
SEASON: 10 sites; toil, electric hookup,
store, f, cga. MISC.: Reservations ac-
cpeted. Pets on leash.

EAGLE RIVER

Windsor Dam (Nicolet NF). 17 mi E of
Eagle River on St Hwy 70; 3 mi S on
FS 2174. SEASON: 4/29-12/1; 14-day lmt.
FACILITIES: 8 sites (tr -22); tbls, toil,
cga, f, well drk wtr. Store/ice/gas (5
mi). ACTIVITIES: Berry-picking; picnic-
ing; fishing. MISC.: Elev 1600 ft; 5
acres; stream; scenic; pets.

EAU GALLE

Lakeview Resort (Dunn County Park).
In the village of Eau Galle. [Informa-
tion: 715-283-4882.] SEASON: All year.
FACILITIES: 15 sites; toil, cga, f,
store, playground. ACTIVITIES: Boating,rl; swimming. MISC.: Pets on leash.
On Lake Eau Galle.

FIFIELD

Fishtrap Campground (Chequamegon NF).
16½ mi E of Fifield on St Hwy 70; 5
mi N on FS 144; 3/10 mi E on FS 1955.
SEASON: 5/15-9/15; 14-day lmt. FACILI-
TIES: 2 sites (tr -22); tbls, toil, cga,
no drk wtr, f. Ice/food/gas (3 mi).
ACTIVITIES: Berry-picking; picnicking;
fishing. Boating,rl (3 mi). Swimming/
waterskiing (5 mi). MISC.: Elev 1600
ft; 2 acres; pets; river. Adjacent to
South Fork of Flambeau River.

Smith Rapids (Chequamegon NF). 12½
mi E of Fifield on St Hwy 70; 1-7/10
mi N on FS 148. SEASON: 5/15-9/15; 14-
day lmt. FACILITIES: 2 sites (tr -22);
toil, cga, f. ACTIVITIES: Fishing; boating,l. Adjacent to South Fork of Flambeau River. MISC.: Elev 1600 ft;pets.

FLORENCE

Campsite #5 (Wisconsin Michigan Power
Company). 6-4/5 mi SE of Florence on
US 1/141; 4-3/10 mi S on Co Rd to campground. SEASON: All year (probably
not plowed out in winter). FACILITIES:
Primitive sites; no drk wtr, tbls, toil,
cga. ACTIVITIES: Hunting in season
(whitetail deer, ruffed grouse); picnic-
ing; fishing; boating,l. Ice fishing
and cross-country skiing in winter.
MISC.: Pets on leash. On Pine River.

Perch Lake (Nicolet NF). 13-2/5 mi W
of Florence on St Hwy 70; 3/5 mi N on
FS 2150; 3/10 mi W on TRAIL 3533. SEA-
SON: 4/28-12/2; 14-day lmt. FACILITIES:
5 tent sites; tbls, toil, cga, f, no drk
wtr. ACTIVITIES: Boating; picnicking;
fishing; hiking. MISC.: Elev 1600 ft;
10 acres; nature trails; scenic; pets.

FREDERIC

Village Park (City Park). In Frederic
on Coon Lake, approximately 6 blocks
from the business district (of a town
of approximately 1000 in population).
SEASON: All yr; 5-day lmt. FACILITIES:
Undesignated primitive sites; tbls, toil,
cga, water from a faucet. ACTIVITIES:
Baseball; picnicking. Fishing is available in surrounding lakes, many of which
are less than 10 mi from Frederic.
MISC.: Lake is not used for swimming
or fishing. Baseball diamond. 9-hole
golf course (1 mi). Pets on leash.

GILMAN

Gilman Swinging Bridge Park (City Park).
In the village of Gilman. [Information:
715-937-2682.] SEASON: All year. FACILI-
TIES: 7 sites; toil, cga, f, store. ACTIV-
ITIES: Picnicking. MISC.:Pets;playground.

GRANTSBURG

Highway 70 Campground (St. Croix National Scenic Riverway). 4 mi W of
Grantsburg on St Hwy 70 to the St. Croix
River. Before crossing the river into
Minnesota, the campground is on your
left at the Wisconsin end of the bridge.
Accessible by FOOT, or by traveling
downriver BY CANOE. Overnight parking
of vehicles at the campground is not
allowed. SEASON: 4/1-10/31; 14-day lmt.
FACILITIES: 15 tent sites; toil, cga.
Water is available across the river at
a Ranger Station, a distance of about
¼ mile. ACTIVITIES: Hiking; boating.
MISC.: Pets allowed if kept on leash.

GURNEY

Potato River Falls (County Park). 1½
mi N of Gurney on St Hwy 169. SEASON:
5/15-11/1; 14-day lmt. FACILITIES: 10
sites (tr -30); tbls, toil, cga, f, drk
wtr. ACTIVITIES: Fishing; picnicking.
MISC.: Pets on leash. Located on the
Potato River.

HAYWARD

Tomahawk Lake Park (City Park). 22
mi N of Hayward just off Co Hwy "N"
on Tomahawk Lake. SEASON: All year.
FACILITIES: 10 sites; toil. ACTIVITIES:
Swimming. MISC.: Beach; pets.

HOLCOMBE

Lake Holcombe Sportsmen's Park. 3 mi
N of Holcombe on St Hwy 27; 2 mi W

on town road, on Lake Holcombe. SEA-
SON: 5/1-10/15. FACILITIES: 35 sites;
toil, cga, f, store, playground. ACTIVI-
TIES: Swimming; boating,d. MISC.:
Donations requested. Reservations avail-
able. Beach; Lake Holcombe. Pets.

HORICON

Horicon Ledge Park (County Park).
2 mi E of Horicon with access from St
Hwy 28 to Raasch Hill Road. SEASON:
5/1-10/1. FACILITIES: Sites; tbls, toil,
cga. ACTIVITIES: Picnicking. MISC.:
On Rock River. Interesting rock formations of the Niagara Escarpment extend
the length of the park. 60 acres.
Camping permits can be obtained free
from the park ranger who is in attendance at all times during the season.
Pets on leash.

IRON RIVER

Brule River (Nicolet NF). 8½ mi SW of
Iron River on St Hwy M73; 1 mi SW on
St Hwy W55. SEASON: 4/25-10/15; 14-day
lmt. FACILITIES: 11 sites (tr –22); tbls,
toil, cga, well drk wtr. Store/ice/gas
(5 mi). ACTIVITIES: Canoeing; picnicking; fishing. Boating,l/waterskiing
(1 mi). MISC.: Elev 1700 ft; 5 acres;
pets. Swimming (1 mi). Brule River
is a fine canoeing and trout fishing
stream.

KENNAN

Big Falls (County Park). 12 mi S of
Kennan on Co Rd "N". SEASON:5/15-11/15;
14-day lmt. FACILITIES: 5 sites; tbls,
toil, cga, f, playground, drk wtr. AC-
TIVITIES: Swimming; boating,rd; picnicking; fishing. MISC.: Pets. Jump River.

LaCROSSE

LaCrosse District of the Upper Mississippi National Wildlife Refuge. Maps
and information on Pool 7 & 8 are available at Room 208 of the Post Office
building, 425 State Street, downtown
LaCrosse. [Information: PO Box 415;
54601.] SEASON: All yr; 14-day lmt. FACI-
LITIES: Undesignated primitive camping.
No facilities. ACTIVITIES: Fishing; hunting; boating; canoeing. MISC.: Pets.

LADYSMITH

Bruce Park (Municipal Park). 8 mi W
of Ladysmith on US 8. SEASON: 5/1-10/1.
FACILITIES: 20 sites; tbls, toil, cga,
electric/water hookups, drk wtr. Store/
ice/laundry/food nearby. ACTIVITIES:
Boating,l; picnicking. Golf/fishing nearby. MISC.: River. Pets on leash.

LA FARGE

LaFarge Village Park (City Park). In
LaFarge on the Kickapoo River. [Infor-
mation: 608-625-2180.] SEASON: April-

October. FACILITIES: 2 sites; toil, electric hookup, cga, f, store, sewer hookup,
playground. MISC.: Pets on leash. Store.

LAONA

Big Joe Canoe Landing (NF). 7 mi N of
Laona on US 8; 4/5 mi N on St Hwy W139;
1/5 mi SW on FS 2500. SEASON: 4/30-12/1;
14-day lmt. FACILITIES: 2 sites (no tr);
tbls, toil, cga, f, no drk wtr. Store/gas/
ice/laundry/food (2 mi). ACTIVITIES:
Boating,l; canoeing; berry-picking; picnicking; fishing. MISC.: Elev 1600 ft;
3 acres; river; scenic; pets on leash.

LORETTA

Brunet River (NF). 2½ mi N of Loretta
on Co Hwy GG; 1/10 mi N on FS 621.
SEASON: 5/1-11/30. FACILITIES: 3 sites;
tbls, toil, cga, no drk wtr. Store/gas/
ice/food (3 mi). ACTIVITIES: Fishing;
picnicking. Boating,l/swimming/waterski-
ing (3 mi). MISC.: Location of old CCC
camp. River. Pets on leash.

LUCK

Luck Village Park (City Park). In village of Luck on Big Butternut Lake.
[Information: 715-472-2610.] SEASON:
Spring through Fall. FACILITIES: 25
sites; tbls, toil, cga, electric hookup;
cold showers; playground. ACTIVITIES:
Boating,rld; swimming; picnicking; fishing; softball; waterskiing. MISC.: Pets.

MANITOWOC

Maribel Caves (County Park). 18 mi
N of Manitowoc on St Hwy 141 on W Twin
River. SEASON: MD-10/1. FACILITIES:
Sites; toil, playground. MISC.: Pets.

MARSHFIELD

City Park. On St Hwy 13, west, in
Marshfield. SEASON: All year. FACILI-
TIES: Sites. MISC.: Pets.

Wildwood Park (City Park). In Marshfield on Wildwood Pond. [Information:
715-384-3606.] SEASON: April-October.
FACILITIES: 18 sites; flush toil, electric
hookups, playground. ACTIVITIES: Swimming. MISC.: Pets; zoo.

MAUSTON

Kennedy Park (Juneau County Park).
New Lisbon exit on I-90, 94, N of New
Lisbon, 3 mi, on Lemonweir River, in
Mauston. [Information: 608-843-4352.]
SEASON: 4/1-11/1. FACILITIES: 50 sites;
toil, cga, f. ACTIVITIES: Boating,l.
MISC.: Reservations accepted; pets.

MEDFORD

Chelsea Conservation Club (Taylor County
Park). 9 mi N of Medford on St Hwy
13. SEASON: May-November. FACILITIES:
10 sites; toil, electric hookup, cga,
f, playground. MISC.: Pets on leash.

Horseshoe Boat Landing (Taylor County Park). 6 mi N of Medford to Whittlesey; NW on town roads. [On Horseshoe Lake.] [Information: 715-748-3475.] SEASON: May-November. FACILITIES: 4 sites; toil. ACTIVITIES: Boating,l. MISC.: Pets.

MINONG

*Howell Bridge Campground (St. Croix National Scenic Riverway). 14 mi W of St Hwy 53 in Minong on St Hwy 77; 2 mi S (left) on Burian Road to the Namekagon River. Campground is accessible by FOOT or by CANOE. SEASON: 4/1-10/31. FACILITIES: 8 sites; toil, cga, treated well water. ACTIVITIES: Picnicking; hiking; canoeing. MISC.: Pets permitted if kept on leash.

NECEDAH

Necedah Park (Juneau County). 1/3 mi W of Necedah on St Hwy 21 (on S side of St Hwy 21). SEASON: All year. FACILITIES: 20 sites; tbls, toil, cga, electric hookup, f, playground.

NEW AUBURN

Rest Area. 5 mi N of New Auburn on US 53 N. SEASON: All yr; 1-night lmt. FACILITIES: Spaces for self-contained RVs. Tbls, toil, cga, dump, phone. ACTIVITIES: Picnicking. MISC.: Pets on leash.

LAONA

*Big Joe Canoe Landing (Nicolet NF). 7 mi N of Laona on US 8; 4/5 mi N on St Hwy W139; 1/5 mi SW on FS 2500. SEASON: 5/1-11/15; 14-day lmt. FACILITIES: 3 sites (no tr); tbls, toil, cga, f. ACTIVITIES: Berry-picking; canoeing; boating; picnicking; fishing. MISC.: Scenic; pets. River canoeing campsite. No river boats.

NORWALK

Norwalk Village Park. ¼ block off St Hwy 71, in Norwalk. SEASON: All year. FACILITIES: Sites. MISC.: Pets on leash.

OSSEO

Stoddard Park (Trempealeau County Park). In Osseo, on Lake Martha. [Information: 715-597-3172.] FACILITIES: 10 sites; toil, cga, f, electric hookup, store, playground. ACTIVITIES: Boating,ld. MISC.: Reservations accepted. Pets on leash.

PEPIN

Pepin Public Campground (City Park). At the west end of Pepin on St Hwy 35. SEASON: 5/1-9/10. FACILITIES: 10 sites (tr -17); tbls, toil, cga, playground, drk wtr. Store/ice/food/laundry nearby. ACTIVITIES: Boating,rld; snowmobiling; picnicking. Fishing/swimming nearby. MISC.: On Lake Pepin. Pets on leash.

PORT WING

Lake Park (City Park). ¼ mi N of Port Wing. SEASON: All year. FACILITIES: 12 sites; toil, cga, f, store. ACTIVITIES: Boating,d; swimming. MISC.: On Lake Superior; beach; pets on leash.

Twin Falls Park (City Park). ¼ mi W of Port Wing on St Hwy 13. SEASON: All year. FACILITIES: 3 sites; toil, cga, f. ACTIVITIES: Hiking. MISC.: Falls; pets. On Twin Falls Creek.

PORTAGE

County Fairgrounds. 4 blocks S of Portage on St Hwy 51. SEASON: All year. FACILITIES: Sites. MISC.: Pets on leash.

Veterans Memorial Field (City Park). In Portage. Inquire locally for directions. SEASON: 6/1-9/31; 2-day lmt. FACILITIES: Sites; toil, store, dump, playground. MISC.: Pets on leash.

POTOSI

Grant River (COE; Mississippi River PUA). 2 mi S of Potosi on Co Rd; W on first improved rd across the railroad tracks. SEASON: All yr; 14-day lmt. FACILITIES: 200 sites; tbls, toil, cga, dump, playground, drk wtr. ACTIVITIES: Boating,l; swimming; picnicking; fishing. MISC.: Pets on leash.

READSTOWN

Tourist Park (City Park). In Readstown, on Kickapoo River. [Information: 608-629-2373.] SEASON: 5/1-10/15. FACILITIES: 100 sites; toil, electric hookup ($), cga, f, store, playground. ACTIVITIES: Boating,rld. MISC.: Reservations accepted. Pets on leash.

RICHLAND CENTER

Pier County Park. 9 mi N of Richland Center on St Hwy 80. SEASON: All yr; 7-day lmt. FACILITIES: 23 sites; tbls, toil, cga, gas, playground. ACTIVITIES: Hiking; picnicking; fishing; canoeing; boating. MISC.: Pets on leash.

SAND CREEK

Sand Creek Community Park (City Park). West of the Red Cedar River on Co Rd "U" and "V". [Information: 715-658-1325.] SEASON: All year. FACILITIES: 6 sites; toil, cga, f, store. ACTIVITIES: Swimming; boating,ld. MISC.: Pets on leash. Red Cedar River.

SEELEY

Silverthorn Lake (City Park). ¼ mi N of Seeley on St Hwy 63. SEASON: 6/1-9/30. FACILITIES: Sites; toil, cga, f, playground. ACTIVITIES: Swimming; boating,d. MISC.: Pets on leash.

SHELDON

Sheldon Community Park (City Park). On the S edge of Sheldon. [Information: 715-452-2635.] SEASON: All yr. FACILITIES: 12 sites; toil, electric hookup, cga, f, store, playground. ACTIVITIES: Swimming; boating,ld. MISC.: On Jump River. Pets permitted if kept on leash.

SPRING VALLEY

Eau Galle Dam and Reservoir (COE; St. Paul District). SEASON: 5/15-11/30; 14-day lmt. FACILITIES: 34 sites (tr -32); toil, f, playground. ACTIVITIES: Swimming; picnicking; fishing; boating,l. MISC.: Change house; overlook; pets.

STEUBEN

Steuben Landing (County Park). At Arco station in Steuben. SEASON: All year. FACILITIES: 20 sites; tbls, toil, cga, gas. ACTIVITIES: Swimming; picnicking; fishing; boating; softball. MISC.: Pets.

SUPERIOR

Lake Minnesuing Park (County Park). 25 mi SE of Superior on St Hwy P. SEASON: 5/1-11/30. FACILITIES: Sites; toil, f. ACTIVITIES: Boating,rd; swimming.

Radigaw Dam (County Park). 32 mi S of Superior on St Hwy 35. SEASON: 5/1-11/30. FACILITIES: Sites; toil, f, store. ACTIVITIES: Swimming. MISC.: Pets.

Rest Area. 2 mi SE of Superior on US 2 and St Hwy 53. SEASON: All year; 1-night lmt. FACILITIES: Spaces for self-contained RVs; tbls, toil, cga, dump, phone. ACTIVITIES:Picnicking. MISC.:Pets.

THREE LAKES

Pine River (Nicolet NF). 6 mi E of Three Lakes on St Hwy 32; 1½ mi N on FS 2178; 7½ mi E on FS 2182. SEASON: 5/1-12/1; 14-day lmt. FACILITIES: 5 sites (tr -22); tbls, toil, cga, f, well drk wtr. ACTIVITIES: Berry-picking; boating,ld; picnicking; fishing. Canoeing in May and first half of June. MISC.: Elev 1600 ft;8 acres; stream; scenic; pets.

TONY

Big Falls Dam (Rusk County Park). 1 mi E of Tony on St Hwy 8; take Co Rd "X" 5 mi N. [Information: 715-322-4636.] SEASON: All year. FACILITIES: 10 sites; toil, cga, f, playground. ACTIVITIES: Boating,l; swimming. MISC.: On Big Falls Flowage. Pets allowed if kept on leash.

TREMPEALEAU

Trempealeau NWR. Maps of the Refuge (Pools 4/5 and 5a/6) and additional information is available at the Refuge Office in Trempealeau. [Information: RR 1; Box 308; Trempealeau, WI 54661; 608/539-3620.] SEASON: All year; 14-day

lmt. [At or within 100 yards of any site.] FACILITIES: Primitive undesignated sites. ACTIVITIES: Hunting; boating; canoeing; fishing. MISC.: Pets.

VIOLA

Viola Park (Richland County Park). 1 mi E of Viola on St Hwy 56. SEASON: 5/1-9/30. FACILITIES: 25 sites; tbls, toil, cga, f, drk wtr, playground. Store/ice/laundry/food/bottled gas nearby. ACTIVITIES: Picnicking. MISC.: On Camp Creek. Pets on leash allowed.

WARRENS

Wazeda Park (County Park). 2 mi NW of Warrens on Town Road. [On Cranberry Flowage.] SEASON: 5/1-11/30. FACILITIES: 16 sites; toil, electric hookup, cga, f. ACTIVITIES: Boating,ld.

WAUZEKA

Plum Creek (County Park). 4 mi N of Wauzeka, along Kickapoo River. FACILITIES: Sites; toil, cga, f. ACTIVITIES: Boating,d; swimming. SEASON: All year.

WESTBORO

Eastwood (Taylor County Park). 9 mi W of Westboro on Co Rd "D"; ½ mi S on FS 104. SEASON: 4/15-12/14; 14-day lmt. FACILITIES: 22 sites; toil, cga, f. ACTIVITIES: Swimming; boating,l.

North Twin Lake (Taylor County Park). 9 mi W of Westboro on Co Rd "D" to Mondeaux Dam; 5 mi SW on FS 107/566. SEASON: April-December; 14-day lmt. FACILITIES: 6 sites; toil, cga, f. ACTIVITIES: Boating,l. MISC.: North Twin Lake. Pets allowed on leash.

WHEELER

Wheeler Village Park (City Park). In the village of Wheeler on Hay River. [Information: 715-632-2523.] SEASON: Summer months. FACILITIES: 7 sites; toil, cga, f, store. ACTIVITIES: Boating,ld; swimming. MISC.: Hay River.

WINNECOUNE

Lake Poygan (County Park). 8 mi W of Winnecoune on Co Rd "B". SEASON: 5/1-9/15. FACILITIES: Sites; toil. ACTIVITIES: Swimming; boating,rd. MISC.: Pets.

WOODFORD

Blackhawk County Park. 1 mi N of Woodford; 12 mi W of Monroe; 5 mi N on St Hwy 11. SEASON: All yr. FACILITIES: 25 sites; toil, electric hookups, cga, f. ACTIVITIES: Boating,ld. MISC.: Pecatonica River. Pets on leash.

WYOMING

Miscellaneous

Toll-Free Number for Travel Information:
  1-800-443-2784 [calling from outside WY]
Right Turns on Red: Permitted after
  full stop, unless otherwise posted.
STATE CAPITOL: Cheyenne
STATE NICKNAME: Equality State
STATE BIRD: Meadowlark
STATE FLOWER: Indian Paintbrush
STATE TREE: Cottonwood

State Parks

Overnight camping fees, $2.00-5.00. Pets are permitted if kept on a leash. Further information: Wyoming Recreation Commission; Box 309; Cheyenne, WY 82002.

Rest Areas

Overnight stops by self-contained vehicles are not prohibited but are discouraged.

BACKCOUNTRY AND WILDERNESS CAMPING

Black Hills NF Backcountry Camping

Camping is permitted throughout the National Forest outside of developed campgrounds, except at signed locations around Pactola, Sheridan, Bismarck and Deerfield Lakes. Open fires in the South Dakota portion of the forest are permitted only in grates in developed campgrounds and picnic areas, unless a fire permit is obtained in advance from the local District Ranger's office. Fire is an ever-present danger in the hills, and violators of the no-open-fires law are subject to stiff penalties. Further information: Forest Supervisor; Bearlodge District; Black Hills NF; PO Box 608; Sundance, WY 82729.

Bridger Wilderness (Bridger-Teton NF)

383,300 acres of scenic wildland. More than 1300 lakes. Fishing. Moose, bighorn sheep, elk, and deer are found in this area. Gannett Peak, the highest point in Wyoming, is 13,785 feet above sea level. Many glaciers are located in the Wind River Range, including the seven largest in the continental U.S. outside of Alaska. Rugged mountain climbing. Hiking. Approximately 500 miles of trails. Further information: Forest Supervisor; Bridger-Teton NF; Box 1888; Jackson, WY 83001.

Grand Teton NP Backcountry Camping

Over 200 miles of trails. The beginning elevation for most trails is 6800 feet. A written FREE permit is required for all overnight, backcountry use. This permit is available at the Moose Visitor Center which is open all year, or at Jenny Lake Ranger Station and Colter Bay Visitor Center during the summer months. Camping permits are not available by mail. They must be picked up in person. A few designated camping sites still remain below the 7000-foot level. They are located on Jackson, Bearpaw, Trapper, Leigh and Phelps Lakes only. Wood fires are allowed in the fire grates provided at these lakeside sites, fire danger permitting. No pets or firearms.

Reservations may be made for some of the backcountry camping areas with 30% of these areas available for this purpose. Reservations are accept BY MAIL ONLY from 10/1-6/1. Submit your FINAL itinerary indicating where you wish to stay each night and your group total to: Permits Office; Grand Teton NP; PO Box 170; Moose, WY 83012. No reservations accepted after 6/1. Group size is limited to a MAXIMUM of 12 people per group in any given canyon per night. Further information: Superintendent; Grand Teton NP; Box 67; Moose, WY 83012.

Yellowstone NP Backcountry Camping

Free permit is required; however, there is a $2.00 park entrance fee from May–October; $1.00 the rest of the year. Or use your Golden Eagle or Golden Age Passport.** 3-day limit per site; all year; no pets. Approximately 1000 miles of hiking trails; 420 backcountry campsites. Large population of grizzly (250) and black (500) bears. Do not hike alone. Further information: Superintendent; Yellowstone NP; PO Box 168; Yellowstone NP, WY 82190.

INFORMATION SOURCES

Maps

The following maps are available from **Forsyth Travel Library** (see order form in Appendix B):

> **State of Wyoming** [Up-to-date, showing all principal roads, points of interest, sports areas, parks, airports, mileage, etc. Full color.]
>
> Completely indexed city maps, including all airports, lakes, rivers, etc., of: **Casper; Cheyenne; Lander; Rawlings; Riverton; Sheridan.**

Gold Mining and Prospecting

Geological Survey of Wyoming; University of Wyoming; Laramie; WY 82070.

State Information

Wyoming Travel Commission; 2320 Capitol Avenue; Cheyenne, WY 82002.
Wyoming Recreation Commission; Box 309; Cheyenne, WY 82002.
Wyoming Game and Fish Commission; PO Box 1589; Cheyenne, WY 82001.
Wyoming Highway Department; Box 1708; Cheyenne, WY 82002.
Department of Economic Planning and Development; 720 West 18th Street; Cheyenne, WY 82002.
Wyoming Archives and Historical Department; State Office Building; Cheyenne, WY 82002.

City Information

Buffalo Chamber of Commerce; PO Box 927; Buffalo, WY 82834.
Casper Area Chamber of Commerce; Box 399; Casper, WY 82601.
Cheyenne Chamber of Commerce; 122 East 17th Street; Cheyenne, WY 82001.
Cody Area Chamber of Commerce; Box 1221; Cody, WY 82414.
Greater Cheyenne Chamber of Commerce; PO Box 1147; Cheyenne, WY 82001.
Jackson Hole Chamber of Commerce; Box E; Jackson, WY 83001.
Laramie Chamber of Commerce; Box 1166; Laramie, WY 82070.

National Forests

Regional Forester; US Forest Service; Federal Center, Building 85; Denver, CO 80225.
U.S. Forest Service; PO Box 129; Douglas, WY 82633.
Bighorn NF; Columbus Bldg; PO Box 2046; Sheridan, WY 82801.
Black Hills NF; PO Box 608; Sundance, WY 82729.
Bridger-Teton NF; Forest Service Bldg; Box 1888; Jackson, WY 83001.
Medicine Bow NF In Wyoming; US Forest Service; Rocky Mountain Region; Federal Center Building 85; Denver, CO 80225.
Shoshone NF; PO Box 961; Cody, WY 82414.
Teton NF; Jackson, WY 73001.

Miscellaneous

Devils Tower National Monument; Devils Tower, WY 82714.
National Park Service; PO Box 168; Yellowstone NP, WY 82190.
Grand Teton NP; Box 67; Moose, WY 83012.
John D. Rockefeller, Jr., Memorial Parkway; c/o Grand Teton NP; Box 67; Moose, WY 83012.
Bighorn Canyon NRA; 454 Nevada Avenue; Lovell, WY 82431.
Flaming Gorge NRA; 1450 Uinta Drive; Green River, WY 82935.
Wyoming [plus Kansas and Nebraska] BLM; 2515 Warren Avenue; PO Box 1828; Cheyenne, WY 82001.

**See page 5.

FREE CAMPGROUNDS

ALPINE

Wolf Creek (Bridger-Teton NF). 8-1/10 mi E of Alpine on US 89. **SEASON:** 5/25-9/5. **FACILITIES:** 10 sites; tbls, toil, cga, f, no drk wtr. **ACTIVITIES:** Picnicking; fishing. Horseback riding (1 mi). **MISC.:** Elev 5800 ft; 4 acres reiver. Pets permitted if kept on leash.

ALTON

Salt River (Lincoln Cty). 9 mi N of Alton, G.F. **SEASON:** 5/1-10/31; 5-day lmt. **FACILITIES:** 10 sites; tbls, toil, cga, no drk wtr. **ACTIVITIES:** Picnicking; fishing; hunting. **MISC.:** Special Attraction: Star Valley. Pets permitted.

ALVA

Bearlodge (Black Hills NF). 7-1/5 mi SE of Alva on St Hwy 111. **SEASON:** 6/1-10/1; 10-day lmt. **FACILITIES:** 7 sites (tr -22); tbls, toil, cga, piped drk wtr. **ACTIVITIES:** Picnicking. **MISC.:** Elev 4700 ft; 1 acre. Pets.

BASIN

Basin Chamber of Commerce CG (City Pk). 1/2 block W of US 16/20 in Basin. **SEASON:** 5/1-10/1; 30-day lmt. **FACILITIES:** 20 sites; tbls, flush toil, cga, elec hkup, pull-thru sp. Store/food/ice/laundry nearby. **ACTIVITIES:** Swimming($); hunting; picnicking; fishing; hiking. Golf (nearby). **MISC.:** Elev 3840 ft; 2 acres. Pets; river.

Basin City Park Behind City hall; paved access rds. Sites need blocking. **SEASON:** 5/1-10/1; 30-day lmt. **FACILITIES:** 25 pull-thru spaces; tbls, flush toil, cga, elec/wtr hkups. **ACTIVITIES:** Picnicking; playground. **MISC.:** Elev 3850 ft. Pets.

BEULAH

Sand Creek (Crook Co.). 4 mi S of Beulah. **SEASON:** 5/1-11/30; 5-day lmt. sites; tbls, toil, cga, no drk wtr. **ACTIVITIES:** Hunting; picnicking; fishing **MISC.:** Spec. Attraction: Black Hills. Pets permitted if kept on leash.

BIG HORN

* **Coffeen Park** (Bighorn NF). 9-3/10 mi SW of Big Horn on Co Rd 335; 8 mi SW on FS FH 631; 8 mi SW on TRAIL FH592. **SEASON:** 7/1-9/15; 7-day lmt. **FACILITIES:** 5 tent sites (no trailers); tbls, toil, cga, no drk wtr. **ACTIVI-TIES:** Picnicking; fishing. **MISC.:** Elev 8500 ft; 2 acres. Borders Cloud Peak Primitive Area. 4-wheel drive needed.

* **Cross Creek** (Bighorn NF). 9-3/10 mi SW of Big Horn on Co Rd 335; 8 mi SW on FS Rd FH631; 6 mi S on TRAIL FH592. **SEASON:** 6/15-9/15; 14-day lmt. **FACILI-TIES:** 3 sites; tbls, toil, cga, no drk wtr. **ACTIVITIES:** Picnicking; fishing. **MISC.:** Elev 8400 ft; 2 acres. 4-wheel drive needed last 6 miles. Pets.

East Fork (Bighorn NF). 9-3/10 mi SW of Big Horn on Co Hwy 335; 8 mi SW on FS FH631; 1/2 mi S on FS F6311. **SEASON:** 6/15-9/15; 7-day lmt. **FACILI-TIES:** 11 sites (tr -16); tbls, toil, cga, no drk wtr. **ACTIVITIES:** Picnicking; fishing. **MISC.:** Elev 7600 ft; 6 acres; stream. Pets permitted if kept on leash.

* **Little Goose** (Bighorn NF). 9-3/10 mi SW of Big Horn on Co Rd 335; 1 mi W on FS Rd 631; 1½ mi S on TRAIL FH275. **SEASON:** 6/15-9/15; 14-day lmt. **FACILI-TIES:** 3 sites; tbls, toil, cga, no drk wtr. **ACTIVITIES:** Picnicking; fishing. **MISC.:** Elev 7000 ft; 2 acres; stream. Pets permitted if kept on leash.

Ranger Creek (Bighorn NF). 9-3/10 mi SW of Big Horn on Co Hwy 335; 10 mi SW on FS FH631. **SEASON:** 6/15-9/15; 7-day lmt. **FACILITIES:** 11 sites (tr -16); tbls, toil, cga, piped drk wtr. **ACTIVI-TIES:** Picnicking; fishing. **MISC.:** Elev 7800 ft. 5 acres. Steep grades-trailers no advised from Big Horn side. Pets.

Middle Piney Lake (Bridger Teton NF). 20 mi W of Big Piney on Co Hwy 350; 6-3/5 mi W on FS 10046. **SEASON:** 7/1-9/30; 14-day lmt. **FACILITIES:** 5 sites (no trailers); tbls, toil, cga, f, well drk wtr. **ACTIVITIES:** Hunting; pic-nicking; fishing. Horseback riding (1 mi). **MISC.:** Elev 8600 ft; 3 acres; lake. On E shore of Middle Piney Lake. Pets permitted if kept on leash.

Sacajawea (Bridger Teton NF). 20 mi W of Big Piney on Co Hwy 350; 4-3/10 mi W on FS 10046. **SEASON:** 7/1-9/30; 14-day lmt. **FACILITIES:** 26 sites (tr -22); tbls, toil, cga, f, piped drk wtr. **ACTIVITIES:** Hiking; picnicking; fishing. Horseback riding (1 mi). Boating,d (2 mi). **MISC.:** Elev 8200 ft; 5 acres. Pets.

BONDURANT

Kozy (Bridger Teton NF). 8 mi NW of Bondurant on US 189. **SEASON:** 6/1-9/30. **FACILITIES:** 8 sites (tr -32); tbls, toil, cga, f, no drk wtr. Food/gas (2 mi). **ACTIVITIES:** Picnicking; fishing. Horseback riding/rental (3 mi). **MISC.:** Elev 6400 ft; 4 acres. 30 mi East of Jackson, Wyo. Pets.

See page 7 for KEY TO ABBREVIATIONS.

BOULDER

Big Sandy (Bridger-Teton NF). 15 mi SE of Boulder on St Hwy 353; 21 mi SE on Co Rd 23118; 6 mi N on FS 116 SEASON: 6/20-9/10; 10-day lmt. FACILITIES: 12 sites (tr -22); tbls, toil, cga, f, piped drk wtr. ACTIVITIES: Swimming; picnicking; fishing; hiking. MISC.: Elev 9100 ft; 18 acres. Trail entrance to Wilderness Big Sandy Creek. Trailhead to Bridger Wilderness Pets permitted if kept on leash.

Boulder Lake (Bridger-Teton NF). 2 mi E of Boulder on St Hwy S353; 6 mi N on Co Hwy 114; 3 mi E on FS 114. SEASON: 6/1-10/15; 10-day lmt. FACILITIES: 20 sites (tr -22); tbls, toil, cga, f, well drk wtr. ACTIVITIES: Hiking; picnicking; fishing; boating; swimming; waterskiing; horseback riding. MISC.: Elev 7300 ft; 11 acres; scenic; river. Trailhead to Bridger Wilderness. Pets.

Burnt Lake (Bridger-Teton NF). 1 mi NW of Boulder on US 187; 9½ mi NE on Co Rd; 1 mi E on FS Rd. SEASON: All yr; 14-day lmt. FACILITIES: Unltd sites; no drk wtr. ACTIVITIES: Hunting; fishing. MISC.: Burnt & Meadow Lakes. Pets permitted if kept on leash.

BUFFALO

Buffalo Municipal CG. 3 blks W of I-25. SEASON: 5/1-10/31; 5-day lmt. FACILITIES: 20 sites; tbls, toil, cga, drk wtr. ACTIVITIES: Hunting; picnicking; fishing; swimming; boating. MISC.: Elev 4800 ft. Municipal pool. Big Horn Mtns. Pets permitted if kept on leash.

Buffalo Tourist Park Hwy 16 (Fort St) turn left on N Desmet St. SEASON: All yr. FACILITIES: No des. sites, toil, cga. ACTIVITIES: Swimming; fishing; tennis; playground. MISC.: Pets.

Canyon (NF). 25½ mi W of Buffalo on US 16; 2 mi E on FS 570. SEASON: 6/1-9/15; 7-day lmt. FACILITIES: 4 tent sites (no trailers); tbls, toil, cga, f. Store/food/gas (2 mi). ACTIVITIES: Hunting; picnicking; fishing. MISC.: Elev 7400 ft; 2 acres. Pets permitted.

Circle Park (Bighorn NF). 14½ mi W of Buffalo on US 16; 2½ mi W on FS 697. SEASON: 6/1-9/15; 7-day lmt. FAC: 10 sites (tr -16); tbls, toil, cga, f, no drk wtr. Store/food/gas (4 mi). MISC.: Elev 7900 ft; 5 acres. Pets permitted if kept on leash. ACTIVITIES: Picnicking; fishing.

Crazy Woman (Bighorn). 26 mi W of Buffalo on US 16; 3/10 mi W on FS 148. SEASON: 5/15-9/15; 7-day lmt. FACILITIES: 5 tent sites (no trailers); tbls, toil, cga, f, no drk wtr. Store/;food/gas (1 mi). ACTIVITIES: Picnicking; fishing. MISC.: Elev 7600 ft; 2 acres; stream. Pets permitted if kept on leash.

Doyle (Bighorn NF). 27 mi W of Buffalo on US 16; 5½ mi SW on FS 571; 3/10 mi SE on FS 645. SEASON: 6/1-9/15; 14-day lmt. FACILITIES: 19 sites (tr -22); tbls, toil, cga, f, no drk wtr. ACTIVITIES: Picnicking; fishing MISC.: Elev 8100 ft; 8 acres; stream. Pets permitted if kept on leash.

Lost Cabin (Bighorn NF). 26 mi SW of Buffalo on US 16; ½ mi N on FS 647 SEASON: 6/1-9/15. FACILITIES: 20 sites; tbls, toil, cga, no drk wtr. ACTIVITIES: Picnicking; fishing. MISC.: Elev 8200 ft; 5 acres; stream. Pets permitted if kept on leash.

* **North Fork Trailhead** (Bighorn NF). 12 mi W of Buffalo on US 16; 2 mi NW on FS Rd; 5 mi W on TRAIL. SEASON: 7/1-9/15. FACILITIES: 3 tent sites; tbls, toil, cga, no drk wtr. ACTIVITIES: Picnicking. MISC.: Adjacent to Cloud Peak Wilderness Area. 4-wheel drive needed. Pets.

South Fork (Bighorn NF). 15 mi W of Buffalo on US 16; 1/5 mi E on FS 556. SEASON: 5/15-9/15; 7-day lmt. FACILITIES: 8 tent sites; tbls, toil, cga, f, no drk wtr. Store/food/gas (1 mi). ACTIVITIES: Picnicking; fishing. MISC.: Elev 7800 ft; 4 acres; stream. Pets permitted if kept on leash.

Tiehack (Bighorn NF). 14-1/2 mi W on US 16; 3/5 mi E on FS 555. SEASON: 5/15-9/15; 14-day lmt. FACILITIES: 8 sites (tr -16); tbls, toil, cga, f, no drk wtr. Store/food/gas (2 mi). ACTIVITIES: Picnicking; fishing. MISC.: Elev 7500 ft; 3 acres; stream. Pets permitted if kept on leash.

CASPER

Alcova Lake CG (County Park). 35 mi SW of Casper off Wyo 220 NCPB. SEASON: 4/15-11/15; 3-day lmt. FACILITIES: 12 sites; tbls, toil, cga, elec/wtr/sewer hookup, dump, store, gas, ice. ACTIVITIES: Hiking; picnicking; fishing; boating,rd; swimming; waterskiing. MISC.: Elev 5500 ft; scenic boat trips; Alcova Dam; playground; lake. Pets permitted if kept on leash.

Beartrap Meadow Park (County Park). 11 mi S of Casper on St. Secondary 1301 (gravel access rds). SEASON: All yr; 3-day lmt. FACILITIES: 15 sites; toil, cga, drk wtr. ACTIVITIES: Picnicking; horseback riding; rockhounding; sledding; snow shoeing; playground; snow skiing. MISC.: Elev 8000 ft. Braille trail (for the blind). 27 mi of snowmobile trails. Pets permitted.

Casper Mtn Park (County Park). 11 mi S of Casper on St. Sec. 1301 (gravel access rds). SEASON: 4/15-11/15; 3-day lmt. FACILITIES: 175 sites; tbls, toil, cga, drk wtr. **ACTIVITIES:** Horseback riding; picnicking; hunting; hiking; sledding; snow shoeing; rockhounding; snow skiing. **MISC.:** Elev 8000 ft; Casper Mtn NCPB. 27 mi of snowmobile trails. Pets permitted if kept on leash.

Gray Reef Reservoir (Co. Pk.) 20 mi SW of Casper off St Hwy 220 (paved access rds). **SEASON:** 4/15-11/15; 3-day lmt. **FACILITIES:** 30 sites; tbls, toil, cga, pull-thru sp. **ACTIVITIES:** Swimming; picnicking; fishing. **MISC.:** Elev 6000 ft. Pets.

Lodgepole (BLM). 17 mi S of Casper on Co & BLM Rds. **SEASON:** 7/1-10/31; 14-day lmt. **FACILITIES:** 15 sites; tbls, toil, cga. **ACTIVITIES:** Picnicking. **MISC.:** Pets permitted.

Pathfinder (Co. Pk.) 37 mi SW of Casper on St Hwy 220, then 2 mi S on Co Rd (paved access rds). **SEASON:** 4/15-11/15; 3-day lmt. **FACILITIES:** 100 sites; toil, cga. **ACTIVITIES:** Swimming; fishing; boating,d. **MISC.:** Elev 6000 ft. Pets permitted if kept on leash.

Ponderosa Park (County Park). 11 mi S of Casper on Wyo 251. **SEASON:** Winter **FACILITIES:** Unltd sites; tbls, toil, cga, no drk wtr. **ACTIVITIES:** Hunting; picnicking; snowmobiling. **MISC.:** Pets.

Rim CG (BLM) 17 mi S of Casper on Co & BLM Rds. **SEASON:** 7/1-10/31; 14-day lmt. **FACILITIES:** 8 sites; tbls, toil, cga. **ACTIVITIES:** Hunting; picnicking. **MISC.:** Muddy Mtn. Pets permitted.

Rotary Park (County Park). 3½ mi S of Casper Mtn Rd. NCPB. **SEASON:** All yr; 3-day lmt. **FACILITIES:** 20 sites; tbls, toil, cga, no drk wtr. **ACTIVITIES:** Picnicking; fishing. **MISC.:** Pets.

CENTENNIAL

Libby Creek-Aspen (Medicine Bow NF). 2-3/10 mi NW of Centennial on St Hwy W; 1/10 mi W on FS Rd 351. **SEASON:** 6/1-9/30; 7-day lmt. **FACILITIES:** 8 sites (tr -22); tbls, toil, cga, f, drk wtr. Store/ice/food/gas/laundry/showers (2 mi). Visitor Ctr/dump (1 mi). **ACTIVITIES:** Picnicking; fishing. Horseback riding (1 mi); rental (5 mi). **MISC.:** Elev 8600 ft; 3 acres; historical interest; stream. Pets.

Libby Creek-Fir (Medicine Bow NF). 1-7/10 mi NW on St Hwy 130; 1/5 mi W on FS 351. **SEASON:** 6/10-9/15; 1-day lmt. **FACILITIES:** 4 tent sites (no trailers); tbls, toil, cga. **ACTIVITIES:** Picnicking; fishing. **MISC.:** Elev 8600 ft; stream. Pets permitted.

Libby Creek-Pine (Mecicine Bow NF). 2 mi NW of Centennial on St Hwy 130; 1/2 mi W on FS 35. **SEASON:** 6/1-9/30; 7-day lmt. **FACILITIES:** 6 sites (tr -16); tbls, toil, cga, no drk wtr. Store/food/gas/ice/laundry/showers (2 mi). Visitor Ctr/dump (1 mi). **ACTIVITIES:** Picnicking; fishing. Horseback riding (1 mi); rental (5 mi). **MISC.:** Elev 8600 ft; 4 acres; stream. Pets.

Libby Creek-Willow (Medicine Bow NF). 2 mi NW of Centennial on St Hwy 130; 1/2 mi W on FS 351. **SEASON:** 6/1-9/30; 7-day lmt. **FACILITIES:** 13 sites (tr -22); tbls, toil, cga, f, drk wtr. Visitor center (1 mi). Store/food/gas/ice/laundry/showers (3 mi). **ACTIVITIES:** Picnicking; fishing. Horseback riding (1 mi); rental (5 mi). **MISC.:** Elev 8600 ft; 9 acres; stream. Pets.

Mirror lake (Medicine Bow NF). 12½ mi W of Centennial on St Hwy 130. **SEASON:** 7/1-9/15; 7-day lmt. **FACILITIES:** 12 sites (tr -32); tbls, toil, cga, drk wtr **ACTIVITIES:** Boating,d; picnicking; fishing; mtn climbing; hiking. **MISC.:** Elev 10,600 ft; 12 acres. Trailhead to Medicine Bow Peak. Pets permitted.

North Fork (Medicine Bow NF). 3½ mi NW on St Hwy 130; 1-7/10 mi NW on FS 101. **SEASON:** 6/1-9/30; 14-day lmt. **FACILITIES:** 16 sites (tr -16); tbls, toil, cga, drk wtr. Dump (5 mi). Visitor Ctr (4 mi). **ACTIVITIES:** Picnicking; fishing. **MISC.:** Elev 8600 ft; 3 acres; stream. Pets permitted if kept on leash.

Silver Lake (Medicine Bow NF). 16 mi W of Centennial on St Hwy 130. **SEASON:** 7/1-9/15; 14-day lmt. **FACILITIES:** 21 sites (tr -32); tbls, toil, cga, piped drk wtr. **ACTIVITIES:** Boating,d; picnicking; fishing. **MISC.:** Elev 10,400 ft: 8 acres; lake. Pets permitted.

CODY

Dead Indian (Shoshone NF). 17 mi N of Cody on St Hwy 120; 8-3/5 mi NW on Co Hwy 70; 11-4/5 mi NW on FS 14100. **SEASON:** 5/15-10/15; 14-day lmt. **FACILITIES:** 6 sites (tr -32); tbls, toil, cga, well drk wtr. **ACTIVITIES:** Picnicking; fishing. **MISC.:** Elev 6100 ft; 11 acres; stream; scenic. Pets permitted.

Deer Creek (Shoshone NF). 42 mi SW of Cody on St Hwy 1501. **SEASON:** 6/15-9/30; 14-day lmt. **FACILITIES:** 7 sites (tr -16); tbls, toil, cga, f, no drk wtr. **ACTIVITIES:** Picnicking; fishing. Horseback riding (5 mi). **MISC.:** Elev 6400 ft; 2 acres; stream; scenic. Trailhead to Washakie Wilderness, access to Toton Wilderness & Thorndfare Country. Pets permitted if kept on leash.

See page 7 for KEY TO ABBREVIATIONS.

Pahaska Trailhead (Shoshone NF). 49-1/5 mi W of Cody on US 16. SEASON: 6/15-9/30; 14-day lmt. FACILITIES: 4 sites (tr -16); tbls, toil, cga, f, no drk wtr. Store/gas/food (1 mi). ACTIVITIES: Picnicking; fishing. Horseback riding/rental (1 mi). MISC.: Elev 6800 ft; 1 acre. Horse corral & parking lot for overnite use by wilderness users only. Pets permitted if kept on leash.

Legion Park (County Park). On 1-25, N edge of town. SEASON: Summer only; 1-day lmt. FACILITIES: 12 sites; tbls, toil, cga, drk wtr. ACTIVITIES: Picnicking. MISC.: Pets on leash.

COKEVILLE

Hams Fork (Bridger Teton NF). 12 mi N of Cokeville on St Hwy 232; 4 mi NE of Cokeville on Co Hwy; 13 .mi E on FS 10062. SEASON: 6/15-9/10; 14-day lmt. FACILITIES: 10 sites (tr -16); tbls, toil, cga, f, piped drk wtr. ACTIVITIES: Picnicking; fishing; hunting. MISC.: Elev 8000 ft; 7 acres; scenic; stream. Pets.

Spring Lake Creek (Bridger-Teton NF). 12 mi N of Cokeville on St Hwy 232; 4 mi NE on Co Hwy 232; 2 mi N on FS 10062; 9/10 mi N on FS 10070. SEASON: 7/1-9/1; 14-day lmt. FACILITIES: 5 sites; toil, f, drk wtr. ACTIVITIES: Swimming; fishing; horseback riding; boating. MISC.: Elev 7300 ft; 3 acres; stream; scenic. Lake Alice Rd closed to motorized vehicles at CG. Pets.

CORA

Green River Lake (Bridger-Teton NF). 24 mi N of Cora on St Hwy 352; 18 mi NE on FS 91. SEASON: 6/15-9/10; 10-day lmt. FACILITIES: 23 sites (tr -22); tbls, toil, cga, f, piped drk wtr. ACTIVITIES: Hiking; picnicking; fishing. Boating/swimming/horseback riding (1 mi). MISC.: Elev 8000 ft; 19 acres; scenic. Wilderness entrance. Pets permitted if kept on leash.

Narrows (Bridger-Teton NF). 9 mi N of Cora on St Hwy 352; 4-3/5 mi E on FS 107; 2½ mi E on FS. SEASON: 6/1-9/10; 10-day lmt. FACILITIES: 19 sites (tr -32); tbls, toil, cga, f, drk wtr. ACTIVITIES: Picnicking; hiking. Boating,l/swimming/fishing/wtrski/horseback riding (1 mi). MISC.: Elev 7800 ft; 16 acres; scenic; lake. Pets permitted if kept on leash.

New Fork Lake (Bridger-Teton NF). 11 mi N of Cora on St Hwy 352; 4-3/5 mi E on Co Hwy; 2-4/5 mi SE on FS 107. SEASON: 6/1-9/10; 10-day lmt. FACILITIES: 15 sites (tr -22); tbls, toil, cga, f, piped drk wtr. ACTIVITIES: Picnicking; fishing; boating (ld, 1 mi); swimming; fishing; waterskiing. MISC.: Elev 7800 ft; 9 acres; lake. Pets permitted.

Whiskey Grove (Bridger-Teton NF). 20 mi N of Cora on St Hwy 352; 2-9/10 mi N on FS 91; 2/5 mi W on FS. SEASON: 6/15-9/10; 10-day lmt. FACILITIES: 9 sites (tr -16); tbls, toil, cga, f, piped drk wtr. ACTIVITIES: Picnicking; fishing. MISC.: Elev 7800 ft; 3 acres. On Green River. Pets.

DAYTON

Dead Swede (Bighorn NF). 34 mi SW of Dayton on US 14; 3 mi SE on FS FH641. SEASON: 6/15-9/30; 14-day lmt. FACILITIES: 22 sites (tr -22); tbls, toil, cga, no drk wtr. ACTIVITIES: Picnicking; fishing. MISC.: Elev 8400 ft; 10 acres; river. Pets permitted if kept on leash.

Game & Fish Commission CG (County Park). 4 mi SW of Dayton off US 14. SEASON: 5/1-10/31; 5-day lmt. FACILITIES: 5 sites; tbls, toil, cga. ACTIVITIES: Picnicking; fishing. MISC.: Big Horn Mtns. Pets permitted.

North Tongue (Bighorn NF). 29 mi SW of Dayton on US 14; 1 mi N on FS FH532. SEASON: 6/1-9/30; 7-day lmt. FACILITIES: 11 sites (tr -16); tbls, toil, cga, no drk wtr. Store/food/gas/ice/dump (1 mi). ACTIVITIES: Picnicking; fishing. Horseback riding; rental (1 mi). MISC.: Elev 7900 ft; 6 acres. Pets.

South Tongue (Bighorn NF). 27 mi SW of Dayton on US 14. SEASON: 6/1-9/30; 4-day lmt. FACILITIES: 7 sites; tbls, toil, cga, no drk wtr. ACTIVITIES: Picnicking; fishing. Boating,l (2 mi). MISC.: Elev 7700 ft. Pets permitted.

Tie Flume (Bighorn NF). 34 mi SW of Dayton on US 14; 2 mi E on FS FH 631. SEASON: 6/15-9/30; 14-day lmt. FACILITIES: 25 sites (tr -22); tbls, toil, cga, no drk wtr. ACTIVITIES: Picnicking;

DOUGLAS

Ayres Natural Bridge Park (County Pk.).12 mi W of Douglas on 1-25, 5 mi S on Co Rd 12W. SEASON: 4/1-11/1; 1-day lmt. FACILITIES: 16 sites; tbls, toil, cga, drk wtr. ACTIVITIES: Picnicking; fishing. MISC.: Elev 5300 ft; scenic mtn drives. Pets permitted.

Camel Creek (Medicine Bow NF). 1 mi W of Douglas on 1-25; 20 mi SW on St Hwy 91; 13 mi SW on Co Hwy 24. SEASON: 6/1-10/15. FACILITIES: 8 sites (tr -22); tbls, toil, cga, f, well drk wtr. ACTIVITIES: Picnicking; fishing. Horseback riding (2 mi). MISC.: Elev 8200 ft; 3 acres; stream. Pets.

Curtis Gulch (Medicine Bow NF). 1 mi W of Douglas on 1-25; 20 mi SW on

St Hwy 91; 14½ mi S on Co Hwy 16; 4 mi NE on FS 658. **SEASON:** 7/1-10/15. **FACILITIES:** 6 sites (tr -22); tbls, toil, cga, f, well drk wtr. **ACTIVITIES:** Picnicking; fishing. Horseback riding (2 mi). **MISC.:** Elev 7500 ft; 1 acre. Pets permitted.

Esterbrook (Medicine Bow NF). 1 mi W on I-25; 17 mi S on Co Hwy 94; 11 mi S on Co Hwy 5; 3 mi E on FS FH653. **SEASON:** 6/1-10/15. **FACILITIES:** 12 sites (tr -22); tbls, toil, cga, f, well drk wtr. Store/food/gas (3 mi). **ACTIVITIES:** Picnicking. Horseback riding (1 mi). Fishing (2 mi). **MISC.:** Elev 6500 ft; 10 acres. Pets permitted.

Friend Park (Medicine Bow NF). 17 mi S on St Hwy 94; 11 mi S on Co Hwy 5; 15 mi SW on FS 653; 3½ mi SE on FS 671. **SEASON:** 6/15-10/15. **FACILITIES:** 6 sites (tr -22); tbls, toil, cga, f, well drk wtr. **ACTIVITIES:** Picnicking. Horseback riding and fishing (1 mi). **MISC.:** Elev 7400 ft; 3 acres; stream; scenic; pets.

Riverside Park (County Park). W edge of Douglas on US 20M, 26M, 87. **SEASON:** 5/1-10/1; 4 pm-10 am. **FACILITIES:** 75 sites; tbls, toil, cga, f, drk wtr. **ACTIVITIES:** Swimming; hunting; **MISC.:** Elev 4900 ft. Jackalope Plunge. Wyo. Pioneer Mus. – 6 mi (paved access rds). Some pull-thru spaces. Pets.

DUBOIS

Double Cabin CG (Shoshone NF). 29 mi N of Dubois on FS 14508. **SEASON:** 6/1-9/30; 14-day lmt. **FACILITIES:** 15 sites (tr -22); tbls, toil, cga, f, piped drk wtr. **ACTIVITIES:** Rockhounding; picnicking; fishing. **MISC.:** Elev 9300 ft; 8 acres. Entrance to primitive area. Geological interest. The nearby Wiggins Fork is a source of petrified wood & the area is a favorite for rockhounds. Pets permitted if kept on leash.

East Fork (County Park). 20 mi NE of Dubois off US 26-287. **SEASON:** 5/1-1/31; 5-day lmt. **FACILITIES:** 4 sites; tbls, toil, cga. **ACTIVITIES:** Hunting; picnicking; fishing. **MISC.:** Wind Rive Mtns. Pets permitted if kept on leash.

Horse Creek (Shoshone NF). 12 mi N of Dubois on FS Rd 14507. **SEASON:** 6/1-10/31; 14-day lmt. **FACILITIES:** 9 sites (tr -22); tbls, toil, cga, f, no drk wtr. **ACTIVITIES:** Picnicking. Horseback riding; (rental 4 mi). **MISC.:** Elev 7500 ft; 6 acres; stream; scenic. Pets.

Pinnacles (Shoshone NF). 23 mi W of Dubois on I-287; 5 mi N on FS 14515. **SEASON:** 6/20-9/30. **FACILITIES:** 22 sites -22); tbls, toil, cga, f. **ACTIVITIES:** Boating; picnicking; fishing. Horseback riding/rental (1 mi). **MISC.:** Elev 9200 ft; 14 acres; scenic. Pets permitted.

Ring Lake (County Park).Take US 26/287 4 mi E of Dubois; follow signs to Ring Lake along very rough 8-mi dirt rd. **SEASON:** 5/1-10/31; 5-day lmt. **FACILITIES:** 10 sites; tbls, toil, cga, no drk wtr. **ACTIVITIES:** Hunting; picnicking; fishing; boating (no motors). **MISC.:** Lake; Wind River Mtns. Pets permitted.

Trail Lake (County Park). 9 mi SE of Dubois off US 26-287. **G.F. SEASON:** 5/1-10/31; 5-day lmt. **FACILITIES:** 5 sites; tbls, toil, cga, no drk wtr. **ACTIVITIES:** Hunting; picnicking; fishing. **MISC.:** Wind River Mtns. Pets permitted.

EDEN

Dills Overnite CG (County Park). US 187, Eden. **SEASON:** Summer; 1-day lmt. **FACILITIES:** 12 sites; toil, drk wtr; elec hookup($). **ACTIVITIES:** Fishing; rockhounding. **MISC.:** Center of Eden Valley. Rock Springs (36 mi). Pets permitted if kept on leash.

ELK MOUNTAIN

Bow River (Medicine Bow NF). 14 mi S of Elk Mtn on Co Hwy 101; 1-3/10 mi SE on FS 1013A; 1/5 mi S on FS 101. **SEASON:** 6/15-9/15; 14-day lmt. **FACILITIES:** 13 sites (tr -32); tbls, toil, cga, f, drk wtr. **ACTIVITIES:** Picnicking; fishing; rockhounding. **MISC.:** 6 acres. Sand Lake. Pets.

Deep Creek (Medicine Bow NF). 14 mi S of Elk Mtn on Co Hwy 101; 1-3/10 mi SE on FS 1013A; 9-2/5 mi SE on FS 101. **SEASON:** 7/1-9/15; 14-day lmt. **FACILITIES:** 12 sites (tr -22); tbls, toil, cga, well drk wtr. **ACTIVITIES:** Picnicking; rockhounding. Boating, rld/fishing/swimming/horseback riding and rental/waterskiing (1 mi). **MISC.:** Elev 10,200 ft; 7 acres; pets; stream; scenic. 1/2 mi from Sand Lake Lodge.

ENCAMPMENT

Bottle Creek (Medicine Bow NF). 7-1/10 mi SW of Encampment on St Hwy 70. **SEASON:** 6/15-10/15; 14-day lmt. **FACILITIES:** 8 tent sites; tbls, toil, cga, piped drk wtr. **ACTIVITIES:** Picnicking; fishing (1 mi). **MISC.:** Elev 8800 ft; 4 acres. Pets permitted.

French Creek (Medicine Bow NF). 4½ mi E of Encampment on St Hwy 230; 11 mi NE on Co Hwy 660. **SEASON:** 6/1-10/1; 14-day lmt. **FACILITIES:** 15 sites (tr -32); tbls, toil, cga, f. **ACTIVITIES:** Rockhounding; picnicking; fishing. **MISC.:** Elev 8000 ft; 3 acres. Pets permitted if kept on leash.

Haskins Creek (Medicine Bow NF). 15-3/10 mi SW of Encampment on St Hwy 401. SEASON: 6/15-10/31; 14-day lmt. FACILITIES: 11 sites (tr -22); tbls, toil, cga, piped drk wtr. ACTIVITIES: Picnicking; fishing. MISC.: Elev 9000 ft; 5 acres. Pets.

Lakeview (Medicine Bow NF). 6 mi W of Encampment on St Hwy 70; 22 mi SW on FS 550. SEASON: 6/15-10/31; 14-day lmt. FACILITIES: 34 sites (tr -22); tbls, toil, cga, piped drk wtr. ACTIVITIES: Boating,ld; waterskiing; picnicking; fishing. Horseback riding (1 mi). MISC.: Elev 8400 ft; 33 acres; lake. Pets permitted if kept on leash.

Lost Creek (Medicine Bow NF). 17-3/10 mi SW of Encampment on St Hwy 401. SEASON: 6/15-10/31; 14-day lmt. FACILITIES: 14 sites (tr -22); tbls, toil, cga, piped drk wtr. ACTIVITIES: Picnicking; fishing. MISC.: Elev 8800 ft; 8 acres; stream. Pets permitted if kept on leash.

Six Mile Gap (Medicine Bow NF). 24-3/5 mi SE of Encampment on St Hwy 230; 2 mi SE on FS 492. SEASON: 6/1-10/15; 14-day lmt. FACILITIES: 7 sites (tr -32); tbls, toil, cga, f, piped drk wtr. ACTIVITIES: Picnicking. Boating,ld/fishing (1 mi). MISC.: Elev 8000 ft; 2 acres. Access to N Platte River. Pets.

EVANSTON

Evanston City Park. 1/2 mi E on US 30. SEASON: 6/1-9/1; 1-day lmt. FACILITIES: 20 sites; tbls, toil, cga, no drk wtr. ACTIVITIES: Picnicking. MISC.: Pets permitted if kept on leash.

Hamblin Park (Municipal Park). ½ mi E of Evanston on St Hwy 30; off I-80. SEASON: All yr; 1-day lmt. FACILITIES: 6 self-contained sites; tbls, toil, cga, f, drk wtr. Store/ice/laundry/food nearby. Playground. ACTIVITIES: Picnicking; snowmobiling; softball. Golf nearby. MISC.: Elev 7000 ft; 5 acres; pets on leash.

FLAMING GORGE

Marsh Creek (NRA). From Utah border 1 mi N on St Hwy 373; 5½ mi N on FS 10106; 16¼ mi N on FS; 2¼ mi W on FS 60022. SEASON: 5/1-9/15; 14-day lmt. FACILITIES: 3 back-in sites, toil, cga. ACTIVITIES: Fishing; boating,l; waterskiing. MISC.: Elev 6100 ft; lake; dirt access rds. Pets permitted.

Upper Marsh Creek (NRA). 5¼ mi NW of Flaming Gorge on St Hwy 260; 5¼ **Upper Marsh Creek** (cont.) mi N on FS 10106; 16¼ mi N on FS 60106; 2¼ mi W on FS 60022. SEASON: 5/1-9/15. FACILITIES: 3 sites (tr -22); tbls, toil, cga. ACTIVITIES: Boating,l; picnicking; fishing; waterskiing. MISC.: Elev 6100 ft; lake. Pets permitted.

FT LARAMIE

Ft. Laramie Municipal Park. SW part of town. From Ft Laramie, 1 block W on Rd, 1 blk S of jct. US 85/26. SEASON: All yr; 1-day lmt. FACILITIES: 25 sites (some pull-thru); tbls, toil, cga, drk wtr. ACTIVITIES: Hunting; picnicking; fishing. MISC.: Elev 4200 ft; 3 acres. Lake Guernsey; Old Ft Laramie; Register Cliff; Hartville; Sunrise mine; playground. Pets.

FOXPARK

Bobbie Thomson (Medicine Bow NF). 11-1/5 mi NW of Foxpark on FS 512. SEASON: 6/1-10/15; 14-day lmt. FACILITIES: 10 sites (tr -32); tbls, toil, cga, well drk wtr. ACTIVITIES: Picnicking; fishing. MISC.: Elev 8900 ft; 3 acres. Pets permitted.

Evans Creek (Medicine Bow NF). 1/2 mi S of Foxpark on FS 512; 1/10 mi SW on FS 5121A. SEASON: 6/1-10/15; 14-day lmt. FACILITIES: 10 sites (tr -16); tbls, toil, cga, well drk wtr. Store/gas (1 mi). Food (5 mi). ACTIVITIES: Picnicking. Fishing (1 mi). MISC.: Elev 9000 ft; 3 acres. Pets.

Miller Lake (Medicine Bow NF). 1/2 mi S of Foxpark on FS 512; 3/10 mi SW on FS 5121B. SEASON: 6/1-10/1; 14-day lmt. FACILITIES: 7 sites (tr -16); tbls, toil, cga, well drk wtr. Store/gas (1 mi). Food (5 mi). ACTIVITIES: Picnicking; fishing. MISC.: Elev 9100 ft; 2 acres; lake. Pets.

Pickaroon (Medicine Bow NF). 23 mi W of Foxpark on FS 512. SEASON: 6/15-10/1; 14-day lmt. FACILITIES: 9 sites (tr -16); tbls, toil, cga, f, no drk wtr. ACTIVITIES: Boating,d; horseback riding; picnicking; fishing. MISC.: Elev 7800 ft; 2 acres. Pets. Adjacent to North Platte River.

Pike Pole (Medicine Bow NF). 23-½ mi W of Foxpark on FS 512. SEASON: 6/15-10/1; 14-day lmt. FACILITIES: 6 sites (tr -16); tbls, toil, cga, f, no drk wtr. ACTIVITIES: Picnicking; fishing. MISC.: Elev 7800 ft; 4 acres. Adjacent to Douglas Creek and N Platte River. Pets permitted if kept on leash.

FREEDOM

Pinebar (NF). 1 mi N on Cty Hwy 34; 9¼ mi W on St Hwy 34. SEASON: 6/15-9/30; 14-day lmt. FACILITIES: 5 sites (tr -16); tbls, toil, cga, f, piped drk wtr. ACTIVITIES: Hunting; picnicking; fishing; hiking; bike trails. MISC.: Elev 6300 ft; 4 acres; river; stream Pets permitted if kept on leash (smal only).

Tincup (NF). 1 mi N on Cty Hwy 34; 2-3/5 mi W on St Hwy 34. SEASON: 6/15-9/30; 14-day lmt. FACILITIES: 3 sites (tr -16); tbls, toil, cga, f, piped drk wtr. Store/gas/ice (4 mi). ACTIVITIES: Hunting; picnicking; fishing; rock-hounding; bike trails. Horseback riding (1 mi). MISC.: Elev 6100 ft; 3 acres; river; stream. Pets.

GILLETTE

Gillett City Park (County Park). End of Main St in Gillette. SEASON: 5/1-11/30; 3-day lmt. FACILITIES: 10 sites; tbls, toil, cga, drk wtr. ACTIVITIES: Swimming; picnicking; fishing; play-ground. MISC.: Pets.

GLENDO

Rest Area. 5 mi S of Glendo on I-25 (paved access rd). SEASON: All yr. FA-CILITIES:Undesig. sites; tbls, toil, cga, dump. ACTIVITIES: Picnicking. MISC.: Elev 6000 ft. Pets.

GLENROCK

Boxelder Converse Co. Park. 10 mi S of Glenrock, Boxelder Rt. SEASON: Summer. FACILITIES: 2 sites; drk wtr. ACTIVITIES: Swimming; fishing. MISC.: Scenic area. Pets permitted.

GREEN RIVER

County Picnic Ground (County Park). 3¼ mi W of town on US 30. SEASON: 5/1-11/30. FACILITIES: 10 sites; tbls, toil, cga, no drk wtr. ACTIVITIES: Picnicking; fishing. MISC.: Pets.

Seedskadee Wildlife Refuge (NWR). 34 mi NW of Green River on St Hwy 372. SEASON: All yr; 7-day lmt. FACILI-TIES: Prim., TENTS ONLY. MISC.: Pets.

Squaw Hollow (Flaming Gorge NRA). 35 mi S of Green River on St Hwy 530. SEASON: All yr; 16-day lmt. FACILI-TIES: 12 sites; tbls, toil, cga, no drk wtr. Nearest supplies - Buckboard Crossing Marine Store, 10 mi N on St Hwy 530. ACTIVITIES: Picnicking; boating,l; water sports. MISC.: Pets.

JACKSON

South Park (County Pk.).7 mi S on US 189. SEASON: All yr. FACILITIES: 4 tent sites; tbls, toil, cga, no drk wtr. ACTIVITIES: Hunting; picnicking; fishing; boating. MISC.: Pets per-mitted if kept on leash.

JEFFREY CITY

Cottonwood (BLM). 6 mi E of Jeffrey City on US 287; 10 mi S on gravel road. SEASON: 6/1-10/1; 14-day lmt. FACILI-TIES: 19 sites (tr -18); drk wtr. AC-TIVITIES: Hunting; fishing (1 mi). MISC.: Elev 8500 ft; 80 acres. Pets.

Jeffrey City Park. W edge of town on US 287 (paved access rds). SEASON: All yr. FACILITIES: 6 pull-thru spaces; tbls, wtr hkup. ACTIVITIES: Hiking; picnicking; softball; play-ground. MISC.: Elev 6000 ft. Pets.

KAYCEE

Kaycee Town Park (City Park). Just off I-25 & US 87; 1/2 blk off Main St in Kaycee. SEASON: All yr; 5-day lmt. FACILITIES: 10 pull-thru sites; tbls, toil, cga. Store/food/ice/laundry (near-by). ACTIVITIES: Picnicking; hunting; fishing. MISC.: Hole-in-the-Wall Outlaw Cave. Pets permitted if kept on leash.

KELLY

Crystal Creek (Bridger Teton NF). 13-1/10 mi E of Kelly on FS 30015. SEASON: 6/5-9/5; 14-day lmt. FACILITIES: 6 sites (tr -22); tbls, toil, cga, no drk wtr. ACTIVITIES: Picnicking; fish-ing. Horseback riding (1 mi). MISC.: Elev 7300 ft; 2 acres; scenic. On banks of Gros Ventre River. Pets.

Red Hills (Bridger Teton NF). 12-4/5 mi E of Kelly on FS 30015. SEASON: 6/5-9/5; 14-day lmt. FACILITIES: 5 sites (tr -16); tbls, toil, cga, f, no drk wtr. ACTIVITIES: Swimming; picnicking; fishing. Horseback riding (1 mi). MISC.: Elev 7300 ft; 2 acres; lake; scenic. On banks of Gros Ventra River. Pets permitted if kept on leash.

LANDER

Atlantic City (BLM). 30 mi S of Lander on St Hwy 28 (Atlantic City Rd). SEA-SON: 6/1-10/31; 14-day lmt. FACILI-TIES: 22 sites (tr -24); tbls, toil, cga, drk wtr. ACTIVITIES: Hunting; picnicking; fishing. MISC.: Historical area. Pets permitted if kept on leash.

Big Atlantic Gulch (BLM). 30 mi S of Lander on St Hwy 28 (Miner's Delight Rd). SEASON: 6/1-10/31; 14-day lmt. FACILITIES: 10 sites (tr -24). ACTIVI-TIES: Hunting; fishing. MISC.: His-torical area. Pets.

Dickinson Creek (Shoshone NF). 15 mi NW of Lander on US 287; turn W at Hines Genl Store; 5 mi SW on Co Hwy; 14 mi SW on FS 167; 3 mi SW on FS 303. SEASON: 7/1-9/30; 14-day lmt. FACILITIES: 15 sites (tr -16); tbls, toil, cga, f, no drk wtr. ACTIVI-TIES: Picnicking; fishing. MISC.: Elev 9400 ft; 7 acres; pets; stream.

Fiddlers Lake (Shoshone NF). 8-7/10 mi SW of Lander on St Hwy 701; 14-7/10 mi SW on FS 307. SEASON: 7/1-9/30; 14-day lmt. FACILITIES: 8 sites (tr -22); f, drk wtr. Store/gas (5 mi). ACTIVITIES: Boating,rld (no motors); fishing. MISC.: Elev 9400 ft; 4 acres. Pets.

See page 7 for KEY TO ABBREVIATIONS.

Louis Lake (Shoshone NF). 8-7/10 mi SW of Lander on St Hwy 701; 21-2/5 mi SW on FS 308. SEASON: 7/1-9/30; 14-day lmt. FACILITIES: 5 sites (tr -22); f, drk wtr. ACTIVITIES: Fishing; boating,rld; waterskiing. MISC.: 3 acres; scenic. Pets.

Popo Agie (Shoshone NF). 8-7/10 mi SW on St Hwy 701; 17-3/5 mi SW on FS 300. SEASON: 7/1-9/30; 14-day lmt. FACILITIES: 3 sites (tr -16); tbls, toil, cga, f, well drk wtr. Store. Picnicking; fishing. Boating,rl/waterskiing/horseback riding/rental (2 mi). MISC.: Elev 8400 ft; 1 acre. Good brook troup fishing in the Little Popo Agie River. Scenic area. Pets.

LARAMIE

Boswell Creek (Medicine Bow NF). 38 mi SW of Laramie on St Hwy 230; 3 mi E on FS 526. SEASON: 6/1-9/15; 14-day lmt. FACILITIES: 9 sites (tr -16); tbls, toil, cga, piped drk wtr. Store/gas (3 mi). Food (5 mi). ACTIVITIES: Picnicking; fishing. MISC.: Elev 8900 ft; 6 acres; stream. Pets.

Holmes (Medicine Bow NF). 22 mi W on St Hwy 130; 11 mi SW on St Hwy 11; 11 mi W on FS 500; 1/10 mi S on FS 543. SEASON: 6/15-9/15; 14-day lmt. FACILITIES: 10 sites (tr -22); tbls, toil, cga, piped drk wtr. ACTIVITIES: Picnicking. Fishing (1 mi). Boating,1/waterskiing (3 mi). MISC.: Elev 9700 ft; 5 acres. 1 mi W of Rob Roy Reservoir. Pets permitted if kept on leash.

Laramie River Mgmt. Area (St. G & F). From Wyo. line, 4 mi S on Laramie Riv. Rd., W to Riv. Bridge. SEASON: 5/1-10/1 FACILITIES: 25 tent sites; no drk wtr. ACTIVITIES: Fishing.   MISC.: Pets.

Pelton Creek (Medicine Bow NF). 40 mi SW of Laramie on St hwy 230; 8 mi NW on FS 898. SEASON: 6/1-10/15; 14-day lmt.   FACILITIES: 11 sites (tr -16); tbls, toil, cga, f, well drk wtr. ACTIVITIES: Picnicking; fishing. Horseback riding (1 mi). MISC.: Elev 8100 ft; 3 acres; stream. Pets permitted.

Rest Area. 9 mi E of Laramie on I-80 (paved access rds). SEASON: All yr. FACILITIES: Undes sites; tbls toil, cga ACTIVITIES: Picnicking. MISC.: Elev 8000 ft. Pets.

Woods Creek (Medicine Bow NF). 31 mi SW of Laramie on St Hwy 230. SEASON: 5/30-9/7; 14-day lmt. FACILITIES: 9 sites (tr -22); no drk wtr. Store/food/gas (5 mi). ACTIVITIES: Picnicking; fishing. Horseback riding (5 mi). MISC.: Elev 8900 ft; 8 acres. Pets permitted if kept on leash.

LONETREE

Hoop Lake (Wasatch NF). 1-4/5 mi E on St Hwy 2414; 10½ mi S on FS 4058. SEASON: 6/15-9/15; 14-day lmt. FACILITIES: 44 sites (tr -16); tbls, toil, cga, f, piped drk wtr. ACTIVITIES: Boating,ld; waterskiing; picnicking; fishing. Horseback riding (1 mi). MISC.: Elev 9000 ft; 35 acres. Pets.

LOVELL

Five Springs Falls (BLM). 25 mi E on US 14A. SEASON: 5/1-10/1; 14-day lmt. FACILITIES: 8 sites; tbls, toil, cga, drk wtr. ACTIVITIES: Swimming; picnicking; fishing; hunting; rockhounding; hiking. MISC.: Elev 8500 ft. Pets permitted if kept on leash.

Lovell Camper Park (City Park). On Quebec Avenue in Lovell. SEASON: 5/1-9/30; 4-day lmt. FACILITIES: 20 sites; flush toil, showers. Store/laundry/ice/food nearby. ACTIVITIES: Swimming; picnicking; fishing; golfing. MISC.: Pets permitted if kept on a leash.

LUSK

North Side CG. N edge of town on US 85 (paved access rds). FACIL.: 10 sites; tbls, toil, cga, elec/wtr/sewr hkups. ACTIVITIES: Swimming; picnicking; fishing. MISC.: Elev 5100 ft. Museum. Rodeos. SEASON: May to cold weather.

Lusk North Park. 2 blks from Main shopping district. SEASON: May to cold weather. FACILITIES: 30 sites; toil, cga, drk wtr. ACTIVITIES: Picnicking; fishing; swimming. MISC.: Rawhide Buttes. Cheyenne - Deadwood Stage. Pets permitted if kept on leash.

Rest Area. 1 mi W of town on US 20; paved access rds. SEASON: All yr. FACILITIES: Tbls, toil, cga, dump. nicking; playground. MISC.: Elev 5100 ft. Pets permitted if kept on leash.

LYMAN

Town of Lyman Public CG. Main St & Lincoln Way. SEASON: 5/1-10/1; 1-day lmt. FACILITIES: 10 pull-thru sites; tbls, toil, cga, drk wtr. ACTIVITIES: Swimming; picnicking; fishing; boating; playground. MISC.: Municipal pool; Vinta Mtns. Pets.

MEDICINE BOW

Bow River (Medicine Bow NF). 14 mi S of Elk Mtn on Co Hwy 101; 1-3/10 mi SE on Co Hwy 101(3A). SEASON: 6/15-9/15; 14-day lmt. FACILITIES: 13 sites (tr -32); toil. MISC.: Pets permitted.

MEETEETSE

Brown Mountain (Shoshone NF). 6 mi SW of Meeteetse on St Hwy 290; 15-4/5 mi SW on Co Hwy 200; 3-1/5 mi W on Fs 14200. SEASON: 6/1-9/15; 14-day lmt.

FACILITIES: 5 sites (tr -16); tbls, toil, cga, f, well drk wtr. ACTIVITIES: Picnicking; fishing. MISC.: Elev 7600 ft; 2 acres; river. Pets.

MOORCRAFT

City CG (County Pk.). 1 mi W of Moorcraft on US 14-16 & I-90. SEASON: All yr; 1-day lmt. FACILITIES: 25 sites; tbls, toil, cga. ACTIVITIES: Picnicking,

Upper Wood River (Shoshone NF). 13-1/5 mi SW of Meeteetse on Wyo. 1200; then 8-3/5 mi SW on Co Rd & 3/10 mi W on FS 14200. SEASON: 6/1-9/15; 14-day lmt. FACILITIES: 4 sites (tr -16); tbls, toil, cga, drk wtr. ACTIVITIES: Picnicking; fishing. MISC.: Elev 8000 ft; 1 acre. Pets permitted if kept on leash.

Wood River (Shoshone NF). 6 mi SW of Meeteetse on St Hwy 290; 15-4/5 mi SW on Co Hwy 200; 3/10 mi W on FS 14200. SEASON: 6/1-9/15; 14-day lmt. FACILITIES: 5 sites (tr -16); tbls, toil, cga, f, well drk wtr. ACTIVITIES: Picnicking; fishing. MISC.: Elev 7300 ft; 1 acre; river. Pets.

Rest Area. W of Moorcraft exit on I-90; paved access rds. SEASON: All yr. FACILITIES: Undesig. sites; tbls, toil, dump. ACTIVITIES: Picnicking. MISC.: Pets permitted if kept on leash.

MORAN

Lava Creek (Bridger Teton NF). 2½ mi E of Moran on US 26. SEASON: 6/15-9/15; 14-day lmt. FACILITIES: 5 sites (tr -16); tbls, toil, cga, no drk wtr. Food/store/ice (4 mi). ACTIVITIES: Hiking; picnicking. Fishing (1 mi). MISC.: Elev 7000 ft; 2 acres. Pets.

MOUNTAIN VIEW

Bridger Lake (Wasatch NF). 7 mi SW of Mtn View on St hwy 2410; 15-2/5 mi S on FS 4072; 9/10 mi S on FS 4126. SEASON: 6/15-9/15; 14-day lmt. FACILITIES: 19 sites (tr -16); tbls, toil, cga, f, no drk wtr. ACTIVITIES: Boating,d; picnicking; fishing. Horseback riding (1 mi). MISC.: Elev 9400 ft.

China Meadows (Wasatch NF). 7 mi SW of Mtn View on St Hwy 2410; 18-2/5 mi S on FS 4072. SEASON: 6/15-9/15; 14-day lmt. FACILITIES: 9 sites (tr -16); tbls, toil, cga, f, piped drk wtr. ACTIVITIES: Boating,d; picnicking; fishing. Horseback riding (1 mi) MISC.: Elev 9500 ft; 4 acres; lake. Pets permitted if kept on leash.

Marsh Lake (Wasatch NF). 7 mi SW of Mtn View on St Hwy 2410, 17-4/5 mi S on FS 4072. SEASON: 6/15-9/15; 14-day lmt. FACILITIES: 33 sites (tr -16); tbls, toil, cga, f, no drk wtr. ACTIVITIES: Boating; fishing; picnicking; horseback riding (1 mi). MISC.: Elev 9300 ft; 15 acres; lake. Pets permitted.

Wilderness Trailhead 7 mi SW of Mtn View on St Hwy 2410; 19-2/5 mi S on FS 4072. SEASON: 6/15-9/15; 14-day lmt. FACILITIES: 4 sites (tr -22); tbls, toil, cga, f, no drk wtr. ACTIVITIES: Picnicking; fishing. Horseback riding (1 mi). Swimming (2 mi). MISC.: Elev 10,000 ft; 2 acres. Trailhead into high Vintas prim. area, horse loading dock. Pets permitted if kept on leash.

NEWCASTLE

Beaver Creek (Black Hills NF). 18 mi N of Newcastle on US 85; 6 mi E on FS 811. SEASON: 6/1-10/1; 10-day lmt. FACILITIES: 8 sites (tr -22); tbls, toil, cga, f, well drk wtr. ACTIVITIES: Picnicking; fishing. MISC.: Elev 6400 ft; 2 acres; pets.

OSAGE

Osage Park (Co. Park). 2 blks SW of St Hwy 16 in town. SEASON: All yr. FACILITIES: 5 sites; tbls, toil, cga. ACTIVITIES: Picnicking. MISC.: Pets.

PINE BLUFFS

Rest Area. 1/10 mi S of Parsons St. exit (paved access rds). SEASON: All yr. FACILITIES: Undesig. sites, tbls, toil, cga, dump. ACTIVITIES: Picnicking. MISC.: Elev 4000 ft. Pets.

PINEDALE

Green River Lake (Bridger Teton NF). 25 mi N of Pinedale on St Hwy 352; 31 mi N on FS rd. SEASON: 6/15-9/15; 14-day lmt. FACILITIES: 24 tent sites; toil. ACTIVITIES: Water sports on Green River Lakes. MISC.: Trailhead entrance to wilderness. Pets permitted.

Half Moon (Bridger Teton NF). 1 mi E on St Hwy 187; 5-1/10 mi NE on Co Hwy 111; 1 mi E on FS 134. SEASON: 6/1-9/10; 10-day lmt. FACILITIES: 8 sites (tr -16); tbls, toil, cga, f, no drk wtr. ACTIVITIES: Picnicking. Fishing/swimming/boating, rl/horseback riding/rental/waterskiing (1 mi). MISC.: Elev 7600 ft; 6 acres; lake. Pets.

Little Halfmoon (Bridger-Teton NF). 1 mi S of Pinedale on US 187; 10 mi E on Co Hwy T112; 1 mi NE on FS F112. SEASON: 6/15-10/1. FACILITIES: 1 site (tr -32); toil, no drk wtr. ACTIVITIES: Boating; swimming; fishing. MISC.: Elev 7600 ft; 10 acres; scenic. Pets.

Narrows (Bridger-Teton NF). 21 mi N of Pinedale on St Hwy 352; 4-3/5 mi E on Co Rd; 2½ mi E on FS Rd. SEASON: 6/15-9/16; 14-day lmt. FACILITIES: 16 tent sites; toil, drk wtr. ACTIVITIES: Hiking. MISC.: Trailhead entrance to wilderness. Access to New Fork Lakes. Pets.

See page 7 for KEY TO ABBREVIATIONS.

New Fork Lake (Bridger-Teton NF). 21 mi N of Pinedale on St Hwy 352; 4-3/5 mi E on Co Rd; 2-4/5 mi SE on FS Rd. SEASON: 6/15-9/15; 14-day lmt. FACILITIES: 15 tent sites; toil, drk wtr. MISC.: Access to New Fork Lakes and boat ramp. Pets permitted.

Trails End (Bridger-Teton NF). 1 mi E on US 187; 2½ mi N on Cty Hwy 111; 8 mi NE on FS 0111. SEASON: 6/25-9/10. FACILITIES: 8 sites (tr -22); tbls, toil, cga, f, piped drk wtr. ACTIVITIES: Picnicking. Horseback riding (1 mi). Fishing (2 mi). MISC.: Elev 9100 ft; 16 acres. Overlook to Wind River Mtns & Fremont Lake. Trail entrance to wilderness area. Scenic; nature trails; visitor center. Pets.

★ **Upper Fremont** (Bridger-Teton NF). 1 mi E of Pinedale on St Hwy S187; 4 mi N on Co Hwy TR111; 3 mi N on FS FS111; 5 mi N, BY BOAT. SEASON: 6/1-9/10. FACILITIES: 3 tent sites; tbls, toil, cga, f, no drk wtr. ACTIVITIES: Picnicking; hiking; fishing; boating,d; swimming; waterskiing; rockhounding. Horseback riding (1 mi). MISC.: Elev 7400 ft; 2 acres; scenic; stream; Pets.

Warren Bridge (BLM). 25 mi N of Pinedale on US 187/189. SEASON: 5/15-10/31; 14-day lmt. FACILITIES: 18 sites (tr -24); drk wtr. ACTIVITIES: Hiking; boating,d; fishing. MISC.: Elev 7500 ft; 80 acres. Pets permitted.

Whiskey Grove (Bridger-Teton NF). 36 mi N of Pinedale on St Hwy 352 & FS Rd. SEASON: 6/15-9/15; 14-day lmt. FACILITIES: 9 tent sites; toil, drk wtr. ACTIVITIES: Fishing. MISC.: Access to Green River. Pets permitted.

Willow Lake (Bridger-Teton NF). 3/10 mi W of Pinedale on US 187; 8 mi N on Co Hwy T110; 2½ mi N on FS F110. SEASON: 6/1-10/1. FACILITIES: 2 sites (tr -32); toil, no drk wtr. NO TBLS. ACTIVITIES: Boating; swimming; fishing. MISC.: Elev 7700 ft; 10 acres; lake; scenic. Pets permitted.

POWELL

Rest Area. US 14A E of town (paved access rds). SEASON: All yr. FACILITIES: 10 sites; tbls, toil, cga, dump. ACTIVITIES: Picnicking; playground. MISC.: Elev 4560 ft; pull-thru sp. Pets.

Scout Cabin Park (Park Co.) US 14A & Day St. SEASON: 5/1-10/31; 1-day lmt. FACILITIES: 2 sites; tbls, toil, cga, drk wtr. ACTIVITIES: Picnicking; swimming. MISC.: Pets.

South Park (Park Co.). Hamilton & Jefferson Sts. SEASON: 5/1-10/31; 1-day lmt. FACILITIES: 3 sites; tbls, toil, cga, drk wtr. ACTIVITIES: Picnicking; swimming; softball; playground. MISC.: Groceries (½ blk). Pets.

Veterans Park (Park Co.). 5th & Gilbert St. SEASON: 5/1-10/31; 1-day lmt. FACILITIES: 3 tent sites; tbls, cga, drk wtr. ACTIVITIES: Picnicking. MISC.: Adjacent to Park Co. Fairgrounds. Pets.

Washington Park (Park Co.). 2nd & Cheyene St. SEASON: 5/1-10/31; 1-day lmt. FACILITIES: 2 sites; tbls, toil, cga, drk wtr. ACTIVITIES: Picnicking; swimming. MISC.: Playground. Pets.

RIVERSIDE

Bennett Peak (BLM). 4 mi E of Riverside on St Hwy 230; 12-1/5 mi NE on French Creek Rd; 6½ mi N on Bennett Park Road. SEASON: 6/1-10/31; 14-day lmt. FACILITIES: 12 sites (tr -20); tbls, toil, cga, drk wtr. ACTIVITIES: Picnicking; fishing; swimming; hunting; boating; canoeing. MISC.: 60 acres; N Platte River Snowy Range Mtns. Pets.

RIVERSIDE

Corral Creek (BLM). 4 mi E of Riverside on St Hwy 230; 12 mi E on French Creek Road; 6 mi N on Bennett Park Road. SEASON: 6/1-10/31; 14-day lmt. FACILITIES: 12 sites (tr -20); drk wtr. ACTIVITIES: Swimming; hunting; boating; canoeing; fishing. MISC.: 30 acres. N Platte River. Snowy Range Mtns. Pets.

RIVERTON

East Side of Ocean Lake (Fremont Co.). 20 mi W of Riverton off US 26-287. SEASON: 5/1-10/31; 5-day lmt. FACILITIES: 20 sites; toil, no drk wtr. ACTIVITIES: Picnicking; swimming; fishing; hunting. MISC.: Bass fishing. Pets permitted if kept on leash.

ROCK SPRINGS

Upper Marsh Creek (Flaming Gorge NRA). 14 mi S of Rock Springs on St Hwy 373; 8 mi W on Co Rd 34; 24 mi S on Co Rd 33; 2½ mi on FS Rd. SEASON: All yr; 16-day lmt. FACILITIES: 24 sites; no drk wtr. ACTIVITIES: Boating,l; water sports. MISC.: Desert camping; antelope habitat. Pets.

SARATOGA

Jack Creek (Medicine Bow NF). 19-1/10 mi W of Saratoga on Co Hwy 500; 8-1/10 mi S on FS 405. SEASON: 6/15-10/15; 14-day lmt. FACILITIES: 12 sites (tr -22); tbls, toil, cga, f, well drk wtr. ACTIVITIES: Picnicking; fishing. MISC.: Elev 8500 ft; 5 acres; stream. Pets.

See page 7 for KEY TO ABBREVIATIONS.

North Platte River (Carbon Co.) 9 mi S of Saratoga at St Hwy 30. SEASON: 5/1-10/31; 5-day lmt. FACILITIES: 26 sites; tbls, toil, cga, no drk wtr. ACTIVITIES: Picnicking; fishing. MISC.: Medicine Bow NF. Pets.

Saratoga Lake (Carbon Co.). 1 mi N of Saratoga on St Hwy 130. SEASON: All yr. FACILITIES: 75 sites; tbls, toil, cga, drk wtr. ACTIVITIES: Picnicking; swimming; fishing. MISC.: Elev 6728 ft. Hot springs & pool; lake Pets permitted if kept on leash.

SAVERY

Battle Creek (Medicine Bow NF). 22-9/10 mi E of Savery on St Hwy 70 (2 mi of unimproved rd, muddy during wet periods); 2 mi S on FS 807. SEASON: 6/1-10/31; 14-day lmt. FACILITIES: 4 sites (tr -16); tbls, toil, cga, drk wtr. ACTIVITIES: Picnicking; fishing. MISC.: Elev 7800 ft; 2 acres. Pets permitted if kept on leash.

Little Sandstone (Medicine Bow NF). 23-3/5 mi NE of Savery on Hwy 401 (7½ mi of unimproved rd). SEASON: 6/1-10/31; 14-day lmt. FACILITIES: 9 sites (tr -22); tbls, toil, cga, well drk wtr. ACTIVITIES: Picnicking; softball/volleyball field. Fishing (1 mi). MISC.: Elev 8400 ft; 3 acres. Pets.

SHELL

Cabin Creek Trailers (Bighorn NF). 15-4/5 mi NE of Shell on Us 14; 1/2 mi E on FS 548. SEASON: 6/1-10/31; 14-day lmt. FACILITIES: 26 sites (tr -32); no tbls, no drk wtr. ACTIVITIES: Fishing (1 mi). MISC.: Reservations required. Pets.

Lower Paintrock Lake (Bighorn NF). 15-4/5 mi NE of Shell on US 14 then 25-7/10 mi SE on FS Rd 610. SEASON: 6/20-9/15; 14-day lmt. FACILITIES: 4 sites; tbls, toil, cga, no drk wtr. ACTIVITIES: Picnicking; fishing; boating; rockhounding. MISC.: Elev 9300 ft; 3 acres. Poor roads trailers not advised. No wake boating. Pets.

Medicine Lodge Lake. 15-4/5 mi NE of Shell on. US 14; 25 mi SE on FS Rd 548. SEASON: 6/20-9/15; 14-day lmt. FACILITIES: 8 sites; tbls, toil, cga, f, no drk wtr. ACTIVITIES: Boating; picnicking; fishing; rockhounding. MISC.: Elev 9300 ft; 5 acres. Poor roads trailers not advised. Pets.

Shell Creek (Bighorn NF). 15-4/5 mi NE of Shell on US 14; 1-1/5 mi S on FS 548. SEASON: 6/15-9/15; 14-day lmt. FACILITIES: 11 sites (tr -22); tbls,

Shell Creek (cont.) toil, cga, f, no drk wtr. ACTIVITIES: Picnicking; fishing; horseback riding; (rental 1 mi). MISC.: 7 acres. Pets.

* **Shell Reservoir** (Bighorn NF). 15-4/5 mi NE of Shell on US 14 then 9 mi SE on FS Rd & 6 mi E on TRAIL. SEASON: 6/20-9/15. FACILITIES: 2 tent sites; tbls, toil, cga, no drk wtr. ACTIVITIES: Picnicking; fishing. MISC.: 4-wheel drive last 6 mi. Pets permitted.

Upper Paintrock Lake (Bighorn NF). 15-4/5 mi NE on US 14; 25-7/10 mi SE on FS 610. SEASON: 6/20-9/15; 14-day lmt. FACILITIES: 6 tent sites (no trailers); tbls, toil, cga, f, no drk wtr. ACTIVITIES: Picnicking; fishing; boating,d. MISC.: Elev 9300 ft; 2 acres. Poor roads-trailers not advised. Pets.

SHERIDAN

Washington Park (Co. Park). US 87-14 on Coffeen Ave. (paved access rds). SEASON: All yr; 1-day lmt. FACILITIES: 25 sites; toil, pull-thru sp. ACTIVITIES: Picnicking. MISC.: Elev 3800 ft; Pets permitted if kept on leash.

SHOSHONI

Shoshoni Park (City Park). 1 blk N & E of center of town (dirt access rd). SEASON: All yr. FACILITIES: Undesignated sites (tr -28); tbls, toil, cga. ACTIVITIES: Picnicking; playground. MISC.: Elev 6000 ft. Pets.

SUNDANCE

Cook Lake (Black Hills NF). 2-1/10 mi W on US 14; 14 mi N on FS 838; 5 mi E on FS 843; 1 mi NW on FS 842. SEASON: 5/15-10/1; 10-day lmt. FACILITIES: 13 sites; tbls, toil, cga, drk wtr. ACTIVITIES: Swimming; picnicking; fishing. MISC.: Elev 4800 ft; 2 acres. Pets.

Reuter (Black Hills NF). 2-1/10 mi W of Sundance on US 14; 2-1/5 mi N on FS 838. SEASON: 10/2-6/1, FREE ($2 rest of yr); 10-day lmt. FACILITIES: 24 sites (tr -16); tbls, toil, cga, piped drk wtr. Store/gas/ice/laundry/ food (4 mi). ACTIVITIES: Picnicking; fishing (4 mi); horseback riding/ rental (5 mi). MISC.: Elev 4900 ft; 5 acres. During FREE season, water is shut off. Pets.

TEN SLEEP

Boulder Trailer Park (Bighorn NF). 20 mi NE of Ten Sleep on US 16; 2 mi S on FS Rd. SEASON: 6/15-9/30; 7-day lmt. FACILITIES: 34 sites (tr -22); tbls, toil, cga, drk wtr. Store/ food/ice (2 mi). ACTIVITIES: Picnicking; fishing; boating,rld (5 mi). MISC.: Elev 8000 ft; 1 acre. 22 units avail. on monthly permit basis only. Pets permitted if kept on leash.

Bull Creek (Bighorn NF). 25 mi NE of Ten Sleep on US 16; ¼ mi N on FS 600. SEASON: 6/15-9/30; 14-day lmt. FACILITIES: 10 sites (tr -16); tbls, toil, cga, f, no drk wtr. Store/gas/food/ice (1 mi). Dump (4 mi). ACTIVITIES: Picnicking; fishing. Boating,rld/horseback riding/rental (1 mi). MISC.: Elev 8400 ft; 4 acres. Pets permitted.

Deer Park (Bighorn NF). 20 mi NE of Ten Sleep on US 16; 6 mi N on FS 604. SEASON: 6/15-9/30; 14-day lmt. FACILITIES: 5 sites (tr -22); tbls, toil, cga, f, no drk wtr. ACTIVITIES: Picnicking; fishing. Boating (2 mi). MISC.: Elev 8900 ft; 3 acres; stream. Pets permitted if kept on leash.

Island Park (Bighorn NF). 20 mi NE of Ten Sleep on US 16; 6 mi N on FS 604. SEASON: 6/15-9/30; 14-day lmt. FACILITIES: 10 sites (tr -22); tbls, toil, cga, f, no drk wtr. Store/gas/ice/food (4 mi). ACTIVITIES: Picnicking; fishing. Boating (3 mi). Horseback riding/rental (4 mi). MISC.: Elev 8600 ft; 4 acres. water sports. Pets.

Leigh Creek (Bighorn NF). 8 mi NE of Ten Sleep on US 16; 1 mi E on FS 265. SEASON: 6/1-9/30; 14-day lmt. FACILITIES: 10 sites (tr -16); tbls, toil, cga, f, no drk wtr. Store/food/gas (2 mi). ACTIVITIES: Picnicking; fishing. MISC.: Elev 5400 ft; 5 acres; stream. Pets.
Leigh Creek (cont.)

Ten Sleep Creek (Bighorn NF). 8 mi NE of Ten Sleep on US 16; 2 mi E on FS 265. SEASON: 6/1-9/30; 14-day lmt. FACILITIES: 5 sites (no trailers); tbls, toil, cga, f, no drk wtr. Store/food (3 mi). ACTIVITIES: Picnicking; fishing. MISC.: Elev 5400 ft; 2 acres; stream. Pets permitted if kept on leash.

West Ten Sleep. 20 mi NE of Ten Sleep on US 16; 7½ mi N on FS 604. SEASON: 6/15-9/30; 14-day lmt. FACILITIES: 10 sites (tr -16); tbls, toil, cga, f, no drk wtr. ACTIVITIES: Picnicking; fishing; boating; water sports. MISC.: Elev 9100 ft; 4 acres; lake. Pets permitted.

THERMOPOLIS

Hot Springs State Park (Hot Spgs Co) NE of town on US 20 N. SEASON: 5/1-10/31; 14-day lmt. FACILITIES: 40 sites; toil, laundromat. ACTIVITIES: Picnicking; swimming; fishing. MISC.: Buffalo Herd. Mineral hot spgs & baths; playground. Pets.

Thermopolis State Park. On E edge of town, W of river (paved access rds). SEASON: All yr; 14-day lmt. FACILITIES: 40 sites; toil, dump, pull-thru

spaces. ACTIVITIES: Swimming. MISC.; Elev 4200 ft. Hot mineral baths at state bath house. Pets.

TORRINGTON

Pioneer Park (Municipal Pk.). From Torrington, US 85 S to 15th St., 5 blks W, 1 blk S. (Paved access rds.) 15th & W. "D" St. SEASON: All yr. FACILITIES: 25 sites; wtr/sewer hkups, f, flush toil, drk wtr. Store/ice/laundry/food (nearby). ACTIVITIES: Golf; boating,d; fishing; swimming (all nearby). MISC.: Elev 400 ft; 4 acres. River; pets on leash.

Springer Reservoir (Goshen Co). SEASON: 5/1-9/30; 5-day lmt. FACILITIES: 10 sites; no drk wtr. ACTIVITIES: Picnicking; swimming; fishing; hunting; boating. MISC.: Pets permitted if kept on leash.

WHEATLAND

Festo Lake (Platte Co). 2 mi W; 1 mi N of Wheatland. SEASON: All yr. FACILITIES: 4 sites; tbls, toil, cga, drk wtr, elec/wtr/swr hkups. ACTIVITIES: Picnicking; swimming; fishing; boating. MISC.: Pets.

Lewis Park (Municipal Pk.). 1 blk E & 4 blks S on center of Wheatland. (600-9th St.). SEASON: All yr; 3-day lmt. FACILITIES: 12 sites; elec/wtr hkups; flus toil, showers. Store/food/ice/laundry (nearby). ACTIVITIES: Golf/swimming/tennis (nearby). MISC.: Pets permitted if kept on leash.

Rest Area. 13 mi N of Wheatland on I-25 S (paved access rds). SEASON: All yr. FACILITIES: tbls, toil, cga. MISC.: Pets. permitted if kept on leash.

Lewis City Park (Platte Co) 1 blk E & 4 blks So of ctr of town (paved access rds). SEASON: All yr; 3-day lmt. FACILITIES: 18 sites; tbls, toil, cga, drk wtr, elec/wtr hkup, dump. ACTIVITIES: Picnicking; golf (9-hole); tennis; softball; playground. MISC.: Elev 5500 ft; 30 acres. Pets permitted.

YELLOWSTONE

Mammoth Campground (Yellowstone NP). At Mammoth Hot Springs, near the N entrance to the park. SEASON: 10/15-5/15, FREE ($3 rest of yr). During free season, entrance fee is $1; rest of year, $2 (or Golden Eagle/Age Passport).** FACILITIES: 87 sites (tr -34); tbls, flush toil, cga, f. Store/food/ice/laundry/showers (nearby). ACTIVITIES: Picnicking; fishing; horseback riding. MISC.: Pets.

See page 7 for KEY TO ABBREVIATIONS.

APPENDIX A

FORSYTH TRAVEL LIBRARY

MAPS
UNITED STATES
AND
CANADA

ALABAMA
- Birmingham •
- Huntsville
- Mobile
- Montgomery
- Muscle Shoals/Florence

ALASKA
- Ketchikan

ARIZONA
- Flagstaff
- Phoenix/Scottsdale •
- Sun City/Youngtown
- Tucson •
- Yuma

ARKANSAS
- Fayetteville
- Fort Smith
- Hot Springs
- Little Rock

CALIFORNIA
- Anaheim/NW Orange Co. •
- Bakersfield/Kern County
- Barstow
- Chico
- Contra Costa County/East San Francisco Bay Area •
- El Segundo
- Fresno/Southern Sierra
- Long Beach
- Los Angeles •
- Los Angeles Freeways
- Marin County/North San Francisco Bay Area •
- Merced/Merced Co.
- Modesto/Turlock
- Monterey/Carmel/Pacific Grove/Pebble Beach/Salinas
- Napa & Sonoma Counties/Wine Country
- Oakland/East Bay Cities •
- Palm Springs
- Sacramento •
- San Bernardino/Riverside Redlands/Colton/Rialto •
- San Bernardino Mountains/Big Bear/Lake Arrowhead
- San Clemente
- San Diego/Coronado/Del Mar •
- San Diego County—North
- San Fernando Valley/Northern Los Angeles •
- San Francisco/Southern Penninsula •
- San Gabriel Valley/Eastern Los Angeles •
- San Jose/Mountain View/Santa Clara/Sunnyvale •
- San Luis Obispo/Morro Bay/Pismo Beach/Paso Robles
- Santa Barbara
- Santa Cruz & County
- Santa Maria
- Stockton/Northern Sierra
- Ventura/Oxnard/Simi/Ojai/Thousand Oaks/Camarillo

COLORADO
- Alamosa/Monte Vista
- Arvada
- Broomfield
- Cortez
- Denver/Colorado Springs/Pueblo/Boulder •
- Fort Collins
- Grand Junction
- Loveland
- Salida

CONNECTICUT
- Bradford
- Bridgeport/Westport
- Danbury
- Hartford
- New Britain/Bristol
- New Haven
- Stamford/Norwalk/Greenwich/New Canaan/Wilton/Darien
- Waterbury

DELAWARE
- Wilmington/New Castle Co.
- Newark

DISTRICT OF COLUMBIA
- Washington, D.C. •

FLORIDA
- Apollo Beach/Ruskin/Sun City Cntr/Sundance/Wimauma
- Cocoa/Melbourne/Merritt Island/and Beaches
- Daytona/Ormond and New Smyrna Beaches
- Deltona
- Ft. Lauderdale/Hollywood/Pompano/N. Miami Beach
- Fort Myers
- Jacksonville •
- Lakeland/Winter Haven
- Miami/Miami Beach/Coral Gables •
- Ocala
- Orlando
- Palm & W. Palm Beach/Lake Worth/Boca Raton/Delray Beach
- Panama City
- Pensacola
- Sarasota/Bradenton
- Tallahassee
- Tampa/St. Petersburg •

GEORGIA
- Athens
- Atlanta •
- Augusta
- Columbus/Fort Benning
- Macon
- Savannah

IDAHO
- Moscow

ILLINOIS
- Chicago Streets
- Chicago & Vicinity •
- Joliet/Bolingbrook
- Peoria
- Springfield
- Waukegan & Lake County

INDIANA
- Evansville
- Fort Wayne
- Indianapolis •
- South Bend/Mishawaka

IOWA
- Davenport & Rock Island/Moline, Illinois
- Des Moines
- Sioux City

KANSAS
- Great Bend
- Hutchinson
- Junction City
- Liberal
- Olathe
- Topeka
- Wichita

KENTUCKY
- Lexington/Bluegrass Area
- Louisville •
- Paducah

LOUISIANA
- Baton Rouge/Port Allen
- New Orleans •
- Shreveport

MAINE
- Bangor

MARYLAND
- Baltimore •

MASSACHUSETTS
- Amhert/Northampton
- Boston •
- Holyoke
- Pittsfield/Berkshire
- Worcester

MICHIGAN
- Detroit •
- Kalamazoo
- Ypsilanti

MINNESOTA
- Minneapolis/St. Paul •
- New Ulm
- St. Cloud

MISSISSIPPI
- Jackson/Clinton

MISSOURI
- Joplin
- Kansas City/Kansas City, Kansas/Overland Park •
- St. Louis •
- Sedalia
- Springfield

MONTANA
- Billings
- Butte

NEBRASKA
- Kearney
- Lincoln
- North Platte
- Omaha/Council Bluffs •

NEVADA
- Las Vegas •
- Reno

NEW MEXICO
- Alamogordo
- Albuquerque •
- Carlsbad
- Gallup
- Las Cruces
- Los Alamos/White Rock
- Roswell
- Silver City

NEW YORK
- Albany/Schenectady/Troy
- Binghamton/Endicott/Johnson City
- Buffalo/Niagra Falls •
- Corning/Elmira/Watkins Glen
- Ithaca
- Long Island/Metro NY
- New York Streets/All 5 Boroughs •
- New York/Metro Area •
- Rochester
- Syracuse
- Utica/Rome

NORTH CAROLINA
- Asheville
- Chapel Hill
- Charlotte
- Durham
- Fayetteville/Fort Bragg
- Greensboro
- Greenville
- Raleigh
- Rocky Mount
- Salisbury
- Wilmington & Beach Area
- Winston/Salem

NORTH DAKOTA
- Fargo/Morehead
- Jamestown
- Minot

OHIO
- Akron
- Bowling Green
- Canton
- Cincinnati
- Cleveland •
- Columbus
- Dayton
- Lorain/Elyria
- Sandusky
- Toledo
- Warren

OKLAHOMA
- Oklahoma City/Tulsa •
- Stillwater

OREGON
- Ashland
- Coos Bay/North Bend
- Klamath Falls
- Portland •

PENNSYLVANIA
- Allentown/Easton/Bethlehem
- Erie
- Harrisburg
- Lancaster
- Philadelphia •
- Pittsburgh •
- Reading
- State College
- Wilkes-Barre
- York

RHODE ISLAND
- North Kingston
- Providence
- Warren

SOUTH CAROLINA
- Anderson/Clemson
- Charleston
- Columbia
- Greenville
- Myrtle Beach & Beach Area
- Rock Hill
- Spartanburg
- Sumter

SOUTH DAKOTA
- Aberdeen

TENNESSEE
- Chattanooga
- Johnson City
- Kingsport
- Knoxville
- Memphis •
- Nashville

UNITED STATES & CANADA—Continued—Only $1.39 each

TEXAS	TEXAS (cont.)	UTAH	WEST VIRGINIA (cont)	UNITED STATES MAPS
___ Abilene	___ Lubbock	___ Cedar City	___ Wheeling	
___ Amarillo	___ Orange	___ Salt Lake City/Ogden/Provo •	WISCONSIN	___ United States
___ Amistad Lake	___ San Antonio •	WASHINGTON	___ Cedarburg	___ Interstate Road Map
___ Austin	___ Waco	___ Bellingham	___ De Pere	
___ Beaumont/Port Arthur	VERMONT	___ Federal Way	___ Green Bay	SECTIONAL MAPS
___ Brownsville	___ Burlington	___ Kennewick/Pasco/Richland	___ Madison	
___ Corpus Christi/North	VIRGINIA	___ Olympia/Lacey/Tumwater	___ Milwaukee •	___ Eastern United States
Padre Island	___ Bristol	___ Seattle •	___ Oshkosh	___ Central & Western U.S.
___ Dallas •	___ Charlottesville	___ Spokane	WYOMING	
___ El Paso	___ Danville	___ Tacoma	___ Casper	
___ Fort Hood	___ Lynchburg	___ Yakima	___ Cheyenne	
___ Fort Worth	___ Norfolk/Hampton Roads/	WEST VIRGINIA	___ Lander	
___ Houston •	Newport News/Portsmouth •	___ Charleston	___ Rawlings	
___ Kingsville	___ Richmond	___ Huntington	___ Riverton	
___ Laredo	___ Roanoke/Salem	___ Parkersburg	___ Sheridan	

U.S. STATE MAPS — All are up-to-date and show all principal roads. scenic & country roads. points of interest. sports areas. campsites. parks. airports. mileage. etc
Full color Folded Indexed **indicate quantity desired in front of each name**

_ Alabama	_ Del./Md./Va./W Va	_ Iowa	_ Nevada/Utah	_ Pennsylvania
_ Alaska	. Florida	_ Kansas/Nebraska	. New Jersey	_ Texas
_ Arizona/Nev. Mexico	_ Georgia	_ Kentucky/Tennessee	_ New York	_ Washington/Oregon
_ Ark./Louis./Miss.	_ Hawaii/Honolulu	_ Maine/ N H./Vermont	_ No & So Carolina	_ Wisconsin
_ California	_ Idaho/Montana	_ Michigan	_ No. & So Dakota	**Note:** These maps are
_ Colorado/Wyoming	_ Illinois	_ Minnesota	_ Ohio	produced by
_ Conn./Mass./R.I.	_ Indiana	_ Missouri	_ Oklahoma	Rand McNally

CANADIAN PROVINCES — Completely indexed with major city insets. attractions. etc. Full color.

_ Alberta/British Columbia/Manitoba/Saskatoon	_ Quebec & Atlantic Provinces	_ Ontario	_ Yukon Territory

CANADIAN CITIES — Indicate quantity desired in front of each title.

_ Calgary/Edmonton	_ Moncton. N.B.	_ Ottawa	_ Saint John. N.B.	_ Quebec City
_ Halifax/Dartmouth	_ Montreal	_ Portage LaPrairie. Man.	_ St. John's Newfoundland	_ Vancouver/Victoria
_ Hamilton/Burlington	_ Oakville/Mississauga	_ Regina/Saskatoon	_ Sydney/Glace Bay, N.S.	_ Winnipeg
			_ Toronto	

PRICES & DISCOUNTS
U.S. — Canadian Maps

___ 1 to 25 Assorted Total Maps ...... $1.39 each = $ _____	___ 25 copies of the same Map .... $.99 each = $ _____
___ 26 to 50 Assorted Total Maps .. $1.22 each = $ _____	(price applies to multiples of 25 only)
___ 51 or More Assorted Total Maps .. $1.12 each = $ _____	___ 100 copies or More of Same Map $.93 each = $ _____

SPECIAL OFFERS:
___ All 32 State Maps offered — Covers all 50 States
(equals to $.94 per map) .... Only $29.95 = $ _____
___ All 20 Canadian Province & City Maps
(equals to $1.11 per map) .... Only $22.19 = $ _____
___ Top 50 American Metropolitan Areas — All produced by Rand McNally (indicated with this
code • on the above list (equals to $.99 per map) .... Only $49.49 = $ _____

BEST BUY!
___ All 332 U.S. & Canadian—
State/Province/City & Sectional
Maps offered in this catalog—
A complete library!
Only $299.99 = $ _____
(equal to $.90 per map)

CANADIAN ORDERS: We are happy to accept Canadian checks. but please convert to U.S. Dollar equivalent...Please add $1.00 for each $20 in purchases to cover increased postal charges. Maps may be subject to Canadian Customs Duty and Taxes and such charges are the responsibility of the purchasers and may be collected on delivery.

Other catalogs available on request — please check:

☐ Worldwide—Travel Books & Maps; Lists hundreds of current books, guides, maps and special publications—Covers U.S. + overseas.

☐ European Rail Travel Guides, RailPasses and Rail Tours—plus details on the Thomas Cook Continental Timetable . . . and much more!

Check catalogs desired and send 25c to cover postage. All our catalogs are returned free with every order. Thank You!

Send this complete catalog with payment to:
Forsyth Travel Library
9154 West 57th Street
P.O. Box 2975, Dept. SA
Shawnee Mission, Kansas 66201

FORSYTH TRAVEL LIBRARY

Name _____

Company _____

Address _____

City _____ State _____ Zip _____

PLEASE COMPLETE PAYMENT INFORMATION:

☐ Check or Money Order Enclosed.
(Payable to: FORSYTH TRAVEL LIBRARY)

☐ Master Charge   ☐ Visa/BankAmericard
(Minimum Charge — $10.00)

Card No. ☐☐☐☐ ☐☐☐☐ ☐☐☐☐ ☐☐☐☐

Expires _____   Interbank No. - Master Charge Only ☐☐☐☐

Signature _____

DOUBLE CHECK! Enter total number of maps ordered from this catalog in box at right. ☐

PLEASE CALCULATE ORDER

TOTAL COST

SHIPPING CHARGES: $1.00 Minimum/$4.00 Maximum - Calculate cost based on 10c per map. Minimum—$1.00.

Thank you **TOTAL REMITTANCE**

Kansas Residents
Please Include 4% Sales Tax

All Prices Are Subject to Change

APPENDIX B

ADDITIONAL SOURCES OF CAMPING INFORMATION

Adirondack Mountain Club; Gabriels, NY 12939.

American Canoe Association; National Office; 4260 East Evans Avenue; Denver, CO 80222.

American Forestry Association; 919 – 17th Street NW; Washington, D.C. 20006.

Appalachian Mountain Club; 5 Joy Street; Boston, MA 02108.

Appalachian Trail Conference; 1718 "N" Street, NW; Washington, DC 20036.

Bureau of Land Management; US Dept. of the Interior; Washington, DC 20240.

Federation of Western Outdoor Clubs; Route 3; Box 172; Carmel, CA 93921.

Forest Service; US Dept. of Agriculture; Washington, DC 20250.

Friends of the Wilderness; 3515 East Fourth Street; Duluth,MN 55804.

Green Mountain Club; 108 Merchants Row; Rutland, VT 05701.

Mazamas; 909 NW 19th Avenue; Portland, OR 97209.

National Campers and Hikers Association; 7172 Transit Road; Buffalo, NY 14221.

National Parks Association; 1701 – 18th Street, NW; Washington, DC 20036.

Sierra Club; 1051 Mills Tower; San Francisco, CA 94104.

Wilderness Society; 729 – 15th Street NW; Washington, DC 20005.

Office of Advertising and Promotion; US Dept. of Commerce; United States Travel Service; Washington, DC 20230.

ABOUT OUR ILLUSTRATOR AND
DIRECTOR OF RESEARCH

A former high school teacher and active businessman, **Leo VanMeer** is the prolific author of numerous articles on travel as well as other topics. His most recent books are A PENNY FOR YOUR THOUGHTS and HOW TO GARDEN ORGANICALLY ON A CITY LOT.

His wife, **Ruth VanMeer**, is an internationally-known watercolor artist and freelance photographer, who also illustrates many of Leo's books and articles with her drawings and photographs.

Together they travel three or four months each year in their recreational vehicle. When they are not traveling, they reside in Clearwater, Florida, where they contribute substantially with their time and excellent ideas in their daughter, **Mary VanMeer's**, corporation, VanMeer Publications, Inc.

ABOUT OUR EDITORIAL STAFF

Originally from Alma, Michigan, **Mary VanMeer** traveled extensively throughout the United States and Europe for several years before making Clearwater, Florida, the headquarters of VanMeer Publications, Inc. In addition to being a freelance writer and photographer, Mary worked in the Los Angeles Regional Publicity Department of Circus Vargas ("the largest traveling circus under a big top") and had a French tutoring/translating business in New York City.

A University of Florida (Gainesville) graduate, she also attended Michigan State University, and the Sorbonne University in Paris, France.

Mary has previously authored four other books: FREELANCE PHOTOGRAPHER'S HANDBOOK; TRAVELING WITH YOUR DOG - U.S.A.; HOW TO SET UP A HOME TYPING BUSINESS; and TRAVELING FREE IN CALIFORNIA.

In 1980, Mary edited and published SEE AMERICA FREE, the predecessor of FREE CAMPGROUNDS, U.S.A., of which William D. Laffler (United Press International) said, "This book belongs in every camper's library." In 1981, joined by the expertise of writer/researcher **Michael Anthony Pasquarelli**, she updated the guide to free campgrounds, as well as co-edited, with Michael, FREE ATTRACTIONS, U.S.A.

Originally from Painesville, Ohio, **Michael Anthony Pasquarelli** has traveled extensively throughout the United States for several years. During these travels, he became acutely aware of the necessity to find economical travel alternatives. During his research into money-saving travel ideas for the public, as a freelance writer, Michael joined forces with **Mary VanMeer** of VanMeer Publications, Inc. Enthusiastically supported by his Number One Fan, his daughter Roxanne, Michael worked with Mary on the book FREE CAMPGROUNDS, U.S.A. Soon thereafter, they co-edited FREE ATTRACTIONS, U.S.A.

Notes

Notes

Notes

Another money-saving guidebook by Mary VanMeer!

FREE ATTRACTIONS, USA

Edited by Mary VanMeer and Michael Pasquarelli

Inveterate researcher Mary VanMeer has turned up thousands of free attractions across the United States, from California to Florida and Alaska and Hawaii.

With this new guide in hand, you can visit an endless variety of activities, such as museums, galleries, parks, gardens, natural wonders, zoos, historical sites, tours and exhibits. Most are located in easily accessible places and all are FREE!

FREE ATTRACTIONS, USA takes you to thousands of places, including:
- The old state capitol in Springfield, Illinois, where Lincoln gave his "House Divided" speech.
- The Reed Gold Mine, near Charlotte, North Carolina, site of the first gold discovery in the United States.
- Thermopolis, Wyoming, where you can take a free bath at a hot spring that is 35 feet in diameter.
- Lyndon B. Johnson Historical Park, in Texas, where you can see the LBJ Ranch and Johnson City.
- Ybor City in Tampa, Florida, a historical district and Cuban community with small shops in and around one of the oldest cigar factories in the world.

Each attraction includes a description, detailed directions for reaching the attraction, hours, season, and other information of interest. A special section of the guide offers a listing of numerous additional addresses for even more detailed information.

In these cost-conscious days, FREE ATTRACTIONS, USA guarantees an interest-filled vacation at a price everyone can afford!
ISBN 0-914788-51-5 $8.95 quality paperback

Ask your local bookseller for a copy of FREE ATTRACTIONS, USA or use the coupon below to order directly from the publisher:

The East Woods Press
429 East Boulevard
Charlotte, NC 28203
(704) 334-0897

Please send me _____copies of FREE ATTRACTIONS, USA @ $8.95 each.

Please add $1.30 postage for first book, 50¢ each additional book.

My check for _____is enclosed.

Charge my Visa_____ Exp. Date_____

Charge my MasterCard_____ Exp. Date_____

Signature_____

Send to_____

_____

_____

The East Woods Press, 429 East Boulevard, Charlotte, NC 28203 (704) 334-0897

East Woods Press Books

Order from:
The East Woods Press
429 EAST BOULEVARD
CHARLOTTE, NC 28203